The United Nations and the Iraq-Kuwait Conflict, 1990-1996

The United Nations
Blue Books Series, Volume IX

The United Nations and the
Iraq-Kuwait Conflict
1990-1996

**With an introduction by
Boutros Boutros-Ghali,
Secretary-General of the United Nations**

Department of Public Information
United Nations, New York

Published by the United Nations
Department of Public Information
New York, NY 10017

Editor's note:

Each of the United Nations documents and other materials reproduced in this book ("Texts of documents", pages 165-824) has been assigned a number (e.g. Document 1, Document 2, etc.). This number is used throughout the Introduction and other parts of this book to guide readers to the document texts. For other documents mentioned in the book but not reproduced, the United Nations document symbol (e.g.,S/22172, A/47/367) is provided. With this symbol, such documents can be consulted at the Dag Hammarskjöld Library at United Nations Headquarters in New York, at other libraries in the United Nations system or at libraries around the world which have been designated as depository libraries for United Nations documents. The information contained in this volume is correct as at 6 February 1996.

Copyright © 1996 United Nations

The United Nations and the Iraq-Kuwait Conflict, 1990-1996
The United Nations Blue Books Series
Volume IX
ISBN 92-1-100596-5
United Nations Publication
Sales No. E. 96.I.3

Printed by the United Nations Reproduction Section
New York, NY

Contents

Section One:
Introduction by Boutros Boutros-Ghali, Secretary-General of the United Nations

Section Two:
Chronology and Documents

Section One
Introduction

I   Overview

1   Few events in the history of the United Nations have demonstrated the far-reaching ability of the Organization to act as a powerful instrument for international peace and security as its sustained and decisive response to Iraq's August 1990 invasion of Kuwait. The breadth of actions taken by the United Nations in more than five years of work—from the immediate, intense worldwide diplomatic activity aimed at ensuring universal support for the restoration of Kuwaiti sovereignty, to the ongoing challenge of building long-term peace and stability in the region—have confirmed the extraordinary relevance of the United Nations in addressing the most complex political issues facing the international community. A principal concern for the Organization throughout its involvement has been to alleviate the hardships the conflict has visited upon the Iraqi civilian population.

2   The Iraqi invasion and occupation of Kuwait was the first instance since the founding of the Organization in which one Member State sought to completely overpower and annex another. The unique demands presented by this situation have summoned forth innovative measures which have given new practical expression to the Charter's concepts of how international peace and security might be maintained. By the use of sanctions and other enforcement measures, through efforts to institute a programme of disarmament and weapons control, in the provision of humanitarian assistance, and with programmes in areas such as boundary demarcation, compensation for damages caused by the invasion and the promotion and protection of human rights, the United Nations has broken new ground as peacemaker, peace-keeper and peace-builder.

3   The United Nations' central role began at the very outset of the crisis. Within hours of the invasion on 2 August 1990, the Security Council met to demand Iraq's withdrawal from Kuwait. Acting incrementally in addressing Iraq's aggression and its aftermath, the Council by late November had adopted 12 resolutions under Chapter VII of the Charter covering various aspects of the situation. No other crisis in the history of the United Nations had elicited such attention and action from the Council in such a compressed span of time. The international outcry extended to the General Assembly, where virtually all Member States participating in the general debate during September and October 1990 deplored the invasion and occupation of Kuwait and called for the restoration of Kuwait's Government and respect for its territorial integrity.

4   These extraordinary measures were accompanied by a military build-up in the region of exceptional speed, scale and international scope by a coalition of United Nations Member States cooperating in the defence of Kuwait. The coalition, which included the United States of America, the United Kingdom of Great Britain and Northern Ireland, France, other European States, a number of Arab States and several other United Nations Member States, deployed their forces in Saudi Arabia, other Gulf States and adjacent waters. The stage was thus set for the use of military power to enforce Iraqi compliance with the will of the international community as clearly and forcefully expressed in Security Council resolutions. Resolution 678 of 29 November 1991 was of particular significance in this regard: it authorized Member States to use "all necessary means to uphold and implement" all relevant Council resolutions if Iraq did not withdraw from Kuwait by 15 January 1991.

5   Parallel to the military build-up, the United Nations actively sought a negotiated end to the crisis. Indeed, it was only when various appeals, diplomatic initiatives and explicit warnings from the Council went unheeded that armed force was finally utilized. Acting in accordance with the Council's authorization, but not under the direction or control of the United Nations, the coalition—in a campaign of aerial bombardment followed by a ground offensive—successfully ousted Iraqi forces from Kuwait and restored Kuwaiti sovereignty. Since the suspension of hostilities on 28 February 1991, a multi-faceted United Nations operation has sought to restore full peace to the region.

6   The primary basis for the wide range of actions that the United Nations has taken to accomplish this goal is Security Council resolution 687 (1991), adopted on 3 April 1991, which imposes numerous obligations on Iraq and, in doing so, constitutes one of the most comprehensive sets of decisions ever taken by the Council. Relying heavily on United Nations bodies and the Secretary-General for implementation, resolution 687 (1991) has involved new subsidiary organs and articulations of the Council's powers. Together with subsequent Council resolutions, as well as those of the General Assembly, this extensive body of decisions has given rise to a striking array of operations and activities, among them:

7   **The United Nations Iraq-Kuwait Observation Mission (UNIKOM).** Established immediately after the cease-fire in April 1991, the UNIKOM force monitors a demilitarized zone (DMZ) along the Iraq-Kuwait border, serving as a vital buffer and confidence-building mechanism.

8   **The United Nations Iraq-Kuwait Boundary Demarcation Commission (IKBDC).** The IKBDC demarcated the boundary between Iraq and Kuwait for the first time, the first instance in which the United Nations performed such a task for two Member States, thereby provid-

ing a precedent to which other nations are looking for possible application to their own circumstances. Further, under resolution 687 (1991), the Security Council decided to guarantee the inviolability of the Iraq-Kuwait border.

9   **The United Nations Special Commission (UNSCOM).** Since April 1991, UNSCOM and the Action Team of the **International Atomic Energy Agency (IAEA)** have carried out the difficult work of documenting and dismantling Iraq's programmes aimed at developing and acquiring weapons of mass destruction and long-range missile capabilities which are prohibited to Iraq under resolution 687 (1991). The cornerstone of this effort has been the right of UNSCOM and the IAEA to conduct rigorous, no-notice, on-site inspections anywhere in Iraq—the only such inspections ever by a United Nations body and the most intrusive ever devised in the field of international arms control. UNSCOM and the IAEA have also worked to establish a comprehensive system of ongoing monitoring and verification, as mandated by resolution 687 (1991).

10   **The United Nations Compensation Commission (UNCC) and Compensation Fund.** Iraq is liable under Security Council resolutions and international law for any loss, damage (including environmental damage) or injury caused by its invasion, and to pay compensation to Governments, individuals and corporations for the harm inflicted. The Commission is processing more than 2.6 million claims with an estimated value exceeding $160 billion—the largest such programme in history.

11   **The United Nations Consolidated Inter-Agency Humanitarian Programme in Iraq.** The response of the United Nations system to the humanitarian emergency in Iraq has involved several innovations. The first was the deployment, some 47 years after Secretary-General Trygve Lie first proposed the idea, of a United Nations Guards Contingent to protect humanitarian workers and property. A second innovation was the use of so-called "blue routes", protected by United Nations Guards, for the transit and repatriation of refugees and displaced persons, which avoided the construction and long-term administration of camps. Another was the adoption by the Security Council of a resolution offering Iraq the opportunity to use the proceeds from the limited sale of Iraqi petroleum and petroleum products to pay for foodstuffs, medicines and other essential civilian needs (and to fund other United Nations activities concerning Iraq mandated by the Council)—the "oil-for-food" formula. And a fourth was the Council's decision to locate proceeds from the sale of Iraqi oil abroad and apply these funds towards the same purposes.

12   **Special rapporteurs for the situation of human rights in occupied Kuwait and in Iraq.** In March 1991, the Commission on Human

Rights condemned violations of human rights by Iraqi forces in occupied Kuwait and by the Government of Iraq in Iraq itself. The Commission decided to assign two separate special rapporteurs, respectively, to investigate violations of human rights committed by Iraqi forces in occupied Kuwait against Kuwaitis and nationals of other States, and to make a thorough study of the violations of human rights in Iraq by the Government of Iraq. The Special Rapporteurs have submitted reports to both the Commission and the General Assembly.

13   Implementation of Security Council resolution 687 (1991) and the other resolutions relating to the Iraq-Kuwait situation has not always proceeded smoothly. Iraq accepted the terms of resolution 687 unconditionally but with considerable reluctance, contending that these terms were an unjust assault on Iraq's sovereignty. Since then it has provided, for the most part, incomplete cooperation in fulfilling its obligations, although by early 1996 that cooperation had improved measurably. Members of the Security Council and other Member States, for their part, have insisted that Iraq, to attain its stated goals of an end to sanctions, normalization of its relations with other States and reintegration into the international community, must comply fully and unconditionally with the relevant resolutions.

14   This volume chronicles the Organization's involvement in the Iraq-Kuwait situation as of February 1996. Following this Overview, Part II of the Introduction recounts events from 1961 to 1963, when the territorial dispute between Iraq and Kuwait was first addressed by the Security Council. Part III recounts the invasion, the imposition by the Council of an arms embargo and other sanctions and efforts to negotiate an end to the crisis prior to the 15 January 1991 deadline set by the Council. Part IV covers the period in which the coalition, pursuant to resolution 678 (1990), took military action to restore the legitimate Government of Kuwait.

15   The provisions of the landmark cease-fire resolution—resolution 687 (1991)—are the focus of Part V. Part VI discusses efforts to strengthen security in the border area. Part VII covers efforts to restore normalcy to Iraq and Kuwait through humanitarian assistance, the repatriation of Kuwaiti and third-State nationals and of Iraqi nationals, the return of Kuwaiti property seized by Iraq, the mitigation of the environmental consequences of the conflict and payment of compensation to the victims of the invasion and occupation. Part VIII describes the work of UNSCOM and the IAEA pursuant to the weapons-related provisions of resolution 687 (1991).

16   Part IX discusses efforts to implement the "oil-for-food" formula and the work of the Special Rapporteurs for human rights, and Part X discusses the sanctions regime. Finally, in Part XI, I offer some

preliminary conclusions on the experience of the United Nations in carrying out its difficult, precedent-setting mandates.

17   The documentation in Section Two, which makes up the bulk of this volume, includes the essential United Nations materials relating to the Iraq-Kuwait crisis: resolutions of the Security Council and statements by its President, resolutions of the General Assembly, major reports of UNSCOM and the IAEA, the final report of the Iraq-Kuwait Boundary Demarcation Commission, periodic progress reports on UNIKOM, reports assessing the humanitarian situation in Iraq and Kuwait and selected communications from Iraq and Kuwait. The "Other documents of interest" listing on pages 157-164 guides readers to additional United Nations documents of value; the United Nations document symbol for some of these "Other documents" is also provided, parenthetically, in the text.

II Background

18 The territorial dispute at issue when Iraq invaded Kuwait in
1990 first came before the Security Council in 1961, when Kuwait
gained its independence from the United Kingdom. Iraq, reasserting its
long-standing position that Kuwait was historically and legally an integral part of Iraq's Basrah province, massed troops on the border. The
Security Council was unable to take action at the time because of a lack
of unanimity among its permanent members. None the less, the clear
commitment of United Nations Member States to a settlement by peaceful means set the stage for the dispute to move to the Arab League, when
a solution was devised that eased the threat of military confrontation.
The involvement of the international community undoubtedly helped
foster the relative calm that governed relations between Iraq and Kuwait
until 1990.

Origins of the dispute

19 The territorial dispute between Iraq and Kuwait has its origins
in the history of the two entities during the Ottoman Empire. The land
which was to become modern Iraq was conquered by the Ottoman
Empire in 1535 and was governed thereafter as three provinces, except
for an interval of Persian rule in the seventeenth century. In 1914, the
Ottoman Empire entered the first World War as one of the Central
Powers, all of which were defeated in 1918. As part of the post-war
arrangements, the Allies stipulated at the Conference of San Remo on
25 October 1920 that Iraq be administered by the United Kingdom as a
Mandate Territory under the League of Nations. Although Iraq subsequently obtained a degree of self-government with respect to its internal affairs, it remained a Mandate Territory until it became independent
on 3 October 1932 and joined the League of Nations. On 21 December
1945, Iraq became an original Member of the United Nations.

20 Kuwait was a sheikhdom during the time of the Ottoman
Empire, and the degree to which it was integrated with the Empire
fluctuated, based in part on shifting trade patterns in the Gulf region.
Thus at times there did exist a link between Ottoman authorities in the
city of Basrah (now part of Iraq) and Kuwait. However, in 1899, under
the threat of nomadic warlords and of increasing Ottoman domination,
the Sheikh of Kuwait had sufficient independence to be able to seek
defensive arrangements with the British Government. These arrange-

ments were codified in a secret treaty which gave the United Kingdom control over Kuwait's foreign affairs but did not establish a formal British protectorate.

21   In 1913, the British Government and the Ottoman Empire entered into an agreement which recognized a semi-autonomous status for Kuwait within the Empire—including a defined boundary—but the agreement was never ratified by either side owing to the outbreak of the first World War. After the war and the dissolution of the Ottoman Empire, the British Government administered Kuwait as a self-governing protectorate. In the early 1920s, a redefining by the British Government of the boundaries between Iraq and Najd, the predecessor kingdom to Saudi Arabia, and between that kingdom and Kuwait, caused Kuwait to lose some two thirds of its territory to Najd. In 1923, the British Government agreed to recognize the border with Iraq claimed by Kuwait, which was identical to that stipulated in the unratified Anglo-Ottoman agreement of 1913.

22   It was in the context of Iraq's pending independence in 1932 that the British Government initiated an exchange of letters from Iraq, dated 21 July 1932, and from Kuwait, dated 10 August 1932,[1] addressed to the British authorities in Baghdad and Kuwait, respectively. The letters confirmed the Iraq-Kuwait border as defined in 1913 and 1923 and subsequently became a main reference point for any discussion of the boundary between the two States. However, Iraq as an independent State continued to claim that Kuwait was a part of its territory.

1/Document 1
See page 165;
Document 2
See page 165

Issue brought before the United Nations

23   As part of the great wave of decolonization in the early 1960s, Kuwait and the United Kingdom re-examined their relationship. Although under the 1899 treaty the United Kingdom had maintained nominal control over Kuwait's external relations, in practice Kuwait had for some time exercised most functions of State. Moreover, Kuwait enjoyed *de jure* and de facto recognition from a large number of countries and, although not a United Nations Member State, was a member of the International Telecommunication Union (ITU), the Universal Postal Union (UPU), the International Civil Aviation Organization (ICAO), the International Labour Organization (ILO), the World Health Organization (WHO) and the United Nations Educational, Scientific and Cultural Organization (UNESCO). On 19 June 1961, Kuwait and the United Kingdom agreed to terminate the 1899 arrangements which had permitted a British military presence in Kuwait, thus formally establishing Kuwait's independence.

24   Once the United Kingdom withdrew its forces as part of the

19 June 1961 agreement, Iraq arrayed troops near the border. This in turn prompted British forces to return to Kuwait on 1 July 1961. That same day, Kuwait cabled the United Nations requesting an urgent meeting of the Security Council. Kuwait made this request pursuant to Article 35, paragraph 2, of the Charter, which allows any State not a Member of the United Nations to bring a dispute to which it is a party before the Security Council if it accepts in advance the obligations of pacific settlement provided for in the Charter.

25 The United Kingdom supported Kuwait's request for a Security Council meeting. On 2 July, Iraq requested that the Council convene to consider the "armed threat by the United Kingdom to the independence and security of Iraq which is likely to endanger the maintenance of international peace and security" (S/4847). Iraq also contended that Kuwait lacked the standing to bring a question before the Security Council under the provisions of Article 35, because Kuwait "is not and has never been an independent State" (S/4848).

26 The Security Council met to consider both complaints on 2, 5, 6 and 7 July 1961. In the debate, Iraq affirmed its commitment to employ only peaceful means to resolve the question. However, Iraq also restated its intention to recover its legitimate rights in Kuwait and objected strenuously to the military presence of the United Kingdom in Kuwait. Kuwait asserted that the forces made available by the United Kingdom would be withdrawn as soon as sufficient guarantees were given that Kuwait's independence would not be violated. The United Kingdom, the United States and France, along with a majority of the other Council members, spoke in support of Kuwait's right to exist as an independent State and also noted with satisfaction Iraq's assurances of its peaceful intentions. However, the United Arab Republic (the union of Egypt and Syria) and some other States also wanted the Council to require a withdrawal of all British forces and suggested that the dispute be settled through a body such as the League of Arab States. The Union of Soviet Socialist Republics supported Iraq's position and asserted that the concentration of British forces in the area was a threat to peace.

27 On 6 July 1961, Kuwait applied formally for membership in the United Nations. Also on that day, the United Kingdom submitted a draft resolution by which the Security Council would call upon all States to respect the independence and territorial integrity of Kuwait and urge that all concerned work for peace and tranquillity in the area. In its preambular paragraphs, the draft resolution noted the statement by the United Kingdom that British forces would be withdrawn as soon as Kuwait considered that the threat to it was removed. On 7 July, the United Arab Republic, which regarded the text as incomplete because it did not require the withdrawal of British forces, submitted its own draft resolution by which the Council would urge that the question be solved

Iraq and Kuwait

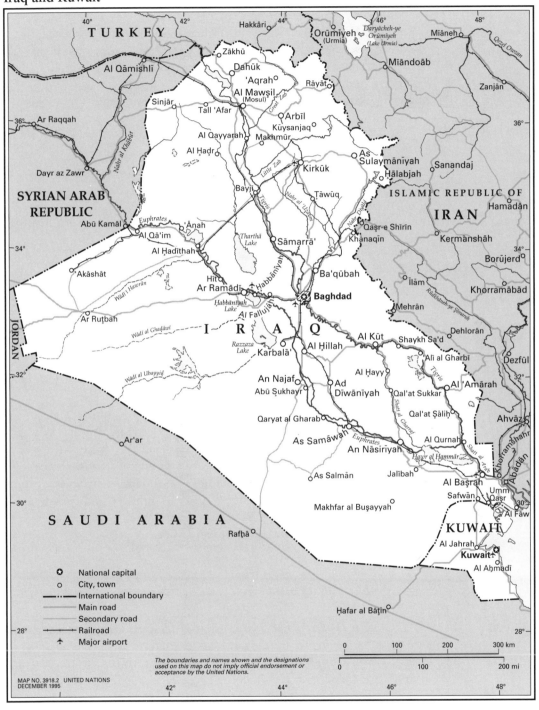

○ National capital
○ City, town
▪▪ International boundary
— Main road
— Secondary road
▪▪▪ Railway
✈ Major airport

The boundaries and names shown and the designations
used on this map do not imply official endorsement or
acceptance by the United Nations.

MAP NO. 3918.2   UNITED NATIONS
DECEMBER 1995

by peaceful means and call upon the United Kingdom to withdraw its forces from Kuwait immediately.

28   Both draft resolutions came to a vote on 7 July. The United Kingdom draft was not adopted owing to the negative vote of the Soviet Union. The United Arab Republic draft was not adopted because it failed to obtain the required seven affirmative votes (the Council having a total of 11 members at that time). After the voting, the President of the Security Council appealed to all parties to abstain from any action that might aggravate the situation and stated that he would reconvene the Council if circumstances made it necessary to do so.

29   Meeting at the same time as the Security Council on 5 July 1961, the Council of the League of Arab States voted to admit Kuwait to membership in the League subject to Kuwait's requesting the withdrawal of British forces, and further agreed to deploy a League force along the Iraq-Kuwait border. The League mandated that Iraq undertake not to use force to annex Kuwait and also agreed to assist Kuwait in joining the United Nations. Having accepted the provisions relating to the British withdrawal and the stationing of a League force, Kuwait was admitted to the Arab League on 30 July 1961, despite Iraqi objections.

30   On 12 August 1961, an agreement was reached between the League and Kuwait governing the disposition of Arab League Security Forces in Kuwait. These forces, composed of contingents drawn from Jordan, Saudi Arabia, the Sudan and the United Arab Republic, began to take up positions along the Kuwaiti side of the border on 10 September. Accordingly, the United Kingdom began to remove its forces from Kuwait, finishing the withdrawal by 19 October.

31   On 30 November 1961, the Security Council met at the request of the United Arab Republic to consider Kuwait's earlier application for United Nations membership. During the debate, Iraq, supported by the Soviet Union, contested Kuwait's eligibility for membership on the grounds that it had no standing as an independent State. A draft resolution sponsored by the United Arab Republic which would have had the Council recommend Kuwait for membership was not adopted owing to the negative vote of the Soviet Union.

Kuwait admitted as United Nations Member State

32   On 20 April 1963, after more than a year of general stability along the Iraq-Kuwait border and following the withdrawal of Arab League forces from Kuwait, Kuwait wrote again to the United Nations to apply for membership. When the Security Council met on 7 May to consider Kuwait's request, Iraq restated its position that Kuwait was an integral part of its territory and requested postponement of Kuwait's

application. This time, however, the Council voted unanimously to recommend that the General Assembly act favourably on Kuwait's request. The Assembly, at its fourth special session, endorsed the recommendation by acclamation on 14 May 1963, thereby admitting Kuwait as the Organization's 111th Member State.[2]

2/Document 3
See page 166

Iraq and Kuwait sign "Agreed Minutes"

33   In February 1963, just prior to Kuwait's renewed request for United Nations membership, a military coup in Iraq brought to power new leaders who declared themselves dedicated to the ideals of Arab unity and socialism. Though the new Iraqi Government had maintained its predecessor's position during the Council's consideration of Kuwait's application for United Nations membership, some months later the Iraqi stance had changed, allowing for a major breakthrough. On 4 October 1963, high-level delegations from Iraq and Kuwait led by the Prime Ministers of both countries met in Baghdad. At that meeting, Iraq recognized the independence and complete sovereignty of Kuwait with its boundaries as specified in the 1932 exchange of letters.[3] In addition, according to the "Agreed Minutes" of that meeting, both countries agreed to immediately establish diplomatic relations.[4] The Agreed Minutes also made reference to a statement by the Government of Kuwait on 9 April 1963 concerning Kuwait's intention to seek, in due time, termination of its 1961 defence arrangements with the United Kingdom. This was accomplished on 13 May 1968. Except for one significant Iraqi incursion into Kuwaiti territory in March 1973, when Iraqi forces briefly occupied Samtah, the Iraq-Kuwait border was calm until 1990.

3/Document 1
See page 165;
Document 2
See page 165

4/Document 4
See page 166

III   Invasion and response

34   Between 2 August 1990, the first day of the crisis, when the Security Council met just 11 hours after Iraqi forces crossed the Kuwaiti frontier, and 29 November 1990, when the Council, in what it termed a "pause of goodwill", gave Iraq until 15 January 1991 to end its occupation of Kuwait, the Council actively sought a peaceful resolution to the crisis. Parallel to these efforts, a coalition of Member States led by the United States assembled a military force in the region, and the Security Council authorized Member States to use "all necessary means" to ensure Iraqi compliance with the relevant Council resolutions. When diplomatic initiatives failed to achieve the desired objectives, the international coalition, acting in accordance with the Council's authorization but not under the control or direction of the United Nations, decided to exercise the power granted to it by the Council and to reverse Iraq's invasion and occupation of Kuwait through military action.

Build-up to the events of 2 August 1990

35   From February through July 1990, statements by President Saddam Hussein of Iraq and other Iraqi officials advanced several political, territorial and financial claims against Kuwait. Among Iraq's charges were that Kuwait had extracted Iraqi crude oil worth $2.4 billion by "slant-drilling" into the Rumaila oilfield; that Kuwait's illegal possession of Warba, Bubiyan and Failaka islands in the Persian Gulf obstructed Iraq's access to Gulf waters; and that Kuwait and other members of the Organization of Petroleum Exporting Countries (OPEC) were not adhering to OPEC's oil-export quotas, thereby depressing worldwide oil prices and depriving Iraq of resources it needed to pay its debts and facilitate its recovery from the devastating eight-year war with the Islamic Republic of Iran. In the latter part of July, Iraq deployed military forces along the border with Kuwait.

36   Kuwait responded that these and other allegations had no basis in truth. On 31 July, the Crown Prince of Kuwait and the Vice-Chairman of Iraq's Revolution Command Council met in Saudi Arabia in an attempt (by Egyptian President Hosni Mubarak) to avert a serious confrontation. However, the talks were unproductive, and on 2 August, at 1 a.m. local time, Iraqi troops crossed the international frontier and began their invasion and occupation of Kuwait.

International condemnation and imposition of sanctions

37   Pursuant to requests from Kuwait and the United States, the Security Council convened within hours of the initial reports of Iraq's invasion and unanimously adopted resolution 660 (1990), in which, invoking articles 39 and 40 of Chapter VII of the United Nations Charter, it condemned the invasion, demanded that Iraq immediately and unconditionally withdraw all its forces to the positions they had occupied the previous day and called on Iraq and Kuwait to begin intensive negotiations to resolve their differences.[5] Each of the five permanent members of the Council voiced opposition to the invasion (S/PV.2932): the United States called it a "heinous act", the Soviet Union expressed "profound concern and alarm", France "most firmly" deplored Iraq's use of force, China stated that Iraqi troops should be withdrawn, and the United Kingdom said, "This is an ugly moment in world affairs." Each also stressed the need for negotiation. Iraq's representative, for his part, stated that Iraqi troops had entered Kuwait solely in response to a request from the "Free Provisional Government of Kuwait" to assist it "to establish security and order so that Kuwaitis would not have to suffer", and he declared that the Iraqi forces would withdraw "as soon as order has been restored". Later that day, 2 August 1990, my predecessor, Secretary-General Pérez de Cuéllar, met with the permanent representatives of Kuwait and Iraq to the United Nations and appealed to the latter for full implementation of resolution 660 (1990).

5/Document 5
See page 167;
Document 6
See page 167

38   The outcry beyond the Security Council was just as strong. On 3 August, the Gulf Cooperation Council condemned the "brutal Iraqi aggression against the fraternal State of Kuwait" and called upon Iraq to withdraw its forces immediately and unconditionally. The League of Arab States, the Organization of the Islamic Conference, the European Community, other regional groups and individual United Nations Member States representing the breadth of world opinion also voiced their opposition.

39   The Security Council returned to action on 6 August when it adopted resolution 661 (1990), imposing under Chapter VII of the Charter comprehensive and mandatory sanctions on Iraq and deciding not to recognize any regime set up in Kuwait by the occupying Power.[6] The Council also established a committee (known informally as the Sanctions Committee) to monitor implementation of the sanctions, which covered the sale and supply of all products and commodities, including weapons and other military equipment, as well as the transfer of funds. Exceptions to the sanctions regime were made for supplies intended strictly for medical purposes and, in humanitarian circumstances, foodstuffs. None the less, Iraq, in a letter to the Secretary-General, described

6/Document 7
See page 168

7/Document 10
See page 170

the sanctions resolution as "unjust", "precipitous", "iniquitous" and designed to "starve the Iraqi people".[7] In order to verify implementation of the sanctions, and at the request of Jordan, my predecessor in December 1990 dispatched the Secretary of the Sanctions Committee to monitor the flow of traffic between Jordan and Iraq.

40   On 7 August, in response to requests from Kuwait, Saudi Arabia, Bahrain and other Governments in the region, and in accordance with Article 51 of the Charter, which recognizes Member States' "inherent right" of "individual or collective self-defence", the United States, followed by the United Kingdom and other European countries, began dispatching air and naval forces to the region. This operation eventually grew into a multinational effort involving more than 30 nations. Arab participation was decided upon at an Extraordinary Arab Summit Conference held in Cairo on 10 August at which the League of Arab States adopted a resolution calling upon Iraq to withdraw its forces from Kuwait, insisting on the restoration of the legitimate Kuwaiti Government and stating that the League would comply with the request of Saudi Arabia and the other Arab States of the Gulf that "Arab forces should be deployed to assist" their armed forces in defending their "soil and territorial integrity against any external aggression" (S/21500).

41   On 12 August, Kuwait wrote to the President of the Security Council and, invoking its inherent right of individual and collective self-defence and Article 51 of the Charter, informed him that Kuwait "has requested some nations to take such military or other steps as are necessary to ensure the effective and prompt implementation of Security Council resolution 661 (1990)".[8] Kuwait, whose leaders had escaped their occupied country and issued a decree that the Government of Kuwait would be convened temporarily in Saudi Arabia, also forwarded a series of reports rejecting Iraq's claims against Kuwait as well as the "Government" set up by Iraq in Kuwait. The Kuwaiti communications charged that Iraq, in systematically taking over the country, was ransacking houses, plundering public facilities and private homes alike, desecrating houses of worship, stealing vehicles, looting banks and businesses, terrorizing civilians and taking steps to alter the demographic nature of the country so as to buttress its political and territorial claims.

8/Document 9
See page 169

42   On 7 August, Iraq had declared its "comprehensive, eternal and inseparable merger" with Kuwait. In an initiative announced on 12 August, President Saddam Hussein of Iraq linked any Iraqi withdrawal from Kuwait to the immediate and unconditional withdrawal of Israel from the occupied Arab territories, the withdrawal of Syrian troops from Lebanon, a mutual withdrawal by Iraq and the Islamic Republic of Iran from territory occupied during the war between those two countries, and the withdrawal of United States forces from the Gulf region. President Hussein proposed that the same principles be applied to achieving each

of these withdrawals, but added that "prior cases of occupation" had to be resolved before addressing the Iraq-Kuwait question (S/21494).

43   On 18 August, Iraq announced it had begun to detain third-State nationals (mostly Americans and Europeans) in Iraq and Kuwait. Of the nearly 13,000 persons so detained, a large number were subsequently placed at strategic sites as "human shields" against the threat of foreign military aggression. In a second initiative announced on 19 August, President Hussein proposed that if the United States committed to withdraw it forces and those of its allies from the wider Middle East region, or if the Security Council guaranteed such a withdrawal, Iraq would release the detainees (S/21651). Neither of Iraq's proposals was deemed an acceptable basis for negotiations by the Security Council. However, between 12 October and 20 December 1990, the Council adopted resolutions 672 (1990), 673 (1990) and 681 (1990) addressing the issue of Palestinian civilians under Israeli occupation.

44   With no sign that Iraq planned to withdraw from Kuwait or otherwise comply with resolutions 660 (1990) and 661 (1990), the Security Council took action on three further occasions during the first month of the crisis. On 9 August, the Council stated in its resolution 662 (1990) that Iraq's annexation of Kuwait had no legal validity and was "null and void".[9] On 18 August, in resolution 664 (1990), the Council demanded that Iraq permit and facilitate the departure of third-country nationals, grant immediate and continuing access of consular officials to them and take no action to jeopardize their safety, security or health.[10] And on 25 August, in resolution 665 (1990), the Council called upon Member States cooperating with the Government of Kuwait which were deploying maritime forces to the area to use such measures as might be necessary "to halt all inward and outward maritime shipping, in order to inspect and verify their cargoes and destinations and to ensure strict implementation of the provisions related to such shipping laid down in resolution 661 (1990)".[11] The Council also requested Member States to use, "as appropriate", the Council's Military Staff Committee to coordinate their actions. Under the Charter, the Military Staff Committee was established to advise and assist the Council on all questions relating to the Council's military requirements. On 9 August, the Ministry for Foreign Affairs of the Soviet Union had expressed its readiness to begin consultations within the Military Staff Committee, urging that the Council deal with the "very critical" Iraq-Kuwait question "on a permanent basis" (S/21479). The Committee, however, was never convoked.

9/Document 8
See page 169

10/Document 11
See page 170

11/Document 12
See page 171

Secretary-General in Amman

45   As the build-up of coalition forces in the Gulf region continued, my predecessor travelled to Amman from 30 August to 2 September

to meet with the Deputy Prime Minister and Minister for Foreign Affairs of Iraq, Mr. Tariq Aziz, to explore prospects for a peaceful end to the crisis. During several hours of discussion over two days, the Secretary-General told the Minister that the United Nations was committed to the approach adopted by the Security Council and that his initiative in travelling to Amman had to be viewed in that framework. The Minister, in his comments to the Secretary-General, placed particular emphasis on the need for an "Arab solution". The Secretary-General replied that the international dimension to the conflict had to be acknowledged. The global interests involved, the large build-up of forces in the area and the presence in Iraq and Kuwait of many third-country nationals made it clear, said the Secretary-General, that the United Nations as well as Arab Governments would have to be involved in resolving the many issues at stake. At the end of the talks, the Secretary-General expressed disappointment that real progress had not been made and voiced the hope that the search for a peaceful solution to the crisis would continue (SG/SM/4487).

Assistance to people uprooted by the Gulf crisis

46   Events in the Gulf led hundreds of thousands of migrant workers from developing countries to flee the region, thereby losing their livelihoods overnight and abandoning savings and possessions. Estimates of the numbers of foreign workers affected by the crisis have varied (E/1991/102). It was reported that several hundred thousand Egyptians returned to Egypt, and that most of the 850,000 Yemenis also had to return. Estimates of the number of returnees to Jordan vary from 330,000 to 400,000. Repatriations were also very high for a number of countries in South and East Asia: India (200,000), Pakistan (140,000), Bangladesh and Sri Lanka (about 100,000 each) and the Philippines (60,000). According to the International Labour Organization (ILO), some 2 million of the 2.8 million migrant workers and their families in Iraq and Kuwait had fled by early February 1991. The United Nations Relief and Works Agency for Palestine Refugees in the Near East (UNRWA) reported that 150,000 of the 350,000 Palestinians working in Kuwait were also uprooted.

47   During the period from early August to the beginning of November 1990, more than 700,000 of these third-country nationals entered Jordan, most of them having no funds, nowhere to go in Jordan and no means of repatriation (UNDRO/1991/1). The Government of Jordan opened its border to this rapid and unexpected influx, and on 23 August requested international help in alleviating the situation. The Office of the United Nations Disaster Relief Coordinator (UNDRO)

was the lead coordinating agency for this emergency operation. The International Organization for Migration (IOM) was asked by UNDRO to assume the lead role in providing transportation and repatriation services. Also involved were the Food and Agriculture Organization of the United Nations (FAO), the United Nations Development Programme (UNDP), the Office of the United Nations High Commissioner for Refugees (UNHCR), the United Nations Children's Fund (UNICEF), the United Nations Relief and Works Agency for Palestine Refugees in the Near East (UNRWA), the World Food Programme (WFP), the World Health Organization (WHO), the International Committee of the Red Cross (ICRC), the League of Red Cross and Red Crescent Societies and a number of non-governmental organizations. On 12 September, my predecessor appointed a Personal Representative for humanitarian assistance relating to the crisis between Iraq and Kuwait.

48   The emergency operation had two components: facilitating the evacuation of the displaced peoples to their countries of origin, and providing assistance—water, food, medicine, shelter and sanitation materials—to those who could not be transported immediately. By 27 August 1990, 200,000 people had entered Jordan, and by early September, an average of 14,000 people were arriving daily. By mid-September an effective logistical operation had started to function, with reception/transit camps set up throughout Jordan. Overland transport and airlifts were organized by the IOM, by the European Community and by Governments of affected countries, and hundreds of thousands of people were repatriated to Asia and Africa so rapidly that their average stay in Jordan was five days. At the peak of the operation, more than 7,000 people of various nationalities were flown out of Amman daily. Others were evacuated overland or by ship.

49   By mid-October, the number of people remaining in the transit centres was approaching zero (UNDRO/1991/1). Although about 80 people lost their lives when the buses transporting them to the airport had accidents, there were no deaths attributed to camp conditions, no outbreaks of diseases or epidemics and no disruption of the social fabric in Jordan. The transit of a smaller number of evacuees through the Islamic Republic of Iran, the Syrian Arab Republic and Turkey was equally smooth. (For more about humanitarian assistance, see paragraphs 112-120, 170-184 and 317-332.)

States affected by sanctions

50   The massive displacements of people, and the sanctions regime decided upon by the Security Council, created economic and other problems for many States. In addition to the loss of worker remittances

and costs associated with repatriation, resettlement, subsistence and job creation for returnees, these countries were experiencing oil shortages and other problems associated with the cessation in oil exports from Iraq and Kuwait of more than 4 million barrels of oil per day—some 7 per cent of world consumption. According to the United Nations *World Economic Survey* for 1991, the halt in exports and subsequent market speculation resulted for a time in "a doubling and tripling of oil prices, with consequent shock effects on many national economies".

51   Under Article 50 of the Charter, countries which find themselves confronted with special economic problems arising from the carrying out of enforcement measures taken by the Security Council can consult with the Council about a solution to their problems. Eventually, 21 States addressed the Council on this basis—the first time in United Nations history that a large number of States had taken such a step. The 21 States were: Bangladesh, Bulgaria, Czechoslovakia, Djibouti, India, Jordan, Lebanon, Mauritania, Pakistan, the Philippines, Poland, Romania, Seychelles, Sri Lanka, the Sudan, Syrian Arab Republic, Tunisia, Uruguay, Viet Nam, Yemen and Yugoslavia.

52   Jordan, having had close economic relations with Iraq prior to the invasion, was particularly hard-hit by the imposition of sanctions and was thus the first of the Article 50 applicants to have its case considered by the Sanctions Committee and acted upon by the Council. On 18 September 1990, the Committee appealed to States to provide immediate assistance and, on 24 September, based on the Committee's recommendation, the Security Council asked the Secretary-General to undertake an immediate assessment of Jordan's problems, which he did by dispatching a special representative to visit Jordan from 10 to 15 October (S/21938). With regard to the other States experiencing difficulties, the Security Council, in its resolution 669 (1990), entrusted the Sanctions Committee with the task of examining requests for assistance and making recommendations to the Council for appropriate action.[12] On 27 September, the Committee decided in principle to set up an open-ended working group for this purpose. (For more about action under Article 50 and the Sanctions Committee, see paragraphs 349-352.)

12/Document 15
See page 174

Further Security Council action

53   The Security Council addressed the humanitarian situation in Iraq and Kuwait in its resolution 666 (1990), adopted on 13 September 1990, in which it instructed the Sanctions Committee to keep the situation regarding foodstuffs in Iraq and Kuwait under constant review, paying particular attention to children under 15 years of age, expectant mothers, maternity cases, the sick and the elderly.[13]

13/Document 13
See page 172

54   On 16 September, the Council responded to Iraq's decision to order the closure of diplomatic and consular missions in Kuwait and to withdraw the immunity and privileges of those missions and their personnel, as well as to Iraq's abduction of foreign nationals who were present in those premises. In resolution 667 (1990), the Council said it was "outraged" at these violations, declared that such acts "strike at the root of the conduct of international relations in accordance with the Charter", strongly condemned Iraq's aggressive acts, demanded the immediate release of the abductees and decided to consult urgently on what further measures to take "in response to Iraq's continued violation of the Charter of the United Nations, of resolutions of the Security Council and of international law".[14]

14/Document 14
See page 173

55   On 25 September, in its resolution 670 (1990), the Security Council explicitly confirmed that the sanctions against Iraq applied "to all means of transport, including aircraft" and elaborated further measures affecting shipping and air transport.[15] Specifically, the Council decided that States would "deny permission to any aircraft to take off from their territory if the aircraft would carry any cargo to or from Iraq or Kuwait other than food in humanitarian circumstances" and that States were to deny overflight permission to any aircraft destined to land in Iraq or Kuwait, and called upon States to detain any ships of Iraqi registry which entered their ports and were in violation of the sanctions resolution.

15/Document 16
See page 174

56   For the vote and the debate on tightening sanctions against Iraq, 13 of the Council's 15 members, including all five permanent members, were represented at the Foreign Minister level—only the third time in United Nations history that Foreign Ministers of all permanent members had attended a Security Council meeting. In statements, each stressed the need for a peaceful, political settlement to the crisis (S/PV.2943). Mr. Pérez de Cuéllar also addressed the Council on 25 September, emphasizing that the manner and scale in which the Council was employing Chapter VII enforcement provisions in Iraq was unprecedented and that, therefore, the United Nations needed to demonstrate, among other things, "that the way of enforcement is qualitatively different from the way of war . . . that it strives to minimize undeserved suffering . . . and that it does not foreclose diplomatic efforts to arrive at a peaceful solution . . ." (SG/SM/4495-SC/5215).

57   In October 1990, the Security Council returned to the issue of Kuwaiti and third-State nationals, including diplomatic and consular personnel, who were being held hostage and/or mistreated by Iraq. In its resolution 674 (1990) adopted on 29 October 1990, the Council demanded that the Iraqi authorities and occupying forces cease and desist from such actions, permit the immediate departure of the detainees and ensure their access to food, water and other basic services.[16] The Council also invited States to collate "substantiated information" on the grave

16/Document 17
See page 176

breaches by Iraq of Council decisions, the Charter, international law, the Fourth Geneva Convention and the Vienna Conventions on Diplomatic and Consular Relations. Further, the Council entrusted the Secretary-General with making available his good offices and, "as he considers appropriate, to pursue them and to undertake diplomatic efforts in order to reach a peaceful solution to the crisis".

58   In resolution 674 (1990), the Council also condemned Iraq for the destruction of Kuwaiti demographic records, the forced departure of Kuwaitis and the relocation of population in Kuwait. These actions were part of what the Council subsequently described, in resolution 677 (1990) of 28 November, as an attempt by Iraq to "alter the demographic composition of Kuwait and to destroy the civil records maintained by the legitimate Government of Kuwait".[17] In response, the Council mandated the Secretary-General to take custody of a copy of the population register of Kuwait, "the authenticity of which has been certified by the legitimate Government of Kuwait". The following day, the Minister for Foreign Affairs of Kuwait gave to the Secretary-General 32 computer tapes containing the official population register of Kuwait as of 1 August 1990. Under the provisions of resolution 674 (1990), the Secretary-General was to establish, in cooperation with the legitimate Government of Kuwait, an Order of Rules and Regulations governing access to and use of this register.

17/Document 18
See page 177

Authorization to use "all necessary means"

59   Convinced of the need to apply even greater pressure on Iraq and determined to secure full compliance with its decisions, the Security Council convened again at the ministerial level on 29 November 1990 and took a decision my predecessor subsequently described as one of "immense portent". Acting under Chapter VII of the Charter, the Council adopted resolution 678 (1990), which contained a clear choice for Iraq. Under paragraph 1, the Council decided to allow Iraq "one final opportunity, as a pause of goodwill", to fully implement on or before 15 January 1991 Security Council resolution 660 (1990) and all subsequent relevant resolutions.[18] Should Iraq fail to do so, said the Council in paragraph 2, the Member States cooperating with the Government of Kuwait were authorized "to use all necessary means"—words understood to mean military force—to uphold and implement the resolutions and to "restore international peace and security in the area".

18/Document 19
See page 178

60   The vote on resolution 678 (1990)—12 in favour, 2 against (Cuba, Yemen) and 1 abstention (China)—represented only the fourth time in United Nations history that the Security Council had decided to authorize Member States to use military force. The first was in 1950, in response to the situation on the Korean peninsula. The second was declared in resolution 221 (1966), in which the Council authorized the United Kingdom to intercept tankers carrying oil to Southern Rhodesia. And the third was the Council's authorization in resolution 665 (1990) of measures to enforce the sanctions imposed on Iraq and occupied Kuwait.

61 Speaking after the vote, the United States said, "Today's resolution is very clear. The words authorize the use of force." (S/PV.2963). The Soviet Union said the text was "one last sincere attempt to give common sense a chance to prevail", but cautioned that there should not be "any mistake about the collective will of the international community as expressed here, or about its resolve and its readiness to act." France said that if Iraq chose to remain "locked into the use of force", the Security Council had no other choice "but to resort to this same means, which would appear to be the only one it recognizes". The United Kingdom said the resolution went "the last mile in search of peace" and that "the military option is reality, not bluff".

62 China, in explanation of its abstention from voting, said that it was neither in favour, because the resolution permitted the use of military action, nor against, since China supported the call for Iraqi compliance with relevant Security Council resolutions. Both Yemen and Cuba, opposing the resolution, objected to the Council's authorization of military action that would not be subject to the command or control of the United Nations.

Diplomatic efforts prior to 15 January 1991

63 The 45-day period between the adoption of Security Council resolution 678 (1990) and the deadline for Iraqi compliance saw a number of initiatives aimed at averting an outbreak of war. Among them were a plan (S/21986) submitted by four non-permanent members of the Security Council (Colombia, Cuba, Malaysia and Yemen), separate initiatives by the Movement of the Non-Aligned Countries, the League of Arab States and the European Community, and a French proposal for an international conference addressing all outstanding questions relating to the Middle East. However, these plans lacked sufficient international support to serve as viable solutions to the crisis.

64 On 9 January 1991, the United States Secretary of State and Iraq's Deputy Prime Minister and Minister for Foreign Affairs held six hours of talks in Geneva. The meeting did not make any headway and my predecessor's subsequent mission to Iraq in the days that followed was carried out amid dim prospects for a diplomatic breakthrough. To gain support for his initiative, Mr. Pérez de Cuéllar first held discussions with

United States President Bush, the representative of the Non-Aligned Movement, and members of the European Community before flying to Baghdad. Meeting with Minister Aziz on 12 January and with President Hussein on 13 January, the Secretary-General urged full compliance with the relevant Security Council resolutions. President Hussein reiterated his country's positions on various issues, including its claims to Kuwait and its call for "an Arab solution" to the crisis, and reaffirmed the linkage Iraq had made between the Iraq-Kuwait situation and other Middle East questions. Returning to New York just before the 15 January deadline, the Secretary-General stated that the talks in Iraq had been "polite but, unfortunately, unsuccessful".

65   On 15 January 1991, the international coalition arrayed in the Gulf included approximately 680,000 troops, of which some 410,000 were from the United States. Estimates of the number of Iraqi troops in occupied Kuwait ranged from 300,000 to 600,000. However, because of differing norms for calculating the composition of Iraqi divisions, such estimates were not verifiable.

66   In a statement that day, the Secretary-General noted that "the world stands poised between peace and war", and he appealed to President Hussein "to turn the course of events away from catastrophe and towards a new era of justice and harmony based on the principles of the Charter of the United Nations".[19] The Secretary-General also said that if Iraq signified its readiness to comply with the Security Council's resolutions and took clear and substantial steps to implement them, a "just peace" would follow.

19/Document 21
See page 179

67   The Secretary-General further stated that with the commencement of an Iraqi troop withdrawal he would be prepared, with the consent of the parties concerned and the agreement of the Security Council, to deploy United Nations observers and, if necessary, United Nations forces to certify Iraq's withdrawal; urge the Security Council to review its decisions imposing sanctions against Iraq; and encourage a process whereby foreign forces deployed in the area would be phased out. He also indicated, based on assurances he had received from various Governments involved, that with a settlement of the Iraq-Kuwait crisis every effort would be made to address, in a comprehensive manner, the Arab-Israeli conflict, including the Palestinian question. "No one", said the Secretary-General, "and no nation can—except with a heavy heart—resort to the other 'necessary means' implied by resolution 678 (1990), knowing in advance that tragic and unpredictable consequences can follow."

IV Coalition action

68   The campaign of aerial bombardment launched by the international coalition against Iraq on 16 January 1991, followed by a ground offensive into Kuwait and south-eastern Iraq commencing on 24 February, achieved the goal of ousting Iraqi forces from Kuwait and reinstating the legitimate Government of Kuwait. Iraq's agreement on 27 February to comply fully with all relevant Security Council resolutions led the coalition to suspend its military operations and created the long-sought opportunity to restore international peace and security to the region.

Air campaign

69   On the evening of 16 January 1991, President George Bush of the United States telephoned the Secretary-General of the United Nations to express appreciation for the latter's efforts in seeking to find a peaceful solution to the Iraq-Kuwait crisis and to inform him that United States fighter aircraft would soon move into action against Iraqi targets in both Iraq and Kuwait. In a televised address that same evening, the President stated that the countries with forces in the Gulf area had "exhausted all reasonable efforts to reach a peaceful resolution" and had no choice but to drive Iraq from Kuwait by force. "When peace is restored", said President Bush, "it is our hope that Iraq will live as a peaceful and cooperative member of the family of nations, thus enhancing the security and stability of the Gulf".

70   The United States reported the launching of the military offensive against Iraq to the President of the Security Council in a letter dated 17 January (S/22090), stating that further delay would only have prolonged the suffering of the Kuwaiti people and increased the risks to the coalition military forces. The purpose of the actions, said the United States, was the liberation of Kuwait, not the destruction, occupation or dismemberment of Iraq, and every effort would be made to minimize civilian casualties. Kuwait wrote to the President of the Security Council on 17 January, informing him that, with the expiry of the deadline set by the Council in resolution 678 (1990) and Iraq's continuing occupation of Kuwait, Kuwait was exercising its right of self-defence and that Kuwaiti forces were cooperating with the forces of "fraternal and friendly States which are equally determined" to end the Iraqi occupation.[20] Other States, including Egypt, France, Italy, Saudi Arabia and the

20/Document 22
See page 180

United Kingdom, likewise reported having taken military action. (See "Other documents of interest", page 157, for a list of communications from Member States taking part in the implementation of resolution 678 (1990).)

71 During the roughly six weeks of the air campaign, the international military coalition targeted Iraq's air defence system, communications infrastructure, electricity-delivery grid, military production and storage facilities and the bridges and supply lines running between the northern and southern parts of Iraq. With these damaged, disrupted or destroyed, coalition forces isolated the Kuwaiti theatre of operations and effectively achieved control of the airspace over Iraq and Kuwait. However, Iraq launched dozens of surface-to-surface missiles over the course of the Gulf war, mostly against Saudi Arabia and Israel, but also against Bahrain and Qatar.

Further diplomatic efforts

72 On 22 January 1991, Mr. Pérez de Cuéllar reiterated his 15 January appeal to Iraq to comply with the relevant resolutions of the Security Council (SG/SM/4537). In a letter, dated 30 January, to the Deputy Prime Minister and Minister for Foreign Affairs of Iraq he urged that the Iraqi Government make "a serious effort to put this tragic situation on the road to a peaceful solution" (S/22172).

73 As the air campaign continued, the Security Council held almost continual informal consultations. States of the Arab Maghreb Union—Algeria, the Libyan Arab Jamahiriya, Mauritania, Morocco and Tunisia—as well as Yemen and Cuba, requested an urgent session of the Security Council to consider options other than the military action being taken against Iraq, but some Council members, including coalition leaders, opposed such a move. On 13 February 1991, the Council adopted a compromise proposal put forth by the United Kingdom under which the Council would discuss the matter in formal but private meetings.

74 The private meetings, held on 14, 15, 16, 23 and 25 February and on 2 March, marked the first time the Security Council had met in private on a substantive issue since 1975, when it convened to consider the situation in Western Sahara. No formal action was taken at any of the 1991 meetings, although Cuba submitted three draft resolutions, one of which called for the immediate dispatch of a United Nations military observer mission to supervise the suspension of offensive combat operations and for the deployment of a peace-keeping force in the area. A communiqué issued after the private sessions indicated that all Council

members, Kuwait, Iraq, other Member States and the Secretary-General had spoken at the session.

75   On 15 February, Iraq informed the Council of its "readiness to deal on the basis of Security Council resolution 660 (1990) with a view to reaching an honourable and acceptable political solution", including withdrawal from Kuwait (S/22229). That readiness was linked, however, to a complete and comprehensive cease-fire; to a retroactive annulment of the remaining 11 Council resolutions on the situation between Iraq and Kuwait; to a withdrawal from the Middle East of forces "participating in the aggression"; to Israel's withdrawal from Palestine and other occupied Arab territories; to a guarantee of Iraq's "full and undiminished historical territorial and maritime rights in any political solution"; and to a political arrangement to be agreed upon based on "the will of the people in accordance with genuine democratic practice".

76   On 18 February, Soviet President Mikhail Gorbachev and Iraq's Deputy Prime Minister and Minister for Foreign Affairs discussed in Moscow a Soviet peace proposal aimed at achieving Iraq's withdrawal from Kuwait in conjunction with lifting all sanctions and constraints imposed by the Security Council against Iraq. Although the Soviet Union addressed letters to the Security Council and to the Secretary-General stating that on the basis of the Soviet plan, Iraq was prepared to withdraw all its forces from Kuwait immediately and unconditionally, the plan failed to gain wider support, mainly because of disagreements over the timing of its various elements (S/22241, S/22265).

Ground offensive and suspension of hostilities

77   At 4 a.m. local time on 24 February, coalition forces launched ground operations, moving hundreds of tanks and tens of thousands of troops from positions in Saudi Arabia into Iraq and Kuwait. That day, Iraq informed the Security Council that it endorsed the Soviet peace initiative (S/22262). The President of the Security Council, following consultations on 25, 26 and 27 February, indicated that many Council members wanted from Iraq a clear, formal and written acceptance of all resolutions.

78   Coalition forces, attacking on several fronts in a combined surface, naval and air offensive, met little resistance from Iraqi forces and succeeded in liberating Kuwait on 27 February. That day, at 9 p.m. Eastern Standard Time (EST), the United States announced that the coalition, its forces by then arrayed throughout Kuwait as well as in south-eastern parts of Iraq, would suspend offensive combat operations as of midnight, EST. "This war is now behind us", said United States

President Bush. "Ahead of us is the difficult task of securing a potentially historic peace." With Iraq's military routed from Kuwait, the Security Council awaited Iraq's diplomatic response.

79   On 27 February, Iraq informed the Security Council that it would comply fully with resolution 660 (1990) and, subject to some conditions, with resolutions 662 (1990)—demanding rescission of Iraq's actions purporting to annex Kuwait—and 674 (1990)—demanding that Iraq ensure the protection and well-being of Kuwaiti and third-State nationals, including diplomatic and consular personnel, being held hostage in Iraq and Kuwait (S/22273). Iraq also said that its armed forces had started to withdraw to the positions they had held prior to 1 August 1990, and promised to release all prisoners of war immediately after a cease-fire was concluded. Later on 27 February, Iraq informed the Council and the Secretary-General that all Iraqi forces had withdrawn from Kuwait, adding that "American and other pro-aggressor forces" were continuing to attack Iraqi forces during their withdrawal.[21]

21/Document 24
See page 181

80   Offensive combat operations were suspended as scheduled at midnight on 27-28 February. "We hope", said my predecessor the morning of 28 February, "it is the beginning of the end of this terrible tragedy." Later that day, by identical letters to the President of the Security Council and the Secretary-General, Iraq stated officially that it agreed to comply fully with Security Council resolution 660 (1990) and all the other Council resolutions.[22] With this notification, the Council embarked on a month of intensive diplomatic consultations on the terms of a permanent cease-fire and other post-war arrangements. On 4 March, Kuwait informed the Secretary-General that its Government was resuming the functions of State and directing the nation's affairs from Kuwait City.[23]

22/Document 25
See page 181

23/Document 29
See page 185

V   Resolution 687 (1991)

81   Security Council resolution 687 (1991) represents one of the most complex and far-reaching sets of decisions ever taken by the Council. The longest text ever adopted by the Council, it sought to involve Iraq cooperatively in post-war measures to build lasting peace and stability in the region. At the same time, enforcement measures remained in effect, including the sanctions regime and the Council's authorization to Member States to use "all necessary means" to uphold Iraqi compliance. Implementation of resolution 687 (1991) sent the United Nations into uncharted territory in many areas, among them the Organization's work in demarcating the international boundary between Kuwait and Iraq, its collaboration with the IAEA in the nuclear area, its administration of a compensation fund and the use by the Security Council of subsidiary bodies such as the Special Commission (UNSCOM) and the Sanctions Committee. Not long after taking office as Secretary-General in January 1992, I met with the Deputy Prime Minister of Iraq and stressed the importance I attach to full implementation of all the provisions of resolution 687 (1991).

Resolution 686 (1991)

82   The path to resolution 687 (1991) began with the adoption of resolution 686 (1991), which brought a provisional end to hostilities.[24] Adopted on 2 March 1991 by a vote of 11 in favour, 1 against (Cuba) and 3 abstentions (China, India, Yemen), resolution 686 (1991) reaffirmed that all 12 resolutions concerning the Iraq-Kuwait situation continued to have "full force and effect" and set out a number of obligations for immediate implementation by Iraq.

24/Document 26
See page 182

83   In resolution 686 (1991), the Security Council demanded in particular that Iraq rescind its actions purporting to annex Kuwait; accept its liability for loss, damage or injury arising from its invasion and occupation of Kuwait; release all detainees and return the remains of any deceased detainees; return all Kuwaiti property; cease hostile or provocative actions by its forces against all Member States; release all prisoners of war under the auspices of the International Committee of the Red Cross (ICRC); and assist the coalition in identifying the location of Iraqi mines, booby traps and other explosives as well as any chemical and biological weapons and material in Kuwait and in areas of Iraq where coalition forces were present, and in the adjacent waters. In resolution 686 (1991), the Council affirmed that all preceding 12 resolutions on the Iraq-Kuwait crisis continued to have full force and effect, and, in paragraph 4, explicitly recognized that during the period required for Iraq to comply with the resolution's demands, the provisions of resolution 678 (1990) authorizing Member States to use "all necessary means" would "remain valid".

84   Before voting to adopt resolution 686 (1991), the Security Council rejected 17 amendments put forward by Cuba which proposed, among other things, declaring an immediate cease-fire without preconditions and deleting all references to the "all necessary means" provisions of resolution 678 (1990) (S/PV.2978).

85   On 3 March 1991, in identical letters to the President of the Security Council and the Secretary-General, Iraq agreed to fulfil its obligations under resolution 686 (1991).[25] Two days later, again in identical letters to the Council President and the Secretary-General, Iraq stated that it had decided to return Kuwaiti gold, paper currency, museum objects and civilian aircraft seized during the occupation (S/22330). Also on 5 March, the Revolution Command Council of Iraq decided that all decisions regarding Kuwait taken subsequent to 2 August 1990 were "null and void"; this decision was published in the Official Gazette of Iraq on 18 March.[26]

86   With Iraq's implementation of resolution 686 (1991) under way, the members of the Security Council began consultations aimed at agreeing on a resolution setting the terms for a definitive cease-fire. The Council's five permanent members, in their statements following the vote, agreed that resolution 686 charted the course for this work, that the United Nations faced a prodigious undertaking in shouldering its post-conflict responsibilities and that the international community had entered the most difficult and most important phase of the crisis.

Adoption of resolution 687 (1991)

87   Resolution 687 (1991), drafted during the month of negotiations following the successful liberation of Kuwait, and adopted on 3 April 1991, was the fourteenth adopted by the Security Council in response to Iraq's invasion.[27] Sponsored by Belgium, France, Romania, the United Kingdom, the United States and Zaire, the text received 12 votes in favour, 1 against (Cuba) and 2 abstentions (Ecuador, Yemen).

88   In the resolution's 26 preambular paragraphs, the Security Council welcomed the restoration to Kuwait of its sovereignty, independence and territorial integrity and the return of its legitimate Government; restated the Council's objective of restoring international peace and security to the region; stressed the importance of various interna-

25/Document 27
See page 183

26/Document 30
See page 185

27/Document 35
See page 193

tional agreements, to which Iraq was a party, covering conventional and nuclear weapons; and expressed grave concern about the humanitarian situation in both Kuwait and Iraq.

89   The 34 operative paragraphs of the resolution were divided into nine parts and set out in great detail the terms for a formal cease-fire to end the conflict and restore security and stability to the area. These requirements are as follows:

90   **Boundary settlement.** In section A of resolution 687 (1991), the Security Council demanded that Iraq and Kuwait respect the inviolability of the international boundary and the allocation of islands set out in the Agreed Minutes of 1963[28] and called upon the Secretary-General of the United Nations to assist in the demarcation of that boundary. The Council also decided to guarantee the inviolability of the international boundary and to take, as appropriate, all necessary measures to that end in accordance with the Charter.

28/Document 4
See page 166

91   **Peace-keeping.** Under section B, the Council requested the Secretary-General to submit a plan for the immediate deployment of a United Nations observer unit to monitor the Khawr 'Abd Allah waterway in the Persian Gulf and a demilitarized zone (DMZ), established under the resolution, extending 10 kilometres into Iraq and 5 kilometres into Kuwait from the boundary referred in the Agreed Minutes.[29] Once the observers were deployed, said the Council, the conditions would be established for the Member States cooperating with Kuwait to "bring their military presence in Iraq to an end consistent with resolution 686 (1991)".

29/Document 4
See page 166

92   **Weapons of mass destruction.** Under section C, the Security Council decreed that Iraq was to eliminate, under international supervision, its chemical and biological weapons stockpiles and its ballistic missiles with a range greater than 150 kilometres. Iraq was to submit to the Secretary-General, within 15 days of the resolution's adoption, a declaration of the locations, amounts and types of such weapons, and the Secretary-General was to develop a plan for creating a special commission to carry out immediate on-site inspections in order to take possession of these weapons and supervise their destruction. The Council further asked the Secretary-General to develop, in consultation with the Special Commission, a plan for the future ongoing monitoring and verification of Iraq's compliance with the ban on these weapons and missiles.

93   **Nuclear-weapon capability.** Also under section C of resolution 687 (1991), the Council decided that Iraq would undertake unconditionally not to acquire or develop nuclear weapons or nuclear-weapons-usable material as well as any subsystems or components or any research, development, support or manufacturing facilities. Iraq was to submit to the Secretary-General and the Director General of

the International Atomic Energy Agency, within 15 days of the resolution's adoption, a declaration of the locations, amounts and types of such items. Based on this declaration, the Director General of the IAEA, through the Secretary-General and with the assistance of the Special Commission, was requested to carry out immediate on-site inspection of Iraq's nuclear capabilities and to develop a plan for the destruction, removal or rendering harmless of all prohibited items. The Secretary-General, the Director General of the IAEA and the Special Commission were also requested to develop a plan, taking into account the rights and obligations of Iraq as a State party to the Treaty on the Non-Proliferation of Nuclear Weapons (1968), for the future ongoing monitoring and verification of Iraq's compliance with the nuclear ban imposed by the resolution.

94   **Kuwaiti property.** In section D, the Council requested the Secretary-General to report to it on the steps taken to facilitate the return of all Kuwaiti property seized by Iraq.

95   **Compensation Fund.** The Security Council in section E of resolution 687 (1991) reaffirmed Iraq's liability under international law for any direct loss, damage (including environmental damage and the depletion of natural resources) or injury to foreign Governments, nationals and corporations as a result of its unlawful invasion and occupation of Kuwait and decided to create a fund to pay compensation for relevant claims. The fund was to be financed from a portion of Iraq's petroleum export revenues. The Council asked the Secretary-General to develop recommendations for setting up the fund as well as a commission to administer it, and to recommend mechanisms for determining the appropriate level of Iraq's contribution to the fund, taking into account the humanitarian needs of the Iraqi people and Iraq's payment capacity. Also in section E of the resolution, the Council demanded that Iraq "adhere scrupulously" to its foreign debt obligations.

96   **Oil and arms embargoes and sanctions against exports to Iraq.** Under section F, the Security Council decided that the sanctions first imposed under resolution 661 (1990) against exports to Iraq would not apply to foodstuffs and to materials and supplies for essential civilian needs, and that it would review this part of the sanctions regime every 60 days, taking into account the policies and practices of the Government of Iraq, including the implementation of all relevant resolutions of the Council, for the purpose of determining whether to reduce or lift the prohibitions. The Council also stated that the ban on Iraqi oil exports would be lifted once the Council approved the programme for the Compensation Fund called for in section E, and once it agreed that Iraq had completed all the actions pertaining to the weapons provisions of resolution 687 (1991). In the mean time, exceptions to the oil embargo would be approved by the Sanctions Committee when needed to assure

adequate financial resources to provide for essential civilian needs in Iraq. Also in section F, the Council specified the categories of weapons to which the arms embargo mandated by resolution 661 (1990) should continue to apply. The provisions relating to both the oil and the arms embargoes would be reviewed by the Council every 120 days, taking into account Iraq's compliance with the resolution and the general progress towards the control of armaments in the region.

97   **Repatriation.** Under section G, Iraq was called upon to extend all necessary cooperation to the International Committee of the Red Cross (ICRC) to facilitate the repatriation of all Kuwaiti and third-State nationals.

98   **Terrorism.** Section H required Iraq to inform the Council that it would not commit or support any act of international terrorism.

99   **Acceptance and cease-fire.** Under section I, the Council declared that a formal cease-fire between Iraq, Kuwait and the countries cooperating with Kuwait would come into effect once Iraq had officially notified the Secretary-General and the Council of its acceptance of the provisions of the resolution.

100   In deciding upon these and other measures in resolution 687 (1991), the Security Council acted under Chapter VII of the Charter of the United Nations, which sets out the various measures the Council may take in response to threats to the peace, breaches of the peace and acts of aggression, such as the imposition of sanctions and the use of military force. The Council, in paragraph 1 of resolution 687 (1991), affirmed that all previous resolutions relating to the crisis continued in force, except as expressly changed in resolution 687 (1991) itself. Thus the provisions of resolution 678 (1990) authorizing Member States to use "all necessary means to uphold and implement" relevant Council resolutions "and to restore international peace and security to the area" remained in force.

Statements in the Council

101   Statements in the Security Council on 3 April 1991 reflected the momentous nature of the resolution and of the broader circumstances surrounding its adoption (S/PV.2981).

102   The Permanent Representative of the United States to the United Nations stated: "This resolution is unique and historic. It fulfils the hope of mankind to make the United Nations an instrument of peace and stability . . . It establishes clear incentives for rapid implementation and trade-offs which will in stages produce a return to normalcy and non-belligerency in the Gulf . . . This is a time of testing for the United Nations and a time of destiny as well. The international community

acted through the United Nations to bring an end to aggression and lawlessness. It must now act as well to restore international peace and security."

103 The Permanent Representative of the Soviet Union stated: "The Kuwait crisis and the process of eliminating it were a serious test of the soundness of the new thinking, the new system of international relations. I think we can state with some gratification today that the international community, in the person of the United Nations and its Security Council, has passed that test and demonstrated that a considerable path has been travelled between the cold war and the new system of international relations. The Security Council has proved in practice its ability to implement its obligation under the Charter of the United Nations to maintain and restore international peace and security."

104 The Permanent Representative of the United Kingdom said that "the expulsion of Iraq from Kuwait and the latter's liberation are of far greater and of far more positive significance for all countries in the world, and for this Organization as a whole, than the many regional conflicts with which we have tried to grapple over recent decades. They have marked a clear, firm and effective determination of the world community not to allow the law of the jungle to overcome the rule of law. They have shown that the Security Council, with not only the solidarity of its permanent members but also supporting votes from countries representing every region of the world, has been able to act to repel aggression in the way its founding fathers intended it to do."

105 The Permanent Representative of China emphasized the importance of an "early realization of a formal cease-fire" as a main factor in his country's affirmative vote. France, said its Permanent Representative, viewed as essential the provisions of resolution 687 (1991) which were aimed at contributing "in the longer term to re-establishing regional security", and stressed that the "heavy responsibilities" entrusted to the Secretary-General and the United Nations responded to France's "desire to see our Organization play an important role in re-establishing peace in the region." Both China and France, in their statements of support for the resolution, also drew attention to the plight of the civilian population in Iraq.

106 Kuwait said that the liberation of Kuwait proved that the United Nations, with its Security Council, "is an effective instrument for collective security and the maintenance of world peace and security". Iraq stated that the "destruction wreaked upon Iraq by the United States and its partners went beyond the limits and the objectives of resolution 678 (1990)", and that the maintenance of economic sanctions against Iraq was in contravention of the Charter.

107 The provisions of resolution 687 (1991) calling on the United Nations to demarcate the Iraq-Kuwait boundary were among the reasons cited by Cuba for its vote against the resolution, and by Ecuador and Yemen for their abstentions. Each contended that the Security Council lacked authority under the Charter to undertake a role that rightfully should either be exercised by the parties themselves or, with their agreement, be brought before the International Court of Justice. In addition, these three States questioned the legality of maintaining the sanctions regime which, Cuba and Yemen stated, had been explicitly tied by resolution 661 (1990) to achieving Iraq's withdrawal from Kuwait. Cuba and Yemen further rejected the provisions of resolution 687 (1991) concerning compensation, on the grounds that determining reparations fell within the exclusive purview of the International Court of Justice under the provisions of Article 36 of its Statute.

108   Among other countries addressing the Council, India stated that its attitude throughout the crisis was governed by two basic considerations: "to bring about the speediest possible liberation of Kuwait, and to minimize, to the maximum extent possible, the loss of life and the human suffering in all the countries directly involved in the crisis". Côte d'Ivoire said, "Throughout this crisis Côte d'Ivoire would have wished war to be avoided. Unfortunately, we had to wage war. The Council was obliged to ensure that law would prevail. It now remains for the Council to ensure that peace will prevail throughout the region."

Acceptance of resolution 687 (1991)

109   In identical letters dated 6 April 1991 addressed to the Secretary-General and to the President of the Security Council, Iraq's Deputy Prime Minister and Minister for Foreign Affairs criticized the text of resolution 687 (1991), calling it "unjust" and alleging that it contained "iniquitous and vengeful measures" and constituted "an unprecedented assault" on the sovereignty and rights of his country.[30] The United Nations, he claimed, was employing harsh and extensive measures to bring about Iraq's compliance with the Council's resolutions while other countries experienced little or no such pressure *vis-à-vis* resolutions pertaining to their actions, and he accused the Organization of applying a "double standard" to Iraq in the form of "criteria of duality" in international relations. None the less, the Minister stated, Iraq had no choice but to accept the resolution's provisions. In a letter dated 10 April, Iraq transmitted the text of a decision taken by the Iraqi National Assembly on 6 April formally accepting resolution 687 (1991).[31]

110   On 11 April 1991, the President of the Security Council, on behalf of its members, formally acknowledged receipt of Iraq's letter. Noting that Iraq's acceptance of resolution 687 (1991) was "irrevocable

30/Document 39
See page 203

31/Document 41
See page 207

32/Document 42
See page 207

33/Document 36
See page 198

and without qualifying conditions", the Council President added that, this precondition having been met, the formal cease-fire was therefore in effect.[32] Kuwait had accepted the provisions of resolution 687 (1991) on 4 April.[33]

Post-war situation in Iraq and Kuwait

34/Document 33
See page 189

111 One month after the suspension of hostilities, in a letter dated 27 March 1991, Mr. Pérez de Cuéllar wrote to the Secretary of State for External Affairs of Canada, who had reported to my predecessor on his recent visit to the Middle East region, of how important it was in his view that the United Nations actively participate in reconstruction and rehabilitation efforts in the Gulf region.[34] He stressed that this was necessary in order not only to deal with the immediate consequences of the hostilities, but also to retain the trust of all the peoples of the world, whom the Organization is meant to serve. Consequently, in the immediate post-war period, the Secretary-General dispatched a series of United Nations inter-agency missions to Iraq and Kuwait in order to document the immense suffering and damage caused by the invasion and its consequences and to assess the two countries' needs in terms of both emergency assistance and longer-term reconstruction. The findings of these missions provided a comprehensive basis upon which the United Nations mobilized a major international response to an enormous humanitarian crisis.

Report on humanitarian needs in Iraq

112 On 1 March 1991, my predecessor announced his decision to dispatch the Under-Secretary-General for Administration and Management on a short mission to Iraq and Kuwait to report on the various actions that the United Nations could take to provide help to those urgently in need. "Every effort must be made", said the Secretary-General, "to avoid further human suffering and to prevent catastrophes from occurring, notably in the fields of health and nutrition" (SG/SM/4548-IK/2).

113 The mission, which also included representatives of UNDP, UNDRO, UNHCR, UNICEF, WHO and FAO, visited Iraq from 10 to 17 March 1991 with a mandate to determine the extent of needs in the primary areas of humanitarian concern—safe water and sanitation, basic health and medical support, food and shelter. In its report of 20 March 1991, the mission stated that virtually all of Iraq's power plants, oil refineries, oil storage facilities and other previously viable sources of fuel and power had been rendered inoperative by the war.[35] Water-treatment stations had ceased to function, and raw sewage was being dumped

35/Document 31
See page 186

directly into the Tigris River, the source of much of the nation's water supply. The lack of fuel to pump irrigation water and drive agricultural equipment threatened the June 1991 harvest. The refrigeration and transport of food were impeded, contributing to a sharp reduction in food supplies and boosting prices beyond the purchasing reach of most families. The distribution of medical supplies was similarly disrupted. Approximately 90 per cent of industrial workers had been reduced to inactivity and, by the end of March, were expected to be deprived of income.

114   The mission recommended, among other things, that international sanctions not be applied to food supplies, agricultural equipment and supplies such as fertilizers, pesticides and veterinary drugs. It also called for the urgent provision of essential drugs and vaccines, fuel and spare parts for the sewage disposal system as well as a variety of items to ensure a minimum quantity of safe water through the hot season from April to September. However, said the report, it would be "difficult, if not impossible, to remedy these immediate humanitarian needs" without emergency oil imports and the rapid patching up of a limited refining and electricity production capacity, with essential supplies from other countries. Otherwise, the report concluded, the Iraqi people could soon face a "further imminent catastrophe".

115   The Sanctions Committee carefully considered the mission's report, as well as an ICRC report dated 19 March. On 22 March, pursuant to resolution 666 (1990), which empowers the Committee to determine that there is "an urgent humanitarian need to supply foodstuffs" to Iraq or Kuwait in order to relieve human suffering, the Committee decided to make "a general determination" that such humanitarian circumstances applied "with respect to the entire civilian population of Iraq in all parts of Iraq's national territory".[36] The Committee also concluded that the imports identified in the Under-Secretary-General's report were to be allowed with immediate effect—the first relaxation of the sanctions for humanitarian purposes prior to the adoption of resolution 687 (1991).

36/Document 13
See page 172;
Document 32
See page 188

Report on humanitarian needs in Kuwait

116   The inter-agency mission to Kuwait, undertaken from 23 to 27 March 1991, saw "prolific evidence of arson, looting, malicious destruction of homes, businesses, markets, museums, libraries and all that a nation cherishes".[37] Some 600 to 700 oil wells, torched in what the report called "a final deliberate onslaught by retreating troops", remained on fire, belching flames and smoke and generating potentially injurious effects on the health, environments and economies of Kuwait and other countries in the area. Power stations, oil refineries and pipelines, communications facilities and water-desalination plants had been

37/Document 34
See page 190

destroyed by war or vandalized to such a degree that they were irreparable. Medical equipment, including ambulances, had been removed, and mainframe computers had been ripped out of government offices and carried off. Enormous quantities of unexploded mines and other ordnance had been left behind, posing a hazard to the resumption of normal life.

117 The mission was able to say of Kuwait that much had already been done since the liberation to deal with the immediate needs of the population. Water was available and supplies were returning to normal, although it remained necessary to monitor water quality given the uncertain environmental conditions. The country's three major sanitation plants required only superficial repairs. Large amounts of imported food were being distributed, although some logistical bottlenecks were occurring and the spread of oil across the land towards the sea, as well as the heavy mining of the coast, were thought to have bleak implications for the future of the domestic agricultural and fishing industries. Kuwaiti medical, surgical and dental facilities were handling the most urgent needs, but a very large number of medical personnel had left Kuwait as a result of the invasion, leaving a critical post-war shortage of nursing and technical staff, and many hospitals, clinics and health centres had closed down or were operating at reduced capacity.

Report on damage to Kuwait

118 On 27 February 1991, the Government of Kuwait requested that a mission be dispatched to assess the loss of life incurred during the Iraqi occupation, examine the practices by the Iraqi occupation forces carried out against the civilian population in Kuwait and assess the damage inflicted on the general infrastructure in the country. With the concurrence of the Security Council, my predecessor decided to send a high-level mission led by a former Under-Secretary-General and including representatives and technical advisors from UNESCO, UNICEF, WHO, the United Nations Environment Programme (UNEP), the Centre for Human Rights and the Departments of International Economic and Social Affairs and of Technical Cooperation for Development in the United Nations Secretariat.

119 The mission visited Kuwait from 16 March to 4 April 1991. According to its report, conservative estimates of overall losses amounted to at least $30 billion—more than Kuwait's gross domestic product for 1989.[38] This total included $10 billion in lost economic output for the period of the occupation and $5 billion for the rehabilitation of Kuwait's petroleum industry. Major damage was also sustained by Kuwait's ports, national airport, electricity-generating systems, petrochemical and other industrial facilities, satellite system, telephone/telecommunications network, media installations and cultural sites. The

38/Document 45
See page 212

country's road transport fleet had been reduced by half, with nearly 300,000 buses, trucks and other vehicles either destroyed or removed to Iraq. Some 170,000 households had been ransacked or vandalized, with losses totalling approximately $2.5 billion. Repair of government buildings and other urban infrastructure was expected to cost at least $500 million. The financial system was severely disrupted, foreign trade suspended, manufacturing paralysed and inventories plundered.

120   The deliberate torching of the oilfields, said the report, represented Kuwait's most pressing problem in the environmental sector. (For more on the environment, see paragraphs 203-210.) In the area of education, virtually every facility, public and private, had been partly destroyed. In libraries and other institutions—such as the Central State Library, the Kuwait Institute for Scientific Research and the Department of Arab Heritage of the National Council for Culture, Arts and Literature—collections containing several hundred thousand volumes, periodicals, papers, technical reports, recordings, computer databases, antiquities and other artifacts had been looted, burned, destroyed by what the report described as "malicious water damage" or reduced to litter. The impact of these and other unquantifiable losses, said the report, such as the "irreplaceable school year lost to all students", would be felt by Kuwait "for generations to come."

Report on Iraqi practices during the occupation

121   The mission reported separately on the human rights abuses that were said to have occurred during the period of occupation.[39] The mission met with representatives of professional associations, neighbourhood cooperatives, members of the diplomatic community and representatives of expatriate national groups, and had extensive contacts with the Kuwaiti Red Crescent Society, the Kuwaiti Human Rights Committee and the Kuwaiti Association for the Defence of War Victims. Among the practices alleged against Iraq were various violations of the Fourth Geneva Convention, including ill-treatment of detainees, arbitrary arrest and/or detention, deportation and collective punishment. Widespread arrests and the use of torture were reported to have occurred in an attempt to extract information on the Kuwaiti resistance network. In the last week of the occupation, beginning on 21 February 1991, several thousand civilians were said to have been indiscriminately picked up from outside their homes, mosques and other public places and taken to Iraq. The mission, in its report, stated that interviews with various Kuwaiti individuals and groups conducted during the mission tended to suggest that the incidence of violent death, including a number of summary executions, was relatively high, with responsibility attributed to the activities of two Iraqi intelligence bodies and elements of Iraq's army.

122   Reports of these and other abuses circulating well before the

39/Document 46
See page 229

mission to Kuwait had led the General Assembly, in December 1990, to condemn the Iraqi authorities and occupying forces for "their serious violations of human rights against the Kuwaiti people and third-State nationals" and to express its "serious concern" about "the systematic dismantling and pillaging of and attacks on the economic infrastructure of Kuwait".[40] In March 1991, the Commission on Human Rights decided to appoint a Special Rapporteur to study the situation of human rights in occupied Kuwait and another Special Rapporteur to study the situation of human rights in Iraq (Resolutions 1991/67, 1991/74). The Assembly, in December 1991, endorsed the Commission's actions.[41] (See paragraphs 333-340 for more details on the activities and findings of the two Special Rapporteurs.)

40/Document 20
See page 178

41/Document 96
See page 370;
Document 97
See page 371

Adoption of resolution 688 (1991)

123   The decision of the Commission on Human Rights to appoint a Special Rapporteur for Iraq stemmed in part from a wave of unrest that struck the north and south of the country immediately after the multinational coalition suspended its military operations. By early April 1991, the fighting had triggered a vast humanitarian calamity, with an estimated 1.5 million Iraqi citizens, mostly Kurds, fleeing towards and across bleak mountain borders with Turkey and the Islamic Republic of Iran.

124   At the request of France and Turkey, which considered these developments to be a threat to international peace and security in the region, the Security Council met on 5 April 1991. Of the 31 Member States which spoke at the meeting, the majority viewed with alarm the magnitude of the human suffering, the massive exodus of Iraqi civilians and the Government's treatment of its own citizens (S/PV.2982). Turkey stated that Iraq's armed forces, in their attempt to quell the two insurgencies, were indiscriminately using deadly fire-power. The Islamic Republic of Iran stated that the horrifying accounts of those who had crossed into that country pointed to the Iraqi military's indiscriminate methods and use of unconventional weapons. Iraq, for its part, stated that it had firm evidence of attempts by some neighbouring States to foment dissent through saboteurs throughout Iraq, thereby to destabilize the country and perhaps even to partition it into mini-States.

125   As a result of its deliberations, the Security Council that day adopted resolution 688 (1991), in which it demanded that Iraq end the repression of the Iraqi civilian population, "including most recently in Kurdish-populated areas", and allow immediate access by international humanitarian organizations to all those in need of assistance.[42] Resolution 688 (1991) was not adopted under Chapter VII of the Charter. Two days later, on 7 April, the United States began to airlift relief aid to

42/Document 37
See page 199

northern Iraq. Several Member States, including France, Italy, the Netherlands, the United Kingdom and the United States, subsequently sent troops to the area to build and protect refugee camps there. In view of the exceptional dimensions of the human tragedy unfolding in the region and the need for urgent measures by the United Nations system, on 9 April my predecessor requested that his Personal Representative for humanitarian assistance relating to the Iraq-Kuwait crisis now serve as his Executive Delegate to coordinate a much broader programme of emergency relief in Iraq. (For more about the United Nations Inter-Agency Humanitarian Programme for Iraq, Kuwait and the Iraq/Turkey and Iraq/Iran Border Areas, see paragraphs 170-184.)

126   Some of the coalition countries, in what they stated was an effort to enforce and monitor compliance with resolution 688 (1991), created two "no-fly" or "exclusion" zones in Iraq. The northern zone was created in June 1991 and covers territory above the 36th parallel; the southern zone was established in August 1992 and extended the flight ban to territory below the 32nd parallel. According to these coalition countries, the cease-fire agreement ending the war empowered them to impose such controls over Iraqi military flights. Iraq has objected to both exclusion zones, saying that they were not adopted on the basis of any United Nations resolution and that their aim was of a political nature, namely to interfere in Iraq's internal affairs and to dismember it on an ethnic and religious basis (S/25523).

VI   Maintaining a secure border

127   Within days of adopting resolution 687 (1991), the Security Council approved a plan for the creation and deployment of the United Nations Iraq-Kuwait Observation Mission (UNIKOM) to monitor the demilitarized zone (DMZ) on both sides of the border and the Khawr 'Abd Allah waterway in the northern end of the Persian Gulf. In May 1991, the United Nations Iraq-Kuwait Boundary Demarcation Commission was established, again with the Council's approval, to demarcate the boundary set out in the Agreed Minutes of 1963.[43] Both operations faced obstacles in carrying out their assigned tasks. But with the support of the Security Council they were able to put into place arrangements that succeeded in restoring conditions of peace and security at the frontier.

43/Document 4
See page 166

The United Nations Iraq-Kuwait Observation Mission (UNIKOM)

128   Under the plan for UNIKOM proposed by my predecessor on 5 April 1991 and approved on 9 April by the Security Council in resolution 689 (1991), the mission was given a threefold mandate: to monitor the 40-kilometre-long Khawr 'Abd Allah waterway and a DMZ 200 kilometres long and extending 10 kilometres into Iraq and 5 kilometres into Kuwait; to deter violations of the boundary through its presence in and surveillance of the DMZ; and to observe any hostile or potentially hostile action mounted from the territory of one State against the other.[44] In addition to its peace-keeping duties, UNIKOM has provided technical support to the United Nations Special Commission (UNSCOM) and logistic support to the United Nations Iraq-Kuwait Boundary Demarcation Commission and to the United Nations Coordinator for the Return of Property from Iraq to Kuwait.

44/Document 38
See page 200;
Document 40
See page 206

129   UNIKOM's initial authorized strength was a maximum of 1,440 armed and unarmed military personnel, including infantry, a field engineer unit, an air unit and a logistic unit. The contingents were fully deployed by 6 May 1991, and monitored the withdrawal of the armed forces still deployed in UNIKOM's assigned zone.[45] On 9 May, with this withdrawal complete, the demilitarized zone established by the Security Council came into effect and UNIKOM assumed its observation responsibilities in full. For operational purposes, the DMZ was divided into three sectors: southern, central and northern. The Mission's headquar-

45/Document 50
See page 245;
Document 60
See page 265

ters were located at Umm Qasr, and it maintained liaison offices in Baghdad and Kuwait City. A logistic base, located first at Doha, Qatar, was later moved to Kuwait City. The Governments of Iraq and Kuwait agreed to afford UNIKOM full freedom of movement across the border.

130   In the early phase of its operations, the Mission numbered 1,385 military personnel, a total that included five infantry companies drawn temporarily from the United Nations Peace-keeping Force in Cyprus (UNFICYP) and the United Nations Interim Force in Lebanon (UNIFIL) to provide additional security. These troops were withdrawn by the end of June 1991, and, as of October 1991, UNIKOM had a total strength of 295 observers, supported by 441 administrative and logistic personnel and 177 civilian staff. Since its inception, the force has been composed of military personnel from more than 30 nations, and for the first time in the history of United Nations peace-keeping, each of the five permanent members of the Security Council has contributed military personnel to the same operation.

131   UNIKOM's concept of operations is based on a combination of patrol and observation bases, observation points, ground and air patrols, investigation teams and liaison with the parties at all levels. The Mission verifies that no military personnel and equipment are within the DMZ and that no military fortifications and installations are maintained in it. The observers patrol their sectors and visit temporary observation posts established in areas of particular activity or where roads and tracks enter the DMZ. UNIKOM monitors the Khawr 'Abd Allah waterway from the land using radar and night-vision equipment and also patrols the area by helicopter. Air patrols are also carried out in the DMZ.

132   In accordance with resolution 689 (1991), the Security Council reviews the modalities of UNIKOM's activities and the question of the Mission's termination or continuation every six months. The Mission's mandate is open-ended; that is, for it to be terminated, a decision of the Council is required. During the period from May 1991 until the latter part of 1992, the situation was generally calm, notwithstanding several shooting incidents as well as some armed and unarmed incursions into the demilitarized zone. In my progress reports to the Council, I noted that despite the calm, UNIKOM continued to maintain a high level of vigilance because full peace had yet to be established in the area.[46] Indeed, the second half of 1992 and the early days of 1993 were marked by a gradual heightening of tension in the DMZ.

Incursions by Iraq

133   The main source of this tension was the issue of the status and property rights of Iraqi farmers who were going to be affected by the demarcation of the boundary between Iraq and Kuwait.[47] Some of the

46/Document 77
See page 296;
Document 86
See page 319;
Document 113
See page 431;
Docume~
See ~

areas farmed by these Iraqis in the northern sector of the DMZ were actually on Kuwaiti territory. Moreover, the Kuwaiti authorities alleged that these farmers were Iraqi military or security personnel. This situation gave rise to a number of incidents, during one of which (on 30 August 1992) a UNIKOM military observer was shot while trying to restore calm. Given the risk that further violence could occur once the boundary was demarcated, UNIKOM stepped up its activities in the area and as an interim measure asked Iraq for a register of local farmers. (For more on Iraqi farmers found to be on Kuwaiti territory, see paragraphs 161-166.) The demarcation of the boundary, which as of December 1992 was almost complete, also showed that six Iraqi police posts, some well-heads of the Ratqah oilfield and part of the Iraqi town of Umm Qasr were on Kuwaiti territory. I brought these issues to the attention of the Security Council in a letter to the Council President dated 23 December.[48]

48/Document 147
See page 513

134 Subsequent Iraqi activities at the former Iraqi naval base at Umm Qasr created a crisis which, ultimately, involved the use of force by Member States and led the Security Council to reinforce UNIKOM's strength.

135 Since the summer of 1991, under close UNIKOM monitoring, Iraq had retrieved Iraqi-owned equipment and other items from the base, which was located in the northern sector of the DMZ. On 24 December 1992, UNIKOM alerted the Iraqi authorities that the retrieval of items would have to come to an end, and requested that all such activity cease by 15 January 1993. However, on 2 January 1993, in a serious violation of the DMZ, some 250 Iraqis entered the base, without UNIKOM authorization, to retrieve Iraqi property. The Iraqi personnel drove military vehicles and about half of them wore military uniforms. Iraqi personnel in civilian clothes and without military vehicles continued to retrieve property from the former naval base during the first days of January. On 10 January 1993, some 200 Iraqi personnel with trucks and heavy loading equipment forced entry into six ammunition bunkers located at the Umm Qasr base and took away most of their contents, which the Security Council had previously determined should be destroyed under the supervision of UNIKOM.

136 Meanwhile, on 8 January, Iraqi authorities informed UNIKOM, as they had separately informed the Special Commission, that the United Nations would no longer be permitted to use its own aircraft to transport UNSCOM and UNIKOM personnel into Iraqi territory. (For more on Iraq's prohibition of UNSCOM flights, see paragraphs 269-273.) Further, there was an increase of Iraqi military activity in the no-fly zones. And on 9 January, the Iraqi official responsible for liaison with UNIKOM informed the Mission's Chief Military Observer that, on 11 January, the Iraqis would dismantle prefabricated housing units at Umm Qasr that Iraq had earlier made available to UNIKOM, and asked that UNIKOM evacuate the premises.

137   UNIKOM reacted immediately and vigorously to each of Iraq's actions within the DMZ and made strong representations to the Iraqi military authorities. In reporting to the President of the Security Council on these developments, I observed in particular that they cast doubt on Iraq's continued willingness to cooperate with UNIKOM and to abide by the commitments it had undertaken in this respect.[49]

49/Document 147
See page 513

138   The Security Council, seeking to restore calm and ensure that United Nations operations in Iraq would be able to carry out their mandates, responded in stages. On 8 January, in a statement by its President, the Council demanded that Iraq not interfere with United Nations flights and that it abide by its obligations under all relevant Council resolutions.[50] Also on 8 January, in a letter addressed to me, the Council President expressed the concern of the members of the Council at the continued presence of six Iraqi police posts on Kuwaiti territory and the members' insistence on the speedy removal of those posts, by 15 January at the latest.[51] On 11 January, following the second Iraqi move into Umm Qasr, the President of the Security Council condemned Iraq's action to remove equipment by force from the Kuwaiti side of the DMZ and warned that such actions were "a direct challenge to the authority of UNIKOM".[52] Stressing that recent Iraqi actions with regard to both UNIKOM and UNSCOM constituted "further material breaches of resolution 687 (1991)", the Council President again warned Iraq of the serious consequences that would flow from such "continued defiance".

50/Document 146
See page 512

51/Document 154
See page 526

52/Document 148
See page 516

139   Iraq, on 12 January, stated that there could be no disputing the fact that the items retrieved from Umm Qasr belonged to it, and contended that what it described as "the clamour surrounding the matter" had been "systematically escalated by the United States and its allies so as to depict Iraq's position as one of flouting Council resolutions" (S/25097).

140   On 13 January, with no indication from Iraq that it was prepared to guarantee the safety and free movement of United Nations aircraft or remove its six police posts from the Kuwaiti side of the DMZ, and pursuant to the Security Council's 11 January determination that Iraq was in material breach of resolution 687 (1991), the United States, the United Kingdom and France staged air raids on anti-missile sites and radar bases in southern Iraq. On 17 January, the United States fired missiles at the Zaafaraniya industrial complex in suburban Baghdad, but also hit a hotel in downtown Baghdad, killing two Iraqis and wounding a number of Iraqis and foreigners. On 18 January, additional air raids

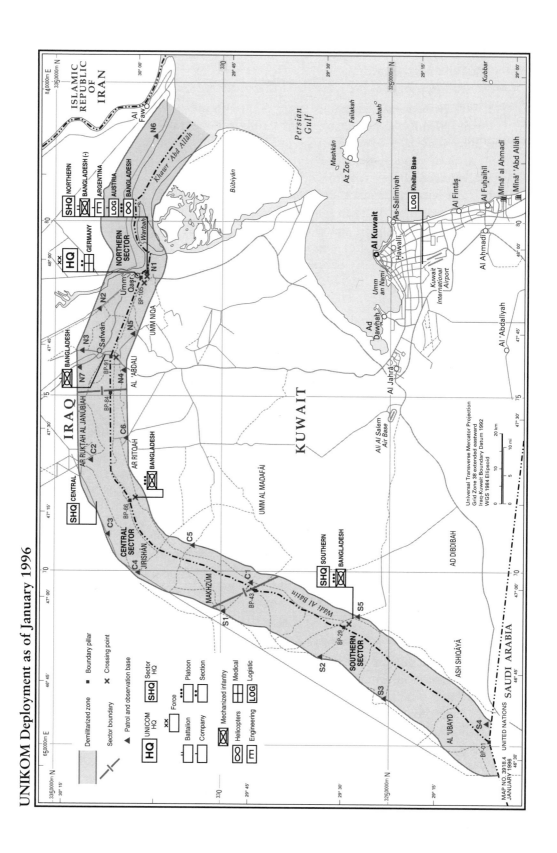

UNIKOM Deployment as of January 1996

by the United States and the United Kingdom targeted radar defence sites in southern and northern Iraq.

141 Iraqi retrieval of property from Kuwait ended on 13 January. The six Iraqi police posts located on Kuwaiti territory were withdrawn on 17-18 January. And on 19 January, Iraqi authorities agreed to a resumption of UNSCOM's flights.

Council decides to strengthen force

142 The Security Council's response to the January incidents culminated on 5 February 1993 in its resolution 806 (1993), which gave UNIKOM a new, extended mandate.[53] UNIKOM was to be made capable of preventing or redressing small-scale violations of the demilitarized zone and the boundary between Iraq and Kuwait, problems that might arise from the presence of Iraqi installations and Iraqi citizens and their assets in the demilitarized zone on the Kuwaiti side of the boundary demarcated by the Boundary Demarcation Commission, and other such violations as had occurred in January. UNIKOM was not, however, authorized to initiate enforcement action.

53/Document 152
See page 525

143 I estimated that with the infantry battalions, support personnel and headquarters elements required to perform these additional functions, UNIKOM would need to comprise some 3,645 military personnel—or a tenfold increase over the Mission's strength at the time the resolution was adopted.[54] Still, I pointed out, even a force of this magnitude would not have enough capacity to prevent a significant military incursion.

54/Document 149
See page 517

144 The strengthening of the force under resolution 806 (1993) was to be executed in phases. For the first stage of this process, I decided to retain the military observers and to reinforce them by one mechanized infantry battalion to be deployed in the northern sector of the DMZ, which includes the towns of Umm Qasr and Safwan. However, the Organization encountered difficulty in identifying a Member State that was in a position to provide the necessary battalion. It was not until October that I was able to notify the Council that Bangladesh, which was already providing military observers to the Mission, had offered to provide an infantry battalion, and that Kuwait had offered to provide the necessary armoured vehicles, heavy transport and other equipment.[55] After a period of training, the battalion became operational on 5 February 1994.

55/Document 171
See page 596

56/Document 170
See page 592;

Document 186
See page 630;

Document 192
See page 663;

Document 204
See page 725;

Document 212
See page 765

A return to relative calm

145 Since the spring of 1993, the DMZ has been generally calm.[56] Farming and the exploration for and exploitation of oil have increased noticeably, as have shipping and fishing activities in the Khawr 'Abd Allah waterway. The completion by Kuwait of a border security system,

comprising a trench, an earthen embankment and a patrol road through these areas, has contributed to the overall quiet in the area by creating a physical barrier to unauthorized border crossings. As a result of this relative calm, and especially after the Iraqi farmers found to be on Kuwaiti territory were relocated, the strengthening of the force authorized by Security Council resolution 806 (1993) was stopped after the first phase of implementation.

57/Document 170

See page 592;

Document 186

See page 630;

Document 194

See page 685;

Document 196

See page 694;

Document 197

See page 695;

Document 204

See page 725;

Document 212

See page 765

146   None the less, some incidents have occurred on either side of the border which threatened the security of UNIKOM personnel.[57] On the Iraqi side, during the period from 1 October 1993 to 31 March 1994, these included the hijacking of a United Nations vehicle and two attempted robberies of a UNIKOM patrol and observation base. On 12 August 1994, a three-man UNIKOM mobile patrol was ambushed, resulting in the death of one soldier and the injury of two others. On the Kuwaiti side, during the night of 28-29 December 1994, gunmen fired on a UNIKOM patrol vehicle, wounding a military observer.

147   Tension also manifested itself when, following the demarcation of the Iraq-Kuwait boundary, Kuwait in June 1993 began construction of its border security system. In one incident, Iraqi nationals crossed into Kuwait during two protest demonstrations and, in a separate incident in November 1993, a security guard for the Kuwaiti border trench project shot two Iraqi policemen who were on Kuwaiti territory, reportedly resulting in the death of one policeman and the injury of the other. Reports about the deployment of Iraqi troops north of the DMZ in October 1994 prompted the Security Council to condemn the action, demand an immediate and complete troop withdrawal and call on UNIKOM to redouble its vigilance. The Iraqi forces were subsequently redeployed away from the border area. On 13 March 1995, two United States citizens mistakenly crossed the border from Kuwait into Iraq, where they were apprehended by Iraqi police. On their way to the border they had crossed a Kuwaiti checkpoint at the edge of the DMZ, as well as a UNIKOM checkpoint at the border. The two men were allowed to pass the UNIKOM checkpoint because, with darkness having just fallen, the sentries on duty mistook their white vehicle for one belonging to the United Nations. Procedures at the checkpoint have since been tightened. The two men were freed on 16 July 1995, following efforts by the United States Government and myself to obtain their release.

148   As of 1 January 1996, the overall strength of UNIKOM was approximately 1,331, including 244 military observers from 32 countries, an infantry battalion of 775 and a helicopter unit of 29, both from Bangladesh, an engineer unit of 50 from Argentina, a logistics unit of 35 from Austria, a medical team of 12 from Germany and 227 civilian staff. During an official visit to Kuwait in late December 1995, I visited

UNIKOM forces on the Kuwaiti side of the Kuwait-Iraq border and thanked them for the effective and efficient manner in which they have carried out their mandate.

The United Nations Iraq-Kuwait Boundary Demarcation Commission

149   The demarcation by the United Nations of the border between Iraq and Kuwait was a technical rather than a political task. This work consisted of the technical steps necessary to demarcate for the first time, in precise geographic coordinates of latitude and longitude, the international boundary set out in the Agreed Minutes of 4 October 1963 and to make arrangements for the physical representation of the boundary through the erection of boundary pillars or monuments.[58]

150   On 2 May 1991, my predecessor reported to the Security Council on arrangements for the creation of a United Nations Iraq-Kuwait boundary demarcation commission.[59] Under the proposed plan, the commission would be composed of one representative each from Iraq and Kuwait and three independent experts appointed by the Secretary-General, one of whom would serve as Chairman. The geographic coordinates established by the commission would constitute the final demarcation of the boundary and would be lodged in the archives of both States, with a certified copy retained in the archives of the United Nations. To carry out the demarcation, the commission would draw upon appropriate material, including a series of topographic maps of Kuwait produced by the United Kingdom Director General of Military Survey on the basis of the 1932 exchange of letters between Iraq and Kuwait and transmitted to the Secretary-General on 28 March 1991. All costs related to the commission's work were to be shared between the interested parties.

151   The Security Council approved the plan on 13 May 1991 (S/22593). The first of the Commission's 11 meetings was held on 23 May 1991.

152   In carrying out its work, the Commission considered the delimitation formula as contained in the 1932 Exchange of Letters[60] and referred to in the 1963 Agreed Minutes,[61] deliberated on the relevant demarcation issues, took account of earlier clarifications, heard statements of position and examined all available documentation and evidence. Such sources included maps, graphics, aerial photographs, diplomatic correspondence, notes and archival documents. Work was carried out through closed meetings, visits to the border area and field assignments. All members of the Commission participated in the first five sessions held between 23 May 1991 and 16 April 1992, at which the

58/Document 4
See page 166

59/Document 48
See page 235

60/Document 1
See page 165;
Document 2
See page 165

61/Document 4
See page 166

Commission adopted its rules of procedure, took decisions on the land boundary and considered the Khawr 'Abd Allah (offshore) section. The representative of Iraq did not attend the subsequent six sessions that were held between 15 July 1992 and 20 May 1993 but was sent all relevant Commission documents and minutes of the meetings.

153 Iraq's decision to cease participation in the Commission's meetings was rooted in its belief that the Commission's work was political—that the Governments of the United States and United Kingdom in particular were seeking to deprive Iraq of its rights and justify the ongoing presence in the region of their armed forces and military bases. At the time of the adoption of resolution 687 (1991), Iraq had objected that the Security Council lacked legal competence to act on border questions, an objection Iraq repeated in letters of 1 June, 13 July and 27 August 1992 specifically addressing the work of the Boundary Demarcation Commission (S/24044, S/24275, S/24496). Still, Iraq had also reconfirmed its acceptance of the relevant provisions of resolution 687 (1991) and indicated its readiness to cooperate with the Secretary-General and to participate in the Commission's work.

154 The Security Council, in June and August 1992, responded to Iraq's decision to end its participation in the Boundary Demarcation Commission's meetings by expressing its complete support for the work of the Commission and recalling that the Commission was "not reallocating territory between Kuwait and Iraq" but was "simply carrying out" a "technical task".[62] The Council also firmly rejected any suggestion by Iraq that tended to "dispute the very existence of Kuwait, a State Member of the United Nations", and expressed concern that Iraq's position could be interpreted as rejecting the finality of the Commission's decisions despite Iraq's acceptance of the terms of resolution 687 (1991).

62/Document 120
See page 458;
Document 129
See page 474

155 The Commission issued its final report at its 11th session, on 20 May 1993.[63] The report outlined the Commission's two years of work, including its consideration of the historical background to the border question, and contained the list of geographic coordinates demarcating the international boundary between Iraq and Kuwait (see map, page 53). I forwarded certified copies of this list to the Governments of Iraq and Kuwait, in order to be lodged in their archives; a third certified copy was retained for safe-keeping in the archives of the United Nations.

63/Document 158
See page 540

156 Among the many questions the Commission was called upon to resolve during its work were those relating to the location of several oil wells and of the Umm Qasr port complex. With regard to the former, the Commission noted that the oil wells in the fields between Safwan and Wadi Al Batin, which Iraq had exploited in the past, fell within Kuwaiti territory according to the boundary shown on the map referred to in Security Council resolution 687 (1991). With regard to the Umm Qasr port complex, the Commission noted that the demarcation left the complex, including all the warehouses, crane installations, deep-water anchorage and two side berths, as well as the whole of Umm Qasr village, the Navy hospital and the sulphur works, within Iraqi territory, although the former naval base was found to be within Kuwaiti territory.

157   The Commission also recognized the importance of navigational access for both parties, and in this connection adopted a statement prepared by the Office of Legal Affairs of the United Nations Secretariat that read in part: "The Commission views navigational access for both States to the various parts of their respective territories bordering the demarcated boundary as of importance for ensuring an equitable character and for promoting stability and peace and security along the border . . . The Commission notes that this right of navigational access is provided for under the rules of international law as embodied in the 1982 United Nations Convention on the Law of the Sea ratified by both Iraq and Kuwait".[64]

64/Document 158
See page 540

158   The Commission also made recommendations for the maintenance of the physical representation of the boundary, proposing that the pillars and markers of the boundary be inspected on an annual basis and that a cleared road giving access to the pillars be created. The maintenance programme was initiated in April 1994 and is the responsibility of UNIKOM.

159   I addressed the Commission's final session on 20 May 1993 and congratulated its members for the excellent work they had performed in producing a precise, well-documented and verifiable demarcation of the entire boundary.[65] I noted that, in completing the physical demarcation of the land part of the boundary, satellite technology had enabled the Commission to position each of the markers with a margin of error of only 1.5 centimetres. "Law, technology, diplomacy and security have come together in a unique United Nations endeavour", I stated, one which constituted "a strong contribution to peace and stability for the region and the world". I also called on Iraq to respect the objectivity and impartiality of the results.

65/Document 157
See page 539

160   In its resolution 833 (1993) of 27 May 1993, the Security Council reaffirmed that the Commission's decisions on the demarcation of the boundary were final; underlined and reaffirmed the Council's decision to guarantee the inviolability of the boundary; and demanded that Iraq and Kuwait respect the inviolability of the boundary and the right to navigational access.[66] Kuwait, in a letter, affirmed that it would honour and be bound by resolution 833 (1993) and reaffirmed that the Commission's decisions were final.[67] Iraq restated its previous positions on the Commission's work, including its opposition to the Commission's decision to demarcate the Khawr 'Abd Allah (offshore) boundary, which

66/Document 161
See page 567

67/Document 163
See page 571

68/Document 162
See page 568

69/Document 167
See page 591

Iraq considered beyond the Commission's terms of reference or mandate, as well as the way in which the boundary had been determined.[68]
The Council, in response, reminded Iraq of its previous acceptance of
resolution 687 (1991), stressed the inviolability of the international
boundary demarcated by the Commission and stressed as well "the
serious consequences that would ensue from any breach thereof".[69]

Iraqi farmers and good offices

161   Well before the release of the Commission's final report in
May 1993, preliminary information about the Commission's demarcation of the boundary revealed that a number of Iraqi citizens and their
assets in the town of Umm Qasr and in the farming area of Al Abdaly
were located on the Kuwaiti side of the border, as were the Ratqah oil
well-heads and other installations. In addition, it became known that six
Iraqi police posts were situated on Kuwaiti territory, while three Iraqi
police posts and two Kuwaiti police posts were shown to be closer to the
boundary than the 1,000 metres earlier established by UNIKOM with
the concurrence of the parties as a reasonable distance to prevent
incidents.

162   Aware of the substantial political and security implications of
these issues, I initiated contacts with the Governments of Iraq and
Kuwait to determine how the United Nations might help to bring about
a settlement. I specifically requested that Iraq withdraw the six police
posts from Kuwaiti territory as soon as possible, and I instructed
UNIKOM's Chief Military Observer to contact the Iraqi authorities to
make the necessary arrangements. I informed both parties that the
matter of the other police posts fell within the mandate of UNIKOM,
and I instructed the Chief Military Observer to arrange with the authorities concerned to have all posts moved to an appropriate distance from
the boundary at an early date.[70] With regard to the presence of Iraqi
civilians on Kuwaiti territory, I wrote to the Government of Kuwait on
17 December 1992 that because of the danger of an escalation of tension
along the border, a recommended course of action would be to permit
the Iraqi farmers and residents of Umm Qasr to remain, at least for an
interim period, on their lands and in their dwellings.[71]

163   In a letter to the President of the Security Council on 23 December, I conveyed to the Council my view that these issues were apt to give
rise to increased tension and friction unless resolved soon, and I outlined
the efforts I had taken to mitigate that risk.[72] Regrettably, my assessment
proved accurate as tensions flared in January 1993, as I have described
(see paragraphs 133-144 above).

164   On 10 January 1993, Kuwait informed me that the Iraqi
nationals would not be permitted to remain in Kuwait, but would be
compensated for their property and assets on the basis of an assessment

70/Document 147
See page 513

71/Document 140
See page 491

72/Document 147
See page 513

Demarcation of the international boundary between Iraq and Kuwait

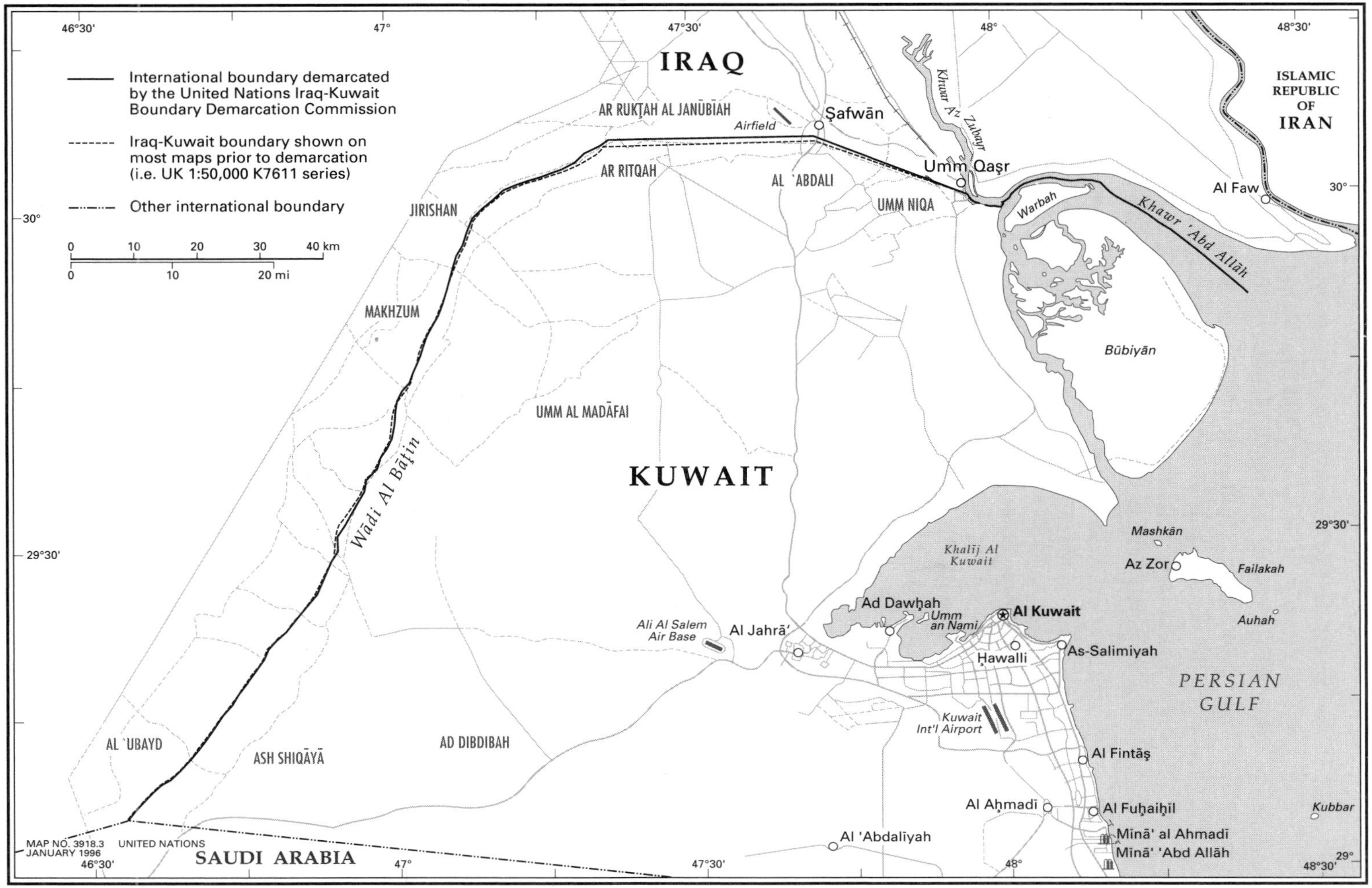

Legend:

— International boundary demarcated by the United Nations Iraq-Kuwait Boundary Demarcation Commission

- - - Iraq-Kuwait boundary shown on most maps prior to demarcation (i.e. UK 1:50,000 K7611 series)

—··— Other international boundary

Scale:
0   10   20   30   40 km
0   10   20 mi

Labels on map:

ISLAMIC REPUBLIC OF IRAN

IRAQ

KUWAIT

SAUDI ARABIA

PERSIAN GULF

Al Faw

Khawr 'Abd Allāh

Būbiyān

Warbah

Khwar Az Zubayr

Umm Qaṣr

Ṣafwān

Airfield

AL 'ABDALI

UMM NIQA

AR RUKĀH AL JANŪBIAH

AR RITQAH

UMM AL MADĀFAI

JIRISHAN

MAKHZUM

Wadi Al Bāţin

AD DIBDIBAH

ASH SHIQĀYĀ

AL 'UBAYD

Mashkān

Az Zor

Failakah

Auhah

Kubbar

As-Salimiyah

Al Fintās

Al Fuḩaiḩil

Minā' al Aḩmadi

Minā' 'Abd Allāh

Al Aḩmadi

Al 'Abdaliyah

Al Kuwait

Khalīj Al Kuwait

Hawalli

Ad Dawḩah

Umm an Namil

Kuwait Int'l Airport

Ali Al Salem Air Base

Al Jahrā'

UNITED NATIONS

MAP NO. 3918.3
JANUARY 1996

by a neutral party nominated by the United Nations. Iraq responded to this suggestion on 1 March by indicating that it would "take no action that might tend to recognize the injustice deliberately inflicted on Iraq" but, at the same time, would "take no action that might provoke dispute or contention with the United Nations".[73] Because I continued to accord utmost importance to re-establishing conditions of security and stability along the border, I offered the full involvement of the United Nations to assist the parties in implementing the repatriation of the Iraqi citizens, an offer which I am gratified to report both Governments accepted.

73/Document 181
See page 623

165   As for the question of compensation, in accordance with a September 1993 arrangement between the United Nations and Kuwait, I appointed an independent contractor to assess the value of the property and assets, on the basis of which I decided on an amount which Kuwait was then asked to pay into a United Nations trust fund for disbursal to the Iraqi citizens. The Security Council, in resolution 899 (1994), approved this approach as an exception to the general prohibition against the remittal of funds which was part of the sanctions regime set out in resolution 661 (1990).[74]

74/Document 183
See page 627

75/Document 181
See page 623

166   At the end of February 1994, I reported to the Council that, with support from UNIKOM, all Iraqi nationals had been relocated to Iraq without disturbance.[75] A representative of the United Nations met with many of the Iraqi individuals prior to their relocation to Iraq and provided them with information as to the amount of compensation that would be available to them and the steps they should take to claim it. Compensation information was also disseminated in the form of press releases and paid notices in the local and regional media. However, none of the Iraqis agreed to accept compensation payments at that time, and additional efforts in 1995 to meet with the Iraqi beneficiaries of the proposed compensation scheme were not successful. The funds—amounting to 56 million Iraqi dinars for 95 farmers, and 15.5 million Iraqi dinars for 206 residential houses—were deposited into a United Nations escrow account, where they have remained at the disposal of the beneficiaries.

Iraqi recognition of the international boundary

167   Iraq's respect for the inviolability of the Iraq-Kuwait boundary is one of its main obligations under Security Council resolutions, and as such is one of the primary factors in the Council's deliberations over any easing or lifting of the sanctions regime. On 10 November 1994, Iraq issued a Revolution Command Council decree and a National Assembly declaration confirming its irrevocable and unqualified recognition of the sovereignty, territorial integrity and political independence of the State of Kuwait and of the international boundary between Iraq and Kuwait, and confirming Iraq's respect for the inviolability of that boundary.[76]

76/Document 198
See page 696

168   Coming so soon after Iraq's October 1994 troop deployments in the direction of the Kuwait border, which had brought the Council's condemnation, the decree and the declaration were widely viewed as signalling an encouraging turn of events. The Council, in a statement by its President on 16 November, called it "a significant step in the direction towards implementation of the relevant Security Council resolutions".[77] The decree and the declaration, as well as a letter to the Secretary-General from Iraq's Minister for Foreign Affairs and a copy of the Official Gazette of the Republic of Iraq dated 10 November 1994, were subsequently deposited in the official archives of the United Nations.

77/Document 199

See page 698

VII   Restoring normalcy in the region

169   The initial focus on security at the Iraq-Kuwait frontier, through the work of UNIKOM and the Boundary Demarcation Commission, was only one dimension of a much wider United Nations objective: the restoration of regional peace and security in all respects. The control and elimination of Iraq's weapons of mass destruction is the subject of Part VIII (see page 74). Other components of this United Nations system-wide effort have included the provision of humanitarian assistance; the repatriation of Kuwaiti and third-State nationals taken prisoner, arrested or otherwise detained during the invasion and occupation and of Iraqi nationals; the return of Kuwaiti property seized by Iraq; the mitigation of the environmental damage caused by the conflict; and the work of the United Nations Compensation Commission.

United Nations Consolidated Inter-Agency Humanitarian Programme in Iraq

78/Document 66
See page 273

170   At the time of its invasion of Kuwait, Iraq was, in certain key economic and social respects, approaching a standard comparable to that of some highly industrialized countries.[78] Iraq had put in place a sophisticated health system, the provision of clean drinking-water was the norm, sewage treatment plants kept water quality in the Tigris and Euphrates rivers at reasonable levels, and while poverty and moderate malnutrition remained a problem in some areas, severe malnutrition and related syndromes were not major public health concerns. Iraq had also built modern power-generation and telecommunications networks to serve both urban and rural areas. Much of the country's food need was met through imports paid for primarily through revenue from the sale of oil.

171   This situation changed abruptly with the imposition of comprehensive sanctions against Iraq following its invasion and occupation of Kuwait. Further, as documented by United Nations missions to the area, the war in January and February 1991 brought about the massive destruction of many elements of Iraq's physical and service infrastruc-

79/Document 31
See page 186

ture.[79] Even before the end of hostilities, a joint WHO/UNICEF mission visited Iraq from 16 to 21 February to deliver a 54-ton shipment of emergency medical supplies, assist in the care of children and mothers, and ascertain essential health needs for the future. The civil conflicts within Iraq that followed the end of hostilities caused further damage and provoked one of the largest and most rapid refugee movements in recent history. In a three-week period, from March to April 1991, more than 400,000 Iraqis—mainly Kurds—fled to the Turkish border, and by mid-May approximately 1.5 million persons had taken refuge either in the Islamic Republic of Iran or in the eastern border area of Iraq. With the exception of some 70,000 Shiites from the southern region around Basrah, the overwhelming majority were Iraqi Kurds.

172   The sudden, massive population outflow prompted a humanitarian relief operation of great scope and intensity, beginning with the commencement by the United States and other coalition members of an airlift of emergency aid to northern Iraq. On 8 April 1991, my predecessor issued an appeal for $178 million to cover the initial needs of vulnerable groups in Iraq. A new appeal for $400.2 million was launched on 12 April for aid to refugees and displaced persons on the borders of Iraq and Turkey and in the Islamic Republic of Iran. These two appeals were then consolidated on 15 May and augmented to provide for emergency needs not previously covered.[80]

80/Document 51
See page 246

Memoranda of Understanding and deployment of a United Nations Guards Contingent

173   A legal framework for UNHCR and other United Nations relief agencies working in Iraqi territory was established with the signing on 18 April 1991 of a Memorandum of Understanding (MOU) between the Executive Delegate of the Secretary-General and the Government of Iraq.[81] The terms of the agreement stipulated that the United Nations and the Government of Iraq would promote the voluntary repatriation of Iraqi displaced persons and take humanitarian measures to avert new flows of refugees and displaced persons from Iraq. To do so, United Nations offices and Humanitarian Centres (UNHUCs) would be established and routes for the return of refugees (known as "blue routes"), with relay stations, would be created. The blue routes were an innovation that permitted the direct and relatively rapid return of refugees and displaced persons to their homelands, thereby avoiding the need for the construction and long-term administration of refugee camps. From an initial request for a three-month emergency programme of assistance to displaced Iraqis, UNHCR extended its programme for more than one year. It assisted in the rehabilitation of more than 1,200 villages through its "winterization programme", and helped in the first phase of agricultural rehabilitation. It implemented health, water and sanitation programmes and coordinated United Nations agencies and other international and non-governmental organizations in this humanitarian effort.

81/Document 44
See page 209

174   The volatile conditions in Iraq led to another United Nations innovation: the deployment of a United Nations Guards Contingent to protect United Nations personnel and assets as well as non-governmental organizations working under the umbrella of the United Nations pro-

gramme. The presence of the Contingent, agreed to in an annex to the MOU dated 25 May 1991, was crucial in ensuring the successful handover of humanitarian operations in the north from the coalition forces to the United Nations.[82] Moreover, by their presence, the Guards were able to defuse tensions and greatly increase security in areas in which the Inter-Agency Humanitarian Programme is being implemented. The first 10 Guards arrived in May 1991 and were stationed near the city of Zakho, and the full complement of 500 Guards, representing 35 nationalities, was deployed by 1 October 1991.

82/Document 57
See page 199

175   Throughout 1991, Iraqi military activities in northern Iraq resulted in new displacements. During October and December, military operations and clashes in the Suleimaniyah and Erbil governorates forced some 200,000 people to leave their homes. The clashes led Government forces and administrators to withdraw from the area, leaving the majority of the three governorates of Erbil, Suleimaniyah and Dohuk under the control of the Kurdish leadership. Nearly all Iraqi civil servants were ordered to withdraw from their posts to Government-controlled territory, and electricity supply to the Kurdish areas was cut. Serious restrictions on the supplies of essential commodities, in particular food and fuel, to these areas followed in November. On 9 December, the Executive Delegate of the Secretary-General and the heads of UNHCR, UNICEF, WFP and WHO expressed their concern about the overall situation to the Government of Iraq, noting that United Nations humanitarian agencies were not in a position to replace essential services and assure the provision of goods denied to the population in the north.

176   A second Memorandum of Understanding had been signed on 24 November 1991, allowing a continuation of the inter-agency programme until 30 June 1992.[83] Modifications to the first Memorandum of Understanding were introduced to reflect changed circumstances, in particular the return of the majority of displaced persons from neighbouring countries. Other amendments to the earlier agreement included the incorporation of measures governing assignment of the Guards Contingent as an integral component of the humanitarian programme, the establishment of a new coordinating mechanism, and the provision of monthly cash contributions in local currency by the Government of Iraq.

83/Document 93
See page 361

177   The extension of the Memorandum of Understanding beyond 30 June 1992 was delayed when Iraq stated that some of the exceptional measures provided for under the two earlier agreements were no longer applicable. Taking the position that the humanitarian programme should be based on transitional arrangements moving from an emergency phase towards "normalization" and regular cooperation with United Nations agencies, Iraq sought, among other things, to close United Nations sub-offices and field stations designed to facilitate the provision of humanitarian assistance, and to limit both the number of

United Nations Guards and the areas of the country in which they could be deployed. On 4 August, I wrote to the Deputy Prime Minister of Iraq, stating my view that the continuation of the humanitarian programmes for the affected populations was imperative.[84] Later that month, however, I informed the Security Council that the various measures taken by Iraq had prevented the United Nations from providing effective assistance, particularly in the north.[85] The Council expressed its deep concern on 2 September, saying that it was "particularly disturbed by Iraq's continuing failure to ensure the safety of United Nations personnel and the personnel of non-governmental organizations", and that it considered "unrestricted access throughout the country and the assurance of adequate security measures" to be essential prerequisites for the effective implementation of the humanitarian programme.[86]

84/Document 126
See page 470

85/Document 127
See page 471

86/Document 129
See page 474

87/Document 135
See page 483

178   After several rounds of intensive negotiations, a third Memorandum of Understanding was signed in New York on 22 October 1992 between the Permanent Representative of Iraq and the United Nations Under-Secretary-General for Humanitarian Affairs.[87] The agreement allowed the continued presence of the Guards Contingent up to a maximum level of 300 Guards in the three northern governorates and in Baghdad. Since 31 March 1993, the arrangements reached under the 1993 Memorandum of Understanding have been renewed by tacit agreement through an exchange of correspondence between both parties.

Inter-agency appeals

179   As of 1 January 1996, in addition to the appeals of April and May 1991, five inter-agency humanitarian appeals had been launched:

	Total appeal requirements	Funds received by United Nations organizations	Funds received by other programmes (NGOs, IGOs, etc.)
	(Millions of United States dollars)		
January 1992–June 1992	143.2	89.1	...
July 1992–March 1993	201.7	134.7	...
April 1993–March 1994	467.1	95.2	77.9
April 1994– March 1995	288.5	61.2	53.4
April 1995–March 1996	138.8	39.4	34.3

(Estimates based on data/information provided by donors and recipient organizations.)

180   In March 1993, an inter-agency mission visited Iraq to assess needs for the period from April 1993 to March 1994. The mission found that conditions in all sectors covered by the programme had deteriorated to such an extent that considerable humanitarian assistance was required, mainly for destitute individuals and others considered the most vulnerable groups of Iraq's civilian population. A one-year plan was developed, focusing on relief and rehabilitation projects promoting self-

reliance in the sectors of energy and municipal services for the north, and in food aid, agriculture, basic health, water and sanitation, education, shelter and road repair for both the north and the south. For the period from April 1994 to March 1995, most of the contributions received by United Nations agencies, NGOs and other programmes were earmarked for the northern governorates. In addition, the volatile security situation continued to justify maintaining the presence of the United Nations Guards Contingent there.

181　The presence of an estimated 10 million land-mines in the northern governorates was also a focus of humanitarian concern. However, no comprehensive de-mining operation has been implemented in Iraq so far, owing to the absence of approval by the Government. The Mine Advisory Group, a non-governmental organization, is implementing mine-awareness education programmes and limited mine-clearance projects in northern Iraq.

182　Since the launching of the appeal covering the period from 1 April 1995 to 31 March 1996, the humanitarian situation in Iraq has deteriorated further in all respects, particularly in the areas of nutrition and health, and living conditions have become increasingly precarious for at least an estimated 4 million persons. With basic drugs and essential supplies lacking throughout the country, health services were nearing a total breakdown. Public health was also being adversely affected by the inadequate supply of clean water, as waste-water treatment plants, dependent on increasingly unavailable spare parts, had ceased to function in most urban areas. More than half the rural population lacked potable water.

183　In the absence of sufficient contributions from the donor community, the distribution of food by WFP was drastically reduced, and only one half to one third of the more than 1 million targeted beneficiaries received monthly assistance. In addition to the growing number of vulnerable groups and destitute families in northern Iraq, approximately 140,000 internally displaced persons were unable to return to their homes in Government-controlled areas, and relief assistance was needed by more than 250,000 persons living in "collective towns" and by some 200,000 pensioners unable to support themselves. In September 1995, WFP reported that more than 4 million people, including 2.4 million children under five and 600,000 pregnant and nursing mothers, were "at severe nutritional risk". And an evaluation of the food and nutrition situation in Iraq issued by FAO in December 1995 stated, among other things, that shortages of basic foods were enormous, that prices of basic food stuffs had risen phenomenally and that sewage disposal had deteriorated. In Baghdad, severe and mild malnutrition were noted among children, and child mortality had risen nearly fivefold since 1990.

184　The sharp rise in human misery throughout Iraq prompted the

Under-Secretary-General for Humanitarian Affairs to write to United Nations Member States and other potential donors, asking them to contribute "urgently and substantially" to fund United Nations humanitarian activities throughout Iraq. In a letter dated 6 December 1995, the Under-Secretary-General described the situation throughout the country as "increasingly disastrous". In January 1996, Iraq's Government agreed to negotiate on the implementation of the plan contained in Security Council resolution 986 (1995) authorizing the use of proceeds from the limited sales of Iraqi oil for the purchase of humanitarian goods (see paragraphs 317-332).

Repatriation of Kuwaiti and third-State nationals and of Iraqi nationals

185 During the fighting that accompanied Iraq's invasion of Kuwait, many Kuwaitis and non-Kuwaitis were taken prisoner, and a significant number were taken to Iraq. A second broad group of persons was arrested as the occupation continued, and a third group was arrested at the very end of the occupation. After the withdrawal of the Iraqi occupying forces, the Kuwaiti Human Rights Committee (instituted by Kuwait's Council of Ministers to centralize the registration of missing persons) informed the United Nations that an initial list of more than 11,700 missing persons had been established as of 20 March 1991.[88]

88/Document 46
See page 229

186 Following the suspension of hostilities, Security Council resolution 686 (1991) of 2 March 1991 gave immediate priority to repatriating persons seized in Kuwait as well as personnel captured from the coalition forces.[89] The Council demanded that Iraq immediately release under the auspices of the ICRC and affiliated societies all Kuwaiti and third-State nationals detained by Iraq and return the remains of any deceased Kuwaiti and third-State nationals. The Council further demanded that Iraq arrange for immediate access to and release of all prisoners of war under the auspices of the ICRC, and that Iraq return the remains of any deceased personnel of the forces of Kuwait and of Member States cooperating with Kuwait. The Council also welcomed the decision of Kuwait and the coalition States to provide access to, and commence immediately the release of, Iraqi prisoners of war, also under the auspices of the ICRC.

89/Document 26
See page 182

187 One month later, when the Security Council adopted resolution 687 (1991), many Kuwaiti and third-State nationals remained in detention or unaccounted for. Section G of the cease-fire resolution thus obligated Iraq, in furtherance of its commitment to facilitate repatriation, to provide lists of such persons, to facilitate ICRC access to them

wherever they might be located or detained, and to facilitate the search by the ICRC for those still unaccounted for. By mid-August 1991, however, the repatriation called for in resolutions 686 (1991) and 687 (1991) had not yet been fully carried out, prompting the Council, in resolution 706 (1991) of 15 August 1991, to express its concern and request that the Secretary-General, in consultation with the ICRC, submit a report on the situation.[90]

90/Document 72
See page 285

188   In response, my predecessor reported on 12 September 1991 that large-scale repatriation operations had been carried out between 6 March and 6 April 1991 in which 4,178 prisoners of war and 2,056 civilian internees had returned to Kuwait.[91] Since then, the ICRC had registered in Iraq a further 3,506 persons wishing to return to Kuwait (although many were deemed ineligible by Kuwait); supervised the repatriation of prisoners of war, civilian internees and other civilians to the United States, the United Kingdom, Italy and Saudi Arabia; and transmitted to Iraq lists from Kuwait and from coalition States of persons missing and believed to be detained in Iraq. In addition, the Special Rapporteur on the situation of human rights in Iraq reported that a number of detainees, possibly including missing Kuwaitis, had been freed when Iraqi rebels attacked jails in such areas as Basrah during the March 1991 hostilities in southern Iraq. In communications annexed to the Secretary-General's September report, Iraq stated that it was cooperating fully with the ICRC, while Kuwait accused Iraq of continuing to detain thousands of prisoners of war, some of whom, said Kuwait, had been transferred to undisclosed locations to which the ICRC was denied access. The Security Council, in a statement of 5 February 1992, declared that there was "serious evidence of Iraqi non-compliance" regarding repatriation.[92]

91/Document 79
See page 302

92/Document 101
See page 390

189   Beginning on 7 March 1992, meetings involving representatives of Iraq, of Kuwait, and of France, Saudi Arabia, the United Kingdom and the United States, with the ICRC as a neutral intermediary, began to establish modalities for identifying and effecting the release of missing persons. The Security Council took note of this development on 11 March, but reported that none the less the ICRC had not yet received any information as to the whereabouts of the persons reported missing in Iraq, or on the search conducted by the Iraqi authorities, or on persons who had died while in custody.[93] Meetings between the countries involved in the repatriation effort continued under ICRC auspices through March and April 1992, and then resumed in October. Still, by late November the Security Council could report no significant progress concerning repatriation, with the ICRC still unable to obtain information as to the whereabouts of persons reported missing in Iraq or to visit Iraqi prisons and detention centres in accordance with standard ICRC criteria. Very few missing persons had been released since March 1992,

93/Document 108
See page 421

the Council President reported on 23 November, while hundreds were believed still to be inside Iraq.[94]

94/Document 137
See page 486

190   On 2 March 1993, Kuwait stated in a letter to the President of the Security Council that it had recently handed over to the ICRC the individual files of 627 prisoners, detainees and missing persons. These files were also submitted to the Special Rapporteur on the situation of human rights in Iraq. Kuwait reiterated its demands that Iraq provide information on all persons deported from Kuwait during the occupation and release without delay those who might still be in detention or return the remains of those deceased. Kuwait also asked that Iraq search for persons listed as missing. In several subsequent communications, Kuwait reported that none of the requested information had been received from Iraq and that Iraq had thwarted various diplomatic efforts aimed at securing the release of Kuwaiti prisoners and detainees (S/25790, S/26103, S/26449, S/26740). Iraq responded by emphasizing its position that there were no so-called Kuwaiti detainees in Iraq (S/25758, S/25928).

191   After unproductive consultations in Geneva in early 1993 between representatives of Iraq, of Kuwait, and of France, Saudi Arabia, the United Kingdom and the United States under ICRC auspices, the ICRC informed the coalition States that Iraq had decided to stop attending these meetings and that it had provided no substantive answers on individual case files. In a series of communications thereafter, Kuwait asserted that Iraq was in fundamental breach of its humanitarian obligations with respect to repatriation, and noted with concern that Iraqi officials and newspapers had begun referring to prisoners and detainees as "the missing" (S/1994/284).

192   Meetings under ICRC auspices of the countries involved in the repatriation effort—now referred to as the Tripartite Commission—resumed with Iraqi participation on 1 July 1994. On 8 December, Iraq, Kuwait and the coalition countries agreed to form a Technical Subcommittee on Military and Civilian Missing Prisoners of War and Mortal Remains to expedite the repatriation process. Both the Tripartite Commission and its Technical Subcommittee have continued to meet. As of November 1995, the total number of files on individual missing persons submitted by Kuwait was 603; Iraq had submitted 29; and there were 25 files concerning Saudi nationals (including 13 submitted by Kuwait). For 70 of these dossiers, the Government of Iraq subsequently provided preliminary replies, but these replies have been characterized as "evasive" and "pro forma" by the Special Rapporteur on the situation of human rights in Iraq.[95] Except for the return to Kuwaiti authorities of the mortal remains of one missing person, little concrete progress has been achieved since the Tripartite Commission process resumed.

95/Document 216
See page 793

193   By its resolution 50/191 of 22 December 1995, the General

96/Document 221

See page 821

Assembly called on Iraq to "improve its cooperation with the Tripartite Commission with a view to establishing the whereabouts or resolving the fates of the remaining several hundred missing persons and prisoners of war" who remain "victims of the illegal Iraqi occupation of Kuwait".[96]

Iraqi prisoners and detainees

194　The repatriation process has extended as well to the cases of Iraqi prisoners of war and civilians and other persons detained in Saudi Arabia and Kuwait. In October 1991, the ICRC supervised a general repatriation of Iraqi prisoners. Upon completion, such repatriation operations had effected the return of 70,067 prisoners of war and 23 mortal remains of Iraqi soldiers. In addition, according to its 1994 annual report, the ICRC, acting under the Fourth Geneva Convention, maintained a delegation in Saudi Arabia to monitor the treatment of the roughly 20,000 Iraqi civilians on record as being interned, some of whom had been prisoners of war who lost that status after the general repatriation. The ICRC terminated these activities in January 1994. The ICRC is continuing to monitor the treatment in Kuwait of a number of people held in connection with the Gulf crisis. These include nationals of Iraq, Jordan, Yemen and the Sudan, as well as Palestinians with travel documents and stateless persons. In 1995, the ICRC saw 620 such individuals.

Efforts of the Special Rapporteur

195　The Commission on Human Rights has made the fate of persons missing as a result of the Gulf conflict part of the mandate of the Special Rapporteur on the situation of human rights in Iraq. After sufficient resources became available in the summer of 1994 to investigate this issue, monitors from the United Nations Centre for Human Rights were sent to Kuwait in 1994 and 1995 to receive and gather information on missing persons. The Special Rapporteur concluded in his 1995 report to the General Assembly that there could be "no doubt of the general responsibility of Iraq under international law" for the fate of the disappeared persons and the effects on their families. Although the Special Rapporteur viewed Iraq's resumed participation in the Tripartite Commission as "a positive step", he emphasized that Iraq was "under an obligation to provide substantive replies on the individual files without further delay".[97]

97/Document 216

See page 793

Return of Kuwaiti property

196　Soon after the invasion of 2 August 1990, Kuwaiti authorities began reporting the extensive seizure by Iraq of public and private property in Kuwait. The Security Council condemned these seizures in

October.[98] Following the suspension of hostilities in February 1991, the Council demanded in resolution 686 (1991) that Iraq immediately begin to return all Kuwaiti property in the shortest possible period. It was the Council's view, set out in a letter from the Council President to my predecessor, that the modalities for this return of property should be arranged through the Secretary-General's office in consultation with the parties, who were in agreement with this procedure (S/22361).

197 The Security Council returned to the matter in resolution 687 (1991), noting that Kuwaiti property had not been returned and requesting the Secretary-General to report on the steps taken to resolve the issue. The Secretary-General was also directed to include with his report a list of property that Kuwait claimed had not been returned or had not been returned intact. In its resolutions 706 (1991) and 778 (1992), the Security Council decided that the programme should be financed with funds contributed to the United Nations escrow account established under those resolutions.

198 Once the programme for the return of property became operational in July 1991, Iraq returned significant amounts of gold, Kuwaiti paper currency, commemorative and commercial coins, civilian aircraft and spare parts, and museum and library items. However, six months later, large quantities of property, particularly military equipment and private property, still remained unreturned. On 5 February 1992, the President of the Security Council made a statement in which he referred to the amount of Kuwaiti property still unreturned as one example of Iraq's "disturbing" lack of cooperation in meeting its obligations under Security Council resolutions.[99] Again, on 23 November 1992, the Council President stressed that much property remained to be returned.[100] After little significant change in this situation, on 25 January 1994, the President of the Security Council asked me to submit a report on the return of all Kuwaiti property seized by Iraq.

199 In my report, which I submitted to the Council on 2 March 1994, I described the organizational details and modalities of the operation and annexed a list of property that had been handed over thus far.[101] An addendum to that report contained Kuwait's list of property that had not been returned or had not been returned intact, as called for by Security Council resolution 687 (1991). I explained that the role of the Coordinator for the return of property was one of receiving, registering and submitting to Iraq claims presented by Kuwait, and of facilitating the return of property declared by Iraq to be in its possession and ready for return. The responsibility for actually returning the property has rested with Iraq, while Kuwait has been responsible for receiving it. At no time has the property been in the custody of the United Nations, nor has it been within the scope of the Coordinator's mandate to investigate or verify claims from either party.

98/Document 17
See page 176

99/Document 101
See page 390

100/Document 137
See page 486

101/Document 182
See page 624

102/Document 182
See page 624

200   To date, properties returned have included those belonging to Kuwait's Ministries of Communication, Defence, Health, Information, Oil, Public Works, Social Affairs and Labour, and Transportation, as well as to the Central Bank of Kuwait, Kuwait Airways, the Arabic Institute for Planning in Kuwait, the Kuwait National Assembly, the Kuwait National Museum, the Kuwait Central Library, the Kuwait News Agency and the Kuwait Institute of Arabic Manuscripts.[102] However, according to the Government of Kuwait, a significant amount of property belonging to Kuwaiti Ministries and organizations has not been returned, or has been returned in unserviceable condition (S/25790, S/26103, S/26449, S/1994/243/Add.1). In addition, Iraq has returned no items of seized private property, valued by Kuwait at hundreds of millions of dollars.

201   In a letter dated 26 September 1994, Iraq stated that, once it had handed over a last C-130 aircraft, Iraq would have returned all the Kuwaiti property in its possession, thus fulfilling all its obligations in this respect under Security Council resolutions 686 (1991) and 687 (1991) (S/1994/1099). Kuwait responded by transmitting a list of Kuwaiti property still to be returned (S/1994/1126).

202   In a subsequent operation lasting from April through July 1995, Iraq returned additional military equipment to Kuwait, although the latter claimed that many of the items were returned in a state of disrepair or were not of Kuwaiti ownership. On 2 August, Kuwait reiterated its position that a significant quantity of military and private property items had not yet been returned, and expressed the hope that the Coordinator would continue his efforts to facilitate the return of all property by Iraq to Kuwait. Kuwait, in its communications on this issue, has emphasized the particular importance it attaches to the return of property which is irreplaceable, especially official archives. Although the Coordinator has remained at the disposal of the parties, little property has been returned since July 1995.

Mitigation of the environmental consequences of the conflict

203   Even before the suspension of hostilities, the United Nations system mobilized an international response to the environmental damage being caused by the crisis. In February 1991, within days of the first reports that Iraq had released 6 to 8 million barrels of oil into the Gulf, the United Nations Environment Programme (UNEP) dispatched an expert mission to the region to make a preliminary impact assessment. At the same time, UNEP encouraged and facilitated the revitalization of the Regional Organization for the Protection of the Marine Environment (ROPME), to which all eight States in the Gulf region belong, so that

ROPME could become a focal point for coordinating emergency activities and the environmental mitigation and rehabilitation efforts in the region (A/CONF.151/PC/72, A/49/207-E/1994/92).

204   Also in February 1991, UNEP launched an Inter-Agency consultation process through which an Inter-Agency Plan of Action was developed to assess the impact of the war on the atmosphere, terrestrial ecosystems, marine and coastal areas and the creation of hazardous wastes, and to propose a comprehensive programme of environmental rehabilitation. The first phase of the Plan of Action was completed on 21 July 1991 and involved extensive surveying by land, air and sea by some 50 experts from 12 United Nations agencies and international organizations, including UNEP, FAO, IAEA, WHO, the International Maritime Organization, the World Meteorological Organization, the United Nations Industrial Development Organization (UNIDO), the United Nations Centre for Human Settlements, UNESCO's Intergovernmental Oceanographic Commission, the World Conservation Union, the World Wildlife Fund and ROPME as well as some 20 other institutions from both within and outside the region (A/47/265-E/1992/81). In early October 1991, a representative of the Secretary-General, serving as the focal point for the United Nations system's activities related to the environmental crisis, conducted a fact-finding visit to Kuwait.

205   Iraq's responsibility for damage to the region's environment was specifically addressed by the Security Council in resolution 687 (1991), paragraph 16, which affirms that Iraq is "liable under international law" for the "environmental damage and the depletion of natural resources" which resulted from its unlawful invasion and occupation of Kuwait.

206   The General Assembly, for its part, cited this paragraph of resolution 687 (1991) in two resolutions calling upon the United Nations system to pursue its efforts to assess and counteract the short- and long-term environmental consequences of the conflict, and upon Member States to provide assistance.[103] The Assembly specifically cited the "disastrous situation caused in Kuwait and neighbouring areas by the torching and destruction of hundreds of its oil wells and of the other environmental consequences on the atmosphere and on land and marine life". The Assembly also expressed its profound concern at the adverse impact that the environmental damage had had on the economic activities of Kuwait and other countries of the region, including the effects on livestock, agriculture and fishing, as well as on wildlife.

207   The rapid response by the international community and private companies brought the short-term environmental consequences of the war under control in far less time than initially estimated. With the direct assistance and involvement of the International Maritime Organization, the massive oil spills, which had their greatest impact on Saudi

103/Document 99
See page 373;
Document 144
See page 509

Arabia's marine and coastal areas, were controlled by successive containment and clean-up programmes. The hundreds of Kuwaiti oil wells set on fire by Iraq, releasing contaminants into the air and onto the ground, were successfully capped by 6 November 1991.

208 Disruption of the terrestrial ecosystem caused by the movement of military vehicles, explosions, defensive constructions, unexploded ordnance and land-mines has taken longer to counter, and the overall long-term environmental impact of the war on the health and well-being of the people of the region remains a cause for concern. My personal representative visited Kuwait during 1992 to keep international attention focused on these issues. Since then, responsibility within the Secretariat for the environmental crisis in the Gulf region has passed on to the Department of Humanitarian Affairs, which, with UNEP, has continued to monitor the long-term environmental impact of the Gulf conflict on the region's ecosystems.

Protection of the environment in times of conflict

209 Iraq's actions during its invasion and occupation of Kuwait also led the General Assembly to adopt a resolution on the "protection of the environment in times of conflict". Following initial consideration in December 1991 of the issue of "exploitation of the environment as a weapon in times of armed conflict", the Assembly adopted resolution 47/37 in November 1992 stressing that "destruction of the environment, not justified by military necessity and carried out wantonly, is clearly contrary to international law". The resolution also urged States to comply with existing international law applicable to protection of the environment in times of armed conflict, including the Hague Convention respecting the Laws and Customs of War on Land (1907), the Geneva Convention relative to the Protection of Civilian Persons in Time of War (1949) and the Convention on the Prohibition of Military or Any Other Hostile Use of Environmental Modification Techniques (1976).

210 In a related initiative, in 1993 and 1994, the ICRC prepared Guidelines for military manuals and other instructions on the laws of war relating to the protection of the environment in times of armed conflict. Drawn from existing international legal obligations and from State practice, the Guidelines stated that the general prohibition against destroying civilian objects also protects the environment, and that the indiscriminate laying of land-mines is prohibited. (See paragraph 181 above for more concerning land-mines.) In December 1994, the General Assembly in resolution 49/50 invited all States to disseminate the Guidelines widely and to "give due consideration to the possibility of incorporating them into their military manuals and other instructions addressed to their military personnel".

United Nations Compensation Fund and Compensation Commission

211 The Security Council first affirmed that Iraq was liable under international law for any loss, damage or injury as a result of its invasion and illegal occupation of Kuwait in resolution 674 of 29 October 1990, which invited States to "collect relevant information regarding their claims, and those of their nationals and corporations, for restitution or financial compensation by Iraq, with a view to such arrangements as may be established in accordance with international law".[104] The Council returned to the subject in resolution 687 (1991) and, in resolution 692 (1991) of 20 May 1991, established the United Nations Compensation Commission (UNCC) and the United Nations Compensation Fund for the processing and payment of claims against Iraq.[105]

104/Document 17
See page 176

105/Document 35
See page 193;
Document 49
See page 240;
Document 54
See page 255

212 The Commission's functions are twofold: first, to administer the Compensation Fund, including determining the allocation of funds on hand and the payment of claims; and second, to organize the procedures and the resolution of claims. The Commission functions under the authority of the Security Council and is a subsidiary organ thereof. Its principal body is the Governing Council, which is composed of representatives of the current members of the Security Council at any given time. The Governing Council is the policy-making organ of the UNCC and, as such, has the responsibility for establishing guidelines on matters such as the administration and financing of the Compensation Fund and the procedures to be applied to the processing of claims. The Governing Council also has the final word as to the payments to be made from the Fund. It is assisted by a number of Commissioners who are experts in fields such as finance, law, accountancy, insurance and environmental damage assessment. A secretariat services and carries out the tasks assigned to it by the Governing Council and the Commissioners and is also responsible for the technical administration of the Compensation Fund.

213 As of 1 October 1995, the UNCC had become responsible for the largest compensation claims programme in history, having received more than 2.6 million claims with an asserted value exceeding $160 billion. The claims, which are submitted by Governments in the form of consolidated claims rather than by individual claimants, have been divided into six different categories:

- Category "A": departure from Iraq or Kuwait (924,937 claims)

- Category "B": serious personal injury or death (6,009)

- Category "C": individual claims for damages up to $100,000 (423,680)

- Category "D": individual claims for damages above $100,000 (10,414)

- Category "E": claims of corporations and other legal entities (6,098)

- Category "F": claims of Governments and international corporations (234)

The Commission has also received 1.24 million Egyptian workers' claims submitted in a consolidated fashion by the Central Bank of Egypt.

214   From its very beginning, in July and August 1991, the Governing Council of the Commission demonstrated particular concern for the more than 1.5 million individuals from Kuwait and more than 100 other countries who were displaced from both Iraq and Kuwait by the invasion and its consequences. In its very first decision, the Council provided the criteria for "simple and expedited procedures" by which Governments could submit consolidated claims and receive payments on behalf of individuals who suffered personal losses as a result of the displacements and related consequences.[106] Moreover, priority was given to individuals rather than corporations and Governments. The Governing Council's concern for individuals also led to the establishment of more practical evidentiary standards by which these claimants were to prove the existence of their losses, particularly since most of these individuals had departed Iraq and Kuwait in chaotic conditions, in many cases losing possession of their passports and important documents.[107]

215   Another matter to which the Governing Council gave early consideration was the situation of Palestinians and other persons who were not in a position to have their claims submitted by a Government. After extensive consultations, the Council decided that the United Nations Relief and Works Agency for Palestine Refugees in the Near East (UNRWA) would assume responsibility for submitting claims on behalf of Palestinians resident in several countries of the Middle East, and that the United Nations Development Programme (UNDP) would present the claims of Palestinians living in territories occupied by Israel. UNDP ultimately accepted similar proposals for the submission of claims by Palestinians residing in other countries. UNHCR offices in various parts of the world also agreed to file such claims.

216   A major concern of the Governing Council was to find a way to ensure that funds made available to Governments by the Commission are indeed passed on to the successful claimants. To that end, the Governing Council adopted decision 18, which, among other things, requires Governments to distribute the funds to claimants within six months of receiving payment from the Commission and to provide information to the Governing Council on the arrangements made for the funds' distribution.[108] Decision 18 also limits the amounts of fees that

106/Document 67
See page 280;
Document 68
See page 281

107/Document 106
See page 411;
Document 121
See page 459;
Document 145
See page 510

108/Document 185
See page 629

Governments may charge to claimants to offset the costs of claims processing.

217   The Government of Iraq has made useful contributions to the work of the Commission throughout its proceedings. Representatives of the Government of Iraq have addressed the Governing Council at each of its 19 sessions; members of the Commission's Secretariat meet regularly with Iraqi representatives to discuss technical matters; and the Government of Iraq has filed written information and views in response to all 12 of the Reports of the Executive Secretary issued pursuant to Article 16 of the Commission's Rules for Claims Procedure.[109] In its presentations to the Governing Council as well as in its written communications, Iraq has requested wider participation in the work of the Commission and access to more detailed information.

109/Document 121
See page 459

218   As the claims processing evolves towards the resolution of the more complex claims in categories "D", "E" and "F", the Commission's Rules provide for a more extensive participatory role for Iraq. Indeed, the Commission has already experienced more direct Iraqi involvement in the consolidated claim filed by the Government of Egypt. In the jurisdictional phase of this claim, the Panel of Commissioners, pursuant to Article 36 of the Rules, invited Iraq to file a "responsive written pleading" and to attend an oral hearing. The Government of Iraq filed its response and, although it was unable to attend the oral hearing, it did provide additional written views that were accepted by the Panel of Commissioners in lieu of Iraq's "hearing presentation". The Governing Council and the Commission's secretariat are currently discussing several procedural measures to facilitate the timely submission of additional information and views by the parties to claims and to accelerate the processing of claims. These measures should further enhance Iraq's role with regard to the resolution of category "D", "E" and "F" claims.

Decisions on awards

219   As of mid-December 1995, the Commission had issued awards to nearly 800,000 category "A" claimants worth more than $2.8 billion. (It should be noted that decisions on awards are a precursor step to the actual payment of those awards.) The Governing Council's decision covering the last 120,000 category "A" claims was scheduled to be issued in mid-1996, at which time the category "A" claims unit was to close down, having fulfilled its mandate to resolve more than 920,000 departure claims on an expedited basis.

220   The category "B" Panel of Commissioners completed its review of such claims in October 1995, and its "Report and Recommendations" was approved by the Governing Council at its 19th session, in December 1995. At that time, the category "B" Claims Unit within the Commission's secretariat ceased functioning, having resolved all serious

personal injury and death claims filed with the Commission with the exception of approximately 600 claims put forward on behalf of missing persons and prisoners of war, whose fate has yet to be determined. The total amount of compensation awarded in category "B" is more than $13 billion.

221   Approximately 300,000 category "C" awards were expected to have been issued by the Commission by the end of 1996, and the final work on such claims was expected to be concluded in mid-1997. The claims units responsible for the resolution of the claims in categories "D", "E" and "F" have begun the preliminary assessment of such claims and were scheduled to begin putting them before a number of Panels of Commissioners in 1996. As a result, it was expected that by the end of 1996 the bulk of the Commission's work will have shifted from the resolution of the "urgent claims" to a concentration on the analysis of the claims in the latter three categories.

Funding and payment of awards

222   Under the provisions of Security Council resolutions 687 (1991), 692 (1991) and 706 (1991), the expenses of the Commission and the resources necessary for the payment of awards to successful claimants are to be borne by the United Nations Compensation Fund, which is to be financed by a percentage of the proceeds from the sale of Iraq's exports of petroleum and petroleum products.[110] Since the sanctions imposed on Iraq by the Security Council remain in place and, to date, the Government of Iraq has not accepted the opportunities provided by the Security Council in its resolutions 706 (1991), 712 (1991) and 986 (1995) for the limited export of petroleum and petroleum products (see paragraphs 317-332), the Compensation Fund has not been adequately financed.[111] This situation improved with the adoption in October 1992 of Security Council resolution 778 (1992), under which Iraqi oil assets frozen abroad were to be transferred by Governments to a United Nations escrow account (see paragraphs 323-327). Pursuant to that resolution, the Commission has been able to finance its operations from 30 per cent of funds representing Iraqi oil-related assets transferred to the escrow account.

223   Because of the limited financing made available, the Governing Council has, to date, given priority to the payment of awards to successful claimants in category "B" for serious personal injury and death claims. In June 1994, the Commission paid $2.7 million to 670 category "B" claimants from 16 countries; in October 1995, the Commission paid an additional $8.2 million to 2,577 category "B" claimants from 41 countries and from three international organizations filing Palestinian claims.[112] At its final session in 1995, the Governing Council also authorized the payment of an additional $2.4 million to 720 cate-

110/Document 35
See page 193;
Document 54
See page 255;
Document 72
See page 285

111/Document 7
See page 168;
Document 72
See page 285;
Document 81
See page 308;
Document 207
See page 754

112/Document 215
See page 793;
Document 218
See page 809

gory "B" claimants from 19 Governments and international organizations. In total, by the end of 1995 more than $13.3 million had been paid to category "B" claimants. However, the Commission still does not possess the resources necessary to pay the bulk of its outstanding compensation awards, a shortfall that will only be exacerbated as the Commission continues its functions of processing claims and issuing awards.

Provisions of resolution 687 (1991) relating to terrorism

224   In the preamble to resolution 687 (1991), the Security Council deplored the threats made by Iraq during the Gulf conflict to "make use of terrorism against targets outside Iraq". The Council also deplored the taking of hostages by Iraq, recalling in this regard that the International Convention against the Taking of Hostages, which was opened for signature in New York in 1979, categorizes such acts as manifestations of international terrorism. Consequently, paragraph 32 of resolution 687 (1991) specifically required Iraq to inform the Security Council that it would "not commit or support any act of international terrorism or allow any organization directed towards commission of such acts to operate within its territory and to condemn unequivocally and renounce all acts, methods and practices of terrorism".[113]

225   To fulfil this requirement, Iraq wrote letters on 11 June 1991 and 23 January 1992 to the Secretary-General and the President of the Security Council, stating Iraq's commitment to refrain from terrorism in the exact language set out in resolution 687 (1991), paragraph 32 (S/23472).[114] These letters were noted by the Security Council President in his statements of 11 March and 23 November 1992 evaluating Iraq's implementation of the obligations imposed on it by Security Council resolutions.[115] No further action concerning terrorism was required of Iraq by the Council.

113/Document 35
See page 193

114/Document 59
See page 264

115/Document 108
See page 421;
Document 137
See page 486

VIII Disarmament and weapons control

226   Iraq's invasion of Kuwait led the Security Counci, to embark on a far-reaching programme of Iraqi disarmament and weapons control to ensure that Iraq would never again, through the possession of weapons of mass destruction and long-range missiles, pose a threat to its immediate neighbours. To carry out this complex and unprecedented work, the Security Council in April 1991 established a subsidiary body, the United Nations Special Commission (UNSCOM), and endowed it with a mandate to implement the provisions of section C of resolution 687 (1991) relating to chemical and biological weapons and ballistic missiles, and to assist the Director General of the International Atomic Energy Agency with similar work in the nuclear area. The IAEA Director General, in turn, established an Action Team to implement section C's nuclear-related provisions.

UNSCOM/IAEA *mandate*

116/Document 35
See page 193

227   Section C of resolution 687 (1991)[116] defined the mandate of the United Nations Special Commission as follows:
- To "carry out immediate on-site inspection of Iraq's biological, chemical and missile capabilities";
- To take possession for their destruction, removal or rendering harmlessof "all chemical and biological weapons and all stocks of agents and all related subsystems and components and all research, development, support and manufacturing facilities";
- To supervise the destruction by Iraq of all its "ballistic missiles with a range greater than one hundred and fifty kilometres, and related major parts and repair and production facilities";
- To monitor and verify Iraq's compliance with its undertaking "not to use, develop, construct or acquire any of the items specified";
- To assist and cooperate with the Director General of the International Atomic Energy Agency in the elimination of Iraq's nuclear-weapon capabilities and in the subsequent monitoring of non-proscribed nuclear activities; and

- To designate for inspection "any additional locations" as deemed necessary by UNSCOM to ensure the elimination of all Iraq's banned capabilities—nuclear as well as non-nuclear.

228   In parallel, the Director General of the IAEA was mandated:
- "To carry out immediate on-site inspections of Iraq's nuclear capabilities" and additional sites as designated by UNSCOM;
- To destroy, remove or render harmless Iraq's nuclear weapons, any subsystems or components or any research, development, support or manufacturing facilities related to such items and nuclear-weapons-usable materials;
- To take exclusive control of all of Iraq's nuclear-weapons-usable materials for custody and removal, with the assistance and cooperation of the Special Commission;
- To monitor and verify Iraq's compliance with its undertaking "not to use, develop, construct or acquire any of the items specified"; and
- To inventory "all nuclear material in Iraq subject to the Agency's verification and inspections to confirm that Agency safeguards cover all relevant nuclear activities in Iraq".

UNSCOM/IAEA organization

229   After Iraq had formally accepted the provisions of resolution 687 (1991), on 18 April 1991 my predecessor submitted to the Security Council a plan for the creation of a United Nations special commission.[117] Following acceptance of the plan by the Security Council on 19 April, the Secretary-General appointed the Executive Chairman and the Deputy Executive Chairman of UNSCOM. Since its establishment, the Commission has been made up of representatives of: Australia, Austria, Belgium, Canada, China, Czechoslovakia (later, the Czech Republic), Finland, France, Germany, Indonesia, Italy, Japan, the Netherlands, Nigeria, Norway, Poland, the Soviet Union (later, the Russian Federation), Sweden, the United Kingdom, the United States and Venezuela.

117/Document 43
See page 208

230   Full sessions of the Commission are held twice yearly to assess the results of operations to date and developments in relations between UNSCOM and Iraq and, in the light of both of these, to discuss policy issues relating to future activities. The work of UNSCOM is planned and managed, under the direction of the Executive Chairman, from United Nations Headquarters in New York. A Field Office in Bahrain serves as the assembly and training point for inspection teams and as the base for UNSCOM's transport aircraft. With the commencement of the ongoing

monitoring and verification regime, the Baghdad Field Office was upgraded in the summer of 1994. It is now the Baghdad Monitoring and Verification Centre (BMVC).

231   UNSCOM staff have been provided by Member States, WHO and the United Nations Secretariat, in particular the Centre for Disarmament Affairs. In addition, large numbers of technical experts—including members of UNSCOM, the Secretariat and personnel made available by Governments, WHO and the provisional secretariat of the Organization for the Prohibition of Chemical Weapons—have served as inspectors and field support officers and on disposal teams. By the end of October 1995, more than 1,000 individuals from some 60 countries had served with UNSCOM and the IAEA.

232   The Director General of the International Atomic Energy Agency, in order to implement resolution 687 (1991), established within the IAEA secretariat in Vienna a small Action Team (hereafter referred to as the IAEA). With the assistance and cooperation of UNSCOM, the Action Team plans and conducts the inspection, disposal and monitoring activities in the nuclear field. The IAEA Action Team has its own offices within the Baghdad Monitoring and Verification Centre, while its inspection and monitoring teams utilize UNSCOM's transportation, communication, Field Office and logistics capabilities.

233   Every six months, in June and in December, both the Secretary-General and the Director General of the International Atomic Energy Agency submit separate reports to the Security Council on implementation of the plans to implement the relevant provisions of resolution 687 (1991).[118] In addition, every April and October, the Secretary-General and the Director General of the IAEA submit reports on the implementation of the plans for ongoing monitoring and verification.[119]

UNSCOM/IAEA privileges and immunities

234   While resolution 687 (1991) mandated UNSCOM and the IAEA to conduct inspections in Iraq, it was necessary to establish the detailed modalities and legal basis on which such inspections would be conducted. This was achieved through an exchange of letters in May 1991 involving my predecessor, the Executive Chairman of UNSCOM and the Minister for Foreign Affairs of Iraq. The letters constituted an agreement between the United Nations and Iraq under which Iraq was to accord to members of UNSCOM, to officials of the United Nations, the IAEA and specialized agencies of the United Nations system, and to technical experts and specialists in Iraq for the purposes of fulfilling the mandate all rights contained in the pertinent provisions of the Convention on the Privileges and Immunities of the United Nations (1946) and the Convention on the Privileges and Immunities of the Specialized

Agencies (1947). As agreed in the exchange of letters, Iraq was also to accord to UNSCOM:

- "Unrestricted freedom of entry and exit without delay or hindrance of its personnel, property, supplies, equipment, spare parts and other items as well as of means of transport, including expeditious issuance of entry and exit visas";
- "Unrestricted freedom of movement without advance notice within Iraq of the personnel of the Special Commission and its equipment and means of transport";
- "The right to unimpeded access to any site or facility for the purpose of the on-site inspection [pursuant to the mandate] whether such a site be above or below ground . . . Any number of sites, facilities or locations may be subject to inspection simultaneously";
- "The right to request, receive, examine and copy any record, data or information or examine, retain, move or photograph, including videotape, any item relevant to the Special Commission's activities and to conduct interviews";
- "The right to designate any site whatsoever for observation, inspection or other monitoring activity and for storage, destruction or rendering harmless" of the items described above;
- "The right to install equipment or construct facilities for observation, inspection, testing or other monitoring activity and for storage, destruction or rendering harmless" of those items;
- "The right to take photographs, whether from the ground or from the air, relevant to the Special Commission's activities";
- "The right to take and analyse samples of any kind as well as to remove and export samples for off-site analysis"; and
- "The right to unrestricted communication by radio satellite or other forms of communication".

235   Iraq was also to:

- "Provide at no cost to the United Nations . . . all such premises as may be necessary for the accommodation and fulfilment of the functions of the Special Commission", to be under the exclusive control of the Executive Chairman of the Special Commission; and
- "Without prejudice to the use by the Special Commission of its own security, . . . ensure the security and safety of the Special Commission and its personnel".

236   These privileges and immunities have proved to be essential to the effective fulfilment of the mandate. They remain in force and have

Document 114
See page 434
Document 116
See page 438;
Document 134
See page 480;
Document 136
See page 484;
Document 155
See page 531;
Document 156
See page 535;
Document 172
See page 596;
Document 173
See page 599;
Document 187
See page 634;
Document 188
See page 641;
Document 193
See page 665;
Document 195
See page 685;
Document 205
See page 727;
Document 206
See page 746;
Document 213
See page 766;
Document 214
See page 771

120/Document 73
See page 287;

Document 82
See page 309;

Document 88
See page 325

since been clarified and supplemented by specific provisions of Security Council resolution 707 (1991) and of UNSCOM's and the IAEA's plans for ongoing monitoring and verification.[120]

Concept of operations

237   The implementation of section C of resolution 687 (1991) by UNSCOM and the IAEA has involved a two-stage process: identification of proscribed capabilities and their disposal; and identification of dual-purpose capabilities and their monitoring.

238   The two stages, implemented concurrently, are interdependent and mutually reinforcing. Indeed, without full disclosure of Iraq's prohibited programmes, and without adequate accounting for the disposal or current disposition of capabilities associated with those programmes, there can be no confidence that the ongoing monitoring and verification system is comprehensive. Conversely, the process of identifying dual-purpose capabilities—and the sources from which Iraq acquired them—has helped in identifying elements of the banned programmes that Iraq did not declare and in building confidence that banned capabilities have been fully accounted for.

239   The implementation process has relied on whatever Iraqi cooperation has been forthcoming and on the enforcement powers of the Security Council. There are two instruments of enforcement immediately available to the Council: the maintenance of sanctions and the oil embargo until Iraq complies with the disarmament provisions of resolution 687 (1991); and an interpretation that failure to comply constitutes a material breach of the terms of the cease-fire and hence opens the way to resumed military action by the coalition or certain of its members. Both means have been used.

Proscribed capabilities

240   Under resolution 687 (1991), the Security Council requires Iraq to declare the locations, amounts and types of all banned capabilities, and calls on UNSCOM and the IAEA, on the basis of Iraq's declarations, to inspect the declared locations and others designated for inspection by UNSCOM in order to verify the accuracy and completeness of the declarations. UNSCOM and the IAEA are also called upon to ensure the destruction, removal or rendering harmless of these banned capabilities.

Dual-purpose capabilities

241   Monitoring of Iraq's dual-purpose capabilities is of indefinite duration since it is to continue until the Security Council decides other-

wise. The purpose is to monitor Iraq's compliance with its obligations not to use, develop, construct or acquire banned items through the diversion of dual-purpose capabilities towards proscribed ends. Consequently, UNSCOM and the IAEA have designed two separate but interlocking systems for monitoring Iraq's ongoing compliance with its obligations in this area: one for dual-purpose capabilities and activities within Iraq, and another—an export/import monitoring mechanism—to monitor Iraq's trade in such capabilities once sanctions are eased or lifted (S/1994/341, S/1995/215).[121] (See paragraphs 311-312, under the subheading "Future activities", for a full description of the export/import monitoring mechanism.)

121/Document 82
See page 309;
Document 88
See page 325;
Document 193
See page 665

242   The operational concept for implementing the UNSCOM and IAEA plans for ongoing monitoring and verification (OMV) involves regular inspections of dual-purpose capabilities, maintenance of accurate inventories of all dual-purpose items and materials and close tracking of the use to which all inventoried items and materials are put. Underpinning this endeavour is an array of interrelated activities: aerial surveillance with a variety of sensors, remote ground-based sensors, tags and seals, sample-taking and analysis, a variety of detection technologies, information obtained from other sources and, at such time as sanctions on Iraq's trade in dual-purpose capabilities are eased or lifted, notifications under the export/import monitoring mechanism. No one of these elements on its own would suffice to provide confidence in the system, but together they constitute the most comprehensive international monitoring system ever established in the sphere of arms control.

Developments in the course of implementation

243   Relations between Iraq and UNSCOM and the IAEA can be characterized as having passed through four phases: an initial phase lasting until September 1991, during which Iraq consistently sought to deny access; a second period, lasting until November 1993, during which Iraq generally did not impede inspections physically but did not provide accurate accounts of its prohibited programmes and did not accept ongoing monitoring and verification activities in accordance with Security Council decisions; a third period, lasting until August 1995, during which Iraq actively cooperated in the establishment and operation of ongoing monitoring and verification mechanisms but continued to provide inadequate disclosures about the extent of its prohibited programmes and to deny access to its archives; and the current period, during which UNSCOM and the IAEA have been evaluating the mass of documentation handed over by Iraq in mid-August 1995 to assess whether Iraq has yet fully revealed its prohibited capabilities.

244   It was initially expected that Iraq would make full and accurate declaration within the time-frame required by resolution 687 (1991), primarily because the lifting of the sanctions and the oil embargo imposed on Iraq was dependent on Iraq being judged in compliance with the terms of the cease-fire. Iraq had explicitly accepted resolution 687 (1991) in a 6 April 1991 letter from its Minister for Foreign Affairs to my predecessor and to the President of the Security Council, in which he stated, with regard to the resolution's provisions on weapons of mass destruction, that Iraq was in compliance with the Treaty on the Non-Proliferation of Nuclear Weapons (1968), that it had adhered to the 1925 Geneva Protocol for the Prohibition of the Use in War of Asphyxiating, Poisonous and Other Gases, and that it had signed the Declaration issued by the Conference of the States Parties to the 1925 Geneva Protocol and Other Interested States held in Paris from 7 to 11 January 1989.[122]

122/Document 39
See page 203

245   On 18 April 1991, pursuant to its obligations under resolution 687 (1991), Iraq made declarations that it had no proscribed nuclear items and that, therefore, monitoring should remain confined to materials under the IAEA's safeguards; that it had no items related to biological weapons or superguns; that it had only some 11,000 chemical munitions; and that it had only 52 Scud missiles remaining and 10 mobile launchers.

Interference with IAEA inspection

246   The first instance in which Iraq created serious obstacles to the work of UNSCOM and the IAEA occurred in June 1991, during the second nuclear inspection conducted by the IAEA (S/22739, S/22743). On three occasions, Iraq sought to deny the Action Team access to sites designated for inspection, and in the third of these incidents, when IAEA inspectors sought to intercept vehicles leaving a site against the express wishes of the team, Iraqi personnel fired warning shots in the air to prevent the inspectors from approaching the vehicles. Furthermore, in contradiction of Iraq's 18 April 1991 declaration, the team found small quantities of plutonium and evidence of a programme to enrich uranium to weapons grade.

247   As a result of these events, the Security Council dispatched, at the end of June 1991, a special mission to Iraq composed of the Executive Chairman of UNSCOM, the Director General of the International Atomic Energy Agency and the United Nations Under-Secretary-General for Disarmament Affairs.[123] The mission obtained assurances of full future cooperation on the part of Iraq, assurances that were subsequently confirmed in writing to my predecessor (S/22762).[124] Pursuant to these assurances, and amid growing evidence that Iraq's initial declaration about its nuclear capabilities was false, Iraq made a new nuclear declaration on 7 July 1991, admitting to three programmes to

123/Document 63
See page 268

124/Document 64
See page 269

enrich uranium: electromagnetic isotope separation, gas centrifuge and chemical exchange. However, Iraq continued to maintain that these three programmes were for peaceful purposes and that it had no programme to acquire or develop nuclear weapons.

248   During this same period of June-July 1991, UNSCOM's missile, chemical and biological inspections were also discovering undeclared capabilities. These included an assembled supergun and parts for four others, missiles and launchers, missile production facilities, chemical munitions at undeclared sites, and a facility which Iraq admitted was for biological warfare research (S/23615).

249   In June 1991, UNSCOM sought, in accordance with the Status Agreement on Privileges and Immunities, to introduce its own helicopters for aerial surveillance and for transporting the inspection teams to sites for no-notice inspections. Iraq, however, refused to ensure the safety of such flights or to provide support facilities for their operation. On 11 August, aircraft with crew and support personnel made available by the United States began to fly, under the direction of UNSCOM, high-altitude reconnaissance flights over Iraq.

Council reaction to Iraqi non-compliance

250   The various discoveries and events of the early months of UNSCOM's and the IAEA's work in Iraq led the Security Council to adopt, on 15 August 1991, resolution 707 (1991).[125] Stating that it was gravely concerned by Iraq's "flagrant violation" and "material breaches" of its obligations under resolution 687 (1991), the Council banned Iraq from conducting any nuclear activities other than those relating to the use of isotopes for medical, industrial or agricultural purposes, and further clarified UNSCOM's right to use whatever means of air transport it deemed necessary, anywhere in Iraq, for the purposes of both transportation and aerial surveillance.

125/Document 73
See page 287

251   In September 1991, the sixth IAEA on-site inspection found, on successive days, large amounts of documentation relating to Iraq's undeclared efforts to acquire nuclear weapons. On the first day of the inspection, Iraqi officials accompanying the team confiscated documents uncovered by the team. The next day, the IAEA team refused to yield a second set of documents. In response, Iraq refused to allow the team to leave the inspection site with these documents. There then ensued a four-day stand-off during which the team remained in the parking-lot of the site. It was only after a statement by the President of the Security Council demanding that the inspection team be immediately allowed to leave the site with all documents they deemed appropriate,[126] and under the threat of enforcement action by members of the Security Council, that Iraq permitted the team to leave with the documents. While Iraq

126/Document 84
See page 319

subsequently returned some of the confiscated documents, certain key documents were never recovered.

252 Following this incident, UNSCOM's Executive Chairman and the IAEA Action Team leader visited Iraq in early October 1991 to obtain assurances of future cooperation—both in relation to access to sites and in relation to UNSCOM's right to introduce its own helicopters. During this visit, Iraq provided assurances in both regards (S/23604, S/23070).

Obstruction of destruction and monitoring activities

253 On 11 October 1991, in fulfilment of paragraphs 10 and 12 of resolution 687 (1991), the Security Council adopted resolution 715 (1991), in which it approved UNSCOM's and the IAEA's plans for ongoing monitoring and verification of Iraq's dual-purpose capabilities.[127] These plans, which entered into effect immediately, required Iraq to submit initial declarations as to its dual-purpose capabilities within 30 days. Instead, however, on 19 November, Iraq's Minister for Foreign Affairs informed the President of the Security Council that Iraq considered the plans for ongoing monitoring and verification to be unlawful.[128] In response, the Executive Chairman of UNSCOM dispatched a special mission to Iraq in late January 1992. Although the mission reported some progress in eliciting information on Iraq's programmes to acquire or produce weapons of mass destruction and ballistic missiles, it was not able to obtain assurances that Iraq would comply with resolution 715 (1991).[129]

254 As a result, I decided to dispatch a special mission to visit Iraq immediately to secure from the highest levels of Government Iraq's unconditional agreement to implement all of Iraq's relevant obligations under resolutions 687 (1991), 707 (1991) and 715 (1991). On 19 February 1992, the Security Council supported this decision and stated that the mission "should stress the serious consequences if such agreement to implement is not forthcoming".[130] The Council declared that by failing to acknowledge its obligations under resolutions 707 (1991) and 715 (1991), Iraq was in material breach of resolution 687 (1991).

255 The high-level mission, headed by the Executive Chairman of UNSCOM, visited Iraq from 21 to 24 February 1992 (S/23643). During the visit, Iraq stated that it accepted only the *principle* of ongoing monitoring and verification, subject to considerations of sovereignty, territorial integrity, national security and non-infringement of Iraq's industrial capabilities. Iraq further informed the mission that it intended to dispatch a high-level delegation to New York to convey Iraq's position on resolutions 707 (1991) and 715 (1991).

256 Initially, Iraq had also prevented the start of the destruction of equipment associated with its ballistic missile production programme.

127/Document 89
See page 339

128/Document 94
See page 363;
Document 100
See page 374

129/Document 102
See page 391

130/Document 104
See page 409

On 14 February 1992, the Executive Chairman of UNSCOM had addressed a letter to Iraq concerning the destruction of certain missile facilities and related items (S/23673). After a period of discussion, however, Iraq refused to comply. Instead, Iraq's Minister for Foreign Affairs sent a letter to the Executive Chairman reiterating an earlier Iraqi proposal to reuse equipment for the BADR-2000 ballistic missile project for "civilian purposes" and for the manufacture of missiles having a range of 100 kilometres. On 28 February 1992, the Security Council condemned the failure by Iraq to comply with its obligations to destroy equipment as directed by the Council and to make the declarations required under the Council's resolutions.[131] The Council also reiterated its statement that Iraq was in material breach of resolution 687 (1991).

131/Document 105
See page 410

257   On 11 and 12 March 1992, a high-level Iraqi delegation, headed by the Deputy Prime Minister, appeared before the Security Council, which met in formal session. In an introductory statement, the President of the Council reiterated the Council's position on the state of Iraqi compliance with its various obligations under the relevant Council resolutions.[132] The Deputy Prime Minister addressed the Council on 11 March, and on 12 March he responded to questions addressed to him by members of the Council (S/PV.3059, S/PV.3059 (Resumption 2)). However, the unconditional assurances which the Council had been seeking were not forthcoming on either occasion.

132/Document 108
See page 421

258   In his initial statement, the Deputy Prime Minister said that Iraq had already provided UNSCOM with all the necessary information on its proscribed weapons and production facilities. He further disclosed for the first time that Iraq had unilaterally destroyed 270,000 proscribed items after the adoption of resolution 687 (1991). He also stated that Iraq was ready to agree to a practical mechanism regarding equipment proscribed by resolution 687 (1991), with a view to rendering that equipment harmless. In regard to ongoing monitoring and verification, the Deputy Prime Minister stated that Iraq was prepared to cooperate, while underlining the need for respect for Iraqi dignity, sovereignty and national security. The President of the Council, in a concluding statement on 12 March, called on Iraq to take immediate steps to comply fully and unconditionally with its obligations.[133]

133/Document 109
See page 425

New Iraqi declarations

259   Subsequent to the Council meeting, Iraq made additional declarations concerning the numbers of ballistic missiles, chemical weapons and associated items that it had destroyed unilaterally. It also said that destruction of buildings and equipment could proceed, and promised shortly to submit both the "full, final and complete disclosures" required of it on all aspects of its proscribed programmes and, in the area

of dual-purpose capabilities, the initial declarations required to establish ongoing monitoring and verification.

260 With the issue of the destruction of production facilities effectively resolved, a ballistic missile team oversaw the destruction of nine items of equipment from 21 to 30 March 1992, and a team supervised the destruction of the majority of the remaining items from 13 to 21 April 1992. In May 1992, the IAEA also supervised the destruction of the Al Atheer facility for the design and construction of a nuclear device.

Threats against UNSCOM aircraft

261 Iraq, however, remained opposed to UNSCOM's aerial surveillance flights. In a letter to UNSCOM dated 9 April 1992, Iraq's Minister for Foreign Affairs called for a halt to all such flights "in order to avoid any unfortunate incidents" and made reference to the possibility that the flights might "endanger the aircraft itself and its pilot".[134] In his response, the Executive Chairman expressed the gravest concern at these remarks, which appeared, he said, "to constitute a threat to the security of the Commission's aerial surveillance flights which . . . are expressly authorized under Security Council resolutions 707 (1991) and 715 (1991)".

134/Document 118
See page 441

262 Upon receipt of this correspondence, the Security Council held consultations on 10 April 1992, after which the President issued a statement reaffirming UNSCOM's right to conduct such flights.[135] The Council called upon the Government of Iraq to give assurances on the security and safety of the flights and warned of "serious consequences" if Iraq did not comply with its obligations in this regard. On 12 April, the Minister for Foreign Affairs of Iraq addressed a letter to the President of the Security Council in which he affirmed that the Government of Iraq "did not intend and does not intend to carry out any military operation aimed at" UNSCOM's aerial surveillance flights (S/23806).

135/Document 115
See page 438

Attempts to secure full declarations from Iraq

263 On 12 March 1992, Iraq, responding for the first time to the demand in resolution 707 (1991) to make "full, final and complete disclosure of all aspects" of its prohibited programmes, handed over to the Director General of the International Atomic Energy Agency what it called its "full, final and complete report" on its nuclear programme. The IAEA expressed deep dissatisfaction with the quality of the document and requested that Iraq revise the report by filling gaps and providing additional detailed information. On 5 June 1992, a revised version of the report was transmitted to the IAEA by a letter from the Iraqi Minister for Foreign Affairs.[136] He explained that the omissions and the lack of scientific and technical details in the first version of the report reflected the Iraqi authorities' "deep concern over the possibility

136/Document 73
See page 287;
Document 118
See page 441;
Document 136
See page 484

that such details could reach various quarters which would use them as a source for establishing and developing a nuclear programme". The IAEA, while acknowledging a few improvements, concluded that the revised version of the report was still totally inadequate.

264   On 5 June 1992, Iraq made what it called its "full, final and complete reports" on chemical and biological weapons and ballistic missiles. The Executive Chairman of UNSCOM, upon analysis of these declarations, described them as "grossly inadequate" and stated that they contained "inaccuracies, inconsistencies and major gaps". They were, he said, "tailored to what Iraq considered UNSCOM to know already, rather than constituting a frank and open disclosure of all the facts".[137]

137/Document 141
See page 492

265   In response to UNSCOM's subsequent attempts to rectify omissions in Iraq's reports, Iraq denied that it had ever used chemical weapons, despite internationally verified evidence to the contrary. Iraqi declarations about imports and production were not supported by tangible or documentary evidence and there was insufficient and misleading information about the evolution of the various programmes and about the links between them. Furthermore, Iraq failed to substantiate information provided to UNSCOM on its prohibited programmes, claiming that it had destroyed all documents related to prohibited activities after the adoption of resolution 687 (1991), a claim which UNSCOM did not accept. Iraq also informed UNSCOM that it had issued an order to protect or conceal certain types of documents unrelated to resolution 687 (1991) from inspection by UNSCOM. Indeed, inspection teams had visited a number of sites which appeared to them to have been "sanitized".

266   In mid-June 1992, Iraq submitted the initial declarations it considered sufficient for the purposes of monitoring, but the reports contained little new information and little about facilities with dual capability. Consequently, they were deemed by UNSCOM to be inadequate for the purposes of initiating full-scale ongoing monitoring and verification in accordance with resolution 715 and the plans adopted by the Security Council. Furthermore, Iraq maintained its objections to the monitoring plans.

Incident at the Ministry of Agriculture

267   A major political problem developed on 5 July 1992 when Iraq refused an inspection team access to the Iraqi Ministry of Agriculture.[138] UNSCOM had reliable information from two sources that the building contained archives related to proscribed activities, in contradiction to Iraq's assertion that all such documents had been destroyed. Iraq, however, claimed that UNSCOM had no right to enter the building as it contained nothing of relevance and that to allow access would be to undermine Iraq's sovereignty and national security. Iraq failed to respond to attempts to resolve the issue at the field level, leading the

138/Document 141
See page 492

Executive Chairman to visit Baghdad from 17 to 19 July 1992. At the end of the visit, Iraq's Deputy Prime Minister offered to permit an inspection independently of UNSCOM, by persons from what he described as the "neutral" members of the Security Council. This idea was rejected by the Council.

268   After a delay of more than three weeks, and following the threat of enforcement action by members of the Security Council, access to the Ministry was obtained. No relevant documents were found, although there was evidence that items had recently been removed from offices. At Iraq's request, the Executive Chairman visited Iraq during the inspection and met with Iraqi officials to discuss future relations. During these talks, the Deputy Prime Minister of Iraq promised a new chapter of cooperation and openness in relations between UNSCOM and Iraq.

Iraq blocks UNSCOM flights

269   On 7 January 1993, Iraq informed UNSCOM that henceforth it would be denied the use of the airfield at Habbaniyah and should either use Iraqi aircraft to fly between Iraq and Bahrain or travel by land from Amman.[139] Such prohibitions would have prevented UNSCOM from conducting short-notice inspections, and the Security Council, in a statement of 8 January, noted that this was an "unacceptable and material breach" of resolution 687.[140]

270   UNSCOM notified Iraq on 9 January of its intention to fly its aircraft over the next days, but Iraq directly linked the continuation of UNSCOM flights with the lifting of the restrictions placed on the international operations of Iraqi Airways by the sanctions regime. The Security Council responded on 11 January by demanding that Iraq cooperate fully with UNSCOM and by warning Iraq of the "serious consequences" that would flow from its "continued defiance".[141] That defiance also included Iraqi incursions into the demilitarized zone between Iraq and Kuwait and increased Iraqi military activity in the no-fly zones (see paragraphs 133-144). Iraq informed the Council on 13 January that it would allow UNSCOM flights on a case-by-case basis but stated that it would not bear responsibility for the safety of such flights. That same day, in accordance with the Security Council's determination of 11 January that Iraq was in material breach of resolution 687 (1991), the United States, the United Kingdom and France staged air raids on sites in southern Iraq.

271   On 16 January, Iraq offered to ensure the safety of UNSCOM flights, but only if they entered Iraqi airspace from Jordanian airspace. UNSCOM responded that it did not have the operational capability to re-route its flights through Jordanian airspace and reminded Iraq of its obligations to cooperate with UNSCOM. While continuing to block all UNSCOM flights, Iraq stated on 17 January that UNSCOM aircraft could enter Iraqi airspace from Bahrain if UNSCOM ensured that no

139/Document 151
See page 519

140/Document 146
See page 512

141/Document 148
See page 516

aircraft of the coalition States flew in the no-fly zones over Iraq whenever UNSCOM aircraft were in Iraqi airspace. UNSCOM immediately informed Iraq that it did not have the wherewithal to comply with these conditions and again reminded Iraq of its obligations. That same day, the United States again took military action against Iraq, launching missiles at a site in the south of Baghdad that had been associated with Iraq's nuclear-weapon programme.

272   On 18 January, Iraq reiterated the same conditions for UNSCOM flights that it had communicated the previous day. Later that afternoon, air raids by the United States and the United Kingdom attacked radar sites in southern and northern Iraq. On 19 January 1993, Iraq informed UNSCOM that it would be able to resume its flights on the basis of established procedures.

273   In February 1993, in an echo of the events of early January, Iraqi officials threatened to shoot down a helicopter providing supporting overhead surveillance for an inspection team if the aircraft did not leave the vicinity of the site. The helicopter left the area temporarily but returned to complete the inspection after UNSCOM raised the issue with higher-level Iraqi authorities.

Iraqi refusal, and then acceptance, of its monitoring obligations

274   In the spring of 1993, problems of non-compliance arose in relation to two new issues: the removal of certain precursor chemicals and production equipment from the Al Fallujah sites to Al Muthanna for destruction; and the installation of remote-controlled monitoring cameras at two rocket engine test stands. Iraq sought to link these two issues with its demand to have a "dialogue" between Iraq, on the one hand, and UNSCOM and the IAEA, or the Security Council, on the other.

275   There followed an intensive series of written and oral exchanges between UNSCOM and Iraq. Iraq explained its objection to the planned destruction of the chemicals and equipment on the grounds that it was possible for them to be redeployed. It objected to the installation of the cameras on the grounds that this would in effect constitute ongoing monitoring and verification under resolution 715 (1991), a resolution whose terms, Iraq contended, were still the subject of discussion between it and the Security Council. Instead, Iraq proposed that action on each of these items await the conclusion of the "dialogue" on how the relevant resolutions should be implemented.

276   These developments led the Security Council, on 18 June 1993, to demand that Iraq accede to the removal and destruction of the chemicals and equipment in question and cease its obstruction of the installation of the cameras.[142] Iraq acceded to the removal and destruction of the chemicals and equipment, which proceeded without further

142/Document 164
See page 572

incident in early July 1993, but it continued to refuse the installation of the cameras.

277   In order to resolve this impasse, the Executive Chairman of UNSCOM visited Baghdad in July 1993. During the visit, Iraq stated for the first time its readiness to comply with the provisions of the plans for ongoing monitoring and verification as contained in resolution 715 (1991). The Executive Chairman subsequently reported that both sides had agreed to hold high-level technical talks in New York at which one of the prime subjects would be the nature and implementation of ongoing monitoring and verification (S/26127). All outstanding issues, including the activation of the cameras, were to be addressed. In the meantime, the cameras were to be installed, tested and maintained. UNSCOM would send inspectors to the two test sites as and when it wished, and Iraq would inform UNSCOM of each rocket test sufficiently in advance for it to send observers. This arrangement was observed.

278   The first round of high-level technical talks was held in New York from 31 August to 9 September 1993 (S/26451). During the talks, UNSCOM and the IAEA explained to Iraq precisely what ongoing monitoring and verification would entail. Iraq stated that its principal concerns related to how the intrusive rights and privileges of UNSCOM would be implemented so as not to endanger the safety of the Iraqi leadership, infringe on Iraq's sovereignty or hinder its economic or technical development. For UNSCOM and the IAEA, key questions were identified, the answers to which were necessary if they were to be in a position to conclude their work on the identification phase of their operations. Most of these key questions related to foreign suppliers and technical advice although, in the chemical weapons area, some related to past production levels.

279   It was agreed at the end of the talks to conduct a further round in Baghdad shortly thereafter in order to resolve all outstanding issues. Iraq promised that it would, in this second round, provide answers to all the questions identified but not answered during the New York meetings. However, UNSCOM stipulated that there would be no second round unless the monitoring cameras were activated. The cameras were activated on 25 September 1993.

280   In the second round of talks, begun on 1 October 1993 in Baghdad, Iraq provided a more detailed account of its past chemical weapons production and, for the first time, details about the disposal of chemical weapons and the suppliers of critical equipment, materials and technical advice in each of the categories (S/26571). However, verification of this new information remained difficult, as Iraq continued to claim that all relevant documentation about its past programmes had been destroyed.

281   Iraq also gave to UNSCOM during the October 1993 talks a

set of declarations updating information it had provided in July 1992 and February 1993 in relation to ongoing monitoring and verification, including names and locations of sites that should be subject to baseline inspections under the monitoring regime. However, UNSCOM advised Iraq that to fulfil its reporting obligations, Iraq would need both to acknowledge its obligations under resolution 715 (1991) and the plans approved thereunder, and to submit the required declarations formally in accordance with the resolution.

282   The next round of talks took place in New York from 15 to 30 November 1993 (S/26825). UNSCOM and the IAEA informed Iraq that, at that stage, the information available in all areas had been deemed to be credible and that they would deploy their best efforts to expedite the process of further verifying that information with a view to arriving at a definitive conclusion in the shortest possible time. They once again pressed Iraq to provide further information and to facilitate, by retrieving documents, the task of verifying its new declarations. In subsequent working groups, Iraq provided additional information on its proscribed programmes and on sites, equipment and materials to be monitored pursuant to the plans for ongoing monitoring and verification. Given Iraq's claims to have unilaterally destroyed items as well as relevant documentation, thereby precluding verification along traditional lines, discussions were held on finding alternative means of verification, on a process to address past difficulties in verification and on how ongoing monitoring and verification would be implemented.

283   During the talks, the Deputy Prime Minister of Iraq met the Executive Chairman of UNSCOM and the leader of the IAEA Action Team and held consultations with members of the Security Council. Following these consultations, Iraq announced, in a letter from its Minister for Foreign Affairs to the President of the Security Council, that the "Government of Iraq has decided to accept the obligations set forth in resolution 715 (1991) and to comply with the provisions of the plans for ongoing monitoring and verification as contained therein".[143] In welcoming this development, UNSCOM requested that Iraq submit as soon as possible consolidated declarations under resolution 715 (1991) and the plans for ongoing monitoring and verification. Iraq, in response, submitted a statement confirming that declarations it had previously made were to be considered to have been made under resolution 715 (1991) and the plans for ongoing monitoring and verification (S/26825). While this addressed the question of the legal status of Iraq's earlier declarations, it did not address the problems arising from the declarations' inadequacies. Consequently, UNSCOM demanded that Iraq submit yet further initial declarations, this time in a format prepared by UNSCOM and designed to elicit the data required to implement its plan for ongoing monitoring and verification.

143/Document 176
See page 604

Establishment of ongoing monitoring and verification (OMV)

284 In January 1994, Iraq submitted new initial declarations for each of the weapons areas which, together with information obtained from other sources, proved sufficient to initiate the baseline inspection process. However, throughout 1994, UNSCOM encountered major problems in the biological area, where incomplete declarations, the failure to declare all equipment and materials subject to monitoring and a failure to declare movement, repair or modification of equipment between inspections resulted in a situation in which the establishment of reliable baseline data was not possible, delaying the initiation of monitoring in that area.

285 The political situation deteriorated sharply during further talks in New York in March 1994. The Deputy Prime Minister of Iraq accused UNSCOM—by virtue of its not having already recommended the immediate lifting of the oil embargo—of acting for political motives not related to its mandate and of being directly under the influence of one Member State. He stated that Iraq had lost confidence in UNSCOM and threatened that cooperation would be withdrawn if the Commission would not set a date for the lifting of the oil embargo. The meeting broke up with no date set for a further round of high-level talks. However, no change was noted in the level of support and assistance being proffered to inspection teams on the ground.

286 In the second week of April 1994, immediately following the Security Council's consideration of UNSCOM's and the IAEA's semi-annual reports, Iraq requested a further round of high-level talks, citing "important developments" since the previous round. In a markedly improved atmosphere, this round of talks resulted in a further joint statement, in which Iraq publicly committed itself to continuing to cooperate with UNSCOM and the IAEA in the conduct of ongoing monitoring and verification and to respect their rights and privileges throughout this stage of their work.

Threats to end cooperation

287 On 22 September 1994, Iraq again threatened to block the work of UNSCOM and the IAEA. In an effort to normalize the situation, the Executive Chairman of UNSCOM visited Baghdad in early October. However, Iraq rejected all appeals to withdraw the threats and started deploying troops in the direction of Kuwait, a move which, in turn, led the United States to begin deploying troops to Kuwait. On 6 October, a joint meeting of Iraq's Revolution Command Council and the Iraqi Command of the Ba'ath Party issued a statement declaring that, unless the Security Council's consideration of UNSCOM's and the IAEA's semi-annual reports on the implementation of ongoing monitoring and verification, scheduled to be held on or about 10 October 1994, were favourable to Iraq, it might withdraw its cooperation with UNSCOM and the IAEA.[144] This condition was rejected by the Council on 8 October 1994.[145] One week later, the Security Council adopted resolution 949 (1994), which, invoking Chapter VII of the Charter, demanded that Iraq "cooperate fully" with UNSCOM and that it withdraw "all military units recently deployed to southern Iraq to their original positions".[146] Iraq did not follow through on its threats and, throughout the period of troop movements of October 1994, UNSCOM and the IAEA were able to continue their normal operations.

144/Document 193
See page 665

145/Document 194
See page 685

146/Document 196
See page 694

Disclosure of Iraq's biological weapons and VX programmes

288   As a result of UNSCOM's difficulties in obtaining accurate and full declarations from Iraq concerning its current dual-purpose biological capabilities, the Commission undertook, beginning in December 1994, a series of extremely rigorous inspections in Iraq and also took up the matter with the supplier companies. These efforts not only yielded information about dual-purpose capabilities but also provided the first tangible evidence that Iraq had in fact undertaken a full-scale programme to produce biological weapons within the country. At first, Iraq denied the programme, but in March 1995, it indicated that the issue might be resolved. However, expectations that Iraq would admit to such a biological weapons programme in time for the progress to be noted in UNSCOM's April report to the Security Council were not met.

289   In the meantime, UNSCOM's analysis of Iraq's March 1995 declaration of its chemical programmes indicated that Iraq had also progressed further in the production of the nerve agent VX than it had yet admitted.

290   During a visit to Baghdad by UNSCOM's Deputy Executive Chairman from 14 to 17 May 1995, Iraqi officials stated that they would resolve UNSCOM's concerns relating to biological weapons only after UNSCOM agreed that all other areas were closed. The Executive Chairman visited Baghdad from 29 May to 1 June 1995 for technical talks on ballistic missiles and on chemical weapons, concerning which some significant progress was made. However, Iraq refused to engage in efforts to resolve the biological weapons issues.

291   During these meetings, the Deputy Prime Minister of Iraq stated that Iraq's sole reason for cooperating with UNSCOM and the IAEA was that it sought reintegration into the international community through the lifting of the sanctions and the oil embargo, leading to the normalization of relations with Member States.[147] If there were no prospect of such reintegration, he said, it would be difficult for Iraq to justify the expense and the effort of such cooperation. The Minister added that, for Iraq, prospects for the desired reintegration would be improved if UNSCOM and the IAEA reported clearly to the Security

147/Document 210
See page 758;

Document 214
See page 771

Council that the essential provisions of resolutions 687 (1991) and 715 (1991) had been implemented. At the current stage, Iraq required statements, on the one hand from UNSCOM that the chemical weapons and missile files were closed and that the ongoing monitoring and verification system was operational, and on the other from the IAEA that the nuclear file was closed. If Iraq thus deemed the prospects of reintegration to be positive, it would be ready in late June 1995 to address to UNSCOM's satisfaction the sole outstanding issue of significance—the biological weapons issue. If the prospects were not good, said the Minister, Iraq would have to reassess its cooperation with the United Nations.

292   Under pressure from Council members to reveal its biological weapons programme, and in the light of Iraq's positive reading of UNSCOM's report to the Security Council in June, Iraq invited the Executive Chairman to visit Baghdad again from 30 June to 2 July 1995 in order to review outstanding issues relating to the biological weapons programme. In an oral statement, Iraq admitted for the first time the offensive nature of its biological weapons programme. Its admissions included: that biological agents for weapons purposes were produced at Al Hakam; that production of the biological warfare agents *Clostridium botulinum* and *Bacillus anthracis* (anthrax) started at Al Hakam in 1989 and continued until 1990; and that large quantities of these agents were produced and stored in concentrated form at Al Hakam. Iraq claimed that the produced agent had never been weaponized and had been destroyed by October 1990 in view of the imminence of hostilities.

293   Until that statement, Iraq had insisted that its military biological programme was limited in scope to defensive research and that no weapons or agents had ever been produced. Iraq undertook to provide, by the end of July 1995, a full, final and complete disclosure of all aspects of the biological weapons programme, in a format which UNSCOM elaborated and explained in detail to Iraq's experts.

294   The positive trend established by Iraq's disclosure of its biological weapons programme and its agreement to destroy equipment related to missile production was reversed by a speech by President Saddam Hussein on 17 July 1995 in which he threatened to end all cooperation with UNSCOM and the IAEA if there were no progress towards the lifting of sanctions and the oil embargo. In a speech in Cairo a few days later, Iraq's Minister for Foreign Affairs added a deadline of 31 August 1995 to this threat.

295   On 4 August 1995, the Executive Chairman again visited Baghdad to receive Iraq's "full, final and complete disclosure" of its biological weapons programme. However, the new document added little to what Iraq had declared on 1 July 1995, and still denied weaponization. The Deputy Prime Minister of Iraq also stressed twice in the first

week of August that the deadline of 31 August for action on sanctions and the oil embargo still stood and was to be taken seriously. He asked the Executive Chairman to convey this message to the Security Council.

August 1995 disclosures

296   On 7 August 1995, General Hussein Kamel Hassan, at that time Minister for Industry and Minerals and formerly Director of Iraq's Military Industrialization Corporation, with responsibility for all of Iraq's weapons programmes, left Iraq for Jordan. On 13 August, the Executive Chairman and the Director General of the International Atomic Energy Agency were invited to return to Baghdad as it had been ascertained, according to Iraq, that General Hassan had hidden from UNSCOM and the IAEA important information on the prohibited programmes. UNSCOM was also informed on 14 August that the 31 August deadline no longer stood.

297   The Executive Chairman and the leader of the IAEA Action Team arrived in Baghdad on 17 August 1995. Iraq, claiming that General Hassan, without the knowledge of the senior Iraqi leadership, had hidden information on the prohibited programmes, said that it wished to cooperate fully with UNSCOM and the IAEA and that there were no longer any time-limits to this cooperation. In subsequent meetings, Iraq disclosed a far more extensive biological weapons programme than previously admitted, including weaponization of agents into 166 bombs and 25 missile warheads. It admitted achieving greater progress in its efforts to produce missile engines in Iraq and that its VX programme, in sharp contrast to its denials in May 1995, was larger and more advanced than previously stated.[148]

298   In the nuclear area, Iraq admitted that a crash programme to produce nuclear weapons had been initiated in September 1990 with the aim of extracting, from safeguarded materials, sufficient highly enriched uranium for a nuclear device by April 1991. Iraq claimed that the extraction programme had never started because of damage sustained in the air war in January 1991. Iraq handed over to the IAEA a report, written on 10 September 1991 and covering the period from 1 June 1990 to 7 June 1991, on progress made towards weaponizing a nuclear device which indicated that work on weaponization had continued until mid-January 1991. Iraq made further disclosures about progress achieved in relation to centrifuge enrichment and gaseous diffusion methods for obtaining weapons-grade nuclear materials. This was especially notable as it was the first occasion on which Iraq had admitted that its nuclear activities were aimed at the production of a nuclear device.[149]

299   On 20 August 1995, as the Executive Chairman and the leader of the IAEA Action Team were leaving Baghdad, Iraqi authorities took them to a farmhouse on the outskirts of Baghdad which Iraq claimed had

148/Document 214
See page 771

149/Document 213
See page 766

belonged to General Hassan and at which it claimed to have found documentation, previously asserted to have been destroyed, relating to banned programmes. These materials—amounting to some 680,000 pages of printed documents as well as computer disks, videotapes, microfilms and microfiches—were handed over to the United Nations. As of January 1996, the formidable task of translating, collating and analysing the information contained in these documents, as well as its subsequent verification, was continuing.

Achievements

Prohibited programmes

300 While the process of verifying the recent cache of documents is still continuing, neither UNSCOM nor the IAEA can state that it has a definitive knowledge of the full scope of Iraq's prohibited programmes. However, both are confident that they now know the "big picture" in each area, although concerns remain about fully accounting for all the capabilities associated with the programmes. These programmes included:

•Efforts at five clandestine uranium enrichment programmes (electromagnetic isotope separation, centrifuge, chemical exchange, laser isotope separation and gaseous diffusion) as well as laboratory-scale plutonium separation and the facilities for a comprehensive nuclear-weapon development programme, aimed at an implosion-type nuclear weapon and linked to a surface-to-surface missile project;

•The production or import of more than 212,000 filled and unfilled munitions, 4,000 tonnes of bulk agent and 17,000 tonnes of precursor chemicals. Iraq's facilities included the substantial chemical weapons production complex of the Al Muthanna State Establishment and three chemical-weapons-related production plants in the Al Fallujah area aimed at developing an indigenous capability to produce the nerve agents sarin, tabun and VX, mustard agent and their precursor chemicals;

•Three separate biological weapons programmes (human bacterial pathogens, human viral pathogens and plant pathogens), involving five facilities in the research, development and production of these weapons. Iraq admits having filled 166 bombs and 25 missile warheads with biological warfare agents (anthrax and botulinum); and

•The import of 819 Scud missiles, mobile launchers, support vehicles and components; indigenous efforts to build both fixed and mobile missile launchers; three programmes to produce longer-range missiles in Iraq (reverse engineering of the extended-range Scud derivatives, two-stage solid fuel missiles and a space re-entry vehicle system); and efforts to develop a parachute system for missiles to give an air burst capability.

301   Much has been achieved in the elimination of Iraq's banned capabilities. In the nuclear area, the IAEA has overseen or verified (given that many of the facilities were badly damaged in the war) the destruction of Iraq's facilities and equipment for the enrichment of uranium and the facility at Al Atheer for the design and construction of a nuclear device. In 1991, the IAEA removed from Iraq its stocks of plutonium and highly enriched uranium; the remaining stocks of irradiated uranium were removed from Iraq in February 1994.

302   UNSCOM has destroyed, removed or rendered harmless the following:

- An assembled supergun;
- The components for four other such guns and one tonne of propellant;
- 151 Scud-variant missiles, 19 mobile launchers, 76 chemical and 113 conventional warheads for Scud-variant missiles, 9 conventional warheads for Al-Fahd missiles, more than 130 missile storage supports and a number of support vehicles, a substantial amount of rocket fuel and component chemicals, 28 operational fixed Al-Hussein missile launch pads and a further 32 fixed launch pads under construction and at various stages of completion, 11 decoy missiles and 9 Scud decoy vehicles, 2 SS-21 guidance-and-control sets and more than 200 imported guidance-and-control components;
- Equipment for the production of missiles and components;
- More than 480,000 litres of chemical warfare agents (including mustard agent and the nerve agents sarin and tabun);
- More than 28,000 filled and nearly 12,000 empty chemical munitions (involving 8 types of munitions ranging from rockets to artillery shells, bombs and ballistic missile warheads);
- Nearly 1,800,000 litres, more than 1,040,000 kilograms and 648 barrels of some 45 different precursor chemicals for the production of chemical warfare agents;
- Equipment and facilities for chemical weapons production; and
- Biological seed stocks used in Iraq's biological weapons programme.

303   UNSCOM has also undertaken extensive efforts to verify Iraq's accounts of how other prohibited capabilities were disposed of (e.g., through use or war damage). In December 1995, an inspection team visited the Al Hakam biological warfare production facility—declared as such by Iraq only in August 1995—to identify equipment to be destroyed.

Ongoing monitoring and verification

304   Once Iraq's formal acceptance of resolution 715 (1991) was obtained on 26 November 1993, UNSCOM immediately reallocated the bulk of its resources to, and obtained additional resources for, the establishment of the system of ongoing monitoring and verification. The system is a large and complex undertaking entailing the inspection of entire categories of sites and industries not previously visited by UNSCOM. In addition, new methods have had to be designed for conducting baseline inspections and assessing the feasibility of monitoring methods, while new applications of technologies have had to be developed to serve the monitoring needs identified in the baseline inspection process.

305 In the first nine months of 1994, UNSCOM analysed the data from Iraq's declarations and from other sources concerning Iraq's dual-purpose capabilities, conducted several hundred baseline inspections of sites to be monitored, drew up monitoring protocols for these sites, tagged and inventoried more than a thousand pieces of equipment and installed some 111 cameras and 20 chemical sensors at more than two dozen sites. UNSCOM further installed a communications system to link these cameras in real time with televisions in the Baghdad Monitoring and Verification Centre.

306 By October 1994, UNSCOM was able to announce that the system was provisionally operational, subject to a period of testing. In April 1995, UNSCOM reported that the system was operational. However, Iraq's failure to declare fully and accurately all aspects of its proscribed programmes meant that UNSCOM could not guarantee that the system was monitoring all the capabilities it should, and uncertainties about the levels of technologies achieved by Iraq in its prohibited programmes raised questions as to whether the monitoring was most effectively focused. These uncertainties remained as of January 1996.

307 Since August 1994, the IAEA has maintained a continuous presence in Iraq for the implementation of its plan for the ongoing monitoring and verification of Iraq's compliance with its obligations under Security Council resolutions. The IAEA Nuclear Monitoring Group (NMG) is accommodated in the Baghdad Monitoring and Verification Centre. Iraq, for its part, has established a National Monitoring Directorate (NMD) in Baghdad to facilitate inspection and reporting in accordance with the OMV.

308 The IAEA's work in this field differs somewhat from UNSCOM's in that there are more clearly definable single-purpose "choke-points" in the development of nuclear weapons than other weapons systems, where most aspects of a weapons capability could be argued to have a dual purpose. In addition, the "signature" of nuclear activity (e.g., radioactivity, heat signatures, the size of facilities) is higher than for the other areas and hence is more easily detected. Information from any source which, after assessment, indicates that nuclear-weapons-related activities might have occurred or be ongoing at a location would make that location a *target* site and arrangements would be made by the IAEA to assemble an expert team to carry out an on-site inspection. As a complementary and perhaps even higher-priority activity, sites judged to have certain characteristics that could contribute to nuclear-weapons-related activities are designated as *capable* sites and are inspected by cross-disciplinary teams made up from members of the various monitoring groups resident in the Baghdad Monitoring and Verification Centre.

309   Inspections under the OMV are usually carried out with no notice to the facility operator or the NMD counterpart. More than 300 sites are currently subject to monitoring inspection. In the first year of operation, the NMG carried out almost 300 inspections at some 85 facilities, including some 40 facilities not previously inspected. Few of these monitoring inspections involve activities directly related to nuclear material.

310   In his report to the Security Council dated 10 October 1994, the Director General of the International Atomic Energy Agency concluded that with the establishment at the end of August 1994 of the IAEA's continuous presence in Iraq all elements of the Agency's OMV plan were in place.[150]

150/Document 195
See page 685

Future activities

311   At such time as the sanctions in effect on Iraq under resolution 661 (1990) are eased or lifted in accordance with paragraph 21 of resolution 687 (1991) to the extent that the export to Iraq of dual-purpose items is again permitted, the export/import monitoring mechanism will enter into effect. This mechanism has been prepared jointly by UNSCOM and the IAEA and was forwarded to the Sanctions Committee on 7 December 1995 for its approval prior to submission to the Security Council for adoption.[151] It would be implemented jointly by UNSCOM and the IAEA.

151/Document 217
See page 804

312   The mechanism as proposed is a dual-notification system. Iraq is required to inform the United Nations in advance of its intentions to import dual-purpose capabilities and, subsequently, of its actual trade in such capabilities. These notifications are to be checked against notifications made by the Governments of the countries from which the capabilities are exported, and will be further checked against information available to UNSCOM and the IAEA from other sources and by inspections in Iraq, both at the border and at the declared end-user site. By this means, UNSCOM and the IAEA will be able to verify, by incorporating the newly imported capabilities into the ongoing monitoring and verification system for the duration of their useful lifetime in Iraq, the actual use to which the imported capabilities are put. In the monitoring of

international trade in dual-purpose capabilities, such verification is unique.

313   Until sanctions are eased or lifted, ongoing monitoring and verification activities will primarily comprise the following:

(*a*)   Inspections to verify the completeness of the list of sites monitored and of the inventories, to verify declarations as to the activities conducted at sites, or to pursue any information obtained which might call into question Iraq's compliance with its obligations under resolution 687 (1991);

(*b*)   Aerial surveillance, from both UNSCOM's high-altitude surveillance aircraft and its helicopters;

(*c*)   Maintenance of the site monitoring and verification protocols by the monitoring experts at the Baghdad Monitoring and Verification Centre;

(*d*)   Monitoring activities conducted by experts dispatched to Iraq to augment the capabilities of the staff of the Centre; and

(*e*)   Review and analysis of the product of the sensors installed at the various sites.

314   These activities are aimed at ensuring that UNSCOM and the IAEA have full knowledge of Iraq's prohibited capabilities and of the level of technology achieved by Iraq in its banned weapons programmes; that the monitoring system is designed and focused at the appropriate dual-purpose technologies and choke-points; and that no dual-purpose capabilities have escaped the monitoring system.

315   The first stage in that process will be to analyse and verify the information contained in the documents obtained in August 1995 to ascertain whether Iraq has fully disclosed, as required, all aspects of its prohibited programmes. Early indications are that the documents point to other, as yet undeclared, banned weapons, items, materials and activities, and that Iraq is continuing to withhold important documents. If this is indeed the case, further efforts will have to be made to elicit the required information and supporting tangible and documentary evidence from Iraq so that the United Nations, in keeping with its mandate under resolutions 687 (1991) and 707 (1991), can be sure that the programmes have been fully disclosed.

IX Caring for the needs of the civilian population

316   In an effort to relieve the suffering of civilians in Iraq and in the Iraq/Turkey and Iraq/Iran border areas, the Security Council devised a scheme—the so-called "oil-for-food" formula—by which exports of Iraqi oil could be used to pay for the provision of foodstuffs and medicines as well as for the Compensation Commission, UNSCOM and other United Nations activities mandated by resolution 687 (1991). However, Iraq has objected to certain aspects of the plan as an infringement of its sovereignty and has refused to allow its implementation. This situation has given rise to fears that an already dire humanitarian situation could deteriorate still further, particularly in the area of public health. These and other conditions in Iraq have been investigated by the Special Rapporteur on the situation of human rights in Iraq as part of the mandate given to him by the United Nations Commission on Human Rights. The persistent and grave nature of abuses he has documented has only compounded concern for innocent civilians in Iraq—and above all the most vulnerable among them—who should not be held hostage to events beyond their control.

Financing "essential civilian needs" and United Nations activities in Iraq

317   To assess essential civilian needs, the United Nations system dispatched a number of missions to the area, beginning with the joint WHO/UNICEF team which visited Iraq at the height of the war, from 16 to 21 February 1991. For two weeks in late June and early July 1991, a United Nations inter-agency mission visited Iraq to assess needs for humanitarian assistance and recommend measures for meeting those needs. The mission concluded that the import of material goods was the primary action required to address "essential civilian needs" in the priority areas of food supply, health services, water, sanitation, power generation, the oil sector and telecommunications.[152] However, the mission reported, the "massive financial requirements" of such imports were of a scale "far beyond" what was, or was likely to be, available under any United Nations–sponsored programme.

152/Document 66
See page 273

318   Even before the adoption of resolution 687 (1991) in April 1991, the international donor community had provided some financial resources to support post-conflict humanitarian programmes. However,

the June-July 1991 mission noted that most available funds had been pledged for the needs of refugees and returnees, and that any additional appeals to the international community would have to compete with other emergency situations around the world. The mission thus concluded that the funds required could be generated only through Iraq's own resources, possibly by unfreezing Iraqi assets held abroad or through the international sale of Iraqi oil, in conformity with the provisions of paragraph 23 of resolution 687 (1991) allowing exceptions to the sanctions as concerns medicine and health supplies, foodstuffs and materials and supplies for "essential civilian needs". Separately, in a report dated 15 July 1991, my predecessor had suggested the sale of some Iraqi petroleum and petroleum products as a means of obtaining the funds required of Iraq by resolution 699 (1991) to cover the full costs of the disarmament and weapons control activities mandated by resolution 687 (1991).[153]

153/Document 65
See page 272

319   On 15 August 1991, the Security Council, acting under Chapter VII of the Charter, adopted resolution 706 (1991), which set out the terms for the limited sale of Iraqi oil and oil products, during a period of six months, primarily to increase the level of funds available for humanitarian programmes and for several of the operations mandated by resolution 687 (1991).[154] Under the resolution, the sum to be produced by these exports could not exceed $1.6 billion. Each purchase would require the approval of the Sanctions Committee. The proceeds would be deposited into an escrow account to be established and administered by the United Nations and would be used not only for humanitarian activities but to cover the full costs of carrying out the tasks authorized by section C of resolution 687 (1991), the full costs of facilitating the return of all Kuwaiti property seized by Iraq and half the costs of the Iraq-Kuwait Boundary Demarcation Commission.[155] Thirty per cent of the value of the exports would be paid to the United Nations Compensation Fund. Speaking before the vote on the resolution, Iraq said that the provisions of the text impinged on its national sovereignty and imposed a foreign guardianship on its people.

154/Document 72
See page 285

155/Document 65
See page 272

320   On 19 September 1991, again acting under Chapter VII of the Charter, the Security Council, in resolution 712 (1991), approved a basic structure for the implementation of resolution 706 (1991).[156] The Council also confirmed that funds from other sources could be deposited in the escrow account as a sub-account and would become immediately available to meet Iraq's humanitarian needs without the deductions specified in the resolutions. By a decision of 15 October, the Sanctions Committee set out a series of procedures to be employed in the proposed scheme of sales.

156/Document 78
See page 298;
Document 81
See page 308

Efforts to secure Iraqi agreement

321   A first round of talks on the implementation of resolutions

706 (1991) and 712 (1991) was held between representatives of Iraq and officials of the United Nations Secretariat from 8 to 10 January 1992 in Vienna. Iraq broke off a scheduled second round of talks, claiming that the conditions being imposed on it by the United Nations were "unnecessary and obtrusive". Iraq subsequently stated that it had satisfied all the conditions specified in paragraph 22 of resolution 687 (1991) and that therefore sanctions should no longer be applied. On 5 February, the Council deplored Iraq's decision to discontinue contacts with the Secretariat, underscoring that Iraq thus bore "the full responsibility" for the humanitarian problems of its civilian population.[157]

157/Document 101
See page 390

322 Though Iraq continued to refuse to accept resolutions 706 (1991) and 712 (1991), the Iraqi authorities decided to resume discussions with the Secretariat on the sale of oil and new rounds of talks were held in Vienna in March and June 1992. However, in July, Iraq reiterated its stance that the proposed plan impaired its independence and interfered in its internal affairs, that it had met its obligations imposed by the Council's resolutions and that it "should be permitted to export oil in a normal and regular manner, with an understanding between Iraq and the United Nations as to the percentage of the proceeds to be deducted for the benefit of the United Nations, in an uncomplicated manner, with the Security Council, if necessary, obliging States not to export a particular kind of goods to Iraq" (S/24276, S/24339). I kept the Security Council abreast of the status of these talks.[158]

158/Document 123
See page 468

Council action on Iraqi oil assets

323 Iraq's refusal to cooperate in the implementation of the Security Council's "oil-for-food" formula, and reports that the humanitarian situation in Iraq was deteriorating further, led the Council to take additional action on 2 October 1992. In the first such action of its kind, the Council, by its resolution 778 (1992), decided that all States in which there were funds representing proceeds from the sale of Iraqi petroleum or petroleum products paid for on or after 6 August 1990—the date on which the Council had imposed sanctions against Iraq—should transfer those funds, with certain exceptions, to the United Nations escrow account provided for in resolutions 706 (1991) and 712 (1991).[159] States in which there were petroleum or petroleum products owned by Iraq were to arrange for the sale of such petroleum at fair market value and then to transfer the proceeds as soon as possible to the escrow account. The Council requested that I ascertain the whereabouts and amounts of such petroleum and petroleum products and of the proceeds of their sale. Later that month, I brought resolution 778 (1992) to the attention of all permanent representatives and permanent observers to the United Nations and also requested all States to provide, by 30 November 1992, all relevant information for the resolution's implementation.

159/Document 132
See page 478

160/Document 160

See page 562

324 I reported to the Security Council on these efforts on 27 May 1993.[160] As of 30 April 1993, 62 States had replied to my October appeal, with two indicating that they held assets subject to the provisions of resolution 778 (1992) which could be transferred to the escrow account. By 30 April, a total of $101.5 million had been received into the account, including voluntary contributions of $30 million from Saudi Arabia, $20 million from Kuwait and $1.5 million from the United Kingdom, and a $50 million transfer of frozen Iraqi assets from the United States. These funds were designated for various purposes specified in resolutions 687 (1991) and 706 (1991). However, projections showing a need for $106.3 million for those activities through the end of 1993, as well as an estimated $489 million to finance the United Nations Inter-Agency Humanitarian Programme for the period from 1 April 1993 to 31 March 1994, gave an indication of the urgent need to locate additional frozen funds and/or for significant new voluntary contributions from Member States.

325 On 29 June 1993, after meeting with the Deputy Prime Minister of Iraq, I announced in Geneva that talks on implementing resolutions 706 (1991) and 712 (1991) would resume at a high level. A fourth round of talks between the United Nations Secretariat and the Government of Iraq was then held at United Nations Headquarters from 7 to 15 July. Though I had hoped at this point to reach an understanding on practical arrangements for the sale of Iraqi oil, the talks were suspended by Iraq, which continued to object to resolutions 706 (1991) and 712 (1991) as unacceptable encroachments on its sovereignty. Throughout the months to come, I continued to maintain the Secretariat's readiness to resume negotiations. It was my view that acceptance of the Council's offer to sell oil was in Iraq's interest, both for alleviating the humanitarian situation in Iraq and for creating a new climate of confidence between Iraq and the Security Council.

326 In 1994, concerned with the financial difficulties of the United Nations Compensation Commission and the lack of sufficient funds being deposited in the United Nations escrow account to finance this and other activities for which Iraq was to pay, I suggested to the Security Council that it might wish to authorize me to seek from oil companies information which would make it possible to identify Iraqi oil-related frozen funds (S/1994/566). As I reported to the Council, information from oil-industry sources indicated that during the weeks immediately preceding the imposition of sanctions by the Council, Iraq had exported hundreds of millions of dollars' worth of oil for which payment would not have been completed when the sanctions took effect on 6 August 1990.

327 It was my assessment that the oil companies concerned might be better equipped than Governments to track and locate the corresponding funds. The Council approved this direct approach on 11 May 1994 (S/1994/567). I subsequently came to the conclusion that the most effective way of obtaining the information required was to address Governments with jurisdiction over the relevant petroleum companies and their subsidiaries, and in letters dated 11 July, I requested the Foreign Ministers of the 20 countries which were, according to the United Nations *Energy Statistics Yearbook* (ST/ESA/STAT/SER.J/33) (1991), the principal importers of Iraqi crude petroleum in 1990 to seek all relevant information.[161] While a number of States provided information on such oil imports, no further funds were identified for deposit into the United Nations escrow account.

161/Document 191
See page 662

New Security Council proposal

328 On 14 April 1995, acting under Chapter VII of the Charter, the Security Council adopted resolution 986 (1995), in which it provided Iraq with another opportunity to sell oil to finance the purchase of humanitarian goods and various mandated United Nations activities concerning Iraq. The new proposal permitted the sale of $2 billion of Iraqi oil—$1 billion in each of two 90-day periods—subject to certain conditions.[162] The resolution also took into account some of Iraq's concerns over resolutions 706 (1991) and 712 (1991) by reaffirming "the commitment of all Member States to the sovereignty and territorial integrity of Iraq" and describing the new exercise as "temporary".

162/Document 207
See page 754

329 Resolution 986 (1995), said many delegations in statements both before and after the unanimous adoption of the text, had achieved a proper balance between, on the one hand, the need to secure Iraq's compliance with international law and, on the other, the need to alleviate the suffering of an unintended target of the sanctions regime—the country's civilian population. Delegations also expressed the hope that Iraq would soon comply with this and all other relevant Security Council resolutions (S/PV.3519).

330 In a statement following the Council's action, I expressed the hope that resolution 986 (1995), if implemented by Iraq, would be a "first step" towards overcoming the "crisis" which existed between Iraq and the international community (SG/SM/5613). I then met with the Deputy Prime Minister of Iraq to discuss its implementation. However, on 15 May 1995, I was informed by the Minister for Foreign Affairs of Iraq that his Government would not implement resolution 986 (1995) because it objected, *inter alia*, to the proportion of petroleum to be exported via the Kirkuk-Yumurtalik pipeline and to the modalities for the distribution of humanitarian relief in three northern governorates.[163] I urged the Government to reconsider its decision and stated the Secretariat's readiness to enter into discussions with Iraq on practical arrangements for implementing the resolution.

163/Document 209
See page 757

331   I met again with the Deputy Prime Minister of Iraq in December 1995 in Geneva, and discussed resolution 986 (1995) as part of more general talks concerning the relationship between the United Nations and Iraq. In January 1996, after an exchange of letters with the Deputy Prime Minister, I was able to announce that the Iraqi Government had accepted my invitation to enter into discussions with the Secretariat regarding implementation of the oil-for-food formula.[164] Those talks began in New York on 6 February 1996.

164/Document 222

See page 823;

Document 223

See page 824

332   As of 31 December 1995, $405.5 million, representing voluntary contributions and Iraqi petroleum assets, had been deposited in the escrow account. This fell far short of what was required to continue to pay compensation claims, and funds were urgently required for the continuation of the inter-agency humanitarian programme, the work of UNSCOM and other activities mandated by the Security Council.

The situation of human rights in Iraq

333   The Special Rapporteur on the situation of human rights in Iraq was appointed after the United Nations Commission on Human Rights in March 1991 expressed "grave concern" at "flagrant" human rights violations by the Government of Iraq. As of January 1996, the Special Rapporteur had produced 12 separate documents detailing a variety of serious human rights violations of a civil, cultural, economic, political and social nature (See "Other documents of interest", page 157).[165] These reports have taken into consideration thousands of pages of testimony, thousands of official Iraqi documents (selected from among approximately 4 million documents to which the Special Rapporteur had access), aerial and satellite photography, almost 100 amateur video recordings, some important audio recordings, scientific studies, medical diagnoses and a variety of physical evidence ranging from flesh wounds to chemical residues in soils. Further, visits were conducted to 10 countries, including Iraq, in order to obtain and verify information of all kinds and from all types of sources.

165/Document 103

See page 394;

Document 216

See page 793

334   According to these reports, human rights violations in Iraq include extrajudicial, summary and arbitrary executions; the routine practice of systematic torture and other cruel, inhuman or degrading treatment or punishment; enforced or involuntary disappearances; and arbitrary arrests and detention. The Government, said the Special Rapporteur, has "terrorized the population into passive submission to the extent that no oppositional opinions, expressions or associations are apparent in the country". Human rights violations are "inevitable" in Iraq, since "guarantees for protection are absent and the scope for abuse of power is enormous. Power is grossly abused on a daily and wide-spread basis" (E/CN.4/1994/58).

335   According to the Special Rapporteur, government attempts to eradicate opposition have also led to violations of the human rights of specific ethnic and religious communities. Policy and actions of the Government since the early 1980s, exacerbated by an internal economic blockade imposed on the northern region in October 1991, have resulted in the systematic destruction of Kurdish villages, the disappearance of thousands of Kurds, unremitting economic hardship and other violations which, said the Special Rapporteur, raise issues of violations of the 1948 Genocide Convention (E/CN.4/1992/31).

336   The Special Rapporteur has also examined the situation of the Marsh Arabs of southern Iraq, whose traditional way of life and survival, he reported, are in jeopardy as a result of the Iraqi Government's actions. Thousands of Marsh Arabs have fled within and beyond Iraq's borders as a result of the Government's military campaign against perceived "criminals" or opponents, which has involved indiscriminate bombardment of villages and arbitrary arrest and detention of large numbers of persons (A/47/367). Forced displacements have also occurred as a result of the Government's "Third River Project", a programme to create a central waterway for irrigation. With respect to Iraq's Shiites, the Special Rapporteur has said that government policy also violates in a systematic way their right to religious freedom, especially in relation to the Shiite religious establishment.

337   Since adding the item to its agenda in 1991, the General Assembly has adopted an annual resolution on the situation of human rights in Iraq.[166] These texts have expressed increasingly strong concern over and condemnation of "massive" violations of human rights by the Government of Iraq. The Assembly has repeatedly called upon Iraq to fulfil the obligations it had undertaken as a party to various international human rights instruments, to cooperate with the Special Rapporteur and to cooperate in the implementation of the "oil-for-food" formula proposed by the Security Council. It has also called for the stationing of human rights monitors throughout the country, as recommended by the Special Rapporteur.

166/Document 96
See page 370;

Document 143
See page 507;

Document 178
See page 607;

Document 202
See page 720;

Document 221
See page 821

338   The Security Council has also given attention to the human rights situation in Iraq, pursuant to its resolution 688 (1991), in which the Council condemned and demanded an end to the repression of the Iraqi civilian population, including in Kurdish-populated areas, and stated that the consequences of the repression threatened international peace and security in the region.[167] In further statements by its President on 11 March and 23 November 1992, the Council said that it remained "deeply concerned" at the grave human rights abuses being perpetrated by the Government of Iraq "against its population, in particular in the northern

167/Document 37
See page 199

168/Document 108

See page 421;

Document 137

See page 486

169/Document 103

See page 394

region of Iraq, in southern Shiite centres and in the southern marshes".[168]

339 On 11 August 1992, at the request of Belgium, France, the United Kingdom and the United States, the Security Council met to consider the human rights situation in Iraq (A/47/367).[169] These four States also invited the Special Rapporteur to participate in the Council's deliberations under rule 39 of the Council's provisional rules of procedure; China, India and Zimbabwe expressed reservations in this connection on the grounds that human rights matters were within the jurisdiction, not of the Security Council, but of the Commission on Human Rights, the Economic and Social Council or the General Assembly. In his statement to the Security Council, the Special Rapporteur expressed his concern about the humanitarian situation in Iraq, and in particular about the Government of Iraq's economic blockade of the northern governorates, the forced relocation of inhabitants of the southern marshes and military attacks on both the north and the south (S/PV.3105).

The situation of human rights in occupied Kuwait

340 In its March 1991 decision to appoint a Special Rapporteur to examine human rights violations by Iraqi forces in occupied Kuwait, the Commission on Human Rights condemned the Iraqi authorities and occupying forces for the grave abuses committed against the Kuwaiti people and nationals of other States, Iraq's failure to treat all prisoners of war and detained civilians in accordance with internationally recognized principles of humanitarian law and Iraq's rejection of the offer by Kuwait and various humanitarian organizations to send emergency assistance to the Kuwaiti people under occupation. The Special Rapporteur submitted a preliminary report in October 1991 (A/46/544) and a final report in January 1992 (E/CN.4/1992/26). He found that Iraq was responsible for a variety of human rights violations during its occupation of Kuwait, including widespread arbitrary and summary executions, torture, arbitrary arrest and detention and the systematic dismantling, pillaging and destruction of health facilities, educational, research and cultural institutions and important parts of the Kuwaiti infrastructure. The General Assembly expressed its "grave concern" at the "grave violations of human rights and fundamental freedoms during the occupation of Kuwait".[170]

170/Document 97

See page 371

X   The sanctions regime

341   The responsibility for monitoring the prohibitions against the sale or supply of arms to Iraq and the related sanctions set out in resolutions of the Security Council was assigned to the Sanctions Committee, a subsidiary body of the Security Council. The Sanctions Committee is not responsible for enforcing the sanctions; such actions are for the Member States to take. Likewise, the Committee was not given the task of determining whether or not Iraq has complied with its obligations under resolutions of the Council to the degree necessary to ease or lift, in part or in whole, the various prohibitions. That decision remains the province of the Security Council.

Sanctions reviews: process

342   Under resolution 687 (1991) and other resolutions relating to the crisis, the Security Council mandated itself to undertake periodic reviews of the status of the sanctions and other procedures established by the Council in connection with the situation between Iraq and Kuwait.[171]

171/Document 35
See page 193

343   **Sanctions against exports to Iraq.** In paragraph 20 of resolution 687 (1991), the Security Council decided that the prohibitions against the sale or supply to Iraq of commodities or products other than medicine and health supplies would not apply to foodstuffs or, under a "no-objection" procedure, to materials and supplies for essential civilian needs. Under paragraph 21, the Council decided to review the provisions of paragraph 20 every 60 days in the light of the policies and practices of the Government of Iraq, including the implementation of all relevant resolutions of the Council, for the purpose of determining whether to reduce or lift the prohibitions.

344   **Oil and arms embargoes against Iraq.** In paragraph 22 of resolution 687 (1991), the Security Council decided that the oil embargo against Iraq would be lifted upon approval by the Council of the programme called for in paragraph 19—relating to Iraq's payment of compensation and of its foreign debt—and upon the Council's agreement that Iraq had completed all actions contemplated in paragraphs 8 to 13, which deal with weapons and weapons-related activities. Under paragraph 23, the Council decided that the Sanctions Committee could approve individual exceptions to the oil embargo when required to assure adequate financial resources to provide essential civilian needs in

Iraq. In paragraphs 24 and 25, the Council decided that all States should maintain the arms embargo against Iraq, and spelt out the items covered by the embargo. And under paragraph 28 of resolution 687 (1991), the Council agreed to review its decisions in paragraphs 22 to 25, except for the items specified and defined in paragraphs 8 and 12, on a regular basis and in any case every 120 days, taking into account Iraq's compliance with the resolution and general progress towards the control of armaments in the region. This sanctions review was distinct from the 60-day review set out in paragraph 21.

345 **Arms and related sanctions against Iraq.** By paragraph 26 of resolution 687 (1991), the Security Council requested the Secretary-General to develop guidelines to facilitate full international implementation of the arms and related sanctions against Iraq. The guidelines, which itemized the types of arms, *matériel* and activities proscribed by the Council and defined the responsibilities of the Sanctions Committee, were approved by the Council in resolution 700 (1991).[172] In paragraph 6 of that resolution, the Council decided to review the guidelines at the same time as it reviewed paragraphs 22 to 25 of resolution 687 (1991)— that is, every 120 days.

172/Document 58
See page 260;
Document 62
See page 268

346 Under the guidelines, actual implementation of the arms and related sanctions would be effected at three levels: by States, by international organizations and through intergovernmental cooperation. The guidelines call on States to institute the necessary controls, procedures and other measures that would prevent any circumvention of the arms and related sanctions, prohibit the export to Iraq of dual-purpose or multi-purpose items that could be used for military purposes, prevent the provision of any arms-related training or technical support services and provide for legal powers to inspect documents and goods and to detain and seize goods where appropriate.

Sanctions Committee

347 The Sanctions Committee was established by resolution 661 (1990). Security Council resolutions 706 (1991), 712 (1991) and 986 (1995) also assigned the Committee additional monitoring tasks relating to the proposed "oil-for-food" formula. Its membership consists of representatives of all members of the Council at any given time.

348 Since September 1991, the Sanctions Committee has reported to the Council at 90-day intervals on implementation of the arms embargo and related sanctions. Each of the 18 reports submitted up to the end of December 1995 stated that, during the periods under review, the Committee had received no information of possible or alleged violations of the arms and related sanctions against Iraq committed by other

States or foreign nationals. Nor had the Committee been consulted by States or international organizations on either the sale or the supply of items to Iraq that might fall within the categories of proscribed items or of dual- or multiple-use items, nor had any allegations of violations in this regard been reported to it. No international organization had reported any relevant information that might have come to its attention. Internal discussions between the Sanctions Committee and UNSCOM staff have been carried out with respect to planning for future post-embargo procedures and to discuss current issues. In addition, it should be noted that the Special Commission pointed out in paragraph 37 of its report of October 1995 that Iraq has acknowledged procurement of missile-related items without notification to the Sanctions Committee.[173]

173/Document 214
See page 771

Economic difficulties of States affected by sanctions

349   Given its authority to recommend exceptions to the sanctions regime, the Sanctions Committee plays a crucial role in helping the international community to reconcile the enforcement measures decided upon by the Security Council with the humanitarian imperative to alleviate humanitarian problems arising from those measures. Those hardships have been felt most acutely, of course, by Iraqi civilians as a result of the Government's refusal to accept the Council's proposed "oil-for-food" plan. But States which were not directly involved in the conflict have also experienced a range of difficulties (as noted in paragraphs 50-52 above).

350   Under Article 50 of the Charter of the United Nations, which provides a recourse for States confronting special economic, social or other problems as a result of the Security Council's use of enforcement measures such as sanctions, the Sanctions Committee was called upon to examine the requests for assistance made by 21 such States. Pursuant to these requests, each of the States involved provided the Committee with explanatory information in the form of statements, letters, memoranda and other materials.

351   In December 1990 and March 1991, the Sanctions Committee adopted decisions launching appeals to the international community to provide technical, financial and material assistance to each of the 21 States on an urgent basis (S/22021, S/22021/Add.1, S/22021/Add.2). Those decisions were then transmitted to the Security Council, which conveyed them to the Secretary-General for implementation.

352   On 22 March 1991, the 21 States addressed a joint memorandum to the President of the Security Council in which they said that the problems affecting them persisted, and in certain respects had been

aggravated, and that the international appeals had not evoked responses commensurate with their urgent needs. Saying that assistance "would reaffirm international solidarity and unity", the 21 States launched a collective appeal for assistance and called upon the Security Council to give renewed attention to their problems. The Council, in a statement by its President on 29 April 1991, made "a solemn appeal to States, international financial institutions and United Nations bodies to respond positively and speedily" to the recommendations of the Sanctions Committee.[174]

Sanctions reviews: results

353   The members of the Security Council held their first sanctions review on 5 August 1991, pursuant to paragraphs 21 and 28 of resolution 687 (1991) and paragraph 6 of resolution 700 (1991). Following informal consultations, the President of the Council made the following statement to the press: "After hearing all the opinions expressed in the course of the consultations, the President of the Council concluded that there was no agreement that the necessary conditions existed for a modification of the regimes established in paragraphs 22, 23, 24 and 25, as referred to in paragraph 28 of resolution 687 (1991); in paragraph 6 of resolution 700 (1991); and in paragraph 20, as referred to in paragraph 21 of resolution 687 (1991)".[175]

354   Similar statements were issued following sanctions reviews carried out by the Council up to and including 18 January 1994.[176] On several of these occasions, the Council added language stressing the need to alleviate humanitarian conditions for the civilian population in Iraq. Since March 1994, no statements have been issued following sanctions reviews. As of January 1996, the full set of sanctions—relating to arms, oil, trade, finance and other economic transactions—remained in place.

XI Conclusion

355   The far-reaching involvement of the United Nations in the Iraq-Kuwait crisis has provided an important test for the world Organization as a force for international peace and security. The extraordinary nature of the situation, the breadth of the Organization's response and the obstacles surmounted since August 1990 all serve to highlight the strengths and abilities of the United Nations and reflect also the continuing relevance and vitality of the Organization. By January 1996, although the situation between Iraq and Kuwait had not been finally resolved, the United Nations had accomplished many of its goals and gleaned a number of valuable lessons.

Conflict resolution

356   The post-cold-war spirit of international cooperation found strong expression in the Security Council throughout the Gulf crisis, enabling the Council to break new ground in several ways.

357   First, it is clear that the Council's decisive actions in the Gulf, including its willingness to use enforcement measures under Chapter VII of the Charter, can serve as a deterrent against comparable acts of aggression or defiance elsewhere. It should be noted, however, that the unanimity of the international response to Iraq's aggression—a classic inter-State conflict in which one large and powerful State sought to dominate and annex a neighbour—has not occurred in subsequent conflicts in which the United Nations has been involved, most of which are internal in nature.

358   Second, the subsidiary bodies created specifically for various aspects of the Iraq-Kuwait crisis, such as the Special Commission (UNSCOM), the Compensation Commission and the Iraq-Kuwait Boundary Demarcation Commission, are new articulations of the Council's powers as set out in the Charter. Third, the Council, through the Special Commission in partnership with the International Atomic Energy Agency, has taken bold steps to control the spread of weapons of mass destruction and other armaments.

359   The experience in the Gulf also focused increased attention on the question of the Organization's wider capacities in the area of preventive diplomacy, peace-keeping and peace enforcement. Less than a year after the successful reversal of Iraq's aggression, the Security Council, at its summit meeting of 31 January 1992, requested an analysis and recom-

mendations on ways of strengthening and making more efficient the capacity of the United Nations for preventive diplomacy, peacemaking and peace-keeping. The Gulf war can thus be said to have led to a valuable dialogue on the issues I raised in *An Agenda for Peace* (1992; A/47/277-S/24111) and its *Supplement* (1995; A/50/60-S/1995/1), including ways to ensure that the Security Council and the Organization in general have the means to discharge their responsibilities under the Charter of the United Nations for the maintenance of international peace and security.

Disarmament

360   The pioneering work of the Special Commission and the IAEA has advanced the cause of disarmament, arms control and non-proliferation on several fronts.

361   In the nuclear area, the on-site inspections carried out by the Action Team of the IAEA in Iraq have improved awareness of the dangers of exporting dual-purpose technologies and led the Agency to review its guidelines and practices for the inspections it performs under safeguards agreements with signatories to the Treaty on the Non-Proliferation of Nuclear Weapons (NPT). Revelations about the advanced nature of Iraq's nuclear programmes also contributed to the May 1995 decision of States parties to the Treaty to extend the NPT indefinitely. Further, the Iraq-Kuwait crisis prompted the Security Council, in resolution 687 (1991), to mention the need to work towards the establishment in the Middle East of a zone free of weapons of mass destruction.

362   With regard to chemical and biological weapons, the practical experience gained by UNSCOM has supported efforts to strengthen international conventions covering these areas, most notably with respect to verification. As for ballistic missiles, investigations of Iraq's capabilities in this area provided information for the multilateral Missile Technology Control Regime, in which nations possessing certain technologies place various limits on their export.

Financing

363   Lack of financial resources has been a serious constraint on the efforts of the United Nations system to carry out some of the various tasks mandated by the Security Council in Iraq. As of January 1996, funds had not yet been identified to meet the needs of UNSCOM for 1996, and the Compensation Commission had been able to pay only a small percentage of the awards it has decided upon. Donor response to the five United Nations inter-agency humanitarian appeals issued since January 1992 has also fallen well short of the funding goals.

The humanitarian situation

364   The breadth of the United Nations role in the Iraq-Kuwait conflict and its aftermath created a unique context for the provision of humanitarian assistance. The Organization was the instrument by which the policy decisions on Iraq/Kuwait were made and enforced and, at the same time, the organization that provided for many of the humanitarian needs of the affected population. Likewise, several prominent donors were part of the community which, as part of the United Nations intergovernmental structure, made and enforced the political decisions and were also major contributors to the work of the humanitarian agencies.

365   None the less, despite the risk that differing views on wider policy questions could disrupt the humanitarian effort, the United Nations was able to work effectively with the Government of Iraq on humanitarian undertakings. Moreover, the work of the humanitarian agencies in Iraq and Kuwait reaffirmed two major principles: namely, humanitarian agencies were granted access to reach the needy population even in the midst of a war, and humanitarian assistance was provided to all sides in the conflict.

366   There has been considerable discussion about the impact and efficacy of sanctions generally as well as how they have been applied specifically in the case of Iraq. Sanctions, as I said in the *Supplement to An Agenda for Peace,* are generally recognized to be a blunt instrument, a case in point being the consequences suffered by non-targeted countries, such as trading partners. With regard to the suffering of Iraqi civilians, the Security Council gave early recognition to this problem and adopted a novel and workable solution—its proposed "oil-for-food" formula, as set in out in resolutions 706 (1991), 712 (1991) and 986 (1995).

367   Since the adoption of resolution 986 (1995), and in accordance with paragraph 13 of that resolution, I have held a series of meetings with Iraqi authorities in order to persuade the Government of Iraq to enter into discussions on the implementation of that resolution. At the latest meeting, held in Geneva on 10 December 1995 with the Deputy Prime Minister of Iraq, I reaffirmed the fact that while the provisions of resolution 986 (1995) itself are not subject to change, it would be in Iraq's interest to agree to discussions on the resolution's implementation. During such discussions, it might be possible to find an acceptable formula for implementation of the resolution.

368   Iraq's interest in accepting the resolution would be in relieving the humanitarian suffering now increasingly affecting its population, as evidenced in recent reports of WFP, FAO and several NGOs. The implementation of resolution 986 (1995) would also release funds for the Compensation Commission to disburse to the millions of workers and others who suffered losses, damage or injury as a result of Iraq's invasion of Kuwait and its consequences. Finally, a small portion of the released funds would be allocated to the financing of relevant United Nations operations such as UNSCOM.

369   During my working visit to Cairo in January 1996, I received the Permanent Representative of Iraq to the League of Arab States on 6 January 1996, who requested the meeting as a Special Envoy of the Deputy Prime Minister. He delivered a message from the Deputy Prime Minister of Iraq proposing that I send a letter to the Deputy Prime Minister inviting the Iraqi Government to enter into a discussion with the United Nations Secretariat concerning the oil-for-food formula, without preconditions.

370   On 18 January 1996, I informed permanent members of the Security Council of my intention to send a letter to the Iraqi Government inviting it to enter into discussions with the United Nations Secretariat on the implementation of resolution 986 (1995). The letter was handed over to the Permanent Representative of Iraq to the United Nations on the same day.[177]

177/Document 222
See page 823

371   I received the Permanent Representative of Iraq at United Nations Headquarters in New York late on 19 January. He delivered a letter from the Deputy Prime Minister informing me that, with reference to my letter of 18 January 1996, the Iraqi Government had accepted my invitation.[178]

178/Document 223
See page 824

372   The discussions on the implementation of resolution 986 (1995) started in New York on 6 February 1996. It is essential that these talks succeed in order to relieve the long suffering of the many victims of this conflict, including the population of Iraq, and I look forward to a positive outcome. This would mark the beginning of a new chapter in the history of relations between the international community and Iraq.

* * *

373   The Iraq-Kuwait conflict occurred at a juncture in history when United Nations Member States had just embarked upon the critical work of assessing ways to confront the challenges of the post-cold-war period and to equip the Organization for the future. In the conflict's immediate aftermath, the successful reversal of Iraq's aggression seemed to herald a new era for the United Nations, and the hope was widely

expressed that the United Nations would and could bring to other global problems the same sustained commitment of political will and material resources that it had summoned in addressing the invasion and occupation of Kuwait.

374 The Organization has indeed compiled a significant list of achievements in the 1990s, in peace-keeping as well as in other areas, owing at least in part to its successful handling of the Iraq-Kuwait situation. At the same time, the experience of the United Nations since 1991, in Iraq and elsewhere, underscores the complex challenges involved in restoring normalcy and promoting long-term stability in areas of conflict. It has been a sobering period for the international community and the United Nations. Nevertheless, this experience has demonstrated anew what can be achieved through collective mechanisms for global peace and security.

BOUTROS BOUTROS-GHALI

Section Two
Chronology and Documents

I   Chronology of events

July-August 1932
In an exchange of letters initiated by the British Government, Iraq and Kuwait confirm the Iraq-Kuwait boundary.
See Document 1, page 165; and Document 2, page 165

19 June 1961
Kuwait gains independence from the United Kingdom.

Late June 1961
The United Kingdom ends its military presence in Kuwait. Iraq deploys troops near the border with Kuwait.

1 July 1961
British forces return to Kuwait.

2, 5, 6 and 7 July 1961
At the request of Kuwait, supported by the United Kingdom, as well as at the request of Iraq, the Security Council meets to consider the dispute between Iraq and Kuwait but does not take any action.

14 May 1963
The General Assembly admits Kuwait as the 111th United Nations Member State.
See Document 3, page 166

4 October 1963
At a meeting in Baghdad, Iraq reaffirms the independence and sovereignty of Kuwait, with boundaries as defined in the 1932 exchange of letters, and the two countries agree to establish diplomatic relations.
See Document 4, page 166

February-July 1990
In statements by President Saddam Hussein of Iraq and other Iraqi officials, Iraq advances political, territorial and financial claims against Kuwait.

Late July 1990
Iraq deploys troops on the border with Kuwait.

31 July 1990
Talks in Saudi Arabia between representatives of Iraq and Kuwait fail to resolve the situation.

2 August 1990
Iraqi troops invade Kuwait. The Security Council adopts resolution 660 (1990), condemning the invasion, demanding the immediate and unconditional withdrawal of all Iraqi forces, and calling upon Iraq and Kuwait to begin intensive negotiations to resolve their differences.
See Document 5, page 167; and Document 6, page 167

6 August 1990
The Security Council adopts resolution 661 (1990), imposing comprehensive mandatory sanctions against Iraq and occupied Kuwait and establishing a committee (the Sanctions Committee) to monitor the sanctions.
See Document 7, page 168

7 August 1990
A coalition of United Nations Member States cooperating in the defence of Kuwait begins to send military forces to the Gulf region.

8 August 1990
Iraq declares the "comprehensive and eternal merger" of Kuwait with Iraq.

9 August 1990
The Security Council adopts resolution 662 (1990), declaring the annexation of Kuwait by Iraq to be "null and void."
See Document 8, page 169

12 August 1990
Kuwait informs the United Nations that it has requested military assistance to ensure the implementation of resolution 661 (1990).
See Document 9, page 169

13 August 1990
In a letter to the Secretary-General, Iraq describes the sanctions imposed by the Security Council as "unjust" and "iniquitous".
See Document 10, page 170

18 August 1990
Iraqi authorities announce that they have detained a number of third-State nationals. The Security Council adopts resolution 664 (1990), demanding that Iraq permit the departure of these individuals from both Iraq and Kuwait.
See Document 11, page 171

25 August 1990

The Government of Jordan requests international help in alleviating the situation of people uprooted from Iraq and Kuwait as a result of the invasion. According to the International Labour Organization, by early February 1991, some 2 million of the 2.8 million migrant workers and their families in Iraq and Kuwait flee, with more than 700,000 entering Jordan. The Office of the United Nations Disiater Relief Coordinator (UNDRO) serves as lead agency for an emergency operation to evacuate displaced people to their countries of origin and provide assistance to those who cannot be transported immediately.

25 August 1990

The Security Council adopts resolution 665 (1990), authorizing maritime forces in the Gulf to use "commensurate" measures to ensure implementation of the sanctions against Iraq.

See Document 12, page 171

30 August–2 September 1990

The Secretary-General of the United Nations meets with Mr. Tariq Aziz, the Deputy Prime Minister and Minister for Foreign Affairs of Iraq in Amman, Jordan.

13 September 1990

The Security Council adopts resolution 666 (1990), requesting the Sanctions Committee to evaluate whether there is an urgent humanitarian need to supply food to Iraq or Kuwait.

See Document 13, page 172

16 September 1990

The Security Council adopts resolution 667 (1990), condemning aggressive acts perpetrated by Iraq against diplomatic missions and the abduction of personnel from those missions, and demanding the immediate release of third-State nationals.

See Document 14, page 173

24 September 1990

The Security Council adopts resolution 669 (1990), requesting the Sanctions Committee to examine requests for assistance from States confronted with special economic problems arising from the imposition of sanctions against Iraq.

See Document 15, page 174

25 September 1990

The Security Council adopts resolution 670 (1990), expanding sanctions against Iraq to include additional measures affecting shipping and air transport.

See Document 16, page 174

28 September 1990

Iraq announces that it will begin releasing detained third-State nationals.

September-October 1990

During the general debate at the forty-sixth session of the General Assembly, a large majority of United Nations Member States voice opposition to Iraq's invasion and occupation of Kuwait and call for the restoration of the legitimate Kuwaiti Government.

11 October 1990

Iraqi authorities release all detained women and children; other third-State nationals continue to be detained at strategic sites.

29 October 1990

The Security Council adopts resolution 674 (1990), demanding that Iraq release all third-State nationals held in Iraq and Kuwait and confirming that Iraq is liable under international law for any loss, damage or injury as a result of its invasion and occupation of Kuwait.

See Document 17, page 176

28 November 1990

The Security Council adopts resolution 677 (1990), condemning Iraq's destruction of Kuwaiti demographic records and its attempts to alter the demographic composition of Kuwait, and mandating the Secretary-General to take custody of a copy of the population register of Kuwait.

See Document 18, page 177

29 November 1990

The Security Council adopts resolution 678 (1990), authorizing Member States cooperating with the Government of Kuwait to use "all necessary means" to uphold and implement the Council's resolutions on the Iraq-Kuwait crisis unless Iraq fully complies with those resolutions on or before **15 January 1991**.

See Document 19, page 178

18 December 1990

The General Assembly calls on Iraq to respect human rights in occupied Kuwait.

See Document 20, page 178

9 January 1991

The United States Secretary of State and the Deputy Prime Minister and Minister for Foreign Affairs of Iraq meet in Geneva.

12-13 January 1991

The Secretary-General meets in Iraq with President Hussein and with the Deputy Prime Minister and Minister for Foreign Affairs to urge Iraq to comply with the Security Council's resolutions.

15 January 1991
In a statement to the press, the Secretary-General appeals to President Hussein for Iraqi compliance with all relevant Security Council resolutions.
See Document 21, page 179

16 January 1991
Coalition forces begin aerial bombardment of Iraq. Kuwait informs the Secretary-General that Iraqi forces continue to occupy Kuwait despite the expiration of the period specified by Security Council resolution 678 (1990) and that Kuwait, with the cooperation of friendly States, is exercising its right of self-defence.
See Document 22, page 180

February 1991
Upon reports of a massive oil slick in the Persian Gulf, the United Nations Environment Programme (UNEP) dispatches a team of experts to the region to assess the preliminary impact.

16-21 February 1991
A joint mission of the World Health Organization (WHO) and the United Nations Children's Fund (UNICEF) to Iraq delivers medical care and 54 tons of medical supplies (including basic health kits, antibiotics for children and oral rehydration salt packs) and assesses future health-care needs.

21-22 February 1991
Iraq sets fire to more than 500 Kuwaiti oil wells.

24 February 1991
Coalition forces begin ground operations, moving into occupied Kuwait and Iraq.

27 February 1991
Kuwait City is liberated. The coalition States declare the end of ground operations. In a letter to the Secretary-General, Iraq states that it will comply fully with relevant Security Council resolutions, provided that certain conditions are met. In a second set of letters, Iraq informs the President of the Security Council and the Secretary-General that all Iraqi forces have been withdrawn from Kuwait. The President of the Security Council confirms the withdrawal.
See Document 24, page 181; and Document 25, page 181

28 February 1991
Hostilities are suspended at midnight, New York time. Iraq officially states its intent to comply fully with resolution 660 (1990) and all other Security Council resolutions relating to the Iraq-Kuwait situation.

Early March 1991
Internal conflict breaks out in both northern and southern Iraq, resulting in large flows of refugees and displaced persons.

2 March 1991
The Security Council adopts resolution 686 (1991), noting the suspension of all offensive combat operations, demanding Iraq's compliance with all 12 relevant Security Council resolutions, giving immediate priority to the repatriation of Kuwaitis, welcoming the decision by the coalition States to commence the release of Iraqi prisoners of war, and requesting the United Nations, specialized agencies and other international organizations in the United Nations system to cooperate with the Government and people of Kuwait in the reconstruction of their country.
See Document 26, page 182

3 March 1991
Iraq agrees to comply with the terms of Security Council resolution 686 (1991).
See Document 27, page 183

3 March 1991
The President of the Security Council welcomes the decision of the Council's Sanctions Committee to facilitate the provision of humanitarian assistance and pledges immediate action on the assessment of a forthcoming mission to the area.
See Document 28, page 184

4 March 1991
The Government of Kuwait returns to Kuwait City and resumes the functions of State.
See Document 29, page 185

6 March 1991
The Commission on Human Rights decides to assign special rapporteurs to study the situation of human rights in occupied Kuwait and in Iraq.

6 March–6 April 1991
Large-scale repatriation of Kuwaitis takes place, including more than 4,000 prisoners of war and more than 2,000 civilians.
See Document 79, page 302

8 March 1991
Iraq's Revolution Command Council declares all decisions regarding Kuwait it had taken since 2 August 1990 to be null and void.
See Document 30, page 185

10-17 March 1991

A United Nations inter-agency mission visits Iraq to assess humanitarian needs and damage to the country's infrastructure.
See Document 31, page 186

16 March-4 April 1991

A United Nations inter-agency mission visits Kuwait to assess the loss of life during the invasion and occupation and the damage done to Kuwait during that period.
See Document 45, page 212; and Document 46, page 229

22 March 1991

The Security Council Sanctions Committee announces its decisions regarding exceptions to the Iraqi sanctions regime in the light of the humanitarian conditions within Iraq following the cessation of hostilities.
See Document 32, page 188

22 March 1991

Twenty-one States confronted with special economic and social problems as a result of the sanctions imposed against Iraq issue a joint memorandum calling for international assistance.

23-27 March 1991

A United Nations inter-agency mission visits Kuwait to assess humanitarian needs and damage done to Kuwait during the Iraqi occupation.
See Document 34, page 190

26 March 1991

The Secretary-General appoints a Coordinator to oversee the programme mandated by resolution 686 (1991) for the return of all Kuwaiti property seized by Iraq during its invasion and occupation of Kuwait.

Early April 1991

The Office of the United Nations High Commissioner for Refugees (UNHCR) reports massive displacements of Iraqi civilians—an estimated 1.5 million refugees and displaced persons—in the aftermath of the internal conflicts in northern and southern Iraq. Large numbers of persons are reported fleeing from northern Iraq to Turkey and the Islamic Republic of Iran.

3 April 1991

The Security Council adopts resolution 687 (1991), detailing the provisions for a cease-fire, including deployment of a United Nations observer unit to monitor a demilitarized zone and the Khawr 'Abd Allah waterway; demarcation of the Iraq-Kuwait boundary; destruction of Iraqi weapons of mass destruction and long-range ballistic missiles under supervision of a Special Commission (UNSCOM) and the International Atomic Energy Agency (IAEA); establishment of a system of future ongoing monitoring and verification of Iraq's compliance with the ban on these weapons and missiles; return of Kuwaiti property; creation of a compensation fund, financed by Iraq, to meet its liability for losses, damages and injuries related to its unlawful occupation of Kuwait; and repatriation of all Kuwaitis and third-State nationals.
See Document 35, page 193

4 April 1991

Kuwait accepts resolution 687 (1991).
See Document 36, page 198

5 April 1991

The Security Council adopts resolution 688 (1991), demanding that Iraq cease repression of its civilian population, including in Kurdish-populated areas, and that it allow immediate access by international humanitarian organizations to all those in need of assistance.
See Document 37, page 199

5 April 1991

The Secretary-General proposes terms of reference and other details for the creation of a United Nations Iraq-Kuwait Observation Mission (UNIKOM). The Security Council approves the plan on 9 April.
See Document 38, page 200; and Document 40, page 206

6 April 1991

Iraq informs the Security Council and the Secretary-General that it has no choice but to accept the terms of resolution 687 (1991).
See Document 39, page 203

8 April 1991

The Secretary-General issues an international appeal for $178 million to cover the initial humanitarian needs of vulnerable groups in Iraq.

9 April 1991

The Secretary-General appoints an Executive Delegate to oversee the United Nations Inter-Agency Humanitarian Programme for Iraq, Kuwait, and the Iraq/Turkey and Iraq/Iran Border Areas.

11 April 1991

The President of the Security Council acknowledges receipt of Iraq's 6 April letter accepting the terms of resolution 687 (1991), and informs the Government of Iraq that, consequently, a formal cease-fire is in effect.
See Document 42, page 207

12 April 1991
A further international appeal is launched for $400.2 million in emergency aid for refugees and displaced persons on the borders of Iraq and Turkey and in the Islamic Republic of Iran.

18 April 1991
A Memorandum of Understanding detailing the conditions of the United Nations humanitarian presence in Iraq is signed in Baghdad.
See Document 44, page 209

18 April 1991
The Secretary-General submits to the Security Council a plan for the establishment of a United Nations Special Commission (UNSCOM) to carry out, with the International Atomic Energy Agency (IAEA), the weapons-related provisions of resolution 687 (1991); the Council approves the plan on **19 April**.
See Document 43, page 208

18 April 1991
Iraq, in its first declaration regarding weapons of mass destruction and ballistic missiles, denies having weapons-grade nuclear material, a biological weapons programme or any superguns. It also declares holdings of ballistic missiles and chemical weapons.

27 April 1991
In a second declaration regarding nuclear weapons, Iraq admits to having some nuclear materials and facilities in addition to those known by the IAEA.

29 April 1991
The Security Council appeals to States, international financial institutions and United Nations bodies to assist countries which find themselves confronted with special economic problems arising from implementing sanctions against Iraq.
See Document 47, page 235

2 May 1991
The Secretary-General submits to the Security Council plans for the creation of the United Nations Iraq-Kuwait Boundary Demarcation Commission, the United Nations Compensation Fund and the United Nations Compensation Commission.
See Document 48, page 235; and Document 49, page 240

9 May 1991
The demilitarized zone comes into effect after UNIKOM monitors the withdrawal of the last armed forces still deployed in UNIKOM's assigned zone.
See Document 50, page 245

15 May 1991
The United Nations issues an international appeal for $415 million in emergency humanitarian assistance for an inter-agency programme covering Iraq, Kuwait and the Iraq/Turkey and Iraq/Iran border areas; the appeal consolidates earlier appeals of 8 April and 12 April.
See Document 51, page 246

15-21 May 1991
The IAEA conducts its first nuclear inspection of Iraqi facilities. By early 1996, the Agency conducts an additional 28 on-site inspections in accordance with the weapons-related provisions of Security Council resolution 687 and other Council resolutions. (*See "Other documents of interest" for a complete listing of the IAEA's inspections and the relevant documentation.*)

16 May 1991
Iraq submits revised declarations covering chemical weapons and ballistic missiles, increasing the number of items declared.

17 May 1991
The Secretary-General submits to the Security Council plans drawn up by UNSCOM and the IAEA for immediate on-site inspections and for the destruction, removal or rendering harmless of weapons of mass destruction and of the facilities for their production.
See Document 52, page 250; and Document 53, page 253

18 May 1991
Iraq accepts the status agreement detailing the facilities, immunities and privileges to be afforded UNSCOM and the IAEA in implementing their mandates.

20 May 1991
The Security Council adopts resolution 692 (1991), establishing the United Nations Compensation Fund and the United Nations Compensation Commission.
See Document 54, page 255; Document 55, page 256; and Document 56, page 258

25 May 1991
The deployment of a United Nations Guards Contingent to protect humanitarian personnel and assets of the United Nations and of non-governmental organizations working in Iraq is agreed to in an annex to the 18 April Memorandum of Understanding.
See Document 57, page 259

May 1991-June 1992
UNHCR assists in the rehabilitation of more than 1,200 villages in northern and southern Iraq and helps in the first phase of agricultural rehabilitation. UNHCR implements health, water and sanitation programmes and

coordinates United Nations and other international agencies and non-governmental organizations participating in the United Nations Humanitarian Programme.

June 1991
A "no-fly zone" barring flights of Iraqi military aircraft above the 36th parallel in northern Iraq is created by coalition States.

2 June 1991
The Secretary-General proposes guidelines and mechanisms for the full implementation of the arms embargo against Iraq.
See Document 58, page 260

9-15 June 1991
UNSCOM conducts its first chemical inspection of Iraqi facilities.

11 June 1991
Pursuant to paragraph 32 of Security Council resolution 687 (1991), Iraq informs the Council that it does not commit or support international terrorism.
See Document 59, page 264

12-20 June 1991
The Special Rapporteur of the Commission on Human Rights on the situation of human rights in Kuwait under Iraqi occupation visits Kuwait.

17 June 1991
The Security Council adopts resolution 699 (1991), approving the Secretary-General's plan of action for eliminating Iraq's banned weapons programmes and determining that Iraq meet the full costs of implementing the provisions of section C of resolution 687 (1991).
See Document 61, page 267

17 June 1991
The Security Council adopts resolution 700 (1991), approving guidelines for monitoring the Iraqi arms embargo.
See Document 62, page 268

23-28 June 1991
During the second IAEA inspection (22 June–3 July 1991), Iraq obstructs access to items prohibited under the terms of the cease-fire. Shots are fired at inspectors trying to intercept a convoy leaving a site during the course of an inspection.

28 June 1991
The Security Council deplores the incidents of 23-28 June, condemns the conduct of the Iraqi authorities and decides to send a high-level mission to Baghdad to obtain assurances that the Government will not in any way prevent UNSCOM or the IAEA from performing their duties.
See Document 63, page 268

30 June–3 July 1991
The high-level United Nations mission reports that Iraq's response falls short of the requirements of Security Council resolution 687 (1991).
See Document 64, page 269

30 June-7 July 1991
UNSCOM, conducting its first ballistic missile inspection of Iraqi facilities, takes inventory of Iraqi stocks and begins the destruction of launchers and missiles.

July 1991
The United Nations programme for the return of Kuwaiti property becomes operational, with Iraq handing over to Kuwait significant amounts of gold, currency and coins, civilian aircraft and spare parts, and museum and library items.

7-18 July 1991
The third IAEA inspection uncovers large stocks of natural uranium and 15 kilograms of highly enriched uranium, and reveals the existence of various uranium enrichment programmes. Iraq maintains that these programmes are for peaceful purposes.

15 July 1991
The Secretary-General recommends the sale of some Iraqi petroleum and petroleum products to finance the destruction or removal of weapons systems mandated by Security Council resolution 687 (1991) and other mandated United Nations activities in Iraq.
See Document 65, page 272

17 July 1991
The Executive Delegate of the Secretary-General for humanitarian assistance in Iraq reports on the extent of humanitarian needs in Iraq.
See Document 66, page 273

18-20 July 1991
The second ballistic missile inspection reveals undeclared decoy missiles and launch support equipment; these items are destroyed.

25 July 1991
The Governing Council of the United Nations Compensation Commission approves guidelines for the conduct of its work.
See Document 67, page 280

27 July-10 August 1991

The fourth IAEA inspection ascertains that there is strong evidence that Iraq had a nuclear weaponization programme.

2 August 1991

The Governing Council of the United Nations Compensation Commission adopts criteria for the expedited processing of urgent claims.
See Document 68, page 281

2-8 August 1991

UNSCOM conducts its first biological inspection of Iraqi facilities and uncovers a major biological programme. Seed stocks of three biological warfare agents are handed over to the team, and the team removes three further potential warfare strains.

5 August 1991

Iraq officially admits that between 1986 and August 1990 it had undertaken biological and bacteriological research, but for only defensive military purposes.

5 August 1991

Following the first review by the Security Council of the sanctions regime in effect on Iraq, the President of the Council states that there is no agreement that the necessary conditions exist for a modification of the sanctions.
See Document 69, page 283

8-15 August 1991

UNSCOM conducts its third ballistic inspection of Iraqi facilities; the Government of Iraq discloses the existence of a supergun and other banned missile-related materials.

11 August 1991

The United States, on behalf of UNSCOM and with prior notification by UNSCOM to the Iraqi authorities, begins to fly high-altitude reconnaissance flights over Iraq.

15 August 1991

The Security Council adopts resolutions 705 (1991), 706 (1991) and 707 (1991). Resolution 705 establishes that compensation to be paid by Iraq shall not exceed 30 per cent of the annual value of its oil exports. Resolution 706 authorizes the export for a six-month period of Iraqi petroleum products sufficient to produce a sum to be determined by the Council but not to exceed $1.6 billion, in order to finance the purchase of humanitarian goods as well as United Nations operations mandated by resolution 687. Resolution 707 de-mands that Iraq halt all nuclear activities of any kind, that it provide full disclosure of its weapons programmes and that it allow UNSCOM and IAEA inspection teams immediate, unconditional and unrestricted access to all sites.
See Document 71, page 284; Document 72, page 285; and Document 73, page 287

16 August 1991

In a letter to the Security Council, Iraq outlines its objections to resolutions 705 (1991) and 707 (1991).
See Document 74, page 289

18-20 August 1991

UNSCOM conducts its third ballistic-missile inspection of Iraqi facilities, focusing on previously undeclared sites suspected of producing missile components. The inspection team reports that, while carrying out an inventory of dual-capacity equipment, it encountered strong opposition by Iraqi authorities.

31 August–6 September 1991

The Special Rapporteur of the Commission on Human Rights on the situation of human rights in Kuwait under Iraqi occupation conducts his second mission to Kuwait.

3 September 1991

In a letter to the Security Council, Iraq further elaborates its objections to resolution 707 (1991).
See Document 76, page 294

4 September 1991

The Secretary-General proposes guidelines and procedures for implementation of the plan to sell Iraqi petroleum and petroleum products authorized by Security Council resolution 706 (1991).
See Document 78, page 298

6-13 September 1991

UNSCOM conducts its fourth ballistic-missile inspection of Iraqi facilities. Iraqi authorities deny UNSCOM inspection teams permission to use United Nations helicopters to inspect sites in western Iraq.

14-20 September 1991

The IAEA conducts its fifth inspection of Iraqi facilities, concentrating on Iraqi declarations concerning nuclear materials and their methods for enriching and extracting plutonium. The team finds 2.2 tons of heavy water.

19 September 1991

The Security Council adopts resolution 712 (1991), addressing various aspects of the proposed plan to sell Iraqi petroleum products authorized by Security Council resolution 706 (1991).
See Document 81, page 308

20 September-3 October 1991
UNSCOM conducts its second biological inspection of Iraqi facilities, and affirms that Iraq had a biological-weapons programme, which must have included plans for weapons development and production.
See Document 92, page 345

21-30 September 1991
The sixth IAEA inspection team is detained in a parking lot for four days after having found documentation describing progress made in Iraq's plan to build nuclear weapons.

23 September 1991
The Security Council calls on Iraq to implement the provisions of resolution 707 (1991) of 15 August.
See Document 83, page 318

24 September 1991
The Security Council strongly condemns the Iraqi authorities for preventing the IAEA inspectors from carrying out their duty.
See Document 84, page 319; and Document 85, page 319

October 1991
The Personal Representative of the Secretary-General responsible for coordinating United Nations activities to mitigate the environmental impact of the Gulf conflict conducts a fact-finding visit to Kuwait.

October 1991
The ICRC supervises the completion of a general repatriation of Iraqi prisoners.

1-9 October 1991
The fifth UNSCOM missile inspection completes the destruction of Iraq's fixed-missile launchers and of the supergun at Jabal Hamran. A start is made on the destruction of the components for the other superguns.

2 October 1991
Following informal consultations, the Security Council announces that there is no agreement that the necessary conditions exist for a modification of the sanctions regime.
See Document 87, page 325

4-6 October 1991
A delegation headed by the Executive Chairman of UNSCOM visits Iraq and obtains agreement on the use of helicopters by UNSCOM for ballistic-missile inspections. UNSCOM starts flying its own helicopters in Iraq for the purposes of transport and logistical support; the aerial support is contributed by Germany.

7 October 1991
The Security Council agrees with the Secretary-General's recommendation that UNIKOM should be maintained for a further six-month period.
See Document 86, page 319

11 October 1991
The Security Council adopts resolution 715 (1991), approving the plans submitted by the Secretary-General and by the Director General of the IAEA for the ongoing monitoring and verification of Iraqi compliance with the weapons-related provisions of Security Council resolution 687 (1991).
See Document 82, page 309; Document 88, page 325; and Document 89, page 339

11-22 October 1991
The IAEA, conducting its seventh nuclear inspection of Iraqi facilities, supervises the destruction of uranium enrichment and reprocessing equipment. On 14 October, Iraq officially acknowledges that research and studies had been under way in the area of nuclear weaponization.

15 October 1991
The Security Council Sanctions Committee establishes procedures to be employed if the plan for the sale of Iraqi oil products authorized by resolution 706 (1991) of 15 August is carried out.
See Document 90, page 340

11-18 November 1991
The eighth IAEA inspection supervises the removal of unirradiated nuclear fuel and investigates the centrifuge programme, intended for the enrichment of uranium.

18 November–1 December 1991
UNSCOM conducts the first joint chemical and biological inspection. The team finds more than 100 items of chemical bomb-making equipment hidden in a sugar factory in Mosul and undeclared materials related to Scud missiles.

19 November 1991
Iraq rejects the plans submitted by the Secretary-General and by the Director General of the IAEA for the ongoing monitoring and verification of Iraqi compliance with the weapons-related provisions of Security Council resolution 687 (1991).

20 November 1991
Iraqi authorities provide the Field Office of UNSCOM with information on nuclear, chemical, biological and conventional weapons, including their delivery sys-

tems, production capabilities and research and development programmes.

24 November 1991
A second Memorandum of Understanding, extending the inter-agency humanitarian programme until 30 June 1992, is signed.
See Document 93, page 361

1-9 December 1991
UNSCOM conducts its sixth ballistic-missile inspection of Iraqi facilities. The team visits fixed Scud launchers, supervises the destruction of supergun components and discovers that Iraq had sought to repair items destroyed during a previous inspection. Further missile-related equipment and transporters are destroyed.

11 December 1991
In the first instance of Iraqi compliance with Security Council resolution 715 (1991) of 11 October, the Iraqi Resident Representative in Vienna transmits to the Director General of the IAEA information on Iraq's nuclear programme.

17 December 1991
The General Assembly expresses its grave concern at the situation of human rights in Kuwait under Iraqi occupation and its deep concern at allegations of widespread violations of human rights in Iraq.
See Document 96, page 370; and Document 97, page 371

20 December 1991
Following informal consultations, the Security Council announces that there is no agreement that the necessary conditions exist for a modification of the sanctions regime. The Council also decides to simplify procedures pertaining to the sanctions regime on items identified as essential to civilian and humanitarian needs by the report of the inter-agency mission which visited Iraq from 10 to 17 March.
See Document 31, page 186; and Document 98, page 372

20 December 1991
The General Assembly calls for international cooperation to mitigate the environmental impact of the Gulf war on the countries in the region.
See Document 99, page 373

January 1992
An Inter-Agency Humanitarian Programme is launched, with requirements amounting to $143.2 million.

3-9 January 1992
The Special Rapporteur of the Commission on Human Rights on the situation of human rights in Iraq visits Iraq.
See Document 103, page 394

8-10 January 1992
A first round of talks is held in Vienna between representatives of Iraq and officials of the United Nations on implementation of resolutions 706 (1991) and 712 (1991); Iraq continues, in the course of subsequent talks, to object to the so-called "oil-for-food" formula contained in those resolutions.

27-30 January 1992
UNSCOM dispatches a special mission to Iraq to elicit Iraqi acknowledgement of its obligations under resolutions 707 (1991) and 715 (1991) and to urge disclosure of information on Iraqi programmes related to chemical and biological weapons and ballistic missiles.

27 January–5 February 1992
During its seventh chemical inspection of Iraqi facilities, UNSCOM verifies the delivery of chemical bomb-making equipment to a central destruction facility under construction at Al Muthanna and concludes that additional tests of the procedure for the destruction of nerve agents would be necessary.

31 January 1992
The Security Council, at its first meeting at the level of heads of State or Government, emphasizes the importance of the full implementation of all relevant Security Council resolutions pertaining to the situation between Iraq and Kuwait and expresses its concern for the humanitarian situation of the civilian population of Iraq.

5 February 1992
Following informal consultations, the Security Council announces that there is no agreement that the necessary conditions exist for a modification of the sanctions regime.
See Document 101, page 390

14 February 1992
The Executive Chairman of UNSCOM, in a letter to Iraq's Minister for Foreign Affairs, identifies ballistic-missile production, repair facilities and related equipment within Iraq and demands their destruction under UNSCOM supervision.

18 February 1992
In a report to the Security Council, UNSCOM concludes that Iraq is not prepared to give its unconditional agreement to implement all of its obligations under

Security Council resolutions 687 (1991), 707 (1991) and 715 (1991), particularly those regarding the destruction of prohibited ballistic-missile-related facilities and equipment.
See Document 102, page 391

19 February 1992
The Security Council states that Iraq's continued failure to acknowledge all of its obligations under resolutions 707 (1991) and 715 (1991), its rejection of the two plans for ongoing monitoring and verification and its failure to provide full disclosure of its weapons capabilities constitute a material breach of the relevant provisions of resolution 687 (1991).
See Document 104, page 409

21-23 February 1992
A special mission, headed by the Executive Chairman of UNSCOM, holds high-level talks with the Government of Iraq in an attempt to secure its unconditional agreement to implement all of its relevant obligations under resolutions 687 (1991), 707 (1991) and 715 (1991).

21-28 February 1992
UNSCOM conducts its eighth ballistic-missile inspection of Iraqi facilities. Teams catalogue prohibited items and attempt to verify the destruction of ballistic-missile production and repair facilities and equipment as directed by the Executive Chairman in his letter of 14 February. Following Iraqi refusal to destroy the specified missiles and components, the inspection team is withdrawn from Iraq and the issue is brought to the attention of the Security Council.

21 February–24 March 1992
The first chemical destruction team destroys 463 nerve-agent-filled rockets, i.e. approximately 2.5 tonnes of agent.

24 February 1992
Iraq reiterates its assertions that it has provided all information required of it by relevant resolutions of the Security Council. Iraq repeats that while it does not reject an ongoing monitoring and verification regime, it objects to the indefinite duration of the privileges, immunities and facilities granted to UNSCOM and the IAEA and the infringement on Iraqi sovereignty they represent.

27 February 1992
The Executive Chairman of UNSCOM reports that he has not secured Iraq's unconditional agreement to implement all of its obligations.

28 February 1992
Iraq questions the authority of UNSCOM to determine the items to be destroyed under resolution 687 (1991). The Security Council reaffirms that it is for UNSCOM alone to determine which items are to be destroyed under resolution 687, and warns Iraq of the serious consequences of its continued non-compliance with its obligations.
See Document 105, page 410

3 March 1992
The Commission on Human Rights expresses its deep concern at the grave violations of human rights and fundamental freedoms committed during the occupation of Kuwait.

5 March 1992
The Commission on Human Rights expresses its strong condemnation of the massive violations of human rights carried out in Iraq.

7 March 1992
Representatives of Iraq, of Kuwait, and of France, Saudi Arabia, the United Kingdom and the United States, with the International Committee of the Red Cross (ICRC) as a neutral intermediary, begin meeting to establish modalities for identifying and effecting the release of persons still reported missing.

11 March 1992
The Security Council expresses its concern at human rights abuses being perpetrated by Iraq against its population.
See Document 108, page 421

11-12 March 1992
The Security Council debates Iraq's compliance with the relevant resolutions. In two presidential statements, the Council reaffirms that the Government of Iraq has not yet complied fully and unconditionally with relevant Council resolutions and states that Iraqi authorities must immediately act to do so.
See Document 108, page 421; and Document 109, page 425

17 March 1992
The Governing Council of the United Nations Compensation Commission adopts criteria for the processing of additional categories of claims covering individuals with losses exceeding $100,000 and the claims of corporations, international organizations and Governments.
See Document 110, page 425

19 March 1992

Iraq, in response to the 12 March statement by the President of the Security Council, declares the existence of as yet undeclared ballistic missiles, chemical weapons and associated material. Iraq reveals that most of these undeclared items were unilaterally destroyed in the summer of 1991, in violation of resolution 687 (1991). Iraq states its willingness to carry out the additional necessary destructions.

19 March 1992

The Security Council informs Iraq of its willingness to authorize the regime governing the sale of Iraqi petroleum and petroleum products as soon as the Secretary-General indicates that the Iraqi authorities are prepared to proceed according to the obligations imposed on them by the regime.
See Document 111, page 430

21-29 March 1992

UNSCOM conducts its ninth ballistic-missile inspection of Iraqi facilities. Teams are charged with verifying the destruction of the facilities and equipment delineated by the Executive Chairman in his letter of 14 February, verifying Iraqi claims of having unilaterally destroyed 89 ballistic missiles and associated equipment in 1991, and conducting undeclared inspections of sites throughout Iraq.

25 March 1992

The IAEA presents to the Government of Iraq a list of buildings and equipment to be destroyed at the Al Atheer-Al Hatteen site.

26-28 March 1992

A second round of discussions is held in Vienna between the United Nations Secretariat and Iraqi representatives on arrangements for the proposed sale of petroleum to finance the purchase of goods for humanitarian purposes.

27 March 1992

Following informal consultations, the Security Council announces that there is no agreement that the necessary conditions exist for a modification of the sanctions regime.
See Document 112, page 430

29-31 March 1992

The Personal Representative of the Secretary-General responsible for coordinating the United Nations response to the environmental crisis in the Gulf region makes a second visit to Kuwait.

4 April 1992

The Executive Chairman of UNSCOM, in a further letter to Iraq, details additional items to be destroyed or to verify as having been destroyed.

5-13 April 1992

UNSCOM teams monitoring preparations for the destruction of chemical weapons at Al Muthanna provide technical guidance for the construction of a mustard-agent incinerator and a large-scale nerve agent hydrolysis plant and supervise the transfer of all chemicals usable for the manufacture of ballistic-missile propellant to the site for destruction.

6 April 1992

The Security Council agrees with the Secretary-General's recommendation that UNIKOM should be maintained for a further six-month period.
See Document 113, page 431

7-15 April 1992

The IAEA conducts its eleventh nuclear inspection of Iraqi facilities and supervises the destruction of equipment and facilities at Al Atheer, Iraq's nuclear weaponization research and development centre.

9 April 1992

Following the incursion of an Iranian aircraft into Iraqi airspace, the Government of Iraq, in a letter to UNSCOM, calls for a halt to all of UNSCOM's aerial surveillance flights, stating that the safety of the pilots and aircraft could be in danger.

10 April 1992

In response to the Iraqi letter of 9 April, the Executive Chairman of UNSCOM expresses his concern at the implied threats to the safety of the Commission's pilots and aircraft. The Security Council reaffirms the right of UNSCOM to conduct aerial surveillance over Iraq, calls upon Iraq to ensure that its military forces do not interfere with or threaten the safety of the Commission's aircraft and personnel and warns the Iraqi authorities of serious consequences should they fail to comply.
See Document 115, page 438

12 April 1992

Iraq asserts that it did not and does not intend to carry out any military operation aimed at UNSCOM surveillance activity.

13-21 April 1992

UNSCOM teams continue to supervise the destruction of ballistic missile production equipment, monitoring the destruction of 45 items and 10 buildings.

15 April 1992
The IAEA plan for the dismantling of uranium enrichment production capabilities at the Tarmiya and Ash Sharqat sites is prepared and communicated to the Government of Iraq.
See Document 114, page 434

15-29 April 1992
During UNSCOM's eighth chemical inspection of Iraqi facilities, UNSCOM teams inspect 14 sites to verify the destruction of chemical-weapon items which Iraq declared it had destroyed unilaterally.

14-22 May 1992
UNSCOM conducts its eleventh ballistic-missile inspection of Iraqi facilities. Teams continue to verify the destruction of the additional chemical warheads and ballistic missiles revealed in Iraq's declaration of 19 March, to inventory material designed for the construction of the BADR-2000 (medium-range ballistic missile), to verify the destruction of additional missile-related items in the Iraqi arsenal, to identify five sets of Iraqi-manufactured missile-guidance components which were to be removed from Iraq, and to find documents related to the construction of facilities associated with the missile programme.

26 May 1992
Iraq informs the Executive Chairman of UNSCOM that it has already disclosed, or is imminently ready to disclose, its full nuclear, chemical, biological and ballistic-missile programmes to the relevant authorities, as required by resolution 687 (1991), and that it is prepared to reach a practical solution to the monitoring programme required by resolutions 707 (1991) and 715 (1991).

26 May-4 June 1992
The twelfth IAEA inspection continues destruction activities at Al Atheer and removes the remaining highly enriched uranium from Iraq.

27 May 1992
Following informal consultations, the Security Council announces that there is no agreement that the necessary conditions exist for a modification of the sanctions regime.
See Document 117, page 441

June 1992
Having fully implemented the Emergency Relief Programme and the first phase of rehabilitation in three northern governorates of Iraq, UNHCR gradually scales down its operations and hands over its activities as well as some assets to other United Nations agencies to enable the continuation of the rehabilitation efforts.

17 June 1992
The Security Council reminds Iraq of its repudiation of all claims to Kuwait and of its obligation under resolution 687 (1991) to accept the inviolability of the international boundary demarcated by the Boundary Demarcation Commission.
See Document 120, page 458

18 June 1992
UNSCOM's Chemical Destruction Group starts its operations in Iraq.

19-22 June 1992
A third round of discussions is held in Vienna between the United Nations Secretariat and Iraqi representatives on arrangements for the proposed sale of petroleum to finance the purchase of humanitarian goods.

21 June 1992
UNSCOM starts using its helicopters for aerial surveillance in Iraq.

26 June 1992
The Governing Council of the United Nations Compensation Commission adopts its Provisional Rules for Claims Procedure.
See Document 121, page 459

26 June-10 July 1992
The second joint chemical and biological inspection team visits undeclared sites and supervises the destruction of chemical bomb-making equipment.

July 1992
A nine-month Inter-Agency Humanitarian Programme (July 1992–March 1993) is launched, with requirements amounting to $201.7 million.

5 July 1992
An UNSCOM inspection team is refused access to Iraq's Ministry of Agriculture.

6 July 1992
The Security Council demands that Iraq grant UNSCOM inspection teams immediate access to the Ministry of Agriculture as required by resolution 687 (1991).
See Document 122, page 467

6-29 July 1992
UNSCOM's ballistic-missile inspection team maintains a watch outside the Ministry of Agriculture building, pending access to the site. The team is withdrawn on **22 July** following an attack on one of its members. Access is finally permitted on **28-29 July**, when a thorough inspection is conducted. Evidence gathered from

the Ministry is consistent with the removal of items during the period the team was denied entry.

14-21 July 1992
The thirteenth IAEA inspection supervises destruction activities at the uranium enrichment plans in Taromiya and Ash Sharqat.

15 July 1992
Iraq refuses to participate in the sixth session of the Iraq-Kuwait Boundary Demarcation Commission; Iraq also does not participate in five subsequent sessions held through the end of the Commission's work on 20 May 1993.

16 July 1992
A member of the United Nations Guards Contingent is murdered in the northern Iraqi Governorate of Dohuk. The Secretary-General calls for an immediate and thorough investigation.

17 July 1992
The Security Council condemns the murder of the United Nations Guard, expresses concern at the deterioration of security conditions affecting United Nations personnel in Iraq and demands the immediate cessation of attacks against United Nations and humanitarian personnel.
See Document 124, page 469

27 July 1992
Following informal consultations, the Security Council announces that there is no agreement that the necessary conditions exist for a modification of the sanctions regime.
See Document 125, page 470

August 1992
A no-fly zone covering Iraqi territory below the 32nd parallel in southern Iraq is created by coalition States.

11 August 1992
The Security Council meets to consider the situation of human rights in Iraq in the light of reports filed by the Special Rapporteur of the Commission on Human Rights. The Special Rapporteur addresses the Council.

17-22 August 1992
A mission led by the Under-Secretary-General for Humanitarian Affairs visits Iraq but fails to reach agreement on the signing of a new Memorandum of Understanding for July 1992 to May 1993.
See Document 127, page 471

24 August 1992
The Secretary-General reports to the Security Council on difficulties encountered in negotiations with the Government of Iraq on renewing the Memorandum of Understanding governing the Inter-Agency Humanitarian Programme in Iraq.
See Document 127, page 471

2 September 1992
The Security Council affirms that the critical humanitarian needs in Iraq demand the continuation of the present humanitarian regime.
See Document 129, page 474

26 August 1992
The Security Council adopts resolution 773 (1992), welcoming the decisions of the Iraq-Kuwait Boundary Demarcation Commission, welcoming the Secretary-General's intention to realign the demilitarized zone to correspond to the international boundary and underlining the Council's guarantee of the inviolability of the international border.
See Document 128, page 473

31 August–7 September 1992
The fourteenth IAEA inspection commences the sampling of Iraqi watercourses as part of its plan to monitor Iraqi compliance with nuclear-weapons-related provisions of Security Council resolutions.

5-12 September 1992
UNSCOM commissions the hydrolysis plant (designed to destroy nerve agent) at Muthanna. Full-scale operation of the plant commences on 24 September.

24 September 1992
Iraq announces it has no objection to the United Nations mounting a relief operation in northern Iraq during the winter.

24 September 1992
Following informal consultations, the Security Council announces that there is no agreement that the necessary conditions exist for a modification of the sanctions regime.
See Document 130, page 474

2 October 1992
The Security Council adopts resolution 778 (1992), directing Governments in possession of the proceeds of the sale of Iraqi petroleum and petroleum products, paid for by or on behalf of the purchaser on or after August 1990, to transfer such funds to the United Nations escrow account.
See Document 132, page 478

9 October 1992

The Security Council agrees with the Secretary-General's recommendation that UNIKOM should be maintained for a further six-month period.
See Document 131, page 475

14-17 October 1992

The Executive Director of UNICEF visits Iraq to expedite the signing of a new Memorandum of Understanding on humanitarian assistance.

15 October 1992

The Security Council expresses support for UNSCOM inspectors in Iraq and concern for their safety.
See Document 133, page 480

22 October 1992

A third Memorandum of Understanding concerning humanitarian assistance is signed with Iraq, allowing the continued presence of the United Nations Guards Contingent in some sectors and extending the agreement on the Contingent until **31 March 1993.**
See Document 135, page 483

10 November 1992

Iraq reiterates its position that the economic sanctions regime imposed upon Iraq should be removed owing both to the high proportion of obligations that Iraq had fulfilled and to the suffering that it was imposing on the Iraqi population. Iraq announces its intention to send a high-level delegation to represent it at the Security Council's November review of Iraqi compliance with its obligations under resolution 687 (1991).

19 November 1992

Iraq submits to the Security Council a detailed account of its activities in conjunction with UNSCOM and IAEA inspections and of measures it has taken to implement section C of resolution 687 (1991).

23-24 November 1992

The Security Council debates Iraq's compliance with the relevant resolutions. At the beginning of the meeting, the Council states that Iraq has not fully complied with all of the obligations placed upon it by all relevant Council resolutions. At the end of the meeting, the Council reiterates its support for the statement made at the opening of the meeting and calls on Iraq to take immediately the appropriate actions to comply fully and unconditionally with its obligations.
See Document 137, page 486; and Document 138, page 490

24 November 1992

Following informal consultations, the Security Council announces that there is no agreement that the necessary conditions exist for a modification of the sanctions regime.
See Document 139, page 491

18 December 1992

The General Assembly condemns the massive violations of human rights reported within Iraq and calls on Member States, international and non-governmental organizations, scientific bodies and individuals to provide assistance for programmes aimed at mitigating the environmental damage resulting from the Iraq-Kuwait conflict.
See Document 143, page 507; and Document 144, page 509

2 January 1993

Some 200 Iraqis enter the former naval base at Umm Qasr in the demilitarized zone without UNIKOM authorization to retrieve Iraqi property.
See Document 147, page 513

7 January 1993

Iraqi authorities inform UNSCOM that the United Nations would no longer be permitted to use its own aircraft to transport personnel and equipment between Iraq and Bahrain.

8 January 1993

The Security Council demands that Iraq permit UNIKOM and UNSCOM to use their own aircraft to transport personnel and equipment and that Iraq abide by its obligations under all relevant Security Council resolutions.
See Document 146, page 512

8 January 1993

The President of the Security Council writes to the Secretary-General concerning Iraqi incursions into the DMZ and expressing Council members' insistence on the removal of six Iraqi police posts on Kuwaiti territory by 15 January.
See Document 154, page 526

10 January 1993

In a further incursion into the demilitarized zone (DMZ), some 200 Iraqis force their way into six ammunition bunkers located at the former naval base at Umm Qasr and remove most of their contents, including weapons and armaments slated for destruction.
See Document 147, page 513

11 January 1993

The Security Council condemns Iraq for removing equipment and other materials from the Kuwaiti side of the DMZ and declares that Iraq's recent actions

towards UNIKOM and UNSCOM constitute material breaches of resolution 687 (1991).
See Document 148, page 516

13 January 1993

Pursuant to the Security Council's 11 January determination that Iraq is in breach of resolution 687 (1991), the United States, the United Kingdom and France stage air raids on Iraqi anti-missile sites and radar bases in southern Iraq.

13 January 1993

Iraqi retrieval of property from Kuwait ends.
See Document 147, page 513

17 January 1993

The United States fires missiles at an industrial complex in suburban Baghdad.

17-18 January 1993

The six Iraqi police posts on Kuwait territory are withdrawn.
See Document 147, page 513; and Document 154, page 526

18 January 1993

The United States and the United Kingdom launch air raids against radar sites in southern and northern Iraq.

18 January 1993

The Secretary-General recommends strengthening UNIKOM to give it the capacity to redress small-scale violations of the DMZ and the border and to deal with problems that might arise from the completed demarcation of the boundary.
See Document 149, page 517

19 January 1993

The Secretary-General reports that Iraq has agreed to a resumption of UNSCOM's flights.
See Document 147, page 513; and Document 154, page 526

25 January 1993

Following informal consultations, the Security Council announces that there is no agreement that the necessary conditions exist for a modification of the sanctions regime.
See Document 150, page 519

February 1993

The ICRC informs the coalition States that Iraq has decided to stop attending consultations concerning repatriation.

February 1993

Iraq submits to UNSCOM updated information relating to compliance monitoring.

5 February 1993

The Security Council adopts resolution 806 (1993), strengthening UNIKOM and widening its mandate to permit it to take direct physical action to prevent or redress violations of the demilitarized zone.
See Document 152, page 525

March 1993

A one-year United Nations Inter-Agency Humanitarian Programme (April 1993–March 1994) is launched with requirements amounting to $489.2 million.

2 March 1993

Kuwait reports that it has handed over to the ICRC the individual files of 627 prisoners, detainees and missing persons about whom it is seeking information from Iraq.

10 March 1993

The Commission on Human Rights reiterates its strong condemnation of the massive violations of human rights in Iraq and requests the Secretary-General, in consultation with the Special Rapporteur, to take the necessary measures in order to send human rights monitors to such locations as would facilitate improved information flows and assessment and would help in the independent verification of reports on the situation of human rights in Iraq.

29 March 1993

Following informal consultations, the Security Council announces that there is no agreement that the necessary conditions exist for a modification of the sanctions regime.
See Document 153, page 526

13 April 1993

The Security Council agrees with the Secretary-General's recommendation that UNIKOM should be maintained for a further six-month period.
See Document 154, page 526

20 May 1993

The Iraq-Kuwait Boundary Demarcation Commission submits its final report on the demarcation of an international boundary between Iraq and Kuwait. The Secretary-General, at the Commission's final session, states that a "precise, well-documented and verifiable demarcation of the entire boundary" has been accomplished.
See Document 157, page 539; and Document 158, page 540

24 May 1993
Following informal consultations, the Security Council announces that there is no agreement that the necessary conditions exist for a modification of the sanctions regime.
See Document 159, page 561

27 May 1993
The Secretary-General reports that as of 30 April, $101.5 million had been deposited into the escrow account set up under resolution 778 (1992) to receive funds for operations mandated by resolution 687 (1991)—$50 million from a transfer of frozen Iraqi assets and the balance from voluntary contributions.
See Document 160, page 562

27 May 1993
The Security Council adopts resolution 833 (1993), reaffirming the decisions of the Iraq-Kuwait Boundary Demarcation Commission and underlining the Council's decision to guarantee the inviolability of the boundary.
See Document 161, page 567

6 June 1993
In a letter to the Secretary-General, Iraq outlines various objections to the work of the Iraq-Kuwait Boundary Demarcation Commission.
See Document 162, page 568

16 June 1993
In a letter to the Secretary-General, Kuwait accepts the decisions of the Iraq-Kuwait Boundary Demarcation Commission.
See Document 163, page 571

16 June 1993
UNSCOM reports on Iraq's non-compliance with monitoring efforts, including its refusal to permit helicopter surveillance during on-site inspections and the installation of monitoring cameras at two test sites.

17 June 1993
Iraqi authorities block the installation of monitoring cameras at two rocket test sites and refuse to transport chemical-weapons-related equipment to a designated site for destruction under UNSCOM supervision.

18 June 1993
The Security Council demands that Iraq accept the installation by UNSCOM of monitoring devices at the rocket-engine test sites and that Iraq transport chemical-weapons-related equipment to the UNSCOM-designated destruction site, and warns the Government of the danger of refusing to comply with the relevant provisions of resolution 687 (1991).
See Document 164, page 572

28 June 1993
The Security Council, in response to Iraq's letter of 6 June, reaffirms the legality and finality of the decisions of the Iraq-Kuwait Boundary Demarcation Commission and reminds Iraq of the inviolability of the international boundary.
See Document 167, page 591

July 1993
Iraq provides UNSCOM with further updates of information relating to compliance monitoring in the missile, chemical and biological areas.

7-15 July 1993
The Secretary-General meets with Iraqi officials in New York to discuss the "oil-for-food" programme; a fourth round of talks is suspended by Iraq.

15-19 July 1993
After high-level meetings between UNSCOM and Iraq, the Executive Chairman of UNSCOM reports to the Security Council that between 18 June and 2 July, Iraq removed all chemical-weapon production equipment and precursor chemicals from its site at Al Fallujah; that, under UNSCOM supervision, it destroyed all of the chemical-weapon equipment; and that the chemical precursors will be destroyed in due course. Iraq agrees to allow installation of monitoring cameras, but not their operation.

21 July 1993
Following informal consultations, the Security Council announces that there is no agreement that the necessary conditions exist for a modification of the sanctions regime.
See Document 168, page 592

31 August–9 September 1993
At talks in New York between Iraq, UNSCOM and the IAEA, Iraq agrees to the operation of the monitoring cameras installed at rocket engine test stands. The cameras are activated on 25 September.

20 September 1993
Following informal consultations, the Security Council announces that there is no agreement that the necessary conditions exist for a modification of the sanctions regime.
See Document 169, page 592

11 October 1993
The Security Council agrees with the Secretary-General's recommendation that UNIKOM should be maintained for a further six-month period.
See Document 170, page 592

15-16 November 1993

In a letter to the President of the Security Council, Kuwait reports acts of provocation by Iraqi nationals.

18 November 1993

Following informal consultations, the Security Council announces that there is no agreement that the necessary conditions exist for a modification of the sanctions regime.

See Document 174, page 603

22 November 1993

In letters to the President of the Security Council, Kuwait reports acts of Iraqi aggression against its nationals, its territory and UNIKOM officers on patrol.

23 November 1993

The Security Council holds Iraq responsible for the recent violations of the Iraq-Kuwait international boundary and demands that Iraq take all necessary measures to prevent any future violation.

See Document 175, page 604

26 November 1993

Iraq accepts resolution 715 (1991), in which the Security Council approved plans for the ongoing monitoring and verification of Iraqi compliance with the disarmament provisions of Security Council resolution 687 (1991).

See Document 82, page 309; Document 88, page 325; and Document 176, page 604

20 December 1993

The General Assembly condemns human rights violations in Iraq.

See Document 178, page 607

January 1994

Iraq makes its first declarations to UNSCOM under resolution 715 (1991) about its dual-purpose capabilities. Iraq notifies the Commission that previous compliance-monitoring declarations should be considered as having been submitted under resolution 715 (1991).

18 January 1994

Following informal consultations, the Security Council announces that there is no agreement that the necessary conditions exist for a modification of the sanctions regime. As called for under resolutions 687 (1991) and 700 (1991), the Council continues to review sanctions every 60 days.

See Document 180, page 623

22 February 1994

The Secretary-General reports to the President of the Security Council on his efforts to resolve the issue of

Iraqi citizens and their assets found to be in Kuwaiti territory following the demarcation of the boundary.

See Document 181, page 623

March 1994

A one-year Consolidated Inter-Agency Humanitarian Programme (April 1994–March 1995) is launched, with requirements amounting to $288.5 million.

2 March 1994

The Secretary-General reports on the return of Kuwaiti property seized by Iraq and includes with his report a 23-page list of properties which Kuwait claims have not been returned, as well as a list of national establishments whose property is also missing.

See Document 182, page 624

4 March 1994

The Security Council adopts resolution 899 (1994), deciding that compensation may be made to Iraqi citizens for loss of assets resulting from the demarcation of the international boundary between Iraq and Kuwait.

See Document 183, page 627

9 March 1994

The Commission on Human Rights expresses for the fourth time its strong condemnation of the massive violations of human rights in Iraq and calls upon Iraq to release all persons arbitrarily arrested and detained, including Kuwaitis and nationals of other States.

12 March 1994

The IAEA completes the removal of all irradiated nuclear fuel from Iraq.

23 March 1994

The Governing Council of the United Nations Compensation Commission adopts decisions concerning the priority of payment, payment mechanisms, distribution of payments and transparency.

See Document 184, page 628; and Document 185, page 629

March–May 1994

In the context of its plan for ongoing monitoring and verification, UNSCOM starts baseline inspections of dual-purpose facilities in Iraq that could be modified for use in acquiring chemical and biological weapons or banned missiles.

8 April 1994

The Security Council agrees with the Secretary-General's recommendation that UNIKOM should be maintained for a further six-month period.

See Document 186, page 630

19 April 1994
Iraq submits to UNSCOM detailed information on its imports of precursor chemicals and equipment for the production of chemical weapons.

24-26 April 1994
A further round of high-level talks between UNSCOM, IAEA and Iraqi officials takes place in Baghdad. Progress made in preparation for ongoing monitoring and verification is assessed and a joint statement is issued.

9-10 May 1994
Following high-level technical talks in Vienna, the IAEA and Iraq issue joint statements acknowledging Iraq's cooperation in facilitating the IAEA's mission.

28 May-7 June 1994
UNSCOM conducts verification inspections of Iraq's biological weapons programme in order to develop an inventory of biological dual-purpose equipment and to mark and photograph relevant equipment in order to provide a baseline of data against which to determine equipment use, modification and transfer.

June 1994
The United Nations Compensation Commission pays $2.7 million to 670 category "B" (serious personal injury or death) claimants from 16 countries

24 June-2 July 1994
Monitors from the United Nations Centre for Human Rights visit Kuwait to gather further information on missing persons.

July 1994
Iraq resumes its participation in the meetings of the Tripartite Commission, which then, in order to expedite the repatriation process, forms a Technical Subcommittee on Military and Civilian Missing Prisoners of War and Mortal Remains.

July 1994
Iraq updates its declarations to UNSCOM of its dual-purpose capabilities in the chemical, biological and missile areas.

11 July 1994
The Secretary-General writes to the Foreign Ministers of the 20 countries which were the principal importers of Iraqi crude petroleum in 1990 to seek information from petroleum companies on any importation of Iraqi petroleum and petroleum products on or after 1 June 1990.
See Document 191, page 662

22 August-7 September 1994
The IAEA conducts its twenty-sixth nuclear inspection of Iraqi facilities. Concurrently with the inspection, the IAEA establishes a continuous presence in Iraq in order to implement the monitoring and verification of Iraq's compliance with its obligations under resolution 707 (1991).

23-26 September 1994
UNSCOM and Iraq resume high-level technical talks in Baghdad to review Iraq's biological-weapon capability and activities since 1986.

2 October 1994
UNSCOM announces that the system for ongoing monitoring and verification of Iraqi compliance with the disarmament provisions of Security Council resolution 687 (1991) is provisionally operational, subject to a period of testing of its effectiveness.

4 October 1994
Kuwait submits to the Secretary-General a list of property which is still to be returned, including property belonging to the Kuwaiti armed forces, Central Bank, Central Library, Government ministries, Government departments and other entities.

6 October 1994
Iraq threatens to cease cooperation with UNSCOM and the IAEA, and moves troops towards the border with Kuwait.

7 October 1994
The Security Council agrees with the Secretary-General's recommendation that UNIKOM should be maintained for a further six-month period.
See Document 192, page 663

8 October 1994
In response to the Iraqi actions of 6 October, the Security Council declares the complete unacceptability of the implication that Iraq may withdraw cooperation from UNSCOM. In response to reports that substantial numbers of Iraqi troops are being redeployed in the direction of the Iraq-Kuwait border, the Council requests the Secretary-General to ensure that UNIKOM redoubles its vigilance and underlines Iraq's full responsibility to comply fully with all relevant Council resolutions.
See Document 194, page 685

14 October 1994
Iraq announces that, as of 12 October, it had withdrawn its troops to their previous positions and affirms its readiness to resolve the issue of its recognition of Kuwaiti sovereignty.
See Document 197, page 695

15 October 1994
The Security Council adopts resolution 949 (1994), condemning Iraq's large-scale deployment of military units towards the Kuwaiti border and demanding their complete withdrawal. The Council also demands that Iraq not redeploy these troops to the south and that Iraq cooperate fully with UNSCOM.
See Document 196, page 694

10 November 1994
An Iraqi Revolution Command Council decree and a National Assembly declaration confirm Iraq's irrevocable and unqualified recognition of the sovereignty, territorial integrity and political independence of the State of Kuwait and of the international boundary between Iraq and Kuwait, as demarcated by the Iraq-Kuwait Boundary Demarcation Commission, and Iraq's respect for the inviolability of that boundary.
See Document 198, page 696

16 November 1994
The Security Council welcomes Iraq's recognition of the State of Kuwait and its commitment to respect Kuwait's sovereignty, territorial integrity and borders.
See Document 199, page 698

23 December 1994
The General Assembly calls on Iraq to release all detained Kuwaitis and third-State nationals and condemns Iraq for its unwillingness to implement the plan to sell oil to provide humanitarian aid, food and health care for its population.
See Document 202, page 720

8 March 1995
The Commission on Human Rights states that it remains concerned at the particularly severe and grave violations of human rights by the Government of Iraq.

21 March 1995
A one-year Consolidated Inter-Agency Humanitarian Programme (April 1995–March 1996) is launched with requirements amounting to $183.3 million.
See Document 203, page 722

6-7 April 1995
A seminar of international biological-weapons experts convened by UNSCOM concludes that Iraq has an undeclared full-scale biological-weapons programme.

10 April 1995
The Security Council agrees with the Secretary-General's recommendation that UNIKOM should be maintained for a further six-month period.
See Document 204, page 725

10 April 1995
UNSCOM reports that the system for ongoing monitoring and verification of Iraqi compliance with the disarmament provisions of Security Council resolution 687 (1991) is operational.

14 April 1995
The Security Council adopts resolution 986 (1995), offering Iraq another opportunity to export petroleum and petroleum products, the proceeds of which would be used to meet the humanitarian needs of the Iraqi people.
See Document 207, page 754

1-3 May 1995
A seminar of international chemical weapons experts is convened by UNSCOM. The panel concludes that Iraq has not adequately disclosed its past chemical-weapons programme.

15 May 1995
Iraq informs the Secretary-General that it will not implement Security Council resolution 986 (1995) authorizing the sale of oil to meet the cost of humanitarian needs.
See Document 209, page 757

22-30 June 1995
Monitors from the United Nations Centre for Human Rights conduct their second mission to Kuwait in order to follow up on the Special Rapporteur's concern for Kuwaiti and third-State nationals who disappeared in the custody of Iraqi authorities during the illegal occupation of Kuwait.

1 July 1995
Iraq admits to having had a full-scale offensive biological-weapons programme.

17 July 1995
President Hussein threatens to end all cooperation with UNSCOM and the IAEA if there is no progress towards the lifting of sanctions and the oil embargo. A deadline of 31 August is subsequently set.

4 August 1995
Iraq gives UNSCOM a written account of its past biological-weapons programme which still denies efforts to weaponize biological warfare agents.

7 August 1995
Gen. Hussein Kamel Hassan, the former Director of Iraq's weapons of mass destruction and ballistic-missile programmes, leaves Iraq for Jordan.

17 August 1995
Iraq admits that it did indeed produce biological weapons, that it had a crash programme to acquire nuclear weapons and that it made greater progress in producing the nerve agent VX and in producing ballistic missiles indigenously than previously declared. It blames the concealment of these data on Gen. Hussein Kamal Hassan. Iraq's threat to end cooperation with UNSCOM and the IAEA by 31 August is removed.

20 August 1995
Iraq hands over to UNSCOM and the IAEA some 680,000 pages of printed documents, computer disks, videotapes, microfilm and microfiche, and various items and materials relating to its past banned weapons programmes.

9-20 September 1995
The twenty-eighth nuclear inspection of the IAEA in Iraq meets with principal Iraqi scientists, engineers and support staff involved in the crash programme and obtains further information and documents.

6 October 1995
The Security Council agrees with the Secretary-General's recommendation that UNIKOM should be maintained for a further six-month period.
See Document 212, page 765

12 October 1995
The Governing Council of the United Nations Compensation Commission pays $8.2 million to 2,577 category "B" (serious personal injury or death) claimants from 41 countries and three international organizations filing Palestinian claims.
See Document 215, page 793

17-24 October 1995
In the twenty-ninth nuclear inspection of IAEA in Iraq, the current state of knowledge of Iraqi scientists and engineers in centrifuge enrichment and weaponization technologies is discussed in order to ensure that ongoing monitoring and verification are properly focused.

6 December 1995
The Under-Secretary-General for Humanitarian Affairs writes to United Nations Member States and other potential donors, asking them to contribute "urgently and substantially" to fund United Nations humanitarian activities in Iraq.

7 December 1995
The Sanctions Committee forwards to the Security Council a proposal for a mechanism to monitor Iraq's exports and imports of dual-purpose capabilities, once sanctions are lifted.
See Document 217, page 804

13 December 1995
The Governing Council of the United Nations Compensation Commission pays $2.4 million to 720 category "B" claimants from 19 Governments and international organizations presenting Palestinian claims.
See Document 218, page 809

22 December 1995
The General Assembly expresses its strong condemnation of human rights violations in Iraq and urges the Government of Iraq to cooperate with the United Nations on the "oil-for-food" formula authorized by Security Council resolution 986.
See Document 221, page 821

26-29 December 1995
The Secretary-General, on an official visit to Kuwait, meets with the Amir of Kuwait, the Crown Prince and Prime Minister of Kuwait, other Government officials, and representatives of Kuwaiti development funds and of other international organizations in Kuwait, and visits UNIKOM forces on the Kuwaiti side of the Iraq-Kuwait border. He also addresses a joint meeting of the National Assembly Committees for Foreign Affairs and for the Protection of Human Rights.

29 January 1996
Following Iraq's acceptance of the Secretary-General's invitation to enter into discussions with the Secretariat on implementation of the "oil-for-food" formula contained in Security Council resolution 986 (1995), the Secretary-General announces that the talks will begin on 6 February.
See Document 222, page 823; and Document 223, page 824

6 February 1996
Discussions on the implementation of Security Council resolution 986 (1995) begin at United Nations Headquarters in New York.

II   List of reproduced documents

The documents reproduced on pages 165-824 include resolutions of the General Assembly and of the Security Council, statements by the President of the Security Council, reports and letters of the Secretary-General, reports of the United Nations Special Commission (UNSCOM), reports of the Director General of the International Atomic Energy Agency (IAEA), reports covering the activities of the United Nations Iraq-Kuwait Observation Mission (UNIKOM), the United Nations Iraq-Kuwait Boundary Demarcation Commission, the United Nations Compensation Commission and the Security Council Sanctions Committee, reports on human rights and humanitarian assistance, communications from Iraq, Kuwait and other States Members of the United Nations, communications from regional organizations, and other materials.

Document 39
Identical letters from the Deputy Prime Minister and Minister for Foreign Affairs of Iraq to the President of the Security Council and to the Secretary-General stating that Iraq has no choice but to accept the provisions of Security Council resolution 687 (1991).
S/22456, 6 April 1991
See page 203

Document 40
Security Council resolution approving the Secretary-General's plan for the creation of UNIKOM.
S/RES/689 (1991), 9 April 1991
See page 206

Document 41
Letter dated 10 April 1991 from the Permanent Representative of Iraq to the President of the Security Council transmitting the National Assembly decision of 6 April 1991 concerning acceptance of Security Council resolution 687 (1991).
S/22480, 11 April 1991
See page 207

Document 42
Letter from the President of the Security Council to the Permanent Representative of Iraq acknowledging receipt of Iraq's communication of 6 April 1991 (Document 39) and noting, this precondition having been met, that the formal cease-fire is therefore in effect.
S/22485, 11 April 1991
See page 207

Document 43
Report of the Secretary-General on setting up a Special Commission (UNSCOM) to carry out on-site inspection of Iraq's biological, chemical and missile capabilities.
S/22508, 18 April 1991
See page 208

Document 44
Letter from the Permanent Representative of Iraq to the Secretary-General transmitting the Memorandum of Understanding dated 18 April 1991 between Iraq and the United Nations concerning humanitarian assistance.
S/22513, 22 April 1991
See page 209

Document 45
Report to the Secretary-General by a United Nations mission assessing the scope and nature of damage inflicted on Kuwait's infrastructure during the Iraqi occupation of the country (extract).
S/22535, 29 April 1991
See page 212

Document 46
Interim report to the Secretary-General by a United Nations mission assessing the loss of life incurred during the Iraqi occupation of Kuwait, as well as Iraqi practices against the civilian population in Kuwait.
S/22536, 29 April 1991
See page 229

Document 47
Statement by the President of the Security Council appealing to States, international financial institutions and United Nations bodies to assist countries which find themselves confronted with special economic problems arising from implementing sanctions against Iraq.
S/22548, 29 April 1991
See page 235

Document 48
Report of the Secretary-General on establishing an Iraq-Kuwait Boundary Demarcation Commission.
S/22558, 2 May 1991
See page 235

Document 49
Report of the Secretary-General regarding creation of a United Nations Compensation Fund and United Nations Compensation Commission as envisaged in Security Council resolution 687 (1991).
S/22559, 2 May 1991
See page 240

Document 50
Report of the Secretary-General concerning UNIKOM.
S/22580, 9 May 1991
See page 245

Document 51
United Nations Inter-Agency Programme relating to Iraq, Kuwait and the Iraq/Iran and Iraq/Turkey Borders: Updated and Consolidated Appeal for Urgent Humanitarian Action (extract).
15 May 1991
See page 246

Document 52
Report of the Secretary-General submitting a plan for immediate on-site inspections by the Special Commission (UNSCOM) and for destruction, removal or rendering harmless of relevant weapons and facilities.
S/22614, 17 May 1991
See page 250

Document 82
Revised plan submitted by the Director General of the IAEA for future monitoring and verification of Iraq's compliance with the requirements of Security Council resolution 687 (1991) for the destruction or removal of specified weapons and with the requirements of resolution 707 (1991) for full disclosure, access to inspection sites and compliance with international obligations (extract).
S/22872/Rev.1, 20 September 1991
See page 309

Document 83
Statement to the press by the President of the Security Council concerning implementation of resolution 707 (1991) and the activities of an UNSCOM inspection team in Baghdad.
UN Press Release SC/5306-IK/54, 23 September 1991
See page 318

Document 84
Statement to the press by the President of the Security Council concerning the activities of an UNSCOM inspection team in Baghdad.
UN Press Release SC/5307-IK/61, 24 September 1991
See page 319

Document 85
Statement to the press by the President of the Security Council concerning the use by UNSCOM of its own helicopters.
UN Press Release SC/5308-IK/62, 24 September 1991
See page 319

Document 86
Report of the Secretary-General on UNIKOM for the period from 9 April to 2 October 1991.
S/23106, 2 October 1991, and addenda: S/23106/Add.1, 4 October 1991, and S/23106/Add.2, 15 October 1991
See page 319

Document 87
Statement by the President of the Security Council concerning the sanctions regime.
S/23107, 2 October 1991
See page 325

Document 88
Report of the Secretary-General transmitting the plan, revised pursuant to the adoption of Security Council resolution 707 (1991), for future monitoring and verification of Iraq's compliance with the destruction or removal of weapons specified in Security Council resolution 687 (1991).
S/22871/Rev.1, 2 October 1991
See page 325

Document 89
Security Council resolution approving the plans submitted by the Secretary-General (Document 88) and the Director General of the IAEA (Document 82).
S/RES/715 (1991), 11 October 1991
See page 339

Document 90
Decision of the Security Council Sanctions Committee on procedures to be employed by the committee relating to the sale of Iraqi oil products.
S/23149, 16 October 1991
See page 340

Document 91
Decision 6 taken by the Governing Council of the United Nations Compensation Commission: Arrangements for ensuring payments to the Compensation Fund.
S/AC.26/1991/6, 23 October 1991
See page 343

Document 92
First report of the Executive Chairman of UNSCOM.
S/23165, 25 October 1991
See page 345

Document 93
Memorandum of Understanding dated 24 November 1991 between Iraq and the United Nations concerning humanitarian assistance.
Not issued as a United Nations document.
See page 361

Document 94
Second report of the Executive Chairman of UNSCOM.
S/23268, 4 December 1991
See page 363

Document 95
First semi-annual report (for the period from 17 June 1991 to 17 December 1991) on the implementation by the IAEA of the plan for the destruction, removal or rendering harmless of items listed in paragraph 12 of Security Council resolution 687 (1991).
S/23295, 17 December 1991
See page 367

Document 96
General Assembly resolution concerning the situation of human rights in Iraq.
A/RES/46/134, 17 December 1991
See page 370

Document 211
Follow-up to the seventh report of the Director General of the IAEA on the implementation of the Agency's plan for future ongoing monitoring and verification of Iraq's compliance with paragraph 12 of Security Council resolution 687 (1991).
S/1995/604, 21 July 1995
See page 763

Document 212
Report of the Secretary-General on UNIKOM for the period from 1 April to 30 September 1995.
S/1995/836, 2 October 1995
See page 765

Document 213
Eighth report of the Director General of the IAEA on the implementation of the Agency's plan for future ongoing monitoring and verification of Iraq's compliance with paragraph 12 of resolution 687 (1991).
S/1995/844, 6 October 1995
See page 766

Document 214
Eighth report of the Secretary-General on the status of the implementation of the plan for the ongoing monitoring and verification of Iraq's compliance with relevant parts of section C of Security Council resolution 687 (1991).
S/1995/864, 11 October 1995
See page 771

Document 215
Decision 32 taken by the Governing Council of the United Nations Compensation Commission: Payment of parts 1 and 2 of the second instalment of claims for serious personal injury or death (category B claims).
S/AC.26/Dec.32 (1995), 12 October 1995
See page 793

Document 216
Report on the situation of human rights in Iraq prepared by the Special Rapporteur of the Commission on Human Rights on the situation of human rights in Iraq (extract).
A/50/734, 8 November 1995
See page 793

Document 217
Letter from the Chairman of the Sanctions Committee to the President of the Security Council forwarding a proposal for a mechanism to monitor Iraq's exports and imports of dual-purpose capabilities.
S/1995/1017, 7 December 1995
See page 804

Document 218
Decision 34 taken by the Governing Council of the United Nations Compensation Commission concerning the third instalment of claims for serious personal injury or death (category B claims) (extract).
S/AC.26/Dec.34 (1995), 13 December 1995
See page 809

Document 219
Letter dated 14 December 1995 from the Director General of the IAEA to the Secretary-General concerning implementation by the IAEA of the plan for the destruction, removal or rendering harmless of items listed in paragraph 12 of Security Council resolution 687 (1991).
S/1995/1040, 18 December 1995
See page 809

Document 220
Tenth report of the Executive Chairman of UNSCOM.
S/1995/1038, 17 December 1995
See page 810

Document 221
General Assembly resolution concerning the situation of human rights in Iraq.
A/RES/50/191, 22 December 1995
See page 821

Document 222
Letter dated 18 January 1996 from the Secretary-General to the Deputy Prime Minister of Iraq inviting Iraq to enter into discussions on implementation of Security Council resolution 986 (1995).
Not issued as a United Nations document.
See page 823

Document 223
Letter dated 18 January 1996 from the Deputy Prime Minister of Iraq to the Secretary-General agreeing to enter into discussions on implementation of Security Council resolution 986 (1995).
Not issued as a United Nations document.
See page 824

The following is a breakdown, by category, of the documents reproduced in this book.

Resolutions of the General Assembly
Documents 3, 20, 96, 97, 99, 143, 144, 178, 202, 221

Resolutions of the Security Council
Documents 6, 7, 8, 11, 12, 13, 14, 15, 16, 17, 18, 19, 26, 35, 37, 40, 54, 61, 62, 71, 72, 73, 81, 89, 128, 132, 152, 161, 183, 196, 207

Statements by the President of the Security Council
Documents 28, 47, 63, 69, 83, 84, 85, 87, 98, 101, 104, 105, 108, 109, 111, 112, 115, 117, 120, 122, 124, 125, 129, 130, 133, 137, 138, 139, 146, 148, 150, 153, 159, 164, 167, 168, 169, 174, 175, 180, 194, 199

Letter from the President of the Security Council to Iraq
Document 42

Communications from Iraq
Documents 1, 10, 24, 25, 27, 30, 39, 41, 55, 59, 74, 76, 162, 176, 197, 198, 223

Communications from Kuwait
Documents 2, 5, 9, 22, 23, 29, 36, 163

Reports and letters of the Secretary-General to the Security Council concerning UNIKOM
Documents 38, 50, 60, 70, 75, 77, 86, 113, 131, 147, 149, 154, 170, 171, 186, 192, 204, 212

Other reports and letters of the Secretary-General to the Security Council
Documents 43, 48, 49, 52, 56, 58, 65, 78, 79, 88, 100, 107, 114, 123, 127, 134, 155, 160, 181, 182, 187, 191, 193, 205, 209, 214

Statements by the Secretary-General
Documents 21, 157

Correspondence of the Secretary-General
Documents 33, 126, 140, 222

Reports of humanitarian missions
Documents 31, 34, 45, 46, 66

Reports and other documents of the IAEA Director General
Documents 53, 82, 95, 116, 119, 136, 142, 156, 166, 172, 177, 188, 190, 195, 201, 206, 211, 213, 219

Reports of the Executive Chairman of the United Nations Special Commission (UNSCOM)
Documents 92, 94, 102, 118, 141, 151, 165, 173, 179, 189, 200, 210, 220

Decisions and reports of the United Nations Compensation Commission
Documents 67, 68, 91, 106, 110, 121, 145, 184, 185, 215, 218

Reports and other documents of the Security Council Sanctions Committee
Documents 32, 80, 90, 217

Memoranda of Understanding
Documents 44, 57, 93, 135

Reports on the situation of human rights in Iraq
Documents 103, 216

Other
Documents 4, 51, 64, 158, 203, 208

III Other documents of interest

Readers seeking additional information about the Iraq-Kuwait situation might wish to consult the following documents, which are available in the Dag Hammarskjöld Library at United Nations Headquarters in New York City, at other libraries in the United Nations system or at libraries around the world which have been designated as depository libraries for United Nations documents. This selective listing is organized by themes, corresponding to those covered in the Introduction to this volume.

BACKGROUND (1961-1963)

Communications from Member States
S/4845, 1 July 1961 (United Kingdom of Great Britain and Northern Ireland)

S/5001, 19 November 1961 (United Arab Republic)

A/5419/Add.1, 9 May 1963 (Costa Rica, Ecuador, Ghana, Honduras, India, Indonesia, Iran, Ireland, Jordan, Liberia, Mali, Morocco, Norway, Pakistan, Philippines, Saudi Arabia, Sierra Leone, Somalia, Sudan, Tanganyika and Tunisia)

Agreement between the League of Arab States and Kuwait on the disposition of League forces in Kuwait
S/5007, 30 November 1961

Communications from Iraq
S/4847, 2 July 1961
S/4848, 2 July 1961
S/4925, 14 August 1961
S/5014, 7 December 1961
S/5043, 28 December 1961
S/5047, 29 December 1961
S/5305, 7 May 1963

Communications from Kuwait
S/4844, 1 July 1961
S/4850, 4 July 1961
S/4852, 6 July 1961
S/4921, 9 August 1961
S/4966, 23 October 1961
S/5011, 4 December 1961
S/5044, 29 December 1961
A/5412-S/5294, 20 April 1963

Letter from the President of the Security Council on the admission of Kuwait to United Nations membership
A/5417, 7 May 1963

Draft resolutions of the Security Council
S/4855, 6 July 1961 (United Kingdom)
S/4856, 7 July 1961 (United Arab Republic)
S/5006, 29 November 1961 (United Arab Republic)

DIPLOMATIC RESPONSE TO IRAQ'S INVASION OF KUWAIT

Communication from the Association of South-East Asian Nations (ASEAN)
A/45/923, 15 January 1991

Communications from the European Community
S/21426, 2 August 1990
A/45/383-S/21444, 6 August 1990
A/45/409-S/21502, 13 August 1990
A/45/433-S/21590, 22 August 1990
A/45/484-S/21721, 7 September 1990
A/45/512-S/21783, 17 September 1990
A/45/522-S/21795, 19 September 1990
A/45/700-S/21920, 1 November 1990

Communications from the Gulf Cooperation Council
S/21430, 3 August 1990
S/21468, 8 August 1990
S/21470, 8 August 1990
A/45/694-S/21916, 30 October 1990
A/45/888-S/22018, 19 December 1990
A/45/908, 27 December 1990
A/45/926-S/22074, 15 January 1991

Communications from the League of Arab States
S/21434, 3 August 1990
S/21500, 13 August 1990
S/21684, 30 August 1990
S/21693, 31 August 1990

Communications from the Movement of Non-Aligned Countries
A/45/585-S/21849, 5 October 1990

Communications from the Organization of the Islamic Conference
S/21448, 6 August 1990
A/45/421-S/21797, 20 September 1990
A/45/923, 15 January 1991

Communication from the Western European Union
A/45/439-S/21455, 7 August 1990

Communications from Iraq
S/21436, 3 August 1990
S/21494, 12 August 1990
S/21499, 13 August 1990
S/21503, 13 August 1990
S/21528, 15 August 1990
S/21563, 20 August 1990
S/21569, 20 August 1990
S/21651, 27 August 1990

Communications from Kuwait
S/21437, 4 August 1990
S/21438, 4 August 1990
S/21439, 5 August 1990
S/21440, 5 August 1990
S/21443, 6 August 1990
S/21450, 6 August 1990
S/21452, 7 August 1990
S/21469, 8 August 1990
S/21505, 13 August 1990
S/21546, 16 August 1990
S/21548, 17 August 1990
S/21559, 17 August 1990
S/21566, 20 August 1990
S/21572, 20 August 1990
S/21586, 22 August 1990
S/21653, 27 August 1990
S/21654, 27 August 1990
S/21663, 28 August 1990
S/21666, 29 August 1990
S/21683, 30 August 1990
A/45/678-S/21914, 30 October 1990
A/45/689, 30 October 1990
A/45/690, 30 October 1990
A/45/691, 30 October 1990
A/45/692, 30 October 1990
A/45/913-S/22048, 4 January 1991

Communications from other Member States
Argentina: A/45/384-S/21445, 6 August 1990; S/21475, 9 August 1990
Belize: S/21484, 10 August 1990
Bolivia: A/45/423-S/21550, 17 August 1990
Brazil: S/21476, 9 August 1990; S/21497, 13 August 1990
Bulgaria: S/21477, 9 August 1990
Canada: A/45/418-S/21519, 14 August 1990
Chile: A/45/396-S/21467, 8 August 1990; S/21469, 8 August 1990; S/21516, 14 August 1990
Costa Rica: A/45/411-S/21521, 15 August 1990; A/45/460-S/21656, 27 August 1990
Cuba: S/21465, 8 August 1990
Cyprus: S/21540, 16 August 1990
Czechoslovakia: S/21488, 10 August 1990
Ecuador: A/45/415-S/21509, 14 August 1990
Egypt: S/21664, 27 August 1990
German Democratic Republic: A/45/377-S/21432, 3 August 1990
Ghana: A/45/391-S/21458, 7 August 1990
Guatemala: S/21533, 15 August 1990
Haiti: A/45/395-S/21466, 8 August 1990; A/45/452-S/21625, 24 August 1990
Honduras: S/21496, 13 August 1990
Hungary: A/45/412-S/21515, 14 August 1990
Iran: S/21428, 2 August 1990; S/21473, 9 August 1990; S/21558, 17 August 1990
Italy: A/45/368-S/21426, 2 August 1990; S/21561, 18 August 1990
Japan: A/45/367-S/21427, 2 August 1990; A/45/386-S/21449, 6 August 1990; A/45/826-S/21979, 4 December 1990
Libya: S/21529, 15 August 1990
Madagascar: A/45/379-S/21435, 3 August 1990
Maldives: A/45/390-S/21456, 7 August 1990
Namibia: A/45/424-S/21555, 17 August 1990
New Zealand: S/21482, 10 August 1990
Nicaragua: S/21457, 7 August 1990
Panama: S/21489, 10 August 1990
Paraguay: S/21446, 6 August 1990
Romania: S/21507, 14 August 1990
Saint Kitts and Nevis: S/21453, 7 August 1990; S/21454, 7 August 1990
Saudi Arabia: S/21554, 17 August 1990
South Africa: S/21433, 3 August 1990
Union of Soviet Socialist Republics: A/45/387-S/21451, 7 August 1990; A/45/400-S/21479, 9 August 1990
United Kingdom: S/21501, 13 August 1990
United States: S/21424, 2 August 1990; S/21537, 16 August 1990; S/21548, 17 August 1990
Uruguay: S/21429, 3 August 1990
Vanuatu: A/45/461-S/21658, 28 August 1990
Yugoslavia: A/45/425-S/21565, 20 August 1990

Joint Communications

European Community and the USSR: A/45/558-S/21834, 18 September 1990

France and the USSR: A/45/468-S/21675, 29 August 1990

USSR and United States: A/45/399-S/21472, 9 August 1990

Statements by the Secretary-General

UN Press Release SG/SM/4474, 2 August 1990

UN Press Release SG/SM/4487, 4 September 1990 (Amman, Jordan)

UN Press Release SG/SM/4495-SC/5215, 25 September 1990

COMMUNICATIONS CONCERNING MILITARY ACTION PURSUANT TO SECURITY COUNCIL RESOLUTION 678 (1990)

Communications from Iraq

S/22154, 28 January 1991

S/22190, 4 February 1991

S/22229, 15 February 1991

S/22262, 24 February 1991

S/22273, 27 February 1991

S/22370, 21 March 1991

Communications from Kuwait

S/22080, 16 January 1991

S/22142, 23 January 1991

S/22172, 30 January 1991

Communications from other Member States

S/22084, 17 January 1991 (Soviet Union)

S/22090, 17 January 1991 (United States)

S/22097, 17 January 1991 (United Kingdom)

S/22100, 17 January 1991 (France)

S/22105, 18 January 1991 (Saudi Arabia)

S/22111, 18 January 1991 (Soviet Union)

A/45/934-S/22113, 18 January 1991 (Egypt)

S/22114, 18 January 1991 (Soviet Union)

S/22115, 21 January 1991 (United Kingdom)

S/22126, 22 January 1991 (Italy)

S/22130, 22 January 1991 (United States)

S/22131, 22 January 1991 (France)

S/22153, 25 January 1991 (Canada)

S/22156, 28 January 1991 (United Kingdom)

S/22160/Rev.1, 29 January 1991 (Israel)

A/45/942-S/22166, 29 January 1991 (Bahrain)

S/22168, 29 January 1991 (United States)

S/22169, 29 January 1991 (France)

S/22173, 30 January 1991 (United States)

S/22180, 31 January 1991 (Saudi Arabia)

S/22191, 4 February 1991 (Canada)

S/22194, 4 February 1991 (Italy)

S/22199, 5 February 1991 (Turkey)

S/22200, 6 February 1991 (Saudi Arabia)

S/22210, 11 February 1991 (France)

S/22215, 11 February 1991 (Soviet Union)

S/22216, 13 February 1991 (United States)

S/22217, 13 February 1991 (New Zealand)

S/22218, 13 February 1991 (United Kingdom)

S/22227, 15 February 1991 (United States)

S/22239, 19 February 1991 (Australia)

S/22241, 19 February 1991 (Soviet Union)

S/22248, 20 February 1991 (Italy)

S/22251, 21 February 1991 (France)

S/22259, 23 February 1991 (Saudi Arabia)

S/22265, 25 February 1991 (Soviet Union)

S/22292, 1 March 1991 (Canada)

S/22295, 1 March 1991 (Israel)

S/22341, 8 March 1991 (United States)

Statement by the Secretary-General

UN Press Release SG/SM/4521-SC/5238, 29 November 1990

UNITED NATIONS IRAQ-KUWAIT OBSERVATION MISSION (UNIKOM)

Composition

S/22488, 12 April 1991

S/22489, 12 April 1991

S/22978, 26 August 1991

S/26622, 24 October 1993

Financing: resolutions and decisions of the General Assembly and reports of the Secretary-General to the General Assembly

A/45/240/Add.1, 22 April 1991

A/45/1005, 29 April 1991

A/45/1006, 2 May 1991

A/RES/45/260, 3 May 1991

A/46/746, 6 December 1991

A/46/769, 12 December 1991

A/46/822, 20 December 1991

A/RES/46/197, 20 December 1991

ST/ADM/SER.B/366, 19 March 1992

ST/ADM/SER.B/388, 12 October 1992

A/47/637, 12 November 1992

A/47/735, 30 November 1992

A/47/823, 21 December 1992

A/RES/47/208 A, 22 December 1992

A/47/637/Add.1, 11 June 1993

A/47/987, 28 July 1993

ST/ADM/SER.B/399, 29 July 1993

A/47/823/Add.1, 9 September 1993

A/RES/47/208 B, 14 September 1993

A/C.5/48/40, 9 December 1993
A/48/772, 17 December 1993
A/DEC/48/466 A, 23 December 1993
A/48/815, 23 December 1993
A/48/844, 12 January 1994
A/48/815/Add.1, 4 March 1994
A/48/897, 8 March 1994
A/48/815/Add.2, 31 March 1994
ST/ADM/SER.B/419, 25 October 1994
A/DEC/48/466 B, 9 March 1994
A/RES/48/242, 5 April 1994
A/49/863, 20 March 1995
A/49/877, 29 March 1995
A/DEC/49/477, 31 March 1995
A/49/902, 19 May 1995
A/49/877/Add.1, 29 June 1995
A/RES/49/245, 12 July 1995

UNITED NATIONS IRAQ-KUWAIT BOUNDARY DEMARCATION COMMISSION

Letters from the Secretary-General
S/22592, 6 May 1991
S/22620, 20 May 1991

Letter from the President of the Security Council
S/22593, 13 May 1991

Communications from Iraq
S/24044, 1 June 1992
S/24275, 13 July 1992
S/24496, 27 August 1992

Communications from Kuwait
S/24060, 9 June 1992
S/24495, 27 August 1992
S/25865, 29 May 1993

Letter from the United Kingdom transmitting
topographic maps
S/22412, 28 March 1991

REPATRIATION OF KUWAITI AND THIRD-STATE NATIONALS AND OF IRAQI NATIONALS

Communications from Iraq
S/22793, 15 July 1991
S/22992, 29 August 1991
S/23264, 3 December 1991
S/23767, 1 April 1992
S/23825, 21 April 1992

S/23909, 13 May 1992
S/1995/197, 10 March 1995

Communications from Kuwait
S/23399, 9 January 1992
S/23661, 28 February 1992
S/23686, 6 March 1992
S/23738, 20 March 1992
S/23779, 3 April 1992
S/25357, 3 March 1993
S/1994/52, 17 January 1994
S/1995/13, 9 January 1995
S/1995/84, 7 March 1995
S/1995/546, 7 July 1995
S/1995/592, 19 July 1995
S/1995/766, 5 September 1995

Communications from France, Kuwait, Saudi Arabia,
the United Kingdom and the United States
S/23686, 6 March 1992
S/1994/52, 19 January 1994

RETURN OF KUWAITI PROPERTY

Communication from the President of
the Security Council
S/22361, 19 March 1991

Letter from the Secretary-General announcing
appointment of a Coordinator for the return
of Kuwaiti property
S/22387, 26 March 1991

Communications from Iraq
S/22330, 5 March 1991
S/22355, 18 March 1991
S/22356, 18 March 1991
S/22375, 21 March 1991
S/23252, 27 November 1991
S/24875, 1 December 1992
S/1994/1099, 27 September 1994
S/1995/197, 10 March 1995

Communications from Kuwait
S/22367, 20 March 1991
S/22394, 22 March 1991
S/22399, 22 March 1991
S/22427, 1 April 1991
S/22433, 2 April 1991
S/22441, 5 April 1991
S/22445, 4 April 1991

S/22458, 8 April 1991
S/22521, 23 April 1991
S/22523, 23 April 1991
S/22557, 1 May 1991
S/22709, 17 June 1991
S/23017, 9 September 1991
S/23018, 9 September 1991
S/23228, 20 November 1991
S/23252, 27 November 1991
S/24806, 13 November 1992
S/25790, 17 May 1993
S/26103, 16 July 1993
S/26449, 15 September 1993
S/1994/25, 11 January 1994
S/1994/545, 6 May 1994
S/1994/1126, 4 October 1994
S/1995/13, 9 January 1995
S/1995/39, 14 January 1995
S/1995/184, 7 March 1995
S/1995/546, 7 July 1995
S/1995/592, 19 July 1995
S/1995/766, 5 September 1995

UNITED NATIONS COMPENSATION COMMISSION

Decisions
[Decisions 1, 6-7, 9-10, 15, 17-18, 32 and 34 are reproduced in this volume.]
2: S/22885, 2 August 1991
3-5, 8: S/24589, 28 September 1992
11: S/24363, 30 July 1992
12-13: S/24611, 5 October 1992
14: S/AC.26/1992/14, 4 January 1993
16: S/AC.26/1992/16, 4 January 1993
19: S/1994/409, 8 April 1994
20: S/1994/792, 5 July 1994
21-23: S/1994/1337, 28 November 1994
24: S/AC.26/Dec.24 (1994), 14 December 1994
25: S/AC.26/Dec.25 (1994), 14 December 1994
26: S/AC.26/Dec.26 (1994), 14 December 1994
27-28: S/1995/285, 29 March 1995
29-30: S/1995/471, 8 June 1995
31: S/AC.26/Dec. 31 (1995), 11 October 1995
33: S/AC.26/Dec. 33 (1995), 13 December 1995
35: S/AC.26/Dec. 35 (1995), 13 December 1995

Statement by the Secretary-General
UN Press Release SG/SM/5319-IK/170, 8 June 1994

Communications from Iraq
S/22629, 21 May 1991
S/22643, 28 May 1991
S/22681, 11 June 1991
S/24989, 20 December 1992
S/1994/348, 26 March 1994

Other
S/1994/566, 13 May 1994
S/1994/567, 13 May 1994
S/1996/41, 19 January 1996

HUMANITARIAN ASSISTANCE

S/22328, 4 March 1991
S/22333, 6 March 1991
S/22334, 6 March 1991

Statement by the Secretary-General
UN Press Release SG/SM/4574-IK/24, 13 June 1991

Communications from Iraq
S/22452, 5 April 1991
S/22460, 8 April 1991
S/24335, 22 July 1992
S/24475, 28 August 1992
S/24757, 3 November 1992
S/25945, 14 June 1993
S/1994/410, 8 April 1994

UNITED NATIONS SPECIAL COMMISSION (UNSCOM) AND INTERNATIONAL ATOMIC ENERGY ASSOCIATION (IAEA)

S/22739, 26 June 1991
S/22743, 28 June 1991
S/22762, 5 July 1991
S/23070, 25 September 1991
S/23673, 4 March 1992
S/23993, 22 May 1992
S/24036, 29 May 1992
S/24056, 3 June 1992
S/24985, 17 December 1992
S/25960, 16 June 1993
S/26584, 14 October 1993
S/26841, 5 December 1993
S/1994/1250, 4 November 1994
S/1995/208, 17 March 1995

Reports of UNSCOM and IAEA missions and high-level talks
S/23643, 26 February 1992
S/24443, 14 August 1992
S/26127, 21 July 1993
S/26451, 16 September 1993
S/26571, 12 October 1993
S/26825, 1 December 1993
S/1994/151, 10 February 1994
S/1994/341, 24 March 1994
S/1994/520, 29 April 1994
S/1994/564, 13 May 1994
S/1994/860, 20 July 1994

IAEA resolutions
A/45/1037-S/22812, 19 July 1991
A/46/509-S/23088, 30 September 1991

Annex 3 of IAEA plan for ongoing monitoring and
verification (Document 82; see page 309)
S/24300, 16 July 1992 (first update and revision)
S/1995/215, 23 March 1995 (second update and revision)

Reports of IAEA on-site inspections
S/22788, 15 July 1991 (consolidated first and second, 15-21
   May 1991 and 22 June-3 July 1991)
S/22837, 25 July 1991 (third, 7-18 July 1991)
S/22986, 28 August 1991 (fourth, 27 July-10 August 1991)
S/23112, 4 October 1991 (fifth, 14-20 September 1991)
S/23122, 8 October 1991 (sixth, 22-30 September 1991)
S/23215, 14 November 1991 (seventh, 11-22 October 1991)
S/23283, 12 December 1991 (eighth, 11-18 November 1991)
S/23505, 30 January 1992 (ninth, 11-14 January 1992)
S/23644, 26 February 1992 (tenth, 5-13 February 1992)
S/23947, 22 May 1992 (11th, 7-15 April 1992)
S/24223, 2 July 1992 (12th, 26 May-4 June 1992)
S/24450, 16 August 1992 (13th, 14-21 July 1992)
S/24593, 28 September 1992 (14th, 31 August-
   7 September 1992)
S/24981, 17 December 1992 (15th, 8-18 November 1992)
S/25013, 22 December 1992 (16th, 5-8 December 1992)
S/25411, 13 March 1993 (17th, 25-31 January 1993)
S/25666, 26 April 1993 (18th, 3-11 March 1993)
S/25982, 21 June 1993 (19th, 30 April-7 May 1993)
S/26333, 20 August 1993 (consolidated 20th and 21st, 25-30
   June 1993 and 24-27 July 1993)
S/1994/31, 14 January 1994 (22nd, 1-15 November 1993)
S/1994/355, 25 March 1994 (23rd, 4-11 February 1994)
S/1994/650, 1 June 1994 (24th, 11-22 April 1994)
S/1994/1001, 26 August 1994 (25th, 22 June-1 July 1994)
S/1994/1206, 22 October 1994 (26th, 22 August-
   7 September 1994)

S/1994/1443, 22 December 1994 (27th, 14-21 October
   1994)
S/1995/1003, 1 December 1995 (28th, 9-20 September 1995)
S/1996/14, 10 January 1996 (29th, 17-24 October 1995)

Communications from Iraq
S/22682, 10 June 1991
S/22749, 29 June 1991
S/22786, 13 July 1991
S/22826, 24 July 1991
S/22912, 8 August 1991
S/23064, 24 September 1991
S/23065, 24 September 1991
S/23102, 1 October 1991
S/23110, 4 October 1991
S/24321, 20 July 1992
S/24336, 22 July 1992
S/24339, 7 August 1992
S/24829, 20 November 1992
S/24964, 14 December 1992
S/25086, 10 January 1993
S/25097, 13 January 1993
S/25979, 21 June 1993
S/26811, 26 November 1993

HUMAN RIGHTS

Reports of the Special Rapporteur on the situation of
   human rights in occupied Kuwait
A/46/544, 16 October 1991
E/CN.4/1992/26, 16 January 1992

Reports of the Special Rapporteur on the situation of
   human rights in Iraq
A/46/647, 13 November 1991
A/47/367, 10 August 1992 (transmitted to the Security
   Council by S/24386)
A/47/367/Add.1, 13 November 1992
E/CN.4/1993/45, 19 February 1993
A/48/600, 18 November 1993
A/48/600/Add. 1, 19 November 1993
E/CN.4/1994/58, 25 February 1994
A/49/651, 8 November 1994
E/CN.4/1995/56, 15 February 1995
E/CN.4/1996/12, 4 September 1995

Communications from Iraq
S/24388, 6 August 1992
A/48/387-S/26424, 9 September 1993

Letter from the United States transmitting a
Government report entitled "Report on Iraqi
war crimes (Desert Shield/Desert Storm)"
S/25441, 19 March 1993

Letter from Iraq referring to S/25441
S/25976, 21 June 1993

ARMS EMBARGO AND RELATED SANCTIONS

Reports of the Secretary-General
S/21536, 15 August 1990
S/21641, 25 August 1990
S/21715, 6 September 1990
S/22884, 1 August 1991 and addenda: S/22884/Add.1,
 10 September 1991 and S/22884/Add.2, 4 December 1991

Reports of the Sanctions Committee
[The first report of the Sanctions Committee, S/23036,
13 September 1991, is reproduced in this volume as
Document 80]
S/23279, 11 December 1991 (second)
S/23708, 12 March 1992 (third)
S/24083, 11 June 1992 (fourth)
S/24545, 10 September 1992 (fifth)
S/24912, 4 December 1992 (sixth)
S/25442, 19 March 1993 (seventh)
S/25930, 11 June 1993 (eighth)
S/26430, 12 September 1993 (ninth)
S/26874, 14 December 1993 (tenth)
S/1994/274, 8 March 1994 (11th)
S/1994/695, 10 June 1994 (12th)
S/1994/1027, 4 September 1994 (13th)
S/1994/1367, 1 December 1994 (14th)
S/1995/169, 1 March 1995 (15th)
S/1995/442, 1 June 1995 (16th)
S/1995/744, 28 August 1995 (17th)
S/1995/992, 28 November 1995 (18th)

Communications from Iraq
S/21568, 20 August 1990
S/24002, 26 May 1992
S/24276, 13 July 1992
S/25523, 5 April 1993

Communication from Kuwait
S/21545, 16 August 1990

ARTICLE 50 OF THE CHARTER OF THE UNITED NATIONS

Communications from affected States
S/21620, 24 August 1990 (Jordan)
S/21686, 31 August 1990 (Lebanon)
S/21695, 4 September 1990 (Sudan)
S/21710, 5 September 1990 (Sri Lanka)
S/21711, 5 September 1990 (India)
S/21712, 5 September 1990 (Philippines)
S/21737, 10 September 1990 (Lebanon)
S/21741, 12 September 1990 (Bulgaria)
S/21748, 13 September 1990 (Yemen)
S/21775, 17 September 1990 (Uruguay)
S/21776, 17 September 1990 (Pakistan)
S/21808, 21 September 1990 (Poland)
S/21821, 26 September 1990 (Viet Nam)
S/21837, 3 October 1990 (Czechoslovakia)
S/21856, 10 October 1990 (Bangladesh)
S/21875, 15 October 1990 (Pakistan)
S/21891, 19 October 1990 (Seychelles)
S/21918, 31 October 1990 (Poland)
S/21984, 6 December 1990 (Sri Lanka)
S/21990, 8 December 1990 (Romania)
S/22011, 18 December 1990 (Philippines)
S/22013, 19 December 1990 (India)
S/22014, 19 December 1990 (Yugoslavia)
S/22015, 19 December 1990 (Tunisia)
S/22019, 19 December 1990 (Czechoslovakia)
S/22023, 20 December 1990 (Seychelles)
S/22026, 20 December 1990 (Uruguay)
S/22193, 4 February 1991 (Syria)
S/22209, 8 February 1991 (Djibouti)
S/22382, 25 March 1991 (Memorandum from
 21 Member States)

Sanctions Committee
S/21786, 18 September 1990
S/22021, 20 December and addenda: S/22021/Add.1,
 21 December 1990, and S/22021/Add.2, 19 March 1991
S/22419, 1 April 1991
S/23108, 24 September 1991

Letter from the Secretary-General to the President of the Security Council: findings of his Special Representative on impact of sanctions on Jordan
S/21938, 22 October 1990

Letter from the President of the Security Council to
the Secretary-General concerning assistance to two
countries affected by sanctions
S/22398, 22 March 1991

EVENTS OF OCTOBER-NOVEMBER 1994

**Letter from Iraq and the Russian Federation transmitting
text of a joint communiqué issued on 13 October 1994**
S/1994/1173, 15 October 1995

**Letter from the President of the Security Council to
Iraq concerning Iraq's recognition of Kuwait's
sovereignty, independence and territorial integrity
and of the international border between Kuwait and Iraq**
S/1994/1297, 16 November 1994

IRAQI COMPLIANCE WITH SECURITY COUNCIL RESOLUTIONS AND RELATED MATTERS

Communications from Iraq
S/22689, 11 June 1991
S/23472, 24 January 1992
S/23636, 24 February 1992
S/24726, 29 October 1992
S/24822, 13 November 1992
S/25064, 8 January 1993
S/25391, 10 March 1993
S/25535, 6 April 1993
S/25758, 12 May 1993
S/26302, 13 August 1993
S/26427, 11 September 1993

Communications from Kuwait
S/25790, 18 May 1993
S/26103, 16 July 1993
S/26449, 16 September 1993

OTHER

Economic consequences of the Gulf crisis: Preliminary
assessment by the United Nations Conference on Trade
and Development (UNCTAD)
TD/B/1272, 25 September 1990

Impact of the Gulf crisis on developing countries:
Report of the Administrator of the United Nations Develop-
ment Programme (UNDP)
DP/1991/60, 9 May 1991

Environmental assessment of the Gulf Crisis: Report
of the Secretary-General of the Conference on
Environment and Development
A/CONF.151/PC/72, 10 May 1991

Economic, social and environmental consequences
of the situation between Iraq and Kuwait and
its short-, medium- and long-term implications:
Note by the Secretariat
E/1991/102, 24 June 1991

**United Nations High Commissioner for Refugees (UNHCR)
Report on Northern Iraq, April 1991-May 1992**
[No document symbol], 1 September 1992

IV Texts of documents

The texts of the 223 documents listed on the preceding pages are reproduced below. The appearance of ellipses (. . .) in the text indicates that portions of the document have been omitted. A subject index to the documents begins on page 825.

Document 1

Letter dated 21 July 1932 from the Prime Minister of Iraq reaffirming the Iraq-Kuwait boundary

Not issued as a United Nations document

Nuri Pasha to Sir F. Humphrys
Office of the Council of Ministers,
Baghdad, July 21, 1932

I think Your Excellency will agree that the time has now come when it is desirable to reaffirm the existing frontier between Iraq and Kuwait.

I therefore request that the necessary action may be taken to obtain the agreement of the competent authority or authorities in Kuwait to the following description of the existing frontier between the two countries:

"From the intersection of the Wadi-el-Audja with the Batin and thence northwards along the Batin to a point just south of the latitude of Safwan; thence eastwards passing south of Safwan Wells, Jebel Sanam and Um Qasr leaving them to Iraq and so on to the junction of the Khor Zoberi with the Khor Abdulla. The islands of Warbah, Bubiyan, Maskan (or Mashjan), Failakah, Auhah, Kubbar, Qaru and Umm-el-Maradim appertain to Kuwait."

Document 2

Letter dated 10 August 1932 from the Ruler of Kuwait to the Political Agent of the United Kingdom in Kuwait reaffirming the Iraq-Kuwait boundary

Not issued as a United Nations document

With the hand of pleasure we have received your confidential letter dated the 7th instant (Rabi Thani 1351 (the 9th August, 1932)), and have noted the contents of same, as well as the translation of the letter dated the 25th July, 1932, of His Excellency the High Commissioner for Iraq to the Hon. the Political Resident in the Persian Gulf, and the translation of the letter dated the 21st July, 1932, of His Excellency Nuri Pasha-as-Said, the Iraq Prime Minister, regarding the Iraq-Kuwait frontier. We also have noted from the Hon. The Political Resident's letter dated the 30th July, 1932, that the frontier proposed by the Iraq Prime Minister is approved of by His Majesty's Government. And, therefore, we beg to inform you that we agree to reaffirm the existing frontier between Iraq and Kuwait as described in the Iraq Prime Minister's letter.

Document 3

General Assembly resolution deciding to admit Kuwait to membership in the United Nations

A/RES/1872 (S-IV), 14 May 1963

The General Assembly

Having received the recommendation of the Security Council of 7 May 1963 that Kuwait should be admitted to membership in the United Nations, 1/

Having considered the application for membership of Kuwait, 2/

Decides to admit Kuwait to membership in the United Nations.

1/ *Official Records of the General Assembly, Fourth Special Session,* annexes, agenda item 8, document A/5417.
2/ A/5412. For the text of this document, see *Official Records of the Security Council, Eighteenth Year, Supplement for April, May and June 1963,* document S/5294.

Document 4

"Agreed Minutes Between the State of Kuwait and the Republic of Iraq Regarding the Restoration of Friendly Relations, Recognition and Related Matters", signed at Baghdad on 4 October 1963***

Document 7063, United Nations, *Treaty Series,* 1964

In response to the desire felt by both parties to eliminate all that blemishes the relations between both countries, the official Kuwaiti Delegation visiting the Republic of Iraq on an invitation from the Iraqi Prime Minister, held a meeting with the Iraqi Delegation in Baghdad on 4th October, 1963.

The Kuwaiti Delegation was constituted as follows:

H.H. Shaikh Sabah Al-Salim Al-Sabah, Heir Apparent and Prime Minister;

H.E. Shaikh Saad Al-Abdullah Al-Salim Al-Sabah, Minister of the Interior and Acting Minister of Foreign Affairs;

H.E. Khalifa Khalid Al-Ghunaim, Minister of Commerce;

H.E. Ambassador Abdulrahman Ateeqi, Under-Secretary of the Ministry of Foreign Affairs.

The Iraqi Delegation was constituted as follows:

Major-General Ahmed Hassan Al-Bakre, Prime Minister;

First General Salch Mahdi Ammash, Minister of Defence and Acting Minister of Foreign Affairs;

Dr. Mahmoud Mohammad Al-Homsi, Minister of Commerce;

Mr. Mohammad Kayyara, Acting Under-Secretary of Foreign Affairs.

The talks between the two delegations were conducted in an atmosphere rich in fraternal amity, tenacity to the Arab bond and consciousness of the close ties of neighbourliness and mutual interests.

Both sides affirming their deep-rooted desire in reinforcing their relations for the welfare of both countries, inspired by the high Arab aims; and

Believing in the need to rectify all that blemished the Iraqi-Kuwaiti relations as a result of the attitude of the past Kassim regime towards Kuwait before the dawn of the blessed revolution of the 14th of Ramadhan;

Convinced with the national duty dictating the inauguration of a new page consistent with the bonds and relations between the two Arab countries which are free from the artificial gap created by the past regime in Iraq;

Spurred by the belief of the two Governments in the entity of the Arab Nation and the inevitability of its Unity;

And after the Iraqi side having seen the statement delivered by the Government of Kuwait at the Kuwaiti National Assembly on the 9th of April, 1963, embodying the desire of Kuwait to work for the termination, in due time, of the Agreement concluded with the United Kingdom;

The two delegations have agreed to the following:

1. The Republic of Iraq recognized the independence and complete sovereignty of the State of Kuwait with its boundaries as specified in the letter of the Prime Minister of Iraq dated 21.7.1932 and which

*Came into force on 4 October 1963 by signature.
**Translation provided by the Government of Kuwait.

was accepted by the ruler of Kuwait in his letter dated 10.8.1932;

2. The two Governments shall work towards reinforcing the fraternal relations subsisting between the two sister countries, inspired by their national duty, common interest and aspiration to a complete Arab Unity;

3. The two Governments shall work towards establishing cultural, commercial and economical cooperation between the two countries and the exchange of technical information.

In order to realize all the foregoing objectives, they shall immediately establish diplomatic relations between them at the level of ambassadors.

IN WITNESS WHEREOF the heads of the two delegations have appended their signatures unto these minutes.

Sabah Al-Salim AL-SABAH   Ahmad Hassan AL-BAKRE
Head of Kuwaiti Delegation   Head of Iraqi Delegation

Document 5

Letter from the Permanent Representative of Kuwait to the President of the Security Council requesting an immediate meeting of the Security Council

S/21423, 2 August 1990

Upon instructions from my Government, I have the honour to request an immediate meeting of the Security Council to consider the Iraqi invasion of Kuwait in the early morning of 2 August 1990.

(*Signed*) Mohammad A. ABULHASAN
Ambassador
Permanent Representative

Document 6

Security Council resolution condemning Iraq's invasion of Kuwait, demanding the immediate and unconditional withdrawal of all Iraqi forces and calling for negotiations for a peaceful resolution of their differences

S/RES/660 (1990), 2 August 1990

The Security Council,

Alarmed by the invasion of Kuwait on 2 August 1990 by the military forces of Iraq,

Determining that there exists a breach of international peace and security as regards the Iraqi invasion of Kuwait,

Acting under Articles 39 and 40 of the Charter of the United Nations,

1. *Condemns* the Iraqi invasion of Kuwait;

2. *Demands* that Iraq withdraw immediately and unconditionally all its forces to the positions in which they were located on 1 August 1990;

3. *Calls upon* Iraq and Kuwait to begin immediately intensive negotiations for the resolution of their differences and supports all efforts in this regard, and especially those of the League of Arab States;

4. *Decides* to meet again as necessary to consider further steps to ensure compliance with the present resolution.

Document 7

Security Council resolution imposing mandatory economic sanctions against Iraq and establishing a committee (the "Sanctions Committee") to monitor those sanctions

S/RES/661 (1990), 6 August 1990

The Security Council,

Reaffirming its resolution 660 (1990) of 2 August 1990,

Deeply concerned that that resolution has not been implemented and that the invasion by Iraq of Kuwait continues, with further loss of human life and material destruction,

Determined to bring the invasion and occupation of Kuwait by Iraq to an end and to restore the sovereignty, independence and territorial integrity of Kuwait,

Noting that the legitimate Government of Kuwait has expressed its readiness to comply with resolution 660 (1990),

Mindful of its responsibilities under the Charter of the United Nations for the maintenance of international peace and security,

Affirming the inherent right of individual or collective self-defence, in response to the armed attack by Iraq against Kuwait, in accordance with Article 51 of the Charter,

Acting under Chapter VII of the Charter,

1. *Determines* that Iraq so far has failed to comply with paragraph 2 of resolution 660 (1990) and has usurped the authority of the legitimate Government of Kuwait;

2. *Decides,* as a consequence, to take the following measures to secure compliance of Iraq with paragraph 2 of resolution 660 (1990) and to restore the authority of the legitimate Government of Kuwait;

3. *Decides* that all States shall prevent:

(a) The import into their territories of all commodities and products originating in Iraq or Kuwait exported therefrom after the date of the present resolution;

(b) Any activities by their nationals or in their territories which would promote or are calculated to promote the export or trans-shipment of any commodities or products from Iraq or Kuwait; and any dealings by their nationals or their flag vessels or in their territories in any commodities or products originating in Iraq or Kuwait and exported therefrom after the date of the present resolution, including in particular any transfer of funds to Iraq or Kuwait for the purposes of such activities or dealings;

(c) The sale or supply by their nationals or from their territories or using their flag vessels of any commodities or products, including weapons or any other military equipment, whether or not originating in their territories but not including supplies intended strictly for medical purposes, and, in humanitarian circumstances, foodstuffs, to any person or body in Iraq or Kuwait or to any person or body for the purposes of any business carried on in or operated from Iraq or Kuwait, and any activities by their nationals or in their territories which promote or are calculated to promote such sale or supply of such commodities or products;

4. *Decides* that all States shall not make available to the Government of Iraq, or to any commercial, industrial or public utility undertaking in Iraq or Kuwait, any funds or any other financial or economic resources and shall prevent their nationals and any persons within their territories from removing from their territories or otherwise making available to that Government or to any such undertaking any such funds or resources and from remitting any other funds to persons or bodies within Iraq or Kuwait, except payments exclusively for strictly medical or humanitarian purposes and, in humanitarian circumstances, foodstuffs;

5. *Calls upon* all States, including States non-members of the United Nations, to act strictly in accordance with the provisions of the present resolution notwithstanding any contract entered into or licence granted before the date of the present resolution;

6. *Decides* to establish, in accordance with rule 28 of the provisional rules of procedure, a Committee of the Security Council consisting of all the members of the Council, to undertake the following tasks and to report on its work to the Council with its observations and recommendations;

(a) To examine the reports on the progress of the implementation of the present resolution which will be submitted by the Secretary-General;

(b) To seek from all States further information regarding the action taken by them concerning the effective implementation of the provisions laid down in the present resolution;

7. *Calls upon* all States to cooperate fully with the Committee in the fulfilment of its tasks, including supplying such information as may be sought by the Committee in pursuance of the present resolution;

8. *Requests* the Secretary-General to provide all necessary assistance to the Committee and to make the

necessary arrangements in the Secretariat for that purpose;

9. *Decides* that, notwithstanding paragraphs 4 to 8 above, nothing in the present resolution shall prohibit assistance to the legitimate Government of Kuwait, and calls upon all States;

(a) To take appropriate measures to protect assets of the legitimate Government of Kuwait and its agencies;

(b) Not to recognize any regime set up by the occupying Power;

10. *Requests* the Secretary-General to report to the Security Council on the progress made in the implementation of the present resolution, the first report to be submitted within thirty days;

11. *Decides* to keep this item on its agenda and to continue its efforts to put an early end to the invasion by Iraq.

Document 8

Security Council resolution deciding that the annexation of Kuwait by Iraq under any form is considered null and void

S/RES/662 (1990), 9 August 1990

The Security Council,

Recalling its resolutions 660 (1990) of 2 August 1990 and 661 (1990) of 6 August 1990,

Gravely alarmed by the declaration by Iraq of a "comprehensive and eternal merger" with Kuwait,

Demanding once again that Iraq withdraw immediately and unconditionally all its forces to the positions in which they were located on 1 August 1990,

Determined to bring the occupation of Kuwait by Iraq to an end and to restore the sovereignty, independence and territorial integrity of Kuwait,

Determined also to restore the authority of the legitimate Government of Kuwait,

1. *Decides* that annexation of Kuwait by Iraq under any form and whatever pretext has no legal validity, and is considered null and void;

2. *Calls upon* all States, international organizations and specialized agencies not to recognize that annexation, and to refrain from any action or dealing that might be interpreted as an indirect recognition of the annexation;

3. *Demands* that Iraq rescind its actions purporting to annex Kuwait;

4. *Decides* to keep this item on its agenda and to continue its efforts to put an early end to the occupation.

Document 9

Letter dated 12 August 1990 from the Permanent Representative of Kuwait to the President of the Security Council reporting that military assistance has been requested for implementation of resolution 661 (1990)

S/21498, 13 August 1990

Upon instructions from my Government, I have the honour to inform you of the following:

Kuwait is grateful to all those Governments that have taken a principled stand in support of Kuwait's position against aggression and occupation by Iraq. It is considered essential that these efforts be strengthened so that the provisions of the relevant Security Council resolutions be fully and effectively implemented.

In the exercise of its inherent right of individual and collective self-defence and pursuant to Article 51 of the Charter of the United Nations, Kuwait should like to notify you that it has requested some nations to take such military or other steps as are necessary to ensure the effective and prompt implementation of Security Council resolution 661 (1990).

I would be grateful if you could circulate this letter as a document of the Security Council.

(*Signed*) Mohammad A. ABULHASAN
Ambassador
Permanent Representative

Document 10

Letter from the Deputy Prime Minister and Minister for Foreign Affairs of Iraq to the Secretary-General concerning Security Council resolutions on Iraq and Kuwait

S/21503, 13 August 1990

Letter dated 13 August 1990 from the Permanent Representative of Iraq to the United Nations addressed to the Secretary-General

On instructions from my Government, I have the honour to transmit to you herewith a letter from Mr. Tariq Aziz, Deputy Prime Minister and Minister for Foreign Affairs of the Republic of Iraq.

I should be grateful if you would have the present letter and its annex circulated as a document of the Security Council.

(*Signed*) Abdul Amir A. AL-ANBARI
Ambassador
Permanent Representative

Annex
Letter dated 13 August 1990 from the Deputy Prime Minister and Minister for Foreign Affairs of Iraq addressed to the Secretary-General

As you know, the Security Council has, within a small number of days, adopted a series of iniquitous resolutions against Iraq with a dispatch that is unprecedented in the history of the Organization.

In the first resolution it adopted, the Council leaped immediately to the stage of invoking the provisions of Chapter VII of the Charter without allowing itself sufficient time to comprehend the situation and to acquaint itself with the facts from the parties concerned and in complete disregard of the position of Iraq and clarifications it could provide. In a period of no more than a few days, the Council then leaped to the stage of adopting a resolution on comprehensive and mandatory sanctions, once again in total disregard of the position of Iraq and any of its clarifications. There has never been such a procedure in the history of the Council, and it renders the resolutions adopted against Iraq unjust and out of keeping with the most elementary procedural notions in accordance with which the Council's work has been conducted in the past.

What has thus far transpired in the Council would not have taken place had it not been for the methods of pressure and deception employed by the United States with a number of Council members in order to induce them to vote for the said resolutions. The United States is thus endeavouring to establish itself as the controller of the world and of its destiny. These unjust resolutions, which were prejudged by certain States members of the Council and which the United States has endeavoured to impose, are evidently an ominous phenomenon in the history of the Organization, namely that of the imposition of double standards and selective judgements by force, intimidation and otherwise.

It is the United States, more than any other country in the world, that has regularly violated the Charter of the United Nations, the resolutions of the Security Council and the General Assembly and international law, and particularly so in our region. The United States has used the big stick in addressing international issues, and it has imposed its tyrannical will by force of arms, intimidation and campaigns of disinformation. We see no need to demonstrate that fact by means of examples drawn from the dark record of the United States in the Security Council, which is well known to the international community and which some fair-minded members of the Council have recently recalled in the course of its meetings.

We view the measures adopted by the Council as a flagrant injustice and as a denial of the facts of history and of contemporary events in the international community.

In this connection, we have an important observation to make. Security Council resolution 661 (1990), unjust and precipitous as it is, stipulates, *inter alia*, that the iniquitous sanctions should not include supplies intended strictly for medical purposes and, in humanitarian circumstances, foodstuffs.

The United States has, however, had the intention from the very outset of preventing the delivery of such supplies for the purpose of starving and intimidating the people of Iraq, which is, however, a proud people, one that has fashioned civilizations throughout history and one which rejects humiliation and subjection. The United States has also incited a number of other States to follow its example, just as it has sought to impose a blockade on Iraq's exports and imports, thereby appointing itself the policeman of the world. Its trifling with words and designations does not alter this fact. Iraq calls upon the international community to reject these hostile and inhuman acts and to refuse to allow the United States to abuse human life in this crude fashion.

In another respect, it must be said that the embargo process itself has the objective from the practical point of view of starving the Iraqi people, which would not alter its stance or affect its staying power. How can the Iraqi people obtain foodstuffs and medical supplies when its major resource, namely oil, is cut off? If the Security Council had been thinking along sound humanitarian lines, it would have been in keeping with a true humanitarian approach, to have allowed a certain amount of oil to be exported which would, at the least, suffice to provide for normal humanitarian needs, principally foodstuffs and medicine.

Reference must be made to the fact that the United States has endeavoured by all possible means to induce certain States to close the pipelines that carry Iraqi oil, although these pipelines represent Iraqi investments made prior to recent events and despite the fact that the decision

on closure does not in any way enter into the scope of the resolutions adopted by the Security Council and that it was resorted to only at the inducement of the United States.

In conclusion, I must say to you, Mr. Secretary-General, and through you to the entire international community that the Iraqi people, the Arab nation and all free peoples of the world who are proud of their sovereignty and independence will reject by all legitimate means the attempts of the United States to extend its domination over the world by force, intimidation and deception.

(*Signed*) Tariq AZIZ
Deputy Prime Minister
Minister for Foreign Affairs of Iraq

Document 11

Security Council resolution demanding that Iraq permit the departure of third-State nationals from Kuwait and Iraq

S/RES/664 (1990), 18 August 1990

The Security Council,

Recalling the Iraqi invasion and purported annexation of Kuwait and its resolutions 660 (1990) of 2 August 1990, 661 (1990) of 6 August 1990 and 662 (1990) of 9 August 1990,

Deeply concerned for the safety and well-being of third-State nationals in Iraq and Kuwait,

Recalling the obligations of Iraq in this regard under international law,

Welcoming the efforts of the Secretary-General to pursue urgent consultations with the Government of Iraq following the concern and anxiety expressed by the members of the Council on 17 August 1990,

Acting under Chapter VII of the Charter of the United Nations,

1. *Demands* that Iraq permit and facilitate the immediate departure from Kuwait and Iraq of third-State nationals and grant immediate and continuing access of consular officials to such nationals;

2. *Also demands* that Iraq take no action to jeopardize the safety, security or health of such nationals;

3. *Reaffirms* its decision in resolution 662 (1990) that annexation of Kuwait by Iraq is null and void, and therefore demands that the Government of Iraq rescind its orders for the closure of diplomatic and consular missions in Kuwait and the withdrawal of the immunity of their personnel, and refrain from any such actions in the future;

4. *Requests* the Secretary-General to report to the Security Council on compliance with the present resolution at the earliest possible time.

Document 12

Security Council resolution expanding the sanctions against Iraq and authorizing maritime forces to take "commensurate" measures to ensure strict compliance

S/RES/665 (1990), 25 August 1990

The Security Council,

Recalling its resolutions 660 (1990) of 2 August 1990, 661 (1990) of 6 August 1990, 662 (1990) of 9

August 1990 and 664 (1990) of 18 August 1990 and demanding their full and immediate implementation,

Having decided in resolution 661 (1990) to impose economic sanctions under Chapter VII of the Charter of the United Nations,

Determined to bring to an end the occupation of Kuwait by Iraq which imperils the existence of a Member State and to restore the legitimate authority and the sovereignty, independence and territorial integrity of Kuwait, which requires the speedy implementation of the above-mentioned resolutions,

Deploring the loss of innocent lives stemming from the Iraqi invasion of Kuwait and determined to prevent further such losses,

Gravely alarmed that Iraq continues to refuse to comply with resolutions 660 (1990), 661 (1990), 662 (1990) and 664 (1990) and in particular at the conduct of the Government of Iraq in using Iraqi flag vessels to export oil,

1. *Calls upon* those Member States cooperating with the Government of Kuwait which are deploying maritime forces to the area to use such measures commensurate to the specific circumstances as may be necessary under the authority of the Security Council to halt all inward and outward maritime shipping, in order to inspect and verify their cargoes and destinations and to ensure strict implementation of the provisions related to such shipping laid down in resolution 661 (1990);

2. *Invites* Member States accordingly to cooperate as may be necessary to ensure compliance with the provisions of resolution 661 (1990) with maximum use of political and diplomatic measures, in accordance with paragraph 1 above;

3. *Requests* all States to provide, in accordance with the Charter of the United Nations, such assistance as may be required by the States referred to in paragraph 1 above;

4. *Also requests* the States concerned to coordinate their actions in pursuit of the above paragraphs of the present resolution using, as appropriate, mechanisms of the Military Staff Committee and, after consultation with the Secretary-General, to submit reports to the Security Council and the Security Council Committee established by resolution 661 (1990) concerning the situation between Iraq and Kuwait, in order to facilitate the monitoring of the implementation of the present resolution;

5. *Decides* to remain actively seized of the matter.

Document 13

Security Council resolution requesting the Council's Sanctions Committee to determine whether there is an urgent humanitarian need to supply foodstuffs to Iraq or Kuwait

S/RES/666 (1990), 13 September 1990

The Security Council,

Recalling its resolution 661 (1990) of 6 August 1990, paragraphs 3 (c) and 4 of which apply, except in humanitarian circumstances, to foodstuffs,

Recognizing that circumstances may arise in which it will be necessary for foodstuffs to be supplied to the civilian population in Iraq or Kuwait in order to relieve human suffering,

Noting that in this respect the Security Council Committee established by resolution 661 (1990) concerning the situation between Iraq and Kuwait has received communications from several Member States,

Emphasizing that it is for the Security Council, alone or acting through the Committee, to determine whether humanitarian circumstances have arisen,

Deeply concerned that Iraq has failed to comply with its obligations under Security Council resolution 664 (1990) of 18 August 1990 in respect of the safety and well-being of third-State nationals, and reaffirming that Iraq retains full responsibility in this regard under international humanitarian law including, where applicable, the Geneva Convention relative to the Protection of Civilian Persons in Time of War, of 12 August 1949, 1/

Acting under Chapter VII of the Charter of the United Nations,

1. *Decides* that in order to make the necessary determination whether or not, for the purposes of paragraphs 3 (c) and 4 of resolution 661 (1990), humanitarian circumstances have arisen, the Security Council Committee established by resolution 661 (1990) concerning the situation between Iraq and Kuwait shall keep the situation regarding foodstuffs in Iraq and Kuwait under constant review;

2. *Expects* Iraq to comply with its obligations under resolution 664 (1990) in respect of third-State nationals and reaffirms that Iraq remains fully responsible for their safety and well-being in accordance with interna-

1/ United Nations, *Treaty Series*, vol. 75, No. 973.

tional humanitarian law including, where applicable, the Geneva Convention relative to the Protection of Civilian Persons in Time of War, of 12 August 1949; 1/

3. *Requests*, for the purposes of paragraphs 1 and 2 above, that the Secretary-General seek urgently, and on a continuing basis, information from relevant United Nations and other appropriate humanitarian agencies and all other sources on the availability of food in Iraq and Kuwait, such information to be communicated by the Secretary-General to the Committee regularly;

4. *Also requests* that in seeking and supplying such information particular attention will be paid to such categories of persons who might suffer specially, such as children under 15 years of age, expectant mothers, maternity cases, the sick and the elderly;

5. *Decides* that if the Committee, after receiving the reports from the Secretary-General, determines that circumstances have arisen in which there is an urgent humanitarian need to supply foodstuffs to Iraq or Kuwait in order to relieve human suffering, it will report promptly to the Council its decision as to how such need should be met;

6. *Directs* the Committee that in formulating its decisions it should bear in mind that foodstuffs should be provided through the United Nations in cooperation with the International Committee of the Red Cross or other appropriate humanitarian agencies and distributed by them or under their supervision, in order to ensure that they reach the intended beneficiaries;

7. *Requests* the Secretary-General to use his good offices to facilitate the delivery and distribution of foodstuffs to Kuwait and Iraq in accordance with the provisions of the present resolution and other relevant resolutions;

8. *Recalls* that resolution 661 (1990) does not apply to supplies intended strictly for medical purposes, but in this connection recommends that medical supplies should be exported under the strict supervision of the Government of the exporting State or by appropriate humanitarian agencies.

Document 14

Security Council resolution demanding that Iraq immediately release foreign nationals abducted from diplomatic premises in Kuwait or Iraq

S/RES/667 (1990), 16 September 1990

The Security Council,

Reaffirming its resolutions 660 (1990) of 2 August 1990, 661 (1990) of 6 August 1990, 662 (1990) of 9 August 1990, 664 (1990) of 18 August 1990, 665 (1990) of 25 August 1990 and 666 (1990) of 13 September 1990,

Recalling the Vienna Convention on Diplomatic Relations of 18 April 1961 1/ and the Vienna Convention on Consular Relations of 24 April 1963, 2/ to both of which Iraq is a party,

Considering that the decision of Iraq to order the closure of diplomatic and consular missions in Kuwait and to withdraw the privileges and immunities of these missions and their personnel is contrary to the decisions of the Security Council, the international conventions mentioned above and international law,

Deeply concerned that Iraq, notwithstanding the decisions of the Council and the provisions of the conventions mentioned above, has committed acts of violence against diplomatic missions and their personnel in Kuwait,

Outraged at recent violations by Iraq of diplomatic premises in Kuwait and at the abduction of personnel enjoying diplomatic immunity and foreign nationals who were present in these premises,

Considering also that these actions by Iraq constitute aggressive acts and a flagrant violation of its international obligations which strike at the root of the conduct of international relations in accordance with the Charter of the United Nations,

Recalling that Iraq is fully responsible for any use of violence against foreign nationals or against any diplomatic or consular mission in Kuwait or its personnel,

Determined to ensure respect for its decisions and for Article 25 of the Charter,

Considering further that the grave nature of Iraq's actions, which constitute a new escalation of its violations of international law, obliges the Council not only to express its immediate reaction but also to consult urgently in order to take further concrete measures to ensure Iraq's compliance with the Council's resolutions,

Acting under Chapter VII of the Charter,

1. *Strongly condemns* aggressive acts perpetrated by Iraq against diplomatic premises and personnel in Kuwait, including the abduction of foreign nationals who were present in those premises;

2. *Demands* the immediate release of those foreign nationals as well as all nationals mentioned in resolution 664 (1990);

1/ United Nations, *Treaty Series*, vol. 500, No. 7310.
2/ Ibid., vol. 596, No. 8638.

3. *Also demands* that Iraq immediately and fully comply with its international obligations under resolutions 660 (1990), 662 (1990) and 664 (1990), the Vienna Convention on Diplomatic Relations of 18 April 1961, 1/ the Vienna Convention on Consular Relations of 24 April 1963 2/ and international law;

4. *Further demands* that Iraq immediately protect the safety and well-being of diplomatic and consular personnel and premises in Kuwait and in Iraq and take no action to hinder the diplomatic and consular missions in the performance of their functions, including access to their nationals and the protection of their person and interests;

5. *Reminds* all States that they are obliged to observe strictly resolutions 661 (1990), 662 (1990), 664 (1990), 665 (1990) and 666 (1990);

6. *Decides* to consult urgently to take further concrete measures as soon as possible, under Chapter VII of the Charter, in response to Iraq's continued violation of the Charter of the United Nations, of resolutions of the Security Council and of international law.

Document 15

Security Council resolution asking the Sanctions Committee to recommend a response to States requesting assistance with economic problems arising from the implementation of those sanctions

S/RES/669 (1990), 24 September 1990

The Security Council,

Recalling its resolution 661 (1990) of 6 August 1990,

Recalling also Article 50 of the Charter of the United Nations,

Conscious of the fact that an increasing number of requests for assistance have been received under the provisions of Article 50 of the Charter,

Entrusts the Security Council Committee established by resolution 661 (1990) concerning the situation between Iraq and Kuwait with the task of examining requests for assistance under the provisions of Article 50 of the Charter and making recommendations to the President of the Security Council for appropriate action.

Document 16

Security Council resolution calling for strict compliance with the sanctions against Iraq and confirming that these sanctions apply to all means of transport, including aircraft

S/RES/670 (1990), 25 September 1990

The Security Council,

Reaffirming its resolutions 660 (1990) of 2 August 1990, 661 (1990) of 6 August 1990, 662 (1990) of 9 August 1990, 664 (1990) of 18 August 1990, 665 (1990) of 25 August 1990, 666 (1990) of 13 September 1990 and 667 (1990) of 16 September 1990,

Condemning Iraq's continued occupation of Kuwait, its failure to rescind its actions and end its purported annexation and its holding of third-State nationals against their will, in flagrant violation of resolutions 660 (1990), 662 (1990), 664 (1990) and 667 (1990) and of international humanitarian law,

Condemning also the treatment by Iraqi forces of Kuwaiti nationals, including measures to force them to leave their own country and mistreatment of persons and property in Kuwait in violation of international law,

Noting with grave concern the persistent attempts to evade the measures laid down in resolution 661 (1990),

Noting also that a number of States have limited the number of Iraqi diplomatic and consular officials in their countries and that others are planning to do so,

Determined to ensure by all necessary means the strict and complete application of the measures laid down in resolution 661 (1990),

Determined also to ensure respect for its decisions and the provisions of Articles 25 and 48 of the Charter of the United Nations,

Affirming that any acts of the Government of Iraq which are contrary to the above-mentioned resolutions or to Articles 25 or 48 of the Charter, such as Decree No. 377 of 16 September 1990 of the Revolutionary Command Council of Iraq, are null and void,

Reaffirming its determination to ensure compliance with its resolutions by maximum use of political and diplomatic means,

Welcoming the Secretary-General's use of his good offices to advance a peaceful solution based on the relevant resolutions of the Council and noting with appreciation his continuing efforts to this end,

Underlining to the Government of Iraq that its continued failure to comply with the terms of resolutions 660 (1990), 661 (1990), 662 (1990), 664 (1990), 666 (1990) and 667 (1990) could lead to further serious action by the Council under the Charter, including under Chapter VII,

Recalling the provisions of Article 103 of the Charter,

Acting under Chapter VII of the Charter,

1. *Calls upon* all States to carry out their obligations to ensure strict and complete compliance with resolution 661 (1990) and in particular paragraphs 3, 4 and 5 thereof;

2. *Confirms* that resolutions 661 (1990) applies to all means of transport, including aircraft;

3. *Decides* that all States, notwithstanding the existence of any rights or obligations conferred or imposed by any international agreement or any contract entered into or any licence or permit granted before the date of the present resolution, shall deny permission to any aircraft to take off from their territory if the aircraft would carry any cargo to or from Iraq or Kuwait other than food in humanitarian circumstances, subject to authorization by the Security Council or the Security Council Committee established by resolution 661 (1990) and in accordance with resolution 666 (1990), or supplies intended strictly for medical purposes or solely for the United Nations Iran-Iraq Military Observer Group;

4. *Decides also* that all States shall deny permission to any aircraft destined to land in Iraq or Kuwait, whatever its State of registration, to overfly its territory unless:

(a) The aircraft lands at an airfield designated by the State outside Iraq or Kuwait in order to permit its inspection to ensure that there is no cargo on board in violation of resolution 661 (1990) or the present resolution, and for this purpose the aircraft may be detained for as long as necessary; or

(b) The particular flight has been approved by the Security Council Committee; or

(c) The flight is certified by the United Nations as solely for the purposes of the Military Observer Group;

5. *Decides further* that each State shall take all necessary measures to ensure that any aircraft registered in its territory or operated by an operator who has his principal place of business or permanent residence in its territory complies with the provisions of resolution 661 (1990) and the present resolution;

6. *Decides moreover* that all States shall notify in a timely fashion the Security Council Committee of any flight between its territory and Iraq or Kuwait to which the requirement to land in paragraph 4 above does not apply, and the purpose for such a flight;

7. *Calls upon* all States to cooperate in taking such measures as may be necessary, consistent with international law, including the Chicago Convention on International Civil Aviation of 7 December 1944, 1/ to ensure the effective implementation of the provisions of resolution 661 (1990) or the present resolution;

8. *Also calls upon* all States to detain any ships of Iraqi registry which enter their ports and which are being or have been used in violation of resolution 661 (1990), or to deny such ships entrance to their ports except in circumstances recognized under international law as necessary to safeguard human life;

9. *Reminds* all States of their obligations under resolution 661 (1990) with regard to the freezing of Iraqi assets, and the protection of the assets of the legitimate Government of Kuwait and its agencies, located within their territory and to report to the Security Council Committee regarding those assets;

10. *Further calls upon* all States to provide to the Security Council Committee information regarding the action taken by them to implement the provisions laid down in the present resolution;

11. *Affirms* that the United Nations, the specialized agencies and other international organizations in the United Nations system are required to take such measures as may be necessary to give effect to the terms of resolution 661 (1990) and of the present resolution;

12. *Decides* to consider, in the event of evasion of the provisions of resolution 661 (1990) or of the present resolution by a State or its nationals or through its territory, measures directed at the State in question to prevent such evasion;

13. *Reaffirms* that the Geneva Convention relative to the Protection of Civilian Persons in Time of War, of 12 August 1949, 2/ applies to Kuwait and that, as a High Contracting Party to the Convention, Iraq is bound to comply fully with all its terms and in particular is liable under the Convention in respect of the grave breaches committed by it, as are individuals who commit or order the commission of grave breaches.

1/ United Nations, *Treaty Series*, vol. 15, No. 102.
2/ Ibid., vol. 75, No.973.

Document 17

Security Council resolution demanding that Iraq release third-State nationals being held in Iraq or Kuwait

S/RES/674 (1990), 29 October 1990

The Security Council,

Recalling its resolutions 660 (1990) of 2 August 1990, 661 (1990) of 6 August 1990, 662 (1990) of 9 August 1990, 664 (1990) of 18 August 1990, 665 (1990) of 25 August 1990, 666 (1990) of 13 September 1990, 667 (1990) of 16 September 1990 and 670 (1990) of 25 September 1990,

Stressing the urgent need for the immediate and unconditional withdrawal of all Iraqi forces from Kuwait and for the restoration of Kuwait's sovereignty, independence and territorial integrity and of the authority of its legitimate Government,

Condemning the actions by the Iraqi authorities and occupying forces to take third-State nationals hostage and to mistreat and oppress Kuwaiti and third-State nationals, and the other actions reported to the Council, such as the destruction of Kuwaiti demographic records, the forced departure of Kuwaitis, the relocation of population in Kuwait and the unlawful destruction and seizure of public and private property in Kuwait, including hospital supplies and equipment, in violation of the decisions of the Council, the Charter of the United Nations, the Geneva Convention relative to the Protection of Civilian Persons in Time of War, of 12 August 1949, 1/ the Vienna Convention on Diplomatic Relations of 18 April 1961, 2/ the Vienna Convention on Consular Relations of 24 April 1963 3/ and international law,

Expressing grave alarm over the situation of third-State nationals in Kuwait and Iraq, including the personnel of the diplomatic and consular missions of such States,

Reaffirming that the above-mentioned Geneva Convention applies to Kuwait and that, as a High Contracting Party to the Convention, Iraq is bound to comply fully with all its terms and in particular is liable under the Convention in respect of the grave breaches committed by it, as are individuals who commit or order the commission of grave breaches,

Recalling the efforts of the Secretary-General concerning the safety and well-being of third-State nationals in Iraq and Kuwait,

Deeply concerned at the economic cost and at the loss and suffering caused to individuals in Kuwait and Iraq as a result of the invasion and occupation of Kuwait by Iraq,

Acting under Chapter VII of the Charter,

Reaffirming the goal of the international community of maintaining international peace and security by seeking to resolve international disputes and conflicts through peaceful means,

Recalling the important role that the United Nations and the Secretary-General have played in the peaceful solution of disputes and conflicts in conformity with the provisions of the Charter,

Alarmed by the dangers of the present crisis caused by the Iraqi invasion and occupation of Kuwait, which directly threaten international peace and security, and seeking to avoid any further worsening of the situation,

Calling upon Iraq to comply with its relevant resolutions, in particular resolutions 660 (1990), 662 (1990) and 664 (1990),

Reaffirming its determination to ensure compliance by Iraq with its resolutions by maximum use of political and diplomatic means,

A

1. *Demands* that the Iraqi authorities and occupying forces immediately cease and desist from taking third-State nationals hostage, mistreating and oppressing Kuwaiti and third-State nationals and any other actions, such as those reported to the Council and described above, that violate the decisions of the Council, the Charter of the United Nations, the Geneva Convention relative to the Protection of Civilian Persons in Time of War, of 12 August 1949, 1/ the Vienna Convention on Diplomatic Relations of 18 April 1961, 2/ the Vienna Convention on Consular Relations of 24 April 1963 3/ and international law;

2. *Invites* States to collate substantiated information in their possession or submitted to them on the grave breaches by Iraq as per paragraph 1 above and to make this information available to the Council;

3. *Reaffirms its demand* that Iraq immediately fulfil its obligations to third-State nationals in Kuwait and Iraq, including the personnel of diplomatic and consular missions, under the Charter, the above-mentioned Geneva Convention, the Vienna Convention on Diplomatic Relations, the Convention on Consular Relations, general principles of international law and the relevant resolutions of the Council;

1/ United Nations, *Treaty Series*, vol. 75, No. 973.
2/ Ibid., vol. 500, No. 7310.
3/ Ibid., vol. 596, No. 8638.

4. *Also reaffirms its demand* that Iraq permit and facilitate the immediate departure from Kuwait and Iraq of those third-State nationals, including diplomatic and consular personnel, who wish to leave;

5. *Demands* that Iraq ensure the immediate access to food, water and basic services necessary to the protection and well-being of Kuwaiti nationals and of third-State nationals in Kuwait and Iraq, including the personnel of diplomatic and consular missions in Kuwait;

6. *Reaffirms its demand* that Iraq immediately protect the safety and well-being of diplomatic and consular personnel and premises in Kuwait and in Iraq, take no action to hinder these diplomatic and consular missions in the performance of their functions, including access to their nationals and the protection of their person and interests, and rescind its orders for the closure of diplomatic and consular missions in Kuwait and the withdrawal of the immunity of their personnel;

7. *Requests* the Secretary-General, in the context of the continued exercise of his good offices concerning the safety and well-being of third-State nationals in Iraq and Kuwait, to seek to achieve the objectives of paragraphs 4, 5 and 6 above, in particular the provision of food, water and basic services to Kuwaiti nationals and to the diplomatic and consular missions in Kuwait and the evacuation of third-State nationals;

8. *Reminds* Iraq that under international law it is liable for any loss, damage or injury arising in regard to Kuwait and third States, and their nationals and corporations, as a result of the invasion and illegal occupation of Kuwait by Iraq;

9. *Invites* States to collect relevant information regarding their claims, and those of their nationals and corporations, for restitution or financial compensation by Iraq, with a view to such arrangements as may be established in accordance with international law;

10. *Requires* that Iraq comply with the provisions of the present resolution and its previous resolutions, failing which the Council will need to take further measures under the Charter;

11. *Decides* to remain actively and permanently seized of the matter until Kuwait has regained its independence and peace has been restored in conformity with the relevant resolutions of the Security Council.

B

12. *Reposes its trust* in the Secretary-General to make available his good offices and, as he considers appropriate, to pursue them and to undertake diplomatic efforts in order to reach a peaceful solution to the crisis caused by the Iraqi invasion and occupation of Kuwait, on the basis of resolutions 660 (1990), 662 (1990) and 664 (1990), and calls upon all States, both those in the region and others, to pursue on this basis their efforts to this end, in conformity with the Charter, in order to improve the situation and restore peace, security and stability;

13. *Requests* the Secretary-General to report to the Security Council on the results of his good offices and diplomatic efforts.

Document 18

Security Council resolution condemning Iraqi attempts to alter the demographic composition of the population of Kuwait

S/RES/677 (1990), 28 November 1990

The Security Council,

Recalling its resolutions 660 (1990) of 2 August 1990, 662 (1990) of 9 August 1990 and 674 (1990) of 29 October 1990,

Reiterating its concern for the suffering caused to individuals in Kuwait as a result of the invasion and occupation of Kuwait by Iraq,

Gravely concerned at the ongoing attempt by Iraq to alter the demographic composition of Kuwait and to destroy the civil records maintained by the legitimate Government of Kuwait,

Acting under Chapter VII of the Charter of the United Nations,

1. *Condemns* the attempts by Iraq to alter the demographic composition of Kuwait and to destroy the civil records maintained by the legitimate Government of Kuwait;

2. *Mandates* the Secretary-General to take custody of a copy of the population register of Kuwait, the authenticity of which has been certified by the legitimate Government of Kuwait and which covers the registration of the population up to 1 August 1990;

3. *Requests* the Secretary-General to establish, in cooperation with the legitimate Government of Kuwait, an order of rules and regulations governing access to and use of the said copy of the population register.

Document 19

Security Council resolution authorizing Member States cooperating with the Government of Kuwait to use "all necessary means to uphold and implement" the Council's resolutions on the situation unless Iraq fully complies with those resolutions on or before 15 January 1991

S/RES/678 (1990), 29 November 1990

The Security Council,

Recalling and reaffirming its resolutions 660 (1990) of 2 August 1990, 661 (1990) of 6 August 1990, 662 (1990) of 9 August 1990, 664 (1990) of 18 August 1990, 665 of 25 August 1990, 666 (1990) of 13 September 1990, 667 (1990) of 16 September 1990, 669 (1990) of 24 September 1990, 670 (1990) of 25 September 1990, 674 (1990) of 29 October 1990 and 677 (1990) of 28 November 1990,

Noting that, despite all efforts by the United Nations, Iraq refuses to comply with its obligation to implement resolution 660 (1990) and the above-mentioned subsequent relevant resolutions, in flagrant contempt of the Security Council,

Mindful of its duties and responsibilities under the Charter of the United Nations for the maintenance and preservation of international peace and security,

Determined to secure full compliance with its decisions,

Acting under Chapter VII of the Charter,

1. *Demands* that Iraq comply fully with resolution 660 (1990) and all subsequent relevant resolutions, and decides, while maintaining all its decisions, to allow Iraq one final opportunity, as a pause of goodwill, to do so;

2. *Authorizes* Member States cooperating with the Government of Kuwait, unless Iraq on or before 15 January 1991 fully implements, as set forth in paragraph 1 above, the above-mentioned resolutions, to use all necessary means to uphold and implement resolution 660 (1990) and all subsequent relevant resolutions and to restore international peace and security in the area;

3. *Requests* all States to provide appropriate support for the actions undertaken in pursuance of paragraph 2 above;

4. *Requests* the States concerned to keep the Security Council regularly informed on the progress of actions undertaken pursuant to paragraphs 2 and 3 above;

5. *Decides* to remain seized of the matter.

Document 20

General Assembly resolution concerning the situation of human rights in occupied Kuwait

A/RES/45/170, 18 December 1990

The General Assembly,

Guided by the principles embodied in the Charter of the United Nations, the Universal Declaration of Human Rights, 1/ the International Covenants on Human Rights, 2/ and the Geneva Conventions of 12 August 1949, 3/

Aware of its responsibility to promote and encourage respect for human rights and fundamental freedoms for all and resolved to remain vigilant with regard to violations of human rights wherever they occur,

Reaffirming that all Member States have an obligation to promote and protect human rights and fundamental freedoms and to fulfil obligations they have freely undertaken under the various international instruments,

Condemning the invasion of Kuwait on 2 August 1990 by the military forces of Iraq,

Noting with grave concern that the Iraqi forces in occupied Kuwait continue to commit acts of violence, leaving large numbers of victims and causing enormous human suffering to the civilian population,

Noting also with grave concern that the treatment of prisoners of war and detained civilians in occupied Kuwait does not conform to the internationally recognized principles of humanitarian law,

Expressing grave concern at the continued refusal of Iraq to receive representatives of humanitarian organizations, especially representatives of the International Committee of the Red Cross and a representative of the

1/ Resolution 217 A (III).
2/ See resolution 2200 A (XXI), annex.
3/ United Nations, *Treaty Series*, vol. 75, Nos. 970-973.

Secretary-General, to help in extending humanitarian assistance to the Kuwaiti people under occupation,

1. *Condemns* the Iraqi authorities and occupying forces for their serious violations of human rights against the Kuwaiti people and third-State nationals and, in particular, the continued and increasing acts of torture, arrests, summary executions, disappearances and abduction in violation of the Charter of the United Nations, the International Covenants on Human Rights, other relevant human rights instruments and the relevant instruments of humanitarian law;

2. *Affirms* that the Geneva Convention relative to the Protection of Civilian Persons in Time of War, of 12 August 1949, 4/ applies to Kuwait and that as a high contracting party to the Convention Iraq is bound to comply fully with all its terms and in particular is liable under the Convention in respect of the grave breaches committed by it, as are individuals who commit or order the commission of such breaches;

3. *Expresses its serious concern* about the systematic dismantling and pillaging of and attacks on the economic infrastructure of Kuwait, which seriously undermine the present and future enjoyment by the Kuwaiti people of their economic, social and cultural rights;

4. *Expresses its grave concern* at the living conditions in occupied Kuwait, especially those of women, children, elderly and third-State nationals, which are becoming increasingly difficult;

5. *Expects* Iraq to guarantee respect for international standards applicable under international law, in particular with reference to the protection of the civilian population, and demands that Iraq cooperate fully with and give access to Kuwait to representatives of humanitarian organizations, especially the International Committee of the Red Cross, working to alleviate the suffering of the civilian population in occupied Kuwait;

6. *Also expects* Iraq to comply with its obligations under the Charter and international law in respect of third-State nationals, and demands that Iraq release all nationals of third States;

7. *Urges* Iraq to treat all prisoners of war and detained civilians in accordance with the internationally recognized principles of humanitarian law and to protect them from all acts of violence, including ill-treatment, torture and summary execution;

8. *Condemns* the rejection by Iraq of the offer of the Government of Kuwait to send humanitarian assistance, especially medicine, to the Kuwaiti people under occupation;

9. *Requests* the Commission on Human Rights at its forty-seventh session to consider the situation of human rights in occupied Kuwait;

10. *Decides* to keep under consideration the situation of human rights in occupied Kuwait.

4/ Ibid., No. 973.

Document 21

Statement by the Secretary-General to the press on 15 January 1991

S/22091, 17 January 1991

Letter dated 16 January 1991 from the Secretary-General addressed to the President of the Security Council

I have the honour to transmit to you herewith the text, in French and English, of the statement which I made yesterday on the situation between Iraq and Kuwait.

I should be grateful if you would bring it to the attention of the members of the Security Council.

(*Signed*) Javier PÉREZ DE CUÉLLAR

Annex
Statement by the Secretary-General to the press on 15 January 1991

As 15 January advances, and the world stands poised between peace and war, I most sincerely appeal to President Saddam Hussein to turn the course of events away from catastrophe and towards a new era of justice and harmony based on the principles of the Charter of the United Nations.

All our efforts in this direction will fail unless Iraq can signify its readiness to comply with the relevant resolutions of the Security Council, beginning with resolution 660 (1990).

If this commitment is made, and clear and substantial steps taken to implement these resolutions, a just peace, with all its benefits, will follow. I therefore urge President Saddam Hussein to commence, without delay, the total withdrawal of Iraqi forces from Kuwait.

Once this process is well under way, I wish to assure him, on the basis of understandings that I have received from Governments at the highest level, that neither Iraq nor its forces will be attacked by those arrayed in the international coalition against his country.

Further, with the commencement of withdrawal, as Secretary-General of the United Nations, I would, with the consent of the parties concerned, and the agreement of the Security Council, be prepared immediately to deploy United Nations observers and, if necessary, United Nations forces to certify the withdrawal and to ensure that hostilities do not erupt on the ground.

In addition, with compliance of the resolutions, I would urge the Security Council to review its decisions imposing sanctions against Iraq. I would also encourage a process whereby foreign forces deployed in the area would be phased out.

Peace in the region requires that all its problems be resolved justly and equitably, in accordance with the principles of the Charter of the United Nations.

I have every assurance, once again from the highest levels of government, that with the resolution of the present crisis, every effort will be made to address, in a comprehensive manner, the Arab-Israeli conflict, including the Palestinian question. I pledge my every effort to this end.

As I stated to the Council last night, all of us are aware of the extreme gravity of the decisions to be made in the period ahead. No one and no nation can—except with a heavy heart—resort to the other "necessary means" implied by resolution 678 (1990), knowing in advance that tragic and unpredictable consequences can follow.

I trust, in the circumstances, that wisdom and statesmanship will prevail in all quarters in order to move decisively away from conflict. In appealing to President Saddam Hussein today, I wish him to know that I will readily devote my every capacity to working with him, and with all others concerned, to this end.

In the tenth and final year of my tenure as Secretary-General of the United Nations, no cause would give me greater satisfaction than to set the Middle East as a whole on the road to just and lasting peace. And no disappointment would be greater and more tragic than to find the nations of the world engaging in a conflict that none of their peoples want.

Document 22

Letter from the Permanent Representative of Kuwait to the President of the Security Council stating that, the deadline of resolution 678 (1990) having expired, it was exercising its right to self-defence with the cooperation of friendly States

S/22094, 17 January 1991

On instructions from my Government, I hereby transmit the following information to you:

Following the expiry of the deadline set by the Security Council in its resolution 678 (1990) for the full implementation of its pertinent resolutions, Kuwait notified the Secretary-General of the United Nations that Iraqi forces continued to occupy all territories of the State of Kuwait. Accordingly, and pursuant to paragraph 4 of resolution 678 (1990), Kuwait wishes to inform you that it is exercising its right to self-defence and to the restoration of its rights, first and foremost among which is the recovery of its territories, occupied by Iraq since 2 August

1990. In doing so, the Kuwaiti forces are cooperating with the forces of fraternal and friendly States which are equally determined to end the obdurate Iraqi occupation.

We shall also transmit to you the statement issued by the Kuwaiti Council of Ministers concerning the beginning of the operation to liberate Kuwait.

I should be grateful if you would have this letter circulated as a document of the Security Council.

Accept, Sir, the assurances of my highest consideration.

(Signed) Mohammad A. ABULHASAN
Permanent Representative

Document 23

Letter from the Permanent Representative of Kuwait to the President of the Security Council reporting Kuwaiti military operations against Iraq

S/22164, 28 January 1991

On instructions from my Government, in accordance with paragraph 4 of Security Council resolution 678 (1990) and pursuant to my letter of 17 January 1991 (S/22094), I have the honour to inform you of the following:

A unit of the Kuwaiti armed forces has, in conjunction with the armed forces of fraternal and friendly States, carried out military operations against Iraqi installations with a view to ensuring the complete and unconditional withdrawal of Iraq from Kuwait, in accordance with the relevant resolutions of the Security Council.

A unit of the Kuwait Navy took part in the attack against the oil rig occupied by Iraq.

Kuwait Air Force aircraft also took part in joint air operations directed primarily against ground-to-ground missile sites, missile launchers, artillery positions and concentrations of Iraqi mechanized units.

I should be grateful if you would have this letter circulated as a document of the Security Council.

(Signed) Mohammad A. ABULHASAN
Permanent Representative

Document 24

Similar letters dated 27 February 1991 from the Permanent Representative of Iraq to the President of the Security Council and to the Secretary-General stating that all Iraqi forces have withdrawn from Kuwait

S/22274, 27 February 1991, and S/22288, 28 February 1991

Upon instruction from my Government I have the honour to inform you that all Iraqi forces have withdrawn from Kuwait at dawn today 27 February 1991 local time. The American and other pro-aggressor forces continued to attack our forces during their withdrawal.

I will appreciate it if Your Excellency would have this letter circulated as a document of the Security Council.

(Signed) Abdul-Amir AL-ANBARI
Ambassador
Permanent Representative

Document 25

Identical letters from the Deputy Prime Minister and Minister for Foreign Affairs of Iraq to the President of the Security Council and to the Secretary-General stating that the Government of Iraq agrees to comply fully with all relevant Security Council resolutions

S/22275 and S/22276, 27 February 1991

On instructions from my Government I have the honour to transmit herewith a letter addressed to you from Mr. Tariq Aziz, Deputy Prime Minister, Minister for Foreign Affairs of the Republic of Iraq.

I should be grateful if you would have this letter and its annex circulated as a document of the Security Council.

(*Signed*) Abdul-Amir AL-ANBARI
Ambassador
Permanent Representative

Annex
Letter dated 28 February 1991* from the Deputy Prime Minister and Minister for Foreign Affairs of Iraq addressed to the President of the Security Council

I have the honour to inform you officially that the Government of Iraq agrees to comply fully with Security Council resolution 660 (1990) and all the other Security Council resolutions.

You are kindly requested to transmit this letter to the members of the Security Council and to have it circulated as an official document of the Security Council.

(*Signed*) Tariq AZIZ
Deputy Prime Minister
Minister for Foreign Affairs
  of the Republic of Iraq

*Baghdad time.

Document 26

Security Council resolution taking note of the suspension of offensive combat operations and demanding that Iraq implement all 12 relevant Security Council resolutions

S/RES/686 (1991), 2 March 1991

The Security Council,

Recalling and reaffirming its resolutions 660 (1990) of 2 August 1990, 661 (1990) of 6 August 1990, 662 (1990) of 9 August 1990, 664 (1990) of 18 August 1990, 665 (1990) of 25 August 1990, 666 (1990) of 13 September 1990, 667 (1990) of 16 September 1990, 669 (1990) of 24 September 1990, 670 (1990) of 25 September 1990, 674 (1990) of 29 October 1990, 677 (1990) of 28 November 1990 and 678 (1990) of 29 November 1990,

Recalling the obligations of Member States under Article 25 of the Charter of the United Nations,

Recalling also paragraph 9 of resolution 661 (1990) regarding assistance to the Government of Kuwait and paragraph 3 (*c*) of that resolution regarding supplies strictly for medical purposes and, in humanitarian circumstances, foodstuffs,

Taking note of the letters dated 27 February 1991 from the Deputy Prime Minister and Minister for Foreign Affairs of Iraq addressed to the President of the Security Council and to the Secretary-General, confirming Iraq's agreement to comply fully with all of the resolutions noted above, 1/ and of his letter of the same date addressed to the President of the Security Council stating Iraq's intention to release prisoners of war immediately, 2/

Noting the suspension of offensive combat operations by the forces of Kuwait and the Member States cooperating with Kuwait pursuant to resolution 678 (1990),

Bearing in mind the need to be assured of Iraq's peaceful intentions, and the objective expressed in resolution 678 (1990) of restoring international peace and security in the region,

Underlining the importance of Iraq taking the necessary measures which would permit a definitive end to the hostilities,

Affirming the commitment of all Member States to the independence, sovereignty and territorial integrity of Iraq and Kuwait, and noting the intention expressed by the Member States cooperating with Kuwait under paragraph 2 of resolution 678 (1990) to bring their military presence in Iraq to an end as soon as possible consistent with achieving the objectives of that resolution,

Acting under Chapter VII of the Charter,

1. *Affirms* that all twelve resolutions noted above continue to have full force and effect;

2. *Demands* that Iraq implement its acceptance of all twelve resolutions noted above and in particular that Iraq:

(*a*) Rescind immediately its actions purporting to annex Kuwait;

(*b*) Accept in principle its liability under international law for any loss, damage or injury arising in regard to Kuwait and third States and their nationals and corporations, as a result of the invasion and illegal occupation of Kuwait by Iraq;

1/ *Official Records of the Security Council, Forty-sixth Year, Supplement for January, February and March 1991*, documents S/22275 and S/22276.
2/ Ibid., document S/22273.

(c) Immediately release under the auspices of the International Committee of the Red Cross, Red Cross Societies or Red Crescent Societies all Kuwaiti and third-State nationals detained by Iraq and return the remains of any deceased Kuwaiti and third-State nationals so detained;

(d) Immediately begin to return all Kuwaiti property seized by Iraq, the return to be completed in the shortest possible period;

3. *Also demands* that Iraq:

(a) Cease hostile or provocative actions by its forces against all Member States, including missile attacks and flights of combat aircraft;

(b) Designate military commanders to meet with counterparts from the forces of Kuwait and the Member States cooperating with Kuwait pursuant to resolution 678 (1990) to arrange for the military aspects of a cessation of hostilities at the earliest possible time;

(c) Arrange for immediate access to and release of all prisoners of war under the auspices of the International Committee of the Red Cross and return the remains of any deceased personnel of the forces of Kuwait and the Member States cooperating with Kuwait pursuant to resolution 678 (1990);

(d) Provide all information and assistance in identifying Iraqi mines, booby traps and other explosives as well as any chemical and biological weapons and material in Kuwait, in areas of Iraq where forces of Member States cooperating with Kuwait pursuant to resolution

678 (1990) are present temporarily, and in the adjacent waters;

4. *Recognizes* that during the period required for Iraq to comply with paragraphs 2 and 3 above, the provisions of paragraph 2 of resolution 678 (1990) remain valid;

5. *Welcomes* the decision of Kuwait and the Member States cooperating with Kuwait pursuant to resolution 678 (1990) to provide access to and commence immediately the release of Iraqi prisoners of war under the auspices of the International Committee of the Red Cross, as required by the terms of the Geneva Convention relative to the Treatment of Prisoners of War, of 12 August 1949; 3/

6. *Requests* all Member States, as well as the United Nations, the specialized agencies and other international organizations in the United Nations system, to take all appropriate action to cooperate with the Government and people of Kuwait in the reconstruction of their country;

7. *Decides* that Iraq shall notify the Secretary-General and the Security Council when it has taken the actions set out above;

8. *Also decides,* in order to secure the rapid establishment of a definitive end to the hostilities, to remain actively seized of the matter.

3/ United Nations, *Treaty Series*, vol. 75, No. 972.

Document 27

Identical letters from the Deputy Prime Minister and Minister for Foreign Affairs of Iraq to the President of the Security Council and to the Secretary-General concerning agreement to fulfil Security Council resolution 686 (1991)

S/22320 and S/22321, 3 March 1991

Letter dated 3 March 1991 from the Permanent Representative of Iraq to the United Nations addressed to the President of the Security Council

On instructions from my Government, I have the honour to transmit to you herewith a letter addressed to you by Mr. Tariq Aziz, Deputy Prime Minister and Minister for Foreign Affairs of the Republic of Iraq, dated 3 March 1991.

I should be grateful if you would have this letter and its annex circulated as a document of the Security Council.

Accept, Sir, the assurances of my highest consideration.

(*Signed*) Abdul-Amir AL-ANBARI
Ambassador
Permanent Representative

Annex
Letter dated 3 March 1991 from the Deputy Prime Minister and Minister for Foreign Affairs of Iraq addressed to the President of the Security Council

I have the honour to inform you that the Iraqi Government has taken note of the text of Security Council resolution 686 (1991) and that it has agreed to fulfil its obligations under the said resolution. We hope that the Council, in its turn, will interact in an objective and honourable manner, pursuant to the provisions of international law and the principles of equity and justice, with our faithful and—to the extent that we are able—speedy fulfilment of those obligations.

You and the members of the Security Council are well aware of the manner in which the American forces and their partners in the military operations against Iraq have implemented Security Council resolution 678 (1990), and of the major losses which Iraq has suffered to its infrastructure, economic, civilian, cultural and religious property, basic public services such as electricity, water, telephones, transport, fuel and other essential requirements of everyday life.

Despite these facts, resolution 686 (1991) has ignored the Iraqi people's suffering and the imposition on Iraq alone of a long series of obligations. A number of members of the Security Council referred to this fact, leading one of them (Cuba) to vote against the resolution, while three States—India, Yemen and China, the latter being a permanent member of the Council—abstained.

We record these facts for history and for the attention of those members of the Security Council and the international Organization—and those elements of international public opinion—who have a conscience. Our agreement to fulfil our obligations under this resolution stems from our determination to refute the pretexts which some may employ in order to persist in their aggression against Iraq and to inflict further harm on its people.

Iraq hopes that the Security Council will ensure the adoption of a resolution proclaiming an official cease-fire and the cessation of all military operations on land, at sea and in the air, as well as the immediate withdrawal of the foreign military forces stationed without any justification in various regions of Iraq. Iraq also hopes that the Security Council will proceed to declare, with all possible speed, the bases for its adoption of Security Council resolutions 661 (1990), 665 (1990) and 670 (1990) as having lapsed, with the result that the resolutions become null and void.

Accept, Sir, the assurances of my highest consideration.

(*Signed*) Tariq AZIZ
Deputy Prime Minister
Minister for Foreign Affairs

Document 28

Statement by the President of the Security Council concerning humanitarian assistance to those affected by the conflict

S/22322, 3 March 1991

The Council welcomes the decisions taken to date relating to food and medical needs by the Committee established under resolution 661 including those just taken to facilitate the provision of humanitarian assistance including infant formula and water purification material.

It calls upon the Committee to continue to act promptly on requests submitted to it for humanitarian assistance.

It urges the Committee to pay particular attention to the findings and recommendations on critical medical/public health and nutritional conditions in Iraq which have been and will continue to be submitted to it by the World Health Organization, UNICEF, the International Committee of the Red Cross and other relevant organizations, consistent with the relevant resolutions, and urges these humanitarian agencies to play an active role in this process and cooperate closely with the Committee in its work.

The Council welcomes the Secretary-General's announcement that he plans to send urgently a mission led by Under-Secretary-General Martti Ahtisaari comprising representatives of the appropriate United Nations agencies to Iraq and Kuwait to assess the humanitarian needs arising in the immediate post crisis environment. The Council invites the Secretary-General to keep it informed in the shortest possible time on the progress of his mission on which it pledges to take immediate action.

Document 29

Letter from the Deputy Prime Minister and Minister for Foreign Affairs of Kuwait to the Secretary-General stating that the Kuwaiti Government is resuming the functions of the State

S/22338, 6 March 1991

Letter dated 6 March from the Chargé d'affaires a.i. of the Premanent Mission of Kuwait to the United Nations addressed to the Secretary-General

I have the honour to transmit herewith a message from His Excellency Sheikh Sabah Al-Ahmad Al-Jaber Al Sabah, Deputy Prime Minister and Minister of Foreign Affairs, addressed to Your Excellency.

I should appreciate it if you would arrange for this message to be circulated as a document of the Security Council.

(*Signed*) Nabeela AL-MULLA
Chargé d'affaires a.i.

**Annex
Letter dated 4 March 1991 from the Deputy Prime Minister and Minister for Foreign Affairs of Kuwait addressed to the Secretary-General**

I have the honour and pleasure to inform you that the Government of Kuwait is resuming the functions of the State and directing the affairs of the nation from Kuwait City.

I should like to seize this opportunity to express our gratitude and appreciation to you personally and to the United Nations system as a whole for the indispensable role played to reverse the Iraqi aggression and to end the occupation of Kuwait.

The contribution of the United Nations system to the restoration of Kuwait's territorial integrity, and the return of the legitimate government to the country has reconfirmed the purposes and objectives of the Charter and the importance of the Organization in maintaining international peace and security.

(*Signed*) Sabah Al-Ahmad Al-Jaber AL SABAH
Deputy Prime Minister
and Minister of Foreign Affairs

Document 30

Identical letters from the Permanent Representative of Iraq to the President of the Security Council and to the Secretary-General transmitting a decision of the Revolution Command Council nullifying all actions regarding Kuwait

S/22342, 8 March 1991

On instructions from my Government, and further to its acceptance of Security Council resolution 686 (1991), as indicated in the letter addressed to you by the Minister for Foreign Affairs of my Government, dated 3 March 1991, I have the honour to transmit to you a copy of Revolution Command Council decision No. 55 of 5 March 1991 concerning the application of paragraph 2 (a) of resolution 686 (1991).

I should be grateful if you would have this letter and its annex circulated as a document of the Security Council.

(*Signed*) Abdul Amir A. AL-ANBARI
Ambassador
Permanent Representative

**Annex
Revolution Command Council decision No. 55
dated 17 Sha'ban A.H. 1411 (5 March A.D. 1991)**

In accordance with the acceptance by the Iraqi Government of Security Council resolution 686 (1991) and with its previous declarations regarding acceptance of the other Security Council resolutions, and pursuant to the provisions of article 42, paragraph (a) of the Constitution,

The Revolution Command Council has decided as follows:

1. All Revolution Command Council decisions subsequent to 2 August 1990 regarding Kuwait are null and void.

2. All laws, decisions, regulations, instructions, directives and measures issued by virtue of the decisions of the Council referred to in paragraph 1 above are abrogated and all the effects arising therefrom are nullified.

3. No text which is contradictory to the provisions of this decision shall have any effect.

4. This decision shall be published in the Official Gazette and shall take effect from 3 March 1991.

5. The competent ministries and authorities shall undertake the implementation of this decision.

(*Signed*) Saddam HUSSEIN
Chairman of the Revolution Command Council

Document 31

Report on humanitarian needs in Iraq in the immediate post-crisis environment by a mission to the area led by the Under-Secretary-General for Administration and Management, 10-17 March 1991 (extract)

S/22366, 20 March 1991

Letter dated 20 March 1991 from the Secretary-General addressed to the President of the Security Council

Further to my decision to dispatch a mission in order to assess the humanitarian needs arising in Iraq and in Kuwait in the immediate post-crisis environment, I have the honour to inform you that the mission, led by Under-Secretary-General Martti Ahtisaari and comprising representatives of appropriate United Nations agencies and programmes, visited Iraq in the period from 10 to 17 March 1991.

In the light of the wish of the members of the Security Council to be kept informed of the progress of the mission (S/22322), I have the honour to transmit herewith, for their consideration, the report prepared by Mr. Ahtisaari concerning his visit to Iraq.

The Mission will commence its visit to Kuwait on 22 March 1991. I shall of course convey to you as soon as possible the report on that visit.

(*Signed*) Javier PÉREZ DE CUÉLLAR

Annex
Report to the Secretary-General on humanitarian needs in Kuwait and Iraq in the immediate post-crisis environment by a mission to the area led by Mr. Martti Ahtisaari, Under-Secretary-General for Administration and Management, dated 20 March 1991

Introduction

1. You asked me to travel, as a matter of urgency, to Kuwait and Iraq to assess humanitarian needs there in the immediate post-crisis environment, and to bring with me a team comprising representatives of the appropriate United Nations agencies and programmes. Your decision was announced in a press statement of 1 March 1991.

2. On 3 March 1991, the President of the Security Council made a statement on behalf of the Council, in which it welcomed your announcement and invited you to keep it informed in the shortest possible time of the progress of this mission, in respect of which it pledged to take immediate action (S/22322).

3. In the days immediately preceding my departure, I consulted with all concerned parties, and met on 4 and 5 March 1991 with the Permanent Representative of Iraq to the United Nations, H.E. Dr. Abdul Amir A. Al-Anbari, and with the Chargé d'affaires of Kuwait to the United Nations, Ambassador Mohammad Saad Al-Sallal. Each pledged the full cooperation of his Government but mentioned logistical difficulties and communication problems with his capital. In my meeting with the representative of Kuwait I expressed a preference to travel there first. He, however, responded that his Government anticipated receiving a mission led by Mr. Abdulrahim Farah to assess losses and damages during the Iraqi occupation of Kuwait. His authorities preferred to receive that mission first. Thus, he believed that it would be more practical for my mission to travel first to Iraq before proceeding to Kuwait. He appreciated my desire to go first to his country and hoped that the mission could be received there in the near future.

4. I departed from New York on 7 March. The mission assembled at Geneva the following day. It comprised representatives not only of the Secretariat, but also of the United Nations Children's Fund (UNICEF), the United Nations Development Programme (UNDP), the Office of the United Nations Disaster Relief Coordinator (UNDRO), the Office of the United Nations High Com-

missioner for Refugees (UNHCR), the Food and Agriculture Organization of the United Nations (FAO) and the World Health Organization (WHO). On my way to the Middle East, I consulted at Geneva with Mr. Claudio Caratsch, Vice-President of the International Committee of the Red Cross (ICRC). The mission travelled to Amman on 9 March and arrived at Baghdad on 10 March. At Amman, I was received by His Highness Crown Prince Hassan and by His Excellency Mr. Taher Al-Masri, Foreign Minister of Jordan. The mission remained in Iraq until 17 March. On that date I travelled to Bahrain while awaiting the outcome of consultations in New York and your further instructions. In Bahrain I met with the Foreign Minister, His Excellency Sheikh Mohamed bin Mubarak Al Khalifa. On 19 March you instructed me to return to New York. Leaving the remainder of the mission in Bahrain whilst awaiting the decision of the Kuwaiti Government, I departed that day and arrived in New York on 20 March. The Kuwaiti authorities have now informed you that the mission is expected to depart Bahrain for Kuwait on or about 22 March.

I. Modus operandi *in Iraq*

5. The mission began its work immediately upon arrival at Baghdad on 10 March, first linking up with local UNDP and UNICEF representatives and, later that day, meeting with His Excellency Mr. Mohamed Sa'eed Al-Sahaf, Minister of State for Foreign Affairs, and senior officials of the relevant government departments and of local authorities. Joint working groups were established with the various United Nations specialist members of the mission. These held their first meetings that same evening to establish work programmes. Field work was undertaken from 11 to 16 March at various locations in and around Baghdad. A longer field trip was made by a group from the mission, led by myself, to Mosul, 400 kilometres north-west of Baghdad, and I myself also inspected numerous locations in Greater Baghdad. I and members of the mission held meetings with representatives of foreign diplomatic missions at Baghdad and with senior representatives of ICRC. Members of the mission also met with representatives of several non-governmental organizations (NGOs) who had made their way to Iraq to see the situation for themselves. I held final meetings in respect of the specialist teams' work with the Foreign Minister, His Excellency Mr. Tariq Aziz, and with the Minister of State and the participating senior officials, on the evening of 16 March.

6. The Iraqi authorities were fully cooperative in regard to the activities of the five specialist working groups. These dealt with: food and agriculture; water, sanitation and health; transportation and communications; energy; and refugees and other vulnerable groups.

Members were able to inspect all locations and facilities that they had requested to see in the Baghdad area and in several other governorates, and could also engage in independent field research in wholesale and retail markets and undertake household surveys. However, the Government was unable to accede to my request that we visit Souera, Moussayeb, Basrah, Nasiriyah and Kirkuk. In respect of some, the problems were said to be logistical; in regard to others, concern for security was conveyed. I expressed regret at our inability to cover the whole country, because it was important that the United Nations should be able to assess the humanitarian needs of the entire population of Iraq in all regions. The authorities also expressed their regret on this subject, and we agreed that locally based United Nations staff would travel to these areas as soon as conditions permitted. It has, however, been possible to infer from information available from various other sources that needs are unlikely to vary greatly from what we ourselves observed, but it is reported that conditions may be substantially worse in certain locations.

II. *Summary of findings and recommendations in regard to Iraq*

7. A summary of the mission's findings and conclusions is set out below. It is based upon a number of internal working papers, technical annexes, visits to sites and oral reports by mission specialists.

A. *General remarks*

8. I and the members of my mission were fully conversant with media reports regarding the situation in Iraq and, of course, with the recent WHO/UNICEF report on water, sanitary and health conditions in the Greater Baghdad area. It should, however, be said at once that nothing that we had seen or read had quite prepared us for the particular form of devastation which has now befallen the country. The recent conflict has wrought near-apocalyptic results upon the economic infrastructure of what had been, until January 1991, a rather highly urbanized and mechanized society. Now, most means of modern life support have been destroyed or rendered tenuous. Iraq has, for some time to come, been relegated to a pre-industrial age, but with all the disabilities of post-industrial dependency on an intensive use of energy and technology.

9. My mandate was limited to assessing the need for urgent humanitarian assistance. It did not extend to the huge task of assessing the requirements for reconstructing Iraq's destroyed infrastructure, much less, to developmental matters. Accordingly, my report to you, in its several technical sections, seeks with as much exactitude as possible to convey the extent of needs in the

primary areas of humanitarian concern: for safe water and sanitation, basic health and medical support; for food; for shelter; and for the logistical means to make such support actually available. Underlying each analysis is the inexorable reality that, as a result of war, virtually all previously viable sources of fuel and power (apart from a limited number of mobile generators) and modern means of communication are now, essentially, defunct. The far-reaching implications of this energy and communications' vacuum as regards urgent humanitarian support are of crucial significance for the nature and effectiveness of the international response.

10. These conditions, together with recent civil unrest in some parts of the country, mean that the authorities are as yet scarcely able even to measure the dimensions of the calamity, much less respond to its consequences, because they cannot obtain full and accurate data. Additionally, there is much less than the minimum fuel required to provide the energy needed for movement or transportation, irrigation or generators for power to pump water and sewage. For instance, emergency medical supplies can be moved to health centres only with extreme difficulty and, usually, major delay. Information regarding local needs is slow and sparse. Most employees are simply unable to come to work. Both the authorities and the trade unions estimate that approximately 90 per cent of industrial workers have been reduced to inactivity and will be deprived of income as of the end of March. Government departments have at present only marginal attendance. Prior to recent events, Iraq was importing about 70 per cent of its food needs. Now, owing to the fuel shortage, the inability to import and the virtual breakdown of the distribution system, the flow of food through the private sector has been reduced to a trickle, with costs accelerating upwards. Many food prices are already beyond the purchasing reach of most Iraqi families. Agricultural production is highly mechanized, and much land depends on pumped-water irrigation. Should the main harvest in June 1991 be seriously affected by a lack of energy to drive machines and pump water, then an already grave situation will be further aggravated. As shown below, prospects for the 1992 harvest could, for combined reasons, be in at least as much jeopardy. Having regard to the nature of Iraq's society and economy, the energy vacuum is an omnipresent obstacle to the success of even a short-term, massive effort to maintain life-sustaining conditions in each area of humanitarian need.

...

F. *Observations*

37. The account given above describes as accurately as the mission has been able, using all sources, including much independent observation, to ascertain the situation, which, within the time available and the travel limitations referred to earlier, was perceived to exist in regard to urgent humanitarian needs in Iraq during the week of 10-17 March. I, together with all my colleagues, am convinced that there needs to be a major mobilization and movement of resources to deal with aspects of this deep crisis in the fields of agriculture and food, water, sanitation and health. Yet the situation raises, in acute form, other questions. For it will be difficult, if not impossible, to remedy these immediate humanitarian needs without dealing with the underlying need for energy, on an equally urgent basis. The need for energy means, initially, emergency oil imports and the rapid patching up of a limited refining and electricity production capacity, with essential supplies from other countries. Otherwise, food that is imported cannot be preserved and distributed; water cannot be purified; sewage cannot be pumped away and cleansed; crops cannot be irrigated; medicaments cannot be conveyed where they are required; needs cannot even be effectively assessed. It is unmistakable that the Iraqi people may soon face a further imminent catastrophe, which could include epidemic and famine, if massive life-supporting needs are not rapidly met. The long summer, with its often 45 or even 50 degree temperatures (113-122 degrees Fahrenheit), is only weeks away. Time is short.

Document 32

Decision of the Security Council Sanctions Committee regarding humanitarian assistance to Iraq

S/22400, 22 March 1991

Note by the Secretary-General

The Secretary-General has received the attached letter from the President of the Security Council. In light of its final paragraph, he is circulating the letter herewith as a document of the Security Council for the attention of all States.

Annex
Letter dated 22 March 1991 from the President of the
Security Council addressed to the Secretary-General

I have the honour to inform you that the members of the Security Council, in consultations of the whole, held on 22 March 1991, took note of the following decision of the Security Council Committee established by resolution 661 (1990) concerning the situation between Iraq and Kuwait, adopted at its 36th meeting, on 22 March 1991, with regard to the determination of humanitarian needs in Iraq:

"1. The Security Council Committee established by resolution 661 (1990) concerning the situation between Iraq and Kuwait has carefully considered Under-Secretary-General Ahtisaari's report of 20 March 1991 on his recent visit to Iraq (S/22366), as well as the report of the ICRC of 19 March 1991 (S/AC.25/1991/COMM.102) summarizing the conclusions of its own delegation in Iraq.

"2. Under paragraph 5 of resolution 666 (1990), the Committee has the power to determine, after receiving all relevant reports and information, that circumstances have arisen in which there is an urgent humanitarian need to supply foodstuffs to Iraq in order to relieve human suffering; and in that event the Committee will report promptly to the Council its decision as to how such needs will be met.

"3. In the light of the new information available to it, the Committee has decided to make, with immediate effect, a general determination that humanitarian circumstances apply with respect to the entire civilian population of Iraq in all parts of Iraq's national territory. The Committee has also concluded that civilian and humanitarian imports to Iraq as identified in Mr. Ahtisaari's report are integrally related to the supply of foodstuffs and supplies intended strictly for medical purposes (which are exempt from sanctions under the provisions of resolution 661 (1990)) and that such imports should also be allowed with immediate effect.

"4. The Committee decides upon a simple notification procedure for foodstuffs supplied to Iraq and a no-objection procedure for those civilian and humanitarian imports (other than supplies intended strictly for medical purposes) described in the preceding paragraph.

"5. Subject to prior notification to the Committee of the flight and its contents, the Committee hereby gives general approval under paragraph 4 (b) of resolution 670 (1990) for all flights which carry only foodstuffs or supplies intended strictly for medical purposes. This procedure applies equally to the civilian and humanitarian imports referred to in paragraph 3 above, the supply of which is subject to the no-objection procedure laid down in paragraph 4.

"6. It notes with satisfaction that the Government of Iraq has assured Mr. Ahtisaari's mission that it would accept a system of monitoring of imports and their utilization. The Secretary-General is requested, in consultation with the Government of Iraq and the ICRC, to arrange for such a system of on the spot monitoring to proceed in conjunction with the despatch of United Nations personnel to Iraq to supervise the effective utilization, for the benefit of the civilian population in all areas, of all imports to be established under the responsibility of the United Nations."

I have the honour to request that you bring the above-mentioned decision to the attention of all States.

(*Signed*) Peter HOHENFELLNER
President of the Security Council

Document 33

Letter dated 27 March 1991 from the Secretary-General to the Secretary of State for External Affairs of Canada concerning the latter's visit to the Middle East

Not issued as a United Nations document

I should like to acknowledge receipt of your letter dated 15 March 1991 and to thank you for informing me of the details of your recent visit to the Middle East.

I greatly appreciate your raising with the Kuwaiti authorities the question of the treatment of the Palestinian population in Kuwait, for, as your are aware, I am concerned at reports that they might be at risk of mistreatment. Last week, Mr. Abdulrahim Farah, the head of the United Nations mission currently in Kuwait, conveyed my hope to the Prime Minister that his Government would do everything possible to prevent injustice against Palestinians. The Prime Minister gave his assurance that the rights of Palestinians living in Kuwait would be safeguarded. Subsequently, on 24 March I sent to Kuwait an official from UNRWA to have a close look at the situation of the Palestinians there and to report back to me. I shall share with you the details of his report.

It was particularly interesting to read the details of your discussions with King Hussein, the Crown Prince and Foreign Minister Masri of Jordan. I firmly believe that the time is ripe for a concerted effort to resolve the long-standing Arab-Israeli conflict and I am confident that Ambassador Edouard Brunner, whom I appointed last Friday as Special Representative to the Middle East, will ably demonstrate the continuing commitment of the United Nations to finding a peaceful solution to this difficult problem.

In informal consultations of the Security Council on 8 February, I expressed my concern about the public perception of this Organization and stressed how important it was for the United Nations to retain the trust of all the peoples of the world whom it is meant to serve.

This Organization did indeed pass through a testing moment, but, through active participation in the efforts at reconstruction and rehabilitation in the Persian Gulf region, I feel that it can justify the high expectations which the international community has for the United Nations. The two missions I have recently dispatched to the region are a first step towards dealing with the immediate consequences of the hostilities.

I agree that much thought should be given to enhancing long-term defences against aggression and establishing lasting peace and security in the region, and I am grateful to you for emphasising to your interlocutors the important role the United Nations can play in this. Your actions are further testimony to the long tradition of cooperation and support, particularly in the realm of peace-keeping and peace-making, which this Organization has enjoyed in its contacts with your country.

Yours sincerely,

(*Signed*) Javier PÉREZ DE CUÉLLAR

Document 34

Report on humanitarian needs in Kuwait in the immediate post-crisis environment by a mission to the area led by the Under-Secretary-General for Administration and Management, 23-27 March 1991 (extract)

S/22409, 28 March 1991

Letter dated 28 March 1991 from the Secretary-General addressed to the President of the Security Council

Further to my letter to you dated 20 March 1991 (S/22366), I have the honour to inform you that the mission led by Under-Secretary-General Martti Ahtisaari to assess the humanitarian needs arising in the immediate post-crisis environment in Iraq and Kuwait visited Kuwait from 23 to 27 March 1991.

The report of the mission is submitted herewith for the consideration of the members of the Security Council.

(*Signed*) Javier PÉREZ DE CUÉLLAR

Report to the Secretary-General on humanitarian needs in Kuwait in the immediate post-crisis environment by a mission to the area led by Mr. Martti Ahtisaari, Under-Secretary-General for Administration and Management, dated 28 March 1991

Introduction

1. You asked me to travel, as a matter of urgency, to Kuwait and Iraq to assess humanitarian needs there in the immediate post-crisis environment, and to bring with me a team comprising representatives of the appropriate United Nations agencies and programmes. Your decision was announced in a press statement on 1 March 1991.

2. On 3 March 1991, the President of the Security Council made a statement on behalf of the Council, in which it welcomed your announcement and invited you to keep it informed in the shortest possible time of the progress of this mission, in respect of which it pledged to take immediate action (S/22322).

3. I submitted a report to you on the first part of my mission, that relating to Iraq, on 20 March 1991 and, in a letter of that date, you transmitted it to the President of the Security Council (S/22366). As noted in your letter, the Mission was to commence its visit to Kuwait on 22 March 1991, and you stated that you would convey to the Council the report on that visit as soon as possible.

4. After consultations at Headquarters, I myself departed for the mission area on 23 March, arriving in Kuwait on 25 March. I was received there by the Minister of Planning of the Kuwaiti Government, Mr. Suleiman Abdul-Razaq Al-Mutawa, and by members of the mission, who had remained in Bahrain after my departure for Headquarters on 19 March and had preceded me to Kuwait on 23 March.

5. In Kuwait, the Mission comprised representatives of the Secretariat, the United Nations Development Programme (UNDP), the Office of the United Nations Disaster Relief Coordinator (UNDRO), the Office of the United Nations High Commissioner for Refugees (UNHCR), the World Food Programme (WFP) and the Food and Agriculture Organization of the United Nations (FAO). It received substantial assistance from Mr. Abdulrahim Abby Farah and members of his mission who were at the time in Kuwait looking into the subject of damages sustained by Kuwait during events subsequent to 2 August 1990 and, in particular, from the technical knowledge and experience of members of Mr. Farah's mission from the United Nations Environment Programme (UNEP). It was also materially assisted by representatives of the United Nations Children's Fund (UNICEF) office in the Arab Gulf States, and by a World Health Organization (WHO) mission that was also in the country at that time. The mission completed its work in Kuwait on 27 March and departed on that date. I returned to New York today, 28 March 1991.

I. Modus operandi *in Kuwait*

6. In close consultation with myself, members of the mission who had remained in Bahrain while I was undertaking consultations in New York began their work immediately upon arrival in Kuwait on 23 March 1991. Teams began to meet with Kuwaiti officials in the fields of food, agriculture, water, sanitation, health, transportation, communications, energy and environmental matters, and to visit various sites and locations throughout Kuwait. Upon my arrival on 25 March 1991 I was briefed

by senior members of the mission and immediately met for a working session with Mr. Suleiman Abdul-Razaq Al-Mutawa, Minister of Planning in the Government of Kuwait. With him, I was then briefed at Camp Freedom by Brigadier-General Mooney, United States Army, and members of the Kuwaiti Joint Task Force. I met that evening with Mr. Sheikh Nasser As-Sabah, Minister of State in the Kuwaiti Foreign Ministry, and other Ministers. On 26 March I was received by His Highness, Sheikh Saad Al-Abdullah As-Salim As-Sabah, Crown Prince and Prime Minister of Kuwait. I also met with Mr. Abdul-Wahab Al-Fozan, Minister of Health, and with representatives of the diplomatic community. I toured the city of Kuwait and by helicopter, many parts of the country and saw conditions there. Members of the mission accompanied me on these visits and inspections and continued and completed their technical work in the country. With the excellent cooperation of Mr. Farah and his team I and my mission had access to relevant aspects of its technical findings, upon which certain parts of this report also draw. I was briefed by Dr. Daniel Tarantola of a WHO mission that had been invited to the country by the Government of Kuwait for an assessment of health conditions and needs.

7. The Kuwaiti authorities afforded the mission their fullest cooperation.

II. *Summary of findings and recommendations in regard to Kuwait*

8. A summary of the mission's findings and conclusions is set out below. It is based upon a number of internal working papers, technical annexes, visits to sites and oral reports by members of the mission and by other United Nations specialists present at the time in Kuwait.

A. *General remarks*

9. Kuwait is scarred by the ravages of illegal occupation and, subsidiarily, of war. At least two thirds of the population present on 2 August 1990 are now scattered throughout the world. Those who remained have fresh memory of a brutal occupation and the sacking and pillaging of their homes, their resources and their environment. Many vividly recount inhuman or degrading treatment undergone by themselves or family members. I and my mission saw for ourselves prolific evidence of arson, looting, malicious destruction of homes, businesses, markets, museums, libraries and all that a nation cherishes. Kuwait's coast is disfigured by broken buildings and rolls of barbed wire; its beaches made lethal by hundreds of thousands of mines. Above it hangs a thick cloud of oily dark smoke that, on some days, brings a chilly twilight at noon, as well as still-uncharted perils to health. No one knows exactly how many of its oil wells are on fire; but at least half, perhaps 600 to 700, are

belching flames and smoke. From the air, the horizon sometimes comprises only black clouds and pillars of fire, torched in a final deliberate onslaught by retreating troops. The environmental havoc still cannot be authoritatively assessed, but its consequences are already felt by neighbouring countries, and may affect yet others still more distant. Rivers, ponds and even lakes of spilling oil lie on the sand and edge towards the wadis, the roads and the sea. Power stations, oil refineries, communications facilities and water-desalination plants have been destroyed by war or vandalized so that they are irreparable. Harbours are blocked, ships sunk, cranes toppled. Life-preserving medical equipment, even ambulances, have been removed; mainframe computers have been ripped out of government offices and carried off.

10. This scene of devastation, some being calculated, much wanton, was, I learned, even worse four weeks ago, when Kuwaitis began to return to their liberated country. For much has already been done, as the following paragraphs will show, to put Kuwait back on the road to reconstruction. Food supplies are being brought in and distributed, although both officials and observers say that such distribution has at times been somewhat uneven. Some water and power have been restored. Petrol is being made available, free of charge, even for private vehicles. Telephone communications have been partly re-established, and international traffic will soon follow. An assessment of damages to homes, businesses and economic facilities and resources is under way, and much contracting for reconstruction has already been completed. Means of internal and external transportation are starting to function, in a limited fashion, even though there may still be limited air- and seaport capability and many vehicles were stolen or destroyed. Teams of specialists are beginning to assess and remedy the oilfield disasters. A Kuwaiti Government is in place (at this time, on a caretaker basis) and, despite vast logistical and all other species of practical problems, is drawing up plans for reconstruction. It is working closely with a joint Kuwaiti task force, comprising elements of the armed forces allied with Kuwait in the recent conflict, which was established in December 1990 to plan for the time when liberation should have taken place. The allied element of the Joint Task Force comprises civil affairs elements of the United States, United Kingdom, French, Canadian and Saudi Arabian armed forces, with medical, communications, police, transportation, intelligence, aviation, finance, engineering and sanitation specialists and teams from those Governments. At a briefing on 25 March 1991 General Mooney of the United States Army and some of his senior staff described the work of the Joint Task Force in regard to water, food and medical supplies, sanitation, power, telecommunications and transportation, as well

as in regard to damage assessment and surveys during the period from December 1990 to date. He said that contracts worth more than US$550 million had already been signed for work in these various areas. The Joint Task Force said that it believed that the country had now largely overcome the emergency phase and that it anticipated that power and communications would be effectively restored by mid-April in Kuwait City and that most services would be functioning throughout the country in between three and six months. The oil industry would take the longest to restore. The Minister of Planning called the burning of the oil wells "the crime of all centuries", because of its multifarious short- and long-term negative consequences—health, environmental, economic—for Kuwait and other countries as well. General Mooney said that the amount of unexploded mines and other ordnance was colossal. There was, he added, a good military programme for clearance, but he said that he had never seen so much of that hazard before. Many members of the mission saw unexploded weaponry during their work in Kuwait. The Task Force said that clearance of the quantities left behind exceeded the capabilities of the allied forces.

11. Kuwaiti government ministers told me that they were taking the opportunity to review questions of population composition and the future of the workforce. Prior to 2 August 1990 the population was about 2.3 million, of whom about 700,000 were Kuwaiti nationals (about 30 per cent). Most of the population had left the country during the period of occupation and conflict. At the time of my mission to Kuwait, estimates of the remaining population varied between 600,000 and 700,000, of whom perhaps one third were Kuwaitis. The authorities have recommended that their exiled countrymen not return to Kuwait for three months to allow essential services to be rehabilitated, and spoke of the possibility that the future permanent population should be limited, with others being in the country on a more or less short-term basis. They planned that return from exile should keep pace with the gradual resumption of economic activity, the re-establishment of basic social amenities and the reduction of environmental health hazards. While the mission was in Kuwait this policy had not yet been finalized.

12. As during the previous mission to Iraq, we focused our initial attention upon the basic areas of humanitarian concern: the need for shelter, food supplies, clean water, sanitation and adequate health support, as well as on the logistical capability to make these effective for the people as a whole. Particular local conditions may create additional hazards. The account which follows regarding the situation in these various areas of basic concern is affected in one form or another by the general factors that I have sketched above. Kuwait, with the assistance of the Governments cooperating with it in

the Joint Task Force, is steadily assessing its needs and seeking to overcome them within the parameters which it is establishing. My recommendations are formulated in the spirit of cooperation with which my mission was received and welcomed, and in the context of the assistance of which the international community is, I believe, capable.

...

G. Observations

41. There can be no doubt that a deliberate attempt was made to extinguish Kuwait, its national identity, the pride of its people in their history and achievements. The manner of destruction, with its coordinated vandalism and massive looting, leaves an indelible image. It was a privilege for me and the members of my team to witness the rebirth of a nation, however painful the circumstances. Already, with the cooperation of its friends and allies, the country has made remarkable progress in dealing with immediate humanitarian needs. It is now moving swiftly towards meeting the major tasks of reconstruction. Therefore, little in the way of traditional humanitarian aid is immediately required of the international community at large. Certain vital assistance, as described above, is, however, urgently necessary so that the suffering of the population of Kuwait is not further prolonged, and so that it and its neighbours can again live in good health and peace.

42. Finally, I should like to place on record my appreciation to the executive heads of UNDP, UNICEF, UNHCR, UNDRO, UNEP, WFP, FAO and WHO for the cooperation which permitted a mission of so wide a range of specializations and experience to work with me in Iraq and Kuwait. I believe it most important that the United Nations family of organizations establish ever-closer coordination, and matters of emergency humanitarian assistance provide an excellent area in which this can be developed further. I was especially fortunate in the members assigned to this mission. Their objectivity, expertise and professionalism, often under trying circumstances, and the excellent spirit of cooperation, reminded me once again of the great reservoir of experience and dedication available to the United Nations.

Document 35

Security Council resolution establishing detailed measures for a cease-fire, including deployment of a United Nations observer unit; arrangements for demarcating the Iraq-Kuwait border; the removal or destruction of Iraqi weapons of mass destruction and measures to prevent their reconstitution, under the supervision of a Special Commission and the Director General of the IAEA; and creation of a compensation fund to cover direct loss and damage resulting from Iraq's invasion of Kuwait

S/RES/687 (1991), 3 April 1991

The Security Council,

Recalling its resolutions 660 (1990) of 2 August 1990, 661 (1990) of 6 August 1990, 662 (1990) of 9 August 1990, 664 (1990) of 18 August 1990, 665 (1990) of 25 August 1990, 666 (1990) of 13 September 1990, 667 (1990) of 16 September 1990, 669 (1990) of 24 September 1990, 670 (1990) of 25 September 1990, 674 (1990) of 29 October 1990, 677 (1990) of 28 November 1990, 678 (1990) of 29 November 1990 and 686 (1991) of 2 March 1991,

Welcoming the restoration to Kuwait of its sovereignty, independence and territorial integrity and the return of its legitimate Government,

Affirming the commitment of all Member States to the sovereignty, territorial integrity and political independence of Kuwait and Iraq, and noting the intention expressed by the Member States cooperating with Kuwait under paragraph 2 of resolution 678 (1990) to bring their military presence in Iraq to an end as soon as possible consistent with paragraph 8 of resolution 686 (1991),

Reaffirming the need to be assured of Iraq's peaceful intentions in the light of its unlawful invasion and occupation of Kuwait,

Taking note of the letter dated 27 February 1991 from the Deputy Prime Minister and Minister for Foreign Affairs of Iraq addressed to the President of the Security Council 1/ and of his letters of the same date addressed to the

1/ *Official Records of the Security Council, Forty-sixth Year, Supplement for January, February and March 1991*, document S/22273.

President of the Council and to the Secretary-General, 2/ and those letters dated 3 March 3/ and 5 March 4/ he addressed to them, pursuant to resolution 686 (1991),

Noting that Iraq and Kuwait, as independent sovereign States, signed at Baghdad on 4 October 1963 "Agreed Minutes between the State of Kuwait and the Republic of Iraq regarding the restoration of friendly relations, recognition and related matters", 5/ thereby formally recognizing the boundary between Iraq and Kuwait and the allocation of islands, which Agreed Minutes were registered with the United Nations in accordance with Article 102 of the Charter of the United Nations and in which Iraq recognized the independence and complete sovereignty of the State of Kuwait with its boundaries as specified in the letter of the Prime Minister of Iraq dated 21 July 1932 and as accepted by the ruler of Kuwait in his letter dated 10 August 1932,

Conscious of the need for demarcation of the said boundary,

Conscious also of the statements by Iraq threatening to use weapons in violation of its obligations under the Protocol for the Prohibition of the Use in War of Asphyxiating, Poisonous or Other Gases, and of Bacteriological Methods of Warfare, signed at Geneva on 17 June 1925, 6/ and of its prior use of chemical weapons, and affirming that grave consequences would follow any further use by Iraq of such weapons,

Recalling that Iraq has subscribed to the Final Declaration adopted by all States participating in the Conference of States Parties to the 1925 Geneva Protocol and Other Interested States, held in Paris from 7 to 11 January 1989, 7/ establishing the objective of universal elimination of chemical and biological weapons,

Recalling also that Iraq has signed the Convention on the Prohibition of the Development, Production and Stockpiling of Bacteriological (Biological) and Toxin Weapons and on Their Destruction, of 10 April 1972, 8/

Noting the importance of Iraq ratifying the Convention,

Noting also the importance of all States adhering to the Convention and encouraging its forthcoming review conference to reinforce the authority, efficiency and universal scope of the Convention,

Stressing the importance of an early conclusion by the Conference on Disarmament of its work on a convention on the universal prohibition of chemical weapons and of universal adherence thereto,

Aware of the use by Iraq of ballistic missiles in unprovoked attacks and therefore of the need to take specific measures in regard to such missiles located in Iraq,

Concerned by the reports in the hands of Member States that Iraq has attempted to acquire materials for a nuclear-weapons programme contrary to its obligations under the Treaty on the Non-Proliferation of Nuclear Weapons of 1 July 1968, 9/

Recalling the objective of the establishment of a nuclear-weapon-free zone in the region of the Middle East,

Conscious of the threat that all weapons of mass destruction pose to peace and security in the area and of the need to work towards the establishment in the Middle East of a zone free of such weapons,

Conscious also of the objective of achieving balanced and comprehensive control of armaments in the region,

Conscious further of the importance of achieving the objectives noted above using all available means, including a dialogue among the States of the region,

Noting that resolution 686 (1991) marked the lifting of the measures imposed by resolution 661 (1990) in so far as they applied to Kuwait,

Noting also that despite the progress being made in fulfilling the obligations of resolution 686 (1991), many Kuwaiti and third-State nationals are still not accounted for and property remains unreturned,

Recalling the International Convention against the Taking of Hostages, 10/ opened for signature in New York on 18 December 1979, which categorizes all acts of taking hostages as manifestations of international terrorism,

Deploring threats made by Iraq during the recent conflict to make use of terrorism against targets outside Iraq and the taking of hostages by Iraq,

Taking note with grave concern of the reports transmitted by the Secretary-General on 20 March 11/ and 28 March 1991, 12/ and conscious of the necessity to meet urgently the humanitarian needs in Kuwait and Iraq,

Bearing in mind its objective of restoring international peace and security in the area as set out in its recent resolutions,

Conscious of the need to take the following measures acting under Chapter VII of the Charter,

1. *Affirms* all thirteen resolutions noted above, except as expressly changed below to achieve the goals of the present resolution, including a formal cease-fire;

2/ Ibid., documents S/22275 and S/22276.
3/ Ibid., documents S/22320 and S/22321.
4/ Ibid., document S/22330.
5/ United Nations, *Treaty Series*, vol. 485, No. 7063.
6/ League of Nations, *Treaty Series*, vol. XCIV (1929), No. 2138.
7/ A/44/88, annex.
8/ General Assembly resolution 2826 (XXVI), annex.
9/ United Nations, *Treaty Series*, vol. 729, No. 10485.
10/ General Assembly resolution 34/146, annex.
11/ *Official Records of the Security Council, Forty-sixth Year, Supplement for April, May and June 1991*, document S/22366, annex.
12/ *Official Records of the Security Council, Forty-sixth Year, Supplement for January, February and March 1991*, document S/22409, annex.

A

2. *Demands* that Iraq and Kuwait respect the inviolability of the international boundary and the allocation of islands set out in the "Agreed Minutes between the State of Kuwait and the Republic of Iraq regarding the restoration of friendly relations, recognition and related matters", 5/ signed by them in the exercise of their sovereignty at Baghdad on 4 October 1963 and registered with the United Nations;

3. *Calls upon* the Secretary-General to lend his assistance to make arrangements with Iraq and Kuwait to demarcate the boundary between Iraq and Kuwait, drawing on appropriate material including the maps transmitted with the letter dated 28 March 1991 addressed to him by the Permanent Representative of the United Kingdom of Great Britain and Northern Ireland to the United Nations, 13/ and to report back to the Council within one month;

4. *Decides* to guarantee the inviolability of the above-mentioned international boundary and to take, as appropriate, all necessary measures to that end in accordance with the Charter of the United Nations;

B

5. *Requests* the Secretary-General, after consulting with Iraq and Kuwait, to submit within three days to the Council for its approval a plan for the immediate deployment of a United Nations observer unit to monitor the Khawr 'Abd Allah and a demilitarized zone, which is hereby established, extending ten kilometres into Iraq and five kilometres into Kuwait from the boundary referred to in the "Agreed Minutes between the State of Kuwait and the Republic of Iraq regarding the restoration of friendly relations, recognition and related matters"; to deter violations of the boundary through its presence in and surveillance of the demilitarized zone and to observe any hostile or potentially hostile action mounted from the territory of one State against the other; and also requests the Secretary-General to report regularly to the Council on the operations of the unit and to do so immediately if there are serious violations of the zone or potential threats to peace;

6. *Notes* that as soon as the Secretary-General notifies the Council of the completion of the deployment of the United Nations observer unit, the conditions will be established for the Member States cooperating with Kuwait in accordance with resolution 678 (1990) to bring their military presence in Iraq to an end consistent with resolution 686 (1991);

C

7. *Invites* Iraq to reaffirm unconditionally its obligations under the Protocol for the Prohibition of the Use in War of Asphyxiating, Poisonous or Other Gases, and of Bacteriological Methods of Warfare, signed at Geneva on 17 June 1925, 6/ and to ratify the Convention on the Prohibition of the Development, Production and Stockpiling of Bacteriological (Biological) and Toxin Weapons and on Their Destruction, of 10 April 1972; 8/

8. *Decides* that Iraq shall unconditionally accept the destruction, removal, or rendering harmless, under international supervision, of:

(*a*) All chemical and biological weapons and all stocks of agents and all related subsystems and components and all research, development, support and manufacturing facilities related thereto;

(*b*) All ballistic missiles with a range greater than one hundred and fifty kilometres, and related major parts and repair and production facilities;

9. *Decides also*, for the implementation of paragraph 8, the following:

(*a*) Iraq shall submit to the Secretary-General, within fifteen days of the adoption of the present resolution, a declaration on the locations, amounts and types of all items specified in paragraph 8 and agree to urgent, on-site inspection as specified below;

(*b*) The Secretary-General, in consultation with the appropriate Governments and, where appropriate, with the Director-General of the World Health Organization, within forty-five days of the adoption of the present resolution shall develop and submit to the Council for approval a plan calling for the completion of the following acts within forty-five days of such approval:

(i) The forming of a special commission which shall carry out immediate on-site inspection of Iraq's biological, chemical and missile capabilities, based on Iraq's declarations and the designation of any additional locations by the special commission itself;

(ii) The yielding by Iraq of possession to the Special Commission for destruction, removal or rendering harmless, taking into account the requirements of public safety, of all items specified under paragraph 8 (*a*), including items at the additional locations designated by the Special Commission under paragraph (i) and the destruction by Iraq, under the supervision of the Special Commission,

13/ Ibid., document S/22412.

of all its missile capabilities, including launchers, as specified under paragraph 8 (*b*);

(iii) The provision by the Special Commission to the Director General of the International Atomic Energy Agency of the assistance and cooperation required in paragraphs 12 and 13;

10. *Decides further* that Iraq shall unconditionally undertake not to use, develop, construct or acquire any of the items specified in paragraphs 8 and 9, and requests the Secretary-General, in consultation with the Special Commission, to develop a plan for the future ongoing monitoring and verification of Iraq's compliance with the present paragraph, to be submitted to the Council for approval within one hundred and twenty days of the passage of the present resolution;

11. *Invites* Iraq to reaffirm unconditionally its obligations under the Treaty on the Non-Proliferation of Nuclear Weapons, of 1 July 1968; 9/

12. *Decides* that Iraq shall unconditionally agree not to acquire or develop nuclear weapons or nuclear-weapon-usable material or any subsystems or components or any research, development, support or manufacturing facilities related to the above; to submit to the Secretary-General and the Director General of the International Atomic Energy Agency within fifteen days of the adoption of the present resolution a declaration of the locations, amounts and types of all items specified above; to place all of its nuclear-weapon-usable materials under the exclusive control, for custody and removal, of the Agency, with the assistance and cooperation of the Special Commission as provided for in the plan of the Secretary-General discussed in paragraph 9 (*b*); to accept, in accordance with the arrangements provided for in paragraph 13, urgent on-site inspection and the destruction, removal or rendering harmless as appropriate of all items specified above; and to accept the plan discussed in paragraph 13 for the future ongoing monitoring and verification of its compliance with these undertakings;

13. *Requests* the Director General of the International Atomic Energy Agency, through the Secretary-General and with the assistance and cooperation of the Special Commission as provided for in the plan of the Secretary-General referred to in paragraph 9 (*b*), to carry out immediate on-site inspection of Iraq's nuclear capabilities based on Iraq's declarations and the designation of any additional locations by the Special Commission; to develop a plan for submission to the Council within forty-five days calling for the destruction, removal or rendering harmless as appropriate of all items listed in paragraph 12; to carry out the plan within forty-five days following approval by the Council and to develop a plan, taking into account the rights and obligations of Iraq under the Treaty on the Non-Proliferation of Nuclear Weapons, for the future ongoing monitoring and verification of Iraq's compliance with paragraph 12, including an inventory of all nuclear material in Iraq subject to the Agency's verification and inspections to confirm that Agency safeguards cover all relevant nuclear activities in Iraq, to be submitted to the Council for approval within one hundred and twenty days of the adoption of the present resolution;

14. *Notes* that the actions to be taken by Iraq in paragraphs 8 to 13 represent steps towards the goal of establishing in the Middle East a zone free from weapons of mass destruction and all missiles for their delivery and the objective of a global ban on chemical weapons;

D

15. *Requests* the Secretary-General to report to the Council on the steps taken to facilitate the return of all Kuwaiti property seized by Iraq, including a list of any property that Kuwait claims has not been returned or which has not been returned intact;

E

16. *Reaffirms* that Iraq, without prejudice to its debts and obligations arising prior to 2 August 1990, which will be addressed through the normal mechanisms, is liable under international law for any direct loss, damage—including environmental damage and the depletion of natural resources—or injury to foreign Governments, nationals and corporations as a result of its unlawful invasion and occupation of Kuwait;

17. *Decides* that all Iraqi statements made since 2 August 1990 repudiating its foreign debt are null and void, and demands that Iraq adhere scrupulously to all of its obligations concerning servicing and repayment of its foreign debt;

18. *Decides also* to create a fund to pay compensation for claims that fall within paragraph 16 and to establish a commission that will administer the fund;

19. *Directs* the Secretary-General to develop and present to the Council for decision, no later than thirty days following the adoption of the present resolution, recommendations for the Fund to be established in accordance with paragraph 18 and for a programme to implement the decisions in paragraphs 16 to 18, including the following: administration of the Fund; mechanisms for determining the appropriate level of Iraq's contribution to the Fund, based on a percentage of the value of its exports of petroleum and petroleum products, not to exceed a figure to be suggested to the Council by the Secretary-General, taking into account the requirements of the people of Iraq, Iraq's payment capacity as assessed in conjunction with the international financial institutions taking into consideration external debt service, and

the needs of the Iraqi economy; arrangements for ensuring that payments are made to the Fund; the process by which funds will be allocated and claims paid; appropriate procedures for evaluating losses, listing claims and verifying their validity, and resolving disputed claims in respect of Iraq's liability as specified in paragraph 16; and the composition of the Commission designated above;

F

20. *Decides*, effective immediately, that the prohibitions against the sale or supply to Iraq of commodities or products other than medicine and health supplies, and prohibitions against financial transactions related thereto contained in resolution 661 (1990), shall not apply to foodstuffs notified to the Security Council Committee established by resolution 661 (1990) concerning the situation between Iraq and Kuwait or, with the approval of that Committee, under the simplified and accelerated "no-objection" procedure, to materials and supplies for essential civilian needs as identified in the report to the Secretary-General dated 20 March 1991, 11/ and in any further findings of humanitarian need by the Committee;

21. *Decides* to review the provisions of paragraph 20 every sixty days in the light of the policies and practices of the Government of Iraq, including the implementation of all relevant resolutions of the Council, for the purpose of determining whether to reduce or lift the prohibitions referred to therein;

22. *Decides also* that upon the approval by the Council of the programme called for in paragraph 19 and upon Council agreement that Iraq has completed all actions contemplated in paragraphs 8 to 13, the prohibitions against the import of commodities and products originating in Iraq and the prohibitions against financial transactions related thereto contained in resolution 661 (1990) shall have no further force or effect;

23. *Decides further* that, pending action by the Council under paragraph 22, the Security Council Committee established by resolution 661 (1990) concerning the situation between Iraq and Kuwait shall be empowered to approve, when required to assure adequate financial resources on the part of Iraq to carry out the activities under paragraph 20, exceptions to the prohibition against the import of commodities and products originating in Iraq;

24. *Decides* that, in accordance with resolution 661 (1990) and subsequent related resolutions and until it takes a further decision, all States shall continue to prevent the sale or supply to Iraq, or the promotion or facilitation of such sale or supply, by their nationals or from their territories or using their flag vessels or aircraft, of:

(a) Arms and related *matériel* of all types, specifically including the sale or transfer through other means of all forms of conventional military equipment, including for paramilitary forces, and spare parts and components and their means of production for such equipment;

(b) Items specified and defined in paragraphs 8 and 12 not otherwise covered above;

(c) Technology under licensing or other transfer arrangements used in the production, utilization or stockpiling of items specified in paragraphs (a) and (b);

(d) Personnel or materials for training or technical support services relating to the design, development, manufacture, use, maintenance or support of items specified in paragraphs (a) and (b);

25. *Calls upon* all States and international organizations to act strictly in accordance with paragraph 24, notwithstanding the existence of any contracts, agreements, licences or any other arrangements;

26. *Requests* the Secretary-General, in consultation with appropriate Governments, to develop within sixty days, for the approval of the Council, guidelines to facilitate full international implementation of paragraphs 24, 25 and 27, and to make them available to all States and to establish a procedure for updating these guidelines periodically;

27. *Calls upon* all States to maintain such national controls and procedures and to take such other actions consistent with the guidelines to be established by the Council under paragraph 26 as may be necessary to ensure compliance with the terms of paragraph 24, and calls upon international organizations to take all appropriate steps to assist in ensuring such full compliance;

28. *Agrees* to review its decisions in paragraphs 22 to 25, except for the items specified and defined in paragraphs 8 and 12, on a regular basis and in any case one hundred and twenty days following the adoption of the present resolution, taking into account Iraq's compliance with the resolution and general progress towards the control of armaments in the region;

29. *Decides* that all States, including Iraq, shall take the necessary measures to ensure that no claim shall lie at the instance of the Government of Iraq, or of any person or body in Iraq, or of any person claiming through or for the benefit of any such person or body, in connection with any contract or other transaction where its performance was affected by reason of the measures taken by the Council in resolution 661 (1990) and related resolutions;

G

30. *Decides* that, in furtherance of its commitment to facilitate the repatriation of all Kuwaiti and third-State nationals, Iraq shall extend all necessary cooperation to the International Committee of the Red Cross by providing lists of such persons, facilitating the access of the International Committee to all such persons wherever

located or detained and facilitating the search by the International Committee for those Kuwaiti and third-State nationals still unaccounted for;

31. *Invites* the International Committee of the Red Cross to keep the Secretary-General apprised, as appropriate, of all activities undertaken in connection with facilitating the repatriation or return of all Kuwaiti and third-State nationals or their remains present in Iraq on or after 2 August 1990;

H

32. *Requires* Iraq to inform the Council that it will not commit or support any act of international terrorism or allow any organization directed towards commission of such acts to operate within its territory and to condemn unequivocally and renounce all acts, methods and practices of terrorism;

I

33. *Declares* that, upon official notification by Iraq to the Secretary-General and to the Security Council of its acceptance of the above provisions, a formal cease-fire is effective between Iraq and Kuwait and the Member States cooperating with Kuwait in accordance with resolution 678 (1990);

34. *Decides* to remain seized of the matter and to take such further steps as may be required for the implementation of the present resolution and to secure peace and security in the region.

Document 36

Letter dated 4 April 1991 from the Deputy Prime Minister and Minister for Foreign Affairs of Kuwait to the Secretary-General accepting the provisions of Security Council resolution 687 (1991)

S/22457, 8 April 1991

Letter dated 4 April 1991 from the Permanent Representative of Kuwait to the United Nations addressed to the Secretary-General

I enclose the text of a letter from the Deputy Prime Minister and Minister for Foreign Affairs of Kuwait, Sheikh Sabah Al-Ahmad Al-Jaber Al Sabah, concerning Kuwait's acceptance of resolution 687 (1991), adopted by the Security Council on 3 April 1991.

I should be grateful if you would have the text of this letter circulated as a document of the Security Council.

(*Signed*) Mohammad A. ABULHASAN
Permanent Representative

Annex
Letter dated 4 April 1991 from the Deputy Prime Minister and Minister for Foreign Affairs of Kuwait addressed to the Secretary-General
I have the honour to refer to resolution 687 (1991) adopted by the Security Council on 3 April 1991, a copy of which you transmitted to me by your note dated 3 April 1991. We wish to inform you that we welcome the adoption of this resolution, which aims to eliminate the causes and effects of the occupation, and that we undertake, for our part, scrupulously to comply with all its provisions and to cooperate with you with a view to ensuring its implementation.

It is our hope that, in accordance with paragraph 33 of the resolution, Iraq will officially and unambiguously accept its provisions and make a sincere attempt to put them into practice.

(*Signed*) Sheikh Sabah Al-Ahmad Al-Jaber AL SABAH
Deputy Prime Minister
and Minister for Foreign Affairs

Document 37

Security Council resolution demanding that Iraq end repression of the civilian population in many parts of Iraq and insisting that it allow immediate access by international humanitarian organizations to all those in need of assistance

S/RES/688 (1991), 5 April 1991

The Security Council,

Mindful of its duties and its responsibilities under the Charter of the united Nations for the maintenance of international peace and security,

Recalling the provisions of Article 2, paragraph 7, of the Charter,

Gravely concerned by the repression of the Iraqi civilian population in many parts of Iraq, including most recently in Kurdish-populated areas, which led to a massive flow of refugees towards and across international frontiers and to cross-border incursions which threaten international peace and security in the region,

Deeply disturbed by the magnitude of the human suffering involved,

Taking note of the letters dated 2 and 4 April 1991, respectively, from the representatives of Turkey and France to the United Nations addressed to the President of the Security Council, 1/

Taking note also of the letters dated 3 and 4 April 1991 from the Permanent Representative of the Islamic Republic of Iran to the United Nations addressed to the Secretary-General, 2/

Reaffirming the commitment of all Member States to respect the sovereignty, territorial integrity and political independence of Iraq and of all States in the region,

Bearing in mind the report transmitted by the Secretary-General on 20 March 1991, 3/

1. *Condemns* the repression of the Iraqi civilian population in many parts of Iraq, including most recently in Kurdish-populated areas, the consequences of which threaten international peace and security in the region;

2. *Demands* that Iraq, as a contribution to removing the threat to international peace and security in the region, immediately end this repression, and in the same context expresses the hope that an open dialogue will take place to ensure that the human and political rights of all Iraqi citizens are respected;

3. *Insists* that Iraq allow immediate access by international humanitarian organizations to all those in need of assistance in all parts of Iraq and make available all necessary facilities for their operations;

4. *Requests* the Secretary-General to pursue his humanitarian efforts in Iraq and to report forthwith, if appropriate on the basis of a further mission to the region, on the plight of the Iraqi civilian population, and in particular the Kurdish population, suffering from the repression in all its forms inflicted by the Iraqi authorities;

5. *Also requests* the Secretary-General to use all the resources at his disposal, including those of the relevant United Nations agencies, to address urgently the critical needs of the refugees and displaced Iraqi population;

6. *Appeals* to all Member States and to all humanitarian organizations to contribute to these humanitarian relief efforts;

7. *Demands* that Iraq cooperate with the Secretary-General to these ends;

8. *Decides* to remain seized of the matter.

1/ *Official Records of the Security Council, Forty-sixth Year, Supplement for April, May and June 1991,* document S/23300.
2/ Ibid., documents S/22436 and S/22447.
3/ Ibid., document S/22366, annex.

Document 38

Report of the Secretary-General proposing terms of reference for an observer unit to be known as the United Nations Iraq-Kuwait Observation Mission (UNIKOM)

S/22454, 5 April 1991, and addenda: S/22454/Add.1, 5 April 1991,
S/22454/Add.2, 5 April 1991, and S/22454/Add.3, 9 April 1991

**Report of the Secretary-General on the
implementation of paragraph 5 of Security
Council resolution 687 (1991)**

1. The present report is submitted in pursuance of Security Council resolution 687 (1991) of 3 April 1991. In paragraph 5 of that resolution, the Council established a demilitarized zone along the boundary between Iraq and Kuwait and requested the Secretary-General to submit to the Council, within three days, for approval a plan for the immediate deployment of a United Nations observer unit.

Terms of reference

2. In accordance with paragraph 5 of resolution 687 (1991), the terms of reference of the unit, which I propose should be called the "United Nations Iraq-Kuwait Observation Mission" (UNIKOM), would be:

(a) To monitor the Khor Abdullah and a demilitarized zone extending 10 kilometres into Iraq and 5 km into Kuwait from the boundary referred to in the Agreed Minutes between the State of Kuwait and the Republic of Iraq regarding the Restoration of Friendly Relations, Recognition and Related Matters of 4 October 1963; 1/

(b) To deter violations of the boundary through its presence in and surveillance of the demilitarized zone;

(c) To observe any hostile or potentially hostile action mounted from the territory of one State to the other.

General principles

3. Four essential conditions would have to be met for UNIKOM to be effective: first, it would need to have at all times the confidence and backing of the Security Council. Second, it would have to be given the necessary cooperation of the parties. Third, it would have to function as an integrated and efficient military unit. Fourth, adequate financial arrangements would have to be made to cover its costs.

4. In accordance with established principles,

(a) UNIKOM would be under the command of the United Nations, vested in the Secretary-General, under the authority of the Security Council. Command in the field would be exercised by a Chief Military Observer appointed by the Secretary-General with the consent of the Security Council. The Chief Military Observer would be responsible to the Secretary-General. The Secretary-General would report regularly to the Security Council on the operations of UNIKOM and immediately if there were serious violations of the demilitarized zone or potential threats to peace. All matters that might affect the nature or the continued effective functioning of UNIKOM would be referred to the Council for its decision;

(b) UNIKOM would be composed of military contingents provided by Member States at the request of the Secretary-General. The military contingents would be selected in consultation with the parties and with the concurrence of the Security Council, bearing in mind the accepted principle of equitable geographic representation;

(c) As recommended below, the contingents would comprise armed and unarmed military personnel. UNIKOM and its personnel would be authorized to use force only in self-defence;

(d) UNIKOM would proceed on the assumption that the parties would take all the necessary steps to comply with the decisions of the Security Council. It would have to have the freedom of movement and communication and other rights and facilities that would be necessary for the performance of its tasks. UNIKOM and its personnel would also have to be granted all relevant privileges and immunities provided for by the Convention on the Privileges and Immunities of the United Nations; agreements with the host Governments concerning the status of UNIKOM would have to be concluded without delay. The Governments of Iraq and Kuwait would be expected to provide, free of charge, the land and premises required by UNIKOM.

Considerations relevant to the discharge of the mandate

5. As an observation mission, UNIKOM would be required to monitor and observe and would not be expected and, indeed, would not be authorized to take physical action to prevent the entry of military personnel or equipment into the demilitarized zone. Further, it is my understanding that the clause requiring UNIKOM to "observe any hostile or potentially hostile action mounted from the territory of one State to the other" refers to activities that can be observed in or from the Khor Abdullah and the demilitarized zone.

1/ United Nations, *Treaty Series*, vol. 485, No. 7063.

6. UNIKOM would not assume responsibilities that fall within the competence of the host Governments and would avoid unnecessary interference in the normal civilian life of the area. It is assumed that the Governments of Iraq and Kuwait would each carry out all aspects of civilian administration in their respective part of the demilitarized zone, including the maintenance of law and order. At the same time, if UNIKOM is to be effective, it would need to have certain powers and facilities. In this connection, the two Governments would be expected to extend to UNIKOM full freedom of movement, on land and through the air, across the border and throughout the demilitarized zone; to control movement into and out of the demilitarized zone by requiring all traffic to be routed past United Nations observation posts; to notify UNIKOM in advance of sea and air traffic in the demilitarized zone and the Khor Abdullah; and to establish limitations on the right of their citizens to bear arms in the demilitarized zone. Further details regarding the regulation of activities in the demilitarized zone and the Khor Abdullah would be worked out in consultation with the two Governments, including the number and armament of police deployed in the area.

Area of operation

7. The demilitarized zone is about 200 km long, the Khor Abdullah about 40 km. For the most part, the zone is barren and almost uninhabited, except for the oilfields and two towns, Umm Qasr and Safwan. A small airfield is at Safwan. A port and airfield are at Umm Qasr, which became Iraq's only outlet to the sea after the Shatt al-Arab was blocked. A number of roads cross the demilitarized zone, most of them in the eastern part, but the terrain makes cross-country travel easy, and the inhabitants, particularly the bedouins, are accustomed to moving freely throughout the area and across the border.

Concept of operation

8. In order to carry out the mandate defined by the Security Council, UNIKOM would monitor the situation (on a continuing basis) to ensure that no military personnel and equipment were within the demilitarized zone and that no military fortifications and installations were maintained in it. To this end, it would:

(a) Monitor the withdrawal of any armed forces now in the zone which is to be demilitarized;

(b) Operate observation posts on the main roads to monitor traffic into and out of the demilitarized zone;

(c) Operate observation posts at selected locations in the demilitarized zone;

(d) Conduct patrols throughout the demilitarized zone by land and by air;

(e) Monitor the Khor Abdullah from observation posts set up on its shores and from the air;

(f) Carry out investigations.

Requirements

9. The tasks defined above are essentially tasks for military observers. However, in the circumstances obtaining in the UNIKOM area of operations, they could not be carried out by military observers alone. This is for three main reasons.

10. First, the area of operations, apart from Umm Qasr and territory to the east of it, is currently controlled by the forces of Member States cooperating with Kuwait. As those forces bring their military presence in Iraq to an end, in accordance with paragraph 6 of resolution 687 (1991), there is a risk that disorder would ensue, at least for a period of time. In particular, the forces of Member States cooperating with Kuwait are at present providing humanitarian assistance to some tens of thousands of refugees and displaced persons, many of them in what will become the UNIKOM area of operations. I am taking urgent steps to arrange for the United Nations system to provide such humanitarian support as may be needed by these people. It is also hoped that the host Governments' police forces would soon be in a position to maintain law and order in their respective parts of the demilitarized zone. Nevertheless, during this delicate transitional phase there might well be a threat to the security of UNIKOM personnel, equipment and supplies. My plan therefore includes the provision of an infantry element to ensure UNIKOM's security at that stage.

11. Second, I have been informed by Member States cooperating with Kuwait that mines and unexploded ordnance are a serious hazard in the area. Considerable effort would be required to clear areas required for UNIKOM observation posts and other installations, to make existing roads and tracks safe for patrolling and to establish additional tracks to enable UNIKOM to patrol the length and breadth of the demilitarized zone. Unless satisfactory arrangements can be made to complete this work before UNIKOM is deployed, the mission would have to include a field engineer unit.

12. Third, the demilitarized zone is barren and sparsely populated, the climate is harsh and the infrastructure in the area has suffered greatly. The military observers would therefore need a greater degree of logistic support than is the case in areas that are more settled and have less severe climates. There would thus be a continuing need for a logistic unit.

13. To carry out the tasks described in paragraph 8 above, a group of 300 military observers would be required initially, although this number would be reviewed as the mission gained experience and refined its methods. As regards support for the observers, my plan

would be to assign temporarily to UNIKOM five infantry companies drawn from existing peace-keeping operations in the region, with the agreement of the troop-contributing Governments concerned. These units would provide essential security for UNIKOM during the setting-up phase. The Chief Military Observer would be instructed to advise me, approximately four weeks after the beginning of the operation, whether he foresaw a continuing need for an infantry element. If he did, I would seek the Council's authority to replace the units temporarily assigned to UNIKOM with one or more battalions on a more permanent basis. As indicated in paragraph 11 above, a field engineer unit would also be required if the necessary clearance of mines and unexploded ordnance had not been completed by the time UNIKOM was deployed. In addition, UNIKOM would have an air unit with fixed-wing aircraft and light helicopters, a logistic unit responsible primarily for medical care, supply and transport, and a headquarters unit. The maximum initial strength of UNIKOM would be approximately 1,440 all ranks, of which the infantry temporarily attached to it from already established missions would be approximately 680, and the field engineer unit, if it is deployed, approximately 300.

14. UNIKOM's headquarters would need to be within the demilitarized zone, where Umm Qasr would seem to be the most suitable location. A logistic base would be established in Kuwait. The military observers and the infantry units would be deployed throughout the demilitarized zone. Liaison offices would be maintained at Baghdad and Kuwait City. At the start of the mission, liaison would also need to be maintained with the forces of the Member States cooperating with Kuwait, whose withdrawal through the demilitarized zone would need to be coordinated with UNIKOM.

15. A preliminary estimate of the cost of UNIKOM and my observations on its financing will be circulated in an addendum to the present report.

Consultations with the parties

16. As already stated, UNIKOM would be able to function effectively only with the full cooperation of the parties. In accordance with resolution 687 (1991), I have informed the Permanent Representatives of Iraq and Kuwait of the plan contained in the present report and requested their urgent confirmation that their respective Governments would cooperate with the United Nations on this basis. I will report further to the Security Council as soon as this has been received.

Addendum (S/22454/Add.1, 5 April 1991)

Estimated cost and method of financing

1. Should the Security Council establish the United Nations Iraq-Kuwait Observation Mission (UNIKOM) on the basis set out in the main part of the present report, it is estimated that the cost of the Mission for the first six months would be approximately $83 million. The costs of continuing UNIKOM for the following six months would be approximately $40 million. These estimates do not include additional costs that would be incurred if the infantry units temporarily assigned to UNIKOM are replaced with infantry battalions on a more permanent basis; nor do they include the costs that would be incurred if the engineer unit had to be continued beyond six months. These are preliminary estimates, which might be subject to revision as further details are clarified and/or as a result of decisions taken by the Security Council.

2. It would be my recommendation that the costs of the Mission be considered an expense of the Organization to be borne by Member States in accordance with Article 17, paragraph 2, of the Charter. I would recommend to the General Assembly that the assessments to be levied on Member States be credited to a special account that would be established for this purpose.

3. The capacity of the United Nations to deploy UNIKOM would depend in large measure on the availability of the financial resources necessary to meet the start-up costs of the operation. This in turn would depend not only on the appropriation of the necessary funds by the Assembly but, equally importantly, on the receipt from Member States of their assessed contributions. As is known, the payment of assessed contributions for peace-keeping operations established by the Security Council has been at rates far lower than were necessary to meet cash-flow requirements. In order to meet the start-up costs of UNIKOM, I would therefore appeal to Member States to make voluntary payments, which would be repaid as soon as sufficient assessed contributions have been received. I would also appeal to Member States to make voluntary contributions in cash and in kind for setting up and maintaining the Mission.

4. I take this opportunity to point out that the above cost estimate covers only paragraph 5 of resolution 687 (1991). The financial implications of the resolution's other provisions will become clearer after the necessary detailed examination of the manner in which these provisions may be implemented by the Secretary-General and of the various commissions to be established under the resolution. It is already apparent, however, that the aggregate financial implications of the resolution are likely to be quite substantial.

Addendum: Map (S/22454/Add.2, 5 April 1991)

[Not reproduced here.]

1. In reference to paragraph 16 of my report of 5 April 1991 (S/22454), the Permanent Representative of Iraq informed me on 8 April 1991 that his Government accepted the plan contained in my report and would cooperate with the United Nations on that basis.

2. On 9 April 1991, the representative of Kuwait conveyed to me his Government's acceptance of the plan and its undertaking to cooperate with the United Nations on its implementation.

Document 39

Identical letters from the Deputy Prime Minister and Minister for Foreign Affairs of Iraq to the President of the Security Council and to the Secretary-General stating that Iraq has no choice but to accept the provisions of Security Council resolution 687 (1991)

S/22456, 6 April 1991

Identical letters dated 6 April 1991 from the Permanent Representative of Iraq to the United Nations addressed respectively to the Secretary-General and the President of the Security Council

On instructions from my Government, I have the honour to enclose the text of a letter dated 6 April 1991 addressed to you by the Minister for Foreign Affairs of the Republic of Iraq.

I should be grateful if you would have the text of this letter and its annex circulated as a document of the Security Council.

(*Signed*) Abdul Amir A. AL-ANBARI
Ambassador
Permanent Representative

Annex
Identical letters dated 6 April 1991 from the Minister for Foreign Affairs of the Republic of Iraq addressed respectively to the Secretary-General and the President of the Security Council

I have the honour to inform you that the Iraqi Government has taken note of the text of Security Council resolution 687 (1991), the authors of which are the first to recognize that it is unprecedented in the annals of the Organization, and wishes, before stating its official position, to make a number of fundamental comments regarding certain concepts and provisions contained therein:

I. While in its preamble the resolution reaffirms that Iraq is an independent sovereign State, the fact remains that a good number of its iniquitous provisions impair that sovereignty. In fact, the resolution constitutes an unprecedented assault on the sovereignty, and the rights that stem therefrom, embodied in the Charter and in international law and practice. For example, where the question of boundaries is concerned, the Security Council has determined in advance the boundary between Iraq and Kuwait. And yet it is well known, from the juridical and practical standpoint, that in international relations boundary issues must be the subject of an agreement between States, since this is the only basis capable of guaranteeing the stability of frontiers.

Moreover, the resolution fails to take into account Iraq's view, which is well known to the Council, that the provisions relating to the boundary between Iraq and Kuwait contained in the "Agreed Minutes Between the State of Kuwait and the Republic of Iraq Regarding the Restoration of Friendly Relations, Recognition and Related Matters" dated 4 October 1963 have not yet been subjected to the constitutional procedures required for ratification of the Agreed Minutes by the legislative branch and the President of Iraq, thus leaving the question of the boundary pending and unresolved. The Council has nevertheless imposed on Iraq the line of its boundary with Kuwait. By acting in this strange manner, the Council itself has also violated one of the provisions of resolution 660, which served as the basis for its subsequent resolutions. In its paragraph 3, resolution 660 calls upon Iraq and Kuwait to resolve their differences through negotiation, and the question of the boundary is well known to be one of the main differences. Iraq officially informed the Council that it accepted resolution 660 and was prepared to apply it, but the Council has gone beyond this legal position, contradicting its previous resolution, and adopted an iniquitous resolution which imposes on Iraq, an independent and sovereign State and a Member of the United Nations, new conditions and a boundary line which deprive it of its right to establish its territorial rights in accordance with the principles of international law. Thus the Council is also depriving Iraq of its right to exercise its free choice and to affirm that it accepts that boundary without reservation. Where the question of the boundary is concerned, the Council resolution is an iniquitous resolution which constitutes a dangerous precedent, a first in the annals of the international Organization and—as some impartial members of the Council indicated in their statements when the resolution was voted on—an assault on the sovereignty of States.

It is also to be noted that the United States of America, the author of the draft resolution on which resolution 687, which imposes a solution to the boundary-related and other differences between Iraq and Kuwait, was based, refuses to impose any solution whatsoever on its ally, Israel, in accordance with conventions, United Nations resolutions and international law.

Furthermore, the United States of America is preventing the Security Council from assuming the responsibilities incumbent upon it with respect to the Arab-Zionist conflict, the Israeli policy of annexation of the occupied Arab territories, the establishment of settlements, the displacement of populations and the disregard for the rights of the Palestinian people and the neighbouring Arab countries, by vetoing any draft resolution approved by the remaining members of the Council, for the simple reason that Israel does not want a resolution which favours a just settlement of the conflict.

II. Iraq's position with regard to the prohibition of chemical and bacteriological weapons is clear. It is indeed a party to the Protocol for the Prohibition of the Use in War of Asphyxiating, Poisonous or Other Gases, and of Bacteriological Methods of Warfare, signed at Geneva in 1925. In a statement issued in September 1988, Iraq reiterated its attachment and adherence to the provisions of that Protocol. It also participated in the Conference of States Parties to the 1925 Geneva Protocol and Other Interested States, held at Paris from 7 to 11 January 1989, and signed the Declaration issued by the participating States. On that occasion, Iraq took a position which was unanimously shared by all the Arab countries, namely that all weapons of mass destruction, including nuclear weapons, must be eliminated from the Middle East region.

Iraq is also a party to the Treaty on the Non-Proliferation of Nuclear Weapons, of 1 July 1968. As the many reports of the International Atomic Energy Agency confirm, it is applying all the provisions of the Treaty. The Security Council resolution obliges only Iraq, and it alone, to undertake the destruction of the non-conventional weapons left to it after the heavy destruction inflicted both on these weapons and on the related installations by the military operations launched against Iraq by the 30 countries of the coalition. It does not deprive the other countries of the region, particularly Israel, of the right to possess weapons of this type, including nuclear weapons. Moreover, the Council has ignored its

resolution 487 (1981), which calls on Israel to place all its nuclear facilities under international safeguards, and has not sought to ensure the implementation of that resolution in the same way as it is now seeking to impose the position it has taken against Iraq. It is thus clear that a double standard is being applied with respect to the elimination of weapons of mass destruction in the region, and an attempt being made to disrupt the military balance there, and this is, all the more apparent in that Iraq has not had recourse to weapons of this type.

The application of this provision of the resolution cannot but seriously endanger the regional balance, as indeed was confirmed by certain impartial members of the Security Council in their statements when the resolution was voted upon. There can be no doubt that Israel, an expansionist aggressor country which is occupying the territory of neighbouring countries, usurping the right of the Palestinian Arab people against which it daily commits the most horrible atrocities, and refusing to comply with the resolutions of the Security Council, which it holds in contempt, as well as all the resolutions of the international Organization, will be the first to benefit from this imbalance.

Whereas the resolution emphasizes the importance of all States adhering to the Convention on the Prohibition of the Development, Production and Stockpiling of Bacteriological (Biological) and Toxin Weapons, of a Convention on the Universal Prohibition of Chemical Weapons being drafted and of universal adherence thereto, it makes no mention whatsoever of the importance of universal adherence to the convention banning nuclear weapons or of the drafting of a convention on the universal prohibition of such weapons in the region. Instead, it emphasizes the importance of instituting a dialogue among the States of the region with a view to achieving a so-called balanced and comprehensive control of armaments in the region.

Proof of the resolution's biased and iniquitous nature is afforded by the Council's use of what it terms unprovoked attacks using ballistic missiles as grounds for calling for the destruction of all ballistic missiles with a range greater than 150 kilometres and of all repair and production facilities. The term unprovoked attacks is used of attacks against Israel, a country which itself launched an unprovoked attack in 1981, destroying Iraqi nuclear installations which were used for peaceful purposes and were under international safeguards. In this connection, the Security Council considered in its resolution 487 (1981), adopted unanimously, that that attack constituted a serious threat to the entire safeguards regime of the International Atomic Energy Agency, which is the foundation of the Treaty on the Non-Proliferation of Nuclear Weapons.

It should be pointed out as well that the Council had also considered in the same resolution that Iraq was entitled to appropriate redress for the destruction it had suffered. The Council has to date taken no steps for the implementation of that resolution, whereas it imposes particularly severe and iniquitous terms and mechanisms when it comes to the redress referred to in resolution 687 (1991), without taking into account even the basic humanitarian needs of the Iraqi people.

III. Furthermore, Iraq's internal and external security has been and remains seriously threatened, in that continuing efforts are being made to interfere, by force of arms, in the country's internal affairs. Thus the measures taken by the Council against Iraq to deprive it of its lawful right to acquire weapons and military *matériel* for defence directly contribute to the intensification of these threats and to the destabilization of Iraq, thus endangering the country's internal and external security and hence peace, security and stability throughout the region.

IV. Whereas the Council resolution provides for mechanisms for obtaining redress from Iraq, it makes no reference to Iraq's rights to claim redress for the considerable losses it sustained and the massive destruction inflicted on civilian installations and infrastructures as a result of the abusive implementation of resolution 678 (1990), which were testified to by the delegation sent by the Secretary-General which visited Iraq recently, and have been referred to by the President of a permanent member of the Security Council (Soviet President Mikhail Gorbachev) and by all impartial observers who have seen with their own eyes the consequences of the military operations launched against Iraq. The Council has not explained to world public opinion and the conscience of mankind what the relationship is between its resolution 678 and the deliberate destruction of Iraq's infrastructure—generating stations, water distribution networks, irrigation dams, civilian bridges, telephone exchanges, factories producing powdered milk for infants and medicines, shelters, mosques, churches, commercial centres, residential neighbourhoods, etc. Moreover, the resolution authorizes third parties to claim compensation from Iraq for damage that may have been caused to them, even when such damage resulted from unfulfilment of their commitments to Iraq immediately following the adoption of resolution 661.

Further evidence of the resolution's biased and iniquitous nature is that it holds Iraq liable for environmental damage and the depletion of natural resources, although this liability has not been established; on the other hand, it makes no mention of Iraq's own right to obtain compensation for the established facts of damage to its environment and depletion of its natural resources as a result of more than 88,000 tons of explosives, or for the destruction of water distribution networks, generating stations and the road network, which has spread disease and epidemics and caused serious harm to the environment.

These provisions partake of a desire to exact vengeance and cause harm, not to give effect to the relevant provisions of international law. The direct concrete consequences of their implementation will affect the potential and resources of millions of Iraqis, and deprive them of the right to live in dignity.

V. After imposing compulsory and universal sanctions against Iraq by adopting resolution 661 (1990) in consequence, according to it, of Iraq's refusal to comply with the provisions of resolution 660 (1990), the Council has maintained most of them in force despite Iraq's acceptance of all the Council's resolutions and the implementation of a good number of their provisions. The Council resolution provides for the progressive lifting of sanctions over an unspecified period, thus leaving broad discretionary authority to certain influential members of the Council which have drawn up the Council's resolutions in an arbitrary manner in order to impose them for political purposes which bear no relation to the Charter or to international law.

In essence, this procedure means that the Council has contradicted the initial resolution under which it imposed sanctions against Iraq, and moreover has not taken account of the offensive launched against Iraq, whereas the interests of the other parties have been taken into account, despite their wealth and their considerable resources.

VI. The Council does not deal clearly and directly with the question of withdrawal of the foreign forces occupying part of Iraqi territory, although the resolution declares a formal cease-fire.

The very conditions invoked in support of the declaration of a formal cease-fire also necessitate the withdrawal. The fact that the withdrawal is not explicitly mentioned is tantamount to authorizing the occupation of Iraqi territory for a period whose duration is at the discretion of the occupying countries, which make no secret of their intention to exploit the occupation for political purposes and to make use of it as a trump card in their hand. This position on the part of the Council constitutes a flagrant violation of Iraq's sovereignty, independence and territorial integrity, and cannot be justified by any provision of resolution 678 (1990). Under this same selective, premeditated and totally unjustifiable approach, the resolution stipulates that the observer forces will be deployed in Iraq to a distance of 10 kilometres from the boundary, and only five kilometres into the territory of the other party, despite the fact that the terrain in the region is flat everywhere, with no relief features that would justify this difference of treatment.

VII. Numerous mechanisms are envisaged which will necessitate consultation in the context of the implementation of the resolution's provisions, but the resolution is not at all clear about Iraq's participation in these consultations. The fact that Iraq is concerned to the highest degree in the application of the resolution makes its effective participation in all consultations bearing on the implementation of these provisions essential. However, the Council has once again opted for an arbitrary and inequitable method.

The questions raised in the resolution and discussed in the foregoing preliminary comments constitute, in substance, an injustice, a severe assault on the Iraqi people's right to life and a flagrant denial of its inalienable rights to sovereignty and independence and its right to exercise its free choice.

In practice, the provisions of the resolution embodying the criteria of duality in international relations and the application of a double standard to questions of the same kind hold Iraq and its population hostage to the designs harboured by certain Powers to take control of their resources, set quotas for their food and clothing needs, and deprive them of their right to live in dignity in the modern society to which they aspire.

Such injustices and such assaults on the rights of a member country of the United Nations and its people cannot under any circumstances be in conformity with the purposes and objectives of the Charter. The Council had a duty to discuss the issues before it with objectivity and in accordance with the provisions of international law and the principles of justice and equity.

By adopting this unjust resolution and by this selective treatment of the Iraqi people, the Council has merely confirmed the fact that we have never ceased to emphasize, namely that the Council has become a puppet which the United States of America is manipulating in order to achieve its political designs in the region, the prime objective being to perpetuate Israel's policy of aggression and expansion, despite the empty words about peace and justice in the Middle East uttered by one or another of the Council members which voted for this resolution.

It could not be more clear to all men of honour and justice that these iniquitous and vengeful measures against Iraq are not a consequence of the events of 2 August 1990 and the subsequent period, for the essential motive underlying these measures stems from Iraq's rejection of the unjust situation imposed on the Arab nation and the countries of the region for decades, a situation which has enabled Israel, a belligerent Power heavily armed with the most modern and fearsome conventional weapons and with weapons of mass destruction, including nuclear weapons, to exercise hegemony in the region. This reality confirms what Iraq had stated before the events of 2 August 1990, namely that it was the target of a plot aimed at destroying the potential it had deployed with a view to arriving at a just balance in the region which would pave the way for the institution of justice and of a lasting peace.

It is unfortunate that States whose intention was not in any way to help the United States of America and Israel attain their objectives should involuntarily have contributed to their attainment by voting for this iniquitous resolution.

As Iraq makes its preliminary comments on the juridical and legal aspects of this resolution, so as to encourage men of conscience in the countries members of the international community and world public opinion to make an effort to understand the truth as it is and the need to ensure the triumph of justice, it has no choice but to accept this resolution.

I should be grateful if you would have this letter circulated as a document of the Security Council.

(*Signed*) Ahmed HUSSEIN
Minister for Foreign Affairs of Iraq

Document 40

Security Council resolution approving the Secretary-General's plan for the creation of UNIKOM

S/RES/689 (1991), 9 April 1991

The Security Council,

Recalling its resolution 687 (1991) of 3 April 1991,

Acting under Chapter VII of the Charter of the United Nations,

1. *Approves* the report of the Secretary-General of 5 and 9 April 1991 on the implementation of paragraph 5 of Security Council resolution 687 (1991); 1/

2. *Notes* that the decision to set up an observer unit was taken in paragraph 5 of resolution 687 (1991) and that the unit can be terminated only by a further decision of the Council; the Council shall therefore review the question of its termination or continuation every six months;

1/ *Official Records of the Security Council, Forty-sixth Year, Supplement for April, May and June 1991*, document S/22454 and Add.1 to 3.

3. *Decides* that the modalities for the initial six-month period of the United Nations Iraq-Kuwait Observation Mission shall be in accordance with the above-mentioned report and shall also be reviewed every six months.

Document 41

Letter dated 10 April 1991 from the Permanent Representative of Iraq to the President of the Security Council transmitting the National Assembly decision of 6 April 1991 concerning acceptance of Security Council resolution 687 (1991)

S/22480, 11 April 1991

In accordance with your request, we transmit herewith the National Assembly decision adopted on 6 April 1991 concerning acceptance of Security Council resolution 687 (1991).

(*Signed*) Abdul Amir A. AL-ANBARI

Ambassador

Permanent Representative

Annex

In the Name of God, the Merciful, the Compassionate

Republic of Iraq	No.:
National Assembly	Date:

Decision

The National Assembly has decided at its session held on 6 April 1991 to agree to United Nations Security Council resolution 687 (1991).

(*Signed*) Saadi Mehdi SALIH
President of the National Assembly

Document 42

Letter from the President of the Security Council to the Permanent Representative of Iraq acknowledging receipt of Iraq's communication of 6 April 1991 (Document 39) and noting, this precondition having been met, that the formal cease-fire is therefore in effect

S/22485, 11 April 1991

I have the honour to acknowledge receipt of your communication dated 6 April 1991 (S/22456).

You thereby transmit to me the letter addressed to me by the Minister for Foreign Affairs of Iraq, the penultimate paragraph of which contains official notification of the acceptance, irrevocable and without qualifying conditions, by Iraq of resolution 687 (1991), in accordance with paragraph 33 of that resolution.

You have subsequently confirmed to me on behalf of your Government, during our meeting on 8 April 1991, that the above-mentioned letter constitutes Iraq's irrevocable and unqualified acceptance of resolution 687 (1991) in accordance with paragraph 33 of that resolution. You have also transmitted to me the acceptance by Iraq's National Assembly on 6 April 1991 of the aforesaid resolution (S/22480), and confirmed to me, in the name of your Government, that the Revolution Command Council has used its constitutional powers to make this decision legally binding in the Republic of Iraq.

The members of the Security Council have, accordingly, asked me to note that the conditions established in paragraph 33 of resolution 687 (1991) have been met and that the formal cease-fire referred to in paragraph 33 of that resolution is therefore effective.

The members of the Council welcome this development as a positive step towards the full implementation of resolution 687 (1991).

(*Signed*) Paul NOTERDAEME
President of the Security Council

Document 43

Report of the Secretary-General on setting up a Special Commission (UNSCOM) to carry out on-site inspection of Iraq's biological, chemical and missile capabilities

S/22508, 18 April 1991

1. The present report is submitted in pursuance of Security Council resolution 687 (1991) of 3 April 1991. In paragraph 9 (b) (i) of that resolution the Council decided that the Secretary-General should submit to it for approval a plan calling *inter alia* for the forming of a Special Commission to carry out the tasks enumerated in paragraphs 9 (b) (i-iii), 10 and 13.

2. To enable the Special Commission to play its proper part in assessing information and preparing and planning the activities envisaged in Section C of the resolution, including assisting the Director-General of the International Atomic Energy Agency to present a plan within his designated area, there is an urgent need for the Special Commission to be established. The implementation, within or near the time-frames indicated by the resolution, of all the mandates in Section C will in fact depend on the existence of the Commission, and its advice in the early stages would be essential.

3. Subject to the approval of the Security Council, it is my intention to set up the Special Commission as described below and to make all necessary arrangements for it to begin implementation of its tasks.

4. In setting up the structure for the Special Commission I wish to emphasize the need for an efficient and effective executive body. I propose that it should have an Executive Chairman with a Deputy Executive Chairman to assist the Chairman in carrying out his functions. Following the appointment of these two individuals the remainder of the Special Commission would be established on an expanding basis as appropriate individuals are found to fill the positions. Under the Executive Chairman and Deputy Executive Chairman, the planning and operational direction of the functions of the Commission should be carried out by five groups, each under a head of group with appropriate executive experience in the assigned field and each consisting of a small number of experts. The major areas of responsibility would be: biological and chemical weapons; ballistic missiles; nuclear-weapons capabilities; future compliance and operations support. Thus the formal membership of the Special Commission would be of the order of 20 to 25 persons.

5. Although the specific timing of the Special Commission's activities have yet to be determined, under the provisions of Section C of the resolution, most of the Commission's functions are time-limited. With the accomplishment of the tasks entrusted to four of the five groups, the major active phases would be completed and those four groups would cease to exist. The fifth group would continue in order to implement the activities relating to future compliance.

6. In carrying out its various tasks the Special Commission would be assisted by a number of technical experts serving as inspectors, disposal teams and field support officers. These experts would be either specially engaged for this purpose or made available to the Commission by Member States. Their total number would have to be determined in relationship to the size of the task to be carried out. This can be fully assessed only after the baseline field inspections have been completed by the Special Commission, but it is likely that the personnel involved will number in the several hundreds.

7. As soon as the baseline field assignments of the Special Commission and of the International Atomic Energy Agency have been completed, I intend to work out, in consultation with the Commission, a detailed plan for the implementation of the various tasks entrusted to it, and to submit it to the Security Council for its approval.

8. Following the acceptance by the Government of Iraq of Security Council resolution 687 (1991), expressed in the penultimate provision of the letters addressed respectively to me and to the President of the Security Council on 6 April 1991 by the Minister for Foreign Affairs of the Republic of Iraq, the execution of the baseline field inspections and the subsequent implementation plan is predicated on the assumption of full cooperation by the Iraqi authorities. The Special Commission would enjoy the relevant privileges and immunities provided for in the Convention on the Privileges and Immunities of the United Nations. Members of the Special Commission, experts attached to it and other specialists assigned to assist it in the implementation of Section C of Security Council resolution 687 (1991), would be regarded as experts on mission within the meaning of Article VI of the Convention on the Privileges and Immunities of the United Nations, relevant Annexes to the Convention on the Privileges and Immunities of the Specialized Agencies and Article VII of the Agreement on the Privileges and Immunities of the IAEA, respectively. Taking into account the tasks to be performed by the Special Commission, it may be necessary to conclude special

agreements covering the status, facilities, privileges and immunities of the Commission and its personnel. The existing agreements mentioned above would equally apply to tasks to be performed in Iraq by the IAEA and could be supplemented by special agreements, should the need arise.

9. While the financial implications relating to the establishment and functioning of the Special Commission cannot at this stage be assessed with accuracy, it is anticipated that certain start-up funds will be required. This sum will defray the initial costs of establishing the Headquarters of the Special Commission in New York as well as a field office in the region and the early deployment of advanced elements of the operation in the field. This sum will also defray some of the initial costs to be borne by the IAEA in carrying out the assignments entrusted to it under Section C of the resolution. Comprehensive cost estimates will, of course, be provided to the Security Council as soon as possible. It is my intention, however, to proceed in this regard on the basis of the following principles: (a) that Member States whose nationals will serve on the Commission or assist it in the discharge of its responsibilities should be responsible for their salaries, while the United Nations will bear the costs of travel and daily subsistence, and (b) that the whole exercise will be carried out in the shortest possible time, with a progressive decrease in the number of technical experts and of members of the Special Commission as various operations are completed.

Document 44

Letter from the Permanent Representative of Iraq to the Secretary-General transmitting the Memorandum of Understanding dated 18 April 1991 between Iraq and the United Nations concerning humanitarian assistance

S/22513, 22 April 1991

Letter dated 21 April 1991 from the Permanent Representative of Iraq to the United Nations addressed to the Secretary-General

On instructions from my Government, I have the honour to transmit herewith the letter dated 21 April 1991 addressed to you by the Minister for Foreign Affairs of Iraq, Mr. Ahmed Hussein, together with its annex containing the memorandum of understanding signed with your representative on 18 April 1991. In the letter, Iraq requests the United Nations, in accordance with the agreement concluded at Baghdad on 18 April 1991 between the Government of Iraq and the United Nations, to assume responsibility for the relief centres established in the Zakhou region in northern Iraq by United States armed forces and the forces of other foreign States cooperating with them.

I should be grateful if you would arrange for the text of this letter and its annex to be circulated as a document of the Security Council.

(Signed) Abdul Amir A. AL-ANBARI
Ambassador
Permanent Representative

Annex
Letter dated 21 April 1991 from the Minister for Foreign Affairs of Iraq addressed to the Secretary-General

As you are certainly aware, United States armed forces and the forces of other foreign countries cooperating with them have entered the Zakhou region in northern Iraq. The objective of this operation has been stated to be the establishment in Iraqi territory of centres for assisting displaced Iraqi citizens in Turkey. You are also aware that the Government of Iraq is opposed to this measure, since it would constitute a serious, unjustifiable and unfounded attack on the sovereignty and territorial integrity of Iraq.

This measure was announced at a time when the Iraqi Government had made significant progress in its negotiations with Prince Sadruddin Aga Khan, the representative to whom you have entrusted responsibility for relief operations. Steps to carry out the above-mentioned measure were taken on 20 April 1991, even though the Government of Iraq had signed a comprehensive agreement with your representative on 18 April, which provided for the establishment of humanitarian centres throughout Iraq, and in particular in the northern part of the country, with a view to undertaking the assistance operations necessary to induce Iraqi citizens displaced outside Iraq's frontiers to return in complete security to their places of residence in Iraq. It should be pointed out that the Government of Iraq, while opposing the steps taken by United States forces and the foreign forces cooperating with them for the reasons stated above, has not hindered these operations because it is not opposed to the provision of humanitarian assistance to Iraqi citizens who are in need of it and because it wishes to avoid any complication that may prevent the return of all Iraqi citizens in security to their places of residence.

Because the measures taken by the United States forces and the forces cooperating with them constitute a flagrant violation of Iraq's sovereignty and territorial integrity, and bearing in mind our opposition to the creation of centres under United States control inside Iraqi territory and our belief that the agreement which our Government concluded with your representative on 18 April 1991 has made it possible to define all relief operations in Iraq in an integrated and balanced manner, particularly those targeted to Kurds who are Iraqi citizens in such a way as to avoid the realization of the alleged objectives of the United States centres and to remove any justification for the establishment of such centres, which would in one way or another impair Iraq's sovereignty, the Government of Iraq, in pursuance of the above-mentioned agreement, is approaching you to request the United Nations to assume responsibility for the centres referred to above and to have the coordinator appointed by your representative, who is at the present time in Baghdad, immediately to take the measures necessary for the achievement of the purpose which we have described above. I can assure you that my Government will provide you with all necessary assistance in accordance with the above-mentioned agreement. Please find enclosed the memorandum of understanding signed with your representative on 18 April 1991.

(*Signed*) Ahmed HUSSEIN
Minister for Foreign Affairs of Iraq
Baghdad, 21 April 1991

Enclosure

Memorandum of Understanding
signed on 18 April 1991

This memorandum summarizes the results of discussions held in Baghdad between the Government of the Republic of Iraq, in the context of its request to the Secretary-General of the United Nations in relation to the suffering of the Iraqi population affected by recent events and Security Council resolution 688 of 5 April

1991, which has not been accepted by the Government of Iraq, and:

(a) From 13 to 18 April 1991, the United Nations Mission led by Mr. Eric Suy, Personal Representative of the United Nations Secretary-General, and

(b) From 16 to 18 April, the United Nations Inter-Agency Mission led by Prince Sadruddin Aga Khan, Executive Delegate of the United Nations Secretary-General for the United Nations Humanitarian Programme for Iraq, Kuwait and the Iraq/Iran and Iraq/Turkey Border Areas.

Both Missions have been welcomed by the Government of Iraq.

1. Both sides recognize the importance and urgency of adequate measures, including the provision of humanitarian assistance, to alleviate the suffering of the affected Iraqi civilian population.

2. The Government of the Republic of Iraq welcomes the United Nations efforts to promote the voluntary return home of Iraqi displaced persons and to take humanitarian measures to avert new flows of refugees and displaced persons from Iraq. It pledges its full support to and cooperation with the United Nations and its specialized agencies and programmes in this regard.

3. Both sides agree that the measures to be taken for the benefit of the displaced persons should be based primarily on their personal safety and the provision of humanitarian assistance and relief for their return and normalization of their lives in their places of origin.

4. For this purpose, the Government of the Republic of Iraq agrees to cooperate with the United Nations to have a humanitarian presence in Iraq, wherever such presence may be needed, and to facilitate it through the adoption of all necessary measures. This shall be ensured through the establishment of United Nations sub-offices and Humanitarian Centres (UNHUCs), in agreement and cooperation with the Government of Iraq.

5. Each Centre will be staffed by United Nations civilian personnel which, in addition to the regular staff members of the relevant United Nations agencies, may also include staff co-opted from the non-governmental organizations, the International Committee of the Red Cross and the League of Red Cross and Red Crescent Societies. The Red Crescent Society of Iraq shall be called upon to play a role in the implementation of humanitarian assistance and relief projects.

6. UNHUCs shall facilitate the provision of humanitarian assistance to the needy and would include, *inter alia*, food aid, medical care, agricultural rehabilitation, shelter and any other humanitarian and relief measures geared to the speedy normalization of life, in conformity with the principles of this memorandum. UNHUCs shall also monitor the overall situation in this

regard to advise the Iraqi authorities regarding measures needed to enhance their work.

7. Routes of return, with relay stations along the way as well as logistic back-up capabilities, will be set up urgently in cooperation with the Iraqi authorities to provide to civilians, particularly the women and children as well as the aged and the sick going back to their home areas, the food aid, shelter and basic health care they will need along the way. United Nations staff will accompany such groups, as required.

8. The United Nations shall take urgent measures, in cooperation with the Government of Iraq, for the early stationing of staff as well as the provision of assistance and relief in all designated centres and, as a matter of priority, those close to the Iraqi borders with its neighbouring countries. For this purpose, the United Nations may, in agreement and cooperation with the Government of Iraq, organize air lifts to the areas concerned, as required, as well as transportation by road of humanitarian assistance and relief goods from and through the neighbouring countries under United Nations or other humanitarian auspices. The Government of the Republic of Iraq shall adopt the necessary measures in order to render such aid in a speedy and effective manner.

9. United Nations humanitarian assistance and relief shall be provided simultaneously to the displaced persons, returnees as well as all other populations covered by the relief Programme in order to encourage a speedy normalization of life.

10. The basic framework for United Nations humanitarian action outlined above is intended to facilitate the task of coordination, effective implementation and monitoring of humanitarian assistance and relief operations. Further specifications are contained in the paragraphs which follow.

11. It is agreed that humanitarian assistance is impartial and that all civilians in need, wherever they are located, are entitled to receive it.

12. All Iraqi officials concerned, including the military, will facilitate the safe passage of emergency relief commodities throughout the country.

13. The Government will establish forthwith, together with the United Nations, a relief distribution and monitoring structure to permit access to all civilians covered by the relief Programme, as soon as possible.

14. A Coordinator, at the Assistant Secretary-General level, has been assigned to Baghdad to coordinate, under the Executive Delegate's direction, the implementation of the Humanitarian Relief Programme. He will have permanent access to a high-level government official responsible for emergency activities in the country, to discuss and resolve policy and operational issues that may arise during the implementation of the Programme.

15. The Government of Iraq shall cooperate in granting United Nations field staff access to the parts of the country requiring relief, by air or road as needed, to facilitate the implementation and monitoring of the Programme.

16. Intergovernmental organizations, NGOs and other relief agencies will be encouraged to participate in the implementation of the Programme, in close cooperation with the United Nations and under clearly defined terms of association agreed with the Government.

17. The Government of Iraq will help in the prompt establishment of United Nations sub-offices in support of UNHUCs and other programmes in towns. These will be selected so as to facilitate the relief Programme when required, to encourage the voluntary return of, and to provide essential assistance to, internally and externally displaced, as well as to local populations covered by the Programme.

18. A United Nations radio communication system which is an indispensable instrument for the success of relief and rehabilitation activities will be set up. The system will cover communications requirements within Baghdad and other cities covered by the relief Programme and within and outside the country, as appropriate.

19. In order to facilitate implementation of, and resource mobilization for, the relief Programme, the Government will make available cash contributions in local currency to help cover in-country operational costs while pursuing discussions regarding the establishment of a special exchange rate for relief operations carried out by the agencies and organizations participating in the Programme.

20. The implementation of the above-mentioned principles shall be without prejudice to the sovereignty, territorial integrity, political independence, security and non-interference in the internal affairs of the Republic of Iraq.

21. The above-mentioned principles shall apply for a period ending on 31 December 1991. Two weeks before the expiration of the said period, the principles and their operational modalities shall be reviewed with a view to assessing any further need for their operation.

Done at Baghdad on 3 Shawal 1411 of the Hijri, corresponding to 18 April 1991 A.D.

FOR THE GOVERNMENT OF THE
REPUBLIC OF IRAQ

(*Signed*) H.E. Ahmed HUSSEIN
Minister of Foreign Affairs of the Government of the Republic of Iraq

FOR THE UNITED NATIONS

(*Signed*) H.E. Sadruddin Aga KHAN
Executive Delegate of the United Nations
Secretary-General for the United Nations
Humanitarian Programme for Iraq, Kuwait
and the Iraq/Iran and Iraq/Turkey Border Areas

Document 45

Report to the Secretary-General by a United Nations mission assessing the scope and nature of damage inflicted on Kuwait's infrastructure during the Iraqi occupation of the country (extract)

S/22535, 29 April 1991

Letter dated 26 April 1991 from the Secretary-General addressed to the President of the Security Council

In my letter of 1 March 1991 to the President of the Security Council (S/22333), I brought to his attention a letter I had received from the Permanent Representative of Kuwait requesting that a mission be dispatched immediately to that country to assess the losses of life incurred during the Iraqi occupation of Kuwait and to examine the practices by the Iraqi occupation forces against the civilian population in Kuwait. He had also requested that the team assess the damage inflicted on the general infrastructure in Kuwait.

In his letter of 6 March 1991 (S/22334), the President of the Security Council informed me that members of the Council would welcome my responding positively to that request, recognizing the importance of taking all actions possible to facilitate Kuwait's reconstruction and reintegration into the international economic system.

Accordingly, I requested Mr. Abdulrahim A. Farah, former Under-Secretary-General, to lead a high-level United Nations mission to Kuwait. The mission visited that country from 16 March to 4 April 1991. The report of the mission on the damage sustained by the infrastructure and economy of Kuwait during the Iraqi occupation is submitted herewith for the attention of members of the Security Council.

(*Signed*) Javier PÉREZ DE CUÉLLAR

INTRODUCTION

A. *Mandate and composition of the mission*

1. On 6 March 1991, the Secretary-General decided to dispatch a United Nations mission to Kuwait with the following terms of reference:

   (a) To receive pertinent information from the Kuwaiti authorities, as well as non-governmental organizations (NGOs), for an assessment of the losses in life incurred during the Iraqi occupation of Kuwait;

   (b) To receive pertinent information from the Kuwaiti authorities, as well as NGOs, on Iraqi practices against the civilian population in Kuwait;

   (c) To assess the scope and nature of the damage that was inflicted on Kuwait's infrastructure during the period.

2. The present report is confined to the assessment of the damage to the infrastructure. The information called for in parts (a) and (b) of the terms of reference are the subject of a separate report (S/22536).

3. In his instructions to the leader of the mission, Mr. Abdulrahim Abby Farah, the Secretary-General emphasized the necessity of the mission proceeding without delay and, given the situation prevailing in Kuwait, that its report be completed as soon as possible.

4. Before leaving for Kuwait, Mr. Farah met in New York with the Acting Permanent Representative of Kuwait to the United Nations, Mr. Mohammad Saad Al-Sallal, and was provided with information that would enable the mission to identify specifically the areas and sectors on which the Government of Kuwait wished the mission to focus attention.

5. Sectoral work was assigned among the substantive members of the mission as follows: Mr. Cristian Ossa (Department of International Economic and Social Affairs of the United Nations Secretariat), macroeconomics; Mr. Michael Douglas Gwynne and Mr. Makram Gerges (United Nations Environment Programme (UNEP)), environment, agriculture and fisheries; Mr. John Beynon (United Nations Educational, Scientific and Cultural Organization (UNESCO)), education, culture and information; Dr. Daniel Tarantola (World Health Organization (WHO)), health; Mr. G. H. Connor (Department of Technical Cooperation for Development of the Secretariat), transport and municipal services; Mr. Ola Gunnes (Department of Technical Cooperation for Development), power and telecommunications; Mr. Kamal Mohamed Abou-Hamda, consultant for housing and urban infrastructure; and Mr. John Philip Thomas, consultant for oil industry, assisted by Mr. Johan Schölvinck (Department of International Economic and Social Affairs). Mr. Ramu Damodaran of the United Nations Secretariat served as Secretary of the mission. In view of the abnormal conditions in Kuwait and the absence of any United Nations back-up presence there, it was necessary for the mission to be assisted by a self-contained staff.

6. Members of the mission based in New York convened on 7, 8 and 11 March for preliminary consultations. In accordance with a programme drawn up in consultation with the Government of Kuwait, the main

party reached Bahrain on 13 March, where they were joined by colleagues based elsewhere.

7. Logistical constraints made it necessary for the mission to spend two days in Bahrain before it could proceed to Kuwait. Fortunately, this provided an opportunity for senior members of the mission to be received by His Highness, the Prime Minister of Bahrain, Sheikh Khalifa Bin-Salman Al-Khalifa. Meetings were also held with His Excellency, the Foreign Minister of Bahrain, Sheikh Mohamed Bin-Mubarak, and the Minister for Information, Mr. Tarek Al-Moayyed. Discussions centred on the situation in Kuwait, its impact on the Gulf region and the role of the United Nations. The Government of Bahrain expressed its strong support for Kuwait and its determination to provide that country all possible assistance in the task of national reconstruction.

8. The mission reached Kuwait on 16 March by a special aircraft provided by the Government of Kuwait. It was received at the airport by His Excellency, Mr. Nasser Mohammed Al-Sabah, the Minister of State for Foreign Affairs of Kuwait, and other senior government officials. The same afternoon, the mission discussed its work programme with Mr. Abdullah Al-Dikheel, former Minister for Public Works of Kuwait, who had been designated by the Government as Mr. Farah's counterpart.

9. On 20 March, Mr. Farah was received by His Highness, Sheikh Saad Al-Sabah, Crown Prince and Prime Minister of Kuwait. The Crown Prince expressed his country's deep appreciation to the Secretary-General for his prompt response to its request that a mission be dispatched to look into the question of damage sustained by Kuwait during the country's occupation by Iraq.

10. The mission completed its work in Kuwait on 4 April 1991.

B. *General setting*

11. The mission's mandate made clear that it should confine its study and assessment to the situation that prevailed in Kuwait during the period of occupation, that is, from 2 August 1990 to 26 February 1991. The complexity of the task confronting the members of the mission became apparent once it had the opportunity to witness for itself the realities on the ground and the abnormal conditions that had been created as a result of the occupation.

12. Before 2 August 1990, Kuwait was a society characterized by a highly capitalized, urban infrastructure. The mission arrived in Kuwait just two weeks after the return of the Government. It found itself obliged to begin its task in a country where the electric power, telecommunications and transportation systems had been wrecked, government buildings and other public institu-

tions heavily damaged and most official records and equipment either destroyed or looted. Moreover, very few civil servants had resumed duty, and the vast majority were still outside the country.

13. Despite its acute shortage of senior and experienced staff, the Government did manage, in most cases, to assign counterparts to work with members of the mission in their respective areas of competence. This was particularly considerate since the stay of the mission occurred at a time when the Government was intensely occupied in restoring the administrative machinery and attending to the immediate needs of the people. Because of the staff situation, government counterparts were often called upon to fulfil other tasks while doing their best to assist the mission.

14. Members of the mission travelled extensively throughout the country, by land and by helicopter, making frequent and detailed visits to particular locations, sites and institutions essential to their task. The constraints of time and limitation of facilities necessitated the adoption of sample surveys in all sectors. The mission did not assess the damage sustained by defence infrastructure although it did observe damage to military airfields, barracks and defence installations.

15. Extensive contacts were maintained with members of the diplomatic community in Kuwait, with whom Mr. Farah held two meetings through the courtesy of the Ministry of Foreign Affairs of Kuwait. He also had talks with a number of ambassadors individually.

16. The mission wishes to record its appreciation of the contribution of a number of national and international agencies and groups who provided logistical support, as well as access to data, records and maps. In particular, it should like to mention the Embassies of France, the United Kingdom of Great Britain and Northern Ireland and the United States of America, as well as the Corps of Engineers and the 352nd Civil Affairs Command of the United States Army, the Explosives Ordnance Disposal Coordination Group of the coalition forces, the Environmental Protection Agency of the United States and the Kuwait Petroleum Corporation. Interaction between the mission and these, and other, organizations facilitated a sharing of assessments and ideas and an exchange of expertise, as well as cross-checking and verification of information obtained.

C. *Methodology*

17. Its terms of reference required the mission "to assess the scope and nature of the damage that was inflicted on Kuwait's infrastructure during the period". Since "infrastructure" has a broad meaning, the mission's assessment at the sectoral level has focused on three interrelated elements:

(a) Permanent structures such as roads, ports, hospitals, educational institutions, factories, water plants and government and residential buildings;

(b) Machinery, equipment and other support facilities, including stock, that enabled the structures to perform the functions for which they were designed;

(c) Materials and software (e.g., books, archives, historical artifacts, research data) that were integral to the effective functioning of the service or activity of which they were a part.

18. The report comments on, and attempts to provide, a broad assessment of the impact of events during the Iraqi occupation on the welfare of the population of Kuwait, in particular on the social sectors, as well as on the air and marine environment and terrestrial ecosystems.

19. In the light of its initial findings, the mission also felt it necessary to comment on the extensive loss of output after 2 August 1990 as a result of the damage to the economy during the occupation, and on the nature and scale of the loss of goods, equipment and materials deriving from the deliberate destruction and organized looting and removal of property.

20. The mission was shown numerous sites where moveable property had been removed. According to testimony it received, such removal had been carried out by the Iraqi occupation authorities or on their specific order. Some instances reported to the mission appeared to be prima facie cases of looting, pillaging or plundering and these have so been described in the text. In other cases, property was not physically taken away but simply destroyed on site. In still other instances there is clear evidence of vandalism and ransacking. Accounts given to the mission during its survey attributed responsibility to the occupation forces in all such cases. It was also explained to the mission that during the occupation a number of areas had been declared off-limits to Kuwaiti residents, thus facilitating the removal of goods without their knowledge.

21. While the seizure of some moveable property—particularly from warehouses, factories and plants—appeared premeditated and planned, at the shop or household level the pillaging of goods was said to have been carried out by individual Iraqi soldiers. In a number of cases the Iraqi authorities issued receipts to some institutions and factories from which goods had been taken, and even vouchers to be redeemed subsequently in Iraqi currency.

22. In reading the present report it should be understood that references to the removal of goods, in whatever manner, are intended to mean that they were removed by the Iraqi occupation forces either for their use in Kuwait or for transportation to Iraq.

23. Given the urgent and hence limited time-frame for the mission's work in Kuwait and the very difficult circumstances under which the assessment had to be undertaken, the mission decided to concentrate on the main sectors having a major bearing on Kuwait's economic activity—the oil industry, for example—or on those sectors that substantially affect the welfare of the population, such as health and the environment. The mission also examined the petrochemical and other manufacturing industries, electricity and water, agriculture, livestock and fisheries, sewerage and waste disposal, transport and communications, education and culture, housing and urban infrastructure, banking and commerce, as well as information and other services.

24. The mission established certain guidelines to achieve a uniform approach in all sectors. The approach involved the following steps:

(a) An appraisal of the conditions of each sector before 2 August 1990, together with an identification of the central or core elements in each sector;

(b) Preliminary discussions between the sectoral leaders of the mission and their Kuwaiti counterparts on current conditions in each sector and, in particular, possible damage inflicted on core elements during the period of occupation;

(c) On-site inspection by the sectoral leaders of core elements and of other areas heavily affected, as well as an assessment of loss and damage to the infrastructure, machinery, equipment, support facilities, materials, etc.;

(d) Cross-checking of information with government officials, national and international agencies, technical experts, in particular from the multinational forces (e.g., mine-clearing experts and United States Army Corps of Engineers), and, in relevant cases, executives from the Kuwaiti private sector;

(e) On-site inspection of secondary elements (e.g., electrical substations, local health clinics) and geographical areas moderately damaged or undamaged. This was done on a selective basis, endeavouring to ensure adequate representativity. In a few cases, this was supplemented by a catalogue or inventory from the Kuwaiti authorities;

(f) Discussions with the Kuwaiti authorities, sectoral representatives and other experts in the area to ascertain possible gaps in the assessment of damage and on-site inspection of gaps so identified.

25. Since the mission was not intended to provide, and indeed was not in a position to suggest, an exhaustive, quantified evaluation of damage, the sectoral assessment involves only a characterization of the damage and an indication of its extent. The latter is assessed, wherever possible, in percentage terms. For most estimates, the margin of error is plus or minus 10 per cent.

26. Particular difficulties arose in making accurate assessments of the current inventory of raw materials, spare parts, finished goods and equipment, as well as of intellectual and cultural property (books, archives, historical artifacts, research data, notes and texts) in the various institutions and facilities visited.

27. Since most files were destroyed or removed, it will be particularly difficult for the public and private sectors to reconstitute the lists of their inventory at the time of the invasion. Similarly, it will be some time before exact lists can be established of assets that remained after the withdrawal of the occupation forces, since few, if any institutions or factories show any semblance of normal functioning. Many facilities are wholly deserted and in those cases where some staff have reported for work, they are primarily engaged in the most basic tasks of restoring a semblance of order by sifting through the few remaining documents.

28. The mission visited many premises, inspecting storage rooms and warehouses of each institution in order to verify conditions at the time of its visit. The mission's awareness of the inventory normally required for the proper functioning of the various facilities helped it to gain a good idea of the extent of the losses. It should be borne in mind that Kuwaiti institutions, because of the relatively generous availability of resources, were often in a position to keep large stocks of supplies in hand.

29. Four categories were used to quantify damage or loss of assets: (a) less than 20 per cent, slight damage or slight loss; (b) 20 to 50 per cent, moderate damage or moderate loss; (c) 50 to 80 per cent, heavy damage or heavy loss; and (d) 80 to 100 per cent, completely damaged, total destruction or total loss. The corresponding categories used in the environmental assessment were: light; moderate; severe; very severe. In the case of major infrastructure items, a brief description of the damage to each item has also been included in the text.

30. In surveying the damage to the infrastructure in Kuwait, the mission took into account the fact that some areas, sites and locations in the country had been the scene of armed conflict and engagement, while others had been the target of military action by one side or the other. This was particularly the case with airfields and telecommunication installations. However, the overwhelming majority of sites visited and inspected by the mission suggested damage that was not war-related but the result of wanton and deliberate acts, some intended to destroy specific national assets and vital services.

31. The basic approach to the assessment of the environment was essentially the same as in other sectors. None the less, it is important to highlight its special features. First, it was broad-based, covering all the geography of the country, including coastal areas and environment-related sectors, such as agriculture, livestock and fisheries. Secondly, environmental conditions were still changing rapidly, with further deterioration in some areas and improvement in others. Thus, the mission tried to collect all data on environmental conditions compiled from different sources since the withdrawal of the occupation forces, including data and measurements that were becoming available on an almost daily basis while the mission was in Kuwait.

I. ECONOMIC AND SOCIAL CONDITIONS IN MID-1990 AND EARLY MARCH 1991

A. *Situation before 2 August 1990*

32. In mid-1990, the population of Kuwait was 2.1 million, of whom about 800,000 were Kuwaiti citizens. More than half of the population was under 25 years of age. Well over 90 per cent of the total population lived in urban areas along the coast, giving the whole country a metropolitan character. Life expectancy for men was 71 and for women 75 years, with an infant mortality rate of the order of 15 per 1,000. Kuwaiti citizens enjoyed a developed welfare system backed by a well-equipped infrastructure.

33. Education, including secondary education, was provided free to both Kuwaitis and non-Kuwaitis. Health services were also virtually free and of quite a high standard, as was housing, which was heavily subsidized for the low- and middle-income groups of the population.

34. Per capita income amounted to about US$14,700, while the per capita gross domestic product (GDP) amounted to $11,600 in 1989. The difference was due to large revenues in the form of interest and dividends from accumulated investments abroad. Crude oil production and related activities made up for a large part of total output: 40 to 50 per cent of GDP.

35. The economy had remained fairly vulnerable to oil prices in international markets, since petroleum and petroleum products accounted for 90 per cent of total exports. It had, however, continued to expand, albeit modestly, in the 1980s. The rate of inflation during this period was remarkably low.

36. A cautious balance-of-payments policy and a very large export sector ensured a steady surplus in the balance on current account, leading to increased investments abroad and a strong dinar. Between 1985 and 1989, average annual exports of goods and services amounted to $8,800 million and imports to $4,670 million. According to International Monetary Fund (IMF) figures at the end of June 1990, the level of total reserves minus gold had reached $2,128 million and gold reserves stood at 2.5 million fine troy ounces.

37. The share of gross fixed capital formation in GDP, a major determinant of the potential for economic

growth, could be compared to that of States members of the Organization for Economic Cooperation and Development (OECD): slightly below 20 per cent in the late 1980s. The investment level in 1989 was close to $5 billion. Government policies and the comparatively high investment rates led to a gradual diversification of the economy, despite the enormous potential of the oil industry. Indeed, the country's proven recoverable oil resources were quite high in mid-1990. They had been estimated at 94,500 million barrels, which measured the equivalent of about 200 years of output at a rate of 1.3 million barrels a day.

38. The steady stream of oil export revenues allowed the country not only to attain a high level of material prosperity, but also to channel a large volume of resources through the public budget. In the 1988/89 budget, expenditures reached $11 billion, mainly for industrial diversification, the increased provision of social services and the gradual establishment of a major reserve fund for future generations, as well as aid to low-income developing countries. In fact, in relation to its GDP, Kuwait was among the international community's largest aid donors in the 1980s.

39. In the late 1980s, annual per capita public expenditure in education and health was about $500 and $350 respectively. The number of university graduates was growing at a rate exceeding 8 per cent a year—twice the rate of growth of the population. The number of graduates in petroleum engineering, medicine and allied health services was growing at an even more rapid pace.

40. In brief, Kuwait, in mid-1990, had a solid balance-of-payments position, public finances were under control and the process of industrialization and improved development of human resources was proceeding apace. Economic instability was still somewhat inherent in the development process of the country because of the volatility of oil prices and the unusually high reliance on migrant labour. However, Kuwait had a functioning economy and was clearly poised to attain even higher living standards and still greater social development in the years ahead.

B. *Conditions in March 1991*

41. The invasion of Kuwait in August 1990 brought about a dramatic change. By the end of Iraq's occupation on 26 February 1991, the outlook had been radically transformed. Kuwait City, previously a modern, urban centre with thriving bazaars and a busy commercial district, had become a ghost town. The same was true of other urban areas across the country, where major social dislocations had occurred during the occupation of the country: two thirds of Kuwaiti nationals had sought refuge abroad; three quarters of the labour force had been

obliged to leave Kuwait; and the quality and availability of health services had been dramatically downgraded and education had come to a halt.

42. The effect of the occupation on Kuwait's economic and commercial life was even more devastating. Managerial capacity to run corporate activities and carry out government tasks had been depleted. The occupation authorities, through a web of administrative and financial restrictions, had prevented the few executives who had remained in Kuwait from taking any initiative.

43. The physical infrastructure supporting basic services—electricity, water, waste disposal—had been rendered inoperative; ports largely destroyed; oil production and refining and related offloading activities crippled; the financial system severely disrupted; foreign trade suspended; commerce considerably diminished; manufacturing paralysed; and inventories plundered. The marine environment had been severely affected by the flow of crude oil into the Persian Gulf, while the beautiful waterfront in Kuwait City had been devastated and its entire beach turned into a minefield.

44. From an economic point of view, no less than from an environmental perspective, the greatest damage was that inflicted on the oil industry. The destruction of refineries and pipeline and storage systems and, above all, the firing of more than 600 oil wells had brought unprecedented catastrophe to the economy and the environment of Kuwait. Moreover, numerous mines laid by the occupation forces continued to pose a persistent threat to human lives.

45. At the time of the arrival of the mission in mid-March 1991, economic, social and environmental conditions bore no resemblance to the situation that prevailed only eight months earlier.

46. The fall in aggregate output and the losses of income were staggering. The decrease in Kuwait's GDP between early August 1990 and late February 1991 was more than 70 per cent. Capital formation came to a halt as virtually all new projects, and projects under implementation, were stopped.

47. Even an enormous drop in output and investment paralysis can be a transitory phenomenon. In Kuwait, however, the widespread destruction of capital assets and the supporting infrastructure, as well as the looting of equipment and inventories, could only make recovery difficult and protracted. Output losses remained quite substantial in March and will continue to be very large in the coming months.

48. Despite the unprecedented economic setback and social dislocation, the mission witnessed some significant improvements during the short period it was in Kuwait. Electric power and telephone services had been restored to parts of the country and food and other

essential goods were becoming increasingly available. A few retail shops that had escaped damage had been opened and street vendors had appeared. But the essential process of repair and rehabilitation was still very much at its initial stage. Succeeding generations will continue to be endangered by unexploded ordnance, particularly mines. The physical infrastructure could well require a great part of the present decade to recover. The harm to the population from a polluted environment, although not easily identifiable today, may become manifest in a pervasive way only with the passage of time. Plans for the restoration of social and administrative services are being formulated on an urgent basis. But it will take months, even years, before the country recovers from the damage and losses inflicted by the Iraqi occupation.

II. SUMMARIZED ASSESSMENT OF MAJOR DAMAGE

49. As explained in the introduction to the present report, the mission carried out a very broad assessment of the damage inflicted on the economy of Kuwait as the result of the country's occupation by Iraq.

50. Based upon data presented by the Kuwaiti authorities, as well as on estimates made by expert members of the mission, it was possible to arrive at a very broad approximation of damage and loss sustained in several areas. A summary quantification is presented below.

51. The GDP of Kuwait was of the order of $24 billion in 1989. The invasion led to a virtual paralysis in many economic activities and a major reduction in the delivery of service. The corresponding loss in output, and consequently income, amounted to about $10 billion between August 1990 and February 1991.

52. The rehabilitation of the oil industry, including the capping and control of oil wells, the repair of gathering centres and the reconstruction of refineries is expected to exceed $5 billion. In addition, nearly 4 million barrels were being lost daily at the time of the mission's visit. This loss will accumulate until the wells are controlled and capped.

53. Critical parts of the electrical generating capacity and also part of the distribution grid were destroyed during the occupation. The cost of restoring the electrical system to the standard prevailing before the invasion will be of the order of $1 billion.

54. The damage suffered by the transport infrastructure was heavy in the case of ports and harbours. The national airport also suffered major damage. Air transport services not only sustained damage to their facilities they also experienced a major theft in equipment. The overall losses sustained by ports, the airport and the national airline amount to more than $2 billion.

55. The country's road transport fleet, including private and public vehicles, needs to be restored to its former level. The occupation resulted in at least half of the country's transport fleet (buses, long-haul vehicles, tankers, trucks, cars, etc.) being lost, either by their appropriation and removal from the country or by destruction. Restoring the fleet to its former level of 560,000 vehicles is estimated to cost over $5 billion.

56. The country's satellite system and the internal telephone and telecommunications network will need a considerable amount of replacement equipment and will take some time to repair. It is estimated that $1 billion will be required to bring these essential services back into full operation.

57. In the case of radio, television and press services, another $500 million will be required to rebuild damaged transmitter stations, to replace the powerful transmitters that were either removed or destroyed and to re-equip studios, control rooms and printing establishments.

58. It is difficult to estimate the cost to the housing sector since the losses were not so much the result of structural damage as of ransacking and vandalism that were inflicted on a great number of houses, particularly those that were unoccupied during the seven-month period. At a conservative average figure of $15,000 per dwelling unit, it is estimated that total losses to 170,000 housing units will be approximately $2.5 billion.

59. The reconstruction and refurbishing of two large resort complexes and of 800 rooms in damaged de luxe and first-class hotels will exceed $100 million. The group of hotel owners contacted has made an estimate of $100,000 per room, which includes the restoration of restaurant and catering areas, equipment and all other facilities.

60. To rebuild, repair and refurbish other urban infrastructure, major expenditures will need to be incurred. To restore government buildings, including the National Assembly, and to repair the waterfront, reconstruct the International Trade Fair and rehabilitate the sporting clubs and other recreational facilities, at least $500 million will be required.

61. In the banking sector, Kuwait will need to recover valuables taken from a very large number of commercial banks. Moreover, 1.3 million troy ounces of gold valued at close to $500 million were removed from the Central Bank.

62. The looting of wholesale and retail establishments was massive and spared virtually no commercial centre, warehouse or large store. Estimates in this area can only be very tentative, yet losses (excluding vehicles) could easily approach $1 billion.

63. The damage to the petrochemical industry and other manufacturing activities was large and often characterized by the complete removal of modern machinery and equipment and the looting of inventories (raw materials, spare parts and finished products). Owing to the very large number of affected industrial establishments, an accurate quantification will take considerable time. However, an amount of damage bordering on $1 billion appears reasonable.

64. The above estimates do not cover all damage sustained. Destruction of installations and considerable losses of equipment were sustained in other sectors, in particular education and health, as well as the road network and maintenance equipment, water supply and garbage disposal systems, agricultural stations and fisheries.

65. Moreover, in a number of areas surveyed by the mission there was damage or "hidden losses" whose precise scale and nature were not evident on the surface but which, nevertheless, might represent a further erosion of Kuwait's infrastructural base. These include damage resulting from inadequate care and maintenance, the rusting and disintegration of metal components, the solidification of liquids or extraneous materials obstructing or blocking pipes and ducts in refineries, industrial plants and public utilities. Among the most important of the unassessed losses is the damage to the oil reservoirs. None of these could be assessed at the time of the mission's visit.

66. Related to this is the continuous loss in output, and consequently of income. In March 1991, the economy remained at a standstill. To return to production levels prevailing in early 1990, let alone to surpass them, would require not only enormous investments of money but also manpower.

67. Finally, but by no means the least important, is the range of unquantifiable losses arising from the downgrading of health facilities, the depletion of the national cultural heritage, the irreplaceable school year lost to all students and, of course, the degradation of the environment. Not one of these can even remotely be assessed in finite figures but their impact will be felt by Kuwait for generations to come.

III. OIL INDUSTRY

A. *An overall view*

68. Kuwait's petroleum industry was a fully vertically integrated operation covering all facets of exploration, drilling, production, refining and marketing, both domestically and internationally.

69. During the occupation of Kuwait, much of the country's petroleum industry was pillaged and sabotaged. The latter is perhaps most graphically evidenced by the hundreds of fires that were set off by the blowing up of the oil wells.

70. The mission's assessment of the damage takes into account not only the degree of destruction but also the interdependence and interrelationship of each separate and distinct function of the petroleum industry. In order to facilitate the understanding of the nature of its vertical integration, two block flow schematics are reproduced at the end of the present section. Figure 1 depicts the petroleum production network and figure 2 shows the gas production network [not reproduced here].

B. *Crude oil production facilities*

1. *Situation before 2 August 1990*

71. At the beginning of 1990, Kuwait's oil wells had an installed capacity of 2.9 million barrels per day with maximum technically sustainable capacity of 2.5 million barrels per day. According to some estimates, this latter figure could have been increased to 4 million barrels per day within 24 to 36 months. Proven reserves stood at 94,525 million barrels by the end of the 1980s (or about 130 years of production at a rate of 2 million barrels per day).

72. At the time of the invasion, crude oil production in Kuwait amounted to about 1.5 million barrels per day. Crude oil production and associated offloading facilities were carried out by the Kuwait Oil Company (KOC), a subsidiary of the Kuwait Petroleum Corporation (KPC).

73. There are four areas in Kuwait that are in use for producing crude oil: north Kuwait, west Kuwait, south-east Kuwait and Wafrah. The first three areas are wholly owned and operated by KOC, while the crude oil production in the Wafrah area was shared equally by Kuwait and Saudi Arabia.

74. North Kuwait consisted of four fields with 316 wells and produced 400,000 barrels per day. West Kuwait contained three fields with 134 wells and produced 150,000 barrels per day. South-east Kuwait was the "jewel in the crown" of Kuwait's oil production and contained the multi-reservoir Greater Burgan field, the second-largest oilfield in the world. There were 661 wells in south-east Kuwait and it produced 1.1 million barrels per day. Of the total of 1,111 wells in these three areas, 980 were in production on 1 August 1990. Of the 900 wells in the Wafrah area, 350 were active and produced between 170,000 and 180,000 barrels per day. Half of Wafrah's production was transported through underground pipelines to a refinery at Mina Az Zawr, which is owned and operated by Texaco for the benefit of Saudi Arabia. Part of the other half (heavy crude or eocene) went by underground pipelines to the refinery at Mina

Abd Allah, but was processed at the Al Ahmadi refinery. The rest was normally stored in tanks at Ahmadi town.

75. Wafrah differs from the other three areas in that there was very little pressure in its fields and in many instances oil was pumped out by means of suckerrod pumps. As a result of the pressure in the other three fields, oil and the associated natural gas flowed freely through surface gathering lines to gathering stations for processing.

76. After separating the oil and gas, the oil was conveyed by underground pipelines and manifolds to two storage tank farms at Ahmadi, which had a combined storage capacity of 14 million barrels. The tank farms are located 120 metres above sea-level, which made it possible for the oil to flow by natural gravity through an intricate system of manifolds and underground pipelines to Kuwait's three refineries at Mina al Ahmadi, Mina Abd Allah and Mina Shuaiba as well as to its crude offloading facilities at Mina al Ahmadi and, through marine pipelines, to an offshore sea-island and a single point mooring facility.

77. On 1 August 1990, KOC was operating a modern, sophisticated crude oil production system requiring highly developed managerial and engineering skills and employing some 5,000 people. Its crude oil exports alone (excluding export of refined products) generated about $13 million per day for the Kuwaiti economy.

2. Assessment of damage

78. After almost seven months of occupation, this prosperous situation dramatically changed. Kuwait's oil industry was reduced to a shambles. Excluding the Wafrah area, there were 980 active crude oil and associated natural gas producing wells. Of these, some 550 were in flames. Many other wells, which were not on fire, were gushing tens of thousands of barrels of oil each day, flooding the desert and creating lakes and rivers of oil. If one takes into account the Wafrah area, the total number of active wells increases to 1,330, of which approximately 700 were on fire at the time of the mission's visit.

79. Estimates vary, but there is general agreement that from 2 million to 6 million barrels are lost in this manner each day. On the basis of $20 per barrel, this represents a loss ranging from $40 million to as much as $120 million each day. As a result of the occupation and the consequent loss of production during the period, Kuwait suffered an additional loss of $8.5 billion.

80. Today, no production of crude oil is possible, and it may take as much as 12 to 18 months to bring all the burning and gushing wells under control. Efforts to extinguish the fires have been initiated. These efforts are being helped by four undamaged underground pipelines leading from the tank farms to the Persian Gulf, which can be used to pump sea water to the oil fields in a reverse flow mode. This process will save considerable time,

money and effort. As soon as the reverse flow pumping system is in place the fire fighting effort can start.

81. Since the end of March, three fire-fighting teams have arrived in Kuwait. By the end of May, 15 to 18 teams are expected to be in place. The operation would cost approximately $45 million to $50 million per month. Consequently, bringing all wells under control is estimated to range from $600 million to $850 million, or about $1 million to $1.5 million per well.

82. It is extremely difficult to establish the exact number of wells damaged as a number of areas have not been declared safe to enter because of mines and ordnance. However, taking the situation in the Maqwa and Al Ahmadi fields (both surveyed by the mission by helicopter and located in the Greater Burgan field) as a guide, only 5 out of 239 wells were free of damage. In addition, as the fires continue to rage out of control, major damage may be inflicted on the reservoirs. A number of wells are already yielding water mixed with oil and gas, turning the smoke from black soot to a grey mixture of soot and steam. Wells undergoing this process may be rendered useless for future production and the drilling of replacement wells, expensive remedial drilling techniques or other types of rehabilitation may be required to recover the oil. Furthermore, pressure in the reservoirs is also diminishing, thereby lessening considerably the ease by which the oil is currently produced.

83. In order to determine the extent of the damage to the reservoirs, simulation models must be developed. Fortunately such models have been made in the past for all KOC oil fields. It appears that they can be readily adapted for analysing the present production problems that may exist at the wells. In the event of wells having to be replaced because of irreparable damage, the average cost of completely restoring a shallow well (3,400-9,000 feet) would amount to up to $1.5 million and for a deeper well (9,000-15,000 feet) up to $5 million. Most of the wells in the Greater Burgan and Wafrah fields are shallow, ranging in depth from 3,400 to 4,700 feet, while in the northern and western fields they range from 7,500 to 11,000 feet.

84. At the same time there are 681 wells (550 in the Wafrah area and 131 in the other three areas) and gathering stations that are basically intact and could be brought on stream rather quickly, thus making it possible to produce as much as 50,000 barrels per day within two months and as much as 150,000 barrels per day within six months. These production rates are contingent upon the removal of other bottlenecks downstream from the wells but they are, of course, well below those prevailing before the occupation.

85. The upstream facilities of KOC, consisting of 26 gathering stations (excluding 1 main station and 23

substations at Wafrah), which separate the oil and gas at the well areas, were heavily damaged or destroyed. Of the 26 stations, which cost about $200 million each, the condition of only half could be ascertained since smoke, fire, mines and ordnance precluded visits on foot or surveys by helicopter. Eight of the 13 stations surveyed were severely damaged; 1 of these, located near the crest of the Greater Burgan field, where the smoke and fire conditions are infernal, can be considered representative of another 7, making a total of 15 that are highly likely to have sustained severe damage. Of the remaining five stations visited, three are out of commission because either their tanks or control rooms have been destroyed; at one of the stations, one tank was on fire and the other was slightly damaged. In general, it appears that at least a minimum 31 to 58 per cent of the stations were severely damaged (for a total loss of between $1.6 billion and $3.0 billion) and 12 per cent cannot be operated.

86. The mission's inspection showed that the downstream facilities of KOC also incurred heavy damage. They consist of various manifolds, two tank farms (north and south), pipelines to the refineries and offloading facilities, as well as the crude export facilities.

87. The central mixing manifold was heavily damaged but the filling manifolds for the south and north tank farms are intact. Damage to the two tank farms is major. Of the 35 tanks comprising the south tank farm, with a total storage capacity of 6 million barrels, 14 tanks were destroyed and 2 were damaged, for a lost capacity of about 3.3 million barrels, or 55 per cent. The south tank farm is mostly used to service the refineries but it is also connected to the north tank farm and the crude export facilities through a spur manifold. Of the 24 tanks that comprise the north tank farm, with a total storage capacity of 8 million barrels, 8 tanks were destroyed and 1 was damaged, for a lost capacity of about 3.7 million barrels, or 46 per cent. The north tank farm is basically dedicated to offloading crude for export. The two loading manifolds, which are downstream from the tank farms, were said to have been destroyed by Allied precision bombing in an effort to stem the flow of large quantities of crude oil that was being released into the Persian Gulf.

88. From the above it becomes clear that the KOC operations have been strangled: no oil can enter into its system and no oil, even if it were available, can leave it. The stranglehold is aggravated by the destruction at the crude export facilities. To make matters worse, the time required for rehabilitation will be lengthened since most of the KOC employees fled Kuwait during the occupation, leaving a minimal workforce of about 1,400 people, or only 28 per cent of its normal level.

...

IV. ENVIRONMENT

A. *Oil wells*

1. *Burning*

136. The first reports of oil facilities ablaze in Kuwait came in late January as fire was set to oil installations in the Wafrah oil field. Subsequent news reports suggested that just prior to the ground war, about 150 wells were ignited. This was followed by reports that between 500 and 600 wells had been set afire.

137. The deliberate torching of the oilfields represents Kuwait's most pressing environmental problem of today, beside which all else pales into insignificance. There has never been anything like it in history before. The burning of the oil fields and the environmental effects of the burning are a direct consequence of Iraq's occupation of Kuwait.

138. KOC officials have reportedly concluded that Iraqi soldiers set explosives around the mouth of every oil well in the country immediately after the invasion but did not prime or detonate the charges until two or three days before the Allied ground offensive began on 24 February 1991. The exact number of oil wells burning is still not known officially but the mission estimates that it may have been about 700 at its maximum. Some have started to cone and go out and others are now being put out by fire fighters. The coning of a burning oil well occurs when oil is burned off faster than replacement oil can move in from surrounding oil strata. This allows the less viscous water in the strata below to move into the rock below the well intake and to be drawn up the pipe. The water-oil mixture does not burn properly so the flame goes out. A coned well cannot be restarted and the well has to be redrilled to below the point of water intake. This phenomenon means that the oil discharge pattern is changing as the number of oil wells on fire gradually decreases, while the number of wells gushing unburnt oil increases. This in turn results in the release of more oil on to the land.

139. Estimates of the amount of oil burned each day vary but are commonly thought to be between 2 million and 6 million barrels per day.

140. Each oilfield in Kuwait is producing its own emission cloud, mainly of particulates (including soot) and combustion gases. For practical purposes, there are three basic smoke plumes—southern, central and northern—of which the central is the largest and most dense, being produced by the Ahmadi, Maqwa and Greater Burgan fields. Although adjacent to others, each well fire seems to have its own individuality—a feature recognized by oil-well firemen—reflecting different conditions at the oil entry point and making smoke and gas emission variable.

141. By the end of March 1991, there was little factual information as to the nature and composition of the emissions into the atmosphere from the burning oil wells.

2. Gaseous and particulate emissions

142. Electricity was restored to parts of Kuwait City on 26 March 1991, which enabled one of the three fixed atmospheric sampling stations run by the Kuwait Environment Protection Department and that survived the occupation to begin operations again. Once calibration tests are completed, this station will be able to make authoritative statements on gaseous air quality in Kuwait City.

143. Few atmospheric composition measurements of any sort have been made in Kuwait since the occupation. A United States Environment Protection Agency team measured hydrogen sulphide and sulphur dioxide levels during the week of 11 March at Rawdatayn, Maqwa, Al Ahmadi and Greater Burgan oil fields. All gave low levels of both gases. If sulphur dioxide levels continue to be low, acid rain is unlikely to become a problem. Initial measurements of total hydrocarbons in the air suggest that levels of these substances are high. As yet, it is not possible to give information on individual hydrocarbon species. There are also no analyses yet of emitted particulate composition, especially in relation to heavy metals such as nickel and vanadium, which are present in Kuwait crude oil.

144. Medical opinion in Kuwait does not think that, at the moment, there is a serious environmental problem from the well emissions. In view of the little real information available, however, caution is advised until there has been an airborne investigation of the smoke plumes and a regular, ground-based air-monitoring programme has been re-established.

145. As stated in paragraph 140 above, there are three basic smoke plumes. Each of the main plumes is relatively narrow. On 24 March, affected by southerly winds, the plume from the Maqwa field was approximately 5 kilometres wide where it crossed the coast, while the very dense black cloud from the Al Ahmadi and Greater Burgan fields was about 15 kilometres wide in total, with an inner, very black, core about 5 kilometres wide. This black core completely obscured the sun, making it look like midnight at mid-morning. Over the oil fields, the emission plume can, depending on the winds, be almost on the ground. More normally, the lower plume boundary is, over Kuwait, some 70 to 150 metres above the ground. The plumes gradually rise as distance from the emission source increases. In general, from unmeasured observations, plumes over the central Gulf area seem to have a lower level at about 1,300 metres and an upper level at about 2,500 metres. Smoke layers from the Kuwait fires have been observed in Bahrain and over the Islamic Republic of Iran, depending on wind direction. Eventually, the smoke plume will be dispersed by weather, with the particulates falling or being washed out by rain. Detailed profiling by a specially instrumented research aircraft is necessary to establish the shape of the plumes and their constituents.

146. Ground observations suggest that the visible elements of the emission have not gone into the upper atmosphere. This may be because the oil fires were insufficiently close to create firestorm effects, which could have carried particles into the upper atmosphere. On 24 March 1991, eight fires in the Greater Burgan field were seen to swing towards each other in what could have been the start of a firestorm, but this effect lasted only a very short time. The apparent relatively large sizes of the particles may also be a limiting factor with regard to the height to which they are carried. Global climate change effects of the magnitude envisaged by some scientists are, therefore, probably unlikely.

147. Climatic effects will most likely be confined to the region, and more locally in Kuwait, where the sun-shield effects of the smoke clouds are more pronounced. When the plumes are at their most dense, sunlight does not penetrate and so is unable to heat the land in the normal fashion. Sandy desert areas do not retain heat for very long so that a few days of heavy smoke cover leads to appreciable local cooling beneath the cloud—perhaps 10°C or more. This is a temporary phenomenon, and when the plume swings away, the land heats again and air temperatures eventually rise. Kuwait authorities suggest that local air temperature lowering may have delayed the onset of spring flowering by as much as four weeks in many areas. There is, however, no quantified evidence for this and such a seasonal delay could still be within the range of natural variability.

148. Particulates from fires have been deposited on both land and sea over wide areas. In the Persian Gulf, as surveyed by the mission, they form a surface skin, which wind and currents shape into whorls and kilometre-long strands that resemble oil-slicks. The effects and consequences of these carbon deposits on the sea are not known. On land, the particles cover the ground surface and plants. In the proximity of well fields, this is mixed with unburnt oil given off as a fine spray.

149. Nothing is so far known about the composition of these particles. Samples have been collected but the analyses are not yet complete. It is not possible, therefore, to comment on the likely health and environmental consequences of these deposits.

150. The long-term consequences of this surface deposition are not known, including its effects on ground-

water quality and on the soil seedbank. It is possible that it may help to improve the water retention capabilities of the soil.

3. Crude oil on land

151. A number of burning wells have begun to extinguish themselves naturally through the coning process (see para. 138 above). At the present time, it is believed that some 30 to 40 wells in the central and northern fields may already have extinguished themselves. The mission visited three such wells in the Maqwa field. For some time after their extinction, these wells continue to gush crude oil, pouring huge amounts on to the land. This outpouring of crude oil increased dramatically in the last two weeks of March 1991. As a result, there are now large lakes of crude oil.

152. Deep, 70-metre wide, torrents of oil have blocked roads. Oil rivers flow everywhere from the wells to newly formed oil lakes. The mission observed oil erosion of land where oil rivers scour erosion gulleys in the soil—a phenomenon that may be unique in environmental observation. Natural drainage of the land is towards the coast so that steps are being taken to stop vast amounts of surface oil flowing into the Persian Gulf. Engineers are, therefore, constructing earth-containment dams across valleys to make new oil lakes and to protect roads from oil flooding. Attempts have been made, with limited success, to reignite extinguished wells in order to reduce the oil flood. The potential input into the Persian Gulf from this flood was estimated at 60,000 barrels per day from the central fields and 20,000 barrels per day from the northern fields. Although once a danger, this is no longer considered a real threat since the earth-dam containment policy is working and the gushing wells are starting to be capped, thus reducing the oil flood.

153. The oil on the land will have to be taken off most areas by pumping, scooping or other means and retained in special oil-holding areas until suitable disposal can be arranged. Rehabilitation treatment of the remaining oil-soaked areas is still uncertain. Proposals under consideration include ploughing or harrowing to mix the oil layer with sub-surface soil and sand. It is not known how successful such measures may be and the future of these oil-soaked lands will be one of Kuwait's more obvious environmental problems arising from the occupation.

154. Another major problem that must be faced urgently is the measurement of sulphur dioxide, hydrogen sulphide, carbon monoxide, nitrogen oxides, ozone, carbon dioxide, specific volatile compounds such as benzene, phenols, toluene and formaldehyde, as well as particulates from gaseous and particulate emissions. Also specific health-effect studies will be needed since the range of pollutants in the atmosphere of Kuwait could cause serious respiratory illnesses or have long-term carcinogenic and mutagenic effects.

B. Oil and the marine environment

1. Conditions in the Persian Gulf

155. In late January 1991, a massive amount of oil was reported in the Persian Gulf off the coast of Kuwait. The exact origins of this release and its volume are still matters of some controversy. A special UNEP mission to Saudi Arabia overflew the slick on 7 February and estimated its volume at 1 million barrels or less. It concluded that the oil slick along the Saudi Arabian coast was most likely the main oil slick from the January release, although it did not rule out the possibility of other slicks being in northern Persian Gulf waters. It was not able, for security reasons, to overfly this part of the Persian Gulf to make a determination.

156. The present mission had, therefore, as a major objective to determine whether any major oil slicks were present in adjacent areas of the Persian Gulf. It found no indication of a major oil slick anywhere along the Kuwaiti coast and offshore as far as about 30 kilometres seaward. However, several patches of thin oil sheen of limited size were observed at different localities closer to the coast, within a range of 2 to 3 kilometres. In one place only, a small slick of heavy-looking oil was observed within 1 kilometre of the coast, extending between Al Fuhayhil and Ra's al Mangaf, i.e., for about 3 kilometres along the coast. The only relatively large amount of heavy black oil was found contained in the commercial harbour of the Kuwait Fisheries Company at Mina Shuaiba.

157. During the mission's aerial surveys of the coast (20 and 22 March 1991), narrow bands of black carbon particles extending over varying distances were observed, obviously resulting from atmospheric deposits of carbon emitted with the soot from the burning oil wells.

158. There was no indication of any massive fouling of beaches. Only in a few scattered sites along the Kuwaiti coast visited by the mission were oil traces and deposits found. For example, accumulated black oil was observed on the beach inside coastal embayments where oil is likely to be trapped (in Al Fuhayhil, e.g.). In the southern part of the coast, near Umm-Qusubah, oil was found on the beach under 10 centimetres of sand. Also during the mission's aerial survey on 20 March 1991, some black oil was noted onshore in two small stretches of the shoreline close to the amenity facilities in the Al Khiran area.

159. KOC officials, in their briefing to the mission at KOC headquarters at Al Ahmadi, stated that the occupation authorities had begun to build up the storage quantities for release into the Gulf. According to the KOC log books, there were 10.7 million barrels in storage at

22 January 1991. Shortly after that date, the Iraqis reportedly released the oil from the tank farms to the sea through the pipelines leading to the KOC sea-island. A few days later, an Allied precision bombing air raid destroyed the two loading manifolds downstream from the tank farms as well as the KOC sea-island, thereby effectively halting the flow of crude oil into the Persian Gulf. There were only 1.5 million barrels left in the tank farms. It is estimated that at least 6 million barrels of oil were released. The balance (3.2 million barrels) may have been partly removed to fill in the defensive trenches along the Kuwait-Iraq border and the rest probably burnt.

160.   The above statement by the KOC officials accounts for 6 million barrels of crude oil released into the sea. They further confirmed that there were three Iraqi oil tankers anchoring off the north pier, each of 200,000 tons of crude oil capacity, with a total maximum of 600,000 tons, or 4.2 million barrels. These ships were said to have deliberately unloaded crude oil into the Persian Gulf, as the ships were seen rising gradually as they released their oil contents. One of these ships was damaged by the same air raid described above, which stopped its release of oil.

161.   A satellite image taken on 25 January 1991 shows a long plume of smoke originating from two close-by sources about 16 kilometres off-shore: the bombed sea-island and the tanker. This means that the spillage occurred sometime during the period from 22 to 25 January, sufficiently long to achieve the 6 million barrel quantity dumped. By means of scaling from the same image, it is possible to determine that the oil-slick was about 50 kilometres long and 8 kilometres wide on 25 January. Assuming that the slick had an average thickness of 0.5 centimetres, the resulting volume could be as large as 2 billion litres (13 million barrels) or more than sufficient to contain the 6 million barrels released from the tank farms and the 4.2 million barrels from the tankers.

162.   In the light of the above, it seems reasonable to assume that such an oil-slick was formed on or about 24 January 1991. However, it is evident that a large portion (about 50 per cent) of the slick has quickly evaporated. The remainder, under weathering effects and degradation, has diminished and broken into small patches which moved southwards and reached the Saudi Arabian waters in a much lesser amount of approximately 1 million barrels. This was clearly observed and confirmed by a UNEP expert mission to Saudi Arabia.

2.   *Effects on the marine environment and
      related activities*

163.   The "sheen" effects on the sea surface appear when the oil surface film is less than 1.5×10^{-4} millimetres in thickness. At this thickness, the oil film probably reflects more light than it absorbs but no work appears to have been done to examine the light effects of oil pollution upon phytoplankton primary production.

164.   Perhaps of greater concern are macrophytes such as seagrasses. These will be affected both by toxic hydrocarbons and contamination of sediments. Oils penetrate stomata and can lead to death of the plants. Seagrass beds provide the nursery grounds for commercially important shrimps. So, even if the seagrass beds are not subject to direct oil pollution because of their depth, the young shrimp may be affected by the toxic residues of partially degraded oil. Shrimp, which breed in spring, live for little more than a year, so contamination of the seagrass beds now could severely reduce shrimp catches for a whole year and lead to significant reductions in the following year. Apart from their importance to shrimps, the extensive seagrass beds provide food and a habitat for a wide variety of marine organisms and are a major contributor to the productivity of the Persian Gulf.

165.   Another fragile ecosystem existing in the Kuwaiti marine environment is the coral reef communities that occur at the three coral islands—Kubbar, Qaru and Umm Al Maradim. The parts of these reefs that are very close to the surface will be at risk from direct oil impact, especially if oil coats the corals during extreme low tides. The polyps of which the reefs are formed are also highly sensitive and easily killed, either by direct smothering with oil or ingestion of oil droplets in the water column or toxic oil derivatives. Recovery will be slow because corals are already at the limit of their distribution in the high salinities and temperatures of the Persian Gulf waters.

166.   Furthermore, in the coastal waters of Kuwait, particularly in the north and around Bubiyan Island, there is a very broad inter-tidal zone, with extensive mudflats coated with blue-green algae which provide the basic input for the food chains of many fish and crustaceans. These mudflats also provide the feeding grounds for numerous species of wading birds. The beaching of oil on such mudflats will not only smother the surface algae, but will also kill the fauna of worms and crustaceans upon which both fish and birds feed.

C.   *Land degradation*

1.   *General considerations*

167.   In its overflights and ground surveys, the mission found that large parts of rural Kuwait showed land degradation dating to before the occupation. Overgrazing effects were widespread. Other areas known to be favoured for seasonal camping showed vegetation reduction, while vegetation composition suggested that woody shrubs were less prevalent in these areas than might be expected. Environmental factors resulting from the war

enhanced impacts on these areas because they have been subjected to stress from prior forms of land usage.

168. Land degradation is taken here to mean all forms of land disturbance that have altered the basic surface soil structure and its overlying vegetation cover. All data on land degradation were gathered by the mission during overflights and ground field trips. The mission also held discussions with Kuwaiti Environment Protection Department staff.

2. Military fortifications

169. The Iraqi military fortified many areas of Kuwait prior to the Allied ground offensive. These fortifications were particularly well developed along the southern border of Kuwait and along the entire coastline but especially in the central part where sea-borne Allied landings were expected. However, defensive constructions abound in most parts of the country, being most abundant along roads, around military and communication centres and on most high ground.

170. Those constructions, made of stone and concrete, will persist unless they are removed. Such removal will be necessary in urban areas and in scenic and tourist regions such as at points along the coast and on the escarpment in the Jal Az Zawr National Park.

3. Off-the-road vehicle movement

171. The movement of large numbers of wheeled and tracked vehicles over desert lands can break up the upper sand and soil horizons leading to subsequent wind and water erosion. Repeated damage by vehicles can cause mortality of perennial desert herbs and tussock grasses such as *Panicum turgidum*. Tanks and other tracked vehicles are generally thought to be more destructive in these respects than vehicles with wheels.

172. During the ground war, several thousand Iraqi and Allied vehicles were driving across the desert plains of Kuwait. Several engagements were fought, involving manoeuvring of heavy tracked vehicles, often at speed. The potential for soil and plant damage was, therefore, considerable.

173. Aerial surveys by the mission showed that in many areas, particularly in western Kuwait, there were sets of old tracks made by wheeled vehicles, as well as newer tracks from the recent war. The old tracks were presumably from pre-war camping, hunting or oil survey parties. They stood out as twin bands of very green, often shrubby, vegetation resulting from the current widespread rains. The early wheel tracks functioned here like the hollows described above, with resultant increased plant growth in the wheel ruts. In some areas, the newer wheel and tracked vehicle traces will heal through vege-

tation growth. In other areas, however, the tracks will erode owing to wind action blowing sand and soil particles into the air. Kuwait is known for its seasonal dust storms and dust fall-out onto Kuwait is perhaps the highest in the world. The number of dust storms and their severity may well increase as a result of the abundance of loose sand and soil particles within newly formed wheel tracks. Some of these additional wind-blown particles may be deposited on coastal marine ecosystems. These problems will persist until the re-establishment of a soil stabilizing vegetative cover.

4. Geographical distribution

Coastal zone

174. This zone consists of the beach together with a strip of land fronting the shore. The width of this strip varies according to locality, reaching in places up to some 300 metres from the shoreline.

175. The Iraqi occupation forces constructed very heavy defence lines along the entire length of the sea coast. Bubiyan Island has substantial defences around its south and east coasts but not its west and north, which face Iraq. Faylakah Island is entirely ringed by coastal defences. As far as could be determined, none of the other islands overflown had sea defences (Umm Al Maradim, Kubbar, Quhat and Mashkan). The normal pattern of coastal defences involves one or more outer lines of barbed wire in the sea as fences or coils, a mixture of stakes in the sand and concrete blocks, followed by more barbed wire on land. These are backed by machine-gun positions, gun emplacements and armoured vehicle revetments. Obstacles impeding vision and field of fire have been removed and buildings converted to firing positions. Shoreline defences are intermingled with minefields. These defences are most complex in the southern part of the country and along the coastline of the whole urban complex. On the very southern coastline there are some vehicle disturbances and some craters. From Al Jahrah northwards the coastal defence works became less complex, being reduced to lines of barbed wire with, in places, trenches behind. These defences are in association with minefields. Vehicle track disturbances and crater formation are not extensive. The environmental disturbance from Al Jahrah to the Saudi Arabian border can in general be classed as severe to very severe. There are a few patches, however, where disturbance is only light to moderate. From Al Jahrah northwards disturbance is mainly moderate but light in some places.

South-east zone (south of the Manaqish-Al Jahrah line)

176. Gun emplacements, armoured vehicle revetments, trenches and the like are commonplace every-

where, particularly on raised areas and at points commanding roads, communication centres and other strategic locations. Disturbance is moderate to severe in areas where constructions occur. Crater damage and vehicle track disturbances are severe to very severe in areas near the Saudi Arabian border and in zones bordering the main road to Kuwait City. The international border in the south is marked by fences and two parallel 4 to 6 metre high sand berms separated by a wide, deep ditch that was intended to be filled with oil. Elsewhere vehicle track damage is slight to light and there are relatively few craters.

North-east zone (east of the Al Jahrah-al-Abdali line, excluding Bubiyan Island)

177.   Constructions are found along all roads, on all elevated positions and around all oil fields, military camps and harbours. Constructions are extensive on top of, and behind, the Az Zawr ridge. On open sandy areas, particularly near the periphery of the zone, there is tracked vehicle damage. Craters occur near all military positions. In strategic areas, disturbance is severe, but elsewhere it is moderate. Trenches and vehicle revetments can be found in the remotest of areas, although they are not normally extensive.

Bubiyan Island

178.   There is some defensive construction but only moderate vehicle track and crater disturbance in some places. In general, Bubiyan Island seems not to have been greatly disturbed.

North-west zone

179.   There are scattered constructions throughout, becoming very prevalent in the north close to the Iraqi border. Ammunition dumps, fuel-bowser centres, vehicle revetments, trenches and bunkers of many types abound. Vehicle track damage in the north is severe in places. There are very disturbed areas where large numbers of heavy tracked vehicles manoeuvred, churning the soil in the process. Elsewhere such vehicles advanced cross-country in line-abreast formations, creating extensive parallel tracks. Where military constructions occur, craters abound. In the northern part of the zone, the disturbance in places is severe to very severe; elsewhere, it is moderate. In the southern zone, disturbance seemed mainly light, except along main roads. Some mainly east-west oriented oil trenches were found in a number of places.

South-west zone

180.   Scattered constructions occur on high ground and along the extensive minefield that crosses the south-ern part of the zone from east to west. The southern border of Kuwait has parallel lines of sand berms and trenches to contain soil. There are few cratered areas. Where pathways were cleared through the border defences and the minefields, there is severe local disturbance of the soil where vehicles funnelled into and out of crossing points cleared of mines. Over most of the zone vehicle tracks are sparse or absent, making this zone, overall, the least affected of all the zones.

Other land degradation types

181.   In the time available to the mission, it was not possible to examine all forms of land degradation. Based on documented experience in other war zones, the following are land degradation activities that are likely to have occurred: cutting of shrubs and trees for firewood and camouflage; damage to anti-desertification greenbelt plantations; and the burning of vegetation, both deliberately and inadvertently through ordnance explosions, burning vehicles and ignited fuel. Other likely adverse environmental activities include the shooting or killing of wildlife for sport or food and the contamination of soil and groundwater through seepage of fuel and oils, toxic camouflage paints and other similar substances.

National parks and reserves

182.   Before August 1990, Kuwait was in the final stages of preparing a detailed protected areas system. Three sites had been officially established from a series of nature conservation areas which were proposed in its marker action plans, the most well-known of which is the Jal Az Zawr National Park near Kuwait City.

183.   The Wadi Al Batin Desert Park is crossed by the main east-west minefield and its associated structures. Scattered earthworks and other constructions occur in some areas, especially on high ground, but most of the park seems to remain unaffected by the war.

184.   The Umm-Nigga Desert Park is difficult to locate on the ground from the air. It is crossed by tracks, roads and pipelines (some damaged). Structures of various types are along roads and on high ground or near strategic points. Trenches and bunkers have been built along parts of the shore of the Khawr as Subiyah.

185.   The Jal Az Zawr National Park, the ridge crest and areas to the north of it contain extensive substantial military constructions. Those on the ridge area are obtrusive and should be removed. The foreshore has defensive constructions but these are not extensive. The trenches and other earthworks will gradually disappear. The barbed wire, particularly that in the water, should be removed. On the whole, the foreshore and adjacent marshes are in good condition.

D. *Mines and other unexploded ordnance*

1. *Background*

186. During its seven-month occupation of Kuwait, the Iraqi military took steps to fortify the country against invasion by the opposing Allied forces. An important part of their fortification was the laying of minefields, on land and in the sea, across likely invasion routes and around installations and positions considered to be of strategic significance.

187. The Allied aerial bombardment of Iraqi forces in occupied Kuwait lasted from 17 January 1991 until their final withdrawal from Kuwait on 27 February 1991. Both this aerial bombardment and the accompanying military movement into Kuwait, and subsequent engagement of Iraqi forces, by Allied ground units (24-27 February 1991) involved very considerable use of explosive ordnance by both sides. For a variety of reasons a proportion of this ordnance did not explode and a large part was abandoned by Iraqi forces.

188. Mines and other unexploded ordnance together constitute a major and perhaps long-lasting threat to the environment of Kuwait and to the security and well-being of its people.

189. Both anti-tank and anti-personnel mines were used. The standard anti-tank mine is the VS 2.1 kilograms. Anti-personnel mines include the VS 50, SB 33 and the Valmara 69 jumping mine. The mines are constructed almost entirely of plastic with only the firing pin of metal. They are, therefore, very difficult to locate with most mine-detecting equipment. International agreement calls for the mine-laying party to insert metal pellets in special pockets in the explosive mass as an aid in mine detection at the end of hostilities. The metal pellets were not inserted by the Iraqi forces.

2. *Location of minefields*

190. All information on geographical distribution of the minefields is based on *Kuwait Danger Areas* maps, 19 March 1991 edition.

Coastal zone

191. With minor exceptions, the whole Persian Gulf coast of Kuwait from Iraq to Saudi Arabia was sown with a combination of anti-tank and anti-personnel mines. The minefields form part of an overall coastal defence system involving submerged offshore marine mines and an onshore arrangement of barbed wire, stakes, blocks, trenches and gun and tank emplacements. The mines have been laid both above high tide levels and in the inter-tidal zone. To avoid them floating, mines placed in the inter-tidal zone are sometimes individually tied to a mesh net that is itself pegged to the ground

surface. In most cases, the mines are covered by sand or only slightly protrude from the surface. Operations at the Shuwaikh port, which has a very narrow access, were rendered particularly dangerous because of the proliferation of sea mines.

Southern zone

192. The most extensive minefields in Kuwait are in the south of the country behind its border with Saudi Arabia. Between Al Khiran on the coast and the Manaqish oilfields in the west, the minefields are in solid, roughly parallel lines three or four minefields deep. From the Manaqish oilfields to the Hudud As Salmi custom post in the extreme west of Kuwait, and beyond into Iraq, there is a single continuous set of minefields with outlier fields in front and behind. Very large numbers of mines were used in these fields. On those crossed by the Wafrah road where the mines were visible, the mission estimated the density as 2 to 6 mines per square metre depending on mine type. In Kuwait a mixture of anti-personnel and anti-tank mines was used. In those Wafrah fields examined, most of the mines seen were anti-personnel and linked by trip-wires.

Central zone

193. Extensive minefields (anti-personnel and anti-tank) were set along the north coast of Kuwait Bay and in a south-west/north-east line just to the north-west of Al Jahrah. This defensive line is backed by secondary lines just behind the Az Zawr heights and by areas near a few centres of strategic interest, such as the air bases, army barracks and communication centres.

Other areas

194. Minefields occur at sites of strategic concern in and around Kuwait City and at a few isolated locations in the south and central areas. Faylakah Island has three known minefields in its central area away from the coast—two in the west of the island and one in the east—all containing predominantly anti-personnel mines. Apart from the minefield that crosses the western border of Kuwait in the extreme south-west, there are no other known minefields in the west and north of Kuwait along its borders with Iraq.

3. *Unexploded ordnance*

195. Unexploded devices can be found anywhere in Kuwait, particularly where battles took place or targets were attacked. *Kuwait Danger Areas* maps show the locations of some abandoned tanks or military equipment, but not all. Buildings in Kuwait City and other urban areas still contain many explosive devices. By 28 March 1991, 3 million such devices, including mines, had been cleared from Kuwait City and adjacent areas. No

information was obtained by the mission on unexploded bombs and missiles.

196. Commonly encountered devices include cluster bombs/bomblets and unused ammunition ranging from small arms to rocket-propelled grenades and large artillery mortar shells. These are normally found in ammunition dumps or with abandoned guns, tanks and other military equipment. Booby traps were still being encountered at the time of the mission.

4. *Unexploded ordnance disposal*

197. The military of six nations (United States of America, United Kingdom of Great Britain and Northern Ireland, France, Canada, Saudi Arabia and Kuwait) were coordinating their search, detection and removal operation through the EOD group from their headquarters with the Combined Civil Affairs Task Force (Camp Freedom). By 19 March 1991, a few areas had been cleared, including the runways and aprons of Kuwait International Airport, Shuaiba harbour and a few lengths of beach and seafront in Kuwait City (*Kuwait Danger Areas* maps, 19 March edition).

198. The military have experienced casualties in these clearance operations. In the future, it is expected that most clearance operations will be done by specialist civilian companies under contract to the Government of Kuwait. The question of insurance liability for those injured by explosive devices in areas said to have been cleared remains to be solved.

199. Mines and other explosive devices pose a hazard to the civil population that will persist for some time to come. Kuwait currently has a much smaller population than its pre-war level. Even with this low population, injuries from ordnance explosions are occurring at the rate of 4 or 5 per day, usually involving severe injuries to arms and legs according to reports from emergency rooms at hospitals. Souvenir hunting among abandoned Iraqi military vehicles and among the quite large number of small ammunition depots all along the coast had by 20 March 1991 reportedly led to more than 50 deaths.

5. *Future implications*

200. All the mine and ordnance experts consulted stated that there is no guarantee that swept areas are entirely free of explosive devices. *Kuwait Danger Areas* maps mark the cleared areas in green and accompany them with the following warning legend: "Area swept—approach with caution". These same experts were unanimous that large areas of Kuwait have so many mines that it is impractical to lift them, particularly the vast minefields that cross the southern part of the country. Mine experts recommend that these areas be clearly indicated

and very securely fenced. A number of passageways will have to be cleared through these minefields where they form a barrier to the seasonal movement of pastoralists and their livestock or to recreational and leisure safaris.

201. Several of the actual and proposed protected areas of Kuwait contain minefields and unexploded ordnance. These dangerous areas could be securely fenced to exclude the public and overseas visitors. The Jal Az Zawr National Park on the north of Kuwait Bay is particularly affected since minefields have been set along its coastal flats and marshes, and along parts of the top of the escarpment—both areas of prime interest to visitors. Other proposed national parks or reserves that now contain minefields include the Wadi Al Batin Desert Park (large minefields in its southern area) and the Umm Al Maradim Marine Park (mines and unexploded ordnance along much of the coast; some minefields may also be found in the land part of the reserve). The Faylakah Marine Park should be free of mines, although they may be encountered in other parts of the island.

202. The beaches of Kuwait—and to a considerable extent mined coastal waters also—pose the biggest environmental hazard from munitions because they provide one of the main recreational areas for the people. Although some parts can be fenced off, the majority will have to be swept as effectively as time and resources allow. It must be recognized, however, that there are likely to be injuries from explosions from time to time for several years to come. Because of the large concentration of mines placed it will be virtually impossible to achieve full guarantees after the cleaning.

203. A programme is required to educate the people, including the pastoralists, to the dangers of entering fenced-off minefields and of encountering unexploded devices. In addition, medical services must be prepared to cope with this new form of injury and the public must be educated as to how to respond when explosion injuries occur, and on how to summon the most immediate help.

E. *Environment-related infrastructure*

204. The Environmental Protection Council of Kuwait is the body that oversees the collection and interpretation of environmental data and advises the Government on its direction and policies with regard to the environment headed by the Minister of Public Health.

205. The Environmental Protection Department has five sections (research, finance, administration, public relations and information) and a computer centre. The research programme carried out by the technical divisions includes monitoring and assessment activities in air pollution, water pollution, soil pollution, terrestrial ecology and marine science. Technical facilities operated by the Department include three fixed air pollution monitoring

stations (at Mansouriya, Rabia and Reqqa), which have produced monthly reports since 1984. In addition, the Department operated five mobile air pollution monitoring laboratories to cover general air pollution as well as some specialized pollutants such as hydrogen sulphide, particulates and noise. There were also some 10 dust-sampling stations. Three well-equipped marine research vessels were operated, together with a small but well-equipped marine laboratory at Al Bidaa.

206. During the occupation, three mobile air pollution monitoring laboratories were removed by occupation forces. The three marine research vessels were either removed or destroyed. The marine research station at Al Bidaa, on the waterfront, had soldiers living in it who swept all the equipment outside to make room for their crew's accommodation needs. The station is now completely wrecked and the equipment ruined. The Industrial Medicine Centre in the Shuaiba Industrial Area was also completely vandalized.

207. Another centre at Shuaiba, which is run by the Shuaiba Area Authority, has been reported as completely looted and destroyed. The centre included several laboratories that were fully equipped for industrial pollution monitoring, including continuous air and water pollution monitoring by fixed stations.

208. The Department's Computer Centre, with its mainframe Vax and its supporting microcomputers, survived intact. It is not operating because of a lack of electricity; the computers have also been without maintenance for several months. The three fixed air monitoring stations also survived intact but need electricity to make them functional. Each station when operational monitors wind direction and speed, temperature, relative humidity, NO_2, methane, non-methane hydrocarbons, ozone, carbon monoxide, NO, NO_x. One station also monitors ultraviolet and infrared. One station in the industrial sector was visited. It is situated on top of a local medical clinic. The clinic had all its equipment removed. The air monitoring station was left because the Technical Adviser to the Department told the removal crews that the instruments were fixed and would break if moved and that they would be in trouble if they delivered broken equipment to Baghdad. They contented themselves by pulling out all the computer paper and stealing the three fixed air-conditioning units.

209. Some staff trained to operate the stations are available locally. Most were expatriates who have left Kuwait. Several expatriates have indicated their willingness to return as soon as the situation improves and they are allowed to enter Kuwait.

210. The mission was also informed that all the stockpile of equipment and material for combating oil pollution had been removed and transferred to Basra during the early days of the occupation. The equipment, partially imported and partially produced locally, was an essential part of the Kuwaiti national contingency plan for cases of oil pollution emergency. The equipment included 14 oil skimmers; 10,138 metres of booms of different types; 9 oil pumps; 782 barrels of chemical dispersants of different types, 3 boats, 2 cleaning cars; training equipment; 1 generator; and several other items. This equipment had on several occasions been used for the training of regional experts during courses organized by the Regional Organization for the Protection of the Marine Environment.

211. The mission was provided with seven lists of items looted or destroyed during the occupation, covering fixed and mobile air and water quality monitoring stations, marine research stations and laboratories, office supplies, research vessels, transport and communication facilities and the oil pollution combating equipment.

...

X. CONCLUDING OBSERVATIONS

532. The present report has attempted to present a broad assessment of damage and losses inflicted on Kuwait based primarily on personal inspection and survey by members of the mission, and, in the absence of relevant records and data, on oral and written information provided to them. The mission reached Kuwait less than three weeks after the withdrawal of Iraq's occupation forces. Preceding sections of the present report have detailed the constraints with which it was faced. The mission is aware of the fact that its assessment is not exhaustive. However, it is hoped that its broad findings, arrived at through selective sampling in some sectors and random sampling in others, will provide a representative illustration of the nature and scope of the damage inflicted upon the economy of Kuwait.

533. Today, Kuwait struggles to recover from the consequences of its occupation by Iraq, which have left no section of its population or sector of its economy untouched. Innocent lives have been lost and suffering caused to countless others. The damage inflicted on the economy almost seems incalculable. Over two thirds of the Kuwaiti population was obliged to flee the country and is now widely dispersed, while nearly a million foreign technicians and workers who were the mainstay of the service sector have been forced to abandon their jobs and return to their countries. The oil industry, which is the nerve centre of the economy, is in shambles, while other vital sectors of the infrastructure have been systematically sabotaged and plundered.

534. When the mission arrived in Kuwait, public utilities were not functioning and basic social services were non-existent. The awesome dimensions of the damage inflicted on the country, together with the efforts needed to repair and reconstruct the wrecked infrastruc-

ture, had imparted a feeling of helplessness and despair. The Government and people were faced with a situation of compelling and yet competing priorities. The most visible, and undoubtedly the most significant, of the sectors affected by the occupation was the oil industry.

535. The unprecedented catastrophe of hundreds of burning and gushing oil wells and the consequent pollution of the environment, overshadows the damage sustained by the rest of the industry. In monetary terms the current situation represents a daily loss to Kuwait of between $40 million and as much as $120 million. It is only by the capping of these wells that it would be possible to bring the industry back into operation, particularly since the country's refineries and export facilities have not been entirely destroyed but rather strategically crippled. There is every hope that within two months local demand could be met from domestic oil production. What remains unknown is the condition of the oil reservoirs which it is strongly feared have been damaged.

536. At the time of the mission's departure from Kuwait and six weeks after the start of the oil fires, no one was in a position to define with certainty the composition of the fire emissions. No one can be complacent over the hundreds of burning oil wells that continue to scar the countryside, emitting dense black clouds of smoke that hover ominously over Kuwait—clouds that frequently blot out the sun, turning day into night and causing abnormally sharp drops in temperature. This would point to a serious gap in response mechanisms. It has precluded the mission from saying very much about

the resulting effect on human health and on ecosystems. To remedy this it would appear vitally necessary to establish an international emergency response service.

537. The oil-fire problem in Kuwait has also highlighted the need to consider environmental problems in the Gulf on a regional basis. The smoke plumes from the fires have cast their pall over many other Gulf States. Likewise, oil-slicks originating in one country may move through the Gulf and affect the waters and coastlines of neighbouring countries. There is a need for cooperation in data and information exchange as well as in remedial management actions. The role of regional organizations such as the Regional Organization for the Protection of the Marine Environment cannot be overstressed.

538. Certainly, the most lasting environmental problem facing Kuwait will be that of mines and other unexploded ordnance. It will hit at the social behavioural patterns of all residents of Kuwait as well as the nomadic people who seasonally move across Kuwait's borders. The danger posed to life will continue for a long time to come.

539. Education has suffered across the board. A generation of children and youth have lost at least one school year and virtually every educational facility, public and private, has been ransacked, defiled and partly destroyed. The country has been robbed of its intellectual base. Printed material can be replaced, but not the unpublished materials, lecture notes, correspondence with other researchers and computer databases. As one professor commented, "We are left with nothing except that which is stored in our heads."

Document 46

Interim report to the Secretary-General by a United Nations mission assessing the loss of life incurred during the Iraqi occupation of Kuwait, as well as Iraqi practices against the civilian population in Kuwait

S/22536, 29 April 1991

Letter dated 29 April 1991 from the Secretary-General addressed to the President of the Security Council

It will be recalled that, in his letter of 27 February 1991 addressed to me (S/22333, annex), the Permanent Representative of Kuwait had requested that a United Nations mission be sent to his country, *inter alia*, to assess the losses of life incurred during the Iraqi occupation of Kuwait and to examine the occupation forces' practices against the civilian population of that country.

Consideration of these questions was included in the terms of reference of the high-level United Nations mis-

sion, led by Mr. Abdulrahim A. Farah, which visited Kuwait from 16 March to 4 April 1991. However, the Government of Kuwait requested the mission to defer the preparation of a full report on these aspects until a later date and to issue an interim report at this stage. The present interim report is, accordingly, submitted herewith for the attention of members of the Security Council.

(*Signed*) Javier PÉREZ DE CUÉLLAR

Annex
Interim report to the Secretary-General by the
United Nations mission led by Mr. Abdulrahim A.
Farah, former Under-Secretary-General, assessing
the losses of life incurred during the Iraqi occupation
of Kuwait, as well as Iraqi practices against the
civilian population in Kuwait

Introduction

1. On 27 February 1991 the Permanent Representative of Kuwait to the United Nations addressed a letter to the Secretary-General requesting the dispatch of a United Nations mission to Kuwait which would, *inter alia*, assess the losses of life and examine the practices of the Iraqi forces during the occupation of Kuwait. On 6 March 1991, the Secretary-General appointed a mission under the leadership of Mr. Abdulrahim Abby Farah, former Under-Secretary-General, with the following terms of reference:

(a) To receive pertinent information from the Kuwaiti authorities, as well as non-governmental organizations (NGOs), for an assessment of the losses of life incurred during the Iraqi occupation of Kuwait;

(b) To receive pertinent information from the Kuwaiti authorities, as well as NGOs, on Iraqi practices against the civilian population in Kuwait;

(c) To assess the scope and nature of the damage that was inflicted on Kuwait's infrastructure during the period.

2. A separate report on part (c) of these terms of reference is being issued as document S/22535.

3. On the human rights aspects of the mission's mandate, Mr. Farah was assisted by Mr. Victor Sukhodrev, Special Assistant to the Secretary-General, and Mr. John Pace, Chief, Legislation and Prevention of Discrimination Branch in the Centre for Human Rights of the United Nations Secretariat.

Interim report

4. The mission arrived in Kuwait on 16 March 1991, less than three weeks after the withdrawal of Iraqi forces from the country. It remained in Kuwait until 4 April 1991. Soon after the mission's arrival, Mr. Farah was received by the Crown Prince and Prime Minister of Kuwait. The mission also held a series of meetings with the Minister of State for Foreign Affairs, the Minister of State for Cabinet Affairs and the Minister of Justice and Legal Affairs. These meetings provided an opportunity to discuss matters relating to the human rights situation in Kuwait during the occupation, as well as the requirements of the mission to carry out its mandate.

5. At the time of the mission's arrival in Kuwait, the Government had barely begun to re-establish its administration and to restore basic community services. This situation created considerable difficulties for the mission in making contact with the concerned sections of the community and in publicizing its mandate and programme of work. The national press, radio and television had only begun to resume their activities and their reach was limited. Moreover, the mission discovered on its arrival that inadequate publicity had been disseminated locally concerning its schedule, terms of reference and methods of work. Accordingly, after consultations with the Ministry of Information, arrangements were made for the mission's spokesman to be interviewed over radio and television to explain its mandate.

6. Many persons in Kuwait who may have had information relevant to this mandate were understandably preoccupied with putting their own lives in order and were not able to meet the mission. However, it was the considerable displacement of Kuwait's population outside the country that posed the principal difficulty in obtaining information. Over two thirds of the civilian population had been forced into exile; of an original 650,000 Kuwaitis, only 200,000 were estimated to have remained during the occupation period. Over 1 million foreign nationals, representing more than two thirds of their original number, had been compelled to leave the country. Additionally, there were large numbers of persons who could not be accounted for. The mission was informed, for instance, that a complete list of missing persons said to have been forcibly abducted and taken to Iraq was still being compiled and would probably be completed only when members of their families now abroad returned to their homes.

7. Although the mission did succeed in collecting information pertinent to its mandate from various individuals and groups in Kuwait, it was clear that a report of the type called for in its terms of reference would not be definitive or comprehensive if all who wished to do so were not given the opportunity of presenting their testimony. The Government of Kuwait also felt that the issuance of a definitive report should be delayed by three or four months, by which time it was envisaged that the majority of Kuwaitis abroad would have returned and Iraq would have released those believed to be in its custody.

8. For the reasons stated above, it was agreed that the present report of the mission should be of an interim nature. The mission would resume consideration of matters relating to human rights on a date to be agreed upon by the Government of Kuwait and the Secretary-General.

9. The Government of Kuwait conveyed to the mission its need for the services of a United Nations expert to advise on the modalities and machinery necessary for the collection, coordination and presentation of

information pertinent to the mission's terms of reference. Accordingly, the Secretary-General has made arrangements with the Centre for Human Rights of the United Nations Secretariat to provide the services of an expert to undertake this task.

10. The work of the mission was facilitated by the Government's decision to assign a prominent member of the community, Abdullah Al-Dikheel, former Minister of Public Works, to serve as the government counterpart to the leader of the United Nations mission during its stay in Kuwait. The Government also designated Abd al-Aziz al-Dikheel, Under Secretary of the Ministry of Justice and Legal Affairs, who is also the Chairman of the Kuwaiti Human Rights Committee, to act as the principal focal point for contacts between the mission and the Government in the coming months.

Method of work

11. Two types of information relating to human rights were included in the mission's terms of reference. The first related to the loss of life incurred during the occupation; the second dealt with the question of Iraqi practices against the civilian population during that period.

12. Information furnished under the first category was considered within the framework of existing international human rights norms, including the Universal Declaration of Human Rights a/ and the International Covenant on Civil and Political Rights. b/ The term "loss of life" was also interpreted to cover cases of enforced or involuntary disappearance if such a distinction was made in the information submitted to the mission.

13. Information received under the second category was viewed within the context of the Geneva Convention relative to the Protection of Civilian Persons in Time of War, of 12 August 1949, c/ the Fourth Geneva Convention.

14. The mission categorized information it received within eight broad types of measures or practices that are prohibited by the Fourth Geneva Convention in so far as they relate to the status and treatment of protected persons. These included:

(a) Arbitrary arrest and or detention;
(b) Ill-treatment whilst in detention;
(c) Ill-treatment of civilians;
(d) Deportation;
(e) Non-observance of the right to life;
(f) Expropriation of property;
(g) Destruction of property;
(h) Reprisals/collective punishment.

15. Through a press statement released on 18 March 1991 (see appendix), the mission advised interested parties that the information submitted should conform to the "best-evidence" principle. This required that it should come from sources closest to the alleged occurrences. Basic data, including the indication of place and time and other corroborative elements, would complement the information thus presented.

16. As the human rights team formed an integral part of the overall United Nations mission, its members were able to derive considerable benefit from the information exchanged on the various aspects of the mission's mandate. This helped to identify several important sources of information pertinent to the human rights aspect, particularly those relating to the expropriation, looting or destruction of private property. Such information is incorporated in the damage assessment report, which has been issued separately.

17. The mission conducted 87 interviews, including 75 with individuals. It had extensive contacts with the Kuwaiti Red Crescent Society, the Kuwaiti Human Rights Committee and the Kuwaiti Association for the Defence of War Victims. It also held meetings with professional associations and groups as well as with representatives of neighbourhood cooperatives, which are a distinctive feature of Kuwaiti society. The mission also interviewed members of the diplomatic community in Kuwait and representatives of expatriate national groups.

18. Although the mission was to address itself primarily to non-governmental groups, many individuals were interviewed, their experience being directly relevant to the nature of the mandate and, indeed, essential given the limited number of NGOs operating at the time of the mission's visit. It also took note of reports prepared by some externally based NGOs; these were useful as indicators of prima facie relevant sectors of inquiry. Amnesty International submitted a detailed report in New York on the eve of the mission's departure for Kuwait. During its stay in Kuwait, other international NGOs contacted the mission, including representatives of Physicians for Human Rights and Middle East Watch.

Assessment of the general situation

19. The mission received allegations of a wide range of human rights abuses that were said to have occurred during the period of occupation. The interviews conducted by the mission provided many instances where one or more of the practices prohibited by the Fourth Geneva Convention had allegedly taken place. These included 40 cases of ill-treatment whilst in detention, 33 of arbitrary arrest and or detention, 15 of loss of life, 14 of expropriation of property, 11 of ill-treatment of civil-

a/ General Assembly resolution 217 A (III).
b/ General Assembly resolution 2200 A (XXI), annex.
c/ United Nations, *Treaty Series*, vol. 75, No. 973.

ians, 8 of destruction of property, 3 of deportation and 3 of reprisals or collective punishment.

20. The information received by the mission suggested that, in the early stages of the occupation, the Iraqi authorities had resorted to stringent measures with a view to suppressing any signs of resistance. This was followed at a later stage by the intensive searching of houses for any foreigners and members of the resistance movement who might be concealed there and punishment for those found to be harbouring them. Widespread arrests and the use of torture were reported to have occurred in an attempt to extract information on the resistance network. It was alleged that terror tactics against the civilian population were intensified towards the end of the occupation period. These took the form of arbitrary arrest and, in several cases, killing of people in front of their homes or families as well as the dumping of bodies in public places. In the last week of the occupation, from about 21 February 1991, several thousand civilians were said to have been indiscriminately picked up from outside their homes, mosques and other public places and taken to Iraq.

21. In the absence of documentary evidence, it was not possible for the mission to form a complete picture of the legal regime in force during the occupation. The mission did receive oral evidence citing specific legislation that was said to have been promulgated and enforced in Kuwait. For instance, on or about 21 August 1990, looting was said to have been made a capital offence and, on 25 August 1990, the death penalty was allegedly instituted for harbouring civilian expatriates from Western States.

22. Statements made to the mission contained several references to laws concerning changes in identification papers, currency, ownership documents and other similar evidence of the "Iraqization" of Kuwait. The information received by the mission shows negligible recourse by the Iraqi authorities to judicial procedures, particularly in regard to alleged criminal matters.

23. According to statements made by several persons who lived in Kuwait throughout the occupation, the entire period was characterized by a consistent pattern of resistance, both passive and active. Active resistance included acts of violence, sabotage and harassment of occupation forces. Passive resistance was aimed at frustrating the Iraqi policy of annexation of Kuwait at virtually every level, including the political, commercial, cultural and educational levels.

24. An important feature of this passive resistance was the ability of the civilian population to organize itself through the adaptation of the neighbourhood cooperatives system. In normal times, this system provided essential commodities at subsidized prices to the civilian population. The system continued during the occupation period, thereby ensuring the availability of a regular supply of food and money, which made it possible for the civilian population, Kuwaiti and non-Kuwaiti, to survive independently of the occupation authorities. The mission was also told of successful efforts by some expatriate groups to form their own self-help cooperatives and sources of supply.

Losses of life incurred during the occupation

25. The mission was not provided with any official records or data relating to the loss of life in Kuwait incurred during the occupation. The Government explained that the departments that normally maintained such statistics had ceased to function during the occupation and that any information would have to be obtained eventually through public inquiry. In the circumstances, no precise figure can be given for the losses of life incurred during the occupation until it is possible firmly to establish the whereabouts and condition of persons held by Iraq in its territory as well as those displaced elsewhere. The mission was informed by the Kuwaiti Red Crescent Society that in the first weeks of occupation it had maintained records of deaths, but these were seized after its leadership was detained by the occupation forces on 17 September 1990.

26. The mission received testimony from senior hospital staff about several cases, which they professed to have seen, where persons bore all the signs of having died violent deaths. These submissions were, in some cases, accompanied by photographs. The mission was informed that the neighbourhood cooperatives, which were eminently placed to obtain information in this regard, were conducting their own inquiries in their respective residential areas. This is an ongoing task and the mission was informed that the results would not be available until a later date.

27. Interviews conducted during the visit tended to suggest that the incidence of violent death was relatively high throughout the occupation period. For the most part, responsibility was attributed to the activities of the two Iraqi intelligence bodies known as Istahbarat and Muhabarat. A number of summary executions were also said to have been carried out by army elements. Although the mission put the question regularly, it received no evidence of any form of trial or other judicial or quasi-judicial process.

Iraqi practices during the occupation

28. The Fourth Geneva Convention establishes acceptable international standards of behaviour towards the treatment of the civilian population in times of war

and conflict. Considerable information received by the mission related specifically to articles 27 and 31 to 34.

29. The Kuwaiti Human Rights Committee, established by the Council of Ministers to centralize the registration of missing persons, informed the mission that, as of 20 March 1991, it had recorded applications in respect of over 11,700 persons reported as missing. The Kuwaiti Red Crescent Society informed the mission that a list of 10,500 names had been furnished to the International Committee of the Red Cross (ICRC) at Riyadh for the purpose of negotiations with Iraqi authorities in the repatriation process. During the mission's stay in Kuwait, it was reported that a large number of prisoners-of-war (POWs) and civilian detainees had been repatriated from Iraq. However, it was believed that some 5,000 remained unaccounted for.

30. Allegations were made of several cases of arbitrary arrest and detention, usually followed by deportation or "transfer" to Iraq. These referred to persons of various ages and occupations. The mission was informed of the case of a family with young children that was said to have been detained in reprisal for the alleged involvement of one of its members in resistance activities. The family interviewed by the mission said it had been held at Basra, in Iraq, together with six other families.

31. The mission received several indications of resort to the use of cruel and inhuman treatment and torture. This included information on torture having been practised at a number of specific locations, including police stations, a juvenile detention centre, a sports club and public buildings. Four of these places were visited and at two of them the visit was conducted in the presence of an alleged victim who provided the mission with additional details.

32. The mission was shown tools, instruments and electronic devices said to have been used for torture. Some persons interviewed by the mission still bore evident signs of having been subjected to such an ordeal. A number of medical personnel told the mission that they had attended to patients who had been tortured and who had subsequently died.

33. Among the places where torture was said to have been practised was the Embassy of Iraq in Kuwait. The Dean of the Diplomatic Corps told the mission that, on 16 August 1990, he had witnessed five prisoners being dragged out of the premises, propped up by guards, blindfolded and their bodies bloodied.

34. The mission was informed of several alleged instances of rape, both by persons who said that they were victims and others who were eye-witnesses. Doctors and medical personnel corroborated such information. The mission was told that social and religious taboos often prevented women from reporting instances of rape. How-ever, in many cases the rape had led to pregnancies, making it no longer possible to conceal the fact. The mission was also told of cases of suicide as a result of rape trauma.

35. Information about incidents of reprisals and of collective punishment was also brought to the attention of the mission. The mission visited an area where some 18 houses, on the periphery of a school compound, had been partially destroyed. This was stated to have been an act of reprisal against the local community after the bodies of two Iraqi soldiers had been discovered in the school compound.

Expatriate nationals

36. At the time of the occupation, expatriates in Kuwait could broadly be divided into two categories, namely, the Arab-Asian community and nationals of countries members of the Organisation for Economic Cooperation and Development (OECD). The mission received information from the former category, many of whose members had remained in Kuwait throughout the occupation and had been exposed to Iraqi policies and practices. No contact was possible with members of the latter category, since the overwhelming majority had left Kuwait during the occupation. The United Kingdom Ambassador in Kuwait did, however, provide the mission with the text of a statement recorded by members of his community on their experiences as well as a statement which he himself had delivered to the United Nations Commission on Human Rights at its forty-seventh session held at Geneva from 28 January to 8 March 1991.

37. Repeated reference was made to the mission about the hardships and experiences of the large number of foreign workers who were forced to flee the country under conditions of duress during the occupation as well as those who remained during the entire occupation period. For example, only 5,000 Pakistani nationals remained out of a community of 92,000. The conditions under which the foreign workers departed is reflected in the situation that occurred at the Embassy of the Philippines, where at one point 22,000 persons sought the safety and assistance of their diplomatic mission for a number of weeks until their departure could be arranged.

38. The mission was informed that, during this period of flight, foreign nationals were denied food supplies, even though stocks existed in sufficient quantities at the time. Departure conditions were rendered particularly difficult as people were not allowed to leave Kuwait except by routes prescribed by the occupation authorities. Those of limited or no means were obliged to travel to their homes in south Asia overland, through Iraq or Turkey. This intensely arduous and hazardous journey

was said to have resulted in considerable suffering and even loss of life.

39. With regard to those expatriates who remained, problems were reported to the mission concerning their status *vis-à-vis* the occupation authorities, particularly in matters concerning identity papers, currency exchange and other measures taken by the Iraqi authorities in the context of the purported annexation of Kuwait. Several cases of arbitrary detention, ill-treatment, rape and looting of property were reported to have occurred and these were described in the course of the interviews conducted by the mission.

Diplomatic community

40. On 9 August 1990, the diplomatic community in Kuwait was informed of the "acceptance by Iraq of Kuwait's request for unity" with it and that all diplomatic and consular missions in Kuwait should close by 24 August. The very same day, the United Nations Security Council, in its resolution 662 (1990) decided that "annexation of Kuwait by Iraq under any form and whatever pretext has no legal validity, and is considered null and void". In its subsequent resolution 664 (1990), the Security Council demanded that "the Government of Iraq rescind its orders for the closure of diplomatic and consular missions in Kuwait and the withdrawal of the immunity of their personnel". However, as the Dean of the Diplomatic Corps told the mission, the message from Iraq "was clear: come 24 August, we would no longer be treated as diplomats but would be treated as any civilians whose only protection would be the Fourth Geneva Convention".

41. He continued:

"While the conduct of Iraqi authorities violated norms and custom of diplomatic privilege and immunity, the much more dramatic human impact could be felt in the resulting incapacity of many diplomatic missions in Kuwait to fulfil their primary responsibility, that of protecting the interests of their own nationals."

42. Some ambassadors stated that diplomatic and consular missions that did not comply with the order to close were subject to deliberate acts of harassment, including the suspension of water and electricity as well as telephone communications. Diplomats who stayed on in Kuwait after the 24 August deadline were interned in their premises, which were themselves, on occasion, transgressed. The mission was told of forcible entry into specific diplomatic residences. Privileges and immunities of diplomatic personnel at the highest level were violated.

Concluding remarks

43. The mission was able during its short stay to gather important information required as a basis for its future work. However, a great deal still needs to be recorded and certain aspects will require to be further clarified in order to complete the picture. In particular, the mission will need to obtain more information on the laws that were enforced during the period of occupation and to examine the compatibility of those laws, as well as of actual Iraqi practices, with the provisions of the Fourth Geneva Convention. On the basis of information received so far, there would not appear to have been any law that regulated the conduct of the occupation of Kuwait.

Appendix

18 March 1991

PRESS RELEASE

The U.N. Special Mission to Kuwait will receive information on Iraqi practices during the occupation.

The U.N. Special Mission currently in Kuwait, as part of its mandate will receive pertinent information from Kuwaiti authorities, as well as from non-governmental sectors, on certain issues relating to human rights. This information will cover two aspects:

a. Loss of life incurred during the Iraqi occupation of Kuwait; and

b. Iraqi practices affecting the civilian population in Kuwait during the occupation.

Information furnished under the first heading will be considered within the framework of existing international human rights norms such as the Universal Declaration of Human Rights and the International Covenant on Civil and Political Rights. The term "loss of life" would also cover cases of enforced or involuntary disappearances, if such a distinction is made in the information submitted.

Information received under the second heading would be viewed within the context of the Geneva Convention relative to the Protection of Civilian Persons in Time of War, of 12 August 1949 (the Fourth Geneva Convention).

Interested parties are advised that the information submitted should conform with the "best evidence" principle, i.e., it should come from sources closest to the occurrences alleged. Basic data, such as indication of places, dates and other corroborative elements would complement the information thus presented.

The Mission may be contacted at the SAS Hotel, Kuwait or at the office of the Red Crescent Society of Kuwait.

Document 47

Statement by the President of the Security Council appealing to States, international financial institutions and United Nations bodies to assist countries which find themselves confronted with special economic problems arising from implementing sanctions against Iraq

S/22548, 29 April 1991

The members of the Security Council have considered the memorandum dated 22 March 1991 (S/22382) which was addressed to the President of the Security Council by the 21 States which have invoked Article 50 of the United Nations Charter owing to the special economic problems arising from the implementation of the sanctions imposed against Iraq and Kuwait under Council resolution 661 (1990).

The members of the Security Council have taken note of the Secretary-General's oral report to them on 11 April 1991, in which he supported the appeal launched by the 21 States that have invoked Article 50. The Secretary-General further informed the Council on 26 April 1991 of the conclusions reached by the Administrative Committee on Coordination (ACC) at the session it has just held in Paris, where members of ACC agreed to vigorously pursue their efforts to respond effectively to the needs of countries most affected by the implementation of resolution 661. The Secretary-General will coordinate through ACC, within the framework of this assistance, the activities of organizations of the United Nations system.

The members of the Security Council have taken note of the replies from a number of States (Austria, Belgium, Denmark, France, Germany, Greece, Ireland, Italy, Japan, Liechtenstein, Luxembourg, Luxembourg on behalf of the European Community and its 12 member States, Netherlands, New Zealand, Norway, Portugal, Spain, Switzerland, United Kingdom, United States and the USSR) which have furnished specific information on the assistance they have provided to various affected countries; they have also taken note of the replies from officials of international financial institutions, such as those received from the President of the World Bank and the Managing Director of IMF. They invite other Member States and international financial institutions and organizations to inform the Secretary-General as soon as possible of the measures that they have taken on behalf of the States which have invoked Article 50.

The members of the Security Council make a solemn appeal to States, international financial institutions and United Nations bodies to respond positively and speedily to the recommendations of the Security Council Committee, established under resolution 661, for assistance to countries which find themselves confronted with special economic problems arising from the carrying out of those measures imposed by resolution 661 and which have invoked Article 50.

The members of the Security Council note that the procedure established under Article 50 of the Charter remains in effect.

Document 48

Report of the Secretary-General on establishing an Iraq-Kuwait Boundary Demarcation Commission

S/22558, 2 May 1991

1. The present report is submitted pursuant to Security Council resolution 687 (1991) of 3 April 1991. In paragraph 3 of the resolution, the Security Council called upon me to lend assistance to make arrangements with Iraq and Kuwait to demarcate the boundary between Iraq and Kuwait, drawing on appropriate material, including the map transmitted by Security Council document S/22412, and to report back to the Security Council within one month.

2. In lending my assistance to Iraq and Kuwait with a view to making the arrangements to demarcate the boundary between them, I have borne in mind that, in paragraph 2 of Security Council resolution 687 (1991), the Council demanded "that Iraq and Kuwait respect the inviolability of the international boundary and the allocation of islands set out in the 'Agreed Minutes between the State of Kuwait and the Republic of Iraq regarding the Restoration of Friendly Relations, Recognition and

Related Matters', signed by them in the exercise of their sovereignty at Baghdad on 4 October 1963 and registered with the United Nations and published by the United Nations in document 7063, United Nations, *Treaty Series*, 1964". I have also taken into account that, in a letter dated 4 April 1991 addressed to me by the Deputy Prime Minister and Minister for Foreign Affairs of Kuwait, Kuwait has expressed its intention to scrupulously comply with all the provisions of resolution 687 (1991) and to cooperate with me with a view to ensuring its implementation (S/22457, annex) and that, in accordance with paragraph 33 of Security Council resolution 687 (1991), the Minister for Foreign Affairs of Iraq in the penultimate paragraph of a letter dated 6 April 1991 (S/22456) has notified the Security Council and the Secretary-General of Iraq's acceptance of the provisions of that resolution. The text of the Agreed Minutes referred to in paragraph 2 of Security Council resolution 687 (1991) is contained in Security Council document S/22432.

3. After consultations with the Governments of Iraq and Kuwait, I will now establish an Iraq-Kuwait Boundary Demarcation Commission, to be composed of one representative each of Iraq and Kuwait and three independent experts who will be appointed by me, one of whom will serve as the Chairman. The Council will be informed as soon as the Commission is established. The terms of reference of the Commission will be to demarcate in geographical coordinates of latitude and longitude the international boundary set out in the Agreed Minutes between Kuwait and Iraq referred to above. In view of the fact that one of the main purposes of the demarcation of the boundary between Kuwait and Iraq is to promote stability and peace and security along the border, the Commission will also make arrangements for the physical representation of the boundary. The coordinates established by the Commission will constitute the final demarcation of the international boundary between Iraq and Kuwait in accordance with the Agreed Minutes of 4 October 1963. They will be lodged in the archives of both Governments and a certified copy will also be submitted to me, which I will communicate to the Security Council and will retain for safe-keeping in the archives of the United Nations.

4. The demarcation of the boundary between Iraq and Kuwait will be accomplished by drawing upon appropriate material, including the map transmitted by Security Council document S/22412, and by utilizing appropriate technology. The physical representation of the boundary will be carried out through the erection of an appropriate number and type of boundary pillars or monuments. The Commission will provide for arrangements for maintenance on a continuing basis and locational accuracy (including repositioning, if necessary) of the surficial boundary representation.

5. As soon as the Commission is constituted and after an initial assessment of the resources required for the demarcation of the boundary has been made, the Commission will transmit to me an estimate of costs, which I will communicate to the Security Council; simultaneously, I will make a proposal that all costs, including the initial costs of the Commission, should be shared between the two interested parties.

6. The Commission will be assisted by a small staff that will adopt its own rules of procedure and working methods and make the necessary arrangements for the identification and examination of appropriate material relevant to the demarcation of the boundary. The Commission will be responsible to me in the conduct of its work and will report regularly to me on the progress of its work with a view to the earliest possible finalization of the demarcation of the boundary. The Commission will take its decisions by majority. Its decisions regarding the demarcation of the boundary will be final.

7. The Commission shall enjoy unimpeded freedom of movement in the area of the demarcation of the international boundary as well as all necessary privileges and immunities for the fulfilment of its task. The three independent experts shall enjoy the status of experts on missions within the meaning of article VI of the Convention on Privileges and Immunities of the United Nations of 1946. 1/

8. In the exercise of its task of demarcating the boundary, with respect to physical security and clearance of mines the Commission will rely on the relevant arrangements made for the United Nations Iraq-Kuwait Observer Mission (UNIKOM).

Annex I
Letter dated 19 April 1991 from the Permanent Representative of Kuwait to the United Nations addressed to the Secretary-General

I should like to refer to the report regarding paragraph 3 of Security Council resolution 687 (1991) and to convey the acceptance by the Government of Kuwait of the terms set out in the report and its readiness to cooperate with the United Nations in implementing those terms.

(*Signed*) Mohammad A. ABULHASAN
Ambassador
Permanent Representative

1/ General Assembly resolution 22 A (I).

Annex II
Letter dated 23 April 1991 from the Permanent Representative of Iraq to the United Nations addressed to the Secretary-General

On instructions from my Government and with reference to the meeting that we held with the Legal Counsel of the United Nations, Mr. Fleischhauer, on 17 April 1991, I have the honour to transmit herewith a letter addressed to you by Mr. Ahmed Hussein, Minister for Foreign Affairs of the Republic of Iraq, dated 23 April 1991 concerning the Iraq-Kuwait Boundary Demarcation Commission.

(*Signed*) Abdul Amir A. AL-ANBARI
Ambassador
Permanent Representative

Enclosure
Letter dated 23 April 1991 from the Minister
for Foreign Affairs of Iraq addressed to
the Secretary-General

With reference to the meeting held between our Permanent Representative and the Legal Counsel of the United Nations on 17 April 1991 and your draft report which you intend to submit to the Security Council concerning paragraph 3 of Security Council resolution 687 (1991) and regarding which you asked for the view of my Government, I have the honour to state the following.

Part I of the letter that I addressed to you on 6 April 1991 explained that, although in its preamble Security Council resolution 687 (1991) affirms that Iraq is an independent sovereign State, many of its iniquitous provisions do not respect this sovereignty but constitute an unprecedented assault on it and on the rights that stem therefrom, embodied in the Charter and in international law and custom. With regard to the question of the boundary, the Security Council has imposed a specific position with regard to the Iraqi-Kuwaiti boundary, whereas the custom in law and in practice in international relations is that boundary questions are left to an agreement between States, because this is the sole basis that can guarantee the principle of the stability of boundaries.

Furthermore, the Council resolution does not take into account the viewpoint of Iraq, namely, that the "Agreed Minutes between the State of Kuwait and the Republic of Iraq regarding the Restoration of Friendly Relations, Recognition and Related Matters" of 4 October 1963 have not yet been subjected to the constitutional procedures required for their ratification by the legislative authority and the President of Iraq, thus leaving the question of the boundary pending and unresolved. The Council has nevertheless imposed on Iraq the line of its boundary with Kuwait. By acting in this strange manner, the Council itself has also violated one of the provisions of resolution 660 (1990), which was the basis for the subsequent resolution adopted by the Council. In its paragraph 3, resolution 660 (1990) called upon Iraq and Kuwait to resolve their differences through negotiations, and the question of the boundary is well known to be one of the main differences. Iraq officially informed the Council that it accepted resolution 660 (1990) and was prepared to implement it, but the Council has disregarded this legal position, contradicting its previous resolutions, and adopted an iniquitous resolution that imposes new conditions on Iraq. It has imposed a border situation on Iraq, an independent sovereign State and Member of the United Nations, and has deprived it of its right to establish its territorial rights in accordance with the principles of international law. Thus the Council would also deprive Iraq of the right to exercise its free choice and to affirm that it accepts that boundary without reservation. Where the question of the boundary is concerned, the Council resolution is an iniquitous resolution, which constitutes a dangerous precedent, a first in the annals of the international Organization and—as some impartial members of the Council indicated in their statements when the resolution was voted on—an assault on the sovereignty of States.

The Iraqi Government remains convinced of the legitimate character of the position reflected in the above observations. This legitimate character is especially borne out by the mission entrusted to you by virtue of paragraph 3 of resolution 687 (1991). The above-mentioned paragraph calls upon you to lend your assistance to make arrangements with Iraq and Kuwait to demarcate the boundary between Iraq and Kuwait, drawing on appropriate material, including the map transmitted by Security Council document S/22412.

Accordingly, my Government wishes to make the comments set forth below concerning your draft report to which I referred above.

1. My Government wonders on what legal foundation the Council based its resolution 687 (1991) and you your draft report in considering the map that was transmitted by Security Council document S/22412, dated 28 March 1991, at the request of the Permanent Mission of the United Kingdom and which your Legal Counsel described to our Permanent Representative as a United Kingdom map mentioned in the Agreed Minutes of 1963. The Agreed Minutes did not refer to any map, as is clear from the text published in the United Nations *Treaty Series*, vol. 485, No. 7063. It is blatantly true also that the sole mention of the map in question in paragraph 3

of Council resolution 687 (1991) was introduced without any legal grounds.

The Government of my country was not a party to the drawing of that map. It did not recognize the map, nor is there any proof of its having extended such recognition. Accordingly, the fact that you and the Council consider the map to be a part of the material to be drawn upon for the demarcation process constitutes an iniquitous and unilateral imposition against the will of Iraq, a sovereign State Member of the United Nations, and a prejudgement of the course of the land boundary before any commission embarks on the process of demarcating that boundary.

2. In addition, the assistance that you have offered in making arrangements for the demarcation of the boundary between Iraq and Kuwait must ensure a perfect balance between the positions that either side may adopt with regard to the demarcation process, together with a just and equitable approach to the settlement of any differences that might arise between them concerning technical matters. The Iraqi Government therefore believes that, if the Commission entrusted with the demarcation process is constituted in accordance with your proposal, the result cannot be just and equitable, particularly in view of our comments in paragraph 1 above. You have suggested that the Commission consist of five members, of whom two would represent Iraq and Kuwait respectively, together with three independent experts to be chosen by you, one of whom would be appointed as the Chairman. You have also suggested that the Commission's decisions should be taken by a majority vote. Although it has no doubts as to your credibility with respect to the selection of the three independent experts, my country's Government nevertheless believes that, since it will play no part in the selection of the three experts, it will have no way of ensuring in advance that they are truly independent. Its views with regard to the demarcation process will thus be represented only by one of the five members.

3. You mention in the draft report that the demarcation of the boundary will be accomplished by drawing upon appropriate material, including the map transmitted by Security Council document S/22412, as referred to in paragraph 3 of resolution 687 (1991). However, you add that the Commission may "utilize appropriate technology" (para. 4 of the draft report) and that it will "make the necessary arrangements for the identification and examination of appropriate material relevant to the demarcation of the boundary" (para. 6 of the draft report). The Government of Iraq believes that the terms "appropriate material", "appropriate technology" and "identification and examination of appropriate material relevant to the demarcation of the boundary" must be explained.

This explanation will permit my Government to express its views, if such views are welcome, on a solid basis. The requested explanation will also help to reduce the possibilities of disagreement in the future when the Commission begins its work.

4. You propose in paragraph 5 of the draft report that the costs of the demarcation process should be shared between the two parties. The Government of Iraq fails to understand the basis for this proposal, since the overall thrust of the proposals contained in the draft report amounts—in the opinion of my Government—to a virtual "act of capitulation" in which Iraq is denied any freedom to join in the harmonious agreement on its contents. Accordingly, and in the light of my comments at the beginning of this letter, the suggestion seems to be that Iraq should bear half the costs of the demarcation process without any account being taken of its views on the boundary question as a whole, with respect to either demarcation or delimitation. The Iraqi Government cannot therefore see any justification, based on principles of justice or equity, for bearing any costs relating to a process which is imposed upon it.

I should like, in conclusion, to assure you that the Iraqi Government is fully prepared to consult with you concerning the comments contained in this letter, either in New York or elsewhere. In this connection, I also wish to note that, just as we accepted resolution 687 (1991) despite our objections to and criticism of its provisions, we will cooperate with you and will nominate a representative of our Government to participate in the Demarcation Commission, even if you take no account of the views and comments we have expressed above. We do this because the circumstances forcing our acceptance persist.

(*Signed*) Ahmed HUSSEIN
Minister for Foreign Affairs

Annex III
Letter dated 30 April 1991 from the Secretary-General addressed to the Minister for Foreign Affairs of Iraq

I have the honour to refer to your letter dated 23 April 1991, which was transmitted to me by a letter of the same date from the Permanent Representative of Iraq to the United Nations and which contained comments on the proposals made with regard to the implementation of paragraph 3 of Security Council resolution 687 (1991) and on which I must report to the Security Council no later than 2 May 1991. In informing me of your Government's readiness to cooperate with me and to nominate a representative of Iraq to participate in the proposed Boundary Demarcation Commission, a decision which I welcome, the letter nevertheless contains a number of comments to which I would like to respond.

The first comment of your Government is that, in international law, a boundary demarcation between two States can be carried out only by agreement between the parties and that the Security Council has no competence to impose such a demarcation. In this connection, I would like to recall that, in paragraph 2 of resolution 687 (1991) the Security Council, acting under Chapter VII of the Charter of the United Nations, demanded that Iraq and Kuwait respect the inviolability of their international boundary and the allocation of islands "set out in the 'Agreed Minutes between the State of Kuwait and the Republic of Iraq regarding the Restoration of Friendly Relations, Recognition and Related Matters', signed by them in the exercise of their sovereignty at Baghdad on 4 October 1963". In paragraph 3 of that resolution the Council called upon me to lend my "assistance to make arrangements with Iraq and Kuwait to demarcate the boundary between Iraq and Kuwait". In identical letters dated 6 April 1991 addressed to me and to the President of the Security Council (S/22456), your Government formally notified its acceptance of the provisions of that resolution. You further reconfirmed your Government's acceptance of paragraph 3 of resolution 687 (1991) at the end of your letter of 23 April 1991 (see annex II, enclosure). Therefore, the element of agreement as far as Iraq is concerned, is provided by your Government's official notifications of acceptance. Since the Government of Kuwait has also expressed to me its willingness scrupulously to comply with all provisions of the resolution and to cooperate with me to ensure its implementation (S/22457), the necessary element of consent has been provided by the two parties.

Secondly, your Government states that the proposed demarcation would be prejudged by a specific reference to a map made available by the United Kingdom and which, according to the letter, the Legal Counsel described as "a United Kingdom map mentioned in the agreed minutes of 1963". On a purely factual point, I wish to state that the Legal Counsel of the United Nations did not describe the map as having been mentioned in the 1963 agreed minutes. In response to a question as to which map was referred to in document S/22412, your Permanent Representative was informed that the map in question was "a United Kingdom map". On a substantive level, however, I am obliged to point out that the resolution provides that the demarcation of the boundary should be based on "appropriate material, *including* the

map transmitted by Security Council document S/22412" [emphasis added]. In the light of this wording, I have proposed that the Commission will have to make "necessary arrangements for the identification and examination of appropriate material relevant to the demarcation of the boundary".

Thirdly, your Government queries the independence of the experts to be appointed by me to serve on the Boundary Commission and comments on the proposed decision-making by majority. I would like to assure you that, in appointing the independent experts of the Commission, I shall, as always, base my decisions on the need to ensure independence, competence and integrity. Furthermore, to ensure an equitable approach and the effective functioning of the Commission, I have proposed that neither Government should be able to frustrate the work of the Commission.

Fourthly, your Government has requested me to explain such terms as "appropriate material", "appropriate technology" and "identification and examination of appropriate material relevant to the demarcation of the boundary". It is up to the Commission to examine and identify the relevant documentation and to determine which technology or combination of methods can best be used for the fulfilment of its mandate. In my view it would prejudice the work of the Commission, and even hinder its independence, if at this stage I were to go beyond the level of detail concerning the working methods of the Boundary Commission set out in my draft report.

Finally, your Government objects to paying half of the costs of the demarcation on the ground that its views on the boundary question are not fully being taken into account. However, through your Government's participation in the work of the Boundary Commission its views will find such expression. Together with your Government's acceptance of paragraph 3 of resolution 687 (1991), both in its letter of 6 April 1991 (S/22456) as well as in the letter of 23 April 1991, I can see no basis for objections to the paying of its share of the costs, which will be determined by the Commission.

In the light of your Government's expressed readiness to cooperate with me, I intend to proceed immediately with the establishment of the Commission and will accordingly convey my proposals, together with this exchange of correspondence, to the Security Council.

(*Signed*) Javier PÉREZ DE CUÉLLAR
Secretary-General

Document 49

Report of the Secretary-General regarding creation of a United Nations Compensation Fund and United Nations Compensation Commission as envisaged in Security Council resolution 687 (1991)

S/22559, 2 May 1991

INTRODUCTION

1. The present report is submitted pursuant to paragraph 19 of Security Council resolution 687 (1991) of 3 April 1991. In paragraph 16 of that resolution, the Council reaffirmed that Iraq "is liable, under international law, for any direct loss, damage, including environmental damage and the depletion of natural resources, or injury to foreign Governments, nationals and corporations, as a result of Iraq's unlawful invasion and occupation of Kuwait". In paragraph 17 of the resolution, the Council decided "that all Iraqi statements made since 2 August 1990 repudiating its foreign debt are null and void", and demanded that "Iraq adhere scrupulously to all of its obligations concerning servicing and repayment of its foreign debt". The Council also decided, in paragraph 18 of the resolution, "to create a fund to pay compensation for claims that fall within the scope of paragraph 16 ... and to establish a Commission that will administer the fund".

2. In paragraph 19 of the resolution, the Security Council directed the Secretary-General "to develop and present to the Security Council for decision, no later than 30 days following the adoption of the present resolution, recommendations for the fund to meet the requirement for the payment of claims established in accordance with paragraph 18 ..., and for a programme to implement the decisions in paragraphs 16, 17 and 18 ..., including: administration of the fund; mechanisms for determining the appropriate level of Iraq's contribution to the fund based on a percentage of the value of the exports of petroleum and petroleum products from Iraq not to exceed a figure to be suggested to the Council by the Secretary-General, taking into account the requirements of the people of Iraq, Iraq's payment capacity as assessed in conjunction with the international financial institutions taking into consideration external debt service, and the needs of the Iraqi economy; arrangements for ensuring that payments are made to the fund; the process by which funds will be allocated and claims paid; appropriate procedures for evaluating losses, listing claims and verifying their validity and resolving disputed claims in respect of Iraq's liability as specified in paragraph 16 ...; and the composition of the Commission designated [in paragraph 18]". In making the following recommendations, I have borne in mind the need for maximum transparency, efficiency, flexibility and economy in the institutional framework that will be required for the implementation of the decisions contained in paragraphs 16, 17 and 18 of the resolution.

I. INSTITUTIONAL FRAMEWORK

A. *The Fund*

3. The Fund created by paragraph 18 of Security Council resolution 687 (1991) will be established by the Secretary-General as a special account of the United Nations. The Fund will be known as the United Nations Compensation Fund (hereinafter referred to as "the Fund"). The Fund will be operated in accordance with the United Nations Financial Regulations and Rules. As a special account of the United Nations, the Fund, therefore, will enjoy, in accordance with Article 105 of the Charter and the Convention on the Privileges and Immunities of the United Nations of 13 February 1946, 1/ the status, facilities, privileges and immunities accorded to the United Nations. The Fund will be used to pay compensation for "any direct loss, damage, including environmental damage and the depletion of natural resources, or injury to foreign Governments, nationals and corporations, as a result of Iraq's unlawful invasion and occupation of Kuwait" as provided for in paragraph 16 of resolution 687 (1991).

B. *The Commission*

4. The Fund is to be administered by the Commission established by the Security Council in paragraph 18 of resolution 687 (1991). The Commission, which is to be known as the United Nations Compensation Commission (hereinafter referred to as "the Commission"), will function under the authority of the Security Council and be a subsidiary organ thereof. In accordance with the terms of paragraph 19 of resolution 687 (1991), in carrying out its functions, the Commission will be required to address a variety of complex administrative, financial, legal and policy issues, including the mechanism for determining the level of contribution to the Fund; the allocation of funds and payments of claims; the procedures for evaluating losses, listing claims and veri-

---

1/ General Assembly resolution 22 A (I).

fying their validity; and resolving disputed claims. In the light of the multifarious nature of the tasks to be performed by the Commission, it will, in my view, be necessary to distinguish between questions of policy and the functional aspects of the Commission's work. The Commission should, therefore, operate at a policy-making level and a functional level. A secretariat will be necessary for servicing the work of the Commission at both the policy-making and the functional levels.

C. Structure and composition of the Commission

5. The principal organ of the Commission will be a 15-member Governing Council composed of the representatives of the current members of the Security Council at any given time. The Governing Council will be assisted by a number of commissioners who will perform the tasks assigned to them by the Governing Council. The precise number of commissioners will be determined by the Governing Council in the light of the tasks to be performed. The commissioners will be experts in fields such as finance, law, accountancy, insurance and environmental damage assessment, who will act in their personal capacity. They will be nominated by the Secretary-General and appointed by the Governing Council for specific tasks and terms. In nominating the commissioners, the Secretary-General will pay due regard to the need for geographical representation, professional qualifications, experience and integrity. The Secretary-General will establish a register of experts which might be drawn upon when commissioners are to be appointed.

6. A secretariat, composed of an Executive Secretary and the necessary staff, will be established to service the Commission. The Executive Secretary's primary responsibility will be the technical administration of the Fund and the servicing of the Commission. He will be appointed by the Secretary-General after consultation with the Governing Council. The staff of the secretariat will be appointed by the Secretary-General. The Executive Secretary and staff will serve under the United Nations Staff Regulations and Rules.

D. Status, privileges and immunities of the Commission

7. The Convention on the Privileges and Immunities of the United Nations of 13 February 1946 1/ will apply to the Commission and its secretariat. The members of the Governing Council will have the status of representatives of States, the commissioners will have the status of experts on missions within the meaning of article VI of the Convention and the Executive Secretary and the staff of the secretariat will have the status of officials within the meaning of articles V and VII of the Convention.

E. Expenses of the Commission

8. The expenses of the Commission will be borne by the Fund. More detailed recommendations regarding the budgetary administration of the Commission are set out in paragraph 29 below.

F. Headquarters of the Commission

9. For reasons of economy and practicality, particularly in the secretariat servicing of the Governing Council and the commissioners, the headquarters of the Commission should be in New York. Alternatively, it might be located at the site of one of the two Offices of the United Nations in Europe, i.e. Geneva or Vienna. The Governing Council may decide whether some of the activities of the Commission should be carried out elsewhere.

G. Functions of the Commission

1. *The Governing Council*

10. As the policy-making organ of the Commission, the Governing Council will have the responsibility for establishing guidelines on all policy matters, in particular, those relating to the administration and financing of the Fund, the organization of the work of the Commission and the procedures to be applied to the processing of claims and to the settlement of disputed claims, as well as to the payments to be made from the Fund. In addition to its policy-making role, the Governing Council will perform important functional tasks with respect to claims presented to the Commission. Except with regard to the method of ensuring that payments are made to the Fund, which should be decided upon by consensus, the decisions of the Governing Council should be taken by a majority of at least nine of its members. No veto will apply in the Governing Council. If consensus is not achieved on any matter for which it is required, the question will be referred to the Security Council on the request of any member of the Governing Council. The Governing Council may invite States that it considers to have particular interest in its work to participate without a vote in its discussions. It may also invite members of the United Nations Secretariat or other persons to supply it with information or to give other assistance in examining matters within its competence. The Governing Council will, on behalf of the Commission, report periodically to the Security Council.

2. *The commissioners*

11. The commissioners will, under the guidelines established by the Governing Council, carry out such tasks and responsibilities as may be assigned to them by the Governing Council.

3. The secretariat

12. Under the direction of the Executive Secretary, the secretariat will carry out such tasks as may be assigned to it by the Governing Council and the commissioners, in particular the technical administration of the Fund, and the provision of secretariat services to the Governing Council and the commissioners.

II. THE IMPLEMENTATION OF THE DECISIONS CONTAINED IN PARAGRAPHS 16, 17 AND 18 OF RESOLUTION 687 (1991)

A. Mechanisms for determining the appropriate level of Iraq's contribution to the Fund

13. In accordance with the institutional framework outlined in section I above, it would be for the Governing Council to establish the mechanisms for determining the appropriate level of Iraq's contribution to the Fund in accordance with the criteria laid down in paragraph 19 of Security Council resolution 687 (1991). In carrying out this task, the Governing Council should consider the probable levels of future oil export revenues of Iraq, the amounts of military spending and arms imports in the past, the service of Iraq's foreign debt and the needs for reconstruction and development in the country. The objective should be to settle compensation claims within a reasonable period of time. The Governing Council will, of course, be free to draw upon expert advice as it sees fit. It might wish to be assisted by one or more commissioners who, under the guidance of and within the terms of reference provided by the Governing Council, might give advice with regard to the appropriate level of Iraq's contribution to the Fund as well as to the periodic monitoring of that level of contribution. Simultaneously with the establishment of the Governing Council, I will undertake the appropriate consultations as required by paragraph 19 of resolution 687 (1991) so that, as soon as possible, I will be in a position to suggest the figure not to be exceeded by the Iraqi contribution.

B. Arrangements for ensuring that payments are made to the Fund

14. The arrangements for ensuring payments to the Fund are among the most technical and difficult of the tasks that have been entrusted to the Commission. The decisions taken in this regard will determine, *inter alia*, the financial viability of the Fund and its capacity to meet the compensation claims decided upon by the Commission as well as the size and organization of the secretariat.

15. In addressing the question of the possible arrangements for ensuring payments to the Fund, there is an obvious necessity for securing constant and reliable financing of the Fund, without which the essential purpose of the Fund will be defeated. It is also desirable to seek modalities for the financing of the Fund that avoid the necessity of legal and other proceedings in a multiplicity of third countries and jurisdictions.

16. The legal basis for the payments by Iraq to the Fund is to be found in paragraph 19 of resolution 687 (1991). Iraq has officially notified the United Nations of its acceptance of the provisions of the resolution, including paragraph 19, in accordance with paragraph 33 of the resolution. It follows from paragraph 19 of resolution 687 (1991) that the method envisaged by the Security Council for the financing of the Fund is a contribution by Iraq based on a percentage of the value of its exports determined in accordance with the mechanism referred to in paragraph 13 above. It also follows from the resolution that the Security Council did not envisage using "frozen assets" of Iraq held in third countries for the financing of the Fund.

17. Under these circumstances, there are several options for ensuring that Iraq makes payments to the Fund. These options include the following:

(a) Iraq would pay to the Fund the established percentage of the market value of its exports of petroleum and petroleum products; the market value to be calculated on the day of the export. The payment would be effected in United States dollars and made within 30 days of the export from Iraq;

(b) An escrow account would be opened into which Iraq would deposit advance payments of lump sums equivalent to the estimated quarterly or semi-annual contribution required of it. These lump-sum payments would be re-evaluated periodically;

(c) A physical share of the exports would be taken and sold on the market on behalf of the Fund;

(d) The Fund would be designated as either the sole or co-beneficiary on the bill of lading or other title document and any letter of credit issued. The Fund, in turn, would retain its share and remit the remainder to Iraq;

(e) An escrow account provided with the appropriate privileges and immunities (e.g. at a central bank or an appropriate international institution) would be designated as beneficiary on the bill of lading or other title document and any letter of credit issued. The escrow agent would remit to the Fund the sum designated to be used to satisfy claims and the remainder to Iraq.

It would be for the Governing Council to decide among these various options.

18. All of these methods presuppose cooperation by Iraq and strict supervision of the exports of petroleum and petroleum products from Iraq. To this end, the Commission should arrange for appropriate monitoring. Whatever approach is adopted, should Iraq fail to meet

its payment obligation, the Governing Council would report the matter to the Security Council.

19. It must be recognized that, in all probability, it may be some time before Iraq is able to resume oil exports. In the short term, the Fund is therefore unlikely to receive revenues, and some consideration will have to be given to the financing of the work of the Commission, a problem which is addressed in paragraph 29 below, but more particularly to the financing of the Fund in the near term from assets other than resumed oil exports by Iraq.

C. Claims procedure

20. The process by which funds will be allocated and claims paid, the appropriate procedures for evaluating losses, the listing of claims and the verification of their validity and the resolution of disputed claims as set out in paragraph 19 of resolution 687 (1991)—the claims procedure—is the central purpose and object of paragraphs 16 to 19 of resolution 687 (1991). It is in this area of the Commission's work that the distinction between policy-making and function is most important. The Commission is not a court or an arbitral tribunal before which the parties appear; it is a political organ that performs an essentially fact-finding function of examining claims, verifying their validity, evaluating losses, assessing payments and resolving disputed claims. It is only in this last respect that a quasi-judicial function may be involved. Given the nature of the Commission, it is all the more important that some element of due process be built into the procedure. It will be the function of the commissioners to provide this element. As the policy-making organ of the Commission, it will fall to the Governing Council to establish the guidelines regarding the claims procedure. The commissioners will implement the guidelines in respect of claims that are presented and in resolving disputed claims. They will make the appropriate recommendations to the Governing Council, which in turn will make the final determination. The recommendations that follow have been divided for the sake of convenience under three main headings: the filing of claims; the processing of claims; and the payments of claims.

1. Filing of claims

21. With regard to the filing of claims, the Governing Council must first decide in what manner the claims of foreign Governments, nationals and corporations are to be filed with the Commission. It is recommended that the Commission should entertain, as a general rule, only consolidated claims filed by individual Governments on their own behalf or on behalf of their nationals and corporations. The filing of individual claims would entail tens of thousands of claims to be processed by the Commission, a task which could take a decade or more and could lead to inequalities in the filing of claims disadvan-

taging small claimants. It will be for each individual Government to decide on the procedures to be followed internally in respect of the consolidation of the claim having regard to its own legal system, practice and procedures. The Governing Council may, in addition, consider whether, in exceptional circumstances involving very large and complex claims, a somewhat different procedure could apply. The question might be considered whether such claims, the character of which, of course, would have to be defined by the Governing Council, could be filed individually with the Commission by Governments, nationals or corporations and whether the individual Government, national or corporation could be authorized to present these claims.

22. In this context, there is another matter that requires consideration by the Commission and regarding which the Governing Council should establish guidelines, namely the question of the exclusivity or non-exclusivity of the claims procedure foreseen in paragraph 19 of the resolution. It is clear from paragraph 16 of the resolution that the debts and obligations of Iraq arising prior to 2 August 1990 are an entirely separate issue and will be addressed "through the normal mechanisms". It is also clear from paragraph 16 that the resolution and the procedure foreseen in paragraph 19 relate to liability under international law. Resolution 687 (1991) could not, and does not, establish the Commission as an organ with exclusive competence to consider claims arising from Iraq's unlawful invasion and occupation of Kuwait. In other words, it is entirely possible, indeed probable, that individual claimants will proceed with claims against Iraq in their domestic legal systems. The likelihood of parallel actions taking place on the international level in the Commission and on the domestic level in national courts cannot be ignored. It is, therefore, recommended that the Governing Council establish guidelines regarding the non-exclusivity of claims and the appropriate mechanisms for coordination of actions at the international and domestic levels in order to ensure that the aggregate of compensation awarded by the Commission and a national court or commission does not exceed the amount of the loss. A particular problem might arise in this regard concerning default judgements obtained in national courts.

23. In addition to deciding on the consolidation of claims, the Governing Council may also wish to establish a categorization of claims according to both type and size. The categorization of claims according to type might, for example, distinguish between claims for loss of life or personal injury and property damage, environmental damage or damage due to the depletion of natural resources. The categorization of claims by size might for example, differentiate between small-, medium- and large-sized claims. A further categorization might be to

distinguish between losses incurred by Governments, on the one hand, and losses incurred by nationals and corporations, on the other hand.

24. Governments could be requested by the Governing Council to use these categorizations when filing their consolidated claims. The Governing Council should also establish guidelines regarding the formal requirements for the presentation of claims such as the type of documentation to be presented in support of the claim and the time-delays for the filing of claims. The time-delays should be of sufficient length to permit Governments to establish and implement an internal procedure for the assembling and consolidation of claims. It is recommended that a fixed time period be established for the filing of all claims. A period of two years from the adoption of the filing guidelines would appear to be adequate. Alternatively, the Governing Council could set different filing periods for different types of claims in order to ensure that priority is given to certain claims, for example, loss of life or personal injury. In this respect, I am of the opinion that there would be some merit in providing for a priority consideration of small claims relating to losses by individuals so that these are disposed of before the consideration of claims relating to losses by foreign Governments and by corporations.

2. Processing of claims

25. The processing of claims will entail the verification of claims and evaluation of losses and the resolution of any disputed claims. The major part of this task is not of a judicial nature; the resolution of disputed claims would, however, be quasi-judicial. It is envisaged that the processing of claims would be carried out principally by the commissioners. Before proceeding to the verification of claims and evaluation of losses, however, a determination will have to be made as to whether the losses for which claims are presented fall within the meaning of paragraph 16 of resolution 687 (1991), that is to say, whether the loss, damage or injury is direct and as a result of Iraq's unlawful invasion and occupation of Kuwait. It is recommended that the Governing Council establish detailed guidelines regarding what constitutes such direct loss for the guidance of all claimants as well as the commissioners.

26. Claims will be addressed to the Commission. The Commission will make a preliminary assessment of the claims, which will be carried out by the Secretariat, to determine whether they meet the formal requirements established by the Governing Council. The claims would then be submitted to verification and evaluation by panels normally comprised of three commissioners for this purpose. In carrying out these tasks, it is recommended that the commissioners be given the necessary powers to request additional evidence, to hold hearings in which individual Governments, nationals and corporations can present their views and to hear expert testimony. The Governing Council might wish to address the question of possible assistance to ensure the adequacy of the representation of countries of limited financial means. Iraq will be informed of all claims and will have the right to present its comments to the commissioners within time-delays to be fixed by the Governing Council or the Panel dealing with the individual claim. Recommendations of the commissioners regarding the verification and evaluation of claims will be final and subject only to the approval of the Governing Council, which shall make the final determination. The Governing Council should have the power to return claims to the commissioners for further revision if it so decides.

27. Where a dispute arises out of the allegation made by a claimant that the Panel of Commissioners, in dealing with its claims, has made an error, whether on a point of law and procedure or on a point of fact, such disputes will be dealt with by a board of commissioners who for this purpose should be guided by such guidelines as have been established by the Governing Council and the Arbitration Rules of the United Nations Commission on International Trade Law (UNCITRAL). The UNCITRAL Arbitration Rules will be modified as necessary. The final decision will be made by the Governing Council.

3. Payment of claims

28. It is to be anticipated that the value of claims approved by the Commission will at any given time far exceed the resources of the Fund. It will, therefore, be incumbent upon the Commission to decide on an allocation of funds and a procedure for the payment of claims. It is recommended that the Governing Council establish criteria for the allocation of funds, taking into account the size of claims, the scope of the losses sustained by the country concerned and any other relevant factors. In this connection, it might be necessary to distinguish between Kuwait, on the one hand, and other countries on the other hand. As far as the payment of claims is concerned, it follows from the consolidation of the claims and their filing by individual Governments that payments will be made exclusively to Governments. Individual Governments will be responsible for the appropriate distribution to individual claimants. The Governing Council should establish further guidelines regarding the payment of claims, for example, whether claims should be paid in full or whether percentages should be paid. In the latter case, the unsatisfied portions of the claims will remain as outstanding obligations.

D. *Expenses of the Commission*

29. The expenses of the Commission, including those of the Governing Council, the commissioners and the secretariat, should in principle be paid from the Fund. However, as some time will elapse before the Fund is adequately financed, consideration must be given to the financial implications of the programme outlined. It is recommended that urgent consideration be given to the means by which the initial costs of the Commission will be met.

Document 50

Report of the Secretary-General concerning UNIKOM

S/22580, 9 May 1991

1. The present report is submitted in pursuance of paragraph 5 of resolution 687 (1991) of 3 April 1991, by which the Security Council established a demilitarized zone (DMZ) along the Iraq-Kuwait border and decided to set up an observer unit to monitor the zone and resolution 689 (1991) of 9 April 1991, by which the Council approved my plan (S/22454 and Add.1-3) for the establishment of the United Nations Iraq-Kuwait Observation Mission (UNIKOM).

2. On 13 April, the UNIKOM advance party, comprising the Chief Military Observer, Major-General Günther Greindl, and a number of military and civilian staff, arrived at Kuwait City, established liaison with the Kuwaiti authorities and set up a temporary headquarters. On 15 April, General Greindl travelled to Baghdad and established liaison with the Iraqi authorities.

3. Over the next three weeks, UNIKOM deployed in the zone assigned to it, with the cooperation of the Governments of Iraq and Kuwait and with substantial logistic support from the forces of Member States cooperating with the Government of Kuwait. As of this date, five observation posts have been established in each of the north, centre and south sectors of the zone, with two additional observation posts planned in the north sector and one additional observation post in the south sector.

4. The Governments of Iraq and Kuwait have both agreed to afford UNIKOM full freedom of movement across the border; the DMZ is thus one undivided area of operation for the Mission. For operational purposes, the DMZ has been organized into three sectors. The headquarters is being readied for occupation at Umm Qasr, as originally envisaged, and a logistic base and liaison office have been established at Doha in Kuwait. UNIKOM also maintains a liaison office at Baghdad.

5. At present, UNIKOM comprises 280 military observers from the following countries:

Argentina	7	Nigeria	7
Austria	7	Norway	7
Bangladesh	7	Pakistan	9
Canada	1	Poland	7
China (20) a/	16	Romania	7
Denmark	7	Senegal (7) a/	-
Fiji	8	Singapore	7
Finland	7	Sweden	7
France	20	Thailand	7
Ghana	8	Turkey (7) a/	-
Greece	7	United Kingdom of	
Hungary	6	Great Britain and	
India	8	Northern Ireland	20
Indonesia	7	Uruguay	8
Ireland	8	United States of America	20
Italy	7	Union of Soviet	
Kenya	8	Socialist Republics	20
Malaysia	8	Venezuela	7

a/ Figures in brackets indicate planned strength.

An additional five military observers from the United Nations Truce Supervision Organization (UNTSO) are temporarily attached to the Mission.

6. Administrative and logistic support is provided by the following units:

Movement control (Denmark)	20
Post (Denmark)	5
Engineers (Canada)	297
Medical (Norway)	50
Logistics (Sweden)	134 a/
Aircraft (Switzerland)	3
Helicopters (Chile)	47
Total	556

a/ Includes 99 temporarily detached from the United Nations Interim Force in Lebanon (UNIFIL).

United Nations international civilian staff provide transport, communications and administrative support.

7. In addition, UNIKOM is supported by five infantry companies temporarily assigned from UNIFIL (from Fiji, Ghana and Nepal) and the United Nations Peace-keeping Force in Cyprus (UNFICYP) (from Austria and Denmark), one of which is deployed in each of the three sectors, one at the headquarters at Umm Qasr and one at the logistic base at Doha. Their total strength is 544 all ranks. The total strength of military personnel of UNIKOM at present is 1,385.

8. UNIKOM's deployment was completed on 6 May. UNIKOM then monitored the withdrawal of the armed forces that were still deployed in its assigned zone. That withdrawal having been completed, the DMZ established by the Security Council came into effect at 2000 hours GMT today, 9 May 1991, and UNIKOM assumed in full the observation responsibilities entrusted to it by the Security Council.

9. I shall present a further progress report to the Security Council in approximately four weeks' time, by when I shall have received from the Chief Military Observer the recommendations foreseen in my report of 5 April 1991 (S/22454, para. 13).

Document 51

United Nations Inter-Agency Programme relating to Iraq, Kuwait and the Iraq/Iran and Iraq/Turkey Borders: Updated and Consolidated Appeal for Urgent Humanitarian Action (extract)

15 May 1991

Foreword by the Executive Delegate of the Secretary-General in the context of a United Nations inter-agency humanitarian programme for Iraq, Kuwait and the Iraq/Iran and Iraq/Turkey border areas

At this critical time, it is essential that the initial momentum achieved by the United Nations Inter-Agency Humanitarian Programme be sustained and its impetus extended throughout the region so as to alleviate the suffering of the refugees and displaced persons, as well as the burdens facing their hosts.

At this point, close to 200,000 refugees have returned to Iraq from Turkey and the Iraq/Turkey border, although a further 300,000 remain in the latter area. Such voluntary repatriation demonstrates the significant effect of a combination of reassurance, a United Nations presence and appropriate relief assistance, which can together bring about major breakthroughs. The opening of a United Nations Humanitarian Centre (UNHUC) in Zakho has also substantially contributed to this development.

The most vivid proof of progress is given by Iskiveren camp, the bleak mountain top which the world media transformed into the symbol of tragedy. I am pleased to report that Iskiveren has been virtually emptied of its population and will soon be closed.

Since the 1st of May, UN (WFP) food assistance has been delivered to 106,000 people in 7 towns throughout Northern Iraq. An UNHUC has been opened at Zakho, while UN Sub-offices have been set up in Mosul, Basrah, Erbil, Sulaimaniah and Dohuk.

The Office of the Executive Delegate working with NGOs and concerned member states has developed the "Blue Route" strategy to guide returnees from Iskiveren to Zakho, as well as from Uzumlu/Cukurca through Kani Masi to Zakho and Dohuk. Along the "Blue Route" relay stations are being established with the assistance of concerned member states. These have been and continue to be instrumental in assisting returnees. Meanwhile, three UN convoys, one from Baghdad to Zakho, one from Silopi to Zakho and one from Zakho to Dohuk have laid the basis for a United Nations relief distribution system.

The key to the solution of the bulk of the remaining caseload in Turkey, as well as the massing of displaced persons near Zakho (where 25,000 people are in the US-built transit centre awaiting a chance to return) is the creation of confidence in the greater Dohuk area.

In this context I decided that a convoy be sent to Dohuk: it arrived on the 13th of May, with 117 tons of food for the approximately 20,000 people remaining out of the pre-war population of 185,000. The Dohuk UN sub-office will distribute these essential supplies and maintain the UN flag that could provide a stimulus to refugees returning home.

I am pleased to announce that on 13th May overall responsibility for the transit centre in Zakho was accepted by UNHCR.

The Islamic Republic of Iran still hosts 900,000 refugees. Discussions have already been initiated to lay the ground for additional "Blue Routes" to transit centres and UNHUCs on the Iraqi side of the Iraq-Iran border.

The needs of vulnerable groups in Iraq, as well as preventive measures for health and nutrition, cannot be forgotten. If unmet, moreover, they could well lead to a further mass population exodus.

In Kuwait the plight of displaced persons and the health sector should be addressed with the utmost urgency. Ecological damage caused by the oil fires in Kuwait and oil slicks in the Persian Gulf will spill over far beyond the borders of the region: they call for a immediate international response.

To date, funds contributed to the appeals have been limited and have not matched the magnitude of the crisis. To allow the crucial work already started by the United Nations to continue, to expand throughout the region and on a larger scale and to help initiate new and critical United Nations projects, the international community is urged to respond generously and rapidly to this revised appeal.

(*Signed*) Sadruddin AGA KHAN

Introduction

In April 1991 two separate appeals were made by the United Nations in response to the urgent needs of Iraqi people affected by the Gulf War and its aftermath. The first totalled US$178 million to cover initial emergency needs in Iraq. The second, based on an earlier appeal for start-up funds, was for US$400 million and included the needs of an estimated 1.8 million people fleeing from Iraq into Iran and Turkey.

Since these appeals were launched there have been a number of major initiatives. As a result, some spontaneous repatriation of refugees from the border of Iraq and Turkey and from Iran is occurring. Although a major pre-occupation of refugees is that their safety in Iraq be assured, it is clear that the security zone created in Northern Iraq has offered hope—albeit without long-term guarantees—to many. The establishment by the United Nations on 1 May of a large and highly operational UNHUC in Zakho has significantly contributed to facilitate the return of large numbers of refugees and to support them during their first period of re-integration in their cities and villages of origin. While the situation is highly fluid, since 1 May, an estimated 200,000 persons have spontaneously left their inhospitable mountain refuge.

On 18 April 1991, the Government of Iraq and the Executive Delegate agreed on a framework to meet the mammoth humanitarian needs of civilians affected by the recent upheavals. This document reflects the current situation and its anticipated evolution in coming months. It details urgent actions required to ensure the well-being of refugees who decide to return to Iraq. The document, which consolidates the two previous United Nations appeals, re-emphasises the need for emergency humanitarian assistance in Iraq to avert fresh calamities and further displacements of people. A number of urgent health and environmental-related projects to alleviate the suffering of the people of Kuwait, upon which appalling damage has been inflicted, are also included.

In reviewing this document, several factors must be considered. Firstly, the document reflects a scenario which is based on assumptions that current conditions in regard to the safety and security in areas of return will prevail or that other forms of arrangements are put into place. The representatives of the United Nations and other humanitarian organisations can not by themselves provide the same type of guarantees as the concerned member states provide for the safety of returning nationals. Secondly, actions proposed in the document rely on the full cooperation of the Governments of Iraq, the Islamic Republic of Iran and Turkey, as well as on continued mobilisation of substantial resources by concerned countries.

The third issue concerns financing. The massive mobilisation of financial and human resources has already saved countless lives. The dimensions of the tasks which lie ahead and the exceedingly large numbers of people still in need of assistance, however, will require considerable and additional financial support from the international community. To date, the response to both of the April United Nations appeals has been very much below expectations. Contributions received between January and the end of April 1991 have largely been spent on urgent ongoing activities and little is left over for the tasks ahead.

Executive summary

1. In spite of the massive financial, logistic and human resources which have been mobilised since early April, largely on a bilateral basis, the misery of the peoples of Iraq and Kuwait continues. In human, economic and social terms, the devastation resulting from the war and the displacement of large numbers of people in the civil conflict which followed is incalculable.

2. Since late March 1991, over 1.8 million people, mostly of Kurdish origin, have left their homes in Iraq. Thousands have died during the long arduous trek to the inhospitable border areas of Iraq and Turkey and into Iran. In some areas, deaths due to malnutrition and disease have been as high as 800 a day. In some camps in Iran, where women and children comprise 80% of the refugee populations, only a third still have access to shelter.

3. Inside Iraq, food rationing for those who remained in their homes continues at a level well below the minimum required to sustain normal life. This has resulted in a steady increase in malnutrition. Reconstruc-

tion is taking place in the larger towns and cities, but in many parts of the country the war has robbed civilians of basic health and sanitation services and clean water supplies. Coupled with poor nutrition, the lack of such services threaten the lives of the most vulnerable groups.

4. In good years, harvests inside Iraq account for 30% of the total food requirements, the remainder being covered by food imports, costing approximately US$2 billion. With the disruption of this year's harvests because of war and displacements of populations, substantial additional amounts of food from the international community will be required. Without agricultural assistance, such as seeds and machinery to replace lost assets, the harvest of 1992 will also be disrupted. If government financial assets for such imports can not be used, massive international assistance totalling many billions of dollars may well be required in order to avert major famine.

5. Since the two United Nations appeals in April 1991, a number of events and initiatives have led to the need to revise priority activities in coming months. In the first of these initiatives, several nations joined together to create a security zone in Northern Iraq. Massive logistics operations were mounted through rapid mobilisation of financial and human resources.

6. Further to this, on 18 April 1991 the Executive Delegate of the Secretary-General, Prince Sadruddin Aga Khan, and the Minister of Foreign Affairs of the Republic of Iraq, signed a Memorandum of Understanding aimed at facilitating urgent humanitarian assistance and the voluntary return home of those who wish to go back to their places of origin. The United Nations was further requested both by the Iraqi authorities and concerned member states to take over camps set up bilaterally. Parallel to these events, negotiations have taken place in Baghdad between the President of Iraq and the Kurdish leadership. Various proposals are also being explored in relation to security in the area, including re-deployment of United Nations personnel.

7. As these events were unfolding and the first UNHUC in northern Iraq established, the earlier trickle of spontaneous repatriation from both the Turkish and Iranian borders gained momentum. By 14 May, an estimated 200,000 people had departed from the Iraq/Turkey border, with a further 5,000 a day leaving camps in Iran. Some estimates are that up to 300,000 people may already have returned or are *en route* to Iraq.

8. Given the rapidity of developments, and the overriding pre-occupation amongst refugees that their safety be assured upon return to Iraq, it is difficult to predict the overall pattern of repatriation of the Iraqi refugees. Although no such assurances of safety can be given at this point in time, it is evident that the hopes of many refugees have been raised. Other factors, such as economic considerations and the imminent start of the Iraqi harvest are also believed to be strong incentives for refugees to return home quickly. The onset of fall and the harsh winter which follows will equally have an impact on the numbers of people deciding to go home.

9. While it would be premature to assume that the spontaneous repatriation which has occurred means that a solution is at hand, massive repatriation, at short notice, can not be excluded. Of the refugees who fled to Iran, 50% own a vehicle and thus could very easily and quickly move back. Initial indications from the camps are that up to half of the 1.3 million refugees in Iran and most of the remaining 200,000 refugees on the Iraq/Turkey borders are considering repatriation.

10. UNHCR has primary responsibility for facilitating voluntary repatriation. Given prevailing circumstances, UNHCR is rapidly expanding its traditional role of providing up-to-date information to refugees on conditions inside Iraq and ensuring that returns are purely voluntary. Such returns must be conducted in safety and dignity, with adequate assistance delivered *en route* and in the areas of origin.

11. To ensure the safety and well-being of refugees who are unwilling to repatriate, at least immediately, new sites must be established or existing camps significantly upgraded to provide better conditions for temporary asylum. For planning purposes, it is estimated that large numbers of refugees could remain in Iran and that between 20,000-50,000 people could remain on the Iraq/Turkey border. Activities which must be undertaken without delay are the identification of new sites or the upgrading of existing ones. Additional shelter, safe water supplies and sanitation services are also required, as are supplementary foods to address the poor nutritional condition of many mothers and children. Accelerated immunisation programmes must be carried out to protect women and children from common but killer diseases.

12. Due to the large numbers of refugees returning to Iraq, and the worsening conditions in some parts of the country, emergency assistance must be expanded in Iraq to meet the needs of returning refugees, and to stave off new calamities. Cholera outbreaks are already occurring in some areas. In the south, which is of particular concern, severe food rationing and lack of health and sanitation services have led to increased malnutrition and the likelihood of major epidemics. The plight of women and the newborn is particularly serious. If the situation is allowed to deteriorate, it is feared that further migration from the south will be inevitable. Emergency interventions needed for vulnerable groups are provision of health, water, medical and sanitation services and high protein foods for infants and mothers, many so poorly nourished they have stopped lactating.

13. As a first step to gradually taking over the transit centre in Zakho and refugee camps on the borders, including activities currently being carried out by certain member states, and to facilitate emergency repatriation activities in Iraq, five United Nations sub-offices are being established in the provincial capitals of Basrah, Mosul, Dohuk, Erbil and Suleimaniya. These sub-offices will service a number of field offices and relay stations under the responsibility of United Nations teams. While UNHCR has the lead operational role for refugee and returnee matters and will concentrate its activities in the northern and eastern parts of Iraq from which most of the refugees originate, UNICEF will share the organisational responsibility for setting up this network of United Nations Humanitarian Centres (UNHUCs) in other areas. Non-Governmental Organisations (NGOs) are being encouraged to make use of the logistic facilities that such centres can provide. NGOs will work alongside the United Nations under terms of association which will enhance their participation in humanitarian programmes, which giving them sufficient flexibility so as not to hamper their field activities. This has, in fact, already been successfully established by the Zakho UNHUC with 19 NGOs in the area.

14. In respect of the emergency humanitarian needs and provision of emergency short-term material assistance which is so urgently required by large numbers of the Iraqi people, overall responsibility for the coordination of efforts lies with the Executive Delegate who has been appointed by the Secretary-General as his representative to oversee the implementation of a United Nations Inter-Agency Humanitarian Programme for Iraq, Kuwait and the Iraq/Turkey and Iraq/Iran border areas, and his Coordinator in Baghdad. Operational support has been undertaken by UNICEF, UNHCR, WHO, WFP, FAO, and the International Organisation for Migration (IOM). UNDP is assisting the Executive Delegate and his Coordinator with the provision of professional staff. UNDRO will provide coordination support at Headquarters level.

15. In order for the United Nations to carry out the huge task ahead in regard to refugees, returnees and the most vulnerable inside Iraq, a inter-agency task force has been established. Although the inter-agency team of United Nations personnel is supplemented by personnel from Non-Governmental Organisations (NGOs), bilateral support is also required. Some Governments have already made available to the United Nations fully equipped teams of their countrymen with skills in the areas of water, sanitation and relief camp management. Additional similar assistance is urgently required.

16. In Kuwait, the health care system, which prior to August 1990 compared very favourably with those of industrialised countries, lies in disarray. The departure of large numbers of health professionals, following the invasion of the country, has created major difficulties in managing curative and preventive health services. In addition, large quantities of medical equipment have been damaged or removed. The unprecedented situation caused by the burning of oil wells and the uncontrolled spilling of oil over large areas are also matters of grave environmental concern. Vast resources have been made available by Kuwait itself but funds are required to begin tackling some of the urgent health-related problems, without delay.

17. The cost of carrying out the tasks detailed in this document is considerable. The total budget is US$415,080,737 to cover a four-month period until the end of August 1991. Of this total, US$64,970,099 is required for food supplies. Assistance to refugees and returnees amounts to US$235,478,158.

18. For vulnerable groups in Iraq, US$43,032,480 is required. This will enable the provision of foodstuffs, such as high protein biscuits, immunisation, health and sanitation services and installation of clean water supplies. Also included is US$64 million for short-term material assistance, such as seeds, protection of livestock and agricultural machinery, and re-establishment of a basic communication system. An additional US$7.6 million is required for environmental and health-related programmes in Kuwait.

19. The activities and budgets proposed are the minimum basic requirements for the four months ahead. To ensure that efforts are not duplicated and to complement the activities of other agencies, interventions detailed in this appeal have been coordinated with the International Committee of the Red Cross and the League of Red Cross and Red Crescent Societies. Regular meetings will be held with ICRC/LRCSCS to further enhance efforts in the field.

20. The time-frame proposed by this appeal takes into account that significant movement of returnees is and will continue to occur through the summer of 1991. It must be noted, however, that this plan and estimates of likely repatriation are based upon prevailing conditions and trends. Should major changes occur, many of the proposed activities will have to be reconsidered and eventually expanded. Secondly, the document assumes the complete cooperation of the Governments of Iraq, Turkey and the Government of the Islamic Republic of Iran. Such cooperation and freedom of access between borders is essential if further suffering is to be alleviated. Plans also assume the continuation of bilateral efforts in the humanitarian field.

...

Document 52

Report of the Secretary-General submitting a plan for immediate on-site inspections by the Special Commission (UNSCOM) and for destruction, removal or rendering harmless of relevant weapons and facilities

S/22614, 17 May 1991

Plan for the implementation of relevant parts of section C of Security Council resolution 687 (1991)

Report of the Secretary-General

Introduction

1. The present report is submitted in pursuance of Security Council resolution 687 (1991) of 3 April 1991. In paragraph 9 (b) of that resolution, the Council decided that the Secretary-General, within 45 days of the adoption of the resolution, should develop and submit to it for approval a plan calling for the completion of the tasks enumerated in paragraphs 9 (b) (i to iii) and 10.

2. For the purpose of developing this plan, consultations were held with appropriate Governments, as called for in paragraphs 9 (b) and 13 of the resolution, and, where appropriate, with the Director General of the International Atomic Energy Agency (IAEA) and the Director-General of the World Health Organization (WHO). Furthermore, in order to assess the information submitted by the Government of Iraq and to assist me in developing the plan for the implementation of the tasks enumerated in section C of the resolution, I set up a Special Commission as described in my report of 18 April 1991 to the Security Council (S/22508), which the Council accepted on 19 April.

3. I appointed 21 experts as members of the Special Commission. I have requested Ambassador Rolf Ekéus (Sweden) to serve as its Executive Chairman and Dr. Robert Gallucci (United States of America) to serve as its Deputy Executive Chairman. The other members of the Special Commission are as follows: Dr. Paal Aas (Norway), Lieutenant General (ret.) Ken Adachi (Japan), Professor B. N. C. Agu (Nigeria), Lieutenant-Colonel Andrzej Badek (Poland), Professor Bryan C. Barrass (United Kingdom of Great Britain and Northern Ireland), Mr. Peter von Butler (Germany), Colonel Armando Caputo (Italy), Mr. Ronald Cleminson (Canada), Dr. John Gee (Australia), Professor Helmut Hönig (Austria), Mr. B. A. Kuvshinnikov (Union of Soviet Socialist Republics), Dr. A. J. J. Ooms (Netherlands), Dr. Marjatta Rautio (Finland), Mr. Michel Saint Mleux (France), Mr. Roberto Sanchez (Venezuela), Lieutenant Colonel B. Simandjuntak (Indonesia), Dr. Miroslav Splino (Czechoslovakia), Mr. Emile Vanden Bemden (Belgium), Dr. Yuan Renfeng (China).

4. In order to enable the Special Commission as well as IAEA to discharge their responsibilities properly, a number of technical arrangements are being made to facilitate their work. They include the establishment of a field operations office and a support office. After consultations with the Governments concerned, the Field Operations Office is being set up in Bahrain. The Office will become fully operational by the end of May 1991. The Support Office is being established at Baghdad, Iraq.

I. THE PLAN

5. The provisions of section C of resolution 687 (1991) lend themselves to a three-stage implementation procedure: gathering and assessment of information; disposal of weapons and facilities and all other items specified in paragraphs 8 and 12 of resolution 687 (1991); and monitoring and verification of Iraq's compliance in the future.

A. *Gathering and assessment of information*

6. The first stage of the plan is of crucial importance for the success of the entire operation. It requires input from both the Iraqi Government and the Special Commission. Pursuant to paragraphs 9 (a) and 12, Iraq is responsible for the submission, within fifteen days of the adoption of the resolution, of information on the locations, amounts and types of all items specified in paragraphs 8 and 12, which are to be destroyed, removed or rendered harmless. The Special Commission, pursuant to paragraphs 9 (b) (i) and 13, is responsible for designating any additional locations of these items in Iraq. In carrying out the immediate on-site inspections envisaged in paragraphs 9 (b) (i) and 13 of the resolution, the Special Commission and IAEA respectively must retain the right to choose the timing and locations of the inspection.

7. On 18 and 28 April and 4 May 1991, the Government of Iraq forwarded to the Secretary-General information relating to its chemical and biological weapons and ballistic missiles. On 18 April, the Government of Iraq also forwarded to the Director General of IAEA information of relevance to the responsibilities entrusted to the Agency as stated in paragraphs 12 and 13 of resolution 687 (1991). Further information was communicated to the Agency on 27 April. In communications both to the Secretary-General and the Director General, the Government of Iraq also conveyed its acceptance of

on-site inspections as called for in paragraphs 9 (a) and 12. There has also been a continued exchange of communications between the Special Commission and the Government of Iraq with a view to obtaining additional information and clarifications.

8. Based on the information received so far from the Iraqi authorities, as well as taking into account additional locations designated by the Special Commission, the process of on-site inspections by the Special Commission and IAEA has been initiated. In the course of the inspections, the Special Commission will check the information that has been gathered earlier against the actual situation in the field (i.e. establishing a database); assess the magnitude of the task of disposal of weapons and facilities that it will perform in the second stage of the plan; and determine, with the advice of WHO, the requirements and modalities for carrying it out. The Special Commission is also rendering assistance and cooperation to the Director General of IAEA in connection with on-site inspections for which the Agency is responsible.

9. The on-site inspections to be carried out by both the Special Commission and IAEA cover a large number of sites with different numbers of facilities at each site. For the purpose of ensuring safe access to sites subject to the measures specified in paragraphs 9 (b), 12 and 13 of resolution 687 (1991), teams of explosive ordnance disposal (EOD) experts, construction engineers and security personnel have been engaged to assist the Special Commission and IAEA in the process of carrying out the on-site inspections. The safety of all such personnel is a major consideration. Detailed arrangements covering these and related aspects and governing the precise modalities for carrying out the inspections are embodied in an agreement between the United Nations and the Government of Iraq. The volume of work as well as the physical state of the various objects, installations and facilities subject to inspection, and the paramount concern regarding the safety of the inspection teams and the local population, make it difficult to establish, at the present stage, the exact time-frame within which the first stage can be concluded. Early assessments of the tasks involved make it possible, nevertheless, to outline the general framework of the second stage of the plan, which is described below.

B. *Disposal of weapons and facilities*

10. The main purpose of the second stage of the plan, as specified in paragraphs 8, 9 and 13 of resolution 687 (1991), is to dispose of weapons, facilities and all other items specified in paragraphs 8 and 12 of the resolution. Owing to the highly different nature of the weapons, material and facilities involved, separate proce-

dures are envisaged for their actual disposal, with different teams of experts carrying them out.

11. Regarding chemical weapons and biological weapons-related items and facilities, technical modalities are being worked out with a view to ensuring the complete and safe yielding of possession by Iraq of all items referred to in paragraph 8 (a) of the resolution, for their subsequent destruction, removal or rendering them harmless. Regarding ballistic missiles, procedures for the identification and securing of all items referred to in paragraph 8 (b) of the resolution are being developed with a view to ensuring the supervision of their complete destruction by Iraq. The Special Commission will further assist and cooperate with IAEA in carrying out inspections and in the destruction, removal or rendering harmless of all items referred to in paragraph 12 of the resolution.

12. As far as the disposal process itself is concerned, Iraq will destroy, under the supervision of the Special Commission, all its missile capabilities, including launchers, as specified under paragraph 8 (b) of resolution 687 (1991). The Special Commission and IAEA respectively, with appropriate Iraqi assistance, will dispose of all other items specified under paragraphs 8 (a) and 12 of the same resolution, including missile warheads fitted with chemical warfare agents. It should be noted that under the resolution the Special Commission has the authority to conduct activities related to inspection, yielding and disposal of the items specified in paragraph 8 (a) of the resolution and the inspection and disposal of the items specified in paragraph 8 (b) of the resolution after the expiration of the 45-day period that follows the approval of this plan, if such activities have not been completed.

1. *Ballistic missiles*

13. The disposal of ballistic missiles and related items and facilities raises a relatively smaller number of problems as compared to other types of weapons and facilities. In principle, their disposal should not pose any danger to public safety as it involves a largely mechanical operation. Consequently, the disposal of missiles and related major parts including launchers will be carried out *in situ* and, if possible, it will be done concomitantly with the initial on-site inspection process. Those items not disposed of immediately will be secured, sealed and appropriately documented for later disposal. Furthermore, items such as warheads and fuel might be moved to a special destruction location or facility and disposed of there.

14. As regards repair and production facilities, many of them appear no longer operational as a result of the hostilities. The Special Commission will ascertain the extent to which these facilities are permanently affected, with a view to determining what other steps, if any, are necessary to comply with paragraph 9 (b) (ii) of the resolution.

15. In order to carry out the responsibilities regarding this category of weapons and related facilities, the Special Commission will require individuals with expertise in such fields as launching and guidance systems, propellants and warheads. Teams of experts will be needed to conduct both the on-site inspections and the supervision of the disposal process. The number of teams and their exact composition is currently under study.

2. *Chemical weapons*

16. As regards chemical weapons, in view of the practical problems inherent in their destruction, including possible safety and environmental hazards, the Special Commission, in consultation with WHO, has focused its attention on determining the best methods for their disposal. Taking into account the paramount importance of maintaining acceptable safety standards for the disposal teams and for the local population, the Special Commission will identify and evaluate safe destruction techniques that could be made operable within stringent time-frames.

17. Given the danger chemical weapons represent, their disposal will be initiated only after thorough on-site inspection and assessment of the conditions of stocks and facilities. In this connection, the Special Commission has requested the inspection teams to mark munitions and relevant facilities, to the extent possible, with tamper-indicating devices. In addition, the Special Commission foresees monitoring, between the time of the inspections and the disposal process, by inspectors at relevant locations.

18. The disposal methods will involve neutralization and/or incineration. Movement of chemical weapons and agents will be minimized. In this connection the Special Commission is investigating the use of transportable or mobile destruction equipment. The Special Commission may also consider the possibility of the construction of a destruction facility which would have greater capacity than that offered by transportable or mobile equipment. In this and other options the question of costs will need to be kept under review.

19. As regards research, development, support and manufacturing facilities in connection with chemical weapons, information available to the Special Commission at present suggests that a number of them may have been destroyed as a result of the hostilities. Upon establishing firm data the Special Commission will determine its requirements, both in terms of equipment and human resources, for complying with provisions of paragraph 9 (b) of resolution 687 (1991).

3. *Biological weapons*

20. In the area of biological weapons, it is noted that, in accordance with paragraph 7 of Security Council resolution 687 (1991), Iraq has become a party to the Convention on the Prohibition of the Development, Production and Stockpiling of Bacteriological (Biological) and Toxin Weapons and on Their Destruction. 1/ The Government of Iraq deposited, on 8 April, its instrument of ratification in Moscow.

21. However, as required by the Security Council in its resolution 687 (1991), the Special Commission is seeking to determine whether Iraq possesses any biological weapons-related items that should be disposed of pursuant to the resolution and whether there remains in Iraq a capability to produce such weapons that would also be subject to disposal. In this context, the Special Commission has brought to the attention of the Government of Iraq the report of the Ad Hoc Meeting of Scientific and Technical Experts from States Parties to the Biological Weapons Convention held at Geneva from 31 March to 15 April 1987 and contained in document BWC/CONF.II/EX/2 of 21 April 1987 and has requested the information called for in section II of that report.

22. Biological warfare agents can be destroyed through either standard laboratory equipment or special mobile units.

4. *Nuclear-weapons-related items*

23. In the area of nuclear-weapons-usable material and related items and facilities, the Special Commission will assist IAEA in the removal of weapons-usable material from Iraq and in the disposal of all other relevant items and facilities covered by resolution 687 (1991), by removal or destruction as appropriate.

24. An inspection team, composed of experts from IAEA and the Special Commission, is currently in Iraq to carry out a first inspection based on declarations by the Government of Iraq and the designation by the Special Commission of additional locations. Further inspections will follow prior to the disposal of weapons-usable material and other items subject to paragraph 12 of resolution 687 (1991).

C. *Monitoring and verification of compliance*

25. The third stage of the plan represents a long-term operation. Its main purpose is to ensure ongoing monitoring and verification of Iraq's compliance with paragraphs 8, 9, 10 and 12 of resolution 687 (1991). A detailed plan, as called for in paragraph 10 of resolution 687 (1991), will be submitted to the Security Council for its approval, subsequent to the establishment of a complete database. In developing the plan, the Special Commission will also take into account the provisions for

---

1/ General Assembly resolution 2826 (XXVI).

permitted activities in the framework of the Biological Weapons Convention and by the monitoring/verification methods under discussion in the context of a future Convention on the Prohibition of Chemical Weapons. With the eventual entry into force of such a Convention, the inspectorate envisaged in it should at an appropriate time take over the function of monitoring and verification of compliance in the area of chemical weapons.

26. The verification will be conducted through full and effective on-site inspections including those on short notice. The inspections will cover, as appropriate, military bases, production facilities and storage, as well as research facilities and laboratories. The frequency of on-site inspections will vary considerably for each category of weapons, facilities and activities in question. It will be contingent on previous findings and also on Iraq's clear and continuous demonstration of compliance with resolution 687 (1991).

II. GENERAL CONCEPT OF OPERATIONS

27. The Special Commission, under the guidance of its Executive Chairman, will use a small staff at United Nations Headquarters in New York to prepare detailed plans for field operations in Iraq with regard to all items related to chemical and biological weapons and to ballistic missiles, and together with IAEA with regard to items related to nuclear weapons and nuclear-weapons-usable materials. The plans will describe the composition of teams of experts, drawn from a number of countries, and their movements and activities in Iraq—whether survey, inspection or disposal. The teams will assemble for briefing at the field office in Bahrain and move by dedicated aircraft to Baghdad or some other point-of-entry in Iraq. Vehicles or rotary-winged aircraft will be used to move the teams within Iraq to the sites concerned. Teams will leave the area via Bahrain following debriefing and initial analysis of any samples or data collected in Iraq.

Document 53

Plan developed by the Director General of the International Atomic Energy Agency (IAEA) for the destruction, removal or rendering harmless of nuclear-weapons-usable materials in Iraq

S/22615, 17 May 1991

Note by the Secretary-General

The Secretary-General has the honour to submit to the members of the Security Council the attached letter addressed to him under paragraph 13 of Security Council resolution 687 (1991) by the Director General of the International Atomic Energy Agency (IAEA), and its enclosure containing a plan for the destruction, removal and rendering harmless of items specified in paragraph 12 of that resolution.

Annex
Letter dated 16 May 1991 from the Director General of the International Atomic Energy Agency (IAEA) addressed to the Secretary-General

Under paragraph 13 of Security Council resolution 687 (1991), the Director General of the IAEA is requested, through the Secretary-General of the United Nations, to develop within forty-five days of the adoption of the resolution a plan for the destruction, removal and rendering harmless of the items specified in paragraph 12 of the resolution.

May I accordingly kindly ask you to submit the attached plan to the Security Council.

(Signed) Hans BLIX

Enclosure
Plan for the destruction, removal and rendering harmless of the items specified in paragraph 12 of Security Council resolution 687 (1991)

Introduction

1. Paragraph 13 of Security Council resolution 687 (1991) *inter alia* requests the Director General of IAEA through the Secretary-General, with the assistance and cooperation of the Special Commission ... to develop a plan for submission to the Security Council within 45 days calling for the destruction, removing or rendering harmless of all items listed in paragraph 12 of the resolution.

2. In order to implement the actions required of the Agency pursuant to paragraphs 12 and 13 of the resolution, the Director General of IAEA established on 15 April 1991 an action team placed under the direction of an Agency Deputy Director General and composed of a

Deputy Director for Administration and Management and a Deputy Director for Operations.

3. The Agency established contact with the Special Commission set up by the Secretary-General following the approval by the Security Council on 19 April 1991 of the Secretary-General's report submitted to it in document S/22508. Assistance and cooperation is being rendered by the Special Commission and certain modalities for this cooperation have been agreed upon.

Immediate on-site inspection

4. On 18 April 1991, the Government of Iraq submitted to the Director General of IAEA a declaration required by paragraph 12 of resolution 687 (1991). Further information was provided on 27 April 1991.

5. The first on-site inspection, based on the Iraqi declaration to IAEA and additional designations by the Special Commission, started on 15 May 1991. The inspection team on this occasion was headed by a Chief Inspector appointed by IAEA and consisted of 34 persons, including Agency officials and experts as well as representatives and other personnel of the Special Commission. The team's expertise covers all areas of nuclear technology as well as supporting specialties such as radiation protection, explosive ordnance disposal, communications and field security.

The plan

Nuclear-weapons-usable material

6. Nuclear-weapons-usable material or, as it is referred to in Agency practice, "direct-use material" a/ cannot be destroyed or rendered harmless in Iraq. The Agency will have to take exclusive control of this material for custody and removal from Iraq pursuant to paragraph 12. This is considered to be the foremost task to be undertaken. Known amounts of direct-use material, located in the Tuwaltha area and listed in the Iraqi statement of 27 April 1991, are contained in fresh or irradiated fuel assemblies. Part of this material appears to be stored in accessible conditions. The on-site inspection, which is now under way, is verifying declared quantities and conditions of this material. Further direct-use material, according to the Iraqi declaration, consisting of irradiated fuel assemblies for the IRT 5000 nuclear research reactor,

is buried under the rubble of the reactor building. In all probability, a complex and costly decommissioning operation will be needed to render this material accessible for removal and disposal.

7. Following the preliminary on-site verification now under way of the existence of irradiated direct-use material in the damaged reactor building, it is intended to begin the early removal of easily accessible direct-use material, the decommissioning of the building and the removal of the irradiated fuel assemblies, once their accessibility is achieved.

8. In the event that any additional sites are designated by the Special Commission under paragraphs 9 (b) (ii) and 13 of resolution 687 (1991) further inspections will be carried out.

9. The Agency will take custody, through the application of Agency verification, containment and surveillance methods, of the direct-use material in Iraq. Agency safeguards will be applied to all direct-use material removed from Iraq.

10. Negotiations with countries possessing the technology for the transportation and storage of direct-use material to ascertain their willingness to receive this material are under way. Consideration is being given to various options for the long-term disposal or rendering harmless of this material.

Other items subject to paragraph 12
of resolution 687 (1991)

11. The declaration of Iraq listed only direct-use material and a yellow-cake production unit. Inspection of sites for other items subject to paragraph 12 of resolution 687 (1991) that may be designated by the Special Commission will aim to determine if such items exist and, if so, to remove, destroy or render them harmless.

12. Identification of research, development, support or manufacturing facilities and materials relevant or connected to reprocessing of irradiated fuel and isotopic enrichment of uranium will be given priority as they are capable of producing additional direct-use material.

a/ Direct-use material is nuclear material that can be converted into nuclear explosives components without transmutation or further enrichment, as for instance plutonium containing less than 80 per cent plutonium-238, high-enriched uranium (HEU) (uranium enriched to 20 per cent uranium-235 or more) and uranium-233.

Document 54

Security Council resolution establishing the United Nations Compensation Fund and the United Nations Compensation Commission

S/RES/692 (1991), 20 May 1991

The Security Council,

Recalling its resolutions 674 (1990) of 29 October 1990, 686 (1991) of 2 March 1991 and 687 (1991) of 3 April 1991 concerning the liability of Iraq, without prejudice to its debts and obligations arising prior to 2 August 1990, for any direct loss, damage, including environmental damage and the depletion of natural resources, or injury to foreign Governments, nationals and corporations as a result of Iraq's unlawful invasion and occupation of Kuwait,

Taking note of the report submitted by the Secretary-General on 2 May 1991 pursuant to paragraph 19 of resolution 687 (1991), 1/

Acting under Chapter VII of the Charter of the United Nations,

1. *Expresses its appreciation* to the Secretary-General for his report of 2 May 1991; 1/

2. *Welcomes* the fact that the Secretary-General will now undertake the appropriate consultations requested by paragraph 19 of resolution 687 (1991) so that he will be in a position to recommend to the Council for decision as soon as possible the figure which the level of Iraq's contribution to the United Nations Compensation Fund will not exceed;

3. *Decides* to establish the Fund and the United Nations Compensation Commission referred to in paragraph 18 of resolution 687 (1991) in accordance with section I of the Secretary-General's report, and decides also that the Governing Council of the Commission will be located at the United Nations Office at Geneva and that the Governing Council may decide whether some of the activities of the Commission should be carried out elsewhere;

4. *Requests* the Secretary-General to take the actions necessary to implement paragraphs 2 and 3 in consultation with the members of the Governing Council;

5. *Directs* the Governing Council to proceed in an expeditious manner to implement the provisions of section E of resolution 687 (1991), taking into account the recommendations in section II of the Secretary-General's report;

6. *Decides* that the requirement for Iraqi contributions will apply in the manner to be prescribed by the Governing Council with respect to all Iraqi petroleum and petroleum products exported from Iraq after 3 April 1991 as well as such petroleum and petroleum products exported earlier but not delivered or not paid for as a specific result of the prohibitions contained in resolution 661 (1990) of 6 August 1990;

7. *Requests* the Governing Council to report as soon as possible on the actions it has taken with regard to the mechanisms for determining the appropriate level of Iraq's contribution to the Fund and the arrangements for ensuring that payments are made to the Fund, so that the Security Council can give its approval in accordance with paragraph 22 of resolution 687 (1991);

8. *Requests also* that all States and international organizations cooperate with the decisions of the Governing Council taken pursuant to paragraph 5, and further requests that the Governing Council keep the Security Council informed on this matter;

9. *Decides* that, if the Governing Council notifies the Security Council that Iraq has failed to carry out decisions of the Governing Council taken pursuant to paragraph 5, the Security Council intends to retain or to take action to reimpose the prohibition against the import of petroleum and petroleum products originating in Iraq and financial transactions related thereto;

10. *Decides also* to remain seized of this matter, and requests the Governing Council to submit periodic reports to the Secretary-General and the Security Council.

1/ *Official Records of the Security Council, Forty-sixth Year, Supplement for April, May and June 1991,* document S/22559.

Document 55

Letter from the Permanent Representative of Iraq to the President of the Security Council transmitting a letter dated 27 May 1991 from the Minister for Foreign Affairs of Iraq commenting on Security Council resolution 692 (1991)

S/22643, 28 May 1991

Letter dated 27 May 1991 from the Permanent Representative of Iraq to the United Nations addressed to the President of the Security Council

On instructions from my Government, I have the honour to transmit herewith a letter dated 27 May 1991 from Mr. Ahmed Hussein, Minister for Foreign Affairs of the Republic of Iraq, concerning Iraq's position with regard to Security Council resolution 692 (1991).

I should be grateful if you would have this letter and its annex circulated as a document of the Security Council.

(Signed) Abdul Amir A. AL-ANBARI
Ambassador
Permanent Representative

Annex
Letter dated 27 May 1991 from the Minister for Foreign Affairs of Iraq addressed to the President of the Security Council

After taking note of Security Council resolution 692 (1991), I see it as my duty to inform you of my country's position with regard to that resolution, since it includes provisions which endanger not only Iraq but all concepts of justice and equity, as well as the essence of international law.

Security Council resolution 692 (1991) adds a further dangerous precedent to the series of precedents established by the Council's resolutions against Iraq since 2 August 1990. Although the resolution is of a procedural nature, its consequences and repercussions on the future of the Iraqi people and succeeding generations make it my duty and responsibility formally to notify you of Iraq's position. The Council's refusal to permit open discussion before the adoption of the resolution denied us the opportunity to express our views and prevented international public opinion and the States Members of the Organization from acquainting themselves with the facts which upholders of justice helped to record.

I am adding nothing new when I mention the Security Council's inability to adopt resolutions restoring the usurped right of the Palestinian people and recognizing its inalienable rights to self-determination and the estab-lishment of its own State. Even in the notable exceptional circumstances when the United States voted in favour of Security Council resolution 487 (1981), which condemned Israel for its aggressive attack on the Tammuz nuclear reactor (used for peaceful purposes), the United States did not show any zeal in urging the Security Council to take the measures required to implement that resolution and to oblige Israel to pay the reparations thus provided for.

As a result of the developments in international relations between the Eastern and Western camps, the United States has become the dominant element in the Security Council. It has exploited its influence by forcing the Council to adopt unjust resolutions for the purpose of bestowing international legitimacy on the plan of aggression which it implemented together with its allies against Iraq, without any control or supervision over the military operations by the Council. The United States and its allies were thus left free to destroy Iraq and to shatter its potential and economic infrastructure.

Under resolution 692 (1991), the Council established a political body to take decisions on judicial matters. It made this body both an adversary of Iraq and, at the same time, an arbitrator of its affairs. While the essential task of the Security Council, as a principal organ of the United Nations, is to maintain international peace and security, the Charter entrusts the International Court of Justice, as a separate principal organ of the Organization, with the task of rendering judgements on judicial cases and determining levels of reparations. The Council has thus, under great pressure from the United States of America, Britain and France, been converted from a political into a judicial authority. While the International Court of Justice is an independent authority composed of a body of independent judges, elected regardless of their nationality from among persons of high moral character, who possess the qualifications required in their respective countries for appointment to the highest judicial offices, or are jurisconsults of recognized competence in international law, the Reparations Fund and its Governing Council, established under resolution 692 (1991), reflect the political composition of the Security Council, the object of which—following the end of the Second World War—was to achieve political equilibrium between the victorious allied Powers. Is it right that the Security Council should be converted from a principal organ for the maintenance of international peace and security into an organ which establishes judicial organs subsidiary to itself? It is not empowered to do so under the Charter and, in so doing, encroaches on the authority of another principal organ, namely, the International Court of Justice.

Iraq's responsibility for reparations under paragraph 16 of resolution 687 (1991) must be determined in accordance with the rules and procedures established by international law rather than on the basis of the general policy laid down by the "Governing Council" of the Reparations Fund established under resolution 692 (1991). This Council is to take decisions on claims for compensation which may exceed tens of billions.

The political composition of this Council will make the criterion for consideration of compensation based on the interests and policies of the States members of the Council, not on the principles of international law, without according Iraq the right to defend itself or consult its current and future economic interests. The first proof of this is the Security Council's failure to take into consideration the request made by Iraq for a five-year moratorium on the payment of compensation in the light of its current economic circumstances and the need to meet the basic requirements of the Iraqi people and to repair the damage which Iraq has suffered as a result of the aggression against it. A further proof is that the Security Council has ignored the damage suffered by Iraq—which was many times more than the damage suffered by other countries—as a result of the intensive aerial bombardment aimed at civilian centres and economic and cultural installations, which wrought, according to the description in the report of Mr. Martti Ahtisaari, Under-Secretary-General for Administration and Management, on the situation in Iraq, contained in document S/22366 of 20 March 1991, near-apocalyptic results upon "what had been ... a rather highly urbanized and mechanized society. Now, most means of modern life support have been destroyed or rendered tenuous. Iraq has, for some time to come, been relegated to a pre-industrial age, but with all the disabilities of post-industrial dependency on an intensive use of energy and technology".

This neutral report gave a true picture of the effects of the aggression of the United States of America and its allies on food, agriculture, water, sanitation, health, power, transportation, communications and logistics. What has the Security Council done to deal with these effects that arose out of a grave and unprecedented excess in the implementation of objectives of a Security Council resolution that were not specified therein?

The main features of this destruction were pinpointed by a Harvard University mission, a neutral body, which visited Iraq and published a report on 22 May 1991. It perceived by itself, without any intervention by the Iraqi authorities, the truth of the situation with regard to health and living conditions in Iraq. Its report drew up future death certificates for 170,000 Iraqi children who would die in the course of the year as a result of the effects left by the Gulf War on sanitation in Iraq and the destruction of power generating and water purifying centres, which would lead to the spread of epidemics of cholera, typhoid and communicable diseases. Where are the human rights that the United States upholds? Is it human rights for them to impose an embargo on the Iraqi people for a period close on one year without permitting Iraq to export its oil to meet its basic requirements? The Committee on sanctions has even refused Iraq's request to export a limited amount of oil and petroleum products on the basis of paragraph 23 of resolution 687 (1991), which was drafted by the United States and its allies.

The Security Council's response to the efforts of the United States and its allies to impose proportional appropriations from Iraqi oil revenues means indirectly giving the Council powers of disposal over the oil resources of the people of Iraq with regard to the level of production. The United States and the biased States will thereby realize another objective, namely, the smashing also of the Organization of Petroleum Exporting Countries (OPEC) and the elimination of its right to control its oil resources and determine its exports of crude oil and petroleum products.

Resolution 692 (1991) has opened the door wide to all greedy and crafty parties to submit various false or exaggerated claims without Iraq having any right to establish their lack of legitimacy.

The sure results of this resolution will be to impoverish the Iraqi people and future generations for decades to come and to punish the current Iraqi generation, which has suffered and is still suffering the effects of the economic embargo and military aggression. The resolution will lead to the creation of favourable conditions for the spread of epidemics and social problems and the spread of crime. These results will lead to destabilization in the region and the creation of new foci of conflict and tension, and that will have a far-reaching effect on world peace.

The actions of the Security Council and its Committee on sanctions point to the existence of deliberate dilatoriness and obfuscation aimed at prolonging the term of the embargo and not lifting it for the purpose of realizing political objectives of certain States to the detriment of Iraq at a time when Iraq is fulfilling all its obligations.

Resolution 692 (1991) is unprecedented and has no basis in the United Nations Charter or any international convention. The absolute powers that were given to the

Governing Council of the Fund have never been given to any international organization in modern history.

By this resolution, the Security Council has sown the seed of the destruction of the body which it has created without any legal and just basis. This has made the credibility of the Council and its responsibility for the maintenance of international peace and security the subject of profound doubt. The history of the United Nations will, unquestionably, contain black pages full of condemnation of all the unjust and biased resolutions which were adopted by the Security Council against Iraq under United States pressure and which constitute precedents involving not only the demolition of Iraq's rights but also the destruction of the values of justice and fairness and the defacing of the foundations and content of international law.

Accept, Sir, the assurances of my highest consideration.

(*Signed*) Ahmed HUSSEIN
Minister for Foreign Affairs of the Republic of Iraq

Document 56

Note dated 30 May 1991 from the Secretary-General to the President of the Security Council concerning Iraq's contribution to the United Nations Compensation Fund

S/22661, 31 May 1991

As I indicated in paragraph 13 of my report (S/22559) to the Security Council, pursuant to paragraph 19 of its resolution 687 (1991), I attach herewith a note suggesting a percentage figure of the value of Iraq's petroleum exports which should not exceed its contribution to the Fund.

(*Signed*) Javier PÉREZ DE CUÉLLAR

Annex

30 May 1991

Note of the Secretary-General pursuant to paragraph 13 of his report of 2 May 1991 (S/22559)

1. On 2 May 1991 I presented to the Council, in compliance with Security Council resolution 687, a report (S/22559) pursuant to paragraph 19 of Security Council resolution 687 (1991). In the same paragraph 19 it was stipulated that Iraq's contribution to the fund based on a percentage of the value of the exports of petroleum and petroleum products from Iraq should not exceed a figure to be suggested to the Council by me. In paragraph 13 of the report, I informed the Council that I will undertake the appropriate consultations as required so that, as soon as possible, I will be in a position to suggest this figure.

2. Authoritative data necessary for the preparation of this communication to the Security Council is not readily available. However, given that Iraq derives almost its entire exports earnings from the export of one single commodity (oil) and that the unit price and export volume of Iraqi oil are monitored by OPEC, it is possible to estimate the size and functioning of its economy in general and of its external trade and payments structure in particular. Data available for this exercise have been taken from various sources including the Government of Iraq, the International Monetary Fund, ESCWA, OPEC, and the United Nations Statistical Office.

3. Paragraph 16 of resolution 687, in defining the extent of Iraq's liability, states that it is "liable under international law for any direct loss, damage, including environmental damage and the depletion of natural resources, or injury to foreign government, national and corporations, as a result of Iraq's unlawful invasion and occupation of Kuwait". As paragraph 16 states, this liability is "without prejudice to the debts and obligations of Iraq arising prior to 2 August 1990, which will be addressed through the normal mechanisms". Thus, this communication has to limit itself to dealing with the economic and financial possibilities and constraints of Iraq to compensate for the damage defined in paragraph 16.

4. Iraq's oil production quota, as agreed to within OPEC in July 1990, is of 3.14 million barrels per day. With an estimated internal consumption of about 300,000 barrels per day, the Iraqi Government intends to reach its most recent 1989 level of exports of 2.85 million barrels per day in 1993, as communicated by the Permanent Representative to the United Nations to me in his letter of 29 April 1991. If the reference price of $21 per barrel agreed to by OPEC in July 1990 were to be used during 1993, which after adjustment for quality would result in a price of $20.04 for Iraqi crude, total Iraqi

export earnings for 1993 can be expected to reach $21 billion, surpassing its 1989 export revenue. Such earnings could conceivably be higher, given that global demand for oil increases by 2 per cent annually, that production in large industrial countries has been declining over the last four years, and that only a few countries have the reserves and even fewer the production capacity to offset the resulting shortfall. These calculations also assume that all OPEC member countries would return to roughly similar production quotas as those agreed to in July 1990, thus allowing Iraq to reach this level of exports without causing a price collapse.

5. Estimates for foreign exchange expenditures of the Iraqi economy for strictly civilian purposes during the 1980s vary. By taking account of historical relationships of consumption and investment to GDP and their import intensity, and data on net service imports as provided by Iraq, it is estimated that about $8 billion may be required to sustain a level of civilian imports in 1991 consistent with the needs of the Iraqi economy.

6. Iraq's total external debt and obligations have been reported by the Government of Iraq at $42,097 million as of 31 December 1990. However, the exact figure of Iraq's external indebtedness can only be ascertained following discussions between Iraq and its creditors. To estimate debt servicing requirements it is assumed that Iraq reschedules its debts at standard Paris Club terms.

7. With oil exports expected to reach about $21 billion by 1993 imports should absorb about 48 per cent of export earnings and debt servicing approximately 22 per cent. I suggest, therefore, that compensation to be paid by Iraq (as arising from section E of resolution 687) should not exceed 30 per cent of the annual value of the exports of petroleum and petroleum products from Iraq.

8. The above calculations are based on data and a number of assumptions that have to be kept under review.

Document 57

Letter from the Secretary-General to the President of the Security Council transmitting the annex dated 25 May 1991 to the 18 April Memorandum of Understanding between Iraq and the United Nations (Document 44) concerning the deployment of a United Nations Guards Contingent (extract)

S/22663, 31 May 1991

Letter dated 30 May 1991 from the Secretary-General addressed to the President of the Security Council

I have the honour to convey to you the agreement reached on 25 May 1991 between my Executive Delegate's Coordinator in Iraq, Mr. Bernt Bernander, and the Minister of State for Foreign Affairs of Iraq, Mr. Mohamed Said Al-Sahaf, regarding the deployment in Iraq of a United Nations Guard Contingent. That agreement constitutes an Annex to the Memorandum of Understanding signed on 18 April 1991 by my Executive Delegate and the Minister of Foreign Affairs of Iraq. For ease of reference, I am also enclosing a copy of the Memorandum of Understanding. [Not reproduced here; see Document 44.]

I should be grateful if you could bring this letter to the attention of the members of the Security Council.

(*Signed*) Javier PÉREZ DE CUÉLLAR

Annex

1. Following the agreement in principle for the deployment of a United Nations Guards Contingent, discussions were held on 17 and 18 May 1991 to clarify the principal elements associated with the deployment of such guard units, within the framework of the existing Memorandum of Understanding, signed on 18 April 1991 in Baghdad by H.E. Mr. Ahmed Hussein, Minister of Foreign Affairs of the Republic of Iraq and Prince Sadruddin Aga Khan, Executive Delegate of the Secretary-General of the United Nations for the Humanitarian Programme for Iraq, Kuwait and the Iraq-Iran and Iraq-Turkey border areas.

2. As a first step, ten United Nations Guards have been dispatched to Dohuk, on 19 May 1991, in order to establish a United Nations presence at the sub-office and depots in the town. This unit also liaises with the transit camps in the Zakho plain, with a view to enabling the United Nations to assume control thereof. In addition, the unit collaborates with the local civilian administration which is stepping up the rehabilitation of services in the town. The Dohuk/Zakho-based unit of the Contingent will be built to a strength of 50-60 Guards as soon as possible.

3. In addition to transit camps in the Zakho plain, transit centres/zones (which can best be described as strengthened and enlarged humanitarian centres) will be established along communications routes in other areas of Iraq, wherever such presence may be needed, in agreement with the Government of Iraq. United Nations Guards will be assigned as needed to any transit centres, United Nations sub-offices and Humanitarian Centres (UNHUCs) which may be established by the United Nations in Iraq.

4. The number of Guards in the Contingent will be kept under review as further units are dispatched, but will not exceed a total strength of 500. In order to ensure their mobility, special arrangements will be made to import the required number of suitable vehicles. Arrangements will be made to ensure that United Nations-marked helicopter(s) will be allowed to land in Dohuk, Zakho and Mosul, as well as in the other areas, for the movement of United Nations personnel. Necessary arrangements will also be made to provide the Contingent with the required means of communication and the necessary logistical back-up.

5. The number of Guards assigned to the various regions will be decided in consultation with the Government authorities concerned, but would not exceed 150 in any one region. They will move freely, as their duties require, between humanitarian reception points, transit centres and relay stations, as well as sub-offices, using appropriate existing accommodation facilities in the provincial capitals, other towns and villages, or ad hoc field accommodation at transit centres.

6. United Nations Guards will be authorized to carry side-arms (pistols/revolvers), which will be provided by the Iraqi authorities (subject to the approval of the United Nations with respect to make, model, calibre and munitions). While it is not anticipated that all Guards will be so armed, United Nations guidelines and practices will be followed in this regard.

7. The Iraqi authorities will appoint a Chief Liaison Officer to facilitate the Contingent's operations and a liaison officer at each centre to facilitate their work with the Iraqi authorities. The Iraqi authorities will grant appropriate facilities in Baghdad and elsewhere, including office space, maintenance and repair support, maps, etc.

8. This annex shall be an integral part of the Memorandum of Understanding signed on 18 April 1991. It shall be governed by the terms of that Memorandum; it shall be implemented in cooperation and coordination with the Iraq authorities and expire at the end of the period stated therein (31 December 1991).

Document 58

Report of the Secretary-General proposing guidelines and mechanisms for full international implementation of the arms embargo and related sanctions against Iraq

S/22660, 2 June 1991

1. The Security Council, acting under Chapter VII of the Charter of the United Nations, adopted on 3 April 1991 resolution 687 (1991), paragraph 1 of which affirmed all 13 resolutions (660 (1990) of 2 August 1990, 661 (1990) of 6 August 1990, 662 (1990) of 9 August 1990, 664 (1990) of 18 August 1990, 665 (1990) of 25 August 1990, 666 (1990) of 13 September 1990, 667 (1990) of 16 September 1990, 669 (1990) of 24 September 1990, 670 (1990) of 25 September 1990, 674 (1990) of 29 October 1990, 677 (1990) of 28 November 1990, 678 (1990) of 29 November 1990 and 686 (1991) of 2 March 1991) concerning the situation between Iraq and Kuwait, except as expressly changed by resolution 687 (1991). By paragraph 26 of resolution 687 (1991) the Security Council requested the Secretary-General, in consultation with appropriate Governments, to develop within 60 days, for its approval, guidelines to facilitate full international implementation of paragraphs 24, 25 and 27 of resolution 687 (1991), and to make them available to all States and to establish a procedure for updating those guidelines periodically.

2. Paragraphs 24, 25 and 27 of resolution 687 (1991) read as follows:

"*The Security Council,*

"...

"24. *Decides* that, in accordance with resolution 661 (1990) and subsequent related resolutions and until a further decision is taken by the Security Council, all States shall continue to prevent the sale or supply, or the promotion or facilitation of such sale or supply, to Iraq by their nationals, or from their territories or using their flag vessels or aircraft, of:

"(a) Arms and related *matériel* of all types, specifically including the sale or transfer through other means of all forms of conventional military equipment, including for paramilitary forces, and spare parts and components and their means of production, for such equipment;

"(b) Items specified and defined in paragraphs 8 and 12 above not otherwise covered above;

"(c) Technology under licensing or other transfer arrangements used in the production, utilization or stockpiling of items specified in subparagraphs (a) and (b) above;

"(d) Personnel or materials for training or technical support services relating to the design, development, manufacture, use, maintenance or support of items specified in subparagraphs (a) and (b) above;

"25. *Calls upon* all States and international organizations to act strictly in accordance with paragraph 24 above, notwithstanding the existence of any contracts, agreements, licences or any other arrangements;

"...

"27. *Calls upon* all States to maintain such national controls and procedures and to take such other actions consistent with the guidelines to be established by the Security Council under paragraph 26 above as may be necessary to ensure compliance with the terms of paragraph 24 above, and calls upon international organizations to take all appropriate steps to assist in ensuring such full compliance".

3. Implementation of paragraph 24 of resolution 687 (1991) is to be effected in accordance with resolution 661 (1990) and subsequent related resolutions. Resolution 661 (1990) established a comprehensive set of sanctions to be implemented by all States against Iraq and occupied Kuwait, including the sale or supply of weapons or any other military equipment, whether or not originating in their territories, and any activities that promoted or were calculated to promote such sale or supply of such items. Under paragraph 3 of resolution 661 (1990), the Security Council established a committee consisting of all the members of the Council to undertake the tasks set out in that paragraph. By resolution 665 (1990), the Council called upon those Member States cooperating with the Government of Kuwait and deploying maritime forces to the area to use such measures commensurate to the specific circumstances as might be necessary under the authority of the Security Council to halt all inward and outward maritime shipping in order to inspect and verify their cargoes and destinations and to ensure strict implementation of the provisions related to such shipping laid down in resolution 661 (1990). By resolution 670 (1990) the Council confirmed that resolution 661 (1990) applied to all means of transport, including aircraft. With the specific purpose of preventing the carriage of any commodities or products prohibited under resolution 661 (1990) to or from Iraq or occupied Kuwait, resolution 670 (1990) established mandatory provisions concerning flights. Under those provisions the Council required all States, *inter alia*, to deny any aircraft permission to take off from or overfly their territory if such aircraft was destined to land in Iraq or occupied Kuwait, unless certain conditions were met, as specified in paragraphs 3 and 4 of the resolution. The Committee established by resolution 661 (1990) concerning the situation between Iraq and Kuwait was vested with specific responsibilities, including notification or approval procedures for such flights.

4. On the basis of the above observations, the Secretary-General undertook consultations with appropriate Governments, in accordance with paragraph 26 of resolution 687 (1991). The input from those consultations has been taken into particular account by the Secretary-General in the preparation of the draft guidelines called for by paragraph 26 of that resolution. The draft guidelines are herewith transmitted for the consideration of the Security Council (see annex).

Annex
Draft guidelines to facilitate full international implementation of paragraphs 24, 25 and 27 of Security Council resolution 687 (1991)

Introduction

1. The present guidelines have been developed in accordance with paragraph 26 of Security Council resolution 687 (1991), to facilitate full international implementation of paragraphs 24, 25 and 27 of that resolution.

I. *Categories of prohibited items and activities*

2. For the purpose of the present guidelines, the items and activities proscribed are those referred to in paragraph 24, in conjunction with paragraphs 8 and 12, of resolution 687 (1991) and are the following:

(a) Arms and related *matériel* of all types, specifically including the sale or transfer through other means of:

(i) All forms of conventional weapons and military equipment, including for paramilitary forces, and spare parts and components and their means of production, for such equipment;

(ii) All chemical and biological weapons and all stocks or agents and all related subsystems and components;

(iii) All ballistic missiles with a range greater than 150 kilometres and related major parts;

(iv) Nuclear weapons or nuclear-weapons-usable material or any subsystems or components;

(b) All research, development, support and manufacturing facilities for the items as specified and defined in paragraphs 8 (a) and 12 of resolution 687 (1991);

(c) Repair and production facilities for all ballistic missiles with a range greater than 150 kilometres and related major parts;

(d) Technology under licensing or other transfer arrangements used in the production, utilization or stockpiling of items as specified in paragraphs 24 (a), 8 and 12 of resolution 687 (1991);

(e) Personnel or materials for training or technical support services relating to the design, development, manufacture, use, maintenance or support of items as specified in paragraphs 24 (a), 8 and 12 of resolution 687 (1991).

II. *United Nations mechanism for monitoring the arms and related sanctions*

3. The Committee established by resolution 661 (1990) concerning the situation between Iraq and Kuwait (hereinafter referred to as "the Committee") will be the organ of the Security Council responsible for monitoring the prohibitions against the sale or supply of arms to Iraq and related sanctions established in paragraph 24 of resolution 687 (1991) (hereinafter referred to as "arms and related sanctions"). The Committee will carry out its functions in accordance with the mandate provided in resolutions 661 (1990), 665 (1990) and 670 (1990) in so far as it relates to the items proscribed under paragraph 24 of resolution 687 (1991).

4. The Committee will closely cooperate and coordinate its activities with any present and future bodies that will, pursuant to paragraphs 10 and 13 of resolution 687 (1991), be responsible for the monitoring and verification of Iraq's compliance with the obligations set forth in paragraphs 10 and 12 of that resolution, in so far as they concern the acquisition of the items referred to in those paragraphs. The bodies referred to above will therefore have access to the Committee and will draw its attention to any problems that they may encounter in pursuing their mandate.

5. In discharging its tasks as regards the items referred to in paragraphs 8 (a) and 12 of resolution 687

(1991), the Committee will work in close cooperation with the Special Commission established under paragraph 9 of the resolution and with the International Atomic Energy Agency. In carrying out its work, the Committee will also be able to make use of any expertise or information relevant to its functions available elsewhere within the United Nations system.

6. For the purposes of the present guidelines, the functions of the Committee will be the following:

(a) To meet at regular intervals to examine reports submitted by the Secretary-General on the implementation of the relevant resolutions;

(b) To provide guidance to States and to international organizations, either upon their request or at its own initiative, on matters concerning the implementation of paragraph 24 of resolution 687 (1991), *inter alia*, through the elaboration, as necessary, of relevant criteria;

(c) To reach, in connection with subparagraph (b) above, when needed, agreed interpretations of items falling within the specified categories of proscribed items and activities;

(d) To seek information and maintain contact with States, international organizations and those non-governmental organizations whose activities and or expertise are likely to promote strict implementation of the arms and related sanctions against Iraq;

(e) To bring to the attention of the States and international organizations concerned information reported to it of alleged violations of the arms and related sanctions against Iraq for appropriate action by those States and international organizations;

(f) To report at 90-day intervals to the Security Council on the implementation of the arms and related sanctions against Iraq contained in the relevant resolutions.

III. *Principles of implementation*

7. The actual implementation of the arms and related sanctions against Iraq will be effected at three levels: by all States, by international organizations and through intergovernmental cooperation. States and international organizations are called upon to act strictly in accordance with the arms and related sanctions, notwithstanding the existence of any contracts, agreements, licences or any other arrangements.

A. *States*

8. All States should report to the Secretary-General within 45 days of the approval by the Security Council of the present guidelines on the measures they have instituted for meeting the obligations set out in paragraph 24 of resolution 687 (1991).

9. All States should ensure the institution or maintenance of national controls, procedures and other measures consistent with the present guidelines as may be necessary to ensure compliance with the terms of paragraph 24 of resolution 687 (1991). On that basis, States should ensure that these measures:

(a) Prevent any circumvention of the arms and related sanctions against Iraq, including but not limited to direct circumvention, indirect or clandestine circumvention, and circumvention through subcontracts to companies within the State itself or in other States;

(b) Prohibit the export to Iraq of those dual-purpose or multi-purpose items that States may have reason to believe will be used for military purposes;

(c) Ensure against the provision of any technology, research, personnel or materials for training or technical support services relating to the production, utilization, stockpiling, design, development, manufacture, use, maintenance or support for any of the items as described in paragraph 2 of the present guidelines;

(d) Require that the sale, licensing or other contracts with States or foreign companies contain end-user transfer assurances that ensure no transfer, retransfer, transshipment or servicing to Iraq or to individuals or bodies inside Iraq or to individuals or bodies outside Iraq acting for the benefit of Iraq or of individuals or bodies inside Iraq of any of the items described in paragraph 2 of the present guidelines;

(e) Require from exporters and other commercial intermediaries a declaration that the items for export described in paragraph 2 of the present guidelines are not destined for Iraq directly or through third-party arrangements;

(f) Provide for legal powers to inspect documents and goods and to detain and seize goods where appropriate;

(g) Impose appropriate penalties for non-compliance in their territories and by their nationals elsewhere, and to notify the Committee of all incidents of such non-compliance.

10. Nothing in the present guidelines will preclude any State or group of States from adopting further measures aimed at achieving effective implementation of the arms and related sanctions against Iraq, in accordance with the relevant provisions of resolution 687 (1991).

11. States should ensure that the provisions of the national measures instituted by them are adequately publicized and disseminated within their territories and among their nationals elsewhere, particularly to arms technology developers, producers, traders and exporters and to the transport sector. In implementing the present guidelines, States should pay particular attention to com-

panies known to have been involved in illegal arms procurement activities on behalf of Iraq.

12. States are requested to report to the Committee any information that may come to their attention relating to possible violations of the arms and related sanctions against Iraq committed by other States or foreign nationals. In this regard, States are reminded of their duties under paragraph 7 of resolution 661 (1990) to cooperate fully with the Committee in the fulfilment of its task, including supplying such information as may be sought by the Committee.

13. States ought to consult the Committee on the question whether certain items fall within the provisions of paragraph 24 of resolution 687 (1991), as well as in cases relating to dual-use or multiple-use items, that is to say, items meant for civilian use but with potential for diversion or conversion to military use.

B. *International organizations*

14. In accordance with paragraphs 25 and 27 of resolution 687 (1991) international organizations should take all appropriate steps to assist in ensuring full compliance with the arms and related sanctions against Iraq, including providing to the Committee any relevant information that may come to their attention.

15. International organizations having any dealings with, or activities in, Iraq should carefully review their programmes to make sure that they do not facilitate any of the activities prohibited under paragraph 24 of resolution 687 (1991). Paragraph 13 above shall also apply to international organizations.

C. *Intergovernmental cooperation*

16. States are encouraged to cooperate with each other bilaterally or within the framework of existing regional or other appropriate intergovernmental organizations or through other appropriate intergovernmental arrangements in the implementation of the arms and related sanctions against Iraq. Such cooperation would be particularly useful in matters, among others, of verification of the origin and destination of the items specified in paragraph 24 of resolution 687 (1991), as well as in the exchange of documentary evidence relating thereto.

IV. *Review of the guidelines*

17. Taking into account Iraq's compliance with resolution 687 (1991), the general progress towards the control of armaments in the region, information received from States and international organizations and from the Committee, the Security Council may wish to review the guidelines at the same time as its regular reviews of paragraphs 22, 23, 24 and 25 of resolution 687 (1991),

as set out in paragraph 28 of the same resolution, that is to say, with the first review being undertaken 120 days after the adoption of that resolution.

18. The Security Council may also wish to consider, in the light of any comments or reports that the Committee may make to it, what further action may be necessary to ensure the implementation of the arms and related sanctions against Iraq.

Document 59

Identical letters from the Chargé d'affaires a.i. of the Permanent Mission of Iraq to the United Nations to the President of the Security Council and to the Secretary-General transmitting a letter from the Minister for Foreign Affairs of Iraq concerning Iraq's commitments under the terms of international agreements against terrorism

S/22687, 11 June 1991

Identical letters dated 11 June 1991 from the Chargé d'affaires a.i. of the Permanent Mission of Iraq to the United Nations addressed respectively to the Secretary-General and the President of the Security Council

On instructions from my Government, I have the honour to enclose a letter dated 11 June 1991 addressed to you by the Iraqi Minister for Foreign Affairs, Mr. Ahmed Hussein, on the subject of Iraq's commitments under the terms of the international agreements on crimes of international terrorism.

I should be grateful if you would have the text of this letter and its annex circulated as a document of the Security Council.

(*Signed*) Samir K. K. AL-NIMA
Chargé d'affaires a.i.

Annex
Identical letters dated 11 June 1991 from the Minister for Foreign Affairs of Iraq addressed respectively to the Secretary-General and the President of the Security Council

With reference to paragraph 32 of Security Council resolution 687 (1991), I have the honour to inform you that Iraq has already made known its position with respect to the crime of international terrorism. Iraq rejects all forms of violence which endanger the lives, liberty, security and peace of innocent persons, while reaffirming the right of peoples to self-determination and the need to eliminate colonialism in all its forms in accordance with the Charter of the United Nations.

The Iraqi Government has not hesitated to join with the international community in combating international terrorism and contributing effectively to the international efforts aimed at the attainment of that objective.

You are certainly aware that Iraq was occupying the chairmanship of the Sixth Committee when the General Assembly adopted by consensus, at its fortieth session, resolution 40/61 of 9 December 1985 on international terrorism, and that on that occasion a large number of representatives praised the efforts made by the representative of Iraq with a view to achieving that end.

It should also be emphasized that Iraq is a party to the most important international conventions regarding crimes which can be classed as acts of terrorism, in particular the Convention on Offences and Certain Other Acts Committed on Board Aircraft, signed at Tokyo in 1963; the Convention for the Suppression of Unlawful Seizure of Aircraft, signed at The Hague in 1970, the Convention for the Suppression of Unlawful Acts against the Safety of Civil Aviation, signed at Montreal in 1971 and the Convention on the Prevention and Punishment of Crimes against Internationally Protected Persons, Including Diplomatic Agents, of 1973. In addition, Iraq participated actively in the final phases of the drafting of the International Convention against the Taking of Hostages, of 1979, and has signed that Convention.

Moreover, in dealing with the problem of acts of terrorism Iraqi legislation both ensures the protection of its citizens against such acts and punishes those responsible for them. It should be pointed out in this connection that the Iraqi Penal Code does not regard acts of terrorism as political crimes.

The Government of the Republic of Iraq has never pursued a policy favourable to international terrorism as defined by international law. In this respect, its position is fully in line with that of the majority of Members of the international community.

In view of the foregoing, I wish to inform you, with reference to paragraph 32 of Security Council resolution 687 (1991), that Iraq will not commit or support any act of international terrorism or allow any organization directed towards commission of such acts to operate within its territory, and that it condemns unequivocally and renounces all acts, methods and practices of international terrorism.

Document 60

Report of the Secretary-General on UNIKOM

S/22692, 12 June 1991

1. This is a further progress report on the United Nations Iraq-Kuwait Observation Mission (UNIKOM); it follows my report of 9 May 1991 (S/22580).

Organizational aspects

2. Following the arrival of seven observers each from Senegal and Turkey, UNIKOM now has its full complement of military observers, as follows:

Argentina	7	Nigeria	7
Austria	7	Norway	8
Bangladesh	7	Pakistan	9
Canada	1	Poland	7
China	20	Romania	7
Denmark	7	Senegal	7
Fiji	7	Singapore	7
Finland	7	Sweden	7
France	20	Thailand	7
Ghana	8	Turkey	7
Greece	7	Union of Soviet Socialist	
Hungary	7	Republics	20
India	8	United Kingdom of	
Indonesia	7	Great Britain and	
Ireland	8	Northern Ireland	20
Italy	7	United States of America	20
Kenya	8	Uruguay	8
Malaysia	8	Venezuela	7
		Total	299

3. Administrative and logistic support is provided by the following units:

Engineers (Canada)	293
Logistics (Sweden)	31
Movement control/postal (Denmark)	23
Helicopters (Chile)	50
Medical (Norway)	50
Total	447

Two fixed-wing aircraft from Switzerland are operated by civilians. In addition, UNIKOM has had the use of chartered aircraft for the movement of troops and equipment and for communications between Baghdad and Kuwait. The Government of Sweden provided free airlift at the beginning of the Mission.

4. Two infantry companies (Fijian, Nepalese) and one logistic company (Swedish) temporarily assigned from the United Nations Interim Force in Lebanon (UNIFIL) and one infantry company (Danish) from the United Nations Peace-keeping Force in Cyprus (UNFICYP) have returned to their parent missions. Two infantry companies, one from UNFICYP (Austrian) and one from UNIFIL (Ghanaian), remain with UNIKOM; their combined strength is 217 all ranks. As a result, the overall strength of the Mission has been reduced to 963 all ranks.

5. Logistic support for the Mission is still difficult, given the lack of normal infrastructure in the area. However, thanks to assistance from the United States Army and forces of other Member States cooperating with the Government of Kuwait, UNIKOM is now able to meet its requirements as regards rations, vehicles and accommodation. Conditions in the field, however, remain austere, with all personnel living under canvas and subsisting largely on field rations. The situation is expected to improve gradually, with the provision of fresh rations and prefabricated accommodation.

6. UNIKOM headquarters has remained in a hotel annex south of Kuwait City, which was made available by the Government of Kuwait. By 15 June, the headquarters will be moved, as an interim measure, to the logistic base at Doha, pending completion of the necessary refurbishment of the premises at Umm Qasr, which still lack basic facilities such as electricity, water and sewerage.

7. UNIKOM has maintained contact with and provided logistic support to other United Nations missions working in Iraq and Kuwait.

Demilitarized zone

8. The situation in the demilitarized zone (DMZ) has been calm. It is sparsely populated; the main population centres are the towns of Umm Qasr and Safwan, both

on the Iraqi side. South of Safwan, on Kuwaiti territory, some 5,000 displaced persons still live in the Abdali camp. They are being assisted by the International Committee of the Red Cross (ICRC) and the League of Red Cross Societies. The camp is guarded by Kuwaiti police.

9. The Governments of Iraq and Kuwait, which are responsible for civil administration on their respective sides of the DMZ, have deployed border police to maintain law and order. Iraq currently has some 250 police in the DMZ. Kuwait is in the process of restoring its police presence and plans to rebuild and man some 30 police stations along the border. Both Governments have agreed to limit the armament of their police to sidearms.

10. Much of the DMZ is littered with unexploded ordnance and mines, particularly in the south. UNIKOM maintains maps delineating cleared routes; only on these routes is movement authorized.

Deployment and concept of operations

11. For operational purposes, UNIKOM has divided the DMZ into three sectors. Each sector has a headquarters and six observation posts, of which one in the southern sector has not yet been established. The Austrian security company has platoons in the central and northern sectors and at Umm Qasr; the Ghanaian security company has platoons in the southern sector, the Doha Logistic Base and at the temporary UNIKOM headquarters. The deployment of UNIKOM is shown on the attached map [not reproduced here].

12. In addition to its fixed observation posts, UNIKOM deploys temporary observation points, mobile patrols (on land and in the air) and investigation teams. The temporary observation points are established from the fixed observation posts, either in areas of particular activity or where roads and tracks enter the DMZ. They are augmented by mobile ground patrols and by aerial reconnaissance. The latter is the only means of maintaining adequate observation of the Khor Abdullah waterway and the southern sector of the DMZ, where mines and unexploded ordnance severely limit UNIKOM's ability to carry out ground patrols. The security companies serve as a quick reaction force and maintain a high state of readiness in order to provide protection to the military observers.

13. UNIKOM maintains close liaison with the Governments of Iraq and Kuwait. Both have given the Mission all the support and cooperation necessary for it to carry out its mandate.

Violations and complaints

14. Since the DMZ was established on 9 May, there have been a number of instances in which personnel of the armed forces of both Iraq and Kuwait and personnel of the Saudi Arabian forces stationed in Kuwait were observed in the DMZ. These observations have been brought to the attention of the parties concerned, which have explained that the majority were due to errors of navigation or misunderstandings over the boundaries of the DMZ. UNIKOM has posted signs on all major access roads and tracks leading into the DMZ and it is hoped that this will help to prevent future incursions.

15. UNIKOM has also observed a number of overflights of the DMZ by military aircraft. Most of them have been by F-15 and F-16 type aircraft flying along the Iraq-Kuwait border. UNIKOM has brought these overflights to the attention of the Government of Kuwait.

16. Since 9 May, UNIKOM has received two complaints from the Kuwaiti authorities and three from the Iraqi authorities. The complaints of Kuwait arose from reports of Iraqi policemen carrying rifles in the DMZ and of the massing of Iraqi military formations south of Basra. After investigation by UNIKOM both were considered unfounded. Of the Iraqi complaints, one concerned an air violation that could not be substantiated. Another concerned the alleged establishment of a Kuwaiti military checkpoint within the DMZ south of Safwan; this was in fact a police post. The last complaint was that weapons were being kept at the Abdali camp and flags were being flown in a provocative manner. This complaint has been brought to the attention of the Kuwaiti authorities for appropriate action.

Infantry companies

17. The task of the infantry companies temporarily assigned from UNIFIL and UNFICYP was to provide essential security for UNIKOM during the setting-up phase, in view of the uncertainties at that time and the potential risks that might arise (see S/22454, paras. 10 and 13). After 30 days in the Mission, these companies were reduced from 5 to 2. Major General Greindl, the Chief Military Observer, has now recommended that 1 company of some 150 all ranks continue to be assigned to provide security for the Mission; 1 platoon would be deployed to each of the 3 sectors, and 1 at the headquarters in Umm Qasr. This company would also provide the basis for expansion should this be required for security reasons. General Greindl has based his recommendation on his assessment that the area is still in transition and there remains, for the time being, a risk to UNIKOM personnel.

18. I have weighed the above recommendation most carefully. In addition to General Greindl's military assessment, I have taken into consideration the excellent cooperation received from all concerned in the area and the fact that the perceived threats to the security of UNIKOM personnel during the setting-up phase did not in practice materialize. I have also borne in mind the

financial implications and the growing financial burden on Member States as a result of the expansion of peace-keeping activities. In the light of these considerations, I have decided not to recommend, in the present circumstances, that UNIKOM be provided with an infantry element on a permanent basis. I intend, however, to explore with Member States the possibilities of rapid reinforcement of UNIKOM in case of emergency. I will monitor developments carefully and revert to the Security Council on this matter, should it become necessary.

Observations

19. As will be apparent from the above report, UNIKOM is now established and fully able to carry out the tasks assigned to it by the Security Council. It only remains for it to occupy its headquarters at Umm Qasr, which will be done as soon as possible. The mission area has now entered the season of great heat and this will be a testing period for UNIKOM's personnel and equipment. In the light of its experience during the remaining months of the current mandate period, I will, in October, undertake a further review of its strength and make appropriate recommendations to the Security Council. Meanwhile I take this opportunity to pay tribute to the determination and professionalism which General Greindl and all under his command have shown in setting up UNIKOM in difficult circumstances.

Document 61

Security Council resolution determining that the full cost of the weapons destruction programme should be borne by Iraq

S/RES/699 (1991), 17 June 1991

The Security Council,

Recalling its resolution 687 (1991) of 3 April 1991,

Taking note of the report submitted by the Secretary-General on 17 May 1991 pursuant to paragraph 9 (*b*) of resolution 687 (1991), 1/

Also taking note of the Secretary-General's note of 17 May 1991 2/ transmitting to the Council the text of the letter addressed to him by the Director General of the International Atomic Energy Agency under paragraph 13 of the above-mentioned resolution,

Acting under Chapter VII of the Charter of the United Nations,

1. *Approves* the plan contained in the report of the Secretary-General of 17 May 1991; 1/

2. *Confirms* that the Special Commission and the International Atomic Energy Agency have the authority to conduct activities under section C of resolution 687 (1991) for the purpose of the destruction, removal or rendering harmless of the items specified in paragraphs 8 and 12 of that resolution, after the forty-five-day period following the approval of this plan until such activities have been completed;

3. *Requests* the Secretary-General to submit to the Council progress reports on the implementation of the plan referred to in paragraph 1 every six months after the adoption of the present resolution;

4. *Decides* to encourage the maximum assistance, in cash and in kind, from all Member States to ensure that activities under section C of resolution 687 (1991) are undertaken effectively and expeditiously; decides also, however, that the Government of Iraq shall be liable for the full costs of carrying out the tasks authorized by section C; and requests the Secretary-General to submit to the Council within thirty days for approval recommendations as to the most effective means by which Iraq's obligations in this respect may be fulfilled.

1/ *Official Records of the Security Council, Forty-sixth Year, Supplement for April, May and June 1991,* document S/22614.
2/ Ibid., document S/22615.

Document 62

Security Council resolution approving guidelines for monitoring the arms embargo against Iraq (Document 58)

S/RES/700 (1991), 17 June 1991

The Security Council,

Recalling its resolutions 661 (1990) of 6 August 1990, 665 (1990) of 25 August 1990, 670 (1990) of 25 September 1990 and 687 (1991) of 3 April 1991,

Taking note of the report submitted by the Secretary-General on 2 June 1991 pursuant to paragraph 26 of resolution 687 (1991), 1/

Acting under Chapter VII of the Charter of the United Nations,

1. *Expresses its appreciation* to the Secretary-General for his report of 2 June 1991; 1/

2. *Approves* the guidelines to facilitate full international implementation of paragraphs 24, 25 and 27 of Security Council resolution 687 (1991); 2/

3. *Reiterates* its call upon all States and international organizations to act in a manner consistent with the guidelines;

4. *Requests* all States, in accordance with paragraph 8 of the guidelines, to report to the Secretary-General within forty-five days on the measures they have instituted for meeting the obligations set out in paragraph 24 of resolution 687 (1991);

5. *Entrusts* the Security Council Committee established under resolution 661 (1990) concerning the situation between Iraq and Kuwait with the responsibility, under the guidelines, for monitoring the prohibitions against the sale or supply of arms to Iraq and related sanctions established in paragraph 24 of resolution 687 (1991);

6. *Decides* to remain seized of the matter and to review the guidelines at the same time as it reviews paragraphs 22 to 25 of resolution 687 (1991) as set out in paragraph 28 thereof.

1/ *Official Records of the Security Council, Forty-sixth Year, Supplement for April, May and June 1991*, document S/22660.
2/ Ibid., document S/22660, annex.

Document 63

Statement by the President of the Security Council deploring Iraq's denial of access to an inspection site and asking the Secretary-General to send a high-level mission to Baghdad immediately

S/22746, 28 June 1991

The members of the Security Council have learnt with grave concern of an incident which occurred today when the Iraqi military authorities denied a joint IAEA/Special Commission Nuclear Inspection Team immediate and unimpeded access to a site designated for inspection by the Special Commission under paragraphs 9 and 13 of Security Council resolution 687 (1991). In the course of this incident, the Iraqi military did not comply with a request by the Acting Chief Inspector that there should be no movement of transport or equipment pending inspection. The Iraqi military fired small arms into the air when members of the Team were endeavouring to photograph loaded vehicles leaving the site. This incident followed earlier incidents on 23 and 25 June 1991 when the Iraqi military authorities denied the Nuclear Inspection Team access to certain facilities at another designated site.

On 26 June 1991, the Security Council held a meeting to consider the incidents of 23 and 25 June at which time the Permanent Representative of Iraq confirmed that Iraq had accepted Security Council resolution 687 (1991) and was doing its best to implement all the requirements and obligations imposed on it by the resolution. He further asserted that Iraq was cooperating with all United Nations missions, including the Special Commission. The President subsequently conveyed the Council's serious concern regarding the incidents to the Government of Iraq.

The members of the Council strongly deplore the incidents of 23, 25 and 28 June, and in this connection condemn the conduct of the Iraqi authorities. All these incidents constitute flagrant violations of Security Council resolution 687 (1991) and of the undertakings contained in the exchange of letters between the Secretary-General of the United Nations and the Foreign Minister of Iraq governing the status, privileges and immunities of the Special Commission and of the Inspection Teams mandated under the Security Council resolution. Furthermore, these incidents demonstrate Iraq's failure to abide by its solemn undertakings to comply with all the provisions of Security Council resolution 687 (1991).

The members of the Security Council have decided to ask the Secretary-General to send a high-level mission to Baghdad immediately to meet with the highest levels of the Iraqi Government to convey the Council's urgent demand for unequivocal assurances that the Government will take all necessary measures to ensure that no hindrances are placed in the way of the discharge of the Special Commission's mandate and that it will accord full cooperation, including immediate and unimpeded access, to the inspection teams in compliance with Iraq's obligations and commitments *vis-à-vis* the United Nations and the IAEA. The members of the Council have also stressed that the Government must furnish the high-level mission with unconditional guarantees for the safety and security of all personnel engaged in the performance of functions in connection with Security Council resolution 687 (1991). The mission, composed of the Director-General of the International Atomic Energy Agency (IAEA), the Executive Chairman of the Special Commission and the Under-Secretary-General for Disarmament Affairs, will depart New York this evening, 28 June 1991.

At this time, the members of the Council call upon Iraq to grant the IAEA/Special Commission Nuclear Inspection Team currently in Iraq immediate and unimpeded access to the objects which the Team had endeavoured to inspect on 28 June 1991 and any other site deemed necessary.

The members of the Security Council request the high-level mission to report to it at the earliest opportunity, through the Secretary-General, on the results of its meetings with the highest levels of the Iraqi Government and, in particular, on such further undertakings by the Government to ensure compliance at all levels, including local military and civilian authorities, with Iraq's obligations under Security Council resolution 687 (1991).

The members of the Council wish to make it clear that the Council remains seized of this matter and that any recurrence of non-compliance would have serious consequences.

The members of the Council reiterate their views expressed in resolution 687 (1991) of the threat that all weapons of mass destruction pose to peace and security in the Middle East and of the need to work towards the establishment in the Middle East of a zone free of such weapons.

Document 64

Report of a high-level mission sent to Iraq from 30 June to 3 July 1991

S/22761, 5 July 1991

Letter dated 4 July 1991 from the Secretary-General addressed to the President of the Security Council
I have the honour to transmit to you herewith the report of the high-level mission, composed of Mr. Hans Blix, Director-General of the International Atomic Energy Agency, Mr. Rolf Ekéus, Executive Chairman of the Special Commission established under Security Council resolution 687 (1991), and Mr. Yasushi Akashi, Under-Secretary-General for Disarmament Affairs, which I sent to Iraq at the request of the members of the Security Council, as noted in the statement by the President of the Council of 28 June 1991 (S/22746).

(*Signed*) Javier PÉREZ DE CUÉLLAR

Annex
Report of the high-level mission to Iraq

A. *Introduction*

1. The report of the high-level mission is submitted to the Security Council, through the Secretary-General,

within the context and the framework of the statement by the President of the Council of 28 June 1991 (S/22746), pursuant to which the mission was constituted. Furthermore, the mission has understood that it was to proceed against the background of the three incidents of 23, 25 and 28 June 1991 covered in the President's statement. The report, therefore, does not deal with the experience of three other teams dispatched to Iraq under the provisions of section C of Security Council resolution 687 (1991). The cooperation extended by the Iraqi authorities to these inspection and disposal teams was found to be satisfactory and gave rise to no complaints in respect of the granting of immediate and unimpeded access or of other rights of the Special Commission established under Security Council resolution 687 (1991) and the International Atomic Energy Agency (IAEA) under the resolution.

B. *Composition of the high-level mission*

2. The high-level mission was composed of Mr. Hans Blix, Director-General of IAEA, Mr. Rolf Ekéus,

Executive Chairman of the Special Commission and Mr. Yasushi Akashi, United Nations Under-Secretary-General for Disarmament Affairs. The Secretary-General requested Mr. Ekéus to lead the mission.

3. The mission was assisted by a team of experts: Mr. M. El Baradei (IAEA); and Mr. Johan Molander and Mr. John Scott (Office of the Special Commission).

C. *Itinerary of the high-level mission*

4. The mission assembled in Bahrain on 29 June 1991. On 30 June, the mission proceeded to Baghdad, where it remained until 3 July. On 3 July, the mission travelled to Geneva, reported orally to the Secretary-General on 4 July on the outcome of its work and adopted its report.

D. *Meetings in Baghdad with high-level members of the Iraqi Government*

1. *Schedule of meetings*

5. During its stay in Baghdad, the mission held six meetings with the following members of the Iraqi Government:

30 June 1991

8 p.m. - 9.45 p.m.	Mr. Ahmed Hussein, Minister for Foreign Affairs

1 July 1991

11.15 a.m. - 1.30 p.m.	Mr. Tariq Aziz, Deputy Prime Minister
	The Minister for Foreign Affairs
8.30 p.m. - 9.15 p.m.	The Minister for Foreign Affairs

2 July 1991

10.30 a.m. - 1.30 p.m.	The Deputy Prime Minister
	The Minister for Foreign Affairs
	General Hussein Kamel Hassan, Minister of Defence
	Dr. Homan Abdul Khaliq, Chairman of the Atomic Energy Commission of Iraq
7.35 p.m. - 8.30 p.m.	Mr. Saadoun Hammadi, Prime Minister
10.35 p.m. - 11.30 p.m.	The Minister for Foreign Affairs

6. At the final meeting with the Foreign Minister, the mission presented in broad outline the findings it intended to present to the Secretary-General and to the Security Council. On the request of the Foreign Minister for another meeting the following day, the mission stated that

at that point no new developments of significance to its tasks could be expected. The mission recalled that it had already extended its visit by one day and that the Security Council had requested the mission to report to it at the earliest opportunity. If, however, further developments from the Iraqi side were to be forthcoming, they could be communicated to and presented in New York or Vienna.

2. *Presentation of the demands of the Security Council*

7. During its meetings, the mission emphasized that it had been sent to Iraq in order to convey the urgent demand of the Security Council for unequivocal assurances that the Government of Iraq would take all the necessary measures to ensure that no hindrances were placed in the way of the discharge by the Special Commission of its mandate under Security Council resolution 687 (1991) and would accord, in compliance with Iraq's obligations and commitments *vis-à-vis* the United Nations and IAEA, full cooperation, including immediate and unimpeded access to sites declared or designated under paragraphs 9 and 13 of Security Council resolution 687 (1991), to the inspection teams sent to Iraq by the Special Commission and IAEA. The mission further emphasized that it was under instructions from the Council to obtain unconditional guarantees for the safety and security of all personnel engaged in the performance of functions in connection with Security Council resolution 687 (1991). It was also under instructions to seek detailed information on undertakings and measures by the Government to ensure compliance at all levels, including local military and civilian authorities, with Iraq's obligations under Security Council resolution 687 (1991).

8. In transmitting the Security Council's demands, the mission stressed the Council's grave concern over the incident of 28 June, in particular the use of firearms by Iraqi personnel, and drew attention to the fact that the members of the Council had strongly deplored the incidents of 23, 25 and 28 June 1991 and had condemned the conduct of the Iraqi authorities in this connection. It also underlined that the President's statement recorded the unanimous view of the members of the Council.

9. The mission drew attention to the fact that the Security Council remained seized of the matter. The mission underlined the importance of full compliance by Iraq so as to enable the United Nations to continue to carry out resolution 687 (1991) and that any non-compliance by Iraq would have serious consequences. The mission reiterated the view of the Security Council on the threat that weapons of mass destruction pose to peace and security in the Middle East and on the need to work towards the establishment in the Middle East of a zone free of such weapons.

3. Assurance given by the Government of Iraq

10. The mission received from the Ministers with whom it met the various assurances indicated below:

(a) A decision by the President of Iraq, which had been conveyed to the Security Council in New York by the Permanent Representative of Iraq to the United Nations (S/22749), to the effect that the President had ordered all the Iraqi authorities concerned to extend full cooperation to the United Nations representatives and to facilitate their tasks in line with the obligations undertaken by Iraq. The President had also instructed that all bureaucratic problems arising in the cooperation process should be overcome and had authorized the Minister for Foreign Affairs to issue immediate instructions to all authorities and departments which the United Nations representatives desired to visit and inspect to give access without hesitation;

(b) A further statement by the President of Iraq which, *inter alia*, contained the assurance that Iraq had abandoned all activities that might be in contravention of Security Council resolution 687 (1991);

(c) An assurance that Iraq would take all necessary measures to ensure that no hindrances were placed in the way of the inspection activities of the Special Commission and IAEA and that it would accord full cooperation to the inspection teams, including immediate and unimpeded access, and the right to stop and inspect vehicles in movement;

(d) The information that, in order to implement the assurances of cooperation at all levels, orders had been issued to all Iraqi military and civilian personnel to that effect "and so as to ensure the safety and security of all personnel engaged in the performance of functions in connection with Security Council resolution 687 (1991);"

(e) The information that full authority had been given to the Minister for Foreign Affairs to issue directives relating to compliance with Special Commission and IAEA requests under resolution 687 (1991), and that a high-level military liaison officer was, as of that point, placed in the Ministry of Foreign Affairs with authority to grant immediate access to any military site or installation.

4. Access to the objects observed by the nuclear inspection team

11. The mission insisted throughout on the call by the members of the Security Council that Iraq grant the nuclear inspection team, present in Iraq, immediate and unimpeded access to the objects which the team had endeavoured to inspect on 23, 25 and 28 June 1991. The mission reiterated this call when it was reported to it that materials which the team was invited to inspect at Fallujah on 1 July and on 2 July did not comprise objects which the team had observed on 28 June.

12. The Iraqi side explained that some equipment and material belonging to the Atomic Energy Commission of Iraq had been transferred to the Ministry of Defence for purposes of destruction of items that might be in contravention of Security Council resolution 687 (1991) and of redistribution of other items which could be used for the civilian reconstruction programme in Iraq. It was further stated that some of this equipment and material had been present at the Fallujah site. No specification of these items was given, but the Chairman of the Atomic Energy Commission of Iraq promised to provide, in the near future, a list of all items that had been destroyed. Following these explanations, in the afternoon of 2 July the inspection team, accompanied by the Director-General of IAEA, was taken to a destruction site and was shown certain destroyed equipment. The large pieces of equipment which were thus inspected were related to nuclear research and could not have had relevance for the production of weapons-usable material. No meaningful explanation was given why they had been destroyed.

13. The mission stated that if Iraq had interpreted Security Council resolution 687 (1991) in such a way as not to cover research or other facilities, or equipment for the enrichment of uranium or the separation of plutonium, an additional declaration would be needed to include such items as centrifuges, calutrons, facilities for production of uranium tetrachloride or uranium hexafluoride. The Chairman of the Atomic Energy Commission of Iraq stated categorically that there had not been and there was currently no programme under the Commission for the enrichment of uranium in Iraq. The Deputy Prime Minister added that there was only one nuclear programme in Iraq.

5. Observations by the Government of Iraq

14. The Iraqi side, while reiterating the Government's acceptance of the Security Council's resolutions, none the less considered the resolutions to be harsh and unjust. In this connection, reference was made in particular to Security Council resolution 699 (1991), regarding the liability of Iraq for the costs incurred under section C of Security Council resolution 687 (1991) and their offer to undertake the destruction of chemical weapons. The mission stated that this offer was under serious consideration in the Special Commission.

15. The Iraqi side, when referring to the incidents of 23, 25, and 28 June 1991, complained that insufficient notice of inspection had been given. Furthermore, insistence on undertaking the inspections during the Muslim religious holiday of Eid, when the civilian or military officers concerned could not be easily contacted, was inappropriate. Iraq's industrial base had been badly damaged during the conflict and serious communications

and logistical problems existed. All these factors had contributed to the incidents. The mission stated that appropriate notice would always be given, but that the Special Commission and IAEA had the right to inspect mobile objects with short or no notice. The inspection teams had no intention to disregard the religious feelings of the people of Iraq. However, it was now a common feature of verification under modern arms control agreements that inspections might take place at any time when there were reasons for believing that otherwise the purposes of the inspection might be frustrated. Furthermore, on 23 June, it was noticed that considerable Iraqi activity was under way at the inspection site, despite the religious holiday.

16. The Iraqi side referred to its reservations concerning the composition of certain inspection teams and expressed the hope that in the future they would be more widely drawn. The mission stated that, in composing the teams, primary emphasis had to be put on technical competence. Most teams were composed of personnel of many nationalities. A restricting factor existed in the nuclear weapons and related fields, where the available expertise was largely limited to the five nuclear-weapons States. It was agreed that the selection of the members of the inspection teams was the sole prerogative of the Special Commission and of IAEA.

E. Findings of the high-level mission

17. In spite of their unambiguous character, the general assurances given and the specific measures promised can only be evaluated in the light of present and future implementation by the Iraqi authorities. As described in the present report, the Iraqi response to the request for access to the objects which the inspection team had endeavoured to inspect on 28 June falls short of what has been called for by the Security Council.

Geneva, 4 July 1991

(*Signed*) Rolf EKÉUS

(*Signed*) Hans BLIX

(*Signed*) Yasushi AKASHI

Document 65

Report of the Secretary-General recommending the sale of some Iraqi petroleum and petroleum products to finance the destruction or removal of weapons systems stipulated in Security Council resolution 687 (1991)

S/22792, 15 July 1991

1. The present report is submitted pursuant to paragraph 4 of Security Council resolution 699 (1991), of 17 June 1991, which reads as follows:

"*Decides* to encourage the maximum assistance, in cash and in kind, from all Member States to ensure that activities under section C of resolution 687 (1991) are undertaken effectively and expeditiously; further decides, however, that the Government of Iraq shall be liable for the full costs of carrying out the tasks authorized by section C; and requests the Secretary-General to submit to the Council within 30 days for approval recommendations as to the most effective means by which Iraq's obligations in this respect may be fulfilled".

I

2. The fulfillment by the Government of Iraq of the obligations set out in paragraph 4 quoted above is contingent upon both the availability of funds to meet the financial requirements, as well as concrete arrangements to ensure that the necessary resources are channelled to the United Nations.

3. It will be recalled that the Security Council, in deciding upon the financing of the Compensation Fund, did not envisage the use of "frozen assets" of Iraq held in third countries (see paragraph 16 of the Secretary-General's report dated 2 May 1991 pursuant to paragraph 19 of Security Council resolution 687 (1991), document S/22559). It is therefore assumed that the Council would not wish these assets to be used to meet Iraq's obligations in connection with the fulfillment of paragraph 4 of this resolution.

4. The Secretary-General considers that the most obvious way of obtaining financial resources for this purpose would be the sale of some Iraqi petroleum and petroleum products. The net proceeds of such sales would be deposited in a United Nations account to be used to reimburse the costs of carrying out the tasks authorized under section C of Security Council resolution 687 (1991). The quantities to be sold would therefore have to be established in the light of these costs.

5. While the approach outlined above might ensure that Iraq can meet these financial obligations, it would, at the same time, reduce the resources available for the Compensation Fund and/or those remaining for the Government of Iraq. In this connection, the Secretary-General, in determining the appropriate level of Iraq's contribution to the Compensation Fund, had taken account of: (a) the requirements of the people of Iraq; (b) Iraq's payment capacity, taking into consideration external debt servicing; and (c) the needs of the Iraqi economy.

6. The approach proposed in paragraph 5 above would also necessitate that the sanctions imposed on Iraq under Security Council resolution 661 (1990) be lifted, for a limited period and under clearly defined conditions. It may be necessary to repeat this process in the light of the ultimate costs to be reimbursed.

7. This arrangement presupposes cooperation by Iraq as well as strict supervision of the sale of petroleum and petroleum products from Iraq. To this end, appropriate monitoring would have to be ensured. Should Iraq fail to meet its payment obligations, the Secretary-General would need to report the matter to the Security Council.

II

8. Following the adoption of Security Council resolution 699 (1991), the Secretary-General requested the Permanent Representative of Iraq to inform him by 10 July 1991 of the manner in which the Government planned to meet its obligations under paragraph 4 of that resolution. The reply of the Government of Iraq, dated 7 July 1991, reads as follows:

> "With reference to your letter dated 26 June 1991 I have the honour to inform you that my Government still believes that its offer to take an initiative and destroy the weapon systems would have reduced the costs of destroying the weapons and reduced the related risks and time and would have been the safest solution, but the Security Council did not favour this offer and issued its rash and unfair resolution 699 (1991). Nevertheless, Iraq has recently received encouraging signals from the Special Commission concerning this offer to destroy the chemical weapons, and this offer is still valid and it together with Iraq's experience in this area should help in carrying out the tasks assigned to the Special Commission and the IAEA under part C of resolution 687 (1991)."

9. It should be noted in this connection that the Special Commission is considering the Iraqi offer and no decision has yet been taken on this matter.

10. As far as assistance in cash and in kind is concerned, it may be of interest to the Security Council to note that as of 15 July 1991, voluntary contributions in the amount of US$2 million have been received from Member States in response to paragraph 4 of Security Council resolution 699 (1991).

Document 66

Report to the Secretary-General dated 15 July 1991 on humanitarian needs in Iraq prepared by a mission led by the Executive Delegate of the Secretary-General for humanitarian assistance in Iraq (extract)

S/22799, 17 July 1991

I have the honour to transmit herewith for the attention of the members of the Council the report of the inter-agency mission headed by my Executive Delegate for the United Nations Inter-Agency Humanitarian Programme for Iraq, Kuwait and the Iraq/Turkey and Iraq/Iran border areas, Sadruddin Aga Khan.

The task entrusted to the mission, which visited Iraq from 29 June to 13 July 1991, was to assess current needs for humanitarian assistance and recommend measures for meeting those needs.

(*Signed*) Javier PÉREZ DE CUÉLLAR

Annex
Report to the Secretary-General dated 15 July 1991 on humanitarian needs in Iraq prepared by a mission led by Sadruddin Aga Khan, Executive Delegate of the Secretary-General

Foreword by the Executive Delegate

The aftermath of the Persian Gulf war of January and February 1991 presented a compelling spectacle of suffering and devastation to the international community. The tragic consequences of conflict, the untold loss of life and destruction were compounded by massive displacements of ill-prepared populations, by ecological disasters of unprecedented magnitude, by the collapse of the structures that sustain life in today's human societies. The region continues to face an enormous challenge in its attempt to recover from the ravages of war. In Iraq itself, the upheaval's insidious effects are leading to the gradual but inexorable collapse of essential services, leading to the risk of a humanitarian crisis whose eventual dimensions would dwarf today's difficulties.

When we decided, last month in Geneva, to try to confront these urgent issues, we knew that speed was vital. We were also aware that our findings had to be factual, precise and credible. The expert team from the United Nations programmes and agencies concerned—the United Nations Children's Fund (UNICEF), the World Health Organization (WHO), the Food and Agriculture Organization of the United Nations (FAO), the World Food Programme (WFP), the Office of the United Nations High Commissioner for Refugees (UNHCR) and the United Nations Development Programme (UNDP)—carried out a most professional and effective assessment, well supported by their colleagues already in Iraq. The mission fanned out throughout the country, revealing both pockets of destitution and the full scale of the problems in all regions. This was a field-based mission; the observations and conclusions were drawn from on-the-spot country-wide evaluation, not imposed from the vantage point of predetermined opinion.

As well as our United Nations partners and their colleagues based in Iraq, we benefited from a third tier of expertise: a very distinguished group of non-United Nations specialists and personalities participated in the mission and its activities. I am deeply grateful to Donato Chiarini, Thomas Hammarberg, Arve Johnsen, Jean-Daniel Levi, Sir John Moberly, Edwin Moore, Elliot Richardson and Nico Schrijver for having accepted my invitation to join us. They made a contribution of outstanding intellectual, moral and technical value, which undoubtedly enhances the report's scope and credibility. Needless to say, it represents a consensus view to which all of us subscribe, while not committing every member to every single phrase and sentence written.

Our aim has been to be sober, measured and accurate. We are neither crying wolf nor playing politics. But it is evident that for large numbers of the people of Iraq, every passing month brings them closer to the brink of calamity. As usual, it is the poor, the children, the widowed and the elderly, the most vulnerable amongst the population, who are the first to suffer. This cannot leave us unconcerned, whatever the solution proposed. In the pages of this report we have tried, in accordance with the purely humanitarian remit that was ours, to diagnose the problem and suggest remedies. It will be for the international community to decide how to respond further.

(*Signed*) Sadruddin Aga KHAN

Introduction

1. The decision to undertake the present mission was made by the Secretary-General, his Executive Delegate Sadruddin Aga Khan, and the executive heads of United Nations specialized agencies and programmes responsible for the humanitarian programmes in Iraq, Kuwait and the Iraq/Turkey and Iraq/Islamic Republic of Iran borders at a meeting held at Geneva on 13 June 1991. Extensive first-hand reports had been received in previous weeks indicating that the conditions of the civilian population in many parts of Iraq were steadily deteriorating. The onset of summer was likely to exacerbate the situation further, while the return of large numbers of those displaced was also having a considerable impact on severely strained food, medical, water and infrastructural resources.

2. Given the indications of the worsening plight of the majority of Iraq's population, the meeting decided that a high-level mission should proceed to Iraq to assess the current humanitarian needs and recommend measures to address them. The mission was to be action- and field-oriented, should be carried out rapidly and should focus in particular on the emergency needs of vulnerable groups. Within its overall framework, the mission would concentrate on four main sectors: food supply; water and sanitation; health; and energy (with special reference to power generation).

3. The mission was led by the Secretary-General's Executive Delegate, Sadruddin Aga Khan, and was composed of experts from the relevant United Nations programmes and agencies, namely, UNICEF, WHO, FAO, WFP, UNHCR and UNDP, as well as consultants, specialists and eminent personalities from outside the United Nations system. The latter comprised participants from Canada, France, the Netherlands, Norway, Sweden, the United Kingdom of Great Britain and Northern Ireland, the United States of America and the Commission of the European Communities. While not part of this mission, a separate team from the International Telecommunication Union (ITU) was in Iraq at the same time. Several of their findings are noted in the present report and a summary of their own mission report is included as appendix X.

4. Mission members received briefings at Geneva from the Executive Delegate before flying to Baghdad on 29 June to join with staff from United Nations agencies already in the country. The first part of the mission was devoted to information collection and analysis in Iraq. At Baghdad mission members were briefed by United

Nations staff, non-governmental organizations (NGOs), and the International Committee of the Red Cross (ICRC) and were welcomed by the Minister of State for Foreign Affairs and members of the National Committee for the Coordination of Relief and Assistance. After meetings and discussions with staff of the relevant technical ministries on 1 July, mission members visited various sites, mainly outside Baghdad, from 2 to 7 July. The mission divided into four teams, which visited sites in 16 of the 18 governorates (including Baghdad).

5. The Executive Delegate and additional mission members arrived in Baghdad on 8 July. Together with certain members of his team, he met with various government officials, including the Deputy Prime Minister, the Foreign Minister, ministers of relevant technical Ministries and other senior officials. The Executive Delegate also visited the southern region in order to further the provision of relief assistance to vulnerable groups and displaced persons in the area of the marshes. The mission team departed for Geneva on 13 July.

6. The Executive Delegate and members of the mission greatly appreciated the support and cooperation extended to them by the Iraqi authorities throughout the course of their stay in the country.

. . .

II. *Summary of main findings and recommendations*

13. The mission members concluded that the scale of damage and decline in Iraq in the past year had indeed been dramatic. Eight years of war with the Islamic Republic of Iran had taken their toll even before the destruction of the Persian Gulf war. In significant parts of the country, the destruction caused by the internal civil conflicts that followed the war was comparable or even greater. A final factor had been the consequence of economic and financial sanctions imposed on Iraq, including the freezing of its foreign assets and a ban on the international sale of its oil. It was clear to the mission that the impact of the sanctions had been, and remains, very substantial on the economy and living conditions of its civilian population. The mission was informed that the last reserves of food commodities that are included in the ration basket are in the process of being exhausted.

14. During the past several months major efforts have been made by the Government of Iraq to restore the country to some semblance of its pre-war situation. These efforts have been only partially successful. For example, a number of bridges have been repaired, and with the limited pumping of oil for local consumption, internal transport capabilities have in large part been restored.

15. However, the mission found that in the sectors of concern to it, the process of restoration had in many crucial respects reached its limit. Indeed, there are a number of problem areas that are likely to worsen in the foreseeable future. A review of several of the main findings within each of the sectors, which are discussed in more detail in the later sections of this report, gives reason for alarm.

16. As far as water is concerned, damage to water-treatment plants and the inability to obtain needed spare parts have cut off an estimated 2.5 million Iraqis from the government system they relied upon before the war. The perhaps 14.5 million Iraqis who continue to receive their water through this system are now provided on average with one quarter the pre-war amount per day. Much of this water is of doubtful quality, owing to such problems as defective treatment and lack of sufficient hours of electric power. Major damage was also suffered by the national sewerage system owing to the loss of electric power during the war. Most of this damage has not been repaired, with raw sewage now flowing in some city streets and into the rivers. Diarrhoeal diseases, thought to be mainly caused by water and sewage problems, are now at four times the level of a year ago. The country is already experiencing outbreaks of typhoid and cholera.

17. The health of the population in Iraq is now challenged by growing environmental hazards, insufficient access to quality medical care and inadequate nutrition. Public health programmes have reduced their activities for lack of supplies. Hospitals and public health centres are severely affected by lack of electricity, water and medicines. Medical, surgical, dental and laboratory equipment suffer from the lack of spare parts, reagents and maintenance. The fleet of vehicles that once assured the effectiveness of the health services has been reduced to a few units. Iraq used to import annually approximately US$360 million worth of drugs and medical appliances alone. It is highly improbable that international humanitarian aid will be able to meet this demand. Mechanisms need to be established urgently for the country to procure its own medical supplies and to maintain its equipment in operation. Failing this, the health situation will further worsen. Vulnerable groups, each day more numerous, will be the first victims.

18. As for the food supply, the position is deteriorating rapidly in virtually all parts of the country. Preliminary forecasts for the current main harvest indicate that this year's aggregate cereal production will be around one third of last year's. This will further increase the country's dependence on imports, which even in good years has meant that approximately 70 per cent of its food needs must be imported. Data collected on prices throughout the country show tremendous levels of inflation. For example, current retail prices for wheat and rice—the two normal staple food items—remain 45 and 22 times their corresponding price levels of last year, while average

incomes have shown only moderate gains. The government rationing system, even if basically equitable in its distribution, can provide only about one third of the typical family's food needs, resulting in a strikingly low level of dietary intake. The situation is particularly alarming with respect to the nutritional status of children, pregnant and lactating mothers as well as households headed by widows. Several independent studies and direct observation by the mission confirmed the high prevalence of malnutrition among children. There are numerous, reliable reports of families resorting to sales of personal and household items to meet their immediate needs. Taken collectively, this information clearly demonstrates a widespread and acute food supply crisis which, if not averted through timely intervention, will gradually but inexorably cause massive starvation throughout the country.

19. The current emergency feeding programmes, such as those being implemented by WFP for vulnerable groups, refugees, returnees and internally displaced persons, accordingly acquire special significance and need to be maintained for at least the next few months. The process of repatriation must be encouraged by the continued provision of timely and adequate amounts of relief aid, not least to ensure that the situation in the areas to which the refugees are returning reverts to normal as quickly as possible. It should be noted that the economic sanctions also lessen the ability of the returning refugees to resume their ordinary lives and traditional economic activities. Indeed, the mission was informed by the Kurdish leadership that the sanctions were taking an unfortunately harmful toll upon the living conditions of the Kurdish population.

20. In terms of power generation, Iraq's capacity had been reduced to a negligible level by the end of February 1991. At present, the power generating capacity has been restored to 25 per cent of the pre-war level. As it is operating continuously, electricity production is about 40 per cent of the 1990 level. However, this restoration process has been accomplished through such methods as cannibalizing parts from damaged units, making risky makeshift repairs and operating the remaining plants without the normal breaks for maintenance and repairs. At this point, little more can be done to increase power generation further unless major imports of new parts are allowed. Barring this, power output can be expected to decline from now on. The mission has also assessed the situation of the oil sector. The requirements of the internal market can essentially be met with the current production and refining capacity, although with repairs needed soon for some refineries that are in precarious condition. The main concern is the oil export capacity, which is now only one third of the pre-war level.

21. As for telecommunications, the ITU team noted that at least 400,000 of the original 900,000 telephone lines were damaged beyond repair, while additional ones were partly damaged. The main microwave links connecting most of the cities were also damaged. This has had an obvious negative impact on the operation of health and social services as well as on humanitarian assistance programmes. All international telecommunications were put out of service. Even after restoration work, the system can still handle only 30 per cent of its pre-war internal service, while international telecommunications remain out of service.

22. Clearly, the situation described above is one that deserves urgent attention and immediate response. In considering what actions to recommend, the mission came to a series of additional conclusions.

23. As spelled out in the specific sector reports, the primary action that is needed to address these needs is the import of material goods. This includes such items as drugs, vaccines, medical equipment, ambulances, spare parts and replacements for water and sewerage equipment, food and agricultural inputs and equipment and parts for power generation plants and the oil sector, as well as for the telecommunications network.

24. A review of the relevant Security Council resolutions and decisions by the Security Council Committee established by resolution 661 (1990) concerning the situation between Iraq and Kuwait indicates that the sale or supply to Iraq of most of these items is not restricted, although for most items notification to or prior approval by the Sanctions Committee would be required. Many fall under the clauses exempting "medicine and health supplies" and "foodstuffs" from the sanctions (see resolutions 661 (1990), 666 (1990) and 687 (1991)). Others fall under the category of materials and supplies for "essential civilian needs" as exempted in resolution 687 (1991), as well as the clause contained in the 20 March 1991 Sanctions Committee decision. The latter provides that civilian and humanitarian imports to Iraq, as identified in the report of that date to the Secretary-General, are integrally related to the supply of foodstuffs and supplies intended strictly for medical purposes ... and that such imports should also be allowed ..., subject to approval by the Sanctions Committee under its no-objection procedure. So far, the relevance to the humanitarian programme of the import of spare parts and equipment for the restoration of electric power plants and for the telecommunications network has not been recognized.

25. In this context, the mission observed that, in most of the cases that came to its attention, problems to date with importing the above items had more to do with the financing of such imports than actual prohibitions.

The question of financing becomes even more crucial in relation to future importations that need to be made.

26. The mission members utilized the best information available to them to estimate the costs of returning the systems in each of the four sector areas to their pre-war condition. This proved possible for most sectors, with the estimates being US$12 billion for the power-generating capacity, US$6 billion for the oil sector, US$450 million for the water and sanitation systems, US$2.64 billion for food imports and US$500 million for agricultural imports. While these calculations were not possible for health, an indicative figure would be the typical level of international imports for the health sector for one year, which has been approximately US$500 million.

27. The principal criterion adopted by the mission in evaluating these needs has been that it is concerned not only with addressing immediate requirements of humanitarian scope and nature, but also with averting a crisis in the next 6 to 12 months. To illustrate this point, urgent measures must be taken now to ensure that the next agricultural planting season can be completed under reasonably normal conditions.

28. Consequently, the mission attempted to determine the costs for some lower level of actions, over a one-year time-frame. Figures were calculated for providing approximately two fifths of the pre-war per capita levels of clean drinking water and putting a corresponding proportion of the damaged sewage-treatment capacity back in operation. Expenditures for imports for health services were calculated at the pre-war level. Food import calculations were based on the ration level that WFP provides to sustain disaster-stricken populations. Special supplemental feeding programmes to support the nutritional needs of malnourished children and pregnant and lactating mothers for one year were calculated. Power generation estimates were based on restoring approximately one half of the pre-war capacity of the country. For the oil sector, the mission worked out a cost based on the consolidation of existing refineries, the restoration of lubrication units, the repair of the Iraq-Turkey pipelines, and of the oil facilities in the Kirkuk areas. This would not include repair of the southern oil fields.

29. The total estimated costs for this greatly reduced level of services came to approximately US$6.8 billion over a one-year period. This includes US$180 million for water and sanitation, US$500 million for health services, US$53 million for supplemental feeding, US$1.62 billion for general food imports, US$300 million for essential agricultural needs, US$2 billion for the oil sector and US$2.2 billion for power generation. If this analysis is applied to a four-month time-frame, the requirements would come to US$60 million for water and

sanitation, US$167 million for health services, US$18 million for supplemental feeding, US$540 million for food imports, US$100 million for essential agricultural imports, US$667 million for the oil sector, and US$1.1 billion for power generation. The power and oil sectors include allowances for the front-end costs occurring in these sectors. Thus, the total for an initial four-month period would be US$2.63 billion.

30. The massive financial requirements to establish even this reduced level of service are of a scale far beyond what is, or is likely to be, available under any United Nations-sponsored programme. The current United Nations appeal for humanitarian assistance for Iraq, Kuwait and the border areas with the Islamic Republic of Iran and Turkey has received only some US$210 million to date. Most of these funds are pledged for the needs of refugees and returnees. Further, any additional requests for aid to Iraq must compete with a continually lengthening list of other emergency situations around the world with very compelling needs.

31. It is evident that the Iraqi Government itself will have to revise its priorities and mobilize all internal resources. It will also have to finance the import of the type of materials under discussion, for which it has already requested approval from the Security Council Committee established by resolution 661 (1990). It certainly appeared that the Iraqi Government has the potential itself to generate the funds required to cover the needs identified by the team. This could be done either by the unfreezing of substantial amounts of Iraqi assets now held abroad or through the pumping and subsequent international sale of oil. The mission was informed that foreign exchange reserves of only US$14.75 million were on hand in the central bank and that the Government's holding of gold bullion in support of the national currency had remained constant for the last 20 years.

32. With respect to the possible sale of oil by the Iraqi Government to finance such imports, paragraph 23 of Security Council resolution 687 (1991) empowers the Security Council Committee established by resolution 661 (1990) to approve exceptions to the prohibition against the import of commodities and products originating in Iraq, with the explicit purpose of assuring "adequate financial resources" on the part of the Iraqi Government to procure medicine and health supplies, foodstuffs and materials and supplies for "essential civilian needs".

33. According to the Government, the current oil-production capacity of the country is 1,455 million barrels per day. Taking into account internal consumption requirements, the production available for export could be about 1 million barrels per day. This would mean a potential net revenue of US$5.5 billion over one year. Furthermore, in order to increase the production to the

pre-war level, extensive repairs and rebuilding would have to take place, particularly in the Basra area. The mission therefore recommends that Iraq be allowed to import over a four-month period US$1 billion worth of equipment, spare parts and consumable materials to start restoration of the oil sector.

34. If the Security Council Committee were to decide that Iraq should be allowed to use funds from oil sales or facilitate the use of blocked accounts in order to meet urgent humanitarian needs, the Government indicated that it would cooperate in making available documentation relating to sales of crude oil as well as purchases of the authorized imports. It noted that all revenues accruing from oil sales were normally held in United States banks and that a suitable device for monitoring such credit balances could be established. This procedure could include information on the use of unfrozen accounts. In addition, the staff of the United Nations and other humanitarian agencies present in Iraq, as well as special missions designated by the Secretary-General as required, might for instance submit periodic assessments and in particular report on the changes in the composition of the rations of foodstuffs and the provision of health and social services brought about by increased imports. The staff concerned would also obtain up-to-date information on the repair and improvement of power-generating capacity, the operation of water and sewerage plants and the like. The envisaged procedure would thus help to ensure the actual receipt of the civilian and humanitarian goods in Iraq and their utilization by the intended beneficiaries.

35. In summary, the mission recommends that:

(a) Immediate steps be taken to alleviate the priority needs identified by the mission in the areas of food supply, health services, water and sanitation, power generation, the oil sector and telecommunications;

(b) To meet these needs, essential goods and materials should be imported, including:

(i) Food to meet the minimum consumption requirements, in part to reduce and shorten the emergency relief operation now in operation at donors' expense;

(ii) Agricultural inputs, including fertilizers, pesticides, animal feed and drugs, machinery and spare parts needed to repair the damaged irrigation and drainage system;

(iii) Drugs, including raw materials needed for local pharmaceutical production, vaccines, medical supplies and medical, surgical, dental and diagnostic equipment for the health system;

(iv) Vehicles (and spare parts for them) needed by the health system, including ambulances;

(v) Spare parts, supplies and equipment and replacement pumps and other heavy equipment needed by water-treatment and pumping facilities and by the sewage treatment system;

(vi) Equipment, materials and spare parts for the electric power system, the oil sector and for the telecommunication sector;

(c) A monitoring system should be instituted for this purpose. The relevant commercial transactions relating to the export of oil and the import of the above-mentioned goods and services could be made sufficiently transparent at the international level to allow adequate controls with respect to their shipment and entry into Iraq. The monitoring arrangements in the context of the United Nations humanitarian presence in Iraq, as outlined in paragraph 13 of the Memorandum of Understanding of 18 April 1991, could be further developed and strengthened so as to provide adequate information on the destination and use of the goods in question.

. . .

IV. Concluding remarks

130. None of us on the mission team could overlook a glaring paradox: at a time when the international community is beset with disasters of daunting dimensions around the globe, we continue to appeal to the same donors to fund emergency programmes in Iraq that the country could pay for itself. With considerable oil reserves in the ground, Iraq should not have to compete for scarce aid funds with a famine-ravaged Horn of Africa, with a cyclone-hit Bangladesh.

131. We saw with our own eyes the scenes already reported at length: the raw sewage pouring into the Tigris and the Euphrates, the children afflicted by malnutrition. Our report is inevitably but a photograph in time, fast obsolete, yet the urgency of relief from suffering remains. Further, the hard statistics speak for themselves. Conditions are already grave in all of the essential sectors assessed and can only worsen in the weeks ahead. We must achieve a breakthrough to avert the looming crisis.

132. We have not set our sights on the optimum but no doubt unrealistic goal of full restoration of services to pre-war levels. We have not even aimed at funding for a full year. Instead, more modest objectives for the key sectors, for a limited initial four-month period (September to December 1991), have been quantified. Essential civilian needs must be assured for this immediate future.

133. To fund even this partial endeavour is far beyond the capacity of the United Nations system. Nor should the resources emanate exclusively from international programmes, given the dictates of common sense and of solidarity with those needs elsewhere I referred to

above. Iraq's own national resources, whether material or human, must obviously be put to good use.

134. The mandate assigned to me as the Secretary-General's Executive Delegate is of a humanitarian nature: political determinations are not in my purview. Indeed, we have consistently focused upon the needs of the most vulnerable groups, wherever they may be identified and located throughout the country. The United Nations presence in Iraq, which for the purposes of our operation has been managed through United Nations humanitarian centres with their accompanying complement of United Nations guards, has monitored and reported on the provision of humanitarian assistance and advised the authorities in this respect. This will continue to constitute a major priority. The right to food, water, shelter and adequate health care are amongst the most fundamental of all human rights and must be assured to all people in all areas. As with all the key rights and freedoms set out in the Universal Declaration of Human Rights and the International Covenants, there can be no discrimination whatsoever in their enjoyment. Due note was taken, during our stay in Iraq, of the authorities' declared objective of fostering the democratic process, with its intrinsic attributes of political pluralism and freedom of the press. The present negotiations with the Kurdish leadership were cited as an example of this trend.

135. Events of earlier years and, more recently, the civil strife that followed the Persian Gulf war, brought harmful consequences for vulnerable groups, for displaced populations, which must continue to be redressed. Those affected must be reassured and encouraged to return to their homes. The amenities so commendably accorded to those involved in the civil unrest must be extended. Where mines have been sown as indiscriminate seeds of death around refugees' home regions, they must be detected and removed. Where original habitats have been destroyed, they must be rebuilt: this is particularly true of the Kurdish villages and towns that had been razed in previous years. It takes on an added urgency with the approach of winter. Indeed, massive transformations inflicted upon the human and natural environment in any region are unacceptable and can only be injurious to all concerned in the long term.

136. The creation of confidence, which is sadly lacking in some parts of the country, is crucial. It is in the interest of Iraq, of the displaced populations and of the international community. The United Nations presence in the country has welcomed the cooperation it has received from the authorities in pursuing this shared interest. In the coming weeks, as the need to maintain confidence in the equitable distribution of goods and services throughout all segments of the population takes on critical importance, such transparency and cooperation will be essential. We will have to be assured, in particular, of the maximum distribution to the civilian population, whose proportion can indeed only grow as the time of conflict and the militarization of society recedes.

137. This mission has addressed the current humanitarian needs in Iraq and has concluded that their magnitude requires funding that exceeds international aid and short-term palliatives and can be met only from the country's own resources. How this finding is to be reconciled with the Security Council's imposition of sanctions is a determination that is not ours to make. On the basis, however, of our deliberations and meetings with the authorities in Iraq, it would appear feasible to institute arrangements whereby Iraq's requests for imports to meet the needs outlined in this report would be submitted to the United Nations and subjected to appropriate monitoring. The precise mechanism need not be specified here. The formula agreed upon would provide for clear records of all transactions to be furnished to the Organization. Constant accountability would be assured, as would the humanitarian purposes of imports financed by oil sales. As for the question of equitable distribution, a functioning food rationing system is already in place. Other aspects have been mentioned in preceding paragraphs and concern the United Nations presence in the country.

138. It remains a cardinal humanitarian principle that innocent civilian—and above all the most vulnerable—should not be held hostage to events beyond their control. Those already afflicted by war's devastation cannot continue to pay the price of a bitter peace. It is a peace that will also prove to be tenuous if unmet needs breed growing desperation. If new displacements of Iraq's population result from hunger and disease, if relief is again sought across national frontiers, the region's stability will once more be set at risk with unforeseeable consequences. Humanitarian and political interests converge in the aversion of catastrophe. It is clearly imperative that Iraq's "essential civilian needs" be met urgently and that rapid agreement be secured on the mechanism whereby Iraq's own resources be used to fund them to the satisfaction of the international community.

Document 67

Letter from the President of the Governing Council of the United Nations Compensation Commission transmitting guidelines for the conduct of the Commission's work (extract)

S/22885, 2 August 1991

Letter dated 2 August 1991 from the President of the Governing Council of the United Nations Compensation Commission to the President of the Security Council

In accordance with a decision taken by the Governing Council of the United Nations Compensation Commission, at its tenth meeting, held on 2 August 1991, I have the honour to transmit the following for the information of the members of the Security Council.

The Governing Council of the United Nations Compensation Commission established by Security Council resolution 692 (1991), of 20 May 1991, held its first session at Geneva from 23 July to 2 August 1991.

At its fourth meeting, held on 25 July 1991, the Governing Council approved Guidelines for the conduct of its work (see annex I), a copy of which is attached. In accordance with paragraph 5 of its Guidelines, the Governing Council invited the representatives of Bangladesh, Iraq, Kuwait, Pakistan, the Philippines and Sri Lanka to address the Council and reply to questions put to them by the members.

At its ninth meeting, held on 1 August 1991, the Governing Council decided to hold informal consultations the week beginning 16 September 1991 and to convene its second session the week beginning 14 October 1991.

At its tenth meeting, held today, 2 August 1991, the Governing Council adopted the attached criteria for expedited processing of urgent claims, a copy of which is attached [see Document 68]. The criteria will be issued as a document of the Governing Council for general distribution (S/AC.26/1991/1).

At the same meeting, the Governing Council approved the proposals contained in a working paper submitted by the United States of America on arrangements for ensuring payments to the Compensation Fund (S/AC.26/1991/WP.4/Rev.1), as orally revised. The text of that decision is contained in document S/AC.26/1991/2 of the Governing Council, which is being given general distribution (see annex III [not reproduced here]).

(Signed) Philippe J. BERG
President of the Governing Council of the
  United Nations Compensation Commission

Annex I
Guidelines for the conduct of the work of the Governing Council of the United Nations Compensation Commission

1. The mandate of the Governing Council is defined in the report of the Secretary-General pursuant to paragraph 19 of Security Council resolution 687 (1991) (S/22559). By paragraphs 3 and 5 of its resolution 692 (1991) the Security Council decided to establish the Fund and the Commission referred to in paragraph 18 of resolution 687 (1991) in accordance with section I of the Secretary-General's report, and directed the Governing Council to implement the provisions of section E of resolution 687 (1991), taking into account the recommendations in section II of the Secretary-General's report.

2. The Governing Council will hold its meetings in private but will open them to the public as and when it deems it necessary for the enhancement of the effectiveness of the Governing Council.

3. As provided for in paragraph 10 of the Secretary-General's report, decisions of the Governing Council on the method of ensuring that payments are made to the Fund should be taken by consensus. Other decisions will be taken by a majority of at least nine of its members. No veto will apply in the Governing Council.

4. As provided for in paragraph 10 of the Secretary-General's report, if consensus is not achieved on any matter for which it is required, the question will be referred to the Security Council on the request of any member of the Governing Council.

5. The Governing Council may invite States that it considers to have particular interest in its work to participate without a vote in its discussions. It may also invite members of the United Nations Secretariat or other persons to supply it with information or to give other assistance in examining matters within its competence.

6. Information on the work of the Governing Council will be made publicly available by the President when so decided in consultation with the members of the Governing Council.

7. The Governing Council will be provided with summary records of all its meetings in all official languages.

8. The success of the work of the Governing Council depends upon the cooperation of all States.

9. Prior to the close of each session, the Governing Council will decide on the dates and duration of its next session. In between sessions, if any member of the Governing Council or the Executive Secretary raises a matter that requires prompt consideration by the Governing Council, the President will hold consultations with the members of the Governing Council and could decide to convene it. Members will be informed of the opening date of the session as well as the provisional agenda at least five days in advance.

10. The Governing Council will, on behalf of the Commission, report periodically to the Security Council.

. . .

Document 68

Decision 1 taken by the Governing Council of the United Nations Compensation Commission: Criteria for expedited processing of urgent claims

S/AC.26/1991/1, 2 August 1991

1. The following criteria will govern the submission of the most urgent claims pursuant to resolution 687 (1991) for the first categories to be considered by the Commission. It provides for simple and expedited procedures by which Governments may submit consolidated claims and receive payments on behalf of the many individuals who suffered personal losses as a result of the invasion and occupation of Kuwait. For a great many persons these procedures would provide prompt compensation in full; for others they will provide substantial interim relief while their larger or more complex claims are being processed, including those suffering business losses.

2. These criteria are without prejudice to future Council decisions with respect to criteria for other categories of claims, which will be approved separately as promptly as possible, with expert advice from Commissioners as may be required.

3. The following criteria are not intended to resolve every issue that may arise with respect to these claims. Rather, they are intended to provide sufficient guidance to enable Governments to prepare consolidated claims submissions. It will likely be necessary for the Council to make further decisions on the processing of claims after receiving expert advice where needed.

4. Each Government may submit one or more consolidated claims for each category established by the Council. Thus, each Government may make separate consolidated submissions covering claims in each of the categories set forth below; and it may later submit separate consolidated claims for each additional category to be established by the Council.

5. The Council will promptly establish criteria for additional categories of claims, to permit consolidated submissions by Governments for all losses covered by paragraph 16 of resolution 687 (1991). Business losses of individuals may be part of consolidated claims under the expedited procedures set forth below. The Council will provide further advice on an urgent basis as to the types of business losses eligible for consideration under the expedited procedures. Business losses of corporations and other legal entities will be covered in other criteria to be established. The Council will also separately consider claims on behalf of third parties, such as Governments, insurance companies, relief agencies and employers, which have made payments or provided relief to persons suffering compensable losses.

6. The Council will consider promptly, after receiving expert advice, the circumstances in which claims for mental pain and anguish may be admitted, the amounts to be awarded, and the limits to be imposed thereon.

7. The Council will separately examine the question of the eligibility or otherwise of claims by or in respect of members of the allied coalition armed forces; the Executive Secretary will have available, *inter alia*, the provisions of the relevant national legislation of the Governments concerned.

8. The Commission will process the claims in the initial categories in paragraphs 10 to 16 on an expedited basis. While decisions on the precise method of processing these claims will be made at a later stage, the following steps are contemplated. As the claims are received they would be submitted to a panel of Commissioners for review within a set time limit. If, as expected, the volume of claims in these categories is large, the Commissioners would be instructed to adopt expedited procedures to process them, such as checking individual claims on a sample basis, with further verification only if circum-

stances warranted. The Commissioners would be asked to report to the Council on the claims received and the amount recommended for the claims submitted by each Government. The Council would then decide on the total amount to be allocated to each Government. To the extent necessary, the Council would seek expert advice (for example, on what constitutes serious personal injury) at any stage of the process.

9. As contributions are made to the Fund, the Council will allocate those funds among the various categories of claims. If resources of the Fund are insufficient with respect to all claims processed to date, *pro rata* payments would be made to Governments periodically as funds become available. The Council will decide on the priority for payment of various categories of claims.

Payment of fixed amounts

10. These payments are available with respect to any person who, as a result of Iraq's unlawful invasion and occupation of Kuwait: (a) departed from Iraq or Kuwait during the period of 2 August 1990 to 2 March 1991; (b) suffered serious personal injury; or (c) whose spouse, child or parent died.

11. In the case of departures, $2,500 will be provided where there is simple documentation of the fact and date of departure from Iraq or Kuwait. Documentation of the actual amount of loss will not be required. Claims submitted under this procedure for departure from Iraq or Kuwait cannot be resubmitted for a greater amount in any other category. If the loss in question was greater than $2,500 and can be documented, it may instead be submitted under paragraph 14 and in other appropriate categories.

12. In addition, in the case of serious personal injury not resulting in death, $2,500 will be provided where there is simple documentation of the fact and date of the injury; and in the case of death, $2,500 will be provided where there is simple documentation of the death and family relationship. Documentation of the actual amount of loss resulting from the death or injury will not be required. If the actual loss in question was greater than $2,500, these payments will be treated as interim relief, and claims for additional amounts may also be submitted under paragraph 14 and in other appropriate categories.

13. These amounts are payable cumulatively where more than one situation applies with respect to a particular person. However, no more than $10,000 will be paid for death, and no more than $5,000 for departure, with respect to any one family (consisting of any person and his or her spouse, children and parents).

Consideration of claims for up to $100,000 of actual losses per person

14. These payments are available with respect to death or personal injury, or losses of income, support, housing or personal property, or medical expenses or costs of departure, as a result of Iraq's unlawful invasion and occupation of Kuwait. The Commission will give expedited priority consideration to claims for such losses up to $100,000 per person.

15. (a) Such claims must be documented by appropriate evidence of the circumstances and the amount of the claimed loss. The evidence required will be the reasonable minimum that is appropriate under the circumstances involved, and a lesser degree of documentary evidence would ordinarily be required for smaller claims, such as those below $20,000.

(b) If the loss in question was greater than $100,000, claims for additional amounts may also be submitted in other appropriate categories. Criteria for the submission of claims in excess of $100,000 will be approved separately. Claims larger than $100,000 may be submitted in their entirety at a later date under those separate procedures, or the first $100,000 may be submitted at this time and the remainder separately.

16. Compensation will not be provided for losses suffered as a result of the trade embargo and related measures, nor will costs of attorneys' fees or other expenses for claims preparation be compensated under this category. Any compensation, whether in funds or in kind, already received from any source will be deducted from the total amount of losses suffered.

Requirements applicable under both categories

17. Claims will not be considered on behalf of Iraqi nationals who do not have bona fide nationality of any other State.

18. Claims must be for death, personal injury or other direct loss to individuals as a result of Iraq's unlawful invasion and occupation of Kuwait. This will include any loss suffered as a result of:

(a) military operations or threat of military action by either side during the period 2 August 1990 to 2 March 1991;

(b) departure from or inability to leave Iraq or Kuwait (or a decision not to return) during that period;

(c) actions by officials, employees or agents of the Government of Iraq or its controlled entities during that period in connection with the invasion or occupation;

(d) the breakdown of civil order in Kuwait or Iraq during that period; or

(e) hostage-taking or other illegal detention.

19. Claims will be submitted by Governments. Each Government will normally submit claims on behalf of its nationals; each Government may, in its discretion, also submit the claims of other persons resident in its territory. In addition, the Council may request an appropriate person, authority or body to submit claims on behalf of persons who are not in a position to have their claims submitted by a Government. Each Government shall make one or more consolidated submissions of all such claims for each category. The Council encourages the submission of such claims within six months from the date on which the Executive Secretary circulates to Governments the claims forms described below; and the Commission will thereupon give consideration to such claims as provided herein. The Council will consider at a later time the period within which all such claims must be submitted.

20. Each consolidated claim must include:

(a) a signed statement by each individual covered containing:

(i) his or her name and address, and any passport number or other identifying national number;

(ii) for claims under paragraph 14, the amount, type, and reason for each element of the loss, and any compensation, whether in funds or in kind already received from any source for the claim asserted;

(iii) any documents evidencing the matters set forth in the definition of each category, as well as the items set forth in the preceding subparagraph; and

(iv) his or her affirmation that the foregoing information is correct, and that no other claim for the same loss has been submitted to the Commission;

(b) the affirmation of the Government submitting the claim that, to the best of the information available to it, the individuals in question are its nationals or residents, and the affirmation of the Government or of the person, authority or body as referred to in paragraph 19 that it has no reason to believe that the information stated is incorrect.

21. The Executive Secretary (or a Commissioner) will prepare and the Executive Secretary will distribute a standard form for submission of claims within each category, incorporating the above elements in a clear and concise manner. Except as may otherwise be agreed between the Executive Secretary and the Government in question, claims will be submitted to the Executive Secretary by Governments or by persons, authorities or bodies as referred to in paragraph 19 on the standard form and must include the information in an official language of the United Nations. Each Government may adopt such procedures as it finds appropriate in preparing its consolidated claim. The Executive Secretary (or a Commissioner) will be available to answer questions or provide assistance to any Governments which may request it.

Document 69

Statement dated 5 August 1991 by the President of the Security Council concerning the sanctions regime

S/22904, 7 August 1991

Letter dated 6 August 1991 from the President of the Security Council addressed to the Secretary-General

I should be grateful if you would kindly arrange to circulate as a document of the Security Council the text of the following statement which I, in my capacity as President of the Council, made to the press on 5 August 1991, following the informal consultations held that same day:

"The members of the Security Council held informal consultations on 5 August pursuant to paragraph 28 of resolution 687 (1991), paragraph 6 of resolution 700 (1991) and paragraph 21 of resolution 687 (1991).

"After hearing all the opinions expressed in the course of the consultations, the President of the Council concluded that there was no agreement that the necessary conditions existed for a modification of the regimes established in paragraphs 22, 23, 24 and 25, as referred to in paragraph 28 of resolution 687 (1991); in paragraph 6 of resolution 700 (1991); and in paragraph 20, as referred to in paragraph 21 of resolution 687 (1991)."

(Signed) José AYALA LASSO
President of the Security Council

Document 70

Letter dated 6 August 1991 from the Secretary-General to the President of the Security Council concerning reductions in the strength of UNIKOM

S/22916, 9 August 1991; original in Spanish

I have the honour to refer to Security Council resolution 689 (1991), in which the Council approved my report of 5 April 1991 (S/22454), and in particular to its paragraph 13 concerning the strength of the United Nations Iraq-Kuwait Observation Mission (UNIKOM). I also refer to my report of 12 June 1991 to the Council (S/22692), in which I indicated my intention to undertake a further review of UNIKOM's strength and to make appropriate recommendations.

In the course of that review, Major-General Greindl, the Chief Military Observer of UNIKOM, has recommended that the following adjustments be made in the Mission, with a view to achieving greater efficiency and economy:

- reduce the number of military observers from 300 to 250;
- reduce the size of the medical unit;
- consolidate and reassign the tasks performed by the logistic units, with a small reduction in their strength;
- reduce the strength of the engineer unit from the present level of 293 to 85, with a subsequent reduc-

tion to 50 after the completion of work in support of the Boundary Demarcation Commission.

I have considered the above recommendations and have found them to be well-based. The situation within UNIKOM's area of operations remains calm, the number of border incidents and violations has decreased and the Mission continues to receive the cooperation of all concerned in the area. The eventual reduction of some 45 per cent in the Mission's strength will produce appreciable financial savings.

Accordingly, it is my intention to approach the troop-contributing countries in order to effect these adjustments as quickly as possible but in such a way as to minimize administrative and personal inconvenience for all concerned. Needless to say, I will continue to monitor the situation closely and revert, if necessary, to the Council on the question of the Mission's strength.

I should be grateful if you would bring this matter to the attention of the members of the Security Council.

(Signed) Javier PÉREZ DE CUÉLLAR

Document 71

Security Council resolution endorsing the Secretary-General's suggestion that compensation to be paid by Iraq should not exceed 30 per cent of the annual value of its oil exports

S/RES/705 (1991), 15 August 1991

The Security Council,

Having considered the note of 30 May 1991 which the Secretary-General submitted pursuant to paragraph 13 of his report of 2 May 1991 1/ and which was also annexed to his letter of 30 May 1991 addressed to the President of the Security Council 2/,

Acting under Chapter VII of the Charter of the United Nations,

1. *Expresses its appreciation* to the Secretary-General for his note of 30 May 1991;

2. *Decides* that, in accordance with the suggestion made by the Secretary-General in paragraph 7 of his note, compensation to be paid by Iraq, as arising from

section E of resolution 687 (1991) of 3 April 1991, shall not exceed 30 per cent of the annual value of its exports of petroleum and petroleum products;

3. *Decides also,* in accordance with paragraph 8 of the Secretary-General's note, to review the figure established in paragraph 2 above from time to time in light of data and assumptions contained in the Secretary-General's letter of 30 May 1991 2/ and other relevant developments.

1/ *Official Records of the Security Council, Forty-sixth Year, Supplement for April, May and June 1991,* document S/22559.
2/ Ibid, document S/22661.

Document 72

Security Council resolution authorizing the import of oil products originating from Iraq for a six-month period in order to finance United Nations operations mandated by Security Council resolution 687 (1991)

S/RES/706 (1991), 15 August 1991

The Security Council,

Recalling its previous relevant resolutions and in particular resolutions 661 (1990) of 6 August 1990, 686 (1991) of 2 March 1991, 687 (1991) of 3 April 1991, 688 (1991) of 5 April 1991, 692 (1991) of 20 May 1991, 699 (1991) of 17 June 1991 and 705 (1991) of 15 August 1991,

Taking note of the report dated 15 July 1991 of the inter-agency mission headed by the Executive Delegate of the Secretary-General for the United Nations Inter-Agency Humanitarian Programme for Iraq, Kuwait and the Iraq/Turkey and Iraq/Iran border areas, 1/

Concerned by the serious nutritional and health situation of the Iraqi civilian population as described in the report and by the risk of a further deterioration of this situation,

Concerned also that the repatriation or return of all Kuwaitis and third-State nationals or their remains present in Iraq on or after 2 August 1990, pursuant to paragraph 2 (*c*) of resolution 686 (1991) and paragraphs 30 and 31 of resolution 687 (1991), has not yet been fully carried out,

Taking note of the conclusions of the above-mentioned report, and in particular of the proposal for oil sales by Iraq to finance the purchase of foodstuffs, medicines and materials and supplies for essential civilian needs for the purpose of providing humanitarian relief,

Taking note also of the letters dated 14 April, 31 May, 6 June, 9 July and 22 July 1991 from the Minister for Foreign Affairs of Iraq and the Permanent Representative of Iraq to the United Nations to the Chairman of the Security Council Committee established by resolution 661 (1990) concerning the situation between Iraq and Kuwait, in regard to the export by Iraq of petroleum and petroleum products,

Convinced of the need to ensure equitable distribution of humanitarian relief assistance to all segments of the Iraqi civilian population through effective monitoring and transparency of the process,

Recalling and reaffirming in this regard its resolution 688 (1991), and in particular the importance which the Council attaches to Iraq's allowing unhindered access by international humanitarian organizations to all those in need of assistance in all parts of Iraq and making available all necessary facilities for their operation, and

in this connection stressing the continuing importance of the Memorandum of Understanding between the United Nations and the Government of Iraq signed on 18 April 1991, 2/

Recalling that, pursuant to resolutions 687 (1991), 692 (1991) and 699 (1991), Iraq is required to pay the full costs of the Special Commission and the International Atomic Energy Agency in carrying out the tasks authorized by section C of resolution 687 (1991), and that the Secretary-General, in the report of 15 July 1991 that he submitted to the Council pursuant to paragraph 4 of resolution 699 (1991), 3/ expressed the view that the most obvious way of obtaining financial resources from Iraq to meet those costs would be to authorize the sale of some Iraqi petroleum and petroleum products; recalling also that Iraq is required to pay its contributions to the United Nations Compensation Fund and half the costs of the Iraq-Kuwait Boundary Demarcation Commission; and recalling further that, in its resolutions 686 (1991) and 687 (1991), the Council demanded that Iraq return in the shortest possible time all Kuwaiti property seized by it and requested the Secretary-General to take steps to facilitate this demand,

Acting under Chapter VII of the Charter of the United Nations,

1. *Authorizes* all States, subject to the decision to be taken by the Security Council pursuant to paragraph 5 and notwithstanding the provisions of paragraphs 3 (*a*), 3 (*b*) and 4 of resolution 661 (1990), to permit, for the purposes specified in the present resolution, the import, during a period of six months from the date of adoption of the resolution pursuant to paragraph 5, of a quantity of petroleum and petroleum products originating in Iraq sufficient to produce a sum to be determined by the Council following receipt of the report of the Secretary-General requested in paragraph 5, a sum, however, not to exceed 1.6 billion United States dollars, subject to the following conditions:

1/ *Official Records of the Security Council, Forty-sixth Year, Supplement for July, August and September 1991*, document S/22799, annex.
2/ Ibid., *Supplement for April, May and June 1991*, document S/22663, annex.
3/ Ibid., *Supplement for July, August and September 1991*, document S/22792.

(a) Approval of each purchase of Iraqi petroleum and petroleum products by the Security Council Committee established by resolution 661 (1990) concerning the situation between Iraq and Kuwait, following notification to the Committee by the State concerned;

(b) Direct payment of the full amount of each purchase of Iraqi petroleum and petroleum products by the purchaser in the State concerned into an escrow account to be established by the United Nations and administered by the Secretary-General exclusively to meet the purposes of this resolution;

(c) Approval by the Council, following the report of the Secretary-General requested in paragraph 5, of a scheme for the purchase of foodstuffs, medicines and materials and supplies for essential civilian needs as referred to in paragraph 20 of resolution 687 (1991), in particular health related materials, all of which to be labelled to the extent possible as being supplied under this scheme, and for all feasible and appropriate United Nations monitoring and supervision for the purpose of assuring their equitable distribution to meet humanitarian needs in all regions of Iraq and to all categories of the Iraqi civilian population, as well as all feasible and appropriate management relevant to this purpose, such a United Nations role to be available if desired for humanitarian assistance from other sources;

(d) The total sum of purchases authorized in the present paragraph is to be released by successive decisions of the Committee in three equal portions after the Council has taken the decision provided for in paragraph 5 on the implementation of the present resolution; notwithstanding any other provision of the present paragraph, the Council may review the maximum total sum of purchases on the basis of an ongoing assessment of the needs and requirements;

2. *Decides* that a part of the sum in the account administered by the Secretary-General shall be made available to him to finance the purchase of foodstuffs, medicines and materials and supplies for essential civilian needs, as referred to in paragraph 20 of resolution 687 (1991), and to cover the cost to the United Nations of its activities under the present resolution and of other necessary humanitarian activities in Iraq;

3. *Decides also* that a part of the sum deposited in the account administered by the Secretary-General shall be used by him for appropriate payments to the United Nations Compensation Fund and to cover the full costs of carrying out the tasks authorized by section C of resolution 687 (1991), the full costs incurred by the United Nations in facilitating the return of all Kuwaiti property seized by Iraq, and half the costs of the Iraq-Kuwait Boundary Demarcation Commission;

4. *Decides further* that the percentage of the value of exports of petroleum and petroleum products from Iraq authorized under the present resolution to be paid to the Compensation Fund, as called for in paragraph 19 of resolution 687 (1991) and as defined in paragraph 6 of resolution 692 (1991), shall be the same as the percentage decided by the Council in paragraph 2 of resolution 705 (1991) for payments to the Fund, until such time as the Governing Council of the Fund decides otherwise;

5. *Requests* the Secretary-General to submit to the Council, within twenty days of the date of adoption of the present resolution, a report suggesting decisions to be taken on measures to implement paragraphs 1 (a), (b) and (c), on estimates of the humanitarian requirements of Iraq set out in paragraph 2 and on the amount of Iraq's financial obligations set out in paragraph 3 up to the end of the period of the authorization in paragraph 1, as well as on the method for taking the necessary legal measures to ensure that the purposes of the present resolution are carried out and the method for taking account of the costs of transportation of Iraqi petroleum and petroleum products;

6. *Also requests* the Secretary-General, in consultation with the International Committee of the Red Cross, to submit to the Council within twenty days of the date of adoption of the present resolution a report on activities undertaken in accordance with paragraph 31 of resolution 687 (1991) in connection with facilitating the repatriation or return of all Kuwaiti and third-State nationals or their remains present in Iraq on or after 2 August 1990;

7. *Calls upon* the Government of Iraq to provide to the Secretary-General and appropriate international organizations on the first day of the month immediately following the adoption of the present resolution and on the first day of each month thereafter until further notice, a detailed statement of the gold and foreign currency reserves it holds, whether in Iraq or elsewhere;

8. *Calls upon* all States to cooperate fully in the implementation of the present resolution;

9. *Decides* to remain seized of the matter.

Document 73

Security Council resolution demanding that Iraq provide full disclosure of its weapon programmes as required by Security Council resolution 687 (1991) and allow UNSCOM, the IAEA and their inspection teams immediate, unconditional and unrestricted access to sites they wish to inspect

S/RES/707 (1991), 15 August 1991

The Security Council,

Recalling its resolution 687 (1991) of 3 April 1991 and its other resolutions on this matter,

Recalling also the letter of 11 April 1991 from the President of the Security Council to the Permanent Representative of Iraq to the United Nations, 1/ in which he noted that on the basis of Iraq's written agreement 2/ to implement fully resolution 687 (1991), the preconditions for a cease-fire established in paragraph 33 of that resolution had been met,

Taking note with grave concern of the letters dated 26 and 28 June and 4 July 1991 from the Secretary-General to the President of the Security Council, conveying information received from the Executive Chairman of the Special Commission 3/ and from the high-level mission to Iraq 4/ which establishes Iraq's failure to comply with its obligations under resolution 687 (1991),

Recalling further the statement issued by the President of the Security Council on 28 June 1991 5/ requesting that a high-level mission consisting of the Executive Chairman of the Special Commission, the Director General of the International Atomic Energy Agency and the Under-Secretary-General for Disarmament Affairs be dispatched to meet with officials at the highest levels of the Government of Iraq at the earliest opportunity to obtain written assurance that Iraq will fully and immediately cooperate in the inspection of the locations identified by the Special Commission and present for immediate inspection any of those items that may have been transported from those locations,

Having taken note with dismay of the report of the high-level mission to the Secretary-General on the results of its meetings with the highest levels of the Iraqi Government, 6/

Gravely concerned by the information provided to the Council by the the International Atomic Energy Agency on 15 7/ and 25 July 1991 8/ regarding the actions of the Government of Iraq in flagrant violation of resolution 687 (1991),

Gravely concerned also by the letter of 7 July 1991 from the Minister for Foreign Affairs of Iraq addressed to the Secretary-General and subsequent statements and findings that Iraq's notifications of 18 and 28 April were incomplete and that certain related activities had been concealed, facts both of which constitute material breaches of its obligations under resolution 687 (1991),

Noting, having been informed by the letters dated 26 and 28 June and 4 July 1991 from the Secretary-General, that Iraq has not fully complied with all of its undertakings relating to the privileges, immunities and facilities to be accorded to the Special Commission and the Agency inspection teams mandated under resolution 687 (1991),

Affirming that in order for the Special Commission to carry out its mandate under paragraphs 9 (*b*) (i-iii) of resolution 687 (1991) to inspect Iraq's chemical and biological weapons and ballistic missile capabilities and to take possession of the elements referred to in that resolution for destruction, removal or rendering harmless, full disclosure on the part of Iraq as required in paragraph 9 (*a*) of resolution 687 (1991) is essential,

Affirming also that in order for the International Atomic Energy Agency, with the assistance and cooperation of the Special Commission, to determine what nuclear-weapon-usable material or any subsystems or components or any research, development, support or manufacturing facilities related to them need, in accordance with paragraph 13 of resolution 687 (1991), to be destroyed, removed or rendered harmless, Iraq is required to make a declaration of all its nuclear programmes, including any which it claims are for purposes not related to nuclear-weapon-usable material,

Affirming further that the aforementioned failures of Iraq to act in strict conformity with its obligations under resolution 687 (1991) constitute a material breach of its acceptance of the relevant provisions of that reso-

1/ S/22485.
2/ *Official Records of the Security Council, Forty-sixth Year, Supplement for April, May and June 1991*, document S/22456.
3/ Ibid., documents S/22739 and S/22743.
4/ Ibid., *Supplement for July, August and September 1991*, document S/22761.
5/ S/22746.
6/ *Official Records of the Security Council, Forty-sixth Year, Supplement for July, August and September 1991*, document S/22761, annex.
7/ Ibid., document S/22788.
8/ Ibid., document S/22837.

lution which established a cease-fire and provided the conditions essential to the restoration of peace and security in the region,

Affirming, moreover, that Iraq's failure to comply with the safeguards agreement it concluded with the International Atomic Energy Agency pursuant to the Treaty on the Non-Proliferation of Nuclear Weapons of 1 July 1968, 9/ as established by the Board of Governors of the Agency in its resolution of 18 July 1991, 10/ constitutes a breach of its international obligations,

Determined to ensure full compliance with resolution 687 (1991), and in particular its section C,

Acting under Chapter VII of the Charter of the United Nations,

1. *Condemns* Iraq's serious violation of a number of its obligations under section C of resolution 687 (1991) and of its undertakings to cooperate with the Special Commission and the International Atomic Energy Agency, which constitutes a material breach of the relevant provisions of that resolution which established a cease-fire and provided the conditions essential to the restoration of peace and security in the region;

2. *Also condemns* non-compliance by the Government of Iraq with its obligations under its safeguards agreement with the International Atomic Energy Agency, as established by the Board of Governors of the Agency in its resolution of 18 July 1991, 10/ which constitutes a violation of its commitments as a party to the Treaty on the Non-Proliferation of Nuclear Weapons of 1 July 1968; 9/

3. *Demands* that Iraq:

(*a*) Provide without further delay full, final and complete disclosure, as required by resolution 687 (1991), of all aspects of its programmes to develop weapons of mass destruction and ballistic missiles with a range greater than one hundred and fifty kilometres and of all holdings of such weapons, their components and production facilities and locations, as well as all other nuclear programmes, including any which it claims are for purposes not related to nuclear-weapon-usable material;

(*b*) Allow the Special Commission, the International Atomic Energy Agency and their inspection teams immediate, unconditional and unrestricted access to any and all areas, facilities, equipment, records and means of transportation which they wish to inspect;

(*c*) Cease immediately any attempt to conceal, move or destroy any material or equipment relating to its nuclear, chemical or biological weapons or ballistic missile programmes, or material or equipment relating to its other nuclear activities, without notification to and prior consent of the Special Commission;

(*d*) Make available immediately to the Special Commission, the Agency and their inspection teams any items to which they were previously denied access;

(*e*) Allow the Special Commission, the Agency and their inspection teams to conduct both fixed-wing and helicopter flights throughout Iraq for all relevant purposes, including inspection, surveillance, aerial surveys, transportation and logistics, without interference of any kind and upon such terms and conditions as may be determined by the Special Commission, and to make full use of their own aircraft and such airfields in Iraq as they may determine are most appropriate for the work of the Commission;

(*f*) Halt all nuclear activities of any kind, except for use of isotopes for medical, agricultural or industrial purposes, until the Council determines that Iraq is in full compliance with the present resolution and with paragraphs 12 and 13 of resolution 687 (1991) and the Agency determines that Iraq is in full compliance with its safeguards agreement with the Agency;

(*g*) Ensure the complete enjoyment, in accordance with its previous undertakings, of the privileges, immunities and facilities accorded to the representatives of the Special Commission and the Agency and guarantee their complete safety and freedom of movement;

(*h*) Immediately provide or facilitate the provision of any transportation and medical or logistical support requested by the Special Commission, the Agency and their inspection teams;

(*i*) Respond fully, completely and promptly to any questions or requests from the Special Commission, the Agency and their inspection teams;

4. *Determines* that Iraq retains no ownership interest in items to be destroyed, removed or rendered harmless pursuant to paragraph 12 of resolution 687 (1991);

5. *Requires* the Government of Iraq forthwith to comply fully and without delay with all its international obligations, including those set out in the present resolution, in resolution 687 (1991), in the Treaty on the Non-Proliferation of Nuclear Weapons and in its safeguards agreement with the International Atomic Energy Agency;

6. *Decides* to remain seized of this matter.

9/ United Nations, *Treaty Series*, vol. 729, No. 10485.
10/ *Official Records of the Security Council, Forty-sixth Year, Supplement for July, August and September 1991*, document S/22812, annex, appendix.

Document 74

Letter from the Permanent Representative of Iraq to the President of the Security Council concerning Iraq's views on Security Council resolutions 705 (1991) and 707 (1991)

S/22957, 16 August 1991

Letter dated 16 August 1991 from the Permanent Representative of Iraq to the United Nations addressed to the President of the Security Council

I have the honour to refer to the statement that I made before the Security Council at its meeting held on 15 August 1991. At that time I stated that, because of the time constraint and the length of the statements that I had prepared on the draft resolutions subsequently adopted by the Council on the same day as its resolutions 705, 706 and 707 (1991), I would present only a summary of Iraq's position with regard to resolutions 705 and 707.

Accordingly, I am sending you the full texts of the statements relating to our position on the two aforementioned resolutions.

I should be grateful if you would have these two statements circulated as a document of the Security Council.

(Signed) Abdul Amir A. AL -ANBARI
Ambassador
Permanent Representative

Annex I
Statement by Mr. Abdul Amir A. Al-Anbari to the Security Council at its meeting on 15 August 1991

Mr. President,

I should like to tell you once again how much my delegation appreciates the wisdom with which you have been directing the Council's work since you became President for the month of August.

The Council is meeting today to consider the recommendation made by the Secretary-General in his letter dated 31 May 1991 (S/22661), namely that the contribution to be levied on Iraq's petroleum reserves should be limited to 30 per cent. It also appears that the contribution would begin to be deducted as soon as petroleum exports resume. In this connection, I would like to reiterate what the Iraqi Minister for Foreign Affairs said in the letter which he sent to the President of the Security Council for May 1991, and also what was said in note No. 124 dated 27 May 1991 from the Iraqi Mission, annexed thereto, before explaining to the Council why it should lower the level of the contribution and defer the date on which the contribution would begin to be levied.

The Iraqi Mission has already sent the Secretary-General an official report (annexed to its note No. 72 of 29 April 1991) on Iraq's economic situation, for him to take into account in calculating the contribution referred to in paragraph 19 of Security Council resolution 687 (1991).

The Iraqi Mission also requested the Secretary-General, in its note No. 77 of 1 May 1991, to bring the aforesaid report to the attention of members of the Council. We appreciate the fact that, in proposing a 30 per cent ceiling, the Secretary-General has sought to take account both of the report and of the considerations mentioned in paragraph 19 of resolution 687 (1991). None the less, my Government, which is a daily witness to the sufferings endured by the Iraqi population of all social classes and to the economic difficulties faced by Iraq as a society and a State as a result of the continuation of the embargo imposed on Iraq on 6 August 1990, considers it useful to recall the three considerations which must, according to paragraph 19 mentioned above, be taken into account in determining the level of the contribution, namely:

– the requirements of the people of Iraq;
– Iraq's payment capacity in the light of its external debt service;
– the needs of the Iraqi economy.

These considerations are neither static nor fixed; on the contrary, they are constantly evolving: the situation is in fact becoming increasingly critical and is deteriorating steadily both as a result of the continued embargo on Iraqi imports and on Iraq's petroleum exports and because certain States members of the Sanctions Committee have managed to prevent the implementation of paragraph 23 of resolution 687 (1991) providing for exceptions to be made to the prohibition against the export of Iraqi petroleum in order to finance the purchase of foodstuffs and other products. The international press, in particular *The Washington Post* of 23 June 1991 and *The New York Times* of 25 June 1991, and also the study published by a Harvard University medical mission which visited Iraq, the exhaustive report entitled "Modern warfare and the environment: a case study of the Gulf war" published by Greenpeace last May and the even more detailed report of the mission headed by Prince Sadruddin

Aga Khan, Executive Delegate of the Secretary-General, have established objectively and impartially, with supporting facts and statistics, that the 42 days of air raids against Iraq inflicted damage on the economic and industrial infrastructure and on the means of modern life which, like the social, economic and health consequences of the bombing, was far more serious than reported in the military communiqués and preliminary assessments issued during and after the cessation of military operations. Likewise, the continuation of economic sanctions despite Iraq's acceptance of all the relevant Council resolutions and its full cooperation with the commissions and missions sent by the United Nations, and the failure of the Sanctions Committee to approve the resumption of petroleum exports under the exception provided for in paragraph 23 of resolution 687 (1991), are likely to perpetuate the consequences of the savage bombing raids on Iraq, thereby affecting future generations, the environment and Iraq's economic means of development. We are forced to ask ourselves, therefore, what is the real purpose of continuing the embargo against the Iraqi people and insisting that Iraq may not benefit from the exception provided for in paragraph 23 of resolution 687 (1991).

It is no exaggeration to say that continuing the embargo goes beyond the goals pursued by the Security Council and that the serious consequences of such a course, which include the spread of epidemics, will sooner or later affect the other countries of the region at the least.

Let me now give a conservative assessment of Iraq's financial obligations with respect to servicing its external debt, as well as of the basic needs of the Iraqi population in terms of food, medical and other supplies and the requirements for the reconstruction of the country's economic infrastructure as provided for in paragraph 19 of resolution 687.

On 31 December 1990, Iraq's external debt and financial commitments amounted to more than 13,118,000,000 dinars or more than $42,097,000,000, not taking into account the interest on these debts, namely an outstanding amount of $3.4 billion (one dinar equals about $3.20 at the official rate). These debts represent for the Iraqi economy 65 per cent of GDP, and 97 per cent of them are scheduled for repayment over the coming five years. For this reason, we have requested—as I shall explain below—a five-year grace period in order to enable us to honour these debts.

As for the basic needs, which relate also to imports or the replenishment of food reserves, primary commodities and the expenditures to be incurred on partially repairing the damaged facilities in the civilian and public sector and relaunching the development projects that were under way before the embargo, these are estimated at $140 billion, or $28 billion a year over the period

1991-1995. This figure represents only 60 per cent of the total expenditure, i.e. solely the portion in foreign currency.

Before concluding, I should like to recall paragraph 21 of resolution 687, which provides that the Security Council shall review the embargo on Iraqi imports, with a view to easing or lifting it in the light of the policies and practices of the Government of Iraq in terms of the implementation of all relevant resolutions of the Security Council. Despite its reservations regarding some of these resolutions, my Government has accepted them all and has sought to implement them in good faith and in full cooperation with the United Nations and the commissions and missions it has sent to Iraq with a view to the implementation of the resolutions in question. My Government has done practically everything called for in these resolutions, although their final implementation depends on the work programmes of the international commissions and missions established for this purpose. This may take a long time where certain aspects are concerned, such as the elimination of weapons of mass destruction, the demarcation of the international frontiers and other issues for which the Security Council has assigned responsibility to the Secretariat or the commissions or other bodies established for this purpose.

The measures taken by my Government in implementation of the Security Council resolutions have been described in detail by the Iraqi Minister for Foreign Affairs in his letter dated 8 June 1991 addressed to the Ministers for Foreign Affairs of some countries members of the Council; that letter is annexed hereto as an integral part of my statement.

Iraq accordingly has high hopes that the Council will review the provisions of the embargo—since more than 130 days have elapsed since the adoption of resolution 687 on 3 April 1991—and that it will take a decision on this subject in the light of the considerations set forth above.

Annex II
Letter dated 8 June 1991 from the Minister for Foreign Affairs of Iraq addressed to a number of the Ministers for Foreign Affairs of the States members of the Security Council

As you are well aware, the Iraqi Government accepted Security Council resolution 687 (1991) and gave notice of its acceptance in its letter of 6 April 1991 addressed to both the President of the Security Council and the Secretary-General. I should like on this occasion to confirm to you that the Iraqi Government has complied with the said resolution and adopted a positive attitude towards it ever since its adoption. Allow me to review for you the measures taken in this connection by the Government of Iraq.

1. In connection with section A of the resolution, concerning demarcation of the boundary between Iraq and Kuwait, the Iraqi Government has appointed its representative to the Boundary Demarcation Commission, which held its first session of meetings in New York from 23 to 24 May 1991. Iraq's representative participated actively, in a constructive and cooperative spirit, in the work of that session.

2. In connection with section B of resolution 687 (1991), concerning deployment of the United Nations Iraq-Kuwait Observation Mission (UNIKOM), the competent Iraqi authorities have received the Chief Military Observer, Major-General Günther Greindl, on several occasions in Baghdad since his appointment, together with his assistants. Agreement was reached at these meetings on all the requirements for the deployment of UNIKOM in the demilitarized zone established under the resolution, which came into effect on 9 May 1991.

Cooperation between the competent Iraqi authorities and UNIKOM continues through the channels designated for that purpose between, respectively, the Iraqi Government, UNIKOM headquarters and the United Nations Secretariat.

3. In connection with section C of the resolution, which calls for a series of undertakings to dispense with weapons of mass destruction and neither to use, develop, construct nor acquire any such weapons, Iraq has deposited the instrument whereby the Republic of Iraq ratifies the Convention on the Prohibition of the Development, Production and Stockpiling of Bacteriological (Biological) and Toxin Weapons and on Their Destruction, of 10 April 1972. Iraq has also affirmed its unconditional commitment to its obligations under the Geneva Protocol for the Prohibition of the Use in War of Asphyxiating, Poisonous or Other Gases, and of Bacteriological Methods of Warfare, signed at Geneva on 17 June 1925. In addition, the Iraqi Government has provided details of the locations, amounts and types of items relating to chemical weapons and ballistic missiles specified in the resolution and agreed to an inspection of the sites concerned, as laid down in the resolution.

Iraq has also unconditionally undertaken not to use, develop, construct or acquire any of the items specified in the resolution. It has affirmed its obligations under the Treaty on the Non-Proliferation of Nuclear Weapons of 1 July 1968 and unconditionally agreed not to acquire or develop nuclear weapons or nuclear-weapons-usable material. Iraq informed the International Atomic Energy Agency (IAEA), in a letter dated 27 April 1991 from the Minister for Foreign Affairs, that it was prepared to cooperate with the Agency in implementing the provisions of the resolution: the letter was accompanied by tables providing information on Iraq's nuclear facilities.

Iraq has also provided detailed information on the situation with regard to other weapons covered by the resolution to the Special Commission established to implement section C.

In a letter dated 17 May 1991, Iraq agreed to the proposals contained in the Secretary-General's letter of 6 May 1991 concerning the privileges and immunities of the Special Commission and its visiting teams.

The nuclear weapons inspection team visited Iraq from 14 to 22 May 1991. On 23 May 1991, IAEA issued a statement affirming that Iraq had cooperated fully and responded to all the requests submitted by the inspection team. A chemical weapons inspection team, accompanied by the Chairman of the Special Commission, is to visit Iraq from 9 to 15 June in order to begin its mission. Iraq has made all the necessary arrangements to ensure that the inspection team's mission is a success.

4. In connection with section D of the resolution, which relates to the return of Kuwaiti property, Mr. J. Richard Foran, Assistant Secretary-General and official responsible for coordinating the return of such property, visited Iraq twice during the month of May 1991. The competent Iraqi authorities expressed their readiness to hand over the Kuwaiti property of which Iraq had already notified the Secretariat of the United Nations. A Kuwaiti civilian aircraft was, in fact, handed over at Amman on 11 May 1991. Mr. Foran also undertook a wide-ranging field visit and saw for himself the gold, coins, banknotes, civilian aircraft, museum antiquities and books that will be returned to Kuwait immediately an agreement is reached establishing a location for the handing over, it being understood that it is this property whose handing over Mr. Foran has determined should have priority at the present stage. The same procedures will doubtless be applied to other Kuwaiti property.

5. In connection with sections E and F, which relate to compensation and the lifting of sanctions, no measures are required on the part of Iraq.

6. In connection with section G of the resolution, the competent Iraqi authorities have taken and are continuing to take measures to repatriate all Kuwaiti and third-country nationals, and they have provided lists of their names and have facilitated the access of the delegation of the International Committee of the Red Cross (ICRC) in Baghdad to all such persons wherever detained. It should be mentioned that the number of those freed and repatriated has reached 6,366 (6,289 Kuwaitis, 36 Americans, 5 Italians, 13 Saudis, 17 Frenchmen, 1 Spaniard, 2 Brazilians, 1 Norwegian, 1 Uruguayan and 1 Irishman). The competent Iraqi authorities are still diligently searching for missing subjects of coalition countries with a view to finding them and repatriating them following registration by the ICRC delegation. The com-

petent Iraqi authorities have directly facilitated all matters relating to the work of the ICRC delegation in the registration of Kuwaiti nationals present in Iraq, thereby enabling the delegation to register more than 3,000 Kuwaitis, and they have endeavoured to return the remains of 15 subjects of the coalition countries.

7. In connection with section H, which relates to international terrorism, it should be mentioned that Iraq is a party to the international conventions relating to numerous aspects of this matter and that it abides by the obligations set forth therein. Iraq has not supported any terrorist activities.

In providing you with these clarifications, we are prompted by the hope that you will deem it appropriate to take account of the facts set forth above in any review that the Security Council might intend to make of Iraq's position on the implementation of Security Council resolution 687 (1991).

(*Signed*) Ahmed HUSSEIN
Minister for Foreign Affairs of the Republic of Iraq

Annex III
Statement of the Permanent Representative of Iraq to the United Nations concerning the draft resolution contained in document S/22942 of 14 August 1991, made to the Security Council on 15 August 1991

It is to be noted that the draft resolution is based on two underlying elements which feature in all of its preambular and operative paragraphs and which can be summed up as follows: the circumstances that presented themselves to the second inspection team in the course of its visit to Iraq from 22 June to 3 July 1991, as referred to in the third, fourth, fifth, eighth, ninth and tenth preambular paragraphs; and the resolution of the Board of Governors of the International Atomic Energy Agency (IAEA) of 18 July 1991, as mentioned in the twelfth preambular paragraph.

1. Iraq has already explained in a clear and unequivocal manner and on more than one occasion the circumstances encountered by the second inspection team. The high-level mission led by Mr. Rolf Ekéus was informed during its visit to Iraq of the details of these circumstances, and the Iraqi Government, at the highest levels, provided unambiguous assurances that the Iraqi authorities would provide all possible facilities to the inspection teams. In its report, the high-level mission referred to these assurances and stated that the future would show the extent to which the Government of Iraq would give effect to them. Since that time, several teams have visited Iraq, and a nuclear inspection team and a biological inspection team are still there at this moment.

Iraq provided the third nuclear inspection team with all possible facilities and furnished it with an enormous amount of information, as was stated by the Director-General of IAEA at the news conference he held at United Nations Headquarters in New York on 30 July 1991. The leader of the fourth team, Mr. David Kay, has told the news agencies in Baghdad that his team is making progress, that it has obtained much information and that the Iraqis are cooperating with it. The other teams that have visited Iraq have given no indication that they encountered obstacles or any significant problems in their work.

Is it then reasonable, more than a month after the circumstances experienced by the second inspection team and given the excellent experience of cooperation with all the teams that have visited Iraq during this month, to maintain that Iraq is not cooperating and that it is not meeting its obligations? We had been hoping that the Security Council would express its satisfaction at the cooperation that the United Nations teams are receiving from Iraq rather than anticipating that it would adopt a new resolution condemning Iraq because of one incident. Most of the members of the same second inspection team are now in Iraq; they are receiving unparalleled cooperation; information is being exchanged on an immediate basis; and the Council can solicit the opinion of the team leader presently in Baghdad. Is this not one more indication of Iraq's commitment to the Security Council resolution in question? The Council must take this into account.

2. The Board of Governors of IAEA adopted a resolution on 18 July 1991 condemning Iraq for non-compliance with the Agency's safeguards system and informed the Security Council accordingly under the provisions of article XII.C of the Agency's statute. IAEA did not make this notification because it was a task assigned to it under the terms of Security Council resolution 687 (1991), and the notification is therefore no part of that resolution. The situation recorded by the Board of Governors is one that existed before the adoption of Security Council resolution 687 (1991), and that situation came to an end owing to the destruction inflicted on Iraq's nuclear installations. From the legal point of view, therefore, it is not valid that the present draft resolution, which has the appearance of being intended for the purpose of following up the implementation of Security Council resolution 687 (1991), should be based on a situation that existed prior to the adoption of that resolution. In no legal system does a law or a resolution have retroactive effect. The twelfth preambular paragraph cannot therefore be a consideration for the present draft resolution, and the same applies to operative paragraphs 2 and 3.

Moreover, the resolution adopted by the Board of Governors on 18 July contains two operative paragraphs that should be taken into account. The first, paragraph 3, calls upon Iraq to take remedial measures, and it has done this by means of the letters it addressed to the Director-General of IAEA on 10 and 12 July 1991 and the letters exchanged by the chief of the third United Nations inspection team and his Iraqi counterpart. There are no longer in Iraq any nuclear materials, installations or sites that have not been declared. Another operative paragraph of the same resolution, paragraph 7, refers the matter to the next regular session of the IAEA General Conference. This is the supreme authority of the Agency, and most of the world's countries are represented there. Does the present draft resolution seek to prejudge any resolution that might be adopted by the IAEA General Conference and thus deprive the General Conference of the right to decide on a matter that is within its jurisdiction? Under the terms of the Agency's statute, it can take any necessary measures against any of its members. Operative paragraph 2 of the present draft resolution prejudges a matter that is before the next session of the IAEA General Conference by virtue of a resolution of the Board of Governors.

3. With regard to paragraph 3 of the present draft resolution, we should like to assure the Council that the technicians on both sides, the members of the United Nations teams and their Iraqi counterparts, have reached agreement on clear procedures and have put them into effect in such a way as to ensure the convenience of the members of the teams and the speedy completion of the inspection task and to reduce the number of inspection sites to the extent possible so as to facilitate the future task of the teams. Agreement is reached between the two sides on the movement of materials and parts, and times and locations are established before movement is begun. This happened while the third inspection team was there, and it is now taking place while the fourth team is there, without any complications or superfluous bureaucratic formalities. The Council should welcome and record its satisfaction at the establishment of this mechanism, one that is facilitating the work of the inspection teams and reducing the amount of time lost.

4. In light of the foregoing, we feel that the resolution has no substance since it is largely covered by the agreement on the status, privileges and immunities of the Special Commission, IAEA and the inspection teams, an agreement which has been accepted by Iraq. From our point of view, this agreement is workable when the circumstances for cooperation and coordination are present and in our opinion they have come into being and the last month has demonstrated that they have become more firmly established.

5. We should like to ask the Special Commission and the IAEA inspection teams whether they have entered locations that they were previously prohibited from entering or were prevented from inspecting the items that they contain. According to our information, not a single location remains, as is indicated in the reports of the inspection teams, that the teams have not entered and whose contents they have not inspected. More precisely, there was one location around which commotion arose on 28 June 1991. The chief of the third nuclear inspection team agreed to the movement of the items there, equipment and machinery, to the Tuwaitha site. The removal was supervised by two of the members of the United Nations team, the team registered and photographed all of the items, and they were unloaded from the trucks under the supervision of members of the team. The United Nations team released the non-nuclear equipment for use in the reconstruction of basic services in Iraq, and the trucks left the Tuwaitha site under the supervision and with the agreement of the team. All of this is established in the lists and inventories exchanged by the third United Nations team and the Iraqi side. The equipment was stored in an orderly fashion in order to facilitate future inspection by the team. All of this took place quietly and without uproar. So what reason can there now be that the present draft resolution should contain operative paragraph 3? The Council should rather express its satisfaction at the practical steps that have been taken in this regard.

6. With regard to paragraph 3 (v), which refers to the right of inspection teams to use aircraft, we should like to state that Iraq is not against the use of helicopters or fixed-wing aircraft by inspection teams. What it would, however, like to make clear in this respect is that there are difficulties in ensuring the safety of such flights because of the present situation with regard to aspects of logistics, communications and control following the war.

7. Paragraph 4 of the draft resolution determines that Iraq retains no ownership interest in items to be destroyed, removed or rendered harmless. This text is not realistic from the detailed, technical point of view. It is neither wise nor economically feasible to abandon wrecked materials and equipment without returning them to use in other, civilian, industrial roles. Can it be that the scrap metal of a piece of equipment that has been destroyed should be abandoned rather than put to use by melting it down and reusing it for civilian purposes? Can it be that damaged copper piping, for example, should be left lying useless rather than be reused in meeting the Iraqi people's need for basic services? If the inspection teams render a machine harmless, then why cannot Iraq retain its right to use it for another purpose in which there is no harm? From these and other examples, we can see that this paragraph is not realistic and causes unjustifiable material damage to the people of Iraq.

The draft resolution before you not only lacks legal justification but constitutes a fresh violation of Iraq's sovereignty and imposes upon it new burdens under a veil of international legitimacy by seeking to have the Council adopt arbitrary resolutions. This reveals to the entire world that these resolutions are officially adopted by the majority of the Council but are actually part of an iniquitous and hostile policy directed against Iraq by means of which the neo-colonialist States are seeking to make of Iraq a deterrent example to other third world countries and a field of experiment for their schemes to intervene in the affairs of the other countries of the world in order to prevent them from being able to achieve economic development and exercise control over their oil and other natural resources and in order to impose their political hegemony on them.

It is saddening that certain Western States that are permanent members of the Council should make of it an instrument for the pursuit of illegal and hostile actions detrimental to peace and security in the region. They do so under the cover of international legitimacy and by seeking to have new resolutions adopted on one pretext or another in order to tighten their stranglehold on the Iraqi people and hold it hostage to their embargo and their economic sanctions. As long as the Iraqi people does not submit to the wishes of these States, its oil resources are to be held in pawn by them after the countries in question have consolidated their control of other sources of oil in the Arabian Gulf.

Document 75

Letter dated 23 August 1991 from the Secretary-General to the President of the Security Council concerning adjustments in UNIKOM

S/22977, 26 August 1991

Letter dated 23 August 1991 from the Secretary-General addressed to the President of the Security Council

I should like to refer to my letter of 6 August 1991 (S/29916), in which I informed you of my intention to make certain adjustments in the United Nations Iraq-Kuwait Observer Mission (UNIKOM).

Since then, the level of activity on the Iraq-Kuwait border has increased and, as you are aware, an incident in which shots were fired occurred on 14 August. In view of the circumstances, I consider it advisable not to proceed, for the time being, with reducing the strength of the military observers from 300 to 250, as I had intended. I shall continue to monitor the situation closely, and, if necessary, shall report to the Security Council.

I should be grateful if you would inform the members of the Security Council of this matter.

(*Signed*) Javier PÉREZ DE CUÉLLAR

Document 76

Letter from the Chargé d'affaires a.i. of the Permanent Mission of Iraq to the United Nations to the Secretary-General transmitting a letter dated 28 August 1991 from the Minister for Foreign Affairs of Iraq concerning Iraq's views on Security Council resolution 707 (1991)

S/22998, 3 September 1991

Letter dated 1 September 1991 from the Chargé d'affaires a.i. of the Permanent Mission of Iraq to the United Nations addressed to the Secretary-General

On instructions from my Government, I have the honour to transmit herewith a letter from Mr. Ahmad Hussein, Minister for Foreign Affairs of the Republic of Iraq, dated 28 August 1991, concerning Security Council resolution 707 (1991).

I should be grateful if you would have this letter and its annex circulated as an official document of the Security Council.

(*Signed*) Sabah Talat KADRAT
Deputy Permanent Representative

Annex
Letter dated 28 August 1991 from the Minister for
Foreign Affairs of Iraq addressed to
the Secretary-General

I have the honour to refer to Security Council resolution 707 (1991).

The Government of Iraq considers that this resolution is unwarranted and that, like many of the other resolutions of the Council, it was adopted for motives based on the desire of a number of influential parties in the Security Council to harm Iraq and to contrive yet more pretexts for the non-implementation of the particular provisions of the Security Council resolutions from which Iraq may benefit by a lifting or mitigation of the unjust economic embargo imposed upon it. Iraq has fulfilled all of its obligations under the terms of resolution 687 (1991) in the manner requested by the inspection teams in general and the nuclear inspection teams in particular. It has done so by declaring all aspects of the Iraqi nuclear programme, whether in letters addressed to you or in those exchanged by the Chief of the Iraqi team and the Chiefs of the inspection teams that have visited Iraq. This has also been done in the seminars held, by answering all questions asked, and in the direct meetings held with those responsible for the nuclear programme and with research workers. This demonstrates the full cooperation that has been shown by the Iraqi authorities concerned.

For greater precision, we should like to state our view with regard to the provisions of the operative paragraphs of the Security Council resolution in question.

1. With regard to paragraphs 1 and 2, in which Iraq is condemned twice in the same resolution, it must be said that Iraq has adhered to all of its undertakings under the terms of Security Council resolution 687 (1991). It has, moreover, complied with the safeguards agreement concluded with the International Atomic Energy Agency (IAEA). It has done so by means of the full disclosure of all aspects of the Iraqi nuclear programme and the measures it has taken on remedial action in implementation of the resolution adopted by the IAEA Board of Governors on 18 July 1991. We should like once more to ask the question we have addressed to IAEA on more than one occasion: what more is now required of us, after all the measures we have taken and all the information we have provided, so that Iraq may meet all of its obligations under the terms of the resolution?

2. With regard to paragraph 3 (i) of resolution 707 (1991), Iraq has already provided full, final and complete disclosure, as required by resolution 687 (1991), of all aspects of its programmes. There are no programmes of this type, of any kind whatever, that Iraq has not declared.

3. Since 28 June 1991, the inspection teams have noted no obstacle to their work in gaining access to any and all areas, facilities, equipment, records and means of transportation which they wish to inspect, as demanded in paragraph 3 (ii). We should like, in this connection, to refer to the recent reports of the inspection teams, including that of the third nuclear inspection team contained in document GOV/INF/621 of 2 August 1991, in which reference is made to the full cooperation provided by the Iraqi side. We should like to ask once again: what site is there that a team has not been permitted to enter and inspect?

4. With regard to paragraph 3 (iii), the Government of Iraq took the decision, as of 28 June 1991, to cease any movement or destruction of any material or equipment relating to Security Council resolution 687 (1991). With the arrival of the third nuclear inspection team, agreement was reached by the Chief of the team and his Iraqi counterpart on the movement of certain equipment, after it had been seen by the team, to an appropriate location so as to facilitate future monitoring and inspection by the inspection teams. Certain of these measures were taken under the supervision of members of the third team, and the fourth team once again verified them. Agreement was also reached with the Chief of the fourth team on the continued movement and assembly of those materials and equipment that the team had seen and recorded to the collection sites on which the two parties had agreed for the purpose of facilitating future inspections.

5. Paragraph 3 (iv) refers to the concomitants of an issue which has become part of the past and which was over and done with even before the arrival of the third nuclear inspection team in the first week of July 1991. The third team examined all items and, together with the Iraqi side, undertook its removal to the locations agreed on. We therefore wish to ask what items are still outside the supervision of the inspection teams and to what were they denied access.

We should be very grateful if you or the Special Committee would kindly inform us about such items as are referred to in paragraph 3 (iv). Since there were no such items, we wonder what were the grounds for including this paragraph in the resolution.

6. With regard to paragraph 3 (v), Iraq has already given its opinion concerning aircraft flights. Although Iraq has no objections to that in principle, all that Iraq wishes to make clear, for its part, is that there are issues relating to administration, communications and logistics that must be taken into consideration in order to guarantee the safety of the aircraft and their crews and passengers and that Iraq is most concerned about that and hopes that the issue will be resolved by agreement and coopera-

tion with the competent Iraqi authorities, in order to safeguard the security and safety of all.

7. With regard to the halting of all nuclear activities of any kind, as referred to in paragraph 3 (vi), although this goes beyond the measures set forth in resolution 687 (1991), from the scientific and the practical viewpoints there is no longer any nuclear activity, even in the most elementary sense, following the comprehensive destruction of Iraqi nuclear locations—reactors, laboratories, materials and other. This is referred to also in the report of the Director-General of the International Atomic Energy Agency.

I wish to point out that all the requirements of privileges and immunities and travel facilities of the inspection teams and medical care for them, referred to in paragraphs 3 (vii) and 3 (viii), have been made available in full and to the furthest extent possible in the light of the economic embargo imposed on Iraq. The recent reports of the inspection teams are the best testimony to that.

8. With regard to paragraph 5, Iraq reaffirms its full commitment to its international undertakings, including the Non-Proliferation Treaty and the Safeguards Agreement with the International Atomic Energy Agency.

The preambular and operative paragraphs of resolution 707 (1991) are based on the provisions of resolution 687 (1991), but it deliberately overlooks the rights of Iraq set forth in resolution 687 (1991). In this connection, we wish to inquire what is requested of Iraq, in order that it may show even greater good will in demonstrating its compliance with Security Council resolutions.

We wish also to ask how long the Security Council will disregard the rights of Iraq laid down in Security Council resolutions and when the iniquitous economic embargo imposed on its people will be lifted.

(*Signed*) Ahmad HUSSEIN
Minister for Foreign Affairs of the Republic of Iraq
Baghdad, 28 August 1991

Document 77

Report of the Secretary-General on UNIKOM

S/23000, 3 September 1991

1. The present further interim report on the United Nations Iraq-Kuwait Observation Mission (UNIKOM) contains a summary of events since my last report dated 12 June 1991 (S/22692).

2. UNIKOM continued to monitor the demilitarized zone (DMZ) established by the Security Council. This was generally respected and the number of violations decreased. The following violations of the DMZ were recorded:

(a) UNIKOM observed a number of minor incursions by armed and unarmed military personnel. The Iraqi forces accounted for 6, and the Kuwaiti and allied forces for 36 such incursions;

(b) UNIKOM observed 10 violations by Iraqi police and 5 by Kuwaiti police of the limitation on the arms that they are permitted to carry in the DMZ. As previously reported (S/22692, para. 9), both Iraq and Kuwait have agreed to limit such armaments to sidearms only;

(c) UNIKOM observed 36 violations of the DMZ by military aircraft of the type used by the forces allied with Kuwait.

3. UNIKOM raised the violations of the DMZ with the party concerned, usually in writing, with a view to having action taken to prevent a recurrence. Both Iraq and Kuwait gave repeated assurances to this effect and,

in UNIKOM's judgement, they continued to extend their cooperation to the Mission.

4. Both sides indicated misgivings about the limitation on the armament of the police. They pointed out that that made it difficult for the police to deal effectively with smugglers or others who were better armed. While acknowledging that difficulty, UNIKOM nevertheless considered it necessary to maintain the limitation for the time being in order to reduce the potential for serious incidents.

5. UNIKOM received eight written complaints from Iraq and six from Kuwait. It investigated those complaints and was able in 11 cases to establish the facts through its own observations and informed the complaining party accordingly.

6. One of the purposes of UNIKOM is to deter violations of the boundary between Iraq and Kuwait through its presence in and surveillance of the DMZ. Pending demarcation of that boundary by the Iraq-Kuwait Boundary Demarcation Commission established under paragraph 3 of resolution 687 (1991) and in order to avoid friction and incidents, UNIKOM has established the principle that Iraqi and Kuwaiti officials, including police, should maintain a reasonable distance of about 1,000 metres from the boundary line shown on UNIKOM

maps. UNIKOM is using a British map, which it has given to both sides for reference. They have agreed to work with it as a practical arrangement to facilitate UNIKOM's task and without prejudice to their positions concerning the boundary.

7. During the reporting period, Iraq deployed 4 border police centres and 10 border police posts in the DMZ. Five of the posts are on the Kuwaiti side of the boundary line shown on UNIKOM's map; 2 are closer to it than 1,000 metres, on the Iraqi side. UNIKOM made lengthy and intensive efforts to have Iraq move the seven posts further back. However, the Iraqi authorities maintained that those posts had been in place before 2 August 1990 and that pulling them back would prejudice Iraq's position regarding the demarcation of the border. Once the demarcation had taken place, Iraq would comply with the "reasonable distance" principle.

8. Apart from a border post on the main road south of Safwan, Kuwait has deployed only one police post, in the southern sector. The Kuwaiti authorities maintained contact with UNIKOM regarding the deployment of additional posts and reiterated their willingness to comply with the "reasonable distance" principle, if the Iraqi authorities did so too.

9. UNIKOM recorded the following shooting incidents involving Iraqi and Kuwaiti military and police personnel:

(a) On 28 July 1991, three Kuwaiti soldiers in uniform fired a light machine-gun from a military vehicle at an Iraqi police centre in the central sector. The vehicle left when a UNIKOM patrol appeared. The Iraqis did not return fire and there were no casualties;

(b) On 31 July 1991, a Kuwaiti police patrol reported to UNIKOM observers that its vehicle was stuck in the sand about 1 kilometre north-east of an Iraqi police post. The UNIKOM observers found that the vehicle carried two rifles, hand grenades and ammunition. Iraqi police, who had approached the vehicle, claimed that the Kuwaiti personnel had fired at them;

(c) On 14 August 1991, an incident developed between Iraqi personnel stationed at a police post in the southern sector and a convoy of Kuwaiti police and senior officials accompanied by UNIKOM observers on a joint reconnaissance of proposed police posts. This incident was the subject of a communication from the Permanent Representative of Kuwait to the President of the Security Council (S/22950). A UNIKOM team investigated the incident and questioned persons involved on both sides. The Iraqi policemen claimed that the incident began when their post came under fire from the Kuwaiti convoy. The UNIKOM observers accompanying the convoy, which was stretched out over a long distance, were at its very end and did not notice any firing. The investigating team

was unable to confirm that the Iraqi post had been fired upon. It was also unable to establish which side opened fire in an exchange that took place when two of the Kuwaiti vehicles became bogged down in the sand, were left behind and were then approached by a group of 12 to 15 Iraqi policemen. The firing at that location was heard by the personnel of UNIKOM observation post No. S6. There were no casualties and the Kuwaiti policemen were able to depart in one vehicle. UNIKOM observers came to the spot and informed the Iraqi policemen that they were on Kuwaiti territory and should return to Iraqi territory. The Iraqis initially rejected this and attempted to take possession of the remaining Kuwaiti vehicle, but they withdrew upon the arrival of a UNIKOM patrol and helicopter. The disabled vehicle was returned to the Kuwaiti authorities. The UNIKOM team was not able to establish who initiated the exchange of fire. However, UNIKOM has protested to the Iraqi authorities the violation of Kuwaiti territory and of the limitation on the arms to be carried in the DMZ.

10. The maintenance of law and order, notably the enforcement of laws regulating the movement of persons and goods across the border, is the responsibility of the government authorities concerned. However, as a result of illegal movement across the border, some tension has arisen during the reporting period, which has been of concern to UNIKOM.

11. One source of tension and the site of several shooting incidents was an illegal market, which was held in the southern sector of the DMZ. It is known by UNIKOM as the "sheep market", although alcohol and arms are traded as well as livestock. When UNIKOM first discovered the market in May it was located in Iraq. Following a shooting incident on 27 June, in which three Iraqi policemen were fatally injured, the market ceased for two weeks, after which it reappeared in a new location closer to the border. In mid-August, it moved to the Kuwaiti side of the DMZ. UNIKOM has reported its observations to the Governments of Iraq and Kuwait and both have taken measures to curb access to the market.

12. In a new development since the beginning of August, UNIKOM observed on several occasions groups of Iraqis, apparently civilians, collecting weapons, ammunition and other battlefield items on the Kuwaiti side of the DMZ. In addition, UNIKOM was informed by the Kuwaiti authorities that a number of such persons were arrested well inside Kuwaiti territory. UNIKOM raised the matter with the Iraqi authorities, who denied any involvement by Iraqi officials or soldiers but could not exclude the possibility that civilians had crossed the border. The Iraqi authorities explained that they had offered a financial reward to their citizens for the delivery of ammunition and other military items that were still

scattered throughout large areas and posed a danger to the population. The Iraqi authorities undertook to do what they could to curb crossings into Kuwait. For their part, the Kuwaiti authorities informed UNIKOM that they had arranged to have the southern sector cleared of military items and were considering a similar project for the islands of Bubiyan and Failaka.

13. In the afternoon of 28 August 1991, UNIKOM was informed by a Kuwaiti army liaison officer that there had been an incident involving firing between Iraqi and Kuwaiti personnel on, and in the vicinity of, the Kuwaiti island of Bubiyan, outside the DMZ. The incident has been the subject of communications addressed to the President of the Security Council by the Permanent Representative of Kuwait (S/22990) and by the Chargé d'affaires a.i. of the Permanent Mission of Iraq (S/22993).

14. UNIKOM has carried out an investigation, in the course of which Bubiyan Island was visited and some of the Kuwaiti military personnel directly involved, as well as some of the Iraqis taken into custody during the incident were questioned by the investigating team. The UNIKOM team also visited the Al Faw peninsula in Iraq. The following is a summary of its findings:

(a) In the afternoon of 28 August 1991, a Kuwaiti Coast Guard detachment comprising 4 boats took custody of 11 Iraqi fishing boats and 1 speedboat in the waters off Bubiyan Island and of their crews, 45 persons in all. No one was taken from Bubiyan, and UNIKOM received no further information regarding earlier reports that some Iraqis had hidden on Bubiyan;

(b) According to its commander, the Kuwaiti detachment came under small arms fire from Ras al Qaid and Ras al Barshah on Bubiyan. The UNIKOM team was not able to find evidence of firing at those locations. There were no injuries and none of the vessels showed signs of having been hit;

(c) The crew of the speedboat and at least some of the crews of the fishing boats had collected ammunition and other items (e.g. military-style blankets) on Bubiyan. They stated that they had done so for financial gain. UNIKOM has had independent reports of trading in ammunition in southern Iraq. The UNIKOM team did not find, nor was it shown, evidence that there had been weapons on the Iraqi boats;

(d) A senior Kuwaiti army liaison officer stated that, during the incident on 28 August, 12 Iraqi navy speedboats left the Al Faw jetty to come to the assistance of the Iraqi boats off Bubiyan. The jetty mentioned by the Kuwaiti officer is the only marine facility that UNIKOM has observed on the southern shore of the Al Faw peninsula. It offers no protection and can be used only by small craft, which are grounded at low tide. The jetty is about 13 kilometres from UNIKOM observation post No. 6 and is visited by daily patrols from there. Those patrols have not, so far, observed any naval presence. Similarly, the UNIKOM personnel observing the access to the Khowr Abd Allah south of Umm Qasr had not observed any movement of Iraqi vessels;

(e) The UNIKOM team interviewed Kuwaiti air-force pilots, who stated that on the day of the incident, at 1710 hours local time and after the Coast Guard detachment had left the area with the captured vessels, they had engaged and sunk seven boats off Bubiyan. They did not know from where those boats had come. The UNIKOM team saw from the air the wrecks of two boats in the vicinity of Ras al Qayd but was not able to establish their identity or when they had been sunk.

15. Major-General Greindl and his staff are conscious of the implications of the incidents described in this report. They will continue to maintain a high level of vigilance in the performance of the tasks entrusted to them by the Security Council.

Document 78

Report of the Secretary-General recommending procedures for the sale of Iraqi oil and transmitting estimates of humanitarian requirements in Iraq (extract)

S/23006, 4 September 1991

...

I. *Preliminary observations*

2. A careful study of the relevant provisions of Security Council resolution 706 (1991) and consideration of the measures that may be devised to implement them reveals that a number of those provisions necessitate an approach from a policy point of view, while some others require elucidation for administrative or procedural purposes.

3. For success in implementing the programme envisaged in resolution 706 (1991) pursuant to the provisions of paragraphs 1 to 4 thereof, it will be imperative

to secure the fullest cooperation of Iraq and Turkey, two parties most closely connected to the operation of the programme; on the part of the former, in the production and supply of petroleum and petroleum products for sale and in the distribution of foodstuffs, medicines, materials and supplies for essential civilian needs in Iraq, and on the part of the latter in facilitating an uninterrupted flow of Iraqi petroleum for export via the oil pipeline from Iraq through Turkey, bearing in mind that that route is at present the only viable means of moving bulk quantities of Iraqi petroleum for export. Accordingly, informal contacts have been made with the Iraqi and Turkish authorities for the purpose of exploring and establishing such cooperation.

4. Resolution 706 (1991) stipulates the parameters within which proceeds from the sale of Iraqi petroleum and petroleum products would be devoted to providing the humanitarian and other essential civilian requirements so desperately needed by the people of Iraq, as the Government of Iraq has consistently expressed and as the international community fully recognizes.

5. The Turkish authorities have indicated that the Turkish oil pipeline company BOTAS is prepared to reopen the oil flow, storage and loading operations and that there are at present about 1.58 million barrels of Iraqi petroleum in storage at the Turkish port of Yumurtalik ready for immediate marketing. They have also stated that the figure for the transportation costs to BOTAS will have to be calculated on the basis that the pipeline would be working at full capacity, irrespective of how much petroleum would actually be flowing.

6. The Turkish authorities have further expressed the preference that the transportation costs due to BOTAS be defrayed from the escrow account to be established by the Secretary-General and have also indicated that those costs might be met in kind from petroleum supplies by Iraq.

7. The question of the security from seizure of Iraqi petroleum and petroleum products in transit before acquisition of title to them by prospective buyers and from claims by third parties against the proceeds from the sales of the petroleum and petroleum products has been examined. Possible ways for averting such eventualities are considered in paragraphs 30 to 34 below.

8. There may be potential difficulties inherent in the requirement for release of the funds in the escrow account in three equal tranches. The first difficulty is that it will not be possible to obtain release of any funds until the funds in the account have accumulated to at least one third of the total sum to be determined by the Security Council. Moreover, unless the deductions and operational costs are recovered in the same proportions of one third from each successive tranche, it may be found that, at any stage, the balance of funds in a tranche amounts only to a sum insufficient to provide the necessary humanitarian and other essential civilian needs. These difficulties would be overcome if the Committee established by resolution 661 (1990) was to decide immediately after the adoption of the resolution endorsing the present report that the first tranche of one third of the total could be released.

9. Mention of a United Nations role in dealing with humanitarian assistance that may be provided from funds from other sources (see resolution 706 (1991), para. 1 (c)) raises the possibility that funds from such other sources as accounts held in favour of Iraq or voluntary contributions may be deposited into the escrow account. Use of such funds, apart from the proceeds from authorized sales of Iraqi petroleum and petroleum products, would have to be confined exclusively to the procurement and distribution of items of a humanitarian nature in accordance with the provisions of, and procedures established for, paragraph 20 of resolution 687 (1991) and would have to be free from the obligatory deductions and administrative costs specified in paragraphs 2 and 3 of resolution 706 (1991).

10. Resolution 706 (1991) contemplates the possibility of Iraq offering petroleum products for sale, in addition to crude petroleum. On the basis of all available information, it would appear that Iraq is most unlikely to be in a position to offer significant quantities of petroleum products for sale at present. But if Iraq was able to do so, adequate measures could be devised promptly for verifying and monitoring such exports.

11. Finally, it is to be noted that the actual sum from the sale of Iraqi petroleum and petroleum products will have to be determined by the Security Council after its consideration of the present report. Bearing in mind the reports of the Executive Delegate of the Secretary-General for the United Nations Inter-Agency Humanitarian Programme for Iraq, Kuwait and the Iraq/Turkey and Iraq/Iran border areas (see S/22799, annex, and annex I to the present report [not reproduced here]), the Secretary-General deems it necessary to underline that, even if the maximum amount of $1.6 billion was to be the sum authorized by the Security Council under paragraph 1 of resolution 706 (1991), there would be a shortfall of approximately $800 million in the amount estimated by the Executive Delegate of the Secretary-General as necessary to meet the humanitarian and essential civilian requirements after deductions for the other purposes stipulated in the resolution.

II. *Iraq's current oil export capacity*

12. At present Iraq's crude oil production is between 300,000 and 500,000 barrels per day and maxi-

mum production capacity has been estimated at 1.455 million barrels per day. Only the production facilities in the Kirkuk area in the north and one of the pipelines to Yumurtalik in Turkey are operational. Under these conditions Iraq could export up to 1 million barrels a day, which is the current capacity of that pipeline.

13. Current productive capacity is well below the 3.14 million barrels per day that Iraq was producing before 2 August 1990, of which approximately 330,000 barrels per day were consumed domestically. Before 2 August 1990 Iraqi oil sold at a discount of between $1.50 and $2 below the price of the benchmark North Sea Brent crude.

14. At a possible price of $17.00 per barrel, Iraq would have to sell 94 million barrels (515,000 barrels per day for six months) to obtain the $1.6 billion specified in Security Council resolution 706 (1991). If Iraq was allowed to export at the current maximum capacity of 1 million barrels per day, it could generate revenue of $1.6 billion in three months or $3.2 billion during a six-month period.

III. Estimates of humanitarian requirements

15. As concluded by the recent humanitarian inter-agency mission of the Executive Delegate of the Secretary-General (hereafter referred to as "the mission"), the present food, health and nutrition situation in Iraq is critical. The problems of the severely debilitated population are aggravated by widespread shortages of essential medicines and medical supplies. Additionally, a generalized lack of safe water and unreconstructed or insufficient sanitation facilities maintain the incidence of water-borne and endemic diseases at a high level throughout the country.

16. Taking into account the above situation, the mission recommended that the maintenance of food supply and consumption as well as the close monitoring of the nutritional and health status of the Iraqi population over the next few months are absolutely necessary to prevent full-scale famine and major human disaster developing in the country.

17. The mission estimated that food import requirements for six months would amount to $1.1 billion. It also estimated the cost of imports required to re-establish basic health services at $250 million. In addition, $27 million is deemed necessary to initiate an urgent and critically needed supplementary feeding programme for mothers and children. Water and sanitation requirements covering both equipment and supplies were estimated at $120 million. To import the essential agricultural inputs recommended by the mission an additional $300 million is needed.

. . .

V. Recommendations

A. General recommendations

57. The Secretary-General wishes to recommend the following for consideration and decision by the Security Council with a view to facilitating smooth and secure realization of the objectives and purposes of the relevant provisions of resolution 706 (1991):

(a) Problems would arise if the decisions to release the tranches came only at the end of the process of selling a quantity of oil. Authorization of the release of the first tranche by the Committee established by resolution 661 (1990) immediately after the passage of the enabling resolution should resolve this difficulty;

(b) Paragraph 1 (d) of resolution 706 (1991) provides for a regular review by the Security Council of the ceiling of $1.6 billion. In the light of the estimates contained in the reports of his Executive Delegate, the Secretary-General will at the appropriate time recommend to the Council to use its powers under this provision to increase the maximum figure;

(c) The Security Council may wish to address the question of allowing assets held in favour of Iraq or any voluntary contributions to be deposited into the escrow account as a sub-account to be used exclusively in the manner and for the purposes stipulated in paragraph 20 of resolution 687 (1991);

(d) In response to the request to the Secretary-General to find a method for taking account of the costs of transportation of Iraqi petroleum and petroleum products, it is suggested that the transportation costs payable to Turkey be met in cash or kind. For this purpose, the Secretary-General considers that an additional amount of oil may be permitted to be exported from Iraq over and above the quantity necessary to meet the requirements of resolution 706 (1991). The actual transportation costs to BOTAS will have to be established by negotiations on an ad hoc basis. The value of any such oil is to be subject to the requirement that 30 per cent of its value should be paid directly to the Compensation Fund.

B. Specific measures for the implemention of the relevant provisions of Security Council resolution 706 (1991)

58. In accordance with the basic structure set out in section IV of the present report, the Secretary-General recommends the following specific measures for implementing the relevant provisions of resolution 706 (1991) in a manner that would effectively promote and satisfy the objectives and purposes of the resolution:

(a) Iraq, through its oil authority, SOMO, will market and sell the petroleum, f.o.b. Ceyhan;

(b) Every contract must include the following terms:

(i) The contract enters into force only after it has received the approval of the Committee established by resolution 661 (1990), following notification to the Committee by the State in which the purchaser is based;

(ii) The full proceeds from the sale of petroleum are to be deposited by the purchaser into the escrow account established by the United Nations and administered by the Secretary-General, in accordance with the Financial Regulations and Rules of the United Nations;

(iii) The purchaser must open a letter of credit for each transaction providing for payment into the United Nations escrow account;

(iv) The oil will be shipped via the Kirkuk-Yumurtalik pipeline from Iraq to Turkey;

(c) The Security Council Committee established by resolution 661 (1990) will have ultimate responsibility for monitoring the sale of Iraqi oil. It will be assisted in this function by independent inspection agents appointed by the United Nations, who will verify that the above terms are included in every contract and that the price of the oil is reasonable in light of prevailing market conditions. The Committee may also be assisted by other experts as appropriate in all aspects of its work deriving from Security Council resolution 706 (1991);

(d) The Committee established by resolution 661 (1990) should adopt procedures by which approval of each contract can be obtained promptly. Submissions for approval to the Committee can be made only by the Government of the State of the purchaser concerned. The Governments of States where purchasers are located should, where necessary, establish procedures that facilitate prompt submission of the contracts to the Committee for approval;

(e) Inspection agents will be appointed by the United Nations to ensure that the quantity and quality of oil delivered accords with the contract terms and that no oil is delivered without the requisite approval. They will be stationed at the Iraqi access points to the Kirkuk-Yumurtalik pipeline, at the border between Iraq and Turkey to the extent possible and at the loading terminal in Yumurtalik;

(f) The purchaser will open a letter of credit, issued by a reputable bank engaged in international banking, for each transaction providing for payment into the United Nations escrow account;

(g) Explicit language should be included in the Security Council resolution approving the present report setting forth the immunity of the oil. Iraq should be required, in the same resolution, to take all steps necessary to accord immunity to the oil. Additionally, Turkey should be called upon by the resolution to ensure that, while in Turkish jurisdiction, the oil will not be subjected to legal proceedings;

(h) The escrow account should be set up as a United Nations account and as such will be fully protected by the immunities of the United Nations. Additional protection would follow from establishing the escrow account in a bank of a country which, under the national laws of that country, enjoys the maximum protection from third-party claims. It would also come from including language in the Security Council resolution approving the present report reiterating that the escrow account is to be considered a United Nations asset and therefore enjoys the privileges and immunities of the United Nations;

(i) Purchases of the supplies to meet humanitarian needs in Iraq will be undertaken by Iraq. Monitoring of the purchases and deliveries will be undertaken by the Secretariat with the assistance of United Nations-appointed inspection agents;

(j) The Office of the Executive Delegate will receive a list of humanitarian requirements from Iraq and, after revising the list, if necessary, submit it to the Committee established by resolution 661 (1990) for approval;

(k) The Committee established by resolution 661 (1990) should adopt procedures for approving the submitted list. Upon approval, the Committee shall so notify the Secretary-General, who shall authorize payments from the United Nations escrow account. The Office of the Executive Delegate will then notify Iraq that it may commence procedures for the purchases and for arranging deliveries of the goods;

(l) Inspection agents appointed by the United Nations will evaluate, verify and monitor every element of the transaction up to entry points to Iraq. Part-payment may be made to suppliers at the time of delivery. The remainder will be paid after the Office of the Executive Delegate has submitted a report confirming compliance with the terms of the supply contract to the Committee established by resolution 661 (1990) and the Committee approves such payment;

(m) Movement of goods to designated centres and commencement of in-country distribution will be arranged by the government agencies concerned, which will notify the Office of the Executive Delegate of the proposed distribution of incoming consignments in order to enable the United Nations agencies to put in place effective monitoring arrangements;

(n) Monitoring of in-country distribution will be undertaken in accordance with the proposals submitted by the Executive Delegate of the Secretary-General on 27 August 1991, reproduced in annex II to the present report [not reproduced here].

. . .

Document 79

Report of the Secretary-General concerning the repatriation or return of all Kuwaiti and third-country nationals or their remains present in Iraq on or after 2 August 1990

S/23012, 12 September 1991

1. The following report is submitted in accordance with paragraph 6 of Security Council resolution 706 (1991), which was adopted on 15 August 1991. Paragraph 6 reads as follows: "Further requests the Secretary-General in consultation with the International Committee of the Red Cross (ICRC) to submit within 20 days of the date of adoption of this resolution a report to the Security Council on activities undertaken in accordance with paragraph 31 of resolution 687 (1991) in connection with facilitating the repatriation or return of all Kuwaiti and third-country nationals or their remains present in Iraq on or after 2 August 1990."

2. It will be recalled that in the months since the adoption of Security Council resolution 687 (1991) on 3 April 1991, the Secretary-General and the President of the Security Council have received a number of communications regarding the repatriation or return of Kuwaitis and third-country nationals or their remains present in Iraq since 2 August 1990. For ease of reference, those communications which have been issued as documents of the Security Council are reprinted as annexes at the end of this report.

3. In a meeting with the President of the ICRC in Geneva on 28 August 1991, the Secretary-General drew attention to paragraph 6 of Security Council resolution 706 (1991). He recalled also the text of paragraph 31 of Security Council resolution 687 (1991), which reads: "Invites the International Committee of the Red Cross to keep the Secretary-General apprised as appropriate of all activities undertaken in connection with facilitating the repatriation or return of all Kuwaiti and third-country nationals or their remains present in Iraq on or after 2 August 1990."

4. The ICRC has conveyed to the Secretary-General the following information for inclusion in this report:

A. *Repatriation of former residents of Kuwait from Iraq to Kuwait*

	Prisoners of war	Civilian internees
Operation no. 1: 6 March 1991	1	
Operation no. 2: 7 March 1991		1 174
Operation no. 3: 21-27 March 1991	4 176	862
Operation no. 4: 6 April 1991	1	20
	4 178	2 056

The ICRC points out that all but the second of the above repatriation exercises took place under its auspices. The 1,174 individuals that returned to Kuwait on 7 March 1991 were not registered with the ICRC.

B. *Registration and repatriation of persons wishing to return to Kuwait*

From the beginning of April to 18 August 1991 the ICRC registered in Iraq 3,506 names of civilians, civilian internees or prisoners of war wishing to return to Kuwait. Some prisoners of war and civilian internees were registered by ICRC delegates in detention centres. The large majority of the 3,506 persons came spontaneously to the ICRC office in Baghdad where ICRC delegates recorded their personal data for transmission to the Kuwaiti authorities who, in turn, determine eligibility for repatriation. As of 29 August 1991, Kuwait has authorized the return of 206 persons registered by the ICRC (41 prisoners of war, 53 civilian internees and 112 civilians), all of whom have been repatriated to Kuwait under ICRC auspices.

C. *Repatriation of third country nationals*

The ICRC has supervised the repatriation of 23 prisoners of war of the United States, 12 prisoners of war of the United Kingdom and 2 prisoners of war of Italy. The ICRC has also supervised the repatriation to Saudi Arabia of 28 prisoners of war, 33 civilian internees and 49 civilians.

D. *Kuwaiti list of civilians and military personnel missing since 2 August 1990*

On 9 September 1991, the Kuwaiti authorities handed over to the ICRC Delegation in Kuwait a list containing 2,242 names of civilians and military personnel missing since 2 August 1990, and whom they presume have been arrested by the Iraqi authorities. The ICRC is transmitting this list to the Iraqi authorities.

Annex I

Letter dated 19 April 1991 from the Permanent Representative of Kuwait to the United Nations addressed to the President of the Security Council 1/

On instructions from my Government, I should like to convey to you our position concerning the failure by Iraq to abide by the terms of relevant Security Council resolutions, which puts into question the credibility and motives of the Iraqi regime.

In the first instance, it should be indicated that a humanitarian but urgent concern is not being addressed by the Iraqi Government, specifically, the commitment by Iraq to abide by the terms of paragraphs 2 (c) and 3 (c) of resolution 686 (1991) and of paragraph 30 of resolution 687 (1991). Iraq is yet to repatriate the remaining Kuwaiti prisoners of war and detainees estimated at 5,433.

Second, Iraq has not to date declared its acceptance under the terms of paragraph 1 (b) of resolution 686 (1991) of its liability for any loss, damage or injury arising in regard to Kuwait and third States, and their nationals and corporations, as a result of the invasion and illegal occupation of Kuwait by Iraq.

Third, in spite of its declared readiness to return property seized in Kuwait, Iraq has not to date returned to Kuwait any of those items seized by it. Iraq has yet to implement faithfully the terms of paragraph 2 (d) of resolution 686 (1991) which demands that Iraq "immediately begins to return all Kuwaiti property seized by Iraq, to be completed in the shortest possible period".

Annex II

Letter dated 3 June 1991 from the Chargé d'Affaires a.i. of the Permanent Mission of Kuwait to the United Nations addressed to the President of the Security Council 2/

On instructions from my Government, I should like to bring to your attention the following:

First, in spite of the provisions of paragraphs 2 (c) and 3 (c) of Security Council resolution 686 (1991), that Iraq *immediately* release under the auspices of the ICRC all Kuwaiti and third-country nationals and arrange for *immediate* access to all POWs, Iraq is yet to release around 3,800 POWs and detainees of which around 700 are women and 730 are children 15 years old and below. Iraq has also been found wanting in allowing access to all POWs and detainees. Concern about their fate had been communicated to the Security Council in our letter of 20 May 1991.

Second, notwithstanding the provision of paragraph 2 (d) of resolution 686 (1991) that Iraq *immediately* begin to return all Kuwaiti property seized by Iraq, to be completed in the *shortest possible period*, to date, the only item returned to Kuwait is a single aircraft that the Iraqis had kept in Jordan.

Third, while Iraq has declared, in accordance with the provision of paragraph 2 (a) of resolution 686 (1991), that it has rescinded decisions regarding the annexation of Kuwait, recent statements by the Iraqi Vice-President (S/22655) clearly contradict the aforementioned declaration. These statements emphasize that implementation of Security Council resolutions is but a tactical move rather than a change of policy by Iraq.

Lastly, it should be emphasized that failure, to date, to return all POWs and detainees, return property seized from Kuwait, and cease hostile statements are indications that the "policies and practices of the Government of Iraq" are not in implementation of relevant Security Council resolutions. What is required of Iraq is not merely acceptance, but, as described in resolution 686 (1991), *implementation of its acceptance* of Security Council resolutions.

Annex III

Letter dated 2 July 1991 from the Permanent Representative of Saudi Arabia to the United Nations addressed to the Secretary-General 3/

I have the pleasure, further to letter dated 11 June 1991 (S/22689) addressed to Your Excellency from the Chargé d'affaires a.i. of the Permanent Mission of Iraq to the United Nations, in which he transmitted a letter dated 8 June 1991 from the Minister for Foreign Affairs of Iraq, whereby he confirmed the Iraqi Government's undertaking to accept and comply with all the provisions of Security Council resolution 687 (1991) that are linked with the cease-fire in the Gulf War, to convey to Your Excellency, upon instructions from my Government, that Iraq has not complied with the provisions of section G of resolution 687 (1991) concerning the repatriation of all Kuwaitis and third-country nationals, including Saudi Arabian nationals.

According to the information that the Saudi Arabian authorities concerned received from previously released prisoners and Iraqi refugees that are now in Saudi Arabia, it has been confirmed, without doubt, that there are at

1/ See document S/22512, dated 19 April 1991.
2/ See document S/22702 (annex), dated 13 June 1991.
3/ See document S/22760, dated 3 July 1991.

least 15 Saudi Arabians who have not been repatriated to Saudi Arabia until now.

Annex IV
Letter dated 15 July 1991 from the Permanent Representative of Iraq to the United Nations addressed to the Secretary-General 4/

With reference to the letter of the Permanent Representative of the Kingdom of Saudi Arabia to the United Nations, document S/22760 dated 3 July 1991, I wish to explain to you that the competent Iraqi authorities have advised in respect of the contents of the above-mentioned letter that they have notified the mission of the International Committee of the Red Cross (ICRC) in Baghdad of the arrest of 10 Saudi Arabian civilians because they contravened Iraqi laws and that they have been registered with ICRC. The Iraqi authorities have expressed their readiness to repatriate these 10, whose names are annexed hereto, once the above-mentioned authorities have issued them a pardon.

Annex V
Letter dated 17 July 1991 from the Permanent Representative of Kuwait to the United Nations addressed to the President of the Security Council 5/

On instructions from my Government I should like to draw your attention to the failure by Iraq to abide by the terms of relevant Security Council resolutions, in particular those pertaining to the urgent humanitarian demand that Iraq *immediately* release under the auspices of the ICRC *all* Kuwaiti and third-country nationals and arrange for the ICRC *immediate* access to all POWs and detainees. In this regard, I should like to convey the following:

First, there are around 1,890 Kuwaiti POWs and detainees still held by Iraq, in addition to 1,990 non-Kuwaiti POWs and detainees.

Second, a number of the above were detained at a restricted area in Baghdad, Al-Rahwaniya, near the International Airport. Others were detained at General Intelligence (Al-Mukhabarat) building in Al-Athimiya district in Baghdad.

Third, the ICRC confirmed our information on some locations of POWs and detainees, a matter which was brought to the attention of the members of the Council on 20 May 1991.

Fourth, POWs and detainees have recently been transferred to undisclosed locations. The ICRC have been denied information of, let alone access to, these new locations.

Fifth, since the cease-fire formally came into effect on 11 April 1991 only 68 POWs and detainees of different nationalities have been repatriated in five phases, on 15 and 25 May, 12 and 27 June and 14 July.

Sixth, it is noteworthy that before the cease-fire formally came into effect on 11 April 1991, Iraq had released through the ICRC 5,060 POWs and detainees of different nationalities. Around 1,498 more persons of different nationalities have escaped Iraq through various routes.

Seventh, Iraq includes those returned under family reunion in the total number of POWs and detainees thus inflating the number of repatriated POWs and detainees. To illustrate, 56 persons were released to Kuwaiti authorities on 14 July 1991, of which 53 persons qualified for family reunion, 2 were Kuwaiti POWs and the last was a Syrian detainee.

While bringing the above to your attention, Kuwait wishes to emphasize its deep concern at the fate of those still held by Iraq. Our concern is compounded due to the recent transfer of POWs and detainees to undisclosed locations. Lastly, the Iraqi pattern of release of POWs and detainees puts into question the credibility and motives of the regime *vis-à-vis* a humanitarian matter of no apparent strategic asset to it.

Annex VI
Letter dated 5 August 1991 from the Permanent Representative of Kuwait to the United Nations addressed to the Secretary-General 6/

On instructions from my Government, I wish to inform you that the Iraqi regime, in an attempt to mislead the international community and to divert attention from the fact that it is detaining thousands of Kuwaiti and non-Kuwaiti prisoners of war in flagrant violation of Security Council resolutions 686 (1991) and 687 (1991), as well as of the third Geneva Convention, has persisted in submitting requests to the International Committee of the Red Cross (ICRC) on behalf of individuals it claims to be Kuwaiti citizens seeking to leave and return to Kuwait for the purpose of "reunion". In all, there have been 697 requests, listing 3,458 (three thousand four hundred and fifty-eight) individuals. Kuwait has approved the return of 252 (two hundred and fifty-two) Kuwaitis and non-Kuwaitis among those on the list after checking their identities and nationalities and verifying that they were included, before 1 August 1990, in the civilian population register of the State of Kuwait, a copy of which is deposited with the United Nations in accordance with Security

---

4/ See document S/22793, dated 15 July 1991.
5/ See document S/22809, dated 18 July 1991.
6/ See document A/45/1048-S/22893, dated 6 August 1991.

Council resolution 677 (1990). The individuals concerned left Kuwait of their own accord during the brutal Iraqi occupation. They are not detained in Iraq, as may be seen from the fact that they applied to the ICRC office in Baghdad. Approval was given for the return of those whose identities were verified. Needless to say, their situation is entirely unrelated to that of the prisoners of war whose return has been requested by Kuwait and of whose names a full list was submitted to ICRC and transmitted to the authorities of the Iraqi regime. In attempting to mingle the former cases with those of Kuwaiti prisoners and detainees, the Iraqi regime's intention is simply to procrastinate and to confuse international public opinion with respect to Iraq's inhumane practices and failure to comply with the 1949 Geneva Convention relative to the Treatment of Prisoners of War.

We call upon you to draw the regime's attention to these blatant violations of the third Geneva Convention and to affirm that the Iraqi regime, by persisting in its failure to hand over the remaining prisoners, is contravening both the spirit and the letter of Security Council resolutions 686 (1991) and 687 (1991). In doing so, it is guilty of a flagrant breach of the provisions underlying the cease-fire declaration. All members of the Security Council and international humanitarian organizations are also urged to put pressure on the Iraqi regime with a view to ensuring its full and prompt implementation of the pertinent Security Council resolutions.

Annex VII
Letter dated 8 August 1991 from the Permanent Representative of Kuwait to the United Nations addressed to the Secretary-General 7/

On instructions from my Government, and with reference to my most recent letter, dated 5 August 1991 and issued as document S/22893, I have the honour to transmit to you herewith a detailed list, by nationality, of persons imprisoned or detained in Iraq; the total number of such persons is 2,479. A copy of this list has been sent to the International Committee of the Red Cross.

1.	Kuwaitis	1,839
2.	Non-Kuwaitis	462 (of unknown nationality)
3.	Nationals of the United Arab Emirates	2
4.	Saudis	66
5.	Syrians	18
6.	Egyptians	35
7.	Omanis	2
8.	Lebanese	14
9.	Somali	1
10.	Bahrainis	3
11.	Filipinos	7
12.	Indians	13
13.	Pakistanis	4
14.	Iranians	12
15.	Sri Lankan	1

We request that you do everthing within your power to exert pressure on the Iraqi authorities in order to secure the release of those prisoners and detainees and to put an end to their suffering and that of their families. We hope that all States and international organizations will express in no uncertain terms their resolute condemnation of the inhumane practices of the Iraqi authorities in detaining thousands of Kuwaiti nationals and persons of other countries who are residents of Kuwait.

Annex VIII
Letter dated 29 August 1991 from the Minister for Foreign Affairs of Iraq to the United Nations addressed to the Secretary-General 8/

I wish to refer to the letter dated 17 July 1991 from the Permanent Representative of Kuwait to the United Nations, addressed to the President of the Security Council.

I have the honour to notify you of the following information concerning the situation of Kuwaiti nationals in Iraq since the end of the Gulf War.

1. The competent Iraqi authorities repatriated to Kuwait 6,328 Kuwaitis and 5 persons not of Kuwaiti nationality under the supervision of the delegation of the International Committee of the Red Cross (ICRC) during the period from 4 March to the present.

2. The ICRC delegation registered 3,400 Kuwaitis comprising 606 families who were in Iraq in addition to 159 individuals.

3. The Kuwaiti side agreed to the repatriation of 170 of the Kuwaitis referred to in paragraph 2 above. The Kuwaiti side is now attempting to delude Arab and international public opinion into believing that Iraq is concealing large numbers of Kuwaitis.

4. The Kuwaiti authorities are constantly endeavouring to impede the return of Kuwaitis to Kuwait on the pretext that verification procedures have not been completed. They have made a number of errors as testified by ICRC, the most recent of which was on 13 July when it had been decided to hand over a group of Kuwaitis but the Kuwaiti representative did not come to the Ar'ar area in Saudi Arabia to receive them. The handing over opera-

7/ See document S/22921, dated 9 August 1991.
8/ See document S/22992 (annex), dated 29 August 1991.

tion was postponed until 14 July, the ICRC delegation having confirmed that it had informed the Kuwaiti side of the time of the handing over.

We believe that the delay in the repatriation of the Kuwaitis who are still in Iraq, of which ICRC is aware, was directly caused by the Kuwaiti authorities who bear full responsibility for it.

Iraq is cooperating fully on this matter with ICRC and once again affirms its readiness to hand over all Kuwaitis who are in Iraq to the Kuwaiti side through ICRC. I should like the Secretary-General to exert pressure on the Kuwaiti side to receive them and not to exploit this matter for dishonourable publicity purposes.

Document 80

First report of the Security Council Sanctions Committee on implementation of the guidelines concerning the arms embargo against Iraq

S/23036, 13 September 1991

Letter dated 13 September 1991 from the Chairman of the Security Council Committee established by resolution 661 (1990) concerning the situation between Iraq and Kuwait addressed to the President of the Security Council

I have the honour to transmit herewith for the attention of the members of the Council the report of the Security Council Committee established by resolution 661 (1990) concerning the situation between Iraq and Kuwait pursuant to paragraph 6, subparagraph (f) of the Guidelines to facilitate full international implementation of paragraphs 24, 25 and 27 of Security Council resolution 687 (1991).

The report has been approved by the Committee on 13 September 1991.

(*Signed*) Peter HOHENFELLNER
Chairman
Security Council Committee established by resolution 661 (1990) concerning the situation between Iraq and Kuwait

Annex
Report of the Security Council Committee established by resolution 661 (1990) concerning the situation between Iraq and Kuwait pursuant to paragraph 6, subparagraph (f) of the Guidelines to facilitate full international implementation of paragraphs 24, 25 and 27 of Security Council resolution 687 (1991)

1. At its 2994th meeting, held on 17 June 1991, in connection with its consideration of the item entitled "The situation between Iraq and Kuwait", the Security Council, acting under Chapter VII of the Charter, adopted resolution 700 (1991) by which, *inter alia*, it approved the Guidelines for facilitating full international implementation of paragraphs 24, 25 and 27 of Security Council resolution 687 (1991) of 3 April 1991, annexed to the report of the Secretary-General contained in document S/22660.

2. By paragraph 5 of resolution 700 (1991) the Council entrusted the Committee established under resolution 661 (1990) with the responsibility, under the Guidelines, for monitoring the prohibitions against the sale or supply of arms to Iraq and related sanctions established in paragraph 24 of resolution 687 (1991).

3. Paragraph 24 of resolution 687 (1991) reads as follows:

"*The Security Council,*

"...

"24. *Decides* that, in accordance with resolution 661 (1990) and subsequent related resolutions and until a further decision is taken by the Security Council, all States shall continue to prevent the sale or supply, or the promotion or facilitation of such sale or supply, to Iraq by their nationals, or from their territories or using their flag vessels or aircraft, of:

"(a) Arms and related *matériel* of all types, specifically including the sale or transfer through other means of all forms of conventional military equipment, including for paramilitary forces, and spare parts and components and their means of production, for such equipment;

"(b) Items specified and defined in paragraphs 8 and 12 above not otherwise covered above;

"(c) Technology under licensing or other transfer arrangements used in the production, utilization or stockpiling of items specified in subparagraphs (a) and (b) above;

"(d) Personnel or materials for training or technical support services relating to the design, development, manufacture, use, maintenance or support of items specified in subparagraphs (a) and (b) above;"

4. Under paragraph 6 of the Guidelines (S/22660, annex), the functions of the Committee for monitoring the arms and related sanctions are the following:

(a) To meet at regular intervals to examine reports submitted by the Secretary-General on the implementation of the relevant resolutions;

(b) To provide guidance to States and to international organizations, either upon their request or at its own initiative, on matters concerning the implementation of paragraph 24 of resolution 687 (1991), *inter alia*, through the elaboration, as necessary, of relevant criteria;

(c) To reach, in connection with subparagraph (b) above, when needed, agreed interpretations of items falling within the specified categories of proscribed items and activities;

(d) To seek information and maintain contact with States, international organizations and those non-governmental organizations whose activities and/or expertise are likely to promote strict implementation of the arms and related sanctions against Iraq;

(e) To bring to the attention of the States and international organizations concerned information reported to it of alleged violations of the arms and related sanctions against Iraq for appropriate action by those States and international organizations;

(f) To report at 90-day intervals to the Security Council on the implementation of the arms and related sanctions against Iraq contained in the relevant resolutions.

5. At its 43rd meeting, held on 20 June 1991, the Committee took note of the approval of the Guidelines by the Security Council. This report is submitted in accordance with paragraph 6, subparagraph (f) of the Guidelines, as also mentioned in the letter by the Vice-Chairman of the Committee to the President of the Security Council dated 5 August 1991.

6. By paragraph 12 of the Guidelines all States are requested to report to the Committee any information that may have come to their attention relating to possible violations of the arms and related sanctions against Iraq

committed by other States or foreign nationals. In this regard, States were reminded of their duties under paragraph 7 of resolution 661 (1990) of 6 August 1990, to cooperate fully with the Committee in the fulfilment of its task, including supplying such information as might be sought by the Committee. No information, as requested by paragraph 12 of the Guidelines, has yet been received by the Committee.

7. By paragraphs 13 and 15, all States and international organizations are requested to consult the Committee on the question of whether certain items fall within the provision of paragraph 24 of resolution 687 (1991), as well as in cases relating to dual-use or multiple-use items, that is to say, items meant for civilian use but with potential for diversion or conversion to military use. Neither States nor international organizations have yet consulted the Committee on these questions.

8. By paragraph 14 of the Guidelines international organizations are requested to provide to the Committee any relevant information that may come to their attention. No such information has yet been received by the Committee.

9. By a letter dated 6 August 1991 (S/22904), the President of the Security Council informed the Secretary-General that the members of the Council held informal consultations pursuant to paragraphs 21 and 28 of resolution 687 (1991) and paragraph 6 of resolution 700 (1991). After hearing all the opinions expressed in the course of the consultations, the President of the Council concluded that there was no agreement that the necessary conditions existed for a modification of the sanctions regimes.

10. During the period under review, no allegations of violations of sanctions, particularly in connection with paragraph 24 of resolution 687 (1991), have been reported to the Committee.

11. The Committee will continue its efforts to fulfil the mandate entrusted to it. In this context, it suggests that the Secretary-General might send a reminder to those States which have not yet replied in accordance with paragraph 4 of Security Council resolution 700 (1991) on measures they have instituted for meeting the obligations set out in paragraph 24 of Security Council resolution 687 (1991).*

*The States that have replied so far pursuant to paragraph 4 of Security Council resolution 700 (1991) are listed in the reports of the Secretary-General contained in documents S/22884 and Add.1.

Document 81

Security Council resolution confirming the $1.6 billion ceiling for Iraqi oil sales and authorizing the release of funds to meet Iraq's essential civilian needs

S/RES/712 (1991), 19 September 1991

The Security Council,

Recalling its previous relevant resolutions, and in particular resolutions 661 (1990) of 6 August 1990, 686 (1991) of 2 March 1991, 687 (1991) of 3 April 1991, 688 (1991) of 5 April 1991, 692 (1991) of 20 May 1991, 699 (1991) of 17 June 1991, and 705 (1991) and 706 (1991) of 15 August 1991,

Expressing its appreciation for the report submitted by the Secretary-General on 4 September 1991 pursuant to paragraph 5 of resolution 706 (1991), 1/

Reaffirming its concern about the nutritional and health situation of the Iraqi civilian population and the risk of a further deterioration of this situation, and underlining the need in this context for fully up-to-date assessments of the situation in all parts of Iraq as a basis for the equitable distribution of humanitarian relief to all segments of the Iraqi civilian population,

Recalling that the activities to be carried out by or on behalf of the Secretary-General to meet the purposes referred to in resolution 706 (1991) and the present resolution enjoy the privileges and immunities of the United Nations,

Acting under Chapter VII of the Charter of the United Nations,

1. *Confirms* the figure mentioned in paragraph 1 of resolution 706 (1991) as the sum authorized for the purpose of that paragraph, and reaffirms its intention to review this sum on the basis of its ongoing assessment of the needs and requirements, in accordance with paragraph 1 (d) of that resolution;

2. *Invites* the Security Council Committee established by resolution 661 (1990) concerning the situation between Iraq and Kuwait to authorize immediately, pursuant to paragraph 1 (d) of resolution 706 (1991), the release by the Secretary-General from the escrow account of the first one-third portion of the sum referred to in paragraph 1 above, such release to take place as required subject to the availability of funds in the account and, in the case of payments to finance the purchase of foodstuffs, medicines and materials and supplies for essential civilian needs that have been notified or approved in accordance with existing procedures, subject to compliance with the procedures laid down in the report of the Secretary-General 1/ as approved in paragraph 3 below;

3. *Approves* the recommendations contained in paragraphs 57 (d) and 58 of the Secretary-General's report;

4. *Encourages* the Secretary-General and the Committee to cooperate, in close consultation with the Government of Iraq, on a continuing basis to ensure the most effective implementation of the scheme approved in the present resolution;

5. *Decides* that petroleum and petroleum products subject to resolution 706 (1991) shall, while under Iraqi title, be immune from legal proceedings and not be subject to any form of attachment, garnishment or execution, and that all States shall take any steps that may be necessary under their respective domestic legal systems to assure this protection and to ensure that the proceeds of sale are not diverted from the purposes laid down in resolution 706 (1991);

6. *Reaffirms* that the escrow account to be established by the United Nations and administered by the Secretary-General to meet the purposes of resolution 706 (1991) and the present resolution, like the United Nations Compensation Fund established by resolution 692 (1991), enjoys the privileges and immunities of the United Nations;

7. *Reaffirms also* that the inspectors and other experts on mission for the United Nations, appointed for the purpose of the present resolution, enjoy privileges and immunities in accordance with the Convention on the Privileges and Immunities of the United Nations, 2/ and demands that Iraq allow them full freedom of movement and all necessary facilities;

8. *Confirms* that funds contributed from other sources may, if desired, in accordance with paragraph 1 (c) of resolution 706 (1991), be deposited into the escrow account as a sub-account and be immediately available to meet Iraq's humanitarian needs as referred to in paragraph 20 of resolution 687 (1991) without any of the obligatory deductions and administrative costs specified in paragraphs 2 and 3 of resolution 706 (1991);

9. *Urges* that any provision to Iraq of foodstuffs, medicines or other items of a humanitarian character, in addition to those purchased with the funds referred to in paragraph 1 above, be undertaken through arrangements

---

1/ *Official Records of the Security Council, Forty-sixth Year, Supplement for July, August and September 1991,* S/23006 and Corr.2.

that assure their equitable distribution to meet humanitarian needs;

10. *Requests* the Secretary-General to take the actions necessary to implement the above decisions, and authorizes him to enter into any arrangements or agreements necessary to accomplish this;

11. *Calls upon* States to cooperate fully in the implementation of resolution 706 (1991) and the present resolution, in particular with respect to any measures regarding the import of petroleum and petroleum products and the export of foodstuffs, medicines and materials and supplies for essential civilian needs as referred to in paragraph 20 of resolution 687 (1991), and also with respect to the privileges and immunities of the United Nations and its personnel implementing the present resolution, and to ensure that there are no diversions from the purposes laid down in these resolutions;

12. *Decides* to remain seized of the matter.

Document 82

Revised plan submitted by the Director General of the IAEA for future monitoring and verification of Iraq's compliance with the requirements of Security Council resolution 687 (1991) for the destruction or removal of specified weapons and with the requirements of resolution 707 (1991) for full disclosure, access to inspection sites and compliance with international obligations

S/22872/Rev.1, 20 September 1991

Note by the Secretary-General

The Secretary-General has the honour to transmit to the Security Council the attached revised plan for future ongoing monitoring and verification of Iraq's compliance with paragraph 12 of part C of Security Council resolution 687 (1991) and with the requirements of paragraphs 3 and 5 of resolution 707 (1991) submitted by the Director General of the International Atomic Energy Agency (IAEA).

Plan for future ongoing monitoring and verification of Iraq's compliance with paragraph 12 of part C of Security Council resolution 687 (1991) and with the requirements of paragraphs 3 and 5 of resolution 707 (1991)

Submitted by the Director General of the
International Atomic Energy Agency

I. *Introduction*

1. In paragraph 13 of Security Council resolution 687 (1991), adopted on 3 April 1991, the Director General of the International Atomic Energy Agency (hereinafter referred to as the "IAEA" or "Agency") was requested by the Security Council to carry out immediate on-site inspection of Iraq's nuclear capabilities and to develop and carry out a plan for the destruction, removal or rendering harmless of items prohibited to Iraq under paragraph 12 of resolution 687. The Special Commission, established in accordance with paragraph 9 of resolution 687, was given a role in the nuclear area under resolution 687 of assisting and cooperating with the IAEA and designating sites to be inspected.

2. In paragraph 13 of resolution 687, the Director General of the IAEA was further requested—with the assistance and cooperation of the Special Commissions— to submit to the Security Council for its approval a plan for future ongoing monitoring and verification of Iraq's compliance with its obligations under paragraph 12 of resolution 687.

3. The IAEA submitted to the Security Council for its approval on 29 July 1991 the plan referred to in paragraph 2 above. As the plan was originally developed while immediate on-site inspection was still ongoing, and while the plan for the destruction, removal or rendering harmless of proscribed items was still in an early stage of implementation, the plan was, as indicated therein, provisional in nature and subject to modification upon further direction from the Security Council and upon consideration of the results of the ongoing inspections.

4. As a consequence of the adoption by the Security Council on 15 August 1991 of resolution 707 (1991), and based on the results of the on-site inspections performed to date, the Director General of the IAEA now submits a revised plan (hereafter referred to as "the plan") for approval by the Security Council.

5. The plan incorporates the additional obligations of Iraq under resolution 707 and the corresponding monitoring and verification activities of the Agency.

6. Although resolution 687 does not specify the party which should be assigned the responsibility for

implementation of the plan, the Agency's extensive experience with inspection and verification activities in the nuclear field, which led to the Security Council's asking the Agency to take the lead during the first two phases under paragraph 12 of resolution 687, the need for continuity in the implementation of future measures, and the evident cost benefit of being able to draw on an existing infrastructure, suggest that the Agency be assigned the task of carrying out the plan. The plan was drafted accordingly. It is expected that the verification and monitoring activities will be administered and operated by a special unit in the IAEA Secretariat. For technical and practical reasons, the operation by the Agency appropriately coordinated with the Special Commission or its successor, of field offices in Baghdad is also envisaged.

7. In accordance with the Agency's mandate under resolutions 687 and 707, and as provided for in Articles IX and VII of the Agreement Governing the Relationship between the United Nations and the International Atomic Energy Agency (INFCIRC/11) 1/, the Agency will report on the implementation of the plan to the Security Council.

8. Resolution 707 obliges Iraq, *inter alia*, to "halt all nuclear activities of any kind, except for use of isotopes for medical, agricultural or industrial purposes, until the Security Council determines that Iraq is in full compliance with resolution 707 and with paragraphs 12 and 13 of resolution 687, and the IAEA determines that Iraq is in full compliance with its safeguards agreement with that Agency". So long as the proscriptions under resolution 707 remain operational, the Agency will secure the nuclear material, equipment and facilities which Iraq is allowed to keep and use under the terms of resolution 687 and verify that they are not used for any nuclear activity except as permitted under resolution 707. The Agency will also verify that nuclear material and isotopes are not produced indigenously by Iraq, and that isotopes held or imported by Iraq are used only for medical, agricultural or industrial purposes.

9. The comprehensive sanctions established under Security Council resolution 661 (1991) for application by all States against Iraq, the prohibition against Iraq's acquisition of, and research and development related to, nuclear weapons and nuclear-weapons-usable material, as set out in paragraph 12 of resolution 687, and the prohibition in resolution 707 against all nuclear activities in Iraq except the use of isotopes for medical, agricultural or industrial purposes, all of which were imposed under Chapter VII of the Charter of the United Nations, carry with it the obligation of other States to respect the sanctions and prohibitions until such time as they are lifted by the Security Council and entails the acceptance of an obligation to report intended sales or supplies to Iraq of items not proscribed under resolutions 687 or 707.

10. This plan, and the annexes thereto, which constitute an integral part of the plan, will enter into force upon approval by the Security Council. It will govern all Agency activities in Iraq pursuant to resolutions 687 and 707. The duration of the plan, as well as the scope and content of the plan, remain subject to further decisions and directives of the Security Council.

11. Security Council resolution 687 notes that the actions required of Iraq, including those relevant to nuclear weapons and nuclear-weapons-usable material, represent steps toward the goal of establishing in the Middle East a zone free from weapons of mass destruction. While the terms of any such zone agreement would have to be negotiated between the parties to the arrangement, some of the verification features envisaged in this plan may be of interest in future discussions about verification in such a zone.

II. *The plan*

A. *Relevant decisions of the Security Council*

12. In accordance with paragraph 12 of resolution 687, Iraq is obliged:

- not to acquire or develop nuclear weapons or nuclear-weapon-usable material or any subsystems or components or any research, development, support or manufacturing facilities related to the above;
- to submit to the Secretary-General and the Director General of the IAEA within 15 days of adoption of the resolution a declaration of the locations, amounts and types of items specified above;
- to place all of its nuclear-weapon-usable materials under exclusive control, for custody and removal, of the IAEA, with the assistance and cooperation of the Special Commission appointed by the Secretary-General in accordance with paragraph 9(b) of the resolution;
- to accept, in accordance with the arrangements provided for in paragraph 13 of the resolution, urgent on-site inspection and the destruction, removal or rendering harmless, as appropriate, of such items; and
- to accept the plan referred to in paragraph 13 for the future ongoing monitoring and verification of its compliance with these undertakings.

1/ Article IX provides that the Agency "shall cooperate with the Security Council by furnishing to it at its request such information and assistance as may be required in the exercise of its responsibility for the maintenance or restoration of international peace and security."
Article VII provides *inter alia* that, "At the invitation of the Security Council, the Director General may attend its meetings to supply it with information or give it other assistance within the competence of the Agency."

13. Pursuant to paragraph 13 of resolution 687, the Director General of the International Atomic Energy Agency was requested, with the assistance and cooperation of the Special Commission:

- to carry out immediate on-site inspection of Iraq's nuclear capabilities based on Iraq's declarations and the designation of any additional locations by the Special Commission;
- to develop a plan for submission to the Security Council within forty-five days following adoption of the resolution calling for the destruction, removal, or rendering harmless as appropriate of the items proscribed in paragraph 12 of the resolution, and to carry out the plan within forty-five days following its approval by the Security Council; and
- to develop a plan taking into account the rights and obligations of Iraq under the Treaty on the Non-Proliferation of Nuclear Weapons of 1 July 1968, for the future ongoing monitoring and verification of Iraq's compliance with paragraph 12 of the resolution, including an inventory of all nuclear material in Iraq subject to the Agency's verification and inspections to confirm that Agency safeguards cover all relevant nuclear activities in Iraq, to be submitted to the Security Council for approval within 120 days of adoption of the resolution.

14. Under paragraph 3 of resolution 707, the Security Council demands that Iraq:

- provide full, final and complete disclosure, as required by resolution 687 (1991), of all aspects of its programmes to develop weapons of mass destruction and ballistic missiles with a range greater than 150 km, and of all holdings of such weapons, their components and production facilities and locations, as well as all other nuclear programmes, including any which it claims are for purposes not related to nuclear-weapons-usable material, without further delay;
- allow the Special Commission, the IAEA and their Inspection Teams immediate, unconditional and unrestricted access to any and all areas, facilities, equipment, records and means of transportation which they wish to inspect;
- cease immediately any attempt to conceal, or any movement or destruction of any material or equipment relating to its nuclear, chemical or biological weapons or ballistic missile programmes, or material or equipment relating to its other nuclear activities without notification to and prior consent of the Special Commission;
- make available immediately to the Special Commission, the IAEA and their Inspection Teams any items to which they were previously denied access;

- allow the Special Commission, the IAEA and their Inspection Teams to conduct both fixed wing and helicopter flights throughout Iraq for all relevant purposes including inspection, surveillance, aerial surveys, transportation and logistics without interference of any kind and upon such terms and conditions as may be determined by the Special Commission, and to make full use of their own aircraft and such airfields in Iraq as they may determine are most appropriate for the work of the Commission;
- halt all nuclear activities of any kind, except for use of isotopes for medical, agricultural or industrial purposes until the Security Council determines that Iraq is in full compliance with this resolution and paragraphs 12 and 13 of resolution 687 (1991), and the IAEA determines that Iraq is in full compliance with its safeguards agreement with that Agency;
- ensure the complete implementation of the privileges, immunities and facilities of the representatives of the Special Commission and the IAEA in accordance with its previous undertakings and their complete safety and freedom of movement;
- immediately provide or facilitate the provision of any transportation, medical or logistical support requested by the Special Commission, the IAEA and their Inspection Teams;
- respond fully, completely and promptly to any questions or requests from the Special Commission, the IAEA and their Inspection Teams.

15. Paragraph 5 of resolution 707 further requires that the Government of Iraq forthwith comply fully and without delay with all its international obligations, including those set out in resolution 707, in resolution 687, in the Treaty on the Non-Proliferation of Nuclear Weapons of 1 July 1968 (NPT) and in its safeguards agreement with the IAEA (INFCIRC/172, 29 February 1972).

B. *General provisions*

16. Iraq's obligations under paragraph 12 of resolution 687 and paragraph 3 of resolution 707 are broader in scope than the obligations which are undertaken under the Non-Proliferation Treaty and which are verified by the IAEA. While the approaches and techniques to be used under the present plan draw upon the Agency's safeguards experience, the scope and intensity of verification and monitoring under this plan are much greater in order to satisfy the requirements of Security Council resolutions 687 and 707 and to create confidence that the restrictions imposed upon Iraq in the nuclear field are actually complied with.

17. The safeguards agreement concluded with Iraq pursuant to the NPT shall continue to be in force. The

verification activities pursuant to this plan will be carried out in a manner that takes into account the safeguards activities required under the safeguards agreement.

18. The activities under the plan for the future ongoing monitoring and verification of Iraq's compliance with paragraph 12 of resolution 687 and the nuclear aspects of paragraphs 3 and 5 of resolution 707 will be carried out with the assistance and cooperation of the Special Commission, or such other body as may be designated by the Security Council to carry out monitoring and verification activities relevant to Iraq's compliance with paragraph 10 of resolution 687 (chemical, biological and missile). The agency will continue to provide information concerning the conduct and results of Agency inspections and related activities in order to assist the Special Commission in carrying out its tasks under resolution 687, in particular the task to designate sites for nuclear inspection.

19. Financing of the verification and monitoring activities by the Agency in Iraq under the present plan will be secured by United Nations.

C. *Obligations of Iraq*

20. Pursuant to its obligations set forth in the relevant paragraphs of the Security Council resolutions quoted above, Iraq is:

(a) prohibited under paragraph 12 of resolution 687 from acquiring or developing nuclear weapons or nuclear-weapons-usable material or any subsystems or components or any research, development, support or manufacturing facilities related thereto (see annexes 1 and 3);

(b) required under paragraph 3 of resolution 707 to halt all nuclear activities of any kind except for use of isotopes for medical, agricultural or industrial purposes (see annexes 1, 3 and 4); and

(c) required under paragraph 3 of resolution 707 to cease immediately any attempt to conceal, and any movement or destruction without notification to and prior consent of the Special Commission, of material or equipment relating to its nuclear weapons or other nuclear activities. This obligation is without prejudice to the obligation of Iraq to carry out, at the request of the Agency, the movement, destruction or rendering harmless of nuclear material, equipment or other items.

21. Iraq shall accept unconditionally all of the rights of the IAEA enumerated under section E of this plan. Iraq shall take no action to interfere with, impede, or obstruct the exercise of these rights by the Agency. Iraq shall take all measures which, in the view of the Agency, are necessary to facilitate the full exercise by the Agency of its rights under the plan, including, but not limited to:

(a) the designation of the Iraqi authority responsible for liaison with the Agency, and the name or names of the liaison officers within that authority who shall take the necessary measures to secure for the Agency the effective implementation of the Agency's rights laid down in the plan;

(b) notification to the Agency, immediately upon receipt of the name of the IAEA Chief Inspector for an inspection, of the name of the individual who will be the Iraqi Inspection Representative for the inspection;

(c) ensuring the safety and security of Agency personnel and property and the provision, upon request by the Agency, of appropriate escort, medical and other support personnel;

(d) the provision, at no cost to the Agency, of premises that may be necessary for the fulfillment of the Agency's functions in Iraq under the plan; and

(e) the acceptance of United Nations registration of means of transport on land, sea and in the air and United Nations licensing of the operator thereof.

22. Within 30 days of approval of the plan, Iraq shall provide to the Agency, and subsequently maintain current, information in accordance with annex 2 on the following:

(a) an inventory of all nuclear material in Iraq, as defined in annex 1;

(b) an inventory of all facilities, installations and sites in Iraq where nuclear activities of any kind, including but not limited to research facilities, laboratory-scale installations and pilot plants, have been or are carried out, or which are suitable for carrying out such activities;

(c) an inventory of all material, equipment and items in Iraq identified in annex 3;

(d) an inventory of all isotopes in Iraq used for medical, agricultural or industrial applications as identified in annex 4;

(e) information on existing and proposed programmes of nuclear activities in Iraq for the next five year period; and

(f) an inventory of all facilities, installations and sites in Iraq which are provided with any means of supply of electricity exceeding 10 MWe.

23. Iraq shall also provide to the Agency:

(a) complete design information for any planned nuclear facility or installation in Iraq 180 days before the start of construction of any such facility or installation;

(b) advance information on proposed imports and exports of any nuclear materials and isotopes, and non-nuclear material, equipment and items identified in annexes 1, 3 and 4; and

(c) at the request of the Agency, any other information or data which the Agency requires to enable it to monitor Iraq's compliance with resolutions 687 and 707 or any other relevant Security Council resolutions.

24. Nothing in paragraphs 22 or 23 shall be construed as permitting activities, or the import, supply, sale or use of items, to the extent proscribed under Security Council resolutions 687 or 707 or any other relevant resolution of the Security Council.

25. Should Iraq require for use in an activity not prohibited under resolutions 687 and 707 any item in Iraq identified in annex 3 as not proscribed under resolution 687, or require the importation into Iraq of isotopes for use in an activity identified in annex 4, Iraq shall submit, prior to such use or import, respectively, a request to the Director General of the IAEA, specifying precisely the item and the quantities required, the facility, installation or site to be involved in activities with the item, the purpose of its use and the country of the export of the isotopes. The Director General of the IAEA shall examine the request and, with the assistance and cooperation of the Special Commission or its successor, make a decision with regard to the disposition of the request, including any special arrangements which the Director General considers necessary.

26. Should Iraq require the importation for use in an activity not prohibited under resolution 687 or 707 of any item identified in annex 3 as not proscribed under resolution 687, Iraq shall submit prior to import a request to the Committee established by the Security Council under paragraph 6 of resolution 661 (1991), or such other body designated by the Security Council for that purpose, through the Director General of the IAEA, specifying precisely the item and the quantities required, the facility, installation or site to be involved in activities with the item and the purpose of its use. The Director General of the IAEA, with the assistance and cooperation of the Special Commission, shall examine the request and make a recommendation to the Committee with regard to disposition of the request, including any special arrangements considered necessary.

27. At such time as, pursuant to paragraph 3(vi) of resolution 707, the Security Council determines that Iraq is in full compliance with resolution 707 and with paragraphs 12 and 13 of resolution 687 and the IAEA determines that Iraq is in full compliance with its safeguards agreement with the Agency, Iraq may seek to initiate nuclear activities which are not prohibited by resolution 687. To do so, Iraq shall submit a request to the Security Council specifying precisely the activity, the facility, installation or site where it is to be carried out, and the material or other items to be involved. In considering and examining the request, the Security Council may request the advice, assistance and cooperation of the IAEA and the Special Commission or its successor. Iraq shall not undertake any such nuclear activity until the Security Council has approved the activity.

D. Obligations of other States

28. Paragraphs 24, 25 and 27 of Security Council resolution 687, *inter alia,* direct States not to provide to Iraq any of the items proscribed in paragraph 12 of that resolution.

29. Until such time as the Security Council and the IAEA make the determinations called for in paragraph 3 (vi) of resolution 707, States shall also be barred from supplying to Iraq any other nuclear material and any materials, equipment, facilities, other items or training which are especially designed or prepared for use in nuclear activities, except as related to the use of isotopes for medical, agricultural and industrial activities.

30. (a) States shall provide the Agency, 60 days in advance, with full and complete reporting of intended exports to Iraq of isotopes for medical, agricultural and industrial activities to the extent not prohibited by relevant Security Council resolutions as identified in annex 4. States shall also provide the Agency, 60 days in advance, with full and complete reporting of intended exports to Iraq of any item identified in annex 3 as not prohibited under resolution 687 for use in an activity not prohibited under resolutions 687 and 707. Transfers of items identified in annexes 3 and 4 shall be subject to prior approval by the Agency in accordance with the provisions of paragraphs 25 or 26, as appropriate;

(b) At such time as the constraints imposed by resolution 707 are lifted, States shall also provide the Agency, 60 days in advance with full and complete reporting of intended exports to Iraq of any item identified in annex 3 as not prohibited under resolution 687, technological information, including training, and any other relevant items which could be used in nuclear activities not prohibited under resolution 687 (see annex 1). Transfers of such items, information and training shall be subject to prior approval by IAEA, and shall only be transferred for use in activities authorized by the Security Council under the provisions of paragraph 27.

E. Rights of the IAEA

31. Without prejudice to the rights which the Agency has under the safeguards agreement with Iraq, under the Agreement on the Privileges and Immunities of the IAEA, and under the exchange of notes between the Secretary-General and the Foreign Minister of Iraq, which entered into force on 14 May 1991 and which applies to the Agency *mutatis mutandis*, the Agency shall have the following rights:

(a) to carry out inspections, at any time and without hindrance, of any site, facility, area, location, activity, material or other item in Iraq upon designation by the Special Commission or its successor, or upon its own initiative. Iraq shall provide immediate and unimpeded access to, and shall take the measures necessary to enable inspectors to arrive at the location where inspection activities are to be carried out by the time notified by the Agency;

(b) to inspect any number of sites, facilities, areas, locations, activities, materials or items simultaneously or sequentially;

(c) to conduct unannounced inspections and inspections upon short notice;

(d) to secure any site, facility, area, location, activity, material or item to be inspected and prevent any material or other item from being taken to or from the site until the inspection is concluded;

(e) to stop and inspect vehicles, ships, aircraft or any other means of transportation within Iraq. This also includes the right of the Agency to restrict and/or stop movement of suspected material, equipment or other items;

(f) to inspect imports or exports of material and other items upon arrival or departure;

(g) to establish special modes of monitoring and inspection, including prolonged or continuous presence of Inspectors, use of instruments and other arrangements to facilitate monitoring and verification;

(h) to secure full and free access at any time to all sites, facilities, areas, locations, activities, material and other items, including documentation, all persons and all information which, in the Agency's judgement, may be necessary for its monitoring and verification activities. This includes unimpeded access to all nuclear material, facilities and installations, as well as equipment and non-nuclear material relevant to Iraq's undertakings, and all documentation related thereto;

(i) to request, receive, examine, retain, copy and remove any record, data and information, including documentation; to examine and photograph, including by videotaping, any activity or item; and to retain and move any item;

(j) to conduct interviews with any personnel at any site, facility, area or location under inspection, and with any Iraqi official;

(k) to instal containment and surveillance equipment and other equipment and devices and to construct facilities for observation, testing, verification, monitoring and inspection activities;

(l) to verify inventories, and to take and analyse with its own instrumentation, or to request Iraq under the observation of Agency Inspectors to take and/or analyse samples, and to remove and export samples for off-site analysis;

(m) to mark, tag, or otherwise identify any material or other item;

(n) to use its own instrumentation to collect data during inspections and aerial overflights, including photographic, video, infrared and radar data.

32. The Agency shall also have the right:

(a) to unrestricted freedom of entry into and exit from Iraq, without delay or hindrance, of Agency officials and experts, property, supplies, equipment, including means of transport, and other items. No visas shall be required of such personnel travelling on a United Nations laissez-passer or certificate and possessing an inspection assignment document; Iraq shall ensure prompt issuance of visas of entry and exit for such personnel as may not possess a United Nations laissez-passer or certificate;

(b) to unrestricted freedom to move within Iraq, without advance notice, delay or hindrance of Agency officials and experts, property, supplies, equipment, including means of transportation, and other items. Iraq shall, at the request of the Agency, provide means of transportation, maps or other necessary information;

(c) to remove from Iraq any material and any other item, including documentation;

(d) to use its own means of transport, including fixed- and rotary-wing aircraft for overflights throughout Iraq for all relevant purposes, including inspection, surveillance, transportation and/or logistics;

(e) to use airfields in Iraq for purposes determined by the Agency including landing, take-off, basing, maintenance, refuelling and other support. Iraq shall secure priority clearance for aircraft used by the Agency;

(f) to communicate from any place within Iraq, and without censorship or other hindrance, by radio, satellite or other forms of communication and to connect with the IAEA and the United Nations by radio and satellite network, as well as by telephone, telegraph and other means of communication. Iraq shall, upon request of the Agency, provide, appropriate means of communication;

(g) to use codes and receive papers, correspondence and other items by courier or sealed bags; and

(h) to fly the United Nations flag on premises and means of transport.

33. The Agency shall have the right to make its own arrangements to ensure the safety and security of its personnel and property and to take custody of any material or item.

F. *National implementation measures*

34. Iraq shall adopt the necessary measures to implement its obligations under resolutions 687 and 707, and other relevant Security Council resolutions, and the

present plan, in particular to prohibit all natural and legal persons under Iraq's jurisdiction or control from undertaking anywhere any activity that is prohibited for Iraq by resolutions 687 or 707, by other relevant Security Council resolutions or by the present plan. Iraq shall enact penal laws to secure enforcement of these prohibitions.

35. Iraq shall inform the IAEA of the legislative and administrative measures taken to implement resolutions 687 and 707, other relevant Security Council resolutions and the plan not later than 30 days after the approval by the Security Council of the plan and thereafter as determined by the IAEA.

G. *Non-compliance*

36. Should the IAEA discover any item, including documentation, that Iraq, under resolutions 687 or 707, is obliged to yield to the IAEA for destruction, removal or rendering harmless, the IAEA shall have the right to take it into custody and shall provide for its disposal, as appropriate. Iraq shall retain no ownership interest in items to be destroyed, removed or rendered harmless pursuant to resolution 687 or the plan.

37. Should the IAEA discover any activity taking place in contravention of resolutions 687 or 707, it shall have the right to call upon Iraq to halt the activity and to prevent its recurrence. The IAEA shall also have the right to take any prohibited item involved into custody and shall provide for its disposal, as appropriate.

38. Findings by the IAEA that indicate that Iraq is not in compliance with its obligations under resolutions 687 or 707 or the plan shall be brought to the attention of the Security Council.

39. Findings by the IAEA that Iraq is not in compliance with its obligations under the safeguards agreement between Iraq and the IAEA shall, in accordance with the safeguards agreement and the Statute of the Agency, be reported to the Security Council.

H. *Reports*

40. The IAEA shall, through the Secretary-General, report to the Security Council every six months, and at any other time the Security Council may request, on the implementation of the plan.

I. *Revisions*

41. The plan may only be revised by the Security Council. The IAEA may, however, after informing the Security Council, update and revise the annexes in the light of information and experience gained in the course of the implementation of resolutions 687 and 707 and of the plan. The IAEA shall inform Iraq of any such change.

J. *Entry into force and duration*

42. The present plan shall enter into force immediately upon its approval by the Security Council. The duration of the plan shall by determined by the Security Council.

LIST OF ANNEXES

Annex 1 Definitions

Annex 2 Provisions related to information requirements

Annex 3 List of items to be reported to the Agency

Annex 4 List of nuclear activities permitted under Security Council resolution 707

Annex 1
Definitions

For the purposes of UN Security Council resolutions 687 and 707, the following definitions will be adopted:

1. NUCLEAR MATERIAL

1.1 "Source material"

Uranium containing the mixture of isotopes occurring in nature; uranium depleted in the isotope 235; thorium; any of the foregoing in the form of metal, alloy, chemical compound or concentrate.

1.2 "Special fissionable material"

Plutonium-239; uranium-235: uranium-233; uranium enriched in the isotopes 235 or 233; any material containing one or more of the foregoing.

1.3 "Nuclear-weapon-usable material"

Nuclear material that can be used for the manufacture of nuclear explosive components without transmutation or further enrichment, such as plutonium containing less than 80% plutonium-238, uranium enriched to 20% uranium-235 and uranium-233 or more; any chemical compound or mixture of the foregoing. Plutonium, uranium-233 and uranium enriched to less than 20% uranium-235 contained in irradiated fuel do not fall into this category.

2. NUCLEAR ACTIVITIES

2.1-2.9 (inclusive) refer to activities prohibited under both resolutions 687 and 707.

Any activity such as research and development, design, manufacturing, import of systems, equipment and components, pilot plant and plant construction, commissioning and operation, or utilization in one or more of the following:

2.1 Production of nuclear weapons

2.2 Production and any use of nuclear-weapon-usable material

2.3 Production of metals or alloy containing plutonium or uranium

2.4 Weaponization

This covers the research, development, manufacturing and testing required to make nuclear explosives from special fissionable material.

2.5 Nuclear fuel fabrication using plutonium, uranium-233, uranium enriched to 20% or more in uranium-235.

2.6 Import, construction or use of research and power reactors of any kind utilizing uranium enriched to >20% in uranium-235, uranium-233, plutonium or MOX as a fuel or any reactor designed specifically for plutonium production. This includes critical and subcritical assemblies.

2.7 Reprocessing of irradiated fuel

Including the use of hot cells and associated equipment.

2.8 Enrichment of uranium in isotope 235 and any preparatory steps in this process, including the preparation of UCl_4 and UF_6.

2.9 Production and separation of the isotopes of plutonium, hydrogen, lithium and boron

2.10-2.18 (inclusive) refer to activities, permitted under resolution 687 but prohibited under 707.

Any activity such as research and development, design, manufacturing, import of systems, equipment and components, pilot plant and plant construction, commissioning and operation, or utilization in one or more of the following:

2.10 Import, construction or use of research and power reactors of any type utilizing natural uranium or uranium enriched to less than 20% in uranium-235 as a fuel. This includes critical and sub-critical assemblies, but excludes reactors specifically designed for plutonium production.

2.11 Prospecting, mining or processing of ores containing uranium and/or thorium

2.12 Preparation of chemical compounds containing uranium enriched to less than 20% in uranium-235 and thorium, excluding the preparation of UCl_4 and UF_6.

2.13 Nuclear fuel fabrication using natural uranium or uranium enriched to less than 20% in uranium-235.

2.14 Processing and disposal of radioactive wastes

2.15 Nuclear fusion experimental devices based on magnetic or inertial confinement, including diagnostics

2.16 Production of isotopes both radioactive and stable. The production of the isotopes of plutonium, hydrogen, lithium, boron and uranium is prohibited.

2.17 Import, construction and use of neutron sources, electron accelerators, particle accelerators, heavy ion accelerators

2.18 Research on radiation physics and chemistry and on the physical and chemical properties of isotopes except in area relevant to items 2.19, 2.20 and 2.21.

2.19-2.21 (inclusive) refer to activities permitted under resolution 707.

2.19 Application of radiation and isotopes in food and agriculture

2.20 Application of radiation and isotopes in medicine

2.21 Application of radiation and isotopes in industrial processes

Annex 2
Provisions related to information requirements

1. The initial information under paragraph 22 of the plan to be submitted no later than 30 days after the adoption of the plan by the Security Council shall cover the period from 1 January 1989. Subsequent complete information shall be provided each 15 January and 15 July and shall cover the six-month period prior to the provision of the information.

2. Whenever the information that Iraq is required to provide under paragraph 22 of the plan is equal to nil, Iraq shall provide nil returns and confirm this at monthly intervals.

3. The inventory of nuclear material referred to in paragraph 22(a) of the plan shall include the quantity, form, composition, location and current use of such material, including nuclear material containing uranium or thorium which has not reached the composition and purity suitable for fuel fabrication or for being isotopically enriched. For this purpose, the term "use" shall also include storage. The inventory shall be updated at monthly intervals.

4. The information on facilities, installations or sites to be provided under the plan shall, for each facility, installation or site, include:

(a) the name of the facility, installation or site and of the owner, company or enterprise operating the facility, installation or site;

(b) the location of the facility, installation or site;

(c) a meaningful description of all types of activities at the facility, installation or site;

(d) the source(s) of the financing of the facility, installation or site and of its activities;

(e) the design of the facility, installation or site, including blueprints and photos as built;

(f) precise indication where material or other items, including equipment, specified in the plan or in annexes are present, specifying where applicable, building, room, place within the room;

(g) a detailed description of activities related to the material, other items, equipment or processes specified in the plan or in annexes 3 and 4, including as applicable technical characteristics, material flow and process flow diagrams.

5. The location of a facility, installation or site shall be specified by means of the address and a site diagram. Each diagram shall be drawn to scale and shall indicate the boundaries of the facility, installation or site, all road and rail entrances and exits, and all structures on the facility, installation or site, indicating their purpose. If the facility, installation or site is located within a larger complex, the diagram shall specify the exact location of the facility, installation or site within the complex. On each diagram, the geographic coordinates of a point within the facility, installation or site shall be specified to the nearest second.

6. The inventory referred to in paragraph 22(c) of the plan on non-nuclear materials, equipment and items shall include specification of each item, including its packaging, the number and quantity of the item(s), and, where applicable, quantity, form and composition of such items, as well as the location and use (including storage) of all items on the inventory. The inventory shall be updated at monthly intervals.

7. The information to be provided under paragraph 22(d) of the plan on the inventory of all types of isotopes used for medical, agricultural or industrial purposes shall, for each type of isotope, include the quantity, form, composition, location, list of facilities, installations or sites where produced and used (including storage), and the purpose for which used. The inventory shall be updated at monthly intervals.

8. The information on the nuclear programme to be provided under paragraph 22(e) of the plan shall cover the subsequent five years. The information shall be updated on an annual basis, extending until such time as Agency activities under the plan cease. Any proposed changes to the programme shall be notified to, and subject to approval by the Agency before they are made.

9. The information on each import or export to be provided under paragraph 23(b) of the plan shall include quantity, form, and composition of the material, a description of the equipment, and the origin, destination, point and time of entry into Iraq, and proposed use of the item transferred. The information on imports and exports shall be provided at least 60 days before such transaction commences.

10. Iraq shall notify:

(a) any changes in the inventory referred to in paragraph 22 of the plan, one month in advance;

(b) any changes to nuclear programme referred to in paragraph 22 of the plan, one year in advance;

(c) complete description of the design information for any planned nuclear facility, installation or site or any planned modifications of any existing nuclear facility, installation or site, six months before the start of construction or modification of any such facility, installation or site.

11. All information required under the plan should include the corresponding text in English.

Annex 3
List of items to be reported to the Agency

[Editor's note: Annex 3 to document 82 (S/22872/Rev.1) lists equipment, materials and other items that are specifically prohibited to Iraq under resolution 687 or that may be prohibited if they are used in activities prohibited under resolution 687. The original Annex 3 was subsequently revised twice. The first revision was issued on 16 July 1992 as document S/24300. The second revision was issued on 23 March 1995 as document S/1995/215, followed by two corrigenda, S/1995/215/Corr.1, dated 7 April 1995 and S/1995/215/Corr.2, dated 2 August 1995. Annex 3 and its two revisions are not reproduced here but are available at the Dag Hammarskjöld Library at United Nations Headquarters in New York City, at other libraries in the United Nations system or at libraries around the world which have been designated as depository libraries for United Nations documents.]

Annex 4
List of nuclear activities permitted under
Security Council resolution 707

The following peaceful applications of isotopes imported from other States after prior approval by the IAEA are permitted:

1.   AGRICULTURAL APPLICATIONS

1.1   Soil fertility, irrigation and crop production

1.2   Plant breeding and genetics

1.3   Animal production and health

1.4   Insect and pest control

1.5   Food preservation

1.6   Other uses as approved by the IAEA

2. INDUSTRIAL APPLICATIONS

   2.1 Radiography and other non-destructive testing methods

   2.2 Industrial process control and quality control

   2.3 Radiotracer applications in oil, chemical and metallurgical processes

   2.4 Development of water and mineral resources

   2.5 Industrial radiation processing

   2.6 Other uses as approved by the IAEA

3. MEDICAL APPLICATIONS

   3.1 Diagnostic and therapeutic medicine including dosimetry

   3.2 Radiotherapy by teletherapy and brachytherapy

   3.3 Nutrition and health-related environmental studies

   3.4 Other uses as approved by the IAEA

Document 83

Statement to the press by the President of the Security Council concerning implementation of resolution 707 (1991) and the activities of an UNSCOM inspection team in Baghdad

UN Press Release SC/5306-IK/54, 23 September 1991

First, I have just informed the Security Council of the answer given to me yesterday as President of the Council, by the Iraqi Government.

This answer does not meet the requirements set out by the Council. First of all, the Council has received an oral reply whereas it had specifically asked for a formal and written commitment by Iraq that it will implement unreservedly the provisions of resolution 707 (1991). As far as the substance is concerned, the Iraqi Government sticks to the conditions linked to its acceptance of the Security Council resolutions. I must point out that in its answer, the Iraqi Government never referred to resolution 707 but just mentioned resolution 687 (1991).

The members of the Council unanimously thought that this reply falls short of Council's demand and that I should immediately start bilateral consultations to see what further steps the Council might take.

Secondly, the Council has been informed by the Chairman of the Special Commission, Ambassador Rolf Ekéus, of a very serious incident which is currently taking place in Baghdad. The nuclear inspection team, which is now in Iraq, entered with short notice, early this morning in Baghdad, a building suspected to be a centre for records and documents related to Iraq's nuclear programme.

According to the report received by Ambassador Ekéus, the inspectors found in the building a substantial amount of documentation related to Iraq's nuclear activities, *inter alia* Iraq's fissile nuclear programme, and to nuclear weapons. Ambassador Ekéus told the Council that an early assessment by the inspectors indicates that Iraq was engaged in a nuclear weapons development programme.

The Iraqi liaison officer has on instruction from his authorities told the inspectors that they are not allowed to remove the documents and the records. The exit from the building is blocked. The Iraqi authorities have told the team that a decision on the team's request to leave the site with the documents will be given at 7:30 p.m., local time. I have been mandated by the members of the Security Council to get in touch immediately with the Iraqi Foreign Minister and to demand, on behalf of the Council, that the inspectors be given the possibility to leave the site with the documents as it is obliged by Security Council resolutions.

Document 84

Statement to the press by the President of the Security Council concerning the activities of an UNSCOM inspection team in Baghdad

UN Press Release SC/5307-IK/61, 24 September 1991

I have been mandated by the Council to make the four points that follow:

First, the Council gives its full support to the Special Commission and to the inspection team currently present in Iraq which fulfil with exceptional dedication the tasks set out in the relevant resolutions of the Security Council; the Council reiterates that the Special Commission, acting under the authority of the Council, is the sole judge of the definition of the documents, sites or materials subject to inspection.

Secondly, the Council expresses its strong condemnation of the way the Iraqi authorities have repeatedly prevented the inspectors from carrying out their duty. In particular, the Council considers unacceptable the fact that the inspectors are currently denied the possibility to leave freely the premises that they have inspected this morning.

Thirdly, the Council demands that the inspection team be immediately allowed to leave the site where they are kept without any conditions and in particular that they can take with them all the documents they deem appropriate.

Fourthly, the Council asks me to call upon the Ambassador of Iraq to convey to him its serious concerns.

Document 85

Statement to the press by the President of the Security Council concerning the use by UNSCOM of its own helicopters

UN Press Release SC/5308-IK/62, 24 September 1991

The Iraqi Government has sent a letter to the Council on the use by the Special Commission of its own helicopters. I have been instructed to send to the Ambassador of Iraq a letter taking note of the answer that the Council considers as an unconditional acceptance of resolution 707 (1991).

Technical modalities would be set up in the coming days by the Special Commission.

Document 86

Report of the Secretary-General on UNIKOM for the period from 9 April to 2 October 1991

S/23106, 2 October 1991, and addenda: S/23106/Add.1, 4 October 1991, and S/23106/Add.2, 15 October 1991

Introduction

1. By paragraph 5 of its resolution 687 (1991) of 3 April 1991, the Security Council established a demilitarized zone along the Iraq-Kuwait border and decided to set up an observer unit with the following tasks: to monitor the Khawr 'Abd Allah waterway and the demilitarized zone; to deter violations of the boundary through its presence in and surveillance of the demilitarized zone; and to observe any hostile or potentially hostile action mounted from the territory of one State into the other. By its resolution 689 (1991) of 9 April 1991, the Security Council approved my report on the implementation of the above provisions (S/22454 and Add.1-3); noted that the decision to set up the observer unit had been taken in paragraph 5 of resolution 687 (1991) and could only be terminated by the Council's decision; and decided to review the question of termination or continuation as well as the modalities of the United Nations Iraq-Kuwait Observation Mission (UNIKOM) every six months.

2. The purpose of the present report is to provide the Security Council, prior to its review, with an overview of the first six months of UNIKOM activities. It also updates my reports of 9 May (S/22580), 12 June (S/22692) and 3 September 1991 (S/23000), which covered the greater part of the reporting period in some detail.

Setting up of UNIKOM in the field

3. The setting up of UNIKOM in the field began with the arrival of the Chief Military Observer, Major-General Günther G. Greindl, and his advance party in the mission area on 13 April. The advance party comprising military observers temporarily assigned from the United Nations Truce Supervision Organization (UNTSO) and civilian staff. Over the following three weeks, UNIKOM conducted a thorough reconnaissance of its assigned zone, developed a deployment plan, organized its transport, set up a communications network, developed its lines of supply and provided training and familiarization for the incoming personnel. UNIKOM deployment was completed on 6 May. UNIKOM then monitored the withdrawal of the armed forces that were still deployed in its assigned zone. That withdrawal having been completed, the demilitarized zone (DMZ) established by the Security Council came into effect at 2000 hours Greenwich mean time (GMT) on 9 May 1991.

Organization

4. At the beginning of October 1991, UNIKOM comprised the following personnel:

Military observers

Argentina	7	Nigeria	7
Austria	7	Norway	8
Bangladesh	7	Pakistan	9
Canada	1	Poland	7
China	20	Romania	7
Denmark	7	Senegal	7
Fiji	8	Singapore	7
Finland	7	Sweden	8
France	20	Thailand	7
Ghana	8	Turkey	7
Greece	7	Union of Soviet	
Hungary	7	Socialist Republics	20
India	8	United Kingdom of	
Indonesia	7	Great Britain and	
Ireland	8	Northern Ireland	16
Italy	6	United States of America	19
Kenya	8	Uruguay	8
Malaysia	8	Venezuela	7
		Total	295

Administrative and logistic support

Engineers (Canada)	292
Logistics (Sweden)	30
Movement control/post (Denmark)	19
Helicopters (Chile)	50
Medical (Norway)	50
Total	441

UNIKOM includes also 177 civilian staff, of whom 106 are United Nations staff and 71 are locally recruited. Two small fixed-wing aircraft contributed by the Government of Switzerland are operated by civilians. In addition, UNIKOM had the use of chartered aircraft for the movement of troops and equipment and for communications between Baghdad and Kuwait. The Government of Sweden provided free airlift at the beginning of the mission.

5. The plan for UNIKOM, which was formulated in the first days of April, took into account the uncertainties existing at the time and the risks that might arise. For this reason, three infantry companies (Fiji, Ghana, Nepal) from the United Nations Interim Force in Lebanon (UNIFIL) and two infantry companies (Austria and Denmark) from the United Nations Peace-keeping Force in Cyprus (UNFICYP) were temporarily assigned to UNIKOM to provide security. Fortunately the risks perceived in early April did not materialize, and by the end of June the infantry companies returned to their parent missions, as did a logistic company (Sweden) that had also been temporarily detached from UNIFIL.

6. Logistic support for the Mission was difficult at first because the war had resulted in the destruction or severe disruption of the infrastructure in the area. UNIKOM, therefore, relied on substantial support provided by the United States Army and by the forces of other Member States cooperating with Kuwait. The Governments of Iraq and Kuwait also gave support to UNIKOM. The situation has since improved and UNIKOM now has its full complement of transport and communications equipment, much of which came from the United Nations Iran-Iraq Military Observer Group (UNIIMOG). For most of the period, and especially during the summer, living conditions in the DMZ were austere and very demanding, the military personnel being accommodated under canvas. The provision of air-conditioned prefabricated trailers in September has improved conditions greatly. The Mission was launched from and is being supplied through Kuwait, which has the international airport nearest to the DMZ.

7. A serious hazard from the beginning was the large number of mines and unexploded ordnance left over from the war. UNIKOM engineers cleared some 1,100 kilometres of patrol track and the sites for observation

posts, camps and helicopter pads and disposed of some 7,000 mines and pieces of unexploded ordnance. The engineers also carried out construction work on the various camp facilities and on the future headquarters at Umm Qasr. There will be a continuing requirement for explosive ordnance demolition and the maintenance of patrol tracks and facilities in the DMZ. In addition, the Iraq-Kuwait Boundary Demarcation Commission, established under paragraph 3 of resolution 687 (1991), will require significant engineer support. Provision of this has already begun through the clearing of sites and the placing of preliminary survey markers. So far, 121 out of a projected 165 markers have been placed.

8. As I informed the Security Council in my letter of 6 August 1991 (S/22916), a number of adjustments are being made to the logistic support elements. For the reasons mentioned above, 85 engineers will be retained in UNIKOM but their number will be further reduced when the work in support of the Boundary Demarcation Commission has been completed (see S/22916). Further, the Swedish logistic unit, which was made available for six months only, will be withdrawn. Its tasks and that of the movement control staff will be consolidated in one unit of 45 all ranks, which will be provided by Denmark. Finally, the size of the medical unit will be reduced from 50 to 20. These adjustments will be carried out in the next weeks.

9. With the agreement of the Security Council, I have postponed the reduction in the number of military observers that I had intended to effect (S/22977 and S/22978). I shall keep this matter under review and revert to the Council when appropriate.

10. UNIKOM headquarters was initially located south of Kuwait City in a hotel annex made available by the Government of Kuwait. In June, the headquarters moved temporarily to the logistic base at Doha. Work continues at the future headquarters at Umm Qasr to make it habitable.

11. Major-General Greindl and his senior staff have maintained close contact and held regular meetings with the authorities at Baghdad and Kuwait City. In addition, the UNIKOM liaison staff were in daily contact with their Iraqi and Kuwaiti counterparts. UNIKOM maintains liaison offices at Baghdad and Kuwait City. Local liaison with the Iraqi authorities is also effected through an Iraqi liaison office at Umm Qasr.

Demilitarized zone

12. The DMZ is about 200 kilometres long, to which must be added the Khawr 'Abd Allah waterway, with a length of about 40 kilometres. For the most part, the DMZ is barren and almost uninhabited, except for the towns of Umm Qasr and Safwan. There are airfields at Safwan and Umm Qasr and a port at Umm Qasr. A number of roads cross the DMZ, most of them in the eastern part, but the terrain makes cross-country travel easy, and there are numerous tracks, especially in the central and southern sectors. There are few features in the terrain and it is easy to mistake one's location by a wide margin. It is also easy to mistake the location of the border, which remains to be marked.

13. When UNIKOM arrived in the area, a large number of displaced persons were in the Safwan area. Most of these were moved prior to the establishment of the DMZ, and only a small number remain at the Abdali camp on Kuwaiti territory south of Safwan.

Deployment and concept of operations

14. For operational purposes, UNIKOM has divided the DMZ into three sectors. Each sector has a headquarters and six observation posts/patrol bases. UNIKOM enjoys full freedom of movement throughout the DMZ. The deployment of UNIKOM is shown on the attached map [not reproduced here].

15. UNIKOM's concept of operations, which has been further refined during recent months, places emphasis on mobile patrols in order to observe the length and breadth of the DMZ. The fixed observation posts serve as patrol bases from which the military observers patrol their assigned sectors and visit temporary observation points established in areas of particular activity or where roads and tracks enter the DMZ. In addition to the patrols, all other movements, supply runs for example, are also used for observation; investigation teams are frequently dispatched. Observation on the ground is supplemented by air patrols, using helicopters and the two fixed-wing aircraft. Again, all other flights are also used for observation.

Violations and complaints

16. Since the DMZ came into effect on 9 May, UNIKOM has observed three types of violations: minor incursions on the ground by small groups of soldiers, often just one or two; overflights by military aircraft; and the carrying by policemen of weapons other than side-arms. The largest number of ground incursions, 65, occurred in the month immediately after the establishment of the DMZ. UNIKOM then put up signs on the main roads and tracks to mark entry into the DMZ; after that, the number of ground incursions dropped significantly. The overflights were by military aircraft of a type used by the forces of Member States cooperating with Kuwait and, since early September, also of a type used by Kuwait.

17. In order to reduce the risk of incidents and as envisaged from the outset (S/22454, para. 6), UNIKOM obtained the agreement of the Governments of Iraq and Kuwait that their police operating in the DMZ would

carry only sidearms. Both sides have expressed misgivings about this limitation, pointing out that smugglers and other elements with whom the police have to contend are generally armed with rifles and light machine-guns. UNIKOM has observed a number of violations by both sides, including cases in which policemen have kept rifles out of sight in their posts and vehicles.

18. The following table summarizes the violations observed by UNIKOM:

| | Iraq | | | | Kuwait/allied forces | | | |
	Ground	Air	Police weapons	Total	Ground	Air	Police weapons	Total
10 May-9 June	8	-	-	8	57	29	-	86
10 June-9 July	4	-	-	4	29	28	-	57
10 July-9 August	1	-	6	7	9	9	6	24
10 August-9 September	5	-	4	9	13	13	1	27
10 September-2 October	-	-	1	1	6	7	3	16
Total	18	-	11	29	114	86	10	210

All violations were raised in writing with the party concerned, with a view to preventing a recurrence.

19. During the reporting period, UNIKOM received 28 written complaints from Iraq and 10 from Kuwait. It investigated those complaints and was able in 13 cases to establish the facts through its own observation. The results of the investigations were conveyed to the party concerned.

Other matters

20. One of the purposes of UNIKOM is to deter violations of the boundary between Iraq and Kuwait through its presence in, and surveillance of, the DMZ. Pending demarcation of the boundary, UNIKOM has not taken a position concerning its precise location. UNIKOM uses a British map, which it has given to both sides for reference. They have agreed to work with it as a practical arrangement to facilitate UNIKOM's task and without prejudice to their positions concerning the boundary.

21. In order to avoid friction and incidents, UNIKOM has established the principle that the Iraqi and Kuwaiti authorities, including police, should stay a reasonable distance of 1,000 metres from the boundary line shown on UNIKOM maps. It is not intended that this should lead to the creation of a no-man's land. The authorities retain the right to carry out their functions throughout their respective parts of the DMZ, except that they are expected to consult UNIKOM in advance if those functions should require them to approach closer than 1,000 metres to the boundary line shown on UNIKOM's map [not reproduced here]. Such consultation enables UNIKOM to take measures to avoid incidents.

22. Two main problems have arisen in this regard. First, the removal from storage at Umm Qasr of 11 "HY-2G" missiles and later 4 further missiles of the same

type. I informed the Security Council of this matter on 5 July. UNIKOM took it up with the Iraqi authorities, who have since returned 4 of the missiles to the storage at Umm Qasr but not the other 11.

23. Secondly, Iraq has deployed 4 border police centres and 10 border police posts in the DMZ. Five of the posts are on the Kuwaiti side of the boundary line shown on the UNIKOM map; two are closer to it than 1,000 metres, on the Iraqi side. Lengthy and intensive efforts have been made at United Nations Headquarters as well as in the field to persuade Iraq to move the seven posts further back. However, the Iraqi authorities have maintained that they had been in place before 2 August 1990 and that they would not be pulled back because of the political implications. The Iraqi authorities have assured UNIKOM that Iraq will comply with the reasonable distance principle, once the boundary is demarcated. UNIKOM has recently observed harbour and local police at Umm Qasr, and the Iraqi authorities have indicated that they intend to deploy more policemen in the DMZ. They have undertaken to consult UNIKOM in advance of such deployment.

24. For its part, Kuwait has established five police posts and one police observation point in the DMZ. The Kuwaiti authorities have been in touch with UNIKOM about the locations of these posts and of additional posts which they plan to set up. They have also reiterated their willingness to comply with the reasonable distance principle if the Iraqi authorities do so as well.

25. In accordance with the plan approved by the Security Council in its resolution 689 (1991), UNIKOM requires that it be informed in advance of the movement of ships through the Khawr 'Abd Allah waterway (see S/22454, para. 6). In September, UNIKOM observed movements by an Iraqi pilot ship and a maintenance ship between Umm Qasr and the Khawr 'Abd Allah water-

way. UNIKOM had not been informed of these movements and raised them with the Iraqi authorities, who have since complied with the UNIKOM notification requirement.

26. In the course of August, tension rose as a result of incursions from Iraq into Kuwaiti territory by persons collecting weapons, ammunition and other battlefield items. These persons, and others similarly engaged in the Iraqi part of the DMZ, were dressed in civilian clothes and used civilian vehicles. The question has been raised whether they are in fact military personnel but UNIKOM has not been able to establish that this is so. It has, however, been informed by the Iraqi authorities that they offer rewards to persons who retrieve weapons and ammunition from the battlefield. It has also had indications that there is an unofficial market for such items in Iraq. In addition to its own observations, UNIKOM has been informed by the Kuwaiti authorities of such incursions and of arrests they have made. One such incident investigated by UNIKOM occurred on 28 August, when the Kuwaiti Coast Guard took 12 small vessels and detained 45 Iraqis off the Kuwaiti island of Bubiyan. I reported on these matters on 3 September (S/23000, paras. 12-14). Subsequently such incursions subsided. However, on 30 September and 1 October, UNIKOM observed in its southern sector Iraqis collecting mines on the Kuwaiti side of the line shown on the UNIKOM map [not reproduced here], at a minefield that straddles that line.

27. In the Iraqi part of the DMZ the collection of military equipment and ammunition has continued. Recently, mines and unexploded ordnance have also been lifted. It is evident that there are persons engaged in this dangerous activity who are not trained for it; there have been numerous casualties and to UNIKOM's knowledge at least 16 persons have died during the last 10 days. Many of the casualties were brought to UNIKOM posts, from where they were evacuated by helicopter and treated by UNIKOM's medical staff. UNIKOM raised this matter with the Iraqi authorities on humanitarian grounds. On 2 October 1991, the Iraqi authorities informed UNIKOM that they had issued strict instructions to the police to stop civilians from collecting mines in the DMZ. It is hoped therefore that the problems described in this and the preceding paragraph will not recur.

28. I have reported previously about the so-called "sheep market", an illegal market where alcohol and arms are traded as well as livestock (S/23000, para.11). That market has recently moved to a location astride the boundary line in the southern sector. On 15 September, UNIKOM received a complaint from the Kuwaiti liaison staff with the request that it investigate an incident in which 80 armed men from the market had allegedly attacked a Kuwaiti police post with rifles and rocket-propelled grenades and had taken two policemen hostage. The UNIKOM team investigating the incident found no evidence of damage to the police cabins or vehicles, and established that the two missing policemen had been on an errand in Kuwait City. At the sheep market, the traders stated that they had approached the police post to borrow water but the policemen had opened fire, killing one. The UNIKOM team found that man's body some 20 metres from the police post and at the sheep market was shown a water truck with numerous bullet holes.

Financial aspects

29. Should the Security Council continue the mandate of UNIKOM beyond 8 October 1991, the cost of maintaining the Mission for a period of six months would be approximately US $40 million, based on the continuance of its existing strength and responsibilities. The resources needed for maintaining UNIKOM beyond 8 October 1991 will be sought from the General Assembly at its forty-sixth session. In the event that the mandate is extended beyond six months, the Secretary-General will report to the Advisory Committee on Administrative and Budgetary Questions and to the General Assembly during its forty-seventh session on the additional resources needed.

Observations

30. During the last six months, UNIKOM deployed in its area of operation and carried out its tasks pursuant to the mandate entrusted to it by the Security Council in paragraph 5 of its resolution 687 (1991) and in accordance with the implementation plan approved by the Council in its resolution 689 (1991). The DMZ established by the Security Council has been generally respected and the area has been calm. UNIKOM has thus served the purpose for which it was created and, in the light of all the circumstances, I recommend that the Security Council maintain it in the area for a further six-month period.

31. As indicated by the table in paragraph 18 above, there have been rather few violations due to ground incursions by military personnel into the DMZ and their frequency has been falling. The main source of friction during the period under review has been the movement of persons from Iraq to Kuwait across a border which remains to be demarcated. Given Kuwait's recent experience, these unauthorized border crossings have understandably given cause for concern to the Kuwaiti authorities, who have frequently raised them with UNIKOM.

32. Some of these border crossings are by Bedouins and reflect a longstanding practice which has been countenanced by both sides in the past. Others are attributable to the suppliers and customers of the illegal sheep market, which itself changes location from time to time in the

border area. These movements are of some concern to UNIKOM because of the violent incidents to which they sometimes give rise and because those associated with the sheep market are armed with, and trade in, weapons of a higher calibre than those which the police of either side are permitted to carry in the DMZ. This is essentially a law and order problem, which UNIKOM has drawn to the attention of both Governments.

33. A third category of border crossings is caused by persons from Iraq who have penetrated deep into Kuwait in search of weapons, ammunition and other battlefield items. As far as UNIKOM has been able to ascertain, these persons are civilians attracted by the prices which such items fetch, from official or unofficial purchasers, in Iraq. Again, UNIKOM has raised this matter with the Iraqi authorities both because of the tension to which it can give rise and, on humanitarian grounds, because of the carnage suffered by the persons who engage in this very dangerous practice (see para. 27 above).

34. UNIKOM's responsibilities *vis-à-vis* unauthorized border crossings in these various categories have been misunderstood in some quarters. When UNIKOM first deployed it encountered the widely held expectation in the area that it would assume overall responsibility in the DMZ and police it. In the same vein, it was often referred to as the "United Nations forces". To some extent, these expectations have persisted. It is therefore worth repeating that UNIKOM has been constituted as an observation mission and does not have the authority, under the terms of resolution 689 (1991), to assume law enforcement functions. Nor does it have the capacity to do so; the military observers are unarmed and the armed infantry elements have been withdrawn.

35. The continued presence of Iraqi police posts on the Kuwaiti side of the line shown on UNIKOM's map remains a matter of concern. I have instructed the Chief Military Observer of UNIKOM to persevere in his efforts to have these police posts pulled back behind the line.

36. UNIKOM has functioned well, with the cooperation of the parties. Its concept of operations has proven adequate to the task and Major-General Greindl is confident that UNIKOM would detect any significant military movement in or close to the DMZ. With additional experience, the UNIKOM operations will be further refined. There is, however, one aspect of its modalities that seems to require early improvement. This relates to its observation capability, particularly when the weather conditions limit visibility and make air surveillance difficult. Such difficulties cannot be overcome by increasing the number of military observers; UNIKOM is very adequately staffed. Electronic instruments, especially radar, would seem to provide the only means of ensuring continuous observation throughout the DMZ. General

Greindl has made a recommendation to this effect, which is now being studied, taking into account financial as well as operational considerations.

37. Finally, I wish to express my appreciation to the Governments that have contributed personnel to UNIKOM and have provided support in other practical forms. I also wish to pay tribute to Major-General Greindl, to his military and civilian staff, to the military observers and to the soldiers of the support units for the skill and dedication with which they have carried out their tasks in difficult conditions.

Addendum (S/23106/Add.1, 4 October 1991)

1. In paragraph 27 of my report of 2 October 1991 (S/23106) on the United Nations Iraq-Kuwait Observation Mission (UNIKOM), I informed the Security Council that on that day the Iraqi authorities had issued strict instructions to their police to stop civilians from collecting mines in the demilitarized zone (DMZ). However, the Chief Military Observer has since reported that on 2 October 1991 at least 60 Iraqi civilians, with 8 trucks and 40 pick-up vehicles, were observed by UNIKOM collecting mines at a location 15 kilometres south of observation post S-3. Most of the activity was on the Kuwaiti side of the border, both inside and outside the DMZ. Iraqi police, when contacted by UNIKOM observers, said that they had no orders to stop the collection of mines.

2. On 3 October 1991, no mine-collecting activity was observed by UNIKOM. On 4 October, however, the Mission observed a resumption of such activity. Some 50 Iraqi civilians, with 13 trucks and 9 pick-up vehicles, were again observed collecting mines 15 kilometres south of observation post S-3. Once more, they were in the Iraqi and Kuwaiti parts of the DMZ, as well as in Kuwaiti territory outside it. Also, three trucks loaded with mines and four pick-up vehicles with some 30 civilians were observed travelling south at the edge of the DMZ in Kuwait territory, approximately 16 kilometres north-east of observation post S-4.

3. On 3 October 1991 the Chief Military Observer again raised the matter with the Iraqi authorities at Baghdad. He urged them to take immediate action to stop any civilian from crossing the border into Kuwait and, in general, to prevent civilians from undertaking this dangerous practice. The Iraqi authorities expressed astonishment that it was still continuing and assured the Chief Military Observer that strict instructions had been given to the police authorities to prevent mine collecting by civilians. They said that they would take urgent measures to rectify the situation. They also requested UNIKOM to provide them with all dates and locations when Iraqi civilians had been observed collecting mines

in the DMZ. This information was delivered in writing today, 4 October 1991.

4. I have instructed the Chief Military Observer to continue to follow this matter closely and I shall keep the Security Council informed, as necessary.

Addendum (S/23106/Add.2, 15 October 1991)

1. The purpose of this second addendum to my report of 2 October 1991 is to follow up on two issues that had remained pending. The first concerns the Iraqi border police posts that are on the Kuwaiti side of the boundary line shown on the United Nations Iraq-Kuwait Observation Mission (UNIKOM) map [not reproduced here] or closer than 1,000 metres to that line (S/23106, paras. 23 and 35). The second concerns the collecting of mines by Iraqis in the Iraqi as well as the Kuwaiti parts of the demilitarized zone (DMZ) and in some cases well outside the DMZ in Kuwaiti territory (see S/23106/Add.1).

2. On my instructions, Major-General Günther G. Greindl last week again took up both issues with the Iraqi authorities.

3. In the matter of the police posts, the Iraqi authorities reiterated their position that the posts had been in place before 2 August 1990 and that they would not be pulled back because of the political implications. They added that the matter would be settled by the Iraq-Kuwait Boundary Demarcation Commission's decision regarding the course of the border. In the meantime, the border police were under orders to avoid any clashes.

4. With regard to the collecting of mines, the Iraqi authorities undertook to do everything necessary to prevent uncontrolled collection and to notify UNIKOM in advance of any future mine clearing in the DMZ. UNIKOM observed no collecting of mines on Kuwaiti territory after 10 October 1991 and none at all after 11 October.

Document 87

Statement by the President of the Security Council concerning the sanctions regime

S/23107, 2 October 1991

The members of the Security Council held informal consultations on 2 October 1991 pursuant to paragraph 21 of resolution 687 (1991).

After hearing all the opinions expressed in the course of the consultations, the President of the Council con-cluded that there was no agreement that the necessary conditions existed for a modification of the regime established in paragraph 20 of resolution 687 (1991), as referred to in paragraph 21 of that resolution.

Document 88

Report of the Secretary-General transmitting the plan, revised pursuant to the adoption of Security Council resolution 707 (1991), for future monitoring and verification of Iraq's compliance with the destruction or removal of weapons specified in Security Council resolution 687 (1991)

S/22871/Rev.1, 2 October 1991

I. General

A. *Introduction*

1. The present report is submitted in pursuance of Security Council resolution 687 (1991). In paragraph 10 of section C of that resolution, the Security Council requested the Secretary-General, in consultation with the Special Commission, to develop and submit for approval a plan for the ongoing monitoring and verification of Iraq's compliance with its obligations under that paragraph. The Plan is contained in section II of the present report.

2. As outlined in my report to the Security Council of 17 May 1991 (S/22614), the provisions of section C of resolution 687 (1991) lend themselves to a three-stage

implementation procedure: gathering and assessment of information; disposal of weapons and facilities and all other items specified in paragraphs 8 and 12 of resolution 687 (1991); and ongoing monitoring and verification of Iraq's compliance. The first two stages are currently being implemented and will continue until their objectives are fully achieved.

3. The Plan submitted in the present report addresses the third stage, i.e. ongoing monitoring and verification of Iraq's compliance with its unconditional obligation not to use, retain, possess, develop, construct or otherwise acquire any weapons or related items prohibited under paragraphs 8 and 9 of resolution 687 (1991). Thus, monitoring and verification will need to cover not only military but also civilian sites, facilities, material and other items that could be used or activities that could be involved in contravention of Iraq's obligations under resolution 687 (1991). The Plan incorporates the additional obligations of Iraq under Security Council resolution 707 (1991) and the corresponding monitoring and verification activities.

4. The Plan should enter into force directly upon its approval by the Security Council, which means that the early stages of its implementation and the later stages of the disposal of existing prohibited weapons, facilities and related items would take place simultaneously. This would, at an early stage, prevent Iraq from developing new capabilities regarding the relevant weapons categories, thus already closing a potential loophole during the first stages of the implementation of section C of resolution 687 (1991). Carefully managed use of available resources would make it possible to carry out the dual tasks in parallel, to great effect. With the gradual completion of the disposal of Iraq's present weapons capabilities, resources can gradually be transferred and streamlined without therefore, at any stage, compromising the efficiency of the verification of Iraq's compliance with its obligations under resolutions 687 (1991) and 707 (1991). In paragraph 14 of its resolution 687 (1991) the Security Council noted that the actions to be taken by Iraq in paragraphs 8, 9, 10, 11, 12 and 13 of that resolution "represent steps towards the goal of establishing in the Middle East a zone free from weapons of mass destruction and all missiles for their delivery and the objective of a global ban on chemical weapons". The implementation of the Plan, developed pursuant to paragraph 10 of resolution 687 (1991), will contribute to an environment conducive to achieving the above-mentioned goal and objective.

B. Institutional and organizational aspects

5. Bearing in mind that resolutions 687 (1991) and 707 (1991) were adopted by the Security Council acting

under Chapter VII of the Charter of the United Nations, it is assumed that the task of carrying out the monitoring and verification provided for under the Plan should be entrusted to an executive body under the authority of the Security Council. This is particularly important should any situation arise of non-compliance by Iraq with its obligations under section C of resolution 687 (1991) and under resolution 707 (1991).

6. The intrinsic interrelationship between paragraphs 8, 9 and 10 of resolution 687 (1991) requires that this body make direct use of the expertise, the information gathered and assessed and the experience gained by the Special Commission established as a subsidiary organ of the Security Council pursuant to paragraph 9 of resolution 687 (1991).

7. In view of these considerations, it would appear most practical and efficient that a compliance unit be organized under the Special Commission in order to carry out the monitoring and verification tasks provided for under the Plan. The present arrangements for staffing would continue on a revised scale, with appropriate support from the Department for Disarmament Affairs. The financing of the Plan would have to be determined by the competent United Nations organs, possibly in the same way as the arrangements agreed upon for the present phase of the Special Commission's work.

8. The operational requirements will be similar to those now in place for the Special Commission. These include a staff at the United Nations Headquarters in New York to assist the Executive Chairman of the Special Commission, compile and analyse information, schedule, plan and organize inspections and aerial overflights, prepare other field operations and provide general administrative support. A staff will be needed in the region to provide logistic, administrative and other support for field operations in Iraq.

C. Cooperation with the Security Council Committee established by resolution 661 (1990) concerning the situation between Iraq and Kuwait

9. Through resolution 661 (1990) and subsequent related resolutions, including resolution 687 (1991), *inter alia*, its section F, a comprehensive set of sanctions was established to be implemented by all States against Iraq. The prohibition of the acquisition by Iraq of any weapons and related items specified in paragraphs 8 and 12 of resolution 687 (1991) and of the sale or supply to Iraq by other States of these items is of unlimited duration. However, it cannot be excluded that the Security Council, at a future date, may wish to review the present sanctions regarding items with dual use, i.e. items that could be used for prohibited as well as non-prohibited purposes. In order to ensure that such items are not used for prohibited

purposes, the Plan submitted in the present report includes specific provisions for the monitoring and verification, from within Iraq, of any eventual import by Iraq of relevant items with dual use.

10. The efficacy of these provisions would be enhanced if they were complemented by transparency and timely information as regards any future sale or supply by other States to Iraq of relevant items with dual use. Such a comprehensive approach would call for the development of a mechanism that:

(a) Upholds the prohibition on the sale and supply to Iraq by other States of any weapons or related items prohibited under section C of resolution 687 (1991);

(b) Provides for timely information about any sale or supply to Iraq by other States of items that could be used not only for permitted purposes but also for purposes prohibited under resolution 687 (1991).

11. The Plan submitted in the present report contains in its annexes lists of items relevant to the monitoring and verification, from within Iraq, of prohibited items as well as of items with dual use. These should be taken into account in the development of a mechanism related to the sale or supply of items to Iraq by other countries.

12. Such a mechanism should be developed with the cooperation of the Special Commission, the Director General of the International Atomic Energy Agency and the Committee established by resolution 661 (1990) at the earliest possible date, and not later than before the lifting of sanctions covering relevant items.

II. The plan

A. *Scope*

13. In accepting unconditionally Security Council resolution 687 (1991), Iraq has undertaken not to use, retain, possess, develop, construct or otherwise acquire:

(a) Any chemical or biological weapons or any stocks of agents or any related subsystems or components or any research, development, support or manufacturing facilities;

(b) Any ballistic missiles with a range greater than 150 kilometres or any related major parts, including launchers, or any repair or production facilities.

14. In order to ensure Iraq's compliance with these undertakings, the Special Commission, pursuant to resolutions 687 (1991) and 707 (1991), shall, through inspections and through aerial overflights, as well as through the provision of information by Iraq, monitor and verify that activities, sites, facilities, material and other items, both military and civilian, are not used by Iraq in contravention of its obligations under resolutions 687 (1991) and 707 (1991).

15. To this end, the provisions set forth in the Plan and its annexes, which constitute an integral part of the Plan, shall apply.

B. *General provisions*

1. *Information*

16. Iraq shall:

(a) Provide to the Special Commission, on a regular basis, full, complete, correct and timely information on activities, sites, facilities, material and other items, both military and civilian, that might be used for purposes prohibited under paragraph 10 of resolution 687 (1991);

(b) Provide to the Special Commission full, complete, correct and timely information on any additional activities, sites, facilities, material or other items that the Commission may designate for provision of information on a regular basis;

(c) Provide to the Special Commission, fully, completely, and promptly, any additional information or clarification that the Commission may request and respond fully, completely and promptly to any questions or requests from the Special Commission.

Further provisions related to the submission of information are set forth in sections C, D and E and in annexes II, III and IV of the Plan.

2. *Inspections and aerial overflights*

17. The Special Commission shall have the right:

(a) To designate for inspection any site, facility, activity, material or other item in Iraq;

(b) To carry out inspections, at any time and without hindrance, of any site, facility, activity, material or other item in Iraq;

(c) To conduct unannounced inspections and inspections at short notice;

(d) To inspect any number of declared or designated sites or facilities simultaneously or sequentially;

(e) To designate for aerial overflight any area, location, site or facility in Iraq;

(f) To conduct, at any time and without hindrance, both fixed-wing and rotary-wing flights throughout Iraq for all relevant purposes, including inspection, surveillance, aerial overflights (surveys), transportation and logistics without interference of any kind and upon such terms and conditions as may be determined by the Special Commission;

(g) To make full use of its own aircraft with appropriate sensors as necessary and such airfields in Iraq as the Special Commission may determine are most appropriate for its work;

(h) To consider and decide upon requests by Iraq to move or destroy any material, equipment or item relating to its nuclear, chemical or biological weapons or ballistic missile programmes, or material, equipment or any item relating to its other nuclear activities.

18. Iraq shall:

(a) Accept unconditionally the inspection of any site, facility, activity, material or other item declared by Iraq or designated by the Special Commission;

(b) Accept unconditionally aerial overflight of any area, location, site or facility designated by the Special Commission;

(c) Provide immediate and unimpeded access to any site, facility, activity, material or other item to be inspected;

(d) Accept unconditionally and cooperate with the Special Commission in conducting fixed-wing and rotary-wing flights throughout Iraq for all relevant purposes, including inspection, surveillance, aerial overflights (surveys), transportation and logistics upon the terms and conditions determined by the Special Commission;

(e) Accept unconditionally the Special Commission's determinations regarding use of the Commission's aircraft with appropriate sensors as necessary and airfields in Iraq for such aircraft;

(f) Not obstruct aerial overflights or take concealment measures at any area, location, site or facility designated by the Special Commission for inspection or overflight;

(g) Accept unconditionally the inspectors and all other personnel designated by the Special Commission and ensure the complete implementation of the privileges, immunities and facilities of the personnel of the Special Commission and their complete safety and freedom of movement;

(h) Cooperate fully with the Special Commission and facilitate its inspections, overflights and other activities under the Plan;

(i) Accept unconditionally the rights of the Special Commission under the Plan and not take any action to interfere with, impede, or obstruct the exercise by the Special Commission of its functions and rights under Security Council resolutions 687 (1991), 707 (1991) and the Plan;

(j) Designate its Inspection Representative for each inspection to accompany the inspection team in Iraq;

(k) Invite and accept unconditionally the decision of the Special Commission on any requests by Iraq to move or destroy any material, equipment or item relating to its nuclear, chemical or biological weapons or ballistic missile programmes, or material, equipment or any item relating to its other nuclear activities.

19. Further provisions on inspections, aerial overflights, security, privileges and immunities and related provisions are set forth in annex I.

3. *National implementation measures*

20. Iraq shall adopt the necessary measures to implement its obligations under section C of resolution 687 (1991), resolution 707 (1991) and the Plan, in particular:

(a) To prohibit all natural and legal persons under Iraq's jurisdiction or control from undertaking anywhere any activity that is prohibited for Iraq by resolutions 687 (1991), 707 (1991), by other related Security Council resolutions or by the Plan;

(b) To enact penal legislation which, in conformity with international law, shall extend to the activities referred to under subparagraph (a) above undertaken anywhere by any natural or legal persons under Iraq's jurisdiction or control.

21. Iraq shall inform the Special Commission of legislative and administrative measures taken to implement resolutions 687 (1991), 707 (1991), other relevant Security Council resolutions and the Plan, not later than 30 days after the approval by the Security Council of the Plan and thereafter as determined by the Special Commission.

4. *Non-compliance*

22. Should the Special Commission discover any item, including any documentation, that Iraq, under resolution 687 (1991), is obliged to destroy or to yield to the Special Commission for destruction, removal or rendering harmless, the Special Commission shall have the right to take it into custody and shall provide for its disposal, as appropriate. Iraq shall retain no ownership interest in items to be destroyed, removed or rendered harmless pursuant to resolution 687 (1991) and the Plan.

23. Should the Special Commission discover any activity taking place in contravention of resolutions 687 (1991), 707 (1991) or of the Plan, it shall have the right to call upon Iraq to halt the activity and to prevent its recurrence. The Special Commission shall also have the right to take any prohibited item involved, including any documentation, into custody and shall provide for its disposal, as appropriate.

24. Findings by the Special Commission that indicate that Iraq is not in compliance with its obligations under resolutions 687 (1991) and 707 (1991) or the Plan shall be brought to the attention of the Security Council.

5. *Reports*

25. The Special Commission shall, through the Secretary-General, report to the Security Council every six months on the implementation of the Plan and at any other time the Security Council may request.

6. Revisions

26. The Plan may only be revised by the Security Council. The Special Commission may, however, after informing the Security Council, update and revise the annexes in the light of information and experience gained in the course of the implementation of resolutions 687 (1991) and 707 (1991) and of the Plan. The Special Commission shall inform Iraq of any such change.

7. Entry into force and duration

27. The Plan shall enter into force immediately upon its approval by the Security Council. The duration of the Plan shall be determined by the Security Council.

C. Provisions related to chemical items

28. Chemicals, equipment and facilities set forth herein and in annex II could be used for purposes related to chemical weapons. They shall therefore be subject to monitoring and verification in accordance with the following additional provisions in order to ensure that Iraq does not use, develop, produce or otherwise acquire chemical weapons or related items prohibited under resolution 687 (1991).

29. Chemicals that could be used for the development, production or acquisition of chemical weapons but which also have significant uses for purposes not prohibited by resolution 687 (1991) are set forth in list A in annex II. These chemicals may be used, developed, produced, stored or acquired solely for purposes not prohibited by resolution 687 (1991), subject to the provisions under paragraphs 30 and 31 below, and annex II.

30. Iraq shall, not later than 30 days after the adoption of the Plan by the Security Council, and on a regular basis thereafter, provide to the Special Commission information in accordance with annex II regarding:

(a) The total national quantity of the production, processing or consumption of any chemical specified in list A of annex II and of the import and export of any of these chemicals specifying the supplier or recipient countries involved;

(b) Any site or facility that is involved in production, processing, consumption, storage, import or export of one tonne or more per year of any chemical specified in list A of annex II or that at any time has been involved in activities with any of these chemicals for chemical weapons purposes;

(c) Any site or facility that is involved in production or processing of organophosphorus chemicals or is involved in production of organic chemicals by chlorination;

(d) Any site or facility where production, processing, consumption, storage, import or export of one tonne or more per year of any chemical specified in list A of annex II, or where production or processing of organophosphorus chemicals or where production of organic chemicals by chlorination is planned;

(e) Any import or any other acquisition of equipment or technologies intended for production and processing of any chemical specified in list A of annex II, of any organophosphorus chemical or for production of organic chemicals by chlorination.

31. Should Iraq plan any production, processing, consumption, storage, import or export not notified under paragraph 30 (d) above, it may begin such an activity only after providing to the Special Commission a special notification in accordance with annex II.

32. Chemicals that have little or no use except as chemical warfare agents or for the development, production or acquisition of chemical weapons or which have been used by Iraq as essential precursors for chemical weapons are set forth in list B of annex II. Iraq shall not retain, use, transfer, develop, produce, store, import or otherwise acquire these chemicals. Should Iraq require any chemical specified in list B of annex II, it shall submit a request to the Special Commission specifying precisely the chemical and the quantities required, the site or facility where it is to be used and the purpose of its use. The Special Commission will examine and decide on the request and establish the special arrangements it considers consistent with resolution 687 (1991).

33. Further provisions related to chemical items are set forth in annex II.

D. Provisions related to biological items

34. Micro-organisms and toxins, equipment and facilities set forth herein and in annex III could be used for purposes related to biological and toxin weapons affecting humans, animals or plants. They shall therefore be subject to monitoring and verification in accordance with the following additional provisions in order to ensure that Iraq does not use, develop, produce or otherwise acquire biological and toxin weapons or related items prohibited under resolution 687 (1991).

35. Iraq shall, not later than 30 days after the adoption of the Plan by the Security Council, and on a regular basis thereafter, provide to the Special Commission information in accordance with annex III regarding:

(a) Any site or facility at which work with toxins or with micro-organisms meeting the criteria for risk groups IV, III or II according to the classification in the 1983 World Health Organization (WHO) *Laboratory Biosafety Manual* is carried out, or any site or facility at which work with genetic material coding for toxins or genes derived from the aforementioned micro-organisms is carried out;

(b) Any site or facility having a laboratory (unit) meeting the criteria for a "maximum containment laboratory" or "containment laboratory" as specified in the 1983 WHO *Laboratory Biosafety Manual*, such as those designated as biosafety level 4 (BL4) or P4, biosafety level 3 (BL3) or P3 or equivalent standards and any site or facility being constructed or modified so as to possess such containment capabilities;

(c) Any site or facility at which fermentation or other means for the production of micro-organisms or toxins using vessels larger than 10 litres individually or 40 litres in the aggregate is carried out;

(d) Any site or facility for the bulk storage of toxins or of micro-organisms meeting the criteria for risk groups IV, III or II;

(e) Any site or facility for the production of vaccines;

(f) Any research, development, testing or other support or manufacturing facility for equipment and other items specified in paragraph 1 of annex III;

(g) Any imports, other acquisition or exports of micro-organisms meeting the criteria for risk groups IV, III and II, toxins and vaccines, as well as related equipment and facilities, specifying the supplier or recipient countries involved.

36. Iraq shall, not later than 30 days after the adoption of the Plan by the Security Council, and on a regular basis thereafter, provide to the Special Commission:

(a) A list of all documents of a scientific and technical nature published or prepared by any site or facility engaged in work relating to toxins or micro-organisms meeting the criteria for risk groups IV, III and II, including those of a theoretical nature. Full copies of such documents shall be made available by Iraq to the Special Commission upon request. Documents of a purely diagnostic nature relating to risk group II micro-organisms are excepted;

(b) A description of all work on toxins or micro-organisms meeting the criteria for risk groups IV, III or II as well as of all work being conducted on the dissemination of micro-organisms or toxins into the environment or on processes that would lead to such dissemination, specifying the site or facility involved.

37. Iraq shall provide to the Special Commission in accordance with annex III information on all cases of infectious diseases affecting humans, animals or plants, that deviate, or seem to deviate, from the normal pattern or are caused by any micro-organism meeting the criteria for risk groups IV and III and on all cases of similar occurrences caused by toxins.

38. Iraq shall not:

(a) Import items referred to in paragraph 35 (g) above without giving prior notice to the Special Commission in accordance with annex III. As an exception, the emergency import of vaccines may take place with simultaneous notification to the Special Commission;

(b) Conduct any activities in the field of micro-organisms and toxins except by civilian personnel not in the employ of any military organization. Such activities shall be conducted openly; no classified or secret programmes or activities shall be permitted. The sites or facilities engaged in such activities shall not be under the control of, or owned by, any military organization. Should any military organization need to be involved in such activities for prophylactic or therapeutic purposes, Iraq shall submit a request to the Special Commission specifying precisely the toxins, micro-organisms and the quantities required, the site or facility where they are to be used and the purpose of their use. The Special Commission will examine and decide on the request and establish the special arrangements it considers consistent with resolution 687 (1991);

(c) Conduct activities on diseases other than those indigenous to or immediately expected to break out in its environment;

(d) Conduct any breeding of vectors of human, animal or plant diseases. Should Iraq need to conduct any such activity, Iraq shall submit a request to the Special Commission specifying precisely its requirements, the vectors to be bred, the site or facility where the activity is to take place and the purpose of the activity. The Special Commission will examine and decide on the request and establish the special arrangements it considers consistent with resolution 687 (1991);

(e) Possess at any one time more than one facility having a laboratory (unit) meeting the criteria for a "maximum containment laboratory" as specified in the 1983 WHO *Laboratory Biosafety Manual*, such as those designated as biosafety level 4 (BL4) or P4 or equivalent standard. Iraq shall not possess at any one time more than two facilities having a laboratory (unit) meeting the criteria for a "containment laboratory", such as those designated as BL3 or P3 or equivalent standard. Should Iraq require any additional such facilities, Iraq shall submit a request to the Special Commission specifying the precise requirement. The Special Commission will examine and decide on the request and establish the special arrangements it considers consistent with resolution 687 (1991).

39. Further provisions related to biological items are set forth in annex III.

E. *Provisions related to missiles*

40. Facilities, equipment, other items and technologies set forth herein and in annex IV could be used

for the development, construction, modification or acquisition of ballistic missiles with a range greater than 150 kilometres. They shall therefore be subject to monitoring and verification in accordance with the following additional provisions in order to ensure that Iraq does not use, develop, construct or acquire any ballistic missiles with a range greater than 150 kilometres or related items prohibited under resolution 687 (1991).

41. The prohibition applies to any ballistic missiles or missile delivery systems capable of such a range regardless of payload and to any related major parts, which include missile/rocket stages, re-entry vehicles, solid- or liquid-fuel motors, guidance sets, thrust vector controls, warheads and fusing systems, launchers capable of launching ballistic missiles with a range greater than 150 kilometres and related principal launch equipment, missile transporters and other ground support equipment for such missiles. The prohibition also applies to modification of any missile or any missile delivery system to a ballistic missile with a range greater than 150 kilometres. The prohibition also applies to launch technologies such as tube- or gun-type launchers, which enable such ranges to be achieved.

42. Iraq shall not construct, otherwise acquire or operate sites or facilities for the use, development, production, training or other support of ballistic missiles capable of a range greater than 150 kilometres, including sites or facilities for research, development, modification, manufacture, assembly, testing, storage, repair, training, flight simulating and operational use of such missiles, nor acquire related major parts specified in paragraph 41 and the items listed in paragraph 1 of annex IV for such missiles.

43. Iraq shall, not later than 30 days after the adoption of the Plan by the Security Council, and on a regular basis thereafter, provide to the Special Commission the following:

(a) A list of all its missiles designed for use, or capable of being modified for use, in a surface-to-surface role with a range greater than 50 kilometres, specifying their name and type, type of propulsion, number of stages and/or boosters, guidance systems, payload, warhead and re-entry vehicle types, launcher types, airframe and warhead transporter, ground support equipment and the sites or facilities where these missiles, items or equipment are located;

(b) Information on any project and on any site or facility for such missiles, including sites or facilities for production, assembly, repair and maintenance, storage and operational bases, specifying their locations;

(c) Information on any project and on any site or facility for missile research, development, modification or testing, specifying its locations;

(d) Information on the development, production, export, import or other acquisition, training or other services related to the items, equipment and technologies listed in annex IV, specifying sites or facilities where such items, equipment and technologies are located, the purposes and the projects for which they are being used and the supplier or recipient countries involved.

44. Iraq shall notify the Special Commission in accordance with annex IV of the developmental or test launch of any missile, specifying where and when the launch is to take place.

45. Further provisions related to missiles are set forth in annex IV.

Annex I
Detailed provisions related to inspections, aerial overflights, security, privileges and immunities

1. In addition to the basic rights and obligations set forth in paragraphs 17 and 18 of the Plan, the provisions set out in this annex shall apply.

Scope

2. The Special Commission shall have the right:

(a) To secure any site to be inspected and prevent any material or other item from being taken to or from the site until the inspection is concluded;

(b) To stop and inspect vehicles, ships, aircraft or any other means of transportation within Iraq, any material or other item in movement and to restrict and/or stop movement of material or other items;

(c) To inspect imports or exports of material and other items upon arrival or departure;

(d) To establish special modes of monitoring and verification, including prolonged or continuous presence of inspectors, use of instruments and other arrangements to facilitate monitoring and verification;

(e) To secure full and free access at any time to all sites, facilities, areas, locations, activities, material and other items, including documentation, all persons and all information which, in its judgement, may be necessary for its monitoring and verification activities.

Notification

3. The Special Commission shall, at a time it considers appropriate, notify Iraq of:

(a) The site, facility, activity, material or other item to be inspected;

(b) The name of the head of the inspection team (the Chief Inspector) and the estimated number of personnel who will take part in the inspection;

(c) The estimated time of departure and arrival of any flight from, to or within Iraq, and other appropriate details, by any aircraft used by the Special Commission.

4. Iraq shall, upon receipt of the name of the Chief Inspector for an inspection, immediately inform the Special Commission of the name of the individual who will be the Iraqi Inspection Representative for the inspection.

Conduct of inspections or aerial overflights

5. The Special Commission shall have the right:

(a) To request, receive, examine, copy and remove any record, data, information or documentation and to verify inventories;

(b) To examine, retain, move or photograph, including by videotaping, any activity or item;

(c) To conduct interviews with any personnel at a site or facility under inspection, or with any Iraqi official;

(d) To install containment, surveillance and other equipment and devices and to construct facilities for inspection, observation, testing, verification or monitoring activities;

(e) To take samples of any kind and perform on-site analyses of the samples using its own equipment;

(f) To remove and transfer samples outside Iraq for analyses off-site at laboratories of its choice;

(g) To mark, tag or otherwise identify any material or other item;

(h) To use its own instrumentation to collect data during inspections and aerial overflights, including photographic, video, infrared and radar data.

6. Iraq shall:

(a) Provide clarification or explanation of any ambiguity that might arise during an inspection;

(b) Perform, upon request by the Special Commission, analyses of samples in the presence of inspectors, including on-site;

(c) Perform, upon request by the Special Commission, any additional task.

Travel, transport and communications

7. The Special Commission shall have the right:

(a) To unrestricted freedom of entry into and exit from Iraq, without delay or hindrance, for all its personnel, property, supplies, equipment, spare parts, means of transport, material and other items. No visa shall be required of such personnel travelling on United Nations laissez-passer or certificate and possessing an inspection assignment document; Iraq shall ensure prompt issuance of visas of entry and exit for such personnel as may not possess a United Nations laissez-passer or certificate;

(b) To unrestricted freedom of movement within Iraq, without advance notice, delay or hindrance, for all

its personnel, property, supplies, equipment, spare parts, means of transport, material and other items;

(c) To fly the United Nations flag on its premises and means of transport;

(d) To use its own means of transport, including fixed- and rotary-wing aircraft, throughout Iraq for all relevant purposes, including inspection, surveillance, aerial overflights (surveys), transportation and logistics;

(e) To use airfields in Iraq for the purposes determined by the Special Commission including landing, take-off, basing, maintenance, refuelling and other support;

(f) To communicate from any place within Iraq, and without censorship or other hindrance, by radio, satellite or other forms of communication, and to connect with the United Nations by its radio and satellite network, as well as by telefax, telephone, telegraph and other means;

(g) To use codes and receive papers, correspondence and other items by courier or sealed bags;

(h) To unrestricted freedom to remove from Iraq, without delay or hindrance, any material or other item, including any documentation, acquired during inspection or other monitoring and verification activities.

8. Iraq shall:

(a) Permit, without delay or hindrance, the Special Commission's personnel, property, supplies, equipment, spare parts, means of transport, material and other items to move within Iraq, without advance notice, as well as to enter or leave Iraq, promptly issuing entry and exit visas if required on national passports and accepting United Nations laissez-passers or United Nations certificates as valid travel documents without requiring visas;

(b) Accept United Nations registration of means of transport on land, sea and in the air and United Nations licensing of the operators thereof;

(c) Provide priority clearance, as well as the basing and all necessary facilities as determined by the Special Commission for any fixed- or rotary-wing aircraft used by the Commission;

(d) Provide, upon the request of the Special Commission, the means of transport, maps or other information needed;

(e) Take every necessary measure to ensure that the inspection team arrives at the site or facility to be inspected by the time notified by the Special Commission;

(f) Provide, upon the request of the Special Commission, appropriate means of communication;

(g) Provide, upon request of the Special Commission, appropriate escort and/or support personnel;

(h) Provide, upon request of the Special Commission, medical, logistical and/or technical support;

(i) Not interfere with or censor any communication to or from the Special Commission or its personnel;

(j) Permit, without delay or hindrance, the Special Commission to remove from Iraq any material or other item, including any documentation, acquired by the Commission during inspection or other monitoring and verification activities.

Security, privileges and immunities

9. The Special Commission shall have the right to make its own arrangements to ensure the safety and security of its personnel and property and to take custody of any material or other item, including documentation.

10. Iraq shall ensure the safety and security of the personnel and property of the Special Commission and shall provide the arrangements to this end when so requested by the Special Commission.

11. In addition and without prejudice to the foregoing provisions, the Special Commission and any agency of the United Nations system participating in the carrying out of the Plan, its property, funds, assets and personnel shall enjoy the facilities, privileges and immunities provided for in the applicable convention or agreement, namely the Convention on the Privileges and Immunities of the United Nations, the Agreement on the Privileges and Immunities of the International Atomic Energy Agency (IAEA) and the Convention on the Privileges and Immunities of the Specialized Agencies.

12. Iraq shall extend to:

(a) The officers and other members of the Special Commission the privileges and immunities, exemptions and facilities that are enjoyed by diplomatic envoys in accordance with international law;

(b) The officials of the United Nations, of IAEA and any of the specialized agencies of the United Nations, performing functions in connection with the implementation of the Plan, the privileges and immunities applicable to them under articles V and VII of the Convention on the Privileges and Immunities of the United Nations; or articles VI and IX of the Agreement on the Privileges and Immunities of the International Atomic Energy Agency; or articles VI and VIII of the Convention on the Privileges and Immunities of the Specialized Agencies;

(c) The technical experts and other specialists performing functions in connection with the implementation of the Plan the privileges and immunities accorded to experts performing missions for the United Nations, for IAEA or for the specialized agencies of the United Nations under article VI of the Convention on the Privileges and Immunities of the United Nations, article VII of the Agreement on the Privileges and Immunities of the International Atomic Energy Agency, and the relevant annexes to the Convention on the Privileges and Immunities of the Specialized Agencies, respectively.

Other provisions

13. Iraq shall designate the Iraqi authority responsible for liaison with the Special Commission and shall inform the Special Commission of the name or names of the liaison officers within that authority who shall have the full power and shall take the necessary measures to secure for the Special Commission the effective implementation of the Commission's rights laid down in the Plan.

14. The official points of contact between Iraq and the Special Commission during the course of an inspection shall be the Chief Inspector designated by the Special Commission and the Inspection Representative designated by Iraq.

15. Iraq shall provide, at no cost to the Special Commission, in agreement with the Special Commission, all such premises as may be necessary for the accommodation and fulfilment of the functions of the Special Commission in Iraq. All such premises shall be inviolable and subject to the exclusive control and authority of the Special Commission.

16. All information provided by, and communications from, Iraq to the Special Commission under the Plan shall include the corresponding text in English.

17. For the purposes of the performance of the functions of the Special Commission in implementation of the Plan, the rights, facilities, privileges and immunities conferred in the Plan where necessary supplement and elaborate upon the rights, facilities, privileges and immunities provided for in the exchange of notes between the Secretary-General of the United Nations and the Minister for Foreign Affairs of Iraq, which entered into force on 14 May 1991, regarding the status, privileges and immunities of the Special Commission as originally established pursuant to paragraph 9 of Security Council resolution 687 (1991).

Annex II
Provisions related to chemical items

1. The following list contains chemicals that could be used for the development, production or acquisition of chemical weapons, but which also have significant uses for purposes not prohibited by resolution 687 (1991):

	List A	Chemical Abstracts Service (CAS) registry no.
1.	Chemicals, except for those chemicals specified in list B of this annex, containing a phosphorus atom to which is bonded one methyl, ethyl or propyl (normal or iso) group but not further carbon atoms	
2.	Dialkyl (Me, Et, n-Pr or i-Pr) N, N-dialkyl (Me, Et, n-Pr or i-Pr)-phosphoramidates	
3.	Arsenic trichloride	(7784-34-1)
4.	2,2-Diphenyl-2-hydroxyacetic acid	(76-93-7)
5.	Quinuclidin-3-ol	(1619-34-7)
6.	N,N-Dialkyl (Me, Et, n-Pr or i-Pr) aminoethyl-2-chloride and corresponding protonated salts	
7.	N,N-Dialkyl (Me, Et, n-Pr or i-Pr) aminoethane-2-ol and corresponding protonated salts	
8.	N,N-Dialkyl (Me, Et, n-Pr or i-Pr) aminoethane-2-thiol and corresponding protonated salts	
9.	Amiton: O,O-Diethyl S-(2-(diethylamino)ethyl) phosphorothiolate and corresponding alkylated and protonated salts	(78-53-5)
10.	PFIB: 1,1,3,3,3-pentafluoro-2-(trifluoromethyl)-1-propene	(382-21-8)
11.	Phosgene	(75-44-5)
12.	Cyanogen chloride	(506-77-4)
13.	Hydrogen cyanide	(74-90-8)
14.	Trichloronitromethane (chloropicrin)	(76-06-2)
15.	Phosphorus oxychloride	(10025-87-3)
16.	Phosphorus trichloride	(7719-12-2)
17.	Phosphorus pentachloride	(10026-13-8)
18.	Trimethyl phosphite	(121-45-9)
19.	Triethyl phosphite	(122-52-1)
20.	Dimethyl phosphite	(868-85-9)
21.	Diethyl phosphite	(762-04-9)
22.	Sulphur monochloride	(10025-67-9)

	List A	Chemical Abstracts Service (CAS) registry no.
23.	Sulphur dichloride	(10545-99-0)
24.	Thionyl chloride	(7719-09-7)
25.	Cyclohexanol	(108-93-0)
26.	Hydrogen fluoride	(7664-39-3)
27.	Ortho-chlorobenzylidenemalononitrile (CS)	(2698-41-1)
28.	Potassium fluoride	(7789-23-3)
29.	Ammonium bifluoride	(1341-49-7)
30.	Sodium bifluoride	(1333-83-1)
31.	Sodium fluoride	(7681-49-4)
32.	Sodium sulphide	(1313-82-2)
33.	Chloroethanol	(107-07-3)
34.	Dimethylamine	(124-40-3)
35.	Dimethylamine hydrochloride	(506-59-2)
36.	Potassium cyanide	(151-50-8)
37.	Sodium cyanide	(143-33-9)
38.	Tri-ethanolamine	(102-71-6)
39.	Di-isopropylamine	(108-18-9)

2. The following list contains chemicals that have little or no use except as chemical warfare agents or for the development, production or acquisition of chemical weapons, or which have been used by Iraq as essential precursors for chemical weapons:

	List B	Chemical Abstracts Service (CAS) registry no.
1.	O-Alkyl (C_{10}, incl. cycloalkyl) alkyl (Me, Et, n-Pr or i-Pr)-phosphono fluoridates e.g. Sarin: O-isopropyl methylphosphonofluoridate	(107-44-8)
	Soman: O-pinacolyl methylphosphonofluoridate	(96-64-0)
2.	O-Alkyl (C_{10}, incl. cycloalkyl) N,N-dialkyl (Me, Et, n-Pr or i-Pr) phosphoramidocyanidates e.g. Tabun: O-ethyl N,N-dimethylphosphoramidocyanidate	(77-81-6)

3. O-Alkyl (H or C10, incl. cycloalkyl)
   S-2-dialkyl (Me, Et, n-Pr or i-Pr)-
   aminoethyl alkyl (Me, Et, n-Pr or i-Pr)
   phosphonothiolates and corresponding
   alkylated and protonated salts
   e.g. VX: O-ethyl S-2-diisopropylamino-
   ethyl methylphosphonothiolate (50782-69-9)

4. Sulphur mustards:
   2-Chloroethylchloromethylsulphide (2625-76-5)
   bis(2-chloroethyl)sulphide:
   Mustard gas (H) (505-60-2)
   bis(2-chloroethylthio)methane (63869-13-6)
   1,2-bis(2-chloroethylthio)ethane:
   Sesquimustard (Q) (3563-36-8)
   1,3-bis(2-chloroethylthio)-n-propane (63905-10-2)
   1,4-bis(2-chloroethylthio)-n-butane
   1,5-bis(2-chloroethylthio)-n-pentane
   bis(2-chloroethylthiomethyl)ether
   bis(2-chloroethylthioethyl)ether:
   O-Mustard (T) (63918-89-8)

5. Lewisites:
   Lewisite 1: 2-chlorovinyldichlorarsine (541-25-3)
   Lewisite 2: bis(2-chlorovinyl)
      chloroarsine (40334-69-8)
   Lewisite 3: tris(2-chlorovinyl)arsine (40334-70-1)

6. Nitrogen mustards:
   HN1: bis(2-chloroethyl)ethylamine (538-07-8)
   HN2: bis(2-chloroethyl)methylamine (51-75-2)
   HN3: tris(2-chloroethyl)amine (555-77-1)

7. 3-Quinuclidinyl benzilate (BZ) (6581-06-2)

8. Saxitoxin (35523-89-8)

9. Ricin

10. Alkyl (Me, Et, n-Pr or i-Pr)
    phosphonyldihalides
    e.g. methylphosphonyldifluoride (676-99-3)
      methylphosphonyldichloride (676-67-1)

11. Dimethylmethylphosphonate (756-79-6)

12. O-Alkyl (H or C10, incl. cycloalkyl)
    O-2-dialkyl (Me, Et, n-Pr or i-Pr)-
    aminoethyl alkyl (Me, Et, n-Pr or i-Pr)
    phosphonites and corresponding
    alkylated salts and protonated salts
    e.g. QL: O-ethyl O-2-diisopropylami
     noethyl methylphosphonite (57856-11-8)

13. O-Alkyl (C10, incl. cycloalkyl) alkyl
    (Me, Et, n-Pr or i-Pr)-phosphono
    chloridates
    e.g. Chloro Sarin: O-isopropyl
     methylphosphonochloridate (1445-76-7)
     Chloro Soman: O-pinacolyl
     methylphosphonochloridate (7040-57-5)

14. N,N-Dialkyl (Me, Et, n-Pr or i-Pr)
    phosphoramidic dihalides

15. Bis(2-hydroxyethyl)sulphide
    (thiodiglycol) (111-48-8)

16. 3,3-Dimethylbutan-2-ol (pinacolyl
    alcohol) (464-07-3)

3. The initial information under paragraph 30 of the Plan to be provided not later than 30 days after the adoption of the Plan by the Security Council shall cover the period from 1 January 1988. Subsequent information shall be provided each 15 January and 15 July and shall cover the six-month period prior to the provision of the information. The advance notifications under paragraph 30 (d) of the Plan shall cover the subsequent six months. The special notifications under paragraph 31 of the Plan shall be provided not later than 30 days in advance.

4. Whenever the information that Iraq is required to provide under section C of the Plan and this annex is equal to nil, Iraq shall provide nil returns.

5. The information on chemicals to be provided under section C of the Plan shall for each chemical include:

(a) The chemical name, common or trade name used by the site or the facility, structural formula and Chemical Abstracts Service registry number (if assigned);

(b) The purposes for which the chemical is produced, processed, consumed, stored, imported or exported;

(c) The total amount produced, processed, consumed, stored, imported or exported.

6. The information on sites or facilities to be provided under section C of the Plan shall for each site or facility include:

(a) The name of the site or facility and of the owner, company or enterprise operating the site or facility;

(b) The location of the site or facility;

(c) A general description of all types of activities at the site or facility;

(d) The sources and amounts of the financing of the site or facility, and of its activities.

7. The location of a site or facility shall be specified by means of the address and a site diagram. Each diagram shall be drawn to scale and shall indicate the boundaries of the site or facility, all road and rail entrances and exits and all structures on the site or facility, indicating their purpose. If the site or facility is located within a larger complex, the diagram shall specify the exact location of the site or facility within the complex. On each diagram, the geographic coordinates of a point within the site or facility shall be specified to the nearest second.

8. In addition to information specified in paragraph 6 of this annex, the following information shall be provided for each site or facility that is or will be involved in production, processing, consumption, storage, import or export of chemicals specified in list A of this annex:

(a) A detailed description of activities related to these chemicals including, as applicable, material-flow and process-flow diagrams, chemical reactions and end-use;

(b) A list of equipment used in activities related to these chemicals;

(c) The production capacity for these chemicals.

9. In addition to information specified in paragraph 6 of this annex, the following information shall be provided for each site or facility that is or will be involved in production or processing of organophosphorus chemicals or in production of organic chemicals by chlorination:

(a) A detailed description of activities related to the relevant chemicals, and the end-uses for which the chemicals are produced or processed;

(b) A detailed description of the processes used in the production or processing of organophosphorus chemicals or in the production of organic chemicals by chlorination, including material-flow and process-flow diagrams, chemical reactions and a list of equipment involved.

10. The information on each import to be provided under section C of the Plan shall include:

(a) Specification of each item and the quantity imported and the purpose of its use in Iraq;

(b) Country from which the item is imported and the specific exporter;

(c) Point or port and time of entry of the item into Iraq;

(d) Site or facility where it is to be used;

(e) Name of the specific importing organization in Iraq.

Annex III
Provisions related to biological items

1. The following list contains equipment and other items relevant to the acquisition of biological and toxin weapons or biological and toxin weapons capability:

(a) Detection or assay systems specific for risk groups IV, III and II micro-organisms and toxins;

(b) Biohazard containment equipment;

(c) Equipment for the micro-encapsulation of living micro-organisms;

(d) Complex media for the growth of risk groups IV, III and II micro-organisms;

(e) Bio-reactors and fermentation vessels;

(f) Recombinant deoxyribonucleic acid (DNA), equipment and reagents for its isolation, characterization or production and equipment and reagents for the construction of synthetic genes;

(g) Equipment for the release into the environment of biological material;

(h) Equipment for studying the aerobiological characteristics of micro-organisms or toxins;

(i) Equipment for breeding of vectors of human, animal or plant diseases.

2. The initial information under paragraphs 35 and 36 of the Plan to be provided not later than 30 days after the adoption of the Plan by the Security Council shall cover the period from 1 January 1986. Subsequent information shall be provided each 15 January and 15 July and shall cover the six-month period prior to the provision of the information. Notifications under paragraph 38 (a) of the Plan shall be provided not later than 60 days in advance.

3. Whenever the information that Iraq is required to provide under section D and this annex is equal to nil, Iraq shall provide nil returns.

4. The information on each site or facility to be provided under section D of the Plan shall include the following:

(a) The name of the site or facility and of the owner, company, or enterprise operating the facility;

(b) The location of the site or facility (including the address, geographic coordinates to the nearest second, the specific buildings and any structure numbers, location of the facility within any larger complex);

(c) The sources and amounts of financing of the site or facility and of its activities;

(d) The main purpose of the site or facility;

(e) The level of protection, including, as applicable, the number and size of maximum containment or containment laboratories (units);

(f) Scope and description of activities, including, as applicable, a list of types and quantities of micro-organisms, toxins or vaccines and equipment and other items specified in paragraph 1 of this annex;

(g) A list of micro-organisms and toxins, equipment and vaccines imported or uniquely isolated for the use of the site or facility, or exported, indicating the supplier or recipient countries involved.

5. The information on imports to be provided under paragraphs 35 (g) and 38 (a) of the Plan shall cover:

(a) Toxins and micro-organisms meeting the criteria for risk groups IV, III, and II according to the classification in the 1983 WHO *Laboratory Biosafety Manual* and genetic material coding for toxins or genes derived from the aforementioned micro-organisms;

(b) Equipment and facilities for the production, utilization or storage of micro-organisms meeting the criteria for risk groups IV and III according to the classification in the 1983 WHO *Laboratory Biosafety Manual*, genetic material coding for toxins or genes derived from the aforementioned micro-organisms, as well as of toxins or vaccines;

(c) Complex media for the growth of micro-organisms meeting the criteria for risk groups IV and III in quantities greater than 100 kilograms;

(d) Equipment for micro-encapsulation of living micro-organisms;

(e) Personnel or material for training or technical support services related to the design, development, use, manufacture or support of items specified in paragraph 35 (a) of the Plan and paragraphs 1 and 5 (a) of this annex; and shall for each import into Iraq specify:

(a) Types and quantities of micro-organisms, toxins or vaccines;

(b) Quantities of any equipment or other items specified in paragraph 1 of this annex;

(c) Country from which the micro-organisms, toxins, vaccines or items are imported and the specific exporter;

(d) Point or port and time of entry into Iraq;

(e) Site or facility where it is to be used and purpose of its use.

(f) Name of the specific importing organization in Iraq.

6. The information under paragraph 37 of the Plan shall be provided within seven days of the occurrence and the standardized form contained in section III of the annex on confidence-building measures in document BWC/CONF.III/23/II shall be utilized as appropriate.

7. Iraq shall, not later than each 15 April, provide to the Special Commission the copies of the declarations, information and data that Iraq has sent to the United Nations Department for Disarmament Affairs pursuant to the agreements on confidence-building measures, including the exchange of information and data, reached at the Third Review Conference of the Parties to the Convention on the Prohibition of the Development, Production and Stockpiling of Bacteriological (Biological) and Toxin Weapons and on Their Destruction (document BWC/CONF.III/23/II and its annex on confidence-building measures).

Annex IV
Provisions related to missiles

1. The following list contains equipment, other items and technologies relevant to the development and manufacture of missiles that could be used in the development and manufacture of ballistic missiles capable of a range greater than 150 kilometres:

(a) Subsystems usable in missile systems that could be used in the development and manufacture of ballistic missiles capable of a range greater than 150 kilometres:

(i) Individual rocket stages;

(ii) Re-entry vehicles, and specially designed equipment therefor;

(iii) Solid- or liquid-fuel rocket engines;

(iv) Guidance sets;

(v) Thrust vector controls;

(vi) Warhead safing, arming, fuzing and firing mechanisms;

(b) Propulsion components and equipment that could be used in the development and manufacture of ballistic missiles capable of a range greater than 150 kilometres:

(i) Rocket-motor cases and production equipment therefor;

(ii) Staging mechanisms and production equipment therefor;

(iii) Liquid-fuel control systems and components therefor, specially designed to operate in vibrating environments of more than 12g/rms between 20/Hz and 2,000/Hz;

(iv) Propellants and constituent chemicals for propellants;

(v) Production technology or production equipment for the production, handling, mixing, curing, casting, pressing, machining and acceptance testing of the liquid- or solid-fuel missile propellants and propellent constituents;

(c) Guidance and control equipment that could be used in the development and manufacture of ballistic missiles capable of a range greater than 150 kilometres:

(i) Gyroscopes, accelerometers and inertial equipment and software therefor;

(ii) Flight control systems usable in missile systems;

(iii) Avionics equipment specially designed or modified for use in unmanned air vehicles or rocket systems and software and components therefor usable in missile systems;

(d) Equipment and technical data for the production of structural composites usable in missiles and components, accessories and software therefor that could be used in the development and manufacture of ballistic missiles capable of a range greater than 150 kilometres;

(e) Pyrolytic deposition and densification equipment and technology that could be used in the development and manufacture of ballistic missiles capable of a range greater than 150 kilometres;

(f) Launch and ground support equipment and facilities usable for missile systems that could be used in the development and manufacture of ballistic missiles capable of a range greater than 150 kilometres;

(g) Analog computers, digital computers or digital differential analysers usable in air vehicles, rocket systems or missile systems that could be used in the development and manufacture of ballistic missiles capable of a range greater than 150 kilometres;

(h) Test facilities and equipment usable for missile systems, to include vibration test equipment using digital control techniques, wind tunnels and test benches for solid- or liquid-fuel rockets that could be used in the development and manufacture of ballistic missiles capable of a range greater than 150 kilometres;

(i) Specially designed software or components for missile design, production or operation that could be used in the development and manufacture of ballistic missiles capable of a range greater than 150 kilometres;

(j) Materials and devices for reduced observables in missile systems that could be used in the development and manufacture of ballistic missiles capable of a range greater than 150 kilometres;

(k) Material and devices for protecting missile systems against nuclear effects that could be used in the development and manufacture of ballistic missiles capable of a range greater than 150 kilometres.

2. The initial information under paragraph 43 of the Plan to be provided not later than 30 days after the adoption of the Plan by the Security Council shall cover the period from 1 January 1988. Subsequent information shall be provided each 15 January and 15 July and shall cover the six-month period prior to the provision of the information. Notifications under paragraph 44 of the Plan shall be provided not later than 14 days prior to the date of launch.

3. Whenever the information which Iraq is required to provide under section E of the Plan and this annex is equal to nil, Iraq shall provide nil returns.

4. The information on sites or facilities to be provided under section E of the Plan shall for each site or facility include:

(a) The name of the site or facility and of the owner, company or enterprise operating the site or facility;

(b) The location of the site or facility;

(c) The sources and amounts of the financing of the site or facility, and of its activities;

(d) A general description of all types of activities at the site or facility;

(e) List of equipment, other items and technologies specified in paragraph 1 of this annex used or present at the site or facility and their quantities;

(f) A detailed description of activities related to the equipment, other items and technologies specified in paragraph 1 of this annex.

5. The location of a site or facility shall be specified by means of the address and site diagram. Each diagram shall be drawn to scale and shall indicate the boundaries of the site or facility, all road and rail entrances and exits and all structures on the site or facility, indicating their purpose. If the site or facility is located within a larger complex, the diagram shall specify the exact location of the site or facility within the complex. On each diagram, the geographic coordinates of a point within the site or facility shall be specified to the nearest second.

6. The information on each import to be provided under section E of the Plan shall include:

(a) Specification of each item and the quantity imported and the purpose of its use in Iraq;

(b) Country from which the item is imported and the specific exporter;

(c) Point or port and time of entry of the item in Iraq;

(d) Project and site or facility where it is to be used;

(e) Name of the specific importing organization in Iraq.

Document 89

Security Council resolution approving the plans submitted by the Secretary-General (Document 88) and the Director General of the IAEA (Document 82)

S/RES/715 (1991), 11 October 1991

The Security Council,

Recalling its resolutions 687 (1991) of 3 April 1991 and 707 (1991) of 15 August 1991 and its other resolutions on this matter,

Recalling in particular that under resolution 687 (1991) the Secretary-General and the Director General of the International Atomic Energy Agency were requested to develop plans for future ongoing monitoring and verification and to submit them to the Security Council for approval,

Taking note of the report 1/ and note 2/ of the Secretary-General, transmitting the plans submitted by the Secretary-General and the Director General of the Agency,

Acting under Chapter VII of the Charter of the United Nations,

1. *Approves,* in accordance with the provisions of resolutions 687 (1991), 707 (1991) and the present resolution, the plans submitted by the Secretary-General 1/ and the Director General of the International Atomic Energy Agency; 2/

2. *Decides* that the Special Commission shall carry out the plan submitted by the Secretary-General, as well as continuing to discharge its other responsibilities under resolutions 687 (1991), 699 (1991) of 17 June 1991 and 707 (1991) and performing such other functions as are conferred upon it under the present resolution;

3. *Requests* the Director General of the Agency to carry out, with the assistance and cooperation of the Special Commission, the plan submitted by him and to continue to discharge his other responsibilities under resolutions 687 (1991), 699 (1991) and 707 (1991);

4. *Decides* that the Special Commission, in the exercise of its responsibilities as a subsidiary organ of the Security Council, shall:

(*a*) Continue to have the responsibility for designating additional locations for inspection and overflights;

(*b*) Continue to render assistance and cooperation to the Director General of the Agency by providing him, by mutual agreement, with the necessary special expertise and logistical, informational and other operational support for the carrying out of the plan submitted by him;

(*c*) Perform such other functions, in cooperation in the nuclear field with the Director General of the Agency, as may be necessary to coordinate activities under the plans approved by the present resolution, including making use of commonly available services and information to the fullest extent possible, in order to achieve maximum efficiency and optimum use of resources;

5. *Demands* that Iraq meet unconditionally all its obligations under the plans approved by the present resolution and cooperate fully with the Special Commission and the Director General of the Agency in carrying out the plans;

6. *Decides* to encourage the maximum assistance, in cash and in kind, from all Member States to support the Special Commission and the Director General of the Agency in carrying out their activities under the plans approved by the present resolution, without prejudice to Iraq's liability for the full costs of such activities;

7. *Requests* the Security Council Committee established under resolution 661 (1990) concerning the situation between Iraq and Kuwait, the Special Commission and the Director General of the Agency to develop in cooperation a mechanism for monitoring any future sales or supplies by other countries to Iraq of items relevant to the implementation of section C of resolution 687 (1991) and other relevant resolutions, including the present resolution and the plans approved hereunder;

8. *Requests* the Secretary-General and the Director General of the Agency to submit to the Security Council reports on the implementation of the plans approved by the present resolution, when requested by the Security Council and in any event at least every six months after the adoption of this resolution;

9. *Decides* to remain seized of the matter.

1/ *Official Records of the Security Council, Forty-sixth Year, Supplement for October, November and December 1991,* document S/2871/Rev.1.
2/ Ibid., document S/22872/Rev.1 and Corr.1.

Document 90

Decision of the Security Council Sanctions Committee on procedures to be employed by the committee relating to the sale of Iraqi oil products

S/23149, 16 October 1991

Procedures to be employed by the Security Council Committee established by resolution 661 (1990) concerning the situation between Iraq and Kuwait in the discharge of its responsibilities under Security Council resolutions 706 (1991) and 712 (1991)

I. *Preparatory steps:*

1. The Committee will select, upon recommendation by the Secretariat, three independent experts in international oil trade as "overseers" at United Nations Headquarters, and entrust them with the authority to approve or reject oil sale contracts on behalf of the Committee. The overseers will be authorized to correspond with applicants as needed. The nomination of three persons will ensure a 24-hour availability for contract approvals.

2. Other experts, agents and inspectors (as required below) will be appointed by the Secretary-General. The Committee will take note of these appointments.

3. States may, if they so wish, forward to the Committee a list of national oil purchasers (private companies, State-owned companies, State agencies, ministries, etc.) authorized to communicate with the overseer. Once the Committee has taken note of these lists and passed them on to the overseer, these purchasers are entitled to communicate directly with the overseer (see sect. II, part A, para. 3 below). If States do not submit such a list, or if a certain purchaser is not included in the list, the communication with the overseer must go via the Permanent Mission in New York.

4. For the purpose of section II, part A, paragraph 3 below, a Standard Application Form will be elaborated by the Committee and circulated among all States. States and national oil purchasers shall use only these Standard Application Forms.

5. The Secretariat will set up a new fax line to be used exclusively for correspondence with regard to oil transactions. Applicants are requested to send their relevant applications and relating correspondence only via this fax line. Other correspondence with the Committee shall go through the already existing channels.

6. Iraq and Turkey will have to conclude an arrangement on the price and payment modalities for the use of Turkish oil installations. Once this arrangement is concluded, it must be forwarded to the Committee which will take not of it. United Nations agents will check the implementation of this arrangement and report periodically to the Committee.

7. Monitoring of delivery to Iraq of foodstuffs, medicines, and materials and supplies for essential civilian needs will be done by independent inspection agents appointed by an appropriate United Nations programme or organization, such as, for example, the Office for Project Services (OPS). Monitoring of the distribution of these goods will be arranged by the Executive Delegate in cooperation with relevant United Nations programmes and organizations, including appropriate humanitarian non-governmental organizations (NGOs). The Committee will be informed about the relevant arrangements, including those for the purpose of section III, part A, paragraph 11 below.

8. Upon recommendation by the Secretariat, the Committee will nominate an expert (a staff member of one of the United Nations programmes or organizations) who will act as an aide to the Committee for the purposes of section III, part A, paragraph 8 below.

II. *Sales of Iraqi oil and oil products:*

A. *Sales of Iraqi oil:*

1. The Iraqi State Organization for the Marketing of Oil (SOMO) signs a contract with the purchaser. The contract must include the provisions as specified in paragraph 58 of the report by the Secretary-General pursuant to paragraph 5 of Security Council resolution 706 (1991) (S/23006).

2. United Nations agents at SOMO review the contracts to assure compliance with the provisions of paragraph 58 of the Secretary-General's report and forward by fax copies of the approvable contracts, supporting documents, and their independent reports to the overseer in New York.

3. The national oil purchaser or the Permanent Mission of the State of purchase forwards by fax a formal request (Standard Application Form) for approval to the Committee, together with a copy of the contract and all other supporting documents.

4. The overseer reviews the contract and supporting documents to ensure that:
   – they comply with paragraph 58 of the Secretary-General's report, including that a confirmed irrevocable letter of credit is opened providing for payment into the escrow account;
   – the conditions of payment envisaged in the letters of credit are in conformity with existing market practices;

– they do not appear to contain any attempt at fraud or deception;

– the transaction's pricing is consistent with world prices and market trends; and

– the transaction does not exceed the limits imposed by Security Council resolutions 706 (1991) and 712 (1991).

5. If the contract and supporting documents are found to be in order, the overseer, on behalf of the Committee, approves the sale (within the shortest period of time possible, at the maximum 24 hours) and informs by fax the national oil purchaser or the Permanent Mission concerned, as well as SOMO.

6. The overseer sends his notification of sales approval, together with a copy of the contract, supporting documents, and the report of the United Nations agent at SOMO, by fax to the inspector at Ceyhan who will authorize loading only after these documents are in his possession.

7. Depending on the number of applications, the overseer reports to the Committee, in a structured and standardized manner, at least twice a week on contracts approved by him (including the cumulative quantity and value of oil authorized for export), and informs the Secretary-General accordingly.

8. The oil is pumped into storage tanks. Agents at the pipeline check the pumping. Subject to their confirmation, the oil can be loaded on ships and the ships can leave the terminal. The agents will have the authority to prohibit the delivery of the oil if there is any evidence of irregularity.

9. The agents report to the Committee on their assessment of the pumping and loading.

10. The purchaser makes payment into the escrow account.

11. Twice a week, the Secretary-General forwards statements of the escrow account, including outlines of anticipated future obligations, to the Committee.

B. *Sales of Iraqi oil products:*

The regime for the sale of oil products will be broadly similar to that described above, but the precise arrangements will be elaborated at a later stage, as and when the need arises.

III. *Purchase by Iraq of foodstuffs, medicines, and materials and supplies for essential civilian needs:*

A. *Purchase by Iraq of foodstuffs, medicines, and materials and supplies for essential civilian needs, to be financed from the escrow account:*

1. Iraq sends a categorized list of relevant requirements to the Executive Delegate. (Preferably, a two-month list, quantity- and value-oriented.) If Iraq intends also to finance medicines from the escrow account, these too should be mentioned in general terms on the list, together with their value. The overall value of the list must not exceed that part of the amount authorized by the Committee, in accordance with paragraph 2 of Security Council resolution 712 (1991), which is available for humanitarian purchases.

2. The Executive Delegate forwards the list, revised by him if necessary, to the Committee.

3. The Committee takes action on the list and forwards to the Secretary-General and the Executive Delegate the list as approved. (The first list will be taken up at a meeting of the Committee; subject to agreement, later lists might be dealt with under a "no-objection" procedure.)

4. The Secretary-General will make the list known to all States.

5. The Executive Delegate informs Iraq about the clearance.

6. Iraq signs a contract with the exporter, in accordance with normal commercial practice and the relevant Security Council resolutions.

7. (a) *Medicines:*

The Permanent Mission of the exporter's country informs the Committee of the exporter's wish to be paid from the escrow account. A copy of the relevant contract must be attached to this communication.

(b) *Foodstuffs:*

The Permanent Mission of the exporter's country notifies the Committee. This notification must contain the information that the exporter wants to be paid from the escrow account. A copy of the relevant contract must be attached to this notification.

(c) *Materials and supplies for essential civilian needs:*

The Permanent Mission of the exporter's country requests approval, under the "no-objection" procedure, by the Committee. This request must contain the information that the exporter wishes to be paid from the escrow account. A copy of the relevant contract must be attached to this request.

8. An expert (aide to the Committee) checks the contracts, in particular on the price/value relationship, and informs the Chairman. His findings will be attached to the circulation note to Committee members.

9. (a) *Medicines:*

(i) If the contract is found in order, the Committee informs the Permanent Mission concerned and the Secretary-General that the contract has been found in order, i.e. the exporter can expect payment from the escrow account.

(ii) If the contract is not found in order, the Committee informs the Permanent Mission concerned and the Secretary-General that the contract has not been found in order, i.e. the exporter cannot expect payment from the escrow account. However, medical supplies can be shipped anyway if the exporter so wishes.

(b) *Foodstuffs*:

(i) If the contract is found in order, the Committee takes note of the notification and informs the Permanent Mission concerned and the Secretary-General accordingly and states that the contract has been found in order, i.e. the exporter can expect payment from the escrow account.

(ii) If the contract is not found in order, the Committee takes note of the notification and informs the Permanent Mission concerned and the Secretary-General accordingly but states that the contract has not been found in order, i.e. the exporter cannot expect payment from the escrow account. However, foodstuffs can be shipped anyway if the exporter so wishes.

(c) *Materials and supplies for essential civilian needs*:

(i) If the contract is found in order, and if the Committee approves the shipment under the "no-objection" procedure, it informs the Permanent Mission concerned and the Secretary-General of the approval and states that the contract has been found in order, i.e. the exporter can expect payment from the escrow account.

(ii) If the contract is not found in order, and if the Committee nevertheless approves the shipment under the "no-objection" procedure, it informs the Permanent Mission concerned and the Secretary-General of the approval but states that the contract has not been found in order, i.e. the exporter cannot expect payment from the escrow account. However, the goods can be shipped anyway if the exporter so wishes.

(iii) If the Committee cannot approve the shipment, whether or not the contract is found in order, the goods are not allowed to be shipped.

From here on only if the contract has been found in order:

10. The Secretary-General may effect part-payment to the exporter, according to commercial practice.

11. United Nations agents check the delivery (the quality, quantity, labelling, etc.) at the unloading port and the entry points to Iraq and report to the Committee. The agents will have the authority to inspect the shipment documents and, if necessary, to open and examine the contents as needed.

12. The Committee evaluates the reports. If satisfactory, it approves the final payment and informs the Secretary-General.

13. The Secretary-General effects final payment.

14. United Nations agents monitor in-country distribution and report, via the Executive Delegate, in a consolidated manner to the Committee.

15. The Committee evaluates these reports to ensure that equitable internal distribution is being maintained and takes appropriate action if not.

16. Twice a week, the Secretary-General forwards statements of the escrow account, including outlines of anticipated future obligations, to the Committee.

B. *Purchase by Iraq of foodstuffs, medicines, and materials and supplies for essential civilian needs, to be financed from the sub-account of the escrow account*:

1. According to paragraph 8 of Security Council resolution 712 (1991), imports financed from the sub-account of the escrow account, are, apart from the provision of paragraph 1 (c) of Security Council resolution 706 (1991), subject only to the provisions and procedures of paragraph 20 of Security Council resolution 687 (1991).

2. Monitoring (paragraph 1(c) of Security Council resolution 706 (1991)) will be carried out as indicated in annex II of the Secretary-General's report.

3. Twice a week, the Secretary-General forwards statements of the sub-account of the escrow account, including outlines of anticipated future obligations, to the Committee.

Document 91

Decision 6 taken by the Governing Council of the United Nations Compensation Commission: Arrangements for ensuring payments to the Compensation Fund

S/AC.26/1991/6, 23 October 1991

Decision taken by the Governing Council of the United Nations Compensation Commission during its second session, at the 15th meeting, held on 18 October 1991

Arrangements for Ensuring Payments to the Compensation Fund

1. Paragraph 7 of Security Council resolution 692 (1991) requested the Governing Council to report as soon as possible on the actions it has taken with regard to the arrangements for ensuring that payments are made to the Fund, so that the Security Council could give its approval in accordance with paragraph 22 of resolution 687 (1991).

2. The arrangements in the following paragraphs will be revised when circumstances warrant.

3. These arrangements will come into operation only when sanctions are removed pursuant to paragraph 22 of resolution 687 (1991) and are consistent with the approach adopted in resolutions 706 (1991) and 712 (1991) and with the reports of the Secretary-General dated 2 May 1991 (S/22559), and 4 September 1991 (S/23006). The Governing Council will oversee the implementation of these arrangements.

Payment mechanism

4. Purchasers of Iraqi petroleum and petroleum products will continue to be required to make all payments to an escrow account established by the Secretary-General as a special account of the United Nations. This Escrow Account will replace the escrow account established pursuant to resolutions 706 (1991) and 712 (1991). The Executive Secretary and the Secretary-General will consult to establish the appropriate arrangements for the administration of this Escrow Account and on the question of which person or institution should be the Escrow Agent. Use of an escrow account will ensure continuity and predictability for those involved in transactions involving Iraqi petroleum and petroleum products.

5. The Compensation Fund will be a separate account administered by the Executive Secretary under the policy guidance of the Governing Council. The Executive Secretary will report periodically to the Governing Council on the administration of the Fund. The Escrow Agent will transfer from the Escrow Account to the Compensation Fund the percentage due it and remit the remainder to Iraq, without any further deduction except as specifically provided in this paper. The Compensation Fund will bear interest. The Executive Secretary will be authorized to enter into any agreements or arrangements necessary to implement this paragraph and will report to the Governing Council on these agreements or arrangements.

6. Contracts for the sale and purchase of Iraqi petroleum and petroleum products will be made directly by Iraq (SOMO) with purchasers. They must provide that payment will be transferred directly to the Escrow Account. To ensure payment occurs, purchasers will be required to open a confirmed irrevocable letter of credit for each transaction providing that the proceeds will be paid to the Escrow Account, except where the Executive Secretary determines that there is an alternative equivalent guarantee of payment. A letter of credit form will be established. The issuing or confirming bank for each transaction will be required to be a reputable commercial bank notified by the parties to the transaction and acceptable to the Executive Secretary. The amount and timing of payments will be in accordance with normal commercial practice (for crude oil shipments, market price, with payment 10-60 days after loading in Iraq or in a contiguous State). The Escrow Agent will notify the Executive Secretary of each payment into the Escrow Account. In cases where payment to the Escrow Account is not made by documentary letter of credit and is not made within the time period specified in the contract, the Executive Secretary will arrange for the stand-by letter of credit (or alternative equivalent guarantee) to be called.

7. With regard only to exports by truck of Iraqi petroleum and petroleum products, a special system will apply. Iraq's neighbouring States will be required, within five days, to provide the Executive Secretary with copies of the customs documents specifying the volume and value of such shipment. If the petroleum or petroleum products are bought for use in a neighbouring State or for re-export, the purchaser will be required to pay the percentage to the Escrow Account within 30 days after petroleum or petroleum products are exported from Iraq. The Escrow Agent will transfer this full amount to the Compensation Fund. Instead of a letter of credit, if payment is not made within 30 days, the Executive

Secretary will notify the Escrow Agent of the additional amount to be provided on account of the shipment. The Escrow Agent will then transfer such additional amount to the Compensation Fund out of other funds passing through the Escrow Account. Truck shipments for direct sales by Iraq from terminals in neighbouring States will be handled in the same manner as shipments from pipeline terminals, i.e. the requirement for payment of the full purchase price into the Escrow Account, backed up by a letter of credit, will apply.

8. With respect to barter transactions, Iraq will be required to choose either of the following two options for each shipment: (a) arrange another cash sale from which such additional funds will be deducted as are required to make payment for the barter transaction, with these funds being remitted to the Escrow Account in advance of transfer of title of the petroleum or petroleum product, or (b) pay the required percentage from other sources in advance of the transfer of title. Agreements for such barter transactions must indicate a market contract price for the petroleum or petroleum products.

The amount of the required percentage under either of the preceding alternatives will be fixed by reference to this price. If a barter, or other transaction mentioned above occurs without the required payment being made to the Escrow Account, the Executive Secretary will notify the Escrow Agent of the amount to be provided on account of the shipment, and the Escrow Agent will transfer such additional amount to the Compensation Fund out of other funds passing through the Escrow Account.

9. The question of exports of petroleum and petroleum products for debt repayment will be addressed by the Governing Council at a later stage, noting Security Council resolutions 687 (1991) and 692 (1991).

10. The Executive Secretary will report on the status, location and value of the Iraqi petroleum and petroleum products previously exported and subject to the percentage deduction under paragraph 6 of resolution 692 (1991) and, taking into account the results of payments under resolutions 706 (1991) and 712 (1991), will develop, for the consideration of the Governing Council, proposals for assuring that contributions are made to the Compensation Fund with respect to such previous exports.

11. The Escrow Account and Compensation Fund will be special funds of the United Nations with appropriate privileges and immunities. The Compensation Commission will ask the Security Council to reaffirm that the Escrow Account and Compensation Fund enjoy the privileges and immunities of the United Nations. Before the Escrow Account or Compensation Fund are established, a satisfactory legal opinion will be obtained from the institution or institutions in which they are to be held attesting that they will be immune from suit or other form of judicial process, including attachment, garnishment and offsets.

12. The Compensation Commission will ask the Security Council to decide under Chapter VII that exports of Iraqi petroleum and petroleum products, while in transit, are immune from attachment or other legal action. Before Iraqi petroleum or petroleum products transit any State other than Iraq, the Executive Secretary will obtain a satisfactory legal opinion attesting to such immunity from that State or, if he deems it appropriate, may enter into any agreement with that State providing for such immunity. Upon transfer of title to the purchaser, the petroleum and petroleum products will not be subject to garnishment by Iraq's creditors.

13. These arrangements are designed to permit normal commercial marketing of Iraqi petroleum and petroleum products once sanctions are lifted, while both ensuring that the Compensation Fund receives all the payments it is due and protecting the petroleum and petroleum products and the sales proceeds from garnishment by Iraq's creditors. The Escrow Account and Compensation Fund will be immune from garnishment. Payments that purchasers owe the Escrow Account will not be subject to garnishment since the payment will be owed to the account and not to Iraq.

Monitoring

14. The monitoring system is to be implemented with the greatest possible use of existing commercial mechanisms and with a view to imposing the minimum burden on normal commercial activity that is consistent with ensuring payments to the Compensation Fund.

15. The Executive Secretary is requested to hire Commission agents to monitor the flow of petroleum and petroleum products at appropriate points, including any functioning loading terminals and at meters situated at the Iraqi border in any functioning pipeline running into a neighbouring State. Before any loading, Commission agents will check that the contract or barter transaction agreement has the approved content, that the letter of credit has the approved form and content, and that the transaction contains no indication of fraud. This paragraph would not apply to truck shipments; the Commission would essentially rely on the assistance of the Customs authorities in Iraq's neighbouring States to assist in the monitoring, but would have the authority to make spot checks.

16. Commission agents will also check that the pricing is within an acceptable range of the market price as determined by the Executive Secretary, with expert assistance, taking into account other relevant transac-

tions, the commercial usages of the parties to the particular transaction, and other relevant circumstances. If the Commission agents determine that the contract price is below the acceptable range for petroleum or petroleum products that have been loaded and shipped, the Executive Secretary will notify the Escrow Agent of the additional amount needed to cover the resulting shortfall in contributions to the Compensation Fund. The Escrow Agent will transfer such additional amount to the Compensation Fund out of other funds passing through the Escrow Account. Commission agents will have authority to prevent loading and shipment if these matters are not in order. In accordance with standard practice in the industry, the parties to the transaction will be required to provide a report from a recognized independent petroleum inspector of international reputation attesting to quality and quantity. The Commission agents will provide copies of the contracts, letters of credit and the independent inspectors' reports to the Executive Secretary, who will maintain a register of all transactions and of related payments into the Escrow Account and Compensation Fund.

17. Where the loading terminal is outside Iraq, the Executive Secretary is requested to obtain the assistance of the State where it is located in conducting the monitoring and otherwise assisting in the implementation of the decisions of the Governing Council. (Resolution 692 (1991) requested all States and international organizations to cooperate fully with such decisions.) When Iraq's offshore terminal again becomes operational, the Execu-

tive Secretary will make arrangements for monitoring exports from it.

18. The Executive Secretary will consult with the Secretary-General to draw on the relevant experience and staff used by the Secretary-General, to avoid duplication of efforts.

Governing Council and Security Council action

19. The Governing Council requests that the Executive Secretary make all the arrangements, consulting with the Secretary-General as necessary, so that this system can be implemented immediately when the Security Council takes action pursuant to paragraph 22 of resolution 687 (1991). The Governing Council should, when it reports to the Security Council pursuant to paragraph 7 of resolution 692 (1991), request that in the resolution of approval pursuant to paragraph 22 the Security Council include the provisions necessary for the effective implementation of these arrangements, including provisions (a) reaffirming the immunity of the Escrow Account and Compensation Fund, (b) establishing the immunity of the Iraqi petroleum and petroleum products while in transit, until title is transferred to a purchaser, and (c) requiring that all States take any necessary domestic measures to implement the arrangements decided upon by the Governing Council for ensuring payments to the Compensation Fund.

Document 92

First report of the Executive Chairman of UNSCOM

S/23165, 25 October 1991

Note by the Secretary-General

The Secretary-General has the honour to transmit to the Security Council a report submitted by the Executive Chairman of the Special Commission established by the Secretary-General pursuant to paragraph 9 (b) (i) of Security Council resolution 687 (1991).

Enclosure

Letter dated 24 October 1991 from the Executive Chairman of the Special Commission established by the Secretary-General pursuant to paragraph 9 (b) (i) of Security Council resolution 687 (1991) addressed to the Secretary-General

I have the honour to refer to the session of the Special Commission established by the Secretary-General pursu-

ant to paragraph 9 (b) (i) of Security Council resolution 687 (1991), which was held at United Nations Headquarters from 21 to 23 October 1991. In the course of its work, the Special Commission had before it a report submitted by me as Executive Chairman on the activities undertaken by the Special Commission in the initial five months of operational activities under section C of Security Council resolution 687 (1991). The Commission agreed that my report should be transmitted to you with the request that it be circulated as a document of the Security Council.

(*Signed*) Rolf EKÉUS
Executive Chairman
Office of the Special Commission

Annex

Report by the Executive Chairman of the Special Commission established by the Secretary-General pursuant to paragraph 9 (b) (i) of Security Council resolution 687 (1991)

A. *Scope of the report*

1. Six months have elapsed since the adoption by the Security Council on 3 April 1991 of its resolution 687 (1991). Pursuant to section C of that resolution the Special Commission (UNSCOM) was established to perform the functions assigned to it in that section. These relate to the elimination of Iraq's weapons of mass destruction and the means of their production as well as to ensuring that the acquisition of such weapons is not resumed in the future. Pursuant to his executive responsibilities, the present report is presented by the Executive Chairman to give an account of the initial five months of operational activities.

2. This is the first comprehensive account of the work undertaken to implement section C of Security Council resolution 687 (1991) and subsequent related resolutions. Consequently, it touches upon the establishment, composition, organization, mandate and financing of the Special Commission, as well as its operational activities in the chemical, biological and ballistic missile fields and its responsibilities in the nuclear field. Where necessary, separate appendices deal with these various aspects. The report highlights significant issues. It also gives the Executive Chairman's assessment of the results achieved, the difficulties encountered and what remains to be done to secure full implementation of the requirements of the Security Council resolutions.

B. *Servicing of the Special Commission*

3. Immediately upon the establishment of the Special Commission as a subsidiary organ of the Security Council, steps were taken to set up a small, full-time secretariat to assist the Executive Chairman in the exercise of his functions. The secretariat is stationed principally at United Nations Headquarters in New York, with a field office in Bahrain and a support office at Baghdad. The Bahrain office serves as the staging area for the assembly, briefing and report writing of inspection teams, while the Baghdad office provides the required logistical support in the field. The secretariat has been assisted in its work by members of the Commission. Other staff have been provided by Governments, the United Nations Secretariat, in particular the Department for Disarmament Affairs, and the World Health Organization (WHO). Inspection teams have consisted of personnel made available by Governments, members of the Commission, the United Nations Secretariat, WHO and, in the nuclear field, by inspectors and staff of the International Atomic Energy Agency (IAEA). In composing the teams, selection was principally based upon the technical qualifications and expertise of the inspectors with due regard to drawing the members of inspection teams from as many Member States as possible within the range of available capabilities and experience. Nationals of 34 countries have so far served on inspection teams. In briefing team personnel on their assignments, attention is drawn to their responsibilities as experts on mission for the United Nations acting under a mandate from the Security Council. Further information on the Special Commission and the functions of the secretariat is contained in appendix I to the present report.

4. The Executive Chairman wishes to place on record his profound appreciation to the Secretary-General, to Governments and to the agencies concerned for the assistance made available as well as to the able staff placed at his disposal for the dedicated service they have rendered, sometimes in very trying and dangerous circumstances, to carry out the mandate of the Security Council.

C. *Status, privileges and immunities*

5. After extensive and sometimes difficult negotiations, an agreement was concluded with the Government of Iraq concerning the status, privileges and immunities of the Special Commission, the IAEA and United Nations specialized agencies involved in implementation of Security Council resolution 687 (1991). The provisions in the agreement with Iraq are recapitulated, elaborated upon and reinforced in the Special Commission's plan a/ for future ongoing monitoring and verification of Iraq's compliance with relevant parts of section C of Security Council resolution 687 (1991) which was approved by the Council in its resolution 715 (1991) of 11 October 1991. An agreement has also been concluded with the Government of Bahrain in respect of the field office at Manama.

D. *Progress made*

6. The implementation of section C of Security Council resolution 687 (1991) involves what can most conveniently be described as a three-stage process. First, there is the inspection and survey phase, designed to gather the information necessary to make an informed assessment of Iraq's capabilities and facilities in the nuclear, chemical, biological and ballistic missile fields. The second phase is concerned with the disposal of weapons of mass destruction, facilities and other items related thereto through destruction, removal or rendering harm-

a/ S/22871/Rev.1. See, in particular, paras. 17 and 18 and annex I of the plan.

less, as appropriate, as provided for in resolution 687 (1991). Third is the long-term monitoring phase, to ensure ongoing verification of Iraq's compliance with its obligations under section C of resolution 687 (1991). These phases may run concurrently, but they provide a convenient basis for assessing what has been achieved so far.

7. At present, it can be said with some confidence that through rigorous and intensive inspections by the Special Commission in the chemical, biological and ballistic missile fields and by IAEA and the Special Commission in the nuclear field, it has been possible to compile, in the course of the first phase, sufficient information to have a general picture of Iraq's capabilities and facilities in all the areas concerned. However, some important lacunae remain; filling them will be pursued energetically.

8. By the end of October 1991, 20 inspection missions will have been fielded. For a list of the missions, see appendix II to the present report. Thirteen of these missions related to chemical, biological and ballistic missile areas. The other seven missions were nuclear inspection missions undertaken by IAEA with the assistance and cooperation of the Special Commission. Such assistance and cooperation included the provision of persons with expertise in the fields of nuclear weapons, various nuclear-energy-related technologies as well as special materials. It also included broad logistical support, such as explosive ordnance disposal, information, communications, medical, interpretation and photographic support and financing. Furthermore, the Commission has the responsibility, in the absence of declarations by Iraq, for designating locations for nuclear inspections as well as for all other inspections. Such designations are based on assessments made within the Special Commission, or on information received from interested Member States.

9. In the nuclear field, the IAEA-led inspections have disclosed three clandestine uranium enrichment programmes or activities: chemical, centrifuge and electromagnetic isotope separation as well as laboratory-scale plutonium separation. The sixth nuclear inspection finally obtained conclusive evidence of a nuclear weapons development programme, aimed at an implosion-type nuclear weapon linked to a surface-to-surface missile project. Given the information obtained about the advanced nature of Iraqi efforts to develop an implosion system, it appears that it is the availability of adequate amounts of fissile material that would have been the major factor in determining how soon Iraq could have produced a nuclear device. For example, if Iraq would have started with natural uranium using its electromagnetic isotope separation (EMIS) technology, that time could have been as little as 12 to 18 months. Further

information will be found in appendix III to the present report.

10. Subject to confirmation by the completion of the verification phase in the near future, it seems probable that a full assessment of Iraq's chemical weapons capabilities will be achieved. So far Iraq has acknowledged possession of 46,000 pieces of filled munitions. Iraq's facilities include the substantial chemical weapons production complex of the Al Muthanna State Establishment and three planned precursor production plants in the Al Fallujah area. In addition to the central storage of filled chemical munitions, warfare agents and precursor chemicals in bulk at Al Muthanna, filled chemical munitions, often damaged and leaking, are stored at various sites throughout the country. The process of moving these munitions to storage at Al Muthanna prior to destruction has been initiated. Al Muthanna has been designated as the central destruction site for Iraq's chemical weapons. Destruction of filled munitions and bulk agents at Al Muthanna will begin early in 1992 and is expected to continue into 1993. To date, 11,829 unfilled chemical munitions have been destroyed by Iraqi personnel under the supervision of Special Commission inspectors. Further information will be found in appendix IV to the present report.

11. In the area of biological weapons capabilities, the inspection activities initially focused on the major research and development site at Salman Pak, but over 10 additional sites have now been inspected. Conclusive evidence that Iraq was engaged in an advanced military biological research programme has been collected. No evidence of actual weaponization has been found, but the inspections have provided a sound database for future monitoring of biological capabilities in Iraq. Details are given in appendix IV.

12. In the field of ballistic missiles—those with a range greater than 150 kilometres—the Special Commission inspection teams have supervised the destruction of 62 ballistic missiles, 18 fixed Scud missile launch pads, 10 launchers, 11 decoy missiles, 32 ballistic missile warheads, 127 missile storage support vehicles, a substantial amount of rocket fuel, an assembled 350 millimetre supergun, components for 350 and 1,000 millimetre superguns and 1 tonne of supergun propellant. In addition, inspectors have confirmed the destruction by coalition bombing of several missile repair and production facilities. However, important questions remain unresolved, in particular, a satisfactory accounting for all the relevant missiles obtained or constructed by Iraq, and a full disclosure of plans and progress in future ballistic missile development. Further work is required to obtain a full accounting of Iraq's missile capabilities before the Special Commission can certify that all subject items have

been identified. Details will be found in appendix V to the present report.

13. Continuing work on concepts and details of compliance monitoring, in conjunction with IAEA, has resulted in the development of plans for long-term monitoring in the chemical, biological and ballistic missile areas and, separately, on nuclear monitoring. Although these two plans were initially drawn up separately, the drafts have as far as possible been harmonized by the Special Commission and IAEA. A notable factor in the preparation of the plans has been the cooperation from and the inputs submitted by various Governments. Monitoring and verification under the Special Commission's plan will need to cover not only military but also civilian sites, facilities, material and other items that could be used or activities that could be involved in contravention of Iraq's obligations under Security Council resolution 687 (1991). In order to ensure Iraq's compliance with these undertakings, the Special Commission, pursuant to resolutions 687 (1991) and 707 (1991) will, through inspections and aerial overflights, as well as the provision of information by Iraq, monitor and verify these activities, sites, facilities, material and other items.

14. In sum, the activities of the Special Commission and IAEA have been highly effective in the period under review, particularly taking into account that five months ago the Commission was without staff, resources and plans of operation and was required to build up from the very beginning the infrastructure required for its functioning. Account must also be taken of the magnitude of the task with which the Special Commission and IAEA have been faced, given the scope and variety of Iraq's efforts to conduct research and, in certain areas, to produce weapons of mass destruction. These efforts, particularly in the nuclear field, have consumed a significant portion of Iraq's expenditure of billions of dollars derived from its oil revenues, as indicated to the Executive Chairman in his meeting with the Deputy Prime Minister of Iraq, Mr. Tariq Aziz, at Baghdad, on 5 October 1991, when the Deputy Prime Minister, while denying acquisition of nuclear weapons, admitted research in this field.

15. The accomplishments of the Special Commission and the inspection teams, which are described briefly in paragraphs 9-13 above, are thus remarkable. The activities undertaken have resulted in a situation, of significance for the future, where:

(a) Regarding chemical weapons and biological weapons capabilities, a comprehensive database will shortly be at hand;

(b) In the ballistic missile field, it would also seem that a comprehensive understanding should be within reach, even if further inspections and analysis are required to be able to state with full confidence that a complete disclosure of remaining ballistic missiles has been made by Iraq;

(c) In view of the lack of full cooperation by Iraq and its persistent concealment efforts, a complete disclosure of the nuclear weapons programme of Iraq has yet to be made. The sixth nuclear inspection produced important and definitive evidence that much remains to be done;

(d) The Plans for compliance monitoring prepared by the Special Commission (S/22871/Rev.1) and by IAEA (S/22872/Rev.1) have been submitted to the Security Council. They were formally approved by unanimity on 11 October 1991 in Security Council resolution 715 (1991).

E. *Attitude of Iraq*

16. The inspections undertaken have had to be energetic, rigorous and intensive because of the failure of Iraq, particularly in the nuclear field, to adopt the candid and open approach to the disclosure of its capabilities which is called for in section C of resolution 687 (1991). While cooperation from Iraq has generally been forthcoming at the field level—most notably in the chemical and to a degree in the biological areas—in relation to activities and resources declared by Iraq, a totally different attitude of non-cooperation, concealment and sometimes false information has emerged in relation to non-declared activities, resources and sites that have been designated by the Special Commission on the basis of its own assessments or of data supplied to it by States.

17. This has resulted in a number of serious incidents, including those of 23, 25 and 28 June 1991, when a nuclear inspection team was denied access to certain facilities and, on the latter occasion, shots were fired by the Iraqi military to deter the team from photographing trucks transporting materials previously removed from Iraqi nuclear programme sites. These incidents were reported to the Security Council (S/22739 and S/22743), and resulted in the Council dispatching, at the end of June 1991, a high level mission (see S/22746), composed of the Executive Chairman of the Special Commission, the Director General of IAEA and the United Nations Under-Secretary-General for Disarmament Affairs to meet with the highest levels of the Iraqi Government. This mission received various assurances of full cooperation from the Government, which were confirmed to the Secretary-General (S/22762), but, as the mission reported to the Security Council (S/22761, annex, para. 17), "in spite of their unambiguous character, the general assurances given and the specific measures promised can only be evaluated in the light of present and future implementation by the Iraqi authorities".

18. The misgivings thus expressed by the mission have been amply confirmed by the subsequent conduct of

the Iraqi authorities, culminating in the detention of a further nuclear inspection team in a parking lot at Baghdad for four days at the end of September 1991. This serious and material violation by Iraq of its obligations under the relevant Security Council resolutions and its agreement on the status, privileges and immunities of the Special Commission and IAEA does not stand alone. Despite express provisions in the agreement, Iraq refused for almost three months to permit the Special Commission to introduce its own helicopter air-support system into Iraq, a matter that had to be reported to and was the subject of representations by the Security Council (S/23064 and S/23070) and which had to be taken up by the Executive Chairman on a special visit to Iraq early in October 1991. That air-support system is now finally operational in Iraq although certain practical details need to be worked out regarding the most direct flight patterns for particular flights.

19. The elements of misinformation, concealment, lack of cooperation and violation of the privileges and immunities of the Special Commission and IAEA have not created any trust in Iraq's intentions. They have had a negative impact on relations with Iraq and have engendered an atmosphere of profound scepticism, particularly in the nuclear area; this atmosphere has to some degree contaminated the other three areas. It has had for Iraq an effect directly contrary to its professed desire for an early lifting of the sanctions imposed in the relevant Security Council resolutions. It has led to the adoption of Security Council resolution 707 (1991) of 15 August 1991 and it constituted an element that had to be taken most seriously into account in the preparation by the Special Commission and by IAEA of their plans for securing Iraq's future compliance with the provisions of section C of resolution 687 (1991). A change in the attitude of Iraq to one of candour, transparency and cooperation at all levels is probably the one single element that could contribute most substantially to a timely and satisfactory implementation of the mandate of the Special Commission and of IAEA. Only then will it be possible to present a finding by them that Iraq is in substantial compliance with its obligations under section C of resolution 687 (1991).

F. Issues for the immediate future

20. The progress made, despite obstacles placed in the way by Iraq, in completing the first stage of activities under section C of resolution 687 (1991), gives increasing urgency to a number of issues, particularly the destruction, removal or rendering harmless of items proscribed by the resolution; the organization and initiation of compliance monitoring; the compilation and provision of information on suppliers of Iraq in the nuclear, chemical, biological and ballistic missile fields; and some critical administrative issues.

1. The issue of destruction

21. The Special Commission established at an early stage a Destruction Advisory Panel to advise on the particularly difficult and hazardous area of chemical weapons destruction. The Panel met on 24-28 June 1991, 5-9 August 1991 and 10-14 September 1991, and has submitted three substantive reports. A small fact-finding mission also visited Baghdad on 11-14 August 1991 for detailed technical discussions with the competent Iraqi authorities on the role of Iraq in the destruction of their chemical weapons munitions, agents, precursors and intermediates. Final decisions on the technologies to be used to destroy Iraqi chemical warfare agents and the extent of Iraqi involvement in the destruction process now require urgent consideration. The decisions made will have to take account of the need to ensure public safety, to enforce acceptable emission standards and to be as far as possible rapid and cost-effective. A second fact-finding mission to Iraq is under preparation in this connection.

22. Another urgent issue relates to the destruction of equipment and support facilities in prohibited weapons programmes. Decisions will have to be taken on a number of dual-use items that have been used or were acquired in order to be used in the prohibited areas. A balance must be found between the requirements of resolution 687 (1991) to destroy, remove or render harmless all such items, on the one hand, and requests from Iraq, on the other, that such items be used for civilian and peaceful purposes. Team leaders have been issued with provisional guidelines in this regard, but these will have to be refined in the light of experience, also taking due note of any changes in Iraq's attitude to cooperation with the Special Commission and IAEA.

2. Compliance monitoring

23. Following approval by the Security Council of the compliance monitoring plans drawn up by the Special Commission and by IAEA, it is now urgently necessary that the organization, detailed procedures and resources required to implement these plans should be developed and emplaced. Included in this implementation programme is the need for a comprehensive database that will draw together information from various sources. A start has been made on developing this database and this will be pressed forward with vigour.

3. Information on suppliers to Iraq

24. Another issue of importance is the release from the Special Commission and IAEA of information per-

taining to foreign procurement to the Iraqi weapons programmes. Such information, previously acquired sporadically, is now systematically being collected. It indicates a pattern of broad and successful Iraqi procurement efforts in many countries. While many suppliers obviously have carried out perfectly legitimate exports of general purpose or dual-use items, which have thereafter been transferred to weapons programmes, there are also indications of circumvention of national or multinational export controls and non-proliferation regimes. Until information is more complete and a full analysis of the material has been performed, the Special Commission and IAEA have agreed to release specific information only to Governments requesting information on Iraqi procurement efforts in their countries. However, once a comprehensive database has been obtained and fully analysed, relevant information will be made available to the Sanctions Committee in connection with compliance monitoring. Furthermore, the broader objective of preventing the spread of weapons of mass destruction will require an active and open release policy.

4. Administrative issues

25. Two problems of an administrative nature have faced the Commission from its inception, solutions to which are of crucial importance both for the completion of the current phases and for the implementation of the long-term monitoring plans: these are the staffing and financing of the Special Commission.

26. To date, the small staff has been made up of highly qualified experts on loan from Governments and on assignment from other United Nations offices. In the case of experts on loan from Governments, many of them hold positions of high responsibility in their home countries and a pressure is increasingly being felt that they return to their normal workplaces. In the case of United Nations staff, the same pressure exists from releasing departments for staff on assignment to the Commission. Additionally, because of the press of other responsibilities on the limited human resources of the United Nations Secretariat, there has been and continues to be understandable reluctance to release the personnel identified for staffing the field offices in Bahrain and Baghdad, which, as a result, are still not yet staffed to their full agreed levels. Ways must be found to staff fully the Commission on a more long-term basis at the high level of expertise necessary for it to accomplish its demanding tasks, particularly under the regime for ongoing monitoring and verification.

27. The issue of the financing of the Commission's activities has been complex and controversial. It has been the position of the Secretary-General that, to ensure dependability, the financing of the Special Commission should be secured through the assessment of Member States, and a budget was proposed on this basis for submission to the General Assembly through the Advisory Committee on Administrative and Budgetary Questions. Approval of a budget through these regular mechanisms has been considered necessary for the establishment of posts other than on a short-term basis for the personnel of the Commission and for long-term obligations of financial resources.

28. However, this course of action was not supported by all Member States and by its resolution 699 (1991) of 17 June 1991, the Security Council called for the maximum assistance, in cash and in kind, from all States to ensure that activities under section C of resolution 687 (1991) were undertaken effectively and expeditiously. The Council also decided that the Government of Iraq should be liable for the full costs of carrying out the tasks authorized by section C, the Secretary-General being requested to submit a report on the most effective means for the fulfilment of Iraq's obligations in this respect. On the basis of that report (S/22792), which expressed the view that the most obvious way of obtaining the necessary financial resources from Iraq would be to authorize the sale of some Iraqi petroleum and petroleum products, the Council, by its resolution 706 (1991), gave such authorization subject to international controls and restrictions, part of the proceeds to be made available for meeting the costs of the Special Commission and IAEA. So far no sales have taken place and thus no proceeds made available.

29. Until these proceeds are forthcoming, the Special Commission's activities are being financed, on an interim basis, from the Working Capital Fund and, as of 1 October 1991, from trust fund sources containing the voluntary contributions from Member States for activities under Security Council resolution 687 (1991), which at this time total $5.5 million.

30. These resources have been supplemented by contributions in kind from Member States, including personnel, land and air transportation, high altitude aerial surveys, communications, chemical and biological protective and detection equipment, medical supplies and ambulances. For further information on the contributions received see appendix VI to the present report. The Executive Chairman is most grateful for all the assistance thus rendered to the Special Commission by Member States. Without it, the progress made in discharging its mandate would have been impossible.

31. However, the Special Commission remains without a formally approved budget, without a guaranteed assurance of the availability of adequate financial resources and without posts for personnel except on a short-term basis. The United Nations Controller has

ensured that adequate financing has been available and thus activities of the Commission have not so far been constrained to any serious extent. However, the continuing uncertainty has caused difficulties in long-term planning and staffing. From the present time up to 31 March 1992, it is anticipated that the Special Commission will require funds in the neighbourhood of $79 million. The uncertainties that exist need urgent resolution if the Special Commission is to have the financial and budgetary stability required to implement its responsibilities for the destruction, removal or rendering harmless of Iraq's weapons of mass destruction and to prevent any reacquisition of the same through an effective and timely regime of compliance monitoring as defined in the respective plans of the Special Commission and IAEA.

G. *Concluding observations*

32. The success of the Special Commission in carrying out its unique task under section C of resolution 687 (1991) has depended on three factors of crucial importance:

(a) The full political support of the Security Council. The Special Commission is a subsidiary organ of the Council, responsible to it through the Secretary-General. The Council has been kept fully informed of the Commission's activities. Executive summaries of the Special Commission's inspections in the chemical, biological and ballistic missile fields have regularly been made available to the Secretary-General by the Executive Chairman and by the former to the Security Council. Reports by IAEA on its inspections have been circulated in Security Council documents (S/22788, S/22837, S/22986 and Corr.1, S/23112 and S/23122). The Council has also been kept informed of the particular problems and difficulties that have been encountered, and the Council has reacted vigorously and affirmatively. The statement of 27 June (S/22746), whereby the high-level mission was dispatched to Iraq, and Security Council resolutions 707 (1991) and 715 (1991) were adopted unanimously. Finally, the strong position taken by the Council *vis-à-vis* Iraq during the sixth nuclear inspection when team members were detained by the Iraqi authorities (see para. 18 above) further underlined the Council's full support for the activities of the Special Commission and IAEA;

(b) The support of Governments. The detachment from important positions in various countries of highly qualified experts to serve in the Office of the Special Commission and on inspection missions has been of decisive importance for the implementation of a unique programme of elimination of weapons of mass destruction. Of almost equal importance has been the provision of fixed-wing and rotary-wing air support, vehicles, specialized equipment and materials, logistics and information;

(c) The support of the Secretary-General and of other units of the United Nations Secretariat. The contributions of the Secretariat in experienced personnel, operations, logistics and administration, in particular from the Department for Disarmament Affairs, the Field Operations Division, the Department of Administration and Management, the Department of Conference Services and the Department of Public Information have been characterized by resourcefulness, flexibility and dedication in coping with a new and challenging task. They go a long way to demonstrate the capabilities and potentials of the Secretariat, if financial resources are available, to manage new activities rapidly and efficiently.

33. For the successful continuation of the Special Commission's long-term activities in Iraq, it is imperative that the strong support of the Security Council and the commitment of individual Governments and of the Secretary-General and other units of the United Nations Secretariat be maintained.

Appendices to the report

I. Establishment, organization and mandate of the Special Commission

II. List of missions fielded to 31 October 1991

III. Nuclear issues

IV. Chemical and biological weapons

V. Ballistic missiles and long-range guns

VI. Voluntary contributions to the Special Commission

Appendix I
Establishment, organization and mandate of the Special Commission

A. *Establishment*

1. By its resolution 687 (1991) of 3 April 1991, the Security Council, acting under Chapter VII of the Charter of the United Nations, established the terms and conditions for a formal cease-fire between Iraq and Kuwait and the Member States cooperating with Kuwait in accordance with Security Council resolution 678 (1990). Section C of resolution 687 (1991) is concerned with the elimination of Iraq's weapons of mass destruction and the means of their production and with measures to ensure that production is not resumed. For these purposes paragraph 9 of section C called for a report by the Secretary-General on the forming of a Special Commission to perform certain tasks assigned to it in the resolution (see paras. 5-10 below). The Secretary-General submitted his report (S/22508) to the Security Council on 18 April 1991, and it was approved by the Council on 19 April

1991 (S/22509). The Secretary-General's report provided for the appointment by him of the Special Commission, headed by an Executive Chairman with a Deputy Executive Chairman to assist the Chairman.

B. *Composition*

2. The Executive Chairman, the Deputy Executive Chairman and the members of the Special Commission appointed by the Secretary-General are as follows: (a) Executive Chairman: Mr. Rolf Ekéus (Sweden); (b) Deputy Executive Chairman: Mr. Robert L. Gallucci (United States); and (c) members: Mr. Paal Aas (Norway); Mr. Ken Adachi (Japan); Mr. B. N. C. Agu (Nigeria); Mr. Andrzej Badek (Poland); Mr. Bryan C. Barrass (United Kingdom); Mr. Peter von Butler (Germany); Mr. Armando Caputo (Italy); Mr. Ronald Cleminson (Canada); Mr. John Gee (Australia); Mr. Helmut Hönig (Austria); Mr. B. A. Kuvshinnikov (Union of Soviet Socialist Republics); Mr. A. J. J. Ooms (Netherlands); Ms. Marjatta M. Rautio (Finland); Mr. Michel Saint Mleux (France); Mr. Roberto Sanchez (Venezuela); Mr. B. Simandjuntak (Indonesia); Mr. Miroslav Splino (Czechoslovakia); Mr. Emile Vanden Bemden (Belgium); and Mr. Yuan Renfeng (China).

C. *Organization*

3. The report of the Secretary-General (S/22508) provided that, under the Executive Chairman and the Deputy Executive Chairman, the planning and operational direction of the functions of the Commission should be carried out by a number of groups: biological and chemical weapons; ballistic missiles; nuclear weapons capabilities; future compliance; and operations support. Taking this into account, the Special Commission organized its work as indicated below. It associated, where appropriate, experts in the fields concerned with members of the Commission on certain groups and on the destruction advisory panel which was set up by the chemical and biological weapons group.

(a) Nuclear/IAEA Group: Mr. B. A. Kuvshinnikov (USSR) (Coordinator); Mr. B. N. C. Agu (Nigeria); Mr. M. Saint Mleux (France); Mr. E. Vanden Bemden (Belgium); and Mr. Yuan Renfeng (China);

(b) Chemical/Biological Weapons Group: Mr. J. Gee (Australia) (Coordinator); Mr. P. Aas (Norway); Mr. K. Adachi (Japan); Mr. B. C. Barrass (United Kingdom); Mr. H. Hönig (Austria); Mr. A. J. J. Ooms (Netherlands); Mr. R. Sanchez (Venezuela); Mr. J. Santesson (WHO); and Mr. M. Splino (Czechoslovakia);

(c) Destruction Advisory Panel: Mr. R. G. Manley (United Kingdom) (Chairman); Mr. K. Flamm (United States); Mr. A. Leblanc (France); Mr. G. Leonov, (USSR);

Mr. J. McAndless (Canada); Mr. R. Mikulak (United States); and Mr. J. Santesson (WHO);

(d) Ballistic Missiles Group: Mr. A. Caputo (Italy) and Mr. B. Simandjuntak (Indonesia);

(e) Future Compliance Monitoring Group: Mr. P. von Butler (Germany) (Coordinator); Mr. A. Badek (Poland); Mr. R. Cleminson (Canada); Ms. M. M. Rautio (Finland).

4. Responsibilities for operations support have been vested in the Office of the Executive Chairman of the Special Commission (see para. 3 of the report) at United Nations Headquarters and in the Field Office in Bahrain and the Support Office at Baghdad. The secretariat of these offices, under the direction of the Executive Chairman, carries out the day-to-day verification activities; compiles and analyses information; schedules, plans and organizes inspections and aerial overflights; prepares other field operations; provides general administrative support; ensures liaison with IAEA and the relevant Departments of the United Nations Secretariat; answers inquiries from Governments, the press and the public; and performs such other functions as may be required by the Executive Chairman. In addition to staff seconded by Governments, the total number of regular United Nations staff who will be servicing the Commission when all posts are filled will be 66: 13 Professionals and 53 General Service.

D. *Mandate*

5. The mandate of the Special Commission is established by the Security Council in paragraphs 9 (b) and 10 of section C of its resolution 687 (1991). By its resolution 699 (1991) of 17 June 1991, the Council confirmed that a 45-day period mentioned in paragraph 9 (b) did not place a time-limit on the activities to be carried out under section C of its resolution 687 (1991). The mandate of the Commission and its rights were confirmed and clarified by the Council in its resolution 707 (1991) of 15 August 1991. On 11 October 1991, the Council, by its resolution 715 (1991), approved the Special Commission's plan for future ongoing monitoring and verification of Iraq's compliance with relevant parts of section C of Security Council resolution 687 (1991) (S/22871/Rev.1), which provides for the continuation of the Special Commission and for a compliance unit under it to be organized to carry out the monitoring and verification tasks provided for under the plan. At the present time, the plan is not yet operational and thus the mandate of the Commission in the period under review is governed by the pertinent provisions of resolutions 687 (1991), 699 (1991) and 707 (1991).

6. The mandate of the Commission in the period under review has been essentially:

(a) To carry out immediate on-site inspection of Iraq's biological, chemical and ballistic missile capabilities, based on Iraq's declarations and the designation of any additional locations by the Special Commission itself;

(b) To receive from Iraq, possession for destruction, removal or rendering harmless, taking into account the requirements of public safety, of all items specified under paragraph 8 (a) of resolution 687 (1991), including items at the additional locations designated by the Special Commission under paragraph 9 (b) (i) of the resolution and to supervise the destruction by Iraq of all its missile capabilities, including launchers, as specified under paragraph 8 (b);

(c) To provide the assistance and cooperation to the Director General of IAEA required in paragraphs 12 and 13 of resolution 687 (1991);

(d) To consult the Secretary-General in developing a plan for the future ongoing monitoring and verification of Iraq's compliance with paragraph 10 of resolution 687 (1991).

7. Paragraph 8 of resolution 687 (1991), which is directly relevant to the Commission's mandate, provides that Iraq:

"shall unconditionally accept the destruction, removal or rendering harmless, under international supervision, of:

"(a) All chemical and biological weapons and all stocks of agents and all related subsystems and components and all research, development, support and manufacturing facilities;

"(b) All ballistic missiles with a range greater than 150 kilometres and related major parts, and repair and production facilities."

8. Under paragraphs 12 and 13 of resolution 687 (1991), IAEA is vested with responsibilities in the nuclear area substantially similar to those of the Special Commission in the chemical and biological weapons and ballistic missile areas. These responsibilities are to be carried out with the assistance and cooperation of the Special Commission. The Commission also has the responsibility to designate locations for nuclear inspections.

9. Under Security Council resolution 707 (1991), it is, *inter alia*, confirmed that Iraq must notify and obtain prior consent from the Special Commission before any movement or destruction of any material or equipment relating to Iraq's nuclear, chemical or biological weapons or ballistic missile programmes or material or equipment relating to other Iraqi nuclear activities.

10. For the future, by its resolution 715 (1991), the Security Council has entrusted the Special Commission with implementation of the Commission's plan for ongoing monitoring and verification. By the same resolution, the Council, *inter alia*, requires the Commission to extend, by mutual agreement, its assistance and cooperation to the Director General of IAEA in his implementation of the Agency's plan for ongoing monitoring and verification. The Council further decided by that resolution that the Commission should continue to have the responsibility for designating additional locations for inspection and overflights and should perform such other functions, in cooperation in the nuclear field with the Director General of IAEA, as might be necessary to coordinate activities under the two plans, including making use of commonly available services and information to the fullest extent possible in order to achieve maximum efficiency and optimum use of resources.

Appendix II
List of missions fielded to 31 October 1991

Team	Inspection	Dates
IAEA 1/UNSCOM 1	Nuclear	14-22 May
UNSCOM 2	Chemical	9-15 June
UNSCOM 3	Ballistic missile	30 June-7 July
IAEA 2/UNSCOM 4	Nuclear	22 June-3 July
IAEA 3/UNSCOM 5	Nuclear	6-19 July
IAEA 4/UNSCOM 6	Nuclear	27 July-10 August
UNSCOM 7	Biological	2-8 August
UNSCOM 8	Ballistic missile a/	8-15 August
UNSCOM 9	Chemical	15-22 August
UNSCOM 10	Ballistic missile	18-20 July
UNSCOM 11	Chemical	31 August-9 September
UNSCOM 12	Chemical	31 August-5 September
UNSCOM 13	Ballistic missile	6-13 September
IAEA 5/UNSCOM 14	Nuclear	14-20 September
UNSCOM 15	Biological	20 September-3 October
IAEA 6/UNSCOM 16	Nuclear	21-30 September
UNSCOM 17	Chemical	6 October-9 November
UNSCOM 18	Ballistic missile a/	1-14 October
IAEA 7/UNSCOM 19	Nuclear	11-22 October
UNSCOM 20	Chemical	22 October-2 November

a/ UNSCOM 8 and UNSCOM 18 also surveyed and rendered harmless the 350 millimetre and 1,000 millimetre long-range guns and components.

Appendix III
Nuclear issues

(Compiled with the assistance of the International Atomic Energy Agency)

A. *Declarations*

1. On 6 April 1991, Iraq, by action of its National Assembly, agreed to Security Council resolution 687 (1991). Pursuant to this resolution, Iraq declared on 18 April 1991 that it had none of the nuclear-related items referred to in the resolution, so "monitoring shall remain confined to the materials currently declared and used with the knowledge of, under the supervision of and subject to the safeguards of the International Atomic Energy Agency".

2. On 27 April, in response to a letter from IAEA, Iraq declared various forms of safeguarded enriched uranium and various nuclear-related equipment, laboratories and facilities at Al Tuwaitha and Al Qaim.

3. As a result of findings during subsequent inspections, Iraq declared on 7 July 1991 a large number of activities and facilities characterized as being part of its peaceful nuclear programme. Key among these were three methods for enriching uranium: electromagnetic, centrifuge and chemical exchange.

4. Since then, Iraqi admissions of additional nuclear-related activities and facilities have continued—and inspection work has continued. Very recently, indisputable evidence of an extensive Iraqi nuclear weapons development programme has been obtained.

B. *Key findings*

5. The key findings of the first two nuclear inspection teams, during whose inspections (IAEA 1/UNSCOM 1 and IAEA 2/UNSCOM 4) the various forms and quantities of IAEA-safeguarded enriched uranium were located, identified and taken into IAEA custody, were as follows (S/22788):

(a) Much equipment and almost all documentation had been removed by the Iraqi authorities from the Al Tuwaitha Nuclear Research Centre;

(b) The Iraqi authorities had destroyed evidence of some of Iraq's activities or obscured it by grading, concrete pouring and other methods;

(c) 2.26 grams of undeclared plutonium had been separated from a safeguards-exempted reactor fuel element;

(d) A hitherto undeclared electromagnetic isotope separation programme had existed for enriching uranium.

6. In the opinion of the inspecting teams, no more than three kilograms of highly enriched uranium could have been produced at Al Tuwaitha, although a high-capacity production programme was planned for the near future.

7. The key findings of the third nuclear inspection team (IAEA 3/UNSCOM 5) during whose inspection Dr. J. Jaffar, Deputy Chairman of the Iraqi Atomic Energy Commission, denied the existence of a nuclear weapons programme, were as follows (S/22837):

(a) Through procurement abroad and/or the mining and processing of indigenous uranium ores, Iraq had built up a large inventory of natural uranium;

(b) On the basis of data provided by Iraq, 15 kilograms of highly enriched uranium could have been produced each year when the electromagnetic isotope separation (EMIS) facility at Tarmiya became fully operational;

(c) An identical facility at Ash Sharqat was 85 per cent complete when it was destroyed during the war;

(d) On the basis of Iraqi disclosures, equivalent efforts had not been devoted to the centrifuge and chemical exchange methods.

8. The key findings of the fourth nuclear inspection team (IAEA 4/UNSCOM 6) were as follows (S/22986 and Corr.1):

(a) On the basis of an Iraqi declaration, under a clandestine programme carried out in violation of its safeguards agreement with IAEA, three grams of plutonium had been separated from irradiated reactor fuel;

(b) Sufficient natural uranium was available to produce annually 15 kilograms of highly enriched uranium using electromagnetic isotope separators;

(c) On the basis of information provided by the Iraqi authorities, centrifuge production was planned to begin in 1991: a 100-machine cascade would have been operating in 1993 and a 500-machine cascade in 1996;

(d) In the opinion of the inspectors, the centrifuge production facility could have built several thousands of centrifuges a year;

(e) Despite Iraqi denials of the existence of a weaponization programme, evidence of activities such as specialized high-explosive testing and items such as exploding bridge wire detonators indicated that a weaponization programme had existed.

9. The key findings of the fifth nuclear inspection team (IAEA 5/UNSCOM/14) were as follows (S/23112):

(a) According to an Iraqi statement, 2.2 tons of heavy water which had been imported had been lost because of bomb damage to the storage tank (inspectors were shown the damaged tank);

(b) The chemical exchange enrichment facilities shown to the team had been thoroughly cleaned, leaving no evidence of the extent of the programme.

10. Preliminary key findings of the sixth nuclear inspection team (IAEA 6/UNSCOM 16) were as follows (S/23122):

(a) Conclusive documentary evidence was found at two facilities that Iraq had had a programme for developing an implosion-type nuclear weapon;

(b) Other documents linked the nuclear weapons development programme to a surface-to-surface missile project;

(c) An extensive weaponization programme had been carried out at Al Tuwaitha and Al Atheer, including work with internal neutron initiators and plans for external initiators, high-explosive components, exploding bridge wire detonators and firing sets for multiple detonator systems;

(d) Some documents indicated the existence of a project to produce a sizeable amount of lithium-6, an isotope contained in natural lithium. The lithium-6 project was part of the overall Iraqi nuclear weapon development programme. Lithium-6 is a key component of thermonuclear weapons and is also the source material to produce tritium, an isotope of hydrogen. Tritium is employed in nuclear weaponry as a "booster" in nuclear weapons and as a component in certain types of neutron initiators;

(e) The development of internal neutron initiators based on plutonium-238 was being contemplated, which provided a rationale for the Iraqi interest in separating plutonium in quantities inadequate for an explosive device;

(f) One- and two-dimensional hydrodynamic codes based on well-known hydrodynamic models had been developed by Iraq and were used in conjunction with Iraqi-developed neutronic codes;

(g) Gaseous diffusion existed as an enrichment method, in addition to the activities declared on 7 July 1991;

(h) Substantial nuclear weapons-related procurement from foreign sources had been conducted;

(i) The Iraqi authorities had devised cover explanations for external purchases, including a country-wide survey of related equipment needed in the civilian sector;

(j) Employee lists indicated that Dr. Jaffar had had the lead technical and administrative responsibility for the nuclear weapons development programme;

(k) Substantial facilities that had been used in the clandestine programme had not been declared.

C. *Incidents and problems*

11. In addition to the continuing problem of piecemeal revelation of aspects of the nuclear programme, the following incidents stand out:

(a) The concealment of evidence of the EMIS programme went to the extreme of pouring concrete over tell-tale structures and covering the concrete with rubble;

(b) A similar concealment procedure was adopted in the case of chemical facilities where the feed material for the different enrichment processes had been prepared;

(c) Access to designated sites where EMIS equipment was stored was repeatedly denied;

(d) When one of the inspection teams was about to come upon a large quantity of EMIS equipment that the Iraqi authorities were attempting to remove, warning shots were fired in order to impede the team;

(e) Documents collected by inspectors in the course of the sixth nuclear inspection were forcibly confiscated by the Iraqi authorities and some of them were not returned;

(f) The sixth nuclear inspection team was detained for 92 hours during the week of 23 September.

D. *Inventory of nuclear materials*

12. Apart from the safeguarded inventories declared by Iraq on 27 April 1991 and the initial estimates made by the inspection teams of the potential capability of Iraq's EMIS facilities, no evidence was found of an inventory of highly enriched uranium—and certainly none of a quantity sufficient for making an explosive device.

13. Only a few grams of plutonium are known to have been separated.

E. *Plan for the destruction, removal and rendering harmless of nuclear-related items*

14. The plan, developed by IAEA, addressed nuclear weapons-usable material separately from other items. Nuclear weapons-usable material cannot be destroyed or rendered harmless in Iraq. Consequently, the plan stipulated that IAEA will take custody of the material and remove it.

15. Other items will be removed, destroyed or rendered harmless as appropriate.

F. *Plans for future compliance monitoring*

16. The IAEA plan (S/22872/Rev.1) for nuclear monitoring has been closely coordinated with the Special Commission's plan (S/22871/Rev.1) for all other monitoring called for in Security Council resolutions 687 (1991) and 707 (1991). The IAEA's plan takes into account the safeguards agreement concluded with Iraq pursuant to the Treaty on the Non-Proliferation of Nuclear Weapons. It assumes that activities for which the Special Commission is responsible, including site designation and aerial surveillance, will continue in support of IAEA inspections.

17. The plan calls *inter alia* for:

(a) Unconditional Iraqi acceptance of all inspection rights cited in the plan;

(b) The right to carry out inspections in Iraq anywhere and at any time, with or without advance notice;

(c) The right to install continuous containment and surveillance equipment, including unique identifiers for material or items;

(d) A complete inventory of items and activities in the nuclear field that might be relevant in the development of nuclear weapons and/or in the acquisition of nuclear weapons-usable material;

(e) The advance provision of information on nuclear facility construction and imports of nuclear items that might be relevant to the production of nuclear weapons or nuclear weapons-usable material;

(f) The barring of other States from supplying Iraq with proliferation-sensitive equipment and technology.

18. The extent to which Iraq may engage in any nuclear activity is conditioned by the provisions of section C of Security Council resolution 687 (1991) and of paragraph 3 (vi) of resolution 707 (1991), the latter requiring Iraq to halt all nuclear activities of any kind, except for use of isotopes for medical, agricultural or industrial purposes until the Security Council determines that Iraq is in full compliance with resolution 707 (1991) and paragraphs 12 and 13 of resolution 687 (1991), and IAEA determines that Iraq is in full compliance with its safeguards agreement with IAEA.

Appendix IV
Chemical and biological weapons

1. The first chemical weapons inspection (UNSCOM 2) was a survey of the Al Muthanna State Establishment declared by Iraq as its sole chemical weapons research, development, production and filling facility; some chemical weapons munitions and bulk agents were also stored at this site. Since it had been heavily attacked during the hostilities, it was expected that the site would be in a very hazardous condition, not only because of the presence on site of unexploded ordnance but also [due] to damaged and leaking chemical weapons munitions and bulk chemical weapons agent stores. One important task of the survey team, therefore, was to assess the hazards as well as to make a preliminary assessment of the site and of the Iraqi declaration as a necessary preliminary to a subsequent full, detailed and safe inspection of the site; safety considerations were considered to be a priority during this survey because of their unknown nature, magnitude and extent.

2. Other tasks of this survey team were to include, *inter alia*, a general description of the Al Muthanna State Establishment; a detailed description of specific areas (identifying any that would require particular attention during the subsequent full inspection); identification of any particular problems likely to be encountered during the subsequent full inspection; any indicators of undeclared activities relevant to Security Council resolution 687 (1991); any factors relevant to the use of the site for the destruction of chemical weapons; and a brief description of the Iraqi chemical weapons munitions present.

3. The following were the principal outcomes of the inspection:

(a) None of the information gathered was significantly at variance with the Iraqi declarations;

(b) No evidence was found at this site for non-chemical weapons activities relevant to Security Council resolution 687 (1991);

(c) The site was in a highly dangerous condition, which would present problems for the subsequent full inspection, currently being carried out by UNSCOM 17 (see para. 22 below);

(d) The site would provide a suitable location for the centralized destruction of Iraq's chemical weapons agents and munitions, but the technical details regarding the destruction of these items, particularly the involvement of Iraqi personnel, remain to be fully defined.

4. The second chemical weapons inspection (UNSCOM 9) consisted of one day at each of three chemical production sites in the Al Fallujah area, two days inspecting the pilot plants at Al Muthanna and one day inspecting the declared storage site at Tammuz (Al Taqqadum) Air Base at Habbaniyah. Discussions with Iraqi officials during the inspection clarified previous ambiguities about the Al Muthanna State Establishment, also known as the State Enterprise for Pesticide Production (SEPP). These discussions confirmed that the Al Muthanna Establishment comprises the large production complex at Al Muthanna, the three intended precursor production sites at Al Fallujah and the munitions stores at Al Muhammediyat.

5. The inspections of the Al Fallujah sites in general confirmed the Iraqi declarations. Al Fallujah 1 had never been completed and had therefore not been used for the production of chemical weapons-related items. Al Fallujah 2 commenced production of significant quantities of chlorine in mid-1990. Plans for the large-scale production of other materials such as PCl_3, $POCl_3$, $SOCl_2$ and other precursors were not realized. Al Fallujah 3 had never been used for the production of chemical weapons agent precursors; instead it had been used for the formulation of pesticides, the active ingredients being imported. Some commercially available chemicals weapons precursor chemicals were found stored at this site. All three sites were extensively damaged by bombing during the hostilities.

6. The Iraqi authorities stated that chemical weapons agents were neither produced nor stored at any of these sites. The team found no evidence which contradicted this statement.

7. The inspections of the pilot plants at Al Muthanna revealed that one had been destroyed by bombing but two were still in a relatively undamaged condition. These two pilot plants were inspected in detail and it was concluded that they could, as proposed by Iraq, be adapted for use as a pilot-scale facility to develop a method for the destruction of the Iraqi nerve agents based on caustic hydrolysis. The team recommended that Iraq should be given permission to carry out the necessary modifications and the relevant process development.

8. In the course of the inspection of Tammuz (Al Taqqadum) Air Base at Habbaniyah, 200 aerial bombs were counted and recorded. Analysis of air samples from two of these bombs, selected at random, confirmed that they contained mustard agent. These findings were consistent with the Iraqi declaration that 200 mustard-filled aerial bombs were stored at this site.

9. The third chemical weapons inspection (UNSCOM 11) visited declared sites at Dujayl, Al Bakr Air Base and the auxiliary Al Matasim Aerodrome, the Proving Ground at Al Fallujah and undeclared sites designated by the Special Commission at Al Fallujah General Headquarters and Al Taji.

10. In the depot at Al Fallujah General Headquarters, which had not been declared as containing any chemical weapons items, chemical protective equipment and related material was found. A variety of grenades containing the riot control agent CS were found but no other chemical filled munitions were found.

11. The team examined the 30 chemical-filled ballistic missile warheads declared by Iraq and found by UNSCOM 8 in the Dujayl area, albeit some 30 kilometres from the location notified to the Special Commission (see appendix V, para. 6). Iraq had informed the Special Commission that 14 of the warheads were of the so-called binary type, filled only with a mixture of isopropanol and cyclohexanol, the organophosphorus component (DF) required to produce the nerve agent being added only immediately prior to use. The resulting agent would have been a mixture of the nerve agents GB and GF. Fifty-six plastic containers filled with DF were also found; these bore evidence of extensive leakage. Iraq stated that the other 16 warheads were filled with a mixture of nerve agents GB and GF. Analysis of samples taken from the binary warheads, one of the nerve agent filled warheads and DF container, by laboratories outside Iraq confirmed the Iraqi declarations. Iraq was instructed by the team to transport the warheads to Al Muthanna for disposal.

12. At Al Bakr Air Base, 25 type 250 gauge aerial bombs and 135 type 500 aerial bombs filled with mustard agent had been declared by Iraq. These were found at Al Matasim Aerodrome, an airfield auxiliary to the Al Bakr Air Base, situated about 30 kilometres to the north of the Base, they had evidently developed internal pressure since four had already burst spontaneously and mustard agent vapour was detected at the site, necessitating the use of full individual protective equipment when working close to the bombs or downwind of them. Samples were taken from four of the bombs, which were then resealed. Iraq was instructed to transport the bombs to Al Muthanna subject to strict safety precautions and after venting the excess pressure. No other chemical items were found at this site.

13. The site of Al Taji is a large military installation which had been declared in connection with ballistic missiles but not for chemical weapons. Approximately 6,000 empty aluminium containers intended for filling with nerve agent and insertion into 122 millimetre rocket warheads were found. No other chemical items were found at Al Taji.

14. At the Al Fallujah Proving Ground, Iraq had declared the storage of 6,394 mustard-filled 155 millimetre artillery shells. These were seen by the inspection team essentially in accordance with the declaration. They were stored in the open and appeared to be in good condition. Analysis of samples taken from four of the shells confirmed the presence of mustard agent. No evidence was found of any other activities or material relevant to Security Council resolution 687 (1991).

15. In discussions with Iraqi officials towards the end of the inspection contradictory statements were made regarding the marking of chemical munitions. Iraqi officials also failed to respond satisfactorily to requests for information on Iraq's past chemical weapons programme, particularly as regards foreign suppliers of munitions, equipment and precursor chemicals.

16. The two primary tasks of the fourth chemical weapons inspection (UNSCOM 12) were to direct the destruction, by Iraqi personnel, of all unfilled chemical weapons munitions currently at Al Muthanna and to reconnoitre, select and show to Iraqi officials the locations at Al Muthanna where bulk agents, chemical munitions and intermediate, precursor and other chemical weapons-related chemicals would be collected and the locations where future destruction operations would be carried out. These objectives were successfully achieved, although not without incident.

17. The destruction operations were successful. A total of 8,157 unfilled chemical weapons munitions, consisting of six different varieties of bombs, 155 millimetre artillery shells and 122 millimetre rocket warheads

were destroyed either by crushing with a bulldozer or cutting with an oxyacetylene torch. Subsequently, parts of chemical munitions and 3,672 122 millimetre rocket warheads were destroyed. Dies used for making bombs remain to be destroyed.

18. During this destructive work, a supposedly unfilled 122 millimetre rocket warhead burst and a nearby Iraqi worker was exposed to nerve agent. Owing to the prompt action of a member of the inspection team (Lieutenant Colonel T. Van Erp, Netherlands) the casualty was very quickly taken to the site hospital where he received appropriate and timely treatment from Iraqi medical personnel. He recovered over a period of a few days. There were no other casualties but the incident illustrates that Al Muthanna is still an extremely hazardous site and that the recovery and destruction of Iraq's chemical weapons munitions (and agents) will be a protracted and dangerous undertaking.

19. A separate incident occurred in the case of the 30 chemical-filled ballistic warheads removed to Al Muthanna from Dujayl in two separate shipments. In the first shipment, 14 warheads stated by the Iraqis to be filled with the mixture of alcohols, and considered relatively harmless, were moved. Ten were opened, found to contain the alcohols and were drained preparatory to destruction. At this point the senior Iraqi official present said that the remaining four were filled with the nerve agent sarin. Apparently these warheads had been moved during the night prior to dispatch to Al Muthanna and the sarin-filled warheads had been confused with alcohol-filled ones. All 20 remaining warheads are now being treated as sarin-filled until proved otherwise. This was potentially a very serious incident, as the warheads were upwind of a number of Iraqi workers and UNSCOM inspectors.

20. Iraq has declared 6,120 sarin-filled 122 millimetre rocket warheads and their attendant motors. They are stored in the open but have not been counted nor have their contents been verified. They present a significant hazard both from the point of leakage of sarin and instability of the rocket propellant. In order to improve safety the Iraqis were directed to move the warheads to the designated storage area; the rocket motors were to be separated and moved to another storage area separate from the warheads. They will remain in these locations until both warheads and motors have been separately counted and verified.

21. A suitable storage location at Al Muthanna for chemical weapons agents and munitions was identified and the Iraqi officials briefed and given detailed maps of the area. Four possible destruction sites were identified.

22. The fifth chemical weapons inspection (UNSCOM 17) began on 6 October and is expected to continue until 9 November. The large team—over 50 persons—is conducting a detailed and full survey of Al Muthanna in preparation for the destruction phase.

23. The sixth chemical weapons inspection team (UNSCOM 20) entered Iraq on 22 October and will inspect several sites, including some that are widely separated. It will need to make use of the United Nations helicopters in order to complete its tasks in the time allocated.

24. Cooperation by the Iraqis with all the inspection teams has been variable but, in general, it has been good.

25. The first biological weapon inspection (UNSCOM 7) carried out a full, detailed inspection of the site at Salman Pak. There were also detailed technical discussions with Iraqi officials.

26. Although Iraq had previously denied possession of biological weapons and any related items, Iraqi officials admitted on the team's arrival in Iraq to having carried out to a programme of biological research for military purposes which, it was made clear, could have been used for both defensive and offensive purposes. The micro-organisms involved were Clostridium botulinum, Clostridium perfringens and Bacillus anthracis. Iraqi officials informed the team that the research programme had commenced in mid-1986 and had been terminated in August 1990, at which point, it was claimed, all stocks had been destroyed. At a subsequent stage in the inspection, however, the team was given bacterial seed stocks which indicated that Iraq had also possessed the following micro-organisms which are considered as biological warfare agents—Brucellus abortus, Brucella melitensis, Francisella tularensis and various strains of Clostridium botulinum. In addition, three simulants of biological warfare agents were provided by Iraq; these were Bacillus subtilis, Bacillus cereus and Bacillus megaterium. No biological weapons or evidence of weaponization was found.

27. The second biological inspection (UNSCOM 15) visited 10 different declared and undeclared sites. Four of these were inspected without advance notice. These 10 sites included a pharmaceutical plant, a blood bank, vaccine production facilities and research and development laboratories with fermentation capabilities and specially designed facilities to enable work with hazardous disease-causing organisms of humans and animals to be carried out.

28. No biological weapons or facilities for filling weapons were found. However, the inspection team unanimously agreed that the Iraqi biological weapon programme, which consisted of a research component at Salman Pak, logically would have included a plan for a development and production component.

Appendix V
Ballistic missiles and long-range guns

1. Five ballistic missile teams have conducted inspections in Iraq to make an inventory, identify for destruction, and monitor the destruction of all declared ballistic missiles with a range greater than 150 kilometres, related parts and components and all research, development, support and manufacturing capabilities. Ballistic missile inspection planning centred on the inspection and destruction of the declared items, the production facilities, and the fixed launch structures in the Western Zone of Iraq.

2. Destruction of ballistic missiles began with the first inspection team's activities in July 1991 before a comprehensive destruction policy had been established. The first team (UNSCOM 3) carried out the initial inventory and supervision of the destruction of all declared missiles, launchers and support equipment, visiting seven different sites and facilities. Missile systems and components destruction was primarily a straightforward task of crushing by bulldozers readily carried out by the Iraqis. Three of the sites were former production and repair facilities that had been destroyed by coalition bombing.

3. The second ballistic missile inspection (UNSCOM 10) was conducted in mid-July on short notice to investigate information suggesting additional undeclared missiles and support equipment. This team found undeclared decoy missiles and additional support equipment in the vicinity of a site previously inspected by the first ballistic missile team. These were also destroyed.

4. Subsequent inspections of production and repair facilities encountered less enthusiastic cooperation and outright disagreement on destruction of some equipment and structures. In July, the Iraqis finally acknowledged possession of a long-range "supergun" and components to build additional and larger calibre weapons. This type of gun was capable of delivering prohibited munitions beyond 150 kilometres.

5. The third ballistic missile team (UNSCOM 8) in August conducted inspections focusing on declared and undeclared suspected ballistic missile production facilities. In addition, a survey of the declared supergun, propellant and unassembled parts at three different sites was undertaken. A significant number of documents and blueprints related to the construction and development of this system was provided to the inspection team. The information obtained and photographs taken were collected for study and use in a planned later inspection/destruction activity.

6. Production, repair and test equipment and machinery associated with the Scud, Al Hussein and Badr 2000 missiles were inspected and identified for destruction at five declared and seven undeclared sites. All sites suffered damage during the coalition bombing, some

extensively, with structures and equipment being completely destroyed or damaged with others virtually intact. Identification for destruction of specific missile tooling and test equipment was readily accepted by the Iraqis. Machinery and equipment identified for destruction which also had non-missile application (dual use) or use in missile systems not prohibited by Security Council resolution 687 (1991) generated vigorous controversy and opposition. This equipment was sealed and guidance was requested from the Special Commission. An inventory was made of all other equipment to enable the Special Commission to decide on its destruction, removal or rendering harmless in consonance with the policies being developed by the Commission in these respects. After return of the inspection to New York, the destruction of certain equipment was called for in a letter to the Iraqi Government based on the inspection report and the provisional guidelines on destruction, removal or rendering harmless initiated by the Special Commission (see para. 21 of the report).

7. At one undeclared site, the team discovered an additional 187 Scud fuel, oxidizer and starter storage tanks. The team also found 30 Scud warhead canisters containing chemical-filled warheads in the same vicinity (see appendix IV, para. 11). Although the warheads had been declared to the Special Commission, they were not at the location specified in the declaration. Upon completion of this inspection Iraq provided the team with a declaration of additional Scud fuel and oxidizer storage tanks.

8. The fourth ballistic missile team (UNSCOM 13) planned to inspect in September declared fixed launch sites in the Western Zone as well as other undeclared possible missile support facilities using United Nations helicopters in accordance with the provisions of Security Council resolutions 687 (1991) and 707 (1991). Upon arrival in Iraq the team was advised that inspection of the Western Zone using United Nations helicopters would not be permitted. In the expectation that Iraq's approval would be forthcoming before the end of its inspection period, the team was directed by the Executive Chairman of the Special Commission to undertake inspection of the Western Zone only with the use of United Nations helicopters. In the interim the team inspected the destruction of Scud fuel and oxidizer storage tanks located during the third inspection. The oxidizer tanks were leaking toxic level emissions prompting the team to abandon this site until air quality at the site was acceptable. Two inspections at undeclared sites were conducted. Although no missile activity was noted at one facility, at the other site the team found four previously destroyed missile transport vehicles from Al Taji which had been spot welded together and moved to that location. An additional undeclared Scud missile storage support/carrier was ob-

served. All items were destroyed and verified. In the absence of Iraqi agreement to use by the Special Commission of United Nations helicopters, the team's mission was terminated at this stage, and it did not undertake the planned inspection of the Western Zone.

9. Immediately following the resolution of the helicopter issue in the first week of October, the fifth ballistic missile team (UNSCOM 18) successfully conducted inspections of the fixed launch sites in the Western Zone. Although Iraq declared 25 out of a total of 28 as destroyed, additional destruction was prescribed and carried out. A number of partially constructed fixed launch sites were inspected at undeclared sites and destruction procedures agreed upon; destruction has still to be verified. The team also returned to the supergun and supervised the destruction of the gun in the Jabal Hamryn mountains north of Baghdad as well as the propellant for the supergun located south of Baghdad. The destruction of the other supergun components at Iskanderiyah has commenced but is not yet completed and will have to be verified later. Several undeclared sites were inspected and found to contain no observable ballistic missile activity.

10. The geographical areas to be covered and the numbers and extent of military and other installations are large. The Special Commission has yet to be convinced that it has obtained a comprehensive assessment of Iraq's ballistic missile capabilities. Future ballistic missile inspection activities will monitor the destruction of outstanding items identified and inspect various sites to complete the information missing on the ballistic missile programme, both the Scud-related systems and the system believed to be associated with the nuclear weapon development.

Appendix VI
Voluntary contributions to the Special Commission

1. Voluntary contributions in cash and in kind, as listed below, have been received to date:

Type	Government	Amount (United States dollars)	Remarks
In cash	Japan	2 500 000	From a trust fund
	United States	2 000 000	
	Kuwait	1 000 000	
In kind:			
(a) Outright grant	Norway		15 vehicles
			5 satellite global positioning system units
			2 ambulances
	United States		7 vehicles
			4 trucks
			2 ambulances
(b) Loaned for the duration of the operation			
	Finland		2 gas chromatographs
	New Zealand		Medical equipment
	Sweden		Decontamination equipment, chemical weapons protective equipment
	United Kingdom		Laboratory equipment, including a gas chromatograph mass spectrometer and an infrared spectrophotometer
			2 biological weapons agent detection kits
			6 chemical weapons agent vapour monitors
(c) Loaned and returned	Belgium		Medical equipment
	Canada		Global positioning system
	France		Medical equipment
	Germany		Explosive ordnance equipment
	Netherlands		Chemical weapons analysis equipment
	United Kingdom		Vehicles

2. In addition to personnel seconded by the United Nations, the IAEA and WHO, the following Governments have provided personnel services for inspection-related activities: Australia, Austria, Belgium, Canada, Czechoslovakia, Finland, France, Germany, Greece, Hungary, India, Indonesia, Italy, Japan, Netherlands, Norway, New Zealand, Romania, Sweden, Switzerland, Thailand, United Kingdom of Great Britain and Northern Ireland, United States of America, and Union of Soviet Socialist Republics.

3. New Zealand has provided a medical team.

Air support

4. The Commission has been provided with high altitude reconnaissance flights over Iraq. The flights are undertaken on a regular basis by an aircraft with crew and support personnel made available to the Commission by the United States. Flights are directed by the Special Commission. They are notified to Iraq 72 hours in advance and acknowledged by Iraq within 48 hours.

5. The German Government has provided the Commission with two C-160 transport planes, based in Bahrain, and three rotary-wing aircraft, including crews and support personnel, based at the Al-Rashid airfield at Baghdad since 1 October 1991.

Document 93

Memorandum of Understanding dated 21 November 1991 between Iraq and the United Nations concerning humanitarian assistance

Not issued as a United Nations document

The present Memorandum of Understanding summarizes the results of the discussions held in Baghdad on 20-23 November 1991 with the Government of the Republic of Iraq during the mission of the Executive Delegate of the Secretary-General for the UN humanitarian programme for Iraq, Kuwait and the Iraq/Iran and Iraq/Turkey Border Areas, pursuant to paragraph 21 of the Memorandum of Understanding signed on 18 April 1991 by H.E. the Minister of Foreign Affairs of the Government of Iraq and the Executive Delegate.

The parties conducted a thorough joint review of the humanitarian operations carried out under the auspices of the office of the Executive Delegate in cooperation with the Government of Iraq over the past seven months. They noted that the overall context in which these activities were taking place has undergone significant changes. They further concluded that the programme, carried out with the full support of the Iraqi authorities, has substantial achievements to its credit. This includes assisting the repatriation of large numbers of refugees from neighbouring countries, the majority of them to their homes and places of origin. Tangible results have also been attained in providing help to the most vulnerable groups throughout Iraq, thanks to resources donated by the international community in response to the successive appeals that have been issued by the Executive Delegate. These contributions have amounted to more than 290 million dollars, of which 249 million are either spent or obligated. The present Memorandum of Understanding shall constitute a self-contained agreement, and its implementation shall

not be construed as having any relation with other measures not envisaged therein.

The parties have agreed as follows:

1. Both sides affirm the importance of the need to continue to provide humanitarian assistance to Iraq to alleviate the suffering of the affected Iraqi civilian population.

2. The Government of Iraq welcomes the efforts of the United Nations and its specialized agencies in providing humanitarian assistance and relief to the civilian population and undertakes to support and cooperate in those endeavours on the basis of this Memorandum of Understanding.

3. For this purpose, the Government of Iraq agrees to cooperate with the United Nations to continue its humanitarian presence in Iraq, wherever such presence may be needed, and to facilitate it through the adoption of all necessary measures. This shall be ensured through the establishment of UN sub-offices and Humanitarian Centres (UNHUCs), in agreement and cooperation with the Government of Iraq.

4. Each Centre will be staffed by United Nations personnel which, in addition to the regular staff members of the relevant UN agencies, may also include staff co-opted from the non-governmental organizations. The parties are mindful of the special contribution provided by other organizations, such as the International Committee of the Red Cross, the League of Red Cross and Red Crescent Societies and the International Organization for Migration. The Red Crescent Society of Iraq shall be

called upon to play an effective role in the implementation of humanitarian assistance and relief projects.

5. UNHUCs shall facilitate the provision of humanitarian assistance to the needy and would include, inter alia, food aid, medical care, agricultural rehabilitation, shelter and any other humanitarian and relief measures in conformity with the principles of this memorandum.

6. Both sides agree that measures continue to be needed for the benefit of the persons who are still displaced and that such measures should be based primarily on their safe return and the provision of humanitarian assistance to facilitate their return and normalization of their lives in their places of origin.

7. The United Nations Guards Contingent as an integral part of the United Nations humanitarian programme will continue to perform its functions in protecting UN personnel, assets and operations linked with the UN humanitarian programme. The UN Guards will continue to be assigned as needed to any sub-offices and UNHUC's which are or may be established by the United Nations in Iraq.

8. The number of UN Guards will continue to be kept under review, and will not exceed a total strength of 500. The number of UN Guards assigned to the various Governorates will be decided in consultation with the Government authorities concerned, but would not exceed 150 in any Governorate.

9. The UN Guards will continue to be allowed to move freely, as their duties require in accordance with this Memorandum of Understanding, between all places where United Nations humanitarian assistance activities take place.

10. United Nations Guards are authorized to carry side-arms (pistols/revolvers) provided by the Iraq authorities with the approval of the United Nations.

11. The Iraqi authorities will maintain the Chief Liaison Officer appointed to facilitate the Contingent's operations and the liaison officer at each centre to facilitate their work with the Iraqi authorities. The Iraqi authorities will continue to make available the facilities in Baghdad and elsewhere, including office space, maintenance and repair support, maps etc.

12. It is agreed that humanitarian assistance is impartial and that all civilians in need, wherever they are located, are entitled to receive it without discrimination.

13. In order to encourage the normalization of life where required, the United Nations will take all necessary measures, in cooperation with the Government of Iraq, for making the relief items available in all designated Humanitarian Centres, by road or by air as required, including from and through the neighbouring countries. The Government of Iraq will take all required measures on its side to facilitate the safe passage and delivery of emergency relief commodities throughout the country in a speedy and effective manner.

14. The Government of Iraq has established together with the United Nations a relief distribution monitoring structure to permit access to all civilians covered by the relief programme. An appropriate coordinating mechanism will be established between the two parties to meet regularly in order to monitor, review and plan future activities, as well as address any difficulties that may arise in the implementation for the current humanitarian assistance programme.

15. The implementation of the humanitarian assistance programme will continue to be coordinated by a senior UN official assigned to Baghdad, under the Executive Delegate's direction. He will have permanent access to high level government officials responsible for relief activities in the country to discuss policy and operational issues that may arise during the implementation of the programme.

16. Inter-governmental organizations, NGOs and other relief agencies will continue to be encouraged to participate in the implementation of the programme in close cooperation with the United Nations and under clearly defined terms of association agreed upon with the Government of Iraq.

17. The Government of Iraq will help in the prompt establishment in appropriate locations of United Nations sub-offices in support of humanitarian programmes for the civilian population including the returnees where necessary.

18. The Government of Iraq shall continue to cooperate in granting United Nations field staff access to the parts of the country requiring relief, by air or road as needed, to facilitate the implementation and monitoring of the Programme. United Nations staff will be allowed, in coordination with the Government of Iraq, to accompany the returnees to their home areas as required.

19. A United Nations radio communication system, which is an indispensable instrument for the success of relief and rehabilitation activities, will be maintained. The system will cover communications requirements within Baghdad and other cities covered by the relief Programme and within and outside the country, as appropriate.

20. In order to make optimal use of programme resources, the Government of Iraq will consider the establishment of a special exchange rate for relief operations carried out by agencies and organizations participating in the programme. Pending a decision in this regard the Government of Iraq undertakes to make available cash contributions in local currency in the amount of ID 1,000,000 at the beginning of each month, or in accordance with the estimates provided by the United Nations Coordinator, if less. Any unused balances re-

maining at the conclusion of the programme will be refunded to the Government of Iraq.

21. The basic frame for United Nations humanitarian action outlined above is intended to facilitate the task of coordination, effective implementation and monitoring of humanitarian assistance and relief operations.

22. The implementation of the above-mentioned principles shall be without prejudice to the sovereignty, territorial integrity, political independence, security and non-interference in the internal affairs of the Republic of Iraq.

23. This Memorandum of Understanding shall apply for a period of six months beginning on 1 January 1992 and ending on 30 June 1992. Six weeks before the expiration of the said period, the principles of the Memorandum and their operational modalities shall be reviewed with a view to accessing any further need for their operation.

Done at Baghdad on 18 Jamada al-Oula 1412 Hijrah corresponding to 24 November 1991 AD.

FOR THE UNITED NATIONS	FOR THE GOVERNMENT OF THE REPUBLIC OF IRAQ
Signed:	Signed:
Name: Sadruddin Aga KHAN	Name: Ahmed Hussein KHODAIR
Title: Executive Delegate of the United Nations Secretary-General for the UN Humanitarian Programme for Iraq, Kuwait and the Iraq/Iran and Iraq/Turkey Border Areas.	Title: Minister of Foreign Affairs of the Republic of Iraq

Document 94

Second report of the Executive Chairman of UNSCOM

S/23268, 4 December 1991

Letter dated 4 December 1991 from the Executive Chairman, Office of the Special Commission established by the Secretary-General pursuant to paragraph 9 (b) (i) of Security Council resolution 687 (1991), addressed to the Secretary-General

I have the honour to recall paragraph 3 of Security Council resolution 699 (1991) of 17 June 1991, which requests the Secretary-General to submit, every six months after the adoption of the resolution, progress reports on the implementation of the provisions of section C of resolution 687 (1991) relating to Iraq's weapons of mass destruction.

You will further recall that, on 25 October 1991, a first report by the Executive Chairman of the Special Commission established by the Secretary-General pursuant to paragraph 9 (b) (i) of Security Council resolution 687 (1991) was circulated on your instructions to the Security Council in document S/23165. This first report summarized all activities undertaken by the Special Commission and by the International Atomic Energy Agency (IAEA) in the implementation of section C of resolution 687 (1991) up to the middle of October 1991. Additionally, at the request of the Director-General of IAEA, the reports prepared by seven inspection teams led by the Agency have been circulated as Security Council docu-

ments (S/22788, S/22837, S/22986 and Corr.1, S/23112, S/23122 and S/23215). A report of the eighth IAEA-led inspection will be circulated in the course of December.

To comply with the provisions of paragraph 3 of Security Council resolution 699 (1991), I am transmitting herewith the text of a progress report which brings up to date the first report referred to in the previous paragraph.

I would be most grateful if you would circulate the attached second report as a document of the Security Council.

(*Signed*) Rolf EKÉUS
Executive Chairman
Office of the Special Commission

Annex
Second report by the Executive Chairman of the Special Commission established by the Secretary-General pursuant to paragraph 9 (b) (i) of Security Council resolution 687 (1991)

Introduction

1. The present report by the Executive Chairman of the Special Commission established by the Secretary-General pursuant to paragraph 9 (b) (i) of Security Coun-

cil resolution 687 (1991) covers the work of the Commission for the period from 15 October to 4 December 1991. This second report is confined to operational activities and matters directly pertinent thereto as these are the areas which need to be brought up to date to provide, together with the first report by the Executive Chairman (S/23165), a comprehensive picture of the establishment and functioning of the Special Committee since the adoption of Security Council resolutions 687 (1991) and 699 (1991).

Attitude of Iraq

2. The first report by the Executive Chairman contained, in paragraphs 16 to 19, a comprehensive account of the attitude of Iraq. In the period under review this attitude has not changed. In respect of sites and activities declared by Iraq and the issue of Iraq's participation in the destruction of chemical weapons, cooperation at the field level has been forthcoming. However, in respect of sites designated by the Special Commission, where the Commission and IAEA are acting on their own sources of information regarding possible clandestine conduct of proscribed activities, non-cooperation and obstruction continue to be encountered. There is thus no progress to report which would indicate a change of policy on the part of Iraq to one of candour, transparency and cooperation at all levels. As the Executive Chairman remarked in the first report, this is probably the one single element that could contribute most substantially to a timely and satisfactory implementation of the mandate of the Special Commission and of IAEA.

3. The Special Commission has had to remain vigilant in the period under review to prevent implementation of measures proposed by Iraq which could impinge upon the facilities, privileges and immunities of the Commission and of IAEA in matters such as the taking into and out of Iraq of all necessary equipment, materials and other items required for inspections and the analysis of their results and the taking of photographs at sites under inspection. So far the strong position taken by the Commission and the Chief Inspectors involved seems to have been successful in preserving the rights concerned.

4. With respect to ongoing monitoring and verification of Iraq's compliance with paragraphs 10 and 13 of Security Council resolution 687 (1991), the Special Commission has very recently received in New York from Iraq information which the Government states to be "the information required under resolution 687 (1991) that comes within the mandate of the Special Commission". Until the information is translated, the Commission cannot determine the extent to which it meets the substantive requirements of the Special Commission's and IAEA's plans for ongoing monitoring and verification

(S/22871/Rev.1 and S/22872/Rev.1 and Corr.1) which were unanimously approved by the Security Council in its resolution 715 (1991), although it may be observed that certain procedural requirements laid down in the plans as to time-limits and languages of submission have not been met. If the Commission and IAEA are to be in a position to carry out their functions in connection with ongoing monitoring and verification, the Commission deems it to be of great importance that Iraq expressly recognize its obligations under the two plans and Security Council resolution 715 (1991). Such express recognition is still awaited.

Nuclear issues

5. Two more inspections were completed (IAEA 7/UNSCOM 19 and IAEA 8/UNSCOM 22), one each in October (11 to 22 October) and November (11 to 18 November), since the sixth nuclear inspection summarized in the previous report. In addition to the successful removal of unirradiated fuel from Iraq, the inspection teams focused much of their inspection activity on a number of sites associated with (a) Iraq's programme to design and develop the non-nuclear components of a nuclear weapon and (b) centrifuge component manufacture.

6. Significantly, Iraq provided for the first time to the seventh nuclear inspection team formal though incomplete written acknowledgement of its nuclear weapons programme:

> "Various research and studies of the sort to which you refer as 'weaponization' have been carried out. The objective in carrying out such research and studies was to establish the practical, technical and scientific requirements for a programme of this nature in the event that a political decision were to be taken to proceed in that direction."

7. The extensive and detailed documentation of the nuclear weapons programme that was obtained by the sixth inspection team, and its removal from Iraq only after that team's detainment in a parking lot for four days, preceded the Iraqi admission to the seventh team of having conducted research and studies on nuclear weapons. In fact, the seventh and eighth inspection teams visited designated facilities judged to be directly associated with the testing and development of the high-explosive components of the implosion system of a nuclear weapon. The characteristics of these facilities were considered inconsistent with Iraq's explanations of their purpose. Thus, Iraq's position that it conducted studies but had no programme to develop nuclear weapons is inconsistent with both documents and inspection results that reveal a well-funded and broadly based pro-

gramme involving sophisticated facilities for nuclear weapons development.

8. In the area of fissile material production, important questions put to Iraq remain unanswered. While much of the electromagnetic isotope separation (EMIS) equipment has been turned over for destruction, the critical collector pockets which would permit confirmation of Iraq's assertions that only low levels of enrichment were achieved have not been produced for analysis. Substantial uncertainties also remain over the centrifuge programme where Iraq has produced some but not all parts and materials, and failed to reveal the sources of its supply of critical parts and materials. Even less information has been produced by Iraq on their efforts in the diffusion and chemical separation processes. All this is especially troubling in the light of preliminary results of sampling accomplished at Al Tuwaitha, and noted in the IAEA seventh inspection report (S/23215), that provide evidence of uranium enriched to 93 per cent in the isotope U^{235}. Additional sampling was undertaken by the seventh and eighth inspection teams. Analysis and further investigation are clearly required.

9. Iraq's recent record in the nuclear area is consistent with, if less dramatic than, its actions over the last six months that included the concealment of evidence of plutonium separation, of uranium enrichment, and of nuclear weapons development, of refusal to permit inspection teams to enter some sites and exit others, and confiscation of documents from inspectors in the course of an inspection. In sum, Iraq has not cooperated in the critical area of nuclear-weapons-related activity and the Special Commission and IAEA are some distance from achieving the transparency which is sought.

Chemical and biological weapons

10. Since the first report was prepared, two further chemical inspections have been completed, one being the long and detailed inspection of the Al Muthanna State Establishment (7 October to 8 November 1991) while the other visited a series of declared chemical munitions storage sites (22 October to 2 November 1991). There has also been a combined chemical and biological weapons inspection which visited (17 to 30 November 1991), at very short notice, a number of sites designated by the Special Commission as being of potential chemical weapons and/or biological weapons interest in addition to revisiting the original site at Salman Pak.

11. The technically very successful inspection of Al Muthanna (UNSCOM 17) compiled a comprehensive and detailed inventory of the site, including facilities, munitions, agents, agent condition, precursors and intermediates. Among the salient findings were the discovery of small quantities of the nerve agents *sec.*butyl sarin,

n-butyl sarin and ethyl sarin, although Iraq has disputed the identification of the latter two agents. While the quantities found were of no direct military significance, the relevance of the finding lies in the fact that Iraq clearly had carried out research on nerve agents other than those previously declared.

12. Although the mustard agent at Al Muthanna was generally of good quality (typically 90 per cent), the nerve agents were found to have undergone extensive degradation and the agent content was very low, generally below 10 per cent and in some cases below the 1 per cent level. This new information may have significant repercussions for the process finally selected for the destruction of the nerve agents as well as for the safety hazards likely to be encountered during destruction; both aspects will need further consideration.

13. In general, the findings of the inspection at Al Muthanna were in substantial agreement with Iraq's declaration, although in the case of the 122 mm rockets a precise and full count was not possible as the rockets generally were found to be in a very dangerous condition. Explosive demolition was considered to be the safest means of achieving their destruction since opening and draining operations would be particularly hazardous.

14. The inspection of the remaining declared storage sites (UNSCOM 20) was likewise a successful operation. All the declared sites, some of them distant from Baghdad and therefore requiring the use of United Nations helicopter transport, were inspected, the chemical weapons munitions verified, counted and recorded; where it was safe to transport the munitions to Al Muthanna the necessary instructions to this effect were given to Iraq. At Al-Tuz, Khamisiyah and Muhammadiyat numbers of munitions were discovered, including but not restricted to 122 mm rockets, which were considered to be in too unsafe a condition to move and for which a drilling and draining operation would be very hazardous. A recommendation was made on safety grounds that these items should be destroyed *in situ* by explosive demolition. In a few cases, due to extensive destruction by coalition bombing, it was not possible to observe and count all munitions; when the damage had been less extensive the number and types of munitions observed accorded well with the Iraqi declarations.

15. The combined chemical and biological weapons inspection (UNSCOM 21), except for the revisit to Salman Pak, concentrated on short notice inspection of undeclared sites designated by the Special Commission; some 13 sites were inspected.

16. The inspection was completed only very recently and the full official report is therefore not at present available. Field reporting, however, indicates that no chemical- or biological-weapons-related activities were

associated with any of the designated sites. In the course of the inspection a small sub-team was dispatched to Al Muthanna to witness an Iraqi experiment with a simulant to prove the use of the modified pilot plant for exploratory work on the destruction of nerve agents; this was successful.

17. Since the first report was prepared a small (4 person) mission has visited Iraq for detailed technical discussions (11 to 15 November 1991) with Iraqi counterparts on various of the issues related to the destruction of chemical weapons and agents, with particular emphasis on the direct involvement of Iraq in this process and on safety aspects. Issues discussed and on which the Special Commission team made recommendations included an Iraqi design for a mustard agent incinerator, the destruction of nerve agents by caustic hydrolysis, and the breaching and draining of munitions.

18. When, in the very near future, all the data compiled by UNSCOM 17 at the Al Muthanna State Establishment have been analysed, the Special Commission will have a very good understanding of Iraq's declared major primary chemical weapons site. Furthermore, the discussions on the destruction of chemical weapons and agents have resulted in a considerable improvement in technical understanding by both sides, particularly as regards the potential hazards involved in some operations and of the technologies potentially available for implementing the various destruction processes. Commencement of the destruction process early in 1992 can thus be confidently expected.

Ballistic missiles and long-range guns

19. With respect to ballistic missiles, by the end of 1991 two additional Special Commission ballistic missile inspections (UNSCOM 23 and UNSCOM 24) are expected to have been completed. To date, Special Commission inspection teams have, according to the latest revised data, supervised the destruction of 62 ballistic missiles, 18 fixed missile launch pads, 33 ballistic missile warheads, 127 missile storage support racks, a substantial amount of rocket fuel, an assembled 350 mm supergun, components of two 350 and two 1,000 mm superguns, and 1 tonne of supergun propellant.

20. So far, no information has come to light which clearly contradicts Iraq's disclosure of 5 July 1991 with respect to the status of its ballistic missile force. Nevertheless, the fact that Iraq continued to fire ballistic missiles throughout the Gulf war and still had a portion of its force following that war, despite what were, by all public accounts, the intensive efforts of coalition forces to find and destroy them, attests to the relative ease with which they could be concealed even in war. Special Commission inspection teams have found undeclared ballistic missile support equipment and noted Iraqi attempts to reuse previously destroyed missile transport vehicles.

21. The Special Commission is seeking further information, analysis of which may allow a more comprehensive understanding of this issue and increase confidence in any assessments which may emerge. At the present time, however, as pointed out in the first report, important questions still remain unresolved, namely, whether Iraq continues to have any ballistic missiles in its possession, and its plans and progress in future ballistic missile development. The two ballistic missile inspections which are being undertaken this month should shed additional light on these questions.

Administrative issues

22. The administrative issues outlined in paragraphs 25 to 31 of the first report remain unresolved, most particularly the issue of financing. The Special Commission is most grateful to record the receipt of additional voluntary contributions from Kuwait ($1,000,000) and Saudi Arabia ($1,730,000), which have enabled it to continue to function in the period under review. However, the shortage of readily available funds will become critical early next year, particularly if the Special Commission and IAEA are to proceed with the very costly removal of the spent irradiated fuel from Iraq.

Concluding observations

23. In the previous report, the full support of the Security Council, Governments, the Secretary-General and the Secretariat of the United Nations were identified as being of crucial importance in the carrying out of the mandate laid down in section C of Security Council resolution 687 (1991). This will certainly remain to be the case as the Special Commission and IAEA confront the difficult issues which will arise in connection with the destruction, removal or rendering harmless of Iraq's weapons of mass destruction and the facilities for their production and as the plans for ongoing monitoring and verification are put into full effect. Experience to date has shown that results can be achieved only where resolute stands are taken in response to challenges by Iraq to the implementation of various aspects of the mandate of the Special Commission and IAEA. Such resolute stands can be based only on the full support of the United Nations as a whole and its Member Governments in achieving all the basic objectives of section C of Security Council resolution 687 (1991).

Document 95

First semi-annual report (for the period from 17 June 1991 to 17 December 1991) on the implementation by the IAEA of the plan for the destruction, removal or rendering harmless of items listed in paragraph 12 of Security Council resolution 687 (1991)

S/23295, 17 December 1991

Note by the Secretary-General

The Secretary-General has the honour to transmit to the Security Council, pursuant to paragraph 3 of Security Council resolution 699 (1991), the attached first semi-annual report on the implementation by the IAEA of the plan for the destruction, removal or rendering harmless of items listed in paragraph 12 of United Nations Security Council resolution 687 (1991).

Annex
Letter dated 5 December 1991 from the Director General of the International Atomic Energy Agency addressed to the Secretary-General

United Nations Security Council resolution 699 (1991), approved on 17 June 1991, requests, *inter alia*, the Secretary-General to submit to the Security Council progress reports on the implementation of the plan for the destruction, removal or rendering harmless of the items specified in paragraph 12 of resolution 687 (1991). Such reports are to be submitted every six months after the adoption of the resolution and the first report is therefore due on 17 December 1991.

Please find attached an outline of the activities carried out by the Agency during the past six months under the plan for the destruction, removal or rendering harmless, that you might find useful for the preparation of your report.

(*Signed*) Hans BLIX

Enclosure

First semi-annual report (covering the period 17 June – 17 December 1991) on the implementation by the IAEA of the plan for the destruction, removal or rendering harmless of items listed in paragraph 12 of UN Security Council resolution 687 (1991)

Introduction

Security Council resolution 699 of 17 June 1991 approved the plan submitted by the IAEA through the Secretary-General for the destruction, removal or rendering harmless of all items listed in paragraph 12 of Security Council resolution 687. Resolution 699 at the same time called for a report to be submitted every six months on progress in implementing the plan. This is the first such report.

At the same time the plan was drawn up, the first on-site inspection under the terms of resolution 687 had just started. The objectives of that inspection were based on the declarations made by the Government of Iraq on 18 and 27 April 1991. The plan took into account the material and facilities known to exist at the time, but stressed that inspections would have to determine whether items additional to those declared by Iraq existed. As subsequent inspections have shown, the Iraqi nuclear program was far more extensive that what was indicated by the declarations of 18 and 27 April 1991, and the full extent of the program may not even now be know. This report therefore covers not only the items known at the time of submission of the IAEA plan but also items revealed subsequently.

Throughout this period, Iraq's persistent practice of only limited acknowledgement of activities exposed through inspection, its concealment of evidence in such critical areas as uranium enrichment and nuclear weapons development, its denial of unrestricted access to certain sites, its detaining of the Agency's team on one occasion and its confiscating of documents from inspectors have made it rather difficult for the Agency to discharge its duties.

Original Prime Concern

The original prime concern related to the nuclear material known to be in Iraq in a readily nuclear-weapons-usable form (in Agency practice, such material is referred to as "direct-use" material, "directly usable" meaning that no further enrichment or irradiation in a reactor is necessary). Of this material, the most important as regards ease of handling and hence use in weapons production consisted of the stocks of fresh (unirradiated) fuel for the IRT 5000 reactor. These consisted of 68 fuel assemblies of 80% enrichment with a U-235 content of 10.97 kilograms and 10 assemblies of 36% enrichment with a U-235 content of 1.27 kilograms. In addition, there was a set of fresh fuel plates for the Tamus-2 reactor (French

MTR type) with an enrichment of 93% and a total U-235 content of 372 grams.

Other highly enriched material containing a total of 35.58 kg of U-235 had been irradiated and so, owing to its radioactivity, could not be readily utilized in weapons production. Nevertheless, the degree of enrichment, up to 93% meant that this material also had to be considered of high strategic value. The first IAEA inspection team found that the irradiated material was held at two storage locations. One was the fuel pond, which contained both the reactor core and fuel storage racks (and near which was a small subsidiary storage pool); the other was an emergency storage to which the fuel from the Tamuz-2 reactor core and associated pound had been transferred during the bombing campaign. This emergency storage, designated "location B", consisted of pits in a farmland area a few miles from the Tuwaitha Nuclear Centre.

Present Situation

Direct-Use Material

All the fresh fuel for the IRT 5000 reactor, both 80% and 36% enriched, was removed from Iraq on 15 and 17 November 1991. Removal of the strategically most significant material marks an important stage in the implementation of the IAEA plan. 400 grams of unirradiated high-enriched uranium now remains in Iraq. This will be removed soon if current contract negotiations are successful.

The irradiated fuel presented severe problems regarding preparation for safe transport. The fuel at location B is stored under conditions which would be completely unacceptable by normal standards. Radiation levels are high and owing to the lack of water treatment and suitable containing material, corrosion problems cannot be avoided. The pond at the IRT 5000 reactor site was filled with debris when the reactor was destroyed. Careful work was necessary in order to clear the pond and improve conditions sufficiently to verify the fuel without creating an area contamination hazard. This had now been done and plans to prepare the fuel for lifting and transport are being worked out. All fuel elements in location B are presently under the Agency seals.

Initially, no fuel handling organization was willing to enter into a contract for removal of the fuel from Iraq. Later, a consortium of leading transport and reprocessing organizations from two States expressed a willingness to enter into a commercial arrangement, and contract negotiations have been under way for several months. It is hoped that these will be completed shortly. The financial sums involved are large and many legal and safety problems are having to be solved before the parties can conclude a contract. During this period the fuel has been regularly inspected by the IAEA inspection teams.

Plutonium

A total of 6 grams of clandestinely produced plutonium was enventually declared by Iraq. This material was removed from Iraq during the fifth IAEA inspection.

Other Nuclear Material

Since the declarations of 18 and 27 April, inspections have resulted in some 400 tons of additional material being declared by Iraq—natural uranium in many forms, ranging from yellowcake to processed chemicals. Although not directly weapons-usable material, it falls within the scope of Security Council resolution 707. Much of the material had been concealed by dispersion or burial in desert areas. As a result, it took time to recover and assemble all this material at a site where identification and verification could take place. The technical activities involved in verifying the material have now been completed and the material is under seal.

Equipment

The IAEA plan stated that priority would be given to the identification of research, development, support and manufacturing facilities and materials relevant or connected to irradiated fuel reprocessing and isotopic enrichment. The extent of the facilities and equipment revealed has been reported after each inspection and will therefore only be summarized here. The major discovery has been that of the Electromagnetic Isotope Separation (EMIS) program and its extent. A major concealment effort was made by Iraq to hide the existence of its program from inspectors, equipment being dispersed and in many cases buried in remote areas. As far as can be established in these circumstances, the EMIS equipment has now been largely accounted for. The remaining parts have been collected at one site and destruction has been proceeding steadily during recent inspections. Destruction involves cutting the magnet pole pieces (with special plasma torches), the vacuum chambers and associated equipment. A total of eight large magnet poles have been destroyed to date and all the vacuum chambers.

In addition to the EMIS program, a centrifuge program was under way. The equipment for this has also been systematically destroyed or removed. In particular, some rotor and bearing parts have been removed for examination, to establish the extent and nature of the program, while most of the centrifuge components have been crushed. Special machines used to produce the centrifuges have been destroyed or rendered useless by the cutting of key parts.

Weaponization

Recent inspections have concentrated on the nuclear weaponization program—i.e. warhead development and assembly as distinct from nuclear material production. The seventh and eighth inspections revealed special equipment essential to such a program. Two special video cameras ("streak cameras") have been removed from Iraq and other equipment has been sealed pending decision on removal, destruction or monitoring.

Hot Cells

The Tuwaitha Nuclear Centre was extensively equipped with "hot cells" for dealing with radioactive material. Many of these were severely damaged in the bombing, but concern remained about their possible reconstruction and about the possible use of the undamaged cells. During the seventh inspection, these cells were rendered harmless by the cutting of manipulator arms and control wires. Associated glove boxes were rendered useless by having cement poured into them. As a long-term measure, epoxy resin is being used in addition to cement to render harmless the mixers-settlers.

Buildings

To date no buildings have been destroyed by inspection teams. Most buildings used in the clandestine programs were destroyed by bombing. The Iraqi authorities themselves have expressed a desire to demolish many buildings at Tuwaitha so that the sites may be re-used for non-prohibited nuclear activities or for non-nuclear activities. The sites of Buildings B50, B80 and B85, which were destroyed by bombing, have already been completely cleared.

Future Activities

The removal from Iraq of the remaining 35 kilograms of U-235 contained in the irradiated fuel elements of the Tamuz-2 and IRT 5000 research reactors is one of the major tasks still pending. Negotiations with contractors are in progress, and preliminary work to facilitate the extraction of the fuel elements from the damaged reactor building is terminated.

Destruction of the EMIS components will be completed; other key equipment relevant to nuclear weapons development research and to centrifuge manufacturing which is now under Agency seals will be rendered useless or removed.

It is expected that the analysis of samples taken at Al Atheer will indicated which equipment-building still need to be destroyed.

Vienna, 5 December 1991

Summary

The present situation regarding destruction, removal or rendering harmless can be summarized as follows:

Directly usable material (High Enriched Uranium)

68 fuel assemblies 80% enriched   – removed

10 fuel assemblies 36% enriched   – removed

(Remaining – 372 grams of U-235 in 93%-enriched uranium contained in MTR-type fuel plates)

Plutonium

6 grams   – removed

Natural uranium

Approximately 400 tons   – stored under IAEA seal

EMIS equipment

Magnet poles	– 8 destroyed
Vacuum chambers	– all destroyed
Coils	– all destroyed

Centrifuge equipment

Centrifuges	– destroyed (some specimens removed to IAEA)
Manufacturing equipment	– key components destroyed
Hot Cells	– rendered harmless

Document 96

General Assembly resolution concerning the situation of human rights in Iraq

A/RES/46/134, 17 December 1991

The General Assembly,

Guided by the principles embodied in the Charter of the United Nations, the Universal Declaration of Human Rights 1/ and the International Covenants on Human Rights, 2/

Reaffirming that all Member States have an obligation to promote and protect human rights and fundamental freedoms and to fulfil the obligations they have undertaken under the various international instruments in this field,

Mindful that Iraq is a party to the International Covenants on Human Rights;

Recalling Security Council resolution 688 (1991) of 5 April 1991, in which the Council demanded an end to the repression of the Iraqi civilian population and insisted that Iraq should cooperate with humanitarian organizations and ensure that the human and political rights of all Iraqi citizens are respected,

Recalling also the pertinent resolutions of the Commission on Human Rights and the Subcommission on Prevention of Discrimination and Protection of Minorities, which expressed grave concern at the flagrant violations of human rights by the Government of Iraq,

Recalling in particular Commission on Human Rights resolution 1991/74 of 6 March 1991, 3/ in which the Commission requested its Chairman to appoint a special rapporteur to make a thorough study of the violations of human rights by the Government of Iraq, based on all information the special rapporteur may deem relevant, including information provided by intergovernmental and non-governmental organizations and any comments and material provided by the Government of Iraq, and to submit an interim report thereon to the General Assembly at its forty-sixth session and a report to the Commission at its forty-eighth session,

Deeply concerned by the volume and extent of allegations of human rights violations by the Government of Iraq, such as arbitrary arrests and detentions, enforced or involuntary disappearances, torture, inhuman or degrading practices, extrajudicial killings, summary or arbitrary executions, hostage-taking and use of persons as "human shields", the lack of freedom of expression and the absence of an independent judiciary,

Noting the view of the Special Rapporteur that these allegations are each day increasing and necessitate considerable and detailed examination,

Deeply concerned by the fact that chemical weapons have been used on the Kurdish civilian population, by the forced displacement of hundreds of thousands of Kurds and the destruction of Kurdish towns and villages, as well as by the situation of tens of thousands of displaced Kurds living in camps in the north of Iraq and by the deportation of thousands of Kurdish families,

Also deeply concerned by the repressive measures taken by the Government of Iraq against the Shiah communities in the south of Iraq,

Concerned especially by the alleged use of excessive force by the Government of Iraq against Iraqi civilians, in particular the Kurds and the Shiites,

Noting with interest the message conveyed to the Special Rapporteur by the Government of Iraq of its intention fully to cooperate with him, with such cooperation including acceptance of a visit to Iraq to investigate the allegations of violations of human rights in that country,

Regretting, however, that the Government of Iraq has failed to answer a considerable number of specific questions asked by the Special Rapporteur on acts being committed by the Government of Iraq that are incompatible with international human rights instruments that are binding on that Government,

1. *Takes note with appreciation* of the interim report of the Special Rapporteur 4/ and the considerations and observations contained therein;

2. *Expresses its deep concern* about the numerous and detailed allegations of grave human rights violations by the Government of Iraq to which the Special Rapporteur has referred in his report, in particular:

(*a*) Arbitrary detention, including that of women, children and the elderly, as well as the systematic practice of torture and other cruel, inhuman or degrading practices, and of enforced or involuntary disappearances as a part of a general structured programme of repression aimed at quelling opposition;

(*b*) Extrajudicial killings, including political killings and summary or arbitrary executions throughout the country, particularly in the northern Kurdish autono-

---

1/ Resolution 217 A (III).
2/ Resolution 2200 A (XXI), annex.
3/ See *Official Records of the Economic and Social Council, 1991, Supplement No. 2* (E/1991/22), chap. II, sect. A.
4/ A/46/647, annex.

mous region, in southern Shiah centres and in the southern marshes;

(*c*) Hostage-taking and the use of persons as "human shields", a most grave and blatant violation of Iraq's obligations under international law;

3. *Calls upon* the Government of Iraq to release all persons arrested and detained without ever being informed of charges against them, and without access to legal counsel or due process of law;

4. *Also calls upon* the Government of Iraq, as a State party to the International Covenant on Civil and Political Rights, 2/ to abide by its obligations under this Covenant and under other international instruments on human rights, and particularly to respect and ensure these rights for individuals irrespective of their origin within its territory and subject to its jurisdiction, including Kurds and Shiites;

5. *Regrets* the failure of the Government of Iraq to provide satisfactory replies to all the allegations of violations of human rights, and calls upon it to reply quickly in a comprehensive and detailed manner to these allegations so as to enable the Special Rapporteur to form an accurate assessment as a basis for his recommendations to the Commission on Human Rights;

6. *Urges*, therefore, the Government of Iraq to accord its full cooperation to the Special Rapporteur during his forthcoming visit to Iraq to investigate the allegations of violations of human rights;

7. *Requests* the Secretary-General to give all necessary assistance to the Special Rapporteur to fulfil his mandate;

8. *Decides* to continue the examination of the situation of human rights in Iraq during its forty-seventh session under the item entitled "Human rights questions", in the light of additional elements provided by the Commission on Human Rights and the Economic and Social Council.

Document 97

General Assembly resolution concerning the situation of human rights in Kuwait under Iraqi occupation

A/RES/46/135, 17 December 1991

The General Assembly,

Recalling its resolution 45/170 of 18 December 1990,

Guided by the principles embodied in the Charter of the United Nations, the Universal Declaration of Human Rights, 1/ the International Covenants on Human Rights 2/ and the Geneva Conventions of 12 August 1949, 3/

Aware of its responsibility to promote and encourage respect for human rights and fundamental freedoms for all and resolved to remain vigilant with regard to violations of human rights wherever they occur,

Reaffirming that all Member States have an obligation to promote and protect human rights and fundamental freedoms and to fulfil obligations they have freely undertaken under the various international instruments,

Expressing its grave concern at the grave violations of human rights and fundamental freedoms during the occupation of Kuwait,

1. *Takes note with satisfaction* of Commission on Human Rights resolution 1991/67 of 6 March 1991; 4/

2. *Expresses its appreciation* to the Special Rapporteur on the situation of human rights in Kuwait under Iraqi occupation for his preliminary report; 5/

3. *Expresses its deep concern* for Kuwaiti and third-country national detainees and missing persons in Iraq;

4. *Requests* the Government of Iraq to provide information on all Kuwaiti persons and third-country nationals deported from Kuwait between 2 August 1990 and 26 February 1991 who may still be detained and, in accordance with its obligations under article 118 of the Geneva Convention relative to the Treatment of Prisoners of War of 12 August 1949 6/ and article 134 of the Geneva Convention relative to the Protection of Civilian Persons in Time of War of 12 August 1949, 7/ to release these persons without delay;

5. *Also requests* the Government of Iraq to provide, in accordance with its obligations under articles 120 and 121 of the Geneva Convention relative to the Treatment of Prisoners of War and articles 129 and 130 of the Geneva Convention relative to the Protection of Civilian

1/ Resolution 217 A (III).
2/ Resolution 2200 A (XXI), annex.
3/ See *Official Records of the Economic and Social Council, 1991, Supplement No. 2* (E/1991/22), chap. II, sect. A.
4/ United Nations, *Treaty Series*, vol. 75, Nos. 970-973.
5/ A/46/544 and Corr.1.
6/ United Nations, *Treaty Series*, vol. 75, No. 972.
7/ Ibid., No. 973.

Persons in Time of War, detailed information on persons arrested in Kuwait between 2 August 1990 and 26 February 1991 who may have died during or after that period while in detention, as well as on the site of their graves;

6. *Further requests* the Government of Iraq to search for the persons still missing and to cooperate with international humanitarian organizations, such as the International Committee of the Red Cross, in this regard;

7. *Requests* that the Government of Iraq cooperate with and facilitate the work of international humanitarian organizations, notably the International Committee of the Red Cross, in their search for and eventual repatriation of Kuwaiti and third-country national detainees and missing persons.

Document 98

Statement by the President of the Security Council concerning the sanctions regime imposed against Iraq and humanitarian conditions of the civilian population in Iraq

S/23305, 20 December 1991

The members of the Security Council held informal consultations on 6 December 1991 pursuant to paragraph 28 of resolution 687 (1991) of 3 April 1991, paragraph 6 of resolution 700 (1991) of 17 June 1991 and paragraph 21 of resolution 687 (1991). After hearing all the opinions expressed in the course of the consultations, the President of the Council concluded that there was no agreement that the necessary conditions existed for a modification of the regimes established in paragraphs 22 to 25, as referred to in paragraph 28 of resolution 687 (1991), in paragraph 6 of resolution 700 (1991), and in paragraph 20, as referred to in paragraph 21 of resolution 687 (1991).

However, with a view to alleviating the humanitarian conditions for the civilian population in Iraq and in order to facilitate the utilization of paragraph 20 of resolution 687 (1991), the Security Council Committee established under resolution 661 (1990) concerning the situation between Iraq and Kuwait is requested to study immediately those materials and supplies for essential civilian and humanitarian needs as identified in the Ahtisaari report 64 (S/22366) with the purpose of drawing up a list of items which may, with the Council approval, be transferred from the 'no-objection' procedure to a simple notification procedure. Members of the Council may submit proposals of items for this purpose.

With regard to imports of items subject to prior approval under the 'no-objection' procedure by the Committee (i.e. items other than food and medicine), any member of the Committee putting forward an objection to such an import will offer a specific explanation at a meeting of the Committee.

The members of the Council are aware of reports received concerning the approximately 2,000 Kuwaitis believed to be still detained in Iraq, access by the International Committee of the Red Cross to all detainees and places of detention, the return of Kuwaiti property, and particularly the return of Kuwaiti military equipment and their bearing upon the present state of Iraqi compliance with resolution 687 (1991).

In the light of the above, the Council will request the Secretary-General to prepare a factual report on Iraq's compliance with all the obligations placed upon it by resolution 687 (1991) and subsequent relevant resolutions. This report will be made available to the Council in good time before it undertakes its next review under paragraph 21 of resolution 687 (1991).

In the course of consultations it was noted that resolutions 706 (1991) of 15 August 1991 and 712 (1991) of 19 September 1991 gave to Iraq the possibility for oil sales to finance the purchase of foodstuffs, medicines and materials and supplies for essential civilian needs for the purpose of providing humanitarian relief. However, this possibility has not yet been used.

Document 99

General Assembly resolution concerning international cooperation to mitigate the environmental consequences on Kuwait and other countries in the region resulting from the situation between Iraq and Kuwait

A/RES/46/216, 20 December 1991

The General Assembly,

Aware of the disastrous situation caused in Kuwait and neighbouring areas by the torching and destruction of hundreds of its oil wells and of the other environmental consequences on the atmosphere, land and marine life,

Bearing in mind all relevant Security Council resolutions, in particular section E of resolution 687 (1991) of 3 April 1991,

Having taken note of the report submitted by the Secretary-General to the Security Council describing the nature and extent of the environmental damage suffered by Kuwait, 1/

Having also taken note of decision 16/11 A adopted by the Governing Council of the United Nations Environment Programme on 31 May 1991, 2/

Profoundly concerned at the deterioration in the environment as a consequence of the damage, especially the threat posed to the health and well-being of the people of Kuwait and the people of the region, and the adverse impact on the economic activities of Kuwait and other countries of the region, including the effects on livestock, agriculture and fishing, as well as on wildlife,

Acknowledging the fact that dealing with this catastrophe goes beyond the capabilities of the countries of the region and, in that regard, recognizing the need for strengthened international cooperation to deal with the issue,

Noting with appreciation the appointment by the Secretary-General of an Under-Secretary-General as his Personal Representative to coordinate United Nations efforts in this field,

Also noting with appreciation the efforts already undertaken by the Member States of the region, other States, the organizations of the United Nations system, and governmental and non-governmental organizations to study, mitigate and minimize the consequences of this environmental catastrophe,

Bearing in mind the effective work of the Regional Organization for the Protection of the Marine Environment and the inter-agency task force established under the leadership of the United Nations Environment Programme especially for the environmental situation in the region, and the plan of action,

Expressing its special appreciation to the Governments which have extended financial support to the two trust funds established for the purpose by the Secretary-General of the International Maritime Organization and the Executive Director of the United Nations Environment Programme,

Emphasizing the need to continue to take comprehensive measures to study and mitigate these environmental consequences within a framework of sustained and coordinated international cooperation,

1. *Urgently appeals* to all States Members of the United Nations, intergovernmental and non-governmental organizations, scientific bodies and individuals to provide assistance for programmes aimed at the study and mitigation of the environmental deterioration of the region and for strengthening the Regional Organization for the Protection of the Marine Environment and its role in coordinating the implementation of these programmes;

2. *Calls upon* the organizations and programmes of the United Nations system, in particular the International Maritime Organization and the United Nations Environment Programme, to pursue their efforts to assess and counteract the short-term as well as long-term impact of the environmental deterioration of the region;

3. *Requests* the Secretary-General, through his Personal Representative, to render assistance to the members of the Regional Organization for the Protection of the Marine Environment in the formulation and implementation of a coordinated and consolidated programme of action comprising costed project profiles, to help identify all possible resources for the programme of action and, *inter alia*, for strengthening the environmental capacities of the members of the Regional Organization for the Protection of the Marine Environment to surmount the problem, and to allocate, within existing resources, the minimum resources required to enable his Personal Representative to continue to help coordinate the activities of the United Nations system to that end;

4. *Also requests* the Secretary-General to submit to the General Assembly at its forty-seventh session, through the Economic and Social Council, a report on the implementation of the present resolution;

1/ See S/22535 and Corr.1 and 2, annex; see *Official Records of the Security Council, Forty-sixth Year, Supplement for April, May and June 1991*, document S/22535.
2/ See *Official Records of the General Assembly, Forty-sixth Session, Supplement No. 25* (A/46/25), annex.

5. Decides to include in the provisional agenda of its forty-seventh session a sub-item entitled "International cooperation to mitigate the environmental consequences on Kuwait and other countries in the region resulting from the situation between Iraq and Kuwait" under the item entitled "Development and international economic cooperation".

Document 100

Report of the Secretary-General on the status of compliance by Iraq with the obligations placed upon it under certain of the Security Council resolutions relating to the situation between Iraq and Kuwait

S/23514, 25 January 1992

1. The present report is presented to the members of the Security Council pursuant to the request addressed to the Secretary-General in the statement issued by the President of the Council on 20 December 1991 (S/23305). By the President's statement, the Security Council, among other things, requested the Secretary-General "to prepare a factual report on Iraq's compliance with all the obligations placed upon it by resolution 687 (1991) and subsequent relevant resolutions", such a report to "be made available to the Security Council in good time before the Council undertakes its next review under paragraph 21 of resolution 687 (1991)". 1/

2. The Secretary-General proceeded immediately to identify all the applicable obligations under the Security Council's request, and to determine Iraq's compliance with them, to date. While some of the obligations placed upon Iraq are of a rather general nature, many others were clearly specified in the resolutions imposing them. However, there are some obligations for which no monitoring body or mechanism under or outside the United Nations auspices could be readily identified and so approached for contributions in time for preparation of the present report.

3. For the purposes of the present report, the Secretary-General has focused his attention only on those provisions in the relevant resolutions that place mandatory obligations upon Iraq. The comments received from various sources relating to the observations and assessments of Iraq's compliance are reproduced in the annex to the present report.

A. OBLIGATIONS OF A GENERAL NATURE

4. There are two principal, general obligations upon which Iraq's compliance with all its obligations may be based and assessed.

1. *Acceptance by Iraq of the provisions of the entire resolution 687 (1991) (para. 33)*

5. Under paragraph 33 of resolution 687 (1991) Iraq was required to give official notification to the Secretary-General and to the Security Council of its acceptance of the provisions of the entire resolution, as a precondition for a formal cease-fire becoming effective between Iraq and Kuwait and the States cooperating with Kuwait.

6. By a letter dated 6 April 1991 addressed simultaneously to the Secretary-General and the President of the Security Council (S/22456), Iraq signified its unconditional acceptance of Security Council resolution 687 (1991). By a further letter dated 10 April (S/22480) Iraq transmitted the text of a decision adopted by the National Assembly of Iraq on 6 April 1991, accepting the resolution.

2. *Compliance by Iraq with all its international obligations (para. 5 of resolution 707 (1991))*

7. By paragraph 5 of resolution 707 (1991), Iraq is required to comply with all its international obligations, including those set out in resolutions 687 (1991) and 707 (1991), 2/ and in the Treaty on the Non-Proliferation of Nuclear Weapons of 1 July 1968, and Iraq's safeguards agreement with the International Atomic Energy Agency (IAEA). 3/ No specific requirement was made of Iraq to confirm its compliance with the provisions of this paragraph.

1/ The next review under paragraph 21 of resolution 687 (1991) falls due on 28 January 1992.
2/ For the purposes of the present report, the Secretary-General was guided by the President's statement of 20 December 1991 (S/23305) in so far as it referred to Iraq's compliance with the obligations set out only in the resolutions alluded to in that statement.
3/ For proper coverage of Iraq's compliance with the Treaty and the nuclear safeguards agreement, see paragraph 20, below.

B. SPECIFIC OBLIGATIONS

1. *Respect for the inviolability of the international border and allocation of islands between Iraq and Kuwait (para. 2 of resolution 687 (1991))*

8. Under paragraph 2 of resolution 687 (1991) it was demanded of Iraq to respect the inviolability of the previously agreed international border and the allocation of islands between Iraq and Kuwait (cf: document 7063, United Nations, *Treaty Series*, 1964). The comments on this item are contained in the annex to the present report (see annex, sect. A).

2. *Obligations relating to conventional, biological or chemical weapons and such materials for warfare (paras. 8, 9 (a) and 10 of resolution 687 (1991), para. 3 of resolution 707 (1991) and para. 5 of resolution 715 (1991))*

9. The monitoring of Iraq's compliance with, and the implementation of, the obligations as required under the relevant resolutions cited above was entrusted to the Special Commission established under paragraph 9 (b) (i) of Security Council resolution 687 (1991). The Special Commission's comments on this matter are contained in the annex to the present report (see annex, sect. B).

3. *Obligations relating to nuclear capability development programmes (paras. 10 and 12 of resolution 687 (1991), para. 3 of resolution 707 (1991) and para. 5 of resolution 715 (1991))*

10. The monitoring of Iraq's compliance with, and the implementation of, the obligations as required under the relevant resolutions cited above, was entrusted to IAEA. The comments of IAEA on this matter are contained in the annex to the present report (see annex, sect. C).

4. *Obligations relating to repatriation of and access to all Kuwaiti and third-country nationals in Iraq (para. 30 of resolution 687 (1991))*

11. Under the provisions of paragraph 30 of resolution 687 (1991) it was required of Iraq to extend all necessary cooperation to the International Committee of the Red Cross (ICRC) in all matters relating to the location of and access to all Kuwaiti and third-country nationals in Iraq for the purpose of their repatriation. 4/

12. In his report to the Security Council dated 12 September 1991 (S/23012), the Secretary-General included information he had received from ICRC relating, among other things, to repatriation of former residents of Kuwait from Iraq, registration and repatriation of persons wishing to return to Kuwait, repatriation of third-country nationals, and details of a Kuwaiti list of

civilians and military personnel missing since 2 August 1990. In response to the Secretary-General's request for information for the purposes of the present report, ICRC has submitted additional comments on the item, which are contained in the annex to the present report (see annex, sect. D).

5. *Iraq's liability under international law for loss or damage resulting from its unlawful invasion and occupation of Kuwait (para. 16 of resolution 687 (1991))*

13. Information received with regard to this item is contained in the annex to the present report (see annex, sect. E).

6. *Adherence to all obligations concerning the servicing and repayment of Iraq's foreign debt (para. 17 of resolution 687 (1991))*

14. The response from the International Monetary Fund (IMF) indicates that, as of 31 December 1991, Iraq was in arrears to the IMF in the sum of Special Drawing Rights (SDR) 7.3 million. Furthermore, the Chairman of the Paris Club of Creditor Countries has submitted a tabulation of Iraq's indebtedness to some of the Club members amounting to a total of some US$13,420 million due since 1 April 1991. The relevant communications concerning this item are contained in the annex to the present report (see annex, sect. F).

7. *Non-entitlement to claims deriving from the effects of the measures taken by the Security Council in resolution 661 (1990) and related resolutions (para. 29 of resolution 687 (1991))*

15. According to information received with regard to this item, Iraq attempted to enforce a claim under which it would have benefited from a contract frustrated by the coming into effect of the terms of resolution 661 (1990). Communications concerning this item are contained in the annex to the present report (see annex, sect. G).

8. *Liability by Iraq for the full cost of the tasks authorized under section C of resolution 687 (1991) (para. 4 of resolution 699 (1991))*

16. The comments received with regard to this item are contained in the annex to the present report (see annex, sect. H).

4/ In paragraph 31 of the resolution, the Council invited ICRC to keep the Secretary-General apprised, as appropriate, of all the activities undertaken in pursuance of paragraph 30, as well as those relating to the return of the remains of Kuwaiti and third-country nationals present in Iraq on or after 2 August 1990.

9. *Requirement to provide monthly statements of gold and foreign currency reserves holdings (para. 7 of resolution 706 (1991))*

17. To date, the Secretary-General has received no notification from Iraq of the amount of its holdings of gold and foreign currency reserves. Furthermore, IMF has reported that, since the adoption of resolution 706 (1991), it has not received from the Iraqi authorities any information concerning Iraq's holdings of gold and foreign currency reserves. 5/ The text of the letter on comments on this item from the Managing Director of IMF is reproduced in the annex to the present report (see annex, sect. F).

C. OTHER OBLIGATIONS

18. Two other types of obligations placed upon Iraq are drawn to the Council's attention, namely: obligations imposed upon Iraq under Chapter VII of the Charter (mandatory obligations) but for which no monitoring organ has been specifically designated.

1. *Undertaking required on not committing, supporting or abetting commission of any international terrorist acts (para. 32 of resolution 687 (1991))*

19. In the absence of any specifically designated organ for monitoring Iraq's compliance with the above-mentioned obligation, the Secretary-General is unable to offer any guiding information to the members of the Council. However, in a letter dated 11 June 1991 (S/22687) Iraq, with reference to paragraph 32 of resolution 687 (1991), stated that it was a party to the international conventions relating to this item, and affirmed that it had never pursued a policy favourable to international terrorism as defined by international law. In a further letter of the same date (S/22689) Iraq reaffirmed its position.

2. *Compliance with obligations in the Treaty on the Non-Proliferation of Nuclear Weapons of 1 July 1968 (para. 5 of resolution 707 (1991))*

20. In its letter of 6 April 1991 (S/22456), in which it signified its acceptance of resolution 687 (1991), Iraq also stated that it was a party to the Treaty on the Non-Proliferation of Nuclear Weapons of 1 July 1968, adding that many reports of IAEA confirmed that Iraq was applying all the provisions of the Treaty. IAEA for its part, in two letters dated 19 July (S/22812) and 27 September 1991 (S/23088) from the Director-General, informed the Security Council of the finding by the Board of Governors of IAEA that Iraq had not fully complied with its obligations under its safeguards agreements with the Agency. In a resolution adopted on 20 September

1991 (GC/(XXV)/RES/568) the General Conference of IAEA, taking note of Security Council resolution 687 (1991), had, among other provisions, strongly condemned "Iraq's non-compliance with its nuclear non-proliferation obligations", and demanded that Iraq "immediately and fully comply with all of its nuclear non-proliferation obligations".

Annex
Substantive texts of the communications received from various sources indicating their observations and assessments of Iraq's compliance

A. IRAQ'S COMPLIANCE WITH THE PROVISIONS OF PARAGRAPHS 2 AND 5 OF SECURITY COUNCIL RESOLUTION 687 (1991)

In view of the mandate of the United Nations Iraq-Kuwait Observation Mission (UNIKOM), the text below deals with both paragraphs 2 and 5 of resolution 687 (1991).

1. Paragraph 2 of Security Council resolution 687 (1991) requires Iraq and Kuwait to respect the inviolability of the international boundary and the allocation of islands as set out in the "Agreed Minutes" signed by them on 4 October 1963. Paragraph 5 of the same resolution requires the two States to respect a demilitarized zone (DMZ) established by the Security Council. The Council set up the United Nations Iraq-Kuwait Observation Mission (UNIKOM) to monitor the DMZ and the Khor Abdullah; to deter violations of the boundary through its presence in and surveillance of the DMZ; and to observe any hostile or potentially hostile action mounted from the territory of one State to the other.

2. Iraq has respected the DMZ.

3. With regard to respect for the international boundary it should be noted that, pending the boundary's demarcation on the ground, UNIKOM has not taken a position concerning its precise location. UNIKOM uses a British map, which it has given to both sides for reference; they have agreed to work with it as a practical arrangement to facilitate UNIKOM's task and without prejudice to their positions concerning the boundary. In order to avoid friction and incidents, UNIKOM has established the principle that the authorities on both sides should stay a reasonable distance of 1,000 metres from the boundary line shown on UNIKOM's map. However, five Iraqi police posts are on the Kuwaiti side of that line, and two are closer to it than 1,000 metres, on the Iraqi side. In response to repeated requests by UNIKOM to move these

---

5/ Subsequently, a representative of IMF amplified orally that disclosure of such information was obligatory to all signatory members to the Charter of that organization, of which Iraq was one.

posts to positions at least 1,000 metres on the Iraqi side of the line, the Iraqi authorities have declined to do so on the grounds that this could prejudice their position relating to the border. They have said that Iraq will comply with the reasonable distance principle, once the border is demarcated.

4. In August and September 1991, there were a number of incursions from Iraqi into Kuwaiti territory by persons collecting weapons, ammunition and other battlefield items. The question was raised whether they were in fact military personnel but UNIKOM was not able to establish that this was so. The incursions ceased in October after the Iraqi authorities took effective measures to curb them. Since then, the Iraq-Kuwait border has been quiet.

B. EXTRACT FROM LETTER DATED 21 JANUARY 1992 FROM THE EXECUTIVE CHAIRMAN OF THE SPECIAL COMMISSION

As requested in the memorandum of 8 January 1992, I am sending herewith the contribution of the Special Commission to the Secretary-General's report. As you will see, the text submitted herewith provides for a part B of the chapter of the report involved in which the text on nuclear issues which you have received from the Director-General of IAEA can be inserted.

Attachment
Section C of Security Council resolution 687 (1991) and resolutions 707 (1991) and 715 (1991)

Introduction

1. The paragraphs which follow deal with the status of Iraq's compliance with the provisions of section C of Security Council resolution 687 (1991) of 3 April 1991 and resolutions 707 (1991) and 715 (1991) of 15 August and 11 October 1991 respectively. Section C of resolution 687 (1991) relates to the elimination of Iraq's capabilities in regard to weapons of mass destruction and also to ensuring that the acquisition of such weapons is not resumed in the future. Resolutions 707 (1991) and 715 (1991) are concerned with matters directly related to implementation of section C of resolution 687 (1991), including ongoing monitoring and verification of Iraq's compliance with its obligations and the facilities, privileges and immunities of the Special Commission established under resolution 687 (1991) and of the International Atomic Energy Agency (IAEA).

2. The status of Iraq's compliance with the obligations arising from these particular provisions has been addressed in a number of previous reports, circulated by the Secretary-General to the Security Council, covering the period from the adoption of resolution 687 (1991) in April 1991 up to early December 1991. Two reports by

the Executive Chairman of the Special Commission were circulated in documents S/23165 of 25 October 1991 and S/23268 of 4 December 1991. These reports cover all aspects encompassed by section C of resolution 687 (1991) and the subsequent related resolutions. At the request of the Director-General of IAEA, the Secretary-General issued, as documents of the Council, inspection reports prepared by eight of the nuclear inspection teams in Iraq led by the Agency (S/22788, S/22837, S/22986 and Corr.1, S/23112, S/23122, S/23215 and S/23283). A report from the ninth nuclear inspection team, which left Iraq on 14 January 1992, will be forthcoming in the near future. A further report by the Director-General, covering the Agency's operations under the relevant Council resolutions for the period April to December 1991, was circulated on 17 December 1991 in document S/23295.

3. Part A of the present chapter, based upon information provided by the Special Commission, updates the reports of the Executive Chairman listed above, in so far as they relate to paragraphs 8, 9 and 10 of resolution 687 (1991) and related provisions in resolutions 707 (1991) and 715 (1991). Part B is based upon information provided by the Director-General of IAEA, and is concerned with paragraphs 12 and 13 of resolution 687 (1991) and related provisions in resolutions 707 (1991) and 715 (1991).

Part A: Paragraphs 8, 9 and 10 of Security Council resolution 687 (1991) and related provisions in resolutions 707 (1991) and 715 (1991)

Chemical and biological weapons

4. Under paragraphs 8 and 9 of section C of resolution 687 (1991), Iraq is, *inter alia*, required to accept unconditionally the destruction, removal or rendering harmless, under international supervision, of all chemical and biological weapons and all stocks of agents and all related subsystems and components and all research, development, support and manufacturing facilities. It is further required to submit to the Secretary-General a declaration of the locations, amounts and types of the foregoing items and to permit urgent, ongoing inspection thereof by the Special Commission, both at sites declared by Iraq and at any additional locations designated by the Special Commission. Iraq is also required to yield possession of all the foregoing items, both at declared and designated sites to the Special Commission for destruction, removal or rendering harmless, taking into account requirements of public safety.

5. Iraq made declarations under the foregoing provisions of 23 locations. Twenty-three other sites were designated by the Special Commission. Inspections have been carried out by the Special Commission at 43 of these locations. Three sites declared by Iraq, but assessed by the

Special Commission to be of low priority, will be visited shortly on future inspections.

6. Although the Iraqi authorities have been cooperative in efforts to destroy their declared chemical stockpile, they have as yet failed to disclose fully all the information required under resolution 687 (1991) on their chemical weapons programmes despite repeated requests from the Special Commission. Specifically, Iraq has not answered requests to identify the development, support and manufacturing components of those programmes. Such components clearly exist in view of the types of weapons which have been identified.

7. Ten types of weapons have been found in the Iraqi chemical weapons arsenal which, Iraq maintains, were manufactured locally or modified in Iraq for chemical weapons fill. The equipment so far found appears to have been involved in the manufacture of only two of these types, 250 and 500 gauge aerial bombs. Iraq has so far not accounted for the location of equipment for the fabrication of the remaining eight declared types of chemical weapons.

8. Furthermore, there is evidence that Iraq continues to attempt to retain machinery directly involved in the manufacture of chemical weapons by moving it away from its original location at the principal Iraqi chemical weapons facility, the Muthanna State Establishment. An example of this was encountered in December 1991 by the most recent chemical weapons team to visit Iraq (UNSCOM 21). Iraq had been directed by the Special Commission to return to Muthanna all the chemical bomb casing manufacturing equipment which had been removed from that site after the adoption of resolution 687 (1991), and Iraq claimed to have complied with this directive. However, during a short-notice inspection of a sugar factory in Mosul, Special Commission inspectors found almost 100 items of metal-working machinery originating from Muthanna. After attempting to argue that these items were of a general purpose nature for civil use, the Iraqi officials concerned admitted that the items had come from the chemical bomb casing and supporting general maintenance workshops at Muthanna. Iraq was again directed to return the equipment to Muthanna for disposal.

9. Iraq initially denied possession of biological weapons and related items. However, during the Special Commission's first biological weapons inspection of the site at Salman Pak, Iraqi officials admitted to having carried out a programme of biological research for both defensive and offensive purposes. Iraq has not to date disclosed a plan for a development and production component of its activities in this area. The Special Commission considers that such a plan is a logical part of the Iraqi programme and will continue to press for its disclosure.

10. In the absence of a full, complete and final disclosure by Iraq of its chemical and biological weapons programmes, the Special Commission will need to continue first phase inspections and to designate further suspected sites in order to uncover the full scope of those programmes before the Commission is able to conclude that in this area Iraq is meeting its obligations under paragraphs 8 and 9 of resolution 687 (1991).

Ballistic missiles and long-range guns

11. Under paragraphs 8 and 9 of section C of resolution 687 (1991), Iraq is, *inter alia*, required to accept unconditionally the destruction, removal or rendering harmless, under international supervision, of all ballistic missiles with a range greater than 150 kilometres and related major parts, and repair and production facilities. It is further required to submit to the Secretary-General a declaration of the locations, amounts and types of the foregoing items and to permit urgent, ongoing inspection thereof by the Special Commission, both at sites declared by Iraq and any additional locations designated by the Special Commission. Iraq is also required to destroy, under the supervision of the Special Commission, all its missile capabilities, including launchers, as specified in paragraph 8 of the resolution.

12. Iraq has declared under the foregoing provisions some 24 locations. An additional 47 locations were designated by the Special Commission. All these locations have been inspected.

13. Since the second report of the Executive Chairman of the Special Commission was submitted to the Security Council on 4 December 1991 (S/23268), a Special Commission ballistic missile inspection team, in inspecting components of the 1,000 mm "supergun", found that 22 barrel sections and some hydraulic buffers had not been adequately destroyed according to the specifications laid down by the previous inspection team. Iraqi personnel were requested to destroy the components as directed, which was done and subsequently verified. At another site the team found that two SCUD missile trailers that had been previously destroyed had been welded together and outfitted to carry shorter-range FROG-7 missiles. The team requested their complete destruction, together with six unaltered transporters and accepted an Iraqi proposal that they be blown up with explosives. The destruction of these eight trailers was verified by the team. Finally, with the destruction since the second report of the remaining fixed SCUD launchers, all declared missiles and their launchers and major parts have now been destroyed.

14. While the Special Commission is fully satisfied that all of Iraq's declared ballistic missiles have been destroyed, there remains substantial uncertainty whether

all missiles subject to resolution 687 (1991), primarily SCUD or SCUD variants, have been declared as required. The Special Commission is endeavouring, by means of an exchange of information with Member States and by various interactions with Iraq, to attempt to resolve these uncertainties. Further, the Special Commission continues to receive information that various significant components intended for indigenously produced SCUDs were contracted for and received by Iraq. The Special Commission, with the cooperation of Member States, is seeking to confirm this information and to resolve the outstanding issues with the Iraqi authorities.

Ongoing monitoring and verification

15. Under paragraph 10 of section C of resolution 687 (1991), Iraq is, *inter alia*, required to undertake unconditionally not to use, construct or acquire any of the items proscribed in paragraphs 8 and 9 of the resolution relating to ballistic missiles and chemical and biological weapons. The Secretary-General is requested, in consultation with the Special Commission, to develop a plan for ongoing monitoring and verification of Iraq's compliance with that undertaking. Similar provisions in respect of Iraq's nuclear activities are laid down in paragraphs 12 and 13 of section C of the resolution, the plan for ongoing monitoring and verification in this regard to be prepared by the Director-General of the International Atomic Energy Agency, with the assistance and cooperation of the Special Commission.

16. On 11 October 1991, the Security Council adopted resolution 715 (1991), which approved the plans for future ongoing monitoring and verification of Iraq's compliance with relevant parts of section C of Security Council resolution 687 (1991) (S/22871/Rev.1 and S/22872/Rev.1 and Corr.1) submitted in accordance with resolution 687 (1991). Under paragraph 5 of resolution 715 (1991), Iraq is obliged to meet unconditionally all its obligations under the plans and to cooperate fully with the Special Commission and the Director-General of IAEA in carrying out the plans.

17. To ensure Iraq's full compliance, these plans—both in nuclear and non-nuclear areas—cover not only military but also those civilian facilities and items that could be used, or activities that could be involved, in contravention of the relevant Iraqi obligations. The plans provide for inspections, aerial overflights in Iraq and submission of information by Iraq so that the Special Commission, or in the nuclear area IAEA with the assistance and cooperation of the Commission, would be able to monitor and verify that no nuclear, chemical or biological weapons or ballistic missiles or other items prohibited under resolution 687 (1991) are acquired anew. The first step to be taken by Iraq under these plans was

the submission, by 10 November 1991, of initial information on the specific dual-purpose activities, facilities and items outlined in the plans and their annexes.

18. Only in late November did the Special Commission receive from Iraq a document that was stated in the letter of transmission to be the information requested of Iraq in accordance with resolution 687 (1991). This document does not recognize that Iraq has any obligations under resolution 715 (1991) and the Special Commission's plan approved thereunder. Instead it arrogates to Iraq the right to decide what information it will provide to the Special Commission and, in this respect, does little more than repeat information already supplied. It thus falls well short of the information required under the Special Commission's plan adopted by resolution 715 (1991).

19. On 20 December 1991, the Chairman of the Special Commission sent a letter to the Permanent Representative of Iraq to the United Nations in which he stated that the present Iraqi attitude constituted a serious obstacle to the implementation of the monitoring and verification of Iraq's compliance with its obligations under resolution 687 (1991). He requested Iraq to rectify this situation immediately and fulfil its obligations under resolution 715 (1991) and the plan for ongoing monitoring and verification (S/22871/Rev.1). The Chairman requested Iraq to provide by 15 January 1992 all the information and data specified in that plan.

20. As of the time of the writing of this report no response has been received from Iraq to the Chairman's letter. Furthermore Iraq has not provided its first semi-annual declaration which was due from it on 15 January under the Special Commission's plan approved by the Security Council.

21. The Special Commission is sending a special mission to Iraq scheduled for 27 to 29 January 1992. The mission will be led by two members of the Special Commission and its objectives will be twofold: first, to underline the most serious concern with Iraq's failure to provide required information under Security Council resolution 715 (1991) and, second, to urge Iraq, in accordance with resolution 707 (1991), to disclose, fully and completely, information on its programmes in areas related to chemical and biological weapons and ballistic missiles with a range greater than 150 kilometres.

Iraq's reporting obligations under Security Council resolution 707 (1991)

22. Under paragraph 3 (i) of Security Council resolution 707 (1991) Iraq is required to provide, without further delay, full, final and complete disclosure of all aspects of its programmes to develop weapons of mass destruction and ballistic missiles with a range greater than

150 kilometres, and of all holdings of such weapons, their components and production facilities and locations, as well as all other nuclear programmes, including any which it claims are for purposes not related to nuclear-weapons-usable material.

23. As will have been seen from the preceding sections, while Iraq has made a number of declarations relating to its weapons of mass destruction and the facilities for their production, these declarations have been far from complete. The Special Commission has found it necessary to make numerous designations of undeclared sites, and such designations are continuing in the absence of the full, final and complete disclosure called for by paragraph 3 (i) of resolution 707 (1991). Particularly in the nuclear field the Special Commission can have no confidence that Iraq has disclosed the full scope and nature of its programmes for fissile material production and of its research and development efforts in respect of nuclear weapons.

24. Since making its initial declarations, Iraq has consistently maintained that it has no further declarations to make except when confronted with evidence of the inadequacy of its prior declarations. At a meeting with the Minister of State for Foreign Affairs on 12 January 1992, in which the Deputy Executive Chairman of the Special Commission participated, the position was again taken by Iraq that it would not make any further declarations but would respond only to information, such as that reported above in part B of this chapter concerning its acquisition of large quantities of components for centrifuges for its gas centrifuge enrichment programme, when directly confronted with that information. This approach does not discharge Iraq's obligation to provide the full, final and complete disclosure called for in paragraph 3 (i) of resolution 707 (1991).

25. Under paragraph 3 (ix) of resolution 707 (1991), Iraq is required to respond fully, completely and promptly to any questions or requests from the Special Commission, IAEA and their inspection teams.

26. On a number of previous occasions, particularly as a result of inspection activities, specific questions on the relevant Iraqi capabilities have been put to the Iraqi authorities. Many of these questions remain unanswered, and thus Iraq is not meeting all its obligations to provide information to the Special Commission and IAEA at their request. Consequently, despite the inspection efforts undertaken by the Special Commission, some important lacunae remain which preclude full understanding of the Iraqi programmes concerned. There is therefore a need to seek from Iraq further information so that a more comprehensive understanding may be arrived at of the issues involved which would increase confidence in any assessments to be prepared for the Security Council.

Issues relating to the obligations of Iraq in connection with the facilities, privileges and immunities of the Special Commission and of IAEA

27. On 14 May 1991 an agreement between the United Nations and Iraq on the facilities, privileges and immunities of the Special Commission, contained in an exchange of notes between the Secretary-General and the Minister for Foreign Affairs of Iraq entered into force. This agreement spelled out the requirements for the Special Commission, IAEA and their inspection teams to discharge effectively the functions conferred on them in resolution 687 (1991). These requirements included unrestricted freedom of entry into and exit from Iraq for personnel, equipment and means of transport; unrestricted freedom of movement without advance notice in Iraq; unimpeded access to any declared or designated site; the right to request, receive and copy any record, data or other information; the right to take photographs from the ground or the air relevant to the Special Commission's activities; the right to operate the Special Commission's own means of transport, both on the ground and in the air and various other facilities, privileges and immunities, including ensuring the security and safety of inspectors and other personnel.

28. Difficulties encountered by the Special Commission and IAEA in the conduct of inspections, and the failure of Iraq on a number of occasions to abide by the terms of the agreement, have been reported in several documents submitted to the Security Council (see, for example, S/22739, S/22743, S/23165, para. 17 and appendix III, paras. 5 and 11, and S/23268, para. 3). These difficulties have included denial of access to certain sites; threats to the security of inspectors, on one occasion by means of rifle fire; detention of an inspection team in a parking lot for four days; destruction or movement for purposes of concealment of equipment and documentation from designated sites; forcible removal and refusal to return documentary evidence found by an inspection team and refusal for over three months to permit the Special Commission to introduce its own helicopters into Iraq for the transportation of inspection teams and for other official inspection activities.

29. Among the measures adopted by the Council in response to these violations are a number of provisions contained in paragraph 3 of resolution 707 (1991) confirming the facilities, privileges and immunities of the Special Commission and IAEA. These provisions demand, *inter alia*, that Iraq grant immediate, unconditional and unrestricted access to sites, facilities, equipment and records; cease attempts to conceal and to move or destroy any proscribed material or equipment without prior consent from the Special Commission; make immediately available items to which access was

previously denied; and permit the operation of fixed-wing and helicopter flights in Special Commission or IAEA aircraft for all relevant purposes, including inspection, surveillance, aerial surveys, transportation and logistics. Resolution 707 (1991) further demands that Iraq ensure the complete implementation of the privileges, immunities and facilities of representatives of the Special Commission and IAEA and their complete safety and freedom of movement.

30. Since the second report of the Executive Chairman of the Special Commission was circulated to the Security Council on 4 December 1991, there have been no significant violations of the facilities, privileges and immunities of the Special Commission and of IAEA. Access has been granted to inspection teams at both declared and designated sites. There have been no threats to the security and safety of inspectors while engaged on official inspections, and the Special Commission has continued to operate its own fixed-wing and helicopter flights.

31. However, Iraq continues to protest, as a violation of its sovereignty, each aerial surveillance flight undertaken by the Special Commission despite the clearly established right of the Commission to undertake such flights. This right derives from resolution 687 (1991) and is expressly laid down in the agreement that entered into force on 14 May 1991 and in paragraph 3 of resolution 707 (1991). Moreover, the issue referred to in the Executive Chairman's report of 4 December 1991 regarding the possible application of control measures at Habbaniya airport which would interfere with the Commission's rights to unimpeded entry into and exit from Iraq of equipment, materials and other items has not been resolved definitively. Furthermore, Iraq has so far failed to deliver to IAEA documentation which was forcibly removed from a nuclear inspection team during the period of its detention in a parking lot in September 1991.

32. Resolution 707 (1991) also requires Iraq to provide or facilitate the provision of transportation, medical or logistical support requested by the Special Commission and IAEA. Iraq has responded readily to such requests.

33. The obligations of Iraq in respect of the facilities, privileges and immunities of the Special Commission and of IAEA are of a continuing nature. Those obligations are repeated and reinforced in the plans for ongoing monitoring and verification which were approved by the Security Council in its resolution 715 (1991), and their implementation in this context remains to be tested. Past experience has shown that the Special Commission and IAEA have to be vigilant and to take a strong stand in defence of the facilities, privileges and immunities to which they are entitled and this will continue to be the policy.

Summary

34. In the almost 10 months that have elapsed since the adoption of Security Council resolution 687 (1991), significant progress has been made in the implementation of section C of that resolution but much remains to be done.

35. In the first report of the Executive Chairman of the Special Commission (S/23165, para. 6) it was pointed out that this implementation involved a three-stage process—inspection and survey, disposal of weapons of mass destruction and the facilities for their production, and ongoing monitoring and verification of Iraq's compliance with its obligations under section C of resolution 687 (1991).

36. The inspection and survey phase has not yet been completed. It would have been completed by this time if Iraq had met in a comprehensive manner its obligations on reporting and had made the full, final and complete disclosure of all aspects of its programmes to develop weapons of mass destruction which is called for by resolution 707 (1991). Furthermore, the Special Commission has no confidence that such full, final and complete disclosure will be forthcoming in the immediate future as the Iraqi authorities have indicated very recently that they will respond only to specific items of evidence of undisclosed weapons, facilities and materials.

37. The disposal phase is being implemented with significant progress in the area of ballistic missiles where Iraq has, under Special Commission supervision, destroyed its declared missiles and launchers. Planning in relation to the destruction of chemical weapons is now in an advanced stage, with the active cooperation of Iraq under Special Commission supervision. In the nuclear area the fresh uranium fuel has been removed from Iraq, and arrangements are under negotiation for the removal of irradiated fuel and the long-term storage of nuclear wastes. Destruction, removal or rendering harmless of the facilities, materials and equipment involved in proscribed activities is now a matter of increasing urgency where difficult questions will arise in regard to dual or multi-purpose items. This process may thus be protracted.

38. In respect of the third phase relating to ongoing monitoring and verification, while the Special Commission's and IAEA's plans have been approved by the Security Council in resolution 715 (1991), the Iraqi authorities have not made a clear acknowledgement of their obligations under these plans and resolution 715 (1991). Instead, they have adopted an approach which arrogates to themselves the determination of what they consider to be required of them under paragraphs 10, 12

and 13 of resolution 687 (1991). In the view of the Special Commission, Iraq is thus not in compliance with its obligations under resolution 715 (1991) and for this reason the Special Commission is dispatching a special mission to Iraq at the end of January to discuss the Commission's serious concern in this regard with the Iraqi Government. In the previous reports by the Executive Chairman of the Special Commission to the Security Council stress has been placed on the need for a change of policy on the part of Iraq to one of candour, transparency and cooperation at all levels. The experience of the Special Commission in the last two months has confirmed this need.

Part B: Paragraphs 12 and 13 of Security Council resolution 687 (1991) and related provisions in resolution 707 (1991) and 715 (1991)

(See sect. C of the present annex)

C. ATTACHMENT TO THE LETTER DATED 20 JANUARY 1992 FROM THE DIRECTOR GENERAL OF THE INTERNATIONAL ATOMIC ENERGY AGENCY

Report of the Director General on Iraq's compliance with its obligations under Security Council resolutions as they relate to nuclear activities

I. Introduction

1. This report summarizes the compliance to date by Iraq with its obligations under Security Council resolutions 687 (1991), 707 (1991) and 715 (1991) as they relate to nuclear activities.

II. Iraq's obligations related to nuclear activities

2. Pursuant to paragraph 12 of Security Council resolution 687 (1991), Iraq is obliged not to acquire or develop nuclear weapons or nuclear-weapons-usable material or any related sub-systems, components or facilities, including research, development, support or manufacturing facilities. Iraq was required to submit by 18 April 1991 a declaration of the locations, amounts and types of all such items. Iraq is under a continuing obligation to accept urgent on-site inspections and to place all of its nuclear-weapons-usable material under the exclusive control of the International Atomic Energy Agency (IAEA) for custody and removal. Iraq is further obliged to accept the destruction, removal or rendering harmless, as appropriate, of all proscribed items and to accept the Agency's plan for the future ongoing monitoring and verification of its compliance with these undertakings.

3. Pursuant to its obligations under resolution 687 (1991), and in accordance with the 14 May 1991 exchange of letters between the Secretary-General and the Foreign Minister of Iraq, Iraq is obliged, *inter alia*, to extend to IAEA and personnel assigned to carry out inspections and other activities under resolution 687 (1991), the privileges and immunities necessary for the fulfilment of such functions, in particular, but not limited to those privileges and immunities identified in the exchange of letters. These included unrestricted freedom of entry, exit and movement without advance notice, unimpeded access to any site or facility for on-site inspection and the right to request, receive, examine and copy records and examine, return, move or photograph any relevant items.

4. Affirming Iraq's failure to act in strict conformity with its obligations under resolution 687 (1991), the Security Council on 15 August adopted resolution 707 (1991), which imposed additional obligations on Iraq. These include the requirement that Iraq make a declaration of all of its nuclear programmes, including any which it claims are for purposes not related to nuclear-weapons-usable material, and to halt all nuclear activities of any kind, except for the use of isotopes for medical, agricultural or industrial purposes. Iraq was specifically directed to cease immediately any attempt to conceal, and on its own initiative to move or destroy, any material or equipment relating to its nuclear programme. Resolution 707 (1991) reiterated Iraq's obligation to provide immediate, unconditional and unrestricted access to all items and locations the inspection teams wished to inspect, and to ensure the complete implementation of privileges and immunities of the representatives of IAEA and of the Special Commission. Resolution 707 (1991) further requires Iraq to comply fully with its obligations under the Treaty on the Non-Proliferation of Nuclear Weapons and its safeguards agreement with IAEA.

5. Pursuant to resolution 715 (1991), adopted on 11 October, by which the Security Council approved the Director General's plan for future ongoing monitoring and compliance with paragraph 12 of resolution 687 (1991) and paragraphs 3 and 5 of resolution 707 (1991), Iraq is required to meet unconditionally all of its obligations under the plan and to cooperate fully with the Director General in carrying out the plan. The plan itself calls for the submission by Iraq within 30 days of approval of the plan inventories of all nuclear material in Iraq; of all facilities, installations and sites in Iraq where nuclear activities have been, can be or are carried out; of material, equipment and items in Iraq required to be reported to the Agency; of all isotopes in Iraq used for medical, agricultural or industrial applications, of information on existing or proposed nuclear programmes; and

of all facilities, installations and sites in Iraq which have electricity supplies greater than 10 mwe.

III. Compliance

A. Declaration of a nuclear-weapons programme

6. Iraq consistently denied the existence of any work related to nuclear-weapons development until 14 October, when, in the course of the seventh inspection it was acknowledged that research studies in weaponization had been under way. Inspection activities revealed that Iraq had gone to great lengths to conceal or destroy any evidence of such a programme, a fact later confirmed by Iraqi authorities. The inspection team had a strong component of nuclear-weapons experts who had become convinced as a result of a number of repeated visits that the Al Altheer site was involved in investigations related to nuclear-weapons design. Iraq maintained that this was a materials production development centre until, finally, on 21 October, it admitted that Al Altheer was also built to serve the weaponization programme.

B. Declaration of nuclear-weapons-usable material

7. In accordance with resolution 687 (1991), Iraq was to have submitted by 18 April a declaration of the locations, amounts and types of all nuclear-weapons-usable material. On 18 April 1991, Iraq submitted to IAEA a letter stating that there was no nuclear-weapons-usable material in Iraq. Based on information concerning material under Agency safeguards, which included nuclear-weapons-usable material, clarification was requested by IAEA. A revised declaration was received by IAEA on 27 April reflecting only the safeguarded material.

8. Following the visit to Iraq in June of a high-level mission sent under the authority of the Security Council on account of the repeated failure of Iraq to fully reveal its nuclear programme and its denial of access to inspectors (see paras. 12-14 below), a new declaration giving details on different aspects of the Iraqi nuclear programme and a variety of nuclear material was submitted on 7 July. In response to follow-up questions, clarifications were provided on 14 July and on 27 July indicating, *inter alia*, the existence of additional nuclear material.

9. The July declaration and clarifications showed that Iraq had further processed material to chemical forms suitable for enrichment and for production of plutonium, material which Iraq was required to have declared to the Agency in accordance with the Safeguards Agreement between Iraq and IAEA and by resolution 687 (1991). Also revealed for the first time in the July communications was the existence of gram quantities of plutonium which had been clandestinely separated from irradiated fuel at the Tuwaltha nuclear centre. Associated

with this was the clandestine production, irradiation and reprocessing of fuel assemblies fabricated from the previously undeclared uranium stocks.

C. Declaration of facilities

10. Prior to the first inspection, the only known nuclear facilities in Iraq were those in the Tuwaltha nuclear centre, where nuclear material was being safeguarded. No other facilities were declared in the initial Iraqi statements. As a result of the second inspection, the Tarmiya industrial centre was revealed as the site for the electromagnetic isotope separation process (EMIS), a facility capable of producing nuclear-weapons-usable material. This was a large site still in the installation stage, but with some production units having started operation and produced enriched uranium. It was declared to the first team as a plant for manufacturing transformers, an implausible claim. When its true nature was established, later inspections showed that extensive deception had taken place, including laying fresh concrete to hide evidence of the machinery that had been installed and to the painting of walls to impede the verification of the presence of uranium. Iraqi authorities also admitted that a facility at Ash Sharqat, which had initially been declared to be a non-nuclear plastic coating plant, was in reality, intended to be a duplicate of the plant at Tarmiya.

11. The Mosul chemical plant that produced the uranium oxide and tetrachloride material used as feed material in the enrichment programme was only declared on 7 July. Extensive subterfuge and deception had taken place to hide its true nature from inspectors.

D. Declaration of equipment

12. Most of the equipment for the EMIS process had been buried prior to the first inspection. It was then excavated and moved between various sites by convoy to hide it from detection. The second inspection team located the equipment, but was refused access a number of times to the military camps to which it had been moved. Photographs were eventually obtained as the convoy attempted to escape by a back entrance as inspectors were denied access at the front. In this incident warning shots were fired by Iraqi security personnel.

13. When this irrefutable evidence was obtained, and following the high-level mission, on 7 July the Iraqi authorities gave a detailed account of the EMIS programme, but denied any major progress in a centrifuge enrichment programme. As evidence accumulated, admissions were made of a small number of centrifuges and components as the first stages of a research and development programme, then of the intention to build a small (100 machine) cascade. A facility was located which was

judged by the experts on the inspection team to be capable of producing a few thousand machines a year. Iraq denied such intentions.

14. Lately more openness has been shown by the Iraqi authorities in discussions held on this programme where some important inconsistencies remaining from previous inspections were resolved and important admissions were made as to the progress, objectives, and dimensions of the programme. These discussions took place in January 1992 when an inspection team visited Iraq to discuss evidence of the importation of key components sufficient for a few thousand centrifuges. This information was discussed at the Iraqi Ministry of State level in the presence of technical experts from both sides. As a result of this discussion, the Iraqi authorities acknowledged the procurement of these materials and components and explained that all these supplies had been destroyed or "rendered harmless" by melting and crushing prior to the beginning of nuclear inspections in Iraq under resolution 687 (1991). Iraqi authorities further acknowledged the procurement of 100 tons of the special high tensile strength steel (maraging steel) sufficient to produce a few thousand centrifuge rotors and rotor internal fittings and the procurement of several thousand aluminium forgings for the vacuum housing flanges. The Iraqi authorities stated that these materials had also been destroyed or rendered harmless by melting prior to the commencement of inspections.

E. *Access and inspection rights*

15. In addition to the denial of access and inspection rights referred to under paragraphs 12 to 14 above, a serious incident also occurred during the sixth inspection, when the inspection team attempted to remove documents relating to the nuclear programme from two sites at Baghdad. A confrontation took place resulting in the team being confined within a parking lot for four days. Some documents were forcibly removed from the team's vehicles. Most of the documents seized were returned, but some were not. Iraq claimed that these related to sensitive personnel matters such as salaries and health and were not relevant to the inspection work. Among the documents that were finally obtained by the team were two reporting progress on the Iraqi nuclear-weapon programme, making it clear that a large well-funded research programme had been under way to develop an implosion-type nuclear explosive.

F. *Removal and rendering harmless*

16. According to a number of statements made by Iraq, actions were taken prior to the beginning of inspections under resolution 687 (1991) to dismantle and/or destroy components, equipment and material related to the clandestine nuclear programmes. Components of the EMIS process together with centrifuges and related components have been destroyed by the Agency with the assistance of Iraqi personnel. The hot cells and glove boxes at the Tuwaltha nuclear centre have been rendered harmless by cutting the manipulator arms and pouring in cements or epoxy resin. The Iraqi authorities cooperated in the carrying out of this work.

17. Iraq has cooperated in the removal of the un-irradiated high-enriched fuel for the IRT-5000 reactor. This was flown from Iraq on 15 and 17 November. The security and transport arrangements were undertaken by Iraq. Two streak video cameras and related equipment, equipment suitable for nuclear-weapons development, were removed from Iraq.

IV. *Summary*

18. The response of Iraq to the inspection work of IAEA has largely followed a pattern of denial of clandestine activities until the evidence is overwhelming, followed by cooperation until the next case of concealment is revealed. As a consequence of this behaviour, it is not possible to be confident that the full extent of prohibited nuclear activities in Iraq has been disclosed. Continuation of the inspection activities, in parallel with the monitoring programme, is deemed necessary.

D. LETTER DATED 16 JANUARY 1992 FROM THE PRESIDENT OF THE INTERNATIONAL COMMITTEE OF THE RED CROSS

1. In his letter dated 8 January 1992, the Under-Secretary-General for Political and Security Council Affairs draws our attention to paragraphs 30 and 31 of United Nations Security Council resolution 687 (1991) and asks ICRC to inform your office accordingly, with a view to the preparation of your report in this connection to the Security Council.

2. In response to the Under-Secretary-General's request I have the honour to send you herewith an updated report covering activities related to the search for and repatriation of missing persons believed to be in Iraq. Earlier information on the subject was conveyed to your predecessor by ICRC in September 1991.

3. To summarize efforts to date, since the end of the war ICRC has invited representatives of Iraq, France, Kuwait, Saudi Arabia, the United Kingdom and the United States to six meetings, where pending issues related to the implementation of the Geneva Conventions of 1949 have been discussed, such as the repatriation of prisoners of war, civilian detainees and persons missing in action, and the return of mortal remains. Over the last 10 months ICRC has supervised the repatriation of thou-

sands of military personnel and civilians captured or arrested by either side during the conflict.

4. Despite all these efforts, both during negotiations and in the field, there are still thousands of persons reported missing by the parties to the conflict.

5. I none the less remain confident that by pursuing our efforts as a neutral intermediary and implementing the provisions of the Geneva Conventions, methods and operational procedures will be found to achieve tangible results in the search for and repatriation of persons reported missing after the conflict.

Attachment
Report on activities related to the search for missing persons in Iraq and their repatriation

1. To date, the International Committee of the Red Cross (ICRC) has supervised the repatriation from Iraq of 4,299 prisoners of war, i.e. 4,233 Kuwaiti, 29 Saudi, 23 American, 12 British and 2 Italian nationals, including 2 Kuwaiti prisoners of war who were repatriated during the last three months.

2. It has furthermore supervised the return from Iraq of 1,436 civilians: 1,291 to Kuwait, 128 to Saudi Arabia, 11 to Egypt, 1 to the Syrian Arab Republic, 1 to the Philippines, 1 to Austria and 3 to the United States. These figures include the 112 civilians who have been returned over the last three months in eight separate operations to Kuwait (81), Saudi Arabia (26) or other countries (5). However, the 1,174 civilian internees who returned on 7 March 1991 to Kuwait via Safwan are not included in these statistics, since that repatriation did not take place under the auspices of ICRC.

3. Thus, a total of 6,909 persons (prisoners of war and civilians) have returned from Iraq to their home countries since the beginning of March 1991.

4. In the period from 13 March to 7 July 1991, three separate operations were carried out under ICRC supervision to repatriate the mortal remains of 8 British nationals, 7 Americans and 1 Kuwaiti.

5. In Iraq, ICRC has furthermore registered about 3,700 persons whose nationality could not be established with certainty. These persons claimed that they had been living in Kuwait and expressed their wish to return to their former place of residence. They are living in different locations and are free to move around within Iraqi territory. The large majority of them reported spontaneously to the ICRC office at Baghdad, where ICRC delegates recorded their personal data for transmission to the Kuwaiti authorities who, in turn, determine the applicants' eligibility for repatriation.

6. The Kuwaiti authorities have submitted a list of missing persons, the latest update of which contains 2,101 names (12 October 1991). The Kuwaiti authorities

have repeatedly stressed that the names on that list are not identical with those mentioned under paragraph 5 above. They have also told ICRC that information from returning Kuwaiti prisoners has induced them to believe that many Kuwaiti nationals are still being held in Iraq.

7. The Saudi authorities have reported 17 Saudi nationals as missing in Iraq. Through ICRC, the Saudi military authorities have sent the Iraqi Government detailed testimonies by former Saudi prisoners, according to whom some of the missing Saudi nationals, including Colonel Nadira, a military pilot, had been seen in Iraqi captivity.

8. Pursuant to a decision taken by Iraq and the Coalition Forces, pending issues related to the implementation of the Geneva Conventions of 1949, such as the repatriation of prisoners of war, civilian detainees and persons missing in action and the return of mortal remains, are being dealt with by a special Commission made up of representatives of Iraq, France, Kuwait, Saudi Arabia, the United Kingdom and the United States. The Commission meets periodically under the auspices of ICRC.

9. At its last meeting, held at Geneva on 16 and 17 October 1991, the Commission discussed methods and operational procedures for achieving, in the shortest possible time, tangible results in the search for and repatriation of persons reported missing by both Saudi Arabia and Kuwait. Three different but complementary approaches were then considered and submitted as proposals to the Government of Iraq:

(a) Publishing of Saudi and Kuwaiti lists of missing persons in the Iraqi media;

(b) ICRC visits to places of detention in Iraq, in accordance with ICRC standard procedures, in order to assist the Iraqi authorities in the tracing of protected persons;

(c) Constitution of individual inquiry files by the Iraqi authorities in order to meet the request of the parties concerned for well-documented replies.

10. The Permanent Mission of Iraq to the United Nations at Geneva thereupon informed ICRC, in a diplomatic note dated 11 November 1991, of Iraq's position as regards the proposals mentioned under paragraph 9 above. It can be summarized as follows:

(a) The competent Iraqi authorities agreed to publish the names of the missing Kuwaiti and Saudi nationals in a newspaper in Iraq;

(b) Iraq is willing to provide ICRC with a list of prisons and places of detention in order to facilitate ICRC visits to these places. The visits will be restricted to one per site;

(c) The sole objective of these visits is to search for missing Saudi and Kuwaiti nationals;

(d) Iraq requests that the principle of reciprocity be applied, namely that the above-mentioned procedures in the search for missing persons be applied also in Kuwait and Saudi Arabia.

11. The representatives of the Coalition Forces responded officially to ICRC and Iraq on 21 November 1991 by expressing dissatisfaction with regard to three points in the Iraqi statement. First, they considered that publication in only one Iraqi newspaper was insufficient. Secondly, they objected to ICRC visits being limited to one per site. Thirdly, they objected to reciprocity being the basis for further action.

12. Five weeks after the October meeting, when no tangible results had been achieved in the search for and repatriation of missing Kuwaiti and Saudi military personnel and civilians, ICRC Delegate General for the Middle East and North Africa travelled to Baghdad for discussions with the Minister of Defence, Mr. Ali Hassan Al-Majid, the Minister of State for Foreign Affairs, Mr. Mohammad Sayed Al-Sahaf, and the Head of the Legal Department at the Ministry of Foreign Affairs, Dr. Akram Al-Witry. The discussions were inconclusive.

13. In a diplomatic note dated 17 December 1991, the Ministry of Foreign Affairs informed ICRC of its latest position. In addition to reiterating its previous position, outlined under paragraph 10 above, Iraq invited ICRC to prepare a plan containing methods and procedures for the tracing of missing Kuwaiti, Saudi, Iraqi or other nationals in accordance with the Geneva Conventions.

14. ICRC has not yet received any information as to the whereabouts of the persons reported missing in Iraq. Nor has it received detailed and documented information on the search conducted by the Iraqi authorities. Finally, it is also still awaiting information on persons who have died while in custody.

15. ICRC regrets that no substantive agreement could be reached between the Parties and that it has consequently not been possible hitherto to implement any of the proposals set out in Point 9 above.

16. This report is a specific response to the letter of the Under-Secretary-General for Political and Security Council Affairs, dated 8 January 1992, and is therefore confined to activities related to the search for and repatriation of persons protected by the Geneva Conventions in Iraq. Activities based on the Geneva Conventions and related to the search for and the repatriation of Iraqi prisoners of war and civilians in the Kingdom of Saudi Arabia and the State of Kuwait are consequently not covered by this report.

E. INFORMATION RECEIVED WITH REGARD TO IRAQ'S COMPLIANCE WITH THE PROVISIONS OF PARAGRAPH 16 OF RESOLUTION 687 (1991)

The text reproduced below includes a contribution received from the Secretariat of the Governing Council of the United Nations Compensation Commission.

1. In resolution 674 (1990) of 29 October 1990, the Security Council reminded Iraq "that under international law it is liable for any loss, damage or injury arising in regard to Kuwait and third States, and their nationals and corporations, as a result of the invasion and illegal occupation of Kuwait by Iraq". The liability of Iraq under international law was reaffirmed in paragraph 2 (b) of resolution 686 (1991), in which the Security Council demanded that Iraq, *inter alia*, "accept in principle its liability under international law for any loss, damage, or injury arising in regard to Kuwait and third States, and their nationals and corporations, as a result of the invasion and illegal occupation of Kuwait by Iraq". Paragraph 16 of resolution 687 (1991) again reaffirmed and further specified "... that Iraq ... is liable under international law for any direct loss, damage, including environmental damage and the depletion of natural resources, or injury to foreign Governments, nationals and corporations, as a result of Iraq's unlawful invasion and occupation of Kuwait".

2. In order to implement Iraq's obligation to compensate losses, damages and injuries arising out of Iraq's unlawful invasion and occupation of Kuwait, the Security Council decided in paragraph 18 of resolution 687 (1991) to create a Fund and to establish a Commission to administer the Fund. In paragraph 19 of the same resolution the Council provided, *inter alia*, that Iraq's contribution to the Fund would be based on a percentage of the value of the exports of petroleum and petroleum products from Iraq not to exceed a figure to be suggested to the Council by the Secretary-General.

3. Iraq communicated its acceptance of the provisions of resolution 687 (1991) with identical letters dated 6 April 1991 addressed to the Secretary-General and the President of the Security Council (S/22456). Iraq's unconditional acceptance also covered paragraphs 16 and 19 of the resolution, and in particular commits Iraq to accepting the decisions taken pursuant to paragraph 19 concerning the percentage of its exports of petroleum and petroleum products to be paid to the Fund. In paragraph 2 of resolution 705 (1991) the Security Council decided that in accordance with the suggestion made by the Secretary-General in paragraph 7 of his note of 30 May 1991 (S/22661), compensation to be paid by Iraq (as

arising from section E of resolution 687 (1991)) should not exceed 30 per cent of the annual value of the exports of petroleum and petroleum products from Iraq.

4. The Compensation Fund and Compensation Commission referred to in paragraph 18 of resolution 687 (1991) were established by resolution 692 (1991) in accordance with part I of the report of the Secretary-General of 2 May 1991 (S/22559). Paragraph 5 of the resolution directed the Governing Council of the Commission to implement the relevant provisions of resolution 687 (1991), and paragraph 8 requested all States and international organizations to cooperate with the decisions of the Governing Council taken pursuant to paragraph 5. The Governing Council of the Compensation Commission has held three sessions to date and has adopted decisions, *inter alia*, on the expedited processing of claims by individuals, arrangements for ensuring payments to the Compensation Fund, and criteria for processing additional categories of claims. These decisions are not addressed directly to Iraq and do not impose new obligations upon it; they are rather intended to provide guidance to States and Commissioners. The decision concerning arrangements for ensuring payments to the Compensation Fund will only become binding upon Iraq after its approval by the Security Council pursuant to paragraph 7 of resolution 692 (1991). The delegation of Iraq has addressed the Governing Council on several occasions and has expressed Iraq's willingness to fully cooperate with its decisions. The comments and observations contained in those statements do not seem to qualify or contradict Iraq's pledge to cooperate with the Governing Council.

5. Iraq's compliance with its obligation under paragraph 16 of resolution 687 (1991) is dependent upon the resumption of its exports of petroleum and petroleum products. This has not yet taken place because the economic sanctions imposed by resolution 661 (1990) are still in force. In view of the persistence of the economic sanctions, albeit in the attenuated form provided for by paragraph 20 of resolution 687 (1991), and in view of the serious nutritional and health situation of the Iraqi civilian population, the Security Council deemed it appropriate to partially lift the prohibitions against the import of commodities and products originating in Iraq and against financial transactions related thereto, in order to generate financial resources to meet such humanitarian requirements. This was achieved with resolution 706 (1991), which authorized all States to permit the import, during a period of six months, of petroleum and petroleum products originating in Iraq sufficient to produce a sum to be determined by the Council following receipt of a report of the Secretary-General, but not to exceed US$1.6 billion. Resolution 712 (1991) approved the recommendations contained in paragraph 57 (d) and 58 of the report of the Secretary-General of 4 September 1991 (S/23006) on the implementation of resolution 706 (1991), and confirmed the figure of $1.6 billion. The sum so produced would be destined to finance the purchase of the items referred to in paragraph 20 of resolution 687 (1991) as well as various activities undertaken by the United Nations in implementation of resolution 687 (1991), including appropriate payments to the United Nations Compensation Commission. Iraq has not yet agreed to sell petroleum and petroleum products under this regime. Iraq has objected to resolutions 706 (1991) and 712 (1991), stating that it had satisfied all conditions specified in paragraph 22 of resolution 687 (1991) and therefore sanctions should no longer be applied against Iraq.

F. (i) EXTRACT FROM LETTER DATED 16 JANUARY 1992 FROM THE MANAGING DIRECTOR OF THE INTERNATIONAL MONETARY FUND

With reference to paragraph 17 of resolution 687 (1991), Iraq is currently in arrears to IMF in the special drawing rights (SDR) department. As of 31 December 1991 the overdue obligations amounted to SDR 7.3 million. The Iraqi authorities have indicated to the Fund that although willing to meet their financial obligations to the Fund, their attempts to do so have failed because of the international sanctions in place. With reference to paragraph 7 of resolution 706 (1991), the Fund has not received since the adoption of the resolution any information from the Iraqi authorities concerning their holdings of gold and other foreign currency reserves.

(ii) LETTER FROM THE CHAIRMAN OF THE PARIS CLUB OF CREDITOR COUNTRIES

... In order to complete the United Nations information on Iraq's debt, please find enclosed some data that some creditor countries from the Paris Club asked me to convey to you.

The Paris Club Secretariat remains at the disposal of your services for any complementary information they would need.

Iraq's debt summary

Some of the creditor countries asked me to convey to you these figures (outstanding amounts as of 1 April 1991):

(In millions of United States dollars)	
Japan	3 482
France	2 327
Germany	1 914
Italy	1 433
United Kingdom	1 194

Austria	926
Australia	499
Spain	366
Canada	296
Belgium	276
Sweden	226
Finland	171
Netherlands	132
Switzerland	119
Ireland	41
Denmark	18

G. Information Received From The Security Council Committee Established By Resolution 661 (1990) Concerning The Situation Between Iraq And Kuwait

In connection with the Secretary-General's forthcoming report on Iraq's compliance with all of the obligations placed upon it by resolution 687 (1991) and subsequent relevant resolutions, the Security Council Committee established by resolution 661 (1990) concerning the situation between Iraq and Kuwait has no information to offer with respect to paragraphs 10 and 12 of resolution 687 (1991) at this stage. With respect to paragraph 29 of the same resolution, attention is drawn to the letter dated 30 September 1991 from the Permanent Representative of Denmark to the United Nations addressed to the Chairman, and the Chairman's reply thereto dated 23 October 1991, copies of which are attached hereto.

Attachments

1. *Letter dated 30 September 1991 from the Permanent Representative of Denmark to the United Nations addressed to the Chairman of the Security Council Committee established by resolution 661 (1990) concerning the situation between Iraq and Kuwait*

On instructions from my Government I have the honour to submit to the Committee the enclosed statement dated 24 September 1991 by the Danish shipping company A. P. Moller concerning a violation by Iraq of Security Council resolution 687 (1991), in particular its paragraph 29.

It appears from the statement that the company has been presented with a legal claim of approximately US$ 4 million by the "Agricultural Supplies Company of Baghdad", an Iraqi Government subsidiary. The claim has been raised in connection with a contract the performance of which was affected by reason of the measures taken by the Security Council in resolution 661 (1990) and related resolutions. In the opinion of the Danish

company the claim represents a violation of Security Council resolution 687 (1991).

I should be grateful if you would have this question considered by the Committee, and I should appreciate to receive any views which the Committee might have on the matter.

Enclosure
Statement dated 24 September 1991 from A. P. Moller Company addressed to the Ministry of Foreign Affairs, Denmark

Application to the European Community and to the Security Council of the United Nations for the violation by Iraq, *inter alia*, of resolution 687 (1991).

We refer to our meeting on 13 September 1991 and should like to submit the following matter to you.

1. On 9 July 1990, the vessel in question was time chartered to a company domiciled in Switzerland.

Pursuant to the time charterers' instructions and to the terms and conditions of the governing time charter party, the vessel loaded a cargo of 61,450 tons of corn in the port of Westwego, Louisiana. The loading was completed on 20 July 1990.

The bills of lading and the further shipping documents all provided for the discharge to be carried out in the port of Aqaba, Jordan, but expressly stated that the cargo was "in transit to Iraq" and was to be delivered to an Iraqi company. The time charterers consequently gave order for the vessel to proceed to Aqaba.

2. At the time when the Iraq/Kuwait war had started and the Embargo Rules of the United Nations and the EEC came into force (including resolution 661 (1990)) in the month of August 1990, the vessel was en route to the port of discharge.

The owners of the vessel and the Ministries and lawyers consulted all concluded that it would be a severe violation of the governing international Embargo Rules now in force to deliver the cargo as set out in the shipping documents. Consequently, the owners asked the time charterers and the Iraqi cargo interests for new but legitimate discharging orders, but in vain. Instead, the time charterers cancelled the time charter party.

3. In compliance with the Embargo Rules and in order to mitigate damages, the owners of the vessel applied to the Italian courts and were granted a legal order to discharge and to store the cargo in various Italian ports. The bill of lading holders were invited to be represented, but omitted to attend to their interests.

The Italian courts subsequently arranged for a local sale of the cargo and the proceeds were deposited with the courts. In the meantime, the owners of the vessel had unfortunately suffered considerable consequential losses.

4. In connection with the subsequent cease-fire, the Government of Iraq agreed, *inter alia*, to respect and acknowledge the international Embargo Rules and on 3 April 1991, the United Nations Security Council passed resolution 687 (1991), in which paragraph 29 provides:

> "that all States, including Iraq, shall take the necessary measures to ensure that no claim shall lie at the instance of the Government of Iraq, or of any person or body in Iraq, or of any person claiming through or for the benefit of any such person or body, in connection with any contract or other transaction where its performance was affected by reason of the measures taken by the Security Council in resolution 661 (1990) and related resolutions."

5. Nevertheless, the managers of the relevant vessel have received a writ apparently taken out by the alleged cargo owners, Agricultural Supplies Company of Baghdad, an Iraqi Government subsidiary. The plaintiffs seem to raise a claim of approximately US$ 4 million equal to the alleged cargo value less the proceeds deposited in Italy. The action seems to be based on the Iraqi resolution No. 377 dated 16 September 1990, according to which it is said to be a violation of Iraqi law to comply with the international Embargo Rules. In the aforesaid writ, the defendant carriers are apparently called upon to appear before the courts of Baghdad on 5 October 1991.

6. The defendant carriers have, however, returned the Iraqi writ as being incorrectly served, and according to advice given also by the Danish Ministry of Foreign Affairs the defendants will have to refrain from appearing in the action before the Iraqi courts.

7. It is our opinion that the aforesaid Iraqi claim and proceedings constitute a clear violation of the terms and conditions of the cease-fire and of resolution 687 (1991).

We are aware of the fact that the European Commission has recently put forward a proposal for an EEC regulation to implement paragraph 29 of United Nations Security Council resolution 687 (1991) addressing especially the problems of bonds and contracts whose performance have been affected by the Embargo.

With due respect, we find the draft EEC resolution somewhat insufficient and unclear to protect all parties, who have duly complied with the Embargo Rules such as the owners of the vessel in this particular matter. These owners are especially concerned that a judgement by default may be granted by the Iraqi courts, which judgement may be enforced by the Government of Iraq or by the courts in a country which is friendly towards Iraq. This may be done by way of arresting, detaining or perhaps of confiscating the relevant vessel, a sister vessel or other assets which are owned or managed by the same carriers.

While such enforcement procedure, if any, is being carried out, considerable losses may be suffered. It may even be regarded as a violation of the governing international rules if in such case the owners or their underwriters decide to honour the Iraqi claim to mitigate losses.

8. In consideration thereof, we call upon the Danish Government, as well as EEC, to see to it that the forthcoming Council regulation be drafted so properly and clearly as to protect and indemnify the law-abiding companies and individuals who have been put in situations like this.

We also request EEC to bring up this matter in the United Nations Security Council, in which France is a permanent member. The matter is of considerable importance and urgency.

We shall, of course, be ready to provide any supplementary information on the matter in question which you may require and we look forward to hearing from you.

2. *Letter dated 25 October 1991 from the Chairman of the Security Council Committee established by resolution 661 (1990) concerning the situation between Iraq and Kuwait addressed to the Permanent Representative of Denmark to the United Nations*

On behalf of the Security Council Committee established by resolution 661 (1990) concerning the situation between Iraq and Kuwait, I have the honour to acknowledge receipt of your letter dated 30 September 1991 concerning a legal claim against a Danish company by the Agricultural Supplies Company of Baghdad.

In that connection, pursuant to a decision of the Committee taken after considering this matter at its 52nd meeting, held on 18 October 1991, I have the honour to draw your attention to paragraph 29 of resolution 687 (1991).

H. SITUATION CONCERNING THE FINANCING OF OPERATIONAL COSTS

1. Security Council resolution 699 (1991) of 17 June 1991 established the principle that "... the Government of Iraq shall be liable for the full cost of carrying out the tasks authorized by section C [of resolution 687 (1991)] ...".

2. On the other hand, Security Council resolution 706 (1991) of 15 August 1991 covered in a comprehensive manner the question of Iraq's financial obligations, both in the military/political and the humanitarian fields. The former included:

(a) Appropriate payment to the United Nations Compensation Fund;

(b) The full costs of carrying out the destruction of Iraq's weapons of mass destruction (sect. C of Security Council resolution 687 (1991));

(c) The full costs incurred by the United Nations in facilitating the return of all Kuwaiti properties;

(d) Half the costs of the Boundary Commission.

3. The Council also required the Government of Iraq to provide the Secretary-General with a monthly statement of the gold and foreign currency reserves it holds in Iraq or elsewhere (para. 7 of resolution 706 (1991)).

4. In its resolution 706 (1991), the Council decided that the cost of the specific activities undertaken by the United Nations as a consequence of resolution 687 (1991) should be financed from the proceeds of the authorized sales of Iraqi petroleum and petroleum products.

5. However, the Government of Iraq has yet to signify its willingness to comply with the provisions of Security Council resolutions 706 (1991) and 712 (1991).

6. The Iraqi Government has indicated that it is not prepared to resume the production and export of petroleum and petroleum products on the basis of the procedures outlined in above-mentioned resolutions.

7. Notwithstanding the foregoing, the Secretary-General has authorized the appropriate departments and offices of the Secretariat to initiate the implementation of the tasks set forth in Security Council resolutions 706 (1991) and 712 (1991). As of 31 December 1991, financial commitments for the implementation of these four tasks amounted to $17.2 million. This amount was provided through a commitment authority of $10 million by the Advisory Committee on Administrative and Budgetary Questions under the provisions of General Assembly resolution 44/203 of 2 December 1989 on unforeseen and extraordinary expenses, as well as by contributions from certain Member States in the amount of $7.2 million.

8. These amounts, as well as all future amounts to be disbursed in connection with the implementation of the aforementioned Security Council resolutions, are to be reimbursed to the United Nations by Iraq from the proceeds of the authorized sales of Iraqi petroleum and petroleum products.

9. To this end, the Secretary-General has entered into discussions with the Iraqi authorities with a view to devising practical arrangements that would make it possible to achieve the objectives of Security Council resolutions 706 (1991) and 712 (1991). Two rounds of discussions have been held so far: in Baghdad, on 22 and 23 November 1991, and at the United Nations Office at Vienna, from 8 to 10 January 1992. While these discussions have been constructive, no concrete decision has been arrived at regarding the resumption of Iraqi oil production. A further round of discussions is due to be held in early February 1992.

Document 101

Statement by the President of the Security Council concerning the sanctions regime imposed against Iraq, Iraq's compliance with Security Council resolution 687 (1991) and humanitarian conditions of the civilian population in Iraq

S/23517, 5 February 1992

The members of the Security Council held informal consultations on 28 January and 5 February 1992 pursuant to paragraph 21 of resolution 687 (1991). The members of the Council express their thanks to the Secretary-General for his factual report on Iraq's compliance with all the obligations placed upon it by resolution 687 (1991) and subsequent relevant resolutions (S/23514).

After taking note of the Secretary-General's report and hearing all the opinions expressed in the course of the consultations, the President of the Council concluded that there was no agreement that the necessary conditions existed for a modification of the regime established in paragraph 20 of resolution 687 (1991), as referred to in paragraph 21 of that resolution.

In the context of compliance, the Council members note with concern the recent incident at Baghdad, which demonstrates a lack of Iraqi cooperation in complying with the resolutions of the Council.

In connection with the Secretary-General's factual report on Iraq's compliance with all the obligations placed upon it by resolution 687 (1991) and subsequent relevant resolutions, the members of the Security Council note that while much progress has been made, much remains to be done. There is serious evidence of Iraqi non-compliance over its programmes for weapons of mass destruction and the repatriation of Kuwaitis and other third-country nationals detained in Iraq. There is still much Kuwaiti property to be returned. The members of the Council are disturbed by the lack of Iraqi cooperation. Iraq must implement fully resolution 687 (1991) and subsequent relevant resolutions as was stated in the statement read out by the President of the Council on behalf of its members in the meeting held on 31 January 1992 with the participation of the heads of State and Government (S/23500).

The members of the Security Council note that with a view to alleviating the humanitarian conditions of the civilian population of Iraq and facilitating the utilization of paragraph 20 of resolution 687 (1991), the Security Council Committee established by resolution 661 (1990) had been requested to prepare a study of those materials and supplies for essential civilian and humanitarian needs, other than medicines which have not been subject to sanctions and food shipments which have been permitted to move freely, that might be transferred from the "no objection" procedure to a simple notification procedure. The members of the Council also note the report of the Chairman of the Committee in this

regard. They express their appreciation for the efforts the Chairman has made to reach a conclusion and encourage him to continue his consultations with the members of the Committee on the study and to report to the Council at an early date.

The members of the Council strongly deplore that the Iraqi authorities have decided and communicated that decision to the Secretariat to discontinue contacts with the Secretariat regarding implementation of resolutions 706 (1991) and 712 (1991), which give to Iraq the possibility for oil sales to finance the purchase of foodstuffs, medicines and materials and supplies for essential civilian needs for the purpose of providing humanitarian relief. They underscore that the Government of Iraq, by acting in this way, is forgoing the possibility of meeting the essential needs of its civilian population and therefore bears the full responsibility for their humanitarian problems. They hope that a resumption of these contacts may lead to the early implementation of the scheme set out in those resolutions to enable humanitarian supplies to reach the Iraqi people.

Document 102

Special report of the Executive Chairman of UNSCOM

S/23606, 18 February 1992

Note by the Secretary-General

The Secretary-General has the honour to transmit to the Security Council a report submitted by the Executive Chairman of the Special Commission established by the Secretary-General pursuant to paragraph 9 (b) (i) of Security Council resolution 687 (1991).

Annex
Special report by the Executive Chairman of the Special Commission established by the Secretary-General pursuant to paragraph 9 (b) (i) of Security Council resolution 687 (1991)

A. *Introduction*

1. In the Secretary-General's report circulated to the Security Council on 25 January 1992, the Special Commission expressed its most serious concern 1/ at the failure of Iraq to provide full, final and complete disclosure of all aspects of its programmes to develop weapons of mass destruction and to accept its obligations in respect of ongoing monitoring and verification of its compliance with its obligations under section C of Security Council resolution 687 (1991). In the light of the report which the

Executive Chairman has received from a special mission which he sent to Baghdad on 27 January 1991, 2/ this failure of Iraq is now clearly tantamount to a rejection by the Government of Iraq of any obligations imposed on it by Security Council resolutions 707 (1991) and 715 (1991), both of which were adopted under Chapter VII of the Charter (see para. 14 below). Instead, Iraq recognizes only its own understanding of obligations imposed on it by paragraphs 10 and 12 of Security Council resolution 687 (1991) which falls far short of what is necessary for the implementation of the plans for ongoing monitoring and verification approved by resolution 715 (1991).

2. For the Special Commission this is a matter of very great importance as the Commission, in the discharge of its responsibilities under the resolutions of the Council, now has to commence in Iraq ongoing monitoring and verification activities. However, monitoring and verification of Iraq's unconditional obligation not to use, develop, construct or acquire any weapons of mass destruction can only be done effectively if Iraq acknow-

1/ S/23514, paras. 15 to 26.
2/ See para. 14 below.

ledges and abides by its obligations under resolution 707 (1991) and the plans for ongoing monitoring and verification approved by Council resolution 715 (1991).

B. *The basic requirements for ongoing monitoring and verification: Security Council resolutions 707 (1991) and 715 (1991)*

(i) *Resolution 707 (1991)*

3. Ongoing monitoring and verification can only be carried out effectively if the monitoring authorities have the clearest possible picture of what Iraq's capabilities have been in the development and production of weapons of mass destruction and what industrial facilities and materials remain at its disposal or are from time to time acquired which, while devoted to civilian activities, could be converted with relative ease to proscribed military uses. On 15 August 1991, in its resolution 707 (1991), the Security Council demanded that Iraq provide the full, final and complete disclosure of its weapons capabilities required for the clearest possible picture of what those capabilities have been. Iraq has so far failed to provide that disclosure, although some progress has been made through a procedure of interrogation where specific questions are addressed to Iraq to which it replies.

4. This is not the procedure called for by the resolution, but it is the only way in which it has proved possible to make any progress. This procedure will not achieve the desired result. Experience to date has borne this out. For example, in response to questions put by the special mission dispatched recently to Iraq by the Special Commission, Iraq has admitted that originally it had declared under resolution 687 (1991) only a part of the ancillary equipment for its ballistic missile force. It explained that the undeclared equipment had been destroyed without notification to the Commission in the summer of 1991. The Commission had previously requested Iraq to provide the list of all items that fell under resolution 687 (1991), but which had been destroyed by Iraq without the supervision of the Commission. Up to now no such list has been provided so it is not possible to assess the full implications of these actions by Iraq. However, it is clear that concealment of the destruction of items covered by resolution 687 (1991) has considerably complicated the inspection process and distorted the picture of Iraq's programme of relevant ballistic missiles which has not been completely disclosed under resolution 707 (1991). Furthermore, the unilateral destruction of these items carried out by Iraq without the supervision and consent of the Commission and without prior or subsequent notice is not in accordance with resolution 687 (1991).

5. Iraq is also required to provide a proper accounting for all items that fall under resolution 687 (1991), both under that resolution and under resolution 707 (1991). An example of Iraq's failure in this regard is to be found in Iraq's insistence that its chemical weapons production did not start until 1984, when the United Nations itself concluded that Iraq had used chemical weapons against Iran in 1983. Given that Iraq also inconsistently claims that all its chemical weapons were produced indigenously, this completely undermines the credibility of the figures that Iraq has given for chemical weapons production and use and the material balance that it has provided to the Special Commission. Furthermore, neither documentary nor complete physical supporting evidence has been provided for Iraqi responses to questions concerning the import or production of chemical weapons, chemical warfare agents, related subsystems and production facilities, equipment, etc. In relation to the biological weapons, Iraq clearly violated its obligations to hand over to the Commission all its biological weapons-related items when it destroyed buildings at Salman Pak immediately prior to the first Commission inspection there. Explanations provided to date, including those given most recently to the special mission, have not been convincing.

6. Much of the information obtained recently should have been provided by Iraq on its own initiative as part of its compliance with resolutions 687 (1991) and 707 (1991). The examples of Iraq withholding information from the Special Commission until specifically asked to show that full, final and complete disclosure of all aspects of its programmes has not been provided as required by resolution 707 (1991). These examples also show that the interrogative approach will not lead to disclosure of all information.

7. A further matter regarding Iraq's compliance with certain provisions of Security Council resolution 707 (1991), other than those relating to reporting, and which impinge upon the privileges and immunities of the Special Commission, has recently become a matter of growing concern. Under that resolution Iraq is required to allow the Commission "to make full use of ... such airfields in Iraq as (it) may determine are most appropriate for the work of the Commission". To date inspection teams entering and leaving Iraq have been required to use the Habbaniyah airfield 100 kilometres from Baghdad, ostensibly because it was the only undamaged operational field available. However, there are now two airfields (Muthanna and Rasheed) within Baghdad city limits which are operational. Iraqi Airways is operating scheduled internal flights out of Muthanna and United Nations helicopters are based at Rasheed. At Habbaniyah Iraq is imposing increasingly onerous requirements on incoming and outgoing United Nations flights to and from Kuwait or Bahrain which considerably delay loading and off-

loading and which have come close to harassment. Aircraft are also required to use a runway several kilometres away from the airport ground facilities.

8. Given the distance of Habbaniyah from the Special Commission's centre of operations in Baghdad and the onerous conditions now there imposed, the Commission, on 23 January 1992, made an official approach to the Government recalling the relevant provisions of resolution 707 (1991) and proposing that the Commission's incoming and outgoing flights use Rasheed or Muthanna airports. So far no response has been received and persistent follow-up attempts by the Commission's staff in Baghdad have met with evasive and temporizing replies.

9. The Secretary-General's report of 25 January 1992 refers not only to the difficulties at Habbaniyah airport, but also to Iraq's constant objections to the Special Commission's aerial surveillance flights and to the failure of Iraq to deliver to IAEA part of the documents forcibly removed from a nuclear inspection team in Baghdad on 23 September 1991. The protests on aerial surveillance continue; while the documents have been promised they have not yet been delivered. These two further examples demonstrate Iraq's refusal to acknowledge its obligations under resolution 707 (1991).

10. In the light of past experience, a positive outcome to these matters will only be achieved if a very firm stand is taken.

(ii) *Resolution 715 (1991)*

11. The most serious difficulty, however, which confronts those responsible for implementing section C of resolution 687 (1991), is Iraq's apparent rejection of the plans for ongoing monitoring and verification submitted to the Council by the Secretary-General and by the Director-General of IAEA (S/22871/Rev.1 and S/22872/Rev. 1 and Corr. 1). These plans were approved by the Council in its resolution 715 (1991). By the same resolution, the Council demanded that Iraq meet unconditionally all its obligations under the two plans and cooperate fully in carrying them out. It is of great importance that Iraq expressly recognize its obligations under the two plans and resolution 715 (1991).

12. Iraq's position on resolution 715 (1991), and the plans approved thereunder, was formally stated in a letter of 19 November 1991 which the Foreign Minister of Iraq addressed to the President of the Security Council. In the letter Iraq strongly attacked the plans for ongoing monitoring and verification, claiming that they were "aimed at objectives incompatible with the letter and spirit of the United Nations Charter, the norms of international law and international and humanitarian pacts and covenants". The letter further asserted that the plans

"constituted a dangerous precedent, causing the gravest damage to the credibility of the United Nations and its fundamental role in the protection of the independence and territorial sovereignty of Member States".

13. With the letter of 19 November 1991, Iraq transmitted "information required under resolution 687 (1991)". This information, however, did not correspond to the declarations required under the plans approved by resolution 715 (1991). This failure by Iraq to comply with the plans was reported to the Council in the Secretary-General's report of 25 January 1992, where detailed information was provided on the steps being taken by the Special Commission to seek Iraq's compliance with Security Council resolution 715 (1991). As was indicated in that report, the Commission was sending a special mission to Baghdad, at the end of January 1992, to underline the Commission's most serious concern with Iraq's failure to provide the full, final and complete disclosure of its programmes in the field of weapons of mass destruction demanded by resolution 707 (1991) and to comply with resolution 715 (1991).

14. That special mission has now returned and reported to the Executive Chairman. While it obtained some of the information which should previously have been supplied under resolution 707 (1991), this had to be done by the interrogative procedure referred to above. On resolution 715 (1991), the special mission met with absolutely no success. Iraq, at the level of the Minister of State for Foreign Affairs, reiterated that the Government maintained its position expressed in the letter of 19 November 1991.

15. It is now completely clear that Iraq has arrogated to itself the determination of how paragraphs 10 and 12 of section C of Security Council resolution 687 (1991) should be applied. The Special Commission has thus regretfully concluded that, despite the Commission's best endeavours, Iraq has no intention of meeting its obligations under the plans approved under, and the provisions included in, Security Council resolution 715 (1991).

C. *Conclusions*

16. As such a position is contrary to the Security Council resolutions, the Special Commission and the IAEA would be precluded from carrying out effectively a programme of ongoing monitoring and verification of the nature and scope approved by the Council. Should the Commission now seek to initiate the ongoing monitoring and verification phase of its mandate under these circumstances, it will be sending a message that, in fact if not in law, it is prepared to operate this phase of its responsibilities under Iraq's, not the Council's conditions. Past experience has demonstrated the very serious inadequa-

cies of such an approach. The Commission is therefore not legally able nor is it prepared to adopt it. In such circumstances the Commission has felt that it had no alternative but to report this matter immediately to the Council for its instructions.

17. The statement issued on behalf of the Council on 31 January 1992, at the conclusion of the 3046th meeting of the Council held at the level of Heads of State and Government, stresses that all of the resolutions adopted by the Council on this matter remain essential to the restoration of peace and stability in the region and must by fully implemented. The circumstances above show that the longer firm action is delayed, in the face of Iraq's repeated refusal to acknowledge any obligations under Security Council resolutions 707 (1991) and 715 (1991), the more intransigent the Government's position is likely to become. If this attitude is not changed the third and final phase of the responsibilities of the Special Commission under paragraph 10 of resolution 687 (1991) cannot be implemented, nor can resolutions 707 (1991) and 715 (1991).

Document 103

Report on the situation of human rights in Iraq prepared by the Special Rapporteur of the Commission on Human Rights on the situation of human rights in Iraq (extract)

E/CN.4/1992/31, 18 February 1992 (transmitted to the Security Council by S/23685 as S/23685/Add.1 on 9 March 1992)

...

II. ALLEGED HUMAN RIGHTS VIOLATIONS

A. *Issues affecting the population as a whole*

1. *Summary or arbitrary execution*

40. Regular and consistent reports of executions have reached the Special Rapporteur throughout the period of his mandate. Allegations have ranged from inadequate judicial review to orchestrated mass executions and burials. With respect to this last issue, the use of weapons of mass destruction and the issue of mass graves will be discussed. However, the problem of "normal" summary of arbitrary executions will first be addressed here.

41. Executions continue to be routinely carried out. This conclusion is fully justified in the light of the Special Rapporteur's visit in January 1992 to Abu Graib prison where, in one wing of the "heavy" section 96, he found prisoners awaiting execution. This figure (from just one prison) is to be compared with the figure given by the Government in its reply of 23 January 1992, in which it is stated that there were only 24 death sentences proclaimed for the whole of 1978.

42. While it is apparent that the death penalty is regularly administered, this fact is all the more disconcerting in view of the failings of the due process of law described below. Moreover, information and testimony received by the Special Rapporteur make it clear that executions have routinely been carried out without judicial review. In fact, according to the documents repro-duced in annex II and said to have been found in the Security Department offices of Arbil, Sulaimaniya and various other offices now under Kurdish control, the security service reporting to the President and other officers of the State (or simply to the Baath Party) has carried out executions on executive or party authority without judicial review. Most significantly, arbitrary executions were carried out on thousands of families of those thought to have been "saboteurs".

43. Information and testimony received by the Special Rapporteur affirm that there have been practices of mass execution. A report of a recent medical fact-finding mission, sent by Middle East Watch and Physicians for Human Rights, provides further evidence of the practices of the Iraqi security forces. Of particular interest is the following statement attributed to a grave digger from Arbil:

"It was in the autumn of 1986. I was called to the morgue soon after the attempted assassination of the governor of Arbil, Ibrahim Z'angang. In fact, it was the fourth attempt. An Iraqi officer met me at the morgue entrance and took me to a security police vehicle. Inside were the corpses of about 19 young men. Their bodies were riddled with bullets, their hands were tied behind their backs, and they were blindfolded. The officer said I was to bury these 'dogs'. Later, the morgue workers told me that these young men were students who had been randomly rounded up and shot by a firing squad only a few hours earlier. It was nothing more than retaliation for the botched execution attempt, a way of warning the Kurds... So I went with the officer and the bodies to the cemetery. Traditionally, we wash the dead before burial and then wrap them in a white cloth. But the officer wouldn't allow it. He said it had to be done quickly. So I buried them with their clothes on. However, I did manage to place stones around the bodies and to turn their heads toward Mecca."

Exhumation of one of the graves indicated by the grave digger provided corroborative evidence of the story's accuracy.

44. In Sulaimaniya, a grave digger made the following statement to the same fact-finding mission:

"I must have buried 600 or maybe up to 1,000 people—all killed by the secret police between 1985 and 1989. Sometimes they were *peshmerga*, sometimes women, sometimes children. Sometimes they'd been tortured. There were other grave diggers but I'm sure I buried most of them."

Exhumation of unmarked graves indicated by the grave digger again provided corroborative evidence of the truth of this story.

45. Testimony received by the Special Rapporteur also confirmed that arbitrary or summary executions were common during and after March 1991 uprisings. House-to-house searches by Government forces were said to have regularly resulted in executions, including of women and children.

46. One particularly disturbing piece of evidence viewed by the Special Rapporteur was a videotaped official and public execution of five men. Blindfolded and tied to poles, the men were placed before a large crowd, including various military officers and public officials. After some statements had been read out, the men were repeatedly shot. With the bodies crumpled to the bottom of the poles, an apparent security officer walked past the corpses placing a bullet from his pistol to each one's head; maintaining his stride, he delivered the five shots in a few seconds. Young children observed these executions from the front rows of the public assembly.

47. With regard to mass killings as a result of the use of chemical weapons and other weapons of mass destruction, the Special Rapporteur refers to paragraphs 22, 23, 74 and 75 of his interim report (A/46/647). After further study including consideration of eye-witness testimony received by the Special Rapporteur, there can be no doubt that Iraq has used excessive force, including chemical weapons, on several occasions during the past few years.

48. With regard to the use of chemical weapons in particular, Mr. Tariq Aziz, then Foreign Minister, stated during a press conference in Bonn on 1 July 1988 that both sides in the Iran-Iraq war had used chemical weap-

ons. It has been established, however, that Iraq also used chemical weapons against civilians. In a report of 19 August 1988 to the Security Council (S/20314, annex), the Secretary-General of the United Nations noted with deep regret the conclusion of an expert group, which had been sent to investigate the matter, that chemical weapons had been used against Iranian civilians in an area adjacent to an urban centre lacking any protection against that kind of attack.

49. But there is also abundant evidence that Iraq used chemical weapons against its own civilians. For instance, a report of a medical mission to Turkish Kurdistan by Physicians for Human Rights dated February 1989 concluded that Iraqi aircraft attacked Kurdish villages in northern Iraq with bombs containing lethal poison on 12 August 1988. This conclusion was based on responses to a systematically administered questionnaire, videotaped eyewitness accounts, and the physical examination of people residing in refugee camps in southeastern Turkey at the time of the mission.

50. The Special Rapporteur has himself spoken with several people in the Kurdish part of Iraq who claimed that members of their families were either killed or severely injured as a consequence of chemical attacks by Iraqi aircraft, or that they had themselves been victims of such attacks. A list of 103 people who were killed during the chemical bombardment of the village of Sheekwassan in the governorate of Arbil on 16 April 1987 was submitted to the Special Rapporteur in this connection. In addition, he received another list with the names of 45 inhabitants of the same village. These people, it was claimed, had been transferred to a hospital after having been injured during the chemical attack. They were subsequently killed by the secret police and buried in mass graves near Arbil.

2. *Torture and other cruel, inhuman or degrading treatment*

51. Throughout the decade of the 1980s, Amnesty International denounced, in several reports, the widespread, systematic torture of detainees by Iraqi Government security forces (both police and military).

52. The use of torture in order to compel prisoners, and also detainees held for any security-related offence, to sign "confessions", to give information regarding themselves as well as other persons, and to force them to renounce their political affiliations, was said to be routine practice. Victims were reportedly most often subjected to torture immediately after their arrest and during interrogation under pre-trial detention, when they were held incommunicado. In many cases, they were suspected of being members of prohibited political parties such as the Kurdistan Popular Democratic party (KPDP), the Kurd-

istan Democratic Party (KDP), the Patriotic Union of Kurdistan (PUK), the Kurdistan Socialist Party-Iraq (KSP-I), the Iraqi Communist Party (ICP) and al-Da'wa al-Islamiya. It has further been alleged that the relatives of such suspects, including children, were held in lieu of such suspects sought by the authorities and were also tortured in the process.

53. Interrogation practices have been described as brutal and have, in some cases, resulted in permanent physical or mental damage to the victims. In its report "Torture in Iraq 1982-1984" of 15 April 1985, Amnesty International provides a list of 30 different methods of torture allegedly used by members of the Iraqi security forces. They include both physical and psychological torture, such as beatings, burnings, extraction of finger-nails, sexual assault including rape, electric shocks, acid baths, deprivation of food, water, sleep or rest, as well as subjection to mock executions. Several of the victims were said to have died as a result of torture, which would explain why government documents brought to the at-tention of the Special Rapporteur frequently speak of "criminals" having "died during interrogation" (see, for example, document No. 5 in annex II). Moreover, it was reported that in several cases of alleged extrajudicial execution the victims were subjected to torture before being killed.

54. In particular, Amnesty International reports that brutal treatment of children has become routine practice in Iraqi prisons. Young people have reportedly often been tortured to force them to reveal information about their relatives. Allegedly, even infants have been ill-treated to compel members of their families to "con-fess" to alleged political offences. According to these reports, some of the 300 children and youths arrested in Sulaimaniya in September and October 1985 had been tortured, and three of them died in custody as a result. Their bodies were said to have been found in the streets on the outskirts of the town, bearing marks of torture. The bodies of 29 others of these children and youths, reportedly executed in January 1987, were returned to their families. They also showed marks of torture.

55. Quoting its Constitution and several other laws prohibiting torture, the Government of Iraq has repeat-edly denied that torture frequently occurs in the country. Allegations submitted to it by Amnesty International have been qualified as "bizarre", "false" and "without foun-dation" since torture is prohibited by the nation's Con-stitution and laws. These allegations were denied even when they had been presented with consistent evidence in the form of detailed medical examination results and other material findings. According to the Government's response to Amnesty International, occasional cases of torture had been investigated and those responsible had

been dealt with. The Special Rapporteur has received similar assurances. However, as torturers remain anony-mous, and only very few (former) prisoners will take the risk of severe retaliation, it must be assumed that the torturers can continue their practices in the knowledge that the chances are extremely small that they will ever be punished for their crimes.

56. The Special Rapporteur has received consider-able testimony from victims of and eye-witnesses to tor-ture; testimony from victims was frequently corroborated by scars remaining on their bodies. The testimony re-ceived recounts a wide variety of methods of torture, although certain practices appear to be routine given the frequency of references and consistency of accounts given by the witnesses. The testimony of victims was also corroborated by that of former security officers, who were able to provide specific information concerning the security apparatus in general and its use of torture in particular.

57. The findings of the Special Rapporteur confirm that torture, including in its most cruel forms, has been used on a large scale as a method of extracting confessions and terrorizing the population throughout the 1980s and to the present day. The summaries of a small number of testimonies are provided below:

(a) In early 1982, the witness's son was taken from the University in Baasra, and for 6 months the witness sought his whereabouts. Finally deciding to ask the officer in charge of the security centre in Baasra about the fate of his son, the witness was taken blindfolded to the General Security Centre in Baghdad in November 1982. There he was interrogated, being told that his son was a "criminal". In an attempt to get him to "confess" his son's criminal activity, the witness was tortured during seven months, having his legs and back burnt and being hit on the back of the head (from which he still bears a scar). Finally, he was brought before a court and released in July 1983. His son was tortured and released in November 1983.

(b) In early March 1991, before the uprising began, the witness was arrested by the intelligence services in Baasra. He was blindfolded and taken to the city's secu-rity centre, where he remained for one month. During his detention, he was beaten and subjected to electric shocks. In April 1991, he was transferred to Radwaniya prison in Baghdad where his interrogation began; he was sub-jected to more electric shocks, suffered burns and was hanged by his hands tied behind his back. He was released some two months later because of lack of evidence. The witness suffers from a weak left leg as a consequence of his tortures.

(c) On 28 December 1985, the security forces and intelligence services stormed the witness's home at 3:00 a.m. He was taken to the General Security Centre in Baghdad and placed in its "Third Section". He subsequently remained in prison for three and a half years, being transferred to many different prisons in the country, including that of Tikrit. During his detention, he was badly tortured, being subjected to beatings, the dripping of acid on his skin, the use of electric shocks, and beatings with cables. He had been charged with slandering Saddam Hussein and with being a member of the al-Da'wa Party, but he was released in 1988 when the Revolution Court could find no evidence against him.

(d) The witness was arrested in 1990 and imprisoned for having deserted from the army. While in prison, he was severely beaten and kicked, was subjected to electric shocks and was burnt with a hot iron.

(e) On 17 July 1988, the witness deserted from the army. He was caught and taken to the Security Centre in Baasra where, from 20 July 1988, he was subjected to various forms of torture, including hangings, electric shocks, sexual assaults, the extraction of his right eye and the removal of his fingernails by pliers; he suffered damage to his left eye as the result of a kick.

(f) The witness was arrested at the University of Mosul in 1985. During his detention, his arm was broken in the course of beatings. Upon an escape attempt, he was shot in the left hand. The witness also suffers stiffness in his fingers which he attributes to electric shocks administered during his detention.

(g) In September 1984, the witness was arrested by the security forces and taken to Najaf Security Centre where, in the course of interrogation, he was hung from a ceiling fan, subjected to electric shocks and beatings to all parts of his body including his genitals, and had hot water poured over him. He also suffered psychological torture as he was placed in solitary confinement, hearing screams and cries. After 11 months, he promised to give names and collaborate with the security forces, whereupon he was released. He fled the city.

(h) In 1985, the witness was arrested with her family and taken to the Karbala Security Centre. She was separated from her family and placed in solitary confinement. During her interrogation, she had her clothes torn off and was sexually assaulted.

(i) The witness had been arrested several times by the Security Forces, beginning in 1979. During his fourth arrest, in 1988, he was severely tortured by the use of electric shocks and sexual assaults. He was witness to other persons having their eyes pulled out and being dragged over broken glass.

(j) On 19 April 1990, the witness was arrested for the second time, having previously been taken to the Security Centre in al-Shanafiya. During his second detention, he was subjected to electric shock and was threat-

ened with the rape of his wife before his eyes in order to extract a confession. Having fainted from torture, he was taken to Saddam Hospital, but the witness refused a suggested injection because his friend had previously been poisoned. On 22 November 1990, the witness was released, but he suffers from a paralysed left hand as a result of his torture.

(k) On 29 May 1984, the witness was arrested and taken blindfolded to the Baasra Security Centre where he remained for 13 months. During his detention, he had his teeth pulled out and lost his hair as a result of scaldings with boiling water.

(l) The witness was arrested for having refused to join the army. During his imprisonment, he suffered various forms of torture (beatings, cablings, electric shocks, being hung from the ceiling) along with 30 other persons who had refused to join the army. The witness reports that some of those 30 persons had teeth and nails pulled out, while others had their tongues cut.

(m) In April 1986, the witness was taken from his house for having refused to join the army. Being told that he must either join the army or be executed, he was tortured by electric shocks and had his nails pulled out. During his detention, the witness also saw a girl being raped.

(n) During the March 1991 uprisings, the witness was arrested with his brother. He and his brother were both subjected to severe beatings, electric shocks, and the removal of their fingernails. As a result, his brother (who was badly tortured) is now emotionally disturbed.

(o) The witness was arrested in 1989 and suffered injuries during interrogation. As a result, he was taken to a military hospital where he was subjected to further torture, having some of his flesh scraped off. He was subsequently transferred to a prison where toxic materials were put on his wounds.

(p) During a military action against "communists" in the governate of Sulaimaniya in September 1988, the witness (then an army medic) covered a body in the street with a cloth, whereupon he was arrested for sympathizing with the saboteurs. He was next charged with being a communist. Taken to the "Fifth Section" of the General Security Centre in Baghdad, he was handcuffed and blindfolded and was then forced to sign various documents. In an effort to extract his confession, he was told that his two sisters would be brought before him and raped. When the sisters were brought before him, he confessed and was thereupon imprisoned.

58. The use of torture by Iraqi security forces violates both national and international law. Torture is prohibited by article 22(a) of the Iraqi Constitution and by article 127 of the Iraqi Code of Criminal Procedure No. 23 of 1971. However, it is reported that no safe-

guarding mechanisms and procedures have been established to ensure respect for the prohibition of torture by security and police forces. Indeed, it would appear that torture is a systematic practice conforming to government directives.

59. The use of torture is a serious violation of several international human rights standards, such as those embodied in: article 5 of the Universal Declaration of Human Rights; article 7 of the Covenant on Civil and Political Rights; and the Declaration on the Protection of All Persons from Being Subjected to Torture and Other Cruel, Inhuman or Degrading Treatment or Punishment. With respect to this last instrument in particular, the Iraqi Government stated officially on 3 September 1979 that it intended to comply with the Declaration and "to continue the implementation, through its national legislation and other effective measures, of the provisions of the said Declaration."

3. Enforced or involuntary disappearances

60. The Commission on Human Rights has been confronted with the phenomenon of disappearance for well over a decade and in that time the phenomenon has come to be considered as one of the most heinous of crimes. Disappearance presents a complex of violations against the individual, the family, and the community in general. The wives and children of disappeared husbands and fathers are particularly hard hit. Often, families are left without support, and in a state of limbo, without being able to take over property rights or have the peace of mind of knowing the fate of their loved ones, and with wives being unable to remarry.

61. From the information received, it is beyond doubt that the problem of disappearances is enormous in Iraq. In receiving testimony from witnesses, the Special Rapporteur was several times reminded that there is hardly a family in Iraq that has not been touched by the phenomenon. Indeed, both the Minister of Interior and the Deputy Prime Minister agreed with the Special Rapporteur that the problem is widespread and complex, while Professor al-Duri of the Consultative Committee on Human Rights of the Ministry for Foreign Affairs offered the information that he had two nephews who had gone missing. While these admissions relate primarily to war losses, it would seem most appropriate and long overdue for the Government to establish an independent body of enquiry and record keeping.

62. In connection with his mandate, the Special Rapporteur takes note of the valuable work of the Working Group on Enforced or Involuntary Disappearances. Specifically, it is interesting to note that of the 3,874 detailed and individual cases transmitted to the Government, the Government has only ever seen fit to respond

to a mere 206, clarifying just 70 of these. Such a response rate does not bode well for the Special Rapporteur, who is at present in possession of over 17,000 names of persons who have allegedly disappeared, of which an estimated 12,000 cases contain sufficient detail to be taken up by the Working Group. In fact, since the submission of the Special Rapporteur's interim report, a steady flow of cases has been received, often accompanied by identity documents and photographs. This has presented logistical problems in so far as most are received in Arabic and Kurdish; the great majority of these cases are still being translated and analysed, and so the Government of Iraq has yet to receive many of these lists. In any event, and judging from the volume of cases already received by the Special Rapporteur, it is within the realm of possibility if not probability that Kurdish estimates of up to 182,000 disappeared are realistic.

63. Many examples of cases of disappearance could be cited. But one case is perhaps revealing; that of a Mr. al-Subeiti who was sentenced to death in absentia for being a member of the al-Da'wa al-Islamiya Party. While working some time later in Jordan in 1981, he was arrested and imprisoned by the local authorities. In 1981, Mr. Barzan al-Tikriti came to obtain him on an extradition order that stipulated that he would not be executed. His children received two personal letters from him thereafter: one in 1982 and the other in 1983. There has been no news from him or of him since then. The terror an event like this transmits, even across borders, is considerable.

64. Annex III [not reproduced here] contains only a sample of cases of disappearance received by the Special Rapporteur. This list of 238 names and particulars has been compiled from seven collective case files received by the Special Rapporteur during his recent visit to Iraqi Kurdistan. In each case detailed information is provided. Viewed together with the thousands of cases submitted to the Working Group on Disappearances in the early 1980s and the large numbers being submitted as a result of the Anfal Operations and in relation to the March 1991 uprisings, the Special Rapporteur can only conclude that there has been and continues to be a systematic policy of enforced disappearance.

4. Arbitrary arrest and detention

65. Testimony received by the Special Rapporteur continues to affirm that arbitrary arrest and detention are routinely practised in Iraq and remain a major contributing factor to the general climate of fear. In the context of other violations, such as torture, enforced disappearance and summary or arbitrary execution, victims are almost always arbitrarily arrested and detained. In fact, arbitrary arrest and detention is often the precursor to such greater

violations. With respect to this subject, the Special Rapporteur refers to his remarks in his interim report (see A/46/647, paras. 14, 15 and 63-65) and to the related matters discussed above.

66. With regard to places of detention, the Special Rapporteur notes that information and testimonies received reveal the use of all sorts of centres of detention, with over 100 places having been identified by witnesses. This information stands in stark contrast to the Government's contention that there are at present only four functioning prisons in Iraq.

5. Due process and the rule of law

67. The notions of "due process of law" and "rule of law" are integrally linked: the rule of law is poorly served and undermined if the requisites of due process are not respected, and the notion of due process becomes meaningless if the rule of law is not secure. As matters of international human rights law, these two notions are defined particularly in terms of articles 10 and 11 of the Universal Declaration of Human Rights and articles 9 and 14 of the Covenant on Civil and Political Rights. However, the rule of law requires more than respect of procedural rights; it requires respect for most if not all rights and a concerted effort to eradicate the scourge of arbitrariness.

68. In Iraq, neither is the due process of law generally respected nor is the rule of law upheld. On the contrary, information and testimony received reveals a consistent if not routine failure to respect due process. At the same time, and perhaps partly because of it, the rule of law has been completely undermined.

69. While numerous testimonies alleged the absence of counsel during trial, the absence of time and support to prepare a defence, and all other such attendant guarantees (assuming any trial in the first place), perhaps examination of an individual case will help demonstrate where the problems lie. In this connection, the case of Mr. Ian Richter, raised in the interim report (paras. 41, 42 and 84, 85), is a useful example, regardless of the fact that he was released some months ago.

70. According to Mr. Richter's own testimony, and contrary to the obligations of Iraq under article 9 (2) of the Covenant, Mr. Richter was never informed of the charges against him. Under the terms of article 14 of the Covenant, Mr. Richter was not given adequate time or facilities to prepare his defence, he was brought before a Revolution Court without benefit of legal representation, he was not permitted to examine any witnesses against him, he was forced to sign documents in Arabic which he did not understand, and he was not allowed the right of appeal. In Mr. Richter's case, however, the arbitrariness may be said to have come full circle as his release has not

been explained in law and it is not certain whether or not he is entitled to any compensation for the five and a half years he spent in prison. Virtually all testimony received by the Special Rapporteur cites the same violations.

71. Turning to the rule of law, the Provisional Constitution of July 1970, which is still essentially in force, speaks neither of "government" nor of "executive power" but refers only to the "Council of Ministers"—an organ "comprised of ministers and presided over by the President of the Republic" (article 61). However, the real power in the country resides (apart from in the Office of the President) in the Revolution Command Council, which is the "State's supreme organ" (article 37). The membership of the Revolution Command Council is constituted by nine persons whose names, including that of Saddam Hussain, are listed in Revolution Command Council Decree No. 836 of 12 July 1982; the said Decree, which is an amendment to article 37 of the Constitution, also appoints the President of the Revolution Command Council who, *ipso facto*, is the President of the Republic. Any modification of the composition of the Revolution Command Council would thus require a modification of the Constitution.

72. The Revolution Command Council holds extensive legislative and executive powers at one and the same time. Significantly, it may establish laws and make decisions that have the force of law (article 42). It supervises the laws voted upon by the National Assembly, which it may dissolve, and pronounces the decisions necessary to bring ordinary laws into force. The Revolution Command Council has exclusive competence to adopt laws and make decisions relating to the Ministry of Defence and to the State Security, particularly those relating to their powers, organization and budgets (article 43 of the Constitution and article 105 of Law No. 55 of 1980, Law on the National Assembly). Moreover, the Revolution Command Council is the only authority that may, by a two-thirds majority decision, modify the Constitution (article 66). Further, without the approval of the Revolution Command Council (which meets *in camera*), no steps can be taken against the President, the Vice-President or any other members of the Revolution Command Council. In sum, the Revolution Command Council and its members are subject to no legislative or judicial constraints: they are accountable to no one.

73. Without being elected, either directly or indirectly, by the people, the President of the Republic holds, at the same time, the offices of: Head of State, President of the Revolution Command Council, President of the Council of Ministers, Commander-in-Chief of the Armed Forces, and Secretary General of the Baath Party. Perhaps most importantly, he is also de facto chief of State Security in as much as it reports directly to him and to no other

minister. The length of the President's mandate is not specified in the Constitution, although it is presumably for life since all other members of the Government are required to believe in the "Qadissiyah of Saddam" (see, for example, article 14 of Law No. 55 of 1980). The Vice-President and Ministers are appointed by the President and are responsible to him. He can dismiss them at will. He is the head of the executive, has wide-ranging diplomatic powers, presides over the meetings of the Revolution Command Council, promulgates the laws passed by the National Assembly, commands the armed forces, decides on national defence policies and conducts military operations in time of war. To carry out his duties, he has full and sole constitutional authority to decree whatever measures he deems appropriate, for which he alone is responsible.

74. Until very recently, there was a "Revolution Court" which decided all cases of crimes against the State's domestic and foreign security as well as a wide variety of other offences (Revolution Command Council Decree No. 1016 of 1978); there was no possibility to appeal decisions of the Revolution Court. While this Court was eliminated by Revolution Command Council Decree No. 140 of 1991, it is interesting to note that in 1985 the Revolution Command Council had given the President of the Republic the right to annul any decision taken by the Revolution Court and to refer cases back to the Court for reconsideration.

75. In view of the vast constitutional and de facto powers of the President, it is clear that there are at least two systems of law operating within Iraq: a "normal" system of ordinary laws that addresses the typical affairs of daily life, such as highway traffic ordinances, and a parallel system of Revolution Command Council and Presidential Decrees that addresses all matters of internal and external security together with whatever other matters the Revolution Command Council and President care to address. In fact, the power lies essentially in this second system of what may be called "extra-judicial legality" (or what Mr. Tariq Aziz has characterized as "Revolutionary legality"). However, beyond these two systems provided for within the Constitution, there may be said to be yet another order of rule—an order that might be called "extra-legal" in as much as it is not provided for in any texts of Iraqi law. This is the order of rule that proceeds from the personal whims and wishes of a few individuals who hold positions in the inner circle of the President. Irrespective of the extent of their legal authority, these persons have a de facto power to instruct the agents and organs of the State. An example of such power may be seen in the words of Mr. Ali Hassan al-Majid (then Secretary General of the Office for the Organization of the North and now Minister of Defence) when he asserted that he "went beyond the instructions of the leadership" in carrying out his tasks in the north—for which he was subsequently decorated by the President (the quoted words were expressed in a taped conversation, in the possession of the Special Rapporteur, involving a person the Special Rapporteur is confident is Mr. al-Majid). In fact, therefore, one is confronted in Iraq with a totalitarian system which does not take into account the rights of the individual. In such a system, human rights violations are inevitable.

6. *The freedoms of thought, expression and association*

76. The freedoms of thought, expression and association are guaranteed, respectively, by articles 18, 19 and 20 of the Universal Declaration of Human Rights and articles 18, 19 and 22 of the Covenant on Civil and Political Rights. Their proximity in these instruments is no accident in as much as these freedoms are so closely related that restrictions on one of these freedoms almost always has an impact on the others. In Iraq, the relationship is clear in so far as it would appear that the Government will not permit any thought, expression or association that significantly conflicts with the ideology of Arab Baath Socialism as interpreted by the party leadership, led by General Secretary Saddam Hussain.

77. While several Ministers maintained before the Special Rapporteur that Iraq is an open and pluralistic society that tolerates all varieties of beliefs in private and in public, the Special Rapporteur cannot ignore the long-standing government policies aimed against members of the al-Da'wa al-Islamiya Party (which follows Shi'a Islamic teachings), the Communist Party and members of all manner of other political parties and religious or philosophical groupings that do not accord with Baath Party ideology.

78. Perhaps the simplest evidence of the holding of a belief is one's private and public statements and affiliations. Here, thought is clearly linked with expression and association. In Iraq, it has been alleged that personal convictions have been captured by a web of government infiltrators and informants present throughout Iraqi society. Other evidence of convictions is given by confessions which, it is alleged, are frequently extracted under torture. But, the clearest evidence of violation of the freedom of expression continues to be found in Iraqi law which, for example, prescribes severe penalties including death for, *inter alia*, anyone slandering or insulting the President or anyone representing him, the Revolution Command Council, the Baath Party, the National Assembly or the Government (see the Special Rapporteur's interim report, A/46/647, paras. 33 and 80, and page 34 for the Government's response, all referring to Revolu-

tion Command Council Decree No. 840 of 4 November 1986). Irrespective of the number of prosecutions under this law, its very existence clearly inhibits freedom of expression in violation of Iraq's obligations.

79. Turning to the issue of freedom of association, violations come in two principal forms: restrictions on associations of a political nature, and restrictions on the right to form and join independent trade unions. As far as associations of a political nature are concerned, several are specifically outlawed, such as the al-Da'wa al-Islamiya Party and the Communist Party. According to the relevant laws, membership in or association with these groups could carry the death penalty. While the Government denies that the law related to al-Da'wa al-Islamiya Party affiliation has ever "been put into practical effect" (A/46/647, page 35), the very existence of such laws has a far-reaching effect and is a violation of obligations under international human rights law. Moreover, information and testimony received by the Special Rapporteur indicates that this law has been regularly used not only against actual Party affiliates but also against anyone that might be considered an "enemy of the State" as determined by any number of security officers. Indeed, information from one source gave the particulars (including personal photographs) of over 50 individuals who had been allegedly executed for being members of the Party.

80. With respect to the right to form and join trade unions, and notwithstanding the fact that Iraq is a Party to International Labour Organisation Convention No. 98 of 1948 concerning Freedom of Association and the Right to Organise (to which article 22, paragraph 3, of the Covenant on Civil and Political Rights specifically refers), Iraq's Trade Union Organisation Law of 2 June 1987 establishes a trade union structure that places all trade unions within the Government's control. Thus, no independent trade union associations may be formed.

7. Access to food and health care

81. Access to food and health care continues to be a problem for a large part of the population. But, while it is clear that the economic sanctions imposed by the United Nations have had a significant impact on the economy as a whole, the Special Rapporteur repeats the note in his interim report (A/46/647, para. 96) that the sanctions specifically exempt "supplies intended strictly for medical purposes, and, in humanitarian circumstances, foodstuffs". It is the Government of Iraq's obligation, therefore, to adjust its food rations and social welfare to address the specific needs of all its people, and to help international relief agencies serving the most vulnerable.

82. Iraq is not a poor country, and so the Security Council has devised the formula of "oil for food" (and medicine) to allow Iraq to utilize its natural wealth to satisfy the minimum needs of the people. While the formula may be somewhat cumbersome, and perhaps not economically advantageous to the Government of Iraq, the issue at hand does not concern economic advantage and the Special Rapporteur remains convinced that an appropriate formula could have been worked out had there been sufficient political will on the part of the Government. Having recently chosen to break off negotiations to find an appropriate formula, and thereby having dismissed an opportunity to enlarge the available resources of food and medicine at a time when the people are in dire need (according to the Government's own argument), the leadership of Iraq has evidently made a political determination that its notions of "sovereignty" are more important than its obligations to respect human rights.

83. Considering the fact that the Government has itself imposed an economic embargo (specifically including medicaments, foodstuffs, gasoline and heating oil) against the portions of its population essentially living in the Autonomous Region of Kurdistan, and so far as it fails to distribute adequately such goods in the southern marshes, the Government cannot reasonably complain about the embargo instituted under the supervision of the United Nations Security Council. According to information received by the Special Rapporteur and confirmed by his own observations on 6 and 7 January 1992, the Government of Iraq has reduced the flow of rations to those in the Autonomous Region of Kurdistan to only 10 per cent of those given to other citizens. Similar controls on distribution are said to be affecting the southern marshes where great numbers of people are reportedly in need of humanitarian relief. In this connection, it has been reported that the use of health clinics, churches and mosques as centres for food distribution has been prohibited, while the issuance of visas for humanitarian aid personnel has been delayed or they have not been extended. Consequently, while the Government's rationing system and social welfare (together with the efforts of international relief agencies, including specialized United Nations bodies) appears to be functioning relatively satisfactorily through most of the country, its internal embargos and reported interference with the work of certain relief agencies in selected areas is evidence of a policy of discrimination in violation of articles 2, 11 and 12 of the Covenant on Economic, Social and Cultural Rights. The violations against those living in the Autonomous Region of Kurdistan are all the more objectionable because they appear to be directly linked to the Government's political goals of exacting concessions in any future autonomy negotiations.

8. *The situation of women and children*

84. Women and children are protected in general by the two Covenants of 1966 and in particular by articles 2 and 24 of the Covenant on Civil and Political Rights. In addition to the provisions of the Convenants, Iraq is obliged to respect the provisions of the Convention on the Elimination of All Forms of Discrimination against Women. As is often the case, however, women and children suffer both violations against themselves as individuals and hardships resulting from the violations committed against their husbands and fathers. Such violations as summary or arbitrary executions and disappearance have had a harsh impact on the lives of Iraqi women and children, if not as the victims, then as the survivors of victims. As the families of alleged "saboteurs", they have suffered the severest penalties; several of the cases of execution and disappearance that have been brought to the attention of the Special Rapporteur involve women and children, including infants.

85. One of the most serious allegations affecting women is that of systematic rape. According to information and testimony received by the Special Rapporteur, security personnel would sometimes rape a young woman in order to later use her as an informant under the threat that her non-compliance would result in the revelation of her rape, thus subjecting her to public disgrace and ostracism. It has been alleged that some of these rapes were recorded on video-cassettes to be given to the victim's family in the event of non-compliance. Other women were reportedly raped simply as an act of insult or vengence directed against their families. Testimony received from former Iraqi security officers corroborates these allegations.

86. Another unconfirmed allegation of discrimination against women is the allegation that women between the ages of 15 and 45 are still required to obtain an exit visa to leave the country, in contrast to men who are not. It has been explained that the purpose of this particular discrimination is to restrict women and their children from leaving the country to reunite with their husbands and relatives abroad or to otherwise escape the order of repression. Such a restriction would constitute violations of articles 2 and article 12, paragraph 2, of the Covenant on Civil and Political Rights and article 2 of the Convention on the Elimination of All Forms of Discrimination against Women.

9. *Property rights*

87. Information received by the Special Rapporteur points to numerous violations of property rights under the terms of article 17 of the Universal Declaration of Human Rights (refers to the right of everyone "to own property alone as well as in association with others" and the right not to be "arbitrarily deprived" of property). In addition, property rights must be respected in so far as they relate to articles 17, 18 and 27 of the Covenant on Civil and Political Rights and article 15, paragraph 1 (a), of the Covenant on Economic, Social and Cultural Rights.

88. Allegations received by the Special Rapporteur focus on the conduct of the Government in four specific areas: action against alleged criminals; expulsion of those said to be of "Persian ancestry"; discrimination against the Turkoman population; and matters relating to religious and cultural property.

89. With respect to Iraqi action against alleged criminals, it appears to be a routine practice to confiscate both the movable and immovable property of persons accused of criminal activity. Whether or not such accusations have been proved in a court of law, and whether or not there have been convictions and sentences in this regard, seems to be irrelevant to the process of confiscation. As evidence of this apparently widespread practice, the Special Rapporteur heard considerable testimony and is in possession of numerous allegedly official government documents which attest to the practice. In this connection, document 6 in annex II to the present report specifically states that "criminals' movable and immovable property was confiscated because of their association with pro-Iranian subversive groups", while documents 3 and 6 specifically refer to the demolition of the houses of the families of criminals. On this last point, it is evident that the property rights of the said families have clearly been violated in an arbitrary fashion. The heavy impact that such confiscations and demolitions would have on the family members is evident.

90. The practice of confiscation attains an entirely different dimension in the context of the long-established practice of expulsion of those said to be of "Persian ancestry". Information and testimony received by the Special Rapporteur alleges that the process of expulsion was normally accompanied by the confiscation of all movable and immovable property belonging to those expelled. Aside from all types of personal property, confiscation extended to houses, real estate, and commercial property, including businesses. Having been stripped of their possessions and livelihood, these persons were then expelled from the country without any form of compensation.

91. The issue of discrimination against the Turkoman population in relation to property was raised by the Special Rapporteur in his interim report (A/46/647, paras. 48 and 89). While the Government of Iraq initially denied the existence of any such discrimination, responding that "all Iraqis are subject to the same legal regulations concerning the disposal of real estate" and justifying certain "administrative procedures" by the argument of halting the "increasing migration from rural areas" (see

page 48 of the interim report), the Special Rapporteur observes in the Government's reply of 23 January 1992 that such "administrative procedures governing the ownership of land in the Iraqi governates, including the governorate of Ta'mim, have been abolished and any citizen living in the latter governorate, regardless of his ethnic affiliation, is now entitled to acquire ownership in real estate without being obliged to follow any of the administrative procedures that were formerly in force". Acknowledging this admission of discrimination having taken place, the Special Rapporteur wonders what steps are being taken by way of restitution or at least compensation for those discriminated against.

92. As regards matters relating to religious and cultural properties, the Special Rapporteur is especially disturbed by reliable reports of expropriation, confiscation and destruction of properties belonging to religious and cultural communities, specifically with regard to the destruction of churches and mosques, the destruction of religious schools, the confiscation of books and artifacts, and the expropriation of titles to real estate and corporate entities. However, in so far as these matters are directly related to other violations affecting these communities, they will be addressed below.

93. While the violations referred to above are serious in their own right, the Special Rapporteur is even more concerned about the reported abuses that their lawful sanction has permitted. Specifically, it has been reported that the large amount of wealth often involved in such violations has caused various authorities to invoke spurious allegations as a means of obtaining desired property or injuring personal enemies. Such abuses appear to have occurred on a large scale, owing largely to the absence of the rule of law, as discussed above.

B. Violations affecting ethnic and religious communities

General observations

94. It should be noted that the observations made elsewhere in this report also cover cases involving the ethnic and religious communities of Iraq, as well as all other parts of the state population. In this chapter, attention is drawn to situations which particularly affect these communities.

95. As noted above, Iraq is a party to the International Convention on the Elimination of All Forms of Racial Discrimination. Paragraph 4 of article 1, paragraph 2 of article 2, and article 5 of this Convention lay down certain duties of States Parties with regard to the undertaking of special measures for the purposes of establishing and maintaining equality between racial and ethnic groups within a country. In this relation, it would

seem that the internal blockade against the Kurds and actions taken by the Government of Iraq to enforce many of the other official activities described in this chapter are contrary to the obligations the Government has accepted under this Convention.

1. Violations affecting the Kurds

96. The Kurdish population in Iraq numbers between 3.5 and 4 million. With its own language, history and cultural identity, the Kurdish population is territorily identified with the north-eastern part of Iraq running from the plains of Kirkuk to the mountainous borders of Turkey and Iran. While clearly identifiable as a cultural and linguistic minority in Iraq, Kurdish identity is not determined by any particular religious belief, although they are generally Sunni Moslems. Especially important, however, is the role of tribe or clan and its identity with traditional lands which have been cultivated for centuries.

(a) Genocidal practices

97. When large-scale violations of human rights are inflicted on one or more communities of a State population, in addition to those violations which have been directed against the population of the country as a whole, the question inevitably arises whether a government has engaged in genocidal practices as defined in article II of the 1948 Convention on the Prevention and Punishment of the Crime of Genocide, to which Iraq is a State Party. In this instance, the inquiry must address allegations brought against the Government of Iraq relating to the mass murder and execution of Kurds, the destruction of Kurdish towns and villages, forced urbanization and internal deportation, limits on ownership of private property by Kurds in areas designated by the authorities for inhabitance by the majority population, restrictions on agricultural activities, and the use of excessive force, including chemical weapons, against the Kurds in times of conflict.

98. The Special Rapporteur has heard in person and received in writing several testimonies about mass executions and murder of Kurdish civilians. A particularly gruesome account describes in detail the mass murder of Kurdish men, women and children during the "Anfal Operations" (see para. 103 below) of the Iraqi armed forces in 1988. An eye-witness, who had served as a governmental employee assisting with the many trucks used to bring victims numbering in the thousands to the execution sites, outlined an operation and identified the location of the resulting mass graves. It is worth noting that this account coincides with the horrifying story told by a young boy who survived a very similar massacre.

99. Several other accounts detail alleged mass executions and other atrocities committed by the Govern-

ment against the Kurds which go beyond the cruelty and brutality directed against the population at large.

100. It is clear that deliberate actions of the Iraqi Government have caused refugee flows, forced urbanization and internal deportation affecting hundreds of thousands of Kurds. Detailed reports allege the destruction of some four thousand villages affecting well over a million people. One such report running into hundreds of pages details with charts and maps the destruction of 3,839 villages, hamlets and towns, 1,757 schools, 2,457 mosques and places of worship and 271 hospitals and clinics, along with the deportation of 219,828 families. However, according to Mr. Jalal Talabani of the Patriotic Union of Kurdistan, 1,732 villages have been rebuilt to some degree during the past year.

101. Another alleged method employed by the Iraqi authorities and leading to Kurdish displacement has been the denial of or placing of limits on the ownership or use of private property by Kurdish civilians, including private homes and farmland, in areas which the authorities have designated for inhabitance by the majority population or have designated "prohibited security zones". The Special Rapporteur has thus received recent reports of houses having been demolished in Kirkuk and of the Government preventing sowing in nearby and other farming districts. A concerted programme of urbanization or "village amalgamization" as the Iraqi authorities called it (see document 2 in annex II [not reproduced here]) has consequently changed the lifestyles and threatened the culture of the hundreds of thousands of persons affected. Information and testimony received allege a policy aimed at ending the traditional agricultural practices of a large part of the Kurdish population; sowing and cultivation has frequently been forbidden in large areas said to cover up to 75 per cent of the arable land, seeds have been stolen, hundreds of poultry farms closed and explosive mines laid over large parts of traditional farmland. These practices (especially the laying of explosive mines which have caused and continue to cause terrible injuries and loss of life) have been instituted in particular in areas under dispute with regard to the delimitation of the proposed autonomous zone.

102. The use of excessive force, including chemical weapons, against the Kurds is an established pattern. The Special Rapporteur heard several eye-witness accounts by survivors of various attacks by the Iraqi armed forces using bombardments from the air and chemical weapons against the unprotected civilian populations, resulting in large numbers of deaths and injuries. Specific attacks have been well-documented (as discussed above). In addition, the Special Rapporteur has heard a number of other accounts concerning indiscriminate shelling and the use of other heavy weaponry against unarmed or lightly

armed Kurds during the various stages of the March 1991 uprisings.

103. Perhaps the most heinous violations against the Kurds involve the systematic execution of the families of so-called "saboteurs". Documents said to be from Security offices in Kurdish cities corroborate the existence of a series of "Anfal" operations administered under the Office for the Organisation of the North between the autumn of 1987 and mid-1989. A great many of these documents would appear to refer only to confiscation of property, control of cattle movement and the closure of poultry farms, or the relocation of people into "amalgamated villages". However, when read as a whole and with the interspersed records of mass executions of "saboteurs" and their families, the scope of these operations becomes more and more apparent. Moreover, in as much as certain documents specify huge numbers of people (such as document 6, para. 5, in annex II [not reproduced here]) and other documents describe "saboteurs" as including the "Barzani group" (referring to the clan of that name), and in so far as none of the actions under these operations were subject to judicial review, it is evident that the scale of the operations was massive. Further, the previously referred to audio-taped conversation of the then Secretary General of the Office for the Organisation of the North (and present Minister of Defence) Mr. Ali Hassan al-Majid, confirms that these operations were indiscriminately aimed against Kurds as such. Hence, and in the light of the already over 15,000 names of disappeared Kurds that have been brought to the attention of the Special Rapporteur, Kurdish claims of some 182,000 disappeared persons cannot easily be dismissed. Thus, it would seem beyond doubt that these policies, and the "Anfal" operations in particular, bear the marks of a genocide-type design.

(b) The internal blockade

104. It is noteworthy that, at a time when the Iraqi Government is adamantly protesting against the embargo imposed by the international community, the same Government has put up an internal blockade on the import of food, fuel and medicines to the Kurdish areas of the country. Referred to by one Kurdish leader as "a siege within the siege", there can be no doubt that the internal blockade has resulted in more hardship for the most vulnerable in this part of the country. Particular hardship has been endured by the Kurdish community during this cold winter as the Government instituted the blockade, including of paraffin for heating, on 23 October 1991, just as the winter started setting in. Implemented through a series of armed checkpoints on every route in and out of that part of the Autonomous Region which is under Kurdish control, scrupulous sentries confiscate the small-

est quantities of food and fuel, leaving half a tank of gas in cars and burning the rest.

105. Apart from imports of basic goods, the blockade involves the wholesale withdrawal of civil services from Kurdish areas, either by removing centrally based civil servants or by withholding the salaries of local civil servants. Obviously, this practice has resulted in the denial or reduction of social and other services which a government is expected to render. Remuneration for pensioners is also being withheld.

(c) Autonomy

106. International human rights law provides for equality for individuals and groups of different national, ethnic, linguistic and religious origins within one and the same State. As a means of achieving this objective, the relevant international instruments prohibit discrimination and lay down rules concerning special measures and special rights for the benefit of those disadvantaged. In certain spheres of national life, such as in the fields of education, language, culture and religion, these rules are quite specific in nature and content, while States, still under the same obligation of guaranteeing and maintaining equality and non-discrimination, have so far enjoyed greater discretion in the regulation of other national sectors, such as those affecting their political and economic order.

107. The Government of Iraq has repeatedly emphasized the fact that it has chosen the path of suggesting autonomy for the Kurds. In itself, such a choice deserves praise because, although practised by many countries, it is not part of international human rights standards. However, in the light of the history and fate of these autonomy regulations and negotiations, not least in the light of recent and indeed current developments, serious doubts arise as to the significance of the autonomy which the Iraqi Government is willing to grant to the Kurds. The peaceful resolution of the conflict and harmonious relations appear low on the agenda of the Government. Its insistence on placing officials from security agencies within the autonomous zone, the arbitrary and unilateral delimitization of the Region's borders, and the ongoing internal blockade of food and fuel defeat the very purpose of the exercise.

108. At present, the negotiations on autonomy seem to have reached a complete impasse. In this context, it is worth repeating the clear and unambiguous statement of Deputy Prime Minister Tariq Aziz in conversation with the Special Rapporteur on 8 January 1992: discussing the issue of the negotiations on autonomy, Mr. Aziz asserted that "Iraq would be the first to recognize Kurdish independence". However, the Special Rapporteur equally notes the expressed will of the Kurdish representatives to

resolve their disputes with the central authority within the framework of an autonomy agreement.

2. Violations affecting the Assyrians

109. According to information and testimony received by the Special Rapporteur, the Assyrians (a community primarily located in northern Iraq) have reportedly suffered continuous persecution since the coming to power of the Baath Party. The majority of the Assyrian population in Iraq belongs to the Christian faiths of Chaldae and Nestor, and, to a lesser extent, the Syrian-Orthodox Jacobites. Their total number is estimated at about one million, though some estimates are considerably higher.

110. Information received alleges that the Iraqi military destroyed large numbers of Assyrian villages throughout the past two decades, killing many of the inhabitants and forcing others to flee. The Assyrian community was also affected by mass internal deportations away from the northern border region. Further, it was reported that, in the course of air raids on Assyrian villages, after massacres, and after forced relocations, but also because of administrative regulations of the Baath Party, numerous Assyrian churches and monasteries (some of them over one thousand years old) were destroyed. In 1987, for example, a total of 85 Chaldean and Nestorian monasteries and churches were reportedly destroyed.

111. In an appeal made to humanitarian and international organizations on 19 September 1988, Bishop Zia Bobo Doubatou, the leader of the Assyrian Eastern Church in northern Iraq, denounced the continuing oppression and persecution of both Kurds and Assyrians in the northern Iraqi governorates of Heenoy, Dohuk, Arbil, Kirkuk and Sulaimaniya. Bishop Doubatou asserted violations ranging from executions, imprisonment for political reasons and destruction of churches and monasteries to the razing of villages. In particular, the Bishop alleged the use of chemical weapons, poisonous gases, and phosphorous and napalm bombs in the regions of Berwari, Afra and Al-Sheikhan, causing the death and injury of thousands of people as well as the loss of their homes of more than 150,000 people who fled to Turkey or Iran. Although the Bishop's letter was written some two months after the cease-fire between Iraq and Iran, he also alleged that a border strip 50 kilometres deep had been evacuated by the military after the destruction of villages.

112. Other information received by the Special Rapporteur includes lists of allegations concerning the destruction of villages and the deportation of people from the regions of Berwari Balla, Nahla ('Oqra), Zakho, Dohuk and Neeroy Reekan between 1969 and 1987. Among these, the case of Soureya village stands out: it is

alleged that the villagers—numbering 700, including children, women and elderly persons—were killed and burnt at the hands of Lieutenant Colonel Abd al-Karim al Jouhaifi.

113. Notwithstanding the testimony to the contrary of three Christian leaders received by the Special Rapporteur in the al-Rashid Hotel in Baghdad on the evening of 8 January 1992, reports of the violations referred to above were corroborated by official documents said to have been found in Iraqi security offices and by testimony received from victims and eye-witnesses. One such testimony was received from a former Iraqi soldier who claimed to have taken part in the destruction of several Assyrian villages in 1988.

3. *Violations affecting the Turkomans*

114. The Turkoman minority is considered to be the third largest ethnic group in Iraq. Originally from Central Asia, they began settling in Iraq one thousand years ago and still inhabit the north and middle of Iraq, concentrated mainly in the provinces of Mosul, Arbil, Kirkuk and Diyala. At present, it is said, they number some two million people.

115. According to information received, a declaration on the rights of ethnic minorities, dated 24 January 1970, originally permitted the use of the Turkoman language in primary education and in newspapers and magazines. The Turkoman community was also granted permission for the broadcasting of radio and television programmes. However, according to reports, all of these rights were withdrawn a year later and the Turkoman population was subjected to systematic discrimination and abuse.

116. Alleged oppression and persecution includes arrest without charge, torture, internal deportation and exile, confiscation of personal and community properties, and execution. Such oppression and persecution is said to originate in a government policy to replace the Turkomans with Arabs in Kirkuk and other cities and towns where the Turkomans are particularly represented. In particular, Turkoman citizens of the Kirkuk and Ta'mim governorates are reported to have been subjected to restrictions on the purchase and sale of real estate (as discussed above): they have been allowed to sell only to Arabs.

117. Other communications addressed to the Special Rapporteur similarly denounce the discrimination suffered by the Turkoman minority, particularly the fact that they have been forced to leave their lands in the regions they have been inhabiting for centuries. It has further been alleged that, contrary to official statements according to which the Turkomans are considered a minority and thus granted the right to exercise all their cultural rights, the Iraqi Government obliges them to be registered either as Kurds or as Arabs. As such, the people are denied their rights as a Turkoman community.

4. *Violations affecting the Shi'as*

118. The Special Rapporteur has received considerable and significant information concerning the destruction, especially after the March 1991 uprisings, of the traditional culture of the Shi'as who constitute a large part of the population of Iraq. The Shi'a of southern Iraq are the descendants of the original population of Mesopotamia. Their culture, especially in their holy cities, has been described as extraordinarily rich.

119. With respect to violations affecting the community as a whole, certain events are relevant. For example, on 23 March 1991, the shrine of Immam Ali at Najaf was sacked and desecrated. This shrine is as sacred to the Shi'a as Mecca, since it contains the tomb of the Imman. All treasures stored in two large rooms of the shrine (jewels, gold and manuscripts) were said to have been taken by the Iraqi army. When the Special Rapporteur visited the vast Wadi al-Salaam cemetery, where Shi'a pilgrims from as far away as India and Afghanistan have been buried for over one thousand years, he noticed that a highway is being constructed over the graves in what is alleged to be an act of deliberate desecration; leaders of the religious community have not been consulted. In addition, the thousand-year-old Houza, the Shi'a university, was closed along with many other schools, private as well as religious, at Najaf, while libraries with manuscripts that constituted part of the Islamic tradition were destroyed.

120. The Government has also been waging a concerted attack against the Shi'a clergy. The number of clergy at Najaf had been reduced from eight or nine thousand twenty years ago to two thousand 10 years later and eight hundred before the uprisings of 1991. It is alleged that virtually all of them are now under arrest or disappeared, as the Baath regime is seeking to destroy Shi'a culture by wiping out its traditional leaders of the *ulema* class. Several of them have allegedly been executed. Among those tortured and murdered was Ayatollah Bakr al-Sadr, a noted poet and author of famous works of Islamic philosophy. Among those who are still under constant surveillance is the 95-year-old Grand Ayatollah Abul Qasim al-Musawi al-Khoei, together with members of his family and staff, as well as teaching clergymen. Thousands of other Iraqis in the south are said to have suffered the same fate as the clergymen: arrests, imprisonment, torture and execution. It has been estimated that 150,000 people have been arrested in southern Iraq, 15,000 people from Najaf alone.

121. In the aftermath of the uprisings in March 1991, the shrine of Immam Hussain in Karbala was shelled, badly damaged and desecrated. The Baathists later claimed that this was the work of the rebels, but it seems inconceivable that the Shi'a would defile their holiest shrine in such a manner.

122. In Samarra, the third among the sacred cities of the Shi'a, the Special Rapporteur was able to establish that the only Shi'a *madrasi* (school) was destroyed and levelled. According to information received, this happened some weeks after the uprisings. In addition to this destruction, all the Shi'a clergy of Samarra, numbering some 48, have reportedly been arrested. Further, the Shi'a call to prayer, reinstated in a limited fashion in Najaf and Karbala, is said to be still prohibited in Samarra, as has been the Muharram mourning for Immam Hussain (the central religious ritual for all Shi'a Muslims) for the last five years.

123. In addition to the aforementioned, the Government's measures to suppress Shi'a religious and cultural rights have allegedly included:

(a) Restrictions on the public practice of Shi'a rites as prescribed by their religious notables;

(b) Seizure from the Shi'a *ulema* of the administration of the Holy Shrines;

(c) Surveillance and intimidation of worshippers in Shi'a mosques and halls;

(d) Closure of Shi'a religious colleges and universities and prohibition of religious seminars except under official sanction;

(e) Restriction on the movements of religious leaders and scholars, both within the country and in terms of travel abroad;

(f) The launching of frequent "informational" campaigns against Shi'aism, accusing it of deviationism and heresy;

(g) Prohibition or strict censorship in the publication of many Shi'a books, magazines and pamphlets, while the Government's own religious affairs units refuse to countenance the publishing of any Shi'a works, contemporary or traditional;

(h) Prohibition of the broadcasting of any radio or television programme with Shi'a content;

(i) The launching of a campaign to prohibit the application of Shi'a law on personal and family matters, such as in the rites of marriage, inheritance, etc.;

(j) Prohibition of communication between Shi'as outside Iraq and the supreme body on religious authority in the city of Najaf al-Ashraf;

(k) Special restrictions affecting the religious students and scholars who remain.

124. Several other measures have been said to have been undertaken by the Iraqi Government in its policy against the Shi'a cultural heritage. These are said to include the following forms of educational repression:

(a) Closure of all Shi'a parochial schools;

(b) Prohibition of the teaching of the Shi'a creed in any form in the State school system which, in its official curriculum, teaches only a variant of the Sunnite creed, despite the fact that the largest number of school children are Shi'a;

(c) Nationalization, expropriation and closure of al-Fiqh College in Najaf (officially part of the state-sponsored University of Kufa); reports indicate that this was the only remaining Shi'a academic religious college in Iraq teaching Shi'a theology and religious studies. According to these reports, its buildings have been converted into a commercial market and all of its students were transferred to the College of Shari'a (teaching Sunni theology) in Samarra, which is registered as part of the state-sponsored University al-Mustansariya;

(d) Nationalization, expropriation and closure of the Faculty of Islamic Jurisprudence and Literature at Baghdad, Department of Religion, which is attached to the Faculty of Shari'a at Baghdad University;

(e) Nationalization of the Faculty of Jurisprudence in order to attach it to the Ministry of Higher Education;

(f) Refusal of visas to foreign Muslim students in order to keep them from contributing to Shi'a religious scientific studies in Iraq, while other students and lecturers have been forced to leave the country under different pretexts, such as violation of the laws of residency.

125. The Special Rapporteur has received several lists containing the names of a large number of people detained by the Government, among them numerous people from the Grand Ayatullah's family, staff, and their relatives, and various Iranian, Lebanese, Indian, Bahraini, Afghani and Pakistani nationals (see, for example, appendix 2 to the interim report) as well as a list of religious scholars killed between 1974 and 1987. He has also received lists of large numbers of holy shrines, mosques, husainiyas and other religious institutions and schools, Muslim cementeries and public libraries destroyed by the Government forces. Evidently, the situation of the Shi'a religious community is extremely serious. However, the situation of the Shi'a community in the southern marshes appears to be more urgent and so warrants particular attention.

126. In connection with the so-called "Marsh Arabs" (an ancient people living in the souther marshes), it is worth noting a series of articles published in *Al-Thawra* (the Baath Party newspaper) in April 1991, in which it was said that the Marsh Arabs are a "monkey-faced" people who are not "real Iraqis" but are rather the descendents of black slaves brought to the south in the Middle Ages. The articles condemn the Marsh Arabs'

culture as "primitive, debased and un-Iraqi". Their habits of personal hygiene and their intellects are said to be inferior.

127. According to information received by the Special Rapporteur, the Iraqi army is said to encircle the region of the marshes at the present time. The army is said to dispose of several helicopter airports within the region. Recent and continuing measures instituted by the Iraqi military forces against the population of the marshes (including Marsh Arabs, internally displaced persons and refugees, and army deserters) are said to include the tightening of control over food destined for the area, the confiscation of boats, and the evacuation of all areas within three kilometres of the marshlands. Further reports indicate that military attacks have been launched against the Marsh Arabs between 4 December 1991 and 18 January 1992, resulting in hundreds of deaths. Animal and bird life have also been said to have been killed in large numbers, while the marsh waters themselves have allegedly been filled with toxic chemicals. The apparent recent and continuing nature of the policy aimed against this particular part of the Shi'a community is most disturbing.

C. Hostage-taking and the use of persons as "human shields"

128. Iraqi acts of hostage-taking and the use of persons as "human shields" are two of the most conspicuous violations and are alarming in the complex of violations they reveal: the taking of hostages is contrary to the terms of article 13 of the Universal Declaration of Human Rights and article 12 of the Covenant on Civil and Political Rights, and it is strictly prohibited by article 34 of the Fourth Geneva Convention of 1949. While the Special Rapporteur has already addressed the issue in relation to the events leading up to the recent Gulf war (A/46/647, paras. 24 and 76), subsequent allegations indicate that these events were not unique, but rather reflect a pattern of behaviour going back to the beginning of the Iran-Iraq war. Specifically, testimony received in refugee camps in southern Iran concerned Iranian civilians who had been taken hostage by attacking Iraqi forces in the southern Iranian border regions as long ago as the early part of the Iran-Iraq war. This testimony asserts that many Iranian civilians were rounded up by occupying Iraqi forces and transported back to Iraqi camps where they were generally mistreated and tortured, if not arbitrarily executed. Witnesses claim that many Iranian were forcibly conscripted into the Iraqi army to return and fight the Iranian army, which would be a "grave breach" under the terms of article 147 of the Fourth Geneva Convention of 1949. Those who refused were subject to summary execution, which would be a "war crime"

under the terms of article 6 of the Charter of Nuremberg. Several of those so brought out of Iran remain missing, while others stripped of their identity documents appear stateless.

129. The story of hostage-taking involving Iranian civilians during the Iran-Iraq war parallels strongly the proven cases of hostage-taking during the occupation of Kuwait. The Government of Iraq originally took some several thousand non-Kuwaiti foreigners hostage in Iraq and Kuwait. The release of these persons before the start of the coalition's attacks was off-set by the taking of Kuwaiti and other civilian hostages (including, among others, Egyptians and Saudis). Although many of these persons escaped during the March 1991 uprisings in southern Iraq and many others were released by the Government of Iraq as part of the cease-fire agreement, allegations remain to the effect that Iraq continues to hold 2,101 Kuwaitis along with small numbers of nationals of other States. For its part, the Kuwaiti Association to Defend War Victims (a non-governmental organization) has a list of 1,053 persons of various nationalities who are allegedly still being held hostage in Iraq; 546 of these cases reportedly involve persons who have either been seen in detention in Iraq or were seen being abducted during the occupation of Kuwait. In reply to these allegations of the continuing detention of hostages in Iraq, the Government has acknowledged that there remain a significant number of Kuwaitis in Iraq, but asserts that they are all at liberty to return and have simply chosen not to do so (E/CN.4/1992/64, para.1).

130. According to reports from former hostages and according to testimonies received, those detained were subject to various forms and degrees of mistreatment. Allegations include: detention in inhumane conditions, lack of access to food and clean water, lack of medical treatment, the cutting of women's hair, beatings, rapes, and mental and physical torture. According to the testimonies of those formerly taken as hostages during the Iran-Iraq war, many were also forced to do labour while many others were arbitrarily or summarily executed. Aside from the clear breaches of human rights law that these allegations entail, such acts as are alleged are violations of article 27 of the Fourth Geneva Convention of 1949 and constitute "grave breaches" under article 147 of that same Convention. It is further to be noted that the killing of hostages constitutes a "war crime" in accordance with article 6 of the Charter of Nuremberg.

131. In as much as certain of those taken hostage were used as "human shields" to protect potential military targets, Iraq committed outrageous acts in violation of a host of human rights norms and in violation of article 28 of the Fourth Geneva Convention of 1949, which

reads as follows: "The presence of a protected person may not be used to render certain points or areas immune from military operations". Article 23 of the Third Geneva Convention of 1949 similarly prohibits the use of prisoners of war as "human shields".

132.   Given that many of the above allegations have been definitely proven, and given that Iraq has in fact admitted to the taking of hostages and the use of certain of them as "human shields", and given further that there can be no excuse for such grave breaches of the norms of international human rights and humanitarian law, the Special Rapporteur expresses the hope that appropriate compensation will be paid to the victims of these violations.

D.   *The plight of refugees*

133.   Undoubtedly the most striking testament to the situation of human rights in Iraq in recent years has been the decision of millions of Iraqi citizens to flee their homes in search of refuge. Perhaps this fact alone speaks volumes about the order of repression suffered for so long by so many. There can be no doubt that these people gave testimony with their feet to the extent of violations of human rights in Iraq.

134.   During his January visits to Iraq and certain of its neighbouring countries, the Special Rapporteur saw with his own eyes the conditions these people had chosen to endure as refugees and heard with his own ears their stories of the outrages and indignities many of them had experienced and virtually all had witnessed. Of the over two million people who fled to the Kurdish hills and southern deserts to escape the indiscriminate attacks in March 1991 and the subsequent repression in April 1991, several hundreds of thousands of whom found temporary refuge in neighbouring countries, some 83,000 persons in Iran and another 33,000 in Saudi Arabia still remained in refugee camps at the time of the Special Rapporteur's visits in mid-January 1992. In the course of their flight many became separated from their families or saw their very young, elderly and sick perish in the escape. Having left their homes and belongings behind them, these people now have to spend their lives as refugees. Many display the physical scars of their tortures, while all carry the deep emotional burden of their experience. Against this background, the Special Rapporteur cannot doubt that these refugees remain outside Iraq owing to a well-founded fear of persecution.

135.   In assessing the causes of this flight of refugees, the Special Rapporteur observes that the arrival of refugees across frontiers corresponds directly with expulsions (forced eviction, confiscation of properties and the stripping of all rights and legal status), the use of chemical weapons against Kurds in 1987 and 1988, and the use of weapons of indiscriminate and mass destruction during the March 1991 uprisings.

136.   It is clear that the Government of Iraq is responsible for the causes of this flight of millions of refugees and remains responsible for the continued suffering of these people, in addition to that of the hundreds of thousands of persons expelled in previous years.

   . . .

Document 104

Statement by the President of the Security Council concerning Iraq's compliance with relevant resolutions of the Council

S/23609, 19 February 1992

The members of the Security Council express their gratitude to the Secretary-General for the report submitted to the Security Council on 18 February 1992 (S/23606).

The members of the Security Council note that while progress has been made, much still remains to be done to implement the relevant resolutions of the Council. The members of the Council are gravely concerned by Iraq's continued failure to acknowledge all its obligations under Council resolutions 707 (1991) and 715 (1991), and its continued rejection of the plans of the Secretary-General and of the Director-General of the International Atomic Energy Agency (S/22871/Rev.1 and S/22872/Rev.1 and Corr.1 as approved by resolution 715 (1991)) for ongoing monitoring and verification of Iraq's compliance with its obligations under paragraphs 10, 12 and 13 of resolution 687 (1991).

Ongoing monitoring and verification of Iraq's obligations is an integral part of Security Council resolution 687 (1991), which established a cease-fire and provided the conditions essential to the restoration of peace and security in the region. Such ongoing monitoring and verification is a step of the utmost importance towards the goal set out in paragraph 14 of that resolution.

Iraq's failure to acknowledge its obligations under resolutions 707 (1991) and 715 (1991), its rejection up until now of the two plans for ongoing monitoring and verification and its failure to provide the full, final and complete disclosure of its weapons capabilities constitute a continuing material breach of the relevant provisions of resolution 687 (1991). Unconditional agreement by Iraq to implement these obligations is one of the essential preconditions to any reconsideration by the Council under paragraphs 21 and 22 of resolution 687 (1991) of the prohibitions referred to in those paragraphs.

The members of the Council support the decision of the Secretary-General to dispatch a special mission headed by the Executive Chairman of the Special Commission to visit Iraq immediately to meet and discuss with the highest levels of the Iraqi Government for the purpose of securing the unconditional agreement by Iraq to implement all its relevant obligations under resolutions 687 (1991), 707 (1991) and 715 (1991). The mission should stress the serious consequences if such agreement to implement is not forthcoming. The Secretary-General is requested to report on the results of the special mission to the Security Council upon its return.

Document 105

Statement by the President of the Security Council concerning UNSCOM's special mission to Baghdad, 21-24 February 1992, and Iraq's compliance with relevant Security Council resolutions

S/23663, 28 February 1992

The members of the Security Council express their gratitude to the Secretary-General for the report submitted to the Council on 27 February 1992 (S/23643), transmitting the results of the special mission dispatched to Iraq by the Secretary-General pursuant to the statement of the President of the Council of 19 February 1992 (S/23609). The members of the Council approve in full the conclusions of the special mission as contained in the report and in particular its finding that Iraq is not prepared to give its unconditional agreement to implement all of its obligations under resolutions 687 (1991), 707 (1991) and 715 (1991).

The members of the Council deplore and condemn the failure of the Government of Iraq to provide the special mission with full, final and complete disclosure, as required by resolution 707 (1991), of all aspects of its programmes to develop weapons of mass destruction and ballistic missiles with a range greater than 150 kilometres, including launchers, and of all holdings of such weapons, their components and production facilities and locations, as well as all other nuclear programmes; and the failure of Iraq to comply with the plans for ongoing monitoring and verification (S/22871/Rev.1 and S/22872/Rev.1 and Corr.1) approved by resolution 715 (1991). In the statement made on 19 February 1992 (S/23609) prior to the dispatch of the special mission to Iraq the Council noted that Iraq's behaviour constituted a material breach of resolution 687 (1991). Regrettably this continues to be the case.

Furthermore, the members of the Council equally deplore and condemn Iraq's failure, within the time prescribed by the Special Commission at the request of Iraq, to commence destruction of ballistic missile-related equipment designated for destruction by the Special Commission. The members of the Council reaffirm that it is for the Special Commission alone to determine which items must be destroyed under paragraph 9 of resolution 687 (1991). Therefore, the Government of Iraq's letter of 28 February 1992 to the Executive Chairman of the Special Commission is unacceptable. Iraq's refusal to implement the determinations of the Special Commission constitutes a further material breach of the relevant provisions of resolution 687 (1991).

The members of the Council demand that Iraq immediately implement all its obligations under Council resolution 687 (1991) and subsequent resolutions on Iraq. The members of the Council require the Government of Iraq to communicate directly to the Council without further delay an authoritative and unconditional acknowledgement of its agreement to accept and implement the above noted obligations, including specifically to comply with the determination of the Special Commission requiring the destruction of ballistic missile-related equipment. The members of the Council emphasize that Iraq must be aware of the serious consequences of continued material breaches of resolution 687 (1991).

The members of the Council note that an Iraqi delegation is prepared to come to New York as soon as it is invited to do so. The members of the Council have asked its President to extend such an invitation to the delegation to come to New York without further delay. The members of the Council intend in any event to continue their consideration of this question no later than the week beginning 9 March 1992.

Document 106

Decision 9 taken by the Governing Council of the United Nations Compensation Commission: Propositions and conclusions on compensation for business losses: types of damages and their valuation

S/AC.26/1992/9, 6 March 1992

Decision taken by the Governing Council of the United Nations Compensation Commission during the resumed Fourth Session, at the 23rd meeting, held on 6th March 1992

Propositions and Conclusions on Compensation for Business Losses: Types of Damages and Their Valuation

1. The propositions and conclusions contained in this Decision shall apply to compensation for the loss of earnings or profits and other business losses covered by Security Council resolution 687 (1991).

2. The basic premise underlying all of the findings concerning business losses is that, pursuant to paragraph 16 of Security Council resolution 687 (1991), Iraq "is liable under international law for any direct loss, damage, including environmental damage and the depletion of natural resources, or injury to foreign Governments, nationals and corporations as a result of Iraq's unlawful invasion and occupation of Kuwait".

3. This Decision does not attempt to describe all of the conceivable factual and legal situations resulting from Iraq's invasion and occupation of Kuwait. Bearing in mind Security Council resolution 687 (1991), other types of losses may have been suffered, and they are eligible for compensation if they result from Iraq's invasion and occupation of Kuwait. Ultimately, it will be up to the Commissioners to identify the applicable principles and apply them to the circumstances of particular cases.

4. The propositions and conclusions contained in this Decision are not intended to be a comprehensive statement of relevant principles. The Governing Council will review the matter and will provide further guidance concerning business losses as required in the future. In particular, the Governing Council will request the Secretariat to consider the question of steps which might be taken to protect against multiple recovery of compensation by claimants, or to confirm that claimants have attempted to avail themselves of particular possible sources of recovery, as a prerequisite to relief from the Commission.

5. When reference is made herein to corporations and other legal entities, it is understood that such corporations or other legal entities may be either publicly or privately owned enterprises.

6. The trade embargo and related measures*, and the economic situation caused thereby, will not be accepted as the basis for compensation. Compensation will be provided to the extent that Iraq's unlawful invasion and occupation of Kuwait constituted a cause of direct loss, damage or injury which is separate and distinct from the trade embargo and related measures. (Where, for example, the full extent of the loss, damage or injury arose as a direct result of Iraq's unlawful invasion and occupation of Kuwait, it should be compensated notwithstanding the fact that it may also be attributable to the trade embargo and related measures). The total amount of compensable losses will be reduced to the extent that those losses could reasonably have been avoided. Further guidance on the matters dealt with in this paragraph will be provided by the Governing Council for the use of the Commissioners when assessing claims.

I. LOSSES IN CONNECTION WITH CONTRACTS OR PAST BUSINESS PRACTICE

(A) *Contracts*

7. The following general conclusions apply with regard to Iraq's liability for contract losses.

Contracts with Iraq

8. Where Iraq itself was a contracting party and breached its contractual obligations, Iraq is liable under general contract law to compensate for all actual losses suffered by the other contracting party, including, *inter alia*, losses relating to specially manufactured goods. Future lost profits may be compensable in such a case if they can be calculated under the contract with reasonable certainty. An alternative measure of damages may apply where a governing contract specifically provides for a particular measure, except that the amount of compensation provided should not exceed the loss actually suffered. Breaches of contract not resulting from the invasion and occupation of Kuwait are not within the jurisdiction of the Commission.

9. Where Iraq did not breach a contract to which it was a party, but continuation of the contract became

---

*The trade embargo and related measures refers to the prohibitions in United nations Security Council Resolution 661 (1990) and relevant subsequent resolutions and the measures taken by states pursuant thereto.

impossible for the other party as a result of Iraq's invasion and occupation of Kuwait, Iraq is liable for any direct loss the other party suffered as a result, including lost profits. In such a situation, Iraq should not be allowed to invoke *force majeure* or similar contract provisions, or general principles of contract excuse, to avoid its liability.

Contracts where Iraq is not a party

10. Where losses have been suffered in connection with contracts to which Iraq was not a party, the following conclusions apply. Iraq is responsible for the losses that have resulted from the invasion and occupation of Kuwait. A relevant consideration may be whether the contracting parties could resume the contract after the lifting of the embargo against Kuwait, and whether they have in fact resumed the contract. Iraq principally cannot be relieved from its responsibility by *force majeure* provisions of contracts to which it is not a party or contract excuse rules of other applicable laws.

(B) *Past business practice*

11. Where a loss has been suffered relating to a transaction that has been part of a business practice or course of dealing, Iraq is liable according to the principles that apply to contract losses. No liability exists for losses related to transactions that were only expected to take place based on a previous course of dealing.

II. Losses Relating to Tangible Assets

12. Where direct losses were suffered as a result of Iraq's invasion and occupation of Kuwait with respect to tangible assets, Iraq is liable for compensation. Typical actions of this kind would have been expropriation, removal, theft or destruction of particular items of property by Iraqi authorities. Whether the taking of property was lawful or not is not relevant for Iraq's liability if it did not provide for compensation.

13. In a case where business property had been lost because it had been left unguarded by company personnel departing due to the situation in Iraq and Kuwait, such loss may be considered as resulting directly from the invasion and occupation.

14. On the other hand, losses that occurred because company personnel was detained by Iraqi authorities, must clearly be considered a direct result. In this context, it is relevant to note the Hague Regulations on Land Warfare annexed to Conventions II of 1899 and IV of 1907 respecting the Laws and Customs of War on Land, which require that an occupying power has to restore and to ensure public order and safety as far as possible (Hague Regulations, Article 43).

15. Depending on the type of asset and the circumstances of the case, one of several valuation methods may be used. Methods typically used to value tangible assets are book value and replacement value. *Book value* is considered to mean value at which an asset is carried on a balance sheet. Book value at any time is cost of an item minus accumulated depreciation. *Replacement value* is considered to mean the amount required to obtain an asset of the same kind and status as the asset damaged or lost. Replacement value would not normally allow for replacement of an old item with a new one.

III. Losses Relating to Income-Producing Properties

16. The following general conclusions apply with regard to losses suffered as a result of Iraq's invasion and occupation of Kuwait in connection with income-producing properties. These include various kinds of businesses whose value is determined not only by the value of their individual assets but also by the greater value they possess due to their capacity to generate income. The conclusions are based on the premise that the business affected was a going concern, i.e. it had the capacity to continue to operate and generate income in the future.

17. In principle, Iraq is liable to compensate for the loss of a business or commercial entity as a whole resulting from Iraq's invasion and occupation of Kuwait. In the event that the business has been rebuilt and resumed, or that it could reasonably have been expected that the business could have been rebuilt and resumed, compensation may only be claimed for the loss suffered during the relevant period.

18. For the valuation of income-producing properties there are several alternative concepts. One is to measure by reference to costs, which leads to the determination of book value. Another is to determine the value of the property as a going concern. This is often done by reference to the market value of similar properties. Where such market value cannot be ascertained, the economic or current value of that asset can be ascertained by the *discounted cash flow (DCF)* method or by the *price/earnings (P/E)* method. The DCF method calculates the value at one specified time of cash flows that are to be received at a different time by discounting the yearly net cash flows to present value, with the discount rate including cost of capital and risk components. The price/earnings method takes as a basis past periods' business results and then capitalises them by the application of a multiple (P/E ratio) which reflects expectations about future performance and growth, or lack of it.

19. In principle, the economic value of a business may include loss of future earnings and profits where they can be ascertained with reasonable certainty. In the case of the loss of businesses and their earning capacity resulting from the invasion and occupation of Kuwait, it can

be expected that a number of such businesses can be or could have been rebuilt and resumed. The method of a valuation should therefore be one that focuses on past performance rather than on forecasts and projections into the future. Compensation should be provided if the loss can be ascertained with reasonable certainty based on prior earnings or profits. For example, the loss of any earnings or profits during the relevant time period could be calculated by a multiple of past earnings and profits corresponding to that time period.

Document 107

Further report of the Secretary-General on the status of compliance by Iraq with the obligations placed upon it under certain of the Security Council resolutions relating to the situation betweeen Iraq and Kuwait

S/23687, 7 March 1992

1. The present report is submitted to the members of the Security Council in response to the request made to the Secretary-General by the members in the course of their informal consultations on 3 March 1992. By the terms of that request, the Secretary-General is providing herein an update, in so far as is available, of the information presented in his report of 25 January 1992 1/ on Iraq's compliance with the obligations placed upon it by resolution 687 (1991) and subsequent relevant resolutions.

2. Under the same terms of the aforementioned request, the Secretary-General is also providing, in so far as is available, information on the status of Iraq's compliance with the provisions relating to the return of Kuwaiti property from Iraq to Kuwait (resolution 686 (1991), para. 2 (d)); information on the status of Iraq's compliance with the provisions relating to the demarcation of the international boundary between Iraq and Kuwait (resolution 687 (1991), para. 3); and information on Iraq's compliance with the relevant provisions of Security Council resolution 688 (1991) concerning the humanitarian situation of the Iraqi civilian population in many parts of Iraq, including in the Kurdish-populated areas. The requested information is presented in the four sections below.

I. UPDATE OF THE SECRETARY-GENERAL'S REPORT OF 25 JANUARY 1991

3. The update of the information in the Secretary-General's report of 25 January 1992, 1/ in so far as is available, is presented herein in such a way as to follow the pattern of that report. Thus, any new or additional information received, or lack of any such information, from the original contributing sources is presented or entered under the corresponding headings and subheadings, as indicated below.

A. Obligations of a general nature

4. In his letter of 23 January 1992 2/ addressed to the President of the Security Council, the Minister for Foreign Affairs of Iraq reiterated the position of his Government, declared in his earlier letter of 6 April 1991, 3/ that Iraq had found itself left with no other alternative but to accept resolution 687 (1991). In the letter of 23 January 1992 the Minister further stated the following:

"During the period between the adoption of resolution 687 (1991) on 3 April 1991 and 31 December 1991, Iraq met a very large part of the conditions, restrictions and measures imposed upon it by resolution 687 (1991). ..."

5. No other information has been received with regard to this item.

B. Specific obligations

1. Respect for the inviolability of the international border and allocation of islands between Iraq and Kuwait (paras. 2 and 5 of resolution 687 (1991))

6. In his letter of 23 January 1992, 2/ the Minister for Foreign Affairs of Iraq specified the measures which he said the Government had undertaken in its dealings with the United Nations Iraq-Kuwait Observation Mission (UNIKOM), indicating that Iraq had "extended everything required to facilitate the work of UNIKOM and fully cooperated with the Mission in order to ensure the success of its tasks and avoid any difficulties".

7. Since the submission of the Secretary-General's report of 25 January 1992, 1/ there has been no change with regard to Iraq's compliance with paragraphs 2 and

1/ S/23514.
2/ S/23472, annex.
3/ S/22456, annex.

5 of resolution 687 (1991) in the context of UNIKOM's mandate.

2. *Obligations relating to conventional, biological or chemical weapons and such materials for warfare (paras. 8, 9 (a) and 10 of resolution 687 (1991), para. 3 of resolution 707 (1991) and para. 5 of resolution 715 (1991))*

8. In his letter dated 23 January 1992, the Minister for Foreign Affairs of Iraq gave an account of the measures taken by the Government of Iraq in implementation of section C of resolution 687 (1991). 4/

9. In a communication dated 6 March 1992, the Executive Chairman of the Special Commission established under section C of resolution 687 (1991) submitted information bringing up to date the activities of the Commission that bear upon the status of Iraq's compliance with its obligations under the relevant Security Council resolutions. That information is reproduced in annex I to the present report.

3. *Obligations relating to nuclear capability development programmes (paras. 10 and 12 of resolution 687 (1991), para. 3 of resolution 707 (1991) and para. 5 of resolution 715 (1991))*

10. The comments in paragraph 8 above apply equally to this item.

11. In a communication dated 5 March 1992, the Director General of the International Atomic Energy Agency (IAEA) provided information on the developments that occurred in the course of the last two inspections carried out in Iraq (11-14 January and 5-13 February 1992). The text of the communication from the Director General of IAEA is reproduced in annex II to the present report.

4. *Obligations relating to repatriation of and access to all Kuwaiti and third-country nationals in Iraq (para. 30 of resolution 687 (1991))*

12. In his letter of 23 January 1992, the Minister for Foreign Affairs gave an account of the measures taken by Iraq with regard to the obligation under this item. 5/

13. In a further letter dated 28 February 1992, 6/ the Minister for Foreign Affairs of Iraq specified the measures taken by Iraq in order to meet its obligations with regard to paragraph 30 of resolution 687 (1991). In that connection, he indicated that Iraq had extended all necessary cooperation to the International Committee of the Red Cross (ICRC) in implementation of the provisions of paragraph 30 of the resolution. The letter also mentioned the visit to Iraq, at Iraq's invitation, of a team from the League of Arab States (LAS), as well as contacts Iraq had made with the "coalition States" under the auspices of ICRC. The attention of members of the Council is also drawn to the letter dated 6 March 1992, 7/ addressed to the Secretary-General by the representatives of France, Kuwait, Saudi Arabia, the United Kingdom of Great Britain and Northern Ireland and the United States of America in response to the letter of 28 February 1992 from the Minister for Foreign Affairs of Iraq.

14. Additional information concerning this item has been received from ICRC in a letter dated 6 March 1992, the text of which is reproduced below:

"The International Committee of the Red Cross (ICRC) is actively pursuing the matter of the above-mentioned resolution and relevant paragraph, along the lines discussed with all the parties concerned during a meeting held in Geneva on 16 and 17 October 1991 under the auspices of ICRC. The procedures laid out during that meeting are an on-going process and the representatives of the coalition have regularly been kept informed of the results.

"Our Delegate General for the Middle East and Northern Africa is in Baghdad right now in an effort to negotiate further progress in the matter of concern to you. A new evaluation on the standing of the issue could therefore be made at a later and more appropriate stage."

5. *Iraq's liability under international law for loss or damage resulting from its unlawful invasion and occupation of Kuwait (para. 16 of resolution 687 (1991))*

15. The contribution from the United Nations Compensation Commission to the Secretary-General's report of 25 January 1992 1/ was included in section E of the annex to that report.

16. Additional information has been received from the Commission in a letter dated 5 March 1992, the text of which is reproduced below:

"The only information that this office can add to our comments forwarded to you on 17 January 1992 is that at the end of the fourth session of the Governing Council held from 20 to 24 January 1992, the Council considered a request made by the Permanent Representative of Iraq asking for a five-year grace period for Iraq's contribution to the Compensation Fund in view of the country's financial obligations and its requirements in food and medicine.

4/ S/23472, enclosure, sects. 3-23.
5/ S/23472, enclosure, paras. 28 and 29.
6/ S/23661, annex.
7/ S/23686.

"The Council decided that 'questions concerning compliance of Security Council resolutions are of the competence of the Security Council and should therefore be addressed to it through the appropriate channels'."

6. *Adherence to all obligations concerning the servicing and repayment of Iraq's foreign debt (para. 17 of resolution 687 (1991))*

17. Information received from the International Monetary Fund (IMF) in a letter dated 6 March 1992 indicates that as of 29 February 1992, Iraq's arrears to IMF had increased to 8.6 million special drawing rights (SDRs). In this connection, the letter again draws attention to the position of the Iraqi authorities that, although willing to meet their financial obligations to the Fund, their attempts to do so have failed because of the international sanctions in place. IMF has also stated that it still had not received any information from the Iraqi authorities concerning their holdings of gold and other foreign currency reserves.

18. The Office of the Paris Club has reported no changes in the figures of Iraq's indebtedness to the members of the Club published in section F (ii) of the annex to the Secretary-General's report of 25 January 1992.

7. *Non-entitlement to claims deriving from the effects of the measures taken by the Security Council in resolution 661 (1990) and related resolutions (para. 29 of resolutions 687 (1991))*

19. No new information has been received with regard to this item.

8. *Liability by Iraq for the full cost of the tasks authorized under section C of resolution 687 (1991) (para. 4 of 699 (1991))*

20. As of 29 February 1992, financial commitments for the implementation of the four tasks listed in the Secretary-General's report of 25 January 1992 amounted to $18.6 million. This amount was provided through a commitment authority of $10 million by the Advisory Committee on Administrative and Budgetary Questions under the provisions of General Assembly resolution 44/203 of 2 December 1989 on unforeseen and extraordinary expenses, as well as by contributions from certain Member States in the amount of $8.6 million.

9. *Requirement to provide monthly statements of gold and foreign currency reserves holdings (para. 7 of resolution 706 (1991))*

21. To date, the Secretary-General has received no notification from Iraq of the amount of its holdings of gold and foreign currency reserves. This has also been confirmed by IMF (see para. 17 above).

C. *Other obligations*

1. *Undertaking required on not committing, supporting or abetting commission of any international terrorist acts (para. 32 of resolution 687 (1991))*

22. In his letter of 23 January 1992, 9/ the Minister for Foreign Affairs reiterated the position of the Government of Iraq regarding this item, as stated in the letters from Iraq mentioned in the Secretary-General's report of 25 January 1992. 10/

23. No other information has been received with regard to this item.

2. *Compliance with obligations in the Treaty on the Non-Proliferation of Nuclear Weapons of 1 July 1968 (para. 5 of resolution 707 (1991))*

24. No new information has been received with regard to this item.

II. COMPLIANCE BY IRAQ REGARDING THE RETURN OF KUWAITI PROPERTY FROM IRAQ TO KUWAIT

(Resolution 686 (1991), para. 2 (d))

25. Pursuant to the adoption of Security Council resolution 686 (1991) of 2 March 1991 and an exchange of letters between the President of the Security Council and the Secretary-General, a Coordinator for the return of property was appointed by the Secretary-General on 26 March 1991. 11/ Since that time a number of discussions and meetings have taken place with the responsible Iraqi and Kuwaiti officials. The return of the property has commenced and, to date, properties of the Central Bank of Kuwait, the Central Library of Kuwait, the National Museum of Kuwait, the Kuwait News Agency, Kuwait Airways Corporation and the Kuwait Air Force have been returned. A number of additional items are ready for return and the process is continuing. In addition, Kuwait has submitted lists of properties from other ministries, corporations and individuals that are being pursued. The Iraqi and Kuwaiti officials involved with the return of property have extended maximum cooperation to the United Nations to facilitate the return.

8/ S/23514, annex, sect H, para. 2.
9/ S/23472, enclosure, para. 30.
10/ S/23514, para. 19.
11/ S/22387.

III. COMPLIANCE BY IRAQ UNDER THE MANDATE OF THE IRAQ-KUWAIT BOUNDARY DEMARCATION COMMISSION

26. The Iraq-Kuwait Boundary Demarcation Commission, which was established pursuant to the provisions of paragraph 3 of resolution 687 (1991), has provided information which states that Iraq has fully participated in the work of the Commission. The information further states as follows:

"Iraq has attended all of the meetings, has participated in the voting procedures of the Commission and has taken an active role in the drafting of the Commission's report to the Secretary-General. The preliminary field work of the Commission, the first stage of surveying and mapping, was concluded in November 1991 without any hindrance on the part of Iraq.

"It is expected that Iraq will fully participate in the next session of the Commission, which is scheduled for 8 to 16 April in New York."

IV. COMPLIANCE BY IRAQ UNDER SECURITY COUNCIL RESOLUTION 688 (1991)

27. In paragraphs 2, 3 and 7 thereof, Security Council resolution 688 (1991) of 5 April 1991 imposed obligations upon Iraq.

28. In 25 June 1991, the Chairman of the Commission on Human Rights, following decision 1991/256 of the Economic and Social Council, appointed a Special Rapporteur (Mr. Max van der Stoel, Minister of State of the Netherlands) for a fact-finding mission to Iraq, the Islamic Republic of Iran and Saudi Arabia. The Special Rapporteur, in accordance with the Commission's resolution 1991/74, prepared a report which was published on 18 February 1992 in document E/CN.4/1992/31. It is also to be circulated as document S/23685. Attention is drawn to the conclusions and recommendations contained in paragraphs 146 to 159 of that report.

29. Also, the Office of the Executive Delegate of the Secretary-General has forwarded observations on the issues identified as falling under its purview relating to paragraphs 2, 3 and 7 of resolution 688 (1991). Those comments are reproduced in annex III to the present report.

Annex I
Information received from the Special Commission

Section C of Security Council resolution 687 (1991) and resolutions 707 (1991) and 715 (1991)

Introduction

1. Since the circulation on 25 January 1992 of the report by the Secretary-General on the status of compli-ance by Iraq with the obligations placed upon it under certain of the Security Council resolutions relating to the situation between Iraq and Kuwait, a/ two notes by the Secretary-General dated 18 and 26 February 1992 respectively, b/, c/ have been issued which contain reports by the Executive Chairman of the Special Commission. These reports bring up to date the information contained in the report of 25 January regarding the status of Iraq's compliance with, in particular, Security Council resolutions 707 (1991) and 715 (1991).

2. The present document contains a brief account of the developments recorded in the reports just mentioned and the Council's actions on those reports. Thereafter it brings up to date the information contained in the report of 25 January 1992 in so far as it relates to the inspection activities undertaken under the aegis of the Special Commission in the discharge of its responsibilities under section C of Security Council resolution 687 (1991).

Security Council resolutions 707 (1991) and 715 (1991)

3. In the report of 18 February, b/ the Executive Chairman of the Special Commission indicated that, despite the Special Commission's best efforts, Iraq was continuing to refuse to make the full, final and complete disclosure called for under Council resolution 707 (1991) of all its programmes and capabilities relating to weapons of mass destruction and ballistic missiles with a range greater than 150 kilometres. While some additional information on Iraq's programmes for the production of weapons of mass destruction had been obtained since 25 January 1992, this had to be done through a procedure of question and answer. The Special Commission was convinced that such a procedure could not result in detection of as yet undeclared elements of the Iraqi programmes and that its usefulness had been exhausted. Information on such elements was essential for a full understanding of Iraq's programmes and could be obtained only if Iraq met its obligations under Council resolution 707 (1991) to provide a full, final and complete disclosure of its programmes (see para. 13 below). In respect of Council resolution 715 (1991), and the plans for ongoing monitoring and verification approved thereunder, Iraq was maintaining the position stated in a letter to the President of the Security Council of 19 November 1991 which constituted an apparent rejection of the plans and thus of the resolution.

a/ S/23514.
b/ S/23606.
c/ S/23607.
d/ S/23609.

4. Consultations held in the Council on 18 and 19 February 1992 on the Executive Chairman's report resulted in the issue by the President on 19 February of a statement on behalf of the members of the Council. d/ In this it was recorded, *inter alia*, that Iraq's failure to acknowledge its obligations under resolutions 707 (1991) and 715 (1991), its rejection of the two plans for ongoing monitoring and verification and its failure to provide the full, final and complete disclosure of its weapons capabilities constituted a continuing material breach of the relevant provisions of resolution 687 (1991). The statement further provided that unconditional agreement by Iraq to implement these obligations was one of the essential preconditions for any reconsideration by the Council under paragraphs 21 and 22 of resolution 687 (1991) of the prohibitions referred to in those paragraphs. In the statement the members of the Council welcomed the decision of the Secretary-General to dispatch a special mission headed by the Executive Chairman of the Special Commission to visit Iraq immediately to meet and discuss with the highest levels of the Iraqi Government for the purpose of securing the unconditional agreement by Iraq to implement all its relevant obligations under resolutions 687 (1991), 707 (1991) and 715 (1991).

5. The report by the Executive Chairman of the Special Commission of 26 February 1992 related to the outcome of the special mission's visit to Baghdad, which had taken place from 21 to 24 February 1992. In the course of the discussions held during that visit, the special mission and the Iraqi side had exchanged written statements of their positions. e/ After a careful review of the statement of Iraq, and taking account of the discussions held, the Executive Chairman indicated that he had regretfully concluded that he had been unable to secure unconditional agreement by Iraq to implement all its relevant obligations under Security Council resolutions 687 (1991), 707 (1991) and 715 (1991). Iraq had indicated, instead, that its delegation to be dispatched to talk to the Security Council in the near future would convey Iraq's position on resolutions 707 (1991) and 715 (1991). In a letter of 24 February 1992 addressed to the Secretary-General, the Minister for Foreign Affairs of Iraq repeated essentially the points made in the written statement that had been given to the special mission. At the request of the Foreign Minister this letter was circulated to the Security Council. f/

6. Consultations in the Council on this report of the Executive Chairman on 27 and 28 February 1992, during which the Council was also informed orally of Iraq's refusal to undertake as directed by the Special Commission destruction of certain of its ballistic missile capabilities (see document S/23673 and para. 12 below), resulted in the issue of a statement of 28 February 1992 by the President of the Council, on behalf of the Council, at its 3058th meeting on 28 February 1992. g/ In this statement the members of the Council approved in full the conclusions of the special mission. They also deplored and condemned the failure of Iraq to provide the special mission with the acknowledgements and undertakings which it had been sent by the Council to obtain and its failure to commence within the prescribed time destruction of ballistic missile-related equipment designated for destruction by the Special Commission. The statement records that this latter refusal constituted a further material breach of the relevant provisions of resolution 687 (1991). In the statement the members of the Council required Iraq to communicate directly to the Council without further delay an authoritative and unconditional acknowledgement of its agreement to accept and implement its obligations under the Council's resolutions.

Inspection activities and other issues arising under section C of Security Council resolution 687 (1991) and related resolutions

Chemical and biological weapons

7. From 27 January to 5 February 1992 the seventh chemical weapons inspection (UNSCOM 26) visited 10 sites, of which 5 were declared and 5 undeclared. The undeclared sites included a chemical-warfare training facility, an ammunition-storage depot, a fertilizer factory, a large military training complex and an ammunition repair facility. The declared sites visited included the Al-Qa'Qa phosgene plant and four commercial sites where fermentation equipment was either currently in use or had been in use at one time. Although there was no evidence of any proscribed items or activities the team determined that the phosgene plant, because of its chemical-warfare potential, required compliance monitoring. Additionally, the team observed a test run of a small-scale nerve agent hydrolysis operation as an ongoing evaluation of the Iraqi destruction proposals. Further test results are required before rendering a decision on the efficacy of the proposed process. The team also verified the return to the Muthanna State Establishment of all remaining chemical bomb-casing manufacturing equipment from a sugar factory in Mosul as directed by a previous inspection team.

8. A special mission headed by two members of the Special Commission was in Iraq at the same time as UNSCOM 26. That mission was able to obtain previously undisclosed information on the development,

e/ S/23643, appendices I and II.
f/ S/23636.
g/ S/23663.

support and manufacturing components of the Iraqi chemical weapons programme. During question-and-answer sessions the Iraqi officials were asked to describe the function of each item of machinery at the Muthanna workshop to the UNSCOM 26 inspection team, allowing the inspectors to determine which of the chemical weapon systems had in fact been manufactured, modified or assembled at Muthanna.

9. During the special mission, Iraqi officials produced statistics for specific types of chemical munitions imported. However, many of these figures are contradictory or show a considerable increase from the previously declared numbers. Iraqi authorities have yet to provide consistent complete answers to fundamental weapon-stockpile issues as required under Council resolution 687 (1991). Without documentary evidence to validate constantly changing figures, the Special Commission cannot conclude that Iraq has complied with its responsibilities for full disclosure.

10. The first chemical destruction mission (UNSCOM 29) is currently in Iraq controlling the destruction of approximately 450 sarin-filled 122 mm rockets at Khamisiyah, which were judged by a previous inspection team (UNSCOM 20) to be too dangerous to move and thus to require destruction in place.

11. With respect to the biological warfare programme, Iraqi officials told the special mission that they had nothing further to add to what had already been provided to the two biological weapons inspection teams. They maintained that all documents and information related to the programme had either been handed over to the first biological inspection team or had been destroyed. The Special Commission remains convinced that this aspect will require watchful monitoring in the future.

Ballistic missiles

12. One ballistic missile inspection (UNSCOM 28) has been conducted since the last report. During the period 21 to 28 February a total of seven sites were inspected, three of which were on a short-notice basis. The team conducted an inventory at four of the sites, validated previous catalogued items and identified for destruction additional items that had been moved to the site or recovered from destroyed structures. The main focus of the inspection was to supervise the destruction of some of the missile repair and production facilities and equipment identified for destruction in a letter of the Special Commission to Iraq of 14 February 1992. h/ The date for destruction was set for 26 February. The Iraqi officials, however, refused to carry out the destruction, referring the issue to higher authority. On 27 February the Iraqi Government, through its Permanent Mission to the United Nations, requested from the Special Commis-

sion a delay of 24 hours for commencing destruction. The delay was granted. However after 24 hours the Iraqi authorities informed the Commission, in a letter of 28 February, i/ and orally the inspection team, that it still refused to carry out the destruction required. The team was then withdrawn from Iraq and the matter referred to the Security Council (see para. 6 above).

13. At one location designated for a short-notice inspection, the team found equipment and machinery clearly designated for an Iraqi declared ballistic missile production activity at another location. This equipment had not been previously declared at any location. At the time this equipment was found the special mission headed by the Executive Chairman of the Special Commission was being informed that Iraq had already provided all necessary information. The concurrence of these two events underlines the importance of the full, final and complete disclosure called for by Council resolution 707 (1991).

14. The team also observed reconstruction of structures at sites declared by Iraq under the provisions of Council resolution 687 (1991).

15. The Special Commission can only conclude that Iraq has yet to provide full disclosure in the area of ballistic missile activity proscribed by Council resolution 687 (1991).

Additional inspections

16. In early February, a Special Commission inspection team (UNSCOM 30), augmented by inspectors from an IAEA inspection team, carried out an inspection at the Ministry of Industry and Minerals, a non-declared site. The purpose was to investigate a report that computers had been moved to that location which were suspected to have been used for activities prohibited by Council resolution 687 (1991). Four mainframe computers were located at the site (referred to as the Al-Rafidien computer centre): three of them appeared non-operational and a random sampling of files present in the fourth revealed nothing related to Council resolution 687 (1991).

Issues relating to the obligations of Iraq in connection with the facilities, privileges and immunities of the Special Commission and IAEA

17. No progress has been made in respect of the issues raised in paragraphs 31 to 33 of the attachment to the Secretary-General's report of 25 January 1992. a/ Regarding the Special Commission's aerial surveillance flights, Iraq continues to protest vigorously such flights

h/ S/23673, annex I, enclosure I.
i/ S/23673, annex III, enclosure.

despite the clear right of the Special Commission to undertake them. The problems at Habbaniyah airport, as the Executive Chairman reported to the Council on 18 February 1992 b/ have led to an official approach to the Government, recalling the relevant provisions of resolution 707 (1991) on the Special Commission's landing rights and proposing that the Commission's incoming and outgoing flights use one of two now operational airports within the city limits of Baghdad. No reply has been received to date. During the visit of the most recent special mission to Baghdad the Executive Chairman of the Special Commission indicated, as he reported to the Council, j/ that he was prepared to discuss with the Government practical arrangements to take account of any legitimate concerns it might have regarding the use of airports. So far this offer has not been taken up.

18. Iraq has still not returned all the documents forcibly removed from a nuclear inspection team in Baghdad on 23 September 1991. b/

Summary

19. Since the Secretary-General's report of 25 January 1992 was issued, a/ strenuous efforts have been made by the Security Council and by the Special Commission to obtain from Iraq acknowledgement of its obligations under Security Council resolutions 707 (1991) and 715 (1991) and its unconditional agreement to implement all of its obligations under resolutions 687 (1991), 707 (1991) and 715 (1991). So far, these acknowledgements and undertakings have not been obtained, much less tested in practice. If this situation persists, and if the high-level Iraqi delegation to meet with the Security Council in the immediate future does not provide the acknowledgements and undertakings demanded in the statements by the President of the Council of 19 and 28 February 1992, the Special Commission will be neither legally nor practically able to initiate the programme for ongoing monitoring and verification of Iraq's compliance with its obligations under section C of Security Council resolution 687 (1991). This programme is an integral part of the cease-fire resolution. The solution to this matter, in accordance with the Security Council resolutions, now lies with Iraq.

20. Among the outstanding matters at this time, the following would appear to be the most important:

(a) Failure by Iraq to acknowledge its obligations under Council resolutions 707 (1991) and 715 (1991) and under the plans approved by resolution 715 (1991);

(b) Failure by Iraq to agree to implement unconditionally all its obligations under section C of Council resolution 687 (1991) and resolutions 707 (1991) and 715 (1991);

(c) Failure by Iraq to provide all the information required under resolutions 687 (1991) and 707 (1991) in order for the Special Commission and IAEA to have a full, final and complete picture of all aspects of Iraq's programmes for weapons of mass destruction and ballistic missiles with a range greater than 150 km; k/

(d) Failure by Iraq to provide the declarations required under the plans for ongoing monitoring and verification;

(e) Failure by Iraq to make arrangements necessary for the implementation, in the interests of efficient performance, of certain of the facilities, privileges and immunities of the Special Commission, such as airport landing rights;

(f) Failure by Iraq to comply with the Special Commission's instructions regarding the destruction of items and facilities used in its proscribed ballistic missile programmes.

j/ S/23643, enclosure, para. 9.
k/ Illustrative of the missing information is the list contained in the statement by the recent special mission delivered to the Government of Iraq on 22 February 1992 which is to be found in appendix I, part B, para. 2, of the special mission's report to the Secretary-General, e/.

Annex II
Information received from the International Atomic Energy Agency

Pages 16 to 20 of document S/23514 contain the report of the Director General of IAEA on Iraq's compliance with its obligations under United Nations Security Council resolutions as they relate to nuclear activities.

Some recent developments, occurring during the ninth (11-14 January 1992) and the tenth (5-13 February 1992) Agency inspections, may warrant an updating of document S/23514. We suggest the addition of the following paragraphs.

"In the course of the two last inspections - IAEA/9 of 11 to 14 January 1992 and IAEA/10 of 5 to 13 February 1992 - the following developments occurred:

(a) During the January inspection, the Iraqi technical team provided important information on the extent of procurement of stock materials needed for the manufacturing of several thousand ultracentrifuges intended for the production of enriched uranium. It stated that those stock materials had been rendered harmless or destroyed prior to the commencement of Agency inspections under resolution 687 (1991). Agency inspectors were taken to the sites where the remains of these materials were stored;

(b) In the course of the February inspection, the Iraqi technical team repeatedly declared that it was anxious to close the present phase of inspection and to start implementing the plan for ongoing monitoring and verification. It proposed to clarify, once and for all, all the oustanding issues concerning past nuclear activities and that IAEA define what is still needed of it;

(c) As to the position of the Iraqi authorities regarding the provision of information pursuant to Security Council resolution 715 (1991) and relevant to the plan for future ongoing monitoring and verification, a/ the Iraqi technical team conceded that the information transmitted so far did not conform with the requirements under the plan, specifically:

(i) Annex II to document S/22872/Rev.1 requires that the initial information to be submitted by Iraq cover the period from 1 January 1989, whereas the information received from Iraq reflects the situation as of the date the information was prepared (November 1991), i.e. after the Persian Gulf War, during which certain facilities and equipment had been damaged, and subsequent to the destruction of items by the Iraqi side itself;

(ii) The list of items to be reported to IAEA, contained in annex III to document S/22872/Rev.1 should not have been limited to items in the possession of the Iraqi Atomic Energy Commission, but should have included all items of the kind in question existing in Iraq.

The Iraqi technical team advised the Agency team that, while modifications of the initial information could be made in order to reflect the situation as of 1 January 1989, it could not comply with the second requirement as it deemed it practically impossible to extend the list to cover all items of the kind in question existing in Iraq."

a/ S/22872/Rev.1.

Annex III
Comments from the Office of the Executive Delegate of the Secretary-General

Paragraph 2 of Security Council resolution 688 (1991) demands that Iraq end the repression (of the Iraqi civilian population in Iraq, including in Kurdish-populated areas).

Since late October 1991, serious restrictions on the supplies of essential commodities, in particular food and fuel, have been imposed by the Government on the three northern Governorates of Dohuk, Erbil and Suleimaniya.

While these restrictions have not affected the three Governorates in a uniform manner, the population has experienced considerable hardship as a result: less than half of the regular food rations were distributed to the northern region during December. At the same time, the salaries of civil servants in the three Governorates have not been paid since November 1991.

On 9 December 1991, the executive heads (the Executive Delegate, the United Nations High Commissioner for Refugees, the Executive Directors of the United Nations Children's Fund and the World Food Programme and the Director General of the World Health Organization) expressed their concern in this respect to the Government of Iraq, noting that United Nations humanitarian agencies were not in a position to replace essential services and assure the provision of goods denied to the Kurdish population at large. The Government's position, as conveyed to the Coordinator and Special Representative in Baghdad, is that the restrictions have been imposed in view of the inability of the Kurdish leadership to maintain security and protect Government personnel and resources. To date, the series of discussions between the Government and representatives of the Kurdish leadership have not succeeded in putting an end to the supply restrictions.

By paragraph 3 of the same resolution, the Council "insists that Iraq allow immediate access by international humanitarian organizations to all those in need of assistance in all parts of Iraq and to make available all necessary facilities for their operations" ... and, by paragraph 7, it "demands that Iraq cooperate with the Secretary-General to these ends".

The Executive Delegate negotiated with the Government of Iraq and signed with the Minister for Foreign Affairs on 18 April 1991 a Memorandum of Understanding for the implementation of the United Nations inter-agency humanitarian programme in Iraq.

Paragraph 15 of the Memorandum provides that the Government of Iraq shall cooperate in granting international humanitarian organizations access to the parts of the country requiring relief, by air or road as needed, to facilitate the implementation and monitoring of the programme. Paragraphs 4 and 8 also provide for the Government's cooperation for the establishment of United Nations sub-offices and relief centres as required for humanitarian assistance.

On 24 November 1991, the Foreign Minister and the Executive Delegate agreed to renew and extend the Memorandum of Understanding up to the end of June 1992. In the new Memorandum of Understanding (paras. 3, 13, 14, 17 and 18), the Government commits itself to the extension of further cooperation for United

Nations relief activities in facilitating access to those in need.

On the basis of this Memorandum, the Government has extended its cooperation in facilitating the access of United Nations agencies and other international organizations where necessary in most parts of Iraq. Repeated endeavours by the Executive Delegate, however, for the establishment of humanitarian centres at Kirkuk, in the north, and at Nasariya and Hammar, in the south, have not yet met with the approval of the Government. The Executive Delegate notified the Government that its refusal failed to comply with the letter and the spirit of the Memorandum of Understanding concluded with the United Nations for the implementation of the inter-agency humanitarian programme.

The Government's position in this respect, as conveyed to the Executive Delegate, is that, according to the Memorandum of Understanding, the establishment of United Nations humanitarian centres and the determination of humanitarian needs is to be undertaken "in agree-ment and cooperation with the Government of Iraq" and with due respect for the latter's independence, sovereignty and territorial integrity; given the need for agreement, the Government's refusal is not to be construed as a unilateral act.

Under the original Memorandum of Understanding, the Government committed itself to make available cash contributions in local currency to help to cover in-country operational costs while pursuing discussions regarding the establishment of a special exchange rate for relief operations carried out by the agencies and organizations participating in the programme. During 1991 Iraq accordingly contributed 1.5 million Iraqi dinar. Under the new Memorandum of Understanding, the Government undertook to make available cash contributions in local currency in the amount of 1 million Iraqi dinar at the beginning of each month. As of 17 January 1992, however, no such contribution had yet been received by the inter-agency programme despite repeated requests to this effect with the respective authorities.

Document 108

Statement by the President of the Security Council concerning general and specific obligations of Iraq under various Security Council resolutions relating to the situation between Iraq and Kuwait

S/23699, 11 March 1992

Note by the President of the Security Council

Following consultations among members of the Security Council, the President of the Council made the following introductory statement, on behalf of the Council, at its 3059th meeting, on 11 March 1992, in connection with the Council's consideration of the item entitled:

"(a) The situation between Iraq and Kuwait

"(b) Letter dated 2 April 1991 from the Permanent Representative of Turkey to the United Nations addressed to the President of the Security Council (S/22435)

"Letter dated 4 April 1991 from the Chargé d'affaires a.i. of the Permanent Mission of France to the United Nations addressed to the President of the Security Council (S/22442)

"Letter dated 5 March 1992 from the Chargé d'affaires a.i. of the Permanent Mission of Belgium to the United Nations addressed to the President of the Security Council (S/23685)".

I. *General obligation*

1. The resolutions concerning the situation between Iraq and Kuwait impose a number of general and specific obligations upon Iraq.

2. As regards the general obligation, Iraq is required, under paragraph 33 of Security Council resolution 687 (1991), to give official notification to the Secretary-General and to the Security Council of its acceptance of the provisions of that entire resolution.

3. Iraq signified its unconditional acceptance in letters dated 6 and 10 April 1991 (S/22456 and S/22480, respectively) and 23 January 1992 (S/23472).

4. When the Security Council met at the level of Heads of State and Government on 31 January 1992 the concluding statement made by the President of the Council, on behalf of its members (S/23500), contained the following passage:

Last year, under the authority of the United Nations, the international community succeeded in enabling Kuwait to regain its sovereignty and territorial integrity, which it had lost as a result of Iraqi aggression. The resolutions adopted by the Security

Council remain essential to the restoration of peace and stability in the region and must be fully implemented. At the same time the members of the Council are concerned by the humanitarian situation of the innocent civilian population of Iraq.'

5. On 5 February 1992, the President of the Security Council issued a statement on behalf of its members (S/23517) in which he stated, among other things:

In connection with the Secretary-General's factual report (S/23514) on Iraq's compliance with all the obligations placed upon it by resolution 687 (1991) and subsequent relevant resolutions, the members of the Security Council note that while much progress has been made, much remains to be done. ... The members of the Council are disturbed by the lack of Iraqi cooperation. Iraq must implement fully resolution 687 (1991) and subsequent relevant resolutions as was stated in the statement read out by the President of the Council on behalf of its members in the meeting held on 31 January 1992 with the participation of the heads of State and Government (S/23500).'

6. In a statement made on behalf of the Council on 28 February 1992 (S/23663), the President said:

The members of the Council demand that Iraq immediately implement all its obligations under Council resolution 687 (1991) and subsequent resolutions on Iraq. The members of the Council require the Government of Iraq to communicate directly to the Council without further delay an authoritative and unconditional acknowledgement of its agreement to accept and implement the above noted obligations, including specifically to comply with the determination of the Special Commission requiring the destruction of ballistic missile-related equipment. The members of the Council emphasize that Iraq must be aware of the serious consequences of continued material breaches of resolution 687 (1991).'

7. I must also draw attention to the further report of the Secretary-General on the status of compliance by Iraq with the obligations placed upon it (S/23687).

8. From the aforementioned statements by the President and in view of the reports of the Secretary-General, it will be seen that, despite Iraq's statements of unconditional acceptance of Security Council resolution 687 (1991), the Security Council has determined that Iraq is not in full compliance with all of its obligations.

II. *Specific obligations*

9. In addition to the general obligation to accept the provisions of resolution 687 (1991) in their entirety, several Security Council resolutions impose specific obligations upon Iraq.

(a) *Respect for the inviolability of the international boundary*

10. By paragraph 2 of resolution 687 (1991) the Security Council demands that Iraq respect the inviolability of the international boundary and the allocation of islands previously agreed upon between Iraq and Kuwait. Pursuant to paragraph 3 of that resolution, the Secretary-General established a Boundary Demarcation Commission to demarcate the boundary between Iraq and Kuwait. Paragraph 5 of the same resolution requires Iraq and Kuwait to respect a demilitarized zone (DMZ) established by the Security Council. The Council has been informed that Iraq has respected the DMZ and that it has fully participated in the work of the Boundary Demarcation Commission. It has also been informed that Iraq refuses to withdraw a number of police posts that are not in line with UNIKOM's principle that both sides should stay 1,000 metres from the boundary line shown on UNIKOM's map.

(b) *Weapons-related obligations*

11. Section C of resolution 687 (1991) imposes certain specific obligations upon Iraq with respect to its chemical and biological weapons programmes, its ballistic missile programmes with a range greater than 150 kilometres and its nuclear programmes. These obligations are elaborated upon in resolutions 707 (1991) and 715 (1991). The obligations are defined in paragraphs 8, 9, 10, 11, 12 and 13 of resolution 687 (1991) and they are elaborated upon in paragraphs 3 and 5 of resolution 707 (1991) and paragraph 5 of resolution 715 (1991).

12. The information relevant to Iraq's compliance with the obligations laid down in the paragraphs of the Security Council resolutions to which I have just referred is reproduced in annex I to the Secretary-General's report (S/23687).

13. By resolution 699 (1991), the Security Council decided that the Government of Iraq shall be liable for the full costs of carrying out the tasks authorized by section C of resolution 687 (1991). No funds have so far been received from Iraq to meet this liability.

14. The Council has noted that since the adoption of resolution 687 (1991) progress has been made in the implementation of section C of that resolution but that much remains to be done. There is serious non-compli-

ance with the obligations concerning the programmes for weapons of mass destruction and ballistic missiles and the members of the Council have found this to be a continuing material breach of resolution 687 (1991).

15. The Special Commission has informed the Council about the outstanding matters that would at the present time appear to be the most important. The Council's attention is invited again to annex I of the Secretary-General's report, S/23687 of 7 March 1992.

16. The Council has also noted the statement by the International Atomic Energy Agency (IAEA) contained in the Secretary-General's report of 25 January 1992 (S/23514, section C of the annex). The attention of the Council is drawn to information annexed to the further report of the Secretary-General, S/23687 (annex II), of 7 March 1992, relative to the two last inspections by the IAEA, on Iraq's compliance with its obligations under United Nations Security Council resolutions as they relate to nuclear activities.

17. In a statement issued on behalf of the members of the Council (S/23609), the President stated on 19 February 1992 that:

'Iraq's failure to acknowledge its obligations under resolutions 707 (1991) and 715 (1991), its rejection up until now of the two plans for ongoing monitoring and verification and its failure to provide the full, final and complete disclosure of its weapons capabilities constitute a continuing material breach of the relevant provisions of resolution 687 (1991).'

18. In a further statement made on 28 February 1992 on behalf of the Council (S/23663), the President said:

'The members of the Council deplore and condemn the failure of the Government of Iraq to provide the Special Commission with full, final and complete disclosure, as required by resolution 707 (1991), of all aspects of its programmes to develop weapons of mass destruction and ballistic missiles with a range greater than 150 kilometres, including launchers, and of all holdings of such weapons, their components and production facilities and locations, as well as all other nuclear programmes; and the failure of Iraq to comply with the plans for ongoing monitoring and verification approved by resolution 715 (1991). ... Furthermore, the members of the Council equally deplore and condemn Iraq's failure, within the time prescribed by the Special Commission at the request of Iraq, to commence destruction of ballistic missile-related equipment designated for destruction by the Special Commission. The members of the Council reaffirm that it is for the Special Commis-

sion alone to determine which items must be destroyed under paragraph 9 of resolution 687 (1991).'

(c) *Repatriation of and access to Kuwaiti and third-country nationals in Iraq*

19. As regards Kuwaiti and third-country nationals in Iraq, Security Council resolutions 664 (1990), 666 (1990), 667 (1990), 674 (1990), 686 (1991) and 687 (1991) impose an obligation on Iraq to release, facilitate repatriation of, and arrange for immediate access to them, as well as the return of the remains of any deceased personnel of the forces of Kuwait and of the Member States cooperating with Kuwait pursuant to resolution 678 (1990). Furthermore, paragraph 30 of resolution 687 (1991) requires Iraq to extend all necessary cooperation to the International Committee of the Red Cross (ICRC) in facilitating the search for Kuwaiti and third-country nationals still unaccounted for.

20. The Security Council was informed by the ICRC in January 1992 that almost 7,000 persons have returned from Iraq to their countries since the beginning of March 1991. The ICRC also stated that despite all its efforts, there are still thousands of persons reported missing by the parties to the conflict.

21. A special commission composed of the representatives of France, Iraq, Kuwait, Saudi Arabia, the United Kingdom and the United States has met under the auspices of the ICRC, to try to reach an agreement on, among other things, the implementation of paragraph 30 of resolution 687 (1991). However, the ICRC has informed the Council that it has not yet received any information as to the whereabouts of the persons reported missing in Iraq. Nor has it received detailed and documented information on the search conducted by the Iraqi authorities. Finally, it is also still awaiting information on persons who have died while in custody.

22. The attention of the Council is drawn to section 4, paragraphs 12 to 14, of the Secretary-General's report contained in document S/23687 of 7 March 1992.

(d) *Iraq's liability under international law*

23. Another obligation concerns Iraq's liability under international law. In resolution 674 (1990), the Security Council reminds Iraq 'that under international law it is liable for any loss, damage or injury arising in regard to Kuwait and third States and their nationals and corporations, as a result of the invasion and illegal occupation of Kuwait by Iraq'. Its liability under international law is reaffirmed in paragraph 2 (b) of resolution 686 (1991) and paragraph 16 of resolution 687 (1991). Resolution 687 (1991) further specifies that it 'is liable under

international law for any direct loss, damage, including environmental damage and the depletion of natural resources, or injury to foreign Governments, nationals and corporations, as a result of Iraq's unlawful invasion and occupation of Kuwait'.

24. By paragraph 18 of the same resolution, the Security Council created a Fund to pay compensation for claims that fall within paragraph 16, to be financed by a percentage of the value of the exports of petroleum and petroleum products from Iraq. In view of the existing economic sanctions against Iraq under resolution 661 (1990), Iraq was permitted by the Security Council under resolutions 706 (1991) and 712 (1991) to sell a limited quantity of oil, as an exception, a portion of the proceeds from which would be used to provide financial resources for the Fund. To date, it has not availed itself of this possibility. The Council notes that this authorization is due to lapse on 18 March 1992. The members of the Council are aware of a request by Iraq for a five-year moratorium on meeting its financial obligations, including payments into the Compensation Fund.

(e) *Repayment and servicing of Iraq's foreign debt*

25. With regard to another obligation, the Security Council, in paragraph 17 of resolution 687 (1991), demands that Iraq scrupulously adhere to all of its obligations concerning servicing and repayment of its foreign debt.

26. The attention of the Council is drawn to paragraphs 17 and 18 of the Secretary-General's report (S/23687) of 7 March 1992.

(f) *Return of property*

27. I now turn to the question of return of property. The Security Council, in paragraph 2 (d) of resolution 686 (1991), demands that Iraq immediately begin to return all Kuwaiti property seized by it, to be completed in the shortest possible period. The members of the Council have noted with satisfaction that, as stated in the further report of the Secretary-General, Iraqi officials involved with the return of property have extended maximum cooperation to the United Nations to facilitate the return.

(g) *Monthly statements of gold and foreign currency reserves*

28. Another obligation is set out by paragraph 7 of resolution 706 (1991), under which the Government of Iraq is required to provide to the Secretary-General and appropriate international organizations monthly statements of its gold and foreign currency reserves. To date,

no such statements have been provided to the Secretary-General or to the IMF.

(h) *Undertaking not to commit or support acts of international terrorism*

29. By paragraph 32 of resolution 687 (1991), Iraq is required not to commit or support acts of international terrorism or allow any organization directed towards commission of such acts to operate within its territory and to condemn unequivocally and renounce all acts, methods, and practices of terrorism.

30. The Council notes Iraq's statements contained in letters dated 11 June 1991 (S/22687 and S/22689) and 23 January 1992 (S/23472) that it is a party to international conventions against terrorism and that it has never pursued a policy favourable to international terrorism as defined by international law.

(i) *Security Council action with respect to the Iraqi civilian population*

31. Resolutions 706 (1991) and 712 (1991) provide a means for Iraq to meet its obligations to supply its civilian population with needed humanitarian assistance, particularly food and medicine. To date, Iraq has refused to implement these resolutions. In fact after initiating discussions with Secretariat representatives on implementation, Iraq abruptly terminated the discussions.

III. *Security council resolution 688 (1991)*

32. I should now like to refer to the demands by the Security Council with respect to the Iraqi civilian population. In paragraph 2 of resolution 688 (1991), the Security Council demands that Iraq, as a contribution to removing the threat to international peace and security in the region, end the repression of its civilian population. In paragraphs 3 and 7, the Security Council insists that it allow immediate access by international humanitarian organizations to all those in need of assistance in all parts of Iraq, and demands its cooperation with the Secretary-General to these ends.

33. The Security Council remains deeply concerned at the grave human rights abuses that, despite the provisions of resolution 688 (1991), the Government of Iraq continues to perpetrate against its population, in particular in the northern region of Iraq, in southern Shi'a centres and in the southern marshes (Commission on Human Rights resolution 1992/71 of 5 March 1992). The Security Council notes that this situation is confirmed by the report of the Special Rapporteur of the Commission on Human Rights (E/CN.4/1992/31, also to be circulated in document S/23685) and by the comments of the Office of the Executive Delegate of the Secretary-General contained in the further report of the Secretary-General.

34. The members of the Council are particularly concerned at the reported restrictions on the supplies of essential commodities, in particular food and fuel, which have been imposed by the Government of Iraq on the three northern governorates of Dohuk, Erbil and Suleimaniya. In this regard, as the Special Rapporteur has noted in his report, inasmuch as the repression of the population continues, the threat to international peace and security in the region mentioned in resolution 688 (1991) remains.

IV. *Concluding observation*

35. In view of the observations on the record of Iraq's performance, the Security Council has considered itself justified in concluding that Iraq has not fully complied with the obligations placed upon it by the Council. It is the Council's hope and expectation that this meeting will prove an invaluable opportunity to advance in the consideration of this issue as required in the interest of world peace and security, as well as that of the Iraqi people.

Document 109

Statement by the President of the Security Council concerning Iraq's compliance with the relevant Council resolutions

S/23709, 12 March 1992

In concluding the present stage of the consideration of the item on the agenda, I have been authorized, following consultations among members of the Security Council, to make the following statement on behalf of the Council:

"The views of the Security Council having been expressed through its President and by the statements of its members on the extent of compliance by the Government of Iraq with its obligations under the relevant Security Council resolutions, the Security Council has listened with close attention to the statement by the Deputy Prime Minister of Iraq and his responses to the questions posed by Council members.

"The members of the Security Council wish to reiterate their full support for the statement made by the President of the Council on their behalf at the opening of the 3059th meeting (S/23699).

"In the view of the Security Council, the Government of Iraq has not yet complied fully and unconditionally with those obligations, must do so and must immediately take the appropriate actions in this regard. It hopes that the goodwill expressed by the Deputy Prime Minister of Iraq will be matched by deeds."

Document 110

Decision 7 taken by the Governing Council of the United Nations Compensation Commission: Criteria for additional categories of claims

S/AC.26/1991/ 7/Rev.1, 17 March 1992

Decision taken by the Governing Council of the United Nations Compensation Commission during its third session, at the 18th meeting, held on 28 November 1991, as revised at the 24th meeting held on 16 March 1992

Criteria for additional Categories of Claims

I. *Criteria for processing of claims of individuals not otherwise covered*

1. The following criteria will govern the submission of all claims of individuals not filed under the criteria adopted by the Governing Council on 2 August 1991, pursuant to resolution 687 (1991).

2. The following criteria are not intended to resolve every issue that may arise with respect to these claims. Rather, they are intended to provide sufficient guidance to enable Governments to prepare consolidated claims submissions.

3. The Commission will process the claims as expeditiously as possible. While decisions on the precise method of processing these claims will be made at a later stage the following steps are contemplated. The Secretar-

iat will make a preliminary assessment of the claims to determine whether they meet the formal requirements established by the Governing Council. The claims would then be submitted to a panel or panels of Commissioners for review within a set time-limit. The Commissioners would be instructed to utilize different procedures appropriate to the character, amount and subject-matter of particular types of claims. In so far as possible, claims with significant common legal or factual issues should be processed together. The Commissioners would be asked to report to the Council on the claims received and the amount recommended for the claims submitted by each Government. The Council would then decide on the total amount to be allocated to each Government. The Council may decide to refer unusually large or complex claims to panels of Commissioners for detailed review, possibly involving additional written submissions and oral proceedings. In such a case, the individual would be allowed to present his or her case directly to the panel.

4. As contributions are made to the Fund, the Council will allocate those funds among the various categories of claims. If resources of the Fund are insufficient with respect to all claims processed to date, *pro rata* payments would be made to Governments periodically as funds become available. The Council will decide on the priority for payment of various categories of claims.

5. Claims may be submitted under this category for the loss of earnings or profits; the Commission will consider at a later time the circumstances in which such claims may be admitted, the amounts to be awarded, and the limits to be imposed thereon.

Claims covered

6. These payments are available with respect to any direct loss, damage, or injury (including death) to individuals as a result of Iraq's unlawful invasion and occupation of Kuwait. This will include any loss suffered as a result of:

(a) Military operations or threat of military action by either side during the period 2 August 1990 to 2 March 1991;

(b) Departure from or inability to leave Iraq or Kuwait (or a decision not to return) during that period;

(c) Actions by officials, employees or agents of the Government of Iraq or its controlled entities during that period in connection with the invasion or occupation;

(d) The breakdown of civil order in Kuwait or Iraq during that period; or

(e) Hostage-taking or other illegal detention.

7. These payments are available with respect to individuals who claim losses in excess of those compensable under claim forms B or C. These payments are also available with respect to individuals who have chosen not to file under claim form A, B, or C because their losses exceed $100,000. In addition, these payments are available to reimburse payments made or relief provided by individuals to others—for example, to employees or to others pursuant to contractual obligations—for losses covered by any of the criteria adopted by the Council.

8. Since these claims may be for substantial amounts, they must be supported by documentary and other appropriate evidence sufficient to demonstrate the circumstances and the amount of the claimed loss.

9. Direct losses as a result of Iraq's unlawful invasion and occupation of Kuwait are eligible for compensation. Compensation will not be provided for losses suffered as a result of the trade embargo and related measures. Further guidance will be provided on the interpretation and application of this paragraph.

10. Any compensation, whether in funds or in kind, already received from any source will be deducted from the total amount of losses suffered.

Submission of claims

11. Claims will not be considered on behalf of Iraqi nationals who do not have bona fide nationality of any other State.

12. Claims will be submitted by Governments. Each Government may submit claims on behalf of its nationals, and may in its discretion also submit the claims of other persons resident in its territory. In addition, the Council may request an appropriate person, authority, or body to submit claims on behalf of persons who are not in a position to have their claims submitted by a Government.

13. Each consolidated claim must include:

(a) For each separate claim, a signed statement by each individual covered containing:

(i) his or her name and address, and any passport number or other identifying national number;

(ii) a description of and documents evidencing the amount, type, and reason for each element of the loss;

(iii) identification of any compensation, whether in funds or in kind, already received from any source for the claim asserted;

(iv) his or her affirmation that the foregoing information is correct, and that no other claim for the same loss has been submitted to the Commission;

(v) a copy of any previously submitted individual claim; and

(b) The affirmation of the Government submitting the claim that, to the best of the information available to it, the individuals in question are its nationals or residents, and the affirmation of the Government or of the person, authority, or body as referred to in paragraph 12 that it has no reason to believe that the information stated is incorrect.

14. The Executive Secretary (or a Commissioner) will prepare and the Executive Secretary will distribute a standard form for submission of these claims, incorporating the above elements in a clear and concise manner. Except as may otherwise be agreed between the Executive Secretary and the Government in question, claims will be submitted to the Executive Secretary by Governments or by persons, authorities, or bodies as referred to in paragraph 12 on the standard form and must include the information in an official language of the United Nations. Each Government may adopt such procedures as it finds appropriate in preparing its claims. The Executive Secretary (or a Commissioner) will be available to answer questions or provide assistance to any Governments which may request it.

15. Governments must submit all claims on behalf of individuals within one year of the date on which the Executive Secretary circulates these claims forms. The Council encourages the submission of such claims within six months from the date on which the Executive Secretary circulates to Governments the claims forms; and the Commission will thereupon give consideration to such claims as provided herein.

II. Criteria for processing claims of corporations and other entities

16. The following criteria will govern the submission of claims of corporations, other private legal entities and public-sector enterprises (hereinafter referred to as "corporations and other entities") pursuant to resolution 687 (1991).

17. The following criteria are not intended to resolve every issue that may arise with respect to these claims. Rather, they are intended to provide sufficient guidance to enable Governments to prepare consolidated claims submissions.

18. The Commission will process the claims as expeditiously as possible. While decisions on the precise method of processing these claims will be made at a later stage the following steps are contemplated. The Secretariat will make a preliminary assessment of the claims to determine whether they meet the formal requirements established by the Governing Council. The claims would then be submitted to a panel or panels of Commissioners for review within a set time-limit. The Commissioners would be instructed to utilize different procedures appropriate to the character, amount and subject-matter of particular types of claims. In so far as possible, claims with significant common legal or factual issues should be

processed together. The Commissioners would be asked to report to the Council on the claims received and the amount recommended for the claims submitted by each Government. The Council would then decide on the total amount to be allocated to each Government. The Council may decide to refer unusually large or complex claims to panels of Commissioners for detailed review, possibly involving additional written submissions and oral proceedings. In such a case, the entity would be allowed to present its case directly to the panel.

19. As contributions are made to the Fund, the Council will allocate those funds among the various categories of claims. If resources of the Fund are insufficient with respect to all claims processed to date, *pro rata* payments would be made to Governments periodically as funds become available. The Council will decide on the priority for payment of various categories of claims.

20. Claims may be submitted under this category for the loss of earnings or profits; the Commission will consider at a later time the circumstances under which such claims may be admitted, the amounts to be awarded, and the limits to be imposed thereon.

Claims covered

21. These payments are available with respect to any direct loss, damage, or injury to corporations and other entities as a result of Iraq's unlawful invasion and occupation of Kuwait. This will include any loss suffered as a result of:

(a) Military operations or threat of military action by either side during the period 2 August 1990 to 2 March 1991;

(b) Departure of persons from or their inability to leave Iraq or Kuwait (or a decision not to return) during that period;

(c) Actions by officials, employees or agents of the Government of Iraq or its controlled entities during that period in connection with the invasion or occupation;

(d) The breakdown of civil order in Kuwait or Iraq during that period; or

(e) Hostage-taking or other illegal detention.

22. These payments are available to reimburse payments made or relief provided by corporations or other entities to others—for example, to employees, or to others pursuant to contractual obligations—for losses covered by any of the criteria adopted by the Council.

23. Since these claims may be for substantial amounts, they must be supported by documentary and other appropriate evidence sufficient to demonstrate the circumstances and the amount of the claimed loss.

24. Direct losses as a result of Iraq's unlawful invasion and occupation of Kuwait are eligible for compensation. Compensation will not be provided for losses

suffered as a result of the trade embargo and related measures. Further guidance will be provided on the interpretation and application of this paragraph.

25. Any compensation, whether in funds or in kind, already received from any source will be deducted from the total amount of losses suffered.

Submission of claims

26. Each Government may submit claims on behalf of corporations or other entities that, on the date on which the claim arose, were incorporated or organized under its law. Claims may be submitted on behalf of a corporation or other entity by only one Government. A corporation or other entity would be required to request the State of its incorporation or organization to submit its claim to the Commission. In the case of a corporation or other private legal entity whose State of incorporation or organization fails to submit, within the deadline established in paragraph 29, such claims falling within the applicable criteria, the corporation or other private legal entity may itself make a claim to the Commission within three months thereafter. It must submit at the same time an explanation as to why its claim is not being submitted by a Government, together with the relevant information specified in paragraph 27. In such a case, any award of the Commission will be paid directly to the corporation or other private legal entity.

27. Each consolidated claim must include:

(a) For each separate claim, a signed statement by an authorized official of each corporation or other entity covered containing:

    (i) documents evidencing the name, address and place of incorporation or organization of the entity;

    (ii) a general description of the legal structure of the entity;

    (iii) a description of and documents evidencing the amount, type, and reason for each element of the loss;

    (iv) identification of any compensation, whether in funds or in kind, already received from any source for the claim asserted;

    (v) his or her name and address and affirmation that the foregoing information is correct, and that no other claim for the same loss has been submitted to the Commission;

(b) The affirmation of the Government submitting the claim that, to the best of the information available to it, the entities in question are incorporated or organized under its law and the affirmation of the Government that

it has no reason to believe that the information stated is incorrect.

28. The Executive Secretary (or a Commissioner) will prepare and the Executive Secretary will distribute a standard form for submission of these claims, incorporating the above elements in a clear and concise manner. Except as may otherwise be agreed between the Executive Secretary and the Government in question, claims will be submitted to the Executive Secretary by Governments on the standard form and must include the information in an official language of the United Nations. Each Government may adopt such procedures as it finds appropriate in preparing its claims. The Executive Secretary (or a Commissioner) will be available to answer questions or provide assistance to any Governments which may request it.

29. Governments must submit all claims on behalf of corporations or other entities within one year of the date the Executive Secretary circulates the claims forms. The Council encourages the submission of such claims within six months from the date on which the Executive Secretary circulates to Governments the claims forms; and the Commission will thereupon give consideration to such claims as provided herein.

III. *Criteria for processing claims of governments and international organizations*

30. The following criteria will govern the submission of claims of Governments and international organizations pursuant to resolution 687 (1991). Each Government will submit claims of its own and those of its political subdivisions, or any agency, ministry, instrumentality, or entity controlled by it.

31. The following criteria are not intended to resolve every issue that may arise with respect to these claims. Rather, they are intended to provide sufficient guidance to enable Governments and international organizations to prepare consolidated claims submissions.

32. The Commission will process the claims as expeditiously as possible. While decisions on the precise method of processing these claims will be made at a later stage the following steps are contemplated. The Secretariat will make a preliminary assessment of the claims to determine whether they meet the formal requirements established by the Governing Council. The claims would then be submitted to a panel or panels of Commissioners for review within a set time-limit. The Commissioners would be instructed to utilize different procedures appropriate to the character, amount and subject-matter of particular types of claims. In so far as possible, claims with significant common legal or factual issues should be processed together. The Commissioners would be asked to report to the Council on the claims received and the

amount recommended for the claims submitted by each Government. The Council would then decide on the total amount to be allocated to each Government. The Council may decide to refer unusually large or complex claims to panels of Commissioners for detailed review, possibly involving additional written submissions and oral proceedings. In such a case, when an international organization is involved, it would be allowed to present its case directly to the panel.

33. As contributions are made to the Fund, the Council will allocate those funds among the various categories of claims. If resources of the Fund are insufficient with respect to all claims processed to date, *pro rata* payments would be made to Governments periodically as funds become available. The Council will decide on the priority for payment of various categories of claims.

Claims covered

34. These payments are available with respect to any direct loss, damage, or injury to Governments or international organizations as a result of Iraq's unlawful invasion and occupation of Kuwait. This will include any loss suffered as a result of:

(a) Military operations or threat of military action by either side during the period 2 August 1990 to 2 March 1991;

(b) Departure of persons from or their inability to leave Iraq or Kuwait (or a decision not to return) during that period;

(c) Actions by officials, employees or agents of the Government of Iraq or its controlled entities during that period in connection with the invasion or occupation;

(d) The breakdown of civil order in Kuwait or Iraq during that period; or

(e) Hostage-taking or other illegal detention.

35. These payments are available with respect to direct environmental damage and the depletion of natural resources as a result of Iraq's unlawful invasion and occupation of Kuwait. This will include losses or expenses resulting from:

(a) Abatement and prevention of environmental damage, including expenses directly relating to fighting oil fires and stemming the flow of oil in coastal and international waters;

(b) Reasonable measures already taken to clean and restore the environment or future measures which can be documented as reasonably necessary to clean and restore the environment;

(c) Reasonable monitoring and assessment of the environmental damage for the purposes of evaluating and abating the harm and restoring the environment;

(d) Reasonable monitoring of public health and performing medical screenings for the purposes of investigation and combating increased health risks as a result of the environmental damage; and

(e) Depletion of or damage to natural resources.

36. These payments will include loss of or damage to property of a Government, as well as losses and costs incurred by a Government in evacuating its nationals from Iraq or Kuwait. These payments are also available to reimburse payments made or relief provided by Governments or international organizations to others—for example to nationals, residents or employees or to others pursuant to contractual obligations—for losses covered by any of the criteria adopted by the Council.

37. Since these claims will be for substantial amounts, they must be supported by documentary and other appropriate evidence sufficient to demonstrate the circumstances and the amount of the claimed loss.

38. Direct losses as a result of Iraq's unlawful invasion and occupation of Kuwait are eligible for compensation. Compensation will not be provided for losses suffered as a result of the trade embargo and related measures. Further guidance will be provided on the interpretation and application of this paragraph.

39. Any compensation, whether in funds or in kind, already received from any source will be deducted from the total amount of losses suffered.

Submission of claims

40. Each consolidated claim must include:

(a) For each separate claim, a signed statement by an authorized official of the Government or international organization containing:

(i) his or her name and address, and government agency instrumentality, or ministry or controlled entity, or the international organization, with which associated;

(ii) a description of and documents evidencing the amount, type, and reason for each element of the loss;

(iii) identification of any compensation, whether in funds or in kind, already received from any source for the claim asserted;

(iv) his or her affirmation t'   ~egoing information is correct, and t   ~ for the same loss has been su'   ~.

(b) The affirmation o'
tional organization submitt'
to the best of the inform
reason to believe that th

41. The Executi
will prepare and the '
standard form for su

above elements in a clear and concise manner. Except as may otherwise be agreed between the Executive Secretary and the Government or international organization in question, claims will be submitted to the Executive Secretary on the standard form and must include the information in an official language of the United Nations. The Executive Secretary (or a Commissioner) will be available to answer questions or provide assistance to any Governments or international organizations which may request it.

42. Governments and international organizations must submit all claims within one year of the date on which the Executive Secretary circulates the standard form. The Council encourages the submission of such claims within six months from the date on which the Executive Secretary circulates to Governments and international organizations the claims forms; and the Commission will thereupon give consideration to such claims as provided herein.

Document 111

Statement by the President of the Security Council concerning implementation of the plan to use the proceeds of sales of Iraqi petroleum and petroleum products to purchase foodstuffs, medicines and materials and supplies for essential civilian needs

S/23732, 19 March 1992

The Security Council welcomes the announcement of the Iraqi authorities that they will resume discussions with the United Nations Secretariat concerning implementation of the scheme of sales of Iraqi petroleum and petroleum products, as provided for in Security Council resolutions 706 (1991) and 712 (1991), and for the use of the proceeds of such sales in accordance with the Secretary-General's report of 4 September 1991 (S/23006) and the above-mentioned resolutions.

The Council also welcomes the Secretary-General's intention that these discussions be organized without delay.

The Council is prepared to authorize the regime for the sale of Iraqi petroleum and petroleum products on the above basis for a like period of time as that specified in these resolutions as soon as the Secretary-General indicates that the Iraqi authorities are prepared to proceed on a date certain with the export of petroleum and petroleum products in accordance with the scheme.

The members of the Council are prepared at an appropriate time to consider possible further extensions of time based upon Iraq's cooperation with the above and the Council's ongoing assessment of the needs and requirements in accordance with paragraph 1 (d) of Security Council resolution 706 (1991).

Document 112

Statement by the President of the Security Council concerning the sanctions regime

S/23761, 27 March 1992

The members of the Security Council held informal consultations on 27 March 1992 pursuant to paragraphs 21 and 28 of resolution 687 (1991) and paragraph 6 of resolution 700 (1991).

After hearing all the opinions expressed in the course of the consultations, the President of the Council concluded that there still was no agreement that the necessary conditions existed for a modification of the regimes established in paragraph 20 of resolution 687 (1991), as referred to in paragraph 21 of that resolution; in paragraphs 22, 23 24 and 25 of resolution 687 (1991), as referred to in paragraph 28 of that resolution; and in paragraph 6 of resolution 700 (1991). The members of the Council expressed the hope that the offers of cooperation recently conveyed by Iraq will be fully matched by actual deeds.

Document 113

Report of the Secretary-General on UNIKOM for the period from 3 October 1991 to 31 March 1992

S/23766, 31 March 1992

Introduction

1. By paragraph 5 of its resolution 687 (1991) of 3 April 1991, the Security Council established a demilitarized zone (DMZ) along the Iraq-Kuwait border and decided to set up an observer unit with the following tasks: to monitor the Khawr Abd Allah waterway and the DMZ; to deter violations of the boundary through its presence in and surveillance of the DMZ; and to observe any hostile or potentially hostile action mounted from the territory of one State into the other. By its resolution 689 (1991) of 9 April 1991, the Security Council approved my predecessor's report on the implementation of the above provisions; 1/ noted that the decision to set up the observer unit had been taken in paragraph 5 of resolution 687 (1991) and could be terminated only by the Council's decision; and decided to review the question of termination or continuation as well as the modalities of the United Nations Iraq-Kuwait Observation Mission (UNIKOM) every six months. In keeping with the above provisions, the Security Council reviewed UNIKOM's mandate on 7 October 1991 and concurred with my predecessor's recommendation that UNIKOM be maintained for a further six-month period. 2/

2. The purpose of the present report is to provide the Security Council, prior to its review, with an overview of the last six months of UNIKOM's activities.

Organization

3. As of April 1992, the composition of UNIKOM was as follows:

Military observers

Argentina	7	Ireland	8
Austria	7	Italy	7
Bangladesh	7	Kenya	8
Canada	1	Malaysia	8
China	20	Nigeria	7
Denmark	7	Norway	8
Fiji	8	Pakistan	9
Finland	7	Poland	7
France	20	Romania	7
Ghana	8	Russian Federation	20
Greece	7	Senegal	7
Hungary	7	Singapore	7
India	8	Sweden	7
Indonesia	7	Thailand	7

Military observers (continued)

Turkey	7	United States	
United Kingdom of		of America	20
Great Britain and		Uruguay	8
Northern Ireland	20	Venezuela	7
		Total	300

Administrative and logistic support

Engineers (Canada)	85
Logistics (Denmark)	45
Helicopters (Chile)	50
Medical (Norway)	20
Total	200

The above figures represent authorized strength. The actual strength is subject to minor fluctuations, particularly in connection with rotation. From 18 December 1991, a number of military observers were temporarily detached to Yugoslavia to serve as United Nations military liaison officers. Their number varied, reaching a peak of 50 during the first week of March 1992. At present, 30 military observers are still in Yugoslavia to assist the United Nations Protection Force (UNPROFOR).

4. UNIKOM also includes 196 civilian staff, of whom 102 are international staff and 94 are locally recruited. In addition to the military helicopters contributed by Chile, UNIKOM has the use of two small fixed-wing civilian aircraft contributed by the Government of Switzerland and a chartered aircraft that is used to carry its personnel and equipment between Baghdad and Kuwait.

5. Command of UNIKOM continues to be exercised by Major-General Günther Greindl (Austria), the Chief Military Observer.

6. During the period under review the Canadian engineers cleared and marked an additional 200 kilometres of patrol track, disposed of 4,850 pieces of unexploded ordnance and reconfirmed the safety of previously cleared routes. They also carried out improvements at the headquarters extension known as Camp Khor and built 3 landing strips and 16 concrete helicopter landing pads in the DMZ. They also provided support to the United Nations Iraq-Kuwait Boundary Demarcation Commission by placing 165 preliminary survey markers and 13

1/ S/22454 and Add.1-3.
2/ S/23106.

survey control points in the DMZ. As planned, the engineers will be further reduced to 50 on 1 April.

7. The Danish logistic unit, which replaced the previous Swedish unit, provided transport, including distribution of logistic supplies, as well as maintenance of heavy-duty vehicles. It also provided security for UNIKOM headquarters and the logistic base at Doha.

8. The Norwegian medical unit was reduced in strength to 20. It provides general medical support, including a sick-bay facility at Umm Qasr and first-aid posts at the central and southern sector headquarters.

9. On 1 November 1991, UNIKOM moved to its permanent headquarters at Umm Qasr in the DMZ. At the same time, the helicopter unit moved to the headquarters extension at Camp Khor, where the northern sector headquarters is also located. The headquarters premises have been refurbished and living conditions for both military personnel and civilian staff working there are now adequate. The provision of air-conditioned prefabricated trailers and other facilities has much improved conditions for the military observers working in the DMZ.

10. Major-General Greindl and his senior staff have held regular meetings with the authorities in Baghdad and Kuwait City. Daily liaison with the authorities is maintained through UNIKOM's liaison offices in the two capitals. In addition, local liaison with the Iraqi authorities is maintained at Umm Qasr. The Governments of Iraq and Kuwait have given the Mission all the support and cooperation necessary for it to carry out its mandate.

11. UNIKOM has maintained contact and provided support to other United Nations missions working in Iraq and Kuwait, in particular to the Boundary Demarcation Commission and to the United Nations Return of Property from Iraq to Kuwait (UNROP).

Demilitarized zone

12. The DMZ is about 200 kilometres long, to which must be added the Khawr Abd Allah waterway, with a length of about 40 kilometres. For the most part, the DMZ is barren and almost uninhabited, except for the towns of Umm Qasr and Safwan. There are airfields at Safwan and Umm Qasr and a port at Umm Qasr.

13. Much of the DMZ is still littered with unexploded ordnance and mines, particularly in the south. Recently the Government of Kuwait contracted with explosive ordnance disposal companies to clear its side of the DMZ and, in consultation with UNIKOM, the companies concerned have started work.

Deployment and concept of operations

14. For operational purposes, UNIKOM has divided the DMZ into three sectors; each sector has a headquarters and six patrol/observation bases. The UNIKOM deployment is shown on the attached map [not reproduced here]. UNIKOM has full freedom of movement throughout the DMZ.

15. UNIKOM's concept of operations revolves around a combination of patrol and observation bases, observation points, vehicular and aerial patrols, investigation teams and liaison with the parties at all levels. UNIKOM's observation capability is enhanced by night observation devices and a range of visual magnifying equipment. The deployment of two maritime radar systems in its northern sector at patrol/observation bases N-1 and N-6 has much improved UNIKOM's surveillance of the Khawr Abd Allah waterway. The observation capability of UNIKOM will be further enhanced by the erection of 17 observation towers, which is currently under way.

16. UNIKOM has conducted trials of ground surveillance radars to complement its existing observation capability in the DMZ. Technical trials have taken place in the DMZ on three types of ground surveillance radar at no cost to the United Nations. These trials have not been fully conclusive and General Greindl has therefore recommended further operational trials.

Violations and complaints

17. The situation in the DMZ has been calm. UNIKOM has observed three types of violations in the DMZ: minor incursions on the ground by small groups of soldiers, often just one or two; overflights by military aircraft; and the carrying by policemen of weapons other than sidearms. The overflights were by military aircraft of types used by Kuwait and by the forces of Member States cooperating with Kuwait. In addition, UNIKOM recorded five violations (overflights) by unidentified aircraft. The table below summarizes the violations observed by UNIKOM [table is on page 433].
All violations were raised in writing with the party concerned, with a view to having action taken to prevent a recurrence.

18. During the reporting period, UNIKOM received 31 written complaints from Iraq and 7 from Kuwait. UNIKOM investigated these complaints and conveyed the results to the parties concerned.

Other matters

19. UNIKOM kept in contact with the Governments of Iraq and Kuwait concerning certain aspects of civilian administration in their respective parts of the DMZ, particularly the maintenance of law and order. Iraq maintained 4 border police centres and 11 border police posts in the DMZ. Five of the police posts remain on the Kuwaiti side of the boundary line shown on the UNIKOM map and two are on the Iraqi side of the boundary but closer than 1,000 metres to it. The Chief

| | Iraq | | | | Kuwait/Member States cooperating with Kuwait | | | |
	Ground	Air	Police weapons	Total	Ground	Air	Police weapons	Total
3 Oct-9 Nov	1	0	0	1	11	7	14	32
10 Nov-9 Dec	0	0	0	0	8	10	5	23
10 Dec-9 Jan	0	0	1	1	5	12	5	22
10 Jan-9 Feb	0	0	1	1	1	1	0	2
10 Feb-9 Mar	0	0	1	1	0	2	2	4
10 Mar-31 Mar	0	0	0	0	6	3	8	17
Total	1	0	3	4	31	35	34	100

Military Observer continued his efforts to have the seven posts pulled back. However, the Iraqi authorities have maintained that the posts must remain until the border between Iraq and Kuwait has been demarcated. Iraq has also deployed harbour police at Umm Qasr port and customs police at Safwan. Kuwait has set up 13 of 20 planned police posts in the DMZ. Both parties have consulted UNIKOM in advance of new police deployments in the DMZ. Separate biweekly meetings with the chiefs of the border police of Iraq and Kuwait were used to resolve minor problems at the local level.

20. During the period under review, UNIKOM observed an increase in the movement of Iraqi civilian ships through the Khawr Abd Allah waterway, in connection with the surveying of maritime channels and the reconstruction of the Al-Bakr oil terminal. Movement of ships is observed from the shore and also by air reconnaissance. Iraq has complied with the requirement to give advance notice of such movements.

21. Activity in the illegal market described in previous reports 3/ has declined. The market remains located astride the boundary line in the southern sector, but the authorities of Iraq and Kuwait have taken effective measures to limit access to it through intensive patrolling, checkpoints and, outside the DMZ, helicopter patrols.

22. During the last six months four incidents took place in UNIKOM's area of operations that gave cause for concern. A brief summary of these incidents follows:

(a) On 10 October 1991, 55 Iraqi fishermen were detained north-east of Failaka Island by the Kuwaiti authorities, which claimed that they were within Kuwaiti territorial waters. This was disputed by the fishermen and by the Iraqi authorities. It has proved impossible for UNIKOM to ascertain the actual location where the fishermen were apprehended. They were eventually returned to Iraq through the International Committee of the Red Cross (ICRC) on 26 October 1991;

(b) On 18 October 1991, Iraq complained that a Kuwaiti patrol entered Iraq near Safwan, wounding a local farmer with rifle fire and forcibly detaining two others, and allegedly firing on an Iraqi police post at Safwan. UNIKOM's investigation concluded that the incident took place on the Kuwaiti side of the DMZ, close to the boundary, in an area where Iraqis had been farming prior to 2 August 1990. UNIKOM could not verify the claim that the Iraqi police post had been fired on;

(c) On 2 November 1991, 12 Iraqi policemen were delivering salary packets, rations and supplies to their police posts Al-Ratqa and Talha, in the central sector of the DMZ. When the policemen finished their task at Al-Ratqa, they drove towards Talha on UNIKOM's Mike Road, which crosses the boundary line in several places. The Iraqis were intercepted by Kuwaiti personnel armed with rifles. The Iraqis were detained for interrogation; Kuwaiti authorities took control of their vehicle, pistols, ammunition and supplies, as well as a sum of Iraqi dinars. The detained Iraqis were repatriated under the supervision of ICRC on 7 December 1991;

(d) On 7 January 1992, two Kuwaiti policemen were apprehended at the Iraqi police post Umm Qasr, which is one of the five on the Kuwaiti side of the boundary line shown on UNIKOM's map. A UNIKOM investigation concluded that the two policemen had lost their way and had approached the Iraqi post by mistake. The two were returned to Kuwait through ICRC on 25 January 1992.

Three of the above incidents occurred near the boundary line. UNIKOM has repeatedly urged both parties to comply with the requirement that they maintain a reasonable distance of about 1,000 metres from the line in order to avoid such incidents.

Financial aspects

23. By its resolution 46/197 of 20 December 1991, the General Assembly authorized the Secretary-General to enter into commitments for the operation of UNIKOM at a rate not to exceed $5,600,000 gross ($5,441,500 net) per month for the six-month period beginning 9 April

3/ S/23000, para. 11, and S/23106, para. 28.

1992, subject to the prior concurrence of the Advisory Committee on Administrative and Budgetary Questions, should the Security Council decide to continue the Observation Mission beyond 8 April 1992. Therefore, assuming continuance of the Mission's existing responsibilities, the costs to the United Nations for maintaining UNIKOM during the six-month period through 8 October 1992 will be within the level of commitment authorized by the Assembly in its resolution 46/197.

24. As at 23 March 1992, unpaid assessed contributions to the UNIKOM Special Account for the period since the inception of the Mission on 9 April 1991 up to 8 April 1992 amounted to $18.2 million.

Observations

25. During the past six months, conditions along the border between Iraq and Kuwait have been calm and the DMZ established by the Security Council has been generally respected. The number of violations has been further reduced and those that occurred have been minor.

26. UNIKOM has continued to maintain a high level of vigilance and has performed its tasks effectively. In this it has had the cooperation of both parties. I have no doubt that the presence and activities of UNIKOM in the area are essential for ensuring respect for the DMZ and maintaining calm in the area. Therefore, I recommend to the Security Council that it maintain UNIKOM for a further six-month period.

27. In order to avoid incidents, UNIKOM requires the authorities on both sides to maintain a reasonable distance from the boundary line drawn on UNIKOM's map. The importance of this principle is underlined by the fact that three of the four incidents reported in paragraph 22 above occurred on occasions when it was not observed. It is my hope that both sides will ensure that there is no recurrence.

28. The continued presence of Iraqi police posts on the Kuwaiti side of the line shown on UNIKOM's map [not reproduced here] remains a matter of concern.

29. Finally, I wish to pay tribute to Major-General Greindl and to all the men and women under his command, both military and civilian, for the skill and dedication with which they have carried out their important task. Their discipline and bearing have been of a high order, reflecting credit on their countries and on the United Nations.

Document 114

First report of the Secretary-General on the status of the implementation of the plan for the ongoing monitoring and verification of Iraq's compliance with relevant parts of section C of Security Council resolution 687 (1991)

S/23801, 10 April 1992

Introduction

1. The present report is submitted in pursuance of paragraph 8 of Security Council resolution 715 (1991) adopted on 11 October 1991. This requests the Secretary-General and the Director General of the IAEA to submit to the Security Council reports, when requested and at least every six months after the adoption of the resolution, on the implementation of the plans approved under resolution 715 (1991), for the ongoing monitoring and verification of Iraq's compliance with relevant parts of Section C of Security Council resolution 687 (1991). The paragraphs below provide information, for the first six-month period, on the implementation of the plan to be carried out by the Special Commission established by the Secretary-General pursuant to paragraph 9 (b) (i) of Security Council resolution 687 (1991). This plan itself contains, in paragraph 25, the same reporting requirements on the implementation of the plan as the Council's resolution 715 (1991).

2. The Special Commission's monitoring and verification plan is contained in document S/22781/Rev.1. It covers the long-term monitoring and verification of Iraq's compliance with its unconditional obligations under Section C of resolution 687 (1991) not to use, retain, possess, develop, construct or otherwise acquire any weapons or related facilities and items prohibited under paragraphs 8 and 9 of that resolution relating to proscribed ballistic missiles, chemical and biological weapons and facilities. Monitoring and verification under the plan will need to cover not only military but also those civilian sites, facilities, material and other items or activities that could be used in contravention of these obligations of Iraq under resolution 687 (1991). For that purpose the plan provides for inspections in Iraq, aerial overflights and submission of information by Iraq so that the Special Commission

would be able to monitor and verify that no chemical or biological weapons, ballistic missiles with a range greater than 150 kilometres, or any other facilities and items prohibited under resolution 687 (1991) were reacquired.

3. Under paragraph 5 of resolution 715 (1991), Iraq is required to meet unconditionally all its obligations under the plan and to cooperate fully with the Special Commission in carrying out the plan.

4. The first practical steps to be taken by Iraq under the plan were the submission, by 10 November 1991, of (a) initial information on the specific dual-purpose activities, facilities and items outlined in the plan and its annexes; and (b) a report on the legislative and administrative measures taken to implement resolutions 687 (1991), 707 (1991), other relevant Security Council resolutions and the plan. Iraq is further obliged to update the information in (a) above each 15 January and 15 July, and to report further on (b) when requested by the Special Commission. Ongoing monitoring and verification can only be carried out effectively if the Special Commission has the clearest picture of what Iraq's capabilities have been in the development, production and acquisition of weapons of mass destruction and prohibited ballistic missiles and what items, facilities and materials were at its disposal or would be from time to time acquired which, while devoted to civilian activities, could be converted with relative ease to proscribed military uses.

Developments during the period
11 October 1991-8 April 1992

5. Iraq's position on resolution 715 (1991) and the monitoring and verification plan approved thereunder was formally stated in a letter of 19 November 1991 which the Minister for Foreign Affairs of Iraq addressed to the President of the Security Council. In the letter Iraq did not recognize any obligations under resolution 715 (1991) and strongly attacked the plan, claiming that it was "aimed at objectives incompatible with the letter and spirit of the United Nations Charter, the norms of international law and international and humanitarian pacts and covenants". In the view of the Special Commission, this position is tantamount to a rejection of the resolution and the plan.

6. Only in late November did the Special Commission receive from Iraq a document that was stated in the letter of 19 November of the Minister for Foreign Affairs of Iraq to be "the information required under resolution 687 (1991) that comes under the mandate of the Special Commission". As described in paragraph 5 above, the letter does not recognize that Iraq has any obligations under resolution 715 (1991) and the plans approved thereunder. Instead Iraq arrogated to itself the right to decide what information it would provide to the Special

Commission and, in this respect, the document transmitted to the Special Commission did little more than repeat information already supplied. It thus fell well short of the information required under the monitoring and verification plan. No information was provided by Iraq, as required by the plan, on the legislative and administrative measures taken to implement resolutions 687 (1991), 707 (1991), other relevant Security Council resolutions and the plan.

7. The Executive Chairman of the Special Commission in a letter, dated 20 December 1991, to the Permanent Representative of Iraq to the United Nations stated that the Special Commission could not accept that the document provided by Iraq with the letter of 19 November constituted the submission of information required under Security Council resolution 715 (1991). He further stressed that Iraq's attitude was a serious obstacle to the implementation of the monitoring and verification of Iraq's compliance with its obligations under resolution 687 (1991). In the letter Iraq was requested to rectify the situation immediately and fulfil its obligations under resolution 715 (1991) and the monitoring and verification plan. The Special Commission asked Iraq to provide by 15 January 1992 all the information and data specified in the plan.

8. Iraq has failed to respond to these requests, and has not provided its first semi-annual declaration which under the plan was due from it on 15 January 1992. No notifications on specific activities, as stipulated by the plan, were communicated by Iraq to the Special Commission.

9. The failure by Iraq to acknowledge its obligations under resolution 715 (1991) and to comply with the monitoring and verification plan was reported to the Security Council in the Secretary-General's notes and reports (S/23268, S/23514, S/23606, S/23643 and S/23687) which also referred to steps taken by the Special Commission to seek Iraq's compliance with Security Council resolution 715 (1991) and the plan.

10. As part of these efforts the Special Commission, at the end of January 1992, sent a special mission headed by two members of the Commission to Baghdad to underline the Commission's most serious concern with Iraq's failure to comply with the resolution 715 (1991) and the plan. Iraq, at the level of the Minister of State for Foreign Affairs, reiterated that the Government maintained its position expressed in the letter of 19 November.

11. In view of the attitude maintained by Iraq the Special Commission reported on 18 February to the Security Council (S/23606) its conclusion that "Iraq has no intention of meeting its obligations under the plans approved under, and the provisions included in, Security Council resolution 715 (1991)".

12. On 19 February 1992, the President of the Security Council issued a statement on behalf of the members of the Council which noted that "ongoing monitoring and verification of Iraq's obligations is an integral part of Security Council resolution 687 (1991), which established a cease-fire and provided the conditions essential to the restoration of peace and security in the region". The statement of 19 February also determined that Iraq's failure to acknowledge its obligations under resolution 715 (1991) and its rejection of the two plans for ongoing monitoring and verification constituted a continuing material breach of the relevant provisions of resolution 687 (1991). The members of the Council supported the decision of the Secretary-General to dispatch a special mission headed by the Executive Chairman of the Special Commission to visit Iraq immediately to meet and discuss with the highest levels of the Government of Iraq for the purpose of securing the unconditional agreement by Iraq to implement all its relevant obligations under resolutions 687 (1991), 707 (1991) and 715 (1991).

13. The special mission headed by the Executive Chairman of the Special Commission was immediately dispatched and held talks with the Government of Iraq on 21, 22 and 23 February. The report on the proceedings and outcome of the mission's visit was communicated to the Security Council by a note of the Secretary-General of 26 February (S/23643). This report contained amongst its conclusions the statement by the Executive Chairman that he was not able to report to the Council that he had secured from the highest levels of the Government of Iraq unconditional agreement by Iraq to implement all its relevant obligations under Security Council resolutions 687 (1991), 707 (1991) and 715 (1991).

14. In order to achieve its objectives, the special mission specifically urged Iraq to acknowledge its obligations under resolution 715 (1991) and the plans approved under it as well as to take specific steps to implement its obligations such as submission of declarations required under the plans and an undertaking that Iraq would cooperate to ensure implementation of the plans. In response, Iraq stated that it did not reject the plans for ongoing monitoring and verification approved under Security Council resolution 715 (1991). In elaborating on this statement, Iraq indicated that it had accepted only the principle of ongoing monitoring and verification, and that this was subject to considerations of sovereignty, territorial integrity, national security and non-infringement on Iraq's industrial capabilities. The Executive Chairman could not conclude that such a statement constituted unconditional agreement by Iraq to implement its obligations under the plans for ongoing monitoring and verification.

15. On 28 February the President of the Security Council issued a statement in which the members of the Council approved in full the conclusions of the special mission, and deplored and condemned, *inter alia*, the failure of Iraq to comply with the plans for ongoing monitoring and verification approved by resolution 715 (1991). The statement reiterated the Council's determination that Iraq's behaviour constituted a material breach of resolution 687 (1991) and demanded that Iraq immediately implement all its obligations under Council resolution 687 (1991) and subsequent related resolutions.

16. Through the report of the Secretary-General on the status of compliance by Iraq with the obligations placed upon it under certain of the Security Council resolutions (S/23687), the Special Commission informed the Council on 7 March that the most important outstanding matters include: failure by Iraq to acknowledge its obligations under Council resolution 715 (1991) and under the plans approved by this resolution; failure by Iraq to agree to implement unconditionally all its obligations under resolution 715 (1991); and failure by Iraq to provide the declarations required under the plans for ongoing monitoring and verification. This information was brought to the attention of the Security Council in the statement made by the President of the Council at the opening of the 3059th meeting on 11 March.

17. The Security Council met on 11 and 12 March to consider all aspects of Iraq's compliance with resolution 687 (1991) and other relevant resolutions. The Executive Chairman of the Special Commission in his statement before the Council reiterated that Iraq's position towards the plans for ongoing monitoring and verification could not be understood otherwise than as rejection.

18. On 11 March, the Deputy Prime Minister of Iraq expressed before the Council Iraq's readiness to reach a practical solution to the question of the Security Council's verification of Iraq's capabilities to produce the weapons prohibited by resolution 687 (1991), while underlining the need for respect for Iraq's sovereignty and national security. He stated that "the understanding by the Security Council of the logical and legitimate principles, basis and requests which we have presented will naturally lead to an objective, equitable and just implementation of the substantive obligations placed upon Iraq in resolutions 707 (1991) and 715 (1991), in a manner which will satisfy the Council".

19. At the conclusion of the meeting of the Security Council on 12 March, the President of the Council made a statement indicating that, in the view of the Security Council, the Government of Iraq had not yet complied fully and unconditionally with its obligations, must do so and must immediately take the appropriate actions in this

regard. The Council expressed its hope that the goodwill expressed by the Deputy Prime Minister of Iraq would be matched by deeds.

20. Following the consideration in the Security Council of Iraq's compliance with the relevant resolutions, officials from the Office of the Executive Chairman of the Special Commission met on 12 and 13 March with an Iraqi technical team. The Commission explained in detail to the team what it expected of Iraq by way of implementation of the plan for ongoing monitoring and verification (S/22871/Rev.1). In response to Iraq's requests the Special Commission provided during the meetings detailed explanations as to the format and modalities required by the plan for its implementation under its different sections and annexes. The delegation of Iraq promised to provide, by early April, the information under the plan except on the sources of imported items and on operational employment or disposition of relevant weapons. The Special Commission stressed that the information should be provided in full as required by the plan. The team handed over, by way of example, certain preliminary material on the content of Iraq's future official declarations. After review of the material, the Special Commission found that information contained therein did not meet the requirements of the plan and it therefore informed Iraq that the material needed further work to ensure that the declarations to be submitted by Iraq corresponded—both in substance and in format—to the requirements of the plan for ongoing monitoring and verification. As of 8 April no declarations or information as required by the plan has been received from Iraq by the Special Commission.

21. The Special Commission communciated on 20 December to Iraq that it would not be in a position to decide upon the requests of Iraq for the reuse of certain dual-purpose items until it received all information and data under the plan for ongoing monitoring and verification, and obtained clear and unequivocal acceptance by Iraq of resolution 715 (1991) and the plan. Any such items that might be released by the Special Commission for reuse, after being rendered harmless, need to be covered by appropriate monitoring and verification procedures envisaged in the plan.

Conclusions

22. At the moment the Special Commission has to report that, despite the Commission's best endeavour, it was not possible to begin the practical implementation of the plan for ongoing monitoring and verification (S/22871/Rev.1) approved by resolution 715 (1991) because of the positions maintained by Iraq since the adoption of this resolution. It is apparent that during the period covered in this report Iraq was not in compliance with Security Council resolution 715 (1991) nor with the plan.

23. Without clear acknowledgement by Iraq of its obligations under Security Council resolution 715 (1991) and the plans approved thereunder, as well as without its agreement to implement unconditionally these obligations, the Special Commission will be neither legally nor practically able to initiate and operate effectively the monitoring and verification plan contained in document S/22871/Rev.1. There would be no assurances on the full implementation of resolution 715 (1991) as envisaged by the Security Council and Iraq's position would still be a matter of great concern. In the absence of these steps on the part of Iraq the credibility of Iraq's declarations on its capabilities related to resolution 715 (1991) would be greatly undermined. As the statement, dated 19 February, of the President of the Security Council on behalf of the Council members indicated, unconditional agreement by Iraq to implement its obligations under resolution 715 (1991) is one of the essential preconditions to any reconsideration by the Council under paragraphs 21 and 22 of resolution 687 (1991) of the prohibitions referred to in those paragraphs.

24. The Security Council in its resolution 715 (1991) demanded that Iraq meet unconditionally all its obligations under the plan for ongoing monitoring and verification (S/22871/Rev.1) and cooperate fully with the Special Commission in carrying out the plan. If Iraq adopts such an approach and abides by its obligations, then the practical implementation of the plan could proceed in a smooth and unobtrusive manner, on a routine basis and without unnecessarily hampering or delaying the normal activities at locations which would be inspected. The full cooperation, complete initial and periodic declarations and goodwill of the Government of Iraq will be the determining factor.

25. Along with a clear acknowledgement by Iraq of its obligations under resolution 715 (1991) and the plans approved thereunder, the immediate step required to start the proper operation of the plan for ongoing monitoring and verification (S/22871/Rev.1) is for Iraq to file with the Special Commission the initial declarations required under the plan. If and when Iraq's declarations are received, the Special Commission will evaluate them in order to determine the extent to which they meet the requirements—both in format and in substance—of the plan. Such declarations are essential so that the Special Commission will be in a position to begin and carry out effectively its inspections and other monitoring and verification activities under the plan of the nature and scope approved by the Security Council.

Document 115

Statement by the President of the Security Council concerning the safety and security of UNSCOM's aerial surveillance flights over Iraq

S/23803, 10 April 1992

The members of the Security Council have learnt with grave concern from the Executive Chairman of the Special Commission of recent developments which appear to call for a halt in and constitute a threat to the safety and security of the Special Commission's aerial surveillance flights over Iraq. The members of the Council wish to point out that the surveillance flights are carried out under the authority of Security Council resolutions 687, 707 and 715 (1991). Reaffirming the right of the Special Commission to conduct such aerial surveillance flights, the members of the Council call upon the Government of Iraq to take all the necessary steps to ensure that the Iraqi military forces will not interfere with or threaten the security of the flights concerned and to comply with its responsibilities to secure the safety of the Special Commission's aircraft and personnel while flying over Iraq. The members of the Council warn the Government of Iraq of the serious consequences which would ensue from any failure to comply with these obligations.

Document 116

First report of the Director General of the IAEA on the implementation of the Agency's plan for the future ongoing monitoring and verification of Iraq's compliance with paragraph 12 of resolution 687 (1991)

S/23813, 15 April 1992

Note by the Secretary-General

The Secretary-General has the honour to transmit to the Security Council the attached report of the Director General of the International Atomic Energy Agency on the implementation of the Agency's plan for future ongoing monitoring and verification of Iraq's compliance with paragraph 12 of resolution 687 (1991).

Annex
Letter dated 11 April 1992 from the Director General of the International Atomic Energy Agency addressed to the Secretary-General

Paragraph 8 of resolution 715 (1991), adopted by the Security Council on 11 October 1991, requests the Director General of the International Atomic Energy Agency to submit to the Security Council reports on the implementation of the Agency's plan for future ongoing monitoring and verification of Iraq's compliance with paragraph 12 of resolution 687 (1991).

These reports are to be submitted when requested by the Security Council and, in any event, at least every six months after the adoption of resolution 715.

Accordingly, I am requesting you to kindly transmit the enclosed first six months' report on the implementation of the plan and remain available for any consultation you or the Council may wish to have.

(*Signed*) Hans BLIX

Enclosure

Report of the Director General of the International Atomic Energy Agency on the Implementation of the Agency's Plan for Future Ongoing Monitoring and Verification of Iraq's Compliance with Paragraph 12 of Resolution 687 (1991)

1. On 11 October 1991, the Security Council adopted resolution 715 (1991) approving, *inter alia*, the plan submitted in document S/22872/Rev.1/Corr.1, by the Director General of the International Atomic Energy Agency for future ongoing monitoring and verification of Iraq's compliance with paragraph 12 of Part C of Security Council resolution 687 (1991) and with the requirements of paragraphs 3 and 5 of resolution 707 (1991). In paragraph 8 of resolution 715, the Security Council requested the Director General of the IAEA to submit to it reports on the implementation of the plan when requested by the Security Council and, in any event, at least every six months after the adoption of resolution 715.

2. Accordingly, the Director General hereby submits the first six-month report on implementation of the plan for future ongoing monitoring and verification related to Iraq's nuclear capabilities.

3. Pursuant to paragraph 22 of the plan, Iraq was obliged to provide to the Agency within 30 days of approval of the Plan (i.e., by 10 November 1991), and in accordance with Annex 2 of the plan:

(a) an inventory of all nuclear material in Iraq;

(b) an inventory of all facilities, installations and sites in Iraq where nuclear activities of any kind, including but not limited to research facilities, laboratory-scale installations and pilot plants, which have been or which are suitable for carrying out such activities;

(c) an inventory of all material, equipment and items in Iraq identified in Annex 3 of the Plan;

(d) an inventory of all isotopes in Iraq used for medical, agricultural or industrial applications;

(e) information on existing and proposed programmes of nuclear activities in Iraq for the next five-year period; and

(f) an inventory of all facilities, installations and sites in Iraq which are provided with any means of supply of electricity exceeding 10 MW.

4. Annex 2 of the Plan, which contains the provisions related to information requirements, sets out in detail the information to be provided with respect to the above. The Annex requires that the initial information be provided, in English, within 30 days of adoption of the plan by the Security Council. It further requires that the initial information cover the period from 1 January 1989, with subsequent complete information to be provided each 15 January and 15 July, covering the six-month period prior to the provision of the information.

5. In a letter of 19 November 1991 addressed to the President of the Security Council, the Minister of Foreign Affairs of Iraq criticized the plans under resolution 715 (1991) as the most recent of "unlawful measures" taken by the Security Council. He described the plans as "arbitrary restrictions on development programmes in Iraq" and a violation of the "principles on which the United Nations was established, including that of safeguarding the independence, sovereignty and territorial integrity of Member States". Specific complaint was made that the plans contained no limitation in time for its implementation. The letter concluded by stating "that Iraq, in accordance with its obligations under resolution 687 (1991) ... is submitting herewith the information required under resolution 687 (1991) that comes under the mandate of the Special Commission." That information was delivered to the field office of the Special Commission in Baghdad on 20 November 1991 for onward transmission to the President of the Council. It

consisted of approximately 190 pages of Arabic text including, *inter alia*, five tables related to Iraq's nuclear capabilities.

6. On 3 December, the Director General of the IAEA met with the Iraqi Resident Representative to the International Atomic Energy Agency in Vienna. He stated that the Agency had not yet received the information specified in paragraph 22 (b-f) pursuant to Annex 2 of the plan and pointed to Iraq's obligations.

7. On 11 December 1991, the Iraqi Resident Representative in Vienna transmitted to the Director General 52 pages (in Arabic) " in compliance with Security Council resolution 715", indicating that these pages had been among those supplied to the Baghdad office of the Special Commission by the Minister for Foreign Affairs at an earlier date (see para. 5 above). The texts submitted by the Iraqi Resident Representative consisted of the following:

(1) Table 1 (11 pages) – "Iraq's obligations and action taken"

(2) Table 2 (7 pages) – "Inventory of nuclear material in Iraq," along with a notation that "In addition to that, uniform tables are being prepared for all information contained in the declarations mentioned in paragraph (a), (b) and (c) of the table

(3) Table 3 (1 page) – "Information on nuclear sites, facilities and installations"

(4) Table 4 (3 pages) – "Inventory of radioactive sources of the Iraqi installations and establishments other than the Iraqi Atomic Energy Commission"

(5) Table 5 (20 pages) – "Inventory of radioactive sources in Iraqi installations and establishments other than the Iraqi Atomic Energy Commission"

(6) Table 6 (10 pages) – Although indicated as a separate table in the covering letter, this table is actually an appendix to table 3.

The letter from the Permanent Representative of Iraq of 11 December is the sole occasion on which reference is made to the submission of information under resolution 715 (1991), the Iraqi authorities at the highest levels having otherwise consistently throughout referred to information as being submitted under resolution 687 (1991).

8. In the course of the ninth IAEA inspection in Iraq, the Head of the Iraqi Inspection Team, Mr. Al-Hajjaj, submitted to the Agency's Chief Inspector, a letter (in Arabic) dated 13 January attaching a supplement to the previous table identifying additional radioactive sources found in the Tuwaitha centre. Simultaneously, Mr. Hajjaj submitted another letter of the same date attaching another table, identified as Table 2, also in Arabic, listing "equipment and devices related to the Iraqi nuclear programme in accordance with Security Council resolution 687 (1991)." In the latter, the Head of the Iraqi

Inspection Team referred to a number of items requested to be included in the table which Iraq considered as exceeding their obligations under resolution 687.

9. During the Tenth IAEA Inspection in Iraq, discussions were held with Iraqi authorities on the plan for ongoing monitoring and verification. The Iraqi side indicated that they were anxious to close the present phase of inspection and to begin implementing the plan. They proposed to clarify, once and for all, all the outstanding issues concerning their past nuclear activities and asked the IAEA to define what was still needed of them. The Iraqi authorities admitted that the information transmitted to date had not conformed with the requirements of the plan in so far as it mainly reflected the situation as of the date the information was prepared (November 1991) rather than covering the period from 1 January 1989 as stipulated in the resolution. This resulted in an understatement of activities, equipment and material owing to the omission of some of the facilities and equipment damaged in the course of the Gulf war and/or destroyed by the Iraqi side. The Iraqi authorities further acknowledged that the list of items to be reported to the IAEA should not have been limited to items in the possession of the IAEC, but rather should have included all such items in Iraq. While agreeing that modification of the information to reflect the situation as of 1 January 1989 could be made, the Iraqi team advised the Agency that, as it would be practically impossible to report to the Agency all items of the kind in question in Iraq, they could not comply with that requirement. The Iraqis also refused to identify facilities, installations and sites provided with an electricity supply exceeding 10MW, except for two such facilities belonging to the IAEC.

10. On 21 to 24 February 1992 the Executive Chairman of the Special Commission visited Baghdad on a special mission in an attempt to secure unconditional agreement by Iraq to implement all of its relevant obligations under Security Council resolutions 687 (1991), 707 (1991) and 715 (1991). Iraq indicated that it would be dispatching shortly a delegation to talk to the Security Council which would convey Iraq's position on resolutions 707 (1991) and 715 (1991). In a letter dated 24 February 1992 addressed to the Secretary-General (S/23636) the Minister of Foreign Affairs of Iraq reiterated the points made in the written statement which had been provided to the special mission (S/23643). The President of the Security Council issued on 28 February 1992 a statement on behalf of the Council, condemning the failure of Iraq to provide the special mission with the acknowledgements and undertakings which the mission had been sent to secure.

11. On 11 March 1992, the Deputy Prime Minister of Iraq, Mr. Tariq Aziz, in his address to the Security Council, asserted Iraq's willingness to comply with resolution 687 and to "reach a practical solution to the question of the Security Council verification of Iraq's capabilities to produce the weapons prohibited by resolution 687." Iraq conditioned its willingness to do so "on the basis of respect to its sovereignty and dignity and of non-infringement upon its national security, and on the basis that not allowing the objectives stipulated in Resolution 687 to be turned into means of preventing our people and country from living its free normal life like all other free people in the world." Mr. Aziz suggested that further negotiation and modification of the two plans approved under resolution 715 were necessary.

12. At the request of Iraq, the IAEA held subsequent meetings with an Iraqi technical team to discuss matters related to the requirements of information under resolution 715 (1991) and on the destruction of nuclear-related items.

13. The analysis by the IAEA of the translation of the tables provided by Iraq is complicated by the fact that, rather than producing a complete detailed inventory as required by Annex 2 of the plan, the Iraqi authorities have so far produced only lists of equipment, facilities and material with cross-references to other communications. Consequently, a determination as to the comprehensiveness and completeness of the information provided by Iraq is difficult to make. A number of inconsistencies and deficiencies have been identified by the Agency. No information was provided, as required by the plan, on the legislative and administrative measures taken by Iraq to implement resolution 687, 707, other relevant Security Council resolutions and the plan.

14. The 11th IAEA Inspection Team to visit Iraq from 7-15 April is scheduled to hold discussions on this matter with a view to securing from Iraq complete information in accordance with the requirements of the plan. It has been made clear to the Iraqi side that the IAEA will not negotiate modifications to the terms of the plans approved by the Security Council pursuant to resolution 715.

15. In conclusion, it is necessary to underscore that, until such time as Iraq provides the Agency with full and complete details of its nuclear programme, as required in accordance with resolution 715 and the relevant underlying plan, the IAEA will be precluded from establishing a firm basis for carrying out effectively monitoring and verification of the scope and nature approved by the Security Council.

Document 117

Statement by the President of the Security Council concerning the sanctions regime

S/24010, 27 May 1992

The members of the Security Council held informal consultations on 27 May 1992 pursuant to paragraph 21 of resolution 687 (1991).

After hearing all the opinions expressed in the course of the consultations, the President of the Council concluded that there still was no agreement that the necessary conditions existed for a modification of the regime established in paragraph 20 of resolution 687 (1991), as referred to in paragraph 21 of that resolution.

Document 118

Third report of the Executive Chairman of UNSCOM

S/24108, 16 June 1992

Note by the Secretary-General

The Secretary-General has the honour to transmit to the Security Council a report submitted by the Executive Chairman of the Special Commission established by the Secretary-General pursuant to paragraph 9 (b) (i) of Security Council resolution 687 (1991).

Annex
Third report by the Executive Chairman of the Special Commission established by the Secretary-General pursuant to paragraph 9 (b) (i) of Security Council resolution 687 (1991)

Introduction

1. The present report is the third report by the Executive Chairman of the Special Commission established by the Secretary-General pursuant to paragraph 9 (b) (i) of Security Council resolution 687 (1991). It is provided in accordance with paragraph 3 of Security Council resolution 699 (1991) to cover the period 4 December 1991 to 10 June 1992. This report summarizes developments since the previous report a/ in order to provide, together with the first report of the Executive Chairman, b/ a comprehensive picture of the establishment and functioning of the Special Commission since the adoption of Security Council resolution 687 (1991).

2. The report itself highlights the principal developments and activities. It also gives the Executive Chairman's assessment of the results achieved, the difficulties encountered and what remains to be done to secure full implementation of the requirements of the relevant Security Council resolutions. Where necessary, separate appendices give a more detailed account of specific aspects of the Commission's work during the period under review.

I. *Organizational and administrative issues*

3. In the period under review, there have been two changes in the composition of the Commission. On 5 February 1992, the Deputy Executive Chairman, Mr. Robert Gallucci (United States of America), resigned to take up important new responsibilities in Washington, D.C. The Executive Chairman would like to take this opportunity to express his thanks to Mr. Gallucci for his invaluable services to the Commission and for his unfailing support and to pay a tribute to his contributions in the field, including participation in some of the most difficult inspections in Iraq, in which he amply demonstrated both his courage and his diplomatic skill. The Secretary-General appointed Mr. Michael Newlin (United States) as Deputy Executive Chairman in succession to Mr. Gallucci. Mr. Newlin, who has served as United States Ambassador to the United Nations Organizations in Vienna, has considerable experience in the nuclear field and the Office of the Special Commission has already benefited greatly from this, particularly in its collaboration with the International Atomic Energy Agency (IAEA).

4. In March 1992, the Executive Chairman learned with great regret of the untimely death of Mr. Ken Adachi (Japan), who had played such a valuable part in the work of the Special Commission and, in particular, the Chemi-

a/ S/23268
b/ S/23165, annex.

cal Biological Weapons Group. The Secretary-General has appointed Mr. Hideyo Kurata (Japan) to replace Mr. Adachi.

5. The organizational structure remains essentially as described in the first report of the Executive Chairman. The Office of the Executive Chairman has been supplemented by the addition of an Information Assessment Unit, which is now operational. The Field Offices in Bahrain and Baghdad continue effectively to service and support the surveillance activities.

6. Finances continue to require attention in the absence of Iraqi agreement to sell oil under the terms of Security Council resolution 706 (1991). The Commission's operations are supported by contributions in cash and in kind from a number of Member States. Further information on organizational and administrative issues is contained in appendix V.

7. The Executive Chairman wishes once again to place on record his profound appreciation to the Secretary-General, to Governments and to the agencies concerned for the assistance made available, as well as to the able staff placed at the disposal of the Commission for the dedicated service they have rendered, sometimes in very trying and dangerous circumstances, to carry out the mandate of the Security Council.

II. *Status, privileges and immunities*

8. The status, privileges and immunities of the Special Commission, IAEA and the United Nations specialized agencies involved in the implementation of Security Council resolution 687 (1991) continue to be regulated by the various agreements and Council resolutions and decisions mentioned in paragraph 5 of the first report. b/ By an exchange of letters between the Secretary-General and the Director-General of IAEA on the one hand, and the Minister for Foreign Affairs of Bahrain on the other, the agreement in respect of the Commission's field office in Manama has been extended for a further period of six months, to 29 September 1992. Issues which have arisen in Iraq in the implementation of the status, privileges and immunities of the Commission have been principally in connection with the operation and landing rights of the Commission's aircraft, where difficulties persist (see appendix I).

III. *Developments*

A. *Political developments: the attitude of Iraq*

9. In the period under review, the Special Commission and IAEA have continued to conduct vigorous inspections of sites declared by Iraq or designated by the Commission. These inspections have served as the main source for compiling a picture of Iraq's weapons of mass destruction and the capabilities for their production.

Although cooperation has been extended, in most instances, to inspectors at the field level, Iraq's authorities have not been uniformly forthcoming in providing information on the weapons programmes as a whole. The problems which were emerging in the first five months of the operation have crystallized, and thus the emphasis of the work of the Commission has shifted in the period under review from concentration on the organization of inspections to seeking compliance with the resolutions and decisions of the Security Council. The major developments in this regard are described in detail in appendix I. Broadly speaking, the problems may be summarized as follows:

(a) The Commission's task has always been viewed as having three phases: inspection and survey; destruction; and long-term ongoing monitoring and verification to ensure that Iraq does not reacquire proscribed weapons. Although these three phases will overlap to a large extent, the intention was that the emphasis should shift with time from the first through to the third phase. However, on 19 November 1991, the Iraqi authorities informed the President of the Security Council that Iraq considered that the Commission's and IAEA's plans for future ongoing monitoring and verification, approved under Security Council resolution 715 (1991), were unlawful.

(b) Furthermore, Iraq has failed to provide the initial declarations required under the plans for future ongoing monitoring and verification, which are important for the identification of which facilities, materials and activities would need to be monitored under the plans. On 5 June 1992, Iraq transmitted to the Commission documents containing what it has characterized as a comprehensive and complete version of its nuclear, chemical, biological and ballistic missiles activities. These documents, which should correspond to the full, final and complete disclosures required under Council resolution 707 (1991), are now being analysed by the Commission and IAEA. An assessment of these documents will be transmitted to the Council as soon as possible to complement the present report.

(c) The situation is further aggravated by the continuing obstructions that the Iraqi authorities have been putting in the way of the Commission's landing rights for fixed-wing aircraft and their increasing criticism of the Commission's high-altitude surveillance flights.

Thus, the realization of the intentions to proceed with the evolution of the Commission's activities from inspection and survey through destruction to ongoing monitoring and verification have so far been in large part delayed by the actions of the Iraqi Government.

10. In response to a special report on the situation by the Executive Chairman, the Security Council declared

that Iraq was in material breach of resolution 687 (1991) and dispatched a high-level mission, headed by the Executive Chairman, to Iraq, armed with a statement demanding that Iraq give the necessary assurances on compliance with the Council's resolutions or face serious consequences. That mission visited Iraq from 21 to 24 February 1992. In its report c/ it concluded that unconditional agreement by Iraq had not been provided and that, therefore, the initiation and practical implementation of resolution 715 (1991) and the plans approved thereunder for ongoing monitoring and verification could not be undertaken in a credible manner. Partly coinciding with the mission, Iraq refused to permit the start of the destruction of equipment associated with its ballistic missile production programme. Upon being apprised of the situation, the Security Council condemned the failure by Iraq to comply with its obligations to destroy equipment as directed by the Council and to make the declarations required under the Council's resolutions. Furthermore, the Security Council reiterated its statement that Iraq was in material breach of resolution 687 (1991).

11. The Security Council met in formal session on 11 and 12 March 1992. In an initial statement, the President of the Council, on behalf of all members, reiterated the Council's position. The Deputy Prime Minister of Iraq, Mr. Tariq Aziz, made two statements, neither of which contained the assurances sought by the Council. The Council furthermore heard statements by all its members, by the Permanent Representative of Kuwait to the United Nations, by the Director-General of IAEA and by the Executive Chairman of the Commission. The Chairman in his statement indicated that, although it was the aim of the Commission to report to the Council as soon as possible that Iraq was in substantial compliance with section C of resolution 687 (1991), no question of this could arise until Iraq had acknowledged and implemented its obligations under all the relevant Council resolutions and decisions. In a concluding statement on 12 March, the President of the Council, on behalf of the Council, stated that Iraq must immediately take steps to comply fully and unconditionally with its obligations under the relevant Security Council resolutions.

12. Following the Council's meeting, Iraq made additional declarations concerning the numbers of ballistic missiles, chemical weapons and associated items. Furthermore, it declared its readiness to go along with the required destruction of buildings and equipment. Subsequently, destruction of such items, relevant to the missile and nuclear weapons programmes, have been carried out. As referred to above, the Iraqi authorities have handed over to the Special Commission what they called "full, final and complete reports" on chemical and bio-

logical weapons and ballistic missiles as well as on its nuclear programme. These reports are now being studied by the Special Commission and IAEA to assess whether they meet the requirements of the relevant Security Council resolutions. However, neither the initial declarations required under the plans for ongoing monitoring and verification nor the acknowledgement of Iraq's obligations have been received.

B. Operational developments

13. With regard to chemical weapons, although verification and survey activities continue, there has been a progressive shift in emphasis with relatively more time and resources being devoted to issues directly related to the destruction of Iraq's identified chemical weapons (CW) assets. At Khamisiyah, the Special Commission has supervised the first destruction of filled chemical munitions, while at the Muthanna site work is progressing to construct chemical agent destruction plants. The aim is to have these plants commissioned during the summer of 1992. A new development was the Iraqi admission of 19 March 1992 that it had omitted to declare 24,470 chemical munitions and that these weapons had been unilaterally destroyed in direct contravention of resolution 687 (1991), which requires that possession of Iraq's chemical weapons should be yielded to the Commission for destruction, removal or rendering harmless under its supervision. An inspection team has since been able to verify, by examining the excavated remains of the munitions, that the numbers contained in the Iraqi declarations were substantially correct.

14. There have been few developments on the biological side. Inspection activities have continued through joint chemical and biological teams.

15. Regarding ballistic missiles, the emphasis has shifted to the destruction of facilities associated with Iraq's production programme. The Executive Chairman informed the Iraqi authorities that destruction should start in February 1992. Initially, as recorded in the report of the Secretary-General of 7 March 1992, d/ Iraq delayed and refused to comply. Only at the end of March 1992 did Iraq allow the destruction of these facilities to begin. This destruction programme is now advanced.

16. Meanwhile, inspection activities also continued, with Iraq maintaining that it no longer had any missiles with a range greater than 150 kilometres and hence that there was no further missile destruction to be done. Confronted, however, with the information that the Special Commission had incontrovertible evidence

c/ See S/23643.
d/ S/23678.

that Iraq's initial declarations of April 1991 had not included a substantial number of ballistic missiles and related equipment then in its possession, Iraq presented on 19 March 1992 a new declaration. In it Iraq admitted that it had failed to declare 92 proscribed ballistic missiles and much associated equipment and vehicles, including mobile missile launchers, and that it had destroyed these unilaterally, in contravention of resolution 687 (1991), in the summer of 1991. Inspection teams since then have been able to verify that the numbers contained in this new declaration were substantially correct.

17. However, although events have proceeded more smoothly at the field level than at the political level, there have been occasions when there has been deliberate interference with inspection activities, e.g. tampering with equipment designated for removal by inspection teams for further analysis and doctoring of documentation. Such interference, coupled with Iraq's failure to date to provide the full, final and complete disclosure required under resolution 707 (1991), can only be interpreted as evidence that Iraq is still seeking to conceal from the Special Commission information directly relevant to section C of resolution 687 (1991).

C. Health and safety

18. A matter of increasing concern as the Special Commission moves into the destruction phase is the fact that many of the activities carried out by the Commission in Iraq are potentially very hazardous. Sufficient information and experience have been gained in the first six months of operations by the Commission to provide a basis for a realistic health and safety policy document. The Chemical and Biological Weapons Working Group, during the course of its discussions of safety issues, decided in December 1991 to prepare such a document and delegated to the Destruction Advisory Panel the task of preparing a draft. The draft was prepared by the Panel during its meeting in February 1992 and was reviewed by the CBW Working Group during its meeting in April 1992.

19. Environmental aspects of the activities of the Special Commission have also been given thorough consideration by the Destruction Advisory Panel. In particular, environmental and safety issues have been at the forefront of their consideration of chemical destruction activities. The situation at many sites, particularly at the Muthanna State Establishment, is already leading to local environmental contamination which requires rapid solutions. A short paper giving details of the factors considered and the technical steps taken to minimize environmental contamination during chemical destruction operations has been prepared for the United Nations Environment Programme (UNEP).

IV. Issues and priorities for the future

20. Although much has been achieved by the Special Commission, clearly much remains to be done. In particular, the following require action before the Commission can report to the Security Council that Iraq is in substantial compliance with its obligations:

(a) The destruction, removal or rendering harmless of Iraq's prohibited weapons capabilities—i.e. equipment and facilities associated with its weapons of mass destruction and ballistic missiles programmes and the successful initiation of destruction of Iraq's stocks of chemical munitions, agents and precursors;

(b) Acknowledgement by Iraq of its obligations under Council resolutions 707 (1991) and 715 (1991);

(c) Verification by the Commission of the accuracy and adequacy of the data provided in Iraq's "full, final and complete report";

(d) Declarations by Iraq under the plans adopted through resolution 715 (1991), with regard to, inter alia, dual capable facilities used for permitted purposes but which could be used for prohibited purposes;

(e) The initiation and smooth functioning of the plans for future ongoing monitoring and verification to ensure that Iraq does not reacquire prohibited capabilities;

(f) Acceptance by Iraq of the Special Commission's aircraft landing rights.

21. The priority at the moment is to obtain from Iraq its acknowledgement of its obligations under resolutions 707 (1991) and 715 (1991), and the declarations due under the plans for ongoing monitoring and verification of its obligations not to reacquire those proscribed items. On the operational side, immediate attention needs to be given to the continuing obstruction facing the Special Commission with regard to landing rights for the fixed-wing aircraft. The verification and assessment of Iraq's reports transmitted on 5 June on its weapons programmes is furthermore already under way.

22. Work progresses on the destruction, removal or rendering harmless, as appropriate, of the items covered by section C of resolution 687 (1991) and thought is being given to which facilities will have to be subject to the plans for ongoing monitoring and verification. As the Special Commission moves further into the verification and monitoring phases, more consideration will have to be given to funding and staffing of these more permanent activities. The issue of import monitoring will, prior to the lifting or easing of sanctions, need to be addressed in coordination with the Sanctions Committee established by the Security Council under its resolution 661 (1990).

Appendix I
Political developments

1. In the period under review it has been necessary to devote much time and effort to seeking to obtain from Iraq three of the essential elements outstanding in the implementation of the Special Commission's mandate, namely:

(a) The full, final and complete disclosure, as required by Security Council resolution 687 (1991), of all aspects of Iraq's programmes to develop weapons of mass destruction and ballistic missiles with a range greater than 150 kilometres, and of all holdings of such weapons, their components and production facilities and locations, as well as all other nuclear programmes;

(b) Acknowledgement of Iraq's obligations under Security Council resolutions 707 (1991) and 715 (1991) and under the plans of the Special Commission and of IAEA for ongoing monitoring and verification of Iraq's obligations approved by resolution 715 (1991); a/

(c) Provision of the declarations called for under the plans for ongoing monitoring and verification.

Much time and effort have also been devoted to seeking to resolve difficulties arising in connection with the second phase of the Special Commission's activities relating to the destruction, removal or rendering harmless of weapons of mass destruction and the relevant associated facilities. Certain difficulties in connection with the Special Commission's air operations have also continued.

A. *Ongoing monitoring and verification*

2. An express acknowledgement by Iraq is necessary, not only of its obligations under resolution 687 (1991) but also under resolutions 707 (1991) and 715 (1991), to ensure Iraq's continued compliance with its obligations not to reacquire prohibited weapons. Ongoing monitoring and verification cannot be implemented without a clear picture and understanding of Iraq's programmes for weapons of mass destruction and ballistic missiles as they existed before the conflict in the Persian Gulf and without full and verified declarations, required under the plans, which cover both military and civilian sites, facilities, materials and other items or activities that could be used in contravention of Iraq's obligations under section C of resolution 687 (1991).

3. The Special Commission's and IAEA's plans for ongoing monitoring and verification called for the submission by Iraq of its initial declarations by 10 November 1991. By letter of 19 November 1991 to the President of the Security Council, the Minister for Foreign Affairs of Iraq criticized the plans as being "aimed at objectives incompatible with the letter and spirit of the United Nations Charter, the norms of international law and international and humanitarian pacts and covenants". Under cover of the same letter, the Minister for Foreign Affairs transmitted "information required under resolution 687 (1991) that comes under the mandate of the Special Commission". This information did not correspond to the declarations required under the plans.

4. The Security Council's attention was drawn by the Executive Chairman to this situation in his second report submitted to the Security Council on 4 December 1991 b/ and it was elaborated upon in the Secretary-General's report to the Council of 25 January 1992 on the status of Iraq's compliance with the relevant resolutions of the Security Council. c/ On 31 January 1992, the Security Council met at the level of Heads of State and Government and, in the President's statement issued at the conclusion of that meeting, d/ it was, *inter alia*, provided, with reference to the Council's resolutions on the situation between Iraq and Kuwait, that those resolutions "remain essential to the restoration of peace and stability in the region and must be fully implemented".

5. Also late in January 1992, the Executive Chairman sent a special mission, headed by two Special Commission members, to Baghdad to seek from the Iraqi authorities the undertakings referred to in paragraph 1 above. Although that mission was able to report some progress in obtaining through an interrogative procedure information on Iraq's programmes to acquire or produce weapons of mass destruction and ballistic missiles, it was not able to obtain the undertakings required and, on resolution 715 (1991), the Government of Iraq affirmed its position as stated in the letter of 19 November 1991 from the Minister for Foreign Affairs.

6. Faced with such a situation, the Executive Chairman, on 18 February 1992, submitted a special report e/ to the Security Council in which he concluded that the position taken by Iraq was such that it was neither legally nor practically possible for the Special Commission to carry out effectively a programme of ongoing monitoring

a/ S/22871/Rev.1 and S/22872/Rev.1 and Corr.1.
b/ S/23268, annex, para.4
c/ S/23514, annex, sect. B, paras. 15-26.
d/ S/23500.
e/ S/23606, annex.

and verification of the nature and scope approved by the Council. On 19 February 1992, the President of the Council issued a statement, on behalf of its members, f/ expressing, *inter alia*, their grave concern at Iraq's position which constituted "a continuing material breach of the relevant provisions of resolution 687 (1991)", and supporting the decision of the Secretary-General to dispatch a high-level mission headed by the Executive Chairman of the Commission "to visit Iraq immediately to meet and discuss with the highest levels of the Iraqi Government for the purpose of securing the unconditional agreement by Iraq to implement all its relevant obligations under resolutions 687 (1991), 707 (1991) and 715 (1991)".

7. The high-level mission, headed by the Executive Chairman, visited Baghdad from 21 to 24 February 1992. In his report submitted to the Council on 26 February, g/ the Executive Chairman concluded that he was not able to secure "from the highest levels of the Government of Iraq unconditional agreement by Iraq to implement all its relevant obligations under Security Council resolutions 687 (1991), 707 (1991) and 715 (1991)". As regards the plans for ongoing monitoring and verification, the Executive Chairman reported that Iraq "accepted only the *principle* of ongoing monitoring and verification, and this is subject to considerations of sovereignty, territorial integrity, national security and non-infringement on Iraq's industrial capabilities". The Executive Chairman's report indicated that the Iraqi authorities had referred to their intention to dispatch a high-level delegation to New York, and that "the Iraqi delegation dispatched to talk to the Security Council will convey Iraq's position on resolutions 707 (1991) and 715 (1991)".

8. On 28 February 1992, the President of the Security Council made a statement on behalf of its members, h/ deploring and condemning Iraq's failure to provide the undertakings sought by the high-level mission, approving in full the conclusions of the mission and demanding "that Iraq immediately implement all its obligations under Council resolution 687 (1991) and subsequent resolutions on Iraq".

9. On 7 March 1992, the Secretary-General submitted to the Security Council, at its request, an update of his report of 25 January 1992 on Iraq's compliance with the obligations placed upon it by resolution 687 (1991) and subsequent resolutions. i/ In annex I to that report, containing information received from the Special Commission, attention was again drawn, *inter alia*, to Iraq's failure to acknowledge and implement its obligations under Council resolutions 707 (1991) and 715 (1991) and under the plans approved by resolution 715 (1991).

10. On 11 and 12 March 1992 an Iraqi delegation, headed by the Deputy Prime Minister, appeared before the Security Council. At the outset of that meeting, the President of the Council made a statement on behalf of its members j/ in which he recalled in some detail the Council statements of 19 and 28 February 1992, referred to above.

11. The Deputy Prime Minister addressed the Council on 11 March 1992, and on 12 March he responded to questions addressed to him by members of the Council. k/ The unconditional assurances which the Council had been seeking were not forthcoming on either occasion. In his initial statement he said that Iraq had already provided the Special Commission with all the necessary information on its proscribed weapons and production facilities. He further disclosed for the first time that Iraq had unilaterally destroyed 270,000 proscribed items after the adoption of resolution 687 (1991). He also stated that Iraq was ready to reach a practical mechanism regarding the issue of equipment proscribed under paragraph 8 of resolution 687 (1991), with a view to rendering that equipment harmless. In regard to ongoing monitoring and verification, the Deputy Prime Minister stated that Iraq was prepared to cooperate, while underlining the need for respect for Iraqi dignity, sovereignty and national security. In his response to questions, he basically affirmed the positions he had set forth the previous day.

12. Speaking in the Council on 11 March 1992 after the Deputy Prime Minister, the Executive Chairman underlined that the fundamental aim of the Commission was to report to the Council that Iraq had met in full all its obligations under section C of resolution 687 (1991) as elaborated upon in resolutions 707 (1991) and 715 (1991). However, the Commission's ability to do so was conditioned by the degree of cooperation which it received from Iraq and the openness and transparency of that State. Although Iraq claimed to have provided all necessary information on its proscribed programmes and weapons, that was not the case. The information given was not complete, systematic or supported by the documentary and material evidence necessary to verify it. With regard to the items declared to have been destroyed unilaterally, the Commission had requested a list fully accounting for all those items but had not received it. Such unilateral destruction had been contrary to resolution 687 (1991) and apparently on a scale which indicated that many gaps remained, which Iraq must fill, in the picture of its prohibited weapons programmes. Turning to the second phase of the Commission's operations, the

f/ S/23609.
g/ S/23643, annex.
h/ S/23663.
i/ S/23687.
j/ S/23699.
k/ S/PV.3059 and S/PV.3059 (Resumption 2).

Executive Chairman acknowledged that Iraq's cooperation had been good in regard to the destruction of actual weapons declared by Iraq. However, another situation prevailed in regard to the production facilities for such weapons where Iraq was, for instance, refusing to comply with the Commission's decisions in respect of the destruction of certain missile-producing facilities. Likewise, regarding the third phase of the Commission's activities, namely ongoing monitoring and verification, the existence of an impasse had now clearly been established. If the plans for ongoing monitoring and verification approved by the Council appeared intrusive, that was in large measure a result of the conduct of Iraq. If Iraq cooperated, the intrusive elements need not be invoked. The Executive Chairman concluded by saying that until Iraq undertook to comply with the Council's decisions in full, and confirmed such an undertaking in practice, the possibility of the Special Commission's certifying Iraq's compliance with its obligations under section C of resolution 687 (1991) did not even arise.

13. On 12 March 1992, the President of the Council made a statement, on behalf of the Council, in which, with reference to "the extent of compliance by the Government of Iraq with its obligations under the relevant Security Council resolutions" he recorded that "the Government of Iraq has not yet complied fully and unconditionally with those obligations, must do so and must immediately take the appropriate actions in this regard". The President's statement concluded with the Council's hope that "the goodwill expressed by the Deputy Prime Minister of Iraq will be matched by deeds".

14. On 12 and 13 March 1992, when the Iraqi delegation appeared before the Security Council, an Iraqi team met with the Executive Chairman and other officials of the Commission. The latter provided to the former detailed explanations as to the format and modalities required by the Special Commission's plan for ongoing monitoring and verification under its different sections and annexes. The Iraqi team promised to provide, by early April, the information required under the plan except on the sources of imported items and on operational deployment or disposition of relevant weapons. The Commission's side stressed, however, that the information should be provided in full as required by the plan.

15. On 10 April 1992, the Secretary-General, as required by paragraph 8 of Security Council resolution 715 (1991), submitted to the Council a report on the status of the implementation of the Special Commission's plan for the ongoing monitoring and verification of Iraq's compliance with relevant parts of section C of Security Council resolution 687 (1991). l/ A similar report on the implementation of IAEA's plan was submitted by the Director-General of the Agency. m/ The Secretary-Gen-

eral's report, after recounting pertinent details on the developments outlined above, concluded that Iraq had not been in compliance with Security Council resolutions nor with the plans. The members of the Council decided that the President of the Council should convey to the Permanent Representative of Iraq to the United Nations that Iraq's compliance with the plans was imperative. He did this on 22 April 1992. No formal reply to this approach has been made. However, on 26 May 1992, the Executive Chairman received a letter from the Minister of State for Foreign Affairs of Iraq n/ in which the latter mentioned drafts of the declarations required under the plan but made no promise of when the final declaration might be received. The letter also reiterated the position taken by the Deputy Prime Minister of Iraq on 11 March 1992 on the issue of Iraq's acknowledgement of its obligations under resolutions 707 (1991) and 715 (1991) and on how the plan for ongoing monitoring and verification should be implemented. The plan itself contains precise methods for implementation which have been approved by the Council acting under Chapter VII of the Charter of the United Nations.

B. Destruction, removal or rendering harmless of proscribed items

16. Another issue to which much time and attention has had to be devoted in the period under review relates to the second phase of the Special Commission's operations, namely the disposal of weapons of mass destruction, facilities and other items related thereto through destruction, removal or rendering harmless, as appropriate, as provided for in resolution 687 (1991). For the Special Commission the issue has arisen mainly in connection with Iraq's ballistic missile production capabilities and for IAEA in connection with the Iraqi complex at Al-Atheer, the technical core of which was intended for the special processes needed for nuclear weapons development and manufacturing. In the area of the disposal of Iraq's chemical weapons and precursors, the Iraqi authorities have continued their earlier cooperation and have been working on the construction of hydrolysis and incineration facilities at the Al-Muthanna site which should be operational and meet the Special Commission's safety and environment requirements in the near future (see appendix II). Throughout the planning, development work and execution of chemical destruction operations, relations with Iraq have generally been much more relaxed, technically detailed and businesslike compared with the inspection activities. The better atmosphere thus generated has undoubtedly con-

l/ S/23801.
m/ S/23813.
n/ S/24002, annex.

tributed to the timely and satisfactory progress made in this area.

17. Under paragraph 9 (b) (ii) of resolution 687 (1991), Iraq is required to destroy, under the supervision of the Special Commission, all its proscribed missile capabilities, including launchers. On 14 February 1992, the Executive Chairman addressed a letter to the Iraqi authorities concerning the destruction of certain missile facilities and transmitting lists of items which must be destroyed and items for further consideration and decision. o/

18. A ballistic missile team sent to Iraq on 21 February met, however, with a request for delay. The Executive Chairman, who was in Baghdad at the time for the high-level mission, agreed to a brief delay in the scheduled date for commencing destruction. After he left Iraq, however, the Iraqi authorities refused to comply, the Minister of State for Foreign Affairs instead sending a letter to the Executive Chairman p/ reiterating his earlier proposal to reuse equipment for the BADR-2000 ballistic missile project for a variety of what were stated to be "civilian purposes" and for the manufacture of 100-kilometre range missiles. Upon receipt of Iraq's decision not to proceed with the destruction of the items concerned, the Executive Chairman ordered the team to withdraw from Iraq.

19. On 28 February 1992, the Security Council met to consider the report by the Executive Chairman g/ on the results of the special mission sent to Iraq pursuant to the statement of the President of the Security Council of 19 February 1992. In introducing his report in Security Council consultations on 27 and 28 February 1992, the Executive Chairman informed the Council orally of Iraq's failure to comply with the Special Commission's decisions on the destruction of the missile capabilities concerned. The President of the Council, in the statement which he issued on 28 February 1992 at the conclusion of those consultations, h/ recorded, *inter alia*, that the members of the Council deplored and condemned Iraq's failure to commence destruction of the equipment concerned and reaffirmed that it was for the Special Commission alone to determine which items must be destroyed under paragraph 9 of resolution 687 (1991), its failure in this regard being a further material breach of the relevant provisions of resolution 687 (1991).

20. An account of the foregoing developments was given in the Secretary-General's further report i/ of 7 March 1992, referred to in paragraph 9 above, and the President's statement of 28 February 1992 was repeated in paragraph 18 of the introductory statement j/ made by the President on behalf of the Council on 11 March 1992, when the Council met with the participation of the Deputy Prime Minister of Iraq. On 19 March 1992, the Minister of State for Foreign Affairs of Iraq, in a letter to the Executive Chairman, confirmed that Iraq was ready to carry out the destruction as required by the Commission.

21. On 7 April 1992, the Executive Chairman sent a letter to the Iraqi authorities transmitting the updated versions of annex A, on items which must be destroyed, and annex B, on items for further consideration and decisions. This update resulted from the findings of UNSCOM inspections and the review of Iraq's suggestions and requests.

22. During the period 21 to 30 March 1992, a ballistic missile team oversaw the destruction of nine items of equipment and, during the period 13 to 21 April 1992 another team supervised the destruction of the majority of the remaining items in the extended List A. q/ Developments up to 1 April 1992 were reported to the President of the Security Council in a letter of 2 April 1992 from the Executive Chairman.

C. Inspection and survey

23. The Iraqi declarations of 19 and 28 March 1992, referred to in paragraph 12 of the present report, while evidencing some shift by Iraq towards greater openness, have at the same time proven that the Iraqi authorities have not only deliberately misled the Special Commission by omission but have also actively falsified the evidence. Thus, perhaps paradoxically, this potential shift towards more transparency, while welcomed if it heralds a real shift towards a fully cooperative attitude on the part of the Government of Iraq, has taken place under circumstances that justify the Commission's scepticism of Iraq's declarations in the past. It also indicates that, at least for the immediate future, new declarations will also have to be closely scrutinized and that the Commission will have to continue with its programme of inspection and survey missions.

24. Throughout the period, relations at the field level between inspection teams and their Iraqi counterparts have been generally satisfactory. However, there have been some instances of obstruction by Iraq and, on one occasion, actual physical harassment. By contrast, the better relations established between those involved in the preparations for chemical weapons destruction prove that a more cooperative approach by Iraq benefits both sides in terms of efficiency and timeliness.

o/ S/23673, annex I.
p/ Ibid., annex III.
q/ List contained in S/23673, annex I, enclosure II, as modified by the Executive Chairman's letter of 4 April 1992 to the Minister of State for Foreign Affairs of Iraq.

D. *The Commission's air operations*

25. Generally speaking, Iraq has complied in the period under review with its obligations in respect of the status, privileges and immunities of the Special Commission. However, Iraq has continued to cause difficulties in respect of the Commission's conduct of its own fixed-wing and aerial surveillance flights. Arrangements in regard to the Commission's helicopter operations have been satisfactory since they were commenced, after considerable difficulty, in October 1991.

26. Throughout the period under review, Iraq has continued to protest vigorously against the Special Commission's aerial surveillance flights, and this matter was reported to the Security Council on a number of occasions. r/

27. The protests from Iraq escalated to the point where, on 10 April 1992, the Executive Chairman transmitted to the President of the Council a letter of 9 April he had received from the Chargé d'affaires a.i. of Iraq in New York and the response of 10 April the Executive Chairman had sent to the Minister for Foreign Affairs. The letter from the Chargé d'affaires referred to a recent incursion by Iranian aircraft into Iraq and called for a halt of all the Special Commission's aerial surveillance flights "in order to avoid any unfortunate incidents" and made reference to the possibility that the flights might "now endanger the aircraft itself and its pilot". In his letter to the Minister for Foreign Affairs, the Executive Chairman expressed the gravest concern at these remarks "which appear to constitute a threat to the security of the Commission's aerial surveillance flights which derive from Security Council resolution 687 (1991) and which are expressly authorized under Security Council resolutions 707 (1991) and 715 (1991) and in the status agreement between the United Nations and Iraq of 14 May 1991". The Executive Chairman indicated that unless the Special Commission received immediate assurances that the Government of Iraq would take all "the necessary steps to ensure that the Iraqi military forces will not interfere with or threaten the security of the flights, the modalities for these unescorted flights will have to be reviewed".

28. Upon receipt of this correspondence, the Council held consultations on 10 April 1992, after which the President issued a statement on behalf of the Council members, s/ in which it was pointed out that "the surveillance flights are carried out under the authority of Security Council resolutions 687 (1991), 707 (1991) and 715 (1991)", and the right of the Commission to conduct such flights was reaffirmed. The Council called upon the Government of Iraq to give the assurances on the security and safety of the flights which the Executive Chairman had sought in his letter of 10 April to the Minister for Foreign Affairs, and warned of serious consequences if Iraq did not comply with its obligations in this regard.

29. On 12 April, the Minister for Foreign Affairs of Iraq addressed a letter to the President of the Security Council, t/ in which he said that the sole purpose of the Chargé d'affaires' letter of 9 April had been to draw attention to the dangers to which surveillance flights might "be exposed by reason of the recent hostile action of the Iranian Air Force in Iraqi airspace and the Iraqi defensive counter-action". He affirmed that the Government of Iraq "did not intend and does not intend to carry out any military operation aimed at" the Commission's aerial surveillance flights.

30. The other issue which remains unresolved is that of landing rights for the Special Commission's fixed-wing aircraft in the Baghdad area. Up to the present, landing facilities have been made available by the Iraqi authorities for these aircraft at Habbaniyah airfield, 100 kilometres from Baghdad, although two airfields within Baghdad city limits have been returned to operational use (Muthanna and Rasheed).

31. At Habbaniyah, from time to time, Iraq has proposed to introduce control measures which would impinge on the rights of the Special Commission and IAEA to take into and out of Iraq all necessary equipment, materials and other items required for inspections and the analyses of their results. In the face of objections from the Commission, these measures have not been enforced. However, Iraq has required the Commission's aircraft to land at greater and greater distances from the airport ground facilities where immigration and other formalities are carried out. This has become increasingly onerous and time-consuming.

32. Reference to these difficulties were made in the Secretary-General's report to the Security Council of 25 January 1992 u/ and the matter was elaborated upon in the Executive Chairman's special report to the Council of 18 February 1992. v/ In that report, the Executive Chairman recalled that, under Council resolution 707 (1991), Iraq is required to allow the Commission "to make full use of ... such airfields in Iraq as [it] may determine are most appropriate for the work of the Commission". He further indicated that on 23 January

r/ S/23514, annex, sect. B, para. 31; S/23606, para. 9; and S/23687, annex I, para. 17.
s/ S/23803.
t/ S/23806.
u/ S/23514, annex, sect. B, para. 31.
v/ S/23606, annex, paras. 7 and 8.

1992, an official approach on behalf of the Special Commission had been made to the Iraqi authorities, proposing that the Commission's incoming and outgoing flights use Muthanna or Rasheed airfield and that discussions be immediately entered into to make the necessary practical arrangements.

33. Repeated attempts to receive a response from the Iraqi authorities both in the field and at the level of the Executive Chairman, during his special mission to Baghdad in February 1992 and discussions with the Iraqi delegation to the Security Council in March 1992, have so far been unsuccessful. The Security Council has been kept informed on a number of occasions, w/ without the Executive Chairman so far requesting specific Council action. However, on 11 April 1992, the Executive Chairman addressed a letter to the Minister of State for Foreign Affairs of Iraq recalling the entire history of the matter. In that letter, the Executive Chairman indicated that the Special Commission will have in the near future to make a determination that Rasheed airfield is the most appropriate for the work of the Commission, unless in the interim the Iraqi authorities propose to the Commission an airport in Baghdad which meets the Commission's requirements. Rasheed would permit consolidation of all the Commission's air operations at one location convenient for its offices and accommodation in Baghdad and would obviate the long delays occasioned by the use of Habbaniyah. At Habbaniyah, the distance from Baghdad has been compounded as a source of delay by the resumption of flights by Iraqi military aircraft requiring the Commission to take long detours to reach the airport facilities.

E. *Conclusions*

34. The conduct of Iraq, as demonstrated above, confirms the invariable experience of the Special Commission that only a resolute and determined attitude by the Commission, backed up by the Security Council, is likely to achieve the necessary cooperation from Iraq in the many areas covered by section C of Security Council resolution 687 (1991), and by resolutions 707 (1991) and 715 (1991) where this cooperation has yet to be forthcoming. Where the Special Commission has sought to adopt a different approach, for example in respect of landing rights for its fixed-wing aircraft, it has met only with evasion or lack of definite response. The Special Commission's repeated calls for a change in the attitude of Iraq to one of candour, transparency and cooperation at all levels remain largely unanswered. While Iraq has referred on a number of occasions to a new spirit of cooperation, words have not, for the most part, yet been translated into deeds.

Appendix II
Chemical and biological weapons

A. *Inspections*

1. At the time of the last report, the first joint chemical and biological inspection team (UNSCOM 21) had very recently completed its work and only a preliminary account of the results was available. The inspection concentrated on possible chemical-weapon (CW) or biological weapon (BW) storage sites, such as airfield bunkers and ammunition depots. A total of 15 sites designated by the Commission were subject to very short-notice inspections. In some cases the notification of inspection was handed to the Iraqi hosts only as the site itself was being approached either by road or by air (helicopter), resulting in virtually no-notice inspections. In addition, a visit was made by a sub-team to Al-Muthanna to witness experiments, using the simulant D4, on the destruction of nerve agents by caustic hydrolysis. At only two of the inspected sites were any items of relevance to Security Council resolution 687 (1991) found. At Karbala, a 12-frame bunker appeared to have had an unusual level of security around it; on questioning, the Iraqi hosts admitted that it had been used for the storage of bulk mustard agent in 1984-1985 but there were no indications that this or any other agents were present when this bunker was destroyed by coalition bombing. Also at Karbala three undeclared, apparently discarded, SCUD triple-frame missile carriers were discovered and reported to the ballistic missile team. Although Iraqi officials stated that four of the buildings at this site had been used for the storage of SCUD missiles during the conflict between the Islamic Republic of Iran and Iraq, there was no evidence of the recent storage of such missiles. At the Mosul Sugar Factory, almost 100 items of metal working machinery from the bomb workshop and general workshop at Muthanna were discovered. This machinery had been used for the manufacture of 250- and 500-gauge bombs. These items were marked and catalogued and the Iraqi officials were requested in writing to return all the items to Muthanna.

2. The seventh CW inspection (UNSCOM 26), which was in Iraq from 27 January to 5 February 1992, inspected 10 sites which had either been declared by Iraq or were designated for inspection by the Executive Chairman. No evidence was found of activities or items relevant to resolution 687 (1991). The team was also able to verify the return to Al-Muthanna site of the bomb-making equipment from Mosul and to observe preparations for and completion of one experimental test run of nerve agent hydrolysis at the pilot plant. Changes to the experimental conditions and procedures were required by

w/ S/23643, annex, enclosure, para. 23; and S/23687, annex I, para. 17.

the team, largely on safety grounds, but also including technical aspects. The team concluded after the test run that further test runs would be required to establish and prove satisfactory operating conditions and procedures.

3. The eighth chemical inspection team (UNSCOM 35) visited 14 sites over the period 15 to 29 April 1992 to verify, to the extent now practicable, Iraq's declarations, handed to the Chief Inspector of UNSCOM 31 on 28 March 1992, relating to CW items unilaterally destroyed by Iraq during July 1991. Additionally, the team carried out a no-notice inspection of a suspected documentation centre. The team also visited the previous headquarters of the Centre for Technical Research. No activity of relevance to Security Council resolution 687 (1991) was seen at either site.

B. *Destruction activities*

4. The destruction of Iraq's chemical agents and filled chemical munitions will certainly be a complex, difficult, time-consuming and potentially hazardous task; arguably it is the most difficult task facing the Special Commission, involving health, safety and environmental aspects in addition to varied technical problems. The planning and preparation for these activities, in New York and in Iraq, continues; destruction of some filled chemical munitions has already been carried out.

5. During the inspections carried out by UNSCOM 20 during October-November 1991, the team concluded that the 122-millimetre rockets at the Khamisiyah site were too unsafe to be moved to Al-Muthanna for destruction there. It was therefore decided that these rockets should be destroyed on site at Khamisiyah. Discussions on the optimum method of destruction involved the Destruction Advisory Panel and the CBW Working Group of the Special Commission. Taking all factors into consideration, it was decided that the rockets were best destroyed by the use of explosive charges to destroy the rocket motors and open the warheads at the same time and to thermally destroy the released agents and degradation products in a fuel fire ignited at the same time the explosive charges were detonated. A team (UNSCOM 29) over the period 21 February to 24 March 1992 directed, controlled and observed the whole operation and provided specialist technical skills and equipment (explosive ordnance destruction expertise, decontamination and medical cover, atmospheric sampling, agent monitoring equipment, etc.) as necessary. Owing to a combination of technical problems, the work experienced initial delays; in addition more rockets were present than expected and further rockets were discovered, buried on the site, some of which were recovered and destroyed during the operation. These set-backs required the team to stay at Khamisiyah for an additional two weeks. The

initial problems were overcome and the team was able to start destroying the rockets. In this way, a total of 463 rockets (389 filled, 36 partially filled and 38 unfilled) were destroyed, approximating to 2.5 tonnes of agent (a GB/GF mixture). Safety and environmental concerns were of paramount importance throughout, and the Special Commission's requirements were strictly observed. A system for atmospheric monitoring was established as two linear arrays, at 200 metres and 1,800 metres, downwind of the destruction area. No evidence was obtained for any significant atmospheric contamination by the nerve agent.

6. Preparations for the destruction of CW agents at Muthanna have been actively continued and a team (UNSCOM 32) was in Iraq over the period 5 to 13 April 1992 to assess progress and to provide expert technical guidance.

(a) *Mustard agent incinerator*. Considerable progress has been made with the construction of this facility and the team estimated that the work is approximately 70 per cent complete. The major elements were in place but further work, including modifications required by the team, were required before commissioning can be considered. Given completion of this work to the standard required, the team saw no reason why the incinerator could not be made to work in a safe, effective and environmentally acceptable manner.

(b) *Nerve agent hydrolysis.* The experimental work on nerve agent hydrolysis carried out to date, together with the four experiments directed and observed by the team, has demonstrated the feasibility of the process. Consistent achievement of the destruction limits set by the Special Commission has yet to be convincingly demonstrated owing to the need to check the analytical procedures. Further experimental runs will be required to fully define operating parameters once the effectiveness of the analytical procedures, based on gas liquid chromatography, has been proven. The construction of the large-scale nerve agent hydrolysis plant has progressed well but further work and modifications requested by the team as a result of their inspection are required. Given completion of all outstanding work to the required standard, and satisfactory definition of the operating parameters as a result of the experimental programme at the pilot plant, the team saw no reason why the large-scale nerve agent destruction facility could not function safely, effectively and in an environmentally acceptable manner.

(c) *Other tasks.* Just prior to UNSCOM 32's departure for Iraq, the Special Commission decided that ballistic-missile-related chemicals (ammonium perchlorate, hexamethylene diisocyanate, tolylene diisocyanate, and aluminum powder—all used in the production of solid rocket propellant) should be transferred from their present locations to the Al-Muthanna site for controlled destruction there. Al-Muthanna is now the site in Iraq where, as far as possible, all of the Special Commission's chemical destruction operations will be carried out. UNSCOM 32 was therefore instructed to reconnoitre Al-Muthanna site to select an area or areas where the ballistic-missile chemicals could be safely stored to await destruction there. The team was also instructed to discuss with Iraq possible means of destruction of these chemicals and also safe transport of the chemicals to Muthanna. These objectives were achieved.

A roller mounted cradle to which was fitted a remotely operated electric drill had been developed by Iraq for the remote drilling of potentially hazardous 155-millimetre shells. The team inspected this and agreed that it would be safe and effective but would be time- and labour-intensive. Drilling and draining of filled munitions was very likely to represent the rate-determining step in the destruction of Iraq's chemical agents.

Advantage was also taken of the presence of UNSCOM 32 at Muthanna to discuss provision of facilities required by the UNSCOM team which will need to be permanently available at Muthanna during the CW destruction operation; a suitable building was identified for use as an operations room, offices, medical room and other facilities.

Appendix III
Ballistic missiles

1. During the period from December 1991 to June 1992, the United Nations Special Commission conducted a further six ballistic missile inspections in Iraq.

2. There have continued to be doubts about initial Iraqi ballistic missile declarations. In particular, there were questions about the numbers provided by Iraq concerning how many Scud and Scud-variant missiles were used in the war between the Islamic Republic of Iran and Iraq and for other purposes. Iraqi declarations of 19 March 1992 and subsequently confirmed that the Special Commission's suspicions were well-founded; 89 Scud-type missiles were claimed by Iraq to have been destroyed unilaterally and buried in the summer of 1991. Iraqi authorities modified earlier declarations by, *inter alia*, reducing by 67 the number they previously asserted had been used in the war with the Islamic Republic of Iran. In the light of this and of Iraq's unwillingness to provide evidence which confirms their latest declarations on the past disposition of its ballistic missiles, the Commission continues to harbour justifiable doubts. It is thus not clear that the latest declarations constitute transparency, cooperation and candour.

3. The Commission is now engaged in studying the 5 June report by Iraq and will strive to arrive early at an assessment of the comprehensiveness of the report. Additional inspections and destruction at declared and undeclared sites are required to fulfil the Commission's responsibility to ensure that all ballistic missiles with a range in excess of 150 kilometres, related major parts, and repair and production facilities have been located and destroyed.

4. UNSCOM 23 was conducted from 1 to 9 December 1991 to verify the destruction of fixed launch sites primarily in the Western Zone and the destruction of "supergun" components. A number of undeclared potential missile sites particularly in the production area were also designated for inspection. The team inspected a total of 17 different locations, of which 7 were undeclared sites. Reconstruction at some sites was fairly advanced. In addition, two sites to which production equipment had been evacuated from a production facility were also visited. At two undeclared sites, equipment assessed by the team to have been primarily intended for use in ballistic missile production and testing was found. Iraqi officials were instructed not to remove this equipment pending further instructions from UNSCOM. Four Scud-missile transporters were inspected once again; two of them had been welded and fitted with a non-prohibited short-range missile cradle. Destruction was required for all these transporters; Iraq agreed to destroy them and proposed to blow up the four similar ones remaining at Al-Taji.

5. UNSCOM 24 was conducted from 9 to 17 December 1991 to inspect a number of suspected ballistic missile sites for documentary evidence relating to missiles and equipment and for suspected missile concealment locations. The team inspected 14 different locations; 1 site was in Baghdad, the remainder were in the Western Zone. The team employed a combination of ground and air transportation to accomplish its task of inspecting 13 undeclared sites and 1 declared site. All inspections were conducted on a short-notice basis with site declaration given either upon arrival at the site, or 30 to 40 minutes before arrival at the site. The team was organized in two elements, tailored to tasks and skills. A document search group was composed for those sites designated for document search.

6. UNSCOM 28 was conducted from 21 to 28 February 1992 to supervise destruction by Iraq of missile repair and production facilities and related equipment which were identified to Iraq in a letter dated 14 February 1992. In addition, all prohibited items discovered were to be catalogued and their exact locations recorded. The team inspected a total of seven different locations. The ballistic missile production and repair facilities for the missile solid propellant project were visited and the team observed that all of them had been extensively rebuilt. A

number of areas which were inaccessible to previous inspection teams owing to war damage were visited and prohibited items were catalogued. However, the Iraqi authorities refused to comply with instructions to destroy the missile production and repair equipment as required in the Executive Chairman's letter of 14 February 1992 to the Minister of State for Foreign Affairs. No items were destroyed but they were recatalogued for a future destruction mission. When it became apparent that the Iraqi authorities would not permit destruction to occur, the Executive Chairman ordered the team to halt its activities and withdraw from Iraq, which it did.

7. UNSCOM 31 was conducted from 21 to 30 March 1992 to verify Iraq's claim to have unilaterally destroyed 89 ballistic missiles during the summer of 1991 along with certain associated equipment, to initiate the destruction of Iraq's ballistic missile production and repair equipment and to carry out a number of undeclared inspections. The team supervised the destruction of some of the missile production equipment that UNSCOM 28 BM8 had not been able to destroy. Among papers given to the Chief Inspector was a revised accounting of the number of missiles Iraq claims to have received from the former Soviet Union, and the uses to which they had been put; in particular, the list revises downward the number of missiles fired against the Islamic Republic of Iran between 1980 and 1988.

8. UNSCOM 34 was conducted from 13 to 21 April 1992 to resume the activities of UNSCOM 28, i.e. the supervision of the destruction by Iraq of facilities and equipment associated with Iraq's ballistic missile production programme. The team supervised the destruction of 45 such items of production equipment and 10 buildings, that is, the majority of the items on List A of the Executive Chairman's letter of 14 February 1992 as extended by his letter of 4 April 1992, both to the Minister of State for Foreign Affairs of Iraq, and continued with the verification of the Iraqi declaration of 19 March 1992.

9. UNSCOM 36, conducted from 14 to 22 May 1992, further continued this process. The team inventoried equipment designed for the production of nozzles for the BADR-2000. All items declared were verified as destroyed, including a second mock-up of the BADR-2000 ballistic missile, miscellaneous components, and missile transport dollies. The team additionally verified the destruction of two horizontal test vehicles, two independent test vehicles, two independent training test vehicles, and one missile maintenance vehicle, the erector arm of the training launcher, nine oxidizer and four propellant vehicles, a spot welder and a rolling machine. UNSCOM 36 identified five sets of Iraqi manufactured missile guidance components which the team had been directed to remove from Iraq for technical analysis. Additional guidance component parts were found; these had been destroyed unilaterally by Iraq and the remains scattered in and around a 10-kilometre stretch of a canal. The team inspected remains of previously destroyed "TONKA" fuel starter systems. Finally, UNSCOM 36 found a number of the documents relating to the construction of facilities associated with, or suspected of being associated with, missile systems. After some discussion, the team removed for further analysis copies of 33 pages of documents concerning construction at Sa'ad 16.

Appendix IV
Special Commission inspection schedule

Nuclear

15 May-21 May 1991	IAEA1/UNSCOM1
22 June-3 July 1991	IAEA2/UNSCOM4
7 July-18 July 1991	IAEA3/UNSCOM5
27 July-10 August 1991	IAEA4/UNSCOM6
14 September-20 September 1991	IAEA5/UNSCOM14
21 September-30 September 1991	IAEA6/UNSCOM16
11 October-22 October 1991	IAEA7/UNSCOM19
11 November-18 November 1991	IAEA8/UNSCOM22
11 January-14 January 1992	IAEA9/UNSCOM25
5 February-13 February 1992	IAEA10/UNSCOM27+30
7 April-15 April 1992	IAEA11/UNSCOM33
26 May-5 June 1992	IAEA12/UNSCOM37

Chemical

9 June-15 June 1991	CW1/UNSCOM2
15 August-22 August 1991	CW2/UNSCOM9
31 August-8 September 1991	CW3/UNSCOM11
31 August-5 September 1991	CW4/UNSCOM12
6 October-9 November 1991	CW5/UNSCOM17
22 October-2 November 1991	CW6/UNSCOM20
18 November-1 December 1991	CBW/UNSCOM21
27 January-5 February 1992	CW7/UNSCOM26
15 April-29 April 1992	CW8/UNSCOM35
21 February-24 March 1992	CD1/UNSCOM29
5 April-13 April 1992	CD2/UNSCOM32

Biological

2 August-8 August 1991	BW1/UNSCOM7
20 September-3 October 1991	BW2/UNSCOM15

Ballistic missiles

30 June-7 July 1991	BM1/UNSCOM3
18 July-20 July 1991	BM2/UNSCOM10
8 August-15 August 1991	BM3/UNSCOM8
6 September-13 September 1991	BM4/UNSCOM13
1 October-9 October 1991	BM5/UNSCOM18
1 December-9 December 1991	BM6/UNSCOM23
9 December-17 December 1991	BM7/UNSCOM24
21 February-29 February 1992	BM8/UNSCOM28
21 March-29 March 1992	BM9/UNSCOM31
13 April-21 April 1992	BM10/UNSCOM34
14 May-22 May 1992	BM11/UNSCOM36

Special missions

30 June-3 July 1991
11 August-14 August 1991
4 October-6 October 1991
11 November-15 November 1991
27 January-30 January 1992
21 February-24 February 1992

Appendix V
Establishment and mandate

1. *Establishment and composition*

1. The establishment, organization and mandate of the Special Commission remains essentially as described in the first report of the Special Commission. a/ Changes in the composition are recorded in paragraphs 3 and 4 of the present report.

2. *Organization*

2. The Office of the Executive Chairman of the Special Commission continues to discharge its responsibilities for operations support, with the assistance of the Field Offices in Bahrain and Baghdad. The number of regular United Na-

tions staff assigned to the Special Commission or specifically recruited for service with it total 45: 14 Professionals and 31 General Service. Staff made available by Governments to serve in the three offices number 14.

3. As the amount of information available to the Special Commission has continued to increase rapidly, it became obvious during the period under review that a capability to manage it more effectively was required. An Information Assessment Unit has thus been established in the Executive Office of the Special Commission. This Unit commenced its operations in early January 1992. The principal functions of the Unit include the systematic,

a/ S/23165, annex.

computer-assisted storage, retrieval and assessment of information pertaining to the Commission's mandate. Other key functions are assisting in the planning and execution of inspections in Iraq, and the direction, on behalf of the Executive Chairman, of aerial surveillance flights over Iraq. The primary sources of information for the Information Assessment Unit include: reports of Commission inspection teams, results of aerial surveillance flights, information provided by States, and information from public media. Iraqi declarations required by Security Council resolutions, when they come to constitute full, final and complete disclosure, will also be an important source of information to the Commission. It is expected that the Information Assessment Unit will play an increasingly important role in the operations of the Commission, particularly in ongoing monitoring and verification.

3. Mandate

4. The mandate of the Special Commission remains unchanged, although further progress has been made in the preparations for the introduction of ongoing monitoring and verification of Iraq's compliance with relevant parts of section C of Security Council resolution 687 (1991). It has not proved possible to initiate such ongoing monitoring and verification in the period under review, given Iraq's failure to acknowledge its obligations under Council resolutions 707 (1991) and 715 (1991) and under the Commission's and IAEA's plans for such monitoring approved by resolution 715 (1991). b/ Furthermore, the declarations by Iraq required under the plans will be needed before ongoing monitoring and verification can commence. (See appendix I for details.)

b/ S/22871/Rev.1 and S/22872/Rev.1 and Corr.1.

Appendix VI
Contributions to the Special Commission

1. The following contributions in cash and in kind (i.e., in addition to materials and equipment provided by Governments to individual inspectors) have been received to date:

(a) *In cash paid into United Nations accounts*

Government	Amount (United States dollars)	Remarks
Japan	1 000 000	From a trust fund
Kuwait	1 000 000	
Saudi Arabia	1 730 000	
United Kingdom	170 000	
United States of America	14 000 000	

The United Nations provided support out of the Working Capital Fund for the first five months of operation to a total of $8 million.

(b) *Outright grant*

Australia	Individual chemical protective equipment
France	Individual chemical protective equipment
Norway	15 vehicles 5 satellite global positioning system units 2 ambulances
United Kingdom	600 tins decontamination agent XLIEI
United States of America	7 vehicles 4 trucks 2 ambulances

(c) *Loaned for the duration of the operation*

France	3 chemical agent detectors (AP2C)
New Zealand	Medical equipment
Sweden	Decontamination equipment Individual chemical protective equipment
United Kingdom	Individual chemical protective equipment 2 biological weapons agent detection kits 24 chemical weapons agent vapour monitors 1 chemical remote agent detection unit

(d) *Loaned and returned*

Belgium	Medical equipment
Canada	Global positioning system Remote chemical detection equipment
Finland	2 gas chromatographs
France	Medical equipment
Germany	Explosive ordnance equipment
Netherlands	Chemical weapons analysis equipment
Switzerland	Chemical detection equipment Protective clothing
United Kingdom	5 vehicles Laboratory equipment, including a gas chromatograph mass spectrometer and an infrared spectrophotometer Portable generators

Personnel

2. In addition to personnel assigned from the United Nations, IAEA and the World Health Organization, the following Governments have provided personnel for the Commission's activities: Argentina, Australia, Austria, Belgium, Canada, Czechoslovakia, Finland, France, Germany, Greece, Hungary, India, Indonesia, Italy, Japan, Netherlands, Norway, New Zealand, Romania, Russian Federation, Sweden, Switzerland, Thailand, United Kingdom of Great Britain and Northern Ireland and United States of America.

3. To date, New Zealand has provided full medical support consisting of a core team of five personnel, augmented as necessary by additional doctors and medical assistants for particularly hazardous inspections or special projects.

4. Several Governments have responded positively to the Commission's request for personnel to be seconded to the chemical destruction programme at Al-Muthanna. The Commission will report on these contributions once the programme is under way.

Air support

5. The Commission has been provided with high-altitude reconnaissance flights over Iraq. The flights are undertaken on a regular basis by an aircraft with crew and support personnel made available to the Commission by the United States. Flights are directed by the Special Commission and the aircraft bear United Nations insignia. They are notified to Iraq 72 hours in advance and acknowledged by Iraq within 48 hours.

6. The Government of Germany has provided full air transport and support for the Commission's ground activities. Two C-160 Transall aircraft, based in Bahrain, transport inspectors and United Nations Special Commission personnel and cargo to and from Baghdad. Thirteen crew and support personnel operate the aircraft. Three CH-53 rotary-wing aircraft, including 28 crew and support personnel, are based at the Al-Rasheed airfield in Baghdad. They ferry teams to and carry out surveillance flights in relation to inspection sites, and act as the primary means of emergency medical evacuation of United Nations Special Commission personnel. They have also provided emergency medical services, on an ad hoc basis, to other United Nations personnel in Iraq.

Facilities

7. The Government of Bahrain generously provides facilities for the Bahrain Field Office at Manama airfield. In addition, it has made available facilities which enabled personnel from the Special Commission to install and use analytical equipment specifically required by one of its chemical inspection teams.

Document 119

Second semi-annual report (for the period from 17 December 1991 to 17 June 1992) on the implementation by the IAEA of the plan for the destruction, removal or rendering harmless of items listed in paragraph 12 of Security Council resolution 687 (1991)

S/24110, 17 June 1992

Note by the Secretary-General

The Secretary-General has the honour to transmit to the Security Council, pursuant to paragraph 3 of Security Council resolution 699 (1991), the attached second semi-annual report on the implementation by the IAEA of the plan for the destruction, removal or rendering harmless of items listed in paragraph 12 of United Nations Security Council resolution 687 (1991).

Annex
Second semi-annual report (covering the period 17 December 1991 - 17 June 1992) on the implementation by the IAEA of the plan for the destruction, removal or rendering harmless of items listed in paragraph 12 of UN Security Council resolution 687 (1991).

Introduction

By resolution 699 of 17 June 1991, the Security Council approved the plan submitted by the IAEA through the

Secretary-General for the destruction, removal or rendering harmless of all items listed in paragraph 12 of Security Council resolution 687. Resolution 699 also called for the Secretary-General to submit every six months a progress report on the implementation of the plan.

The first of these reports was circulated by the Secretary-General to the members of the Security Council in document S/23295 dated 17 December 1991. The Secretary-General also circulated on 29 May 1992 a report (S/24036) submitted by the Director General of the IAEA on the status of Iraq's compliance with its obligations under Security Council resolutions 687 (1991), 707 (1991) and 705 (1991). In this report, the Director General provided information related to destruction activities carried out in Iraq during the 11th inspection mission.

This is the second semi-annual report on the implementation by the IAEA of the plan for destruction, removal or rendering harmless covering the period from 17 December 1991 to 17 June 1992. Its content has been structured in such a way as to facilitate comparison with the previous report and evaluation of progress.

PRESENT SITUATION

Direct-Use Material

Fresh fuel

After the removal of all the fresh fuel for the IRT 5000 reactor, which was accomplished in November 1991, in conjunction with the 8th IAEA inspection, the 12.24 kg of U-235 contained in the fuel was processed in a Russian facility and transformed through isotopic dilution into approximately 61 kg of uranium enriched to slightly less than 20% in U-235. Once the product specifications have been verified by the Agency, this material will be transferred from the processing plant to an agreed facility for storage in Russia. Agency safeguards will continue to be applied during storage.

The French-origin MTR type plates containing a total of 372 grams of U-235, and the Russian-origin pins, containing a total of 116.1 grams of U-235, were removed from Iraq in June 1992 by the inspectors of the 12th team and are now temporarily stored at laboratory of the IAEA in Seibersdorf, Austria.

Irradiated fuel

As referred to in the first report (S/23295), other irradiated enriched research reactor fuel containing a total of 35.58 kg of U-235 is held in storage in two locations, one within Tuwaitha in the Russian reactor building, the second, at a site identified as Location B, a few kilometers north of Tuwaitha in farm land area.

Inadequate storage conditions at Location B led to serious corrosion problems. New containers were brought to this site and filled with demineralized water, into which all of the fuel elements in Location B were transferred with the exception of 6 control rods. The situation is now stable and the corrosion rate should decrease.

Negotiations with the consortium of commercial companies from France and the UK for the removal and reprocessing of this fuel have met with difficulties of a legal, technical and financial nature. Efforts are being made to overcome these difficulties.

Plutonium and other nuclear material

There is nothing further to report on plutonium. As to other nuclear material, the material balance is still not satisfactory. The IAEA is continuing efforts to reconcile discrepancies in the declarations.

Installations, equipment and other materials relevant to enriched uranium production

Information received from Governments of other States and, in particular, from the Government of Germany about the procurement by Iraq of large quantities of special materials and components needed in the manufacturing of gas centrifuges for the production of enriched uranium, was used in the course of the 9th IAEA inspection mission. The Iraqi authorities acknowledged the procurement of these materials and components, but stated that all of them had been destroyed or "rendered harmless" before the start of inspection activities under UN Security Council resolution 687 (1991). In the course of the same mission, the Iraqi side acknowledged the procurement of additional special material and components not included in the information previously received by the Agency from Iraq or other States.

The Iraqi authorities stated that destruction of these materials and components had also occurred prior to commencement of the inspection activities. A detailed description of the material and components in question is contained in document S/23505. The extent and effectiveness of the destruction carried out by the Iraqi authorities of these items is now under assessment by the Agency. Additional measures will be necessary, in some cases, to rule out any possibility of recovery.

The destruction of components specific to the Electromagnetic Isotope Separation (EMIS) program, begun in the previous six-month reporting period, continues. The destruction activities have included the removal to a nearby storage area of 51 return irons (30 tons each) from the alpha calutron pier at Tarmiya.

A plan for the dismantling of EMIS uranium enrichment production capabilities at the Tarmiya and Ash Sharqat sites was prepared and communicated to the Iraqi side on 15 May 1992. The plan included reduction of the electrical power delivery to both sites, removal of general utilities from buildings and destruction of eight key technical buildings.

Implementation of this plan was begun, with full cooperation of the Iraqi Atomic Energy Commission, in the course of the 12th IAEA Inspection (26 May - 4 June 1992) and is presently more than 50% complete. Dismantling operations at Tarmiya and Ash Sharqat will be completed by the time of the next inspection, scheduled to take place in July 1992, in the course of which the destruction of relevant buildings at these sites will also be completed.

Installations and equipment relevant to the weaponization activities

On 25 March 1992, following a series of meetings in Vienna between IAEA officials and an Iraqi technical delegation, a formal communication containing a list of buildings and equipment to be destroyed at the Al Atheer-Al Hatteen site was transmitted to the Iraqi authorities. The Al Atheer-Al Hatteen site had been identified by the IAEA as the main research centre where the IAEC intended to pursue its program for developing nuclear weapons. Eight buildings covering a surface of approximately 35 000 square meters, and 26 major equipment items, some consisting of several components, were destroyed under the supervision of Agency inspectors in the course of the 11th and 12th IAEA inspection missions. In the case of one additional item on the equipment list, essential components were removed to IAEA, Vienna.

The techniques employed for destruction included the use of explosive charges. A total of more than 6 tons of explosives were used. The large bunker at the Al Hatteen site was filled with concrete and scrap iron to prevent its further use (350 cubic meters of concrete were poured), as the use of explosives in this case was judged to be impractical. The bunker's high protective berm was levelled. Cutting torches were used to destroy the steel liner shell of the internal explosion test chamber and to cut off reinforcing bars of the internal explosive test chamber and of the contained firing facility that was part of the physics building. The Iraqi side provided all the equipment, materials and manpower necessary for fulfilling the destruction plan under the supervision of the IAEA teams. Details of the buildings and equipment destroyed at the Al Atheer-Al Hatteen site are given in the inspection reports of IAEA-11 (S/23947) and IAEA-12 (in preparation).

FUTURE ACTIVITIES

The removal from Iraq of the remaining 35 kilograms of U-235 contained in the irradiated fuel elements of the Tamuz 2 and IRT 5000 research reactors is one of the major tasks still pending. It is hoped that negotiations with the contractors can be brought to a successful conclusion and that the financial resources necessary for removal and processing of the irradiated fuel will be found.

The destruction of key buildings and installations at Tarmiya and Ash Sharqat will be completed in the course of the next IAEA inspection in Iraq. Once this operation is finished, Tarmiya, Ash Sharqat, Tuwaitha and Al Atheer-Al Hatteen will not be equipped for undertaking activities proscribed under United Nations Security Council resolution 687 (1991). The verification of compliance by Iraq with the requirements of the resolution at these sites will rest on the IAEA plan for future ongoing monitoring and verification.

Additional destruction, removal or rendering harmless may be necessary in the near term pending the result of ongoing sample analysis. In the long term, as provided for in paragraph 31 of the IAEA plan for future ongoing monitoring and verification, the inspection of any sites designated by the Special Commission or the IAEA in the course of implementation of that plan may also give rise to the need for destruction, removal or rendering harmless not foreseen at this time.

Document 120

Statement by the President of the Security Council concerning the Iraq-Kuwait Boundary Demarcation Commission

S/24113, 17 June 1992

The members of the Security Council have noted the letter of 17 April 1992 from the Chairman of the Iraq-Kuwait Boundary Demarcation Commission to the Secretary-General and express their complete support for the work of the Secretary-General and the Boundary Demarcation Commission in implementing paragraph 3 of resolution 687 (1991). They recall in this connection that through the demarcation process the Boundary Demarcation Commission is not reallocating territory between Kuwait and Iraq, but is simply carrying out the technical task necessary to demarcate the precise coordinates of the boundary between Kuwait and Iraq for the first time. This task is being carried out in the special circumstances following Iraq's invasion of Kuwait and pursuant to resolution 687 and the Secretary-General's report (S/22558) for implementing paragraph 3 of that resolution. They look forward to the completion of the work of the Commission.

The members of the Council have noted with particular concern the letter of 21 May 1992 from the Minister of Foreign Affairs of the Republic of Iraq to the Secretary-General (S/24044) concerning the work of the Boundary Demarcation Commission, which appears to call into question Iraq's adherence to Security Council resolution 687 (1991). The members of the Council are concerned in particular that the letter from Iraq of 21 May 1992 may be interpreted as rejecting the finality of the Boundary Demarcation Commission's decisions notwithstanding the terms of resolution 687 and the Secretary-General's report for implementing paragraph 3 of that resolution, both of which were formally accepted by Iraq.

They note with dismay that the letter recalls past Iraqi claims to Kuwait without also recalling Iraq's subsequent repudiations of these claims, *inter alia* through its acceptance of resolution 687 (1991). The members of the Council firmly reject any suggestion that tends to dispute the very existence of Kuwait, a member State of the United Nations.

The members of the Council remind Iraq of its obligations under resolution 687 (1991), and in particular paragraph 2 thereof, and under other relevant resolutions of the Council.

The members of the Council also remind Iraq of its acceptance of the resolutions of the Council adopted pursuant to Chapter VII of the United Nations Charter, which forms the basis for the cease-fire. The members of the Council wish to stress to Iraq the inviolability of the international boundary between Iraq and Kuwait being demarcated by the Commission and guaranteed by the Council pursuant to resolution 687 (1991), and the grave consequences that would ensue from any breach thereof.

Document 121

Decision 10 taken by the Governing Council of the United Nations Compensation Commission: Provisional rules for claims procedure

S/AC.26/1992/10, 26 June 1992

Decision taken by the Governing Council of the United Nations Compensation Commission at the 27th meeting, Sixth session held on 26 June 1992

The Governing Council decides:

To approve the Provisional Rules for Claims Procedure the text of which is annexed to the present decision.

Annex
Provisional rules for claims procedure

I. *General provisions*

Article 1. *Use of Terms*

The following definitions apply for the purpose of these Rules:

1. "Commission" means the United Nations Compensation Commission.

2. "Compensation Fund" or "Fund" means the United Nations Compensation Fund, created by para-

graph 18 of Security Council resolution 687 (1991) and established by paragraph 3 of Security Council resolution 692 (1991) in accordance with section I of the Secretary-General's Report (S/22559) dated 2 May 1991.

3. "Secretary-General" means the Secretary-General of the United Nations.

4. "Governing Council" or "Council" means the Governing Council of the Commission.

5. "Commissioners" means experts appointed by the Governing Council for the verification and evaluation of claims.

6. "Executive Secretary" means the Executive Secretary of the Commission and includes any Deputy of, or other person, authorized by the Executive Secretary.

7. "Secretariat" means the Secretariat of the Commission.

8. "Standard Forms" means claim forms prepared and distributed to Governments by the Executive Secre-

tary for claims under claims criteria adopted by the Governing Council.

9. "Claim Forms" means standard forms and any other form agreed between the Executive Secretary and the Government or international organization in question for filing claims.

10. "Rules" means the Commission's Provisional Rules for Claims Procedure.

11. "Criteria" means Criteria for Expedited Processing of Urgent Claims (Governing Council's decision No. S/AC.26/1991/1 dated 2 August 1991), and Criteria for Additional Categories of Claims (Governing Council's decision No. S/AC.26/1991/7 dated 4 December 1991) as well as any other criteria that the Governing Council may adopt.

12. "Claimant" means any individual, corporation or other private legal entity, public sector entity, Government or international organization that files a claim with the Commission.

13. "Person or Body" means an individual, corporation or other private legal entity, public sector entity, Government, or international organization.

14. "International Organization" means an international organization of States.

15. "Documents" means all submissions and evidence presented by a claimant in support of a claim, in whatever form, including Statements of Claim in categories E and F.

16. "Database" means computerized information, pertaining to individual claimants and claims, kept by the Commission to assist in the processing of claims.

Article 2. *Scope of the Rules*

These Rules apply to processing of claims submitted to the Commission under the criteria adopted by the Governing Council.

Article 3. *Calculation of Periods of Time*

For the purposes of calculating a period of time under these Rules, such period shall begin to run on the day following the day when the document is received or a notification is made. If the last day of such period is an official holiday or a non-business day at the headquarters of the Commission, the period is extended until the first business day that follows. Official holidays and non-business days occurring during the running of the period of time are included in calculating the period. The Executive Secretary will issue a list of such days.

II. *Submission and filing of claims*

Article 4. *Submission of Claims*

1. Claim forms and documents are to be submitted to the Commission at the Secretariat's headquarters (Palais des Nations, Villa La Pelouse, Geneva, Switzerland).

2. Claim forms shall be deemed to have been submitted when they are physically delivered to and received by the Secretariat.

Article 5. *Who May Submit Claims*

1. Governments and international organizations are entitled to submit claims to the Commission.

(a) A Government may submit claims on behalf of its nationals and, at its discretion, of other persons resident in its territory. In the case of Governments existing in the territory of a former federal state, one such Government may submit claims on behalf of nationals, corporations or other entities of another such Government, if both Governments agree.

(b) A Government may submit claims on behalf of corporations or other entities that, on the date on which the claim arose, were incorporated or organized under the law of that State. If the Governments concerned agree, one Government may submit claims in respect of joint ventures on behalf of the nationals, corporations or other entities of other Governments.

(c) Claims may be submitted on behalf of an individual, corporation or other entity by only one Government.

(d) International organizations may submit claims only on their own behalf.

2. An appropriate person, authority, or body appointed by the Governing Council may submit claims on behalf of persons who are not in a position to have their claims submitted by a Government.

3. A corporation or other private legal entity is required to request the State of its incorporation or organization to submit its claim to the Commission. In the case of a corporation or other private legal entity whose State of incorporation or organization fails to submit, within the time-limit established by the Governing Council, such claims falling within the applicable criteria, the corporation or other private legal entity may itself make a claim to the Commission within three months thereafter. It must provide at the same time an explanation as to why its claim is not being submitted by a Government.

Article 6. *Claim Forms and Language*

1. Except as may otherwise be agreed between the Executive Secretary and the Government or international

organization in question, claims must be submitted on the standard forms prepared and distributed by the Secretariat.

2. Due to the fact that the Commission's computerized software and database system, which is technically required for the processing of a large number of claims, has been designed in English, the working language of the claims procedure before the Commission will be English.

3. Claim forms can be submitted in any of the official languages of the United Nations. However, since English is the working language of the claims procedure and of the Commission's computerized database, in cases where claim forms are not submitted in English, an English translation of the form must be provided. The translation as submitted, will serve as the basis for the evaluation of the claim.

4. With respect to claims in categories A, B and C, the documents supporting the claims are not required to be translated into English at the stage of the submission of the claims. The Secretariat, on the basis of methods adopted for processing and evaluation of claims, will notify each Government as to the extent of the translation required and the time-limit for providing it.

5. With respect to claims in categories D, E and F, all documents supporting the claims must also be submitted in English or be accompanied by an English translation.

6. In the case of oral proceedings, the Executive Secretary shall arrange for interpretation as necessary into and from other official languages of the United Nations.

Article 7. *Format of Claims*

1. Claim forms in category A must be submitted only in the computer format distributed by the Secretariat. Governments will maintain custody of the original paper copies of Form A and supporting documents and will make them available to the Commission upon request.

2. Claim forms and documents in all other categories must be submitted on paper. In addition to filing claims in these categories on paper, Governments may also submit them in a computer format.

3. All claim forms and documents filed with the Commission on paper are to be submitted on paper 8 1/2 inches x 11 inches or on A-4 size paper (21 cm x 29.5 cm) or on paper no larger than A-4. If a document cannot conveniently be reproduced on paper no larger than A-4, it is to be folded to A-4 size, unless the Executive Secretary agrees otherwise in special circumstances.

4. Claims and documents filed with the Commission in a computer format are to be submitted on MS/DOS or UNIX compatible formats, or in such other format as may be agreed to by the Executive Secretary.

Article 8. *Copies*

1. Except as otherwise agreed to by the Executive Secretary, claim forms and documents must be submitted with the following number of copies:

For category A: 3 copies of micro floppy disk

For categories B & C: 1 original and 2 copies

For D & other categories: 1 original and 8 copies

2. The Secretariat, or the Commissioners, may request additional copies or accept a smaller number in exceptional circumstances.

Article 9. *Representatives*

For the purpose of these Rules, all communications between the Commission's Secretariat and a Government concerning claims shall take place through its Permanent Mission in Geneva. Further, except in cases where a specially authorized representative is designated by a Government and notified to the Executive Secretary, the head of the Permanent Mission of a Government shall be considered as its representative before the Commission. Governments that do not maintain Permanent Missions in Geneva and international organizations shall notify the name of their duly authorized representatives to the Executive Secretary.

Article 10. *The Registry*

A registry will be set up within the Secretariat. A member of the Secretariat will be designated by the Executive Secretary as Registry Officer. The Registry Officer will receive the claims and register them.

Article 11. *Receipt of Claims*

1. Upon the submission of a claim, the Registry Officer will issue a delivery receipt identifying the parcel received and confirming the date it was received and the person who presented it.

2. The Registry Officer will in due course verify:

(a) that the claim has been submitted by a person or body who, in accordance with the decisions of the Governing Council, has a right to file claims with the Commission;

(b) that the claim has been submitted within the relevant time-limit established by the Governing Council;

(c) that, in the case of a corporation or other private legal entity making a claim directly to the Commission in accordance with Article 5, paragraph 3, above:

(i) evidence is attached indicating that a request was made by the entity concerned to the State of its incorporation or organization to submit its claim to the Commission;

(ii) explanation is provided as to why the claim was not submitted by a Government.

Article 12. *Unauthorized or Late Submissions*

1. In the case of claims submitted by an unauthorized person or entity, including claims presented by a corporation or other private legal entity without showing that a previous request has been made to the State of its incorporation or organization, the Executive Secretary will return the documents received, and inform the person or entity concerned of the reasons why the claim cannot be registered.

2. In the case of claims submitted by an authorized person or body after the expiration of the time-limit set by the Governing Council for a given category of claims, the Executive Secretary will report to the Governing Council. The Governing Council will decide whether to accept the late-filed claims or not.

Article 13. *Filing Receipt*

If the claim is submitted by an authorized person or body within the established time-limit, the Registry Officer will register the claim and issue a filing receipt indicating:

(a) the claim and its category;

(b) the party who presented the claim;

(c) the number of claims contained in a consolidated claim;

(d) the number assigned to the claim for identification.

Article 14. *Preliminary Assessment*

1. The Secretariat will make a preliminary assessment of the claims received in order to determine whether they meet the formal requirements established by the Governing Council. To this end the Secretariat will verify:

(a) that the claims have been submitted on the appropriate claim forms with the required number of copies, and in English or with an English translation;

(b) that the claims contain the names and addresses of the claimants and, where applicable, evidence of the amount, type and causes of losses;

(c) that the affirmation by the Government has been included in respect of each consolidated claim stating that, to the best of the information available to it, the claimants are its nationals or residents, and that it has no reason to believe that the information stated in the claims is incorrect;

(d) that all required affirmations have been given by each claimant.

2. In the case of claims of corporations and other legal entities the Secretariat will also verify that each separate claim contains:

(a) documents evidencing the name, address and place of incorporation or organization of the entity;

(b) evidence that the corporation or the legal entity was, on the date on which the claim arose, incorporated or organized under the law of the State the Government of which has submitted the claim;

(c) a general description of the legal structure of the entity;

(d) an affirmation by the authorized official for each corporation or other entity that the information contained in the claim is correct.

Article 15. *Claims Not Meeting the Formal Requirements*

If it is found that the claim does not meet the formal requirements established by the Governing Council, the Secretariat will notify the person or body that submitted the claim about that circumstance and will give it 60 days from the date of that notification to remedy the defect. If the formal requirements are not met within this period, the claim shall not be considered as filed.

Article 16. *Reports and Views on Claims*

1. The Executive Secretary will make periodic reports to the Governing Council concerning claims received. These reports shall be made as frequently as required to inform the Council of the Commission's case load but not less than quarterly. The reports shall indicate:

(a) Governments, international organizations or other eligible parties that have submitted claims;

(b) the categories of claims submitted;

(c) the number of claimants in each consolidated claim;

(d) the total amount of compensation sought in each consolidated claim.

In addition, each report may indicate significant legal and factual issues raised by the claims, if any.

2. The Executive Secretary's report will be promptly circulated to the Government of Iraq as well as to all Governments and international organizations that have submitted claims.

3. Within 30 days in case of claims in Categories A, B and C, and 90 days in case of claims in other categories, of the date of the circulation of the Executive Secretary's report, the Government of Iraq as well as Governments and international organizations that have submitted claims, may present their additional information and views concerning the report to the Executive

Secretary for transmission to panels of Commissioners in accordance with Article 32. There shall be no extensions of the time-limits specified in this paragraph.

4. Requirements set forth in Articles 3, 4, 6 (3), 7, 8 and 11 (1) shall apply to such additional information and views.

Article 17. *Categorization of Claims*

In order to facilitate the work of Commissioners and to ensure uniformity in the treatment of similar claims, the Secretariat will proceed to categorize claims according to, *inter alia*, the type or size of the claims and the similarity of legal and factual issues.

III. *Commissioners*

Article 18. *Appointment*

1. Commissioners shall be appointed for specific tasks and terms by the Governing Council upon nomination by the Secretary-General on the basis of recommendations of the Executive Secretary.

2. The Secretary-General has established a Register of Experts which, as stated in his 12 June 1991 invitation for the submission of names of experts, while not limiting his selection, might be drawn upon when Commissioners are nominated for appointment. The Executive Secretary will keep and up-date the register.

Article 19. *Qualifications*

1. In nominating and appointing the Commissioners, due regard shall be paid to the need for geographical representation, professional qualifications, experience and integrity.

2. Commissioners will be experts in fields such as finance, law, accounting, insurance, environmental damage assessment, oil, trade and engineering.

3. Nominations and appointments of Commissioners shall be made paying due regard to the nature of the claims and categories of claims to be assigned to them.

Article 20. *Procedure for Appointment*

1. The Executive Secretary will transmit to the Governing Council the nominations for Commissioners proposed by the Secretary-General, indicating which Commissioners are to serve on each panel and who, within each panel, will act as a Chairman.

2. The Executive Secretary will recommend to the Secretary-General for nomination as many panels of Commissioners as necessary to process claims in an expeditious manner.

3. When transmitting to the Governing Council the nominations for Commissioners, the Executive Secretary

will specify the claims or categories of claims to be assigned to each panel, indicating the expertise and the number of Commissioners required.

4. If the Governing Council does not agree on the appointment of a nominee for a panel, it will request the Secretary-General, through the Executive Secretary, to submit a new nomination.

5. If, at the time the Executive Secretary transmits the new nomination, the Governing Council is not in session, the new nomination will be communicated to the members of the Governing Council. The Governing Council may approve replacement Commissioners at intersessional meetings.

6. The same procedure will apply whenever a new Commissioner must be nominated.

Article 21. *Requirements*

1. Commissioners will act in their personal capacity. Commissioners shall not have financial interests in any of the claims submitted to them or to the panel to which they belong. They may not be associated with or have financial interests in any corporations whose claims have been submitted to them or to the panel to which they belong.

2. Commissioners shall not represent or advise any party or claimant concerning the preparation or presentation of their claims to the Commission during their service as Commissioner or for two years thereafter.

Article 22. *Disclosure*

1. All prospective Commissioners shall file a statement that shall disclose to the Executive Secretary any prior or actual relationship with Governments, corporations or individuals, or any other circumstances, that are likely to give rise to justifiable doubts as to his impartiality or independence with respect to his prospective tasks. This information will be provided to the Governing Council at the time the nomination of the prospective Commissioner is transmitted.

2. A Commissioner, once appointed, shall disclose to the Executive Secretary any new circumstances likely to give rise to justifiable doubts as to his impartiality or independence.

3. When any Commissioner obtains knowledge that any particular claim before his panel involves circumstances likely to give rise to justifiable doubts as to his impartiality or independence with respect to that claim or group of claims, he shall disclose such circumstances to the Executive Secretary and, if appropriate, shall disqualify himself as to that case.

4. If any Government, international organization, individual claimant, or Commissioner becomes aware of

circumstances that give rise to justifiable doubts as to a Commissioner's impartiality or independence, such circumstances must be communicated to the Executive Secretary not later than fifteen days after they became known.

5. The Executive Secretary will inform the Governing Council about the circumstances brought to his attention or of which he learns that are likely to give rise to justifiable doubts as to the impartiality or independence of a Commissioner, transmitting a statement of the Commissioner concerned.

6. In any case in which such circumstances are disclosed to the Governing Council, it may determine whether the Commissioner should cease to act, either generally or with respect to a particular claim or claims. Pending such a determination by the Governing Council, the Commissioner concerned will continue to perform his tasks.

Article 23. *Resignation*

1. A Commissioner who intends to resign from his office shall communicate his decision, through the Executive Secretary, to the Governing Council.

2. A Commissioner who has submitted his resignation shall continue to perform his functions until such time as his resignation is accepted by the Governing Council.

Article 24. *Completion of Work*

If a Commissioner resigns during the course of consideration of any particular claim or group of claims, the Commissioner will continue to serve for the limited purpose of completing work on that particular claim or group of claims, unless excused by the Governing Council.

Article 25. *Failure to Act*

In the event that a Commissioner fails to act or in the event of *de jure* or de facto impossibility of his performing his functions, the Executive Secretary shall inform the Governing Council, which may decide to replace the Commissioner in accordance with the procedures set forth in Article 20 (6).

Article 26. *Privileges and Immunities*

Commissioners, when performing functions for the Commission, will have the status of experts on mission within the meaning of Article VI of the Convention on the Privileges and Immunities of the United Nations of February 13, 1946.

Article 27. *Declaration*

Every Commissioner shall, before taking up his duties, make the following declaration:

"I solemnly declare that I will perform my duties and exercise my position as Commissioner honourably, faithfully, independently, impartially and conscientiously."

This declaration shall be signed and delivered to the Executive Secretary, and attached to the documents pertaining to the Commissioner's appointment.

IV. *Procedures governing the work of the panels*

Article 28. *Constitution of Panels*

1. Unless otherwise decided by the Governing Council, Commissioners will work in panels of three members. Each of the members of a panel shall be of different nationality.

2. Priority is to be given to the establishment of panels of Commissioners to deal with claims in categories A, B and C.

Article 29. *Organization of Work*

Chairmen of the panels will organize the work of their respective panels so as to ensure the expeditious processing of the claims and the consistent application of the relevant criteria and these Rules.

Article 30. *Confidentiality*

1. Unless otherwise provided in these procedures or decided by the Governing Council, all records received or developed by the Commission will be confidential, but the Secretariat may provide status reports to Governments, international organizations or corporations making claims directly to the Commission in accordance with Article 5, paragraph 3, regarding claims that they have submitted.

2. Panels will conduct their work in private.

3. Commissioners shall not disclose, even after the termination of their functions, any information not in the public domain that has come to their knowledge by reason of their working for the Commission.

Article 31. *Applicable Law*

In considering the claims, Commissioners will apply Security Council resolution 687 (1991) and other relevant Security Council resolutions, the criteria established by the Governing Council for particular categories of claims, and any pertinent decisions of the Governing Council. In addition, where necessary, Commissioners shall apply other relevant rules of international law.

Article 32. *Submission of Claims to Panels*

1. Following the appointment of Commissioners by the Governing Council, the Executive Secretary will submit to panels of Commissioners the single claims or categories of claims assigned to each of them together with the related documentation, containing the results of the preliminary assessment made by the Secretariat and any other information deemed to be useful for the work of the Commissioners, as well as the additional information and views submitted in accordance with Article 16.

2. Any information received by the Secretariat after the expiration of the time-limits as established in Article 16 will be submitted when received, but the work of the panel will not be delayed pending receipt or consideration of such information.

3. The Executive Secretary may, after consulting the relevant panel chairmen, reallocate a claim or claims from one panel to another in order to ensure the efficient processing of claims.

Article 33. *Work of the Panels*

1. After receiving claims from the Executive Secretary, Commissioners will examine them and meet to deliberate and prepare their recommendations to the Governing Council.

2. Panels of Commissioners will normally meet at the headquarters of the Secretariat. Meetings will be held to the extent deemed necessary by the Chairman of each panel. Commissioners will continue their work on the claims while away from the headquarters of the Secretariat, conducting the necessary communications among themselves and with the Secretariat.

3. Any recommendation or other decision of the panel shall be made by a majority of the Commissioners.

Article 34. *Assistance by the Executive Secretary*

1. The Executive Secretary and the staff of the Secretariat will provide administrative, technical and legal support to the Commissioners, including the development and maintenance of a computerized database for claims and assistance in obtaining additional information.

2. In considering the claims, the Commissioners will take into account the results of the preliminary assessment of claims made by the Secretariat in accordance with Article 14, as well as other information and views that the Executive Secretary may provide in accordance with Article 32.

3. A member of the Secretariat may attend sessions of the panel and may, if required, provide information to the Commissioners.

Article 35. *Evidence*

1. Each claimant is responsible for submitting documents and other evidence which demonstrate satisfactorily that a particular claim or group of claims is eligible for compensation pursuant to Security Council resolution 687 (1991). Each panel will determine the admissibility, relevance, materiality and weight of any documents and other evidence submitted.

2. With respect to claims received under the Criteria for Expedited Processing of Urgent Claims (S/AC.26/1991/1), the following guidelines will apply:

(a) For the payment of fixed amounts in the case of departures, claimants are required to provide simple documentation of the fact and date of departure from Iraq or Kuwait. Documentation of the actual amount of loss will not be required.

(b) For the payment of fixed amounts in the case of serious personal injury not resulting in death, claimants are required to provide simple documentation of the fact and date of the injury; in the case of death, claimants are required to provide simple documentation of the death and family relationship. Documentation of the actual amount of loss will not be required.

(c) For consideration of claims up to US$100,000 of actual losses, such claims must be documented by appropriate evidence of the circumstances and amount of the claimed loss. Documents and other evidence required will be the reasonable minimum that is appropriate under the particular circumstances of the case. A lesser degree of documentary evidence ordinarily will be sufficient for smaller claims such as those below US$20,000.

3. With respect to claims received under the Criteria for Processing Claims of Individuals not Otherwise Covered, Claims of Corporations and Other Entities, and Claims of Governments and International Organizations (S/AC.26/1991/7/Rev.1), such claims must be supported by documentary and other appropriate evidence sufficient to demonstrate the circumstances and amount of the claimed loss.

4. A panel of Commissioners may request evidence required under this Article.

Article 36. *Additional Information*

A panel of Commissioners may:

(a) in unusually large or complex cases, request further written submissions and invite individuals, corporations or other entities, Governments or international organizations to present their views in oral proceedings;

(b) request additional information from any other source, including expert advice, as necessary.

Article 37. *Review by Commissioners of Urgent Claims*

With respect to claims received under the Criteria for Expedited Processing of Urgent claims (S/AC.26/1991/1), the following expedited procedures may be used:

(a) The Secretariat will proceed to check individual claims by matching them, insofar as possible, against the information in its computerized database. The results of the database analysis may be cross checked by the panel.

(b) With respect to claims that cannot be completely verified through the computerized database, if the volume of claims is large, the panel may check individual claims on the basis of a sampling with further verification only as circumstances warrant.

(c) Each panel will make its recommendations on the basis of the documents submitted, taking into account the preliminary assessment conducted in accordance with Article 14, any other information and views submitted in accordance with Article 32 and any information submitted in accordance with Article 34. Each panel will normally make its recommendations without holding an oral proceeding. The panel may determine that special circumstances warrant holding an oral proceeding concerning a particular claim or claims.

(d) Each panel will complete its review of the claims assigned to it and issue its report as soon as possible but no later than 120 days from the date the claims in question are submitted to the panel.

(e) Each panel will report in writing through the Executive Secretary to the Governing Council on the claims received and the amount recommended to be allocated to each Government or other entity for each consolidated claim. Each report will briefly explain the reasons for the recommendations and, to the extent practicable within the time-limit, contain a breakdown of the recommendations in respect of individual claims within each consolidated claim.

Article 38. *Review by Commissioners of Other Claims*

With respect to claims received under the Criteria for Processing of Claims of Individuals not Otherwise Covered; Claims of Corporations and Other Entities; and Claims of Governments and International Organizations (S/AC.26/1991/7/Rev.1), the following procedures will be used:

(a) In so far as possible, claims with significant common legal and factual issues will be processed together.

(b) Panels may adopt special procedures appropriate to the character, amount and subject-matter of the particular types of claims under consideration.

(c) Each panel will complete its review of any claim or group of claims and report in writing through the Executive Secretary to the Governing Council within 180 days of the date the claims in question are submitted to the panel, except for any unusually large or complex claims referred for detailed review, as described below. Each panel will make its recommendations on the basis of the documents submitted, taking into account the preliminary assessment conducted in accordance with Article 14, any other information and views submitted in accordance with Article 32 and any information submitted in accordance with Article 34.

(d) Unusually large or complex claims may receive detailed review, as appropriate. If so, the panel considering such a claim may, in its discretion, ask for additional written submissions and hold oral proceedings. In such a case, the individual, corporation, Government, international organization or other entity making the claim may present the case directly to the panel, and may be assisted by an attorney or other representative of choice. The panel will complete its review of the case and report in writing through the Executive Secretary its recommendations to the Governing Council within twelve months of the date the claim was submitted to the panel.

(e) Each panel will report in writing through the Executive Secretary to the Governing Council on the claims received and the amount recommended to be awarded for each claimant. Each report will briefly explain the reasons for the recommendations.

Article 39. *Additional Time*

If a panel considering a claim or group of claims cannot complete its work within the allotted time, the panel will notify the Governing Council through the Executive Secretary of the estimated additional time required. The Governing Council will decide whether the panel should continue its work on the claims or group of claims, with a time-limit to be decided by the Council, or should be discharged of the claim or group of claims, which would be given to another panel.

Article 40. *Decisions*

1. The amounts recommended by the panels of Commissioners will be subject to approval by the Governing Council. The Governing Council may review the amounts recommended and, where it determines circumstances require, increase or reduce them.

2. The Governing Council may, in its discretion, return a particular claim or group of claims for further review by the Commissioners.

3. The Governing Council will make its decisions on amounts to be awarded at each session with respect

to claims covered in any reports of Commissioners circulated to members of the Governing Council at least 30 days in advance of the session.

4. Decisions of the Governing Council will be final and are not subject to appeal or review on procedural, substantive or other grounds.

5. Decisions of the Governing Council and, after the relevant decision is made, the associated report of the panel of Commissioners, will be made public, except the Executive Secretary will delete from the reports of panels of Commissioners the identities of individual claimants and other information determined by the panels to be confidential or privileged.

Article 41. *Correction of Decisions*

1. Computational, clerical, typographical or other errors brought to the attention of the Executive Secretary within 60 days from the publication of the decisions and reports, will be reported by the Executive Secretary to the Governing Council.

2. The Governing Council will decide whether any action is necessary. If it is determined that a correction must be made, the Governing Council will direct the Executive Secretary as to the proper method of correction.

Article 42. *Withdrawal of Claims*

A claim pending before the Commission may be withdrawn at any time by the Government or entity that submitted the claim to the Commission. In any case where the claim has been paid, settled or otherwise resolved, it shall be withdrawn.

Article 43. *Additional Procedural Rulings*

Subject to the provisions of these procedures, Commissioners may make such additional procedural rulings as may be necessary to complete work on particular cases or categories of cases. In so doing, the Commissioners may rely on the relevant UNCITRAL Rules for guidance. Commissioners may request the Governing Council to provide further guidance with respect to these procedures at any time. The Governing Council may adopt further procedures or revise these Rules when circumstances warrant.

Document 122

Statement by the President of the Security Council concerning the refusal by Iraq to permit a team of UNSCOM inspectors to enter certain premises

S/24240, 6 July 1992

The members of the Security Council have learnt with concern of the refusal of the Government of Iraq to permit a team of inspectors sent to Iraq by the Special Commission to enter certain premises designated by the Special Commission for inspection.

The members of the Council recall that, under paragraph 9 (b) (i) of section C of Security Council resolution 687 (1991), Iraq is required to permit the Special Commission to undertake immediate on-site inspection of any locations designated by the Commission. This obligation is imposed as a result of a decision of the Council, taken under Chapter VII of the Charter. Furthermore, Iraq has agreed to such inspections as a condition precedent to the establishment of a formal cease-fire between Iraq and Kuwait and the Member States cooperating with Kuwait in accordance with Security Council resolution 678 (1990). The members of the Council further recall that by paragraph 2 (ii) of resolution 707 (1991) the Council has reaffirmed the relevant provision of resolution 687 (1991) and expressly demanded that Iraq "allow the Special Commission ... and their Inspection Teams immediate, unconditional, and unrestricted access to any and all areas, facilities, equipment, records, and means of transportation which they wish to inspect."

Iraq's present refusal to permit access to the Inspection Team currently in Iraq to the premises designated by the Special Commission constitutes a material and unacceptable breach by Iraq of a provision of resolution 687 which established the cease-fire and provided the conditions essential to the restoration of peace and security in the region. The members of the Council demand that the Government of Iraq immediately agree to the admission to the premises concerned of the inspectors of the Special Commission as required by the Chairman of the Special Commission, so that the Special Commission may establish whether or not any documents, records, materials, or equipment relevant to the responsibilities of the Commission are located therein.

Document 123

Letter dated 15 July 1992 from the Secretary-General to the President of the Security Council concerning implementation of Security Council resolutions

Not issued as a United Nations document

In a letter addressed to me on 11 July 1992 and contained in document S/24276, the Minister for Foreign Affairs of Iraq illustrated the point of view of his Government with regard to the implementation of a number of Security Council resolutions as well as some other matters.

With regard to the implementation of Security Council resolutions 706 (1991) and 712 (1991), you are aware that the Secretariat has been involved in talks with the Iraqi side for the purpose of working out procedures which would make possible that implementation. These talks focused on every aspect of the so-called "oil-for-food" scheme, the moral objective of which is to provide humanitarian relief to the Iraqi population and, in particular, to those most affected. The talks conducted by my Secretariat worked out procedures to deal with:

(a) the sale of oil by Iraq and payment for it in accordance with Security Council resolutions and decisions;

(b) the purchase of foodstuffs, medicines, materials and supplies for essential civilian needs, with the proceeds of the sale of that oil in accordance with Security Council resolutions and decisions;

(c) the procedures for the monitoring of the distribution of food throughout the country in accordance with Security Council resolutions and decisions.

Throughout the last few months, the Secretariat has kept members of the Council informally abreast of the status of these talks which, were—as you know—*ad referendum*. The procedures worked out during those talks covered in great detail all the above mentioned aspects of the scheme and were taken for approval to Baghdad by the Iraqi delegation on 22 June 1992. ...

As indicated in the letter of 11 July from the Foreign Minister of Iraq, it would appeared that such an approach is not acceptable to the Government of Iraq.

With regard to Security Council resolution 687, on 5 July, the Special Commission, acting under the explicit rights given to it in the relevant Security Council resolutions, notified the authorities of Iraq of the inspection by its inspection team of certain premises in Baghdad. The Government of Iraq denied and continued to deny up to now access of the inspection team to these premises.

The statement made by the President of the Security Council on 6 July on behalf of the members of the Council has determined that Iraq's refusal to permit access to the inspection team to the premises designated by the Special Commission constituted "a material and unacceptable breach by Iraq of a provision of resolution 687 which established the cease-fire and provided the conditions essential to the restoration of peace and security in the region". The members of the Council also demanded that the Government of Iraq immediately agree to the admission to the premises concerned of the inspectors of the Special Commission as required by the Chairman of the Special Commission, so that the Special Commission may establish whether or not any documents, records, materials, or equipment relevant to the responsibilities of the Commission are located therein.

The Executive Chairman of the Special Commission will visit Iraq immediately to meet with the highest levels of the Iraqi Government for the purpose of securing for the inspection team the immediate and full access to these premises and the unequivocal agreement by Iraq to implement all its relevant obligations under resolutions 687, 705, 715 (1991). The Executive Chairman is to report on the results of his mission upon his return on Monday, 20 July.

As far as the demarcation of the Iraq-Kuwait boundary is concerned, as mandated by section A of Security Council resolution 687 (1991), the Minister for Foreign Affairs of Iraq addressed a letter dated 21 May 1992 to me (S/24044), in which he denounces the decisions adopted by the Iraq-Kuwait Boundary Demarcation Commission concerning the land boundary, as well as the mandate, composition and working methods of the Commission. The Security Council has reacted to that letter with a statement issued by its President on 17 June 1992 (S/24113).

Furthermore, the Permanent Representative of Iraq to the United Nations has transmitted to me on 13 July 1992 a letter dated 12 July 1992 from the Minister of Foreign Affairs of Iraq, in which the Minister informs me that the representative of Iraq will not participate in the sixth session of the Boundary Demarcation Commission, which began at Headquarters on 15 July.

While this is not a matter deriving from a mandate of the Security Council, I wish to mention that the Memorandum of Understanding (MOU) governing the Inter-Agency Humanitarian Programme in Iraq expired on 30 June 1992. In accordance with the provisions of article 23 of the MOU, a formal request for its renewal was conveyed to the Government of Iraq on 9 May 1992. A revised draft text for the renewed MOU was conveyed to the Government of Iraq on 2 June 1992. On 1 July 1992 I issued a statement noting that while discussions are taking place on the MOU, United Nations personnel will continue their humanitarian activities in Iraq under the existing arrangements. During the past two weeks several inconclusive rounds of talks over the renewal of the MOU have taken place between the United Nations Coordinator and representatives of the Government of Iraq. No substantive progress has been achieved: the United Nations Coordinator has reiterated the need to assure the continued provision of humanitarian assistance to vulnerable groups throughout the country by extending the Inter-Agency Programme based upon the MOU, comprising as it does the cardinal principles of equitable distribution of relief assistance, unrestricted access to all parts of the country and the continued deployment of the Guards Contingent. The Government has made clear its position that there was no further reason for the extension of the MOU and that the Guards Contingent had completed its function and was no longer needed.

Notwithstanding the United Nations position that the humanitarian operation should continue under "existing arrangements", visas and travel permits for United Nations staff and NGOs have not been renewed for the current month, despite assurances to the contrary received from the Ministry of Foreign Affairs. Humanitarian operations have accordingly been seriously affected: UNICEF and WFP have been unable to transport relief materials and food assistance in the absence of the necessary papers. Furthermore, no assurance has been received that humanitarian personnel to be rotated in coming days will be issued with the appropriate visas and permits.

Over the past three weeks the security situation has gravely deteriorated. In the most serious of a number of incidents, two members of the United Nations Guards Contingent were injured by a hand grenade attack in their accommodation in the governorate of Arbil. Security incidents have primarily occurred in the Northern governorates but several have also taken place in Baghdad in recent days. On 9 July 1992 I issued a statement demanding that such incidents cease forthwith and expecting the full cooperation of Government authorities in ensuring the safety and well-being of United Nations personnel.

I have pursued discussions with the Government of Iraq towards the extension of the MOU and the continuation of the Humanitarian Programme. These discussions have so far been inconclusive.

In sum, therefore, we are witnessing the absence of progress in negotiations and lack of cooperation by the Government, on one hand, and a deterioration in security conditions for the United Nations and NGO personnel, on the other. Accordingly, I have considered it appropriate to apprise the Security Council's President of the situation and of the serious implications these developments might have.

Please accept, Mr. President, the assurances of my highest consideration.

(*Signed*) Boutros BOUTROS-GHALI

Document 124

Statement by the President of the Security Council concerning the murder of a member of the United Nations Guards Contingent in Iraq on 16 July

S/24309, 17 July 1992

The Security Council deeply deplores the murder of a member of the United Nations Guards Contingent in Iraq on 16 July 1992 in the Governorate of Dohuk. It supports the Secretary-General's decision to order an immediate and thorough investigation of this appalling crime. Members of the Council wish to express their sincere condolences to the family of the victim, Mr. Ravuama Dakia, and to the Government of Fiji.

The Security Council wishes to register its profound concern at the deteriorating security conditions affecting the safety and well-being of United Nations personnel in Iraq. The Council demands that attacks perpetrated against the United Nations Guards Contingent and other humanitarian personnel deployed in Iraq cease immediately and that maximum cooperation be extended by the authorities in the investigation of this crime, as well as in the protection of United Nations personnel.

Document 125

Statement by the President of the Security Council concerning the sanctions regime

S/24352, 27 July 1992

The members of the Security Council held informal consultations on 27 July 1992 pursuant to paragraphs 21 and 28 of resolution 687 (1991) and paragraph 6 of resolution 700 (1991).

After hearing all the opinions expressed in the course of the consultations, the President of the Council concluded that there was no agreement that the necessary conditions existed for a modification of the regimes established in paragraph 20 of resolution 687 (1991), as referred to in paragraph 21 of that resolution; in paragraphs 22, 23, 24 and 25 of resolution 687 (1991), as referred to in paragraph 28 of that resolution; and in paragraph 6 of resolution 700 (1991).

Document 126

Letter dated 4 August 1992 from the Secretary-General to the Deputy Prime Minister of Iraq concerning the work of the Special Commission and humanitarian programmes in Iraq

Not issued as a United Nations document

I should like to express my appreciation for your assistance in helping to resolve the situation regarding the work of the United Nations Inspection Team, and for paving the way for continued and strengthened cooperation between the Government of Iraq and the United Nations.

I had asked Mr. Rolf Ekéus to raise with you separately the question of the extension of the Memorandum of Understanding for the provision of humanitarian assistance throughout Iraq. Prior to that meeting, Under-Secretary-General Eliasson had had contact with Ambassador Al-Anbari in New York and through Coordinator Gualtiero Fulchieri and Assistant Secretary General Foran, with Dr. Al-Qaisi in Baghdad on the same issue. In this regard, the United Nations has presented detailed proposals aimed at reaching an agreement with the Government of Iraq on a number of specific issues.

I was, therefore, disappointed when Mr. Ekéus informed me of your Government's response to the question of the extension of the Memorandum of Understanding. I regret that the difficult circumstances under which that meeting took place may have adversely affected the possibility of any consideration of our detailed proposals in this regard.

I consider the continuation of the humanitarian programmes for the affected populations to be imperative. I believe that it should be possible, building upon our renewed understanding and spirit of cooperation, to reach a mutually satisfactory agreement upon the legal framework for maintaining these programmes.

As the members of the Security Council have continued to express their wish for the extension of the Memorandum of Understanding, I would appreciate being able, in the near future, to inform them that progress has been made in the negotiations to that end. I would, therefore, propose that such discussions take place at an appropriate level in Baghdad or in New York, at your earliest convenience.

Please accept, Excellency, the assurances of my highest consideration.

(*Signed*) Boutros BOUTROS-GHALI

Document 127

Letter dated 24 August 1992 from the Secretary-General to the
President of the Security Council concerning the Memorandum of
Understanding governing the Inter-Agency Humanitarian Programme
in Iraq

S/24509, 2 September 1992

As you are aware, on 4 August 1992 I had addressed a letter to the Deputy Prime Minister of Iraq proposing that discussions on the extension of the Memorandum of Understanding governing the Inter-Agency Humanitarian Programme in Iraq take place at an appropriate level and at the earliest opportunity. On 10 August 1992 I received a reply from the Deputy Prime Minister indicating that his Government would welcome a visit to Iraq by the Under-Secretary-General for Humanitarian Affairs for this purpose. I therefore instructed Mr. Eliasson to proceed with such negotiations, which began upon his arrival in Baghdad on 17 August and concluded on 21 August 1992.

The Under-Secretary-General for Humanitarian Affairs was assisted by the Coordinator and senior officials from the United Nations programmes and agencies participating in the Humanitarian Programme (UNHCR, UNICEF, WFP and WHO). Five extensive rounds of talks were held between the two delegations, chaired on the Iraqi side by Minister for Foreign Affairs Mohammed Al Sahhaf. On 21 August lengthy discussions took place between Deputy Prime Minister Tariq Aziz and Mr. Eliasson. In addition to these talks, several meetings were held at the technical level between the representatives of United Nations programmes and agencies and the respective Government Ministers and officials. A drafting group was also established to work towards an agreed text for the MOU.

The Government of Iraq took the position that in view of the changed circumstances since the adoption of the two preceding Memoranda, the Inter-Agency Humanitarian Programme should be based upon transitional arrangements moving from an emergency phase towards "normalization" and regular cooperation with United Nations agencies. In this context, some of the exceptional measures provided for under the two earlier agreements were no longer applicable:

(a) United Nations sub-offices would no longer be permitted, but access on a functional basis would be granted for project implementation;

(b) NGO participation in the Humanitarian Programme could only be allowed subject to a separate agreement between individual NGOs and the Government of Iraq;

(c) The Guards contingent would be limited to a maximum of 150 Guards to be deployed only in the three northern Governorates with their Chief and "4 or 5 assistants" to be located in Baghdad;

(d) A separate communications system would no longer be accepted for the Humanitarian Programme inside the country;

(e) No further provision for a Government contribution in the local currency could be provided for in the MOU;

(f) The duration of the agreement could not exceed 31 December 1992.

The Government also urged that every effort be made to exempt humanitarian requirements from the imposition of sanctions, stressing the suffering these continued to inflict upon the civilian population.

The United Nations insisted that the critical and priority needs of vulnerable groups in Iraq required the continuation of the Inter-Agency Humanitarian Programme. The United Nations position with respect to the above specific points was as follows:

(a) Sub-offices or field stations were essential to participating United Nations programmes and agencies for the effective implementation of the Humanitarian Programme throughout Iraq;

(b) The participation of NGOs was an important operational requirement: the Government's insistence on separate agreements could be taken into consideration subject to the successful adoption of the MOU;

(c) The Government's limitation upon the overall strength and the location of United Nations Guards was unacceptable. United Nations and NGO participants in the Humanitarian Programme insisted upon the continued deployment of Guards, with a ceiling of 500, in order to ensure their protection, not least in view of the serious deterioration in the current security situation;

(d) The maintenance of the existing radio communications system was an essential component of all United Nations emergency humanitarian operations;

(e) A contribution by the Government in local currency, which had been provided for under previous Memoranda but only paid on three occasions, was necessary for the Programme—in the absence of a special exchange rate for humanitarian operations;

(f) In view of the time lost since the expiry of the last MOU and the importance of the Programme covering the approaching winter months, the duration of the agreement should be until 31 March 1993.

Despite extensive negotiations, wide divergencies remained in the positions of the two parties on the key issues mentioned above. A degree of progress was achieved on certain questions, such as the role of the United Nations Coordinator and the Coordination Committee, as well as on the components to be included in the various sectors covered by the Plan of Action. The United Nations agreed to take into consideration and reflect in the eventual MOU the Government's request for joint preparation of the Plan of Action and for its implementation under the Coordination Committee. Stressing the need to underline the crucial role of NGOs, the United Nations also agreed to take into account and reflect accordingly—subject to an overall consensus on the text—the Government's requirement for the conclusion of separate agreements with NGOs participating in the Programme. Unfortunately, however, the Government was not prepared to modify its position on the question of access and sub-offices and of the deployment of United Nations Guards.

In the course of discussions, particular concern was expressed by the Government of Iraq at the declarations of impending action aimed at imposing an exclusion zone for Iraqi aircraft below the 32nd parallel. An appeal was addressed to me to take up this issue, which the Government maintained to be in contravention of international law. The Deputy Prime Minister explicitly linked the implications of these declarations to the continued presence of the Inter-Agency Humanitarian Programme in the south of the country and the Government's refusal to permit the maintenance of sub-offices under a renewed MOU. The Deputy Prime Minister asserted that sub-offices in the southern region would eventually be misused for inappropriate purposes and maintained that the Inter-Agency Programme was serving political ends. In response, the United Nations strongly emphasized the purely humanitarian mandate of the Programme, the indispensable operational requirement of sub-offices, and the essential need for United Nations Guards in view of the grave security conditions prevailing in the country.

The Deputy Prime Minister further indicated that in the event of such action on an exclusion zone for Iraqi aircraft being put into effect, any eventual MOU would no longer be applicable and the existence of United Nations Guards would no longer be tolerated on Iraqi territory. In addition, the Deputy Prime Minister suggested that any remaining humanitarian personnel in the south be withdrawn as soon as possible to Baghdad so as to ensure their safety in view of the possibility of demonstrations in the Basrah area. Steps were subsequently taken, with my agreement, to recall to Baghdad the eight United Nations Guards and one UNICEF staff member still remaining in Basrah. On 19 August an invitation to visit the southern marshlands was extended to Mr. Eliasson who was authorized to proceed only after the adoption of the MOU. The possibility was accordingly not further explored in view of the lack of agreement on the extension of the MOU.

Mr. Eliasson raised on several occasions the imperative need to ensure the safety of United Nations and NGO personnel, as well as to bring an immediate end to the unacceptable wave of harassment perpetrated against staff based in Baghdad. He also deplored the fact that serious security breaches and incidents of harassment had continued to take place during his own visit. The Minister for Foreign Affairs gave his assurance that every effort would be made to prevent further cases of harassment against United Nations staff.

During the last meeting with the Minister for Foreign Affairs, the latter expressed the view that there would be another opportunity to discuss the Humanitarian Programme and to reach a formula for the extension of the MOU "in a short while". In his view, the door to a practical agreement was not closed: he remained optimistic and hoped that the results achieved, rather than remaining disagreements, would be stressed. He further gave the Government's assurance that "a de facto MOU existed" and that cooperation would be extended to the office of the Coordinator and United Nations programmes and agencies based in Baghdad. The Government would proceed in a "calm, civilized and reasonable manner". Visas and travel permits would be renewed for the staff currently assigned to Iraq but no requests for visas for additional staff would be granted. The "status quo" would apply for the United Nations Guards Contingent: the 120 Guards presently in Iraq could remain but no replacements or additional deployment would be permitted. The Government insisted that offices outside Baghdad and the northern Governorates should be closed forthwith. In addition, the presence of NGOs would not be allowed for the time being.

From the United Nations perspective, the Government's position prevents the Inter-Agency Humanitarian Programme from providing effective humanitarian assistance to vulnerable groups in Iraq. No further United Nations presence, in terms of sub-offices or Guards, is currently permitted in the south of the country. At the same time, the Programme's implementation in the northern Governorates has been brought to a halt: fuel supplies are lacking, thereby preventing the distribution of food from WFP and of supplies for health, sanitation, water and nutrition from UNICEF to a large portion of the population in the north. The latter remain gravely affected by the continued imposition of supply restrictions on food rations, fuel and medical supplies imposed by the Government. The World Food Programme's operations in the north will cease in their entirety in view of the ban imposed on the presence of NGOs, which will prevent the continuation of food distribution currently carried out by CARE.

The discussions in Baghdad on the renewal of the MOU have demonstrated that key issues remain unresolved for the further provision of humanitarian assistance in Iraq. At present, the Programme's staff are making every endeavour to fulfil their mandate from the current locations in Baghdad and the northern region. Under the circumstances indicated above, however, the United Nations will not be in a position to meet the essential humanitarian needs of vulnerable groups: in the absence of a United Nations presence in the south, a reliable assessment of conditions prevailing in that region will not be possible, while in the north, the population will be placed at serious risk if adequate food and fuel supplies are not prepositioned by November and should the Government not reinstate adequate food rations by that date. Such a situation could well lead to a renewed and large-scale displacement of the population.

I would be grateful if you would bring this letter to the attention of the members of the Security Council.

(*Signed*) Boutros BOUTROS-GHALI

Document 128

Security Council resolution concerning the work of the Iraq-Kuwait Boundary Demarcation Commission

S/RES/773 (1992), 26 August 1992

The Security Council,

Reaffirming its resolution 687 (1991) of 3 April 1991, and in particular paragraphs 2 to 4 thereof, and its resolution 689 (1991) of 9 April 1991,

Recalling the report of the Secretary-General of 2 May 1991 relative to paragraph 3 of Security Council resolution 687 (1991), 1/ concerning the establishment of the United Nations Iraq-Kuwait Boundary Demarcation Commission and the subsequent exchange of letters between the Secretary-General and the President of the Security Council of 6 and 13 May 1991, 2/

Having considered the Secretary-General's letter of 12 August 1992 to the President of the Security Council transmitting the further report of the Commission,

Recalling in this connection that through the demarcation process the Commission is not reallocating territory between Iraq and Kuwait but is simply carrying out the technical task necessary to demarcate for the first time the precise coordinates of the boundary set out in the "Agreed Minutes between the State of Kuwait and the Republic of Iraq regarding the restoration of friendly relations, recognition and related matters" 3/ signed by them on 4 October 1963, and that this task is being carried out in the special circumstances following Iraq's invasion of Kuwait and pursuant to resolution 687 (1991) and the Secretary-General's report on the implementation of paragraph 3 of that resolution,

1. *Welcomes* the Secretary-General's letter of 12 August 1992 to the President of the Security Council and the further report of the United Nations Iraq-Kuwait Boundary Demarcation Commission enclosed therewith;

2. *Expresses its appreciation* to the Commission for its work on the demarcation of the land boundary, and welcomes its demarcation decisions;

3. *Welcomes also* the decision of the Commission to consider the eastern section of the boundary, which includes the offshore boundary, at its next session and urges it to demarcate this part of the boundary as soon as possible and thus complete its work;

4. *Underlines* its guarantee of the inviolability of the above-mentioned international boundary and its decision to take as appropriate all necessary measures to that end in accordance with the Charter of the United Nations, as provided for in paragraph 4 of resolution 687 (1991);

5. *Welcomes further* the Secretary-General's intention to carry out at the earliest practicable time the realignment of the demilitarized zone referred to in paragraph 5 of resolution 687 (1991) to correspond to the international boundary demarcated by the Commission, with the consequent removal of the Iraqi police posts;

6. *Urges* the two States concerned to cooperate fully with the work of the Commission;

7. *Decides* to remain seized of the matter.

1/ *Official Records of the Security Council, Forty-sixth Year, Supplement for April, May and June 1991*, document S/22558.
2/ Ibid., *Forty-Seventh Year, Supplement for April, May and June 1992*, documents S/22592 and S/22593.
3/ United Nations, *Treaty Series*, vol. 485, No. 7063.

Document 129

Statement by the President of the Security Council concerning the Inter-Agency Humanitarian Programme in Iraq

S/24511, 2 September 1992

The Security Council is deeply concerned at the current situation of the Inter-Agency Humanitarian Programme in Iraq, as outlined in the Secretary-General's letter of 24 August 1992 to the President of the Council (S/24509), including its reference to Iraq's failure to renew its Memorandum of Understanding with the United Nations.

The Security Council recalls the statement of 17 July 1992 (S/24309), in which the Council expressed its profound concern at the deteriorating conditions affecting the safety and well-being of United Nations personnel in Iraq. The Council is particularly disturbed by Iraq's continuing failure to ensure the safety of United Nations personnel and the personnel of non-governmental organizations (NGOs).

The Security Council expresses its concern regarding the conduct and statements of Iraq on the Inter-Agency Humanitarian Programme which are inconsistent with the previous Security Council resolutions that demand that Iraq cooperate with the international humanitarian organizations.

The Security Council affirms that the critical humanitarian needs of vulnerable groups in Iraq require the speedy conclusion of arrangements that would ensure the continuation of the Inter-Agency Humanitarian Programme. In this respect, the Council considers unrestricted access throughout the country and the assurance of adequate security measures as essential prerequisites for the effective implementation of the programme. To this end, the Council fully endorses the Secretary-General's insistence upon appropriate field offices for participating United Nations agencies and programmes and the continuing deployment of the United Nations Guards. The Council strongly supports the Secretary-General's continuing efforts to sustain a United Nations and NGO humanitarian presence throughout Iraq, and urges him to continue to use all resources at his disposal to help all those in need in Iraq. The Council urges Iraq in the strongest possible terms to cooperate with the United Nations.

Document 130

Statement by the President of the Security Council concerning the sanctions regime

S/24584, 24 September 1992

The members of the Security Council held informal consultations on 24 September 1992 pursuant to paragraph 21 of resolution 687 (1991).

After hearing all the opinions expressed in the course of the consultations, the President of the Council concluded that there still was no agreement that the necessary conditions existed for a modification of the regime established in paragraph 20 of resolution 687 (1991), as referred to in paragraph 21 of that resolution.

Document 131

Report of the Secretary-General on UNIKOM for the period from 1 April to 30 September 1992

S/24615, 2 October 1992

Introduction

1. By paragraph 5 of its resolution 687 (1991) of 3 April 1991, the Security Council established a demilitarized zone (DMZ) along the Iraq-Kuwait border and decided to set up an observer unit with the following tasks: to monitor the Khawr Abd Allah waterway and the DMZ; to deter violations of the boundary through its presence in and surveillance of the DMZ; and to observe any hostile or potentially hostile action mounted from the territory of one State into the other. By its resolution 689 (1991) of 9 April 1991, the Security Council approved the report of the Secretary-General on the implementation of the above provisions; 1/ noted that the decision to set up the observer unit had been taken in paragraph 5 of resolution 687 (1991) and could be terminated only by the Council's decision; and decided to review the question of termination or continuation as well as the modalities of the United Nations Iraq-Kuwait Observation Mission (UNIKOM) every six months. In keeping with the above provisions, the Security Council last reviewed UNIKOM's mandate on 6 April 1992 and concurred with my recommendation that UNIKOM be maintained for a further six-month period. 2/

2. The purpose of the present report is to provide the Security Council, prior to its review, with an overview of UNIKOM's activities during the last six months.

Organization

3. As of September 1992, the composition of UNIKOM was as follows:

Military observers

Argentina	7	Ghana	7
Austria	7	Greece	6
Bangladesh	7	Hungary	6
Canada	1	India	6
China	15	Indonesia	6
Denmark	6	Ireland	6
Fiji	6	Italy	5
Finland	6	Kenya	6
France	20	Malaysia	6

Military observers (continued)

Nigeria	7	Thailand	7
Norway	7	Turkey	6
Pakistan	8	United Kingdom of	
Poland	6	Great Britain and	
Romania	6	Northern Ireland	15
Russian Federation	15	Uruguay	7
Senegal	7	United States	
Singapore	7	of America	15
Sweden	6	Venezuela	6
		Total	254

Administrative and logistics units

CANENG (engineers)	44
Chile Air (helicopters)	50
DANLOG (logistics)	45
NORMED (medical)	20
Total	159
Total military personnel	413

The authorized strength of the military observers is 300, of whom 46 are currently on stand-by in their countries. UNIKOM includes 186 civilian staff, of whom 90 are international staff and 96 are locally recruited.

4. There has been a change in the command of UNIKOM. Major-General T. K. Dibuama (Ghana) took over as Chief Military Observer with effect from 13 July 1992. Major-General Günther Greindl (Austria) returned to his country's service.

5. UNIKOM has the use of two small fixed-wing civilian aircraft contributed by the Government of Switzerland and a chartered aircraft that is used for the transport of personnel and equipment between Baghdad and Kuwait. On 19 August 1992, the Government of Chile informed me of its intention to withdraw its helicopter unit by the end of October 1992. Bids are being solicited from commercial contractors to replace the unit.

6. During the period under review the Canadian engineers cleared and marked 50 kilometres of new patrol tracks, disposed of 1,200 pieces of ordnance and recon-

1/ S/22454 and Add.1-3.
2/ S/23789.

firmed the safety of previously cleared routes. Work was carried out at UNIKOM headquarters Umm Qasr and Camp Khor to improve security and working conditions. Four landing strips were built at UNIKOM positions in the DMZ. In addition, observation towers were erected at some of the patrol and observation bases and a modified version of the towers is on order for the others. For protection, UNIKOM has begun to install shelters at its positions; two such shelters have been built to date.

7. The Danish logistic unit (DANLOG) continued to carry out vehicle maintenance, supply and security tasks, the latter mainly for the headquarters facilities at Umm Qasr and Camp Khor and for the logistic base in Doha.

8. The Norwegian Medical Unit (NORMED) maintained a sick-bay facility at Umm Qasr, serving the headquarters and the northern sector, and first-aid posts at the central and southern sector headquarters. It also assisted a number of civilians injured by exploding ordnance.

9. UNIKOM continued to provide technical support to other United Nations missions in Iraq and Kuwait. In particular, it assisted the United Nations Iraq-Kuwait Boundary Demarcation Commission with air transport and by clearing mines at the border marker sites; it also provided accommodation, transport and communications. Support was further given to the United Nations return of property from Iraq to Kuwait. UNIKOM provided movement control in respect of all United Nations aircraft operating in the area.

Demilitarized zone

10. The length of the DMZ is about 200 kilometres, to which must be added the Khawr Abd Allah waterway, with a length of about 40 kilometres. For the most part, the DMZ is barren and almost uninhabited, except for the towns of Umm Qasr and Safwan. There are airfields at Safwan and Umm Qasr and a port at Umm Qasr.

11. Much of the DMZ is still littered with unexploded ordnance and mines, particularly in the south. Private companies under contract to the Government of Kuwait continued clearing the DMZ on the Kuwaiti side.

12. The edges of the DMZ are marked only in a few places on the main access roads and tracks, and the absence of proper markings elsewhere has been a factor in several violations. Once the United Nations Iraq-Kuwait Boundary Demarcation Commission has completed its work, UNIKOM will realign the DMZ based on the boundary as demarcated by the Commission and mark the edges of the DMZ so that they are clearly identifiable.

Deployment and concept of operations

13. UNIKOM remained deployed in the DMZ, as outlined in previous reports. For operational purposes it has divided the DMZ into three sectors, each with a headquarters and six patrol/observation bases. UNIKOM exercises full freedom of movement throughout the DMZ.

14. UNIKOM's concept of operations remained based on a combination of patrol and observation bases, observation points, ground and air patrols, investigation teams and liaison with the parties at all levels. In carrying out its tasks, UNIKOM employs a set of surveillance aids, which include maritime radar for the Khawr Abd Allah, night vision devices, high-powered binoculars and video cameras. In addition, UNIKOM uses the Global Positioning System, a satellite system which allows a very accurate determination of location, something that is of great value in the terrain of the DMZ. As reported earlier, 3/ UNIKOM also conducted trials of ground surveillance radars; it has since determined that such radars would add only marginally to its observation capability and that the considerable expense would therefore not be justified.

15. The Chief Military Observer and other senior staff of UNIKOM maintained regular contacts with the authorities in Baghdad and Kuwait City. At the local level, liaison continued with the police on both sides, particularly with regard to civilian activity in the DMZ. These contacts again proved useful in dealing with complaints and facilitating UNIKOM's operations. Both Governments continued to extend their cooperation to UNIKOM.

Violations and complaints

16. During the first part of the reporting period, the situation in the DMZ was generally calm. During the second part, there was a heightening of tension in the northern sector and in the Khawr Abd Allah as a result of friction relating to civilian activity (see paras. 19 and 20 below). UNIKOM observed three types of violations of the DMZ: minor incursions on the ground by small groups of soldiers, often just one or two; overflights by military aircraft; and the carrying by policemen of weapons other than side-arms. The following table summarizes the violations observed by UNIKOM:

3/ S/23766, para. 16.

	Iraq				Kuwait			
			Police				Police	
	Ground	Air	weapons	Total	Ground	Air	weapons	Total
1-30 Apr	0	0	0	0	2	1	1	4
1-31 May	1	0	0	1	10	0	4	14
1-30 Jun	1	0	0	1	6	0	4	10
1-31 Jul	0	0	1	1	3	0	2	5
1-31 Aug	0	0	0	0	0	0	2	2
1-30 Sep	1	0	1	2	3	0	1	4
Total	3	0	2	5	24	1	14	39

	Member States cooperating with Kuwait			Unidentified		
	Ground	Air	Total	Ground	Air	Total
1-30 Apr	0	2	2	0	0	0
1-31 May	0	2	2	0	1	1
1-30 Jun	0	1	1	0	0	0
1-31 Jul	0	0	0	0	1	1
1-31 Aug	1	1	2	0	2	2
1-30 Sep	0	4	4	1	15	16
Total	1	10	11	1	19	20

17. UNIKOM raised these violations with the party concerned, with a view to having action taken to prevent a recurrence. Since the declaration of a "no-fly zone" in southern Iraq, UNIKOM has observed a number of overflights of the DMZ at an altitude too high to allow identification. I have asked the Governments that had declared the "no-fly zone" to avoid actions that might compromise the demilitarized status of the DMZ or adversely affect the work of UNIKOM.

18. During the reporting period, UNIKOM received 30 written complaints from Iraq and 28 from Kuwait. UNIKOM investigated each complaint and conveyed its findings to the parties concerned.

Other matters

19. The work of the Boundary Demarcation Commission has drawn attention to the fact that some of the farms operated by Iraqi farmers in the northern sector are actually on Kuwaiti territory. The Kuwaiti authorities view these farmers with suspicion, and there have been repeated allegations that the farmers were actually Iraqi military or security personnel. Tension has accordingly risen in the area and a number of firing incidents have taken place, including an incident on 30 August in which a UNIKOM military observer was injured while trying to restore calm. UNIKOM has stepped up its activity in the area and is keeping it under constant observation. However, there is a risk of further conflict when the boundary has been demarcated. UNIKOM has been in touch with both sides, with a view to maintaining calm and promoting a timely solution. As an interim measure, UNIKOM

has asked the Iraqi authorities to provide a detailed register of all farmers in the area concerned in order to enable it to monitor the activities of the farmers closely and to look into any unusual presence or activity which could cause concern.

20. Fishing by Iraqi fishermen in the Khawr Abd Allah increased during the period. On a number of occasions, UNIKOM was contacted by the Iraqi authorities about fishermen who were overdue, or to help retrieve boats which had been detained by the Kuwaiti authorities. On the other hand, UNIKOM received complaints from the Kuwaiti authorities that Iraqi fishing boats had violated Kuwaiti territorial waters. UNIKOM was able to resolve some of these problems, and it increased its surveillance of the Khawr Abd Allah in order to prevent incidents.

21. Since July 1992, the safety of United Nations staff in Iraq, including UNIKOM staff, has been a matter of some concern. Several incidents occurred in which staff received threatening telephone calls in their hotel rooms, car tyres were slashed and car windows broken. During the period there were also demonstrations against United Nations activities in Iraq. UNIKOM remained in close touch with the United Nations Security Coordinator in Baghdad on this matter and also raised it directly with the Iraqi authorities. In recent weeks the situation has improved.

Financial aspects

22. Should the Security Council continue the mandate of UNIKOM beyond 9 October 1992, the cost of

maintaining the Mission for a further period of six months would be approximately $30 million, based on the continuation of its existing strength and responsibilities. The necessary resources for that period would be sought from the General Assembly at its forty-seventh session.

23. As at 28 September 1992, unpaid assessed contributions to the UNIKOM Special Account amounted to $32.1 million. This represents approximately 26 per cent of the total assessments for the period since the inception of the Mission through 8 October 1992.

Observations

24. As described above, the situation in the DMZ, which continued to be calm during the first weeks of the period under review, has since been marked by a gradual heightening of tension in some areas. Although this trend has not so far become a cause for serious concern, it needs to be carefully watched, and UNIKOM has maintained a high level of vigilance.

25. The main source of tension is the issue of the status and property rights of the Iraqi farmers who will be affected by the demarcation of the boundary between Iraq and Kuwait. This issue has given rise to incidents, in one of which a UNIKOM military observer was injured. I have conveyed to both sides my concern at the situation and urged them to exercise restraint.

26. I wish to draw attention once again to the requirement that the parties maintain a reasonable distance from the boundary line shown on UNIKOM's map. Most minor incidents can be avoided if this simple rule is observed.

27. In the light of all the circumstances, it is evident that the continued functioning of UNIKOM is an indispensable factor in maintaining the DMZ, preventing or containing further incidents and reducing tension. I therefore recommend to the Security Council that it maintain UNIKOM for a further six-month period.

28. I wish to express warm thanks to Major-General Günther Greindl, who led UNIKOM with great skill from its inception until last July. I also wish to pay tribute to his successor, Major-General T. K. Dibuama, and to all the men and women of UNIKOM, both military and civilian, for their devotion and skill in serving the United Nations. Their discipline and bearing reflect credit on their countries and on the United Nations.

Document 132

Security Council resolution concerning Iraq's assets frozen outside Iraq

S/RES/778 (1992), 2 October 1992

The Security Council,

Recalling its previous relevant resolutions and in particular resolutions 706 (1991) of 15 August 1991 and 712 (1991) of 19 September 1991,

Taking note of the letter of 15 July 1992 from the Secretary-General to the President of the Security Council on Iraq's compliance with the obligations placed on it by resolution 687 (1991) of 3 April 1991 and subsequent resolutions,

Condemning Iraq's continued failure to comply with its obligations under relevant resolutions,

Reaffirming its concern about the nutritional and health situation of the Iraqi civilian population, and the risk of a further deterioration of this situation, and recalling in this regard that resolutions 706 (1991) and 712 (1991) provide a mechanism for providing humanitarian relief to the Iraqi population, and that resolution 688 (1991) of 5 April 1991 provides a basis for humanitarian relief efforts in Iraq,

Having regard to the fact that the period of six months referred to in resolutions 706 (1991) and 712 (1991) expired on 18 March 1992,

Deploring Iraq's refusal to cooperate in the implementation of resolutions 706 (1991) and 712 (1991), which puts its civilian population at risk and which results in the failure by Iraq to meet its obligations under relevant Council resolutions,

Recalling that the escrow account provided for in resolutions 706 (1991) and 712 (1991) will consist of Iraqi funds administered by the Secretary-General which will be used to pay contributions to the United Nations Compensation Fund, the full costs of carrying out the tasks authorized in section C of resolution 687 (1991), the full costs incurred by the United Nations in facilitating the return of all Kuwaiti property seized by Iraq, half the costs of the United Nations Iraq-Kuwait Boundary Demarcation Commission and the cost to the United Nations of implementing resolution 706 (1991) and of other necessary humanitarian activities in Iraq,

Recalling that Iraq, as stated in paragraph 16 of resolution 687 (1991), is liable for all direct damages resulting from its invasion and occupation of Kuwait, without prejudice to its debts and obligations arising prior to 2 August 1990, which will be addressed through the normal mechanisms,

Recalling its decision in resolution 692 (1991) of 20 May 1991 that the requirement for Iraqi contributions to the Compensation Fund applies to certain Iraqi petroleum and petroleum products exported from Iraq before 3 April 1991, as well as to all Iraqi petroleum and petroleum products exported from Iraq after 2 April 1991,

Acting under Chapter VII of the Charter of the United Nations,

1. *Decides* that all States in which there are funds of the Government of Iraq, or its State bodies, corporations, or agencies, that represent the proceeds of sale of Iraqi petroleum or petroleum products, paid for, by or on behalf of the purchaser on or after 6 August 1990, shall cause the transfer of those funds (or equivalent amounts) as soon as possible to the escrow account provided for in resolutions 706 (1991) and 712 (1991) provided that this paragraph shall not require any State to cause the transfer of such funds in excess of 200 million United States dollars or to cause the transfer of more than 50 per cent of the total funds transferred or contributed pursuant to paragraphs 1 to 3 of the present resolution and further provided that States may exclude from the operation of this paragraph any funds which have already been released to a claimant or supplier prior to the adoption of the present resolution, or any other funds subject to or required to satisfy the rights of third parties, at the time of the adoption of the present resolution;

2. *Also decides* that all States in which there are petroleum or petroleum products owned by the Government of Iraq, or its State bodies, corporations, or agencies, shall take all feasible steps to purchase or arrange for the sale of such petroleum or petroleum products at fair market value, and thereupon to transfer the proceeds as soon as possible to the escrow account provided for in resolutions 706 (1991) and 712 (1991);

3. *Urges* all States to contribute funds from other sources to the escrow account as soon as possible;

4. *Decides further* that all States shall provide the Secretary-General with any information needed for the effective implementation of the present resolution and that they shall take the necessary measures to ensure that banks and other bodies and persons provide all relevant information necessary to identify the funds referred to in paragraphs 1 and 2 above and details of any transactions relating thereto, or the said petroleum or petroleum products, with a view to such information being utilized by all States and by the Secretary-General in the effective implementation of the present resolution;

5. *Requests* the Secretary-General:

(*a*) To ascertain the whereabouts and amounts of the said petroleum and petroleum products and the proceeds of sale referred to in paragraphs 1 and 2 above, drawing on the work already done under the auspices of the United Nations Compensation Commission, and report the results to the Council as soon as possible;

(*b*) To ascertain the costs of United Nations activities concerning the elimination of weapons of mass destruction, the provision of humanitarian relief in Iraq, and the other United Nations operations specified in paragraphs 2 and 3 of resolution 706 (1991);

(*c*) To take the following actions:

(i) To transfer to the United Nations Compensation Fund, from the funds referred to in paragraphs 1 and 2 above, the percentage referred to in paragraph 10 below; and

(ii) To use the remainder of funds referred to in paragraphs 1 to 3 above for the costs of United Nations activities concerning the elimination of weapons of mass destruction, the provision of humanitarian relief in Iraq, and the other United Nations operations specified in paragraphs 2 and 3 of resolution 706 (1991), taking into account any preference expressed by States transferring or contributing funds as to the allocation of such funds among these purposes;

6. *Decides* that for so long as oil exports take place pursuant to the system provided in resolutions 706 (1991) and 712 (1991) or to the eventual lifting of sanctions pursuant to paragraph 22 of resolution 687 (1991), implementation of paragraphs 1 to 5 above shall be suspended and all proceeds of those oil exports shall immediately be transferred by the Secretary-General in the currency in which the transfer to the escrow account was made, to the accounts or States from which funds had been provided under paragraphs 1 to 3 above, to the extent required to replace in full the amounts so provided (together with applicable interest), and that, if necessary for this purpose, any other funds remaining in the escrow account shall similarly be transferred to those accounts or States, provided, however, that the Secretary-General may retain and use any funds urgently needed for the purposes specified in paragraph 5 (*c*) (ii) above;

7. *Decides* that the operation of the present resolution shall have no effect on rights, debts and claims existing with respect to funds prior to their transfer to the escrow account; and that the accounts from which such funds were transferred shall be kept open for retransfer of the funds in question;

8. *Reaffirms* that the escrow account referred to in the present resolution, like the Compensation Fund, enjoys the privileges and immunities of the United Nations, including immunity from legal proceedings, or any forms of attachment, garnishment or execution; and that no claim shall lie at the instance of any person or body in connection with any action taken in compliance with or implementation of the present resolution;

9. *Requests* the Secretary-General to repay, from any available funds in the escrow account, any sum transferred under the present resolution to the account or State from which it was transferred, if the transfer is found at any time by him not to have been of funds subject to the present resolution; a request for such a finding could be made by the State from which the funds were transferred;

10. *Confirms* that the percentage of the value of exports of petroleum and petroleum products from Iraq for payment to the Compensation Fund shall, for the purpose of the present resolution and exports of petro-leum or petroleum products subject to paragraph 6 of resolution 692 (1991), be the same as the percentage decided by the Security Council in paragraph 2 of resolution 705 (1991) of 15 August 1991, until such time as the Governing Council of the Compensation Fund may decide otherwise;

11. *Decides* that no further Iraqi assets shall be released for purposes set forth in paragraph 20 of resolution 687 (1991) except to the sub-account of the escrow account established pursuant to paragraph 8 of resolution 712 (1991), or directly to the United Nations for humanitarian activities in Iraq;

12. *Decides* that, for the purposes of the present resolution and other relevant resolutions, the term "petroleum products" does not include petrochemical derivatives;

13. *Calls upon* all States to cooperate fully in the implementation of the present resolution;

14. *Decides* to remain seized of this matter.

Document 133

Statement to the press by the President of the Security Council concerning the activities of UNSCOM

UN Press Release SC/5484-IK/125, 15 October 1992

The Security Council this afternoon received an interesting briefing from the Executive Chairman of the United Nations Special Commission (UNSCOM).

Ambassador Rolf Ekéus informed us about UNSCOM 45's general framework and purposes.

In his briefing, the Executive Chairman confirmed his decision to maintain this inspection according to the scheduled timetable. The Security Council expressed its support for this decision.

Chairman Ekéus also drew attention to press reports of a high-level statement made in Iraq, which would constitute a threat to the security of the United Nations inspectors. The Security Council stressed its particular concern for the safety of the inspectors.

Finally, the Council expressed the wish that Iraq will fully cooperate with UNSCOM 45 and will seize the opportunity to demonstrate its willingness to comply fully with Council resolutions.

Document 134

Second report of the Secretary-General on the status of the implementation of the plan for the ongoing monitoring and verification of Iraq's compliance with relevant parts of section C of Security Council resolution 687 (1991)

S/24661, 19 October 1992

Introduction

1. The present report is the second submitted pursuant to paragraph 8 of resolution 715 (1991), adopted on 10 October 1991, in which the Security Council requested the Secretary-General to submit a report to the Council every six months on the implementation of the Special Commission's plan for ongoing monitoring and

verification of Iraq's compliance with relevant parts of section C of Security Council resolution 687 (1991). It updates the information contained in the first report, circulated as document S/23801 on 10 April 1992.

2. Under the Special Commission's ongoing monitoring and verification plan, contained in document S/22871/Rev.1, Iraq is obliged to provide certain declarations. The first were due by 10 November 1991 concerning (a) initial information on the specific dual-purpose activities, facilities and items outlined in the plan and its annexes; and (b) a report on the legislative and administrative measures taken to implement resolutions 687 (1991) and 707 (1991), other relevant Security Council resolutions and the plan. Iraq is further obliged to update the information on (a) above each 15 January and 15 July, and to report further on (b) when requested to do so by the Commission.

3. The first report concluded that, despite the strenuous efforts of the Special Commission, "it was not possible to begin the practical implementation of the plan ... because of the positions maintained by Iraq since the adoption of" resolution 715 (1991). It further concluded that, "without the clear acknowledgement by Iraq of its obligations under Security Council resolution 715 (1991) and the plans approved thereunder, as well as its agreement to implement unconditionally these obligations, the Special Commission will be neither legally nor practically able to initiate and operate effectively the monitoring and verification plan contained in document S/22871/Rev.1".

4. Since the adoption of resolution 715 (1991) the Security Council, in the light of Iraq's non-compliance, has adopted a number of decisions relating to ongoing monitoring and verification which have further served to define the Council's position and provide guidance to the Special Commission in seeking to carry out its mandate. These decisions, embodied in statements issued by the President of the Council on behalf of its members, include the following:

(a) The finding that full implementation of the Council's resolutions on the situation between Iraq and Kuwait is essential to the restoration of peace and security in the region (S/23500 of 31 January 1992);

(b) The finding that Iraq's failure to acknowledge its obligations under resolutions 707 (1991) and 715 (1991) and to provide the necessary declarations constitutes a continuing material breach of resolution 687 (1991) (S/23609 of 19 February 1992);

(c) The finding that Iraq's unconditional agreement to implement its obligations under resolutions 707 (1991) and 715 (1991) and the plans is an essential precondition to any reconsideration of the lifting of sanctions under paragraphs 21 and 22 of resolution 687 (1991) (S/23609 of 19 February 1992);

(d) The finding that unconditional agreement by Iraq to implement all its obligations under resolutions 707 (1991) and 715 (1991) is necessary for initiation and credible practical implementation of ongoing monitoring and verification (S/23663 of 28 February 1992);

(e) The finding that Iraq had not complied fully and unconditionally with all its obligations, must do so and must immediately take appropriate actions in this regard (S/23709 of 12 March 1992).

These Council decisions recognize the preconditions which are essential for the Special Commission to be able to undertake credible full-scale monitoring activities. They are required as much of Iraq's permitted industry in the chemical, biological and ballistic missile areas is dual capable and, as such, will require monitoring under the plan.

Developments during the period 10 April-10 October 1992

5. After receipt of the Secretary-General's report of 10 April, the Council decided that its President should convey to the Permanent Representative of Iraq to the United Nations that Iraq's compliance with the plans was imperative. The President did this on 22 April. No formal response was given to the President of the Council. However, in reply to a letter from the Executive Chairman of the Special Commission to the Iraqi Minister of State for Foreign Affairs concerning the lack of the required declarations and acknowledgements, the latter responded on 26 May (S/24002) setting out Iraq's position. After reiterating the statement of the Deputy Prime Minister of Iraq, Mr. Tariq Aziz, to the Security Council at its meeting on 11 March 1992, Iraq demanded:

> "that agreement be reached between it, UNSCOM and IAEA, under the auspices of the Security Council, on practical guarantees to ensure that the measures and methods of ongoing monitoring will not be of such a nature as to infringe upon Iraq's sovereignty, threaten its internal security, lead to interference in its internal affairs or deny it the prospects of scientific, technological and industrial progress both in civilian fields and in military fields not prohibited under resolution 687 (1991)".

6. On 27 June 1992, Iraq formally submitted what it terms its "report on future compliance verification". This report has been examined by the Office of the Special Commission and by a group of international experts convened by the Office for the specific purpose of evaluating it.

7. This group of experts concluded that the declarations contained in the report were of themselves inadequate for the purposes of commencing effective ongoing monitoring and verification activities but did provide a

base on which to build through further discussions with the Iraqi authorities. In addition to the conditions mentioned in paragraphs 3 and 4 above, the Special Commission has identified a long list of issues that will need to be clarified before ongoing monitoring and verification activities can commence, and will raise these with the Iraqi side during the next series of inspections and in meetings arranged specifically for this purpose.

8. Major general shortcomings in the report made by Iraq include:

(a) Failure to provide unconditional acknowledgement of its obligations under resolution 715 (1991) and the plans approved thereunder;

(b) Lack of clear indication of the basis on which the report was made. The letter from the Iraqi authorities which preceded the delivery of the report stated that:

> "We would like to confirm hereby what the Vice-Premier, Mr. Tariq Aziz, established in his address to the Security Council on 11 March 1992. 'That Iraq is prepared to reach practical arrangements within the framework of the objective defined by the Security Council, and not exceed it to political or intelligence aims ... besides the possibility of reaching a reasonable formula to fulfil the aims of the current plans, guaranteeing at the same time Iraq's legitimate rights, sovereignty and security. The Council's understanding of the principles, basis and legitimate and logical requests we exposed, would naturally lead to a fair, just and objective application of the fundamental commitments required from Iraq in resolutions 707 (1991) and 715 (1991) which would lead to the Council's satisfaction.'

> "On this basis, the competent Iraqi authorities will, in the coming few days, deliver two copies of the report on future compliance verification to ... the Special Commission in Baghdad."

This position is a repetition of that stated in the letter of 26 May 1992 (S/24002—see para. 5 above). Taken with Iraq's strong criticism of the plan and resolution 715 (S/23606, para. 12), its oft-stated position of neither accepting nor rejecting them, and Iraq's failure to make the acknowledgement as in (a) above, suggests that Iraq made the declarations in accordance with its own understanding of what its obligations should be rather than in accordance with the plan adopted by the Security Council and contained in document S/22871/Rev.1;

(c) The absence of a declaration concerning the legislative and administrative measures taken by Iraq to give effect to the plan;

(d) The inadequacy of the declarations on civilian plants with dual capability.

9. A further difficulty relates to the inadequacy of a different set of declarations Iraq is obliged to provide—the full, final and complete disclosure of all aspects of its weapons programmes proscribed under section C of resolution 687 (1991), as required under resolution 707 (1991). In particular, complete information on Iraq's past production, suppliers and consumption of prohibited items and its past capacity to produce such items is necessary in order to plan effective inspection and import control regimes as required under the future ongoing monitoring and verification plans and Security Council resolution 715 (1991). The mechanism foreseen in paragraph 7 of that resolution can only be realistically designed when this information is available to the Sanctions Committee, the Special Commission and the International Atomic Energy Agency.

Conclusions

10. From the above, it is clear that the conditions for the initiation in full of the Special Commission's plan for ongoing monitoring and verification have not yet been met. Furthermore, there has been no movement in Iraq's underlying position on the plan and resolution 715 (1991) to suggest a change in the Commission's assessment that Iraq is seeking to ensure that implementation of the plan proceeds on the basis of its interpretation of its obligations, rather than on the basis of Security Council resolutions and the plan adopted by the Council.

11. As the Special Commission has previously pointed out, while its activities can be conveniently described as consisting of three stages—identification, destruction and monitoring—in actual fact these three stages overlap and merge one into the other. For example, the Commission is already engaged in revisiting or undertaking aerial surveillance of sites where proscribed activities were previously identified in order to ensure that those activities have not been resumed. This is essentially a monitoring function. The Commission is also actively seeking to identify civilian sites which are likely to require future monitoring. It is also seeking to supplement the information provided by Iraq (see para. 7 above) through vigorous questioning and inspection, so that the initiation of full-scale monitoring will not be unduly delayed once Iraq makes the necessary political commitment to full compliance. Nevertheless, for the time being the Commission remains constrained from going beyond preparatory work into full-scale monitoring and verification until it is clear that Iraq will comply with such monitoring on the Council's, not Iraq's, terms. The Council's directives on this point are unequivocal and must be complied with both by the Commission and by Iraq.

Document 135

Memorandum of Understanding dated 22 October 1992 between Iraq and the United Nations concerning humanitarian assistance

Not issued as a United Nations document

1. The present Memorandum of Understanding summarizes the results of discussions held in Baghdad on 17-22 August, in New York on 28 September - 2 October, and in Baghdad on 14-17 October 1992, between the Government of the Republic of Iraq and the United Nations.

2. The parties conducted a thorough review of the humanitarian assistance operations coordinated and implemented by the Inter-Agency Humanitarian Programme, in consultation with the competent Iraqi authorities. Both parties recognised the need for the continuation of the Programme for the provision of humanitarian assistance to alleviate the suffering of the affected Iraqi civilian population throughout the country.

3. The Programme shall be based on the Plan of Action prepared in joint consultation by the parties. Implementation of the Plan of Action shall be coordinated and supervised jointly by the two parties as provided for in this Memorandum of Understanding.

4. The Programme shall comprise the provision of assistance, including, *inter alia*, food aid including the requirements of making it available inside Iraq, nutrition assistance, basic health and medical care including support for public health systems and the provision of health equipment and medical supplies, water purification and sanitation assistance including the provision of equipment and spare parts required for the operation of water and sewerage treatment plants, agricultural assistance, primary education and, in the three northern Governorates, shelter as well as other humanitarian and assistance measures to be undertaken in conformity with the needs of the affected civilian population throughout the country.

5. The Programme shall be implemented by the United Nations and its Specialized Agencies, in close consultation and full collaboration with the Government of Iraq. Field representatives will be assigned to the field in order to coordinate or perform the required activities with their Iraqi counterparts foreseen under the Plan of Action agreed between the two parties and for the duration of the activities envisaged by the Programme under the Plan of Action. To that end, the Government of Iraq shall provide the necessary separate office space as well as accommodation and communication links between the field and the United Nations offices in Baghdad.

6. In this context, the Government of Iraq shall cooperate in granting United Nations field staff, safe and unimpeded access, by air or by road as necessary, to facilitate the implementation of the Programme. It will take all required measures to facilitate the safe and rapid passage as well as delivery of humanitarian assistance commodities throughout the country.

7. The Office of the United Nations Coordinator shall continue to coordinate the work of the United Nations and its Specialized Agencies participating in the activities envisaged by the Programme. Effective and regular coordination between the Government of Iraq and the Programme shall be carried out by a Coordination Committee of representatives of agencies and the Government of Iraq. The Committee shall coordinate the implementation of the Programme. It shall also plan for future activities and resolve any difficulties that may arise in practice.

8. In close consultation with the Government of Iraq, the United Nations Guards Contingent will continue to provide protection for United Nations and NGO personnel, assets and operations linked with the Programme.

9. The United Nations Guards will continue to be assigned as needed in the three northern Governorates of Suleimaniya, Arbil and Dohuk. The number of United Nations Guards required in the country shall not exceed 300, including a small administrative component, not exceeding 8, in their Headquarters in Baghdad. They shall enjoy complete freedom of movement in carrying out their functions. They are authorized to carry side arms provided by the Iraqi authorities with the approval of the United Nations. The Iraqi authorities will maintain the Chief Liaison Officer appointed to facilitate the Contingent's operations and the Liaison Officer in each sector to facilitate its work with the Iraqi authorities. Facilities including office, maintenance and repair support, will continue to be made available by the Government of Iraq where appropriate.

10. Non-governmental organizations will be encouraged to participate in the implementation of projects included in the Plan of Action, as prepared jointly by the competent Iraqi authorities and the United Nations. This participation shall be effected in close cooperation with the United Nations, and in accordance with terms of association between the Specialized Agencies and the NGO concerned, and an agreement between the NGO concerned, presented by the Coordinator, and the Government of Iraq.

11. The Government of Iraq shall ensure the timely issuance and renewal of visas and other necessary official documents to the staff of the relevant United Nations organizations, NGOs and relief agencies which are required for the implementation of the Programme.

12. The Government of Iraq will continue to extend its cooperation in maintaining a United Nations radio communications system with the outside world in Baghdad. The Government of Iraq will ensure the provision of adequate and reliable means of communications between the United Nations field offices and the United Nations Agencies Headquarters in Baghdad. Cooperation will be extended to provide the United Nations radio communications system between United Nations Agencies Headquarters and the three Governorates of Suleimaniya, Arbil and Dohuk, covered by the United Nations Programme. In addition, the Government of Iraq will cooperate with the United Nations in ensuring mobile links between the United Nations humanitarian personnel in the field and their home bases.

13. The Government of Iraq will consider the establishment of a special rate of exchange for assistance operations carried out by the agencies and organizations participating in the Programme. Pending a decision in this regard the Government of Iraq undertakes to make available cash contribution in local currency in the amount of ID 500,000 at the beginning of each month, or in accordance with the estimates provided by the United Nations Coordinator if less. Any unused balance remaining at the conclusion of the Programme will be refunded to the Government of Iraq.

14. The implementation of the Inter-Agency Humanitarian Programme shall be without prejudice to the sovereignty, territorial integrity, political independence, security and non-interference in the internal affairs of the Republic of Iraq.

15. The present Memorandum of Understanding will remain in force until 31 March 1993 and, if necessary, be reviewed six weeks before its expiration with a view to assessing the modalities of further cooperation.

Signed in New York this 22nd day of October 1992.

Jan ELIASSON,
Under-Secretary-General for Humanitarian
Affairs, United Nations

Nizar HAMDOON,
Ambassador Extraordinary & Plenipotentiary,
Permanent Representative of Iraq to the United Nations

Document 136

Second report of the Director General of the IAEA on the implementation of the Agency's plan for the future ongoing monitoring and verification of Iraq's compliance with paragraph 12 of resolution 687 (1991)

S/24722, 28 October 1992

The Secretary-General has the honour to transmit to the Security Council the attached report of the Director General of the International Atomic Energy Agency on the implementation of the Agency's plan for future ongoing monitoring and verification of Iraq's compliance with paragraph 12 of resolution 687 (1991).

Annex
Letter dated 30 September 1992 from the Director General of the International Atomic Energy Agency addressed to the Secretary-General

In paragraph 8 of its resolution 715 (1991), of 11 October 1991, the Security Council requested the Director General of the International Atomic Energy Agency to submit to the Council reports on the implementation of the Agency's plan for future ongoing monitoring and verification of Iraq's compliance with paragraph 12 of resolution 687 (1991). These reports are to be submitted when requested by the Council and, in any event, at least every six months after the adoption of resolution 715 (1991). The first such report was submitted to you on 11 April 1992 and distributed to the Security Council in document S/23813 of 15 April 1992.

Accordingly, I am requesting you to kindly transmit the enclosed second six-month report on the implementation of the plan and remain available for any consultation you or the Council may wish to have.

(Signed) Hans BLIX

Second report of the Director General of the International Atomic Energy Agency on the implementation of the Agency's plan for future ongoing monitoring and verification of Iraq's compliance with paragraph 12 of resolution 687 (1991)

1. On 11 October 1991, the Security Council adopted resolution 715 (1991) approving, *inter alia*, the plan submitted in document S/22872/Rev.1 and Corr.1 by the Director General of the International Atomic Energy Agency for future ongoing monitoring and verification of Iraq's compliance with paragraph 12 of part C of Security Council resolution 687 (1991) and with the requirements of paragraphs 3 and 5 of resolution 707/(1991). In paragraph 8 of resolution 715 (1991), the Security Council requested the Director General of IAEA to submit to it reports on the implementation of the plan when requested by the Security Council and, in any event, at least every six months after the adoption of resolution 715 (1991). The first six-month report submitted by the Director General was circulated on 15 April 1992 as document S/23813.

2. The Director General hereby submits the second six-month report on implementation of the plan for future ongoing monitoring and verification related to Iraq's nuclear capabilities.

3. As reported in S/23813, the Iraqi authorities had submitted to IAEA information declared to be that required pursuant to paragraph 22 of the plan. The scope of the submissions did not conform with the provisions related to information requirements, set forth in annex 2 of the plan, in so far as the Iraqis included only those items belonging to the Iraqi Atomic Energy Commission, rather than all relevant items located in Iraq as required in paragraph 1 of annex 2, and the information provided did not reflect the situation as of 1 January 1989. In addition, the form of the submissions made it difficult to assess the comprehensiveness and completeness of the information.

4. In the course of the eleventh IAEA inspection (7-15 April 1992), the Iraqi authorities agreed to provide revised and updated inventories. The Iraqis also requested clarification of the list of items to be reported to the Agency as identified in annex 3 of the plan.

5. During the eleventh inspection, the Iraqis were also requested to provide information concerning the suppliers of maraging steel, carbon fibre centrifuge rotors and enrichment-related technology. The Iraqi reply suggested that the information could be forthcoming by the next inspection.

6. During the twelfth IAEA inspection (26 May-4 June 1992) the Iraqi authorities provided a revised decla-ration of their nuclear programme, referred to by Iraq as the "full, final and complete" report required by Security Council resolution 707 (1991). The first such declaration, considered as a draft, had been handed over to the Director General in the course of the March 1992 Security Council discussions on Iraq. However, they refused to provide the information concerning the suppliers of the enrichment equipment and technology as requested in the previous inspection. This remains an open question, with no indication from the Iraqi authorities that such infor-mation will be forthcoming. Moreover, stiffeninq resis-tance to certain inspection activities was experienced.

7. As to the updated and revised inventories, the Iraqi authorities were reminded of their obligation to submit semi-annual reports, the next one falling due on 15 July 1992, and were provided with clarifications with regard to items listed in annex 3 of the plan.

8. Following consultations with the Special Com-mission and notification to the Security Council, Iraq was provided with a revision of annex 3 of the plan, as contemplated in paragraph 41 of the plan. Additional clarifications were requested by and discussed with the Iraqi authorities during the thirteenth and fourteenth IAEA inspections (14-21 July and 31 August-7 September 1992), and it is now expected that updated inventories will be submitted by Iraq.

9. On 11 December 1991, IAEA received from Iraq a request that the import of certain radioisotopes for use in nuclear medicine applications be exempted from the sanctions imposed by the Security Council. The request was referred to the Secretary-General. On 28 January 1992, IAEA was advised that the Security Council Com-mittee established by resolution 661 (1990) agreed to the Iraqi request, subject to procedures for each shipment of such material, specifically:

(a) The Iraqi Government must first secure techni-cal clearance from IAEA;

(b) The exporting country must request the Com-mittee's approval, attaching to that request a copy of IAEA's technical approval;

(c) In order to facilitate its own decisions, the Com-mittee invited IAEA to transmit to it copies of all Iraqi requests for approval for the import of radioactive iso-topes, and of the Agency's response thereto.

10. The Iraqi authorities were notified accordingly and on 14 January 1992 submitted to IAEA a letter containing information required pursuant to paragraph 25 of the plan concerning the proposed import by Iraq of radioactive isotopes intended for diagnosis and medical treatment. IAEA concluded that the request complied as a technical matter with the requirements of Security Council resolution 707 (1991), paragraph 3 (vi), and with

the provisions of the plan, and notified the Security Council Committee and the Iraqi authorities.

11. On 26 March 1992, the Iraqi authorities submitted to IAEA a list of research projects involving the use of a number of specified radioisotopes. Following the receipt of certain clarifications and additional information required pursuant to paragraphs 22 and 25 and annex 2 of the plan, IAEA advised Iraq by letter of 7 July 1992 of IAEA's technical approval of 42 of the 44 projects. The two remaining projects, in the opinion of IAEA, could be linked to research and development in the reprocessing area and to site qualification of nuclear power plants, activities proscribed under resolutions 687 (1991) and/or 707 (1991), and therefore could not be approved by IAEA.

12. On 25 September 1992, the thirty-sixth General Conference of IAEA adopted a resolution (GC(XXXVI)/1043) demanding, *inter alia*, that Iraq "fully and immediately comply with all of its obligations under its safeguards agreement with the Agency and under relevant Security Council resolutions, including the requirement under Security Council resolution 707 (1991) that it submit a full, final and complete declaration of Iraq's nuclear programme which includes all information called for by Security Council resolution 687 (1991)". The resolution further requested the Director General to "take, as soon as possible, the necessary measures for the implementation of the long-term moni-

toring plan, in accordance with Security Council resolution 715 (1991)".

13. In conclusion, the full implementation of the plan for future ongoing monitoring and verification of Iraq's compliance with paragraph 12 of resolution 687 (1991) will be possible only once the Iraqi authorities have fully complied with the information requirements laid down in document S/22872/Rev.1 and Corr.1, including the revised annex 3, as indicated in paragraphs 4, 7 and 8 of the present report. There are indications that this information is in the process of being compiled by the Iraqis. In the meantime, the Agency has already started to implement those components of the plan which do not depend on the availability of additional information from the Iraqi authorities, including the following:

– Periodic checks of Agency seals applied to nuclear and other materials, equipment and machine tools;
– Visits to sites where facilities and equipment which had been identified as related to Iraq's nuclear weapons programme during previous inspections, to verify that no nuclear activity is resumed;
– Analysis of high and low altitude imagery of any known nuclear sites in Iraq to identify the purpose of new buildings or to detect other activities which might require further on-site inspection;
– Initiation of a project aimed at periodic radiometric surveys of the main water bodies in Iraq to permit the detection of the presence, or resurgence, of major nuclear activities.

Document 137

Statement by the President of the Security Council concerning general and specific obligations of Iraq under various Security Council resolutions relating to the situation between Iraq and Kuwait

S/24836, 23 November 1992

Note by the President of the Security Council

Following consultations among members of the Security Council, the President of the Council made the following introductory statement, on behalf of the Council, at its 3139th meeting, on 23 November 1992, in connection with the Council's consideration of the item entitled:

"(a) The situation between Iraq and Kuwait

"(b) Letter dated 2 April 1991 from the Permanent Representative of Turkey to the United Nations addressed to the President of the Security Council (S/22435)

Letter dated 4 April 1991 from the Chargé d'affaires a.i. of the Permanent Mission of France to the United Nations addressed to the President of the Security Council (S/22442)

Letter dated 5 March 1992 from the Chargé d'affaires a.i. of the Permanent Mission of Belgium to the United Nations addressed to the President of the Security Council (S/23685 and Add.1)

Letter dated 3 August 1992 from the Chargé d'affaires a.i. of the Permanent Mission of Belgium to the United Nations addressed to the President of the Security Council (S/24386)

Letter dated 19 November 1992 from the Permanent Representative of Belgium to the United Nations addressed to the President of the Security Council (S/24828).

"I. General obligation

"1. The resolutions concerning the situation between Iraq and Kuwait impose a number of general and specific obligations upon Iraq.

"2. As regards the general obligations, Iraq is required, under paragraph 33 of Security Council resolution 687 (1991), to give official notification to the Secretary-General and to the Security Council of its acceptance of the provisions of that entire resolution.

"3. Iraq signified its unconditional acceptance in letters dated 6 and 10 April 1991 (S/22456 and S/22480, respectively) and 23 January 1992 (S/23472).

"II. Specific obligations

"4. In addition to the general obligation to accept the provisions of resolution 687 (1991) in their entirety, several Security Council resolutions impose specific obligations upon Iraq.

"(a) *Respect for the inviolability of the international boundary*

"5. By paragraph 2 of resolution 687 (1991) the Security Council demands that Iraq respect the inviolability of the international boundary and the allocations of islands previously agreed upon between Iraq and Kuwait. Pursuant to paragraph 3 of that resolution, the Secretary-General established a Boundary Demarcation Commission to demarcate the boundary between Iraq and Kuwait. Paragraph 5 of the same resolution requires Iraq and Kuwait to respect a demilitarized zone (DMZ) established by the Security Council.

"6. Iraq did not participate in the work of the Boundary Demarcation Commission at its July 1992 and October 1992 sessions. Iraq has refused up to now to withdraw a number of police posts that are not in line with UNIKOM's principle that both sides should stay 1,000 metres from the boundary line shown on UNIKOM's map. The Council in paragraph 2 of resolution 773 (1992) welcomed the Commission's land demarcation decisions and, by paragraph 5, the intention of the Secretary-General to carry out at the earliest practicable time the realignment of the DMZ to correspond to the international boundary demarcated, by the Commission, with the consequent removal of the Iraqi police posts.

"7. In response to the Iraqi Foreign Minister's 21 May 1992 letter to the Secretary-General (S/24044), the Security Council in a 17 June 1992 statement (S/24113) stressed to Iraq the inviolability of the international boundary between Iraq and Kuwait being demarcated by the Commission and guaranteed by the Council pursuant to resolution 687 (1991). The Presidential statement also noted with dismay that the Iraqi Foreign Minister's letter recalled past Iraqi claims to Kuwait without also recalling Iraq's subsequent repudiation of these claims. The members of the Council firmly rejected any suggestion that tended to dispute the existence of Kuwait. Resolution 773 (1992) underlined the Council's guarantee of the above-mentioned international boundary and its decision to take as appropriate all necessary measures to that end in accordance with the Charter, as provided for in paragraph 4 of resolution 687 (1991).

"(b) *Weapons-related obligations*

"8. Section C of resolution 687 (1991) imposes certain specific obligations upon Iraq with respect to its chemical and biological weapons programmes, its ballistic missile programmes with a range greater than 150 kilometres and its nuclear programmes. These obligations are elaborated upon in resolutions 707 (1991) and 715 (1991). The obligations are defined in paragraphs 8, 9, 10, 11, 12 and 13 of resolution 687 (1991) and they are elaborated upon in paragraphs 3 and 5 of resolution 707 (1991) and paragraph 5 of resolution 715 (1991).

"9. By resolution 699 (1991), the Security Council decided that the Government of Iraq shall be liable for the full costs of carrying out the tasks authorized by section C of resolution 687 (1991). No funds have so far been received from Iraq to meet this liability.

"10. The Council has noted that since the adoption of resolution 687 (1991) progress has been made in the implementation of section C of that resolution but that much remains to be done. In particular, Iraq needs to provide the full, final and complete disclosure of all aspects of its programmes for weapons of mass destruction and ballistic missiles with a range greater than 150 kilometres. There is a particular and vital requirement for complete information, including credible documentary evidence on Iraq's past production, suppliers and consumption of all prohibited items, and its past capacity to produce such items.

"11. Iraq must also acknowledge clearly its obligations under Security Council resolution 715 (1991) and the two plans for ongoing monitoring and verification approved thereunder. It must agree to implement these obligations unconditionally. In this connection the Council notes the letter of 28 October 1992 from Iraq's Minister of Foreign Affairs to the Secretary-General seeking a review of the terms and provisions not only of resolution 715 (1991) but also Security Council resolution 707 (1991). It is accordingly clear that Iraq seems unprepared to comply with the obligations already prescribed.

"12. The Special Commission has informed the Council about the outstanding matters that would at the present time appear to be the most important. The Council has noted document S/24661 of 19 October 1992 entitled 'The Status of the Implementation of the Plan for the Ongoing Monitoring and Verification of Iraq's Compliance with Relevant Parts of Section C of Security Council resolution 687 (1991)'.

"13. The Council has also noted the document S/24722 of 28 October 1992 containing the second report of the Director General of the International Atomic Energy Agency (IAEA) on the implementation of the Agency's plan for the future ongoing monitoring and verification of Iraq's compliance with paragraph 12 of resolution 687 (1991).

"14. In a statement issued on behalf of the members of the Council (S/23803) on the Special Commission's right to conduct aerial surveillance flights in Iraq, the President stated on 10 April 1992 that:

'The members of the Council wish to point out that the surveillance flights are carried out under the authority of Security Council resolutions 687 (1991), 707 (1991) and 715 (1991). Reaffirming the right of the Special Commission to conduct such aerial surveillance flights, the members of the Council call upon the Government of Iraq to take all the necessary steps to ensure that the Iraqi military forces will not interfere with or threaten the security of the flights concerned and to comply with its responsibilities to secure the safety of the Special Commission's aircraft and personnel flying over Iraq.'

The President also said:

'that the members of the Council warn the Government of Iraq of the serious consequences which would ensue from any failure to comply with these obligations'.

"15. The Special Commission, on 15 October 1992, informed the Council of actions endangering the safety and security of the Commission's inspection teams in Iraq, including a systematic campaign of harassment, acts of violence, vandalism to property and verbal denunciations and threats at all levels. The President of the Council issued on the same day a statement to the press stressing the Council's particular concern for the safety of the Commission's inspectors.

"16. In a further statement made on 6 July 1992 on behalf of the Council (S/24240) concerning the Government of Iraq's refusal to permit access to certain premises by a team of inspectors, the President said:

'Iraq's present refusal to permit access to the Inspection Team currently in Iraq to the premises designated by the Special Commission constitutes a material and unacceptable breach by Iraq of a provision of resolution 687 (1991) which established the cease-fire and provided the conditions essential to the restoration of peace and security in the region. The members of the Council demand that the Government of Iraq immediately agree to the admission to the premises concerned of the inspectors of the Special Commission as required by the Chairman of the Special Commission, so that the Special Commission may establish whether or not any documents, records, materials, or equipment relevant to the responsibilities of the Commission are located therein.'

"Security Council resolution 707 (1991) demands that Iraq allow the Special Commission, the IAEA and their inspection teams immediate, unconditional and unrestricted access to any and all areas, facilities, equipment, records and means of transportation which they wish to inspect. Therefore, the Council cannot accept Iraq's insistence that there must be a limit on access by the inspection teams.

"(c) *Repatriation of and access to Kuwaiti and third-country nationals in Iraq*

"17. As regards Kuwaiti and third-country nationals in Iraq, Security Council resolutions 664 (1990), 666 (1990), 667 (1990), 674 (1990), 686 (1991) and 687 (1991) impose an obligation on Iraq to release, facilitate repatriation of, and arrange for immediate access to them, as well as the return of the remains of any deceased personnel of the forces of Kuwait and of the member States cooperating with Kuwait pursuant to resolution 678 (1990). Furthermore, paragraph 30 of resolution 687 (1991) requires Iraq to extend all necessary cooperation to the International Committee of the Red Cross (ICRC) in facilitating the search for Kuwaiti and third-country nationals still unaccounted for.

"18. In spite of ICRC's best ongoing efforts, ICRC has not received information as to the whereabouts of the persons reported missing in Iraq. Nor has it received detailed and documented information on the search conducted by the Iraqi authorities. Following the 11-12 March 1992 Council meeting with the Iraqi Deputy Prime Minister, Iraq published in its press lists of those believed missing/detained inside Iraq. ICRC has still not received permission to visit Iraqi prisons and detention centres in accordance with standard ICRC criteria. Very few missing persons/detainees have been released since March 1992, while hundreds are believed still to be inside Iraq.

"(d) *Iraq's liability under international law*

"19. Another obligation concerns Iraq's liability under international law. In resolution 674 (1990), the Security Council reminds Iraq that under international law it 'is liable for any loss, damage or injury arising in regard to Kuwait and third States and their nationals and corporations, as a result of the invasion and illegal occupation of Kuwait by Iraq'. Its liability under international law is reaffirmed in paragraph 2 (b) of resolution 686 (1991) and paragraph 16 of resolution 687 (1991). Resolution 687 (1991) further specifies that it 'is liable under international law for any direct loss, damage, including environmental damage and the depletion of natural resources, or injury to foreign governments, nationals and corporations, as a result of Iraq's unlawful invasion and occupation of Kuwait'.

"20. By paragraph 18 of the same resolution, the Security Council created a fund to pay compensation for claims that fall within paragraph 16, to be financed by a percentage of the value of the exports of petroleum and petroleum products from Iraq. In view of the existing economic sanctions against Iraq under resolution 661 (1991), Iraq was permitted by the Security Council under resolutions 706 (1991) and 712 (1991) to sell a limited quantity of oil, as an exception, a portion of the proceeds from which would be used to provide financial resources for the fund. To date, it has not availed itself of this possibility. The Council noted that this authorization lapsed on 18 March 1992 but indicated its readiness to authorize the regime for the sale of Iraqi petroleum and petroleum products for a like period of time as that specified in the resolutions and also its readiness to consider possible further extensions (S/23732, 19 March 1992). Since then Iraq has not shown any willingness to resume discussions about implementing these resolutions. The members of the Council are aware of a previous request by Iraq for a five-year moratorium on meeting its financial obligations, including payments into the Compensation Fund.

"21. In view of Iraq's refusal to cooperate in the implementation of resolutions 706 (1991) and 712 (1991) after several rounds of technical discussions with the Secretariat, the Security Council adopted resolution 778 (1992) which mandates that certain frozen Iraqi assets be transferred to a United Nations escrow account. A portion of these funds will be transferred to the Compensation Fund.

"(e) *Repayment and servicing of Iraq's foreign debt*

"22. With regard to another obligation, the Security Council, in paragraph 17 of resolution 687 (1991), demands that Iraq scrupulously adhere to all of its obligations concerning servicing and repayment of its foreign debt.

"(f) Nonentitlement to claims deriving from the effects of the measures taken by the Security Council in resolution 661 (1990) and related resolutions (para. 29 of resolution 687 (1991)) of the Security Council

"23. According to information received with regard to this item, Iraq has attempted to enforce some claims under which it would have benefited from a contract frustrated by the coming into effect of the terms of resolution 661 (1990), in particular, through the confiscation of the property of foreign companies and organizations left in Iraq.

"(g) *Return of property*

"24. I now turn to the question of return of property. The Security Council, in paragraph 2 (d) of resolution 686 (1991), demands that Iraq immediately begin to return all Kuwaiti property seized by it, to be completed in the shortest possible period. The members of the Council have previously noted with satisfaction that Iraqi officials involved with the return of property have extended cooperation to the United Nations to facilitate the return. However, much property, including military equipment and private property, remains to be returned.

"(h) *Monthly statements of gold and foreign currency reserves*

"25. Another obligation is set out by paragraph 7 of resolution 706 (1991), under which the Government of Iraq is required to provide to the Secretary-General and appropriate international organizations monthly statements of its gold and foreign currency reserves. To date, no such statements have been provided to the Secretary-General or to the IMF.

"(i) *Undertaking not to commit or support acts of international terrorism*

"26. By paragraph 32 of resolution 687 (1991), Iraq is required not to commit or support acts of international terrorism or allow any organization directed towards commission of such acts to operate within its territory and to condemn unequivocally and renounce all acts, methods and practices of terrorism.

"27. The Council notes Iraq's statements contained in letters dated 11 June 1991 (S/22687 and S/22689) and 23 January 1992 (S/23472) that it is a party to international conventions against terrorism and that it has never pursued a policy favourable to international terrorism as defined by international law.

"(j) *Security Council action with respect to the Iraqi civilian population*

"28. Resolutions 706 (1991) and 712 (1991) provide a means for Iraq to meet its obligations to supply its civilian population with needed humanitarian assistance, particularly food and medicine. Resolution 778 (1992) mandates that certain frozen Iraqi assets be transferred to a United Nations escrow account and urges States to contribute funds from other sources to the escrow account. A portion of these funds will be used for humanitarian assistance.

"III. Security Council resolution 688 (1991)

"29. I should now like to refer to the demands by the Security Council with respect to the Iraqi civilian population. In paragraph 2 of resolution 688 (1991), the Security Council demands that Iraq, as a contribution to removing the threat to international peace and security in the region, end the repression of its civilian population. In paragraphs 3 and 7, the Security Council insists that it allow immediate access by international humanitarian organizations to all those in need of assistance in all parts of Iraq, and demands its cooperation with the Secretary-General to these ends.

"30. The Security Council remains deeply concerned at the grave human rights abuses that, despite the provisions of resolution 688 (1991), the Government of Iraq continues to perpetrate against its population, in particular in the northern region of Iraq, in southern Shi'a Centres and in the southern marshes (Commission on Human Rights resolution 1992/71 of 5 March 1992). The Security Council notes that this situation is confirmed by the reports of the Special Rapporteur of the Commission on Human Rights (E/CN.4/1992/31, also circulated as document S/23685 and Add.1, and part I of the interim report circulated as document S/24386). The members of the Council recall their public meeting with Mr. Max van der Stoel on 11 August 1992.

"31. The members of the Security Council take note of the renewal on 22 October 1992 of the Memorandum of Understanding providing the framework for urgent humanitarian assistance throughout the country between the United Nations and the Government of Iraq.

"IV. Concluding observation

"32. In view of the observations on the record of Iraq's performance, and without prejudice to further action by the Security Council on the question of the implementation of its relevant resolutions by Iraq, the Security Council has considered itself justified in concluding that Iraq has up to now only selectively and then partially complied with the obligations placed upon it by the Council. It is the Council's hope that this meeting will prove a valuable opportunity to impress once again upon Iraq the imperative need for full compliance and to obtain from Iraq undertakings which would constitute an advance in the consideration of this issue as required in the interest of world peace and security, as well as that of the Iraqi people."

Document 138

Statement by the President of the Security Council concerning Iraq's compliance with the relevant Council resolutions

S/24839, 24 November 1992

In concluding the present stage of the consideration of the item on the agenda, I have been authorized, following consultations among members of the Security Council, to make the following statement on behalf of the Council:

The views of the Security Council having been expressed through its President and by the statements of its members on the extent of compliance by the Government of Iraq with its obligations under the relevant Security Council resolutions, the Council has listened with close attention to the statements by the Deputy Prime Minister of Iraq. The Council regrets the lack of any indication in the statements by the Deputy Prime Minister of Iraq of how the Government of Iraq intends to comply with the resolutions of the Council. It also regrets the baseless threats, allegations and attacks launched by the Deputy Prime Minister of Iraq against the Council, the Special Commission, the International Atomic Energy Agency (IAEA), the Iraq-Kuwait Boundary Demarcation Commission and the Committee established by resolution 661 (1990). The Council rejects *in toto* these threats, allegations and attacks.

Having heard all the interventions in the debate, the Council reiterates its full support for the statement made by the President of the Council on its behalf at the opening of the 3139th meeting (S/24836).

In the view of the Security Council, while there have been some positive steps, the Government of Iraq has not yet complied fully and unconditionally with its obligations, must do so and must immediately take the appropriate actions in this regard.

Document 139

Statement by the President of the Security Council concerning the sanctions regime

S/24843, 24 November 1992

The members of the Security Council held informal consultations on 24 November 1992 pursuant to paragraphs 21 and 28 of resolution 687 (1991) and paragraph 6 of resolution 700 (1991).

After hearing all the opinions expressed in the course of the consultations, the President of the Council concluded that there was no agreement that the necessary conditions existed for a modification of the regimes established in paragraph 20 of resolution 687 (1991), as referred to in paragraph 21 of that resolution; in paragraphs 22, 23, 24 and 25 of resolution 687 (1991), as referred to in paragraph 28 of resolution 687 (1991); and in paragraph 6 of resolution 700 (1991).

Document 140

Letter dated 17 December 1992 from the Secretary-General to the First Deputy Prime Minister and Minster for Foreign Affairs of Kuwait concerning demarcation of the Iraq-Kuwait boundary

Not issued as a United Nations document

I wish to thank you for your letter of 2 December 1992, which was transmitted to me by a letter of the same date from Ambassador Abulhasan. I wish, in this connection, to express my appreciation for your kind words on the role played by the United Nations in contributing to the re-establishment of conditions of security and stability along the border between Iraq and Kuwait.

I am, of course, aware of and concerned by the situation consequential upon the recently completed demarcation of the land portion of the Iraq-Kuwait boundary which you mention in your letter, namely, the presence of Iraqi police posts in Kuwaiti territory or within 1,000 metres of the Iraqi side of the boundary within the demilitarized zone; the presence of a number of Iraqi farmers on the Kuwaiti side of the boundary; and the fact that the Ratqah oil well-heads and other installations are on the Kuwaiti side of the newly demarcated boundary. In addition, the Chief Military Observer of UNIKOM has advised me that two Kuwaiti police posts are within the 1,000 metres area in the demilitarized zone; and that a part of the Iraqi village of Umm Qasr, including a school, is now located on the Kuwaiti side of the boundary.

The location of both the Iraqi and Kuwaiti police posts within the demilitarized zone is a matter that falls within the mandate of UNIKOM, and I have therefore instructed the Chief Military Observer to contact the respective competent authorities with a view to a final resolution of this problem.

The other questions mentioned above deserve, I believe, the most careful consideration. I am sure that you will agree with me that they may have substantial political and security implications. There is little doubt that in the event the Kuwaiti authorities sought to expel the Iraqi farmers and the Iraqi residents of the village of Umm Qasr from Kuwaiti territory, such action would generate tension in the area, for which UNIKOM has certain responsibilities pursuant to Security Council resolution 687 (1991).

It seems to me that it would be in the interest of Kuwait and of all other parties involved if Kuwait would permit the Iraqi farmers and residents of Umm Qasr to remain, at least for the time being, on their lands and in their dwellings after the territorial jurisdiction on the areas in question has passed from Iraq to Kuwait. There is no rule of international law which makes it axiomatic that populations have to be driven out of the territory where they are settled if the territorial jurisdiction changes. Moreover, I am convinced that this would be the only effective way to avert the concrete danger that an escalation of the tension along the border might jeopardize the efforts of the United Nations to achieve stability and security in the area.

I understand that Kuwaiti law allows only Kuwaiti nationals to own land; however, I believe that in such exceptional circumstances the Kuwaiti Government might find alternative legal solutions to avoid the expulsion of the farmers. In this connection, I welcome the statement contained in your letter that Kuwait is ready to arrive at a fair and appropriate settlement. However, I wish to reiterate that it would be preferable if your Government allowed the Iraqi farmers to remain on their lands, as indicated in the preceding paragraph. If your Government deems it useful in the consideration of a possible settlement, the United Nations could seek to determine the numbers of Iraqi farmers and residents of Umm Qasr who are affected by the demarcation.

I consider it my duty in this connection to point out that the responsibility of the Security Council is directly involved since the problems highlighted above are an outgrowth of the implementation of Security Council resolution 687 (1991). It would surely be preferable for all concerned to have this matter handled in such a way that no new crisis arises that might jeopardize peace and security in the area and would have to be brought to the attention of the Security Council.

Accept, Excellency, the assurances of my highest consideration.

(Signed) Boutros BOUTROS-GHALI

Document 141

Fourth report of the Executive Chairman of UNSCOM

S/24984, 17 December 1992

Note by the Secretary-General

The Secretary-General has the honour to transmit to the Security Council, pursuant to paragraph 3 of Security Council resolution 699 (1991), the attached fourth progress report on the implementation of the provisions of section C of resolution 687 (1991) relating to Iraq's weapons of mass destruction.

Annex
Fourth report of the Executive Chairman of the Special Commission established by the Secretary-General pursuant to paragraph 9 (b) (i) of Security Council resolution 687 (1991), on the activities of the Special Commission

Introduction

1. The present report is the fourth on the activities of the Special Commission established by the Secretary-General pursuant to paragraph 9 (b) (i) of Security Council resolution 687 (1991), submitted to the Security Council by the Executive Chairman of the Commission. It is the third such report provided in accordance with paragraph 3 of Security Council resolution 699 (1991). It covers the period from 10 June to 14 December 1992, and is further to the reports contained in documents S/23165, S/23268 and S/24108 and Corr.1.

I. *Organizational and administrative issues*

2. Since the last report, there have been two changes in the composition of the Special Commission. Mr. Michael Newlin resigned as Deputy Executive Chairman on 31 October 1992, for family reasons. Mr. Peter von Butler resigned as the German representative on the Commission, following a new professional assignment. Dr. Pierce S. Corden and Dr. Helmut Frick have been appointed respectively as their replacements. Mr. Newlin's experience and exceptional diplomatic skills were indispensable during a difficult phase of the Commission's work and contributed significantly to progress registered. Mr. von Butler's expert advice and substantial contributions will be missed. The Executive Chairman looks forward to benefiting from the talents and experience that Dr. Corden and Dr. Frick will bring to the Commission.

3. The organizational structure remains that described in the third report. Currently there are 31 staff in the Office of the Executive Chairman; 25 in the Bahrain Field Office; and 74 in the Baghdad Field Office, including the members of the chemical weapons destruction group and helicopter crews.

4. There is still no agreement on the sale of Iraqi oil to finance United Nations operations resulting from the cease-fire resolution. The financing of the Special Commission's work thus remains a matter of concern. Current expenses have been met from contributions from Member States and advances by the United Nations so that operations can be continued. On 2 October 1992, the Security Council adopted resolution 778 (1992) which enables the use of frozen Iraqi assets to pay for the expenditures foreseen in resolutions 687 (1991) and 706 (1991), including the costs of the Commission's operations, and provides for these assets to be paid into the escrow account established pursuant to resolution 706 (1991). It remains to be seen whether this will provide a solution to the financing problems of the activities undertaken pursuant to section C of Security Council resolution 687 (1991). On 10 December 1992, the first contribution to the escrow account, specifically earmarked for the Com-

mission, was received from Saudi Arabia in the amount of $30 million. Given the future commitments for operations under section C of resolution 687 (1991) which the Commission will be required to fund during the course of 1993, further cash contributions by Governments are foreseen to be required.

5. Governments have continued to support the operation of the Special Commission through the contribution of personnel, services and equipment. Resolution 687 (1991) foresaw government support in the form of both voluntary contributions and advances, pending a long-term solution to the financing issue. Supporting Governments are now being asked, in accordance with paragraph 5 (b) of resolution 778 (1992), to inform the Commission of the cost of those contributions that they consider advances. A statement of the Commission's operating costs, together with further information on organizational and administrative issues, can be found in appendix I to the present report.

II. *Status, privileges and immunities*

6. The status, privileges and immunities of the Special Commission, the International Atomic Energy Agency (IAEA) and the United Nations specialized agencies involved in the implementation of Security Council resolution 687 (1991) continue to be regulated by the relevant agreements and Council resolutions and decisions listed in the previous reports to the Council.

7. The Special Commission and IAEA on the one hand, and the Government of Bahrain on the other, have agreed to extend for a further six months, until 31 March 1993, the exchange of letters relating to the facilities, privileges and immunities of the Special Commission and IAEA in Bahrain.

8. In Iraq, there have been continuing problems in the implementation of the Special Commission's status, privileges and immunities. These have related principally to the right of the Commission to operate aircraft anywhere within Iraq, the most serious instance relating to the refusal of the Iraqi authorities to accept that an appropriately notified aerial surveillance flight should take place (see para. 11 (f) below). That incident was notified to the Security Council on 10 December 1992. A disturbing new development has been a sharp deterioration of the security of Commission personnel and property in Iraq. This was first evident during the stand-off that developed over the issue of access to the Ministry of Agriculture (see para. 11 (d) below). The recent inspection teams in Iraq have also experienced security problems. Full details are found in appendix II to the present report.

III. *Developments*

A. *Political developments: the attitude of Iraq*

9. The Special Commission and IAEA have continued to conduct vigorous inspections of sites declared by Iraq or designated by the Commission. Iraq has, in general, continued its cooperation at the field level, with the notable exception of the issue of access to the Ministry of Agriculture. At the time of writing, furthermore, Iraq appears to have ceased to follow the more cooperative approach which it had shown during UNSCOM 45 to the provision of information to an inspection team during seminars on specific outstanding issues conducted in Baghdad with Iraqi officials. Also, as noted in the previous paragraph, Iraq has created a further problem by blocking an aerial surveillance mission by a Commission helicopter over a designated site situated on the outskirts of Baghdad, thus clearly violating Iraq's obligations and the Commission's rights. And, while Iraq has handed over what it terms its full, final and comprehensive reports on its weapons programmes and its declarations in relation to future compliance monitoring, those documents do not provide the information required by the Security Council and needed by the Commission for it to carry out its mandate effectively.

10. On 23 and 24 November 1992, at the request of Iraq, the Security Council held a meeting to discuss the implementation of its resolutions concerning the situation in Iraq. The Iraqi Deputy Prime Minister, Mr. Tariq Aziz, addressed the Council as he had in March 1992, and repeated Iraqi complaints against the Council, the Special Commission and IAEA. He also presented what Iraq referred to as a "factual report", which is a selective résumé of events, subsequently circulated in the annex to document S/24829. It ignores mention of the areas in which Iraq is failing to meet its obligations.

11. The main problems are as follows:

(a) Iraq's position on the plans for ongoing monitoring and verification, approved under Security Council resolution 715 (1991), remains as stated in the letter of 19 November 1991 to the President of the Council from the Foreign Minister of Iraq. This was elaborated upon in the statement of the Iraqi Deputy Prime Minister before the Council on 12 March 1992. Essentially, Iraq's position is that the plans approved by the Council are unlawful and a solution that addresses the substance of the plans but which is acceptable to Iraq should be negotiated between Iraq, the Council, the Special Commission and IAEA. In a letter dated 26 May 1992 (subsequently circulated as document S/24002) from the then Iraqi Minister of State for Foreign Affairs to the Executive Chairman of the Special Commission, Iraq stated that it:

"demands that agreement be reached between it, UNSCOM and IAEA, under the auspices of the Security Council, on practical guarantees to ensure that the measures and methods of ongoing monitoring will not be of such a nature as to infringe upon Iraq's sovereignty, threaten its internal security, lead to interference in its internal affairs or deny it the prospects of scientific, technological and industrial progress both in the civilian fields and in military fields not prohibited under resolution 687 (1991).

"Iraq's basic position on all these issues is also linked to the matter of the resolutions imposing the embargo and sanctions on Iraq, which have remained unchanged by the Security Council despite all the obligations fulfilled by Iraq in accordance with the Council's resolutions.

"We have not ... received from the Special Commission anything which would indicate an understanding of Iraq's just demands ...".

This position was again confirmed in a letter dated 28 October 1992 from the Iraqi Foreign Minister to the Secretary-General (S/24726, annex), which stated that:

"It is ... essential for the Council to conduct a radical review, on the basis of justice and fairness, of the terms and provisions of these two resolutions."

and yet again in the statements to the Council of Mr. Aziz on 23 November (S/PV.3139, resumption 1) and 24 November 1992 (S/PV.3139, resumption 2), in which he said:

"[T]here is a need for all those measures and the provisions of the no longer necessary Security Council's resolutions to be drastically reviewed." (ibid., resumption 1, p. 98)

This position is maintained despite assurances by the Commission that, if Iraq cooperated, its legitimate concerns would be met and the Commission's activities would be carried out in a manner which is not unduly intrusive;

(b) Iraq's full, final and complete disclosures of its proscribed weapons programmes, due under Council resolution 707 (1991), and its initial declarations, due under the plans for ongoing monitoring and verification, contain major shortcomings which will need to be rectified if they are to form the basis for a definite material balance of Iraq's past weapons of mass destruction programmes and for effective monitoring and verification of compliance. The information provided is frequently tailored to what the Iraqi authorities consider the Commission to know already, rather than constituting a frank and open disclosure of all the true facts.

Despite this, the Commission has accepted these declarations as a basis for dialogue with the Iraqi authorities that it is hoped would establish full, final and complete disclosures. However, on 8 December 1992, General Amer, the principal interlocutor on non-nuclear issues, informed the Chief Inspector of UNSCOM 47 that the Commission would "get nothing more, nothing" in the way of information on Iraq's weapons of mass destruction programmes. An account of that interview was communicated to the Security Council by the Deputy Executive Chairman of the Special Commission. That communication was subsequently circulated in document S/24985. A response by Iraq was issued in document S/24964;

(c) Iraq has failed to substantiate information provided to the Special Commission on its prohibited programmes. The Commission has repeatedly urged Iraq to provide access to authentic documents that would substantiate the Iraqi data. In the absence of a positive response from the Iraqi Government, the Commission has had to conduct intrusive inspections, including document searches.

Iraq has claimed that it destroyed all documents related to prohibited activities after the adoption of resolution 687 (1991) and that no records have been kept of the documents destroyed. The Commission has difficulties in accepting this claim. It has welcomed those exceptional occasions where Iraq has produced documents to support data it was providing. This happened, for example, during UNSCOM 45. It is necessary for Iraq to follow this precedent in all areas of proscribed weapons, materials and activities, thus meeting a long-standing requirement for credible and verifiable data on all its prohibited programmes.

Iraq has also informed the Special Commission that the Government has issued an order to protect certain types of documents from inspection by the Commission, including their removal from the sites under inspection and other concealment measures. Inspection teams have visited a number of sites which have clearly been "sanitized". Although Iraq claims that this has involved only documents unrelated to resolution 687 (1991), the Commission has had no opportunity to confirm this.

Within the context of the declarations it has submitted, Iraq has formally informed the Executive Chairman, in the aforementioned 26 May 1992 letter (S/24002, annex), that "Iraq has declined to divulge information indicating the names of foreign companies from which it has purchased ... equipment and materials ... on moral grounds", adding that it would not abandon this position. The letter also stated that "disclosure of the names of companies and individuals will expose ... them to the dangers of liquidation and revenge attacks at the hands of hostile intelligence services ... as has happened in cases such as that of Gerald Bull." Such a position is clearly unacceptable. Although the Commission has some evidence of procurement through elaborate third-party arrangements, it is far from complete. Accurate and full information on Iraq's foreign procurement networks and suppliers is essential if the Commission and IAEA are to be able to establish a complete, coherent and credible picture of Iraq's programmes for weapons of mass destruction as they existed in January 1991 and to decide in a realistic manner whether all proscribed weapons and capabilities have been accounted for. Such information is also necessary to devise the workable and realistic mechanism for import control called for in paragraph 7 of resolution 715 (1991). This is yet another example of where failure to cooperate could lead to much more intrusive and wide-ranging procedures than would otherwise be the case;

(d) A major political problem developed on 5 July 1992 when Iraq refused an inspection team access to the Ministry of Agriculture. The Special Commission had reliable information from two sources that the building contained archives related to proscribed activities. Those archives were clearly of relevance to the Commission's work, and their retention by Iraq was also clearly prohibited. Iraq, in any event, had no justifiable basis on which to refuse access.

Iraq, however, claimed that the Commission had no right to enter the building as it had nothing of relevance to weapons systems proscribed under resolution 687 (1991) and that to allow access would be to undermine Iraq's sovereignty and national security. The Executive Chairman sent the Director of the Bahrain Field Office to Baghdad to try to resolve the situation quietly through the agreement of mutually acceptable modalities of an inspection. Iraq failed to respond to this and so the Chairman visited Baghdad from 17 to 19 July. At the end of the visit, the Deputy Prime Minister offered an inspection by persons from the neutral members of the Council, independently of the Commission. That idea, on the advice of the Chairman, was rejected by the Security Council.

After a delay of over three weeks, and following further discussions in New York between the Executive Chairman and the Permanent Representative of Iraq to the United Nations on modalities, access to the Ministry was obtained.

At the request of the Iraqi authorities, the Executive Chairman visited Iraq during the inspection and met Iraqi officials to discuss future relations. During those talks, Mr. Tariq Aziz promised a new chapter of cooperation and openness in relations between the Commission and Iraq.

Since that incident, the Iraqi Minister of Information has on several occasions sought to establish that Iraqi Ministry buildings are off limits to the Commission. Clearly, that is not the case: the Commission has already inspected two Ministry buildings and the mandate, as laid down in resolution 687 (1991), does not provide for any sanctuaries. Nor may Iraq, or the Commission for that matter, change the terms of the mandate. Only the Security Council has the power to do so. While the Commission refuses to lend any credibility to the statements of the Iraqi Information Minister in this regard, and while it will conduct inspections at such facilities as and when there is an operational requirement to do so, such statements are not helpful and do nothing to promote confidence within the Commission that Iraq is indeed willing to cooperate fully with the Commission in the timely fulfilment of its mandate. In a subsequent inspection, Iraq permitted access to a site for which it had originally claimed sanctuary status. This, it is hoped, should finally dispose of the issue;

(e) A further problem was encountered at the outset of the forty-seventh inspection (UNSCOM 47). An IAEA team, accompanied by Commission inspectors, sought to conduct a document search at a site designated by the Commission. Upon the arrival of the team, persons left the buildings carrying documents, despite the protests of the Chief Inspector. While the Iraqi counterparts promised to return the documents, and indeed did produce some, the inspectors were unable to verify that these were the documents taken from the building. This represents a further clear violation of the Commission's and IAEA's rights of unimpeded and immediate access to documents and to remove or copy them. Protests have been lodged with the Iraqi Foreign Minister by the Commission and with the Permanent Representative of Iraq at Vienna by IAEA. So far the Commission has received no response;

(f) Parallel with this problem is the ongoing problem referred to in paragraph 9 above, namely that Iraq is blocking the conduct of an aerial inspection by helicopter of a site duly designated by the Commission. General Amer has told the Commission's Field Office in Baghdad that its helicopters will never be allowed to overfly Baghdad on surveillance missions "by one metre". Security Council resolution 707 (1991) explicitly sanctions the use by the Commission of fixed- or rotary-wing aerial surveillance over all Iraqi territory. No exceptions are made for Baghdad. The position taken by General Amer not to permit the surveillance flight therefore constitutes a violation of the Commission's rights and Iraq's obligations. A formal complaint has been lodged with the Foreign Minister of Iraq and the Commission expects Iraq to comply forthwith with its obligations to cooperate with the Commission in the fulfilment of its mandate. A reply is still awaited;

(g) Another worrying political development has been the increase in harassment of Commission personnel and damage to Commission property in Iraq. This occurred at the time of the Ministry of Agriculture incident and was evidently part of a centrally organized government campaign to intimidate and humiliate United Nations personnel in general, and Commission personnel in particular. However, while the situation improved for a brief period, the problem has not disappeared. The situation would seem to deteriorate again each time there is a rise in tension between the Commission and Iraq. Statements by the President of Iraq recently referred to inspection teams as "stray dogs" and "wolves tearing at the flesh of the Iraqi nation". This could only serve to inflame the situation and was reported to the Security Council, whereupon the President of the Council issued a statement to the press on 15 October underlining the Council's particular concern for the safety of inspectors. Similar remarks were, however, echoed by the Deputy Prime Minister of Iraq on 22 October 1992. The Foreign Minister of Iraq picked up the same theme in his letter of 28 October 1992 to the Secretary-General (S/24726, annex), in which he alleged that "most of the inspection teams ... behaved in a hostile manner and proceeded to engage in effrontery, provocation and the contrivance of problems". In his statement to the Council on 24 November 1992 (S/PV.3139, resumption 2), the Deputy Prime Minister said some of the teams went to Baghdad "to create problems" and behaved "in a provocative manner". The inspections are, without exception, carried out in strict adherence to the relevant Security Council resolutions and with due regard to Iraq's legitimate concerns. The Commission rejects these allegations, which give rise to an unacceptable situation. The Iraqi press currently refers to the inspectors as "rabid dogs". Iraq has an unambiguous obligation to ensure the safety and security of Commission personnel and property. It has been reminded of this obligation frequently by both the Commission and the Council;

(h) Other problems continue with both the operation of Commission aircraft, in the form of landing rights and flight paths, and with the provision by Iraq of on-site accommodation for inspection teams. Iraq still refuses to allow the use of Rasheed Airbase for the C-160 flights into Iraq. It also sought, upon the imposition by the coalition of the no-fly zone south of the 32nd parallel, to deny Commission aircraft the right to cross that parallel over Iraqi airspace. The Commission made it clear that such a position would not be tolerated and Iraq withdrew its objections. Iraq refused to allow the 14th ballistic missiles team (UNSCOM 45) to set up a base camp at the Rasheed Airbase. Difficulties remain with the unloading of aircraft at Habbaniyah Airbase.

In addition, Iraq continues to protest the use by the Commission of its own high-altitude surveillance aircraft and helicopters. In the letter of 28 October 1992 of the Iraqi Foreign Minister to the Secretary-General referred to above, Mr. Al-Sahaf said that "the use of such aircraft ... was not in fact designed to meet the declared objectives of inspection and technical observation ... The time has come for the Security Council to review these unjust decisions and measures ... and to ensure that each measure has a specific time-frame ... Iraq expects a new style of treatment from the Security Council". During his addresses to the Council on 23 and 24 November 1992, the Iraqi Deputy Prime Minister reiterated Iraq's "call for a halt to the activities of United States U-2 spy planes, which ... use the cover of the United Nations" and said that "the use of foreign helicopters by the inspection teams is no longer justified." This continues a consistent pattern of rejection by Iraq of the Commission's rights and privileges in this regard.

These obstacles taken together impede the Commission's operations and hinder the fulfilment of its mandate.

Thus the situation as regards the level of Iraq's implementation remains essentially unchanged from the time of the last report to the Security Council: the realization of the intention to proceed from inspection and survey through destruction to ongoing monitoring and verification has been in large part delayed further by the actions of the Iraqi Government. It is apparently unwilling to acknowledge that those actions constitute the main impediment to the fulfilment of the Commission's mandate and to the Commission's so reporting to the Council. It remains the case, as noted in the second report of the Commission on the implementation of the plans for ongoing monitoring and verification (S/24661), that while preparations for the implementation of the plans are being made, the conditions for their full-scale implementation have not yet been met.

B. *Operational developments*

12. In the chemical weapons area, the shift in emphasis and resources towards destruction activities has continued. While inspections of declared and undeclared sites proceed, teams have overseen the destruction of most of the chemical bomb-making equipment identified by the Commission; the Chemical Destruction Group has been established in Baghdad; and at the Muthanna State Establishment, the destruction *in situ* of 122 mm rockets too unsafe to drain has continued, the quantities and locations of munitions and agents awaiting destruction or removal have been surveyed and the two chemical destruction facilities at Muthanna have been completed.

The full-scale destruction of nerve agent in the hydrolysis plant has started. Final runs for the destruction of the mustard agent in the incinerator have been successfully concluded and full-scale destruction will commence at the beginning of 1993. A policy for the destruction of the precursor chemicals, which have deteriorated and now pose a safety hazard, will be presented to Iraq shortly.

13. While doubts continue to be expressed about the fullness of Iraq's declarations concerning its biological weapons programme, there has been little development in this area. Inspections have continued through joint chemical and biological teams.

14. All ballistic missiles and items related to their production and development, so far identified as requiring destruction (known as list A), have been destroyed. Certain items (known as list B) have been sealed or tagged, pending either a decision to destroy them or the establishment of full-scale ongoing monitoring and verification activities so that they may be monitored under that regime to ensure that they are only used for permitted purposes. Until the appropriate decisions are taken by the Special Commission, the items concerned cannot be used by Iraq or moved from their locations.

15. During the period under review, considerable progress has been made in obtaining information from Iraq about its operational use of missiles since 1980. Nevertheless, crucial data are still missing, in particular sources of foreign procurement. Until this is obtained, a material balance for missile systems cannot be established.

16. Aerial surveillance activities have intensified. The regular flights of the high-altitude surveillance aircraft (now running at about three per week) have been supplemented with aerial inspections conducted from the Special Commission's helicopters based at Rasheed Airbase. These helicopter inspections commenced on 21 June 1992 and have been used to supplement the high-altitude photography in the planning of inspections, monitoring of sites, preparation of inspection teams and identification of potential inspection targets. In addition, they give the Commission a rapid response capability to transport an inspection team to a site in response to time-sensitive data. A full account of the helicopter surveillance programme is found in appendix V to the present report.

C. Iraq's declarations

17. As noted in paragraph 11 (b) above, Iraq delivered what it terms its "full, final and comprehensive reports" on its weapons programmes and its declarations under the plans for "future compliance monitoring".

18. Both sets of declarations are flawed and incomplete. No information is given on suppliers. Iraq denies that it ever used chemical weapons, despite internation-

ally verified evidence to the contrary. Declarations about imports and production are not backed with adequate supporting documentary evidence and are, in any case, incomplete. There is insufficient and probably misleading information about the evolution of the various programmes and about the links between them. In sum, "full, final and comprehensive report" is a misnomer and these declarations cannot be taken as an adequate base upon which to determine a material balance. However, the Special Commission has accepted that they provide the possibility for dialogue with the Iraqi authorities to arrive at such a base. The Commission looks to the Iraqi authorities to be forthcoming in filling in the gaps and resolving the inconsistencies in these reports.

19. A similar situation exists with the initial declarations due under the plans for ongoing monitoring and verification. While Iraq has deposited substantial reports, the reports contain little new information, and little about facilities with dual capability which would have to be covered by the ongoing monitoring and verification regime. Again, the Special Commission has accepted these reports as a starting point for further discussion. But of themselves, the reports are inadequate for the purposes of initiating full-scale ongoing monitoring and verification.

IV. Issues and priorities for the future

20. The Special Commission continues to carry out its mandate to the best of its ability. That mandate derives essentially from section C of resolution 687 (1991) as elaborated upon in resolutions 707 (1991) and 715 (1991) and the plans approved thereunder. Further responsibilities of the Commission are reflected in certain paragraphs of resolution 687 (1991) other than those of section C. An important example is to be found in paragraph 22 in section F of the resolution which provides that the embargo against imports of commodities and products originating in Iraq and the prohibitions against financial transactions related thereto will have no further force or effect when certain conditions are met, in particular when the Council is in agreement that Iraq has completed all actions contemplated in section C of resolution 687 (1991). Obviously, assessments by the Commission have a primary role to play in assisting the Council in this respect.

21. Further inspection activities are planned in each of the weapons categories. Destruction activities now focus on chemical weapons at Muthanna. Preparations for the implementation of the plans for ongoing monitoring and verification are under way and initial discussions between the Commission, IAEA and certain Governments have taken place on the potential form of an import control regime to apply after the lifting of

sanctions. The intention is to discuss the modalities of the regime in greater depth in the near future with IAEA and the Sanctions Committee, as required by paragraph 7 of resolution 715 (1991).

22. From the above sections of the present report, it can be seen that, despite progress in many areas, no major breakthrough has been achieved which could make it possible to change the conclusion of the previous report to the Security Council. The most important developments have taken place in the areas of destruction of proscribed items and information on missile programmes and use. Nevertheless, much remains to be done. The main areas which require action before the Special Commission will be in a position to report to the Security Council that Iraq is in substantial compliance with its obligations are as follows:

(a) Acceptance and implementation by Iraq of all the Commission's privileges and immunities, including ensuring the safety and security of UNSCOM personnel and property, the operation of and landing rights for UNSCOM aircraft and non-obstruction of the Commission's logistics and aerial surveillance flights;

(b) Unconditional acknowledgement by Iraq of its obligations under Security Council resolutions 707 (1991) and 715 (1991);

(c) Provision by Iraq of the documentation necessary to substantiate the data contained in its declarations and to provide the Commission with a full picture of its foreign procurement networks and suppliers;

(d) Supplementation and revision of Iraq's declarations to the point where, in the view of the Commission, they constitute the full, final and complete disclosures required under resolution 707 (1991) and the initial declarations required under the plans for ongoing monitoring and verification adopted under resolution 715 (1991);

(e) The initiation and smooth functioning of the plans for ongoing monitoring and verification to ensure that Iraq does not reacquire the weapons proscribed to it.

23. The Executive Chairman, during a meeting with the Deputy Prime Minister of Iraq in New York on 25 November 1992, reminded the Iraqi authorities of the actions they must undertake, as indicated in the previous paragraph, if the Commission is to be in a position, after these actions have been carried out, to report to the Council that Iraq has, in the view of the Commission, met the conditions laid down in paragraph 22 of Security Council resolution 687 (1991). Should there be any indication that Iraq is prepared to meet these conditions, the Executive Chairman would consider whether it would be useful for him to visit Baghdad in the early part of 1993. So far no such indications have been forthcoming and, as noted above, at the present time there is little cause for optimism.

Appendix I
Organizational and administrative issues

1. The Special Commission has currently a total of 131 positions distributed amongst its three Offices. The IAEA Action Team comprises seven persons. Forty-eight positions are supported by UNSCOM, including 6 of the IAEA positions. The balance of the staff are on loan from their Governments for assignments ranging from 3 to 12 months. Personnel have been provided for the Commission's activities from Argentina, Australia, Austria, Belgium, Canada, Czechoslovakia, Finland, France, Germany, Greece, Hungary, India, Indonesia, Italy, Japan, the Netherlands, Norway, New Zealand, the Republic of Korea, Romania, the Russian Federation, Sweden, Switzerland, Thailand, the United Kingdom of Great Britain and Northern Ireland and the United States of America.

2. The distribution of the staff of the Commission in each Office and of the IAEA Action Team is as follows:

(a) *Headquarters of the Commission in New York.* The headquarters of the Commission in New York has 31 staff assigned to it: 17 positions (6 in the Professional and 11 in the support staff category) are currently charged to the operating budget of UNSCOM; and 14 positions are filled by staff assigned to the Commission by various Member States. The breakdown of functions is as follows:

Unit	Position
Office of the Chairman	1 Executive Chairman
	1 Deputy Chairman
	1 Senior Counsellor (Legal)
	1 Special Adviser and Spokesman
	2 support staff
Administrative Office	2 Professionals
	6 support staff
Division of Operations	7 Advisers in the chemical, biological, ballistic and nuclear fields
	1 support staff
Information Assessment Unit	5 Advisers in the chemical, biological, ballistic and nuclear fields
	2 Advisers in aerial and photographic support
	2 support staff

(b) *Office of the Commission in Bahrain.* The Bahrain Field Office has 25 staff assigned to it on a regular basis to provide financial, administrative, logistic and training support to the inspection activities of the Special Commission and IAEA pursuant to the relevant Security

Council resolutions. Ten positions (three Professionals and seven local support staff) are charged to the operating budget of the Commission. Functions are broken down as follows:

Administration and logistic support	3 Professionals 7 local staff
Aerial and photographic support	2 Advisers
Air transport	13 Transall C-160 crew members

(c) *Office of the Commission in Baghdad.* Seventy-four persons are currently assigned on a long-term basis to the Commission's Baghdad Office to provide logistic, communication and medical support to the inspection teams of UNSCOM and IAEA and in support of the chemical destruction programme. This number is expected to increase to around 90 persons as soon as the chemical destruction activities in Muthanna are being carried out on a full-scale basis. Fifteen positions (11 Professionals and 4 local support staff) are under the UNSCOM operating budget. The other 59 staff are provided by their Governments. The breakdown of functions is as follows:

Administration and logistic support	10 Professionals 4 local staff
Aerial and photographic support	2 Advisers
Medical support	5 medical staff
Chemical destruction	23 Advisers (including two medical staff dedicated to the chemical destruction programme)
Air transport	30 helicopter crew members

(d) *International Atomic Energy Agency.* The IAEA Action Team has a total of seven staff. Six positions (five Professionals and one support staff) are charged to the operating budget of the Commission, as follows:

| Operational and technical support | 5 Professionals |
| Administrative support | 1 Professional
1 support staff |

Financial situation of the Special Commission

3. Since the inception of its operations in April 1991, a total of US$26.4 million has been allotted by the United Nations to cover the cost of the operations of the Special Commission and IAEA in support of the relevant Security Council resolutions. Funds were provided through a number of cash contributions and from the operating budget of the United Nations and were appropriated as follows:

Object of expenditure	Millions of United States dollars
Staff costs	3.5
Travel-related costs	17.5
IAEA contract for removal of fresh nuclear fuel	2.0
Services: Communications, translation and maintenance of vehicles; offices in New York and Baghdad*	2.0
Supplies and equipment	1.4
TOTAL	26.4

*The Bahrain Field Office at Manama airfield has been provided by the Government of Bahrain free of charge.

4. Operating requirements for 1993 are expected to reach $55.0 million, which includes the estimated IAEA expenditures for the removal of irradiated nuclear fuel from Iraq and for the permanent disposal thereof.

Appendix II
Security issues

1. As noted in paragraphs 8 and 11 (g) of the present report, security for UNSCOM personnel and property sharply decreased during the stand-off over access to the Ministry of Agriculture. While matters improved somewhat after the resolution of this issue, security has worsened each time there has been a period of tension between the Special Commission and the Iraqi authorities. The following summarizes the types of incidents which have occurred, rather than cataloguing each incident.

Demonstrations

2. During the stand-off at the Ministry of Agriculture, there were daily demonstrations of increasing size and hostility. While the Iraqi officials sought to pass these off as spontaneous outbursts of public sentiment, demonstrators arrived in government buses, sometimes from government offices, and, on occasion, threw government-supplied fruit and vegetables. During this period, the hostility of the demonstrations grew, with flags being burned, items being thrown at inspectors,

inspectors being exposed to screamed abuse and demonstrators being allowed within feet of the inspectors and their vehicles. There was one incident of attempted self-immolation.

3. Demonstrations against the United Nations in general and UNSCOM in particular have continued sporadically since. The demonstrations were sufficiently centrally coordinated for the Ministry of Information to be able to inform the press corps in advance of the timing and place of each one.

4. A different kind of demonstration involved the placement of propaganda materials in the rooms of UNSCOM inspectors. Clearly, only hotel staff or government security personnel would have access to the room numbers of the inspectors.

Harassment

5. Harassment of UNSCOM staff has taken many forms. Obscene, nuisance, intimidating and threatening phone calls (including death, bomb and firebomb threats) have been received. On occasion, these calls have been made to each and every member of an inspection team in alphabetical order. Again, only hotel staff or security personnel would have access to the information for the conduct of such an operation.

6. Another form of harassment concerned wrongful entry into inspectors' rooms. Sometimes the contents of drawers were emptied onto the floor; at other times items, such as cameras or money, were stolen. In public, UNSCOM staff have been jostled, threatened with physical abuse, refused service in restaurants and shops, and have had meals and drinks overturned on them while in restaurants.

7. UNSCOM offices in the Sheraton Hotel have also been entered without permission and property stolen, including a computer.

Physical attacks

8. UNSCOM property, particularly its vehicles, has been subject to repeated damage: cars have been sprayed with paint; aerials have been broken; tyres have been stolen, let down, slashed or had their valves removed; and lights, windows and windscreens have been smashed (both overnight and while people were driving the vehicle).

9. Inspectors have had a variety of items thrown at them: fruit, vegetables, eggs, rocks, bottles, light bulbs, rubbish, ink, paint and diesel fuel. They have been physically attacked with punches, shoes and, at the Ministry of Agriculture, with a skewer in an attempted stabbing of one of the inspectors maintaining watch over the exits. On several occasions, persons in cars or on motorcycles

attempted to run over UNSCOM staff crossing the road between the Palestine and Sheraton hotels.

Conclusion

10. Iraq is a country with a formidable security organization. During the Ministry of Agriculture stand-off, Iraqi officials and news agencies made statements that could only be interpreted as inflammatory. Little was done by Iraqi security personnel either to prevent such incidents or to investigate them after the event and to apprehend the perpetrators. Requests for improved security were sometimes heeded, but were generally met by statements that Iraq had ensured and would ensure at all times the safety of UNSCOM staff. This response was frequently used even when an incident had just occurred.

11. Given all the above, it is difficult not to believe that the decrease in security is the result of a centrally coordinated government campaign to intimidate and humiliate UNSCOM staff. While some incidents may be spontaneous, the atmosphere in which such acts might be considered by Iraqi citizens has been fostered by Iraqi officials, presumably with the backing of the Government, and those officials have done little to rectify the situation.

Appendix III
Inspection activities

Chemical activities

1. UNSCOM 39 conducted inspection activities in Iraq from 26 June to 10 July 1992 at declared and undeclared sites, essentially in search of documentation concerning Iraq's proscribed weapons activities. Nothing of relevance to Security Council resolution 687 (1991) was found at those sites. The team also surveyed and recorded reconstruction activity at the Fallujah sites, where chemical weapon precursors were formerly produced. In addition, it supervised the destruction of the majority of the chemical bomb-making equipment identified by the Special Commission to date. The sites visited included some biological weapons sites and, at short notice, some ballistic missile sites. The inspection ended with the stand-off at the Ministry of Agriculture, where the Iraqi authorities refused the team access to the building.

2. UNSCOM 44 conducted its activities in Iraq from 21 to 29 September 1992. Its aim was to verify the location and quantity of chemical munitions and agents awaiting destruction and hence to assess whether Iraq had implemented in full the Commission's instructions to move all identified agents and munitions to the central destruction facility at the Muthanna State Establishment. With the exception of the mortar rounds at Fallujah and whatever may remain in the damaged and unsafe bunkers

at Muhammadiyat, this was found to be the case. A full survey of the agents and munitions at Muthanna is under way and a comprehensive inventory, which will form the baseline for destruction activities, is being drawn up.

3. UNSCOM 47, comprising two sub-teams, one designated CBW3 and the other IAEA 16, has just returned to Bahrain from Baghdad. While all proscribed weapons categories were covered, the main thrust was chemical and bacteriological weapons. The results of the inspection remain to be assessed fully once the inspection report is received.

Biological activities

4. As noted above, UNSCOM 39 conducted inspection of some declared and undeclared biological weapons sites. No new information of note was discovered. Developments at sites known to have been related to Iraq's biological research continue to be monitored through aerial surveillance by both high-altitude aircraft and helicopters.

5. UNSCOM 47, as noted above, undertook some biological weapons inspection activities. Additionally, there were some seminar-type meetings with the Iraqi side. The aim of these had been to resolve differences and to fill gaps in the knowledge of the Special Commission. Very little additional information was obtained, given the attitude of Iraq referred to in paragraph 11 (b) of the present report.

Ballistic missiles

6. Also as noted above, UNSCOM 39 conducted inspection of some declared and undeclared possible ballistic missile-related sites. Prime amongst these was the Ministry of Agriculture. As stated in the main body of the text of the present report, access was denied to UNSCOM 39. The team eventually was withdrawn, due to other engagements elsewhere. Its place outside the Ministry was taken by another team, UNSCOM 40, on 11 July 1992. The task was to maintain a watch outside the building until such time as access was allowed. In the event, the team was forced to withdraw from the vicinity of the building on 22 July 1992, following an attack on one of the inspectors, which the Iraqi security officials did nothing to prevent. The Chief Inspector rightly decided not to endanger the lives of his inspectors. Following discussions on modalities in New York between the Executive Chairman of the Special Commission and the Permanent Representative of Iraq to the United Nations, access was agreed, and the UNSCOM team conducted a full inspection. No proscribed items were found, although there were indications that such items might have been removed.

7. UNSCOM 42 conducted inspection activities in Iraq from 7 to 18 August 1992. Its main purpose was to investigate Iraq's ability to acquire or produce indigenously proscribed ballistic missiles, especially missile guidance-and-control systems. Inspection techniques included document and computer searches and joint helicopter ground operations. Seminar-type meetings were held in order to resolve questions arising from the inspection activities. Virtually all the senior officials known to have been involved in the ballistic missile programmes attended the seminars.

8. UNSCOM 42 discovered no weapons or components prohibited under resolution 687 (1991). Nor was there evidence that Iraq could produce indigenously complete guidance-and-control systems, including gyroscopes, for ballistic missiles, although there had been considerable effort on the part of Iraq in the research, development and prototype manufacture of such systems which apparently never reached fruition. The team obtained important further information relating to:

(a) The scope and extent of Iraq's programmes to acquire or produce prohibited ballistic missiles and components, including information concerning previously undisclosed projects for computer support and missile fuel production;

(b) The interrelationship between the various projects in the ballistic missiles programme and the involvement of different Iraqi organizations in the programme;

(c) Foreign involvement in certain aspects of the programme.

Amongst the sites visited was the newly established Iraqi research-and-development facility, at which all research and development into non-prohibited ballistic missiles (i.e., those with a range of less than 150 km) will be undertaken in the future. The inspection of this site provided much information that will be of use in designing the ongoing monitoring and verification regime.

9. UNSCOM 45 conducted inspection activities from 16 to 30 October 1992. Its objectives were twofold: to determine whether Iraq retained an inventory of or a capability to produce fuels for ballistic missiles, and to obtain information on the operational use of these missiles. Iraq adopted a more open approach during UNSCOM 45 to the provision of data on the operational use of its ballistic missiles since 1980, and the information provided was useful. The team obtained information on Iraq's past plans to acquire fuel and oxidizer for prohibited missiles. The team did not find any evidence that Iraq had the capability indigenously to produce such fuels.

Appendix IV
Destruction of Iraq's chemical agents and munitions

Background

1. As a result of its chemical inspections pro-gramme, UNSCOM now has considerable information on Iraq's chemical agents and munitions. The agents which Iraq had available were mustard agent, the nerve agents GB and GF (and also about 70 tonnes of "spoilt" GA) and small research quantities of three other nerve agents. The total quantities involved are approximately 250-300 tonnes.

2. The munitions identified include various kinds of aerial bombs, CS-filled mortar bombs, artillery shells and rockets, together with a small number of other munitions such as rocket-propelled grenades; 30 SCUD (Al Hussein) missile chemical warheads were also discov-ered and 45 were declared by Iraq to have been destroyed unilaterally. In total the number of unfilled munitions so far discovered is on the order of 90,000, the agent-filled munitions numbering about 50,000. These are approxi-mate figures and may be subject to some revisions in the future.

3. Of the filled munitions, the mortar bombs were filled with CS, the 155 mm shells are filled with mustard agent (and generally are intact and not leaking) and the 122 mm rockets are filled with nerve agents, either GB or a GB/GF mix. The aerial bombs are filled with either mustard agent or nerve agents. Some of the SCUD chemi-cal warheads are filled with GB, the others being designed to use the binary process. These were filled with a mixture of two alcohols (isopropanol and cyclohexanol) to which the organophosphorus compound DF was to be added immediately before use, a mixture of the nerve agents GB and GF being formed during the flight time of the war-head.

Destruction of chemical weapons agents
and munitions

4. The primary site for all chemical destruction activities is Muthanna State Establishment, the Iraqi main chemical warfare research-and-development, produc-tion, filling and storage facility. Although limited explo-sive demolition/incineration has been carried out on 122 mm rockets at one site (Khamisiyah-UNSCOM 29), the munitions discovered at all other sites have now been safely transported to Muthanna and are stored, in the open, to await destruction.

5. All destruction activities are being carried out by Iraqi personnel under the close and direct supervision of an UNSCOM team (UNSCOM 38, Chemical Destruc-tion Group (CDG)). The formation of the Chemical Destruction Group in Iraq commenced with the arrival

of an advance party of three inspectors on 18 June 1992. The numbers increased in two increments to the current strength of 23 persons, including medical support, from 12 countries.

6. CDG will maintain a continuous presence at Muthanna during all destruction activities.

7. The destruction of unfilled munitions, and emptied munitions after thorough and complete decon-tamination, is done by simple physical means, such as crushing or cutting with an oxy-acetylene torch. These activities are coordinated, supervised and recorded by the UNSCOM team.

8. Filled munitions are either drained (aerial bombs) or destroyed by a combination of simultaneous explosive opening and high-temperature incineration if they are assessed as too dangerous to drill and drain. This is the case with most of the 122 mm rockets.

9. Bulk mustard agent will be destroyed by incin-eration in an incinerator specifically built by Iraq to UNSCOM requirements. The plant was commissioned under UNSCOM supervision in November 1992. Other materials will also be destroyed in the incinerator, such as some precursor chemicals, ballistic missile-related chemicals which have been moved to Muthanna and various other chemicals found at Muthanna.

10. The nerve agents GB and GB/GF mixtures are currently being destroyed by controlled hydrolysis in a plant which was constructed by Iraq to UNSCOM re-quirements and commissioned by UNSCOM personnel from the Destruction Advisory Panel in September 1992. The aqueous wastes from the plant will be allowed partially to evaporate and cement will then be added. This will produce concrete blocks, which will be buried on site. The purpose of this is to prevent the leaching of the waste hydrolysis salts into, and hence the degradation of, the surrounding soils. All these operations will be carried out under the supervision of CDG at Muthanna.

11. The number and quantity of munitions and agent destroyed by the Special Commission as of 14 December 1992 were on the order of:
  – 12,000 empty munitions;
  – 5,000 sarin-filled 122 mm rockets, including
    motors and warheads;
  – 350 R.400 aerial bombs;
  – 44,500 litres of GB/GF;
  – 120 litres of GB;
  – 5,000 litres of D4;
  – 1,100 litres of dichlorethane;
  – 16.5 tons of thiodiglycol;
  – 5.5 tons of mustard agent.

12. A strict health-and-safety regime has been es-tablished to minimize the danger of immediate and long-term effects of exposure to chemical warfare agents, their

precursors and other hazardous or toxic materials. Remote agent detector arrays are established at the hydrolysis plant and at the rocket destruction site and have not, as yet, recorded any downwind hazard.

Future plans

13. At present, the time-limiting factor is the provision of a satisfactory solution to the destruction of the 155 mm mustard-agent-filled artillery shells. However, the nerve agent GB/GF and the 122 mm rocket warheads should be destroyed by the end of January 1993 and destruction of all other chemical agents and munitions completed in 1993.

Appendix V
Aerial inspections

1. Following a discussion within the Office of the Executive Chairman on means to improve the operational effectiveness of UNSCOM, it was decided to inaugurate helicopter aerial surveillance flights. The benefits were foreseen to be: increased and better quality aerial photography to supplement that available from the U-2 which, as of 14 December 1992, has carried out 105 surveillance missions over Iraq, and to help in the planning and preparation of inspections; and improved operational efficiency. The first flight took place on 21 June 1992.

2. This operation is supported by an aerial inspection team of three persons in Baghdad and a fully equipped photographic processing laboratory with a full-time technician, located at the UNSCOM Field Office at Muharraq, Bahrain. All missions are tasked from the Office of the Executive Chairman in New York by the Information Assessment Unit. The Unit has recruited, specifically for this task and the task of interpreting and storing the results, two Professional photographic interpreters. Any problems that arise are referred to the Executive Chairman for decision. A recent case of serious non-compliance is described in paragraph 11 (f) of the present report.

3. As of 14 December 1992, 142 sites had been surveyed by the Aerial Inspection Team. These helicopter surveillance flights do not and cannot replace the high-altitude surveillance operation. The U-2 offers advantages of longer flight time, wider surveillance coverage and maintaining uncertainty of the precise sites which are being photographed. The helicopter offers better oblique photography, higher resolution, 360-degree video coverage, faster response time and hence a greater element of surprise and, thus, deterrence. The results of both operations combine to provide much information that is useful in both the planning and the preparation of inspections and in the monitoring of various sites for suspicious activities. The helicopter photography is particularly of use in briefing inspectors prior to the conduct of a ground inspection.

4. The Aerial Inspection Team has thus proved to be of considerable benefit to the Special Commission. It is anticipated that it will be of equal value to the implementation of the plans for ongoing monitoring and verification.

Appendix VI
Special Commission Inspection Schedule

Nuclear

15 May-21 May 1991	IAEA1/UNSCOM1
22 June-3 July 1991	IAEA2/UNSCOM4
7 July-18 July 1991	IAEA3/UNSCOM5
27 July-10 August 1991	IAEA4/UNSCOM6
14 September-20 September 1991	IAEA5/UNSCOM14
21 September-30 September 1991	IAEA6/UNSCOM16
11 October-22 October 1991	IAEA7/UNSCOM19
11 November-18 November 1991	IAEA8/UNSCOM22
11 January-14 January 1992	IAEA9/UNSCOM25
5 February-13 February 1992	IAEA10/UNSCOM27+30
7 April-15 April 1992	IAEA11/UNSCOM33
26 May-4 June 1992	IAEA12/UNSCOM37
14 July-21 July 1992	IAEA13/UNSCOM41
31 August-7 September 1992	IAEA14/UNSCOM43
8 November-19 November 1992	IAEA15/UNSCOM46
6 December-14 December 1992	IAEA16/UNSCOM47

Chemical

9 June-15 June 1991	CW1/UNSCOM2
15 August-22 August 1991	CW2/UNSCOM9
31 August-8 September 1991	CW3/UNSCOM11
31 August-5 September 1991	CW4/UNSCOM12
6 October-9 November 1991	CW5/UNSCOM17
22 October-2 November 1991	CW6/UNSCOM20
18 November-1 December 1991	CBW1/UNSCOM21
27 January-5 February 1992	CW7/UNSCOM26
15 April-29 April 1992	CW8/UNSCOM35
21 September-29 September 1992	CW9/UNSCOM44
26 June-10 July 1992	CBW2/UNSCOM39
6 December-14 December 1992	CBW3/UNSCOM47
21 February-24 March 1992	CD1/UNSCOM29
5 April-13 April 1992	CD2/UNSCOM32
18 June 1992 ongoing	CDG/UNSCOM38

Biological

2 August-8 August 1991	BW1/UNSCOM7
20 September-3 October 1991	BW2/UNSCOM15

Ballistic missiles

30 June-7 July 1991	BM1/UNSCOM3
18 July-20 July 1991	BM2/UNSCOM10
8 August-15 August 1991	BM3/UNSCOM8
6 September-13 September 1991	BM4/UNSCOM13
1 October-9 October 1991	BM5/UNSCOM18
1 December-9 December 1991	BM6/UNSCOM23
9 December-17 December 1991	BM7/UNSCOM24
21 February-29 February 1992	BM8/UNSCOM28
21 March-29 March 1992	BM9/UNSCOM31
13 April-21 April 1992	BM10/UNSCOM34
14 May-22 May 1992	BM11/UNSCOM36
11 July-29 July 1992	BM12/UNSCOM40A+B
7 August-18 August 1992	BM13/UNSCOM42
16 October-30 October 1992	BM14/UNSCOM45

Special missions

30 June-3 July 1991
11 August-14 August 1991
4 October-6 October 1991
11 November-15 November 1991
27 January-30 January 1992
21 February-24 February 1992
17 July-19 July 1992
28 July-29 July 1992
6 September-12 September 1992
4 November-9 November 1992

Document 142

Third semi-annual report (for the period from 17 June 1992 to 17 December 1992) on the implementation by the IAEA of the plan for the destruction, removal or rendering harmless of items listed in paragraph 12 of Security Council resolution 687 (1991)

S/24988, 17 December 1992

The Secretary-General has the honour to transmit to the Security Council, pursuant to paragraph 3 of Security Council resolution 699 (1991) the attached third semi-annual report on the implementation by the IAEA of the plan for the destruction, removal or rendering harmless of items listed in paragraph 12 of United Nations Security Council resolution 687 (1991).

Annex
Letter dated 14 December 1992 from the Director-General of the International Atomic Energy Agency addressed to the Secretary-General

United Nations Security Council resolution 699 (1991), approved on 17 June 1991, requests—*inter alia*—the Secretary-General to submit to the Security Council progress reports on the implementation of the plan for the destruction, removal or rendering harmless of the items specified in paragraph 12 of resolution 687 (1991). Such reports are to be submitted every six months after the adoption of the resolution and the third report is therefore due on 17 December 1992.

Please find attached an outline of the activities carried out by the Agency during the past six months under the plan for the destruction, removal or rendering harmless, that you might find useful for the preparation of your report.

(*Signed*) Hans BLIX

Enclosure
Third semi-annual report (covering the period 17 June 1992 - 17 December 1992) on the implementation by the IAEA of the plan for the destruction, removal or rendering harmless of items listed in paragraph 12 of UN Security Council resolution 687 (1991)

Introduction

By resolution 699 of 17 June 1991, the Security Council approved the plan submitted by the International Atomic Energy Agency (IAEA) through the Secretary-General for the destruction, removal or rendering harmless of all items listed in paragraph 12 of Security Council resolution 687 (1991). Resolution 699 also called for the Secretary-General to submit every six months a progress report on the implementation of the plan.

The first of these reports was circulated by the Secretary-General to the members of the Security Council in document S/23295 dated 17 December 1991, and the second in document S/24110 dated 17 June 1992.

This is the third semi-annual report of the implementation by the IAEA of the plan for destruction, removal or rendering harmless covering the period from 17 June 1992 to 17 December 1992.

Present status

As recently reported by the Director General in his address to the Security Council, the IAEA has carried out, with the assistance and cooperation of the Special Commission, 16 missions in Iraq, which have entailed inspections at more than seventy sites and have resulted in the gradual disclosure of a broadly-based nuclear programme aimed at the production of enriched uranium and at the development of nuclear weapon capabilities. As a result of these inspections, in the course of which the IAEA has interviewed numerous Iraqi authorities and secured thousands of pages of documents, the IAEA has been able to draw a reasonably coherent and consistent picture of Iraq's nuclear programme. However, doubts remain as to whether the picture is complete.

Efforts to implement the destruction, removal and rendering harmless of all items referred to in paragraph 12 of Security Council resolution 687 (1991) are on-going. The IAEA has supervised extensive destruction of facilities and equipment related to the production of enriched uranium and to the weaponization programme. Key buildings and equipment have been demolished by Iraqi personnel at the direction of the IAEA inspection teams, resulting in the destruction of the Al Atheer, Tarmiya and Ash Sharqat sites. All nuclear-related production facilities at Al Jezira and Al Qaim were destroyed during the Gulf War and the Tuwaitha Centre was badly damaged. With regard to nuclear-weapons-usable material, the only such material currently known to remain in Iraq is the highly enriched uranium in irradiated reactor fuel assemblies, removal of which from Iraq awaits conclusion of the necessary arrangements with recipient countries. The material has been verified and is being kept under seal until its removal. In addition, numerous other material, equipment and components have been either destroyed, removed from Iraq or placed under Agency seal in Iraq and are subjected to regular verification. The details of the activities relevant to destruction, removal or rendering harmless carried out since the second report was submitted by the Director General are set out below.

Direct-use material

Fresh fuel

As indicated in the second report, all of the fresh fuel for the IRT 5000 reactor has been transferred to Russia and transformed, through isotopic dilution, into uranium enriched to slightly less than 20% in U-235. This material has been transferred from the processing plant to a storage facility in Russia, pending its resale, where it will remain under IAEA safeguards. The French-origin MTR type plates and the Russian-origin pins which were removed from Iraq in June 1992 remain in storage at the IAEA laboratory in Seibersdorf, Austria.

Irradiated fuel

As indicated in the second report, negotiations with a consortium of commercial companies from France and the UK for the removal, transportation and disposal of this fuel had met with difficulties of a legal, technical and financial nature. Therefore, the IAEA issued on 27 November 1992 a new request for proposals for the removal, transportation and disposal of the material in question. In the course of the recently-completed Fifteenth IAEA inspection, a group of experts identified the operational requirements for removal of the irradiated fuel from Iraq. From their review of the situation, it can be concluded that all fuel assemblies are now accessible and can be removed without major difficulties, and that substantial involvement of Iraq personnel will be necessary. The estimated time for removal is 4 to 6 months once the operation is begun. It is hoped that the removal operation will begin in the first half of 1993.

Plutonium and other nuclear material

The IAEA continued to pursue its inquiry into inconsistencies in the Iraqi nuclear material flow declarations, in particular with regard to activities said by the Iraqi authorities to have taken place in the building 73 complex at the Al Tuwaitha site. Further discussions have been held with Iraqi personnel on this issue, and additional samples have been taken of the filters, declared feed materials and building 73 waste.

Installations, equipment and other materials relevant to enriched uranium production

In the course of the recently-completed Sixteenth IAEA inspection, Iraqi authorities indicated that they would respond positively to requests for procurement-related data. If complied with, this would help to break the impasse that has developed with respect to provision of such information.

The approximately 96 tonnes of 350-grade maraging steel presented and verified at Iskandariya was transferred to Basra and had been melted and diluted with equal amounts of high carbon steel in the furnaces at Basra. The resulting mixture has been sampled and verified. Analysis of the samples indicated that the operation has succeeded in rendering the maraging steel harmless.

The completion of the destruction of the Electro Magnetic Isotopic Separation (EMIS) sites at Tarmiya and Ash Sharqat was verified by the Fourteenth IAEA Inspection Team. At Tarmiya, all of the EMIS production buildings and associated electrical power distribution capability have been destroyed. The electrical power to the site has been reduced by a factor of three. Further reductions in delivered power will depend on an evaluation of the Iraqi proposals for an alternative use of the site. At Ash Sharqat, all EMIS production and associated electrical production distribution facilities have also been destroyed. The electric sub-station supplying power to the site was verified as having been completely dismantled. EMIS components consistent with Iraqi declarations and independently-acquired procurement data have been verified as destroyed.

The R24 EMIS experimental system, a 1 to 5 scale model of the 1200 mm system built to study the separators magnetic field, was destroyed by Iraqi personnel at the direction of the Fifteenth Inspection Team. The items comprising the system included nine double pole magnets, the winding machine and the transport rails for the winding machine.

Installations and equipment relevant to weaponization activities

The Al Atheeer/Hatteen sites have been re-inspected since completion of the destruction of the weaponization-related facilities and equipment located at the sites. At the invitation of the Iraqi authorities, the Fifteenth IAEA Inspection Team saw five Hadland CCD cameras which had been declared to an UNSCOM missile team a year ago. The cameras and associated accessories were inventoried and the details are being evaluated with respect to the camera's utility for high explosives testing.

Approximately 250 tonnes of HMX, a high-melting point explosive, is currently stored under Agency seal at

Al Qa Qaa pending a determination concerning its disposition.

Future actions

As indicated above, arrangements remain to be made for the removal from Iraq of a quantity of U-235 contained in irradiated fuel elements. Priority should be given to concluding this action as promptly as possible out of safety considerations.

The IAEA has identified and inventoried approximately 700 machine tools. Some of these machine tools meet the specifications for Annex 3 (revised) of the IAEA plan for future ongoing monitoring of Iraq's compliance with relevant Security Council resolutions. Disposition of these items is under consideration.

As indicated in the IAEA's second report on these activities, additional destruction, removal or rendering harmless may be necessary.

Document 143

General Assembly resolution concerning the situation of human rights in Iraq

A/RES/47/145, 18 December 1992

The General Assembly,

Guided by the principles embodied in the Charter of the United Nations, the Universal Declaration of Human Rights 1/ and the International Covenants on Human Rights, 2/

Reaffirming that all Member States have an obligation to promote and protect human rights and fundamental freedoms and to fulfil the obligations they have undertaken under the various international instruments in this field,

Mindful that Iraq is a party to the International Covenants on Human Rights and to other human rights instruments,

Recalling its resolution 46/134 of 17 December 1991, in which it expressed its deep concern about the flagrant violations of human rights by the Government of Iraq,

Recalling also Security Council resolution 688 (1991) of 5 April 1991, in which the Council demanded an end to the repression of the Iraqi civilian population and insisted that Iraq should cooperate with humanitarian organizations and ensure that the human and political rights of all Iraqi citizens were respected,

Recalling in particular Commission on Human Rights resolution 1991/74 of 6 March 1991, 3/ in which the Commission requested its Chairman to appoint a Special Rapporteur to make a thorough study of the violations of human rights by the Government of Iraq, based on all information the Special Rapporteur might deem relevant, including information provided by inter-governmental and non-governmental organizations and any comments and material provided by the Government of Iraq,

Bearing in mind the pertinent resolutions of the Commission on Human Rights condemning the flagrant violations of human rights by the Government of Iraq, including its most recent, resolution 1992/71 of 5 March 1992, 4/ in which the Commission decided to extend the mandate of the Special Rapporteur for a further year and requested him in pursuing his mandate to visit again the northern area of Iraq in particular, and to submit an interim report to the General Assembly at its forty-seventh session and a final report to the Commission at its forty-ninth session,

Recalling Security Council resolutions 706 (1991) of 15 August 1991, 712 (1991) of 19 September 1991 and 778 (1992) of 2 October 1992,

Deeply concerned by the massive and grave violations of human rights by the Government of Iraq, such as summary and arbitrary executions, torture and other cruel, inhuman or degrading treatment, enforced or involuntary disappearances, arbitrary arrests and detentions, and lack of due process and the rule of law and of freedom of thought, expression, association and access to food and health care,

Deeply concerned also by the fact that chemical weapons have been used on the Iraqi civilian population, by the forced displacement of hundreds of thousands of Iraqi civilians and by the destruction of Iraqi towns and villages, as well as by the fact that tens of thousands of displaced Kurds had to take refuge in camps and shelters in the north of Iraq,

1/ Resolution 217 A (III).
2/ Resolution 2200 A (XXI), annex.
3/ See *Official Records of the Economic and Social Council, 1991, Supplement No. 2* (E/1991/22), chap. II, sect. A.
4/ Ibid., *1992, Supplement No. 2* (E/1992/22), chap. II, sect. A.

Deeply concerned further by the current severe and grave violations of human rights by the Government of Iraq against the civilian population in southern Iraq, in particular the Shiah communities in the southern marshes,

Expressing concern in particular that there has been no improvement in the human rights situation in Iraq, and welcoming, therefore, the proposal of the Special Rapporteur for the deployment of a team of human rights monitors in Iraq, 5/

Noting that despite the formal cooperation extended to the Special Rapporteur, the Government of Iraq needs to improve that cooperation, in particular by giving full replies to the inquiries of the Special Rapporteur about acts it is committing that are incompatible with the international human rights instruments that are binding on Iraq,

1. *Takes note with appreciation* of the interim report on the situation of human rights in Iraq submitted by the Special Rapporteur of the Commission on Human Rights 6/ and the observations, conclusions and recommendations contained therein;

2. *Expresses its strong condemnation* of the massive violations of human rights of the gravest nature, for which the Government of Iraq is responsible and to which the Special Rapporteur has referred in his recent reports, in particular:

(*a*) Summary and arbitrary executions, orchestrated mass executions and burials, extrajudicial killings, including political killings, in particular in the northern region of Iraq, in southern Shiah centres and in the southern marshes;

(*b*) The widespread routine practice of systematic torture in its most cruel forms, including the torture of children;

(*c*) Enforced or involuntary disappearances, routinely practised arbitrary arrest and detention, including of women and children and consistent and routine failure to respect due process and the rule of law;

(*d*) Suppression of freedom of thought, expression and association, and violations of property rights;

3. *Deplores* the refusal of Iraq to cooperate in the implementation of Security Council resolutions 706 (1991) and 712 (1991) and its failure to provide the Iraqi population with access to adequate food and health care;

4. *Calls upon* the Government of Iraq to release immediately all persons arbitrarily arrested and detained, including Kuwaitis and nationals of other States;

5. *Calls once again upon* Iraq, as a State party to the International Covenant on Economic, Social and Cultural Rights 7/ as well as to the International Covenant on Civil and Political Rights, 7/ to abide by its freely undertaken obligations under the Covenants and under other international instruments on human rights, and particularly to respect and ensure the rights of all individuals irrespective of their origin within its territory and subject to its jurisdiction;

6. *Recognizes* the importance of the work of the United Nations in providing humanitarian relief to the people of Iraq, and calls upon Iraq immediately and fully to implement the Memorandum of Understanding signed on 22 October 1992 between the United Nations and the Government of Iraq and to cooperate with the United Nations programmes, including ensuring the safety and security of United Nations personnel and humanitarian workers;

7. *Expresses special alarm* at the repressive policies and practices directed against the Kurds, which continue to have an impact on the lives of the Iraqi people as a whole;

8. *Also expresses special alarm* at the resurgence of grave violations of human rights against Shiah communities, especially in southern Iraq, which is the result of a policy directed against the marsh Arabs in particular;

9. *Further expresses special alarm* at all internal embargoes, which prevent the equitable enjoyment of basic foodstuffs and medical supplies, and calls upon Iraq, which has sole responsibility in this regard, to remove them;

10. *Welcomes* the proposal of the Special Rapporteur for a system of human rights monitors which would constitute an independent and reliable source of information, and invites the Commission on Human Rights to follow up this proposal at its forty-ninth session;

11. *Urges once more* the Government of Iraq to set up an independent commission of inquiry to look into the fate of tens of thousands of persons who have disappeared;

12. *Regrets* the failure of the Government of Iraq to provide satisfactory and convincing replies concerning the violations of human rights brought to the attention of the Special Rapporteur, and calls upon it to reply without delay in a comprehensive and detailed manner;

13. *Urges*, therefore, the Government of Iraq to accord its full cooperation to the Special Rapporteur to enable him to make the appropriate recommendations to improve the human rights situation in Iraq;

14. *Requests* the Secretary-General to provide the Special Rapporteur with all the assistance necessary to carry out his mandate;

15. *Decides* to continue its consideration of the situation of human rights in Iraq during its forty-eighth session under the item entitled "Human rights questions" in the light of additional elements provided by the Commission on Human Rights and the Economic and Social Council.

5/ See A/47/367, sect. III.
6/ A/47/367 and Add.1.
7/ See resolution 2200 A (XXI), annex.

Document 144

General Assembly resolution concerning international cooperation to mitigate the environmental consequences on Kuwait and other countries in the region resulting from the situation between Iraq and Kuwait

A/RES/47/151, 18 December 1992

The General Assembly,

Aware of the disastrous situation caused in Kuwait and neighbouring areas by the torching and destruction of hundreds of its oil wells and of the other environmental consequences on the atmosphere and on land and marine life,

Bearing in mind all relevant Security Council resolutions, in particular section E of resolution 687 (1991) of 3 April 1991,

Having taken note of the report submitted by the Secretary-General to the Security Council describing the nature and extent of the environmental damage suffered by Kuwait, 1/

Recalling decision 16/11 A adopted by the Governing Council of the United Nations Environment Programme on 31 May 1991, 2/

Recalling also its resolution 46/216 of 20 December 1991,

Taking note of the report of the Secretary-General, 3/

Profoundly concerned at the degradation of the environment as a consequence of the damage, especially the threat posed to the health and well-being of the people of Kuwait and the people of the region, and the adverse impact on the economic activities of Kuwait and other countries of the region, including the effects on livestock, agriculture and fishing, as well as on wildlife,

Welcoming the recent Mount Mitchell Research Cruise, which was organized under the sponsorship of the Intergovernmental Oceanographic Commission of the United Nations Educational, Scientific and Cultural Organization, the Regional Organization for the Protection of the Marine Environment and the United Nations Environment Programme, to make a scientific assessment of environmental conditions in the region,

Awaiting the meetings due to be held in 1993, at which the results of the Mount Mitchell Research Cruise will be discussed and evaluated,

Acknowledging the fact that dealing with this catastrophe goes beyond the capabilities of the countries of the region and, in that regard, recognizing the need for strengthened international cooperation to deal with the situation,

Noting with appreciation the appointment by the Secretary-General of an Under-Secretary-General as his Personal Representative to coordinate United Nations efforts in this field,

Also noting with appreciation the efforts already undertaken by the Member States of the region, other States, the organizations of the United Nations system and governmental and non-governmental organizations to study, mitigate and minimize the consequences of this environmental catastrophe,

Bearing in mind the effective work of the Regional Organization for the Protection of the Marine Environment and the inter-agency task force established under the leadership of the United Nations Environment Programme especially to consider the environmental situation in the region, as well as the plan of action,

Expressing its special appreciation to the Governments that have extended financial support to the two trust funds established for the purpose by the Secretary-General of the International Maritime Organization and the Executive Director of the United Nations Environment Programme, and to the Governments and organizations that supported the recent international research cruise organized under the auspices of the Intergovernmental Oceanographic Commission, the Regional Organization for the Protection of the Marine Environment and the United Nations Environment Programme,

1. *Appeals* to all States Members of the United Nations, intergovernmental and non-governmental organizations, scientific bodies and individuals to provide assistance for programmes aimed at the study and mitigation of the environmental degradation of the region and for strengthening the Regional Organization for the Protection of the Marine Environment and its role in coordinating the implementation of these programmes;

2. *Calls upon* the organizations and programmes of the United Nations system, in particular the International Maritime Organization and the United Nations Environment Programme, to pursue their efforts to assess the short-term as well as the long-term impact of the

---

1/ See S/22535 and Corr.1 and 2, annex; see *Official Records of the Security Council, Forty-sixth Year, Supplement for April, May and June 1991,* document S/22535.
2/ See *Official Records of the General Assembly, Forty-sixth Session, Supplement No. 25* (A/46/25), annex.
3/ A/47/265-E/1992/81.

environmental degradation of the region and to consider measures that may be needed to counteract these effects;

3. *Requests* the Secretary-General, through his Personal Representative, to render assistance to the members of the Regional Organization for the Protection of the Marine Environment in the formulation and implementation of a coordinated and consolidated programme of action comprising costed project profiles, to help identify all possible resources for the programme of action and, *inter alia,* for strengthening the environmental capacities of the members of the Regional Organization for the Protection of the Marine Environment to deal with this problem, and to allocate, within existing resources, the minimum resources required to enable his Personal Rep-

resentative to continue to help coordinate the activities of the United Nations system to that end;

4. *Also requests* the Secretary-General to submit to the General Assembly at its forty-ninth session, through the Economic and Social Council, a report on the implementation of the present resolution;

5. *Decides* to include in the provisional agenda of its forty-ninth session the sub-item entitled "International cooperation to mitigate the environmental consequences on Kuwait and other countries in the region resulting from the situation between Iraq and Kuwait" under the item entitled "Development and international economic cooperation".

Document 145

Decision 15 taken by the Governing Council of the United Nations Compensation Commission: Compensation for business losses resulting from Iraq's unlawful invasion and occupation of Kuwait where the trade embargo and related measures were also a cause

S/AC.26/1992/15, 18 December 1992

Compensation for Business Losses Resulting from Iraq's Unlawful Invasion and Occupation of Kuwait where the Trade Embargo and Related Measures Were also a Cause

Decision taken by the Governing Council of the United Nations Compensation Commission at its 31st meeting, held in Geneva on 18 December 1992

1. Paragraph 16 of United Nations Security Council resolution 687 reaffirms "that Iraq, without prejudice to the debts and obligations of Iraq arising prior to 2 August 1990, which will be addressed through the normal mechanisms, is liable under international law for any direct loss, damage, including environmental damage and the depletion of natural resources, or injury to foreign Governments, nationals and corporations, as a result of Iraq's unlawful invasion and occupation of Kuwait."

2. In paragraph 6 of its Decision S/AC.26/1992/9 on Propositions and Conclusions on Compensation for Business Losses, hereinafter referred to as Decision 9, the Governing Council set out guidelines for awarding compensation for business losses caused by Iraq's unlawful invasion and occupation of Kuwait where the trade embargo and related measures were also a cause, and undertook to provide further guidance on the matter.

3. The two essential elements of admissible losses are (a) that such losses must be the result of Iraq's unlawful invasion and occupation of Kuwait and (b) that

the causal link must be direct. Although the UN trade embargo was imposed in response to Iraq's invasion and occupation of Kuwait, losses suffered solely as a result of that embargo are not considered eligible for compensation because the causal link between the invasion and the loss is not sufficiently direct.

4. The terms of contracts, and transactions that have been part of a business practice or course of dealing, as well as the relevant circumstances will need to be examined by Commissioners to determine whether related claims fall within the scope of the Compensation Commission.

5. In all cases, Commissioners will require evidence that claims fall within the criteria of direct loss as set out in paragraph 16 of resolution 687 in order for them to be eligible for compensation by the Compensation Fund. It will not be enough for claimants to argue that losses were due to the chaotic economic situation following Iraq's unlawful invasion and occupation of Kuwait. There will be a need for detailed factual descriptions of the circumstances of the claimed loss, damage or injury.

6. In its Decisions No. 1 (S/AC.26/1991/1) and No. 7 (S/AC.26/1991/7/Rev.1), the Governing Council decided that compensation payments are available with respect to any direct loss suffered as a result of:

(a) Military operations or threat of military action by either side during the period 2 August 1990 to 2 March 1991;

(b) Departure from or inability to leave Iraq or Kuwait (or a decision not to return) during that period;

(c) Actions by officials, employees or agents of the Government of Iraq or its controlled entities during that period in connection with the invasion or occupation;

(d) The breakdown of civil order in Kuwait or Iraq during that period; or

(e) Hostage-taking or other illegal detention.

These guidelines are not intended to be exhaustive. There will be other situations where evidence can be produced showing claims are for direct loss, damage or injury as a result of Iraq's unlawful invasion and occupation of Kuwait.

7. Commissioners will wish to apply relevant valuation methods to different categories of loss. Paragraph 15 of Decision 9 shows various valuation methods for tangible assets depending on the type of asset and the circumstances of the case. Paragraph 18 of Decision 9 shows various valuation methods for losses relating to income producing properties. When compensation for losses of future earnings and profits is assessed, documentary evidence such as a contract should be presented wherever possible, and where no contract existed, other evidence should be submitted to enable losses of future earnings to be calculated with reasonable certainty. Such evidence should wherever possible be broadly equivalent to contracts that were in existence, or prove that such contracts or projections of future trading patterns existed. Paragraph 17 of Decision 9 states that, in the case of a business which has been, or could have been, rebuilt and resumed, compensation would be awarded for the loss from cessation of trading to the time when trading was, or could have been, resumed. In the case of a business or course of trading which it was not possible to resume, the Commissioners would need to calculate a time limit for compensation for future earnings and profits, taking into account the claimant's duty to mitigate the loss wherever possible.

8. This paper does not address the issues arising from claimants' attempts to avail themselves of particular sources of recovery, such as to claim against the other party to a contract.

Commentary on paragraph 6 of Decision 9

9. The first four sentences of paragraph 6 of Decision 9 are now considered in turn. The object is to provide further guidance for Commissioners when they assess claims in respect of business losses of individuals, corporations and other entities. The guidance is also intended to help claimants in presenting their claims. It will be for Commissioners to draw on the principles in this guidance when making their judgements on actual cases which will stand or fall according to their specific factual and legal situations.

I. "The trade embargo and related measures, and the economic situation caused thereby, will not be accepted as the basis for compensation."

(i) The practical effect of this statement is that any loss, damage, or injury resulting solely from the trade embargo and related measures, and the economic situation caused thereby, is not eligible for compensation. The trade embargo and related measures are the prohibitions in United Nations Security Council resolution 661 (1990) and relevant subsequent resolutions and the measures taken by states in anticipation thereof and pursuant thereto, such as the freezing of assets by Governments. The trade embargo against Kuwait was applied from 6 August 1990 to 3 April 1991 during Iraq's occupation of Kuwait. The trade embargo against Iraq was also applied from 6 August 1990 and is still in force.

(ii) "The economic situation caused thereby" is a broader concept. The trade embargo and related measures had wider economic effects, both on international trade and on economic activity within Kuwait and Iraq. For example, the world price of oil was temporarily higher than it otherwise would have been and, in addition, countries which previously imported oil from Iraq and Kuwait had to find other sources of supply, with effects on transport and transit services and on refinery operating costs. Companies which might have expected to export goods or services to Kuwait or Iraq will have had to look for alternative markets, with potentially depressing effects both on their profits and those of their suppliers.

II. "Compensation will be provided to the extent that Iraq's unlawful invasion and occupation of Kuwait constituted a cause of direct loss, damage, or injury which is separate and distinct from the trade embargo and related measures."

(i) The practical effect of this statement is that compensation will be provided, if and to the extent that loss, damage, or injury resulting directly from Iraq's unlawful invasion and occupation of Kuwait was actually suffered and would have been suffered irrespective of whether the trade embargo and related measures had been in force.

(ii) Particularly in the case of larger and more complex claims, the Commissioners may decide that some losses listed in a claim are a direct result of Iraq's unlawful invasion and occupation of Kuwait and should be compensated and that other losses listed in the same claim resulted solely from the embargo and related measures and are therefore ineligible for compensation. In this situation partial compensation would in principle be payable.

III. "Where the full extent of the loss, damage, or injury arose as a direct result of Iraq's unlawful invasion and occupation of Kuwait, it should be compensated notwithstanding the fact that it may also be attributable to the trade embargo and related measures."

(i) This is intended to show that the full extent of a loss, damage, or injury may be attributed both to Iraq's unlawful invasion and occupation of Kuwait and to the trade embargo and related measures; they are parallel causes.

(ii) Some cases of parallel cause loss may prove difficult to assess. There would be instances at the time of the invasion and embargo when ships diverted because it was unsafe to enter Kuwaiti or Iraqi ports. The Commissioners will need to examine closely the alleged cause of all losses after 6 August 1990 in order to determine the extent to which the loss arose as a direct result of the Iraqi invasion and occupation of Kuwait, and is therefore compensable, even though it could also be considered to have resulted from the embargo and related measures. If the Commissioners decide that a loss had such a parallel cause, full compensation would in principle be awarded.

IV. "The total amount of compensable losses will be reduced to the extent that those losses could reasonably have been avoided."

(i) The duty to mitigate applies to all claims and not simply to those under discussion in paragraph 6 of Decision 9. The subject of mitigation is referred to in paragraphs 10, 17 and 19 of Decision 9.

10. The guidance contained in the present Decision applies to all types of business losses, including losses relating to contracts, transactions that have been part of a business practice or course of dealing, tangible assets and income-producing properties.

Document 146

Statement by the President of the Security Council concerning United Nations flights into Iraqi territory

S/25081, 8 January 1993

The Security Council is deeply disturbed by the Government of Iraq's recent Notes to the Office of the Special Commission in Baghdad and to the Headquarters of the United Nations Iraq-Kuwait Observation Mission (UNIKOM) that it will not allow the United Nations to transport its personnel into Iraqi territory using its own aircraft.

The Security Council refers to resolution 687 (1991) requiring Iraq to permit the Special Commission and the IAEA to undertake immediate on-site inspection of any locations designated by the Commission. The agreement on facilities, privileges and immunities between the Government of Iraq and the United Nations, and resolutions 707 (1991) and 715 (1991) elaborated on Iraq's obligations by demanding, *inter alia*, that the Special Commission and the IAEA be allowed, as they determined necessary, to use their own aircraft throughout Iraq and any airfield in Iraq without interference or hindrance of any kind. Concerning UNIKOM, Iraq is obligated by resolution 687 (1991) and committed by an exchange of letters dated 15 April 1992 and 21 June 1992 respectively to the unrestricted freedom of entry and exit without delay or hindrance of its personnel, property, supplies, equipment, spare parts and means of transport.

The implementation of the measures set out in the recent communications of the Iraqi Government would seriously impede the activities of the Special Commission, the IAEA and UNIKOM. Such restrictions constitute an unacceptable and material breach of the relevant provisions of resolution 687 (1991), which established the cease-fire and provided the conditions essential to the restoration of peace and security in the region, as well as other relevant resolutions and agreements.

The Council demands that the Government of Iraq abide by its obligations under all relevant Security Council resolutions and cooperate fully with the activities of the Special Commission, the IAEA and UNIKOM. In particular, it demands that the Government of Iraq not interfere with the currently envisaged United Nations flights. The Security Council warns the Government of Iraq, as it has done in this connection in the past, of the serious consequences which would ensue from failure to comply with its obligations.

Document 147

Special report by the Secretary-General on UNIKOM

S/25085, 10 January 1993, and addendum, S/25085/Add.1, 19 January 1993

1. I wish to report to the Security Council a number of serious developments concerning the United Nations Iraq-Kuwait Observation Mission (UNIKOM).

2. Firstly, this morning at about 0700 hours local time, a party of some 200 Iraqis with trucks and heavy loading equipment forced entry into the six ammunition bunkers located in a former Iraqi naval base at Umm Qasr, on Kuwaiti territory, and took away most of their contents, including four "HY-2G" anti-ship missiles.

3. UNIKOM, which had maintained a 24-hour guard over the bunkers, made an effort to prevent access to them but was unable to do so. UNIKOM then attempted to prevent the Iraqi trucks loaded with items from the bunkers from leaving the scene by placing United Nations vehicles in their path. After some manoeuvring, the Iraqis surrounded the United Nations vehicles, preventing them from moving without seriously injuring or killing Iraqi personnel. The Iraqis then breached the fence and left.

4. At the first news of this incident, UNIKOM's Chief Military Observer, Major-General Timothy K. Dibuama, summoned the Senior Iraqi Liaison Officer at Umm Qasr and protested to him this serious violation. He also instructed UNIKOM's Chief Liaison Officer in Baghdad to lodge a formal protest with the Iraqi Ministry of Foreign Affairs. In their contacts with the Iraqi authorities, General Dibuama and his representatives pointed out that the Iraqi personnel, without prior clearance, had entered an area which is now known to be Kuwaiti territory and had contravened the Security Council's decision, laid down in the President's letter of 3 November 1992, that the contents of the bunkers should be destroyed by UNIKOM or by a specialized firm acting at UNIKOM's request and under its supervision.

5. Secondly, General Dibuama has reported that up to 500 Iraqi personnel continued today to dismantle prefabricated buildings in the former naval base, also on Kuwaiti territory, and to remove the parts and other items. This activity is in violation of the procedure established by the Security Council and conveyed to me in the President's letter of 8 January 1993. A copy of this letter was sent to the Permanent Representative of Iraq to the United Nations the same day and General Dibuama informed the Senior Iraqi Liaison Officer in Umm Qasr one day later, that is yesterday.

6. General Dibuama has kept the Kuwaiti authorities informed of the above developments. He has stationed observers at the crossing points along the border in the Umm Qasr area with instructions to stop approaching Iraqis, to warn them that they are about to enter Kuwaiti territory, and to describe to them the procedure established by the Security Council for the removal of Iraqi property and assets.

7. Thirdly, I wish to report that in a meeting at Umm Qasr on 4 January 1993, Major-General Abdallah Firas, the Chairman of Iraq's Higher Committee for Coordination which is responsible for liaison with UNIKOM, raised with General Dibuama the question of the retrieval by Iraq of the prefabricated buildings which Iraq had made available to UNIKOM in a part of the former naval base (Camp Khor). General Dibuama referred this question to United Nations Headquarters and my colleagues have raised it with the Permanent Representative of Iraq, asking that his Government stop the workers. They have suggested that the matter be discussed, with a view to finding an agreed solution which would preserve UNIKOM's ability to carry out the mandate entrusted to it by the Security Council. The Permanent Representative had not yet responded when, on 9 January, General Firas informed General Dibuama that on 11 January the dismantling of prefabricated buildings in the former naval base would be extended to include the buildings used by UNIKOM. General Firas suggested that UNIKOM evacuate these premises.

8. The premises in question consist of 19 buildings, which house such elements as the UNIKOM's northern sector headquarters, helicopter support, and transport workshops. Others are used for the accommodation of personnel. Additional prefabricated buildings have been added by UNIKOM. I should like to point out that, by an exchange of letters, respectively dated 15 April and 21 June 1992, the Government of Iraq has agreed that the land and premises it has made available to UNIKOM shall be inviolate and subject to the exclusive control and authority of the United Nations.

9. The above developments are taking place at a time when the Security Council is already actively seized of other aspects of the situation, such as Iraq's ban against United Nations aircraft. They cast doubt on Iraq's continued willingness to cooperate with UNIKOM and to abide by the commitments it has undertaken in this respect. As the Security Council is aware, Iraq's cooperation is essential for UNIKOM to perform its tasks effectively. It is for this reason that I am bringing these matters to the Council's attention.

Annex I
Letter dated 8 January 1993 from the President of the Security Council addressed to the Secretary-General

On behalf of the members of the Security Council, I have the honour to refer to your letter dated 23 December 1992, in which you brought to the Council's attention some issues arising from the demarcation of the boundary between Iraq and Kuwait. The members of the Council considered this matter in the course of consultations of the whole on 5 January 1993 and asked me to convey to you the following:

The members of the Council concur with the general approach outlined in your letter. They are particularly concerned at the continued presence of six Iraqi police posts on Kuwaiti territory and insist on their speedy removal, by 15 January at the latest. They also note the unsafe proximity to the boundary of three other Iraqi posts and two Kuwaiti police posts.

The members have also before them a letter dated 4 January 1993 from the Chargé d'affaires a.i. of the Permanent Mission of Kuwait to the United Nations and they have since taken note of UNIKOM's weekly report for the period 28 December 1992-3 January 1993. They believe the presence of Iraqi military personnel in the demilitarized zone was a serious violation of resolution 687 (1991). They also consider that the removal of the Iraqi property and assets from Kuwait territory should be undertaken only after prior clearance by UNIKOM and by the Kuwaiti authorities through UNIKOM and should be completed by 15 January 1993. The members

of the Council would be obliged if you would keep them informed of development in these matters.

(*Signed*) Yoshio HATANO
President of the Security Council

Annex II
Letter dated 23 December 1992 from the Secretary-General addressed to the President of the Security Council

I have the honour to refer to the situation in the area of operation of the United Nations Iraq-Kuwait Observation Mission (UNIKOM), following the placement of the border pillars along the land boundary between Iraq and Kuwait by the United Nations Iraq-Kuwait Boundary Demarcation Commission. The demarcation of the land boundary is thus nearly complete, except for minor technical matters.

I consider it timely, therefore, to bring to the Council's attention some issues arising from the demarcation of the boundary. These concern six Iraqi police posts, part of the Iraqi town of Umm Qasr, several Iraqi farms along the eastern part of the boundary and some well heads of the Ratqah oil field, all of which have been shown to be on Kuwaiti territory.

The issue of the Iraqi police posts on Kuwaiti territory was first raised with the Iraqi authorities more than one year ago. At that time, the boundary had not yet been demarcated and the Iraqi authorities maintained that they could not withdraw the posts as this might prejudice their position regarding the boundary. They stated, however, that they would abide by the decision of the Boundary Demarcation Commission. This assurance has recently been repeated. I have requested the Iraqi authorities to withdraw the six police posts from Kuwaiti territory as soon as possible and I have instructed Major-General Dibuama, the Chief Military Observer of UNIKOM, to be in touch with those authorities regarding the necessary arrangements.

Three Iraqi police posts and two Kuwaiti police posts are now closer to the boundary than 1,000 metres, which UNIKOM, with the concurrence of both sides, has established as a reasonable distance to prevent incidents. Persistent complaints about shooting incidents involving police posts underline the continuing validity of this rule. I have accordingly instructed Major-General Dibuama to arrange with the authorities concerned that the police posts in question be moved further away from the boundary at an early date.

The issue of the Iraqi citizens and their assets which remain on Kuwaiti territory is potentially volatile and apt to give rise to increased tension and friction unless resolved soon. At the same time, it is clearly in the interest of all involved that this issue be settled in a reasonable way. I am in touch with the Governments of Iraq and Kuwait in order to promote such a settlement and to determine how the United Nations may help to bring it about. I trust that the Security Council concurs with this approach and shall keep it informed of the results of my contacts.

I should be grateful if you would bring the contents of this letter to the attention of the members of the Security Council.

(*Signed*) Boutros BOUTROS-GHALI

Annex III
Letter dated 3 November 1992 from the President of the Security Council addressed to the Secretary-General

The members of the Security Council have examined the question you brought to the attention of the President through your letter dated 23 September 1992. They fully share the concerns expressed by the UNIKOM Commander related to the threats to security linked to the presence of Iraqi and Kuwaiti military equipment in six bunkers within the demilitarized zone, near the headquarters of the Observation Mission. The members of the Security Council deem it necessary, as recommended by the Commander of the Observation Mission, for the bunkers to be emptied of their contents.

The members of the Security Council have noted that UNIKOM has carried out, within the demilitarized zone where it is deployed, destruction of mines and ammunition that might be harmful to the observers (your reports S/22454, approved by resolution 689 (1991), S/23106, S/23766 and S/24615). They are of the opinion that the military equipment referred to in your letter dated 23 September 1992, which also represents a threat to the security of the members of the Observation Mission, should similarly be destroyed by UNIKOM or by a specialized company acting upon the request of the Mission and under its supervision.

In the event of UNIKOM entrusting a specific company with the destruction of the military equipment contained in the six bunkers, the cost of this operation should not be covered by the regular budget of UNIKOM but by Iraq and Kuwait. Each of these two States should support the financial burden related to the destruction of the contents of the bunkers located on its territory, i.e., on its side of the border as demarcated by the Boundary Demarcation Commission.

The members of the Security Council are of the opinion that it would be useful for UNIKOM to consult the Special Commission to enable the latter to check whether any of the military equipment contained in the six bunkers fall into the category mentioned in paragraph 8 of resolution 687. In this case, this equipment should be destroyed by the Special Commission, in coordination with UNIKOM.

(*Signed*) André ERDOS
President of the Security Council

Addendum (S/25085/Add.1, 19 January 1993)
Special report of the Secretary-General on the United Nations Iraq-Kuwait Observation Mission

1. The Chief Military Observer of the United Nations Iraq-Kuwait Observation Mission (UNIKOM) has reported that the Iraqi authorities have withdrawn the six police posts that were located on Kuwaiti territory.

2. The withdrawal was announced to UNIKOM in the afternoon of 17 January. The Iraqi police personnel withdrew with their equipment that evening and dismantled and removed three of the posts. The next morning, they returned and removed the other three posts. This happened under UNIKOM's supervision and with the agreement of the Kuwaiti authorities, which UNIKOM had consulted. UNIKOM has inspected the six sites and has reported that everything has been removed.

3. As of midday on Wednesday, 13 January 1993, the retrieval of Iraqi assets from Kuwaiti territory has ceased.

4. In my letter of 23 December 1992 (see S/25085, annex II), I mentioned that three Iraqi police posts, as well as two Kuwaiti police posts, were closer to the boundary than 1,000 metres, which has been established as a reasonable distance to prevent incidents. Through an oversight, these figures did not include two Iraqi police posts that were set up in the central sector in early December 1992. UNIKOM had asked that these posts also should be moved further from the boundary. In Umm Qasr, where the boundary runs through a built-up area, three police check-points and a border post are also within the 1,000-metre range.

Document 148

Statement by the President of the Security Council concerning various actions by Iraq vis-à-vis *UNIKOM and UNSCOM*

S/25091, 11 January 1993

The Security Council notes that there have been a number of recent actions by Iraq as part of its pattern of flouting relevant Security Council resolutions. One was the series of border incidents involving the United Nations Iraq-Kuwait Observation Mission (UNIKOM); another was the incident concerning the United Nations Special Commission (UNSCOM) and UNIKOM flights.

The Security Council is deeply concerned at the incidents reported in the Secretary-General's special report of 10 January 1993 on UNIKOM (S/25085). The Security Council recalls the provisions of resolution 687 (1991) that established the Demilitarized Zone between Iraq and Kuwait and demanded that both countries respect the inviolability of the international boundary between them. It reaffirms that the boundary was at the very core of the conflict and that, in resolutions 687 (1991) and 773 (1991), it guaranteed the inviolability of the boundary and undertook to take as appropriate all necessary measures to that end in accordance with the Charter of the United Nations.

The Council condemns the action taken by Iraq on 10 January 1993 to remove equipment by force from the Kuwaiti side of the demilitarized zone without prior consultation with UNIKOM, and through UNIKOM with the Kuwaiti authorities, as set out in the letter of 8 January 1993 from the President of the Security Council to the Secretary-General. In particular, the Council draws attention to the removal by Iraq of four HY-2G anti-ship missiles and other military equipment from the six bunkers in the former Iraqi naval base at Umm Qasr on Kuwaiti territory, in spite of the objections of UNIKOM and their efforts to prevent this. This action is a direct challenge to the authority of UNIKOM and amounts to clear-cut defiance by Iraq of the Council, which stipulated in the letter of 3 November 1992 from the President of the Council to the Secretary-General that the military equipment in the six bunkers should be destroyed by or under the supervision of UNIKOM. The Council demands that the anti-ship missiles and other military equipment removed by force from the six bunkers at Umm Qasr in Kuwaiti territory be returned immediately to the custody of UNIKOM for destruction, as previously decided.

The Council also condemns further Iraqi intrusions into the Kuwaiti side of the demilitarized zone on 11 January 1993. It demands that any future retrieval mission be in accordance with the terms set out in the letter of 8 January 1993 from the President of the Council to the Secretary-General. On the UNIKOM facilities at Camp Khor, the Council stresses that the land and premises occupied by UNIKOM shall be inviolate and subject to the exclusive control and authority of the United Nations.

The Council invites the Secretary-General, as a first step, to explore on an urgent basis the possibilities for restoring UNIKOM to its full strength and to consider in an emergency such as this the need for rapid reinforcement as set out in paragraph 18 of his report of 12 June 1991 (S/22692), as well as any other suggestions that he might have to enhance the effectiveness of UNIKOM, and to report back to the Council.

The Council is also alarmed by Iraq's refusal to allow the United Nations to transport its Special Commission (UNSCOM) and UNIKOM personnel into Iraqi territory using its own aircraft. In this connection the Council reiterates the demand in its statement of 8 January 1993 that Iraq permit UNSCOM and UNIKOM to use their own aircraft to transport their personnel into Iraq. It rejects the arguments contained in the letter of 9 January 1993 from the Minister of Foreign Affairs of Iraq to the President of the Security Council (S/25086).

These latest developments concerning the activities of UNIKOM and UNSCOM constitute further material breaches of resolution 687 (1991), which established the cease-fire and provided the conditions essential for the restoration of peace and security in the region, as well as other relevant resolutions and agreements. The Council demands that Iraq cooperate fully with UNIKOM, UNSCOM and other United Nations agencies in carrying out their mandates, and again warns Iraq of the serious consequences that will flow from such continued defiance. The Council will remain actively seized of the matter.

Document 149

Further special report of the Secretary-General on UNIKOM

S/25123, 18 January 1993, and addendum, S/25123/Add.1, 26 January 1993

1. In his statement of 11 January 1993 (S/25091) the President of the Security Council on behalf of the Council invited me, as a first step, to explore on an urgent basis the possibilities for restoring the United Nations Iraq-Kuwait Observation Mission (UNIKOM) to its full strength and to consider in an emergency such as the present one the need for rapid reinforcement as set out in paragraph 18 of the then Secretary-General's report of 12 June 1991 (S/22692), as well as any other suggestions I might have to enhance the effectiveness of UNIKOM, and to report back to the Council.

2. The emergency referred to above arose following a series of incidents involving Iraq, which are mentioned in the statement of the President of the Council. It is accordingly assumed that the Council's objective in enhancing UNIKOM's effectiveness is to prevent a recurrence of such incidents and, should they recur, enable UNIKOM to deal with them effectively.

3. The Security Council in resolution 687 (1991) established UNIKOM as an observation mission with the tasks of monitoring the demilitarized zone (DMZ) along the boundary between Iraq and Kuwait; deterring violations of the boundary through its presence in and surveillance of the DMZ; and observing any hostile or potentially hostile action mounted from the territory of one State to the other. UNIKOM's observers are unarmed. In case of a violation, the observers report and make representations, or representations are made at a higher level either in the field or at United Nations Headquarters. The operation is based on the premise that the Governments of Iraq and Kuwait will take the necessary steps to comply with the decisions of the Security Council and will cooperate with UNIKOM in good faith. UNIKOM has neither the authority nor the means to enforce the Council's decisions.

4. The incidents which have taken place in the area of operation since the beginning of the month were closely monitored by UNIKOM and reported to United Nations Headquarters. In addition, UNIKOM made immediate representations to Iraqi personnel on the spot as well as to the Iraqi military authorities through the established liaison channel. On this occasion, protests and representations were for the most part ineffective because UNIKOM's interlocutors stated that they were powerless to influence a course of events which had been set in motion at the highest levels of the Iraqi Government. Similarly, representations made at United Nations Head-

quarters remained without a positive response until the Security Council itself intervened and, in addition, other measures were threatened by Member States, at which point the President of the Security Council was informed, *inter alia*, that Iraq would suspend its unauthorized retrieval of property from Kuwaiti territory.

5. UNIKOM thus performed the function for which it was designed and for which its strength is sufficient. If, however, the Security Council should decide that UNIKOM's present mandate does not permit an adequate response to such violations as have occurred and that UNIKOM should be able to prevent and redress them, then UNIKOM would require a capacity to take physical action. Such action could be taken to prevent or, if that fails, redress:

(a) Small-scale violations of the DMZ;

(b) Violations of the boundary between Iraq and Kuwait, for example by civilians or police; and

(c) Problems that might arise from the presence of Iraqi installations and Iraqi citizens and their assets in the DMZ on the Kuwaiti side of the newly demarcated boundary.

The above tasks could not be performed by unarmed observers. In their place, UNIKOM would have to be provided with infantry in sufficient numbers. With regard to the third point, I should also recall my letter of 23 December 1992 (S/25085, Annex I) in which I brought to the Security Council's attention some issues arising from the demarcation of the boundary. These concerned the Iraqi police posts on Kuwaiti territory, whose urgent withdrawal I have been seeking and for which the Council has set the deadline of 15 January 1993, and the Iraqi citizens and their assets which remain on Kuwaiti terrritory. In regard to the latter, I have already informed the Council that I am in touch with the Governments of Iraq and Kuwait, with a view to having this issue settled in a reasonable way. I have noted with appreciation the Council's concurrence with this approach. I shall be actively pursuing my contacts and I shall keep the Council informed of their outcome.

6. In his statement the President of the Security Council invited me to consider the need for rapid reinforcement of UNIKOM with infantry units. When this idea was introduced in June 1991, it was based on the assumption that other peace-keeping operations in the region, namely the United Nations Peace-keeping Force in Cyprus (UNFICYP) and the United Nations Interim

Force in Lebanon (UNIFIL), would retain the capacity to detach infantry to assist UNIKOM, as they had done when that Mission was set up. Following the reduction in the military strength of the two peace-keeping forces, this capacity no longer exists. Moreover, their detachments would take some time to reach UNIKOM and they would be available only for a few weeks, after which they would have to return to their parent missions. This would not meet the requirements set out above, which call for infantry to be present on the ground on a permanent basis.

7. It is estimated that three mechanized infantry battalions would be required to perform the functions outlined in paragraph 5 above. In addition, UNIKOM's airlift capability would need to be augmented so that it could lift one company in one wave for rapid reaction. Together with the necessary increase in headquarters and support elements, UNIKOM would then comprise the following military elements:

– Headquarters and communications	225
– infantry battalions (3 x 750)	2 250
– logistic battalion	750
– engineers	200
– medical unit	100
– helicopters (e.g. 20 x Bell 212)	120
Total	3 645

The above assets are those that would be needed to enable UNIKOM to carry out its new mandate with regard to the land boundary. If the Security Council required the force also to prevent violations of the maritime boundary, when demarcated, UNIKOM would need naval assets, with the necessary docking facilities, to enable it to patrol the Khawr Abd Allah and intercept any violating vessels.

8. Following the introduction of the infantry units, it would no longer be necessary or practical to retain the unarmed military observers in the Mission. All their present tasks would be assigned to the infantry, which would be deployed at the existing Patrol and Observation Bases and patrol the DMZ. The units would need to include a sufficient number of officers to carry out liaison, investigations and other special tasks.

9. UNIKOM would not assume responsibilities falling within the competence of the host Governments, which would continue to carry out all aspects of civilian administration in their respective territory. As in the past, both Governments would be expected to consult with UNIKOM on the regulation of their activities within the DMZ. This would be of particular importance with regard to the maintenance of law and order, as UNIKOM would have become an armed force with a mandate which in some respects would overlap that of the local police.

10. UNIKOM would be provided with the weapons integral to its infantry battalions. It would not use its weapons except in self-defence, which would include resistance to attempts by forceful means to prevent it from discharging its duties under the mandate of the Security Council. UNIKOM would thus not be authorized to initiate enforcement action.

11. UNIKOM would need to retain the freedom of movement and the privileges and immunities it now has and the arrangements governing its presence in Iraq and Kuwait should continue to apply *mutatis mutandis*.

12. It is to be emphasized that the above is based on the assumption that the Government of Iraq as well as the Government of Kuwait would undertake to cooperate with the restructured Mission. In the absence of such cooperation, it would become impossible for UNIKOM to carry out its functions, in which case the Security Council would need to consider alternative measures. It is also worth noting that a force on the scale suggested above would not have the capacity to prevent a significant military incursion. Should the Security Council consider that this risk exists, it would be necessary to make other arrangements for dealing with it, while at the same time ensuring the safety of UNIKOM.

Addendum (S/25123/Add.1, 26 January 1993)

1. In my report of 18 January 1993 (S/25123), I outlined in paragraph 5 a possible enlargement of UNIKOM's mandate, in case the Security Council should decide that UNIKOM's present mandate does not permit an adequate response to such violations as have occurred. In paragraphs 7 and 8 of the report, I described the means which UNIKOM would require to carry out this enlarged mandate.

2. It is estimated that the cost associated with the strengthening of the operation as described in my report would amount to some $112 million for an initial six-month period. It is further estimated that the additional monthly cost thereafter would be approximately $12 million. A breakdown of the estimated cost for the first six-month period by main categories of expenditure is provided for information purposes in the annex to this addendum.

3. Should the Security Council decide to enlarge the mandate and strength of UNIKOM, it would be my recommendation to the General Assembly that the associated additional cost should be considered an expense of the Organization to be borne by Member States in accordance with Article 17, paragraph 2, of the Charter of the United Nations and that the assessments to be levied on Member States be credited to the UNIKOM special account.

(Thousands of United States dollars)

Objects of expenditure	Initial six months
1. Military component	
(a) Contingent personnel	38 000
(b) Other costs pertaining to contingents	9 000
2. Civilian staff costs a/	3 000
3. Premises	25 000
4. Air operations	14 000
5. Transport operations	5 000
6. Communications	2 000
7. Miscellaneous equipment	6 000
8. Miscellaneous supplies, services, freight and support costs	10 000
Total	112 000

a/ Provides for 31 additional international staff and 52 additional locally recruited staff.

Document 150

Statement by the President of the Security Council concerning the sanctions regime

S/25157, 25 January 1993

The members of the Security Council held informal consultations on 25 January 1993 pursuant to paragraph 21 of Security Council resolution 687 (1991).

After hearing all the opinions expressed in the course of the consultations, the President of the Council concluded that there was no agreement that the necessary conditions existed for a modification of the regimes established in paragraph 20 of resolution 687 (1991), as referred to in paragraph 21 of that resolution.

Document 151

Report of the Executive Chairman of UNSCOM transmitting an account of the Commission's operations in connection with the events since Iraq first informed the Commission that the Commission would not be allowed to use its aircraft to transport personnel and equipment into Iraq

S/25172, 29 January 1993

Note by the Secretary-General

The Secretary-General has the honour to transmit to the Security Council a report submitted by the Executive Chairman of the Special Commission established by the Secretary-General pursuant to paragraph 9 (b) (i) of Security Council resolution 687 (1991).

Annex
Report by the Executive Chairman of the Special Commission

1. In response to a wish expressed by the members of the Security Council, the Special Commission herewith presents an account of the Commission's operations in connection with the events since Iraq first informed the Commission that the Commission would not be allowed to use its aircraft to transport personnel and equipment into Iraq from the Commission's Field Office in Bahrain. In this context, and for the sake of clarity, brief references to the Commission's rights and obligations are included.

Mandate

2. The Special Commission was established pursuant to paragraph 9 (b) (i) of section C of Security Council resolution 687 (1991), *inter alia*, in order:

(a) To carry out immediate on-site inspections of Iraq's biological, chemical and missile capabilities;

(b) To take possession for the destruction, removal or rendering harmless of all chemical and biological weapons and all stocks of agents and all related subsystems and components and all research, development, support and manufacturing facilities;

(c) To supervise the destruction by Iraq of all its ballistic missiles with a range greater than 150 kilometres and related major parts, including launchers, and repair and production facilities; and

(d) To assist the Secretary-General in developing a plan for the future ongoing monitoring and verification of Iraq's compliance with its obligation not to use, develop, construct or acquire any of the items listed above.

3. In addition, the Commission has been charged with certain duties and responsibilities, such as transportation, communication and logistic support, information and surveillance. These have been enumerated in detail in Security Council resolutions 707 (1991) and 715 (1991).

4. Following the adoption of Security Council resolution 687 (1991), the Office of Legal Affairs was asked to comment on the status of the Special Commission. It stated that the Commission was to be treated as a subsidiary organ of the Security Council.

5. In practical terms, the Special Commission seeks to implement its mandate without reference to the Security Council on operational issues. This includes the decision as to whether conditions are such as to permit continued operations while ensuring the safety and security of Commission personnel and property. If the Commission is blocked in its efforts to fulfil its mandate, it informs the Council, through the President, of the situation forthwith. Responsibility then lies with the Council and its members, not the Commission, i.e., to decide what action is required to rectify the situation. In short, the Commission is given responsibility for implementation, and the Council preserves for itself enforcement.

6. This principle was confirmed during the March 1992 meetings of the Council addressed by the Deputy Prime Minister of Iraq, Mr. Tariq Aziz. During that meeting, Mr. Aziz sought the Council's intervention in differences between Iraq and the Special Commission on such an operational matter as the destruction of certain equipment designated for destruction by the Commission. The members of the Council reaffirmed that it was for the Special Commission alone to determine which items must be destroyed under paragraph 9 of resolution 687 (1991) (S/23663, S/23699, S/PV.3059 and resumption 1).

Recent events

7. On 7 January 1993, the Office of the Special Commission in Baghdad received a note from the Ministry for Foreign Affairs of Iraq stating that henceforth the Commission would be denied the use of the Habbaniyah airfield and that the Commission should use either Iraqi aircraft to transport its personnel and equipment between Bahrain and Iraq or the land route from Amman, Jordan. This was duly reported orally by the Commission to the Council on 8 January, resulting in the relevant parts of the presidential statement issued that day (S/25081), and subsequently supplemented by a letter to the President of the Security Council (see appendix I). The statement noted that the restrictions placed on the Commission's flights constituted an "unacceptable and material breach" of the relevant provisions of United Nations Security Council resolution 687 (1991) and contained a warning to Iraq about serious consequences that would ensue from failure to comply with its obligations.

8. On 9 January 1993, the Executive Chairman of the Special Commission sent, through the Permanent Mission of Iraq to the United Nations, a letter to the Minister for Foreign Affairs (see appendix II), informing him of the content of the presidential statement and attaching new notifications for Special Commission flights in accordance with the established procedures. A third-person note (see appendix III) containing the same message was delivered to the Ministry for Foreign Affairs in Baghdad the next morning. During the meeting in which the note was delivered, the Iraqi official cited a letter, dated 9 January, from the Minister for Foreign Affairs to the President of the Security Council, linking the decision not to permit Special Commission flights to the Sanctions Committee decision not to permit Iraqi Airways to resume its international operations and restating the options offered to the Commission of using Iraqi aircraft or the land route. The Executive Chairman of the Commission was referred to the same letter in a response from the Permanent Representative of Iraq to the United Nations.

9. This response was reported to the Council on 11 January and resulted in the relevant sections of the presidential statement issued that day in which the Council demanded that Iraq cooperate fully with the Special Commission and warned Iraq of "the serious consequences that will flow from such continued defiance" (S/25091). This statement was responded to formally by the Minister for Foreign Affairs of Iraq on 12 January in a letter to the Secretary-General. In a further letter of 13 January to the President of the Security Council, the Minister for Foreign Affairs again refused to allow flights under the normal procedures, stating that flights would be accepted on a case-by-case basis but that Iraq could bear no responsibility for the safety of the Commission's aircraft. Furthermore, the response did not address the issue of the notifications already with Iraq.

10. On 14 January, the Commission delivered a second note (see appendix IV) to the Iraqi authorities together with new notifications for its flights. The Commission stated its expectation that it would receive ac-

knowledgement in writing in good time for the flights to proceed without delay.

11. As of the morning of 15 January, no response to these notifications had been received. The Executive Chairman therefore informed the Permanent Representative of Iraq to the United Nations, Ambassador Nizar Hamdoon, in a telephone conversation that, unless the Commission received a response before 1600 hours EST that afternoon, he would be obliged to inform the Council that a further flight had been blocked by Iraq's actions. At 1300 hours EST, the Commission received a note from the Ministry of Foreign Affairs which reiterated the fact that Iraq would bear no responsibility for the safety of Commission flights and extended that condition to cover any confusion or error on the Iraqi side. Later that evening the Commission sent to the Permanent Mission of Iraq to the United Nations a further note (see appendix V) containing new flight notifications and demanding that they be acknowledged in accordance with Iraq's obligations. This note was also delivered directly to the Ministry in Baghdad the next morning by the Special Commission Field Office there. The note was accompanied by the Executive Chairman's letter to the President of the Security Council (see appendix VI) informing him that the Iraqi response had constituted a refusal on the part of Iraq of the Commission's notifications because it abdicated Iraq's responsibility for ensuring the security and safety of Commission personnel. The letter to the President also stated that the Commission had made new flight notifications to Iraq with the expectation that those notifications would be acknowledged in accordance with Iraq's obligations.

12. On 16 January, the Commission received a further note from the Ministry of Foreign Affairs. It stated that Iraq would guarantee the safety of the Commission's flights to and from Habbaniyah airfield if they entered Iraqi airspace from Jordanian airspace and requested further notifications from the Commission for new flight paths following that route. The Commission responded in a note (see appendix VII) the same evening, reminding Iraq of its obligations under resolutions 687 (1991), 707 (1991) and 715 (1991), and the exchange of leters of May 1991 between the Secretary-General and the Minister for Foreign Affairs of Iraq, informing Iraq that it could not operate using the longer route specified by Iraq, and explaining that it coordinated routinely with the States patrolling the "no-fly zone" so that the aircraft of those States did not represent a threat to the safety of the Commission's aircraft. The Commission informed the Iraqi authorities of its intention to fly using the direct route between its base of operations in Bahrain and Habbaniyah airfield and demanded that Iraq ensure the security and safety of the Commission's flights.

13. On 17 January, the Commission received another note stating that Iraq would guarantee the safety of the Commission's aircraft if the Commission would guarantee that coalition aircraft did not fly in Iraqi airspace while the Commission's aircraft were in the air. In response the same day, the Commission sent a note (see appendix VIII) stating that it was not in a position to provide the guarantees referred to in the Iraqi note. The reply again stressed that the Commission would coordinate with the States concerned to ensure the conditions for safe flight in the "no-fly zone" and again demanded guarantees from Iraq that it would ensure the security and safety of the flights previously notified to Iraq. The Commission also stated that it would coordinate closely with the Iraqi authorities in this matter.

14. In the evening (EST) of 18 January, Iraq sent a note which merely reiterated the condition for Commission flights set the previous day.

15. At 1300 hours on 19 January, Iraq informed the Commission that, on the basis of the statement of the Revolution Command Council, it would allow the resumption of Commission flights in accordance with established procedure as agreed by the two sides. By telephone, a guarantee was given that Iraq would ensure the safety of the Commission's aircraft.

Commentary

16. It can be seen from the above that this recent crisis concerning the flights of the Special Commission's aircraft was brought about by Iraq's initial refusal on 7 January 1993 to permit the Commission to use its aircraft to transport its personnel and equipment into Iraq. This was a most serious breach of Iraq's obligations under the Council's resolutions 687 (1991), 707 (1991) and 715 (1991), all adopted under Chapter VII of the Charter of the United Nations, and the exchange of letters of May 1991 between the Secretary-General and the Minister for Foreign Affairs of Iraq. It should also be noted that Iraq was required to, and did, acknowledge explicitly in writing its acceptance of the provisions of resolution 687 (1991), establishing the cease-fire and providing the conditions essential for the restoration of peace and security in the region, and the agreement on the facilities, privileges and immunities contained in the exchange of letters (S/22456).

17. Upon learning of Iraq's refusal of the Special Commission's right to fly its aircraft, the Commission reported the matter to the President of the Security Council and, in an informal session of the Council, to the members. Upon the statement by the Council, the Commission immediately sought to resume its operations and hence to allow Iraq to erase its breach by allowing the Commission to exercise its rights without conditions. Iraq, as it did on each subsequent occasion until 19

January 1993, again repeatedly refused to allow the Commission to exercise its rights without condition. At each Iraqi refusal, the Commission immediately informed the President of the Council of the situation and subsequent actions. Each time it also responded to Iraq the same day, offering a way for Iraq to meet its obligations, e.g., by stating that, through the Commission's coordination with the States enforcing the "no-fly zone", the conditions for safe flight would be ensured, provided Iraq did not itself threaten the flights.

Appendix I
Letter dated 8 January 1993 from the Executive Chairman of the Special Commission addressed to the President of the Security Council

I have the honour, in agreement with the Director General of the International Atomic Energy Agency (IAEA), to bring to your attention the following adverse development affecting the work of the Special Commission and IAEA in implementation of their mandates under section C of Security Council resolution 687 (1991) and other relevant Security Council resolutions and decisions.

The Special Commission has received the attached note (No. 10/4/92035) from the Iraqi Ministry of Foreign Affairs concerning its use of aircraft in support of its operations in Iraq. The note suggests that the Special Commission might charter Iraqi aircraft for its transport needs or use the land route. It insists that no aircraft, other than chartered Iraqi aircraft, will henceforth be allowed to use Habbaniyah airfield, which has so far served as the sole point of entry into Iraq for the Commission's fixed-wing aircraft.

This prohibition on the Special Commission's use of its own aircraft in support of its operations in Iraq is a most serious breach of Iraq's obligations under the pertinent decisions of the Security Council, including Security Council resolutions 687 (1991), 707 (1991) and 715 (1991), and of Iraq's obligations under its agreement with the United Nations relating to the facilities, privileges and immunities of the Special Commission and IAEA in Iraq. Specific provisions which would be violated if Iraq persists include:

(a) *The exchange of letters between the Minister for Foreign Affairs of Iraq and the Secretary-General of May 1991.* The exchange provides that the facilities, privileges and immunities of the Special Commission shall include:

"(i) Unrestricted freedom of entry and exit without delay or hindrance of its . . . means of transport;

"(ii) Unrestricted freedom of movement without advance notice within Iraq of . . . its equipment and means of transport;

. . .

"(x) Acceptance of United Nations registration of means of transport on land, sea and in the air and United Nations licensing of the operators thereof".

(b) *United Nations Security Council resolution 707 (1991).* Paragraph 3 "Demands that Iraq

...

"(v) allow the Special Commission, IAEA and their inspection teams to conduct both fixed-wing and helicopter flights throughout Iraq for all relevant purposes including inspection, surveillance, aerial surveys, transportation and logistics without interference of any kind and upon such terms and conditions as may be determined by the Special Commission, and to make full use of their own aircraft and such airfields in Iraq as they may determine are most appropriate for the work of the Commission;

. . .

"(vii) ensure the complete implementation of the privileges, immunities and facilities of the representatives of the Special Commission and IAEA in accordance with its previous undertakings and their complete safety and freedom of movement".

(c) *The plan for ongoing monitoring and verification (S/22871/Rev.1), approved by Security Council resolution 715 (1991).* Paragraph 17 states that "the Special Commission shall have the right:

. . .

"(e) To designate for aerial overflight any area, location, site or facility in Iraq;

"(f) To conduct, at any time and without hindrance, both fixed-wing and rotary-wing flights throughout Iraq for all relevant purposes, including inspection, surveillance, aerial overflights (surveys), transportation and logistics without interference of any kind and upon such terms and conditions as may be determined by the Special Commission;

"(g) To make full use of its own aircraft with appropriate sensors as necessary and such airfields in Iraq as the Special Commission may determine are most appropriate for its work".

Paragraph 18 of the plan stipulates that "Iraq shall:

...

"(b) Accept unconditionally aerial overflight of any area, location, site or facility designated by the Special Commission;

...

"(d) Accept unconditionally and cooperate with the Special Commission in conducting fixed-wing and rotary-wing flights throughout Iraq for all relevant purposes, including inspection, surveillance, aerial overflights (surveys), transportation and logistics without interference of any kind and upon such terms and conditions as may be determined by the Special Commission;

"(e) Accept unconditionally the Special Commission's determinations regarding use of the Commission's aircraft with appropriate sensors as necessary and airfields in Iraq for such aircraft;

"(f) Not obstruct aerial overflights ... ;

"(g) ... ensure the complete implementation of the privileges and immunities of the personnel of the Special Commission and their complete safety and freedom of movement;

"(h) Cooperate fully with the Special Commission and facilitate its inspections, overflights and other activities under the plan;

"(i) Accept unconditionally the rights of the Special Commission under the plan and not take any action to interfere with, impede or obstruct the exercise by the Special Commission of its functions and rights under Security Council resolutions 687 (1991), 707 (1991) and the plan".

Taken together with the other instances of Iraq's failure to meet its obligations under the resolutions and decisions of the Security Council, which have been reported to the Council most recently in the Special Commission's semi-annual report on its operations dated 17 December 1992 and circulated in document S/24984, this latest serious breach could bring the Special Commission's and IAEA's activities in Iraq, including on-site inspections pursuant to Security Council resolution 687 (1991), to a virtual standstill unless Iraq immediately accepts the Special Commission's aircraft landing and taking off from appropriate airfields of the Commission's choice, in particular in the Baghdad area, and complies with all its other obligations under the relevant Security Council resolutions and decisions.

I should be grateful if you could have this letter and its enclosure brought to the attention of the members of the Security Council for appropriate action.

(*Signed*) Rolf EKÉUS
Executive Chairman
Office of the Special Commission

Appendix II
Letter dated 9 January 1993 from the Executive Chairman of the Special Commission addressed to the Minister for Foreign Affairs of Iraq

I learnt with alarm of the note 10/4/1/92035 of 7 January 1993 passed from the Ministry for Foreign Affairs to our Field Office in Baghdad, in which the Ministry for Foreign Affairs informed the Special Commission of the decision of the Government of Iraq that the Commission would no longer be able to use its own aircraft for transport into Iraq.

As the Office of the Special Commission has already informed your Permanent Mission to the United Nations, this matter was brought to the attention of the President of the Security Council in the course of 8 January 1993. The Council then considered the issue and, in formal session, adopted a presidential statement. This statement notes that the actions of the Government of Iraq represent an unacceptable and material breach of its obligations. It demands that the Government of Iraq abide by all its obligations arising from United Nations Security Council resolutions and agreements between the Government of Iraq and the United Nations. It also states that failure to abide by these obligations will have serious consequences.

In these circumstances, I have instructed the Special Commission Field Office in Baghdad to present to the Ministry again the flight plans for the UNSCOM C-160 aircraft flights for the coming days. The Special Commission expects to receive acknowledgement in writing of these flight plans in good time for the flights to proceed without delay. Any delay in the receipt of a positive response will be reported to the Security Council forthwith.

(*Signed*) Rolf EKÉUS
Executive Chairman
Office of the Special Commission

Appendix III
Note verbale dated 9 January 1993 from the Special Commission addressed to the Ministry of Foreign Affairs of Iraq

The Special Commission presents its compliments to the Ministry of Foreign Affairs and has the honour to refer to the Ministry's note 10/4/1/92035 of 7 January 1993 which stated that Iraq would no longer permit the Special Commission to use Habbaniyah airport for its own aircraft.

The Special Commission herewith attaches a copy of the presidential statement adopted yesterday by the Security Council meeting in formal session. This statement notes that the actions of the Government of Iraq represent an unacceptable and material breach of its obligations. It demands that the Government of Iraq abide by all its obligations arising from United Nations Security Council resolutions and agreements between the Government of Iraq and the United Nations. It also states that failure to abide by these obligations will have serious consequences.

In these circumstances, the Special Commission presents again flight plans for the UNSCOM/C-160 aircraft flights for the coming days. The Special Commission expects to receive acknowledgement in writing of these flight plans in good time for the flights to proceed without delay. Any delay in the receipt of a positive response from the Government of Iraq will be reported to the Security Council forthwith.

Appendix IV
Note verbale dated 13 January 1993 from the Special Commission addressed to the Ministry of Foreign Affairs of Iraq

The Special Commission presents its compliments to the Ministry of Foreign Affairs and has the honour to present flight plans for the UNSCOM C-160 aircraft for the coming days. The Special Commission expects to receive acknowledgement in writing of these flight plans in good time for the flights to proceed without delay.

Appendix V
Note verbale dated 15 January 1993 from the Special Commission addressed to the Ministry of Foreign Affairs of Iraq

The Special Commission presents its compliments to the Ministry of Foreign Affairs and has the honour to refer to the letter of 15 January 1993 from the Chairman of the Special Commission to the President of the Security Council, a copy of which is attached (see appendix VI). It has the further honour to present the attached notifications of flight plans for the UNSCOM C-160 aircraft for the coming days. The Special Commission expects to receive, on a most urgent basis so that these flights may proceed without delay, acknowledgement of these notifications and of Iraq's obligations for ensuring the security and safety of United Nations Special Commission personnel as provided pursuant to Security Council resolutions 687 (1991), 707 (1991) and 715 (1991) and the exchange of letters of May 1991 between the United Nations Secretary-General and the Minister for Foreign Affairs of Iraq.

Attachment

The following are notifications of flight plans for UNSCOM aircraft, C-160 Transall, from Bahrain to Habbaniyah airport and return to Bahrain:

Date	ETA	Location	ETD	Remarks
17 January 1993	ORIG	BAHRAIN	0500Z	UN566/7
(Sunday)	0730Z	HAB	0830Z	STOPOVER
	1100Z	BAHRAIN	TERM.	RTB
18 January 1993	ORIG	BAHRAIN	0500Z	UN566/7
(Monday)	0730Z	HAB	0830Z	STOPOVER
	1100Z	BAHRAIN	TERM.	RTB
19 January 1993	ORIG	BAHRAIN	0500Z	UN566/7
(Tuesday)	0730Z	HAB	0830Z	STOPOVER
	1100Z	BAHRAIN	TERM.	RTB
20 January 1993	ORIG	BAHRAIN	0500Z	UN566/7
(Wednesday)	0730Z	HAB	0830Z	STOPOVER
	1100Z	BAHRAIN	TERM.	RTB

N.B. All times are Zulu.

Appendix VI
Letter dated 15 January 1993 from the Special Commission addressed to the President of the Security Council

I have the honour to inform you that the Special Commission has received a response from the Ministry of Foreign Affairs of Iraq concerning the United Nations Special Commission's notification to carry out flights into Habanniyah airfield over the coming days. In its relevant paragraphs, the response which states that "Iraq does not oppose the granting of your request as contained in the aforesaid note. However, Iraq affirms that it is not responsible for the safety of aircraft inside Iraqi airspace in the event, God forbid, of confusion or error, since all weapons in Iraq, even at the popular level, are trained on defending Iraq's skies and its sovereignty given that it has been subjected to a series of well-known hostile operations and that hostile aircraft are continuing to violate Iraq's sovereignty and to penetrate its airspace."

This response constitutes a refusal on the part of Iraq of the Commission's notification because it abdicates Iraq's obligations for ensuring the security and safety of United Nations Special Commission personnel as provided pursuant to Security Council resolutions 687 (1991), 707 (1991) and 715 (1991) and the exchange of letters of May 1991 between the United Nations Secretary-General and the Minister for Foreign Affairs of Iraq.

The Commission is providing immediately to Iraq new notifications for flights in the coming days, with the expectation that these notifications will be acknowledged in accordance with Iraq's above-mentioned obligations.

(Signed) Rolf EKÉUS
Executive Chairman
Office of the Special Commission

Appendix VII
*Note verbale dated 16 January 1993 from the Special
Commission addressed to the Ministry of Foreign
Affairs of Iraq*

The Special Commission has the honour to present its compliments to the Ministry of Foreign Affairs of Iraq and to refer to the letter 1/7/22 of 16 January 1993 from the Permanent Representative of Iraq to the United Nations to the Executive Chairman of the Special Commission and the attached note 10/4/2/92107 from the Ministry for Foreign Affairs of Iraq of the same date concerning the notifications for flights of the Commission's aircraft over the coming days.

Under the provisions of United Nations Security Council resolutions 687 (1991), 707 (1991) and 715 (1991) and the exchange of letters of May 1991 between the Secretary-General and the Minister for Foreign Affairs of Iraq, Iraq is responsible for the security and safety of the Special Commission and its personnel. Furthermore, the Commission has the right to unrestricted freedom of entry and exit without hindrance of its personnel and means of transport. It also has the right to conduct both fixed-wing and helicopter flights throughout Iraq for all relevant purposes without interference of any kind and upon such terms and conditions as may be determined by the Commission, and to make such use of its own aircraft and such airfields in Iraq as it may determine are most appropriate for the work of the Commission.

The restrictions imposed by Iraq on the Special Commission would have as a consequence that the Commission cannot effectively carry out its operations in Iraq. Furthermore, this issue has already been addressed in September 1992 when the "no-fly zone" south of the 32nd parallel was established. On that occasion, the Commission informed the Ministry for Foreign Affairs that it would be impractical to operate using the longer route. That remains the case. The Commission has been using the direct route since September 1992 without incident.

The Special Commission informs the Ministry of Foreign Affairs of Iraq that the Commission requires use of the direct route between Bahrain and Habbaniyah airfield and that the Government of Iraq, in accordance with its obligations, ensure the safety and security of the Commission's aircraft and personnel. The Special Commission will coordinate with the States mentioned in the Ministry's note to ensure that they are aware of the flight plans of the Commission's aircraft and hence that they will not represent a threat to the security and safety of the Commission's aircraft and personnel.

Appendix VIII
*Note verbale dated 17 January 1993 from the Special
Commission addressed to the Ministry of Foreign
Affairs of Iraq*

The Special Commission presents its compliments to the Ministry for Foreign Affairs of Iraq and has the honour to refer to the Ministry's note 10/4/2/92112 of 17 January 1993, concerning the notifications of flight plans for the Commission's aircraft.

Since the Special Commission is not in a position to make guarantees for the actions of States, this cannot be the basis for the conduct of flights. However, the Commission can, and does as a matter of course, coordinate with the authorities of the three States mentioned in the Ministry's note so that the conditions for safe flights are ensured. The Commission will, as usual under the established procedures, coordinate closely with the competent Iraqi authorities on this matter.

Consequently, the Special Commission informs the Ministry of its intention to conduct flights already notified to the Ministry. The Commission expects to receive acknowledgement of the relevant notifications.

Document 152

Security Council resolution concerning UNIKOM

S/RES/806 (1993), 5 February 1993

The Security Council,

Reaffirming its resolution 687 (1991) of 3 April 1991, in particular paragraphs 2 to 5 thereof, and its resolutions 689 (1991) of 9 April 1991 and 773 (1992) of 26 August 1992, and its other resolutions on this matter,

Having considered the report of the Secretary-General of 18 and 19 January 1993, 1/

Noting with approval that work is being completed on the realignment of the demilitarized zone referred to in

1/ *Official Records of the Security Council, Forty-eighth Year, Supplement for January, February and March 1993,* documents S/25123 and Add.1.

paragraph 5 of resolution 687 (1991) to correspond to the international boundary demarcated by the United Nations Iraq-Kuwait Boundary Demarcation Commission,

Deeply concerned at recent actions by Iraq in violation of relevant Security Council resolutions, including the series of border incidents involving the United Nations Iraq-Kuwait Observation Mission,

Recalling the statements made by the President on behalf of the Council on 8 2/ and 11 January 3/ 1993,

Acting under Chapter VII of the Charter of the United Nations,

1. *Underlines once again* its guarantee of the inviolability of the international boundary between the State of Kuwait and the Republic of Iraq and its decision to take as appropriate all necessary measures to that end in accordance with the Charter of the United Nations, as provided for in paragraph 4 of resolution 687 (1991);

2. *Approves* the report of the Secretary-General, and decides to extend the terms of reference of the United Nations Iraq-Kuwait Observation Mission to include the functions contained in paragraph 5 of the report;

3. *Requests* the Secretary-General to plan and execute a phased deployment of the strengthening of the Mission, taking into account the need for economy and other relevant factors and to report to the Council on any step he intends to take following an initial deployment;

4. *Reaffirms* that the question of termination or continuation of the Mission and the modalities of the Mission will continue to be reviewed every six months pursuant to paragraphs 2 and 3 of resolution 689 (1991), the next review to take place in April 1993;

5. *Decides* to remain seized of the matter.

2/ S/25081.
3/ S/25091.

Document 153

Statement by the President of the Security Council concerning the sanctions regime

S/25480, 29 March 1993

The members of the Security Council held informal consultations on 23 and 29 March 1993 pursuant to paragraphs 21 and 28 of Security Council resolution 687 (1991) and paragraph 6 of Security Council resolution 700 (1991).

After hearing all the opinions expressed in the course of the consultations, the President of the Council concluded that there was no agreement that the necessary conditions existed for a modification of the regimes established in paragraph 20 of Security Council resolution 687 (1991), as referred to in paragraph 21 of that resolution; in paragraphs 22, 23, 24 and 25 of Security Council resolution 687 (1991), as referred to in paragraph 28 of resolution 687 (1991); and in paragraph 6 of Security Council resolution 700 (1991).

Document 154

Report of the Secretary-General on UNIKOM for the period from 1 October 1992 to 31 March 1993

S/25514, 2 April 1993

Introduction

1. By paragraph 5 of its resolution 687 (1991) of 3 April 1991, the Security Council established a demilitarized zone (DMZ) along the Iraq-Kuwait border and decided to set up an observer unit with the following tasks: to monitor the Khawr Abd Allah waterway and the DMZ; to deter violations of the boundary through its presence in and surveillance of the DMZ; and to observe any hostile or potentially hostile action mounted from the territory of one State into the other. By its resolution 689 (1991) of 9 April 1991, the Security Council approved the report of the Secretary-General on the implementation of the above provisions (S/22454); noted that the decision to set up the observer unit had been taken in paragraph 5 of resolution 687 (1991) and could be terminated only by a decision of the Council; and decided to review the question of termination or continuation as well as the modalities of the United Nations Iraq-Kuwait Observation Mission (UNIKOM) every six months. The

Security Council last reviewed this matter on 9 October 1992 and concurred with my recommendation (S/24615, para. 27) that UNIKOM be maintained for a further six-month period (S/24649). The purpose of the present report is to provide the Security Council, prior to its forthcoming review, with an overview of UNIKOM's activities during the last six months.

I. *Organization*

2. As of March 1993, the composition of UNIKOM was as follows:

Military observers

Argentina	7
Austria	7
Bangladesh	7
Canada	1
China	15
Denmark	6
Fiji	6
Finland	6
France	15
Ghana	6
Greece	6
Hungary	6
India	6
Indonesia	6
Ireland	6
Italy	6
Kenya	6
Malaysia	6
Nigeria	7
Norway	8
Pakistan	7
Poland	6
Romania	6
Russian Federation	15
Senegal	7
Singapore	7
Sweden	6
Thailand	7
Turkey	6
United Kingdom	15
Uruguay	6
United States of America	14
Venezuela	6
Total	247 a/

Administrative and logistic units

Logistics (Denmark	45
Medical (Norway)	20
Total	65
Total military personnel	312

a/ The authorized strength of the military observers is 300, of whom 53 are on stand-by in their countries.

UNIKOM also has 188 civilian staff, of whom 80 are recruited internationally and 108 locally.

3. Major-General T. K. Dibuama (Ghana) continues as Chief Military Observer.

4. The Government of Canada withdrew its engineer unit at the end of March, and I have accepted Argentina's offer to replace it.

5. The Government of Chile withdrew its helicopter unit at the end of October 1992. It was replaced by a civilian unit, under contract to UNIKOM, which provides three helicopters. UNIKOM also has two small fixed-wing aircraft contributed by the Government of Switzerland at no cost to the Organization and it has the use of a chartered aircraft for the transport of personnel and equipment between Baghdad and Kuwait.

6. During the period under review, the Canadian engineers disposed of 10,000 pieces of ordnance, constructed 3,000 metres of security fencing around UNIKOM headquarters and Camp Khor, constructed two new airstrips and maintained 1,500 kilometres of existing patrol routes. They also assisted the United Nations Iraq-Kuwait Boundary Demarcation Commission by clearing and constructing roads into 106 border pillar points, enabling the surveyors and contractors to work in safe areas, and by assisting with the transportation and the emplacement of the border pillars. In preparation for its arrival, the intended campsite for the reinforcement infantry battalion, approximately 3 square kilometres, was cleared and levelled. Also, durable observation towers were erected at all patrol/observation bases.

7. The Danish logistic unit continued to carry out vehicle maintenance, supply and security tasks, the latter mainly for the headquarters facilities at Umm Qasr and Camp Khor and for the logistic base in Doha.

8. The Norwegian medical unit maintained a sick-bay facility at Umm Qasr, serving the headquarters and the northern sector, and first aid posts at the central and southern sector headquarters. The unit also provided emergency assistance to civilians injured by exploding ordnance.

II. *Strengthening of UNIKOM*

9. Following a series of incidents in January (see paras. 18-24 below), the Security Council, on 5 February 1993, adopted resolution 806 (1993), by which it approved my report of 18 January 1993 (S/25123) and extended UNIKOM's terms of reference to include the capacity to take physical action to prevent or redress:

(a) Small-scale violations of the DMZ;

(b) Violations of the boundary between Iraq and Kuwait, for example by civilians or police; and

(c) Problems that might arise from the presence of Iraqi installations and Iraqi citizens and their assets in the

DMZ on the Kuwaiti side of the newly demarcated boundary.

10. In my report of 18 January I had suggested that in order to carry out these tasks, UNIKOM's unarmed military observers should be replaced by three mechanized infantry battalions with appropriate support elements. In approving my report, the Security Council requested me to execute a phased deployment of the strengthening of UNIKOM, taking into account the need for economy and other relevant factors, and to report to the Council on any step I intend to take following the initial deployment. After consulting with members of the Council, I plan in the first phase to retain the military observers and to reinforce them by one mechanized infantry battalion to be deployed in the northern sector of the DMZ, which includes the towns of Umm Qasr and Safwan. UNIKOM's logistic support elements will be reinforced slightly, that is, the Danish logistic unit will be brought up to 50, the incoming engineer unit will also comprise 50, and the medical unit is to be raised to 35, all ranks.

III. *Concept of operations*

11. The DMZ is about 200 kilometres long, to which must be added the Khawr Abd Allah waterway, with a length of about 40 kilometres. For the most part, the DMZ is barren and almost uninhabited, except for the towns of Umm Qasr and Safwan. There are airfields at Safwan and Umm Qasr and a port at Umm Qasr.

12. The boundaries of the DMZ, which extends 10 kilometres into Iraq and 5 kilometres into Kuwait, have been adjusted to align them with the international border as demarcated by the United Nations Iraq-Kuwait Boundary Demarcation Commission. The boundaries of the DMZ have been marked at 1-kilometre intervals and at major entry points; in addition, a road has been constructed along their entire length. The DMZ is now clearly identifiable on both sides.

13. UNIKOM remained deployed in the DMZ as outlined in previous reports. For operational purposes it has divided the DMZ into three sectors. At the end of February 1993, the sectors were slightly adjusted so that there are now seven patrol/observation bases in the northern sector, six in the central sector, and five in the southern sector. The northern sector has thus been strengthened in response to operational requirements.

14. UNIKOM's concept of operations is based on a combination of patrol/observation bases, observation points, ground and air patrols, investigation teams and liaison with the parties at all levels. UNIKOM employs surveillance aids, which include maritime radar for the Khawr Abd Allah, night vision devices, high-powered binoculars and video cameras. In addition, UNIKOM uses the Global Positioning System for the accurate determination of locations in the terrain.

15. UNIKOM has liaison offices in Baghdad and Kuwait City, and the Chief Military Observer and other senior staff of UNIKOM have maintained regular contacts with the authorities in both capitals. At the local level, liaison continued with the police on both sides, particularly with regard to civilian activity in the DMZ. These contacts have been useful in dealing with complaints and facilitating UNIKOM's operations.

IV. *Situation in the DMZ*

16. During the first part of the reporting period, the situation in the DMZ was generally calm. However, considerable tension arose at the beginning of the year as a result of Iraqi activities at Umm Qasr.

17. In the summer of 1991, the Iraqi authorities had begun to retrieve equipment and other items from the former Iraqi naval base at Umm Qasr under arrangements made by UNIKOM in consultation with the Iraqi and Kuwaiti authorities, since the naval base is within 1,000 metres of the boundary line then shown on UNIKOM's map. UNIKOM monitored this activity and, in cooperation with the United Nations Coordinator for the Return of Property from Iraq to Kuwait, satisfied itself about the ownership of the items involved. Towards the end of last year, as the work of the United Nations Iraq-Kuwait Boundary Demarcation Commission progressed, it became known that the newly demarcated boundary placed the naval base on Kuwaiti territory. Although the demarcation had not yet been completed formally, UNIKOM alerted the Iraqi authorities on 24 December 1992 that the retrieval of items on the Kuwaiti side of the newly demarcated boundary would have to come to an end and requested that all such activity cease by 15 January 1993. The Iraqi authorities accepted this deadline. UNIKOM kept the Kuwaiti authorities informed of these exchanges.

18. On 2 January 1993, some 250 Iraqis entered the former naval base at Umm Qasr to retrieve Iraqi property, including prefabricated buildings, fences, street lamps and other items. The Iraqi personnel came with various military vehicles and about half of them wore military uniforms. This was a serious violation of the DMZ, which was immediately and vigorously protested.

19. Iraqi personnel, in civilian clothes and without military vehicles, continued to retrieve property from the former naval base during the first days of January. On 8 January, the President of the Security Council wrote the Secretary-General that the Council's members considered that the removal of the Iraqi property and assets from Kuwaiti territory should be undertaken only after prior clearance by UNIKOM and by the Kuwaiti authorities through UNIKOM and should be completed by 15 Janu-

ary 1993. In the same letter, the President of the Security Council expressed the concern of the members of the Council at the continued presence of six Iraqi police posts on Kuwaiti territory and the members' insistence on those posts' speedy removal, by 15 January at the latest (S/25085, annex I). The Iraqi authorities were informed of this letter both at United Nations Headquarters and in the field.

20. Further, on 8 January, the Iraqi authorities informed UNIKOM, and separately the United Nations Special Commission, that the United Nations would no longer be permitted to use its own aircraft in Iraq. On 8 January, the President of the Security Council made a statement on behalf of the Council, demanding that the Government of Iraq abide by its obligations under all relevant Security Council resolutions and cooperate with the United Nations bodies and, in particular, not interfere with United Nations flights (S/25081).

21. In the morning of 10 January, some 200 Iraqi personnel with trucks and heavy loading equipment forced entry into six ammunition bunkers located in the former naval base, on Kuwaiti territory, and took away most of their contents, which the Security Council had previously ordered destroyed (S/25085, annex III). I described these and related developments in my special report of 10 January 1993 (S/25085). On 11 January, the President of the Security Council made a statement on behalf of the Council (S/25091).

22. Iraqi retrieval of property from Kuwaiti territory ended on 13 January and on 17/18 January the six Iraqi police posts located on Kuwaiti territory were withdrawn (S/25085/Add.1). Since then, the situation in the area has again been generally calm.

23. Apart from the events described above, UNIKOM observed three types of violations of the DMZ: minor incursions by military personnel on the ground, often inadvertently; overflights by military aircraft, most of which were unidentified; and violations involving the carrying and firing of weapons other than sidearms, the majority of which were committed by policemen. The following table summarizes the violations observed by UNIKOM:

	Iraq				Kuwait			
	Ground	Air	Weapon	Total	Ground	Air	Weapon	Total
1-31 Oct.	1	0	2	3	1	0	2	3
1-30 Nov.	1	0	0	1	0	1	0	1
1-31 Dec.	0	0	1	1	1	1	7	9
1-31 Jan.	2	0	2	4	0	0	14	14
1-28 Feb.	0	0	1	1	0	0	4	4
1-31 Mar.	0	1	0	1	0	0	4	4
Total	4	1	6	11	2	2	31	35

	Member States cooperating with Kuwait				Unidentified			
	Ground	Air	Weapon	Total	Ground	Air	Weapon	Total
1-31 Oct.	0	1	1	1	1	8	0	9
1-30 Nov.	0	5	0	5	1	5	0	6
1-31 Dec.	0	0	0	0	0	3	1	4
1-31 Jan.	1	0	0	1	0	8	0	8
1-28 Feb.	0	0	0	0	0	0	0	0
1-31 Mar.	0	0	0	0	0	2	0	2
Total	1	6	0	7	2	26	1	29

UNIKOM raised these violations with the party concerned, with a view to having action taken to prevent a recurrence.

24. During the reporting period, UNIKOM received 27 written complaints from Iraq and 46 from Kuwait. UNIKOM investigated each complaint and conveyed its findings to the parties concerned. Many of the complaints concerned alleged firing at police posts close to the border. UNIKOM's investigation teams have repeatedly seen at these posts rifles and machine-guns, which are prohibited in the DMZ. Increasingly, the police on both sides have denied UNIKOM access to their posts, apparently to prevent them from noticing these weapons.

25. As will be recalled, UNIKOM, with the agreement of both parties, has established 1,000 metres as a reasonable distance to be maintained from the border. UNIKOM requires that it be informed in advance and monitors closely activities within the 1,000-metre zone in order to prevent incidents. The persistent complaints about firing from police posts underline the continuing

validity of this rule. At present, 13 Iraqi facilities of various kinds (customs posts, police posts and control points) and two Kuwaiti police posts are closer to the border than 1,000 metres. Seven of the Iraqi posts are in the towns of Safwan and Umm Qasr, which extend right up to the border and where a presence is required for the maintenance of law and order and to control border crossings. Major-General Dibuama, on my instructions, is in touch with the authorities concerned, with a view to reducing the presence in the 1,000-metre zone to the minimum necessary to perform these functions.

26. Most of the complaints pertain to areas where, as a result of the boundary demarcation, Iraqi citizens and assets have been found to be on the Kuwaiti side of the boundary, including the oil well heads at Ratqah, the farms in the Safwan area, and some assets at Umm Qasr. I am in touch with the Governments of Iraq and Kuwait with a view to having these issues settled in a reasonable way. In the meantime, UNIKOM patrols these sensitive areas by day and by night.

27. During the first part of the reporting period, as an expression of discontent with the impending border demarcation, there was some local agitation and harassment of UNIKOM staff at Umm Qasr. People threw rocks and other objects at passing UNIKOM vehicles, attempted to impede UNIKOM vehicles, inquired after certain nationalities, and refused to sell produce to UNIKOM personnel. These incidents have ceased.

28. UNIKOM continued to provide technical support to other United Nations missions in Iraq and Kuwait. In particular, it assisted the United Nations Iraq-Kuwait Boundary Demarcation Commission with air and ground transport, accommodation, communications and engineer support. Support in the form of accommodation and escorts was also provided to the United Nations Coordinator for the Return of Property from Iraq to Kuwait. UNIKOM continued to provide movement control in respect of all United Nations aircraft operating in the area.

V. *Financial aspects*

29. By its resolution 47/208 of 22 December 1992, the General Assembly authorized the Secretary-General to enter into commitments for the operation of UNIKOM, subject to the review by the Security Council of the mandate of the Mission in respect of the period beyond 8 April 1993, at a rate not to exceed $3.3 million gross ($3.1 million net) per month for the period from 1 May to 31 October 1993. This authorization is subject to the prior concurrence of the Advisory Committee on Administrative and Budgetary Questions.

30. Present indications are that the cost of maintaining UNIKOM during the extension period, including the strengthening of the Mission, may exceed the level of commitment authorized by the Assembly in its resolution 47/208. In such event, the Secretary-General will report to the Advisory Committee and the General Assembly on the additional requirements needed for the maintenance of the Mission.

VI. *Observations*

31. During the last six months, UNIKOM's area of operations has, for the most part, been calm. In January, however, Iraqi actions created a serious situation. UNIKOM reacted promptly to these actions and made strong representations to the Iraqi military authorities. Based on UNIKOM's reports, such representations were also made at United Nations Headquarters in New York. The Security Council was directly involved in these efforts. It is regrettable that Iraq did not respond positively to those *démarches* until Member States had credibly threatened, and then used, force.

32. The events of January have demonstrated the value of the United Nations presence on the border between Iraq and Kuwait as well as the need that it continue. I therefore recommend to the Security Council that it maintain UNIKOM for a further six-month period.

33. I have outlined in paragraph 10 above my plans for the strengthening of UNIKOM in accordance with Security Council resolution 806 (1993). I regret that I cannot report more progress in this matter. However, owing apparently to the increase in commitments to United Nations peace-keeping operations in general, it has not been possible so far to identify a Member State which is in a position to provide the mechanized infantry battalion to be deployed in the first phase. I hope to be able to revert to the Council on this matter in the near future.

34. UNIKOM will continue to depend on the cooperation of the Governments of Iraq and Kuwait in order to carry out the tasks entrusted to it by the Security Council. In this connection, it will be of particular importance in the coming months that both sides exercise the necessary measure of restraint in order to prevent friction along the border so that outstanding issues such as those referred to in paragraph 26 above may be resolved reasonably.

35. In conclusion, I wish to pay a tribute to the Chief Military Observer and to the men and women under his command for the manner in which they have carried out their difficult task. Their discipline and bearing have been of a high order, reflecting credit on themselves, on their countries and on the United Nations.

Document 155

Third report of the Secretary-General on the status of the implementation of the plan for the ongoing monitoring and verification of Iraq's compliance with relevant parts of section C of Security Council resolution 687 (1991)

S/25620, 19 April 1993

Introduction

1. The present report is the third submitted pursuant to paragraph 8 of Security Council resolution 715 (1991), adopted on 11 October 1991, by which the Council requested the Secretary-General to submit a report to the Council every six months on the implementation of the Special Commission's plans for the ongoing monitoring and verification of Iraq's compliance with relevant parts of section C of Security Council resolution 687 (1991). It updates the information contained in the first two reports (S/23801 and S/24661).

2. In brief, in the period under review, Iraq has continued its refusal to provide unconditional acknowledgement of its obligations under resolution 715 (1991) and the plans approved thereunder. It has further underlined its position that the only obligation it recognizes in respect to ongoing monitoring and verification is that contained in paragraph 10 of resolution 687 (1991) and that it does not accept the modalities and arrangements for such monitoring and verification as laid down in the plans approved by the Council in resolution 715 (1991). In these circumstances, no progress has been made in carrying out the ongoing monitoring and verification approved by the Council in resolution 715 (1991).

I. Developments during the period 11 October 1992-10 April 1993

A. Provision of information

3. Under the Special Commission's ongoing monitoring and verification plan (S/22871/Rev.1), Iraq is obliged to provide certain declarations. The first were due by 10 November 1991, concerning (a) initial information on the dual-purpose activities, facilities and items specified in the plan and its annexes; and (b) a report on the legislative and administrative measures taken to implement resolutions 687 (1991) and 707 (1991), other relevant Security Council resolutions and the plan. Iraq is further obliged to update the information on (a) each 15 January and 15 July, and to report further on (b) when requested to do so by the Commission.

4. As was noted in the last report (S/24661), no declarations were received from Iraq until 27 June 1992, i.e., Iraq missed the first two reporting requirements. The product received on 27 June was called by Iraq "Report on future compliance and monitoring". However, a group of international experts convened by the Commission to assess this report deemed it, while providing a basis on which to build, to be inadequate for the purpose of commencing ongoing monitoring and verification activities. Furthermore, the report contained no declaration on the legislative and administrative measures taken by Iraq to give effect to its obligations.

5. On 14 February 1993, Iraq provided a second set of declarations entitled "Updated monitoring information. Report No. 2". These add little to the first set.

6. A further difficulty relates to the inadequacy of a different set of declarations Iraq is obliged to provide—the full, final and complete disclosure of all aspects of its weapons programmes proscribed under section C of resolution 687 (1991), as required under resolution 707 (1991). In particular, complete information on Iraq's past production, suppliers and use of prohibited items and its past capacity to produce such items is necessary in order to plan effective inspection and import control regimes as required under the future ongoing monitoring and verification plans and Security Council resolution 715 (1991). The mechanism foreseen in paragraph 7 of that resolution can only be realistically designed when this information is available to the Sanctions Committee, the Special Commission and the International Atomic Energy Agency (IAEA).

B. Operational developments

7. Due to Iraq's continued refusal to provide unconditional acknowledgement of its obligations under resolution 715 (1991) and the plans for ongoing monitoring and verification approved thereunder, the Special Commission continues to be unable to begin implementation of the plan covering its areas of competence (S/22871/Rev.1). However, the Commission has identified certain facilities and activities in Iraq which clearly need to be monitored in the interim because they could already be put to prohibited use. Consequently, the Commission has instituted a new type of inspection activity, termed "interim monitoring". The introduction of this activity in no way diminishes the requirement to institute

full-scale monitoring as envisaged in the plans and hence does not diminish the importance of Iraq acknowledging unconditionally its obligations under them.

8. The first interim monitoring team was established on 26 January 1993, based at the Ibn Al-Haytham missile research centre to the north of Baghdad. Iraq has declared this centre to be its principal facility for research into and development of missiles with a range of less than 150 kilometres, that is, those not banned under the terms of resolution 687 (1991). The centre employs a significant number of scientists previously employed in Iraq's now proscribed ballistic missile programmes. While its work centred around the Ibn Al-Haytham facility, the team also visited other sites. It completed its work on 23 March 1993.

9. Based on the experience of the team at Ibn Al-Haytham, which in part highlighted the significant amount of ongoing activity in Iraq on solid propellant missile systems, the Commission decided it would be useful to continue this inspection effort. A second team was established on 27 March 1993. While it will continue the task of monitoring the Ibn Al-Haytham centre, other facilities in Iraq conducting work on solid propulsion and related technologies will also be monitored.

C. Political developments

10. On the substance of the plans for ongoing monitoring and verification, Iraq's position remains unchanged. By a letter dated 28 October 1992 from the Iraqi Foreign Minister addressed to the Secretary-General (S/24726, annex), Iraq reiterated its opposition to resolutions 707 (1991) and 715 (1991) by stating that:

"It is ... essential for the Council to conduct a radical review, on the basis of justice and fairness, of the terms and provisions of these two resolutions."

11. In his statements to the Council on 23 November (S/PV.3139, resumption 1) and 24 November 1992 (S/PV.3139, resumption 2), the Deputy Prime Minister of Iraq, Mr. Tariq Aziz, said:

"[T]here is a need for all those measures and the provisions of the no longer necessary Security Council's resolutions to be drastically reviewed." (ibid., resumption 1, p. 98)

12. On 31 January 1993, the Iraqi Government officially informed the Executive Chairman of the Special Commission in writing that Iraq considered the new arrangement of interim monitoring at the Ibn Al-Haytham facility to be conducted under resolution 687 (1991). The Commission understood this to mean that Iraq would prevent this team, or any other team, from

operating under the terms of the plan approved under resolution 715 (1991).

13. As recently as 29 March 1993, during discussions on the modalities for the second interim monitoring team, Commission personnel detected no change on the part of Iraq on the fundamental issues of acknowledgement of resolution 715 (1991) and on the provision of data on suppliers. This was borne out on 1 April 1993, when General Amer met the team. Reading from prepared notes and stressing that this was the official Iraqi position on the issue of monitoring, General Amer is reported by the United Nations Chief Inspector to have said:

"Iraq accepted the first monitoring team to the Ibn Al-Haytham centre in accordance with resolution 687 (1991). However, it appears from the modalities of the monitoring team that the Special Commission is trying to overlap in a discreet fashion Iraqi obligations under resolution 687 (1991) and resolution 715 (1991). This is very clever. Iraq knows that, using Iraqi cooperation under resolution 687 (1991), the Special Commission wants to assert Iraqi obligations under resolution 715 (1991). Iraq is fully aware of this effort. If the objective of the Special Commission is to make sure that no prohibited activities are going on, prohibited items are destroyed and Iraq has no capability to reactivate proscribed programmes, Iraq has no objections as this is part of resolution 687 (1991). However, if the objective is to start a de facto implementation of resolution 715 (1991) without Special Commission testament to the Security Council that Iraq is in full compliance with resolution 687 (1991) and without implementing paragraph 22 of that resolution, Iraq will not welcome this mission. The monitoring missions would not be welcome. But even in this case, Iraq will still cooperate with the Special Commission to see the true objectives of these missions and to explore the intentions of the Special Commission. Iraq told the Special Commission that resolution 715 (1991) could only be discussed in connection with the implementation of paragraph 22 of resolution 687 (1991). You should never think or believe that it could be done otherwise."

14. Iraq's position is maintained despite assurances by the Commission that, if Iraq cooperated, its legitimate concerns would be met and the Commission's activities would be carried out in a manner which is not unduly intrusive.

D. Iraqi conduct

15. In addition to these statements of position, Iraq has, through its conduct over recent months, consistently

demonstrated its desire to limit the Commission's inspection rights and operational capabilities through seeking to place restrictions on inspectors in the course of their work. While many of these Iraqi actions have taken place during the course of inspections under resolution 687 (1991), the Commission has no doubt that they form part of a long-term campaign to establish a practice for the conduct of inspections which would severely restrict the rights provided in the plans and relevant Security Council resolutions. Iraq is thus clearly seeking to assert for itself the right to interpret how the resolutions should be implemented.

16. Included in this campaign have been attempts by Iraq: to restrict the scope of inspections and information gathering; to restrict access and impose delays on inspections; to restrict the exercise of the Commission's aerial rights; to impose limits on the duration, size and composition of inspections; to require advance notice of inspection activities; and to limit the right to take photography. Further details on these incidents can be found in the annex to the present report. Each incident has varied in seriousness. Some might not be significant were they not part of a general trend. However, when taken together, these incidents add up to a major impediment which would effectively impede credible long-term monitoring and verification. This again underlines the need to obtain from Iraq as soon as possible its formal acknowledgement of its obligations under resolution 715 (1991), so that the Council's requirements laid down in that resolution can be met.

II. Conclusions

17. The conditions for the initiation in full of the Special Commission's plan for ongoing monitoring and verification have still not been met. There has again been no movement in Iraq's underlying negative position on the plan and resolution 715 (1991). The Commission's assessment remains that Iraq is seeking to ensure that implementation of the plan proceeds on the basis of its interpretation of its obligations, rather than on the basis of Security Council resolutions and the plan adopted by the Council.

18. Iraq's spurious complaints and allegations about the motives and activities of the Commission, some of which are recorded in the annex, demonstrate Iraq's unwillingness both to comply with its obligations and to facilitate the task of the Commission. Iraq's reluctance to provide willingly the information required by the Commission in order for it to fulfil its mandate means that the Commission has to be more extensive and intrusive in its efforts to obtain that information. This reluctance and Iraq's attempts to limit the Commission's endeavours raise doubts about Iraq's intent. This, in turn, raises the degree of certainty that the Commission requires about Iraq's capabilities and about the use to which it puts its dual-capable facilities before the Commission can report with confidence that Iraq is in substantial compliance with its obligations arising from the relevant resolutions of the Security Council.

19. In the meantime, the Commission continues to revisit or survey from the air sites identified as having been used for activities proscribed by section C of resolution 687 (1991) in order to ensure that those activities have not been resumed. The Commission has already identified many additional sites which will require future monitoring. It continues to seek to supplement the information provided by Iraq through vigorous questioning and inspection, so that the initiation of full-scale monitoring will not be unduly delayed once Iraq makes the necessary political commitment to full compliance. A key element of this process has been the recent initiation of the interim monitoring concept.

20. Nevertheless, the Commission remains constrained from going beyond preparatory and interim work into full-scale monitoring and verification. Iraq's stance on the fundamental issues, its conduct referred to above and its failure to acknowledge its obligations under resolution 715 (1991) only underscore this conclusion. Unless Iraq changes its position, the Commission will not be in a position to ensure that Iraq does not reactivate its proscribed programmes.

Annex
Compendium of incidents

Restrictions on the scope of inspections

1. Paragraphs 13 to 15 of the present report note the Iraqi reaction to the initiation of interim monitoring. During the course of activity of the first interim monitoring team, several other discussions occurred that indicated a misconception, deliberate or otherwise, on the part of Iraq. The Iraqi counterparts questioned the right of the team to make an inventory of or to tag certain items of equipment at the sites monitored, requesting that specific criteria be established and be used to decide which items might be so treated. The team did not accept this position. Iraq indicated that certain items were of no concern to the Special Commission, when clearly the decision as to what is of concern to it lies with the Commission. Furthermore, some of the items involved have the potential to be used for proscribed purposes. The counterparts also complained about the purpose of the team, stating that it was to control, not monitor, Iraq's activities.

2. On four occasions, Iraq has sought to deny the Commission's basic aerial rights—once in relation to entry of transport aircraft into and out of Iraq (see S/25172, annex), and thrice in relation to overflight of sites for aerial surveillance by helicopter. Except for the flight over the two sites on the outskirts of Baghdad (reported in S/24985, annex), the Commission was eventually able to conduct the flights. However, as already reported to the Council, one of these flights had to be conducted with a restricted flight pattern, and not before Iraq had threatened to shoot the helicopter down if it did not leave the vicinity of the site.

3. Iraq has also hindered access for inspection teams, sometimes seeking, on spurious grounds, completely to deny access. One team was initially denied access because inspection would "breach the sanctity of universities and would upset the students". In each instance, the inspection eventually took place. In the period under review, a total of eight Commission inspection activities were seriously delayed, in one case by over four hours. One, the aerial surveillance on the outskirts of Baghdad, has been blocked.

Restrictions on aerial rights

4. Paragraphs 11 (f) and (h) of the six-monthly report of 17 December 1992 (S/24984, annex) described at length the problems faced until that date by the Special Commission. Problems have continued since. In addition to the incidents referred to in paragraph 2 of the present annex, Iraq has created further difficulties in relation to the Commission's aerial rights.

5. In his letter of 5 August 1992, Mr. Al-Zahawi, Adviser in the Iraqi Ministry for Foreign Affairs, informed the Executive Chairman of the Special Commission that his request to use the Al-Rasheed airfield as the point of entry and departure for inspection teams was unworkable, as the airfield was unserviceable. The Deputy Executive Chairman replied the next day, expressing the desire to so use Al-Rasheed airfield as soon as it became operational. Recently, Sudanese Airways Boeing 707 aircraft have been observed using the airfield. However, inquiries by Commission personnel about the possibility of using it as the point of entry and exit have met with the response that such a decision would be political. No progress has been made on this issue.

6. Iraq has created problems in the operation of the Aerial Inspection Team. It has sought: to establish "no go" areas over which the team may not fly and which may not be included in the boxes designated the night before aerial inspections; to prevent the team from taking photographs and using binoculars while flying between designated sites and even over the designated site; and to demand 10 minutes' notice before an aerial inspection starts.

7. Each time the Commission's high-altitude U-2 surveillance aircraft flies, Iraq lodges a formal complaint about its activities. Iraq persists in calling the aircraft a United States spy plane and has recently described it as being used for "despicable criminal purposes", despite its United Nations registration and mandate. On 10 March 1993, the Minister for Foreign Affairs of Iraq, Mr. Al-Sahaf, addressed a letter to the Secretary-General (S/25387, annex), in which he alleged that the aircraft had been used to assist in the planning of an Israeli operation to assassinate President Saddam Hussein.

Limits on the duration, size and composition of inspections

8. Iraq has sought to limit the duration of both monitoring and aerial surveillance activities, indicating, in relation to the former, that they should be of finite duration and, in relation to the latter, that aerial inspections should not last longer than 15 minutes.

9. Iraq has also sought to limit the size of inspection teams at certain sites it deems sensitive, such as universities, and to interfere in the composition of the team by, for example, seeking to exclude the Commission's own interpreters from a team. It has also sought to establish that those involved in the chemical destruction Group at Al Muthanna are not permitted to take part in other inspection activities and to limit the turnover of Commission personnel in the helicopter support staff.

10. It is clear from the Status Agreement of May 1991 that the Commission has the right to decide the expertise it needs to conduct inspections and hence the right to choose the number and the types of experts it needs on each team and to inspect each site. Iraq is obliged to allow personnel named by the Commission access to conduct their tasks.

Advance notice of inspection activities

11. For aerial surveillance activities, Iraq has sought to establish that it should receive advance notice of the site to be surveyed. No-notice inspections are essential to the effectiveness of the Commission.

Provision of data

12. As noted in section A of the present report, Iraq has failed to provide adequate declarations either of its past proscribed programmes or of its dual-capable facilities which would need to be incorporated into the plans for ongoing monitoring and verification. The Commission has sought to supplement those declarations during each of its inspections. However, Iraq refuses to offer

information willingly, or at all, in certain key areas, e.g., on its supplier networks or its previous use of chemical weapons. Consternation has also been expressed by Iraqi counterparts that the Commission continues to ask questions about Iraq's past programmes, despite the fact that these questions were asked because of Iraq's failure to fulfil its obligation to make full, final and complete disclosures on all aspects of its past programmes (see para. 6 of the present report).

13. Furthermore, Iraq has been unable or unwilling to produce specific items of equipment that the Commission has evidence were supplied to Iraq. Teams continue to find equipment and documents containing information pertinent to their mandate under the resolutions and ongoing monitoring and verification plan.

Photography

14. Iraq has sought to limit the Commission's unrestricted right to photograph any item or activity it deems of relevance to its task. Iraq has delayed photography until "permission" has been obtained from more senior officials; it has sought to prevent photography over a designated site; and it has sought to limit aerial photography to items within a set perimeter and inspection team photography to items Iraq deems to be related to resolution 687 (1991). If this last rule were applied, it would open the possibility of Iraq deciding what was "687-related" and could be used by Iraq to exclude all dual-purpose facilities, items and activities covered by the plans approved under resolution 715 (1991).

Security

15. The issue of security was dealt with at length in document S/24984, appendix II. Since that report and in addition to the threats to the Commission's aircraft referred to above, there have been continued incidents of vandalism of Commission vehicles, including the smashing of windscreens, windows and mirrors and the breaking of aerials. Four of these incidents occurred while the vehicles were being driven by Commission personnel. In one incident, the drivers were medics and the vehicle bore Red Crescent markings.

16. Items continue to be taken from the offices and personal quarters of the Commission. Staff continue sporadically to receive threatening and harassing telephone calls in their hotel rooms in the middle of the night.

Document 156

Third six-month report of the Director General of the IAEA on the implementation of the Agency's plan for the future ongoing monitoring and verification of Iraq's compliance with paragraph 12 of Security Council resolution 687 (1991)

S/25621, 19 April 1993

Note by the Secretary-General

The Secretary-General has the honour to transmit to the members of the Security Council the attached communication which he has received from the Director General of the International Atomic Energy Agency (IAEA).

Annex
Letter dated 8 April 1993 from the Director General of the International Atomic Energy Agency addressed to the Secretary-General

Paragraph 8 of resolution 715 (1991), adopted by the Security Council on 11 October 1991, requests the Director General of the International Atomic Energy Agency to submit to the Security Council reports on the implementation of the Agency's plan for future ongoing monitoring and verification of Iraq's compliance with paragraph 12 of resolution 687 (1991). These reports are to be submitted when requested by the Security Council and, in any event, at least every six months after the adoption of resolution 715. The first two reports were submitted to you on 11 April and 30 September 1992, and distributed to the Security Council as S/23813 (15 April 1992) and S/24722 (28 October 1992), respectively.

Accordingly, I am requesting you to kindly transmit to the President of the Security Council the enclosed third six-month report on the implementation of the Plan and remain available for any consultations you or the Council may wish to have.

(*Signed*) Hans BLIX

Third report of the Director General of the International Atomic Energy Agency on the implementation of the Agency's Plan for future ongoing monitoring and verification of Iraq's compliance with paragraph 12 of resolution 687 (1991)

1. On 11 October 1991, the Security Council adopted resolution 715 (1991) approving, *inter alia*, the Plan submitted in document S/22872/Rev.1/Corr.1 by the Director General of the International Atomic Energy Agency for future ongoing monitoring and verification of Iraq's compliance with paragraph 12 of part C of Security Council resolution 687 (1991) and with the requirements of paragraphs 3 and 5 of resolution 707 (1991). In paragraph 8 of resolution 715, the Security Council requested the Director General of the IAEA to submit to it reports on the implementation of the Plan when requested by the Security Council and, in any event, at least every six months after the adoption of resolution 715. The first two reports submitted by the Director General were circulated on 15 April 1992, as S/23813 and 28 October 1992, as S/24722, respectively.

2. The Director General hereby submits the third six-month report on implementation of the Plan for future ongoing monitoring and verification related to Iraq's nuclear capabilities (hereinafter referred to as the Plan).

3. Since the last report of 28 October 1992, the IAEA has carried out four inspection missions in Iraq, the Fifteenth (8-18 November 1992), Sixteenth (5-8 December 1992), Seventeenth (25-31 January 1993) and Eighteenth (3-11 March 1993) Inspections. The Nineteenth Inspection mission is currently scheduled to take place at the end of April 1993.

Declaration of items subject to the Plan

4. In accordance with paragraph 22 of the Plan, Iraq is obliged to declare to the IAEA items subject to the Plan and to provide, *inter alia*, an inventory of all material, equipment and other items in Iraq identified in annex 3 of the Plan. The items in the annex include those specifically prohibited under resolution 687, as well as others which may be prohibited depending on their use or intended use, or subject to monitoring under the Plan. As previously reported to the Security Council, the Iraq authorities' original declaration was inadequate in scope and in form.

5. During the Fifteenth Inspection, the Iraq counterpart provided the IAEA inspection team with a draft of a revised declaration (10 November 1992). The IAEA team provided detailed comments on the inadequacies which remained. Specifically, the Iraqi counterpart was advised as follows:

(a) Iraq is to include in the inventory any relevant items which were present on or after 1 January 1989, even if such items had been destroyed during or after the war.

(b) The declaration should be self-contained in the sense that it should not include vague references to previous correspondence.

(c) Items required to be declared under paragraph 4 of annex 3 (equipment or materials referred to in section 2 of Memorandum B of INFCIRC/209/Rev.1 and in the annex to INFCIRC/209/Rev.1) should be declared separately under paragraph 4, rather than incorporated within paragraphs 5-70 of annex 3. It was explained to the Iraqi counterpart that there are many INFCIRC/209/Rev.1 items which have no corresponding entry in the other paragraphs of the annex and which were therefore missing entirely in the most recent Iraqi draft update of its declaration. Furthermore, because INFCIRC/209/Rev.1 is quite detailed in its description of various, especially designed or prepared components and equipment, reference to it will produce a more specific and useful accounting of centrifuge components, for example, than that which appeared in the Iraqi draft.

(d) The Iraqi counterpart was also advised of specific questions concerning possible omissions or errors in Iraq's draft declaration of 10 November 1992.

(e) The declaration should be comprehensive, including all relevant items in Iraq, not just those belonging to the Iraqi Atomic Energy Commission.

(f) Machine tools should be included in the declaration if the manufacturers' specifications correspond to the specifications set out in annex 3, or if modifications were made in Iraq to meet these specifications. Only the Agency may determine whether the present condition of specific machine tools warrants removal of such machine tools from the inventory.

6. A commitment was made by the Iraqi authorities to submit an amended declaration which would cover the country as a whole, by the end of 1992. At the end of the Seventeenth Inspection, the Iraqi authorities provided the IAEA team a revised list of annex 3 items which the Iraqis described as covering the period from 1 January 1989 and including all annex 3 items which exist or existed in IAEC facilities, universities and State Establishments which supported the IAEC programme. However, the Iraqi counterparts reserved the right to include items which might have been omitted from the list, either through oversight or because they were not thought to be covered by annex 3, in the next update, which is to be submitted in July 1993.

7. Review of the Iraqi list revealed that the Iraqi authorities had not conformed with the condition identified in 5(e) and 5(f) above. For example, a large number of machine tools inventoried by the Agency in the course

of inspections had not been included in the list. During the Eighteenth Inspection mission, 242 additional machine tools were found, a large number of which, in the opinion of the IAEA team, should have been included in the declaration of Iraq under annex 3. The machine tools have been identified and their present conditions are being evaluated to determine which items may fall outside the specifications set out in annex 3.

Radiometric hydrologic survey

8. The first sampling of Iraq waterways, begun during the Fourteenth Inspection (31 August - 7 September 1992), was concluded during the Fifteenth Inspection (8-18 November 1992). 52 sites throughout Iraq were sampled. The objective of the survey of surface waters are detection and characterization: the detection of undeclared nuclear facilities, and the establishment of a baseline for the longer-term monitoring programme.

9. As of the time of this report, final conclusions and recommendations await evaluation of the sample analysis data. However, the current planning for the long-term monitoring regime contemplates ongoing hydrologic sampling at key monitoring sites with spot checks at other locations. In terms of logistics, sampling locations in the Kurdish area north and north-east of Mosul gave rise to some difficulties which could require reconsideration of such locations for the purposes of sample taking.

Periodic inspection activities

10. A number of short-notice and no-notice inspections were carried out in the last six-month period. In the course of one such inspection during the Sixteenth Inspection, which took place at the Military Industrial Commission (MIC) complex (the former PC-3 Headquarters), a series of events involving failure by Iraq to ensure immediate and unrestricted access to all records which the IAEA and the Special Commission wish to inspect and interference with the right of the IAEA and the Commission to copy records, data and information, took place. These actions amounted to violations by Iraq of the rights of the IAEA and the Special Commission under the Security Council resolutions, the plans approved thereunder, and the Status Arrangements of 14 May 1991. The details of these violations were reported to the Security Council in document S/25013 (24 December 1992). Letters from the Director General of the IAEA and from the Executive Chairman of the Special Commission protesting these violations were sent to the Iraqi authorities.

11. During the Eighteenth IAEA Inspection, a visit was made for the first time to the Saddam University in Baghdad, without prior notice. The Iraqi side initially attempted to seriously restrict the access of the inspection team, but subsequently modified its position. The inspection was conducted by six of the IAEA inspectors, subject to the condition that the seven remaining members of the IAEA team could join the six if any proscribed activity or equipment were found on the premises. No such activity or equipment was found.

Nuclear material balance

12. Of immediate concern is the recent uncovering of major inconsistencies between the Iraqi declarations concerning nuclear material and the IAEA's analytical results of samples. Specifically, it appears that the Iraqi authorities may have mischaracterized the origin of certain nuclear material and understated the amounts of material produced and processed in different locations in Iraq or imported from abroad. This gives rise to serious questions about the inventory of nuclear material in Iraq. Iraqi authorities acknowledge the analytical inconsistencies, but have thus far failed to explain the reasons for such inconsistencies and have refused to discuss the matter any further.

In the absence of further clarification by Iraq on this matter, the IAEA must express strong reservations about the completeness of the Iraqi declarations concerning the presence and use of nuclear material.

Equipment and materials

13. Meetings have been held with the Iraqi side to examine the practical arrangements and inspection activities necessary for monitoring the use of various machine tools and other equipment and materials. The Iraqi authorities acknowledged their acceptance of random, short-notice inspections, their willingness to consolidate equipment at a small number of sites to ease the monitoring problem for both sides, their acceptance of the inspection team's right to take samples and to verify the inventory of produced items, and their willingness to create and maintain a system of records and logbooks and to declare in advance and to continuously document the use of monitored equipment.

Enrichment programme

14. During the Fifteenth Inspection, the Agency team was able to interview a number of senior scientists and engineers who had been involved in the Iraqi centrifuge programme. These included individuals who identified themselves as the technical director of the centrifuge programme; a technical advisor on design, manufacturing, material testing and training; a specialist in rotor dynamics who served as a consultant on the mechanical design of rotating components; a material scientist with responsibility in the centrifuge programme for material selection and testing, surface treatment, heat treatment,

welding technology and flow forming; and two process engineers with responsibility for process development for UF6 production and design and operation of centrifuge process testing.

15. The Iraqi authorities acknowledged for the first time a connection between the centrifuge programme and the Rashdiya Engineering Design Centre. However, they insisted that other than computer modelling, no experimentation involving hardware in support of centrifuge design ever occurred or was planned to take place at Rashdiya. While this positive development must be acknowledged, the fact remains that, for over a year, the Iraqi authorities had persistently denied any involvement of the Centre at Rashdiya in the centrifuge development programme.

Procurement-related information

16. During the Fifteenth Inspection, the Iraqi authorities reiterated the Iraqi Government's refusal to provide information regarding specific procurements and procurement networks. This position seemed to have been slightly modified during the Sixteenth Inspection, at which time the Iraqi Minister of Higher Education and Scientific Research and present Chairman of the Iraqi Atomic Energy Committee, Dr. Human Abdel Khaliq Ghaffour, informed the IAEA team that the Iraqi authorities would "deal positively" with inquiries from the IAEA regarding the procurement of equipment and materials for the Iraqi nuclear programme. However, follow-up written requests by the IAEA for such information failed to produce positive responses from Iraq.

17. In the course of the Seventeenth Inspection, the issue was raised again. Although the Iraqi authorities indicated that it was their intention to provide the missing information, they requested a consolidated list of outstanding questions on procurement by the IAEA and the Special Commission, and that such list should only refer to items related to resolution 687. This procedure was objected to by the Chief Inspector, as experience has demonstrated that such an approach produced little information, and, in fact, only generated more questions.

18. The Eighteenth Inspection team did request, once again, in writing, detailed information about foreign procurement and the Iraqi procurement network. The information requested included that related to the procurement of all equipment, components and raw material listed in annex 3 which were used or intended for use in nuclear-related research, development and production;

manufacturers' names; and names of intermediate suppliers and other companies in the procurement chain. Information on companies and individuals which had provided technical advice on procurement, utilization and design information was also requested. As a matter of priority, the Iraqi authorities were requested to provide, as a demonstration of forthcomingness, answers relevant to the procurement of maraging steel, which had been requested in writing in December 1992.

The Iraqi authorities once again refused to provide the information requested, calling the questions too general and aimed at maintaining the conditions for the embargo.

Removal of irradiated nuclear fuel assemblies

19. Negotiations with the Committee of International Relations on behalf of the Ministry of the Russian Federation for Atomic Energy (CIR Minatom) for the removal, processing and sale or storage of the remaining irradiated nuclear material in Iraq are approaching conclusion. It is anticipated the removal operation will be completed by the end of 1993.

Summary and conclusions

20. The Iraqi Government persists in its refusal to provide the IAEA with information related to foreign procurement and procurement network, in particular as it relates to the Iraqi enrichment programme.

21. Renewed resistance by the Iraqi authorities to providing clarification as to the nuclear material declarations makes impossible a conclusion by the IAEA that all such material has been declared and presented to the IAEA.

22. The shortcomings indicated in paragraphs 20 and 21 above and the continuing discovery of additional material and items which should have been declared by Iraq, but which had not been, prevent the establishment of a technical basis for implementing effectively the long-term monitoring of Iraqi activities as foreseen in resolution 715.

23. The problems identified above are compounded by the refusal of the Iraqi Government to formally recognize its obligations under UN Security Council resolutions 701 (1991) and 715 (1991). Iraq has not yet even formally complied with the requirement laid down in paragraph 12 of Security Council resolution 687 (1991), that it accepts the Plan prepared by the Agency and approved by the Security Council.

Document 157

Statement by the Secretary-General to the final session of the Iraq-Kuwait Boundary Demarcation Commission

UN Press Release SG/SM/4999-IK/148, 20 May 1993

Only two years after its creation, the Boundary Demarcation Commission has come to a successful conclusion. I hope that other United Nations commissions will pay attention to this example.

This is an important moment. For the first time in history, the United Nations has demarcated the boundary between two Member States in the context of maintaining international peace and security. Security Council resolution 687 (1991) was adopted as a consequence of Iraq's invasion of Kuwait. The Council demanded respect for the boundary agreed by Kuwait and Iraq in 1963. The Council called upon me to assist in arranging demarcation of the boundary. And the Council decided to take, as appropriate, all necessary measures to guarantee that border.

Resolution 687 was unconditionally accepted by Iraq. On 2 May 1991, the Iraq-Kuwait Boundary Demarcation Commission was established. Its mandate was to demarcate the international boundary under the formula agreed in 1963. Both Iraq and Kuwait unconditionally accepted the terms of reference of the Commission. The Commission was called to perform a technical and not a political task. During its 11 sessions, the Commission examined many sources, such as maps, graphics, aerial photographs, diplomatic correspondence, notes and archival documents. The Commission appealed to the parties to provide all relevant documentation and evidence. Members of the Commission carried out several field visits.

This highly professional work has produced a precise, well-documented and verifiable demarcation of the entire boundary. It includes the offshore area from the Khowrs to the eastern end of the Khowr Abd Allah. A complete set of coordinates was produced. Boundary markers will clearly display the course of the line. Satellite technology has enabled the Commission to position each marker with a margin of error of only 1.5 centimetres. This would have been unthinkable only a few years ago. Other countries already are looking at this precedent to demarcate their boundaries.

I congratulate all members of the Commission for this excellent work. The past and current chairmen have guided the Commission with great diplomatic and personal ability. The two independent experts have performed a complex and delicate undertaking, with results of outstanding quality. I also express my gratitude to the Chief Military Observer and the personnel of the United Nations Iraq-Kuwait Observation Mission (UNIKOM).

Their cooperation with the Commission in the field was indispensable.

It is regrettable that the representative of Iraq, who participated in the land demarcation decisions, has not participated in the demarcation of the offshore boundary. Iraq has criticized the basis and modalities of the Commission's work in a letter of 21 May 1992 from the Minister of Foreign Affairs to me. I have responded to those comments. The President of the Security Council, in a statement of 17 June 1992, expressed the concern and the dismay of the Council at the attitude adopted by Iraq.

The Commission's demarcation of the boundary between Iraq and Kuwait is in conformity with resolution 687 and with the Charter of the United Nations. The decisions of the Commission concerning the demarcation of the boundary are final. I call upon the Government of Iraq to respect the objectivity and impartiality of the results. Certainty and stability of its borders are in Iraq's interest, and in the interest of the entire region.

As instructed by me, the Chief Military Observer of UNIKOM has realigned the demilitarized zone with the demarcated border. As invited by the Commission, I am making arrangements for the future maintenance of the boundary pillars and markers. I am also helping the parties settle some practical problems that have arisen as a consequence of the demarcation. These steps will contribute to stabilizing the security situation in the area.

Certified copies of the demarcated boundary coordinates have been provided to the Governments of Iraq and Kuwait. A copy of these coordinates will be deposited in the archives of the United Nations. These coordinates represent the final and authentic description of the boundary.

I will bring the report of the Commission, with the coordinates and map attached to it, to the attention of the Security Council. The Council, in resolution 773 (1992), expressed its appreciation to the Commission and welcomed its demarcation decisions. Resolution 687 (1991), enacted under Chapter VII, guaranteed the inviolability of the boundary between Iraq and Kuwait.

This session marks a noteworthy international success. Law, technology, diplomacy and security have come together in a unique United Nations endeavour. All those involved can take great pride in this outcome. Together you have made a strong contribution to peace and stability for the region and the world.

Document 158

Final report on the demarcation of the international boundary between the Republic of Iraq and the State of Kuwait by the United Nations Iraq-Kuwait Boundary Demarcation Commission

S/25811, 21 May 1993, and addendum, S/25811/Add.1, 24 May 1993

Letter dated 21 May 1993 from the Secretary-General addressed to the President of the Security Council

I have the honour to transmit to you and through you to the members of the Security Council the "Final Report on the Demarcation of the International Boundary between the Republic of Iraq and the State of Kuwait by the United Nations Iraq-Kuwait Boundary Demarcation Commission" dated 20 May 1993 containing the list of geographic coordinates demarcating the boundary and the map of the area, which forms an enclosure to the report. I also submit a transmittal letter of the same date from the Chairman of the Commission addressed to me.

As indicated in the above-mentioned letter, in addition to the Final Report, the Chairman of the Commission submitted to me three certified copies of the list of geographic coordinates demarcating the international boundary between Iraq and Kuwait. On 20 May 1993, I forwarded two of these certified copies to the Governments of Iraq and Kuwait respectively, in order to be lodged in their archives. I also brought to the attention of both Governments the Final Report of the Commission together with the map. The third certified copy of the list of geographic coordinates demarcating the international boundary between Iraq and Kuwait will be retained for safekeeping in the archives of the United Nations.

As you know, the Iraq-Kuwait Boundary Demarcation Commission was established pursuant to paragraph 3 of Security Council resolution 687 (1991), which called upon the Secretary-General to lend assistance to make arrangements with Iraq and Kuwait to demarcate the international boundary between the two countries. The Commission was entrusted with the task to demarcate in geographic coordinates of latitude and longitude as well as by a physical representation the international boundary as set out in the "Agreed Minutes between the State of Kuwait and the Republic of Iraq regarding the Restoration of Friendly Relations, Recognition and Related Matters" signed at Baghdad on 4 October 1963. The Commission was also asked to provide for arrangements for maintenance on a continuing basis of the physical representation of the boundary.

In accordance with its mandate and terms of reference, the Commission was called to perform a technical and not a political task and as it is stressed in the Final Report, the Commission has made every effort to strictly confine itself to this objective. In the statement of the President of the Security Council dated 17 June 1992 (S/24113), issued on behalf of its members and in Security Council resolution 773 (1992) of 26 August 1992, related to the work of the Commission, it was pointed out that through the demarcation process the Commission was not reallocating territory between Kuwait and Iraq, but it was simply carrying out the technical task necessary to demarcate for the first time the precise coordinates of the boundary set out in the Agreed Minutes referred to above.

As stated in the Final Report the Commission has fulfilled its mandate. It demarcated in geographic coordinates of latitude and longitude the international boundary between Iraq and Kuwait set out in the Agreed Minutes, made arrangements for the physical representation of the boundary through the emplacement of an appropriate number of boundary pillars or monuments and provided for arrangements for continuing maintenance and location accuracy of the surficial boundary representation.

The coordinates established by the Commission thus constitute the final demarcation of the international boundary between Iraq and Kuwait set out in the Agreed Minutes of 4 October 1963. In accordance with paragraph 2 and 4 of Security Council resolution 687 (1991), both Iraq and Kuwait shall respect the inviolability of this international boundary and its inviolability will be also guaranteed by the Security Council.

Fulfilment by the Commission of its mandate to demarcate the international boundary between Iraq and Kuwait has direct implications for the implementation of paragraph 5 of Security Council resolution 687 (1991) relating to the establishment of a demilitarized zone along that boundary. In January 1993 UNIKOM completed the realignment of the demilitarized zone with the demarcated land section of the boundary and I am now instructing UNIKOM to finalize such realignment with the entire international boundary between Iraq and Kuwait demarcated by the Commission.

With regard to Section X (c) of the Final Report, concerning boundary maintenance, I will make the necessary arrangements, as recommended by the Commission, for maintenance of the physical representation of the boundary. The United Nations personnel and personnel of the survey or similar organizations that will be involved in the implementation of the arrangements for maintenance of the surficial representation of the boundary are to enjoy unimpeded freedom of movement in the area of the demarcated boundary as well as all necessary privileges and immunities for the fulfilment of their task.

As stated above, the decisions of the Commission concerning the demarcation of the international boundary between Iraq and Kuwait are final. I believe that the work performed by the Commission will have a beneficial effect on the restoration of international peace and security in the area concerned, in conformity with the purposes of Security Council resolution 687 (1991). The certainty and stability of the boundary are in the best interest of Iraq and Kuwait and I expect the Governments of both countries to respect the objective and impartial results achieved by the Iraq-Kuwait Boundary Demarcation Commission.

(*Signed*) Boutros BOUTROS-GHALI

Annex
Letter dated 20 May 1993 from the Chairman of the Iraq-Kuwait Boundary Demarcation Commission addressed to the Secretary-General

In accordance with paragraph 3 of Security Council resolution 687 (1991) of 3 April 1991, on behalf of the Iraq-Kuwait Boundary Demarcation Commission, I have the honour to submit herewith the report conveying the final results of its work, together with a certified copy of the list of geographic coordinates demarcating the international boundary between Iraq and Kuwait and a map at the scale of 1:250,000 depicting that demarcation. The report and the coordinates are submitted in three copies, two of which are for communication to the Governments concerned.

As indicated in the report, the Commission will communicate to you in due course authenticated copies of the large-scale maps of the boundary along with technical documentation comprised of certified records of survey stations and boundary pillars.

(*Signed*) Nicolas VALTICOS
Chairman

Appendix
Final report on the demarcation of the international boundary between the Republic of Iraq and the State of Kuwait by the United Nations Iraq-Kuwait Boundary Demarcation Commission

I. *Introduction*

1. The Security Council, by its resolution 687 (1991) of 3 April 1991, affirmed the commitment of all Member States to the sovereignty, territorial integrity and political independence of Kuwait and Iraq. In that regard, the Council noted that Iraq and Kuwait, as independent sovereign States, had signed at Baghdad on 4 October 1963 the "Agreed Minutes Between the State of Kuwait and the Republic of Iraq Regarding the Restoration of Friendly Relations, Recognition and Related Matters", thereby formally recognizing the international boundary between Iraq and Kuwait and the allocation of islands. The Agreed Minutes were registered with the United Nations in accordance with Article 102 of the Charter of the United Nations (United Nations, *Treaty Series*, vol. 485, No. 7063).

2. Bearing in mind its objective of restoring international peace and security in the area, the Security Council, by paragraph 2 of its resolution 687 (1991), demanded that Iraq and Kuwait respect the inviolability of the international boundary and the allocation of islands set out in the aforementioned Agreed Minutes. By paragraph 4 of that resolution, the Council decided to guarantee the inviolability of the international boundary between Iraq and Kuwait.

3. Conscious of the need for demarcation of the said boundary, the Security Council, by paragraph 3 of its resolution 687 (1991), called upon the Secretary-General to lend his assistance to make arrangements with Iraq and Kuwait to demarcate the boundary between them, drawing on appropriate material, including the map transmitted by Security Council document S/22412.

4. In a letter dated 4 April 1991 addressed to the Secretary-General by the Deputy Prime Minister and Minister for Foreign Affairs of Kuwait (S/22457), Kuwait expressed its intention to comply scrupulously with all the provisions of resolution 687 (1991) and to cooperate with the Secretary-General with a view to ensuring its implementation. In accordance with paragraph 33 of resolution 687 (1991), the Minister for Foreign Affairs of Iraq, in the penultimate paragraph of a letter dated 6 April 1991 (S/22456), notified the Security Council and the Secretary-General of Iraq's acceptance of the provisions of that resolution.

5. In letters dated 19 and 23 April 1991 respectively, Kuwait and Iraq agreed to cooperate with the Commission and to nominate representatives of their Governments to participate in its deliberations (see S/22558, annexes I and II).

6. After consultations with the Governments of Iraq and Kuwait, the Secretary-General, pursuant to paragraph 3 of resolution 687 (1991), on 2 May 1991 established the United Nations Iraq-Kuwait Boundary Demarcation Commission, composed of five members—three independent experts to be appointed by the Secretary-General, one of whom would serve as Chairman, and

one representative of each Iraq and Kuwait—to carry out the technical tasks necessary to demarcate the boundary between the two countries (S/22558). Iraq nominated Ambassador Riyadh Al-Qaysi and Kuwait nominated Ambassador Tarek A. Razzouki as their representatives on the Commission (see S/22620).

7. In connection with the report conveying the decisions taken by the Commission on the demarcation of the land boundary, the Security Council, by its resolution 773 (1992), expressed appreciation to the Commission for its work and welcomed those decisions. It also welcomed the Commission's decision to consider the eastern section of the boundary and urged the Commission to demarcate that part as soon as possible.

II. *Mandate and terms of reference*

8. The mandate of the Commission and its terms of reference are laid down in Security Council resolution 687 (1991) and in the report of the Secretary-General on the establishment of the Commission pursuant to paragraph 3 of that resolution (S/22558).

9. The report of the Secretary-General provides that the terms of reference of the Commission are to demarcate in geographical coordinates of latitude and longitude as well as by a physical representation the International boundary between Iraq and Kuwait as set out in the Agreed Minutes. This was to be accomplished by drawing upon appropriate material, including the maps transmitted by Security Council document S/22412 (a set of 10 topographic maps at the scale of 1:50,000 by the United Kingdom Director General of Military Survey) and by utilizing appropriate technology. The physical representation will be carried out by the emplacement of an appropriate number and type of boundary pillars and arrangements made for maintenance on a continuing basis.

10. With reference to the boundary, the 1963 Agreed Minutes provide that:

"The Republic of Iraq recognized the independence and complete sovereignty of the State of Kuwait with its boundaries as specified in the letter of the Prime Minister of Iraq dated 21.7.1932 and which was accepted by the Ruler of Kuwait in his letter dated 10.8.1932."

11. The 1932 Exchange of Letters referred to in the Agreed Minutes contains the following description of "the existing frontier between the two countries", which constitutes the delimitation formula for the demarcation of the Iraq-Kuwait boundary by the Commission:

"From the intersection of the Wadi-el-Audja with the Batin and thence northwards along the Batin to a point just south of the latitude of Safwan; thence eastwards passing south of Safwan Wells, Jebel Sanam and Um Qasr leaving them to 'Iraq and so on to the junction of the Khor Zobeir with the Khor Abdullah. The islands of Warbah, Bubiyan, Maskan (or Mashjan), Failakah, Auhah, Kubbar, Qaru and Umm-el-Maradim appertain to Koweit."

12. The report of the Secretary-General states that the Commission will take its decision by majority and that its decisions regarding demarcation will be final. It further states that the coordinates established by the Commission will constitute the final demarcation of the international boundary. They will be lodged in the archives of the Governments of Iraq and Kuwait and a certified copy will be submitted to the Secretary-General for transmittal to the Security Council and for safekeeping in the archives of the United Nations.

13. The Security Council took note of the Secretary-General's report and its provisions for the establishment and terms of reference of the Commission and expressed support for all his efforts in respect of the demarcation of the boundary (S/22593).

III. *Composition and rules of procedure*

14. Pursuant to paragraph 3 of resolution 687 (1991), the Secretary-General appointed Mr. Mochtar Kusuma-Atmadja, former Minister for Foreign Affairs of Indonesia as Chairman; Mr. Ian Brook, then Technical Director, Swedsurvey, National Land Survey of Sweden; and Mr. William Robertson, Surveyor General/Director General of the Department of Survey and Land Information of New Zealand, as independent experts. Iraq is represented by Ambassador Riyadh Al-Qaysi and Kuwait is represented by Ambassador Tarek A. Razzouki (see S/22620). The views of the parties on the constitution of the Commission and the Secretary-General's response thereto are contained in annexes I, II and III to the report of the Secretary-General (see S/22558). Mr. Miklos Pinther, Chief Cartographer of the United Nations Secretariat, was appointed Secretary to the Commission.

15. With effect from 20 November 1992, Mr. Kusuma-Atmadja resigned as Chairman of the Commission for personal reasons. Consequent upon the resignation of Mr. Kusuma-Atmadja, the Secretary-General appointed as his successor Mr. Nicholas Valticos, former Assistant Director-General of the International Labour Office, and member of the Institute of International Law, who assumed his functions on the same date.

16. The Commission established its own rules of procedure (IKBDC/Doc.2). Rule 1 covered the composition of the Commission. Rule 2 provided that the relevant provisions of the report of the Secretary-General (S/22558) would constitute the terms of reference of the Commission. According to these rules, the decisions of

the Commission regarding the demarcation of the boundary are final. The rules of procedure further stipulated that the quorum would be met by the presence of at least three members, including the Chairman and at least one representative (rule 3), and that decisions would be taken by majority (rule 5). The Commission carried out its work in closed meetings (rule 4), by visits to the border area and through field work. The Secretary of the Commission was entrusted with making all arrangements connected with the work of the Commission (rule 8).

17. In his report of 2 May 1991, the Secretary-General proposed that all costs should be shared between the interested parties. The Commission prepared and approved a cost estimate for the totality of its work, which was submitted to the Secretary-General.

IV. *Meetings and field sessions*

18. The Commission held 11 sessions encompassing 82 meetings; these meetings were held either at the United Nations Office at Geneva or at United Nations Headquarters in New York. The Commission was provided with, and approved, minutes of all its meetings and it approved and issued press releases at the conclusion of each session.

19. The Commission conducted an initial inspection tour of the border area between 15 and 19 June 1991, at which time the two independent experts and the Secretary also visited the national survey offices of Kuwait and Iraq. Following a decision by the Commission to undertake new surveying and mapping of the border area, a survey team was formed from the staff of the national survey departments of New Zealand and Sweden. To execute its task, the survey team undertook four sessions of field work, which also included the final emplacement of the boundary pillars, during the autumn of 1991, the spring and autumn of 1992 and the spring of 1993. At the end of each field session, the two independent experts inspected and verified the work of the survey team. The Secretary made eight visits to the border area to participate in site inspections, to make arrangements for the field work and to establish a field office for the Commission. At the conclusion of each major phase of its work, the Commission prepared and submitted a report to the Secretary-General.

V. *Participation*

20. From the beginning of its work, the Commission requested the representatives of Iraq and Kuwait to submit all relevant documents and other materials for its consideration. This was a regular feature of the subsequent work of the Commission, and full opportunity was provided to both parties to submit all relevant materials and express their positions and views throughout the work of the Commission.

21. At the first five sessions, held between 23 May 1991 and 16 April 1992, at which the Commission adopted its rules of procedure, considered the Khowr Abd Allah section and considered and took decisions on the land boundary, all members participated. The representative of Iraq did not attend the subsequent sessions, held between 15 July 1992 and 20 May 1993. However, copies of all documents and of the authenticated minutes were transmitted to the representative of Iraq.

VI. *Organization of work*

22. At its first session, held in New York on 23 and 24 May 1991, the Commission discussed the organization of its work and requested the secretariat to prepare rules of procedure, which the Commission adopted at its second session. It held an exchange of views relating to the schedule of work, the nature of the task, what constituted appropriate material, on-site visits and the possibility of participation by experts from both countries

23. It was affirmed by the Commission at its first session that its work was technical, not political, and that the nature of its task was demarcation. This was later noted by the Security Council in its resolution 773 (1992) of 26 August 1992, which recalled that "through the demarcation process the Commission is not reallocating territory between Kuwait and Iraq, but it is simply carrying out the technical task necessary to demarcate for the first time the precise coordinates of the boundary set out in the [1963] Agreed Minutes . . . "

24. The Commission asked the independent experts to prepare a plan of action for the demarcation. Subsequently, the independent experts presented a discussion paper, the two parts of which dealt with boundary definition issues and with the technical aspects of surveying, mapping and physical representation.

25. Following a discussion on definition issues, the Commission decided to examine the boundary in three sections. The first was labelled the western section, and corresponded to the initial phrase of the delimitation formula, "from the intersection of the Wadi-el-Audja with the Batin and thence northwards along the Batin to a point just south of the latitude of Safwan". The second was labelled the northern section, corresponding to the phrase "thence eastwards passing south of Safwan Wells, Jebel Sanam and Um Qasr leaving them to Iraq and so on to the junction of the Khor Zobeir with the Khor Abdullah". The third section was called the eastern section, later termed the offshore section and finally called the Khowr Abd Allah section. This part corresponds to reference to the junction, together with the final sentence of the delimitation formula: "the islands of Warbah, Bubiyan,

Maskan (or Mashjan), Failakah, Auhah, Kubbar, Qaru and Umm-el Maradim appertain to Koweit".

26. The Commission adopted a *modus operandi* whereby, for each of the above sections, it deliberated on the interpretation of the applicable parts of the delimitation formula, took account of the 1940 and 1951 clarifications (see para. 36 below) and other relevant evidence, discussed the relevant demarcation issues, heard statements of position, took decisions where necessary and instructed its survey team to carry out the requisite technical tasks in the field.

VII. *Preliminary considerations*

A. *Historical background and boundary definition*

27. In its work, the Commission considered the various delimitation agreements dealing with the boundary between 1913 and 1963 as they related to the international boundary in the 1963 Agreed Minutes.

28. The Anglo-Ottoman Convention of 1913 defined a Green Line running from the coast at the mouth of the Khowr Zhobeir in a north-westerly direction, passing immediately south of Umm Qasr (the old fort), Safwan and Jebel Sanam to the Batin, and then south-west down the Batin. It also showed a Red Line down the Khowr Abd Allah. Both lines depicted the limits of Kuwaiti authority.

29. In September 1920, the Ruler of Kuwait claimed the northern territories allocated to him under the Convention. In the following year, he was told by the British High Commissioner for Iraq, Sir Percy Cox, that the territory allocated to him by the Red Line was beyond dispute.

30. In December 1922, Cox suggested that the Green Line be confirmed as the boundary. This was done in 1923 in an exchange of letters between the Ruler of Kuwait, the British Political Agent in Kuwait and the British High Commissioner for Iraq on a description of the territory deemed identical with the Green Line.

31. In 1923 the British Political Agent in Kuwait, More, erected a noticeboard marked "Iraq-Kuwait boundary" south of Safwan. A decade later, the noticeboard was considered to be the only accurate indication of where the boundary ran in the region. In the summer of 1932 it was removed, and subsequently replaced, by the Iraqi authorities.

32. In July 1932, it being considered desirable to reaffirm the existing frontier between Iraq and Kuwait before Iraq's admission to the League of Nations, the Prime Minister of Iraq wrote a letter on 21 July 1932, and the Ruler of Kuwait responded on 10 August 1932. This Exchange of Letters reaffirming the boundary was reconfirmed by the 1963 Agreed Minutes.

33. In August 1935, Dickson, then British Political Agent in Kuwait, giving advice on the depiction of the boundary on a new map, said that those in Kuwait had always understood the northern boundary to run in a due east-west straight line from the Batin centre line to the noticeboard, and thence, also in a straight line, to the junction of the Khowr Zhobeir and the Khowr Abd Allah. The following year the map, containing several errors, of which the underestimated distance between Umm Qasr and the junction of the Khowrs was probably the most important, was published. It was the basis for much of the consideration of the boundary by the British and Iraqis up to 1963.

34. In April 1937, Edmonds, British Adviser to the Iraqi Minister of the Interior, advised his Minister, and the British authorities, that the boundary should follow the thalweg of the Batin, thence run due east to a point one mile south of Safwan palms and onwards, in a straight line, to the junction of the thalwegs of the Khowr Zhobeir and the Khowr Abd Allah. From the junction of the Khowrs, the boundary followed the thalweg of the Khowr Abd Allah to the open sea.

35. In March 1939, the noticeboard was removed; on 9 June 1940 the British Political Agent in Kuwait, Galloway, assisted by a Kuwaiti expert, replaced it; on 25 June the Iraqi Foreign Ministry protested that the noticeboard had been placed 1,000 metres south of the Iraqi customs post, 250 metres north of the Iraqi boundary.

36. Dickson's and Edmonds' descriptions of the boundary formed the basis of two communications, dated 7 October 1940 and 18 December 1951, from the British Ambassador in Baghdad addressed to the Iraqi Foreign Ministry and Foreign Minister respectively, clarifying the 1932 Exchange of Letters. Those, which specify the low-water line on the southern shore of the Khowr Zhobeir as the boundary in that Khowr, differ only in describing the site of the old noticeboard (in the first) and a point 1,000 metres south of the old Iraqi customs post (in the second) as the point south of Safwan.

37. In March 1942, surveyors from the Indian Army reported that they had erected two concrete pillars: one in Safwan Village amid palm trees and the second pillar half a mile south from the first. Coordinates were determined by astronomical observations for the two pillars and for a point on the north-west corner of the wall of the customs post. The first pillar was not specifically stated to be located at the southernmost palm as was reported in the telegram from Hickinbotham, Political Agent in Kuwait, on 19 March 1942.

38. In 1951 the Iraqi Government indicated that it could accept the 1951 delimitation under the condition that Kuwait would agree to cede the island of Warbah.

This proposal was unacceptable to Kuwait and was withdrawn by the Iraqi Government in 1953.

39. In May 1955, the Iraqi Prime Minister proposed that the boundary depicted in a sketch map which he gave to the Ambassador be advanced 4 kilometres southwards between Safwan and the entrance of the Khowr Abd Allah. A draft agreement, indicating that the boundary depicted on the 1936 map was that agreed in 1932, was then negotiated between the British authorities and Iraqi Foreign Minister. The Iraqi Prime Minister thereafter pressed the Kuwaitis to agree to its conclusion, but they declined.

40. In 1959, Coucheron-Aamot, a Norwegian hydrographer, produced a report and a chart, officially authenticated by the Iraqi Ministry of Petroleum, which defined a median line as the boundary in the Khowr Abd Allah. This official chart, taken from an annex to the Coucheron-Aamot report, was transmitted to the Danish Embassy in Baghdad by the Iraqi Foreign Minister on 22 August 1960 and subsequently published in the *Pleadings* of the International Court of Justice (see I.C.J. *Pleadings*, 1968, vol. I, *North Sea Continental Shelf Cases*, figure D).

B. *General discussion*

41. The Commission held a general discussion on the three sections of the boundary as a whole on the basis of the discussion paper presented by the independent experts.

42. Considerable time was devoted to the investigation and discussion of the definition of the point south of Safwan, the general course of the boundary in the Batin, the position of the boundary south of Umm Qasr and the possible position of the boundary at the junction of Khowr Zhobeir and Khowr Abd Allah in the epoch of 1932. The principles to be applied in the demarcation of the boundary beyond the junction of the Khowrs were also considered at length. The language of the delimitation formula was debated extensively. Of particular concern were whether it was technically possible to demarcate the boundary without a turning-point at Safwan, whether the thalweg or the median line concept should be applied in the northern part of the Batin to divide the grazing areas equitably and whether there had been a shift in the junction of the Khowrs over the past decades. With regard to the Khowr Abd Allah section, the principle of the median line, tempered by equity, was considered.

43. The general deliberations were followed by discussions on the various sections of the boundary, which were continued as the work of the Commission progressed. Each question and each section of the boundary received careful consideration from the legal, historical, technical and practical points of view. The

deliberations, statements of position and the work of the Commission are given in considerable detail in its reports to the Secretary-General (IKBDC/Rep.2, Rep.6 and Rep.7).

VIII. *Mapping*

A. *Necessity for new mapping*

44. In the technical sections of the discussion paper, the independent experts proposed methods for new mapping of the border area to provide a proper basis for demarcation. The maps and the related spatial data were, in the opinion of the experts, a necessary supplement to the existing maps and documents and would be required before demarcation on the ground could be carried out, as there were no adequate maps of the boundary area for the purpose of demarcation.

45. It was pointed out that the boundaries shown on the maps transmitted by Security Council document S/22412 could be considered reliable. Those maps, as well as all other recent maps of the area, indicated the general configuration of the boundary and the existence of a turning-point south of Safwan. But, in depicting the boundary, they were not supported by any detailed rationale The comparison of older maps with the 1991 revised editor, of British Admiralty Chart No 1235 and the Commission's new orthophoto mapping revealed significant discrepancies in absolute positions on the older maps, in particular for the junction of the Khowrs.

46. To assist the Commission in its deliberations and to enable it to achieve a precise demarcation, the independent experts therefore proposed a new survey and mapping of the entire border area. The proposal included the establishment of a geodetic control network and ground control points for mapping, using satellite-based (Global Positioning System (GPS) and Doppler) methods, combined with conventional survey techniques, aerial photography and the production of a set of large-scale orthophoto maps at the scale of 1:25,000. Included also were special maps to enable the Commission to study specific areas such as the Batin and the border areas at Safwan and Umm Qasr.

B. *Field work preparation*

47. The field work of the Commission was undertaken in three stages during four field sessions by a survey team composed of geodesists, surveyors and photogrammetrists from the national survey departments of New Zealand and Sweden. During the first stage, the Commission established its own geodetic datum called "IKBD-92", based on World Geodetic System (WGS 84 ellipsoid), and established geodetic network control. Aerial photography and preliminary mapping were carried

out. During the second stage the decisions of the Commission were implemented through the emplacement of preliminary boundary markers and final boundary pillars. The third stage involved the demarcation of the Khowr Abd Allah section of the boundary as well as additional work on the land boundary sections.

48. In all stages of the field work, the United Nations Iraq-Kuwait Observation Mission (UNIKOM) provided essential support on an at-cost basis. Assistance was extended to the surveyors for the preparation of photo control points and for the establishment of the preliminary positions for the boundary pillars. In this regard, UNIKOM also cleared work areas of unexploded ordnance. UNIKOM facilitated transportation and provided procurement, logistic and operational support for the emplacement of pillars.

1. Control surveys

49. Four datum stations, 25 primary control stations and 137 photo control points were established between September and December 1991. The positions were determined by GPS and Doppler observations. The first function of this work was to facilitate the production of the orthophoto maps and accurate transverse height profiles of the Batin to assist the Commission in its deliberations. The second function was to leave a primary control network in place that could be used to set out the boundary pillars once the final location of the boundary had been determined by the Commission. To provide tidal data, the Commission installed two tide gauges at Umm Qasr.

2. Aerial photography

50. The main aerial photography programme was carried out during the first field session by an air photo team and a specially outfitted aircraft from the National Land Survey of Sweden. Photographs at various scales were produced to facilitate the production of orthophoto maps for the entire length of the land boundary, for the preparation of transverse height profiles of the Batin and for large-scale orthophoto maps of the Safwan and Umm Qasr areas (see IKBDC/Rep.6).

51. Additional aerial photographs were taken in February 1993. The purpose of these photographs was to provide false-colour infrared imagery for the determination of the boundary along the low-water-springs line in the Khowr Zhobeir, to evaluate the quality of the 1991 edition of British Admiralty Chart No. 1235 and to assist with the definition of the median line in the Khowr Abd Allah. Additional photographs were also taken for the production of a series of maps at a scale of 1:2,500 of the Rumailah/Ratqa boundary area and the settled areas along the boundary at Safwan and at Umm Qasr. The purpose of these maps was to provide additional detail on the location of the boundary and to assist in resolving any boundary-related issues.

C. Mapping of the border area

52. Initially, a series of 31 orthophoto maps (in English and Arabic) was produced at a scale of 1:25,000. In addition, separate orthophoto maps were produced at the scale of 1:7,500 for the Safwan and Umm Qasr areas.

53. For the Batin, 1,420 transverse photogrammetric height profiles were produced. From these the lowest-point line in the Wadi was determined by examining the elevation contours, by measuring along the profiles and by generating three-dimensional digital terrain models.

54. At a later stage, the aerial photography was extended eastwards to the outer reaches of the Khowr Abd Allah, from which additional orthophoto maps were produced at the scale of 1:25,000. In order to reduce the final number of map sheets and to provide better coverage of the boundary, the size of the sheets was changed. The boundary from the trijunction to the eastern end of the Khowr Abd Allah is thus covered by 18 map sheets.

D. Charting of the Khowr Zhobeir, the Khowr Shetana and the Khowr Abd Allah

55. At the sixth session, the Commission requested the independent experts to investigate further the Khowr Zhobeir and the Khowr Abd Allah and present appropriate material for consideration. Assisted by hydrographers from the Swedish National Maritime Administration and the Royal New Zealand Navy, the independent experts undertook two separate studies of the earliest detailed hydrographic surveys available for the Khowrs.

56. Following an analysis of the charts, both manual and computer interpretations were made to produce maps for the Commission's consideration at the scale of 1:50,000 and 1:100,000 showing the thalweg line and the median line in the Khowr Abd Allah. Bathymetric contour maps and transverse profiles on the same scale were also prepared. In addition, baseline coordinates were identified and listed for the plotting of a median line.

57. During the third field session, two tide gauges were installed at Umm Qasr to assist with the determination of the low-water line in the Khowr Zhobeir, from its intersection with the land boundary to a point opposite the junction of the Khowr Zhobeir and the Khowr Abd Allah.

IX. Decisions on demarcation

58. At an early stage in its work the Commission reached several decisions which provided the broad parameters for demarcation. These decisions also authorized

the new surveying and mapping and the gathering of additional material, which subsequently enabled the Commission to reach conclusions regarding the demarcation of the frontier between Iraq and Kuwait. The Commission reached its decisions after gathering and carefully considering all available material, including the historical record, maps and aerial photography, after surveying and mapping and after conducting the necessary inspections in the field. Each section of the boundary received thorough scrutiny. Final decisions were reached only after extensive deliberations and after the Commission was satisfied that all the evidence had been properly weighed.

A. Western section

59. The western section of the boundary is that part of the existing frontier which leads from the intersection of Wadi El Audja and Wadi Al Batin northwards along the Batin to a point just south of the latitude of Safwan.

60. The basis for the demarcation of this section was the wording of the delimitation formula in the 1932 Exchange of Letters.

"From the intersection of the Wadi-el-Audja with the Batin and thence northwards along the Batin ...".

61. In October 1940 the British Ambassador in Baghdad presented the Iraqi Foreign Minister with a proposal for the demarcation of the boundary as accepted by Kuwait, which clarified the above wording as follows:

"Along the Batin the frontier shall follow the thalweg, i.e. the line of the deepest depression ... ".

62. This was repeated word for word in a note verbale of December 1951 in which reference is made to contacts between the Foreign Minister of Iraq and the British Ambassador regarding the reopening of the boundary issue. In 1940, Iraq requested a delay until its border with Saudi Arabia had been fixed and, in 1952, it announced that it wanted the issue of the cession of Warbah Island settled before proceeding with demarcation.

63. The Commission decided to demarcate the boundary along the Wadi Al Batin in terms of the line of the lowest points (the thalweg). It also took a decision that the boundary would be marked by a series of straight lines, approximately 2 kilometres in length, such that the areal extent by which the thalweg departs from the boundary on the Kuwait side was equally balanced by the departure on the Iraq side.

64. For this exercise, the Commission undertook large-scale orthophoto mapping of the Batin based on specially flown aerial photography. Terrain models and transverse height profiles were generated to permit computer simulation of the lines of lowest points along the Batin.

65. The Commission decided that the point of intersection of the Wadi El Audja with the Wadi Al Batin was to be determined as pillar No. 1 of the Iraq-Saudi Arabia boundary and it then became boundary pillar No. 1 for the western boundary section.

66. The Commission further took a decision that the northern end of the boundary in the Batin be located at the intersection of the thalweg of the Wadi and the latitude of the point south of Safwan.

67. The line the Commission decided upon to demarcate the western section compares well with the general location of the boundary line as drawn by cartographers on earlier maps, including the map transmitted by Security Council document S/22412, and is very similar to the line depicted on other recent maps.

B. Northern section

68. The northern section is that part of the boundary which, from the intersection of the thalweg of the Wadi Al Batin with the parallel of latitude that runs through the point just south of Safwan, eastwards along that parallel south of Jebel Sanam to the point just south of Safwan and thereafter along the shortest (geodesic) line to the port town of Umm Qasr, and from there to the junction of the Khowr Zhobeir with the Khowr Abd Allah.

1. From the Wadi Al Batin to the point south of Safwan

69. In the 1932 Exchange of Letters the boundary between the northern end of the Batin and Safwan is described as running from a point in the Batin to:

"... a point just south of the latitude of Safwan; thence eastwards passing south of Safwan Wells, Jebel Sanam ...".

70. All descriptions and representations of the boundary on maps after 1935 have depicted the boundary in this section as following a parallel of latitude to a point south of Safwan. For some 16 years, this point was marked by a noticeboard, the position of which also determined the latitude of the line between the western boundary in the Batin and Safwan. This is a point which is fundamental to the definition of the northern boundary and which has never been accurately depicted on any map prior to the maps produced for the Commission.

71. From 1923 to 1939 a noticeboard, which marked the boundary between Iraq and Kuwait, stood at a point on the old road just south of Safwan. This noticeboard was erected at the time of the 1923 agreement which was reiterated in the 1932 Exchange of

Letters. Its position was known to both countries at the time of the 1932 Exchange of Letters and was recognized by both over the subsequent seven years as the international boundary. The position of the noticeboard appears not to have been measured. However, Dickson, who was present at Oqair at the time of the 1923 agreement and was the British Political Agent in Kuwait between 1929 and 1936, stated in 1935 that:

"We have always understood the northern boundary of the frontier to run in a due east and west line from the Batin (centre line) to a point one mile south of Safwan Wells, where a large noticeboard exists on the side of the road which today marks the boundary".

72. Attempts to locate the former position of the noticeboard, after its removal in 1939, resulted in several differing estimations of the distance from reference points in and around Safwan, including the old customs post, the wells and the southernmost date palm. When related to each other there was a degree of congruence around the distance of one mile (1,609 metres) from the customs post. However, the re-establishment of the noticeboard in 1940 resulted in an Iraqi protest note which stated that its re-established position was 250 metres north of the boundary at a distance of 1,000 metres from the customs post.

73. The Commission considered that the two most probable positions for the noticeboard were nearly 1,609 metres (1 mile) and 1,250 metres south of the south-west extremity of the customs post. In the absence of other reliable evidence, the Commission gave equal weight to both measurements and decided on the mean distance of 1,430 metres from the south-west extremity of the old customs post along the old road as the most probable location of the noticeboard. The location of the point thus determined by the Commission is 180 metres farther south than the distance specified in the 1940 Iraqi protest note and 430 metres south of the claim made then and later for Kuwait (see map).

74. The general location of the customs post was established, on site, using GPS equipment and coordinates determined in 1942 from astronomical observations. Image interpretation using several aerial photographs, dating from 1945 to the present day, enabled the Commission to determine the south-west extremity of the old customs post with good accuracy as well as the alignment of the old road south of Safwan beside which the noticeboard had been located.

75. The parallel of 30° 06′ 13.3181″, running westward from the re-established position of the old noticeboard, defines the line of this boundary. At the northern end of the Batin the line of deepest depression is less well-defined than farther south. To determine its position on the ground, the Commission used a combination of orthophoto mapping, height measurements and interpretation of vegetation patterns in the bottom of the Batin. The Commission decided that the intersection of this line with the parallel of latitude 30° 06′ 13.3181″ determined the end of the boundary in the Batin and the start of the northern boundary.

2. *Safwan to the intersection of the Khowrs*

76. This section of the boundary is covered in the 1932 Exchange of Letters by:

"... south of Safwan Wells ... and Umm Qasr leaving them to Iraq and so on to the junction of the Khor Zobeir with the Khor Abdullah".

77. In order to determine the location of the junction of the Khowr Zhobeir and the Khowr Abd Allah, the Commission first identified the thalweg of the channels using the most reliable chart produced as close to the year 1932 as possible. A comparison of various charts, maps and aerial photographs after 1945 indicated that little accretion had occurred during the past 60 years. The Commission considered that the position of the thalwegs of the channels would most likely have remained the same had drudging not occurred. Having identified the thalwegs, the Commission determined the location of the junction of the Khowrs.

78. Guided by the 1940 and 1951 clarifications of the delimitation formula in drawing a straight line on the new orthophoto maps from the point south of Safwan passing south of Umm Qasr to the junction of the Khowrs, the Commission found that such a line would have sliced into the northern shore of the Khowr Zhobeir, thereby closing off the mouth of the Khowr.

79. A careful analysis of the various charts and maps, and comparison with the Commission's new orthophoto maps, revealed that the charts contained distortions of the outline and errors in the absolute positions of the Khowrs and that on the 1936 British map the junction of the Khowrs was plotted some 1,000 metres to the south of its correct position. The reason for this was judged to be a misfit between the newer plane-table mapping of the land areas west of the Khowr Zhobeir and the triangulation surveys east of the Khowr, which dated back to 1917.

80. The 1936 map was used as a basis for graphic descriptions of the boundary for many of the deliberations on the subject over the next decades. As a result, the point where the line between the junction of the Khowrs and Safwan is shown as crossing the shoreline of the Khowr Zhobeir at a point which lies some 800 metres to the south of the point that is obtained when the straight

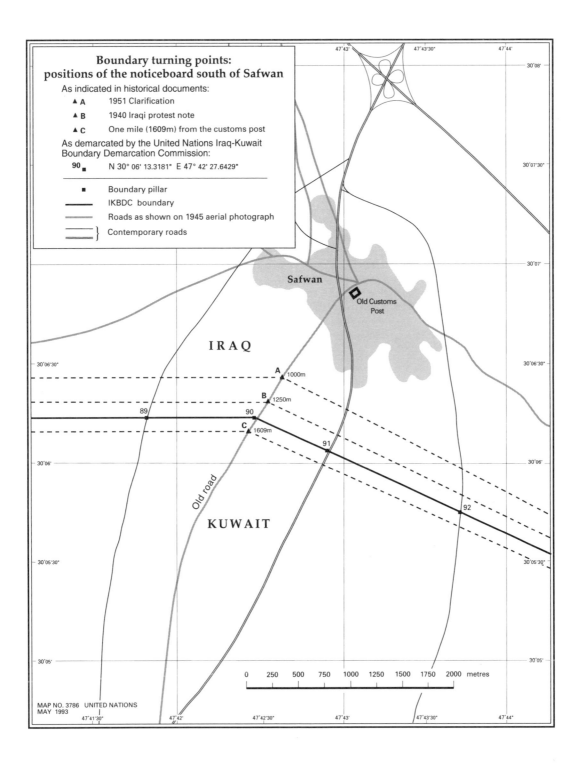

Boundary turning points:
positions of the noticeboard south of Safwan

As indicated in historical documents:

▲ A   1951 Clarification

▲ B   1940 Iraqi protest note

▲ C   One mile (1609m) from the customs post

As demarcated by the United Nations Iraq-Kuwait
Boundary Demarcation Commission:

90 ■   N 30° 06' 13.3181" E 47° 42' 27.6429"

■   Boundary pillar

▬▬   IKBDC boundary

━   Roads as shown on 1945 aerial photograph

⎫
⎬   Contemporary roads
⎭

IRAQ

Safwan

◇ Old Customs
Post

A ▲ 1000m

B ▲ 1250m

89   90

C ▲ 1609m

91

Old road

92

KUWAIT

0   250   500   750   1000   1250   1500   1750   2000 metres

MAP NO. 3786   UNITED NATIONS
MAY 1993

line from the point south of Safwan to the junction is plotted on the Commission's orthophoto maps.

81. The Commission decided that the demarcation of the intersection of the boundary with the shoreline at Umm Qasr should be in terms of the position of the Khowrs as shown on the 1936 map as it was considered that that was the position of the boundary as envisaged and intended from that time. This is also the position shown on the British 1:50,000-scale map transmitted by Security Council document S/22412. This position has now been demarcated as the boundary at Umm Qasr by the Commission, leaving the Umm Qasr port complex and Umm Qasr Village within Iraqi territory.

82. The Commission decided that the position of the junction of the Khowrs should be the position as close as possible to that of epoch 1932. Its position was determined following studies of charts produced between 1907 and 1991, aerial photographs covering a period of some 40 years from 1951 and topographic maps. Although absolute positions varied, there was acceptably good agreement between the shore outlines on the maps and the details on the photographs, which led the Commission to rule out any significant effects of erosion or accretion around the junction of the Khowrs during the period covered by the materials studied.

83. Six identifiable junction points were plotted on the 1:25,000 scale orthophoto map from charts produced in 1907, 1932, 1939, 1948, 1971 and 1991. The best available chart produced closest in time to epoch 1932 was the chart produced by the Basra Port Directorate in 1939. With the exception of the point derived from the 1932 chart and from the 1991 British Admiralty Chart, these points fall within a relatively small circle.

84. The Commission decided also to take into consideration the 1932 chart, despite its lower quality, in fixing the junction point, as it was produced at the time closest to epoch 1932. The final position was a weighted mean position. This has been considered as the most likely location of the position referred to in the British proposal of October 1940 and the December 1951 note verbale.

85. The boundary from the point south of Umm Qasr on the shoreline to the junction of the Khowrs has been depicted on maps in various positions in the Khowr Zhobeir. Specific descriptions are given in the October 1940 and December 1951 clarifications.

86. The Commission decided that the boundary line from the point south of Umm Qasr on the shore should be fixed and should follow the low-water-springs line up to the point directly opposite and nearest to the junction of the Khowr Zhobeir and the Khowr Abd Allah. The Commission further decided to plot the low-water-springs line from the false-colour infrared photographs.

87. The Commission further decided that the boundary from the above point, opposite and nearest to the junction of the Khowrs, to that junction, should be the shortest possible line (see map).

C. *Khowr Abd Allah section*

1. *Boundary line*

88. By the Khowr Abd Allah section, the Commission refers to the maritime, or offshore, boundary from the junction of the Khowr Zhobeir and the Khowr Abd Allah to the eastern end of the Khowr Abd Allah. The Commission felt that the closing statement of the delimitation formula, mentioning the islands of Warbah, Bubiyan, etc. as appertaining to Kuwait, gave an indication that the existing frontier in that section lay in the Khowr Abd Allah.

89. The Commission gave careful consideration to this section of the boundary. Having closely examined the language of the delimitation formula and the historical evidence on this part of the frontier, including earlier proposals for its demarcation, and having taken into account the legal aspects of the matter, the Commission agreed that it had a sufficient basis to proceed with the demarcation of the Khowr Abd Allah section. The Commission noted, moreover, that all the historical evidence pointed to the existence of a general agreement between the two countries on a boundary in the Khowr Abd Allah.

90. The Commission concluded that the existing boundary to be demarcated was the median line, it being understood that navigational access should be possible for both States to the various parts of their respective territory bordering the demarcated boundary.

91. The Commission examined charts that might be used for the selection of base points. To verify the low-water line on the 1991 edition of British Admiralty Chart No. 1235, which had been identified as a chart that could be used for the definition of the median line, infrared false-colour aerial photography was flown at low-water springs. A comparison of the aerial photography with the chart revealed a good degree of agreement. The Commission noted in this connection that an earlier version of that chart had been used by Coucheron-Aamot.

92. After careful comparison between the low-water-springs line on the 1993 aerial photograph, and a preliminary photogrammetric plot based on these photographs, with the 1991 edition of British Admiralty Chart No. 1235, the Commission decided to adopt this chart for defining the median line. Positions on the chart are referred to the WGS 84 datum. For all practical purposes this datum is identical to the Iraq-Kuwait Boundary Datum (IKBD).

93. Established hydrographic techniques were used to identify base points and these were then submitted to

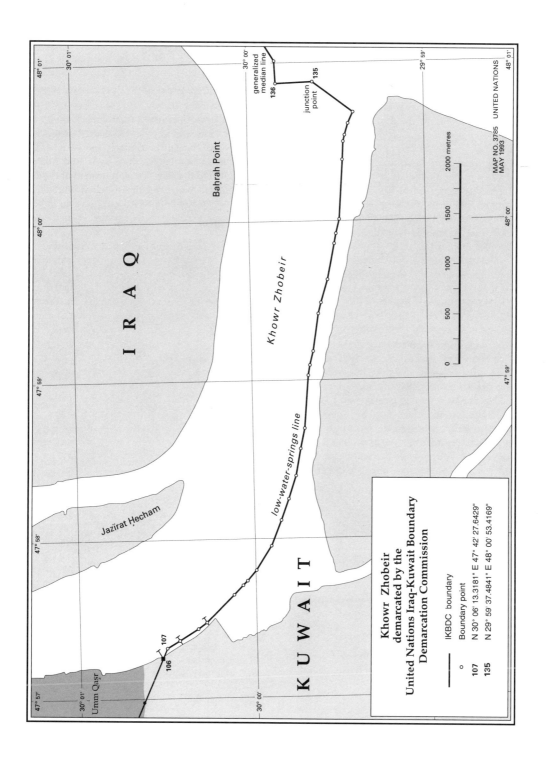

Khowr Zhobeir
demarcated by the
United Nations Iraq-Kuwait Boundary
Demarcation Commission

———— IKBDC boundary

○ Boundary point

107 N 30° 06' 13.3181" E 47° 42' 27.6429"

135 N 29° 59' 37.4841" E 48° 00' 53.4169"

IRAQ

KUWAIT

Bahrah Point

Khowr Zhobeir

Jazirat Hecham

Umm Qaṣr

low-water-springs line

generalized
median line

136

135

junction
point

0   500   1000   1500   2000 metres

MAP NO. 3785
MAY 1993

UNITED NATIONS

107

106

Iraq and Kuwait for approval or the provision of alternatives. Kuwait accepted the base points on its side. No response was received from Iraq either to a request to provide base points or to confirm those suggested by the Commission. Therefore, the Commission proceeded with the demarcation using the base points it had established on the Iraqi side.

94. In considering the terminus point on the median line at the entrance to the Khowr Abd Allah, the Commission sought, in a careful review, to establish the extent of the internationally agreed boundary under the 1963 Agreed Minutes. It therefore examined various representations of the boundary on earlier maps and charts and studied various methods of establishing the end of the agreed boundary to the open sea. It concluded that the entrance to the Khowr Abd Allah from the open sea lay where there was a significant change in the direction of the coastlines of the two States. It determined a precise point on the median line at the entrance.

95. The Commission determined that the boundary connection from the generalized median line to the junction of the Khowrs was the shortest line between them. From that point the median line adopted by the Commission is defined by a set of coordinates which are calculated from the baseline points established on opposite low-water lines as depicted on the 1991 edition of British Admiralty Chart No. 1235. At the eastern end of Warbah, a drying shoal, called the Warbah Spit, that could be subject to major change over the years, had been charted on the British Admiralty chart. Here two median lines were calculated, one taking the shoal into account and the other ignoring it. Equal weight was given to both lines and an average line was calculated between the two medians to decide the demarcation line. The 1959 median line calculated by Coucheron-Aamot at the request of Iraq approximates closely to the demarcation line of the Commission except in the immediate vicinity of Warbah Spit, which Coucheron-Aamot ignored.

2. Navigational access

96. Recognizing the importance of navigational access for both parties, the Commission requested the Office of Legal Affairs of the United Nations Secretariat to prepare a statement on navigational access for its consideration, which was subsequently issued as a Commission document.

97. Following consideration of the note prepared by the Office of Legal Affairs, the Commission adopted the following statement:

"The Commission views navigational access for both States to the various parts of their respective territories bordering the demarcated boundary as of importance for ensuring an equitable character and

for promoting stability and peace and security along the border. In this connection, it is the opinion of the Commission that such navigational access is possible for both States through the Khowr Zhobeir, the Khowr Shetana and the Khowr Abd Allah to and from all their own respective waters and territories bordering their boundary. The Commission notes that this right of navigation and access is provided for under the rules of international law as embodied in the 1982 United Nations Convention on the Law of the Sea ratified by both Iraq and Kuwait. Taking into consideration the particular circumstances of this area, it is also the view of the Commission that the right of access implies a non-suspendible right of navigation for both States."

X. Physical representation of the boundary

A. Physical demarcation of the land boundary

98. Following the establishment of preliminary positions for the pillars demarcating the land boundary, the Commission entered into a contract with the Eastern Asphalt and Mixed Concrete Company (EAMCO) of Bahrain for the manufacture of boundary markers. The pillars were emplaced during the third field session, September-November 1992, by a construction crew contracted from EAMCO and assisted by UNIKOM. The entire operation was under the direction and the supervision of the Commission's survey team.

99. The coordinates for the land boundary are physically demarcated by 106 monuments, approximately 2 kilometres apart, and 28 intermediate markers. The first monument is the existing pillar marking the trijunction point of Iraq, Kuwait and Saudi Arabia. Each boundary monument site consists of a steel-reinforced, silica-mica aggregate concrete boundary pillar, painted yellow and black, 3 metres in height and measuring 45 cm^2 at the top and 90 cm^2 at the base. The pillars are sunk into the ground to an approximate depth of 1.5 metres. A 2 m^2 concrete collar is positioned over them flush with the ground. At each location one witness mark on the Iraqi side and one witness mark on the Kuwaiti side are buried in the ground to facilitate repositioning of the pillar should it become necessary. Small pointer pillars on either side provide a direction towards the site of the next pillar.

100. Before and after the pillars were emplaced, their positions were inspected and checked at each site. During this exercise it was found that intervisibility between pillars was not possible at every location, either because of the terrain or because of structures along the sight-lines. Where the terrain interfered with intervisibility, intermediate pillars were emplaced during the final field session, in April 1993.

B. Physical demarcation of the Khowr Zhobeir and the Khowr Abd Allah

101. The boundary line in the Khowr Zhobeir was not physically demarcated. Instead it was demarcated by geographic coordinates determined photogrammetrically using false-colour infrared photography. During the final field session, a modified pointer pillar was placed on line between pillar No. 106 and the low-water-springs line. Plaques were emplaced on the jetties where the low-water-springs line continued beneath them. An offset mark was emplaced at the southern end of the stone-faced embankment, south of the southernmost jetty. Two pointer poles, which uniquely define the direction between the last point on the low-water-springs line and the junction of the Khowrs, were also emplaced and three witness marks were established close by.

102. Physical demarcation of the Khowr Abd Allah was deemed impractical and not necessary. The boundary line in the Khowr Abd Allah is demarcated by fixed coordinates, ascertained in accordance with the standards followed in general international practice.

C. Recommendations for boundary maintenance

103. With a view to providing for arrangements for maintenance of the physical representation of the boundary, in accordance with the report of the Secretary-General (S/22558, para. 4), the Commission invites the Secretary-General to request the survey organizations that were associated with the Commission or, if not available, similar organizations to provide the following services:

(a) To inspect the pillars and markers of the Iraq-Kuwait boundary on an annual basis;

(b) To report to him after each inspection;

(c) To take appropriate measures for repositioning, repairing or replacing those pillars and markers, as necessary;

(d) To monitor the adequacy of and to emplace any additional boundary markers such as buoys, pilings or other markers, as may be deemed useful.

The Commission considers that, to facilitate future maintenance work, the existence of a cleared road giving access to the pillars is of great importance. It therefore recommends that the Secretary-General should make the necessary arrangements for such a road to be created.

104. The costs incurred for these services should be shared by the two parties concerned.

105. In the opinion of the Commission, such arrangements should remain in force until other technical arrangements are established between Iraq and Kuwait for the purposes of maintaining the surficial representation of their common boundary.

XI. Documentation of demarcation

106. As stated in the Commission's terms of reference (S/22558), the geographic coordinates established by the Commission will constitute the final demarcation of the international boundary between Iraq and Kuwait (see sect. XIII below). (A certified copy of these coordinates is submitted to the Secretary-General, together with the present report.)

107. Documentation of the demarcated boundary also includes a customary set of record sheets of the survey stations and a set of record sheets of each of the boundary pillars.

108. The coverage and layout of the original orthophoto maps of the Commission at the scale of 1:25,000 have been extended and revised and the demarcated boundary plotted on them. Eighteen sheets cover the entire length of that boundary. In addition, orthophoto maps at the scale of 1:2,500 provide further positional information on the boundary in the Rumailah/Ratqa area and the settled areas at Safwan and Umm Qasr.

109. Attached as an enclosure to the present report is a map at the scale of 1:250,000, which provides an overview of the entire length of the boundary.

110. Authenticated copies of all demarcation documentation are to be deposited with the Secretary-General.

XII. Conclusion

111. The United Nations Iraq-Kuwait Boundary Demarcation Commission demarcated in geographic coordinates of latitude and longitude the international boundary set out in the Agreed Minutes between Kuwait and Iraq and made arrangements for the physical representation of the boundary. This latter task included the emplacement of an appropriate number and type of boundary pillars or monuments and provision for arrangements for continuing maintenance and locational accuracy of the surficial boundary representation. The Commission has carried out this mandate, and only this mandate.

112. As noted by the Security Council in its resolution 773 (1992) and by the Commission itself, the Commission has not reallocated territory between Kuwait and Iraq, but has simply carried out the technical task necessary to demarcate for the first time the precise coordinates of the international boundary reaffirmed in the 1963 Agreed Minutes. To this end, the coordinates established by the Commission, as reproduced in section XIII below, constitute the final demarcation of the international boundary between Iraq and Kuwait.

113. The Commission has also made arrangements for the physical representation of the boundary. It has erected 106 boundary pillars and 28 intermediate boundary markers on the international land boundary. It has

demarcated by coordinates a fixed boundary along the low-water line in the Khowr Zhobeir. It has also demarcated the international boundary in the Khowr Abd Allah section by fixed coordinates, following general international practice. It has further recommended a mechanism for ongoing maintenance, which would ensure maintenance of the pillars and markers of the international boundary and would provide some future flexibility for the emplacement of additional markers. Under the Commission's recommendation, this mechanism for continuing maintenance would remain in force until other technical arrangements are made between Iraq and Kuwait for the purposes of maintaining the surficial representation of their common boundary.

114. The Commission has made extensive efforts to obtain all the appropriate material available for this demarcation and has given every opportunity to both parties to submit any appropriate materials and to present their views fully. It is hoped that its work will, in the words of the Secretary-General, in his report of 2 May 1991 (S/22558), "promote stability and peace and security along the border".

XIII. List of coordinates demarcating the international boundary

115. The following [table below] is a list of geographic coordinates for 162 boundary points determined by the United Nations Iraq-Kuwait Boundary Demarcation Commission to demarcate the International boundary between the Republic of Iraq and the State of Kuwait in accordance with the Agreed Minutes of 4 October 1963.

116. Where necessary for the sake of intervisibility, additional intermediate markers have also been established.

117. The coordinates are divided into five sections, each representing a different segment of the boundary.

118. The reference system of the coordinates is the Iraq-Kuwait Boundary Datum 1992 (IKBD-92). The ellipsoid associated with the definition of IKBD-92 is the World Geodetic System 1984 (WGS 84) ellipsoid defined by:

Semi major axis: 6378137.000 metres
Flattening: 1/298.257223563

A. Boundary coordinates in the Wadi Al Batin

119. The boundary in the Wadi Al Batin from pillar No. 1 to pillar No. 72 is a series of straight lines between boundary pillars conforming to the thalweg of the Wadi. Pillar No. 1 on the Iraq-Kuwait boundary is the existing pillar No. 1 on the boundary between Iraq and Saudi Arabia. Pillar No. 72 is located on the intersection of the thalweg of Wadi Al Batin and the line of latitude of the point south of Safwan.

Geographic coordinates:
Boundary

point	Latitude	Longitude	Description
1	N 29° 06' 04.2128"	E 46° 33' 10.9431"	trijunction pillar
2	N 29° 06' 10.6747"	E 46° 33' 25.5664"	pillar
3	N 29° 07' 10.6940"	E 46° 34' 00.8825"	pillar
4	N 29° 08' 00.3923"	E 46° 34' 47.9228"	pillar
5	N 29° 08' 48.6806"	E 46° 35' 39.1756"	pillar
6	N 29° 09' 32.2099"	E 46° 36' 33.5084"	pillar
7	N 29° 10' 07.6002"	E 46° 37' 39.6466"	pillar
8	N 29° 10' 52.0411"	E 46° 38' 32.9901"	pillar
9	N 29° 11' 37.6791"	E 46° 39' 26.1431"	pillar
10	N 29° 12' 26.1698"	E 46° 40' 15.8391"	pillar
11	N 29° 13' 18.1397"	E 46° 41' 01.1813"	pillar
12	N 29° 14' 04.3933"	E 46° 41' 34.9432"	pillar
13	N 29° 15' 02.3669"	E 46° 42' 11.4675"	pillar
14	N 29° 15' 53.3557"	E 46° 42' 58.0267"	pillar
15	N 29° 16' 46.3911"	E 46° 43' 39.2978"	pillar
16	N 29° 17' 37.9173"	E 46° 44' 26.2600"	pillar
17	N 29° 18' 27.7745"	E 46° 45' 13.9179"	pillar
18	N 29° 19' 18.7152"	E 46° 46' 00.4511"	pillar

Boundary point	Latitude	Longitude	Description
19	N 29° 20' 17.8310"	E 46° 46' 32.6872"	pillar
20	N 29° 21' 19.3027"	E 46° 47' 03.3099"	pillar
21	N 29° 22' 08.0505"	E 46° 47' 52.2213"	pillar
22	N 29° 22' 50.5997"	E 46° 48' 52.5327"	pillar
23	N 29° 23' 44.9223"	E 46° 49' 34.5663"	pillar
24	N 29° 24' 34.5568"	E 46° 50' 21.4483"	pillar
25	N 29° 25' 24.2107"	E 46° 51' 09.2409"	pillar
26	N 29° 26' 13.8315"	E 46° 51' 59.1625"	pillar
27	N 29° 27' 18.7699"	E 46° 52' 35.6475"	pillar
28	N 29° 28' 25.3036"	E 46° 53' 04.6798"	pillar
29	N 29° 29' 25.4178"	E 46° 53' 32.9392"	pillar
30	N 29° 30' 22.9330"	E 46° 54' 09.9808"	pillar
31	N 29° 31' 29.9866"	E 46° 54' 16.1735"	pillar
32	N 29° 32' 21.9653"	E 46° 55' 07.3294"	pillar
33	N 29° 33' 20.8033"	E 46° 55' 37.7202"	pillar
34	N 29° 34' 15.5616"	E 46° 56' 20.5211"	pillar
35	N 29° 35' 16.4170"	E 46° 56' 48.3296"	pillar
36	N 29° 36' 14.6575"	E 46° 57' 16.8024"	pillar
37	N 29° 37' 05.4477"	E 46° 58' 12.4297"	pillar
38	N 29° 38' 06.5060"	E 46° 58' 38.8663"	pillar
39	N 29° 38' 58.0957"	E 46° 59' 19.3217"	pillar
40	N 29° 39' 48.4222"	E 46° 59' 53.1945"	pillar
41	N 29° 41' 00.3660"	E 47° 00' 12.2819"	pillar
42	N 29° 42' 13.0994"	E 47° 00' 15.7699"	pillar
43	N 29° 43' 19.5829"	E 47° 00' 24.5714"	pillar
44	N 29° 44' 18.1467"	E 47° 01' 02.8779"	pillar
45	N 29° 45' 08.5000"	E 47° 01' 53.0614"	pillar
46	N 29° 46' 10.2530"	E 47° 02' 17.7614"	pillar
47	N 29° 47' 06.6325"	E 47° 02' 53.8648"	pillar
48	N 29° 48' 09.2729"	E 47° 03' 15.4290"	pillar
48a	N 29° 48' 25.8955"	E 47° 03' 23.7764"	intermediate marker
49	N 29° 49' 08.8932"	E 47° 03' 45.3724"	pillar
49a	N 29° 49' 50.7268"	E 47° 04' 09.6471"	intermediate marker
50	N 29° 50' 06.8587"	E 47° 04' 19.0096"	pillar
50a	N 29° 50' 17.5805"	E 47° 04' 25.4063"	intermediate marker
51	N 29° 51' 05.0040"	E 47° 04' 53.7046"	pillar
52	N 29° 52' 06.7624"	E 47° 05' 19.3202"	pillar
53	N 29° 53' 08.9919"	E 47° 05' 41.6386"	pillar
54	N 29° 54' 11.0843"	E 47° 06' 02.6154"	pillar
55	N 29° 55' 17.0251"	E 47° 06' 16.3831"	pillar
56	N 29° 56' 15.6444"	E 47° 06' 46.8197"	pillar
57	N 29° 57' 11.7890"	E 47° 07' 25.4123"	pillar
58	N 29° 58' 15.1655"	E 47° 07' 46.6825"	pillar
59	N 29° 59' 12.5391"	E 47° 08' 21.9329"	pillar
60	N 30° 00' 00.9556"	E 47° 09' 20.2023"	pillar
60a	N 30° 00' 14.2007"	E 47° 09' 33.2812"	intermediate marker
61	N 30° 01' 02.8841"	E 47° 10' 21.3655"	pillar
62	N 30° 01' 42.1161"	E 47° 11' 22.4627"	pillar
63	N 30° 02' 10.1485"	E 47° 12' 29.9656"	pillar
64	N 30° 02' 35.6610"	E 47° 13' 38.0981"	pillar
64a	N 30° 02' 48.2354"	E 47° 14' 26.0720"	intermediate marker

Boundary point	Latitude	Longitude	Description
65	N 30° 02' 54.8419"	E 47° 14' 51.2858"	pillar
66	N 30° 03' 07.2870"	E 47° 16' 06.4092"	pillar
66a	N 30° 03' 14.7752"	E 47° 16' 27.8149"	intermediate marker
67	N 30° 03' 31.3604"	E 47° 17' 15.2386"	pillar
68	N 30° 04' 07.3734"	E 47° 18' 18.7972"	pillar
69	N 30° 04' 47.7218"	E 47° 19' 18.7703"	pillar
69a	N 30° 05' 16.1844"	E 47° 20' 01.9904"	intermediate marker
70	N 30° 05' 27.9778"	E 47° 20' 19.9024"	pillar
70a	N 30° 05' 40.7090"	E 47° 21' 07.0419"	intermediate marker
71	N 30° 05' 49.7839"	E 47° 21' 40.6563"	pillar
71a	N 30° 06' 05.4691"	E 47° 22' 04.6786"	intermediate marker
72	N 30° 06' 13.3181"	E 47° 22' 16.7010"	pillar (northernmost point in Wadi Al Batin)

B. *Boundary coordinates along the line of latitude of the point south of Safwan*

120. The boundary continuing from pillar No. 72 to pillar No. 90 lies along the line of latitude of the point south of Safwan.

Geographic coordinates:

Boundary point	Latitude	Longitude	Description
72a	N 30° 06' 13.3181"	E 47° 22' 55.4130"	intermediate marker
73	N 30° 06' 13.3181"	E 47° 23' 31.5066"	pillar
73a	N 30° 06' 13.3181"	E 47° 23' 46.0864"	intermediate marker
74	N 30° 06' 13.3181"	E 47° 24' 39.1916"	pillar
74a	N 30° 06' 13.3181"	E 47° 25' 27.5703"	intermediate marker
75	N 30° 06' 13.3181"	E 47° 25' 54.1252"	pillar
75a	N 30° 06' 13.3181"	E 47° 26' 26.1535"	intermediate marker
76	N 30° 06' 13.3181"	E 47° 27' 05.6902"	pillar
76a	N 30° 06' 13.3181"	E 47° 27' 17.4759"	intermediate marker
77	N 30° 06' 13.3181"	E 47° 28' 06.4824"	pillar
77a	N 30° 06' 13.3181"	E 47° 28' 46.6507"	intermediate marker
78	N 30° 06' 13.3181"	E 47° 29' 09.0860"	pillar
78a	N 30° 06' 13.3181"	E 47° 29' 28.6841"	intermediate marker
79	N 30° 06' 13.3181"	E 47° 30' 15.8536"	pillar
79a	N 30° 06' 13.3181"	E 47° 30' 57.6225"	intermediate marker
80	N 30° 06' 13.3181"	E 47° 31' 23.1982"	pillar
80a	N 30° 06' 13.3181"	E 47° 31' 56.6823"	intermediate marker
81	N 30° 06' 13.3181"	E 47° 32' 26.9061"	pillar
81a	N 30° 06' 13.3181"	E 47° 33' 11.3945"	intermediate marker
82	N 30° 06' 13.3181"	E 47° 33' 40.8425"	pillar
82a	N 30° 06' 13.3181"	E 47° 34' 14.5282"	intermediate marker
83	N 30° 06' 13.3181"	E 47° 34' 55.4858"	pillar
83a	N 30° 06' 13.3181"	E 47° 35' 43.1244"	intermediate marker
84	N 30° 06' 13.3181"	E 47° 36' 10.4403"	pillar
84a	N 30° 06' 13.3181"	E 47° 36' 48.9286"	intermediate marker
85	N 30° 06' 13.3181"	E 47° 37' 24.6714"	pillar
85a	N 30° 06' 13.3181"	E 47° 37' 54.5241"	intermediate marker
86	N 30° 06' 13.3181"	E 47° 38' 39.5006"	pillar

point	Latitude	Longitude	Description
86a	N 30° 06' 13.3181"	E 47° 39' 04.1408"	intermediate marker
87	N 30° 06' 13.3181"	E 47° 39' 53.5651"	pillar
88	N 30° 06' 13.3181"	E 47° 40' 45.0226"	pillar
89	N 30° 06' 13.3181"	E 47° 41' 47.4709"	pillar
90	N 30° 06' 13.3181"	E 47° 42' 27.6429"	pillar (turning point south of Safwan)

C. Boundary coordinates along the geodesic between the point south of Safwan and the point south of Umm Qasr

121. The boundary continuing from pillar No. 90 to pillar No. 106 lies along the line of shortest distance (the geodesic).

Geographic coordinates:

Boundary

point	Latitude	Longitude	Description
91	N 30° 06' 03.3807"	E 47° 42' 53.5808"	pillar
92	N 30° 05' 45.0600"	E 47° 43' 41.3864"	pillar
93	N 30° 05' 25.0544"	E 47° 44' 33.5686"	pillar
94	N 30° 05' 02.2409"	E 47° 45' 33.0493"	pillar
95	N 30° 04' 45.0505"	E 47° 46' 17.8514"	pillar
96	N 30° 04' 18.2073"	E 47° 47' 27.7801"	pillar
96a	N 30° 03' 58.9632"	E 47° 48' 17.8893"	intermediate marker
97	N 30° 03' 49.7978"	E 47° 48' 41.7481"	pillar
98	N 30° 03' 21.7283"	E 47° 49' 54.7898"	pillar
99	N 30° 02' 57.8345"	E 47° 50' 56.9334"	pillar
100	N 30° 02' 38.1990"	E 47° 51' 47.9797"	pillar
101	N 30° 02' 10.5648"	E 47° 52' 59.7867"	pillar
102	N 30° 01' 47.7924"	E 47° 53' 58.9307"	pillar
103	N 30° 01' 26.9252"	E 47° 54' 53.1031"	pillar
104	N 30° 01' 13.4491"	E 47° 55' 28.0759"	pillar
104a	N 30° 01' 01.4808"	E 47° 55' 59.1276"	intermediate marker
105	N 30° 00' 55.4621"	E 47° 56' 14.7405"	pillar
105a	N 30° 00' 51.0137"	E 47° 56' 26.2789"	intermediate marker
105b	N 30° 00' 47.0439"	E 47° 56' 36.5746"	plaque on road
105c	N 30° 00' 41.5522"	E 47° 56' 50.8166"	intermediate marker
105d	N 30° 00' 38.2514"	E 47° 56' 59.3757"	plaque on road
106	N 30° 00' 31.8988"	E 47° 57' 15.8470"	pillar south of Umm Qasr

D. Boundary coordinates along the low-water line between Umm Qasr and the junction of the Khowrs

122. Continuing from pillar No. 106, the boundary lies along the extension of the geodesic from pillar No. 90 to pillar No. 106. Boundary point No. 107 is at the intersection of this geodesic and the photogrammetric determination of the line of low water. Boundary point No. 134 lies at the point on the low-water line which is closest to the junction of the Khowrs (boundary point No. 135).

Geographic coordinates:

Boundary

point	Latitude	Longitude	Description
107	N 30° 00' 30.6311"	E 47° 57' 19.1337"	low water point
108	N 30° 00' 25.5597"	E 47° 57' 22.1204"	plaque on jetty
109	N 30° 00' 20.1338"	E 47° 57' 26.6988"	low water point

point	Latitude	Longitude	Description
110	N 30° 00' 17.0202"	E 47° 57' 27.9162"	plaque on jetty
111	N 30° 00' 07.3546"	E 47° 57' 38.5615"	low water point
112	N 30° 00' 04.0223"	E 47° 57' 43.0972"	low water point
113	N 30° 00' 02.4886"	E 47° 57' 45.0878"	low water point
114	N 29° 59' 59.9883"	E 47° 57' 50.2931"	low water point
115	N 29° 59' 54.3048"	E 47° 58' 00.0921"	low water point
116	N 29° 59' 51.1851"	E 47° 58' 07.3891"	low water point
117	N 29° 59' 48.5075"	E 47° 58 15.0012"	low water point
118	N 29° 59' 45.9004"	E 47° 58 23.9522"	low water point
119	N 29° 59' 44.0034"	E 47° 58' 34.7048"	low water point
120	N 29° 59' 42.9652"	E 47° 58' 41.8016"	low water point
121	N 29° 59' 40.8118"	E 47° 59' 01.6401"	low water point
122	N 29° 59' 39.9809"	E 47° 59' 05.2917"	low water point
123	N 29° 59' 38.3873"	E 47° 59' 15.6241"	low water point
124	N 29° 59' 37.0503"	E 47° 59' 26.0722"	low water point
125	N 29° 59' 35.7797"	E 47° 59' 28.9642"	low water point
126	N 29° 59' 33.5772"	E 47° 59' 37.8413"	low water point
127	N 29° 59' 30.9373"	E 47° 59' 51.7876"	low water point
128	N 29° 59' 30.8353"	E 47° 59' 55.2387"	low water point
129	N 29° 59' 29.7002"	E 48° 00' 04.7347"	low water point
130	N 29° 59' 27.9211"	E 48° 00' 23.7886"	low water point
131	N 29° 59' 27.4473"	E 48° 00' 31.1501"	low water point
132	N 29° 59' 27.0442"	E 48° 00' 33.8539"	low water point
133	N 29° 59' 25.6931"	E 48° 00' 37.8351"	low water point
134	N 29° 59' 23.6762"	E 48° 00' 42.0794"	low water point
135	N 29° 59' 37.4841"	E 48° 00' 53.4169"	junction of the Khowrs

E. *Boundary coordinates from the junction of the Khowrs and along the median line of the Khowr Abd Allah*

123. The boundary in the Khowr Abd Allah is the generalized median line as identified by the following

coordinates. Boundary point No. 136 is located at the point on the generalized median line which lies closest to the junction of the Khowrs (boundary point No. 135).

Geographic coordinates:

Boundary

point	Latitude	Longitude	Description
136	N 29° 59' 47.3389"	E 48° 00' 52.6840"	median point
137	N 29° 59' 47.9344"	E 48° 01' 03.2547"	median point
138	N 29° 59' 58.1832"	E 48° 01' 20.7047"	median point
139	N 30° 00' 26.1002"	E 48° 01' 50.4004"	median point
140	N 30° 00' 50.4002"	E 48° 02' 14.4005"	median point
141	N 30° 01' 09.0001"	E 48° 02' 39.0004"	median point
142	N 30° 01' 18.9000"	E 48° 03' 00.0002"	median point
143	N 30° 01' 33.5167"	E 48° 03' 41.3692"	median point
144	N 30° 01' 40.3556"	E 48° 04' 05.2773"	median point
145	N 30° 01' 45.5265"	E 48° 04' 34.0137"	median point
146	N 30° 01' 48.5499"	E 48° 05' 20.2407"	median point
147	N 30° 01' 47.7000"	E 48° 05' 53.7002"	median point
148	N 30° 01' 42.3674"	E 48° 06' 31.1234"	median point
149	N 30° 01' 39.9238"	E 48° 07' 16.8423"	median point
150	N 30° 01' 35.6000"	E 48° 08' 00.9000"	median point
151	N 30° 01' 32.7610"	E 48° 08' 47.0644"	median point

Annex
List of documents and reports of the Commission

I. DOCUMENTS

II. REPORTS

Addendum (S/25811/Add.1, 24 May 1993)
Letter dated 21 May 1993 from the Secretary-General addressed to the President of the Security Council

Demarcation of the international boundary between the Republic of Iraq and the State of Kuwait

(Map at the scale of 1:250,000)

Note: The toponomy on the map corresponds to the orthography found on most recent maps.

[Not reproduced here.]

Document 159

Statement by the President of the Security Council concerning the sanctions regime

S/25830, 24 May 1993

The members of the Security Council held informal consultations on 24 May 1993 pursuant to paragraph 21 of resolution 687 (1991).

After hearing all the opinions expressed in the course of the consultations, the President of the Council concluded that there was no agreement that the necessary conditions existed for a modification of the regimes established in paragraph 20 of resolution 687 (1991), as referred to in paragraph 21 of that resolution.

Document 160

Report of the Secretary-General, pursuant to Security Council resolution 778 (1992), concerning the whereabouts and amounts of Iraqi petroleum and petroleum products and the proceeds of sale

S/25863, 27 May 1993

Introduction

1. The present report is submitted pursuant to paragraph 5 of Security Council resolution 778 (1992) adopted on 2 October 1992, by which the Council requested the Secretary-General to ascertain the whereabouts and amounts of petroleum and petroleum products and the proceeds of sale referred to in paragraphs 1 and 2 of resolution 778 (1992), drawing on the work already done under the auspices of the Compensation Commission, and to report the results to the Security Council as soon as possible.

2. By a note dated 14 October 1992, the Secretary-General brought resolution 778 (1992) to the attention of all Permanent Representatives and Permanent Observers to the United Nations.

3. On 26 October 1992, a note verbale was sent, requesting all States to provide, by 30 November 1992, all relevant information to the Secretary-General for the effective implementation of resolution 778 (1992). By early December 1992 only 33 States had replied, and a reminder was sent on 16 December 1992.

I. Information provided by Member States and observers

4. As of 30 April 1993 the following 62 countries had replied to the Secretary-General's request: Antigua and Barbuda (S/24906), Australia (S/24967), Austria (S/24888), Brazil (S/25737), Brunei Darussalam (S/24927), Botswana (S/25316), Bulgaria (S/24887), Canada (S/25245), Chad (S/25416), Chile (S/24944), China (S/24885), Colombia (S/24994, S/25223), Croatia (S/25060), Cuba (S/25729), Cyprus (S/25073), Denmark (S/24898), Ecuador (S/24903), Estonia (S/25153), Ethiopia (S/24957), Finland (S/24975), France (S/24886), Germany (S/24907), Greece (S/25275), Hungary (S/25173), India (S/24909), Iran (Islamic Republic of) (S/25035), Ireland (S/24890), Israel (S/25323), Italy (S/24911), Japan (S/24993), Kuwait (S/25750), Liechtenstein (S/24899), Luxembourg (S/25348), Malta (S/24896), Mexico (S/25104), Mongolia (S/24910), Morocco (S/24919), Myanmar (S/25119), Netherlands (S/24891), New Zealand (S/24945), Norway (S/24962), Oman (S/24947), Pakistan (S/24972, S/25292), Poland (S/25223), Portugal (S/24920), Republic of Korea (S/24904), Romania (S/25001), Russian Federation (S/24897), Rwanda (S/25083), San Marino (S/25383), Singapore (S/24889), Spain (S/24958), Sweden (S/25138), Switzerland (S/24901), Thailand (S/24908), Trinidad and Tobago (S/25059), Tunisia (S/24998), Ukraine (S/24905), United Arab Emirates (S/25208), United Kingdom of Great Britain and Northern Ireland (S/24995), United States of America (S/24902) and Venezuela (S/25209).

5. The Government of Greece indicated in its note verbale of 3 February 1993 (S/25275) that a number of banks in Greece held a total of $276,000 representing the proceeds of the sale of oil products.

6. In its reply of 15 December 1992 (S/24993), the Government of Japan indicated that the Bank of Tokyo was holding assets totalling $48.88 million. The Government of Japan stated, however, that all of the funds held were subject to, or had to satisfy, the rights of a third party and that consequently no funds could be transferred to the escrow account.

7. The Government of Tunisia, in its note verbale dated 18 December 1992 (S/24998), indicated holdings of Iraqi funds totalling $15.8 million from oil transactions and stated that the funds had already been used in partial settlements of Iraq's debts to Tunisia.

8. The Government of the United States of America, in its note verbale of 30 November 1992 (S/24902), indicated that it held a total of $637.4 million in Iraqi assets subject to the provisions of resolution 778 (1992). It also stated that it was prepared to transfer $200 million of this total to the escrow account, as long as the amount transferred at no time exceeded 50 per cent of the total funds contributed or transferred to the escrow account.

9. None of the remaining 58 States which responded to the Secretary-General's request for information indicated that they had any petroleum or petroleum products or frozen assets subject to the provisions of resolution 778 (1992).

II. Expenditure and estimated costs of United Nations activities

10. Paragraph 5 (b) of resolution 778 (1992) requested the Secretary-General to ascertain the costs of United Nations activities concerning the elimination of weapons of mass destruction, the provision of humani-

tarian relief in Iraq, and the other United Nations operations specified in paragraphs 2 and 3 of resolution 706 (1991).

11. The table below provides the estimated expenditures for the various activities related to the implementation of Security Council resolutions 687 (1991) and 706 (1991) from their inception to 31 December 1993. Also shown are the resources made available from the escrow account or from direct contributions as well as the estimated amount of funding still needed in 1993 for each of these activities. The latter estimates are based on the most current information available and are subject to change as operational requirements and plans are revised or updated.

Table
Estimated expenditures and resources made available, and additional funding needed in 1993, for activities authorized under the provisions of Security Council resolutions 687 (1991) and 706 (1991)
(In millions of United States dollars)

	Estimated expenditure requirements from inception to December 1993 a/	Resources made available from escrow account and contributions	Estimated additional funding necessary
United Nations Compensation Commission	22.6	21.0	1.6
United Nations Special Commission	72.2	37.9	34.3
Return of Kuwaiti property	4.2	4.0	0.2
Iraq-Kuwait Boundary Demarcation Commission	6.7	4.3	2.4
Sale of Iraqi petroleum and miscellaneous	0.6	0.0	0.6
Total	106.3	67.2	39.1

a/ Includes cost estimates for 1993 totalling $72.5 million.

12. Total estimated costs of the United Nations Inter-agency Humanitarian Programme for Iraq, which are summarized in the annex, are projected to be $489.2 million for the period 1 April 1993 to 31 March 1994. These estimates are based on the sum of specific project proposals that represent only the most urgent requirements. They do not constitute an exhaustive list of projects to be implemented as part of this programme, and other project proposals may be identified and examined in the future.

III. *Establishment of the escrow account and receipts to date*

13. A competitive bidding exercise was conducted to select a commercial bank in which to establish the United Nations escrow account. Proposals were sought only from the top credit-rated banks in the world which were also capable of providing for the operational and information needs of the United Nations. Based on its high credit ratings, lack of involvement in South Africa and lowest investment management fees for deposit amounts up to $100 million, Morgan Guaranty Trust Co. of New York was selected. The escrow account was opened at Morgan in December 1992.

14. As of 30 April 1993 a total of $101.5 million had been received into the escrow account. The total includes a $30 million voluntary contribution from Saudi Arabia, a $20 million voluntary contribution from Kuwait, a $50 million transfer of frozen assets from the United States of America and a $1.5 million voluntary contribution from the United Kingdom of Great Britain and Northern Ireland.

15. A bank account for the subaccount of the escrow fund referred to in paragraph 11 of resolution 778 (1992) has also been opened at Morgan Guaranty Trust Co., but this account has not yet received any funds.

IV. *Utilization of the escrow account funds*

16. As of 30 April 1993 the entire total of $101.5 million received into the escrow account had been designated for the purposes specified in Security Council resolutions 687 (1991) and 706 (1991), taking into account preferences expressed by States transferring or contributing funds, as follows:

(a) $33 million had been designated for the United Nations Special Commission authorized under section C of resolution 687 (1991). As of 30 April 1993, a total of $31.5 million had been expended by the Special Commission;

(b) $21 million had been designated for, and the full amount transferred to, the United Nations Compensation Commission. As of 30 April 1993, $6.6 million of this total had been expended;

(c) $4 million had been designated for costs incurred by the United Nations in facilitating the return of Kuwaiti property seized by Iraq. As of 30 April 1993, $2.7 million of this total had been expended;

(d) $2 million had been designated towards Iraq's one half share of the costs of the Boundary Demarcation Commission. As of 30 April 1993, a total of $3.7 million had been expended by the Boundary Demarcation Commission;

(e) $41.5 million had been designated for various humanitarian activities in Iraq. $40 million of this total was for activities in Iraq prior to 31 March 1993; as of 30 April 1993, $38 million of this $40 million total had been expended, primarily by transfer to other executing United Nations agencies. The remaining $1.5 million had been designated for activities commencing after 1 April 1993, and this $1.5 million had been transferred to the United Nations Children's Fund (UNICEF).

V. *Observations and conclusions*

17. The projected cumulative costs through the end of 1993 for the United Nations Special Commission's activities and weapons destruction programme alone totals over $72 million. About $38 million of these costs will be covered from funds already designated in the escrow account and from other contributions, but funding will be needed for at least an additional $34 million over the coming months. A major contract with the International Atomic Energy Agency (IAEA) for approximately $24 million will be ready for signature within the next few days, but there will not be adequate funds to implement the contract unless additional cash is available.

18. The United Nations Compensation Commission has received adequate funds to cover most of its currently projected operational and administrative costs for 1993. No funds are currently available from the escrow account, however, to pay any significant amount of actual claims to injured parties.

19. Cost estimates of the ongoing United Nations Inter-agency Humanitarian Programme for Iraq have not been definitively established, but the projected total for specific project proposals submitted to date by various United Nations agencies and programmes for the period 1 April 1993 to 31 March 1994 comes to $489 million. No further funds are available from the escrow account at the present time for these activities.

20. In the circumstances, additional transfers of frozen funds from Member States that hold such assets and/or significant new voluntary contributions to the escrow account are urgently needed to continue the activities mandated by the Security Council.

Annex
United Nations Inter-agency Humanitarian Cooperation Programme in Iraq

*Listing of projects proposed to date**

1 April 1993-31 March 1994
(In United States dollars)

Activity/projects	Agency/ programme	Total funds required for 1 April 1993- 31 March 1994
Sector 1		
FOOD ASSISTANCE AND NUTRITION		
Project 1 - Food assistance to seriously affected groups	WFP	114 295 650
Project 2 - Food-for-work	WFP	3 700 000
Project 3 - Supplementary feeding for school children	WFP	20 700 000
Project 4 - Nutrition	UNICEF	3 000 000
Subtotal		141 695 650

*The projects listed in the above table are intended to address critical needs identified by the Department for Humanitarian Affairs and United Nations agencies/programmes. The list is not exhaustive, and additional projects will be prepared as required and as funds become available.

Activity/projects	Agency/ programme	Total funds required for 1 April 1993- 31 March 1994
Sector 2		
AGRICULTURAL ASSISTANCE		
Project 1 - Crop protection against sunnpest infestation	FAO	9 350 000
Project 2 - Grain-seed exchange	FAO	4 000 000
Project 3 - Provision of certified wheat seed and fertilizer	FAO	30 950 000
Project 4 - Agricultural machinery and portable pumps	FAO	42 000 000
Project 5 - Improvement of vegetable production in southern governorates	FAO	3 690 000
Project 6 - Provision of vegetable and pulse seeds	FAO	8 700 000
Project 7 - Provision of poultry	FAO	4 250 000
Project 8 - Provision of veterinary inputs and feed concentrates	FAO	15 200 000
Project 9 - Provision of pesticides	FAO	3 445 000
Project 10 - Provision of apiaries	FAO	3 300 000
Project 11 - Rehabilitation of palm dates production	FAO	310 000
Project 12 - Improvement of sugar cane production	FAO	2 175 000
Project 13 - Improvement of irrigation canals	FAO	2 343 000
Subtotal		129 713 000
Sector 3		
HEALTH		
Basic health		
Project 1 - Epidemiological surveillance	WHO	3 000 000
Project 2 - Provision of life-saving drugs and supplies	WHO	23 000 000
Project 3 - Vector control	WHO	8 000 000
Project 4 - Monitoring of inputs	WHO	750 000
Project 5 - Evaluation and training activities	WHO	2 000 000
Project 6 - Basic health	UNICEF	4 000 000
Project 7 - Immunization	UNICEF	3 000 000
Project 8 - Control of diarrhoeal diseases	UNICEF	4 000 000
Project 9 - Control of acute respiratory infections	UNICEF	3 000 000
Project 10 - Childhood disability	UNICEF	1 000 000
Water supply and sanitation		
Project 1 - Water and waste monitoring	WHO	3 250 000
Project 2 - Water supply and sanitation activities	UNICEF	15 000 000
Subtotal		70 000 000

Activity/projects	Agency/ programme	Total funds required for 1 April 1993- 31 March 1994
Sector 4		
COMMUNITY REHABILITATION AND ASSISTANCE		
Education		
Project 1 - Provision of educational assistance	UNESCO/ UNICEF	10 400 000
Shelter		
Project 1 - Shelter	DHA/UNDP-OPS	19 100 000
Road repair and maintenance		
Project 1 - Road repair and maintenance	DHA-IRCU	1 500 000
Mines		
Project 4 - Mines-related activities	DHA/UNDP-OPS	1 250 000
Energy provision		
Project 1 - Fuel provision	UNICEF	45 000 000
Project 2 - Electrical power transmission and generation	DHA/UNDP-OPS	1 500 000
Project 3 - Assessment of electrical power needs	DHA/UNDP-OPS	165 000
Rural women		
Project 1 - Income generation for rural women	UNDP	1 000 000
Rural households		
Project 1 - Rural household food security	UNICEF	1 733 785
Social welfare institutions		
Project 1 - Support for social welfare institutions	UNDP	1 125 000
Municipal services		
Project 1 - Municipal sanitation	DHA/UNOPS	7 473 000
Refugees		
Project 1 - Refugees and returnees	UNHCR	0
Subtotal		90 246 785
Sector 5		
PROGRAMME SUPPORT		
Project 1 - Programme coordination	DHA-SUI/IRCU	5 623 500
Project 2 - United Nations Guards	DHA-SUI/UNFOD	50 665 550
Project 3 - United Nations Volunteers	UNV	1 280 000
Subtotal		57 569 050
Grand total		489 224 485

Document 161

Security Council resolution concerning the Iraq-Kuwait Boundary Demarcation Commission

S/RES/833 (1993), 27 May 1993

The Security Council,

Reaffirming its resolution 687 (1991) of 3 April 1991, in particular paragraphs 2 to 4 thereof, and its resolutions 689 (1991) of 9 April 1991, 773 (1992) of 26 August 1992, and 806 (1993) of 5 February 1993,

Recalling the report of the Secretary-General of 2 May 1991 concerning the establishment of the United Nations Iraq-Kuwait Boundary Demarcation Commission, 1/ the subsequent exchange of letters between the Secretary-General and the President of the Security Council dated 6 and 13 May 1991, 2/ and the acceptance of the report by Iraq and Kuwait,

Having considered the letter dated 21 May 1993 from the Secretary-General to the President of the Security Council 3/ transmitting the final report of the Commission,

Recalling in this connection that through the demarcation process the Commission was not reallocating territory between Kuwait and Iraq, but was simply carrying out the technical task necessary to demarcate for the first time the precise coordinates of the boundary set out in the "Agreed Minutes between the State of Kuwait and the Republic of Iraq regarding the restoration of friendly relations, recognition and related matters" 4/ signed by them on 4 October 1963, and that this task was carried out in the special circumstances following Iraq's invasion of Kuwait and pursuant to resolution 687 (1991) and the report of the Secretary-General regarding implementation of paragraph 3 of that resolution, 1/

Reminding Iraq of its obligations under resolution 687 (1991), in particular paragraph 2 thereof, and under other relevant resolutions of the Council, and of its acceptance of the Council resolutions adopted pursuant to Chapter VII of the Charter of the United Nations, which acceptance forms the basis for the cease-fire,

Noting with approval the Secretary-General's instruction to the United Nations Iraq-Kuwait Observation Mission to finalize the realignment of the demilitarized zone with the entire international boundary between Iraq and Kuwait demarcated by the Commission,

Welcoming the Secretary-General's decision to make the necessary arrangements for the maintenance of the physical representation of the boundary, as recommended by the Commission in section X.C of its report, until other technical arrangements are established between Iraq and Kuwait for this purpose,

Acting under Chapter VII of the Charter,

1. *Welcomes* the letter dated 21 May 1993 from the Secretary-General to the President of the Council 3/ and the 20 May 1993 report of the United Nations Iraq-Kuwait Boundary Demarcation Commission transmitted therewith;

2. *Welcomes also* the successful conclusion of the work of the Commission;

3. *Expresses its appreciation* to the Commission for its work on the land part of the boundary as well as the Khawr 'Abd Allah or offshore section of the boundary, and welcomes its demarcation decisions;

4. *Reaffirms* that the decisions of the Commission regarding the demarcation of the boundary are final;

5. *Demands* that Iraq and Kuwait, in accordance with international law and relevant Security Council resolutions, respect the inviolability of the international boundary, as demarcated by the Commission, and the right to navigational access;

6. *Underlines and reaffirms its decision* to guarantee the inviolability of the above-mentioned international boundary which has now been finally demarcated by the Commission and to take as appropriate all necessary measures to that end in accordance with the Charter of the United Nations, as provided for in paragraph 4 of resolution 687 (1991) and paragraph 4 of resolution 773 (1992);

7. *Decides* to remain seized of the matter.

1/ See *Official Records of the Security Council, Forty-sixth Year, Supplement for April, May and June 1991*, document S/22558.
2/ S/22592 and S/22593 respectively. See *Official Records of the Security Council, Forty-sixth Year, Resolutions and Decisions of the Security Council, 1991*, p. 17.
3/ *Official Records of the Security Council, Forty-eighth Year, Supplement for April, May and June 1993*, documents S/25811 and Add.1.
4/ United Nations, *Treaty Series*, vol. 485, No. 7063.

Document 162

Letter dated 7 June 1993 from the Permanent Representative of Iraq to the Secretary-General transmitting a letter dated 6 June 1993 from the Minister for Foreign Affairs of Iraq concerning the work of the Iraq-Kuwait Boundary Demarcation Commission

S/25905, 8 June 1993

On instructions from my Government, I have the honour to transmit herewith a letter dated 6 June 1993 from Mr. Muhammed Said Al-Sahaf, Minister for Foreign Affairs of the Republic of Iraq, addressed to you on the subject of Security Council resolution 833 (1993).

I should be grateful if you would have this letter and its annex, the letter from the Minister for Foreign Affairs of the Republic of Iraq, circulated as a document of the Security Council.

(*Signed*) Nizar HAMDOON
Ambassador
Permanent Representative

Annex
Letter from the Minister for Foreign Affairs of Iraq dated 6 June 1993 addressed to the Secretary-General

I have the honour to draw attention to the position of my Government on Security Council resolution 833 (1993), adopted on 27 May 1993. Pending our treatment of the matter in detail in the future, after all the completed documentation has arrived from the Commission and been studied by the competent authorities with due care and attention, I should like, on this occasion, to present to you the initial viewpoint of the Government of the Republic of Iraq on this question.

I. First of all, I should like to reaffirm once again what was stated in the letter dated 6 April 1991 from the Minister for Foreign Affairs of the Republic of Iraq addressed to the Secretary-General of the United Nations concerning Iraq's position on Security Council resolution 687 (1991), adopted on 4 April 1991, and what was stated in the letter about the question of the boundary between Iraq and Kuwait (S/22456).

II. I should like to reaffirm once again what was stated in section II of the letter dated 21 May 1992 from the Minister for Foreign Affairs of the Republic of Iraq addressed to you concerning the establishment of the Boundary Demarcation Commission (S/24044).

III. I should like also to reaffirm what was stated in section III of the letter dated 21 May 1992 from the Minister for Foreign Affairs of the Republic of Iraq addressed to you concerning a number of the decisions of the Boundary Demarcation Commission (S/24044).

IV. With regard to the Commission's decision on the demarcation of the offshore boundary in the Khawr Abdullah and its endorsement by the Council in resolution 833 (1993), I should like to draw attention to a number of blatant facts that indicate the great defectiveness characterizing the work of the Commission.

1. When the Commission first discussed the question of the demarcation of the offshore section of the boundary at its third session, held at Geneva from 12 to 16 August 1991, the Chairman of the Commission affirmed—and his understanding was shared by the two independent experts—that there was a difficulty in dealing with the offshore section of the boundary because of the nature or the limits of the mandate given to the Commission, which did not authorize it to deal with the boundary line beyond the junction of the Khawr al-Zubayr and the Khawr Abdullah (i.e., in the sea), unless the two parties so agreed, and that the Commission could, moreover, not confer powers on itself.

2. The representative of the rulers of Kuwait asked the Commission, during its fourth session in New York from 7 to 16 October 1991, that he should be afforded an opportunity to deliver a statement on the offshore section of the boundary at the next session. The Commission decided, in accordance with the adopted rules of procedure, to respond affirmatively to that request. When the representative of the rulers of Kuwait delivered his statement at the fifth session of the Commission, held in New York from 8 to 12 April 1992, the above-mentioned representative discussed the mandate of the Commission and claimed that it included the demarcation of the offshore boundary. At the time when it was assumed that the Chairman of the Commission would announce the conclusion of its work on this question with the position affirmed by the Chairman and the two independent experts at the third session of the Commission, which is stated above, the Chairman of the Commission merely remained silent.

3. At the Commission's sixth session, held in New York from 15 to 24 July 1992, which was essentially devoted to consideration of the Commission's report on its work to the Secretary-General of the United Nations, the Secretariat once again included in the draft agenda

submitted by the Chairman discussion of the offshore section of the boundary. The Commission's minutes, which recorded the facts of the discussions that took place on the subject at this session, clearly revealed to any objective and fair observer the acute differences that prevailed in the discussions of the Commission, particularly between the representative of the rulers of Kuwait and his advisers and the Chairman of the Commission, because of the Kuwaiti pressure on the Chairman and the two independent experts, to adopt the position of the rulers of Kuwait concerning the demarcation of the offshore boundary. The Chairman of the Commission did not hesitate to reveal many of the glaring facts regarding the above-mentioned pressure and the interventions of the Deputy Legal Counsel of the United Nations Secretariat in the work of the Commission.

The final outcome at this session was that the Commission, as stated in its press release issued on 24 July 1992, approved consideration of the Khawr Abdullah sector also and discussion of it at a meeting to be held for this purpose in October.

It should be noted that this press release contained details indicating that the decisions taken by the Commission on the demarcation of what was described as the land boundary did not detach Umm Qasr, oil wells and territory from Iraq for the sake of the opposing policy. It appears that that was done in implementation of what was dictated to the Chairman of the Commission and its two experts regarding the interpretation of the decisions taken by the Commission in order to counter the extensive clamour from the press, which took up the subject and reported a portion of the facts in many newspapers in the West and in the Arab countries. Then the Commission, at its seventh session, held in New York from 12 to 16 October 1992, continued discussion of the matter, in the light of the study submitted by the two independent experts, and requested them to continue collecting data on the question.

4. Two important developments occurred in this series of events. On 12 August 1992, the "further report" of the Boundary "Demarcation" Commission, completed at its sixth session, was transmitted to the President of the General Assembly. The letter of transmittal stated: "As far as the offshore boundary is concerned, the Council might wish to encourage the Commission to demarcate that part of the boundary as soon as possible, and thus complete its work. This statement was made even though the Secretariat knew full well that the Commission had not yet agreed that it was competent under its terms of reference to demarcate the offshore boundary and although its Chairman's position on this matter was very clear to it and reached the point of implied resignation if this matter was imposed on the Commission. This state-ment reinforces the impression that the Rapporteur was prematurely responding to the wish of the rulers of Kuwait and the States which support it in the Security Council and which had planned from the beginning that the outcome of the Boundary Demarcation Commission's work should be what it turned out to be, in spite of opposing views and concepts. In fact, we find that the Security Council hastened to adopt resolution 773 (1992) on 26 August 1992, stating, in paragraph 3, that it welcomed the decision of the Commission to consider the eastern section of the boundary, which included the offshore boundary, and urging the Commission to demarcate that part of the boundary as soon as possible and thus complete its work. This clear correspondence between the language used in the transmittal of the Commission's report to the Security Council and in the language of Security Council resolution 773 (1992) and the background of established facts that emerge from the Commission's discussions reflect beyond any doubt or interpretation a coordinated effort undertaken by the rulers of Kuwait, well-known circles in the Secretariat and certain States members of the Security Council to orient the work of the Commission in a way contrary to the mandate laid down for it by the Council itself in resolution 687 (1991) and in the report of the Secretary-General submitted under paragraph 3 of that resolution (S/22558), without going so far as to expressly amend that mandate, because that would mean an open political and legal scandal that could not be covered up. The Commission's work was guided in this way before it took a specific position on the question, because the utmost it had concerned itself with up to that point had not been more than a study of the topic from the technical viewpoint. That also explains the reiterations of the representative of the rulers of Kuwait, in the minutes of the meetings of the Commission, of his readiness to go to the Secretariat and to the Council for the adoption of the desired position on every occasion that he heard in the Commission a view contrary to what he wanted.

The second development concerns the resignation of the Chairman of the Commission as of 20 November 1992, as he explained in his letter dated 4 November 1992 to the Secretary-General. On 6 November, the Chairman of the Commission addressed another, more detailed, letter on the same subject to the Legal Counsel of the United Nations. This letter made it clear that the resignation was due to two causes, the first being a personal reason and the other being that he had "for some time [had] reservations about the terms of reference of the Commission". The Chairman revealed in the above-mentioned letter how he had several times raised with the Legal Counsel some aspects of the Commission's terms of reference; that the offshore boundary

(Khawr Abdullah) was not specifically referred to in the 1932 Exchange of Letters, which meant that delimitation was lacking for the Commission on which to base the operation of demarcation entrusted to it; and how the Legal Counsel had explained to him "that any change in the mandate of the Commission by the Security Council was out of the question". The letter explained also that the question had been discussed once again by the Chairman and the Legal Counsel in May and had also been discussed at two meetings held between the Chairman and the Legal Counsel, on the one hand, and the Secretary-General, on the other hand, in July and September 1992. And how the Chairman had "described" the situation that made it "impossible" for him to continue in office "unless certain modifications were made to the mandate of the Commission".

In view of the Chairman's realization of the difficulty of changing the Commission's terms of reference, he saw resignation as the only way open to him.

5. Following the resignation of the Chairman of the Commission, Mr. Nicolas Valticos was appointed Chairman, and its eighth session was held at Geneva from 14 to 16 December 1992, when it decided hastily that the basic principle governing the demarcation of the boundary in the Khawr Abdullah must be the median line, it being understood that the main aim and purpose of the adjustment of the boundary was to facilitate navigational access for both parties!

6. The improper intervention and influence on the work of the Commission, which we have mentioned above and which has led to the result already explained, gives rise, in addition to the position that we have indicated, to a number of legal questions that we should like to summarize as follows:

(a) The description of the boundary basically endorsed by the Security Council for demarcation by resolution 687 (1991) and decided on by the report of the Secretary-General submitted under paragraph 3 of the above-mentioned relation in no way touches on a description of the boundary in the Khawr Abdullah area. Accordingly, such description cannot be taken as the basis in any operation of demarcation as carried out by the Commission, because the demarcation must be based on a description, i.e., a delimitation of the boundary agreed on by the parties concerned.

(b) The Khawr Abdullah was not, according to the boundary description adopted by the Security Council in resolution 687 (1991), assigned the characteristic of the territorial sea, for investigation of the principle of its division between States with opposite or adjacent coasts in accordance with the principles of the law of the sea.

(c) The Khawr Abdullah area, even supposing that it were a territorial sea, is correctly described as subject to "special circumstances", as affirmed by the two independent experts also. This, under the 1982 Convention on the Law of the Sea, permits the delimitation of the boundary of the territorial sea to be made by a method other than the principle of the medium line, failing agreement between the two parties on another principle. The provision relating to this case of "special circumstances" gains additional force because of the absence of an agreed formula for the delimitation of the boundary. In other words, the delimitation of the boundary in this area "is being effected for the first time", and thus the "special circumstances" case applies.

(d) Iraq has historic rights in the Khawr Abdullah area, in which the rulers of Kuwait do not carry on substantial navigation, which makes it an exception, according to the 1982 Convention on the Law of the Sea, from the median line rule, as we mentioned in subparagraph (c) above.

(e) The Security Council has no right, pursuant to its functions and powers under the United Nations Charter, to impose a boundary delimitation on a Member State, because, under international law, this sphere of competence is governed by the principle of agreement between the States concerned and because it has, with the precision legally required, no relation to questions of the maintenance of international peace and security that are the sphere of competence of the Council. Thus, the Council has acted *ultra vires*.

V. Iraq has spent billions of dollars over scores of years on excavation works, the extension, improvement and maintenance of the channels, main and secondary navigation lanes leading into and out of the Khawr Abdullah and the erection of maritime installations, ports and wharfs in the Khawr Abdullah area in order to ensure the flow of its overseas trade. The imposition of the boundary in the Khawr Abdullah area, as decided on by the Boundary Demarcation Commission, presents a grave threat to Iraq's right to enjoy freedom of access to the sea by exercising its historic right to unrestricted and safe navigation in the Khawr Abdullah area, to an extent that will, in the future, place it in the position of a landlocked State.

VI. Lastly, I should like, in closing, to reaffirm once again our conclusion stated in the letter dated 21 May 1992 from the Minister for Foreign Affairs of the Republic of Iraq addressed to you (S/24044), because it still holds true, now more than at any previous time, regarding the overall outcome of the work of the Boundary Demarcation Commission and the recent unjust resolution adopted by the Council as resolution 833 (1993):

> "It becomes clear to every impartial observer that the decisions adopted by the Commission represent a purely political decision imposed by the Powers dominating the Security Council and the United Nations at present, particularly the Governments of the United States and the United Kingdom.

"...

"[That] will constitute a very dangerous precedent, contrary in substance and consequences to the duties and responsibilities entrusted to the Council by the Charter of the United Nations. ... It will not have contributed to the preservation of security and stability in the region but will rather have consciously created a continuous hotbed of tension as well as deliberately violated the legitimate and vital interests of a State Member of the United Nations. If there were compelling circumstances which force the Iraqi authorities to take certain positions regarding this decision, the people of Iraq could never be convinced that its historical rights had been respected and its vital interests safeguarded by the Security Council in a manner compatible with the rules of international law and the criteria of justice and fairness. The Arab nation will continue to view this decision as one link in the chain of Western imperialist games which began after the First World War and which have always been the subject of indignation and rejection on the part of the Arab Nation, and which have caused many of the disturbances and changes witnessed in the Arab Nation. The situation which we witness today is not new to the world, and the world knows the outcome resulting from such instances."

(*Signed*) Mohammed Said AL-SAHAF
Minister for Foreign Affairs
    of the Republic of Iraq

Document 163

Letter dated 16 June 1993 from the Permanent Representative of Kuwait to the Secretary-General transmitting a statement issued by the Kuwaiti Council of Ministers concerning the completion by the Iraq-Kuwait Boundary Demarcation Commission of its work

S/25963, 17 June 1993

On instructions from my Government, I am transmitting to you hereunder the text of the statement issued by the Kuwaiti Council of Ministers following the adoption by the Security Council of its resolution 833 (1993) concerning the completion by the Iraq-Kuwait Boundary Demarcation Commission of its work.

"Kuwait affirms that it will honour and be bound by Security Council resolution 833 (1993) and all the relevant Security Council resolutions. The Council has welcomed the final report of the Iraq-Kuwait Boundary Demarcation Commission entrusted with the implementation of paragraph 3 of its resolution 687 (1991). It has reaffirmed that the Commission's decisions are final. It has underlined and reaffirmed its decision to guarantee the inviolability of the international boundary between Kuwait and Iraq and to take as appropriate all necessary measures to that end in accordance with the Charter. It has recalled that, through the demarcation process, the Commission entrusted with the task of demarcating the boundary between Kuwait and Iraq by its resolutions 687 (1991) of 3 April 1991 and 689 (1991) of 9 April 1991 was not reallocating territory between Kuwait and Iraq but was simply carrying out the technical task necessary to demarcate the precise coordinates of the boundary on the basis of the existing agreements and the supporting documentation and evidence provided by the two parties to the Commission, whose decisions are to be considered final as of their adoption. It has demanded that Iraq and Kuwait, in accordance with international law and relevant Security Council resolutions, respect the inviolability of the international boundary, as demarcated by the Commission, and the right to navigational access.

"Kuwait regards the Security Council resolution as an enlightened achievement for the Organization and for international legitimacy and one to be added to its series of achievements contributing to the promotion of international peace and justice. Kuwait takes this opportunity to alert all the countries of the world to the need to maintain pressure on the Iraqi regime to implement all of the relevant Security Council resolutions and particularly those relating to the speedy release of the Kuwaiti prisoners and hostages and third-country nationals that the Iraqi regime is still holding in its prisons and detention camps."

I should be grateful if you would have this letter circulated as a document of the Security Council.

(*Signed*) Mohammad A. ABULHASAN
Permanent Representative

Document 164

Statement by the President of the Security Council concerning the installation of monitoring devices by UNSCOM

S/25970, 18 June 1993

The Security Council is deeply concerned by the Government of Iraq's de facto refusal to accept the United Nations Special Commission's (UNSCOM) installation of monitoring devices at rocket test sites and to transport chemical weapons-related equipment to a designated site for destruction, as set out in a report from the Executive Chairman of the Special Commission to the President of the Security Council (S/25960).

The Council refers to resolution 687 (1991) requiring Iraq to permit the Special Commission and the International Atomic Energy Agency (IAEA) to undertake immediate on-site inspection of any locations designated by the Commission. The agreement on facilities, privileges and immunities between the Government of Iraq and the United Nations, and resolutions 707 (1991) and 715 (1991), clearly establish Iraq's obligation to accept the presence of monitoring equipment designated by the Special Commission, and that it is for the Special Commission alone to determine which items must be destroyed under paragraph 9 of resolution 687 (1991).

Iraq must accept installation by UNSCOM of monitoring devices at the rocket test sites in question and transport the chemical weapons-related equipment concerned to a designated site for destruction.

The Council reminds Iraq that resolution 715 (1991) approved plans for monitoring by the Special Commission and the IAEA which clearly require Iraq to accept the presence of such monitoring equipment at Iraqi sites, designated by the Special Commission, to ensure continuing compliance with its obligations under Security Council resolution 687 (1991).

Iraq's refusal to comply with decisions of the Special Commission, as set out in the report of the Executive Chairman, constitutes a material and unacceptable breach of the relevant provisions of resolution 687 (1991), which established the cease-fire and provided the conditions essential to the restoration of peace and security in the region, as well as violations of Security Council resolutions 707 (1991) and 715 (1991) and the plans for future ongoing monitoring and verification approved thereunder. In this context, it recalls the statements of 8 January 1993 (S/25081) and 11 January 1993 (S/25091), and warns the Government of Iraq of the serious consequences of material breaches of resolution 687 (1991) and violations of its obligations under resolution 715 (1991) and the above-mentioned plans.

The Council reminds the Government of Iraq of its obligations under Security Council resolutions and its undertakings to provide for the safety of inspection personnel and equipment. The Council demands that the Government of Iraq immediately comply with its obligations under Security Council resolutions 687 (1991), 707 (1991) and 715 (1991), and cease its attempts to restrict the Commission's inspection rights and operational capabilities.

Document 165

Fifth report of the Executive Chairman of UNSCOM

S/25977, 21 June 1993

The Secretary-General has the honour to transmit to the Security Council a report submitted by the Executive Chairman of the Special Commission established by the Secretary-General pursuant to paragraph 9 (b) (i) of Security Council resolution 687 (1991).

Annex

Fifth report of the Executive Chairman of the Special Commission, established by the Secretary-General pursuant to paragraph 9 (b) (i) of Security Council resolution 687 (1991), on the activities of the Special Commission

Introduction

1. The present report is the fifth on the activities of the Special Commission, established by the Secretary-General pursuant to paragraph 9 (b) (i) of Security Council resolution 687 (1991), submitted to the Security Council by the Executive Chairman of the Commission. It is the fourth such report provided in accordance with paragraph 3 of Security Council resolution 699 (1991). It covers the period from 14 December 1992 to 14 June 1993. It is further to the reports contained in documents S/23165, S/23268, S/24108 and Corr.1 and S/24984.

I. Organizational and administrative issues

2. Since the last report, there have been further changes in the composition of the Special Commission. Mr. Nicola Circelli has replaced Col. Armando Caputo; Mr. Peter Dunn has replaced Mr. John Gee, who left to take up the position of Director of Verification in the Provisional Technical Secretariat of the Organization for the Prohibition of Chemical Weapons; and Mr. Ron Manley has replaced Professor Bryan Barrass upon the latter's retirement. Mr. Manley has since also submitted his resignation to take up the position of Head of the Chemical Weapons Branch of the Verification Division with Mr. Gee. The Commission hopes to be in a position to submit a nomination for his replacement to the Secretary-General shortly.

3. The organizational structure remains essentially as reported previously. Currently there are 32 staff in the Office of the Executive Chairman in New York, 25 in the Bahrain Field Office and 83 in the Baghdad Field Office.

4. There is still no agreement on the sale of Iraqi oil to finance United Nations operations resulting from the cease-fire resolution. Current expenses have been met from voluntary contributions and advances from Member States and funds made available from frozen Iraqi assets in accordance with Security Council resolution 778 (1992). However, in the absence both of Iraqi agreement to sell oil and of Iraq's acknowledgement of its obligations under resolution 699 (1991) to meet the full costs of the tasks authorized by section C of resolution 687 (1991), the problem of the financing of the Commission's operations remains a matter of great concern and further cash contributions by Governments are urgently required. This is particularly important now as a contract has been concluded to remove from Iraq the irradiated uranium fuel currently stored at Tuwaitha and at Location B, reprocess it and permanently store the wastes. This will involve for the Commission the largest expenditures it has incurred to date. The net contact price amounts to $24,565,000. However, there will be certain ancillary costs for special risk insurance and for radiation protection and other equipment currently estimated to cost in the neighbourhood of $800,000. These items are available at much lower rates to the United Nations and the International Atomic Energy Agency (IAEA) than to the contractor. While the United Nations Controller has given a guarantee that the United Nations has a legal responsibility to meet the costs of this contract, thereby allowing it to go ahead, it has been agreed that meeting the costs of the contract will have first call on all future incoming funds. Consequently, in order to continue operations, the Special Commission must receive funds adequate not only for operations, but also first to meet the outstanding funds for the contract. The funds currently available to finance the contract will have been expended by late August.

5. Governments have continued to support the operation of the Special Commission through the contribution of personnel, services and equipment. Resolution 687 (1991) foresaw government support in the form of both voluntary contributions and advances, pending a long-term solution to the financing issue. Supporting Governments were asked, in accordance with paragraph 5 (b) of resolution 778 (1992), to inform the Commission of the cost of those contributions that they consider advances. Some responses have been received, most of which indicate that the support provided to date should be viewed as voluntary contributions. A statement of the Commission's operating costs, together with further information on organizational and administrative issues, can be found in appendix I.

II. Status, privileges and immunities

6. The status, privileges and immunities of the Special Commission, IAEA and the United Nations specialized agencies involved in the implementation of Security Council resolution 687 (1991) continue to be regulated by the relevant agreements and Council resolutions and decisions.

7. The Special Commission and IAEA, on the one hand, and the Government of Bahrain, on the other, have extended for a further six months, until 30 September 1993, the agreement provided for in the exchange of letters relating to the facilities, privileges and immunities of the Special Commission and IAEA in Bahrain. The formal response from the Government of Bahrain was received by the Secretary-General on 29 April 1993.

8. In Iraq, there have been continuing problems in the implementation of the Special Commission's status, privileges and immunities. The security of Commission personnel and property in Iraq had improved somewhat, but the situation recently deteriorated with attacks on Commission personnel and property (see appendix III). It thus continues to remain a serious concern.

III. Developments

A. Political developments: the attitude of Iraq

9. Inspections of sites declared by Iraq or designated by the Commission have continued. However, Iraq still refuses to cooperate with the Commission and has exhibited a most unwelcome trend in relation to field operations, namely to seek to restrict the manner in which the Commission's rights are implemented. The main problems are as follows:

(a)(i) Iraq continues to maintain its position on the plans approved under Security Council resolution 715 (1991) for ongoing monitoring and verification, stated in the letter of 19 November 1991 from the then Foreign Minister of Iraq addressed to the President of the Council;

(ii) On 31 January 1993, the Iraqi Government officially informed the Executive Chairman of the Special Commission in writing that Iraq considered the new arrangement of interim monitoring at the Ibn Al-Haytham facility to be conducted under resolution 687 (1991). The Commission understood this to mean that Iraq would prevent this team, or any other team, from operating under the terms of the plan approved under resolution 715 (1991);

(iii) On 1 April 1993, General Amer, Chairman of the Iraqi Military Industrialization Corporation, reading from prepared notes and stressing that this was the official Iraqi position on the issue of monitoring, is reported by the Chief Inspector of an inspection team to have said:

> "Iraq accepted the first monitoring team to the Ibn Al-Haytham Centre in accordance with resolution 687 (1991). However, it appears from the modalities of the monitoring team that the Special Commission is trying to overlap in a discreet fashion Iraqi obligations under resolution 687 (1991) and resolution 715 (1991). This is very clever. Iraq knows that, using Iraqi cooperation under resolution 687 (1991), the Special Commission wants to assert Iraqi obligations under resolution 715

(1991). Iraq is fully aware of this effort. If the objective of the Special Commission is to make sure that no prohibited activities are going on, prohibited items are destroyed and Iraq has no capability to reactivate proscribed programmes, Iraq has no objections as this is part of resolution 687 (1991). However, if the objective is to start a de facto implementation of resolution 715 (1991) without Special Commission testament to the Security Council that Iraq is in full compliance with resolution 687 (1991) and without implementing paragraph 22 of that resolution, Iraq will not welcome this mission. The monitoring missions would not be welcome. But, even in this case, Iraq will still cooperate with the Special Commission to see the true objectives of these missions and to explore the intentions of the Special Commission. Iraq told the Special Commission that resolution 715 (1991) could be discussed only in connection with the implementation of paragraph 22 of resolution 687 (1991). You should never think or believe that it could be done otherwise.";

(iv) On 6 June 1993, the Special Commission informed Iraq of its intention to install cameras to monitor rocket test stands at two sites. On 7 June 1993, a senior Iraqi representative informed the chief of the UNSCOM expert team dispatched to Iraq for the installation of the cameras that Iraq would not accept any monitoring activities and would insist that the Special Commission limit itself to inspection activities under resolution 687 (1991). This position was confirmed in a letter of 8 June 1993 from Mr. Riyadh Al-Qaysi, Iraqi Deputy Minister for Foreign Affairs, to the Deputy Executive Chairman of the Special Commission, which stated that the installation of the cameras did not fall within the purview of resolution 687 (1991) "but rather comes within the framework of matters and questions that are still the subject of dialogue between the Iraqi authorities on the one hand and the Special Commission on the other". In a further letter dated 11 June 1993, Mr. Al-Qaysi added that "what we requested ... was a 'postponement of the decision' on the subject" until the proposed dialogue;

(v) Iraq's position is maintained despite assurances by the Commission that, if Iraq cooperated, its legitimate concerns would be met and the Commission's activities would be carried out in a manner which is not unduly intrusive;

(b) Iraq's full, final and complete disclosures of its proscribed weapons programmes, due under Security Council resolution 707 (1991), and its initial declarations, due under the plans for ongoing monitoring and verification, contain major shortcomings that will need to be rectified if they are to form the basis for a definite material balance of Iraq's past weapons of mass destruction programmes and for effective monitoring and verification of compliance. The information so far provided is tailored to what the Iraqi authorities consider the Special Commission to know already, rather than constituting a frank and open disclosure of all the true facts. One set of declarations, concerning the legal and administrative actions taken by Iraq to give effect to its obligations relating to ongoing monitoring and verification, has never been submitted;

(c) Iraq continues to refuse to divulge information indicating the names of foreign companies from which it has purchased equipment and materials. This is clearly unacceptable. Accurate information is essential if the Special Commission is to establish a material balance for proscribed items and, with IAEA and the Sanctions Committee, to devise a workable and realistic mechanism for import control required by paragraph 7 of resolution 715 (1991);

(d) In the period under review, there have been a number of serious incidents of breaches by Iraq of the Commission's rights, privileges and immunities. In January 1993, as reported in document S/25172, Iraq sought to deny the Commission the use of its own aircraft to transport personnel and equipment into and out of Iraq to and from Bahrain. In February 1993, Iraq threatened to shoot down a helicopter providing supporting overhead surveillance for an inspection team if the aircraft did not leave the vicinity of the site. In June, Iraq has blocked the installation of monitoring cameras (see subpara. (a) (iv) above), missed two deadlines for the removal and delivery to the Special Commission of equipment for the production of chemical weapons precursors and delayed an inspection of a site by a full day;

(e) The events referred to in subpara. (d) above also fit into a general pattern of Iraqi conduct. Iraq has, through its conduct since the last report, consistently demonstrated its desire to limit the Commission's inspection rights and operational capabilities through seeking to place restrictions on inspectors in the course of their work. While many of these Iraqi actions have taken place during the course of inspections under resolution 687 (1991), the Commission has no doubt that they form part of a long-term campaign to establish a practice for the conduct of inspections that would severely restrict the rights provided in the plans for ongoing monitoring and verification and relevant Security Council resolutions.

Iraq is thus clearly seeking to assert for itself the right to interpret how the resolutions should be implemented. Included in this campaign have been attempts by Iraq to dispute the Commission's instructions on the destruction of equipment intended for the production of banned weapons; to restrict the scope of inspections and information gathering; to restrict access and impose delays on inspections; to restrict the exercise of the Commission's aerial rights; to impose limits on the duration, size and composition of inspections; to require advance notice of inspection activities; and to limit the right to take photography. Further details on these incidents can be found in appendix III. Each incident has varied in seriousness. Some might not be significant were they not part of a general trend. However, when taken together, these incidents add up to a major impediment that would effectively impede credible long-term monitoring and verification. This again underlines the need to obtain from Iraq as soon as possible its formal acknowledgement of its obligations under resolution 715 (1991), so that the Council's requirements laid down in that resolution can be met.

10. Thus the situation remains essentially unchanged from the time of the last report: the intention to proceed from inspection and survey through destruction to ongoing monitoring and verification has, in large part, continued to be thwarted by the actions of the Iraqi Government. While preparations for the implementation of the plans are being made, the basic conditions for their full-scale implementation have not yet been met.

B. *Operational developments*

11. In the chemical weapons area, further inspection and destruction activities have been conducted, with the emphasis remaining on destruction. Attempts to elicit further information on Iraq's chemical weapons programme through a "seminar" held during an inspection proved unproductive because of the uncooperative attitude of the Iraqi counterparts. No further weapons or associated equipment have been found by inspection teams or declared by Iraq. However, further progress has been made in identifying what equipment and plant need to be destroyed. In this regard, a serious instance of Iraqi obstruction has arisen. Iraq was instructed to move certain items of equipment acquired for chemical weapon precursor production to Muthanna for destruction under Commission supervision there. It replied that it wished to reuse the equipment for the production of pesticides. Iraq, despite the Commission's insistence that its decision is final on the grounds that the equipment was acquired expressly for chemical weapons production and that, even if converted for pesticide production, it could easily and rapidly be reconverted for weapons production, has still not moved all the equipment as instructed. Full

accounts of inspection and destruction activities can be found in appendices IV and V respectively.

12. Further biological inspections were also conducted, as was a "seminar" with Iraqi counterparts on biological weapons issues. The same non-cooperative attitude was met in this area as with chemical weapons. However, inspection activities did assist in identifying additional facilities to be included in the plan for ongoing monitoring and verification.

13. On ballistic missiles, efforts have concentrated on three main aspects: trying to establish a definitive material balance for the SCUDs supplied by the former Soviet Union; trying to account for Iraq's production capacity in the ballistic missiles area; and establishing an interim monitoring regime for Iraq's dual-capable missile research and development facilities. This last has proved necessary because of Iraq's refusal to acknowledge its obligations under the plans for ongoing monitoring and verification (see appendix II).

14. Aerial surveillance activities have continued apace, using both U-2 (a total of 141 missions now flown) and helicopter platforms (236 targets now flown). Helicopter missions continue to be flown in support of ground inspections and to provide a time-series photographic record of sites which will need monitoring under the plans for ongoing monitoring and verification. Plans are also in place to mount additional sensors to the helicopters to give them greater monitoring and deterrence capability. Details of both these operations are contained in appendix V.

C. *Iraq's declarations*

15. Iraq's failure to provide full and honest declarations was touched upon in paragraph 9 (b) above. On 14 February 1993, Iraq provided a second set of declarations entitled "Updated monitoring information. Report No. 2". These add little to the first declarations. Attempts to elicit fuller information on chemical and biological issues were met with a totally unacceptable and uncooperative response, as noted above. Despite internationally verified evidence to the contrary, Iraq denies ever using chemical weapons. It refuses to hand over the missile-firing records essential if the Commission is to verify Iraqi claims to have accounted for all the Soviet-supplied SCUD missiles.

IV. *Issues and priorities for the future*

16. From the above, it can be seen that, despite further progress, no major breakthrough has been achieved that could make it possible to change the conclusion of the previous report. The most important developments have taken place in the area of destruction of proscribed items, but still much remains to be done. The

main areas that require action before the Commission will be in a position to report to the Security Council that Iraq is in substantial compliance with its obligations remain as follows:

(a) Acknowledgement by Iraq of its obligations under Council resolutions 707 (1991) and 715 (1991);

(b) Supplementation and revision of Iraq's "reports" to the point where, in the view of the Commission, they conform with the full, final and complete disclosures required under resolution 707 (1991), particularly as concerns former suppliers, and with initial declarations required under the plans for ongoing monitoring and verification adopted by resolution 715 (1991);

(c) Destruction of all items of equipment identified by the Special Commission as requiring destruction;

(d) The initiation and smooth functioning of the plans for ongoing monitoring and verification to ensure that Iraq does not reacquire the weapons proscribed to it;

(e) Acceptance and implementation by Iraq of all the Commission's privileges and immunities, including ensuring the safety and security of the personnel and property, landing rights for aircraft and non-obstruction of the inspections and logistics.

17. Further inspection activities are planned in each of the weapons categories. Destruction activities now focus on chemical weapons and equipment for their production. Preparations for the implementation of the plans for ongoing monitoring and verification are under way and ideas on the potential form of an import control regime for after the lifting of sanctions have been discussed. New staff recruitment reflects the shift of emphasis towards attempting to establish whether Iraq still has items which should be declared; tracking down Iraq's supplier networks; interim monitoring; preparations for ongoing monitoring and verification activities; and further elaboration of the ideas for import monitoring.

18. The priorities remain to obtain Iraq's acknowledgement of its obligations under resolutions 707 (1991) and 715 (1991) and to obtain satisfactory amendments to the various declarations, especially in relation to suppliers.

Appendix I
Organizational and administrative issues

A. *Staffing of the Special Commission*

1. The Commission currently has a total of 140 positions distributed amongst its three offices. Fifty positions are supported by the Commission. The balance of the staff are on loan from their Governments for assignments ranging from 3 to 12 months. Personnel, equipment and services have been provided for the Commission's activities by Argentina, Australia, Austria, Belgium, Can-

ada, China, the Czech Republic, Finland, France, Germany, Greece, Hungary, India, Indonesia, the Islamic Republic of Iran, Italy, Japan, the Netherlands, Nigeria, Norway, New Zealand, Poland, the Republic of Korea, Romania, the Russian Federation, Spain, Sweden, Switzerland, Thailand, Ukraine, the United Kingdom of Great Britain and Northern Ireland, the United States of America and Venezuela. The responsibilities of the Director General of IAEA are carried out by the Action Team set up within IAEA, the staff of which charged to the Commission's budget are indicated in paragraph 3 below. The Action Team draws upon the part-time services of numerous staff of various IAEA departments, funded under the regular IAEA budget.

2. The staff of the Commission are distributed as follows:

(a) *Headquarters of the Commission in New York*. The headquarters of the Commission in New York has a total of 32 staff assigned to it: 18 positions (8 in the Professional category and 10 in the support staff category) are currently charged to the operating budget of the Commission; and 14 positions are filled by staff assigned to the Commission by various Member States.

Unit	*Position*
Office of the Chairman	1 Executive Chairman
	1 Deputy Chairman
	1 Legal Adviser
	1 Political Adviser and Spokesman
	3 Support staff
Administrative Office	3 Professionals
	2 Support staff
Division of Operations	7 Chemical, biological, ballistic and nuclear experts
	1 Support staff
Information Assessment Unit	5 Chemical, biological, ballistic and nuclear experts
	2 Advisers in aerial photography
	5 Support staff

(b) *Office of the Commission in Bahrain*. The Bahrain Field Office has a total of 25 staff assigned to it on a regular basis to provide financial, administrative, logistic and training support to the inspection activities of the Commission and IAEA pursuant to section C of resolution 687 (1991). Eleven positions (three Professionals and eight local support staff) are charged to the operating budget of the Commission. Functions break down as follows:

Administration and logistic support	3 Professionals
	8 Local staff
Aerial and photographic support	1 Adviser
Air transport	13 Transall C-160 crew members

(c) *Office of the Commission in Baghdad*. A total of 83 persons are currently assigned on a long-term basis to the Commission's Baghdad office to provide logistic, communication and medical support to the inspection teams of the Commission and IAEA and in support of the chemical destruction programme and interim monitoring activities. Fourteen positions (nine Professionals, one international support staff and four local support staff) are under the Commission operating budget. The other 69 staff are provided by Governments.

Administration and logistic support	8 Professionals and Field Service staff
	4 Local staff
	1 International support staff
Aerial and photographic support	4 Advisers
Medical support	5 Medical staff
Chemical destruction	23 Advisers (including 3 medical staff dedicated to the chemical destruction programme)
Monitoring team	8 Advisers
Air transport	30 Helicopter crew members

B. *International Atomic Energy Agency*

3. The Action Team has a total of seven staff charged to the operating budget of the Commission (see also above):

Operational and technical support	5 Professionals
Administrative support	1 Professional
	1 Support staff

C. Financial situation of the Special Commission

4. Under Security Council resolution 699 (1991), Iraq is responsible for meeting the costs of all United Nations operations resulting from section C of resolution 687 (1991). To date, Iraq has made no contribution to the Special Commission's expenses. Indeed, it has rejected two Security Council resolutions, 706 (1991) and 712 (1991), which sought an interim solution to the financing issue.

5. Consequently, the Commission has had to rely on voluntary contributions, in cash and in kind, and on cash advances. Since the inception of its operations in April 1991, a total of $42.4 million has been contributed by a limited number of countries to support the operations of the Special Commission. This amount includes a total of $33 million transferred from the escrow account established under Security Council resolution 778 (1992) and loans to be repaid from Japan, of $2.5 million, and the United States, of $2 million.

6. Resolution 778 (1992) requested the Secretary-General to ascertain the costs of United Nations activities concerning the elimination of weapons of mass destruction. On 3 November 1992, the Special Commission wrote to Governments that have supported the Commission's operations through the provision of equipment, services, personnel and transportation to ascertain whether they considered their support to be voluntary contributions or an advance, for which reimbursement will eventually be required. Germany has indicated that it considers a part of its contributions—$10 million—to be an advance requiring reimbursement. Saudi Arabia made a contribution of $30 million to the escrow account for the Special Commission activities. An additional $3 million has been made available from the escrow account to the Special Commission for a grand total of $33 million.

7. Expenditures crossed the $40 million mark at the end of May 1993. This amount includes the cost of major projects like the successful removal in 1992 of unirradiated nuclear fuel out of Iraq under a contract between IAEA and the Russian Federation for $2 million. The $40 million also includes the first instalment of $6 million for the cost of the contract for the removal of irradiated nuclear fuel which will have to be paid in the coming months. The remaining $32 million have been used to cover the cost of all other activities and operations of the Commission and IAEA.

8. An additional $35 to $40 million will be required between now and the end of 1993 to maintain the current level of activities:

(a) *Removal of nuclear fuel contract*: the balance of $18.565 million will be required to cover the $24.565 million contract. An estimated additional $0.8 million will be needed to cover the cost of spare parts, logistic support, insurance, etc.;

(b) *Ongoing operations*: $10 to $15 million will be needed to maintain the pace of ongoing programmes and to cover the cost of planned operations;

(c) *Loans*: $4.5 million will be needed to cover repayments should the United States and Japanese loans be called. The above amount does not include the $10 million that Germany has disbursed until the end of 1992 for the air support provided to the Special Commission and which it has indicated that it considers an advance to be repaid.

9. The Commission's expenditures have always been kept to the bare minimum and it has essentially been operated on a shoestring budget for lack of an appropriate funding mechanism. The uncertainty of the Commission's financial future currently has an impact on the ability to plan operations effectively. The implementation of Security Council resolution 715 (1991) will require a reassessment of staffing and logistic support requirements both at headquarters and in the field. A full-scale plan of operations could result in at least a doubling of current operational expenditures.

Financial status of the Special Commission

List of contributions	US$
United States	2 000 000
	2 000 000 (loan)
Japan	2 500 000 (loan)
Kuwait	1 000 000
United Kingdom	175 400
Saudi Arabia	1 730 000
(Escrow account)	30 000 000
Various (Escrow account)	3 000 000
Total contributions, including loans	42 405 400
Expenditures, up to 31 May 1993	39 815 000
Estimated requirements for 1 June-31 December 1993	37 810 000
Total	77 625 000
Projected shortfall for 1993 operations	35 219 600

Note: The total shortfall is $50 million when the loans of $4.5 million from Japan and the United States and the contribution of $10 million from Germany are taken into account.

A. *Chemical weapons inspections*

1. UNSCOM47, consisting of two sub-teams, one designated CBW3 and the other IAEA 16, conducted inspection activities during the period from 5 to 14 December 1992, mainly in the chemical and bacteriological weapons field. The last report to the Council under resolution 699 (1991) was prepared before the results of this inspection had been assessed. Seven potential chemical weapons-related sites were visited, including a pharmaceutical plant. Nothing related to Security Council resolution 687 (1991) was found at any of these sites.

2. The two sub-teams jointly conducted a search of the "PetroChemical-3" headquarters. On arrival at the site, an incident occurred: documents were observed being removed from the premises. Some documents were subsequently returned and verified to be unrelated to Security Council resolution 687 (1991). However, the team was unable to establish whether these were the same as those removed.

3. Three question-and-answer "seminars" were held with Iraqi counterparts, specifically on Iraq's "full, final and comprehensive report" on chemical weapons. Little information was obtained. Indeed, the Iraqi side made it clear that it would not answer any question it considered "trivial, unethical or outside the scope of Security Council resolution 687 (1991)".

4. UNSCOM55 conducted chemical inspection activities from 6 to 18 April 1993. A number of potentially chemical weapons-related sites were visited, including the Fallujah sites, formerly part of the Muthanna State Establishment.

5. On 15 April 1993, during the UNSCOM55 inspection, the Chief Inspector handed over to the Iraqi side a letter requiring the removal by 31 May 1993 of certain items of equipment used in the $PCl_3/POCl_3$ production plant at Fallujah to Muthanna for destruction there under Special Commission supervision. These items had been acquired by Iraq specifically for the production of these chemical weapons precursors and as part of Iraq's chemical weapons programme. Consequently, the Commission decided that they needed to be destroyed. Irreversible conversion was not an option and, in any case, Iraq continues not to accept monitoring of dual-purpose equipment under the terms of the plans for ongoing monitoring and verification approved by the Council in its resolution 715 (1991) adopted unanimously under Chapter VII of the Charter. In such conditions, the Commission cannot guarantee the fate of any equipment redeployed by Iraq.

6. Iraq replied to this demand on 29 April 1993 saying that it wished to redeploy this equipment for use in insecticide production. On 14 May 1993, the Commission responded that it had taken into account Iraq's request for reuse of the equipment but that it stood by the earlier decision that, because the items were specifically acquired for the purpose of chemical weapons production, the equipment be removed and destroyed. Iraq responded to this letter on 27 May 1993, saying that the Commission had gone to extremes, adverse to Iraq, in interpreting its mandate, criticizing it, the Sanctions Committee and the Security Council respectively for their decisions relating to the destruction of equipment associated with weapons programmes, to Iraq's requests for imports and to the decisions to maintain sanctions. It accused the Commission and the Committee of following a policy of revenge against the Iraqi people and requested that the Commission change its decision. The Commission again responded on 4 June 1993, reminding Iraq of its obligations under the relevant resolutions and the Commission's rights and duties. It explained that the equipment in question could not be rendered harmless as it was intrinsically capable of being used for prohibited purposes and could quickly be reconverted for such. It gave Iraq until 10 June 1993 to complete the removal of the equipment and warned Iraq that failure to do so would result in the Commission reporting the matter to the Council. On 11 June 1993, Iraq responded that it "remained prepared to give the Special Commission, through bilateral technical consultations, practical guarantees to ensure peaceful use of this equipment in the long term". The Commission has informed Iraq that its decision on destruction is final. As of 14 June, some of the equipment had been removed to Muthanna, but much remained at Fallujah. No formal communication had been received from the Iraqi authorities as to their intentions regarding the remaining equipment. The matter was thus brought to the attention of the President of the Security Council and a formal report made to the Council on 16 June 1993 (S/25960).

B. *Biological weapons inspections*

7. UNSCOM47 also inspected three biological sites, including a visit to the Al Hakim Single Cell Production Facility. Nothing related to Security Council resolution 687 (1991) was found. However, some of the sites will have to be subjected to compliance monitoring.

8. Two question-and-answer "seminars" were held on biological weapons issues. As with the chemical issues, no useful information was obtained.

9. UNSCOM53/BW3 conducted inspection activities from 11 to 18 March 1993. Seven sites were inspected, including one that was undeclared and never

previously visited by the Commission. The items inspected included research equipment, munitions and munition-filling equipment (which transpired to be conventional items). No evidence was found of activities related to Security Council resolution 687 (1991) but, as with most bacteriological weapons-related activities, many sites were found to have a dual-purpose capability. Consequently, the team made recommendations for compliance-monitoring activities.

C. Ballistic missile inspections

10. UNSCOM50 was conducted from 12 to 21 February 1993. This inspection recorded serial numbers of specific machinery and details of raw materials (to assist in the determination of the Iraqi supplier network) and assessed the capabilities of certain establishments and facilities in Iraq, including the Nasser State Establishment, the Yawm Al Azim Facility and the TECO test stand at Zaafaraniyah. The team also supervised the destruction of the dies and molds at Taji used or intended for use in proscribed missile activities.

11. The mission of UNSCOM51 was to check specific information that items proscribed by Security Council resolution 687 (1991) were present in an area west of Baghdad. The items were reported to be related to ballistic missiles with a range greater than 150 kilometres and their associated vehicles. Three undeclared sites, suspected of concealing them, were thoroughly inspected: a large military ammunition production plant and two military units. The Commission designated each site for a short-notice inspection by UNSCOM51. The team conducted its activities on 22 February and mixed proven operational practices with a number of new operational modalities. The inspection team was established and dispatched to Iraq in very short order; it was augmented by the inspection personnel from UNSCOM50, already in Iraq. The designated sites were inspected immediately upon the arrival of the team in Iraq. Helicopter and high-altitude surveillance aircraft were fully integrated into the overall inspection programme. No proscribed items or activities were observed by any of the inspection elements.

12. However, during the inspection, a serious breach of the Commission's aerial surveillance rights occurred. A helicopter was initially prevented from establishing aerial surveillance over one site. Iraqi officials employed repeated and open threats of force to impede the helicopter's mission. On one occasion, this threat was aggravated by Iraqi personnel aiming and training their anti-aircraft guns on the helicopter. These actions on the part of Iraq put Commission personnel in real danger and constituted a gross violation of the Commission's rights and immunities. This serious incident was reported by the

Executive Chairman to the Security Council on 24 February 1993. A full account, in the form of the note handed over to the President of the Council on that occasion, follows.

"Incident involving a Commission helicopter on 22 February 1993

"1. On 22 February 1993, one of the Special Commission's helicopters was flown in support of an inspection of three sites by Special Commission ground inspection teams. This flight had been notified to and acknowledged by the Iraqi authorities under established modalities.

"2. The Special Commission had information that missiles and launchers proscribed by resolution 687 (1991) might be concealed at the sites concerned and the helicopter air surveillance was undertaken so as to ensure that nothing was removed from the sites during the course of the short-notice ground inspection.

"3. At 1320 hours, the crew of the Special Commission's helicopter, on approaching one of the sites, was informed by radio from the accompanying Iraqi helicopter escort that the Commission's helicopter would not be permitted to fly over the site and it was forced to circle 1 to 2 kilometres north-west of the site. The crew contacted the Commission's Chief Inspector on the ground and informed him of the refusal received from the Iraqi authorities. The crew were ordered by the Chief Inspector to proceed again in the direction of the site. As the crew carried out these instructions, they were informed by the Iraqi helicopter escort that, if the Commission's helicopter did not turn away from the site, it would be shot down. Visual observation from the helicopter confirmed that the anti-aircraft guns on the ground were being trained on and were tracking the helicopter. On receipt of this information, the Chief Inspector ordered the helicopter to withdraw to the other inspection sites.

"4. While circling the other inspection sites, the Iraqi authorities ordered the helicopter to return to its base at Rasheed and again threatened to shoot down the helicopter if it did not return to Rasheed. In the circumstances, the captain had no alternative but to proceed in the direction of Rasheed. While *en route* there a new communication was received from the Iraqi authorities that aerial inspection of the site could now take place. The helicopter proceeded to the site where the Iraqi authorities imposed new restrictions, permitting it to fly only over the western side of the area. Shortly thereafter, the helicopter had to return to Rasheed because of lack of fuel, landing there at 1512 hours.

"5. At Rasheed airbase, the Special Commission's Chief Aerial Inspector strongly protested to the local Iraqi officials the above events and indicated that one result had been that the aerial inspection had not been able to complete the tasks assigned to it. He indicated his intention to refuel and to return to the area to complete the assignment. The local Iraqi officials, after checking with higher authorities by telephone, interposed no objection, and the flight thus took place.

"6. In a subsequent interview between the Special Commission's Chief Inspector and General Amer Rashid, in response to the former's strong protest at the Iraqi threats to shoot down a Special Commission helicopter undertaking assigned aerial surveillance in support of a ground inspection under Security Council resolution 687 (1991), General Amer responded that the statements that the helicopter would be shot down were standard military practice."

D. *Interim monitoring*

13. Iraq's continued failure to acknowledge its obligations under resolution 715 (1991) is a major factor preventing the initiation of long-term monitoring by the Commission of Iraq's activities. Meanwhile, as has been ascertained in the course of recent Commission ballistic missile inspections, Iraq is actively pursuing missile-related activities that are covered by the long-term monitoring plan, to include the establishment of a dedicated missile research and design centre north-west of Baghdad.

14. This facility, known as the Ibn Al Haytham Missile Research and Design Centre, was established by Iraq on 4 April 1992 as the main centre for research and design activity in Iraq involving ballistic missiles not prohibited by resolution 687 (1991). This Centre is involved not only in the maintenance of existing permitted missile systems, but also in the design of new missile systems, including the Ababil 100 with a range close to 150 kilometres. The Centre employs many of the scientists and technicians who were involved in the proscribed ballistic missile programmes prior to the Gulf War and adoption of resolution 687 (1991).

15. In the absence of Iraq's acknowledgement of resolution 715 (1991), which delays long-term monitoring efforts across the whole spectrum of Iraqi missile-related activities, interim monitoring of the Ibn Al Haytham Centre was initiated by the Commission to track Iraqi ballistic missile programmes to ensure that no proscribed activity is taking place. The first interim monitoring team, IMT1a, was sent into Iraq on 25 January 1993, where it spent eight weeks investigating the work of the Ibn Al Haytham Centre. The focus of the IMT1a mission was in the area of liquid propulsion systems and related technologies.

16. Based upon the results of IMT1a, the Commission dispatched to Iraq a new team of interim monitors, IMT1b, to relieve IMT1a on 27 March 1993. The purpose of the team was mainly to investigate and assess Iraq's capabilities to produce solid propellant missile systems and to establish the relationships between the various facilities involved in such activities within the Military Industrialization Corporation. It conducted its activities over a 52-day period 27 March to 17 May 1993, centred around 2 facilities: the Al Rasheed Factory, comprising the 3 plants, and the Al Qa'qaa' Establishment. In addition, the team visited the Ibn Al Haytham Research Centre, the focus of the previous monitoring team's activities, and other sites related to missile research and development in and around Baghdad.

17. The main issues discussed with the Iraqi counterparts included details of Iraq's missile designs; Iraq's knowledge of solid propellant technology; Iraq's general capabilities in missile production, both of complete systems and of components; Iraq's ability to increase the range of existing systems; the current status of Iraq's production facilities; and its plans for missile research, development, testing and production.

18. The information obtained by the team has improved the Commission's understanding of Iraq's past weapons programmes and of its technology baseline. It should, furthermore, be of use as and when the Commission is able to commence ongoing monitoring and verification activities in accordance with the plan approved by the Security Council in its resolution 715 (1991).

19. A third interim monitoring team entered Iraq on 5 June 1993. The main focus of this team is Iraq's production capacity in the ballistic missiles area. A full assessment and inventory will be made of Iraq's high-precision machine tools. Accompanying the team was a smaller sub-team whose task was to install cameras to monitor rocket test stands at two sites. Iraq was informed of the Commission's intention to install these cameras on 6 June 1993 but, as noted in the main body of the report, Iraq has to date blocked their installation on the grounds that they comprise sensors for monitoring under resolution 715 (1991), a resolution which Iraq says it will not accept, despite its being adopted unanimously by the Security Council acting under Chapter VII of the Charter.

20. Each interim monitoring team has been initially accompanied by a specialist team from the Commission,

to oversee the establishment of the modalities of inspection and conduct preparatory discussions with Iraqi officials concerning the implementation of the interim monitoring regime. Interim monitoring of Iraqi missile-related facilities will continue as long as the Commission deems necessary.

E. *Removal of nuclear fuels*

21. Under paragraph 12 of Security Council resolution 687 (1991), Iraq is required to place all its nuclear-weapons-usable materials under the exclusive control, for custody and removal, of IAEA, with the assistance and cooperation of the Special Commission. It has already proved possible to remove from Iraq all the fresh uranium fuel assemblies intended for use in the reactors at Tuwaitha.

22. However, the complex legal and practical problems involved in removing, reprocessing and permanently storing the resultant wastes from the irradiated fuel assemblies used in the reactors and now stored at Tuwaitha and Location B, have so far delayed the removal of this nuclear fuel.

23. In late 1992, IAEA again approached the nuclear-weapons States with a request for proposals for removal of the irradiated fuel assemblies, reprocessing and permanent storage of the resultant wastes. On the basis of replies received, negotiations have been entered into with CIR Minatom of the Russian Federation for a contract that would cover all aspects of removal, reprocessing and permanent storage of the resultant wastes. The Special Commission, which will be required to finance the contract, has been actively participating in these negotiations.

24. From 19 to 24 April 1993, an IAEA survey mission, with the participation of representatives of the United Nations, the Special Commission, CIR Minatom and its principal subcontractor for operations in Iraq—the Nuclear Assurance Corporation of the United States—visited Iraq to survey the sites where the removal of the fuel will be undertaken and to arrive at understandings with the Government of Iraq on its provision of services, equipment and manpower for the preparation and removal from Iraq of the 208 irradiated fuel assemblies.

25. A contract was concluded in Vienna on 14 June 1993. IAEA, the United Nations and the Special Commission insisted that the fuel assemblies are to be dealt with in accordance with all requisite international and national safety requirements and that the contract be for a fixed price without the possibility of major cost overruns.

Appendix III
List of incidents

A. *Restrictions on the scope of inspections*

1. During the course of the first interim monitoring team's mission, several other discussions occurred that indicated a misconception, deliberate or otherwise, on the part of Iraq. The Iraqi counterparts questioned the right of the team to make an inventory of or to tag certain items of equipment at the sites monitored, requesting that specific criteria be established and used to decide which items might be so treated. The team did not accept this position. Iraq indicated that certain items were of no concern to the Special Commission, when clearly the decision as to what is of concern to it lies with the Commission. Furthermore, some of the items involved have the potential to be used for proscribed purposes. The counterparts also complained about the purpose of this team, stating that it was to control, not monitor, Iraq's activities.

B. *Denial of, or restrictions on, access and delays to inspection*

2. On four occasions, Iraq has sought to deny the Commission's basic aerial rights—once in relation to entry of transport aircraft into and out of Iraq (see S/25172) and thrice in relation to overflight of sites for aerial surveillance by helicopter. Except for the flight over the two sites on the outskirts of Baghdad (see S/24985), the Commission was eventually able to conduct the flights. However, as already reported to the Council, one of these flights had to be conducted with a restricted flight pattern, and not before Iraq had threatened to shoot the helicopter down if it did not leave the vicinity of the site.

3. Iraq has also hindered access for inspection teams, sometimes seeking, on spurious grounds, completely to deny access. One team was initially denied access because inspection would "breach the sanctity of universities and would upset the students". In each instance, the inspection eventually took place. In the period under review, a total of eight Commission inspection activities were seriously delayed, in one case by over four hours. One, the aerial surveillance on the outskirts of Baghdad, has been blocked.

C. *Restrictions on aerial rights*

4. Paragraphs 11 (f) and (h) of the six-monthly report of 17 December 1992 (S/24984) described at length the problems faced until that date by the Special Commission. Problems have continued since. In addition to the incidents referred to in paragraph 2 above, Iraq has created further difficulties in relation to the Commission's aerial rights.

5. In his letter of 5 August 1992, Mr. Al-Zahawi, Adviser in the Iraqi Ministry for Foreign Affairs, informed the Executive Chairman of the Special Commission that his request to use the Al-Rasheed airfield as the point of entry and departure for inspection teams was unworkable as the airfield was unserviceable. The Deputy Executive Chairman replied the next day, expressing the desire to use Al-Rasheed airfield as soon as it became operational. Recently, Sudanese Airways Boeing 707 aircraft have been observed using this airfield. However, inquiries by Commission personnel about the possibility of using it as the point of entry and exit have met with the response that such a decision would be political. No progress has been made on this issue.

6. Iraq has created problems in the operation of the aerial inspection team. It has sought: to establish "no-go" areas over which the team may not fly and which may not be included in the boxes designated the night before aerial inspections; to prevent the team taking photography and using binoculars while flying between designated sites and even over the designated site; to regulate the altitude at which the helicopters may fly over certain areas; and to demand 10 minutes' notice before an aerial inspection starts.

7. Each time the Commission's high-altitude U-2 surveillance aircraft flies, Iraq lodges a formal complaint about its activities. Iraq persists in calling the aircraft a United States spy plane and has recently described it as being used for "despicable criminal purposes", despite its United Nations registration and mandate. On 10 March 1993, the Minister for Foreign Affairs of Iraq, Mr. Al-Sahaf, addressed a letter to the Secretary-General (S/25387), which alleged that the aircraft had been used to assist in the planning of an Israeli operation to assassinate President Saddam Hussein.

D. *Limits on the duration, size and composition of inspections*

8. Iraq has sought to limit the duration of both monitoring and aerial surveillance activities, indicating, in relation to the former, that it should be of finite duration and, in relation to the latter, that aerial inspections should not last longer than 15 minutes.

9. Iraq has also sought to limit the size of inspection teams at certain sites it deems sensitive, such as universities, and to interfere in the composition of the team by, for example, seeking to exclude the Commission's own interpreters from a team. It has also sought to establish that those involved in the chemical destruction group at Al Muthanna are not permitted to take part in other inspection activities and to limit the turnover of Commission personnel in the helicopter support staff.

10. It is clear from the Status Agreement of May 1991 that the Commission has the right to decide the expertise it needs to conduct inspections and hence the right to choose the number and the types of experts it needs on each team and to inspect each site. Iraq is obliged to allow personnel named by the Commission access to conduct their tasks.

E. *Advance notice of inspection activities*

11. For aerial surveillance activities, Iraq has sought to establish that it should receive advance notice of the site to be surveyed. No-notice inspections are essential to the effectiveness of the Commission.

F. *Provision of data*

12. As noted in paragraphs 9 (b) and 15 of the main body of the report, Iraq has failed to provide adequate declarations either of its past proscribed programmes or of its dual-capability facilities, which would need to be incorporated into the plans for ongoing monitoring and verification. The Commission has sought to supplement those declarations during each of its inspections. However, Iraq refuses to offer information willingly, or at all, in certain key areas, e.g. on its supplier networks or its previous use of chemical weapons. Consternation has also been expressed by Iraqi counterparts that the Commission continues to ask questions about Iraq's past programmes, despite the fact that these questions are asked because of Iraq's failure to fulfil its obligation to make full, final and complete disclosures on all aspects of its past programmes.

13. Furthermore, Iraq has been unable or unwilling to produce specific items of equipment that the Commission has evidence were supplied to Iraq. Teams continue to find equipment and documents containing information pertinent to their mandate under the resolutions and ongoing monitoring and verification plans.

G. *Photography*

14. Iraq has sought to limit the Commission's unrestricted right to photograph any item or activity it deems of relevance to its task. Iraq has delayed photography until "permission" has been obtained from more senior officials; it has sought to prevent photography over a designated site; and it has sought to limit aerial photography to items within a set perimeter and inspection team photography to items Iraq deems to be related to resolution 687 (1991). If this last rule were applied, it would open the possibility of Iraq deciding what was "687-related" and could be used by Iraq to exclude all dual-purpose facilities, items and activities covered by the plans approved under resolution 715 (1991).

H. Security

15. The issue of security was dealt with at length in appendix II to document S/24984. Since that report and in addition to the threats to the Commission's aircraft referred to above, there have been continued incidents of vandalism of Commission vehicles, including the smashing of windscreens, windows and mirrors and the breaking of aerials. Four of these incidents occurred while the vehicles were being driven by Commission personnel. In one such incident, the drivers were medics and the vehicle bore Red Crescent markings. These ambulances have also come under attack whilst parked in hotel car parks.

16. Items continue to be taken from the offices and personal quarters of the Commission. Staff continue sporadically to receive threatening and harassing telephone calls in their hotel rooms in the middle of the night. On 8 June 1993, members of an inspection team had light bulbs thrown at them while they were walking to a restaurant in Baghdad.

Appendix IV
Destruction of Iraq's chemical agents and munitions

1. The present report focuses on developments since the last report.

A. Operations at Muhammadiyat

2. On 21 February 1993, activities started at Muhammadiyat, a chemical weapons storage site west of Baghdad. Most of the stable, filled munitions have been transported to Muthanna (99 250-gauge bombs, 21 500-gauge bombs and 9 DB0 bombs). Destruction on site of unfilled (52 DB0 bombs and 1,105 DB2 bombs) and unstable filled (81 250-gauge bombs and 6 500-gauge bombs) munitions has started. Remaining at Muhammadiyat are 5,127 250-gauge and 1,094 500-gauge bombs (unfilled) and 20 mustard-agent-filled 250-gauge bombs.

B. Incinerator operations

3. The incinerator operates at temperatures in excess of 1,100° C and so meets the specifications set by the Destruction Advisory Panel for the destruction of mustard agent and precursors. During the third week of March 1993, a combustion efficiency monitoring system was installed to monitor performance by continuously measuring concentrations of the combustion gases.

4. Mustard agent is destroyed either by direct injection into the furnace or in a toluene/benzene/diesel mix. Some of the mustard agent has polymerized, complicating the process of extraction and destruction.

C. Hydrolysis operations

5. The neutralization of nerve agents by hydrolysis continued. In early February 1993, hydrolysis of the bulk stocks of the nerve agent sarin was completed, followed shortly after by the completion of the explosive incineration of 122mm sarin-filled rockets on 14 February 1993. On 23 April the destruction of the remaining sarin from the Al Hussein warheads was completed. On 15 February 1993, operation of the hydrolysis plant turned to destruction of the tabun precursor D4.

D. Destruction of munitions

6. During the period covered by the present report, destruction of the following munitions was completed: 122mm rocket motors and components, R400 aerial bombs and tail fin assemblies, unfilled 250-gauge bombs (by cutting) and unfilled DB2 bombs (by crushing). Drainage of 250- and 500-gauge aerial bombs continued and a technique of venting the 155mm mustard-filled projectiles was developed and adopted as the key initial step in the method for their destruction.

E. Status of destruction activities as of 17 June 1993

265 122mm rockets and warheads
6,152 122mm rocket warheads
873 122mm rocket motors
16,885 122mm rocket propellant grains
1,977 122mm rocket motor tubes
1,492 155mm mustard projectiles
21 empty 155mm projectiles
29 Al Hussein warheads for GB/GF
347 R400 bombs
333 R400 tail fin assemblies
1,473 partially filled and polymerized 250- and 500-gauge aerial mustard bombs
120 litres of GB nerve agent
61,273 litres of GB/GF nerve agent
69,328 kg mustard agent
73,005 litres of D4
14,600 litres of DF
1,120 litres dichlorethane
107,148 litres isopropyl alcohol
28,730 litres thio-diethyleneglycol
1,200 litres cyclohexanol/isopropyl alcohol
297,400 litres phosphorous oxychloride
134,200 litres thionyl chloride
415,000 litres phosphorous trichloride
32 2-ton bulk storage containers

Appendix V
Information Assessment Unit

1. During the period under review, the Information Assessment Unit has been strengthened and the Commission has been able to make good use of its improved capabilities.

2. The Unit is mandated to carry out the collection and management of information and to assess available data, in order to create a strong foundation for the Special Commission's implementation of the tasks entrusted to it by the Security Council.

3. With regard to information collection, the Unit is, *inter alia*, identifying information gaps and preparing proposals for how they might be filled using the Commission's collection capabilities. These capabilities include the high-altitude reconnaissance aircraft (U-2), which is currently carrying out up to three surveillance missions per week over Iraq. U-2 imagery is the property of the Commission. It is processed for the use of the Commission (and IAEA) with the help of the United States Government. The Unit is responsible for the tasking of the U-2, coordinating its operations and, with the support of United States specialists, the assessment and interpretation of the imagery.

4. The Unit is furthermore responsible for the aerial inspection activities using the Commission's helicopters in Baghdad as a platform. Thus the Unit identifies targets for aerial inspections carried out by the aerial inspection team permanently based in Baghdad. The aerial inspections utilize first and foremost photography, but other means are also in planning. The imagery resulting from these surveys is analysed by the Unit's photographic interpreters. The imagery, as well as other data acquired through the aerial surveillance activities, are made available for operational planning purposes.

5. The Unit also maintains contacts with relevant agencies within the supporting Governments and requests and obtains from them information of relevance for the work of the Commission.

6. The management of the large amount of data made available to the Commission is a growing responsibility for the Unit. The sources for the data to be dealt with by the Unit are, in addition to Iraq's own declarations, the inspection reports, the aerial surveillance products and the information from Governments.

7. The Unit has spent considerable time in developing ways and means for effective and dynamic management of the wealth of data collected by it. An information management evaluator has been assisting the Commission in developing a data management system corresponding to the needs of the Information Assessment Unit. Inside the Unit, a fully functional data management system is now in place. Some more equipment has to be purchased and recruitment of further operating personnel is under way.

8. The assessment or analytical work on available data carried out in the Unit constitutes, in many respects, the heart of the Commission's activities. This work sets the agenda for the operations side and provides the Executive Chairman with the substance and the technical foundation for reports to the Security Council, for the political evaluation of the extent of Iraq's implementation of its obligations under the cease-fire arrangements and for assessments of the magnitude of the remaining tasks. The significance and importance of the analytical work will only grow with the gradual introduction of monitoring and verification in the activities of the Commission.

9. It is the ambition to keep the Unit, on a continuous basis, staffed with analysts knowledgeable in all the relevant weapons and production categories. However, as there are both practical reasons and reasons of principle for expanding their experience in the field, analysts will regularly participate in inspection teams.

Aerial surveillance programmes

10. As of 15 June 1993, 236 targets had been subjected to helicopter surveillance, and 141 U-2 missions had been flown.

High-altitude surveillance

11. As additional staff has become available to the Unit, particularly additional photographic interpreters, the Unit has been increasingly able to provide specific taskings for U-2 missions. Prior to this, the U-2 operated primarily on the basis of a general priority list, rather than specific taskings to photograph specific sites.

Helicopter surveillance

12. Over the past several months, the focus of the helicopter photographic surveillance programme has been on sites which, at least potentially, are to be subjected to long-term monitoring. Some 60 monitoring missions have been completed. The first such mission at a given site is intended to produce comprehensive photographic coverage of it; subsequent missions would normally involve photography only of changes at the site evident from visual observation.

13. Helicopter surveillance missions continue to be executed in conjunction with ground inspections; typically, the aerial inspection team on board the helicopter is used to "secure" a site subjected to a surprise inspection. In this context, to "secure" a site is to maintain surveillance so as to spot any attempt by Iraqi authorities to remove proscribed items prior to the site being sealed off by the ground inspection team. Subsequently, the

aerial inspection team can conduct a normal photographic mission of the site.

14. During UNSCOM51, for example, both the heliborne aerial inspection team and the U-2 were used for surveillance of the sites being inspected by the ground teams.

Appendix VI
Inspection schedule
(In-country dates)

Nuclear

15 May-21 May 1991	IAEA1/UNSCOM 1
22 Jun-3 Jul 1991	IAEA2/UNSCOM 4
7 Jul-18 Jul 1991	IAEA3/UNSCOM 5
27 Jul-10 Aug 1991	IAEA4/UNSCOM 6
14 Sep-20 Sep 1991	IAEA5/UNSCOM 14
21 Sep-30 Sep 1991	IAEA6/UNSCOM 16
11 Oct-22 Oct 1991	IAEA7/UNSCOM 19
11 Nov-18 Nov 1991	IAEA8/UNSCOM 22
11 Jan-14 Jan 1992	IAEA9/UNSCOM 25
5 Feb-13 Feb 1992	IAEA10/UNSCOM 27
5 Feb-13 Feb 1992	IAEA10/UNSCOM 30
7 Apr-15 Apr 1992	IAEA11/UNSCOM 33
26 May-4 Jun 1992	IAEA12/UNSCOM 37
14 Jul-21 Jul 1992	IAEA13/UNSCOM 41
31 Aug-7 Sep 1992	IAEA14/UNSCOM 43
8 Nov-19 Nov 1992	IAEA15/UNSCOM 46
5 Dec-14 Dec 1992	IAEA16/UNSCOM 47
22 Jan-27 Jan 1993	IAEA17/UNSCOM 49
3 Mar-11 Mar 1993	IAEA18/UNSCOM 52
30 Apr-7 May 1993	IAEA19/UNSCOM 56

Chemical

9 Jun-15 Jun 1991	CW1/UNSCOM 2
15 Aug-22 Aug 1991	CW2/UNSCOM 9
31 Aug-8 Sep 1991	CW3/UNSCOM 11
31 Aug-5 Sep 1991	CW4/UNSCOM 12
6 Oct-9 Nov 1991	CW5/UNSCOM 17
22 Oct-2 Nov 1991	CW6/UNSCOM 20
27 Jan-5 Feb 1992	CW7/UNSCOM 26
15 Apr-29 Apr 1992	CW8/UNSCOM 35
21 Sep-29 Sep 1992	CW9/UNSCOM 44
6 Apr-18 Apr 1993	CW10/UNSCOM 55
18 Nov-1 Dec 1991	CBW1/UNSCOM 21
26 Jun-10 Jul 1992	CBW2/UNSCOM 39

6 Dec-14 Dec 1992	CBW3/UNSCOM 47
21 Feb-24 Mar 1992	CD1/UNSCOM 29
5 Apr-13 Apr 1992	CD2/UNSCOM 32
18 Jun 1992-	CDG/UNSCOM 38

Biological

2 Aug-8 Aug 1991	BW1/UNSCOM 7
20 Sep-3 Oct 1991	BW2/UNSCOM 15
11 Mar-18 Mar 1993	BW3/UNSCOM 53

Ballistic missiles

30 Jun-7 Jul 1991	BM1/UNSCOM 3
18 Jul-20 Jul 1991	BM2/UNSCOM 10
8 Aug-15 Aug 1991	BM3/UNSCOM 8
6 Sep-13 Sep 1991	BM4/UNSCOM 13
1 Oct-9 Oct 1991	BM5/UNSCOM 18
1 Dec-9 Dec 1991	BM6/UNSCOM 23
9 Dec-17 Dec 1991	BM7/UNSCOM 24
21 Feb-29 Feb 1992	BM8/UNSCOM 28
21 Mar-29 Mar 1992	BM9/UNSCOM 31
13 Apr-21 Apr 1992	BM10/UNSCOM 34
14 May-22 May 1992	BM11/UNSCOM 36
11 Jul-29 Jul 1992	BM12/UNSCOM 40A+B
7 Aug-18 Aug 1992	BM13/UNSCOM 42
16 Oct-30 Oct 1992	BM14/UNSCOM 45
25 Jan-23 Mar 1993	IMT1a/UNSCOM 48
12 Feb-21 Feb 1993	BM15/UNSCOM 50
22 Feb-23 Feb 1993	BM16/UNSCOM 51
27 Mar-17 May 1993	IMT1b/UNSCOM 54
5 Jun 1993-	IMT1c/UNSCOM 57

Special missions

30 Jun-3 Jul 1991
11 Aug-14 Aug 1991
4 Oct-6 Oct 1991
11 Nov-15 Nov 1991
27 Jan-30 Jan 1992
21 Feb-24 Feb 1992
17 Jul-19 Jul 1992
28 Jul-29 Jul 1992
6 Sep-12 Sep 1992
4 Nov-9 Nov 1992
13 Mar-22 Mar 1993
19 Apr-24 Apr 1993

Document 166

Fourth semi-annual report (for the period from 17 December 1992 to 17 June 1993) on the implementation by the IAEA of the plan for the destruction, removal or rendering harmless of items listed in paragraph 12 of Security Council resolution 687 (1991)

S/25983, 21 June 1993

Note by the Secretary-General

The Secretary-General has the honour to transmit to the members of the Security Council the attached communication which he has received from the Director General of the International Atomic Energy Agency (IAEA).

Annex
Letter dated 16 June 1993 from the Director General of the International Atomic Energy Agency addressed to the Secretary-General

United Nations Security Council resolution 699 (1991), approved on 17 June 1991, requests—*inter alia*—the Secretary-General to submit to the Security Council progress reports on the implementation of the plan for the destruction, removal or rendering harmless of the items specified in paragraph 12 of resolution 687 (1991). Such reports are to be submitted every six months after the adoption of the resolution and the fourth report is therefore due on 17 June 1993.

Please find attached an outline of the activities carried out by the Agency during the past six months under the plan for the destruction, removal or rendering harmless, which you might find useful for the preparation of your report.

(Signed) Hans BLIX

Enclosure
Fourth semi-annual report (covering the period 17 December 1992 - 17 June 1993) on the implementation by the IAEA of the plan for the destruction, removal or rendering harmless of items listed in paragraph 12 of UN Security Council resolution 687 (1991)

Introduction

By resolution 699 of 17 June 1991, the Security Council approved the plan submitted by the International Atomic Energy Agency (IAEA), through the Secretary-General, for the destruction, removal or rendering harmless of all items listed in paragraph 12 of Security Council resolution 687 (1991). Resolution 699 also called for the Secretary-General to submit every six months a progress report on the implementation of the plan.

The first of these reports was circulated by the Secretary-General to the members of the Security Council in document S/23295 dated 17 December 1991, the second in document S/24110 dated 17 June 1992 and the third in document S/24988 dated 17 December 1992.

This is the fourth semi-annual report of the implementation by the IAEA of the plan for destruction, removal or rendering harmless covering the period from 17 December 1992 to 17 June 1993. During this period, the IAEA, with the assistance and cooperation of the Special Commission of the UN, conducted three on-site inspections in Iraq (IAEA-17, IAEA-18 and IAEA-19, respectively), detailed reports of which have been distributed to the Security Council. 1/

Present status

As of 17 June 1993 the IAEA has carried out, with the assistance and cooperation of the Special Commission, 19 missions in Iraq. These missions have entailed inspections at seventy-five sites and have resulted in the gradual disclosure of a broadly-based nuclear programme aimed at the production of enriched uranium and at the development of nuclear weapon capabilities. As a result of these inspections, in the course of which the IAEA has interviewed numerous Iraqi authorities and secured thousands of pages of documents, the IAEA has been able to draw a reasonably coherent and consistent picture of Iraq's nuclear programme. However, doubts remain as to whether the picture is complete.

Efforts to implement the destruction, removal and rendering harmless of all items referred to in paragraph 12 of Security Council resolution 687 (1991) are ongoing. The IAEA has supervised extensive destruction of facilities and equipment related to the production of enriched uranium and to the weaponization programme. Key buildings and equipment have been demolished by Iraqi personnel at the direction of the IAEA inspection teams, resulting in the destruction of the Al Atheer, Tarmiya and Ash Sharqat sites. All nuclear-related production facilities at Al Jezira and Al Qaim had been destroyed during the Gulf War, and the Tuwaitha Centre was badly damaged.

1/ Document S/25411 (IAEA-17) and document S/25666 (IAEA-18). The IAEA-19 report was sent to the UN Secretary-General for submission to the Security Council, on 10 January 1993.

With regard to nuclear-weapons-usable material, the only such material currently known to remain in Iraq is the highly enriched uranium in irradiated reactor fuel assemblies, removal of which from Iraq awaits conclusion of the necessary arrangements with recipient countries. The material has been verified by non-destructive measures and is being kept under seal until its removal. In addition, numerous other materials, equipment and components have been either destroyed, removed from Iraq or placed under Agency seal in Iraq and are subjected to regular verification. The details of the activities relevant to destruction, removal or rendering harmless carried out since the third report submitted by the Director General are set out below.

Direct-use material

Fresh fuel

As indicated in the second and third reports, all of the fresh fuel for the IRT 5000 reactor has been transferred to Russia and transformed, through isotopic dilution, into uranium enriched to slightly less than 20% in U-235. This material has been transferred from the processing plant to a storage facility in Russia, where it will remain under IAEA safeguards pending its resale. The French-origin MTR type plates and the Russian-origin pins which were removed from Iraq in June 1992 remain in storage at the IAEA Laboratory in Seibersdorf, Austria.

Irradiated fuel

As indicated in the second and third reports, negotiations with a consortium of commercial companies from France and the UK for the removal, transportation and disposal of this fuel had met with difficulties of a legal, technical and financial nature. Therefore, the IAEA issued on 27 November 1992 a new request for proposals for the removal, transportation and disposal of the material in question. The request for proposal was sent to the Governments of China, France, the Russian Federation, the United Kingdom and the United States. By the closing date for the receipt of proposals, only one proposal from CIR-Minatom, an arm of the Russian Federation Ministry for Atomic Energy, had been received. This Russian offer included provision for the removal of the irradiated fuel from Iraq to Russia, reprocessing to recover and isotopically dilute the enriched uranium, and conditioning and permanent storage in Russia of the resulting wastes.

While the final price still remains to be negotiated, every measure has been taken by the Agency and the UN to limit the cost involved and to reduce uncertainties that might lead to cost overruns. Discussions have also been held with the Iraqi authorities to identify in every possible detail the extent of local support needed in Iraq in terms of manpower, equipment and services. Although technically feasible, in full compliance with all relevant safety standards, the packing and removal operations alone are already a major endeavor that will require not less than six months from its commencement until the last fuel element is removed from Iraq. During this time, contractor and Agency personnel will have to stay in Iraq to supervise and direct all operations. The reprocessing of the fuel and the conditioning and permanent storage of the resulting wastes will account for a significant portion of the cost of the contract. If sufficient funds are made available, the contract could be signed—and work could start—in a matter of weeks.

Plutonium and other nuclear material

A primary and continuing objective of the IAEA inspections in Iraq is the verification of the correctness and completeness of Iraqi nuclear material declarations. The nuclear materials subject to safeguards inspection prior to the Gulf War are long since accounted for. None of the safeguard enriched materials had been diverted to the clandestine programme. With the exception of small quantities of natural uranium still to be recovered from waste at the Al Jezira site, all declared bulk uranium stock and intermediate process materials (a total of 550 t uranium) have been verified by chemical analysis and are maintained under seal at a single location. Most of this material, in the form of yellow cake—about one fifth declared after the Gulf War to have come from indigenous production and four fifths from external sources—had not been included in the pre-war safeguards inspection regime.

It is not possible to establish the completeness of Iraqi nuclear material declarations through traditional material accountancy. Efforts to independently confirm quantities of nuclear material not subject to safeguards inspection (much of it in the form of yellow cake delivered to Iraq by external sources) have not been successful. Further, while daily production records for the Al Qaim facility (which produced such material indigenously) have been presented and reviewed by inspection teams, there is not way to verify the completeness of these records. Considerable effort has been expended in an attempt to develop an internally consistent picture of how quantities of nuclear material from the different origins had been utilized. This origin-based accountancy has largely been an effort to match inspection team-measured material, presented in various physical and chemical forms, with Iraqi descriptions of material flows through the declared processes. The matching of quantities of material with the respective origins is carried out through highly precise isotopic and impurity measurements. The resulting picture does not provide assurance that all nuclear materials

FIGURE 1

U-234/U-235 ISOTOPIC RATIOS FOR MATERIALS ASSOCIATED WITH BUILDING 73A

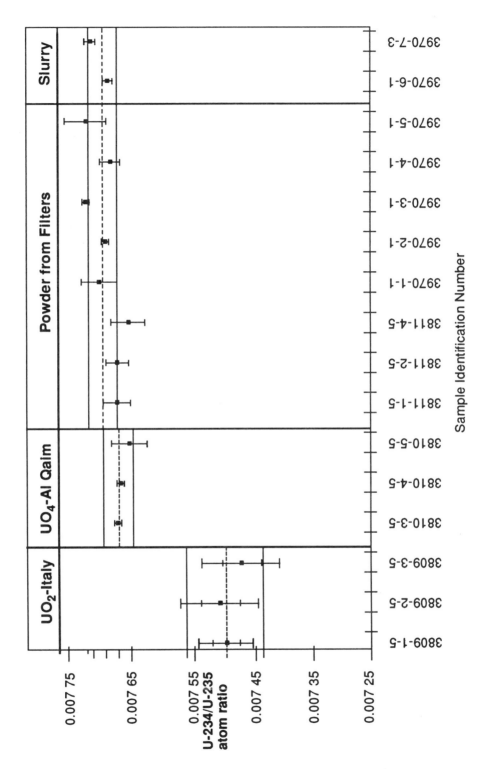

have been declared and presented, but the resulting inconsistencies do provide a technical basis and direction for further investigation.

The Iraqi nuclear material flow chart changed considerably between the time it was first presented and the time that the "full, final and complete" declaration was submitted. The various revisions in the nuclear material flow chart were made by the Iraqi side in response to inconsistencies identified by inspection teams. With the "full, final and complete" declaration of June 1992, the Iraqi response to remaining inconsistencies was that "any differences in weights existing in the chart of nuclear material as verified by the Agency are attributed to either losses of the material during the bombing or mixing of the material during the evacuation or the inaccuracy of the analysis of the samples". Iraqi authorities reported that they now considered that the "nuclear material file is closed" and have declined to provide further clarification. The Agency has consistently rejected this position.

An accumulation of sample analysis data from precise measurements of uranium isotopics and impurities in selected samples are now casting doubt on major elements of the Iraqi side's nuclear material declarations. The declarations in question involve the activities, identified as the "30 July Project", carried out in the building 73 complex at Tuwaitha and a large quantity of UO_2 reportedly imported from Brazil. A description of the specific declarations and the verification findings follows:

Declaration: Building 73a was involved in a variety of fuel fabrication activities utilizing 2,260 kgs of natural uranium (UO_2) from Italy (safeguarded material) and 59 kgs of natural uranium (UO_4) from Akashat/Al Qaim (non-safeguarded material). Thirty-seven air filters containing 50 kg of natural uranium, currently stored under IAEA seal at Location C, were declared to have been installed in building 73a. In addition, waste associated with the activities of buildings 73a and 73b was presented to the IAEA for verification.

Verification findings: The natural concentration of the uranium isotope U-234 is constant within a single uranium ore deposit, but highly variable across geographical separate ore bodies (see for example L. U. Joski, et al., *J. Radioanal. Chem.*, 67 (1981) 47 and 79 (1983) 317). Figure 1 shows U-234/U-235 isotopic ratio measurements for 3 samples of the Italian UO_2, 3 samples of the Akashat/Al Qaim UO_4, samples from 8 of the 37 air filters declared to have been installed in building 73a and 2 samples of waste slurry identified with building 73a activities. The results shown in Figure 1, with further confirmation provided by the impurity

analyses, clearly contradict the Iraqi side's declaration that the bulk of the material utilized in building 73a was of Italian origin. Either the filters had been installed elsewhere than declared (the Iraqi side has indicated that there was no filtration system in building 73c), or the activities carried out in building 73a involved extensive and undeclared utilization of material other than, or in addition to, the Italian UO_2. It is possible that the additional material processed in building 73a was associated with the Iraqi uranium metallurgy programme and this could indicate a greater quantity of material involved in the violation of the safeguards agreement than was disclosed at the time of the eleventh mission.

Declaration: Iraq had received 23.5 tonnes of natural uranium as UO_2 from Brazil. A quantity amounting to 3.4 tonnes of that material had been processed for the enrichment programme. The remaining 20.1 tonnes, contained in 201 drums, was never processed.

Verification findings: The total quantity of uranium verified as contained in the 201 drums is 18.2 tonnes, not the 20.1 tonnes declared. Moreover, when the randomly selected drums were opened for sampling, inspectors noted that material was present in three distinctly different physical forms:
– fine powder;
– granulated material; and
– a mixture of the granulated material and powder.

The Brazilian uranium originates from thorium-bearing ores and, as such, should contain traces of thorium. Impurity analyses indicate that the granulated material contains significant amounts of thorium, while the fine powder contains no thorium. In fact, the broader analytical results suggest that the fine powder is Iraqi UO_2 produced at Al Jezira. During the eighteenth inspection, every one of the 201 drums was opened and the physical form of the material noted. An additional 16 samples were collected. Preliminary results suggest that at least two thirds of the material presented as Brazilian UO_2 was of some other origin.

The verification data concerning the building 73a filters and the Brazilian UO_2 were discussed at length with the Iraqi authorities. They indicated that they could not dispute the results, but could offer no explanation either. They reiterated at length that all nuclear materials in Iraq had been declared and presented. The Iraqi responses to the IAEA's requests for clarifications were along the lines presented by Iraq in connection with the full, final and complete declaration, indicating that part of the material had been recovered under difficult circumstances and that some mixing had been unavoidable. This matter will be further pursued in future inspections.

Installations, equipment and other materials relevant to enriched uranium production and to weaponization activities

In accordance with paragraph 22 of the Agency's plan for future ongoing monitoring and verification of Iraq's compliance with paragraph 12 of part C of the Security Council resolution 687 (1991), contained in document S/22872/Rev.1/Corr.1, Iraq is obliged to declare to the IAEA items subject to the plan and to provide, *inter alia*, an inventory of all material, equipment and other items in Iraq identified in Annex 3 of the plan.

The items in the Annex include those specifically prohibited under resolution 687 (1991), i.e. those items which have to be destroyed, removed or rendered harmless, as well as others which may be prohibited depending on their use or intended use, or subject to monitoring under the plan.

In document S/25621 of 19 April 1993, the Security Council was informed of the Agency's repeated efforts to obtain compliance by Iraq with the requirements of the plan's Annex 3 declaration.

At the end of the seventeenth inspection, the Iraqi authorities provided the IAEA team a revised list of Annex 3 items which the Iraqis described as covering the period from 1 January 1989 and including all Annex 3 items which existed or had existed in IAEC facilities, universities and State Establishments which supported the IAEC programme. However, the Iraqi counterparts reserved the right to include items which might have been omitted from the list, either through oversight or because they were not thought to be covered by Annex 3, in the next update, which is to be submitted in July 1993.

Verification of the correctness and completeness of the new Annex 3 list, started in the course of the eighteenth and nineteenth inspections, will need still some time for completion. Details of this verification are described in the eighteenth inspection report (S/25666) and the nineteenth inspection report (submitted to the Security Council on 10 June 1993).

Future actions

As indicated above, the removal from Iraq of a quantity of U-235 contained in irradiated fuel elements remains one of the major outstanding actions. Priority should be given to concluding this action as promptly as possible.

Efforts to reconcile the major inconsistencies, identified by the inspection teams in the nuclear material flow chart submitted by the Iraqi authorities, have not yet been successful. Discrepancies continue to exist between the Iraqi declarations and the IAEA's findings. This matter will be pursued in future inspections.

Following the January 1993 submission by Iraq of the revised Annex 3 list of the IAEA plan for future ongoing monitoring of Iraq's compliance with relevant Security Council resolutions, verification of the correctness and completeness of this list will continue.

As indicated in the IAEA's third semi-annual report on these activities (document S/25621), additional destruction, removal or rendering harmless may be necessary.

Document 167

Statement by the President of the Security Council concerning the Iraq-Kuwait Boundary Demarcation Commission

S/26006, 28 June 1993

The Security Council has noted with particular concern the letter of 6 June 1993 from the Minister for Foreign Affairs of the Republic of Iraq to the Secretary-General (S/25905) concerning resolution 833 (1993).

The Council recalls in this connection that the Iraq-Kuwait Boundary Demarcation Commission did not reallocate territory between Kuwait and Iraq, but simply carried out the technical task necessary to demarcate the precise coordinates for the first time, on the basis of "The Agreed Minutes between the State of Kuwait and the Republic of Iraq regarding the Restoration of Friendly Relations, Recognition and Related Matters" signed by them on 4 October 1963, which were registered with the United Nations. The Council reminds Iraq that the Boundary Demarcation Commission acted on the basis of resolution 687 (1991) and the Secretary-General's report on implementing paragraph 3 of that resolution, both of which were formally accepted by Iraq. In its resolution 833 (1993), the Council reaffirmed that the decisions of the Commission were final, and demanded that Iraq and Kuwait respect the inviolability of the international boundary as demarcated by the Commission and the right to navigational access.

The Council also reminds Iraq of its acceptance of resolution 687 (1991) of the Council, which forms the basis for the cease-fire. The Council wishes to stress to Iraq the inviolability of the international boundary between Iraq and Kuwait, demarcated by the Commission and guaranteed by the Council pursuant to resolutions 687 (1991), 773 (1992) and 833 (1993), and the serious consequences that would ensue from any breach thereof.

Document 168

Statement by the President of the Security Council concerning the sanctions regime

S/26126, 21 July 1993

The members of the Security Council held informal consultations on 21 July 1993 pursuant to paragraphs 21 and 28 of resolution 687 (1991) and paragraph 6 of resolution 700 (1991).

After hearing all the opinions expressed in the course of the consultations, the President of the Council concluded that there was no agreement that the necessary conditions existed for a modification of the regimes established in paragraph 20 of resolution 687 (1991), as referred to in paragraph 21 of that resolution; in paragraphs 22, 23, 24 and 25 of resolution 687 (1991), as referred to in paragraph 28 of resolution 687 (1991); and in paragraph 6 of resolution 700 (1991).

Document 169

Statement by the President of the Security Council concerning the sanctions regime

S/26474, 20 September 1993

The members of the Security Council held informal consultations on 20 September 1993 pursuant to paragraph 21 of resolution 687 (1991).

After hearing all the opinions expressed in the course of the consultations, the President of the Council concluded that there was no agreement that the necessary conditions existed for a modification of the regimes established in paragraph 20 of resolution 687 (1991), as referred to in paragraph 21 of that resolution.

Document 170

Report of the Secretary-General on UNIKOM for the period from 1 April to 30 September 1993

S/26520, 1 October 1993

Introduction

1. By paragraph 5 of its resolution 687 (1991) of 3 April 1991, the Security Council established a demilitarized zone (DMZ) along the Iraq-Kuwait boundary and decided to set up an observer unit with the following tasks: to monitor the Khawr Abd Allah waterway and the DMZ; to deter violations of the boundary through its presence in and surveillance of the DMZ; and to observe any potentially hostile action mounted from the territory of one State into the other. By its resolution 689 (1991) of 9 April 1991, the Security Council approved the report of the Secretary-General on the implementation of the above provisions (S/22454); noted that the decision to set up the observer unit had been taken in paragraph 5 of resolution 687 (1991) and could be terminated only by a

decision of the Council; and decided to review the question of termination or continuation as well as the modalities of the United Nations Iraq-Kuwait Observation Mission (UNIKOM) every six months. The Security Council last reviewed this matter on 7 April 1993 and concurred with my recommendation (S/25514, para. 32) that UNIKOM be maintained for a further six-month period (S/25588). The purpose of the present report is to provide the Security Council, prior to its forthcoming review, with an overview of UNIKOM's activities during the last six months.

I. *Organization*

2. As of September 1993, the composition of UNIKOM was as follows:

Military observers

Argentina	6
Austria	7
Bangladesh	6
Canada	5
China	15
Denmark	6
Fiji	6
Finland	7
France	15
Guyana	6
Greece	6
Hungary	6
India	6
Indonesia	6
Ireland	6
Italy	7
Kenya	6
Malaysia	6
Nigeria	6
Norway	8
Pakistan	7
Poland	7
Romania	6
Russian Federation	15
Senegal	6
Singapore	6
Sweden	7
Thailand	6
Turkey	7
United Kingdom of Great Britain and Northern Ireland	15
Uruguay	6
United States of America	15
Venezuela	7
Total	252 a/

Administrative and logistic units

Engineers (Argentina)	50	
Logistics (Denmark)	45	
Medical (Norway)	20	
Total		115
Total military personnel		367

a/ The authorized strength of the military observers is 300, of whom 48 are on stand-by in their countries. Four military observers have been temporarily detached to assist the United Nations Observer Mission in Georgia.

UNIKOM also has 185 civilian staff, of whom 79 are recruited internationally and 106 locally.

3. Major-General T. K. Dibuama (Ghana) continued as Chief Military Observer until 20 August 1993. Since then, the UNIKOM Chief of Staff, Brigadier-General Vigar Aabrek (Norway), has been Acting Chief Military Observer. I shall revert to the Security Council concerning the appointment of the new Chief Military Observer.

4. UNIKOM has two small fixed-wing civilian aircraft contributed by the Government of Switzerland at no cost to the Organization and three chartered helicopters. It also has the use of a chartered aircraft for the transport of personnel and equipment between Baghdad and Kuwait.

5. As already reported (S/25514, para. 4), the Canadian engineers were replaced by an Argentinian unit, which reached its full strength in mid-September. The unit arrived without much of the equipment it requires, as it was deemed to be more economical to arrange for the supply of the equipment in the area. Efforts continue to achieve this.

6. The Danish logistic unit continued to carry out vehicle maintenance, supply and security tasks, the latter mainly for the headquarters facilities at Umm Qasr and Camp Khor and for the logistic base at Doha.

7. The Norwegian medical unit continued to provide a sick-bay facility in Umm Qasr, serving the headquarters and the northern sector, and first aid posts at the central and southern sector headquarters. The unit also provided emergency assistance to civilians injured in the DMZ. The Government of Norway has informed me that it intends to withdraw the unit at the end of October. I have approached a number of States for a replacement, so far without result.

8. Concerning the reinforcement of UNIKOM in pursuance of Security Council resolution 806 (1993) of 5 February 1993, it has not been possible, despite strenuous efforts, to identify a Member State which is in a position to provide a suitably equipped mechanized infantry battalion. However, one Member State has offered to provide an infantry battalion if the United Nations would provide the armoured vehicles, heavy transport

and other equipment. Such equipment would normally be integral to the battalion and there is no provision for its purchase in the budget. I am in touch with a Government which has indicated that it would be willing to provide the equipment for the battalion. The Government of Kuwait has also agreed to build the two camps in which the unit is to be accommodated and to make them available to UNIKOM at no charge.

II. *Concept of operations*

9. UNIKOM remained deployed in the DMZ as outlined in previous reports. For operational purposes it has divided the DMZ into three sectors. Its concept of operations is based on a combination of patrol/observation bases, observation points, ground and air patrols, investigation teams and liaison with the parties at all levels. UNIKOM employs surveillance aids, which include maritime radar for the Khawr Abd Allah, night vision devices, high-powered binoculars and video cameras. In addition, UNIKOM uses the Global Positioning System (GPS) for the accurate determination of locations in the terrain.

10. In a letter dated 12 May 1993, the Permanent Representative of Kuwait informed me of his Government's decision to establish a border security system, comprising a trench, an earthen embankment and a patrol road, along the entire length of the land portion of the demarcated boundary between Kuwait and Iraq. This project commenced on 12 June, and at the time of reporting the work was nearly completed in the southern and central sectors. Four crossing points have been constructed for use by UNIKOM, one in each sector and an additional one on the main road at Safwan. UNIKOM will review this arrangement from time to time in the light of its operational requirements.

11. UNIKOM has liaison offices in Baghdad and Kuwait City, and the Chief Military Observer and other senior staff of UNIKOM have maintained regular contacts with the authorities in both capitals. At the local level, liaison continued with the police on both sides, which has been useful in dealing with violations and complaints. Following the recent establishment of a Kuwaiti office in the DMZ, both sides now have liaison facilities within easy reach of UNIKOM's headquarters. The Iraqi authorities have also established liaison offices at the sector level.

III. *Situation in the DMZ*

12. During the period under review, the situation in the DMZ was calm.

13. UNIKOM observed three types of violations of the DMZ; minor incursions by military personnel on the ground; overflights by military aircrafts; and violations involving the carrying and firing of weapons other than sidearms, the majority of which were committed by policemen. The following table summarizes the violations observed by UNIKOM.

	Iraq				*Kuwait*			
	Ground	*Air*	*Weapon*	*Total*	*Ground*	*Air*	*Weapon*	*Total*
April	3	0	0	3	0	0	7	7
May	1	0	0	1	2	0	2	4
June	2	0	0	2	2	0	10	12
July	0	0	1	1	0	0	9	9
August	0	0	1	1	0	0	2	2
September	2	0	2	4	2	0	1	3
Total	8	0	4	12	6	0	31	37

	Member States cooperating with Kuwait				*Unidentified*			
	Ground	*Air*	*Weapon*	*Total*	*Ground*	*Air*	*Weapon*	*Total*
April	2	1	0	3	0	7	0	7
May	1	0	0	1	0	3	0	3
June	0	0	0	0	0	5	0	5
July	0	0	0	0	0	3	0	3
August	0	0	0	0	0	0	0	0
September	0	0	0	0	0	0	0	0
Total	3	1	0	4	0	18	0	18

14. During the reporting period, UNIKOM received eight written complaints from Iraq and none from Kuwait. UNIKOM investigated each complaint and conveyed its findings to the Iraqi authorities. These com-

plaints were about firing at police posts close to the boundary and violations of air space.

15. Much of the DMZ is still littered with unexploded ordnance and debris left over from the war, in particular on the Iraqi side of the border. Private companies under contract to the Government of Kuwait have continued clearing operations on the Kuwaiti side of the DMZ and are currently working in areas along the boundary. The Iraqi authorities also continued to employ civilian work teams inside the DMZ for clearing unexploded ordnance and retrieving equipment damaged during the war. UNIKOM has been kept informed of these activities and monitored them closely.

16. It will be recalled that I have offered my assistance to the Governments of Iraq and Kuwait in the settlement of issues involving Iraqi citizens and their assets found to be on Kuwaiti territory following the demarcation of the boundary. The Government of Kuwait has indicated that it would not be possible for these Iraqi citizens to remain in Kuwait and has offered to pay compensation for their private property and assets. It has requested that the assessment be carried out by a neutral party designated by the United Nations. The Government of Iraq, while rejecting the principle of relocation and compensation, stated that it would take no action that might provoke dispute or contention with the United Nations. I have, in the meantime, selected an experienced land assessor who is in the process of valuing the private Iraqi farms in the Safwan area and the private Iraqi assets at Umm Qasr. On the basis of his assessment and after consultations with the Governments of Iraq and Kuwait, I intend to determine the amount of compensation. I am also ready to assist with the process of compensation. I have appealed to the parties to exercise maximum restraint and to cooperate in the search for a peaceful resolution of all outstanding issues.

17. UNIKOM continued to provide technical support to other United Nations missions in Iraq and Kuwait. In particular, it assisted the United Nations Iraq-Kuwait Boundary Demarcation Commission and the United Nations Coordinator for the Return of Property from Iraq to Kuwait. UNIKOM continued to provide movement control in respect of all United Nations aircraft operating in the area.

IV. *Financial aspects*

18. By its resolution 47/208 B of 14 September 1993, the General Assembly authorized me to enter into commitments for UNIKOM at a rate not to exceed $6,250,825 gross ($6,064,700 net) per month for the four-month period from 1 November 1993 to 28 February 1994. This authorization is subject to the Security Council's review of the mandate of the Mission and to the prior concurrence of the Advisory Committee on Administrative and Budgetary Questions.

19. Should the Security Council continue the mandate of UNIKOM beyond 9 October 1993, the monthly cost of maintaining the Mission will be limited to the commitment authority contained in General Assembly resolution 47/208 B. I shall report to the Advisory Committee and to the General Assembly on the additional requirements needed, if any, for the maintenance of the Mission. In this regard, by letter dated 17 July 1993 and addressed to me, the Permanent Representative of Kuwait conveyed his Government's decision to defray two thirds of the cost of UNIKOM.

20. Unpaid assessed contributions to the UNIKOM Special Account for the period since the inception of the Mission through 31 August 1993 amounted to $26.5 million.

V. *Observations*

21. During the last six months, the UNIKOM area of operations has been calm. Through close monitoring of the area and constant liaison with the Iraqi and Kuwaiti authorities, UNIKOM has played its part in preventing incidents and redressing the minor violations that have occurred. In discharging its responsibilities, UNIKOM has received the cooperation of both sides.

22. The present calm along the Iraq-Kuwait border should not obscure the fact that tensions persist and full peace has yet to be restored to the area. In the circumstances, the presence of UNIKOM remains an important factor of stability along the Iraq-Kuwait border. I therefore recommend that the Mission be maintained for a further six-month period.

23. I regret that it has not been possible to make more progress on the strengthening of UNIKOM. This is the reflection of a recent trend whereby contributions to new United Nations peace-keeping operations are increasingly at the expense of the existing ones, especially those where the situation is reasonably calm. In addition, certain specialized units have become very hard to find and I am having difficulty obtaining a replacement for the Norwegian medical unit. I shall, of course, continue my efforts to overcome these difficulties.

24. In this connection, I note with appreciation the decision of the Government of Kuwait to defray the cost of two thirds of the UNIKOM budget. This will considerably ease the burden on Member States of maintaining the Mission.

25. In conclusion, I wish to pay tribute to the Chief Military Observer and to the men and women under his command for the manner in which they have carried out their difficult task. Their discipline and bearing have been of a high order, reflecting credit on themselves, on their countries and on the United Nations.

Document 171

Letter dated 15 October 1993 from the Secretary-General to the President of the Security Council concerning the composition of UNIKOM

S/26621, 24 October 1993

I have the honour to refer to Security Council resolution 806 (1993) of 5 February 1993, by which the Council extended the terms of reference of the Iraq-Kuwait Observation Mission (UNIKOM) to include the capacity to take action to prevent or redress:

(a) Small-scale violations of the DMZ;

(b) Violations of the boundary between Iraq and Kuwait, for example by civilians or police; and

(c) Problems that might arise from the presence of Iraqi installations and Iraqi citizens and their assets in the DMZ on the Kuwaiti side of the newly demarcated boundary.

In the same resolution the Council requested me to plan and execute a phased deployment of three mechanized infantry battalions in order to carry out these tasks and to report to the Council on any step I intend to take in that regard.

As the Council is aware, in spite of the considerable effort made, it has not been possible for some time to identify a member State which was in position to provide a suitably equipped mechanized infantry battalion. Recently, Bangladesh, which already has contributed military observers to the Mission, has offered to provide an infantry battalion. Kuwait, on its part, has agreed to make the requisite equipment available. Kuwait has also undertaken to build the two camps for the infantry battalion.

Accordingly, I intend to accept the offer of Bangladesh and to expedite, in consultation with the two Governments, the deployment of the first elements of the contingent as soon as the facilities for accommodation and ordnance are ready.

I should be grateful to you if you could bring this matter to the attention of the members of the Security Council.

(Signed) Boutros BOUTROS-GHALI

Document 172

Fourth report of the Director General of the IAEA on the implementation of the Agency's plan for future ongoing monitoring and verification of Iraq's compliance with paragraph 12 of Security Council resolution 687 (1991)

S/26685, 3 November 1993

The Secretary-General has the honour to transmit to the members of the Security Council the attached communication which he has received from the Acting Director General of the International Atomic Energy Agency (IAEA).

Annex
Letter dated 29 October 1993 from the Acting Director General of the International Atomic Energy Agency addressed to the Secretary-General

In paragraph 8 of resolution 715 (1991), adopted on 11 October 1991, the Security Council requests the Director General of IAEA to submit to the Council reports on the implementation of the Agency's plan for future ongoing monitoring and verification of Iraq's compliance with paragraph 12 of resolution 687 (1991) of 3 April 1991. These reports are to be submitted when requested by the Security Council and, in any event, at least every six months after the adoption of resolution 715 (1991).

Accordingly, I am requesting you to kindly transmit to the President of the Security Council the enclosed fourth six-monthly report on the implementation of the plan. The Director General will remain available for any consultations you or the Council may wish to have.

(Signed) David WALLER
Acting Director General

Enclosure
*Fourth report of the Director General of the
International Atomic Energy Agency on the
implementation of the Agency's plan for future
ongoing monitoring and verification of Iraq's
compliance with paragraph 12 of
resolution 687 (1991)*

1. On 11 October 1991, the Security Council adopted resolution 715 (1991) approving, *inter alia*, the plan submitted in document S/22872/Rev.1 and Corr.1 by the Director General of the International Atomic Energy Agency for future ongoing monitoring and verification of Iraq's compliance with paragraph 12 of part C of Security Council resolution 687 (1991) and with the requirements of paragraphs 3 and 5 of resolution 707 (1991). In paragraph 8 of resolution 715 (1991), the Security Council requested the Director General of IAEA to submit to it reports on the implementation of the plan when requested by the Security Council and, in any event, at least every six months after the adoption of resolution 715 (1991). The first three reports submitted by the Director General were circulated on 15 April 1992 (S/23813), 28 October 1992 (S/24722) and 19 April 1993 (S/25621), respectively.

2. The Director General hereby submits the fourth six-monthly report on implementation of the plan for future ongoing monitoring and verification related to Iraq's nuclear capabilities (hereinafter referred to as the plan).

3. Since the last report of 19 April 1993, IAEA has carried out three inspection missions in Iraq, the nineteenth (30 April-7 May 1993), twentieth (25-30 June 1993) and twenty-first (24-27 July 1993) inspections. Detailed reports on the results of these inspections are contained in documents S/25982 and S/26333. The twenty-second mission is currently scheduled to take place in early November 1993.

4. During the period under review high-level technical talks were held in New York (31 August-9 September 1993) and in Baghdad (1-9 October 1993) between delegations from the United Nations Special Commission and IAEA, on the one hand, and, on the other, a delegation from Iraq. Comprehensive reports on these two rounds of talks were circulated to the Security Council as documents S/26451, S/26571 and S/26584.

5. These talks, which grew out of a visit to Iraq by the Executive Chairman of the Special Commission in July 1993 (see S/26127), were intended to address the nature and implementation of the provisions of the plans for ongoing monitoring and verification as approved by Security Council resolution 715 (1991), as well as all other outstanding issues between Iraq, the Commission and IAEA, with a view to resolving such issues.

6. Progress and impediments evidenced in the course of the technical talks are summarized in the relevant sections of the present report.

I. Declaration of items subject to the plan

7. In the course of the high-level technical talks in New York and Baghdad the Iraqi representatives handed over, *inter alia*, statements on additional material (including depleted uranium and heavy water) required to be reported pursuant to annex 3 to the plan, a mid-year update of the declaration of items listed on annex 3 to the plan, a mid-year update of the list of radioisotopes in Iraq as required pursuant to paragraph 22 (d) of the plan and a mid-year update of the information on nuclear-relevant sites and facilities as required under annex 2 to the plan. In addition, the Iraqi officials provided a set of forms developed by the Iraqi Atomic Energy Commission (IAEC) to implement a computerized system of accountancy and reporting, showing status, present location and utilization for all items listed in the declaration required under annex 3 to the plan.

8. The information provided by the Iraqi representatives is being analysed by IAEA to determine whether it satisfies the requirements of the plan. Preliminary results of this analysis show that, while some progress has been made, the overall quality of the documentation still leaves much to be desired in terms of completeness and accuracy. A detailed list of what is needed to bring the IAEC reporting under the plan to the necessary standard has been communicated to the Iraqi Government. Promises have been obtained from IAEC that a further effort will be made to correct the shortcomings and to improve the completeness and accuracy of the documentation. In the course of the technical talks in Baghdad, IAEC informed the IAEA team that additional information required under annex 2 to the plan was in preparation and would be transmitted to the IAEA-22 inspection team.

II. Radiometric hydrologic survey

9. As indicated in the last report on the implementation of the plan, part of the long-term monitoring effort in Iraq involves the periodic radiometric survey of the main water bodies in Iraq. The survey serves as a measure for the timely detection of undeclared nuclear activities as well as for the establishment of a baseline for longer-term monitoring. This requires the collection of surface water, sediment and biota samples. During the nineteenth inspection, such samples were taken at 15 locations along the Tigris-Euphrates watersheds. The next sampling campaign has been scheduled for the beginning of November 1993, in connection with the twenty-second IAEA inspection mission.

III. *Periodic inspection activities*

10. Since the last report on the implementation of the plan, IAEA has conducted three inspection missions, in the course of which it has carried out two no-notice inspections of newly designated sites, as well as a number of inspections of a monitoring nature at previously visited sites. One of these was carried out at a suspected equipment dispersal site near Al Nida (formerly Al Rabiyah), where a number of machines, including one under IAEA seal from Al Nida, were located.

IV. *Nuclear material balance*

11. As indicated above, in the course of the high-level technical talks, the Iraqi authorities made available additional information on nuclear material, in particular as it relates to depleted uranium and imported natural uranium oxide, and on the existence in Iraq of a small amount of heavy water.

12. A complete inventory of all stocks of nuclear material, such as uranium, thorium and plutonium compounds, existing in Iraq is a prerequisite for any meaningful implementation of the plan, since it must provide the starting point of the nuclear material accountancy. Any future variation of the inventory will require a detailed explanation, will entail verification and will have to be thoroughly documented.

13. Major inconsistencies between the Iraqi declarations concerning nuclear material and IAEA's results of samples analysis were mentioned in the last report, which raised serious questions about the completeness of the present inventory of nuclear materials in Iraq. In the course of the high-level technical talks in New York, some clarifications were provided by the Iraqi authorities. If verified, these clarifications could explain these inconsistencies. Such verification will require additional sampling and analysis.

V. *Equipment and materials*

14. In the course of the eighteenth inspection (3-11 March 1993), 242 computer numerical control (CNC) machine tools were seen for the first time during an inspection of the workshops of the Al Hatteen State Establishment. None of the machines had been included previously in the Iraqi declaration with respect to items listed in annex 3 to the plan. The Iraqi authorities asserted that the machine tools had not been included in the list because they had not met the specifications of annex 3. IAEA is currently verifying the correctness of this statement through inquiries with the manufacturers. In IAEA's inventory of CNC machine tools found in Iraq (over 1,000 items), 148 have been identified as Matrix Churchill machine tools. During the nineteenth inspection, the team ascertained that 144 of the 148 Matrix Churchill CNC machine tools did not meet the annex 3 specifications, but that the remaining 4 required further evaluation.

15. Fifty additional Matrix Churchill CNC machine tools were found during the twentieth IAEA inspection in Iraq at the Nahrawan munition factory, following receipt of information provided by a Member State. Again the Iraqi authorities stated that this stock of CNC machine tools did not meet the specifications of annex 3. This statement is being verified by machine tools experts.

16. IAEA has indications suggesting that a considerable number of Matrix Churchill CNC machines exported to Iraq are still missing and this matter will be pursued further.

17. Two hundred fifty-five tons of high explosive of the HMX type are stored under IAEA seal in six bunkers at the Al Qa Qaa site. As a typical dual-use material, HMX is listed in annex 3 to the plan. The present storage conditions of HMX at Al Qa Qaa are inconvenient for monitoring and cause some safety concerns. IAEA has requested that the Iraqi side consolidate the HMX in a safer and more convenient place to facilitate sealing and regular monitoring. The IAEA-20 team evaluated two large bunkers in the Muthanna complex which Iraq had proposed as an alternative storage location. With minor modifications to improve security, these bunkers represent a considerable improvement over the current storage conditions at Al Qa Qaa. The transfer of the HMX is expected to take place during IAEA-22.

VI. *Procurement-related information*

18. A clear understanding of Iraqi procurements and the sources of technical advice for the nuclear programme has been a primary objective since the beginning of inspections in Iraq under resolution 687 (1991). During IAEA-18, following a course well established through previous inspections, a broad range of questions dealing with Iraqi procurements were put to the Iraqi side. The Iraqi side's often stated response was that, with the destruction of records during and following the Gulf war, it had no way to deal with such a general request and, in addition, it believed that most of the requested information was already in the hands of IAEA. While it is true that, through inspection data collected in Iraq, investigations undertaken by Governments of Member States and interviews with personnel of specific companies, most of the programme has been identified and that many of the front organizations and purchasing agents are also known, there still remain uncertainties as to the completeness of the information.

19. A number of important questions, the answers to which remain outstanding, have been put to the Iraqi

aide on several occasions. In December 1992, these questions were put forward in response to an offer from the Chairman of IAEC to deal positively with specific questions. These questions were restated during the first round of high-level technical talks in New York as follows:

(a) What are the identities of the individuals and/or companies from outside Iraq who supplied technical and design information for the Iraqi magnetic centrifuge?

(b) Who were the manufacturers, suppliers, agents and shippers for the 360-grade maraging steel? Please distinguish between the sources of the maraging steel used in the manufacture of centrifuge components outside Iraq and the stock of maraging steel presented inside Iraq. (The Iraqi side expressed concern that, while it can identify the supplier, it has no knowledge of who manufactured the maraging steel);

(c) Who supplied the carbon fibre rotor tubes and how were technical specifications communicated to the manufacturer?

(d) Describe the activities undertaken by the H & H Company with respect to the Iraqi centrifuge enrichment programme;

(e) Identify the manufacturer and describe the procurement procedure for the HMX explosive declared by Iraq to have been intended for conventional armaments.

20. At the end of the second round of high-level technical talks held in Baghdad in October 1993, the Iraqi authorities provided information covering the five areas listed in the previous paragraph. This information is now being verified for correctness and completeness. A preliminary assessment indicates that, while the procurement issues (e.g., the source of supplies and the dealers) have been reasonably covered, the extent of foreign advice concerning the centrifuge uranium enrichment programme has been grossly understated and the information provided in this area is not sufficient to explain the progress made by Iraqi scientists and engineers in developing working centrifuge prototypes. This matter will be further pursued in the course of the November inspection.

VII. *Removal of irradiated nuclear fuel assemblies*

21. Since the last report on implementation of the plan, IAEA was able to conclude a contract with the Committee on International Relations of the Ministry of the Russian Federation for Atomic Energy (CIR Minatom) for the removal, processing and sale or storage of highly enriched uranium still remaining in Iraq, under IAEA's custody, in the form of irradiated fuel assemblies of the Iraqi research reactors. All the complex technical preparations for the removal of the fuel were completed by the end of October. The first of the two shipments to the Russian Federation is currently scheduled to take place in December 1993.

VIII. *Summary and conclusions*

22. Some progress has been made in the last three IAEA inspection missions in Iraq, and during the two rounds of high-level technical talks in New York and Baghdad, in clarifying issues relevant to problems that are still open. Efforts are now focused on completing the technical basis for implementing effectively the ongoing monitoring and verification plan as foreseen in resolution 715 (1991).

23. Remaining problems are compounded by the persistent refusal of the Iraqi Government to formally recognize its obligations under United Nations Security Council resolutions 707 (1991) and 715 (1991). Until Iraq desists in its refusal, it will not have complied with the requirement laid down in paragraph 12 of section C of Security Council resolution 687 (1991) that it accept the plan prepared by the Agency and approved by the Security Council.

Document 173

Fourth report of the Executive Chairman of UNSCOM on the status of the implementation of the plan for the ongoing monitoring and verification of Iraq's compliance with the relevant parts of section C of Security Council resolution 687 (1991)

S/26684, 5 November 1993

Note by the Secretary-General

The Secretary-General has the honour to transmit to the Security Council a report submitted by the Executive Chairman of the Special Commission established by the Secretary-General pursuant to paragraph 9 (b) (i) of Security Council resolution 687 (1991). The present report is submitted pursuant to paragraph 8 of Security Council resolution 715 (1991).

Annex

Status of the implementation of the plan for the ongoing monitoring and verification of Iraq's compliance with relevant parts of section C of Security Council resolution 687 (1991)

Introduction

1. The present report is the fourth submitted pursuant to paragraph 8 of Security Council resolution 715 (1991), adopted on 10 October 1991, which requests the Secretary-General to submit a report to the Council every six months on the implementation of the Special Commission's plan for ongoing monitoring and verification of Iraq's compliance with relevant parts of section C of Security Council resolution 687 (1991). It updates the information contained in the first three reports (S/23801, S/24661 and S/25620).

2. In the first three months of the period under review, developments were not generally positive. Iraq remained adamant in its refusal to acknowledge, during the period covered by the report, its obligations under resolution 715 (1991) and the plans approved thereunder. However, in the last three months, there has been a positive change of attitude on the part of Iraq. The report, in order to be comprehensive, has to cover the entire period and should be read in that light.

3. The inability of the Commission to make any progress during the first three months in the full-scale initiation of ongoing monitoring and verification led to a visit of the Executive Chairman to Baghdad in July 1993. At the conclusion of that visit, the first sign of a change in Iraq's attitude was reflected in a position paper in which Iraq expressed its readiness "to comply with the provisions of the plans as contained in resolution 715 (1991)" (S/26127). Because of this development, the Executive Chairman invited an Iraqi delegation to New York at the beginning of September for high-level technical talks. Based on the results of these talks (S/26451), the Executive Chairman paid a further visit to Baghdad at the beginning of October (S/26571). Considerable progress emerged in the course of these various discussions:

(a) The Commission explained the methods to be used in implementation of the plan for ongoing monitoring which, in large part, Iraq now appears to accept. To the extent that Iraq has voiced concerns, it has indicated to the Commission that it will press, at an early date, for implementation through increasing use of Iraqi facilities, particularly in relation to aerial assets, as a substitute for the independent means now employed and for a realignment of Iraq's obligations in the direction of multilateral conventions in force in similar fields;

(b) Furthermore, Iraq has provided updated information in relation to ongoing monitoring and verification activities and information on sites which should be subject to baseline inspections—declarations that have been welcomed by the Commission. However, these have not been provided under resolution 715 (1991) and hence do not have full legal value and credibility. To be fully effective, baseline inspections and ongoing monitoring and verification activities have to be carried out under the acknowledged regime established by resolution 715 (1991).

4. For the above developments to be of real significance, Iraq must provide unconditional acknowledgement of its obligations under resolution 715 (1991) and the plans approved thereby. Iraq continues to refuse to do so. However, it has indicated that it would do so if it were convinced that that acknowledgement would result in a parallel initiation of full-scale ongoing monitoring and verification and of a process for the lifting of the oil embargo under the terms of paragraph 22 of resolution 687 (1991). The Executive Chairman has repeatedly emphasized to the Iraqi authorities at the highest level that Iraq's acknowledgement must be unconditional. It is unacceptable that Iraq could impose conditions on its preparedness to comply with a decision adopted unanimously by the Security Council under Chapter VII of the Charter.

I. Developments during the period 10 April 1993- 10 October 1993

A. Provision of information

1. Full, final and complete declarations

5. An essential condition for the proper planning of ongoing monitoring and verification is for the Commission to be provided by Iraq with all the information necessary to constitute full, final and complete disclosure of Iraq's past programmes in accordance with Iraq's obligations under resolutions 687 (1991) and 707 (1991). As was noted in annex I to the report on the high-level technical talks, held in New York from 31 August to 10 September 1993 between the Commission and the International Atomic Energy Agency (IAEA) on the one hand and an Iraqi delegation led by General Amer Rashid on the other (S/26451), the two sides identified critical areas, essentially relating to Iraq's past programmes, where further information was required from the Iraqi side if the Commission and IAEA were to be in possession of all the necessary information. It was agreed that those issues not resolved during the New York round of talks would be taken up subsequently in Baghdad. Indeed, during the recent visit of the Executive Chairman of the Commission to Baghdad from 1 to 8 October 1993, he received information from the Iraqi side in response to the Commission's questions. A full report of this visit is to be found

in document S/26571. As noted in that report, the newly provided information must be verified, assessed and confirmed by Commission staff in New York before the Commission could state that Iraq has discharged its obligation, in compliance with paragraphs 8 and 9 (a) of Security Council resolution 687 (1991), to provide the information necessary to constitute full, final and complete disclosures of its past proscribed programmes. During this process, the Commission must draw upon all available information inside and outside the Commission. The Commission is undertaking its assessment as fast as is consistent with the comprehensive and thorough review which the Council would require for any determinations on its part in relation to section C of resolution 687 (1991).

2. Declarations under resolution 715 (1991) and the plans

6. Under the Commission's ongoing monitoring and verification plan (S/22871/Rev.1), Iraq is obliged to provide certain declarations. The first were due by 10 November 1991 concerning (a) initial information on the dual-purpose activities, facilities and items specified in the plan and its annexes; and (b) a report on the legislative and administrative measures taken to implement resolutions 687 (1991) and 707 (1991), other relevant Security Council resolutions and the plan. Iraq is further obliged to update the information each 15 January and 15 July and to report further when requested to do so by the Commission. This is in addition to the information to be provided under resolutions 687 (1991) and 707 (1991) and referred to in paragraph 5 above.

7. In relation to the declarations referred to in paragraph 6 above, Iraq handed to the Commission, during the Executive Chairman's visit to Baghdad in October 1993, a set of declarations which updated the two sets of information provided by Iraq in July 1992 and February 1993 in relation to future ongoing monitoring and verification. It also handed over declarations concerning sites that should be subject to baseline inspections under the monitoring regime. The Commission's experts, who had accompanied the Chairman to Baghdad, discussed these declarations with the Iraqi side and how they could be improved to bring them in line with the requirements of the plan. The Commission's experts also undertook, upon their return to New York, to create a standardized reporting format to facilitate Iraq's reporting and the Commission's handling of the data provided. However, the Commission informed the Iraqi side that, as these declarations had not been made formally under resolution 715 (1991), they could not be accepted by the Commission as meeting Iraq's reporting obligations under the Commission's monitoring plan. Once Iraq acknowledged its obligations under resolution 715 (1991) and the plans approved thereunder, Iraq would need to submit the required declarations formally under and in accordance with the resolution.

8. On the declarations referred to in paragraph 3 (b) above, the Commission has still received nothing from Iraq.

B. Operational and political developments

9. The Commission has stated on several occasions that full-scale initiation of ongoing monitoring and verification cannot proceed without the Council first receiving Iraq's formal acknowledgement of its obligations under resolution 715 (1991). The Council has endorsed this position. In the period under review, as a result of Iraq's continued failure to provide unconditional acknowledgement of its obligations under resolution 715 (1991) and the plans for ongoing monitoring and verification approved thereunder, the Commission has continued to be unable to begin full-scale practical implementation of the plan covering its areas of competence (S/22871/Rev.1).

10. However, the Commission has continued its interim monitoring of certain facilities, along the lines reported to the Council in document S/25620. As noted in that report, the existence of such activity does not diminish the requirement to institute full-scale monitoring as envisaged in the plans and hence does not diminish the importance of Iraq acknowledging unconditionally its obligations under them.

11. The second interim monitoring team conducted its activities over the period 27 March to 17 May 1993. Activities centred around two facilities: the Al-Rasheed Factory, comprising the three plants, and the Al Qa'qaa' Establishment. In addition, the team visited the Ibn Al-Haytham Research Centre and other sites related to missile research and development. The activities monitored included details of Iraq's missile designs; Iraq's knowledge of solid propellant technology; Iraq's general capabilities in missile production, both of complete systems and of components; Iraq's ability to increase the range of existing systems; the current status of Iraq's production facilities; and its plans for missile research, development, testing and production.

12. A third interim monitoring team conducted activities in Iraq over the period 5 to 28 June 1993. The focus of this team was on Iraq's critical industrial manufacturing capabilities, in particular precision machine tools, which have the potential for use in the production of components for banned missiles, especially gyroscope devices and components for liquid fuel rocket engines. The inspection covered 11 sites and continued the monitoring of the Ibn Al-Haytham Missile Research Centre and the Al-Rasheed Factory.

13. On the basis of the experience of the interim monitoring teams and in the absence of Iraq's acknowledgement of Security Council resolution 715 (1991) and the plan, the Commission decided to install remote-controlled monitoring cameras at two rocket-test sites. The purpose would be to verify that no prohibited activities were undertaken at the sites. Iraq was informed of these intentions by letter on 28 May 1993. A small group of experts was despatched to Iraq, arriving on 4 June 1993, to install the cameras and to explain the modalities for their operation to the Iraqi side. However, by letter, dated 8 June 1993 from the Iraqi Under-Secretary for Foreign Affairs to the Deputy Executive Chairman, Iraq stated that:

> "the request [to install monitoring cameras] ... does not fall within the framework of the provisions of the above-mentioned resolution [687 (1991)] but rather comes within the framework of matters and questions that are still being discussed between the Iraqi authorities on the one hand and the Special Commission on the other."

14. The letter suggested that these matters and questions, and by implication all matters related to the implementation of resolution 715 (1991) and the plans approved thereunder, be subject to joint review and that the installation of the cameras should "be postponed until the desired review is conducted". It was further indicated that all monitoring activities also be so delayed. This was in direct contradiction with Iraq's undertaking, in the status arrangements between the United Nations and Iraq, that allow specifically the installation of equipment or the construction of facilities for "observation, inspection, testing or monitoring activity."

15. Iraq continued to maintain its opposition to the installation of the cameras (see S/25960, S/25970, and S/26127 for details). Faced with this position, the Commission proposed to seal the essential equipment at the test sites to ensure that it would not be used without advance notice to the Commission. However, the experts sent to Iraq to fix the seals were denied access to do so.

16. Iraq's blocking of the installation of the monitoring cameras at the two rocket-motor test stands and the sealing of essential equipment at the stands resulted in a visit by the Executive Chairman of the Commission to Baghdad in July 1993. The results of this mission were reported to the Council in document S/26127. Essentially Iraq agreed to the installation of the cameras but not to their immediate activation. Iraq further stated its readiness "to comply with the provisions of the plans of ongoing monitoring and verification as contained in resolution 715 (1991)" and agreed that this matter should be the principal topic for discussion at high-level technical talks to be held in New York in September 1993

(S/26451). During those talks the Commission was able to explain to Iraq in detail how it intended to implement the plan for ongoing monitoring and verification. On the basis of these explanations, Iraq expressed its acceptance, for the most part, of the modalities for implementation.

17. While it was agreed during the high-level technical talks to continue a dialogue between the Commission, IAEA and Iraq, the talks ended without Iraqi acquiescence to the activation of the cameras, despite the Commission's warning that any further dialogue would be dependent on their activation. On 23 September 1993, Iraq agreed to the activation of the cameras and they were so activated on 25 September 1993. Consequently, the Executive Chairman visited Baghdad from 2 to 8 October 1993 to continue the dialogue. During this visit, further considerable progress was made, as reported in document S/26571. However, Iraq continued not to acknowledge its obligations under resolution 715 (1991) and the plans approved thereunder.

C. Iraqi behaviour

18. During the period May to September 1993, the Commission experienced a continuing pattern of obstruction and intimidation from the Iraqi side. Iraq tried to limit inspection activities, discussions and photography to its interpretation of what was "687-related", i.e., to exclude what it considered to be monitoring activities under resolution 715 (1991) or to exclude sites it considered "civilian". There were almost weekly problems over the issue of the taking of photography by the aerial inspection team. In addition, there were sporadic incidents of attacks on the Commission's property and that of inspectors. While this sometimes delayed inspection activities, the Commission at all times insisted on the full respect of its rights.

19. The situation in this regard has greatly improved following the return to Iraq, in mid-September 1993, of the Iraqi delegation to the high-level technical talks in New York. Inspection activities since then, including the activation and operation of the remote-controlled monitoring cameras, have proceeded smoothly without obstruction or delay and there have been no security-related incidents reported.

II. Conclusions

20. While Iraq has been moving recently in a positive direction, the conditions for the initiation in full of the Special Commission's plan for ongoing monitoring and verification have still not been met. Iraq has yet to provide its unconditional acknowledgement of its obligations under resolution 715 (1991) and the plans approved thereunder. However, much time has been spent in discussions between the Commission and Iraq on this subject

and there are signs that Iraq might be moving towards formal acknowledgement.

21. In the meantime, the Commission continues to revisit or survey from the air sites identified as having been used for activities proscribed by section C of resolution 687 (1991) in order to ensure that those activities have not been resumed. This is a monitoring function. The Commission has identified many civilian sites that will require future monitoring and has initiated planning for conducting baseline inspections at these sites. It continues to seek to supplement the information provided by Iraq through vigorous questioning and inspection and has received from Iraq certain additional declarations in this regard, so that the initiation of full-scale monitoring will not be unduly delayed once Iraq makes the necessary political commitment to full compliance. Key elements of this process have been the interim monitoring concept and the installation and operation of monitoring cameras at the two rocket-motor test stands at the Yawm al Azim and Al Rafah sites. They have proven a most reliable and efficient method for monitoring the sites in question. Work has started on the design of an import- and export-monitoring regime, as required under paragraph 7 of Security Council resolution 715 (1991), and will intensify in the next several months.

22. Nevertheless, the Commission remains constrained from going beyond preparatory and interim work into full-scale monitoring and verification because of Iraq's failure to acknowledge the resolution on which ongoing monitoring and verification must be based. Unless these issues are addressed satisfactorily, the Commission will not be in a position to implement effective monitoring and verification of dual-capability facilities on the territory of Iraq, in compliance with the requirements of the plan, with clearly defined rights and with assurances of continuity. Nor could it monitor imports effectively. Hence, it would not be in a position to ensure that Iraq does not reactivate its proscribed programmes. Iraq is now fully aware of the position of the Security Council and of the Commission on this matter, which gives rise to some optimism that Iraq realizes that its acknowledgement of its obligations under resolution 715 (1991) must be unconditional and forthcoming shortly. The Executive Chairman has stressed that this acknowledgement, properly followed by action by Iraq to comply with the plan for ongoing and verification, is an important prerequisite to any favourable assessment by the Commission of Iraq's carrying out its obligations under section C of resolution 687 (1991) and resolutions 707 (1991) and 715 (1991). The undertaking will constitute a significant step towards the goal set out in paragraph 14 of resolution 687 (1991) of establishing in the Middle East a zone free from weapons of mass destruction.

Document 174

Statement by the President of the Security Council concerning the sanctions regime

S/26768, 18 November 1993

The members of the Security Council held informal consultations on 18 November 1993 pursuant to paragraphs 21 and 28 of resolution 687 (1991) and paragraph 6 of resolution 700 (1991).

After hearing all the opinions expressed in the course of the consultations, the President of the Council concluded that there was no agreement that the necessary conditions existed for a modification of the regimes established in paragraph 20 of resolution 687 (1991), as referred to in paragraph 21 of that resolution; in paragraphs 22, 23, 24 and 25 of resolution 687 (1991), as referred to in paragraph 28 of resolution 687 (1991); and in paragraph 6 of resolution 700 (1991).

Document 175

Statement by the President of the Security Council concerning violations of the Iraq-Kuwait boundary

S/26787, 23 November 1993

The Security Council is seriously concerned about recent violations of the Iraq-Kuwait boundary as reported by the United Nations Iraq-Kuwait Observation Mission (UNIKOM), most notably those on 16 and 20 November 1993, when large numbers of Iraqi nationals crossed the boundary illegally. The Council holds the Government of Iraq responsible for these breaches of paragraph 2 of resolution 687 (1991).

The Security Council reminds Iraq of its obligations under resolution 687 (1991), the acceptance of which forms the basis of the cease-fire, and under other relevant resolutions of the Council, including most recently resolution 833 (1993).

The Security Council demands that Iraq, in accordance with international law and relevant Security Council resolutions, respect the inviolability of the international boundary, and take all necessary measures to prevent any violations of that boundary.

Document 176

Letter from the Permanent Representative of Iraq to the President of the Security Council transmitting a letter from the Minister for Foreign Affairs of Iraq conveying Iraq's acceptance of its obligations under Security Council resolution 715 (1991)

S/26811, 26 November 1993

On instructions from my Government, I have the honour to transmit to you herewith a letter dated 26 November 1993 from Mr. Mohammed Said Al-Sahaf, Minister for Foreign Affairs of the Republic of Iraq, conveying Iraq's acceptance of its obligations under Security Council resolution 715 (1991).

I should be grateful if you would have this letter and its annex circulated as a document of the Security Council.

(*Signed*) Nizar HAMDOON
Ambassador
Permanent Representative

Annex
Letter dated 26 November 1993 from the Minister for Foreign Affairs of Iraq addressed to the President of the Security Council

I should like to recall that, among the other positions it communicated during the high-level talks held in Baghdad from 2 to 8 October 1993, Iraq expressed readiness to declare its formal acceptance of the plans for ongoing monitoring in accordance with Security Council resolution 715 (1991) and its agreement to embark on their implementation when it becomes clear that the obligations of the Security Council *vis-à-vis* Iraq under its resolutions and especially under paragraph 22 of its resolution 687 (1991) would be met in full and without obstacles, restrictions or additional conditions.

I should further like to recall that, in the position paper presented by Iraq to the Executive Chairman of the Special Commission on 18 July 1993, in the course of the high-level talks held in Baghdad from 2 to 8 October 1993 and on a number of previous occasions, Iraq affirmed its request that, in the implementation of the monitoring and verification measures set forth in resolution 715 (1991), respect should be ensured for its sovereignty and internal security and the dignity of the Iraqi people and State and for Iraq's right to industrial, scientific and technological advancement and to development in all fields that are not covered by the prohibitions imposed by resolution 687 (1991). It also affirmed its request that in the implementation of the plans for monitoring and verification Iraqi facilities should replace foreign facilities and that the methods to be used in connection with the plans for monitoring and verification should be modified to bring them into line with those used under the international agreements and conventions currently in force.

In a number of documents (the comments on the Iraqi position paper of 18 July 1993 given in document S/26127; the summary of the high-level technical talks held in New York from 31 August to 9 September 1993 contained in document S/26451; and the summary of the talks held in Baghdad from 2 to 8 October 1993 contained in document S/26571), the Executive Chairman of the Special Commission, acting on behalf of the Security Council, made a number of promises and gave a number of undertakings with respect to these legitimate requests.

While Iraq reaffirms these legitimate requests, given its desire to continue its constructive cooperation with the Security Council, the Special Commission and the International Atomic Energy Agency and despite the fact that it has discharged its obligations under paragraphs 8, 9, 11, 12 and 13 of section C of resolution 687 (1991), I should like to inform you that the Government of Iraq has decided to accept the obligations set forth in resolution 715 (1991) and to comply with the provisions of the plans for monitoring and verification as contained therein.

Iraq wishes to remind the Security Council of an essential fact. Despite the discharge by Iraq of its obligations under section C of resolution 687 (1991) and of the other obligations set forth in that resolution and despite the passage of more than three years since the imposition on it of an embargo that has extended to all areas of human life and has caused cruel and bitter suffering to 20 million Iraqis, the Council has yet to take any step towards lifting this unprecedented embargo. With this positive and major step on its part and following the other positive developments as formally recorded in United Nations documents, Iraq accordingly expresses the hope that the Security Council will discharge its obligations towards it as stipulated in resolution 687 (1991) and trusts, above all, that paragraph 22 of that resolution will be implemented speedily and in full and without obstacles, restrictions or additional conditions.

(*Signed*) Mohammed Said AL-SAHAF
Minister for Foreign Affairs of the Republic of Iraq

Document 177

Fifth semi-annual report (for the period from 17 June to 17 December 1993) on the implementation by the IAEA of the plan for the destruction, removal or rendering harmless of items listed in paragraph 12 of Security Council resolution 687 (1991)

S/26897, 20 December 1993

Note by the Secretary-General

The Secretary-General has the honour to transmit to the members of the Security Council the attached communication which he has received from the Acting Director-General of the International Atomic Energy Agency (IAEA).

Annex
Letter dated 10 December 1993 from the Acting Director-General of the International Atomic Energy Agency addressed to the Secretary-General

United Nations Security Council resolution 699 (1991), approved on 17 June 1991, requests, *inter alia*, the Secretary-General to submit to the Security Council progress reports on the implementation of the plan for the destruction, removal or rendering harmless of the items specified in paragraph 12 of resolution 687 (1991). Such reports are to be submitted every six months after the adoption of resolution 699 (1991). The report is therefore due on 17 December 1993.

Please find attached an outline of the activities carried out by the Agency during the past six months under the plan for the destruction, removal or rendering harmless, which you might find useful for the preparation of your report.

(*Signed*) Boris SEMENOV

Acting Director-General

Appendix
Fifth semi-annual report (covering the period 17 June 1993-17 December 1993) on the implementation by the International Atomic Energy Agency of the plan for the destruction, removal or rendering harmless of items listed in paragraph 12 of Security Council resolution 687 (1991)

Introduction

By resolution 699 (1991) of 17 June 1991, the Security Council approved the plan submitted by the International Atomic Energy Agency (IAEA), through the Secretary-General, for the destruction, removal or rendering harmless of all items listed in paragraph 12 of Security Council resolution 687 (1991). Resolution 699 (1991) also called for the Secretary-General to submit every six months a progress report on the implementation of the plan.

The first four reports were circulated by the Secretary-General to the members of the Security Council in document S/23295, dated 17 December 1991; S/24110, dated 17 June 1992; S/24988, dated 17 December 1992; and S/25983, dated 21 June 1993.

This is the fifth semi-annual report on the implementation by IAEA of the plan for destruction, removal or rendering harmless covering the period from 17 June 1993 to 17 December 1993. During this period, IAEA, with the assistance and cooperation of the Special Commission of the United Nations, conducted three on-site inspections in Iraq (IAEA-20, IAEA-21 and IAEA-22), detailed reports of which have been distributed to the Security Council. a/

I. *Present status*

As of 17 December 1993, IAEA has carried out 22 missions in Iraq. The major activities related to the destruction, removal and rendering harmless of proscribed items involved continuing efforts to locate and identify items required to be reported to IAEA.

In addition, a series of high-level technical discussions were held between Iraq, on the one hand, and IAEA and the Special Commission, on the other hand. In the course of these discussions, and of IAEA-22, the Iraqi Government provided information on foreign technical advice received in the centrifuge enrichment area as well as information on procurement from abroad of materials and equipment, including, in particular, maraging steel. Iraq also submitted to IAEA updated and revised declarations pursuant to annexes 2 and 3 of the plan for future ongoing monitoring and verification of Iraq's nuclear activities. Verification of the additional information is under way.

A significant outcome of the high-level talks was the announcement by Iraq, by way of a letter dated 26 No-

vember 1993 addressed to the President of the Security Council (S/26811) from the Minister for Foreign Affairs of Iraq, of Iraq's decision "to accept the obligations set forth in resolution 715 (1991) and to comply with the provisions of the plans for monitoring and verification as contained therein".

Direct-use material

Irradiated fuel

In June 1993, IAEA concluded a contract with the Russian Ministry for Atomic Energy, with the Nuclear Assurance Corporation of the United States of America as a main subcontractor, for the removal, transportation from Iraq and subsequent disposal of the remaining enriched uranium, in the form of 208 irradiated fuel assemblies from the Iraqi research reactors, located in Iraq. Extensive preparatory work was carried out to ensure the safety of the removal operation. These activities included, *inter alia*, the construction of new access roads to the two sites where the fuel assemblies are stored, the installation of cleaning stations and of large reinforced concrete platforms, the securing of adequate heavy-duty lifting equipment and vehicles and the provision of personnel facilities such as offices, decontamination showers and communication equipment.

The first of the two planned shipments was successfully completed on 4 December 1993, with the transport, via air, out of Iraq to a facility in the Russian Federation, of approximately 100 of the fuel assemblies (all of which were manufactured in the former Soviet Union). The removal operations were conducted under the close supervision of IAEA in accordance with all relevant safety standards and measures. The Iraqi authorities have cooperated effectively in providing equipment and utilities and all of the necessary manpower. Preparations for the second shipment will start at the beginning of January 1994, with the objective of completing the total removal by February 1994.

Plutonium and other nuclear material

Efforts have continued to clarify remaining uncertainties in the area of nuclear material, namely the inventory of natural uranium and the detailed utilization of part of this inventory in Iraq's past nuclear activities. Significant progress has been made in the course of IAEA-22 in verifying the origin of the large natural uranium oxide stock declared by the Iraqi authorities to be of Brazilian origin. Also, most of the remaining natural uranium containing slurries from Al Jezira has been re-

a/ S/26333 (IAEA-20 and IAEA-21); the report on IAEA-22 will be forwarded to the Secretary-General for submission to the Security Council as soon as it is ready.

covered—some 59 drums—and is being transferred to location C at Tuwaitha. Verification samples will be taken in the course of the next inspection.

Installations, equipment and other materials relevant to enriched uranium production and to weaponization activities

As indicated above, the Iraqi authorities have submitted an updated list of material, equipment and other items in Iraq identified in annex 3 of the Agency's plan for future ongoing monitoring and verification of Iraq's compliance with paragraph 12 of part C of Security Council resolution 687 (1991). Verification of the correctness and assessment of the completeness of the list, begun in the course of the eighteenth inspection, is continuing. A description of the verification activities carried out during IAEA-20 and IAEA-21 is set out in the consolidated report of the two missions (S/26333). The activities carried out during IAEA-22 will be described in the twenty-second inspection report.

II. *Future actions*

Removal of the remaining irradiated fuel assemblies should be completed by the end of February 1994. Under the contract concluded with the Russian Ministry for Atomic Energy, all the irradiated fuel assemblies removed from Iraq will be reprocessed to recover the highly enriched uranium. The latter will be isotopically diluted to less than 20 per cent enrichment by blending it with natural or depleted uranium. The radioactive waste resulting from reprocessing will be adequately conditioned and permanently stored in a waste repository.

Continuing efforts will be made to resolve remaining uncertainties in the nuclear-material flow chart submitted by the Iraqi authorities.

Verification of the correctness and assessment of the completeness of the revised list of items submitted pursuant to annex 3 of the plan for future ongoing monitoring will continue.

Document 178

General Assembly resolution concerning the situation of human rights in Iraq

A/RES/48/144, 20 December 1993

The General Assembly,

Guided by the principles embodied in the Charter of the United Nations, the Universal Declaration of Human Rights 1/ and the International Covenants on Human Rights, 2/

Reaffirming that all Member States have an obligation to promote and protect human rights and fundamental freedoms and to fulfil the obligations they have undertaken under the various international instruments in this field,

Mindful that Iraq is a party to the International Covenants on Human Rights,

Recalling its resolution 47/145 of 18 December 1992, in which it expressed its deep concern at flagrant violations of human rights by the Government of Iraq,

Recalling also Security Council resolution 688 (1991) of 5 April 1991, in which the Council demanded an end to the repression of the Iraqi civilian population and insisted that Iraq should cooperate with humanitarian organizations and ensure that the human and political rights of all Iraqi citizens were respected,

Recalling in particular Commission on Human Rights resolution 1991/74 of 6 March 1991, 3/ by which the Commission requested its Chairman to appoint a Special Rapporteur to make a thorough study of the violations of human rights by the Government of Iraq, based on all information the Special Rapporteur might deem relevant, including information provided by inter-governmental and non-governmental organizations and any comments and material provided by the Government of Iraq,

Bearing in mind the pertinent resolutions of the Commission on Human Rights condemning the flagrant violations of human rights by the Government of Iraq, including its most recent resolution, 1993/74 of 10 March 1993, 4/ by which the Commission extended the mandate of the Special Rapporteur for a further year and requested him to submit an interim report to the General Assembly

1/ Resolution 217 A (III).
2/ Resolution 2200 A (XXI), annex.
3/ See *Official Records of the Economic and Social Council, 1991, Supplement* No. 2 (E/1991/22), chap. II, sect. A.
4/ Ibid., *1993, Supplement* No. 3 (E/1993/23), chap. II, sect. A.

at its forty-eighth session and a final report to the Commission at its fiftieth session,

Recalling Security Council resolutions 687 (1991) of 3 April 1991, 706 (1991) of 15 August 1991, 712 (1991) of 19 September 1991 and 778 (1992) of 2 October 1992,

Deeply concerned by the massive and grave violations of human rights by the Government of Iraq, such as summary and arbitrary executions, torture and other cruel, inhuman or degrading treatment, enforced or involuntary disappearances, arbitrary arrests and detention and lack of due process and the rule of law and of freedom of thought, of expression, of association and of access to food and health care,

Deeply concerned also by the fact that chemical weapons have been used on the Iraqi civilian population, by the forced displacement of hundreds of thousands of Iraqi civilians and by the destruction of Iraqi towns and villages, as well as by the fact that tens of thousands of displaced Kurds have had to take refuge in camps and shelters in the north of Iraq,

Deeply concerned further by the increasingly severe and grave violations of human rights by the Government of Iraq against the civilian population in southern Iraq, in particular in the southern marshes, a large part of which has sought refuge on the border between Iraq and the Islamic Republic of Iran,

Expressing concern in particular at the fact that there are no signs of improvement in the general situation of human rights in Iraq, and, therefore, welcoming the decision to deploy a team of human rights monitors to such locations as would facilitate improved information flows and assessment and would help in the independent verification of reports on the situation of human rights in Iraq,

Regretting that the Government of Iraq has not seen fit to respond to requests for a visit of the Special Rapporteur on the situation of human rights in Iraq, and noting that, despite the formal cooperation extended to the Special Rapporteur by the Government, such cooperation needs to be substantially improved, in particular by giving full replies to the inquiries of the Special Rapporteur about acts being committed by the Government that are incompatible with the international human rights instruments that are binding on that country,

1. *Takes note with appreciation* of the interim report submitted by the Special Rapporteur of the Commission on Human Rights 5/ and the observations, conclusions and recommendations contained therein;

2. *Expresses its strong condemnation* of the massive violations of human rights of the gravest nature, for which the Government of Iraq is responsible and to which

the Special Rapporteur has referred in his recent reports, in particular:

(*a*) Summary and arbitrary executions, orchestrated mass executions and burials, extrajudicial killings, including political killings, in particular in the northern region of Iraq, in southern Shiah centres and in the southern marshes;

(*b*) The widespread routine practice of systematic torture in its most cruel forms;

(*c*) Enforced or involuntary disappearances, routinely practised arbitrary arrest and detention, including arrest and detention of women, the elderly and children, and consistent and routine failure to respect due process and the rule of law;

(*d*) Suppression of freedom of thought, expression and association and violations of property rights;

(*e*) The unwillingness of the Government of Iraq to honour its responsibilities in respect of the economic rights of the population;

3. *Deplores* the refusal of Iraq to cooperate in the implementation of Security Council resolutions 706 (1991) and 712 (1991) and its failure to provide the Iraqi population with access to adequate food and health care;

4. *Calls upon* the Government of Iraq to release immediately all persons arbitrarily arrested and detained, including Kuwaitis and nationals of other States;

5. *Calls once again upon* Iraq, as a State party to the International Covenant on Economic, Social and Cultural Rights 6/ and to the International Covenant on Civil and Political Rights, 6/ to abide by its obligations freely undertaken under the Covenants and under other international instruments on human rights and, particularly, to respect and ensure the rights of all individuals, irrespective of their origin, within its territory and subject to its jurisdiction;

6. *Recognizes* the importance of the work of the United Nations in providing humanitarian relief to the people of Iraq, and calls upon Iraq to allow unhindered access of the United Nations humanitarian agencies throughout the country, including ensuring the safety of United Nations personnel and humanitarian workers, *inter alia*, through the continued implementation of the Memorandum of Understanding signed by the United Nations and the Government of Iraq;

7. *Expresses special alarm* at the repressive practices directed against the Kurds, which continue to have an impact on the lives of the Iraqi people as a whole;

8. *Also expresses special alarm* at the resurgence of grave violations of human rights in southern Iraq, which is the result of a policy directed against the marsh Arabs

5/ A/48/600, annex.
6/ See resolution 2200 A (XXI), annex.

in particular, many of whom have sought refuge outside the country;

9. *Welcomes* the sending of human rights monitors to the border between Iraq and the Islamic Republic of Iran, and calls upon the Government of Iraq to allow immediate and unconditional stationing of human rights monitors throughout the country, especially the southern marsh area;

10. *Expresses its special alarm* at all internal embargoes, which permit essentially no exceptions for humanitarian needs and which prevent the equitable enjoyment of basic foodstuffs and medical supplies, and calls upon the Government of Iraq, which has sole responsibility in this regard, to remove them and to take steps to cooperate with international humanitarian agencies in the provision of relief to those in need throughout Iraq;

11. *Urges once more* the Government of Iraq to set up an independent commission of inquiry to look into the fate of tens of thousands of persons who have disappeared;

12. *Regrets* the failure of the Government of Iraq to provide satisfactory replies concerning the violations of human rights brought to the attention of the Special Rapporteur, and calls upon the Government fully to cooperate and to reply without delay in a comprehensive and detailed manner so as to enable the Special Rapporteur to formulate the appropriate recommendations to improve the situation of human rights in Iraq;

13. *Requests* the Secretary-General to provide the Special Rapporteur with all assistance necessary to carry out his mandate;

14. *Decides* to continue its consideration of the situation of human rights in Iraq during its forty-ninth session under the item entitled "Human rights questions" in the light of additional elements provided by the Commission on Human Rights and the Economic and Social Council.

Document 179

Sixth report of the Executive Chairman of UNSCOM

S/26910, 21 December 1993

Note by the Secretary-General

The Secretary-General has the honour to transmit to the Security Council a report submitted by the Executive Chairman of the Special Commission established by the Secretary-General pursuant to paragraph 9 (b) (i) of Security Council resolution 687 (1991).

Annex
Sixth report of the Executive Chairman of the Special Commmission, established by the Secretary-General pursuant to paragraph 9 (b) (i) of Security Council resolution 687 (1991), on the activities of the Special Commission

Introduction

1. The present report is the sixth on the activities of the Special Commission established by the Secretary-General pursuant to paragraph 9 (b) (i) of Security Council resolution 687 (1991), submitted to the Security Council by the Executive Chairman of the Commission. It is the fifth such report provided in accordance with paragraph 3 of Security Council resolution 699 (1991). It covers the period from 14 June to 14 December 1993. It is further to the reports contained in documents S/23165, S/23268, S/24108 and Corr.1, S/24984 and S/25977.

I. *Organizational and administrative issues*

2. Since the last report, there have been further changes in the composition of the Special Commission. Mr. Charles Duelfer has been appointed by the Secretary-General as Deputy Executive Chairman in replacement for Mr. Pierce Corden, and Mr. Terrence Taylor has replaced Mr. Ron Manley on the Commission.

3. The organizational structure remains essentially as reported previously. Currently there are 35 staff in the Office of the Executive Chairman in New York, 23 in the Bahrain Field Office and 77 in the Baghdad Field Office.

4. There is still no agreement on the sale of Iraqi oil to finance United Nations operations resulting from the cease-fire resolution. The financing of the Special Commission's work thus remains a matter of concern. Current expenses have been met from voluntary contributions from Member States and funds made available from frozen Iraqi assets in accordance with Security Council resolution 778 (1992). However, in the absence both of Iraqi agreement to sell oil and of Iraq's acknowledgement of its obligations under resolution 699 (1991) to meet the full costs of the tasks authorized by section C of resolution 687 (1991), the problem of the financing of the

Commission's operations remains a matter of great concern and further cash contributions by Governments are urgently required. At the time of writing, the Commission's available funds stood at approximately $1 million, i.e., sufficient to fund operations until mid-January 1994.

5. Governments have continued to support the operation of the Special Commission through the contribution of personnel, services and equipment. A statement of the Commission's operating costs, together with further information on organizational and administrative issues, can be found in appendix I to the present report.

II. *Status, privileges and immunities*

6. The status, privileges and immunities of the Special Commission, the International Atomic Energy Agency (IAEA) and the United Nations specialized agencies involved in the implementation of section C of Security Council resolution 687 (1991) and related resolutions continue to be regulated by the relevant agreements and Council resolutions and decisions.

7. The Special Commission and IAEA, on the one hand, and the Government of Bahrain, on the other, by an exchange of letters dated 20 September and 23 October 1993 respectively, have extended for a further six months, until 31 March 1994, the agreement provided for in the exchange of letters relating to the facilities, privileges and immunities of the Special Commission and IAEA in Bahrain.

8. In Iraq, during the initial part of the period covered by the present report, there were further problems in the implementation of the Special Commission's status, privileges and immunities and with the security of Commission personnel and property. However, since the visit of the Executive Chairman to Iraq in July 1993, the situation has improved considerably and the most recent inspections, including the largest and most intensive yet conducted by the Commission, have passed without incident and with Iraq extending all the facilities requested by the inspection team. However, it should be noted that during UNSCOM65, the investigation into allegations of chemical weapons use by the Government of Iraq against opposition forces, Iraq refused the inspection team's demand to interview army personnel who were in the vicinity of the site of the alleged attack at the time when it was said to have occurred.

III. *Developments*

A. Political developments: the attitude of Iraq

9. The period under review has seen many political developments. The first issue to arise concerned the removal of certain precursor chemicals and production equipment from the Fallujah sites to Muthanna for destruction there. This rapidly became intertwined with two other issues: the installation of remote-controlled monitoring cameras at two rocket engine test stands, and the issue of "dialogue" between Iraq, on the one hand, and the Special Commission and IAEA, or the Security Council, on the other.

10. The fundamental underlying issue for Iraq was its desire to see an end to the first phase of implementation of its obligations under section C of resolution 687 (1991), e.g., the identification and elimination of proscribed weapons and weapons programmes, and for this to be followed by implementation by the Security Council of paragraph 22 of that resolution, i.e., the lifting of the oil embargo, before proceeding to ongoing monitoring and verification activities. Iraq objected to the destruction of the chemicals and equipment on the grounds that they could be redeployed (despite their obvious and direct connection with the chemical weapons programme) and to the installation of the cameras on the grounds that this would, in effect, constitute ongoing monitoring and verification under resolution 715 (1991), a resolution which Iraq had not yet accepted and whose terms, according to Iraq, were still the subject of discussion between Iraq and the Security Council. Instead, Iraq proposed that action on each of these items await the conclusion of a dialogue on all outstanding issues between it and the Special Commission and IAEA.

11. These developments led to the Security Council issuing a statement on 18 June 1993 (S/25970), demanding that Iraq accede to the removal and destruction of the chemicals and equipment in question and cease its obstruction forthwith of the installation of the cameras. Iraq acceded to the removal and destruction of the chemicals and equipment but it continued to refuse the installation of the cameras. In order to resolve this impasse, the Executive Chairman visited Baghdad in July 1993. The result of this visit was a report (S/26127) which recorded position papers of the Commission and Iraq, the Commission's comments on Iraq's position paper and conclusions reflecting common understandings of the two sides.

12. In its paper, Iraq stated for the first time its readiness to comply with the provisions of the plans of ongoing monitoring and verification as contained in resolution 715 (1991). The report noted the agreement of both sides to hold high-level technical talks in New York at which one of the prime subjects would be the nature and implementation of ongoing monitoring and verification. All outstanding issues, including the activation of the cameras, were to be addressed. In the meantime, the cameras were to be installed, tested and maintained. The Commission would send inspectors to the two test sites as and when it wished and Iraq would inform the Commission of each rocket test sufficiently in advance for the Commission to send personnel to observe the test. This

arrangement was observed. Iraq did, during an army manoeuvre in November 1993, launch some short-range missiles without notifying the Commission. On learning of these launches, the Commission informed Iraq that it would also require Iraq to inform it of all such launches. The Iraqi side undertook to set in place procedures for such reporting in accordance with the plan.

13. The first round of high-level technical talks took place in New York from 31 August to 10 September 1993 and resulted in a joint report (S/26451). During these talks, the Commission explained to Iraq precisely what ongoing monitoring and verification would entail and Iraq appeared to accept most of the methods to be used. Its prime concerns related to how the intrusive rights and privileges of the Commission, being extended indefinitely into the future, would be implemented so as not to endanger the safety of the Iraqi leadership, infringe on Iraq's sovereignty or hinder its economic or technical development. For the Commission and IAEA, key questions were identified, the answers to which were necessary if they were ever to be in a position to conclude their work on the identification phase of their operations. Most of these key questions related to foreign suppliers and technical advice although, in the chemical weapons area, some related to past production levels.

14. It was agreed at the end of the high-level technical talks to conduct a further round of high-level talks in Baghdad shortly thereafter in order to resolve all the outstanding issues. Iraq promised, in this second round, to provide answers to all the questions identified but not answered during the New York talks. However, the Commission stipulated that there would be no second round unless the monitoring cameras were activated. Before this happened, a further incident arose when the Iraqi side delayed the installation on board one of the Commission's CH53g helicopters of gamma detection sensors, which the Government of France had made available for surveillance and detection purposes. This dispute was quickly resolved upon the return of General Amer, Director of Iraq's Military Industrialization Corporation, to Baghdad from the New York talks, but this delay resulted in the campaign of survey flights having to be reduced. Furthermore, Iraq did not agree immediately to the activation of the monitoring cameras; agreement was only forthcoming on 23 September 1993, activation being on 25 September 1993.

15. The activation of the cameras and the conduct of the gamma detection surveys permitted the second round of the high-level talks to proceed. A small advance team was sent to Baghdad on 27 September 1993 in order to elicit from the Iraqi side the responses to the questions identified in New York. While Iraq was forthcoming on some of these immediately, most answers were not given

before the arrival of the Executive Chairman on 1 October, as Iraq sought to place conditions on the handing over of the information, i.e., that the Commission side should declare the information adequate before even seeing it.

16. After intensive discussions on all outstanding issues, Iraq did hand over a more detailed account of its chemical weapons production in the past and, for the first time, details on the suppliers of critical equipment or materials in each of the categories, including on those who provided technical advice. However, in exchange for this, Iraq sought to have the information treated as solely confidential to the Commission and requested a statement from the Commission that Iraq was now fully in compliance with section C of resolution 687 (1991), less the future monitoring aspects thereof. This latter statement the Commission could not give, rather wording the report with caveats relating to adequate verification of the newly received information. This did not fully satisfy the Iraqi side, which still sought a definitive statement on the part of the Commission and IAEA to the effect that Iraq was now in full compliance with its obligations. In particular, it sought a statement that the Commission was fully satisfied with the newly provided data. In recognition that the Commission might need some time to study, verify and assess the new data, Iraq accepted instead that there would be a further round of talks in New York.

17. This further round of talks took place in New York from 15 to 30 November 1993, comprising high-level technical talks and, during the second week, parallel political talks. A full report of this round is to be found in document S/26825.

18. In the technical talks, the Commission informed Iraq that, at that stage, the information available in all areas had been deemed to be credible and that the Commission would deploy its best efforts to expedite the process of further verifying that information with a view to arriving at a definitive conclusion in the shortest possible time. In subsequent working groups, Iraq provided information supplementary to that provided in the previous round in Baghdad on its past proscribed programmes and on sites, equipment and materials to be monitored pursuant to the plans for ongoing monitoring and verification. Discussions were held on alternative means of verification, on a process to address past difficulties in verification and on how ongoing monitoring and verification would be implemented.

19. During the political talks, the Deputy Prime Minister of Iraq, Mr. Tariq Aziz, met with the Executive Chairman and held consultations with members of the Security Council. Following these consultations, Iraq announced, by means of a letter from its Foreign Minister to the President of the Security Council (S/26811, annex),

that the "Government of Iraq has decided to accept the obligations set forth in resolution 715 (1991) and to comply with the provisions of the plans for monitoring and verification as contained therein". In welcoming this development, the Commission requested that Iraq submit, as soon as possible, consolidated declarations under resolution 715 (1991) and the plans for ongoing monitoring and verification. Iraq, in response to this request, submitted to the Commission a statement (S/26825, enclosure II) confirming that declarations previously made by Iraq were to be considered to have been made under resolution 715 (1991) and the plans.

20. In conclusion, there have been major positive developments at the political level since the previous report. Iraq has acknowledged its obligations under resolution 715 (1991) and the plans approved thereunder. It has declared its earlier declarations in relation to future monitoring to have been made under and in conformity with resolution 715 (1991) and the plans and it has undertaken to cooperate with the Special Commission in the implementation of the plans in order to arrive, at the earliest feasible time, at the stage where both the Commission and IAEA will be in a position to report to the Council that Iraq was in their view meeting all the requirements of section C of resolution 687 (1991).

B. *Operational developments*

21. Recent operational developments have also been encouraging in that the inspection teams that have conducted activities in Iraq since the September talks have been well received by the Iraqi counterparts and their tasks have been facilitated by Iraq. These inspections have been amongst the most intensive, especially UNSCOM63, which was the largest and longest inspection undertaken by the Commission to date. One, to investigate allegations that Iraq had used chemical weapons against Shiah opposition elements in the southern marshes, was also highly politically sensitive. Nevertheless, Iraq did facilitate this inspection with the exception of refusing to allow the team to interview army personnel as noted in paragraph 8 above.

22. In the chemical weapons area, activities focused on destruction activities. There has been one chemical inspection, the one referred to in the previous paragraph, to investigate allegations of chemical weapons use, and one joint chemical and biological inspection which was able to address satisfactorily concerns that Iraq might have developed a bomb for delivery of chemical or biological weapons (see appendix II, para. 1). Considerable time has been devoted to the development of an updated inventory of chemical production equipment at the Muthanna site. Full accounts of inspection

and destruction activities can be found in appendices II and III respectively.

23. On ballistic missiles, efforts have concentrated on three main aspects: trying to establish a definitive material balance for the SCUDs supplied by the former Soviet Union; trying to account for Iraq's production capacity in the ballistic missiles area; and establishing an interim monitoring regime for Iraq's dual-capable missile facilities. This last has proved necessary because of Iraq's refusal until very recently to acknowledge its obligations under the plans for ongoing monitoring and verification (see appendix II).

24. Aerial surveillance activities have continued apace, using both U-2 (a total of 186 missions flown as of 10 December 1993) and helicopter platforms (335 targets now flown). Helicopter missions continue to be flown in support of ground inspections and to provide a time-series photographic record of sites which shall need monitoring under the plans for ongoing monitoring and verification.

25. Additional sensors (gamma detection, forward-looking infrared radar, ground penetrating radar) have been mounted onto the helicopters for specific missions to give them greater monitoring and detection capability. The gamma detection sensors and the ground penetrating radar have made it necessary that the helicopters operate in a new mode, one of survey. In both cases, the object is to map areas using the sensor: in the case of gamma detection, to map background radiation levels as a reference against which to judge for future gamma surveys and to identify any unusual sources of radiation which might require immediate investigation; in the case of ground penetrating radar, to search for underground chambers or hidden items. Such missions have been flown in and around Baghdad and in central, western and north-western Iraq. Iraq has withdrawn its previous objections to flights within the area which it had claimed to constitute the limits of Baghdad.

26. Details of aerial operations are contained in appendix IV to the present report.

C. *Iraq's declarations*

1. *Full, final and complete declarations*

27. As was noted in annex I to the report of the high-level technical talks, held in New York from 31 August to 10 September 1993, between the Commission and IAEA on the one hand, and an Iraqi delegation led by General Amer Rashid on the other (S/26451), the two sides identified critical areas, which essentially related to Iraq's past programmes, where further information was required from the Iraqi side if the Commission and IAEA were to be able to fulfil their mandates. It was agreed that those issues not resolved during the New

York round of talks would be taken up in Baghdad. Indeed, during the visit of the Executive Chairman of the Commission to Baghdad from 1 to 8 October 1993, he received answers from the Iraqi side to the Commission's questions. A full report of this visit is to be found in document S/26571. As noted in that report, the newly provided information must be verified, assessed and confirmed by Commission staff in New York before the Commission can state that Iraq has discharged its obligation, in compliance with paragraphs 8 and 9 (a) of Security Council resolution 687 (1991), to provide the information necessary to constitute full, final and complete disclosures of its past programmes—an essential condition for the proper planning of ongoing monitoring and verification.

28. In relation to the information provided in the chemical weapons area, Iraq's earlier accounts of its past chemical weapons production had blatantly failed to take into account past disposal of chemical weapons. In Baghdad, the Iraqi side gave for the first time an account of chemical weapons production which addressed the obvious shortfalls of earlier declarations.

29. In each of the weapons areas, the Commission's evaluation of this new information is that it is credible but still incomplete. The quantities for imports and production declared by Iraq are within the Commission's estimate range. However, verification has been rendered difficult as Iraq claims that all relevant documentation about its past programmes has been destroyed. The Commission took the occasion of the high-level talks in New York in November 1993 to press the Iraqi side for further information and to facilitate, to the extent possible, preferably by retrieving documentation, the Commission's task of verifying Iraq's new declarations.

2. Declarations under resolution 715 (1991) and the plans

30. Under the Commission's ongoing monitoring and verification plan (document S/22871/Rev.1), Iraq is obliged to provide certain declarations. The first were due by 10 November 1991, concerning: (a) initial information on the dual-purpose activities, facilities and items specified in the plan and its annexes; and (b) a report on the legislative and administrative measures taken to implement resolutions 687 (1991) and 707 (1991), other relevant Security Council resolutions and the plan. Iraq is further obliged to update the information on (a) each 15 January and 15 July, and to report further on (b) when requested to do so by the Commission. This is in addition to the information to be provided under resolutions 687 (1991) and 707 (1991).

31. In relation to the declarations referred to in (a) in paragraph 30 above, Iraq handed to the Commission,

during the visit to Baghdad in October 1993, a set of declarations which updated the two sets of information provided by Iraq in July 1992 and February 1993, in relation to future ongoing monitoring and verification. It also handed over declarations concerning sites that should be subject to baseline inspections under the monitoring regime. The Commission discussed these declarations with the Iraqi side and how they could be improved to bring them in line with the requirements of the plan. The Commission also undertook, upon the delegation's return to New York, to create a standardized reporting format to facilitate Iraq's reporting and the Commission's manipulation of the data provided. However, the Commission informed the Iraqi side that, as these declarations had not been made formally under resolution 715 (1991), they could not be accepted by the Commission as fulfilment of Iraq's reporting obligations. Once Iraq acknowledged its obligations under resolution 715 (1991) and the plans approved thereunder, Iraq would need to submit the required declarations formally under and in accordance with the resolution.

32. As noted in paragraph 19 above, Iraq has since both accepted the obligations contained in resolution 715 (1991) and stated that earlier declarations made in relation to monitoring should be considered to have been made under and in conformity with resolution 715 (1991) and the plans approved thereunder. While this addresses the question of the legal status of Iraq's earlier declarations, it does not address the problems arising from the declarations' inadequacies, inadequacies that the Commission will have to take up with the Iraqi side before it can fully implement the plan for ongoing monitoring and verification.

33. On the declarations referred to in (b) in paragraph 30 above, the Commission has still received nothing from Iraq. These are clearly required before any determination is made that Iraq is in compliance with its reporting requirements.

IV. Issues and priorities for the future

34. Before the Commission will be in a position to report to the Security Council that Iraq is in substantial compliance with its obligations, the plans for ongoing monitoring and verification to ensure that Iraq does not reacquire the weapons proscribed to it should be initiated and smoothly functioning, i.e., Iraq should:

(a) Supplement and revise its declarations to the point where, in the view of the Commission, they conform with the full, final and complete disclosures required under resolution 707 (1991) and of initial declarations required under the plans for ongoing monitoring and verification adopted by the Council in resolution 715 (1991). In regard to the former, supplementation by supporting documentary evidence clearly provides the most satisfactory solution but, as noted in paragraph 18 above, the Commission has discussed with Iraq alternative means whereby Iraq might assist the Commission in adequately verifying its various declarations;

(b) Establish a track record of accepting and cooperating in the implementation of all aspects of the plans, including compliance with the Commission's privileges and immunities as required for effective and efficient monitoring and verification, ensuring the safety and security of personnel and property, landing rights for aircraft and non-obstruction of inspections and logistics.

For its part, the Commission must, on the basis of Iraq's revised declarations, draw up a list of sites which should be subject to baseline inspections to assess whether and, if so, how each site should be monitored and with what frequency. For each site a monitoring and verification protocol will need to be compiled, containing the information on the site essential for effective monitoring and the details of the monitoring and verification activities to be conducted at the site in question. Once these have been prepared in draft, baseline inspections can proceed and final drafts of the protocols can be submitted by the inspection teams to the Executive Chairman for approval.

35. In addition, the Commission, IAEA and the Sanctions Committee established pursuant to resolution 661 (1990) are required, in accordance with paragraph 7 of resolution 715 (1991), to develop a mechanism for monitoring any future sales of supplies by other countries to Iraq of items relevant to section C of resolution 687 (1991) and other relevant resolutions, including resolution 715 (1991) and the plans approved thereunder.

36. Further inspection activities are planned in each of the weapons categories, albeit with the focus now on ongoing monitoring and verification. Destruction activities currently focus on chemical weapons, chemical precursors and chemical production equipment at Muthanna. Preparations for the implementation of the plans for ongoing monitoring and verification are under way and ideas on the potential form of an import control regime for after the lifting of sanctions have been discussed with IAEA. New staff recruitment reflects the shift of emphasis towards: verifying definitively Iraq's accounts of its past programmes and its supplier networks; preparations for and operations under ongoing monitoring and verification; and further elaboration of the ideas for import and export monitoring.

37. The priorities for the Special Commission are now:

(a) Verification and supplementation of Iraq's declarations to the level at which the Commission can accept them as fulfilling the requirements of the relevant resolutions;

(b) Initiation of monitoring inspections;

(c) Development of the mechanism for import and export monitoring;

(d) Establishment of practice and precedent in the exercise of the Commission's privileges, immunities and facilities necessary for effective and efficient implementation of the plan for ongoing monitoring and verification;

(e) Completion of the destruction activities, essentially in relation to Iraq's former chemical weapons programme at Muthanna.

38. With Iraq's acceptance of resolution 715 (1991) and the plans for ongoing monitoring and verification approved thereunder, the vast majority of the Commission's work will now focus on ongoing monitoring and verification activities. It therefore would make sense to consolidate the Commission's reporting obligations to the Security Council under resolution 699 (1991), which requires the Commission to report each six months on all its activities, and under resolution 715 (1991), which requires it to report each six months on its ongoing monitoring and verification activities. Currently these reporting obligations are for 17 June and 17 December and 10 April and 10 October respectively. Given that Iraq is obliged to make its declarations under the plans for ongoing monitoring and verification each 15 January and 15 July, a reporting requirement for the Commission of each 15 February and 15 August would allow the Commission to incorporate the most recent Iraqi declarations into its reports to the Council. The Special Commission recommends to the Security Council such a consolidated reporting schedule. The Commission would, of course, continue to submit special reports as and when these would be useful, or at the Council's request.

Appendix I
Organizational and administrative issues

A. *Staffing of the Special Commission*

1. The Commission has currently a total of 135 positions distributed amongst its three offices. Fifty positions are fully financed by the Commission. The balance of the staff are on loan from their Governments for assignments ranging from 3 to 12 months. Personnel, equipment and services have been provided for the Commission's activities by Argentina, Australia, Austria, Belgium, Canada, the Czech Republic, Finland, France, Germany, Greece, Hungary, India, Indonesia, the Islamic Republic of Iran, Italy, Japan, the Netherlands, Norway, New Zealand, Poland, the Republic of Korea, Romania, the Russian Federation, South Africa, Sweden, Switzerland, Thailand, the United Kingdom of Great Britain and Northern Ireland and the United States of America. IAEA has a total of seven staff financed by the Commission in

support of the work mandated by section C of Security Council resolution 687 (1991).

B. *Financial situation of the Special Commission*

2. Expenditures until the end of December 1993 will amount to about US$56 million. Out of this, a total of $11.6 million has been used for the 1993 payments required to finance the contract for the removal of nuclear fuel. The 1994 cash required to cover the operations of the Special Commission and IAEA is estimated to be around $35 million, including $9.3 million for the 1994 payments required for the removal of nuclear fuel.

3. In addition, there have been a large number of contributions in kind and in services provided by various Governments. Germany has indicated that it estimates its contribution to UNSCOM, particularly in the provision of aircraft and crews, will be close to $30 million by the end of 1993. Out of this amount, about $17.5 million is considered an advance which will require reimbursement.

C. *Financial status of the Special Commission*

Countries	United States dollars	
United States	2 000 000	
	2 000 000*	
Japan	2 500 000*	
Kuwait	1 000 000	
United Kingdom	175 400	
Saudi Arabia	1 730 000	
	30 000 000	Escrow account
Various	16 647 300	Escrow account
Total contributions	56 052 700	

1991-1992

Expenditures up to 31 December 1992	27 625 200

1993

Estimated 1993 expenditures	28 427 500**

1994

Projected 1994 requirements	35 000 000***

* Loan to be repaid.
** Including US$11.6 million disbursed in 1993 for the removal of nuclear fuel.
*** Including US$9.3 million for the removal of nuclear fuel, to be disbursed in 1994.

Appendix II
Inspection activities

Chemical and biological weapons inspections

1. UNSCOM60, comprising experts already in Iraq, investigated, *inter alia*, indications that Iraq had a larger stock of DB-0 bombs than initially declared and that these munitions might have had a biological warfare application. During this inspection, Iraq declared larger stocks, stating that the bomb was a failed prototype munition for chemical weapons and that the larger numbers represented munitions scrapped during the production and testing phases.

2. UNSCOM63, while primarily focused on searching for possible underground stores of ballistic missiles, also searched for possible hidden stocks of chemical weapons and biological weapons facilities. As reported in paragraph 23 below, no proscribed items or activities were found in this regard.

3. UNSCOM65 was constituted at short notice to investigate persistent reports that chemical weapons had been used by Iraqi Government troops against opposition elements in the southern marshes of Iraq. Initially, the team assembled as a fact-finding mission and visited the Islamic Republic of Iran to obtain clarification about the allegations from persons claiming to have witnessed the incident, specifically to obtain an exact location of the site at which the alleged chemical weapon attack took place. Upon obtaining this information, this team returned to Bahrain for further preparations and entered Iraq, as UNSCOM65, on 19 November 1993.

4. During the inspection, the team conducted a thorough inspection of the site and took a large number of soil, water, flora and fauna samples which will be analysed in various laboratories with expertise in the analysis of such samples. The team also inspected the area around the site of the alleged attack. Vehicles, boats and helicopters were used in this survey. During the inspection the team did not find any immediate evidence of the use of chemical weapons. One unexploded munition was discovered at the site but was in too dangerous a condition for the team to take samples from. Consequently, a second team of explosive demolition experts from the Commission's chemical destruction group at Muthanna was dispatched to the site, on 25 November 1993, and concluded that this munition was not a chemical munition but a high-explosive, rocket-propelled grenade. It was destroyed by these experts.

5. In the course of its investigation the Commission has also obtained some documents, which are now subject to forensic examination and analysis.

6. Analysis of the samples is expected to take some time to conclude. The Commission will not, until the

results of these analyses are available, be in a position to arrive at a definitive conclusion on the question of whether chemical weapons were used or not.

Ballistic missile inspections

7. The Commission has continued intensive and multifaceted inspection efforts in the ballistic missile area. A third interim monitoring mission (IMT-1c) was carried out in June. Monitoring camera systems were installed and activated at two missile test stands and a detailed engineering survey of all known missile test sites in Iraq was conducted. UNSCOM63, the largest inspection team to date, conducted inspections in Iraq in September and October.

Interim monitoring

8. Iraq's persistent refusal, until 26 November 1993, to acknowledge its obligations under Security Council resolution 715 (1991) prevented timely implementation of the plan approved under that resolution for ongoing monitoring and verification by the Commission of relevant activities in Iraq. The plan foresaw immediate implementation as of October 1991. Meanwhile, as had been ascertained in the course of ballistic missile inspections under resolution 687 (1991), Iraq was actively pursuing missile-related activities. Consequently, the Commission initiated, in January 1993, a new type of inspection activity in Iraq, interim monitoring.

9. The prime objectives of interim monitoring were to continue to collect information on missile programmes in Iraq and to deter Iraq from launching covert programmes in prohibited missile systems. Interim monitoring was not intended to substitute for ongoing monitoring and verification under resolution 715 (1991). Instead, the interim monitoring teams were tasked with gathering technical information and providing in-depth assessments in order to assist the Commission in preparation for effective execution of the ongoing monitoring and verification plan, once Iraq acknowledged its obligations under resolution 715 (1991).

10. The activities of the first two interim monitoring teams were given in the previous report (S/25977). A third missile interim monitoring team, UNSCOM57/ IMT-1c, conducted its activities in Iraq from 4 to 28 June 1993. The main objective of this mission was to assess existing Iraqi capabilities in the area of precision machining related to ballistic missiles production, in particular gyroscope devices and liquid-fuel engine manufacture. The team conducted inspection activities at 16 industrial facilities and at two military sites.

11. The interim monitoring inspections provided comprehensive technical assessments of current Iraqi missile programmes of relevance under resolutions 687

(1991), 707 (1991) and 715 (1991), including research, development and production capabilities. The teams were able to collect valuable information and technical data needed for the planning and implementation of ongoing monitoring and verification activities in Iraq under resolution 715 (1991).

Camera systems at missile test stands

12. On 6 June 1993, the Commission informed Iraq of its intention to install remote-controlled camera systems at two missile engine test stands, Al-Yawm Al-Azim and Al-Rafah. The purpose of this inspection effort was to verify that no prohibited activities were taking place at these test stands. The camera system was designed to monitor activities continuously and record all tests at those locations. Iraq responded that it would not accept any monitoring activities and would insist that the Commission limit itself to inspection activities under resolution 687 (1991). In his report to the Council (S/25960), the Executive Chairman stated that Iraq's obstruction was a further failure by Iraq to fulfil its obligations in compliance with the relevant resolutions of the Security Council and agreements with the Commission. On 18 June 1993, the President of the Security Council, on behalf of the Council, stated that Iraq must accept installation by UNSCOM of monitoring devices at the test stands.

13. Even after this statement by the Security Council, Iraq continued its obstruction of the installation of the cameras. On 5 July 1993, after the initial installation team had spent over a month in Iraq awaiting a change in the position of the Government of Iraq which would allow it to proceed with its mission, it was instructed by the Executive Chairman to withdraw. As an interim measure, the Commission, after having informed the Council, dispatched a team (UNSCOM60) to Iraq, on 10 July, to seal the relevant equipment and facilities at both sites so as to ensure that they were not used until the cameras had been installed. The Iraqi authorities blocked this team from carrying out its mission. On 12 July 1993, the Executive Chairman reported these events to the President of the Security Council. The Executive Chairman stated that the matter had been elevated by Iraq from a specific issue of monitoring the missile test sites in question to a level of principle concerning Iraq's acceptance of ongoing monitoring and verification under resolution 715 (1991).

14. The Executive Chairman visited Baghdad from 15 to 19 July 1993, in order to seek full compliance by Iraq with the Council's decision of 18 June 1993. On the issue of the monitoring of the two missile test stands, Iraq, as a result of this visit, agreed on an interim basis to permit the installation of cameras at Al-Yawm Al-Azim and

Al-Rafah. It was also understood that a long-term solution of this issue, including the question of the activation of these cameras, would be one of the topics to be covered during high-level technical talks in New York. Pending the outcome of those talks, the Deputy Prime Minister of Iraq gave the Executive Chairman assurances that Iraq would provide the Commission with sufficient notice of any test firings to permit it to observe those firings and that Iraq would facilitate inspections of the two sites by the Commission at such times and as frequently as the Commission should deem necessary. A full account of this visit is contained in the Executive Chairman's report to the Security Council (S/26127).

15. Pursuant to the above arrangements, the Commission dispatched to Baghdad, on 25 July, a small technical team to install the camera systems at the Al-Yawm Al-Azim and Al-Rafah sites. The installation of the cameras, including their testing, was completed on 3 August 1993. As part of the interim arrangements, the Commission sent a number of missile experts to Baghdad to observe any missile tests that Iraq might declare to the Commission. UNSCOM62 operated in Iraq for this purpose from 23 August till 27 September 1993. UNSCOM62 also performed detailed engineering surveys of test facilities at Al-Yawm Al-Azim, Al-Rafah and five other test stands capable of missile and rocket engine tests.

16. After the first round of high-level talks in New York, the Government of Iraq informed the Commission that it had agreed to the activation of the camera systems at Al-Rafah and Al-Yawm Al-Azim. On 25 September 1993, the cameras were activated. Since then they have been operating on a continuous basis. The cameras are arranged in a manner that enables UNSCOM to assess whether a test was of a prohibited missile, engine or motor. In accordance with operating procedures established by the Commission, these camera systems provide 24-hours-a-day, 7-days-a-week coverage of the missile test stands at Al-Rafah and Al-Yawm Al-Azim. Missile test monitoring handbooks, to include engineering baselines for the test sites, checklists and reporting forms for the Iraqis, were developed. An upgrade of the camera systems, to include radio links and improved lenses, was undertaken from 2 to 10 December 1993.

UNSCOM63

17. UNSCOM63 carried out its mission in Iraq from 30 September to 30 October 1993. The objective was twofold: to investigate reports made available to the Commission concerning suspected prohibited activities in Iraq and the continued concealment of proscribed items, notably missiles; and to verify information provided by Iraq on its past prohibited activities, especially on the operational use of missiles with a range greater than 150 kilometres. These tasks were identified as critical to the Commission's intention to complete the identification phase of its work under resolution 687 (1991).

18. UNSCOM63's objective was such as to require the largest inspection team to date, a long period of detailed preparation and intensive training, in-depth analytical work, innovative use of advanced sensors and deployment of additional UNSCOM aerial assets in Iraq.

19. In addition to utilizing proven inspection procedures, UNSCOM63's mission required the use of new inspection techniques since much of the information to be checked by the team referred to underground storage for prohibited items. As a consequence, ground-penetrating radar (GPR) mounted on helicopters was used to increase the effectiveness of the survey of areas to be inspected. The GPR was custom-designed to maximize its capability to detect prohibited items, especially missiles, missile launchers and possible hide sites.

20. Two additional helicopters were deployed to Iraq to support the inspection. These were Bell 412 helicopters, manned and equipped specifically to meet the requirements of UNSCOM63. The primary mission of these helicopters was to conduct GPR surveys. They also performed aerial inspection of specific sites and provided an additional means of securing sites to be inspected including, as necessary, at night, using forward-looking infrared radar (FLIR).

21. UNSCOM63 started its inspection activities in Iraq on 30 September 1993. Until the arrival of the two Bell helicopters on 3 October 1993, the team conducted ground inspections of a number of sites in and around Baghdad. The first series of inspections utilizing GPR were conducted from 4 to 7 October. Several locations in central Iraq were surveyed to check if prohibited items were present. On 9 October UNSCOM63 relocated to western Iraq. The objective of this phase was to test the veracity of some critical information on the operational use of Al Hussein missiles during the Gulf war. The areas of GPR inspections centred around known launch positions of Al Hussein missiles and varied in size from 20 to 45 square kilometres. Intensive GPR and ground searches were conducted at these locations in order to identify launcher hide sites. In addition, two sites were investigated on the ground and from the air to determine if these were or had been the locations of prohibited activities. On 25 October 1993, UNSCOM63 relocated to an area in north-west Iraq to verify information on past proscribed activities and the presence of prohibited items. This required a search of a very large area (1,000 square kilometres) as well as inspections, including GPR surveys, of specific locations already known to the team or identified through area searches. The inspection in north-west Iraq was completed by 28 October 1993, after intensive

area searches, aerial surveys and ground inspections of specific locations had been accomplished. In parallel with this task, the team visited sites containing declared prohibited items and verified the destruction of these items by Iraq as previously instructed by the Commission.

22. During its deployment in Iraq, UNSCOM63 inspected more than 30 sites and areas. Altogether, 28 GPR missions were flown, totalling more than 56 hours of flying time. The Iraqi authorities were keen to ensure that the inspection proceeded without incident: Iraq provided all the support requested by the inspection team; access to all sites and areas to be inspected was granted; no problems were encountered by the team in execution of its operational plan, including the introduction and use of its aerial assets; and the Iraqi authorities honoured those inspection rights invoked by UNSCOM63.

23. No undeclared prohibited items or activities were identified by UNSCOM63. UNSCOM63 discovered no evidence that contradicted the information provided by Iraq on issues that related to its mission.

Gamma radiation detection surveys

24. The first special aerial inspection team mission which focused on the detection of gamma emissions was flown from 10 to 25 September 1993. Owing to some early obstruction on the part of Iraq, flights did not begin until 15 September and, consequently, the coverage of the mission was considerably reduced. Partial surveys were conducted at Al Tuwaitha, Al Atheer and Al Jezira. Gamma signals were detected from multiple points at all sites. Preliminary analysis indicates the usefulness of this technique in identifying specific locations warranting more detailed ground inspections. Use will be made of this gamma detection capability in the future.

25. The second such aerial inspection using the gamma detection equipment was flown from 2 to 15 December 1993. During this mission, more extensive coverage of previously covered sites was accomplished and additional sites surveyed. Gamma signals were detected from all sites, but the significance of this will not be apparent until the results of the analysis are available.

Appendix III
Destruction of Iraq's chemical agents and munitions

1. A full background report on chemical destruction activities has been given in previous reports. The present report focuses solely on developments since June 1993.

A. *Status and activities of the Chemical Destruction Group*
Personnel

2. Contributing nations have maintained their support for the Chemical Destruction Group (CDG). However, staffing is a permanent problem, as experts with the required qualifications are few and are required for work in the supplying countries. The continued support of these countries will be required until CDG completes its task. As of December 1993, CDG has 27 experts from 12 nations.

Safety and security aspects

3. Safety standards at Muthanna have been kept at the high level established by the Destruction Advisory Panel and the Commission. Recommendations from the Iraqi side to lower some standards in order to speed up destruction activities have been rejected. Regular air sampling has been conducted. Additional warning devices, such as remote-control mustard detectors, have been added to improve safety measures. These high safety standards have paid dividends in ensuring that various minor incidents have been contained. If safety procedures were not followed, the work is of a nature that some of the incidents could have resulted in serious accidents. However, the environment for everyday work remains extremely hazardous due to daily exposure to chemical agents.

Destruction activities

4. The key factors affecting the rate at which CDG destroys chemicals have not changed:

(a) Meteorological/environmental conditions;

(b) Reliability and status of destruction equipment;

(c) Support from the Iraqi side;

(d) Condition of the items to be destroyed (e.g., corroded containers, polymerized mustard, etc.).

5. Figures for the status of destruction at Muthanna, as of 6 December 1993, are listed in section C below. They are listed as absolute figures. However, there is some uncertainty as to the exact amounts of agent actually destroyed because of various factors, such as leakage from containers and deterioration of agent prior to destruction.

6. Over the reporting period, destruction activities went smoothly; the major limitations to continuous destruction were:

(a) Maintenance work to the incinerator and hydrolysis plants;

(b) Spare parts supply problems;

(c) Unfavourable meteorological conditions, mainly wind speed and wind direction.

7. Planning figures for daily destruction rates are approximately 3,500 litres of mustard and 350 litres of tabun. However, the polymerized mustard agent stored in 1-ton containers at Muthanna poses a problem. Destruction is likely to be highly time-consuming.

B. *Future tasks of the Chemical Destruction Group: an outline*

8. Destruction of precursors, chemical agents and munitions will probably be completed by March/April 1994. Other outstanding issues are:

(a) What chemical production equipment should be destroyed;

(b) What destruction methods to use for this equipment;

(c) How to store chemical waste from destruction;

(d) How to seal bunkers that have been identified for sealing;

(e) Which chemicals Iraq should be permitted to use elsewhere;

(f) What final verification of destruction activities will be required prior to the withdrawal of CDG.

A plan for winding down CDG's work, which will address all these questions, is now being developed.

9. The provisional deadline for completing CDG's tasks is set at mid-1994. This estimate is based on CDG's destruction timetable, the time required for the closing-down operations and time built in for slippage. Flexibility will be needed to allow for adjustments to operational needs.

C. *Status of destruction activities as of 6 December 1993*

Munitions

283	122 mm rockets and warheads
6 410	122 mm rocket warheads
863	122 mm rocket motors
16 695	122 mm rocket propellant grains
2 388	122 mm rocket motor tubes
12 638	155 mm mustard-filled artillery shells
34	155 mm empty projectiles
2	155 mm oil-filled projectiles
29	Al Hussein warheads for GB/GF
337	R400 bombs
333	R400 tail fin assemblies
471	250-gauge tail fin assemblies
4	250-gauge bomb, oil-filled
5 172	250-gauge bomb, empty
1 097	250-gauge bomb, polymust a/ (partial)
4	500-gauge bomb, oil-filled
675	500-gauge bomb, polymust (partial)
1 115	DB 2 bomb
61	DB 0 bomb
28 332	Total munitions destroyed

CW agent

17 815	1 b/ GA nerve agent
330	1 GB nerve agent
60 498	1 GB/GF nerve agent
247 966	1 mustard
326 609	1 Total CW agent destroyed

Precursors

123 722	1 D4
14 600	1 DF
1 120	1 dichlorethane
211 023	1 isopropyl alcohol
153 980	1 thio-diethyleneglycol
1 200	1 cyclohexanol/isopropyl alcohol
297 400	1 phosphorus oxychloride
148 800	1 thionyl chloride
415 000	1 phosphorous trichloride
30 000	1 di-isopropylamine
3 000	1 morpholine
53 000	1 chlorobenzaldehyde
1 900	1 ethylchlorohydrine
116 000	1 monoethyleneglycol
1 470 745	1 Total precursors destroyed

a/ I.e., polymerized mustard agent.
b/ Litres.

Appendix IV
Information Assessment Unit

1. Over the past six months the Information Assessment Unit has continued to evolve in response to the changing requirements of the Commission's work. The major activity in this respect concerns preparations for full-scale monitoring activity in Iraq. The preparations have had an impact on all aspects of the work undertaken by the Unit.

2. The Unit's information collection activities have expanded, drawing upon the Commission's own assets, as well as those of external organizations. Supporting Governments and agencies remain a significant source of information and assessment on past proscribed programmes in Iraq. The number of Governments and agencies with whom the Unit has contact has grown over the past six months. These contacts are important not only for gaining information on past activities, but also for establishing links for ongoing monitoring and verification purposes. External organizations also play an important role in providing the Unit with technical data on equipment and systems in Iraq, thus allowing the Unit's analysts to make informed evaluations on their capabilities and functions.

3. The Information Assessment Unit continues to derive great benefit from its aerial surveillance platforms. These have expanded in role and number over the last

few months. The Commission's high-altitude reconnaissance plane (U-2) flies up to three times a week; some 186 missions had been flown as of 13 December 1993. The aircraft's missions are assigned by the Unit and now encompass a number of different roles. The U-2 overflies on a regular basis sites identified as requiring ongoing monitoring and verification and new sites of potential interest as designated by the Unit. In addition, the aircraft has been undertaking photography of areas of Iraq which are of particular relevance to the Commission's work. Mosaics of these areas are being produced and provide the analysts with reference photography of large areas. The final function of the aircraft is to provide aerial surveillance of inspection sites before and during ground teams' visits, in order to ensure that no proscribed or evasion activity has taken place.

4. The second aerial asset available to the Information Assessment Unit is the aerial inspection team. This consists of three inspectors based in Iraq and operating from CH-53g helicopters. Some 215 flights have been undertaken to date by the team covering 335 sites. The emphasis for the team's activities is increasingly focused on sites determined to be of relevance for ongoing monitoring and verification purposes. The detailed photography from these missions provides the Unit's analysts with a means of monitoring changes which take place over time at a particular facility. The aerial inspection team also plays a valuable part in providing aerial surveillance over inspection sites.

5. In September and December 1993, the team undertook a new role with the introduction of a gamma detection programme utilizing equipment mounted on a CH-53g aircraft. A full report on this activity is to be found in paragraphs 24 and 25 of appendix II to the present report. Two other additional types of aerial detection devices have also been introduced into Iraq recently; ground-penetrating radar (GPR) and forward-looking infrared radar (FLIR). Both systems were mounted on Bell 412 helicopters. The GPR, which can detect concealed objects and underground cavities, was the focus of UNSCOM63's inspection activities reported on in appendix II. The FLIR was also used in this inspection for aerial surveillance activities during the first-ever night-time operations. Its main function was to assist in the overnight securing of the sites to be inspected.

6. The photographic product derived from all these aerial assets is held in the Information Assessment Unit in New York where it is assessed by the Unit's photographic interpreters and analysts. Material relating to nuclear facilities is also shared with IAEA. The product now constitutes a very comprehensive library of material which can be drawn upon by the analysts for assessment and monitoring purposes and for use in preparing inspections.

7. The capability for handling written data in the Unit has also expanded with the introduction of new computer hardware and software which offers the analysts a comprehensive means of storing, retrieving and manipulating data.

8. The analytical work undertaken in the Information Assessment Unit continues to be the basis for much of the Commission's activity. In addition to providing assessments on the status of Iraq's compliance with the terms of the cease-fire resolution 687 (1991), the Unit's work also generates the inspection programme. In its assessment role, the Unit is increasingly focusing on defining the sites, facilities and equipment relevant for ongoing monitoring and verification, together with the modalities and techniques to be employed. New staff members have also been recruited to focus on specific aspects of monitoring, such as import control. The Unit continues to benefit from experienced staff who have amassed a wealth of knowledge on Iraq's proscribed programmes.

Appendix V
Ongoing monitoring and verification

1. Work under the ongoing monitoring and verification phase is under way. The ongoing monitoring and verification effort in the three weapons areas for which the Commission has direct responsibility (ballistic missile, chemical and biological) is being coordinated in order to achieve continuity and harmony in approach. Various tasks have already been undertaken.

2. Pending receipt from Iraq of the complete information required under and in accordance with resolution 715 (1991) and the Commission's plan for ongoing monitoring and verification, a list of the sites/facilities which would be subject to baseline inspections has been drawn up. Monitoring and verification protocols for each site to be monitored, containing all relevant materials and information (e.g., name of site/facility, its general function, its location, its geographical coordinates, aerial surveillance data), are being prepared. Concepts for ongoing monitoring and verification inspections have been drawn up, providing for a combination of unannounced and announced inspections. A preliminary assessment of operational and planning requirements has been undertaken in respect of the personnel (length of stay, background, expertise, need for training), equipment (monitoring sensors and technology and standard operational equipment) and assets (ground and air) which will be needed for monitoring purposes. As required by paragraph 8 of resolution 715 (1991), an import/export control mecha-

nism will be put in place, the planning modalities and requirements of which are currently being identified.

3. The monitoring database, which will constitute the backbone of the ongoing monitoring and verification effort, will be organized geographically and will contain all relevant information, whatever its form (aerial imagery, site diagram, floor plan, equipment drawings, photography, inspection reports, texts of Iraqi declarations, etc.).

4. Formats for Iraq's declarations in accordance with its reporting obligations under the plan for ongoing monitoring and verification have been developed. Monitoring and verification protocols for the sites to be inspected are being prepared. These will serve as the basis on which inspections will be conducted at sites identified as requiring regular inspection under the ongoing monitoring and verification regime.

Appendix VI
Suppliers and import monitoring

1. The Commission and IAEA have both long insisted that Iraq provide data on the suppliers of materials and technical expertise for its past banned-weapons programmes. During the high-level technical talks in New York in September, critical items were identified for which details on suppliers were essential if the Commission and IAEA were to be able to fulfil their mandates. Iraq promised to provide details on these at the second round of high-level talks in Baghdad. These were given on the last day of those talks, 8 October 1993.

2. The purpose of insisting on supplier information was twofold:

(a) To discover the full list of who supplied Iraq, thus enabling the Commission and IAEA, by investigating with the supplier companies through the relevant Governments, to establish material balances for each of the weapons programmes. This would be achieved through the rough equation:

items supplied + items locally manufactured

=

items used + items destroyed + items
under UNSCOM/IAEA control

(b) To ascertain the techniques used by Iraq to acquire items which were subject to export controls, thereby enabling the Commission and IAEA better to design, as required under paragraph 8 of resolution 715 (1991), a system for monitoring Iraq's imports and exports to be in place before the lifting of sanctions.

3. The information provided by Iraq responded to the questions identified in New York. In the chemical area, Iraq provided: aggregate quantities of precursors imported against companies and country of origin; aggregate quantities of empty munitions imported against companies and country of origin; and aggregate quantities of production equipment imported by type, capacity, material, company and country of origin. In the biological area, Iraq answered questions about the sources of complex media, toxins, micro-organisms, aerosol generators and incubation chambers, in aggregate quantities by company and country of origin. In the ballistic missile area, the Commission's questions concentrated on critical items essential for the production of ballistic missiles, e.g., gyroscope and fuel components. For these, Iraq provided the name of the company, the country of origin, the quantities supplied, the point of entry into Iraq and the consignee.

4. The Commission is assessing Iraq's declarations, both by seeking confirmation from the named supplying companies, through the relevant Governments, of the items and quantities supplied to Iraq, and by analysing samples of, e.g., maraging steel, to assess whether the material did in fact originate from the source declared by Iraq.

5. It is noticeable that some of the items of concern to the Commission and IAEA did not require export licences at the time. Where such licences were required, Iraq had developed means to circumvent them. Routes of supply can be summarized as follows:

(a) Direct from the manufacturing company to Iraq;

(b) Via a middleman to Iraq. In many of these cases, the manufacturing company did not know the eventual use to which its products would be put, although some of the companies might well have been in a position to suspect the purpose;

(c) Via a third country;

(d) Via a second company in the same country. Transfers of this kind have not generally required export licences.

6. The Commission is required, under paragraph 7 of resolution 715 (1991) and in coordination with IAEA and the Sanctions Committee established pursuant to resolution 661 (1990), to elaborate a mechanism for monitoring Iraq's imports and exports of certain listed items. This will require, in order best to focus the resources and efforts of the Commission, the identification, on the basis of the annexes to the plans for ongoing monitoring and verification, of key choke points in the development and production of the banned weapons capabilities. It should be noted that paragraph 12 of the plan for ongoing monitoring and verification (S/22871/Rev.1) requires that this mechanism should be developed "at the earliest possible date, and not later than before

the lifting of sanctions" covering items relevant to the monitoring plan.

7. The Commission intends to hold in New York, in early 1994, meetings with weapons and export control experts from key supplier countries with the purpose of deriving from the annexes lists of items to be controlled under the regime. On the basis of the results of these meetings, the Commission will consult with IAEA and the Sanctions Committee referred to above on how to proceed with the elaboration of the mechanism and its presentation to the Security Council.

Appendix VII
Inspection schedule
(In-country dates)

Nuclear

15 May-21 May 1991	IAEA1/UNSCOM1
22 June-3 July 1991	IAEA2/UNSCOM4
7 July-18 July 1991	IAEA3/UNSCOM5
27 July-10 August 1991	IAEA4/UNSCOM6
14 September-20 September 1991	IAEA5/UNSCOM14
21 September-30 September 1991	IAEA6/UNSCOM16
11 October-22 October 1991	IAEA7/UNSCOM19
11 November-18 November 1991	IAEA8/UNSCOM22
11 January-14 January 1992	IAEA9/UNSCOM25
5 February-13 February 1992	IAEA10/UNSCOM27
5 February-13 February 1992	IAEA10/UNSCOM30
7 April-15 April 1992	IAEA11/UNSCOM33
26 May-4 June 1992	IAEA12/UNSCOM37
14 July-21 July 1992	IAEA13/UNSCOM41
31 August-7 September 1992	IAEA14/UNSCOM43
8 November-19 November 1992	IAEA15/UNSCOM46
5 December-14 December 1992	IAEA16/UNSCOM47
22 January-27 January 1993	IAEA17/UNSCOM49
3 March-11 March 1993	IAEA18/UNSCOM52
30 April-7 May 1993	IAEA19/UNSCOM56
25 June-30 June 1993	IAEA20/UNSCOM58
23 July-28 July 1993	IAEA21/UNSCOM61
1 November-9 November 1993	IAEA22/UNSCOM64

Chemical

9 June-15 June 1991	CW1/UNSCOM2
15 August-22 August 1991	CW2/UNSCOM9
31 August-8 September 1991	CW3/UNSCOM11
31 August-5 September 1991	CW4/UNSCOM12
6 October-9 November 1991	CW5/UNSCOM17
22 October-2 November 1991	CW6/UNSCOM20
18 November-1 December 1991	CBW1/UNSCOM21
27 January-5 February 1992	CW7/UNSCOM26
21 February-24 March 1992	CD1/UNSCOM29
5 April-13 April 1992	CD2/UNSCOM32
15 April-29 April 1992	CW8/UNSCOM35
18 June 1992-	CDG/UNSCOM38
26 June-10 July 1992	CBW2/UNSCOM39
21 September-29 September 1992	CW9/UNSCOM44
6 December-14 December 1992	CBW3/UNSCOM47
6 April-18 April 1993	CW10/UNSCOM55
27 June-30 June 1993	CW11/UNSCOM59
19 November-22 November 1993	CW12/UNSCOM65

Biological

2 August-8 August 1991	BW1/UNSCOM7
20 September-3 October 1991	BW2/UNSCOM15
11 March-18 March 1993	BW3/UNSCOM53

Ballistic missiles

30 June-7 July 1991	BM1/UNSCOM3
18 July-20 July 1991	BM2/UNSCOM10
8 August-15 August 1991	BM3/UNSCOM8
6 September-13 September 1991	BM4/UNSCOM13
1 October-9 October 1991	BM5/UNSCOM18
1 December-9 December 1991	BM6/UNSCOM23
9 December-17 December 1991	BM7/UNSCOM24
21 February-29 February 1992	BM8/UNSCOM28
21 March-29 March 1992	BM9/UNSCOM31
13 April-21 April 1992	BM10/UNSCOM34
14 May-22 May 1992	BM11/UNSCOM36
11 July-29 July 1992	BM12/UNSCOM40A+B
7 August-18 August 1992	BM13/UNSCOM42
16 October-30 October 1992	BM14/UNSCOM45
25 January-23 March 1993	IMT1a/UNSCOM48
12 February-21 February 1993	BM15/UNSCOM50
22 February-23 February 1993	BM16/UNSCOM51
27 March-17 May 1993	IMT1b/UNSCOM54
5 June-28 June 1993	IMT1c/UNSCOM57
10 July-11 July 1993	BM17/UNSCOM60
24 August-15 September 1993	BM18/UNSCOM62
28 September-1 November 1993	BM19/UNSCOM63

Computer search

12 February 1992	UNSCOM30

Special missions

30 June-3 July 1991
11 August-14 August 1991
4 October-6 October 1991
11 November-15 November 1991
27 January-30 January 1992
21 February-24 February 1992
17 July-19 July 1992
28 July-29 July 1992
6 September-12 September 1992
4 November-9 November 1992

Document 180

Statement by the President of the Security Council concerning the sanctions regime

S/PRST/1994/3, 18 January 1994

The members of the Security Council held informal consultations on 18 January 1994 pursuant to paragraph 21 of resolution 687 (1991).

After hearing all the opinions expressed in the course of the consultations, the President of the Council concluded that there was no agreement that the necessary conditions existed for a modification of the regime established in paragraph 20 of resolution 687 (1991), as referred to in paragraph 21 of that resolution.

Document 181

Letter from the Secretary-General to the President of the Security Council concerning the matter of Iraqi private citizens and their assets which remained on Kuwaiti territory following the demarcation of the Iraq-Kuwait boundary

S/1994/240, 22 February 1994

I have the honour to refer to my letter of 23 December 1992 to the President of the Security Council (S/25085, annex II) in which I brought to the Council's attention some issues arising from the demarcation of the Iraq-Kuwait boundary. Among them was the matter of the Iraqi private citizens and their assets which remained on Kuwaiti territory and about which I had been in touch with the Governments of Iraq and Kuwait to determine how the United Nations might help to bring about a settlement. In a letter dated 8 January 1993, the President of the Council informed me that the members concurred with my general approach.

On 10 January 1993 I received a communication from the First Deputy Prime Minister, Minister for Foreign Affairs of Kuwait which informed me that the Iraqi citizens would not be permitted to remain in Kuwait but would be compensated for their private property and assets on the basis of an assessment by a neutral party nominated by the United Nations. On 1 March 1993 the Permanent Representative of Iraq responded to this suggestion by indicating that his authorities would "take no action that might tend to recognize the injustice deliberately inflicted on Iraq" but, at the same time, would "take no action that might provoke dispute or contention with the United Nations".

Encouraging developments have taken place for the resolution of this issue. All Iraqi nationals in the Umm Qasr area were relocated without disturbance to other dwellings in Iraq by the end of December 1993. Kuwait has permitted the Iraqi nationals in the Al-Abdaly farming area to remain there until the end of February to allow them time to harvest their crops; they are to be relocated to parcels of land in Iraq by 1 March 1994. I should like to take this opportunity to express my appreciation for the cooperation the Governments of Iraq and Kuwait have extended to the Force Commander of the United Nations Iraq-Kuwait Observation Mission (UNIKOM), who has been facilitating this effort which has thus far gone forward without disturbance.

As for the question of compensation, in accordance with an arrangement reached on 22 September 1993 between the United Nations and Kuwait related to the issue of compensation to Iraqi nationals located in Kuwait as a result of the demarcation of the boundary, Kuwait agreed to pay into a trust fund, which I would establish for the purpose, an amount of compensation that I would decide, plus all costs and expenses incurred by the United Nations in connection with this effort. The money would be disbursed after I had made arrangements on the modalities of payment. However, should it not be possible to conclude payment arrangements to my satisfaction, it was also agreed that I would deposit the corresponding amount in an escrow account at the disposal of the beneficiaries. In that event, every effort would be made to inform the Iraqi nationals of the steps they should take to claim their compensation.

Following an assessment of the value of the private property and assets that was carried out by the inde-pendent contractor I appointed for the purpose, I have now decided that the total amount of the compensation shall be 56 million Iraqi dinars for 95 farms and 15.5 million Iraqi dinars for 206 residential houses. The Government of Kuwait has been officially informed of this decision. The amounts of individual payments will be determined in accordance with the recommendations of the contractor.

I trust the Council will concur with my view that the compensation payments would fall within the definition of "payments exclusively for strictly . . . humanitarian purposes" provided for in paragraph 4 of Security Council resolution 661 (1990) as an exception to the general prohibition against the remittal of funds to persons or bodies within Iraq.

I should be grateful, Mr. President, if you would bring the contents of this letter to the attention of the members of the Security Council.

(Signed) Boutros BOUTROS-GHALI

Document 182

Report of the Secretary-General on the return of Kuwaiti property seized by Iraq (extract)

S/1994/243, 2 March 1994

Introduction

1. The present report is submitted in pursuance of paragraph 2 (d) of Security Council resolution 686 (1991) of 2 March 1991, by which the Security Council demanded that Iraq immediately begin to return all Kuwaiti property seized by Iraq, the return to be completed in the shortest possible period; paragraph 15 of Security Council resolution 687 (1991) of 8 April 1991 by which the Council requested the Secretary-General to report to the Security Council on the steps taken to facilitate the return of all Kuwaiti property seized by Iraq, including a list of any property that Kuwait claims has not been returned or which has not been returned intact; and a letter from the President of the Security Council dated 25 January 1994 requesting a report on the return of all Kuwaiti property seized by Iraq.

I. *Organization*

2. By his letter dated 19 March 1991 (S/22361), the President of the Security Council informed the Secretary-General that the members of the Security Council were of the view that the modalities for the return of property from Iraq in accordance with Security Council resolution 686 (1991) should be arranged through the Secretary-General's Office in consultation with the parties, and that that procedure also had the agreement of Iraq and Kuwait. In response, my predecessor informed the Security Council, in a letter to the President dated 26 March 1991 (S/22387), that he had designated Mr. J. Richard Foran, the Assistant Secretary-General, Office of General Services, Department of Administration and Management, as the official responsible for coordinating the return of property from Iraq to Kuwait. Following Mr. Foran's retirement from United Nations service, I designated Mr. Raymond Sommereyns, Director of the West Asia Division of the Department of Political Affairs, as Coordinator for the return of property.

3. The Coordinator has been assisted by a small group of United Nations staff members, including one who acts as his representative in the field. This core group has been augmented by staff members who have served for varying periods of time as members of the teams that facilitated the hand-over operations in Iraq and Kuwait.

4. The responsibility for returning the property rested with Iraq, while Kuwait was responsible for receiv-

ing it. The hand-over operations usually took place from Iraq to Kuwait with the United Nations acting as facilitator, registrar and certifier. At no time was the property in the custody of the United Nations.

5. The Government of Austria generously provided two senior experts from the National Bank of Austria, who acted as advisers on the return of property belonging to the Central Bank of Kuwait.

6. The operation has been financed with funds contributed to the escrow account established under the provisions of Security Council resolutions 706 (1991) and 778 (1992).

II. *Role of the coordinator*

7. The Coordinator has endeavoured to maintain a clear distinction between the mandate entrusted to him and that of the United Nations Compensation Commission.

8. The Coordinator's role has been one of receiving, registering and submitting to Iraq claims presented by Kuwait and facilitating the return of property which Iraq has declared that it has in its possession and is ready to return. Therefore, he has not considered it within the scope of his mandate to investigate or verify claims from Kuwait that specific property items were removed by Iraq or claims by Iraq that specific items were not removed or, if removed, were subsequently destroyed during the hostilities.

9. Members of the United Nations team registered the comments and remarks of the parties in cases where property items were returned in damaged condition. However, they were not involved in assessments as to the scope of the damage or where, when and how it might have occurred.

10. On some occasions, United Nations team members were shown pieces of property items by Iraqi authorities, which explained that they were pieces of items claimed by Kuwait that had been destroyed during the hostilities. With the exception of a few cases where the objects could be clearly identified by numbers or other distinctive markings, it was not possible to verify the authenticity of such information.

III. *Modalities*

11. For want of a procedural precedent, the modalities required were developed specifically for this operation.

A. *Records*

12. The need for a transparent and accurate system of record-keeping was recognized as an important element of a successful operation.

13. Initially, an attempt was made to create a computer programme that could be used uniformly for all commodities and that would provide information that would permit, *inter alia*, a comparison of claims received from Kuwait with deliveries made by Iraq. The system that was developed was used with some success during the first major hand-over operation, namely the return of the property of the Kuwait Central Bank which took place in Ar'ar, Saudi Arabia, during the summer of 1991.

14. However, experience obtained in subsequent hand-over operations demonstrated that it would be difficult to develop a uniform system, since its successful use would require the receipt of data in a uniform manner for all commodities for which a claim was made. In many cases such information was difficult or impossible for Kuwait to provide, as most of its inventory records had been destroyed during the hostilities. On a number of occasions it was necessary to use lists provided by Iraq as the basis for recording the property being returned. Another obstacle was the fact that the lists submitted by the parties differed in format and detail. Records, therefore, had to be developed on a commodity-by-commodity basis, in a similar but not uniform way. This made it impossible to establish a detailed comparison between claims received and property returned.

15. The hand-over forms used in the operation were developed in consultation with the Office of the Legal Counsel. Subject to minor adjustments necessitated by the nature of a specific commodity, they have been used throughout the operation.

B. *Procedures*

16. After consultations with representatives of Iraq and Kuwait, the following procedural arrangements were agreed upon. With minor adjustments, they have been followed during the period of operations:

(a) A commodity-by-commodity approach would be followed;

(b) Kuwait would submit its claims to the Coordinator, who, after registering them, would forward them to Iraq for comments;

(c) When Iraq declared that property related to a specific claim, fully or in part, was in its possession and ready for delivery, the Coordinator, following consultation with the parties, would propose:

(i) The venue and time for the hand-over;

(ii) Procedures for delivery to the hand-over site, the on-site inspection, subsequent inspections at recognized technical institutions where that was deemed necessary, the recording procedure and arrangements for the final transportation of the property items to Kuwait;

(iii) Following approval of the suggested procedures by both parties, the final venue and date for the commencement of the hand-over transaction would be set;

(d) At the time of delivery, members of a United Nations team would record the property delivered and prepare hand-over documents to be signed by the authorized representatives of both parties. These documents would reflect any comments and observations that the parties might wish to make relating to the property, such as its volume or state of repair. A United Nations team leader would then certify by signature that the hand-over had taken place in accordance with the agreed procedures;

(e) Custody of the property would remain with Iraq until the transfer document had been signed, at which time it would revert to Kuwait. At no time would the United Nations take custody of the property;

(f) For practical purposes, all procedures, both oral and in writing, would be carried out in the English language.

C. *Venue*

17. Hand-over operations were carried out at the following venues: a border station near the town of Ar'ar in Saudi Arabia, the use of which was generously provided by the Government of Saudi Arabia; Safwan, a town in southern Iraq; airfields in Iraq; locations in Baghdad; an airport in Amman generously made available by the Government of Jordan; and international waters of the Persian Gulf.

D. *Transportation*

18. Transportation of the property to the hand-over site has been the responsibility of Iraq, while responsibility for transportation from the hand-over site has rested with Kuwait.

19. The means of transportation have varied according to the type of property and its location. Aircraft that were deemed airworthy were handed over at Iraqi airports and airfields, from where they were flown to Kuwait. Sea-going vessels were towed by Iraqi tug-boats to a designated hand-over point in international waters in the Persian Gulf and from there to Kuwait by Kuwaiti tug-boats.

20. Many of the commodities were trucked by Iraq to sites in Ar'ar or Safwan, from where they were moved by vehicles provided by Kuwait. In a number of cases, however, sensitive items such as museum pieces and property belonging to the Kuwaiti Air Force were airlifted out of Iraq.

E. *Inspection and examination*

21. The responsibility for inspecting and examining the property items to be handed over has rested exclusively with Kuwait.

22. On most occasions, inspections took the form of a visual/technical examination at the hand-over site with the methods employed varying from commodity to commodity. For example, during the return of gold bars and museum objects, every item was carefully checked; while in the return of property belonging to a library, only items considered to be of special value or importance were checked individually with others being checked randomly. In some cases, only random checks were carried out, and the items were received and signed for based on the packing lists of each box, crate or container in which they arrived.

23. On a number of other occasions, the parties agreed that specific items such as sophisticated technical or electronic equipment would be subjected to inspections at specialized external institutions in addition to the on-site visual/technical examination that took place at the time of the hand-over. In such cases, the parties generally would agree that Kuwait was to submit the reports from those institutions within a given time-frame for incorporation into the hand-over reports. It would also be agreed that the parties were to recognize those reports as the description of the property at the time of hand-over.

IV. *Summary of the hand-over operations*

24. The decision of the Government of Iraq to return, pursuant to Security Council resolution 686 (1991), quantities of gold, Kuwaiti paper currency and civilian aircraft seized after 2 August 1990 was announced in identical letters dated 5 March 1991 (S/22330) from the Deputy Prime Minister of Iraq to the President of the Security Council and to my predecessor.

25. By letters addressed to the President of the Security Council on 14 March 1991 (S/22427) and to my predecessor on 20 March 1991 (S/22367), the Permanent Representative of Kuwait transmitted partial lists of Kuwaiti property belonging to libraries, the Central Bank of Kuwait, Kuwait Airways Corporation and the Ministry of Justice and Legal Affairs that had been seized by Iraq after 2 August 1990.

26. Following consultations with the parties in April and May 1991, it was agreed to give priority to the following categories: (a) gold, currency notes, commemorative and commercial coins and related items belonging to the Central Bank of Kuwait, (b) civilian aircraft and spare parts belonging to Kuwait Airways Corporation, (c) museum objects belonging to the Kuwait National Museum and (d) the Central Library of Kuwait.

27. At a later stage, arrangements were also made for the hand-over of properties belonging to the following Ministries of the Government of Kuwait: information, defence, transportation, oil, social affairs and labour, health, public works and communication. Properties belonging to the Kuwait News Agency, the Arab Institute for Planning and the Kuwait National Assembly were also handed over. While a number of claims were submitted, no private property has been returned to Kuwait as of this date.

28. A list of all the hand-over operations that have been carried out to date is contained in annex I [not reproduced here].

29. The Coordinator is currently facilitating the return of a structurally damaged C-130 aircraft, which is to be disassembled at the Al-Suwaira airbase by aircraft engineers employed by a private company agreed upon by both parties. The aircraft will then be airlifted out of Iraq for assessment. Discussions are also under way for the return of the Free Art Studio Collection, 80 containers belonging to the Kuwait Airways Corporation and properties of the United Arab Maritime Navigation Company.

30. The Coordinator will continue to be available to the parties to facilitate the return of any other property for which Kuwait may wish to submit a claim. As required, this will be reflected in addenda to the present report.

V. *Observations*

31. Consultations with the parties prior to each hand-over operation required the Coordinator or his representative to act as mediator and communication link in the search for common ground that would lead to a solution acceptable to both sides. The lack of trust between the parties, the absence of a precedent for managing an operation of this kind and the long distances and less than satisfactory telecommunication and travel facilities all added to the complexity of the task. Fortunately, the Coordinator and his staff enjoyed the good will and cooperation of both Iraq and Kuwait throughout the operation.

32. On the whole, the hand-over operations were carried out without major complications, although some were time-consuming and presented considerable logistical problems. As an example, the hand-over of museum objects required two months to complete and entailed detailed inspections of each object as well as arrangements for the packing of some 60 tons of fragile items for transport over almost 100 kilometres of road from Baghdad to Habbaniya airfield, from where they were airlifted to Kuwait.

33. While it was not possible, for reasons already described, to develop a record system that would permit a comparison of deliveries made by Iraq with the claims that had been submitted by Kuwait, the records maintained by the Coordinator have a high degree of accuracy as to the property actually returned. This information will be augmented by Kuwait's list of property that has not been returned or which has not been returned intact, which will be submitted to the Security Council as an addendum to the present report in accordance with paragraph 15 of Security Council resolution 687 (1991).

34. The Coordinator's records of all commodities returned as well as the original hand-over documents will be available for inspection in the Department of Political Affairs.

[Editor's Note: Annex, not reproduced, contains summary of items handed over; addendum (S/1994/243/Add.1), not reproduced contains list from Kuwait of property which it claims has not been returned or not been returned intact.]

Document 183

Security Council resolution concerning compensation for Iraqi citizens affected by the demarcation of the international boundary between Iraq and Kuwait

S/RES/899 (1994), 4 March 1994

The Security Council,

Recalling its resolution 833 (1993) of 27 May 1993,

Having considered the Secretary-General's letter of 22 February 1994 (S/1994/240) concerning the matter of the Iraqi private citizens and their assets which remained on Kuwaiti territory following the demarcation of the international boundary between Iraq and Kuwait, and *welcoming* the developments and arrangements described therein,

Acting under Chapter VII of the Charter of the United Nations,

Decides that the compensation payments to be made pursuant to the arrangements described in the Secretary-General's letter of 22 February 1994 may be remitted to the private citizens concerned in Iraq, notwithstanding the provisions of resolution 661 (1991).

Document 184

Decision 17 taken by the Governing Council of the United Nations Compensation Commission: Priority of payment and payment mechanisms

S/AC.26/Dec.17 (1994)*, 24 March 1994

Priority of payment and payment mechanism

Guiding Principles

Decision taken by the Governing Council of the United Nations Compensation Commission at its 41st meeting, held in Geneva on 23 March 1994

1. In striving to resolve the question of how to allocate the funding available to pay awards to claimants within each category of claims as well as how to allocate available funding among the various categories of claims, Governing Council has been guided by the following basic principles:

A. The Compensation Commission should ensure that similarly situated claimants within each category of claims are treated equally, to the extent feasible, regardless of the chronological order in which their claims are decided;

B. Claimants with claims in the three categories of urgent claims (categories "A", "B" and "C") shall receive priority of treatment, including at both the processing and the payment stages, in accordance with the prior decisions and statements of the Government Council.

Payment Mechanism

2. Payment of an initial amount of US$2,500 (or the principal amount of the award, if less) will be made to each successful claimant in categories "A", "B" and "C".

3. Such payments in respect of successful claimants in categories "A"," B" and "C" will be made by the Compensation Commission to Governments as awards in each category are confirmed by the Governing Council.

4. Such payments will begin when sufficient funds have been accumulated in the Compensation Fund to make payment on all claims approved in the first instalments in categories "A", "B" and "C". Subsequent such payments will also be made when sufficient funds have been accumulated in the Compensation Fund to make payment on all approved claims, within each instalment.

Allocation of Funds

5. For an initial period, successful claimants in categories "A", "B" and "C" will receive all funds available in the Compensation Fund for paying claims, until each has received payment of the initial amount referenced in paragraph 2 above.

6. After the payments in paragraph 2 have been made, the funds available to the Commission for the payment of claims will be allocated as follows:

The Executive Secretary will transfer funds to each appropriate Government in respect of approved claims in all categories. Such transfers will be made when there are funds in the Compensation Fund at least sufficient to make a minimum payment of US$5000 (or the unpaid principal amount of the award, if less) in respect of each approved claim. Amounts transferred in addition to this minimum of US$5000 payment will be proportional to the ratio between the unpaid balance of approved claims submitted by that Government and the unpaid balance of all approved claims.

7. The Compensation Commission will retain an adequate operating reserve consisting of an amount sufficient to cover at least one year's operating expenses.

Revision of the System

8. The Governing Council will monitor the payment system and make revisions wherever and whenever needed in order that the mechanism may evolve and adjust to ongoing circumstances, including the amounts available in the Fund for the payment of claims.

9. If there are insufficient funds to make payments in accordance with the mechanism outlined above, the Governing Council, keeping in mind the principles stated in paragraph 1 above, may decide on how to distribute any limited funds available. In particular, this should not exclude the possibility of distributing the amounts stated in paragraphs 2 and 6 above by successive payments.

Transparency

10. Distribution of compensation will be the responsibility of each Government concerned.

*Decisions of the Governing Council of the United Nations Compensation Commission are now being issued under the symbol S/AC.26/Dec.

Document 185

Decision 18 taken by the Governing Council of the United Nations Compensation Commission: Distribution of payments and transparency

A/AC.26/Dec.18 (1994), 24 March 1994

Distribution of payments and transparency

Decision taken by the Governing Council of the United Nations Compensation Commission at its 41st meeting, held in Geneva on 23 March 1994

I. Governments, exercising their responsibility for the distribution of payments of compensation for direct losses to successful claimants whose claims they have submitted, shall establish their own mechanisms to distribute payments in a fair, efficient and timely manner, subject to the following provisions:

1. Governments may offset their costs of processing claims by deducting a small fee from payments made to claimants. The Governments shall be required to provide explanations satisfactory to the Governing Council for any processing costs so deducted. Such fees shall be commensurate with the actual expenditure of Governments. In the case of awards payable to claimants in categories "A", "B" and "C", the fees should not exceed 1.5 per cent, and for awards payable to claimants in categories "D", "E" and "F", the fees should not exceed 3 per cent. Any commission or charge on compensation received from the UNCC imposed by Governments pursuant to national laws is to be considered a processing cost and may be deducted by the concerned Government. Without prejudice to future decisions concerning eligibility for compensation under category "F", if a Government, that has deducted a processing fee, receives compensation for such costs under category "F", it shall reimburse to claimants those fees deducted.

2. Prior to or immediately following the receipt of the first payment from the Compensation Commission each Government shall provide information in writing through the Executive Secretary to the Governing Council on the arrangements that it has made for the distribution of funds to claimants, and subsequently promptly report any changes to those arrangements.

3. If amounts of awards are specified by the Compensation Commission in respect of each individual claim, Governments should distribute funds to claimants within six months of receiving payment from the Compensation Commission, subject to the provisions of paragraph 5.

4. Not later than three months after the expiration of the time limit for the distribution of each payment received from the Compensation Commission, Governments shall provide information on the amounts of payments distributed. Such reports shall refer to the category of claims and the instalment payment received from the Compensation Commission and shall also include information on the reasons for non-payment to claimants because claimants could not be located or for other reasons, as well as the explanations required on fees deducted under paragraph 1.

5. If a Government fails to distribute funds within six months of their receipt, or indicates that it needs additional time to distribute the funds, or if reports satisfying the requirements of paragraph 4 are not submitted to the Executive Secretary within the prescribed time; and where the Governing Council does not consider that exceptional circumstances exist, or is not satisfied with the reasons given for non-payment or with the adequacy of the reports submitted, the Governing Council may decide to ask for an explanation or further information from the Government concerned. In the absence of a response satisfactory to the Council, it may decide not to distribute further funds to that particular Government.

6. After completing distribution of all payments received from the Compensation Commission, each Government should produce a final summary account of payments made including who was paid, the exact amount received by each claimant and the date of each payment, as well as a report on amounts not distributed. Funds received by Governments from the Compensation Commission that Governments have not disbursed to claimants due to inability to locate such claimants shall be reimbursed to the Compensation Fund, unless otherwise decided by the Governing Council.

7. Governments shall make payments to claimants either in US dollars or in other currencies. If Governments convert US dollar payments received from the UNCC into other currencies for distribution of awards to claimants, they shall notify the Governing Council on the method of conversion and exchange rate to be used, bearing in mind the interests of claimants in receiving full equivalent of their awards.

II. These provisions should also apply to the distribution of payments by any person, authority or body which has been designated by the United Nations Compensation

Commission to collect and submit claims on behalf of persons who are not in a position to have their claims submitted by a Government.

III. The Governing Council will continue to monitor the distribution of payments to claimants and will make revisions and adjustments of the provisions established above, whenever deemed necessary.

Document 186

Report of the Secretary-General on UNIKOM for the period from 1 October 1993 to 31 March 1994

S/1994/388, 4 April 1994

I. Introduction

1. By paragraph 5 of its resolution 687 (1991) of 3 April 1991, the Security Council established a demilitarized zone (DMZ) along the Iraq-Kuwait boundary and decided to set up an observer unit with the following tasks: to monitor the Khawr Abd Allah waterway and the DMZ; to deter violations of the boundary through its presence in and surveillance of the DMZ; and to observe any potentially hostile action mounted from the territory of one State into the other. By its resolution 689 (1991) of 9 April 1991, the Security Council approved the report of the Secretary-General on the implementation of the above provisions (S/22454).

2. On 5 February 1993, the Security Council adopted resolution 806 (1993), expanding UNIKOM's terms of reference to include the capacity to take physical action to prevent or redress small-scale violations of the DMZ; violations of the boundary, for example by civilians or police; and problems that might arise from the presence of Iraqi installations and Iraqi citizens and their assets in the DMZ on the Kuwaiti side of the newly demarcated boundary.

3. By its resolution 689 (1991), the Security Council noted that the decision to set up the observer unit had been taken in paragraph 5 of resolution 687 (1991) and could be terminated only by a decision of the Council; and decided to review the question of termination or continuation as well as the modalities of the United Nations Iraq-Kuwait Observation Mission (UNIKOM) every six months. The Security Council last reviewed this matter in early October 1993 and, in a letter of its President dated 11 October 1993 (S/26566), concurred with my recommendation (S/26520, para. 22) that UNIKOM be maintained for a further six-month period. The purpose of the present report is to provide the Security Council, prior to its forthcoming review, with an overview of UNIKOM's activities during the last six months.

II. Organization

4. On 1 December 1993, Major General Krishna N.S. Thapa (Nepal) assumed his role as the Chief Military Observer from the Acting Chief Military Observer, Brigadier-General Vigar Aabrek (Norway). His appointment was changed to that of Force Commander of UNIKOM on 1 January 1994 to reflect the enhanced capability of the Mission resulting from the addition of a mechanized infantry battalion from Bangladesh. Brigadier-General Yeo Cheng Ann (Singapore) is Chief of Staff and Deputy Force Commander, having arrived in the Mission area on 8 October 1993.

5. A breakdown of UNIKOM military strength as at 14 March 1994 is given in annex I. This has been divided into three main groups: military observers, mechanized infantry battalion and support units. UNIKOM also has 204 civilian staff, of whom 76 are international and 128 are locally recruited.

6. Since the Council last reviewed the Mission's mandate, UNIKOM has implemented the first phase of its reinforcement with the deployment of a mechanized infantry battalion in order to carry out an extended mandate pursuant to Security Council resolution 806 (1993). In response to my request, the Government of Bangladesh agreed to contribute a mechanized infantry battalion (BANBAT) of 775 all ranks to UNIKOM. An advance team arrived in the Mission area in mid-November 1993, followed by the remainder of the battalion during the month of December and early January 1994. After a period of training to familiarize it with equipment provided by Kuwait, the battalion was declared operational on 5 February 1994.

7. The Danish Logistic Unit (DANLOG) has continued to carry out vehicle maintenance, supply and logistics support to the Mission, including the provision

of additional support required by the Bangladesh battalion. This additional support has necessitated some redistribution of tasks and the infantry battalion has taken over some of the guard duties formerly performed by DANLOG.

8. In early November 1993, Austria deployed a 12-member medical team (AUSMED), consisting of 2 doctors and 10 medics, to replace the Norwegian medical unit (NORMED). Some members of NORMED remained in the Mission area until early December 1993 to assist in the transition. In late December 1993 a 16-member medical team arrived from Bangladesh to augment AUSMED. This team, BANMED, arrived with the Bangladesh battalion but is retained as a separate medical unit working in conjunction with AUSMED to provide the required level of medical support to the Mission. It consists of 3 doctors and 13 medics. BANBAT has a small integral medical section of its own.

9. The Argentinian engineer unit (ARGENG) continued its activities aimed at improving security of camps by installing additional fencing, mine-clearing, renovation of helicopter pads and construction of new patrol roads. However, its activity remains limited owing to shortage of equipment. The unit arrived without the equipment it requires and delivery of this equipment, promised by Kuwait, is still awaited. Efforts continue to resolve this problem.

10. UNIKOM retains the two small fixed-wing aircraft contributed by the Government of Switzerland at no cost to the Organization and three chartered helicopters. It also has the use of a chartered AN-26 aircraft for the transport of personnel and equipment between Kuwait and Baghdad.

11. The Government of Kuwait provided the camps at Camp Khor and Al-Abdally for the accommodation of the mechanized infantry battalion at no cost to the Organization.

12. The Government of Kuwait had committed itself to provide 32 armoured personnel carriers (APCs) and 113 other vehicles as well as communications equipment for the battalion, for which the rate of reimbursement for depreciation is still being negotiated. UNIKOM has thus far received all 32 APCs and 83 other vehicles as well as part of the communications equipment, as at 31 March 1994.

III. Concept of operations

13. UNIKOM is deployed in the DMZ as outlined in the attached map [not reproduced here]. For operational purposes, the DMZ is still divided into three sectors (North, Central, South) but, with the addition of the mechanized infantry battalion, UNIKOM's concept of operations has been modified. It is now based on a combination of patrol and observation bases, observation points, ground and air patrols, vehicle check-points, roadblocks, a force mobile reserve, investigation teams and liaison with the parties at all levels.

14. The three sectors continue to be manned by the military observers, who provide the basis for UNIKOM's patrol, observation, investigation and liaison activities within the DMZ, including the Khawr Abd Allah waterway. The mechanized infantry battalion is accommodated in a main battalion camp at Camp Khor and a company at Al-Abdally. From these two locations, it is tasked to provide reinforcement patrols to sectors, in areas where the situation is sensitive and where an infantry force could be required to prevent incidents. The battalion also provides the force mobile reserve capable of rapid redeployment anywhere within the DMZ to prevent or redress small-scale violation of the DMZ and the boundary. Also, where necessary, it provides security for UNIKOM installations. The establishment of vehicle check-points on main roads and the institution of random roadblocks, both considered necessary to prevent the illegal entry of weapons into the DMZ, are subject to further discussions between UNIKOM and the two parties and, therefore, have not yet been implemented.

15. UNIKOM has liaison offices in Baghdad and Kuwait City and, through them, the Force Commander and other senior staff of UNIKOM have maintained regular contacts with the authorities in both capitals. At the local level, liaison continued with the police and the liaison officers of both sides, particularly with regard to civilian activity in the DMZ. These contacts have been useful in dealing with complaints and facilitating UNIKOM's operations.

IV. Situation in the demilitarized zone

16. During the period under review the situation in the DMZ has been generally calm. However, there have been periods of tension.

17. It will be recalled that, as a result of the demarcation of the Iraq-Kuwait boundary, an issue that remained outstanding was the future of private Iraqi citizens who remained on Kuwaiti territory and their assets, in particular in the Al-Abdally farming area and the town of Umm Qasr. When the Kuwaitis started to construct their border security system, comprising a trench, an earthen embankment and a patrol road through these areas, tension manifested itself in two

protest demonstrations in which Iraqi nationals crossed into Kuwait. There was also a serious shooting incident in November 1993 when a member of the security guard for the Kuwaiti trench project shot two Iraqi policemen who were on Kuwaiti territory. This incident is reported to have resulted in the death of one Iraqi policeman and injury to the second.

18. UNIKOM responded to these incidents and quickly restored stability in the area. Through bilateral discussions with Iraqi and Kuwaiti authorities, UNIKOM facilitated arrangements agreeable to both parties for the repatriation of Iraqi nationals living on Kuwaiti territory. Iraqi nationals living in the Umm Qasr area were all repatriated by the end of December 1993 and those living in the Al-Abdally farming area were repatriated by the end of February 1994.

19. It will also be recalled from my previous report (S/26520) that an experienced land assessor was appointed by the Secretary-General to conduct an evaluation of private Iraqi assets in the Umm Qasr and Al-Abdally areas. On the basis of this evaluation, the amount of compensation was determined and a payment scheme was put in place. Subsequently, during the second half of February 1994, compensation notices were delivered to the Iraqi nationals in the farm area. Compensation information was also disseminated in the form of press releases and paid notices in the local and regional media. However, all the Iraqi nationals refused to accept compensation, and the funds contributed by Kuwait were

placed in a United Nations trust fund where they remain at the disposal of the beneficiaries.

20. In the meantime, the Kuwaiti border security system being constructed along its boundary with Iraq has nearly been completed.

21. UNIKOM observed three types of violations: ground violations involving incursions into the DMZ and border crossings by military personnel, resulting in serious incidents; overflights of the DMZ by military aircraft; and violations involving the carrying and firing of weapons other than sidearms in the DMZ. The following table [below] summarizes the violations observed by UNIKOM. UNIKOM raised these violations with the parties concerned, with a view to having action taken to prevent a recurrence.

22. During the reporting period, UNIKOM received a total of 20 written complaints, 13 from Iraq and 7 from Kuwait. UNIKOM investigated each complaint and conveyed its findings to the party concerned. Thirteen of the complaints (2 from Kuwait and 11 from Iraq) concerned shooting incidents inside the DMZ. Three Iraqi civilians were wounded during those incidents in March 1994. However, in all cases, UNIKOM was unable to verify who had fired the shots or who initiated the incidents.

23. There have also been three serious incidents involving the security of UNIKOM's military observers. The incidents involved the hijacking of a United Nations vehicle, which the Iraqi authorities subsequently found completely stripped some 30 kilometres inside Iraq; an

	Iraq				*Kuwait*			
	Ground	*Air*	*Weapon*	*Total*	*Ground*	*Air*	*Weapon*	*Total*
October	0	0	1	1	1	0	5	6
November	2	0	0	2	0	0	11	11
December	2	0	1	3	0	0	0	0
January	0	0	1	1	0	0	2	2
February	1	0	0	1	0	0	0	0
March	0	0	0	0	0	0	0	0
Total	5	0	3	8	1	0	18	19

	Member States cooperating with Kuwait				*Unidentified*			
	Ground	*Air*	*Weapon*	*Total*	*Ground*	*Air*	*Weapon*	*Total*
October	0	0	0	0	0	0	0	0
November	0	0	0	0	0	2	1	3
December	0	0	0	0	0	1	0	1
January	0	0	0	0	0	1	0	1
February	0	0	0	0	0	0	0	0
March	0	0	0	0	0	0	0	0
Total	0	0	0	0	0	4	1	5

attempted robbery of a UNIKOM patrol and observation base; and the robbery of another UNIKOM patrol and observation base, resulting in the theft of personal and United Nations property, including a United Nations vehicle, which has not yet been recovered. All incidents occurred on the Iraqi side of the DMZ. However, the nationality of the perpetrators could not be confirmed. In all three cases, the military observers were threatened with weapons and, in one case, a number of live rounds were fired. No UNIKOM personnel were injured in any of the incidents.

24. During the first two months of the reporting period there was some local agitation and harassment of UNIKOM staff at Umm Qasr. People threw rocks and other objects at the UNIKOM headquarters compound and passing UNIKOM vehicles, slightly injuring some UNIKOM staff and damaging a number of vehicles. These incidents have now ceased.

25. UNIKOM has reminded the parties concerned of their responsibility for maintaining law and order as well as safeguarding United Nations personnel and property. UNIKOM has also increased its patrolling and has reinforced the patrol and observation bases with armed troops from the mechanized infantry battalion to reduce the risks of future incidents of this nature.

26. UNIKOM continued to provide support to other United Nations agencies in Iraq and Kuwait. In particular, it provided assistance in the process of compensation for the Iraqi citizens who were found to be on the Kuwaiti side of the newly demarcated boundary. UNIKOM maintained administrative supervision of the Administrative Unit in Baghdad, which provided administrative and logistic support to other United Nations agencies in Iraq. UNIKOM continued to provide movement controls in respect of all United Nations aircraft operating in the area, as well as medical evacuation assistance to the United Nations Guards Contingent in Iraq. UNIKOM assisted the United Nations Coordinator for the Return of Property from Iraq to Kuwait (UNROP) as well as in the inspections and maintenance of the boundary demarcation monumentation.

V. *Financial aspects*

27. By its decision 48/466 of 23 December 1993, the General Assembly authorized the Secretary-General to enter into commitments for UNIKOM up to the amount of $8,687,800 gross ($8,000,000 net) for the period from 1 November 1993 to 28 February 1994. This amount was in addition to the pledged voluntary contri-

bution of $23,414,800 from the Government of Kuwait of which an amount of $16,000,000 has been received. By its decision 48/466 B of 9 March 1994 the General Assembly also authorized the Secretary-General to enter into commitments for UNIKOM up to the amount of $2,171,950 gross ($2,000,000 net) for the period from 1 to 31 March 1994.

28. Based on the cost estimates 1/ for UNIKOM currently before the General Assembly, the Advisory Committee on Administrative and Budgetary Questions has recommended 2/ that the cost of maintaining the Mission should not exceed $5.5 million gross per month for the period through 31 October 1994. This amount includes the voluntary contribution pledged by the Government of Kuwait in an amount equivalent to two-thirds of the cost of the Mission. Should the General Assembly endorse the recommendation of the Advisory Committee, the monthly cost of maintaining UNIKOM will be limited therefore to $5.5 million gross.

29. Unpaid assessed contributions as at 28 March 1994 to the UNIKOM Special Account for the period since the inception of the Mission amounted to $23,669,133.

VI. *Observations*

30. During the last six months, UNIKOM's area of operations has, for the most part, been calm. Through close monitoring of the area and constant liaison with the Iraqi and Kuwaiti authorities, UNIKOM has played its part in preventing incidents and redressing the violations that have occurred.

31. The outstanding issue arising from the demarcation of the Iraq-Kuwait boundary concerning the Iraqi nationals and their assets remaining on Kuwaiti territory has been resolved by their relocation in Iraq, thus significantly reducing tension in the area. The reinforced capacity of UNIKOM, together with arrangements on the ground, including the completion of the construction of the trench along the Iraq-Kuwait boundary, are factors contributing to stability.

32. However, the present calm along the Iraq-Kuwait boundary should not obscure the fact that tension still persists. There have been incidents, which have demonstrated that full peace has yet to be restored to the area. They also indicate the value of the United Nations presence, as well as the need for it to continue. I therefore

1/ A/48/844.

2/ A/48/897.

recommend to the Security Council that it maintain UNIKOM for a further 12 months.

33. UNIKOM will continue to depend on the cooperation of the Governments of Iraq and Kuwait in order to carry out the tasks entrusted to it by the Security Council. In this connection, I note with appreciation the cooperation by both Governments in helping to resolve issues in a constructive manner. I call upon both Governments to take all necessary measures to ensure the safety of United Nations personnel and property deployed in their respective countries and to prevent the recurrence of incidents that violate the DMZ.

34. In conclusion, I wish to pay tribute to the Force Commander and the men and women under his command for the manner in which they have carried out their difficult task. Their discipline and bearing have been of a high order, reflecting credit on themselves, on their countries and on the United Nations.

Annex I
UNIKOM personnel

14 March 1994

Military observers

Argentina	6	Denmark	6
Austria	6	Fiji	6
Bangladesh	9	Finland	7
Canada	5	France	15
China	15	Ghana	6
Greece	6	Russian Federation	15
Hungary	6	Senegal	6
India	6	Singapore	7
Indonesia	7	Sweden	7
Ireland	5	Thailand	6
Italy	7	Turkey	7
Kenya	6	United Kingdom of	
Malaysia	6	Great Britain and	
Nigeria	6	Northern Ireland	15
Norway	7	United States of America	15
Pakistan	7	Uruguay	6
Poland	7	Venezuela	7
Romania	6		

Total number of military observers deployed
(out of an authorized strength of 300)   254

Infantry battalion (BANBAT)

	Deployed	Authorized
	775	775
Support units:		
Engineers (ARGENG)	50	50
Logistics (DANLOG)	46	50
Medical		
AUSMED	12	
BANMED	16	
Total	124	135
Total UNIKOM	1 153	1 210

Document 187

Fifth report of the Secretary-General on the status of the implementation of the plan for the ongoing monitoring and verification of Iraq's compliance with relevant parts of section C of Security Council resolution 687 (1991)

S/1994/489, 22 April 1994

I. *Introduction*

1. The present report is the fifth submitted pursuant to paragraph 8 of Security Council resolution 715 (1991), adopted on 11 October 1991, which requests the Secretary-General to submit a report to the Council every six months on the implementation of the Special Commission's plan for ongoing monitoring and verification of Iraq's compliance with relevant parts of section C of Security Council resolution 687 (1991). It updates the information contained in the first four reports (S/23801, S/24661, S/25620 and S/26684).

2. Further information concerning developments relating to the implementation of the plan is contained in the reports to the Security Council of the high-level talks, held in November 1993 and March 1994, between the Special Commission and the International Atomic Energy Agency (IAEA) on the one hand and Iraq on the other (S/26825 and Corr.1 and S/1994/341). The attachment to document S/1994/341 contains an outline of the activities planned by the Special Commission to implement ongoing monitoring and verification of Iraq's obligation not to reacquire the weapons banned to it under section C of resolution 687 (1991). Document S/1994/151 con-

tains the text of a joint statement made by the Deputy Prime Minister of Iraq and the Executive Chairman after the February 1994 round of high-level talks in Baghdad.

II. Developments during the period 10 October 1993-10 April 1994

A. Acknowledgement of resolution 715 (1991)

3. The major development in the period under review was Iraq's acceptance of Security Council resolution 715 (1991), received in the form of a letter from the Deputy Prime Minister of Iraq, Mr. Tariq Aziz, to the President of the Security Council (S/26811, annex). This came at the end of a round of high-level talks held in New York between the Special Commission and IAEA, on the one hand, and Iraq, on the other, reported in documents S/26825 and Corr.1.

B. Provision of information

4. At that time, Iraq declared that its previous declarations concerning its current dual-purpose capabilities should be "considered to have been made and submitted in conformity with the provisions of Security Council resolution 715 (1991) and the plans approved thereunder". The Commission responded to Iraq that those previous declarations were deficient in many regards and could not be considered as initial declarations under the plans, nor did they constitute a sufficient basis for the proper planning and implementation of ongoing monitoring and verification.

5. To assist Iraq in the preparation of adequate declarations, the Commission prepared formats in which such declarations should be made. The first of these, covering ballistic missiles and chemical weapons, were provided to Iraq in late December 1993. The Commission received in Baghdad Iraq's first declarations on 16 January 1994. While these new declarations were a considerable improvement on Iraq's earlier reporting, they still were incomplete, particularly those relating to chemical facilities. In some instances, Iraq not only failed to answer some of the questions contained in the formats, but unilaterally rewrote the formats to delete those questions.

6. In parallel with its efforts to elicit full information on current dual-purpose capabilities, the Commission continued its efforts to obtain a complete account of Iraq's programmes banned under the terms of section C of resolution 687 (1991). Only with full information about these programmes and complete information on current dual-purpose capabilities would the Commission be in a position to plan and implement an effective ongoing monitoring and verification system.

7. Efforts here concentrated on information relating to the supply of precursor chemicals, chemical agent production capacity and its utilization, expenditure of SCUD-derivative missiles and suppliers of components for missile production. Discussions on chemical issues took place in the framework of the high-level talks held in Baghdad in February 1994 and in New York in November 1993 and March 1994. Ballistic missile issues were also addressed in the New York meetings. The outcome of these discussions was reported in documents S/26825 and Corr.1 and in the enclosure to document S/1994/341. In the absence of documentation that would assist in the verification of the latest data provided on chemical programmes, the Commission intends to send a team of experts to Iraq in May 1994 in order to interview former senior personnel associated with the programmes.

C. Operations

8. The concept of how the Commission intends to conduct ongoing monitoring and verification is contained in the plan approved by Security Council resolution 715 (1991) (S/22871/Rev.1). It was summarized in the attachment to document S/1994/341.

9. In parallel with the above efforts to elicit further information, the Commission has continued its assessment of Iraq's capabilities, in terms of sites, activities, equipment and materials, which will need to be monitored under the plan for ongoing monitoring and verification. Planning and identification of means for such monitoring is well advanced. These efforts have drawn upon international expertise through the holding of topic-specific seminars in the Commission's headquarters in New York. Trials have been conducted on certain of the tagging and sensor techniques to be deployed for ongoing monitoring and verification purposes. Several inspections focused primarily on ongoing monitoring and verification have already been launched or completed. Details of activities undertaken are contained in annex I to the present report.

10. Plans for further ongoing monitoring and verification activities remain as detailed in the attachment to document S/1994/341 with the following updates:

(a) The ballistic-missile protocol-building team planned to start its tasks on 30 March 1994, is now in Iraq and working smoothly, with good Iraqi cooperation;

(b) The chemical sensors referred to in paragraph 8 of the attachment have now, with the assistance of Iraq, been installed and their performance is being assessed;

(c) The biological protocol-building team started its mission in Baghdad on 8 April 1994;

(d) A team to assess plans for establishing a monitoring centre in Baghdad arrived there on 10 April 1994.

D. *Export/import monitoring mechanism*

11. Paragraph 7 of resolution 715 (1991) requires the Commission, in cooperation with the Committee established under resolution 661 (1990) and the Director General of IAEA, "to develop a mechanism for monitoring any future sales or supplies by other countries to Iraq of items relevant to the implementation of section C of resolution 687 (1991) and other relevant resolutions, including the plans approved hereunder". The Commission and IAEA have prepared a concept paper outlining a mechanism which, in their view, would fulfil the requirements of resolution 715 (1991). It is the intention of the Commission and IAEA to present the paper formally to the Committee established under resolution 661 (1990) before the end of April 1994. Thereafter, the three bodies will need to submit their joint recommendations to the Security Council for its consideration.

Prospects for the future

12. As indicated in the attachment to document S/1994/341, the Special Commission is mobilizing its resources and those of supporting Governments to ensure that an effective ongoing monitoring and verification system will be implemented as soon as feasible. However, in reaching that stage, the Commission is, in large part, dependent on the actions of others, foremost among which is Iraq itself. Without the cooperation of the Iraqi authorities, both in the provision of relevant information and in undertaking the many actions required of them to establish the system, effective implementation of the plan cannot be assured.

13. Iraq has, on several occasions and most notably in the joint statement (S/1994/151) issued at the end of the high-level talks held in Baghdad in February 1994, stated its intention to so cooperate in order to expedite the establishment of ongoing monitoring and verification, thereby enabling the Commission and IAEA to report Iraq's fulfilment of the terms of paragraph 22 of resolution 687 (1991). The Commission hopes and expects this to be the case. However, during the latest round of high-level talks between the Commission and Iraq held in New York in March 1994 and reported in document S/1994/341, Iraq expressed a lack of confidence in the impartiality of the Commission and implied that, unless the Commission reported immediately under paragraph 22 of resolution 687 (1991), cooperation might be withdrawn.

14. It was in the light of these statements that the Commission viewed with great concern an incident involving one of its helicopters, in which a crowd threw stones at the helicopter as it was taking on board two injured soldiers from the United Nations Guards Contingent in Iraq for medical evacuation. A full account is contained in annex II to the present report.

15. This incident placed the aircraft and those on board in severe danger. Iraq is required, under its obligations in respect of United Nations operations in Iraq and, in particular, under the status arrangements through which the Special Commission operates in Iraq, resolution 707 (1991) and the plans for ongoing monitoring and verification approved by resolution 715 (1991), to ensure the safety and security of Special Commission personnel and property. Iraq's failure in this instance to provide adequate security was strongly protested by the Commission to Iraqi authorities in both Baghdad and New York.

16. In response, the Iraqi Government has firmly denied any involvement in the attack, blaming the Commission for the alleged last minute change in landing site. However, the Commission has noted Iraq's assurances that this incident should not be seen as being in any way politically motivated and its undertaking to ensure that similar incidents do not recur.

Annex I
Ongoing monitoring and verification activities

I. *Ballistic missiles*

1. Iraq's acceptance of its obligations under Security Council resolution 715 (1991) led to intensive work to establish a monitoring mechanism of missile-related activities and dual purpose capabilities in Iraq pursuant to the plan for ongoing monitoring and verification in the non-nuclear area (S/22871/Rev.1). These efforts included a number of inspections, assessment of Iraq's declarations submitted under the plan, identification of focal points for monitoring and appropriate monitoring techniques including their field trials, preparation of draft ongoing monitoring and verification protocols, and in-depth discussions with the Iraqi side of monitoring issues, including during the rounds of high-level talks both in New York and in Baghdad. In parallel, the Special Commission continued its investigation into the past prohibited missile programmes of Iraq and of Iraq's compliance with resolution 687 (1991).

A. *UNSCOM 66*

2. UNSCOM 66 carried out an inspection in Iraq over the period from 21 to 29 January 1994. In view of Iraq's acceptance of resolution 715 (1991), UNSCOM 66 was tasked to accomplish the following missions:

(a) To update data collected by previous inspection teams on Iraq's missile research and development (R&D) programme;

(b) To examine issues related to Iraq's reporting on facilities to be monitored under the ongoing monitoring and verification plan in the missile area as approved by resolution 715 (1991);

(c) To conduct a preliminary survey for possible application of appropriate monitoring sensors and technologies.

3. UNSCOM 66 visited a number of R&D and industrial facilities to be monitored under the ongoing monitoring and verification plan. Iraq provided the team with a detailed update of its current missile programmes relevant to surface-to-surface missiles with a range greater than 50 kilometres.

4. UNSCOM 66 carried out extensive work related to Iraq's reporting obligations under the ongoing monitoring and verification plan. This included discussions of Iraq's reporting on facilities to be monitored, examination of declarations submitted by Iraq in January 1994 pursuant to the ongoing monitoring and verification plan and practical on-site investigation of relevant issues. This work resulted in a draft format for Iraq's reporting on those missile R&D and production facilities that would be under the most intensive monitoring regime. During inspection and soon after it, Iraq submitted to the Special Commission reports under this format for all relevant facilities. As a result of UNSCOM 66, Iraq also provided corrections to its January declarations under the ongoing monitoring and verification plan in the missile area.

5. UNSCOM 66 started a survey of sites where installation of sensors and use of other technologies might be appropriate for monitoring purposes. This survey addressed issues of inventory control of dual-purpose equipment, non-removal of equipment from declared facilities and monitoring of activities at facilities. Use of a variety of sensors and recording devices could be an important part of monitoring procedures under the ongoing monitoring and verification plan.

B. UNSCOM 69

6. UNSCOM 69 was in Iraq from 17 to 25 February to accomplish the following missions:

(a) To assess Iraq's dual-purpose missile industrial capabilities that might be used in support of missile production;

(b) To continue compiling the database on Iraq's machine tools and equipment usable for missile production;

(c) To carry out an assessment of possibilities to install sensors and use other technologies to monitor missile-related activities.

7. UNSCOM 69 visited 15 facilities in Iraq, identified a number of focal points for monitoring activities at those sites and carried out a survey for the use of sensors. The machine tool database built by the previous inspection team (UNSCOM 57) was updated, new machines were recorded and some items were tagged.

8. The results of UNSCOM 69 provided the Commission with the necessary background data to refine a scope of facilities for ongoing monitoring and verification under the ongoing monitoring and verification plan.

C. UNSCOM 71

9. Based on the results of UNSCOM 66 and 69, UNSCOM 71 was organized to prepare draft ongoing monitoring and verification protocols for facilities identified so far by the Commission as needing to be subject to ongoing monitoring and verification. A monitoring and verification protocol would incorporate detailed procedures for monitoring activities utilizing a variety of different means at sites in Iraq covered by the ongoing monitoring and verification plan. It would also contain systematized collection of information known about a specific site essential for effective monitoring and verification. Once created, the protocol for a given site would be updated as a result of monitoring and verification activities at that site.

10. UNSCOM 71 started its activities in Iraq on 30 March. The team will continue its work through a succession of rounds of visits to Iraq until the accomplishment of all its tasks. It is anticipated that this will take at least two months.

11. At the time of writing, UNSCOM 71 has completed its first round of activities in Iraq. During this round, the team visited nine facilities to be placed, depending on the nature of their activities, under different regimes of monitoring. UNSCOM 71 also verified on-site Iraq's declarations and reports for monitoring and verification protocols on facilities visited by the team. The team is currently working on the draft protocols for those facilities. UNSCOM 71 will return to Iraq on 18 April to start the second round of its inspection activities. In total, it will visit more than 30 sites.

D. Other activities

12. In support of its efforts to establish a mechanism for ongoing monitoring and verification, the Commission held a number of meetings with international experts. During these meetings, issues were discussed related to the assessment of Iraq's declarations, identification of focal points for monitoring missile-related activities and appropriate monitoring techniques, including sensors, to ensure effective monitoring. Lists of dual-purpose equipment, technologies and other items that could be used for the development, production, modifi-

cation or acquisition of ballistic missiles with a range greater than 150 kilometres were also discussed.

E. *Past prohibited activities*

13. The Commission continued its investigation of the outstanding issues related to the past missile programme proscribed under resolution 687 (1991). This work is essential to establish a solid and verified baseline for ongoing monitoring in accordance with resolution 715 (1991). In particular, this will allow the Commission to have a full and comprehensive picture of the knowledge and know-how Iraq obtained in the missile area through its past activities.

14. Issues related to programmes proscribed under section C of resolution 687 (1991) were discussed with Iraq on a continuous basis, especially during the rounds of the high-level talks in November 1993 and March 1994 in New York. Iraq has furnished additional details on foreign acquisition of critical ballistic missile items as well as its expenditure of ballistic missiles with a range greater than 150 kilometres.

15. The Commission continued to reiterate its request that Iraq provide original documentation that would substantiate the declarations made by Iraq concerning its past prohibited missile programmes. During the February visit of the Executive Chairman of the Special Commission to Baghdad, Iraq finally agreed to hand over to the Commission documentation on the expenditure of prohibited missiles. This documentation covers the period from 1977 to December 1990 and accounts for nearly three quarters of the missiles covered by resolution 687 (1991) and declared by Iraq. Currently, the Commission is conducting an in-depth investigation of these documents and information contained therein. The results of this investigation will be critical for the Commission's reporting to the Security Council under paragraph 22 of resolution 687 (1991).

II. *Chemical*

A. *Data collection*

16. In parallel with the various rounds of high-level political talks, UNSCOM experts have held three technical meetings with Iraq on chemical weapons issues.

1. *Past programmes*

17. In the course of the meeting held in New York in November 1993, Iraq stressed that it had tried to meet all the requirements put forward by the Commission on the provision of information. However, Iraq agreed to endeavour to address any questions that might arise during the Commission's verification activities. The Commission, for its part, informed Iraq that it had as-

sessed as credible the information provided in the talks held in Baghdad in October 1993 regarding Iraq's past chemical weapons programme. However, in the absence of documentation, independent verification of the data remained problematic. The Commission suggested that Iraq, in order to address that problem in part, hold seminars of the officials involved in the chemical weapons programme aimed at stimulating their collective memory to remember details that might facilitate independent verification. The issue of equipment and chemicals left at the Muthanna State Establishment was also discussed. It was agreed that the Commission should send a mission to Baghdad in January 1994 to mark equipment in order to prepare an inventory as to the release or disposal of this equipment. Further discussion was reserved on the release or disposal of chemicals remaining at the site.

18. During the meeting held in Baghdad in February 1994, Iraq informed the Commission of the results of its seminar with senior Iraqi personnel formerly involved in the chemical weapons programme. Additional data on outstanding issues, e.g. the research and development programme and imports of precursor chemicals, were provided.

19. During the meeting held in New York in March 1994, the Commission asked Iraq for additional details to fill in gaps in previously provided information. In response, Iraq presented the results of another seminar it had convened, this time involving retired former officials. These included a breakdown of the quantities of imported precursor chemicals by year and contract. In addition, Iraq was able to present a correlation, on an annual basis, between produced quantities of agents, available precursor chemicals, stored and consumed agents, and available chemical production capacity. A complete overview of its chemical weapons research and development programme, including time-frames, was also provided.

20. The additional information obtained during the course of these meetings was essential to the Commission's efforts to obtain as full a picture of Iraq's chemical weapons programme as possible. For example, in October 1993 Iraq declared 13,221 tons of traceable imported precursor chemicals; in February 1994, 15,037 tons; and in March 1994, 17,657 tons. The declared quantities of produced agents, however, remained unchanged at 4,340.5 tons.

21. The picture created by this additional information is more internally consistent than previous accounts given by Iraq. The order of magnitude of the declared figures appears credible. However, in the absence of supporting documentary evidence, the issue of independent verification remains. In this context, the Commission plans, in April 1994, to interview the personnel involved in Iraq's data recollection seminars.

2. Declarations of dual-purpose facilities

22. In December 1993, the Commission provided Iraq with model formats for the latter's initial declarations, required under the plan for ongoing monitoring and verification, of dual-purpose chemical facilities. On 16 January 1994, Iraq delivered to the Commission's field office in Baghdad partially completed formats. At subsequent meetings of the two sides, Iraq was informed by the Commission of the inadequacies of these returns and of what was required to bring them into conformity with the Commission's requirements. Iraq was told that full initial declarations were one of the main prerequisites for the protocol-building procedure and hence for the initiation of ongoing monitoring and verification.

B. Inspections

23. In the period from 1 to 11 February 1994, UNSCOM 67/CW 13 inventoried and tagged approximately 240 pieces of dual-use chemical production equipment. This equipment had been procured under the auspices of Iraq's chemical warfare programme. On 14 March 1994 Iraq was informed that 44 pieces that had been used for the production of agents and precursor chemicals would have to be destroyed. Iraq was provided with precise descriptions of those items. In addition, Iraq was asked to provide, by 30 April 1994, a detailed description of the intended permitted future use of the remaining tagged equipment for a final decision on their disposal. Those items not destroyed would then be subjected to ongoing monitoring and verification.

24. In the course of UNSCOM 67/CW 13, the team also visited the Ibn al Baytar facility in order to create a monitoring and verification protocol for that site. The purpose of this was to assess whether the general model for monitoring and verification protocols developed in the Commission's headquarters in New York was indeed applicable in practice to dual-purpose chemical facilities.

25. During the period from 20 to 26 March 1994, UNSCOM 70/CW 14 installed four air samplers at the Muthanna site. These samplers are designed to determine the types and levels of chemicals in the air at that site. The team also employed portable samplers that took additional samples for gaining an even more comprehensive survey of the air at Muthanna. The samplers were installed in a pattern that would cover air quality on the site from all wind directions. An Iraqi maintenance and construction crew prepared the mounting poles for the samplers. The samplers were programmed to sample the air around the clock in a discontinuous mode for a 30-day period. The sample tubes are to be removed, replaced with fresh tubes every 30 days and sent to laboratories for analysis. The sampler mechanism is microprocessor-

controlled and is powered by a storage battery charged by a solar panel. A microprocessor-driven meteorological station is mounted on one of the samplers to record hourly wind speed, wind direction, temperature and humidity. The meteorological data are to be down-loaded each time the sampler tubes are changed and will become a part of the permanent record of the sample set.

III. Biological

26. The first biological inspections in the baseline process started with the arrival in Iraq of the fourth biological inspection team on 8 April 1994. The team is scheduled to conduct its activities over a three-week period. The main purpose of this inspection is to verify the declarations submitted by Iraq in January 1994, pursuant to the plan, approved by Security Council resolution 715 (1991), for the ongoing monitoring and verification of Iraq's compliance not to reacquire items prohibited under resolution 687 (1991). Other objectives of this inspection are to provide an assessment of the work being undertaken and of the equipment present at those biological facilities declared by Iraq, many of which have never been visited by the Special Commission; to establish an inventory of said equipment for future tagging; and to draft a format for Iraq's regular reports under the monitoring and verification plan.

A. Talks with Iraq to fill in data gaps

27. In November 1993, discussions that had started in October 1993 regarding formats for reporting under the plan continued. The purpose of these discussions was to provide the Government of Iraq with a frame that would facilitate reporting under the plan by the drafting of limited-text answers, yes/no answers or multiple-choice answers.

28. Following the presentation of Iraqi declarations in January 1994, high-level talks were conducted with Iraqi officials in February and March 1994. These discussions focused upon the information to be provided by Iraq for an efficient and effective monitoring of the biological area. The outcome of these discussions was the provision by Iraq of a new version of the declarations required under the plan in a form that would allow completeness and clarity of the information to be analysed.

B. Seminars of experts in New York

29. In March 1994, a seminar of international experts was held in New York to prepare for inspections connected with establishing the biological baseline. Further seminars to discuss past programmes, Iraq's declarations under the biological provisions of the plan for

ongoing monitoring and verification, sensors and other monitoring technologies, monitoring modalities and requirements for training of monitoring inspectors are planned.

C. *Protocol-building efforts*

30. Efforts to build the protocols for each biological site are under way. The information relating to geographic location has been compiled or will be gathered during the first visit inspection to take place in April 1994. The remaining information will be assembled throughout the baseline process. A draft of the format for information to be provided by Iraq under the protocol will be developed during the inspection in April 1994.

D. *Sensor/tagging trials*

31. A feasibility study of monitoring by cameras will be conducted during the April inspection. Further efforts in this field will be effected by way of seminars in the coming month. Tagging technologies have already been identified and deemed appropriate with respect to biotechnological equipment.

IV. *Nuclear*

32. Activities in the nuclear area since 10 October 1993 are reported in the IAEA report (S/1994/490, appendix). In support of its obligation to designate sites, including in the nuclear area, the Special Commission conducted one gamma survey in the period under review.

33. The second gamma aerial survey mission performed its mission from 2 to 15 December 1993. During this mission, the team surveyed six sites. It obtained detailed gamma spectra at radioactive disposal areas at Tuwaitha as well as two areas at Al Atheer. In addition, gamma surveys were conducted at Rashdiya, Al Hadre, a site near Tikrit and Salah al-Din State Establishment (SAAD-13). While the data are still being analysed, early indications show the power of this capability to survey a relatively large area rapidly and to pinpoint particular sites for more detailed investigation. This system is still being developed, and evident improvements are under way.

V. *Aerial inspections*

34. The Commission's aerial inspections, using both helicopters and high-altitude surveillance aircraft, continued over the period under review. The Commis-

sion's high-altitude reconnaissance aircraft (U-2) now flies once or twice a week, having flown a total of 201 missions since the inception of its use in support of the Commission's operations. The Commission's helicopters have now flown 273 missions, covering some 395 sites. The aerial inspection team currently conducts three to four flights a week.

Annex II
Helicopter-stoning incident

1. While it was undertaking a humanitarian mission to evacuate, at the request of the United Nations Guards Contingent in Iraq, two United Nations soldiers shot in the north of Iraq during an ambush, a Special Commission helicopter was stoned by a crowd that had gathered at the landing site used to take on board the injured.

2. For this operation, the Commission had followed normal procedures, informing the Iraqi authorities first orally and, at 1100 hours on the morning of the mission, in writing of the flight plan and landing site to be used (a playing field adjacent to the Mosul Saddam Hospital). Iraq had officially expressed agreement to these plans. 1/

3. Upon landing at the hospital at 1600 hours, the helicopter was surrounded by a crowd. When the ambulance arrived with the two guards, the crowd sought to hinder its passage to the aircraft and started to throw stones. Only a few of the Iraqi military personnel on hand sought to intervene, ineffectively.

4. Once the injured had been loaded onto the helicopter, the Iraqi soldiers gave up their efforts to control the crowd, who pelted the helicopter with stones. Damage was sustained to all six rotor blades and stones that went into the air intakes damaged the motor bearings and turbine. Further damage was sustained to windows and the fuselage. This damage grounded the aircraft for a period of three weeks while repairs, costing around $1.5 million, were undertaken.

5. The pilot of the helicopter decided that, regardless of the damage sustained by the helicopter, immediate departure was the surest way to safeguard the lives of the crew and passengers and to escape a dangerous situation.

1/ Contrary to an Iraqi press release dated 29 March 1994, there was no last minute change of flight plan or landing site. Indeed, Iraqi personnel in Mosul had assisted in the preparation of the landing site at 1130 hours and in Baghdad had received a written flight path containing flight plan and landing site details.

Document 188

Fifth report of the Director General of the IAEA on the implementation of the Agency's plan for future ongoing monitoring and verification of Iraq's compliance with paragraph 12 of Security Council resolution 687 (1991)

S/1994/490, 22 April 1994

Note by the Secretary-General

The Secretary-General has the honour to transmit to the members of the Security Council the attached communication dated 20 April 1994, which he has received from the Director General of the International Atomic Energy Agency (IAEA).

Annex
Letter dated 20 April 1994 from the Director General of the International Atomic Energy Agency to the Secretary General

Paragraph 8 of resolution 715 (1991), adopted by the Security Council on 11 October 1991, requests the Director General of the International Atomic Energy Agency (IAEA) to submit to the Security Council reports on the implementation of the Agency's plan for future ongoing monitoring and verification of Iraq's compliance with paragraph 12 of resolution 687 (1991). These reports are to be submitted when requested by the Security Council and, in any event, at least every six months after the adoption of resolution 715.

Accordingly, I am requesting you kindly to transmit to the President of the Security Council the enclosed fifth six-monthly report on the implementation of the plan. I remain available for any consultations you or the Council may wish to have.

(Signed) Hans BLIX

Appendix
Fifth report of the Director General of the International Atomic Energy Agency on the implementation of the Agency's plan for future ongoing monitoring and verification of Iraq's compliance with paragraph 12 of resolution 687 (1991)

I. Introduction

1. On 11 October 1991, the Security Council adopted resolution 715 (1991) approving, *inter alia*, the plan submitted by the Director General of the International Atomic Energy Agency for future ongoing monitoring and verification of Iraq's compliance with paragraph 12 of Part C of Security Council resolution 687 (1991) and with the requirements of paragraphs 3 and 5

of resolution 707 (1991) (see S/22872/Rev.1 and Corr.1). In paragraph 8 of resolution 715 (1991), the Security Council requested the Director General of IAEA to submit to it reports on the implementation of the plan when requested by the Security Council and, in any event, at least every six months after the adoption of resolution 715 (1991). The Director General has submitted thus far four reports, circulated on 15 April 1992 (S/23813); 28 October 1992 (S/24722); 19 April 1993 (S/25621); and 3 November 1993 (S/26685), respectively.

2. The Director General hereby submits the fifth six-monthly report on the implementation of the plan for future ongoing monitoring and verification related to Iraq's nuclear capabilities (hereinafter referred to as the plan).

3. Since the last report of 3 November 1993, IAEA has carried out three inspection missions in Iraq, the twenty-second (1-15 November 1993), the twenty-third (4-11 February 1994) and the twenty-fourth (11-22 April 1994). The detailed reports on the results of the twenty-second and twenty-third inspections are contained in documents S/1994/31 of 14 January 1994 and S/1994/355 of 25 March 1994, respectively. The report on the results of the twenty-fourth inspection is expected to be issued shortly.

4. Three more rounds of high-level technical talks were held between IAEA and the United Nations Special Commission, on the one hand, and Iraq, on the other hand. These discussions, which were continuations of the talks held from 1 to 9 September 1993 in New York, and from 27 September to 8 October 1993 in Baghdad, took place from 15 to 30 November 1993 at United Nations Headquarters in New York, from 1 to 4 February 1994 in Baghdad and from 14 to 19 March 1994 again in New York. Comprehensive reports on four rounds of the talks are contained in documents S/26451, S/26571, S/26584 and S/1994/341. Another round of talks will be held in Baghdad from 23 to 26 April.

5. The focus of the talks has been the implementation of the IAEA and Special Commission plans for ongoing monitoring and verification approved by the Security Council in resolution 715 (1991) and the resolution of outstanding issues between Iraq and the two organizations.

6. The most significant progress that took place in the course of the high-level technical talks was the formal acceptance by Iraq, in a letter of 26 November 1993 from the Minister for Foreign Affairs of Iraq to the President of the Security Council (S/26811), of the obligations set forth in resolution 715 (1991) and Iraq's agreement to comply with the provisions of the plans for monitoring and verification as contained therein.

7. The Iraqi representatives continued to press for a definite date by which IAEA and the Special Commission would submit reports to the Security Council indicating Iraq's compliance with the relevant paragraphs of resolution 687 (1991), with a view to achieving the lifting of the oil embargo by operation of paragraph 22 of resolution 687 (1991). However, it is not yet possible or practical for either IAEA or the Special Commission to commit to such a date at this stage.

8. The progress made in the last six months is summarized below in the relevant sections of the present report. As a general comment it must be noted that, since the beginning of the high-level technical talks initiated by a visit of Chairman Ekéus to Baghdad in July 1993, a marked improvement has occurred in the working relationship with the Iraqi side. An evident effort is now deployed by the Iraqi authorities to provide promptly the information needed to fulfil the requirements of the different resolutions, to remove remaining gaps or uncertainties, to reconcile discrepancies between previous Iraqi declarations and IAEA's findings and to provide all the necessary assistance to implement the plan.

II. *Declaration of items subject to the plan*

9. Paragraph 22 and annexes 2 and 3 of the IAEA plan approved by the Security Council in resolution 715 (1991) set forth in detail the information and reporting requirements necessary for satisfactory implementation of the plan. As pointed out in previous reports, the overall quality of the documentation provided under the plan in the past by the Iraqi officials left much to be desired in terms of completeness and accuracy.

10. In order to assist the Iraqi side to bring their reporting to the necessary standard, a set of forms is being developed by IAEA that will cover the various reporting requirements in such a way as to facilitate the electronic processing of the information. Detailed guidelines on the completion of the forms are also being prepared. A first set of these forms, related to information on facilities, locations and sites, and using this improved reporting frame, was completed by Iraq and submitted to IAEA at the end of March 1994. A summary appraisal has shown that, subject to minor improvements, an acceptable reporting standard is now at hand.

III. *Radiometric hydrologic survey*

11. As part of its twice yearly radiometric survey of the surface waters of Iraq, IAEA carried out the second water sample collection of 1993 and the first of 1994. A total of 15 sites along the Tigris-Euphrates watersheds were sampled in each campaign and the results are being analysed.

IV. *Periodic inspection activities*

12. Three inspection missions have been carried out since the last report on the implementation of the plan. In the course of these inspections, monitoring activities were conducted, including short-notice inspections, at the eight "core" sites of the former Iraqi nuclear programme and at a number of other sites, facilities and installations that had supported the programme and where dual-use machine tools and other material and equipment relevant to annex 3 to the plan and subject to monitoring are located. On the average, each inspection has covered 40 facilities, installations and sites. Nothing was observed that was indicative of prohibited activities.

13. In the course of the most recent inspections, IAEA installed video surveillance systems at Um Al Ma'arik, where major components of the electromagnetic isotope separations (EMIS) modules had been fabricated. Preparations were made for future installation of surveillance systems at the Nassr State Establishment in the flow-forming machine workshop.

V. *Nuclear material balance*

14. IAEA is in the process of corroborating, with the assistance of the Brazilian Government, data provided by Iraq on the 20.6 tons of natural uranium in the form of UO_2 declared by Iraq to have come from Brazil. The inspection teams have completed detailed microscopic examination, bulk density assessments and sampling for chemical analysis of the material in question, the preliminary results of which indicate that the material is not indigenous to Iraq.

15. Areas of uncertainty in the total amount of natural uranium contained in the wastes arising from the processing of indigenous Iraqi uranium concentrates in the UO_2-UCl_4 plants at Al-Jezirah are being clarified with the assistance of the Iraqi management of the plant, which has provided additional analytical data. If confirmed by IAEA, the data should permit resolution of this issue.

16. Discrepancies between the inspection findings and the Iraqi declarations are now limited to the sources of uranium processed in Building 73a at Tuwaitha and described in the report of the eighteenth inspection mission (see S/25666, annex). Additional filters said to have been probably taken from elsewhere in complex 73 have

been presented to the inspectors and samples were taken for chemical and isotopic analysis during the twenty-fourth inspection. Despite repeated efforts from both sides, this matter remains open, although it is believed that its resolution will not have a significant impact on the overall accuracy of the uranium material balance.

VI. *Equipment and materials*

17. As described in the previous report, IAEA had indications that a considerable number of Matrix-Churchill CNC machine tools exported to Iraq were still missing and that this matter had to be further pursued. This issue finally was resolved, with the assistance of the Iraqi authorities, during the twenty-third inspection mission. In November 1993 the Iraqi side declared the prior delivery of a total of 278 Matrix-Churchill CNC turning machines. This number closely approaches the figure of 280 communicated to IAEA by the exporting country. To date, 272 Matrix-Churchill CNC turning machines have been located and examined by IAEA inspectors. Machine tool experts who assisted IAEA in the evaluation of the capability of these machines have advised that none of the identified machines supplied to Iraq are of the quality that would require their declaration under annex 3 to the plan. Furthermore, a written statement has been provided by the successor company to Matrix-Churchill certifying that none of the Matrix-Churchill CNC turning machines supplied to Iraq met the annex 3 quality specifications. In consultation with the Special Commission, it was decided that none of the 272 Matrix-Churchill CNC turning machines identified in Iraq fall within the category of items subjected to routine monitoring and verification under either plan and that, therefore, the tagging seals would be removed by IAEA inspectors in the course of the next inspections. This decision was communicated to the Iraqi authorities on 30 March 1994.

18. Comprehensive verification of the inventory of the major components of the Tammuz-1 and Tammuz-2 research reactors was completed during the twenty-third inspection, with the participation and assistance of an expert from the supplier State. It was possible to conclude that all of the sensitive components of the two reactors were now satisfactorily accounted for.

19. A number of requests have been submitted by Iraq for the release, for use in civilian needs, of certain items of equipment and material. Notification and prior consent for such action is required by paragraph 3 (iii) of resolution 707 (1991). The procedures for handling those requests are detailed in paragraph 25 of the IAEA plan, which requires a decision by the Director General, with the assistance and cooperation of the Special Commission. In accordance with paragraph 25 of the plan, the specific procedures for the release of these items subject to the requests have been established and are being implemented.

VII. *Procurement-related information*

20. Since the last report, the Iraqi authorities have provided significant and credible information on procurement related to the Iraqi uranium enrichment programme, in particular as regards the sources of maraging steel and outside technical advice for the centrifuge programme.

21. The Iraqi side identified an individual as Iraq's agent for the procurement of the maraging steel, and provided information on the shipments of material, including quantities, physical configuration and transportation routes. Confirmation of this information awaits further follow-up action by the Governments of the relevant Member States.

22. Significant progress was also achieved in the area of the role played by foreign technical advice in the centrifuge enrichment area. During the twenty-second inspection, interviews were conducted with Iraqi personnel, in the course of which the names of individuals, the circumstances under which they became involved and the details of the technical help they provided were given to IAEA. Information was also provided on the procurement of components of the prototype machines.

VIII. *Removal of irradiated nuclear fuel assemblies*

23. Since the last report, the remaining highly enriched uranium, in the form of irradiated fuel, was removed from Iraq, thus completing the removal of declared stocks of nuclear-weapons-usable material from Iraq. The irradiated fuel was removed under contract with the Ministry of Atomic Energy of the Russian Federation and a United States subcontractor. The irradiated fuel, which was removed in two consignments, on 1 December 1993 and 12 February 1994, was transported by air to the Russian Federation, where it will be treated at a reprocessing plant at Chelyabinsk and the product made available for sale under IAEA safeguards.

IX. *Establishment of a mechanism for future export-import control*

24. Paragraph 7 of Security Council resolution 715 (1991) calls for "... the Committee established under resolution 661 (1990), the Special Commission and the Director General of the International Atomic Energy Agency to develop in cooperation a mechanism for monitoring any future sales or supplies by other countries to Iraq of items relevant to the implementation of section C of resolution 687 (1991) and other relevant resolutions, including the present resolution and the plans approved hereunder".

25. Paragraph 7 of resolution 715 (1991) was adopted within the context of the approval by the Security Council of the plans submitted by the Secretary-General and by the Director General of IAEA for ongoing monitoring and verification of Iraq's undertakings, under paragraphs 10 and 12 of the Security Council resolution 687 (1991), not to reacquire prohibited weapons capabilities. The resolution establishes no fixed duration of such a mechanism, and it has thus been the understanding that the mechanism is intended to make provision for the monitoring of the sale or the supply by other countries to Iraq of items covered by the two plans after the general sanctions imposed by resolution 661 (1991) on those items have been lifted, pursuant to paragraph 21 of resolution 687 (1991). On this understanding, the Special Commission and the Director General of IAEA have prepared, for consideration and approval by the Sanctions Committee, a proposal for a mechanism for export/import monitoring under paragraph 7 of Security Council resolution 715 (1991). The proposal will thereafter be submitted to the Security Council and, once approved, will be applied in the context of the ongoing monitoring activities.

X. *Summary and conclusions*

26. While Iraq has expressed its strong wish for a specific date by which IAEA would submit to the Security Council the report of Iraq's compliance with the relevant paragraphs of resolution 687 (1991), there remain outstanding actions that would need to be completed. IAEA will have to satisfy itself that it is in a position to implement fully the ongoing monitoring and verification plan. It is not at this time possible or practical to provide a specific date by which that will happen. The positive attitude adopted by the Iraqi authorities since the initiation of the high-level talks in the second half of 1993 is bearing fruit, should be continued and must be encouraged. This will permit the acceleration of the full implementation of ongoing monitoring and verification.

Document 189

Seventh report of the Executive Chairman of UNSCOM

S/1994/750, 24 June 1994

Note by the Secretary-General

The Secretary-General has the honour to transmit to the Security Council a report submitted by the Executive Chairman of the Special Commission established by the Secretary-General pursuant to paragraph 9 (b) (i) of Security Council resolution 687 (1991).

Annex
Seventh report of the Executive Chairman of the Special Commission, established by the Secretary-General pursuant to paragraph 9 (b) (i) of Security Council resolution 687 (1991), on the activities of the Special Commission

I. *Introduction*

1. The present report is the seventh on the activities of the Special Commission established pursuant to paragraph 9 (b) (i) of Security Council resolution 687 (1991), submitted to the Security Council by the Executive Chairman of the Commission. It is the sixth such report provided in accordance with paragraph 3 of Security Council resolution 699 (1991). It covers the period from 15 December 1993 to 17 June 1994 and is further to the reports contained in documents S/23165, S/23268, S/24108 and Corr.1, S/24984, S/25977 and S/26910.

2. Building on the Commission's recommendation, contained in paragraph 38 of S/26910, to consolidate its reporting obligations under resolutions 699 (1991) and 715 (1991), this shall be the last report in this series. This recommendation was made as the Commission's work now focuses essentially on ongoing monitoring and verification activities and hence, if the previous reporting sequence were maintained, there would be considerable duplication. A consolidated reporting approach would provide the Security Council with a more concise, comprehensive and continuous written account of all the activities of the Commission on a biannual basis. Unless the Council requests otherwise, a further report under resolution 715 (1991) will be submitted in October 1994 and thereafter consolidated reports under both resolutions will be submitted each February and August. Oral reporting will continue on a monthly basis, as requested by the Council, and special written reports will be submitted as circumstances dictate.

II. *Organizational and administrative issues*

3. Since the last report, there have been no further changes in the composition of the Special Commission. The Commission held its seventh plenary session from 10 to 12 May 1994. This was followed by meetings of the Commission's working groups on Chemical Weapons and Ongoing Monitoring and Verification.

4. Currently there are 41 staff in the Office of the Executive Chairman, 23 in the Bahrain Field Office, and 69 in the Baghdad Field Office.

5. There is still no agreement on the sale of Iraqi oil to finance United Nations operations resulting from the cease-fire resolution. Current expenses have been met from voluntary contributions from Member States and funds made available from frozen Iraqi assets in accordance with Security Council resolution 778 (1992). However, in the absence of Iraqi agreement to sell oil, of Iraq's acknowledgement of its obligations under resolution 699 (1991) to meet the full costs of the tasks authorized by section C of resolution 687 (1991) and of an appropriate mechanism for this purpose, the problem of the financing of the Commission's operations remains a matter of great concern. Further cash contributions by Governments are thus urgently required.

6. Governments have continued to support the operation of the Special Commission through the contribution of personnel, services and equipment. Further information on financial and organizational issues can be found in appendix I to the present report.

III. *Status, privileges and immunities*

7. The status, privileges and immunities of the Special Commission, the International Atomic Energy Agency (IAEA) and the United Nations specialized agencies involved in the implementation of Security Council resolution 687 (1991) continue to be regulated by the relevant agreements and Council resolutions and decisions.

8. The Commission and IAEA on the one hand and the Government of Bahrain on the other have extended for a further six months, until 30 September 1994, the agreement provided for in the exchange of letters relating to the facilities, privileges and immunities of the Special Commission and IAEA in Bahrain.

9. In Iraq, there were fewer problems in the implementation of the Commission's status, privileges and immunities and with the security of Commission personnel and property. Such problems that there were, were minor in comparison with earlier experiences, with two exceptions: an incident in which an Iraqi fired on an UNSCOM vehicle convoy in January 1994 and another in April 1994 in which a crowd stoned an UNSCOM helicopter while it was undertaking a medical evacuation

of two members of the United Nations Guard contingent. Iraq is extending to current inspection teams all the support and assistance requested by them.

IV. *Developments*

A. *Political developments*

10. Iraq's acceptance on 26 November 1993 of resolution 715 (1991) and the plans for ongoing monitoring and verification approved thereunder opened the way for the implementation of the plans, the first stage of which is to establish the baseline data for ongoing monitoring and verification. Immediately upon Iraq's acceptance, the Commission informed Iraq that the latter's earlier reports about its dual-purpose capabilities were inadequate in the light of the requirements of resolution 715 (1991) and so full initial declarations made in conformity with these requirements should be submitted to the Commission. Initial declarations were received in mid-January 1994.

11. On the basis of Iraq's declarations and further information provided by Iraq in response to the Commission's requests for supplementary information, as well as information available to the Commission from other sources (most notably the results of its own inspections) and analysis, the Commission then updated its lists of sites, equipment and materials to be monitored under the Commission's plan. The Commission is now in the process of conducting baseline inspections of each of the sites on the list, the end result of which will be monitoring and verification protocols for each site. In parallel, sensors and tags and seals are being installed in line with decisions made on the basis of the recommendations of baseline inspection teams. Iraq has publicly committed itself to cooperate with the Commission and IAEA in this endeavour and the teams are receiving the support and assistance they request of their Iraqi counterparts. This is a welcome change in Iraq's attitude.

12. The political dialogue initiated as part of the resolution of the camera crisis in July 1993 has also continued. High-level meetings were held in New York in March and May 1994, in Baghdad in February and April 1994 and in Amman in May 1994. A further round is scheduled in Baghdad for July 1994.

13. During an earlier such meeting held in New York in November 1993, technical talks on chemical weapons were held in which the Commission suggested to Iraq that, in order to address concerns about the vagueness of Iraq's account of its imports for its chemical weapons programme, Iraq should conduct brainstorming seminars with the officials involved in the programme to see whether collectively they could improve on the precision and completeness of the data. Iraq agreed to pursue the idea, the results of which were received and further

explored in subsequent contacts during the period from February to April 1994.

14. During the February round of talks, there were some technical discussions, but the major element was the joint statement released by the Deputy Prime Minister of Iraq, Mr. Tariq Aziz, and the Executive Chairman at the end of the meeting. That statement, which called for the expediting of the inspection process and in which Iraq stated that it would welcome inspection teams and facilitate their tasks, reflected the increasingly amenable attitude being adopted by the Iraqi authorities in their dealings with the Commission.

15. However, this trend, on the political level, recorded a severe reverse in the March talks. Mr. Aziz accused the Commission and the Executive Chairman of acting for political motives not related to the mandate and directly under the influence of one Member State. He stated that Iraq had lost confidence in the Commission and saw little reason to continue cooperating with it if the Commission would not set a date for the lifting of the oil embargo. Indeed, he threatened that cooperation would be withdrawn if no date were set. The meeting broke up with no date set for a further round of high-level talks. Meanwhile, no change was noted in the level of support and assistance being proffered to inspection teams on the ground.

16. In the second week of April, Iraq requested a further round of high-level talks, citing "important developments" since the previous round. The atmosphere of this round of talks was in marked contrast with the March talks. The result was a further joint statement, in which Iraq publicly committed itself to continue to cooperate with the Commission and IAEA in the conduct of ongoing monitoring and verification and to respect their rights and privileges throughout this stage of their work. This was welcomed by the Commission and IAEA, continued cooperation and respect of their rights and privileges after the lifting of the oil embargo being the prime concern as to whether they would be able to conduct effective ongoing monitoring and verification.

17. These positive trends were confirmed in the May meetings held in New York and Amman. In addition, at the Amman talks, the Commission and IAEA responded to questions raised by Iraq on the proposed export/import monitoring mechanism required under paragraph 7 of resolution 715 (1991).

B. Operational developments

18. The period under review has seen the most intense inspection activity in the Commission's history. Across the board, with Iraq's acceptance of resolution 715 (1991), activities have focused more on establishing the system of ongoing monitoring and verification than on searching for or destroying weapons capabilities. This process is under way in the form of: efforts to establish the baseline data required for initiation of ongoing monitoring and verification; analysis of Iraqi declarations; and the conduct of inspections at declared and designated sites. In New York, much effort has been devoted to the compilation of site folders which, upon completion of the baseline process, will evolve into monitoring and verification protocols for each site to be monitored.

19. In the chemical weapons area, the activities of the Chemical Destruction Group at Muthanna were concluded on 14 June 1994. This brought to a successful conclusion a unique multinational undertaking, fulfilling the Commission's mandate to eliminate Iraq's declared chemical weapons stockpile and doing so expeditiously, at minimal expense, and with no damage to the environment. This was a two-year operation, involving some 100 experts, in the course of which the following were destroyed: over 480,000 litres of chemical warfare agents (including mustard agent and the nerve agents sarin and tabun); over 28,000 chemical munitions (involving 8 types of munitions ranging from rockets to artillery shells, bombs and ballistic missile warheads); and nearly 1,800,000 litres, over 1,040,000 kilograms and 648 barrels of some 45 different precursor chemicals for the production of chemical warfare agents. The Commission wishes to pay special tribute to the international experts and Iraqi personnel who brought this operation to such a successful conclusion in the harshest of environments.

20. The other main focus of effort in the chemical weapons area lay in pressuring Iraq to provide further information on its chemical weapons programme. This pressure continues to pay off: Iraq's most recent account of its past chemical weapons production is much fuller than earlier versions and, for the first time, is supported by a list of letters of credit issued for the import of equipment and materials purchased for the programme. This should allow the Commission, with the assistance of Governments, to verify large parts of Iraq's explanation of its chemical weapons programme. In addition, the first in a series of baseline inspections has been conducted, resulting in the preparation of monitoring and verification protocols for 15 sites. Detailed accounts of inspection and destruction activities can be found in appendices II and III respectively.

21. Further biological inspections were conducted as part of the baseline inspection process. One team visited over 30 sites, obtaining much information needed to design ongoing monitoring and verification in the biological area. A second inspection team inventoried and tagged dual-purpose biological equipment, particularly equipment related to production. Talks were also held to clarify certain issues in the biological area.

22. On ballistic missiles, efforts have concentrated on three main aspects: trying to establish a definitive material balance for SCUD-type missiles and other prohibited items; conducting baseline inspections of Iraq's dedicated and supporting missile plants and dual-capable facilities; and tagging relevant equipment and missiles (see appendix II).

23. Aerial surveillance activities have continued apace, using both U-2 and helicopter platforms. The U-2 continues to be used both in survey mode and to provide detailed photography of sites in preparation for ground inspections. Helicopter missions continue to be flown in support of ground inspections and to provide a time-series photographic record of sites which will need monitoring under the plans for ongoing monitoring and verification.

C. *Iraq's declarations*

24. Since its acceptance of resolution 715 (1991), Iraq has sought to address the Commission's concerns on the provision of data, both in relation to the full, final and complete disclosures and in relation to the declarations of current and recent dual-purpose capabilities due under the plans for ongoing monitoring and verification. There remains some doubt, however, that Iraq is fully cooperating in this regard, particularly as it maintains its claim to have destroyed all documentation and not to be able to recall certain key facts. The lack of documentation continues to present the Commission with the problem of how to verify Iraq's account of its programmes and with the problem of what confidence it can have that it has fully accounted for Iraq's banned capabilities. In this regard, the lack of documentation has been one of the principal delaying factors. That said, there has been a marked change for the better in Iraq's willingness to address the Commission's concerns, particularly in relation to current dual-purpose facilities.

25. A more detailed description of developments in this regard is to be found in the relevant sections of appendix II.

D. *Export/import monitoring mechanism*

26. By paragraph 7 of its resolution 715 (1991), the Security Council requested "the Security Council Committee established under resolution 661 (1990)... the Special Commission and the Director General of [IAEA] to develop in cooperation a mechanism for monitoring any future sales or supplies by other countries to Iraq of items relevant to the implementation of section C of resolution 687 (1991) and other relevant resolutions, including the present resolution and the plans approved hereunder".

27. A draft proposal for an export/import monitoring mechanism was prepared by the Office of the Special Commission in consultation with the IAEA Action Team. The agreed text was then submitted on 13 May 1994 to the Committee established under resolution 661 (1990) (i.e., the Sanctions Committee). At the time of writing, it is expected that the Sanctions Committee will take action in the near future on the proposal and submit it to the Security Council for adoption in a further resolution under Chapter VII of the Charter of the United Nations.

28. The proposal envisages a system of timely notification, rather than licensing, of exports from States and imports into Iraq of items which are covered in the annexes to the Commission and IAEA plans for ongoing monitoring and verification. Iraq, both as importer and the exporting State, will be required to give advance notice of its acquisition of items covered by the plans. A principal consideration in designing the proposal has been the need for a mechanism robust enough to deter Iraq from potential breaches. Nevertheless, to be workable, the mechanism must also be sufficiently simple so as not to place an undue reporting burden on Governments. The mechanism will be buttressed by the ability of the Commission and IAEA to conduct unlimited inspections throughout Iraq.

V. *Issues and priorities for the future*

29. The situation is very different, generally for the better, from that which obtained at the time of the last report. Iraq has accepted resolution 715 (1991) and the plans for ongoing monitoring and verification. It has provided the Commission much new information about both its past programmes and its dual-purpose facilities. It is committed publicly to cooperate with the Special Commission and IAEA in the implementation of ongoing monitoring and verification and to respect their rights and privileges in doing so. Inspection teams are no longer subjected routinely to obstruction or intimidation, rather as a rule receiving the support and assistance they request from their Iraqi counterparts.

30. However, work remains to be done. In order for the Commission to be able to report to the Council that the requirements of the relevant Security Council resolutions have been fulfilled, it must be able to answer two questions in the affirmative:

– Is the Commission confident that it has accounted for and eliminated all of Iraq's banned capabilities?

– Is the Commission confident that it has an effective ongoing monitoring and verification system in place and operational, i.e., one that could deter or detect in time a clandestine attempt to reactivate the banned programmes?

31. Further work still needs to be done to clarify outstanding issues in relation to the past programmes. The speed with which that can be resolved is primarily dependent on Iraq's openness and honesty and, to a lesser degree, supplier Governments' responses to the Commission's requests for assistance in verifying Iraq's accounts of imports.

32. Establishing an effective ongoing monitoring and verification system is no simple task and allows no short cuts. Each site to be monitored needs to be inspected thoroughly and a monitoring and verification protocol prepared for it. This entails preparation and collation of data and imagery from all previous ground and aerial inspections with the results of the Commission's analysis of these. Sensors and tags have to be identified and installed. So long as Iraq continues to cooperate, however, the system should be established soon.

33. Establishing an export/import monitoring mechanism also requires further work (see para. 27 above). After adoption by the Security Council of the necessary resolution approving the mechanism, States will have to take the steps necessary to give internal effect to the mechanism.

Appendix I
Financial and organizational issues

A. Current and future financial mechanism

1. When the Security Council created the Special Commission in April 1991, the organizational structure and the financing arrangements focused upon the identification and destruction phases of the work of the Special Commission and IAEA. At that time, these phases were seen as being of limited duration. Ad hoc measures for staffing and financing were thus resorted to. These included two Security Council resolutions, 706 (1991) and 712 (1991), permitting limited sales of Iraqi oil. Iraq refused to comply with those resolutions. The Council thus adopted, in October 1992, resolution 778 (1992), calling for the transfer of Iraqi assets under third-party control to an escrow account administered by the Secretary-General. Funds deposited in this account have allowed the Special Commission and IAEA to cover their operating budget, total expenditure reaching $55.2 million by the end of 1993. This amount includes $13 million for the first phase of the contract for the removal of nuclear fuel.

2. To date, the Commission and IAEA have been able to operate on this very uncertain financial basis. However, as the Commission and IAEA move into ongoing monitoring and verification, which will be of indefinite duration, it will be necessary for a solid financial base to be established, which will provide the assurance of adequate and continuous financing free of Iraqi control.

This is an issue to which the Security Council will have to address itself when it contemplates action on paragraphs 21 and 22 of resolution 687 (1991).

B. Organizational issues

3. Following Iraq's acceptance of resolution 715 (1991), the Commission's activities have focused increasingly on the implementation of the plans for ongoing monitoring and verification. These require, *inter alia*, that Iraq provide regular and detailed information on activities, equipment and programmes which fall under the regime. Under a new export/import control regime, Member States will also provide a large volume of data. For the Commission's part, this information will be verified by on-site and aerial inspections, information provided from other sources and through the use of various monitoring devices installed at facilities.

4. The organizational and administrative structure of the Commission in New York and in Iraq is being adapted to allow the Commission to maintain its current level of support for intrusive operations while meeting the requirements for ongoing monitoring and verification.

New York

5. Additional staff in the chemical, biological, ballistic and export/import control areas have been provided to the Commission by supporting Governments to assess Iraq's declarations, to develop monitoring and verification protocols and to draft procedures for the export/import monitoring mechanism. It is anticipated that the Commission will require, for the next six months, six experts in support of chemical activities, six for ballistic and four for biological. The nuclear component of the Commission will remain at two. Data analysis and photographic imagery will have a total of five staff. Additional staff will also be brought in for the development of operational plans for export/import control.

The Baghdad Ongoing Monitoring and Verification Centre

6. The activities of the Commission with regard to ongoing monitoring and verification will require an expansion of its facilities in Baghdad. Plans have been drawn up for the establishment of the Baghdad Ongoing Monitoring and Verification Centre. The Iraqi side was informed of these plans, responding to them positively and designating the premises of the United Nations located in the Canal Hotel as the site for the Centre. This Centre will serve the requirements of both the Commission and IAEA. A Director for the Centre has been recruited.

7. Additional office space to accommodate an expanded presence has been identified. Communication equipment has been ordered to increase the total of telephone lines to New York to five, which will allow transmission of data between Baghdad and New York. Data from sites monitored with cameras and other sensors will be transmitted as required to the operations room via telephone and radio links. For this purpose, a 100-metre communications mast provided by Iraq is being erected at the Canal Hotel. Facilities will be available for analysing the data received from the monitored sites and for archiving essential information required in Baghdad. Computers capable of storing relevant protocol information in an electronic form will be installed. The Aerial Inspection Team will be able to process photographs in Baghdad and integrate imagery into the monitoring and verification protocols.

8. Great attention was given to achieving the highest possible level of security at the Centre in order to protect the information gathered and to allow inspectors and analysts to conduct their work in a protected environment.

9. The Operations Room will be moved from the Sheraton Hotel to the Canal Hotel once the construction work in the Canal Hotel is completed. A secure telephone extension will be maintained at the Sheraton Hotel for the use of inspection teams.

10. The support staff will be increased to maintain and operate communications, data collection and analysis equipment which will be acquired by the Commission. In addition to the support staff, Governments will be requested to provide resident experts in aerial imagery, ballistic missiles, chemical weapons and chemical industry, microbiology, nuclear technology and export/import control. They will be sent to Baghdad for a three- to six-month tour of duty. Training in monitoring techniques and in the maintenance of the monitoring equipment will be organized.

11. The Commission hopes that all equipment required to operate the Centre, i.e., communication equipment, office furniture, video cameras, motion sensors, chemical and biological samplers, photo imagery equipment and the database computers, will be provided by contributing Governments as a donation, on a loan basis, or to be reimbursed upon availability of funds from Iraq.

12. While personnel are being recruited and equipment purchased for the task of ongoing monitoring and verification, the Chemical Destruction Group was disbanded at the completion of its task. Personnel have returned to their countries of origin, as has most of the equipment supplied to the Group.

Appendix II
Inspection activities

A. *Missiles*

1. Iraq's acceptance of its obligations under Security Council resolution 715 (1991) led to intensive work to establish a monitoring mechanism of missile-related activities and dual-purpose capabilities in Iraq pursuant to the Plan for ongoing monitoring and verification in the non-nuclear area (S/22871/Rev.1 of 2 October 1991). These efforts included a number of inspections, assessment of Iraq's declarations submitted under the Plan, identification of focal points for monitoring and appropriate monitoring techniques, including their field trials, preparation of draft monitoring and verification protocols and in-depth discussions with the Iraqi side of monitoring issues, including during the rounds of high-level talks both in New York and Baghdad. In parallel, the Commission continued its investigation into Iraq's past prohibited missile programmes and its compliance with resolution 687 (1991).

1. *Inspection activities*

(a) *BM20/UNSCOM66*

2. BM20/UNSCOM66 operated in Iraq over the period from 21 to 29 January 1994. In view of Iraq's acceptance of resolution 715 (1991), BM20/UNSCOM66 was tasked to accomplish the following:

(a) To update data collected by previous inspection teams on Iraq's missile research and development programme;

(b) To examine issues related to Iraq's reporting on facilities to be monitored under the Plan for ongoing monitoring and verification in the missile area as approved by resolution 715 (1991);

(c) To conduct a preliminary survey for possible application of monitoring sensors and technologies.

3. BM20/UNSCOM66 visited a number of research and development and industrial facilities to be monitored under the ongoing monitoring and verification Plan. Iraq provided the team with a detailed update of its current missile programmes relevant to surface-to-surface missiles with a range greater than 50 kilometres.

4. BM20/UNSCOM66 carried out extensive work related to Iraq's reporting obligations under the Plan for ongoing monitoring and verification. This included discussions of Iraq's reporting on facilities to be monitored, examination of declarations submitted by Iraq in January 1994 pursuant to the Plan and practical on-site investigation of relevant issues. This work resulted in a draft format for Iraq's reporting on those missile research-and-development and production facilities that would be under the most intensive monitoring regime. During in-

spection and soon after it, Iraq submitted to the Commission reports under this format for all relevant facilities. As a result of BM20/UNSCOM66, Iraq also provided corrections to its January declarations under the Plan in the missile area. Iraq has yet to provide required data on some of its missile projects.

5. BM20/UNSCOM66 started a survey of sites where installation of sensors and use of other technologies might be appropriate for monitoring purposes. This survey addressed issues of inventory control of dual-purpose equipment, non-removal of equipment from declared facilities and monitoring of activities at facilities. Use of a variety of sensors and recording devices could be an important part of monitoring procedures under the Plan.

(b) BM21/UNSCOM69

6. BM21/UNSCOM69 was in Iraq from 17 to 25 February to accomplish the following:

(a) To assess Iraq's dual-purpose missile industrial capabilities that might be used in support of missile production;

(b) To continue compiling the database on Iraq's machine tools and equipment usable for missile production;

(c) To carry out an assessment of possibilities of installing sensors and using other technologies to monitor missile-related industrial activities.

7. BM21/UNSCOM69 visited 15 facilities in Iraq, identified a number of focal points for monitoring activities at those sites and carried out a survey for the use of sensors. The machine tool database built by IMT1C/UNSCOM57 was updated, new machines were recorded and some items were tagged.

8. The results of BM21/UNSCOM69 provided the Commission with the necessary background data to refine a scope of facilities for ongoing monitoring and verification under the Plan.

(c) BM22/UNSCOM71

9. Based on the results of BM20/UNSCOM66 and BM21/UNSCOM69, BM22/UNSCOM71 was organized to prepare draft monitoring and verification protocols for facilities identified so far by the Commission as needing to be subject to ongoing monitoring and verification. This was the first protocol-building team sent to Iraq as a part of baseline activities in the missile area under the Plan for ongoing monitoring and verification. Ongoing monitoring and verification protocols incorporate detailed procedures and information required for monitoring activities, using a variety of different means at sites in Iraq covered by the Plan. They will also contain a systematic collection of that information known about sites concerned necessary for effective monitoring and verification. Once cre-

ated, a protocol for a given site would be updated as necessary on the basis of the findings of monitoring and verification activities.

10. BM22/UNSCOM71 carried out its activities in Iraq from 30 March to 20 May 1994 through a succession of rounds of visits to Iraq. The team visited more than 30 facilities to be placed, depending on the nature of their activities, under different regimes of monitoring. During these visits, the team verified on-site Iraq's declarations concerning these facilities. The team also conducted the survey of the sites to identify focal points for monitoring activities. BM22/UNSCOM71 has submitted to the Commission for approval draft ongoing monitoring and verification protocols with recommendations for monitoring arrangements and inspection modalities at the facilities to be monitored. These recommendations, include, *inter alia*, suggestions for the installation of cameras of different types and for tagging and monitoring missile-related and dual-purpose equipment. The recommendations also contain proposals for on-site inspection programmes for each facility, amounting to a total of more than 100 inspection visits per year. Successful completion of BM22/UNSCOM71 marked a large and critical step towards the creation of a monitoring and verification regime in the missile area.

(d) BM23/UNSCOM79 and BM24/UNSCOM80

11. BM24/UNSCOM80 began its mission in Iraq on 10 June. This inspection team is tasked to conduct tagging of a number of operational missile systems in Iraq covered by the Plan for ongoing monitoring and verification. The Plan provides for monitoring of missiles designed for use, or capable of being modified for use, in a surface-to-surface role with a range greater than 50 kilometres.

12. The purpose of this tagging operation is to assist the Commission in effective monitoring of non-modification of a number of missile systems and keep a reliable inventory control of missiles under monitoring. In total, BM24/UNSCOM80 tagged more than 1,300 missiles of different types. All missiles were tagged by UNSCOM inspectors, with Iraq's authorities providing preparations and support necessary for safe and efficient operations. BM24/UNSCOM80 also visited a number of sites to ascertain that they were not suitable for prohibited modification activities.

13. After the baseline activities related to operational missiles are completed, the Commission will request Iraq, up to three times per year, to assemble a limited number of tagged missiles for purposes of inspecting them and making sure that they have not been modified to enable missiles to reach a range greater than 150 kilometres. The Commission will select for each inspection up to 10 per cent of the quantity of tagged missiles.

14. As of this writing, BM24/UNSCOM80 is completing its mission in Iraq, with departure planned for 24 June 1994.

15. Monitoring arrangements for operational missiles, including tagging, required extensive preparations and elaboration of appropriate operational modalities. BM23/UNSCOM79 was in Iraq from 23 to 28 May 1994 to conduct preparations for BM24/UNSCOM80. BM23/UNSCOM79 checked on-site work areas for tagging operations and other preparatory work done by the Iraqi authorities for the tagging activities. Prime attention was paid to the safety aspects of working with live missiles. Special operational procedures were established by the Commission for this purpose.

16. BM23/UNSCOM79 also established a technical reference baseline for Iraq's missile systems of interest to the Commission. Reference data for each missile system was gathered to include measurements and photography of major parts and components. The data collected will be used to establish "official" UNSCOM missile configurations for each missile system for use in future inspections and to support automated processing of data collected from the monitoring cameras.

(e) BM25/UNSCOM81

17. BM25/UNSCOM81 arrived in Baghdad on 14 June 1994 and plans to accomplish its mission by 22 June 1994. The objectives of this team were twofold: to present to Iraq's experts definitions elaborated by the Commission of the dual-purpose items contained in annex IV of the Plan for ongoing monitoring and verification, and to discuss certain aspects of the past prohibited activities in Iraq, including missile production and modification projects.

(f) Sensors and tagging

18. Remote-monitoring cameras remain at the two missile test stands. They continue to work in a satisfactory manner and the data obtained allow UNSCOM to monitor on a continuous basis Iraq's static missile testing programme.

19. During December 1993, a team was sent to Baghdad to upgrade these systems. The upgrade gave UNSCOM a better analysis capability by installing higher-resolution cameras. The team also placed the cameras in different areas of the sites, allowing for a better field of view. Telephone-line transmission of signals from the sites to the UNSCOM office in Baghdad was replaced by radio transmission to allow for reliable communications.

20. As mentioned above, BM20/UNSCOM66, BM21/UNSCOM69 and BM22/UNSCOM71 conducted surveys of the missile research-and-development and production sites in Iraq to determine where to install sensors

and employ tags for monitoring purposes. Their recommendations included the use of monitoring cameras for what was considered to be critical areas of these facilities. The teams made a number of proposals on the use of tags and different types of sensors to help identify and monitor specific activities and equipment.

21. Experts will visit Iraq in July to install cameras and to tag equipment identified for monitoring. They will also install equipment in the Baghdad Ongoing Monitoring and Verification Centre to control these systems. Initially, there will be two basic types of cameras. Both will be time-lapsed video, one with motion sensors and one without. All camera systems will be capable of transmitting data to the Centre.

2. Other activities

22. In support of its efforts to establish a mechanism for ongoing monitoring and verification, the Commission held a number of meetings with international experts. During these meetings, issues discussed related to the assessment of Iraq's declarations, identification of critical points for monitoring missile-related activities and appropriate techniques, including sensors, to ensure effective monitoring. Lists of dual-purpose equipment, technologies and other items that could be used for the development, production, modification or acquisition of ballistic missiles with a range greater than 150 kilometres were also discussed.

3. Past prohibited activities

23. The Commission continued its investigation of the outstanding issues related to the past missile programme proscribed under resolution 687 (1991). This work is essential to establish a solid and verified baseline for ongoing monitoring and verification in accordance with resolution 715 (1991). In particular, this will allow the Commission to have a full and comprehensive picture of the knowledge Iraq obtained in the missile area through its past activities.

24. Issues related to programmes proscribed under section C of resolution 687 (1991) were discussed with Iraq on a continuous basis, especially during the rounds of the high-level talks in November 1993 and March 1994 in New York. Iraq has furnished additional details on foreign acquisition of critical ballistic missile items as well as its expenditure of ballistic missiles with a range greater than 150 kilometres. Verification of this and other information provided by Iraq continued, including through contacts with Governments that possess data of relevance to this work.

25. The Commission continued to reiterate its request that Iraq provide original documentation that would substantiate the declarations made by Iraq con-

cerning its past prohibited missile programmes. During the February visit of the Executive Chairman to Baghdad, Iraq finally agreed to give the Commission files on the expenditure of prohibited missiles. This documentation covers the period from 1977 to December 1990 and accounts for nearly three quarters of the missiles covered by resolution 687 (1991) and declared by Iraq. Currently, the Commission is conducting an in-depth investigation of these documents and the information contained therein. The results of this investigation will be critical for the Commission's reporting to the Security Council under paragraph 22 of resolution 687 (1991).

B. *Chemical weapons*

1. *Inspection activities*

26. CW12/UNSCOM65 was constituted at short notice to investigate persistent reports that chemical weapons had been used by Iraqi Government troops against opposition elements in the southern marshes of Iraq. Initially, the team assembled as a fact-finding mission and visited the Islamic Republic of Iran to obtain clarifications about the allegations from persons claiming to have witnessed the incident, specifically to obtain an exact location of the site at which the alleged chemical weapon attack took place. Upon obtaining this information, this team returned to Bahrain for further preparations and entered Iraq, as CW12/UNSCOM65, on 19 November 1993.

27. During the inspection, the team conducted a thorough inspection of the site and took a large number of soil, water, flora and fauna samples which were analysed in various laboratories expert in the analysis of such samples. The team also inspected the area around the site of the alleged attack. Vehicles, boats and helicopters were used in the survey. During the inspection, the team did not find any immediate evidence of the use of chemical weapons. One unexploded munition was discovered at the site but was in too dangerous a condition for the team to take samples from. Consequently, a second team of explosive demolition experts from the Commission's Chemical Destruction Group at Muthanna was dispatched to the site, on 25 November 1993, and concluded that the munition was not a chemical munition but a highly explosive rocket-propelled grenade. It was destroyed by the experts.

28. In the course of its investigation, the Commission has also obtained some documents, which were examined and retained for forensic examination and analysis.

29. The chemical analysis of the samples, undertaken in laboratories in the United Kingdom of Great Britain and Northern Ireland and the United States of America, showed no evidence of the presence of chemi-cal-weapons agents in the samples and so indicated that chemical weapons had not been used during the previous two years in the inspected area (the southern marshes of Iraq). The environmental conditions (e.g., flora and fauna) observed and documented by the team supported the results of the analysis. Based on these results, the forensic examination of the documents, which Iraqi opposition personnel claimed proved the use of chemical-weapons agents, was cancelled.

30. In the period from 1 to 11 February 1994, CW13/UNSCOM67 inventoried and tagged approximately 240 pieces of dual-use chemical production equipment. This equipment had been procured under the auspices of Iraq's chemical warfare programme.

31. The team also visited the Ibn al Baytar facility in order to create a monitoring and verification protocol for that site. The purpose was to assess whether the general model for monitoring and verification protocols developed in the Commission's headquarters in New York were indeed applicable in practice to dual-purpose chemical facilities.

32. As a result of CW13/UNSCOM67, the Iraqi side received on 14 March 1994 an official letter specifying those items of the chemical production equipment which the Commission had decided should be destroyed. Iraq was provided with precise descriptions of the items. In addition, Iraq was asked to provide, by 30 April 1994, a detailed description of the intended permitted future use of the remaining tagged equipment for a final decision on their disposal. Otherwise, the Commission would also have to consider whether the items would also need to be destroyed. Those items not destroyed would then be subjected to ongoing monitoring and verification.

33. During the period from 20 to 26 March 1994, CW14/UNSCOM70 installed four air samplers at the Muthanna site. These samplers are designed to determine the types and levels of chemicals in the air at that site. The team also employed portable samplers which took additional samples for gaining an even more comprehensive survey of the air at Muthanna. The samplers were installed in a pattern which would cover air quality on the site from all wind directions. An Iraqi maintenance and construction crew prepared the mounting poles for the samplers. The samplers were programmed to sample the air around the clock in a discontinuous mode for a 30-day period. The sample tubes are to be removed, replaced with fresh tubes every 30 days and sent to laboratories for analysis. The sampler mechanism is microprocessor-controlled and is powered by a storage battery which is charged by a solar panel. A microprocessor-driven meteorological station is mounted on one of the samplers to record hourly wind speed, wind direction, temperature and humidity. This meteorological data is to be down-

loaded each time the sampler tubes are changed and will become part of the permanent record of the sample set.

34. CW15/UNSCOM74 conducted its activities in Iraq from 19 to 21 April 1994. Its task was to verify the additional information provided by Iraq in the course of the technical part of the high-level talks held in mid-March 1994 in New York. Owing to Iraq's claim that all documents concerning the past programmes of weapons of mass destruction had been destroyed in 1991 and 1992, the team had to resort to indirect proofs. This included interviews with senior personnel involved in Iraq's past chemical weapons programme as well as in Iraq's data recollection seminars held over the period January-March 1994.

35. The Iraqi side was able to provide a credible overview of the past chemical weapons-activities between 1980 and 1988 and in 1990. A major step forward was the presentation of a handwritten copy of the inventory of the procurement activities between 1982 and 1988. This contained a list of "Letter of Credit" numbers, with additional details on suppliers, values of contracts and general description of goods. Iraq claimed the list covered all procurement activities of the chemical weapons programme. An initial evaluation shows that the Iraqi presentation seems to be credible and possibly complete. However, a thorough examination will require much work and a further round of contacts with the supplier Governments.

36. Iraq, during this inspection, claimed that, when the chemical weapons programme was recommenced in 1980, "the Project" could rely for the first two years on the resources of a previous unsuccessful operating organization which stopped its activities in 1978. It was claimed that all procurement activities related to Iraq's chemical weapons programme were cancelled in summer 1988 at the end of the Iran-Iraq war. In 1989 only pesticides were formulated or produced at SEPP/MSE. Iraq claims that the production of live agents was resumed for only one month in 1990. Iraq also admitted, for the first time, that it received direct support from a foreign country in the chemical weapons programme.

37. During this inspection, Iraq also presented its intentions concerning the reuse of dual-use chemical production equipment in civilian projects, such as the production of phenol and aniline. The Iraqi Ministry of Chemical Industry intends to make use of the infrastructure of the former chemical-weapons-related areas at Fallujahs 1, 2 and 3 by establishing a chemical centre for the production of general chemicals and fine chemicals. Production would be at a rate of several hundred to some thousand tonnes per year. A very preliminary evaluation of this intended use of the equipment is that it seems reasonable. UNSCOM always has the possibility to trace the whereabouts of the production equipment.

38. CW16/UNSCOM75 was a "protocol-building" mission that visited 14 sites of chemical interest between 25 May and 5 June 1994. The protocol for each site is a complete folder containing information on the site, Iraqi declarations, UNSCOM assessments and guidance for future inspectors. The sites visited had varying levels of interest for future chemical weapons inspections. Some sites are of high interest since these sites still retain the potential to revert to chemical weapons precursor production. They have equipment, personnel and know-how which could be brought into a chemical weapons operating mode in a relatively short period. Other sites visited have less potential to be converted for use in a chemical weapons programme. There are a total of 47 sites for which protocols are to be developed. The remaining sites will be covered in two more missions.

39. For information on CW17/UNSCOM76, CW18/UNSCOM77 and the conclusion of CDG/UNSCOM38, see appendix III.

2. *Data collection*

40. In parallel with the various rounds of high-level political talks, UNSCOM experts have held three technical meetings with Iraq on chemical weapons issues.

(a) *Past programmes*

41. In the course of the meeting held in New York in November 1993, Iraq stressed that it had tried to meet all the requirements put forward by the Commission on the provision of information. However, Iraq agreed to endeavour to address any questions that might arise during the Commission's verification activities. The Commission, for its part, informed Iraq that it had assessed as credible the information provided in the talks held in Baghdad in October 1993 regarding Iraq's past chemical weapons programme. However, in the absence of documentation, independent verification of the data remained problematic. The Commission suggested that Iraq, in order to address this problem in part, hold seminars of the officials involved in the chemical weapons programme aimed at stimulating the collective memory to remember details which might facilitate independent verification. The issue of equipment and chemicals left at the Muthanna State Establishment was also discussed. It was agreed that the Commission should send a mission to Baghdad in January 1994 to mark equipment in order to prepare an inventory as to the release or disposal of that equipment. Further discussion was reserved on the release or disposal of chemicals remaining at the site.

42. During the meeting held in Baghdad in February 1994, Iraq informed the Commission of the results of its seminar with senior Iraqi personnel formerly involved

in the chemical weapons programme. Additional data on outstanding issues, e.g., the research-and-development programme and imports of precursor chemicals, were provided.

43. During the meeting held in New York in March 1994, the Commission asked Iraq for additional details to fill in gaps in previously provided information. In response, Iraq presented the results of another seminar it had convened, this time involving retired former officials. These included a breakdown of the quantities of imported precursor chemicals by year and contract. In addition, Iraq was able to present a correlation, on an annual basis, between produced quantities of agents, available precursor chemicals, stored and consumed agents and available chemical production capacity. A complete overview of its chemical weapons research-and-development programme, including time-frames, was also provided.

44. The additional information obtained during the course of these meetings was essential to the Commission's efforts to obtain as full a picture of Iraq's chemical weapons programme as possible. For example, in October 1993 Iraq declared 13,221 tonnes of traceable imported precursor chemicals, in February 1994, 15,037 tonnes, and in March 1994, 17,657 tonnes. The declared quantities of produced agents, however, remained unchanged at 4,340.5 tonnes.

45. CW15/UNSCOM74 considered that, during the April discussions held in Baghdad, Iraq had presented to the best of its ability the history of its chemical weapons programme. The orders of magnitude of the declared figures appear credible and the account presented is now more internally consistent than previous accounts. While little new information was divulged on Iraq's chemical weapons research and development, production and weaponization, some of the Commission's earlier conclusions on these matters were corroborated.

46. As supporting documentary evidence for its declarations, Iraq provided a handwritten extract of a list of letters of credit issued for the purpose of purchases for the chemical weapons programme. The list provides some possibility to verify, through contacts with the Governments of the companies named in the list, Iraq's declared imports for the programme. This process of contacting the Governments concerned is well under way, but here UNSCOM is highly dependent on the timely assistance of the Governments.

(b) Declarations of dual-purpose facilities

47. In December 1993, the Commission provided Iraq with model formats for the latter's initial declarations, required under the plan for ongoing monitoring and verification, of dual-purpose chemical facilities. On 16 January 1994, Iraq delivered to the Commission's Field Office in Baghdad partially completed formats. At subsequent meetings of the two sides, Iraq was informed by the Commission of the inadequacies of these returns and of what was required to bring them into conformity with the Commission's requirements. Iraq was told that full initial declarations were one of the main prerequisites for the protocol-building procedure and hence for the initiation of ongoing monitoring and verification. Since then, several meetings of experts from the two sides have addressed this issue, with the result that the Commission now has a more complete set of declarations for such facilities.

C. Biological weapons

1. Inspection activities

48. The first biological inspections in the baseline process started with the fourth biological inspection team (BW4/UNSCOM72), which conducted its activities in Iraq from 8 to 26 April 1994. This inspection verified the declarations submitted by Iraq in January 1994 pursuant to the Plan for ongoing monitoring and verification. Other objectives of this inspection were: to provide an assessment of the work being undertaken and of the equipment present at those biological facilities declared by Iraq, many of which had not previously been visited by UNSCOM; to establish an inventory of said equipment for future tagging; to draft a format for Iraq's regular reports under the monitoring and verification plan; and to provide a preliminary feasibility study regarding remote monitoring of some of the facilities.

49. During the period from 28 May to 7 June 1994, an inspection (BW5/UNSCOM78) was conducted to construct an inventory of biological dual-purpose equipment. The equipment of interest was located in a variety of facilities involved mainly in biological production or research and development. The inventory was developed in three stages: marking of the items of interest with tamper-proof, bar-coded, polymer-coated tape; close-up photography of these items; and the entry of such items and their codes in the inventory. The inventory will provide an overview of Iraq's biological capabilities through accountability of the equipment's use, transfer or modification.

2. Data collection

50. Following the presentation of Iraq's declarations in January 1994, high-level talks were conducted with Iraqi officials in February and March 1994. These discussions focused upon the information to be provided by Iraq for an efficient and effective monitoring of the biological area. The outcome of these discussions was the provision by Iraq of a new version of the declarations required under the Plan in a form which would allow the

accuracy and completeness of the information to be analysed.

51. During BW4/UNSCOM72, further discussions were held with Iraq concerning additional facilities subject to declarations under the Plan for ongoing monitoring and verification. Subsequently, Iraq made supplementary declarations on these sites. In early June 1994, a team of experts held technical talks in Baghdad with Iraq on biological issues aimed at clarifying or completing information previously provided under the Plan, in order to facilitate the analytical work required to establish a monitoring regime for all the sites.

3. Seminars of experts in New York

52. In March 1994, a seminar of international experts was held in New York to prepare for inspections connected with establishing the biological baseline. In May 1994, a further seminar was held as part of the Commission's efforts to review all declarations and data on Iraq's biological capabilities. Discussions focused on the establishment of criteria for use in assessing data on Iraq's relevant biological activities and on the identification of items to be controlled through the export/import monitoring mechanism. Further seminars are planned to discuss the following aspects of the biological elements of the Plan: sensors and other monitoring technologies; monitoring modalities; and requirements for the training of inspectors.

4. Protocol-building efforts

53. Efforts to build the protocols for each biological site are under way. The information relating to the geographical location has been compiled. Further information will be obtained throughout the baseline process. A draft of the format for information to be provided by Iraq has been developed.

5. Remote monitoring and tagging trials

54. A feasibility study of monitoring by cameras was conducted during BW4/UNSCOM72. Further efforts in this field will be effected initially by way of seminars. Tagging technologies have already been identified and deemed appropriate with respect to bio-technological equipment. Based on the results of these seminars and information from inspections, cameras and additional tags may be installed at a later date.

D. Nuclear

55. Activities in the nuclear area are reported separately by IAEA. However, the Special Commission conducted a second gamma aerial survey from 2 to 15 December 1993. During that mission, the team surveyed six sites. It obtained detailed gamma spectra at radioactive disposal areas at Tuwaitha as well as two areas at Al Atheer. In addition, gamma surveys were conducted at Rashdiya, Al Hadre, a site near Tikrit, and Salah Al Din State Establishment (SAAD-13). While the data are still being analysed, early indications show the power of this capability to survey rapidly a relatively large area and to pinpoint particular sites for more detailed investigation. This system is still being developed, and improvements are under way.

E. Aerial inspections

56. The Commission's aerial inspections, using both helicopters and high-altitude surveillance aircraft, continued over the period under review. The Commission's high-altitude reconnaissance aircraft (U-2) now flies once or twice a week, having flown a total of 209 missions since the inception of its use in support of the Commission's operations. The Commission's helicopters have now flown over 300 missions, covering some 450 sites. The Aerial Inspection Team currently conducts three to four flights a week. In all, the Commission's helicopters have completed over 2,000 flying hours in direct support of the Commission's activities.

Appendix III
Destruction of Iraq's chemical agents and munitions

1. A full background report on chemical destruction activities has been given in previous reports. The present report focuses solely on developments since December 1993 and the closing down of the Chemical Destruction Group.

Safety and security aspects

2. The high level of safety standards at Muthanna has been maintained over the reporting period. As in the past, Iraqi requests to lower some standards in order to speed up work have been rejected. Efforts to educate the Iraqi side about safety standards made some slow progress. However, set-backs occurred from time to time but were all contained without serious accident because of quick action of the Chemical Destruction Group.

3. UNSCOM observed increasing pressure on the Muthanna management since November 1993, when the Iraqis started to speed up the support of destruction activities. Most of the minor incidents occurred between November 1993 and April 1994 and can be seen as a direct result of pressure on the Muthanna management from the Government of Iraq. UNSCOM has provided about 100 protective suits to Iraqi workers at Muthanna. The offer was accepted very reluctantly. In summary, the high safety standards have paid dividends.

4. The destruction of chemical warfare agents and precursors was completed by early April 1994. Destruction figures are listed below. A number of missile solid-propellant components were also destroyed in May 1994.

5. After 6 April 1994, the Chemical Destruction Group concentrated on the destruction of dual-use chemical production equipment. The identification and the tagging of this equipment was the main objective of UNSCOM 67 in January/February 1994. That mission provided the Executive Chairman with recommendations for the categories of equipment to be destroyed or returned to Iraq. As noted in appendix II, section B, on the occasion of high-level talks in New York in March 1994, Iraq received a letter containing the Executive Chairman's decision on the destruction of equipment. This provided the basic reference for the activities of the Chemical Destruction Group. Besides single pieces of equipment, the main installations which have been destroyed and partly sealed off are the hydrolysis plant, pilot plants, the aerosol test chamber, the DF plant, and the mustard plant.

6. Bunkers and specially designed, concrete-lined lagoons which have been used for the storage of chemical waste from destruction activities have been sealed off with reinforced concrete according to the directions given by the Destruction Advisory Panel. The incinerator has been given back to the Iraqi authorities. However, all tubes and valves around the burning chamber have been dismantled and stored in bunkers, as they were heavily contaminated.

Closure of the Chemical Destruction Group

7. The closure of Muthanna comprised the following steps:

(a) An area sweep. The main effort fell on those areas where the Group had conducted its major activities (e.g., incinerator, hydrolysis plant, accumulation areas). In parallel, full documentation on bunker sealing was prepared. This was followed by an extended check and sweep, i.e, a clean-up operation. This stage was completed in mid-May 1994;

(b) Two UNSCOM inspections, the first of which (CW17/UNSCOM76) operated from 31 May to 12 June 1994. Its aim was to take samples and to analyse them in real time at Muthanna in order to provide hard data on the state of the site at Muthanna at the time of handover. These results were incorporated into the Muthanna handover protocol, prepared by the follow-on inspection (CW18/UNSCOM77), which operated from 8 to 14 June 1994. In order to ensure accurate transfer of results and

full coordination, these two inspections overlapped by three days. CW18/UNSCOM77 conducted a final inspection and transferred responsibility for Muthanna back to the Iraqi authorities. On 14 June 1994, the Chemical Destruction Group (UNSCOM38) and CW18/UNSCOM77 left Iraq, and the Chemical Destruction Group was disbanded. In all, 100 experts served with the Group;

(c) Completion of final documentation on the Chemical Destruction Group in New York. All Group files will be kept in New York. A documentation team will cover every aspect of operations of the Group, making observations on lessons to be learnt and recommendations for any similar future operation.

Summary

8. The Chemical Destruction Group has successfully completed its mission. The disbanding of the Group on 16 June 1994 marked the completion of one of the Commission's prime mandates under Security Council resolution 687 (1991).

Totals for items destroyed at Al Muthanna

Description

122 mm rockets and warheads	319
122 mm warheads	6 454
155 mm artillery shells - empty	12
155 mm artillery shells - mustard	12 792
155 mm artillery shells - WP a/	45
Al Hussein warhead (GB/GF)	16
Al Hussein warhead - empty	13
R400 bomb	337
250 gauge bomb - oil-filled	5 176
250 gauge bomb - polymust b/	703
250 gauge bomb - empty	12
250 gauge bomb - WP a/	8
500 gauge bomb - oil-filled	4
500 gauge bomb - polymust b/	980
500 gauge bomb - GA	2
DB 2 bomb - unfilled	1 115
DB O bomb - unfilled	61
Total munitions	28 049
Mustard agent	398 046 litres
Nerve agent (GA)	21 365
Nerve agent (GB/GF)	61 633
Total CW agent	481 044 litres

a/ White phosphorus.
b/ Partially filled with polymerized mustard agent.

Description	
DF	14 600 litres
D4	121 675
Thiodiethyleneglycol	153 980
Phosphorus oxychloride	344 800
Thionyl chloride	169 980
Phosphorus trichloride	415 000
Isopropyl alcohol	250 888
Cyclohexanol/isopropyl alcohol	5 200
Dichlorethane	4 120
Di-isopropylamine	30 000
Morpholine	10 000
Chlorobenzaldehyde	41 800
Ethylchlorohydride	1 900
Monoethyleneglycol	49 600
Malononitrile	200
Ethanol	112 700
Thiokolpolysulphide	60
3-hydroxy 2-methyl piperdine	50
Hydrogen sulphide	160
Methanol	42 000
Toluene	10 800
Pyridine	19 000
Total precursor chemicals	1 798 513 litres
Dimethyl amine HCl	238 500 kg
Sodium cyanide	180 000
Potassium cyanide	3 000
Potassium hydrogen di-fluoride	450 000
Sodium fluoride	135 000
Arsenic trichloride	1 850
Hydrogen fluoride	7 000
Mandelic acid	1 650
Tri-ethanolamine	511
Methyl dichloride	2 250
Glycolic acid	50
Diethylaminoethanol thiol HCl	10
2-ethylaminoethanol	180
Chloroacetic acid	2 500
Dimethyl amine	7 210
Methyl iodide	2 000
Potassium fluoride	600
Sodium chloroacetate	250
Aluminium trichloride	2 800
Potassium iodide	3 000
Arsenic trichloride	75
2,4-dichlorophenol	2 250
Trichlorophenol	150
Total chemical precursors	1 040 836 kg

Description	
White phosphorus	648 barrels
Bulk storage containers	32 (2-tonne)

1. Following Iraq's acceptance of Security Council resolution 715 (1991), the work of the Information Assessment Unit has increasingly focused on the implementation of ongoing monitoring and verification. However, this has not been to the exclusion of work on past programmes, where substantial effort has been devoted to verifying Iraq's declarations concerning its former weapons of mass destruction programmes. The Information Assessment Unit also continues to analyse and assess information from supporting Governments and other sources concerning possible outstanding issues in relation to these programmes.

2. The steps under way in the different areas to implement ongoing monitoring and verification are described in detail elsewhere in the present report. However, from the perspective of the Information Assessment Unit, the main practical consequence of Iraq's acceptance of Security Council resolution 715 (1991) has been a vast increase in the amount and content of declarations provided by the Iraqi side. One set of declarations, for example, contained over 2,000 pages of material.

3. The present declarations are being provided in response to draft formats drawn up by the Commission which describe in detail the content and form of the information required for ongoing monitoring and verification. The declarations received in answer to these draft formats require assessment from a number of perspectives. These include reviewing the accuracy of the data supplied and the range and type of facilities declared. The declarations also contain a number of sites not previously inspected by UNSCOM; these need to be identified and preparations for initial inspections undertaken. An additional element of the review process is to assess whether the formats themselves require modification; this is an important aspect of the analysis process, since the final versions of the formats and the consequent declarations constitute an important part of the architecture for ongoing monitoring and verification.

4. In addition to reviewing declarations, a major project has been undertaken within the Information Assessment Unit to compile records for each site to be monitored, drawing upon, *inter alia*, past inspection reports, information from supporting countries and photography. These records will provide the analysts with a comprehensive record of the history of each site undergoing monitoring.

5. Interface with external organizations and other bodies continues to be of great assistance. As an example, over the course of the next six months a new computer system will be installed in the Unit. It will be capable of handling both textual and graphic material, thus provid-

ing a computerized version of the site records described in paragraph 4 above. The system is being developed by an outside agency for the Commission's current requirements and will be capable of adapting to the changing requirements of data handling which will be generated through ongoing monitoring and verification, for example, the development of a system to process the information which will be provided by Iraq and supplier Governments under the export/import control mechanism.

6. The Commission's aerial assets, the high-altitude surveillance aircraft (U-2) and the helicopter-borne Aerial Inspection Team, continue to fulfil their traditional roles. Both assets also provide a useful source of information for preparing for initial inspections at newly declared ongoing monitoring and verification-related sites. The Aerial Inspection Team plays a particularly useful role by preparing site diagrams for new facilities, in advance of ground inspections of the sites.

7. Following the successful introduction of ground-penetrating radar and gamma detection equipment in 1993, the use of additional airborne sensor devices continues to be explored. Further means of exploiting the Commission's current photographic product, as well as potential new sources of material, are being explored. These include the direct transmission of photography.

8. In order to assist with the greater volume of data and to facilitate the establishment of ongoing monitoring and verification, five additional experts have been seconded to the Information Assessment Unit this year. Two new posts have also been created for collators who will act as the interface between the data-entry clerks and the analysts. A second computer expert is also being recruited. In addition to resident experts, the Information Assessment Unit also benefits greatly from short periods of assistance at the Commission by experts familiar with the inspection process.

Appendix V
Inspection schedule
(in-country dates)

Nuclear

15 May-21 May 1991	IAEA1/UNSCOM 1
22 June-3 July 1991	IAEA2/UNSCOM 4
7 July-18 July 1991	IAEA3/UNSCOM 5
27 July-10 August 1991	IAEA4/UNSCOM 6
14 September-20 September 1991	IAEA5/UNSCOM 14
21 September-30 September 1991	IAEA6/UNSCOM 16
11 October-22 October 1991	IAEA7/UNSCOM 19
11 November-18 November 1991	IAEA8/UNSCOM 22
11 January-14 January 1992	IAEA9/UNSCOM 25
5 February-13 February 1992	IAEA10/UNSCOM 27
7 April-15 April 1992	IAEA11/UNSCOM 33

26 May-4 June 1992	IAEA12/UNSCOM 37
14 July-21 July 1992	IAEA13/UNSCOM 41
31 August-7 September 1992	IAEA14/UNSCOM 43
8 November-19 November 1992	IAEA15/UNSCOM 46
6 December-14 December 1992	IAEA16/UNSCOM 47
22 January-27 January 1993	IAEA17/UNSCOM 49
3 March-11 March 1993	IAEA18/UNSCOM 52
30 April-7 May 1993	IAEA19/UNSCOM 56
25 June-30 June 1993	IAEA20/UNSCOM 58
23 July-28 July 1993	IAEA21/UNSCOM 61
1 November-9 November 1993	IAEA22/UNSCOM 64
4 February-11 February 1994	IAEA23/UNSCOM 68
11 April-22 April 1994	IAEA24/UNSCOM 73
21 June-1 July 1994	IAEA25/UNSCOM 83

Chemical

9 June-15 June 1991	CW1/UNSCOM 2
15 August-22 August 1991	CW2/UNSCOM 9
31 August-8 September 1991	CW3/UNSCOM 11
31 August-5 September 1991	CW4/UNSCOM 12
6 October-9 November 1991	CW5/UNSCOM 17
22 October-2 November 1991	CW6/UNSCOM 20
18 November-1 December 1991	CBW1/UNSCOM 21
27 January-5 February 1992	CW7/UNSCOM 26
21 February-24 March 1992	CDG1/UNSCOM 29
5 April-13 April 1992	CDG2/UNSCOM 32
15 April-29 April 1992	CW8/UNSCOM 35
18 June 1992 ongoing	CDG/UNSCOM 38
26 June-10 July 1992	CBW2/UNSCOM 39
21 September-29 September 1992	CW9/UNSCOM 44
6 December-14 December 1992	CBW3/UNSCOM 47
6 April-18 April 1993	CW10/UNSCOM 55
27 June-30 June 1993	CW11/UNSCOM 59
19 November-22 November 1993	CW12/UNSCOM 65
1 February-14 February 1994	CW13/UNSCOM 67
20 March-26 March 1994	CW14/UNSCOM 70
18 April-22 April 1994	CW15/UNSCOM 74
25 May-5 June 1994	CW16/UNSCOM 75
31 May-12 June 1994	CW17/UNSCOM 76
8 June-14 June 1994	CW18/UNSCOM 77

Biological

2 August-8 August 1991	BW1/UNSCOM 7
20 September-3 October 1991	BW2/UNSCOM 15
11 March-18 March 1993	BW3/UNSCOM 53
8 April-26 April 1994	BW4/UNSCOM 72
28 May-7 June 1994	BW5/UNSCOM 78
24 June-5 July 1994	BW6/UNSCOM 84
5 June-8 June 1994	BW7/UNSCOM 86

Ballistic missiles

30 June-7 July 1991	BM1/UNSCOM 3
18 July-20 July 1991	BM2/UNSCOM 10

Ballistic missiles (continued)		Special missions
8 August-15 August 1991	BM3/UNSCOM 8	30 June-3 July 1991
6 September-13 September 1991	BM4/UNSCOM 13	11 August-14 August 1991
1 October-9 October 1991	BM5/UNSCOM 18	4 October-6 October 1991
1 December-9 December 1991	BM6/UNSCOM 23	11 November-15 November 1991
9 December-17 December 1991	BM7/UNSCOM 24	27 January-30 January 1992
21 February-29 February 1992	BM8/UNSCOM 28	21 February-24 February 1992
21 March-29 March 1992	BM9/UNSCOM 31	17 July-19 July 1992
13 April-21 April 1992	BM10/UNSCOM 34	28 July-29 July 1992
14 May-22 May 1992	BM11/UNSCOM 36	6 September-12 September 1992
11 July-29 July 1992	BM12/UNSCOM 40 A+B	4 November-9 November 1992
7 August-18 August 1992	BM13/UNSCOM 42	4 November-8 November 1992
16 October-30 October 1992	BM14/UNSCOM 45	12 March-18 March 1993
25 January-23 March 1993	IMT1a/UNSCOM 48	14 March-20 March 1993
12 February-21 February 1993	BM15/UNSCOM 50	19 April-24 April 1993
22 February-23 February 1993	BM16/UNSCOM 51	4 June-5 July 1993
27 March-17 May 1993	IMT1b/UNSCOM 54	15 July-19 July 1993
5 June-28 June 1993	IMT1c/UNSCOM 57	25 July-5 August 1993
10 July-11 July 1993	BM17/UNSCOM 60	9 August-12 August 1993
24 August-15 September 1993	BM18/UNSCOM 62	10 September-24 September 1993
28 September-1 November 1993	BM19/UNSCOM 63	27 September-1 October 1993
21 January-29 January 1994	BM20/UNSCOM 66	1 October-8 October 1993
17 February-25 February 1994	BM21/UNSCOM 69	5 October 1993-16 February 1994
30 March-20 May 1994	BM22/UNSCOM 71	2 December-10 December 1993
20 May-8 June 1994	BM23/UNSCOM 79	2 December-16 December 1993
10 June-24 June 1994	BM24/UNSCOM 80	21 January-27 January 1994
14 June-19 June 1994	BM25/UNSCOM 81	2 February-6 February 1994
		10 April-14 April 1994
Computer search		24 April-26 April 1994
12 February 1992	UNSCOM 30	28 May-29 May 1994

Document 190

Sixth semi-annual report (for the period from 18 December 1993 to 17 June 1994) on the implementation by the IAEA of the plan for the destruction, removal or rendering harmless of items listed in paragraph 12 of Security Council resolution 687 (1991)

S/1994/793, 5 July 1994

Note by the Secretary-General

The Secretary-General has the honour to transmit to the Security Council the attached communication of 15 June 1994, which he has received from the Director General of the International Atomic Energy Agency (IAEA).

Annex

Letter dated 15 June 1994 from the Director General of the International Atomic Energy Agency addressed to the Secretary-General

United Nations Security Council resolution 699 (1991), approved on 17 June 1991, requests, *inter alia*, the

Secretary-General to submit to the Security Council progress reports on the implementation of the plan for the destruction, removal or rendering harmless of the items specified in paragraph 12 of resolution 687 (1991). Such reports are to be submitted every six months after the adoption of resolution 699 (1991). The next report is therefore due on 17 June 1994.

Please find attached an outline of the activities carried out by the IAEA during the past six months under the plan for the destruction, removal or rendering harmless, which you might find useful for the preparation of your report.

(Signed) Hans BLIX

Appendix
Sixth semi-annual report (covering the period 18 December 1993 – 17 June 1994) on the implementation by the IAEA of the plan for the destruction, removal or rendering harmless of items listed in paragraph 12 of Security Council resolution 687 (1991)

Introduction

By resolution 699 of 17 June 1991, the Security Council approved the plan submitted by the International Atomic Energy Agency (IAEA), through the Secretary-General, for the destruction, removal or rendering harmless of all items listed in paragraph 12 of Security Council resolution 687 (1991). Resolution 699 also called for the Secretary-General to submit every six months a progress report on the implementation of the plan.

The first five reports were circulated by the Secretary-General to the members of the Security Council in Document S/23295, dated 17 December 1991; S/24110, dated 17 June 1992; S/24988, dated 17 December 1992; S/25983, dated 21 June 1993; S/26897, dated 20 December 1993.

This is the sixth semi-annual report on the implementation by the IAEA of the plan for destruction, removal or rendering harmless covering the period from 18 December 1993 to 17 June 1994. During this period, the IAEA, with the assistance and cooperation of the Special Commission of the United Nations, conducted two on-site inspections in Iraq (IAEA-23 and IAEA-24), detailed reports of which have been distributed to the Security Council. 1/

Present status

As of 17 June 1994, the IAEA has carried out twenty-four missions in Iraq. The major activities related to destruction, removal and rendering harmless of proscribed items involved equipment, materials (nuclear and non-nuclear), components, instrumentation, dedicated buildings, plants and their auxiliaries, directly connected with Iraq's past activities in the field of uranium isotopic enrichment, plutonium separation and nuclear weapons design and development.

The IAEA and the Special Commission continued the high-level technical discussions with Iraq with a view to facilitating the full implementation of the plans for ongoing monitoring and verification in Iraq. Since the last report, meetings have been held in Baghdad (in February and April), New York (in March and May) and Vienna (in May).

In the course of the high-level technical talks, the Iraqi Government continued to press for the submission of reports by the IAEA and the Special Commission which would permit the Security Council to consider the lifting of the oil embargo, in accordance with paragraph 22 of Security Council resolution 687 (1991).

In the present phase of work, most of the activities carried out in Iraq by the IAEA under the relevant Security Council resolutions relate to the establishment of procedures for the full implementation of the ongoing monitoring and verification plan approved in Security Council resolution 715 (1991).

Direct-Use Material

Irradiated Fuel

The second and final consignment of irradiated enriched uranium fuel was successfully packaged and shipped from Iraq at the conclusion of IAEA-23. The remaining irradiated fuel, which had been stored at Location B and at the IRT-5000 reactor site was cleaned and transferred to four shielded transport flasks. The flasks were then tested, sealed and loaded into containers and transported, by road, to Habbaniya Airport on 11 February 1994. IAEA radiation protection staff were in attendance throughout the exercise and an ICAO/IATA Dangerous Cargo Inspector was present to review the documentation and inspect the loaded flasks and ancillary equipment which were loaded onto an Antonov 124 on 12 March and flown to Ekaterinburg the same day.

This shipment completed the task of removing all of the direct weapons-usable nuclear material from Iraq. In accordance with the contract with Minatom, for the removal and disposition of the fuel, the irradiated fuel will be chemically treated to separate the enriched uranium from the radioactive wastes and plutonium. The radioactive waste and plutonium will be embedded in a glass matrix and permanently stored at a Russian repository, while the recovered enriched uranium will be iso-

1/ Documents S/1994/355, dated 25 March 1994, and S/1994/650, dated 1 June 1994.

topically diluted to less than 20% enrichment and kept at the disposal of the IAEA.

Other Nuclear Material

Nuclear source material is not included in the items to be destroyed, removed or rendered harmless under UN Security Council resolution 687 (1991). However, complete knowledge of uranium stocks is essential for a meaningful implementation of the IAEA ongoing monitoring and verification.

The process of gathering and consolidating, in a single location, all nuclear source material (such as uranium concentrates and other uranium compounds) existing in Iraq has continued during the last two inspections. As regards further verification of Iraqi declarations concerning such material, the IAEA is in contact with the Brazilian authorities to verify the amount of uranium oxide of Brazilian origin shipped to Iraq in the early eighties.

Installations, Equipment and Other Materials Relevant to Enriched Uranium Production and to Weaponizing Activities

As indicated in the previous report, the Iraqi authorities have submitted an updated list of material, equipment and other items in Iraq identified in Annex 3 of the Agency's plan for future ongoing monitoring and verification of Iraq's compliance with paragraph 12 of part C of Security Council resolution 687 (1991). Verification of the correctness and assessment of the completeness of the list, begun in the course of the eighteenth inspection, is continuing. A description of the verification activities carried out during IAEA-23 and IAEA-24 is set out in the detailed reports of these two missions. None of the newly included items which have been verified have fallen in the category of proscribed items that are required to be destroyed, removed or rendered harmless under Security Council resolution 687 (1991).

Items identified in IAEA document INFCIRC/209/Rev.1 and its annex are incorporated by reference in Annex 3, item 4 of the IAEA ongoing monitoring and verification plan and are therefore required to be reported by Iraq to the IAEA. INFCIRC/209/Rev.1, established by the Nuclear Suppliers Group (NSG), is a list of equipment or material especially designed or prepared for the processing, use or production of special fissionable material. This document was expanded by the NSG to include additional items related to the production of special fissionable material (INFCIRC/209/Rev.1/Mod.2). A copy of the revision was handed to the Iraqi authorities in Baghdad during the course of the high level technical talks. By letter dated 13 June 1994, the IAEA formally communicated to the Iraqi authorities the text of the document and advised them that any change, amendment or addition to INFCIRC/209/Rev.1, including the Annex to it, are incorporated automatically into Annex 3 of the plan and have the same binding effect on the Iraqi reporting requirements under Annex 3 of the IAEA plan. The Iraqi authorities were advised accordingly that all additional items listed in INFCIRC/209/Rev.1/Mod.2 must be reported in the next periodical update of the list of Annex 3 items.

Future actions

Under the contract concluded with the Russian Ministry for Atomic Energy, all the irradiated fuel assemblies removed from Iraq will be reprocessed to recover the highly enriched uranium. The latter will be isotopically diluted to less than 20% enrichment by blending it with natural or depleted uranium. The radioactive waste resulting from reprocessing will be adequately conditioned and permanently stored in a waste repository, as will the resulting separated plutonium.

Efforts will continue toward resolving remaining uncertainties in the nuclear material inventory and the nuclear material flow chart submitted by the Iraqi authorities.

Verification of the correctness and assessment of the completeness of the revised list of items submitted pursuant to Annex 3 of the plan for future ongoing monitoring will continue.

Document 191

Letter from the Secretary-General to the President of the Security Council transmitting a letter sent by the Secretary-General to 20 Governments requesting information on any Iraqi petroleum imported by their countries on or after 1 June 1990

S/1994/907, 30 July 1994

Letter dated 11 July 1994 from the Secretary-General to the President of the Security Council

I have the honour to refer to the letter dated 11 May 1994 which the then President of the Security Council addressed to me concerning the financial emergency of the United Nations Compensation Commission (S/1994/567).

Having considered the matter further, I have come to the conclusion that the most effective way of obtaining the information required about exports of Iraqi petroleum and petroleum products immediately before the imposition of sanctions by the Security Council on 6 August 1990 will be to address the Governments with jurisdiction over the relevant petroleum companies and their subsidiaries.

I accordingly enclose, for the information of the Security Council, the text of a letter which, with minor variations, I have sent to the Governments of the following Member States: Belgium, Brazil, Canada, Croatia, Federal Republic of Yugoslavia (Serbia and Montenegro), France, Germany, Greece, India, Italy, Japan, Netherlands, Portugal, Russian Federation, Singapore, Spain, Thailand, Turkey, United Kingdom, United States.

(Signed) Boutros BOUTROS-GHALI

Annex
Letter dated 11 July 1994 by the Secretary-General

I should like to refer to Security Council resolution 778 (1992) which, as you will recall, was adopted because of the Government of Iraq's continued refusal to accept resolutions 706 (1991) and 712 (1991). By the latter resolutions the Council permitted the export by Iraq of a limited amount of petroleum which was to be used to finance the purchase of humanitarian goods for the Iraqi civilian population and to meet some of the financial obligations of Iraq arising from its illegal invasion and occupation of Kuwait. Included in those obligations was the payment of claims for any direct loss, damage or injury to foreign Governments, nationals and corporations sustained as a result of Iraq's aggression.

In its resolution 778 (1992) the Council decided that all States in which there were funds of the Government of Iraq, or its State bodies, corporations or agencies, that represented the proceeds of sale of Iraqi petroleum or petroleum products, paid for by or on behalf of the purchaser on or after 6 August 1990 (the date of the imposition of sanctions), should cause the transfer of those funds as soon as possible into an escrow account provided for in resolutions 706 (1991) and 712 (1991).

On 26 October 1992, as requested by resolution 778 (1992), I asked Governments to provide all relevant information that would assist in identifying assets relating to Iraqi petroleum or petroleum products [note verbale SCPC/1/92(12)]. As of this date, I have received information about approximately $1 billion in Iraqi assets subject to the provisions of resolution 778 (1992). However, less than $160 million representing Iraqi frozen oil assets or proceeds from the sale of oil have been deposited to the aforementioned escrow account.

I should also like to refer to my letter of 28 April 1994 (S/1994/566) to the President of the Security Council in which I drew the Council's attention to my concern over the emergency which the United Nations Compensation Commission is facing as a result of its lack of sufficient funds to pay awards to some of the victims of Iraq's invasion of Kuwait which are expected to be issued in October 1994. Those awards will amount to approximately $200 million. Thirty per cent of oil-related funds deposited to the escrow account referred to in resolution 778 (1992) was to be designated for the Compensation Fund.

In my letter to the Security Council I also noted that it was likely that the amount of $1 billion referred to above did not include all Iraqi petroleum and petroleum products exported immediately preceding the imposition of sanctions by the Security Council and for which payment would not have been completed when the sanctions took effect on 6 August 1990. According to oil industry sources, the value of such petroleum and petroleum products may amount to hundreds of millions of dollars. These funds fall under the provisions of resolution 778 (1992) relating to the reporting of petroleum assets subject to transfer to the escrow account. On 11 May 1994, the Security Council agreed to my offer to seek information directly from oil companies in order to identify those funds and to arrange for their transfer to the escrow account.

As your country was one of the principal importers of Iraqi crude petroleum in 1990 (according to the Energy Statistics Yearbook), I should be grateful if you would kindly seek all relevant information from petroleum companies and their subsidiaries under your jurisdiction regarding the whereabouts and amounts of any Iraqi petroleum and petroleum products imported by those companies on or after 1 June 1990. Such information should include the description and quantity of the petroleum and petroleum products as well as their respective values on an FOB and CIF basis. Complete information should also be provided on the disposition of the proceeds of the sale of such petroleum or petroleum products.

I would be most grateful if the requested information could be communicated to me by 30 August 1994.

(Signed) Boutros BOUTROS-GHALI

Document 192

Report of the Secretary-General on UNIKOM for the period from 1 April to 29 September 1994

S/1994/1111, 29 September 1994

I. *Introduction*

1. By paragraph 5 of its resolution 687 (1991) of 3 April 1991, the Security Council established a demilitarized zone (DMZ) along the Iraq-Kuwait boundary and decided to set up an observer unit with the following tasks: to monitor the Khawr Abd Allah waterway and the DMZ; to deter violations of the boundary through its presence in and surveillance of the DMZ; and to observe any potentially hostile action mounted from the territory of one State into the other. By its resolution 689 (1991) of 9 April 1991, the Security Council approved the report of the Secretary-General on the implementation of the above provisions (S/22454). And by its resolution 806 (1993), the Council expanded the tasks of the United Nations Iraq-Kuwait Observation Mission (UNIKOM) to include the capacity to take physical action to prevent or redress small-scale violations of the DMZ or the boundary.

2. By its resolution 689 (1991), the Security Council noted that UNIKOM could be terminated only by a decision of the Council, and decided to review the question of the termination or continuation as well as the modalities of the Mission every six months. The purpose of the present report is to provide the Security Council, prior to its forthcoming review, with an overview of the activities of UNIKOM during the last six months.

II. *Organization*

3. Major-General Krishna N. S. Thapa (Nepal) continued as Force Commander. The composition and strength of the Mission is detailed below:

Military observers

Argentina	6	Malaysia	7
Austria	7	Nigeria	6
Bangladesh	9	Pakistan	7
Canada	5	Poland	6
China	15	Romania	7
Denmark	6	Russian Federation	15
Fiji	7	Senegal	6
Finland	6	Singapore	7
France	15	Sweden	6
Ghana	6	Thailand	6
Greece	7	Turkey	6
Hungary	6	United Kingdom of	
India	6	Great Britain and	
Indonesia	7	Northern Ireland	15
Ireland	7	United States of America	15
Italy	6	Uruguay	6
Kenya	7	Venezuela	2
		Total	245

Infantry battalion (Bangladesh)	775

Support units

Engineers (Argentina)	50
Logistic unit (Denmark)	45
Medical unit (Austria 12/Bangladesh 16)	28
Total	123
Total number of military personnel	1 143

Civilian personnel

International staff	81
Locally recruited staff	130
Total number of civilian personnel	211

4. In view of its commitments in other United Nations peace-keeping operations, the Government of Norway has withdrawn its military observers from UNIKOM. The Government of Austria has informed me that it will not be able to maintain its medical unit in the Mission. At my request, it has agreed to keep it there until February 1995 to allow sufficient time for obtaining a replacement.

5. In my last report (S/1994/388), I mentioned that the activities of the Argentine engineers were limited by the shortage of equipment which the Government of Kuwait had undertaken to supply. The equipment has now been delivered, provided by Kuwait as a voluntary contribution at no cost to the United Nations.

6. UNIKOM's air support comprised two small fixed-wing aircraft contributed by the Government of Switzerland at no cost to the United Nations, and three chartered helicopters. The Mission also had the use of a chartered AN-26 aircraft for the movement of personnel and equipment between Umm Qasr, Kuwait City and Baghdad. The Government of Switzerland has recently informed me that it will not be able to provide the two fixed-wing aircraft beyond the end of 1994.

7. UNIKOM's headquarters is in Umm Qasr. It maintains liaison offices in Baghdad and Kuwait City and a logistic base at Doha. The latter is currently being moved to facilities in Kuwait City, which it will share with the liaison office.

III. *Concept of operations*

8. For operational purposes, the DMZ remains divided into three sectors (North, Central and South), as shown in the attached map [not reproduced here]. UNIKOM's concept of operations is based on surveillance, control, investigation and liaison. Surveillance of the DMZ is based on patrol and observation bases, ground and air patrols, and observation points. Control operations include static checkpoints, random checks and maintenance of a force mobile reserve. Investigation teams are maintained at the level of both sector and UNIKOM headquarters, and continuous liaison is carried out at all levels.

9. The military observers perform UNIKOM's main patrol, observation, investigation and liaison activities. The infantry battalion is deployed in a main camp at Camp Khor, a company camp at Al-Abdaly and platoon camps in the South and Central Sectors. It performs armed patrols within the sectors and provides a mobile reserve, which is deployed as necessary in sensitive situations. The battalion also operates checkpoints at the border-crossing sites and conducts random checks in cooperation with Iraqi and Kuwaiti liaison officers. Since late May 1994, the battalion has manned the easternmost patrol and observation base (N-6) on the Iraqi side of the DMZ. It also provides security for UNIKOM personnel and installations where and when necessary.

IV. *Situation in the demilitarized zone*

10. During the period under review, the situation in the DMZ was very calm. There was a noticeable increase in farming, oil exploration and exploitation, as well as in maintenance and construction works on both sides of the border. Increased shipping and fishing were observed in the Khawr Abd Allah.

11. The completion of the Kuwaiti border trench and earthen embankment established a physical barrier between the two sides, creating an obstacle to unauthorized border crossing and thereby contributing to the overall quiet in the border area. Kuwait has also constructed an asphalt road along the full length of the border, parallel to the trench. This road has improved UNIKOM's mobility.

12. There were only very few and minor violations of the DMZ during the period under review, namely one overflight by a military aircraft and five violations involving weapons other than side-arms. No ground violations by military personnel or border crossings resulting in serious incidents were observed. UNIKOM took up each violation with the party concerned for appropriate action. Iraq and Kuwait each submitted two written complaints; they were investigated.

13. A serious incident occurred on 12 August when three members of the infantry battalion patrolling the DMZ in their vehicle on the Iraqi side of the border, north of Safwan, were ambushed by an unknown and unidentified number of assailants armed with automatic weapons. One Bangladesh soldier was shot and killed. The others escaped, one with a gunshot wound to the leg and the other with minor injuries. The assailants took the vehicle, two rifles and some equipment. The Iraqi authorities expressed their deep regret at the incident, promised to do whatever they could to apprehend the attackers and stepped up their security measures in the DMZ. They later recovered the vehicle, together with another vehicle stolen earlier, both completely stripped of their contents, and returned them to UNIKOM. Following the incident, UNIKOM temporarily replaced night patrols of unarmed military observers by armed infantry patrols. The attackers have so far not been apprehended.

14. UNIKOM continued to provide support to other United Nations agencies in Iraq and Kuwait. The Mission maintained administrative supervision of the Administrative Unit in Baghdad, which provided administrative and logistic support to other United Nations agencies in Iraq. It provided movement control in respect of all United Nations aircraft operating in the area, as well as medical evacuation assistance to the United Nations Guards Contingent in Iraq. It provided support to the United Nations Coordinator for the Return of Property from Iraq to Kuwait; to the International Maritime

Organization during its survey of the Khawr Abd Allah in June; and to a team which inspected and carried out maintenance work on the boundary markers in April/May. UNIKOM has now assumed responsibility for maintaining the boundary markers.

V. *Financial aspects*

15. The General Assembly, by its resolution 48/242 of 5 April 1994, authorized me to enter into commitments up to the amount of $5.5 million gross ($5,312,800 net) per month for the maintenance of UNIKOM for the period from 1 May to 31 October 1994, subject to the review by the Security Council of the Mandate of the Mission. The amount is inclusive of the two-thirds share to be met through voluntary contributions from the Government of Kuwait.

16. For the period from 1 November 1994 to 31 March 1995, the General Assembly decided, on an experimental basis, that I may enter into commitments at the same level each month for the maintenance of UNIKOM, subject to the review by the Security Council and to the prior concurrence of the Advisory Committee on Administrative and Budgetary Questions. One third of the full amount authorized for this period is to be assessed on Member States, and two thirds is to be met

through the voluntary contribution of Kuwait. Subject to the Security Council's review, I shall report to the Advisory Committee and the General Assembly at its forty-ninth session on the additional requirements for maintaining UNIKOM.

17. As at 21 September 1994, unpaid assessed contributions to the Special Account for UNIKOM for the period since the inception of the Mission amounted to $27,715,131. The total unpaid assessed contributions for all peace-keeping operations amounted to $1.9 billion.

VI. *Observations*

18. UNIKOM has continued to exercise a high degree of vigilance and through its patrols and liaison activities has contributed to the calm which has prevailed along the Iraq-Kuwait border. In carrying out its functions, UNIKOM has enjoyed the effective cooperation of the Iraqi and Kuwaiti authorities. It is my recommendation that the Mission be maintained.

19. In conclusion, I wish to pay tribute to the Force Commander and the men and women under his command for the manner in which they have carried out their task. Their discipline and bearing have been of a high order, reflecting credit on themselves, on their countries and on the United Nations.

Document 193

Sixth report of the Secretary-General on the status of the implementation of the plan for the ongoing monitoring and verification of Iraq's compliance with relevant parts of section C of Security Council resolution 687 (1991)

S/1994/1138, 7 October 1994

I. *Introduction*

1. The present report is the sixth submitted pursuant to paragraph 8 of Security Council resolution 715 (1991) which requests the Secretary-General to submit a report to the Council every six months on the implementation of the Special Commission's plan for ongoing monitoring and verification of Iraq's compliance with relevant parts of section C of Security Council resolution 687 (1991). 1/

2. The present report marks a very important stage in the evolution of the Commission's mandate. It is particularly detailed in order to support the conclusion contained in chapter VI below that the Commission's ongoing monitoring and verification system is provisionally operational. While certain elements are not yet in place, so much of the preparatory work is complete, with

gaps being filled for the time being by use of alternative measures, that the Commission can with confidence commence the testing of the thoroughness and efficacy of its

1/ The present report updates the information contained in the first five reports, circulated as documents S/23801, S/24661, S/25620, S/26684 and S/1994/489. Further information concerning developments relating to the implementation of the plan is contained in the reports to the Security Council contained in documents S/1994/520, S/1994/750 and S/1994/860. The first is a joint statement issued at the conclusion of the high-level talks, held at Baghdad from 24 to 26 April 1994, between the Special Commission and the International Atomic Energy Agency (IAEA) on the one hand and Iraq on the other. The second is the sixth report provided in accordance with paragraph 3 of resolution 699 (1991), appendix II of which covers in detail the array of ongoing monitoring and verification activities undertaken by the Commission in the period from December 1993 to June 1994. The third is the text of a letter sent to the President of the Security Council and subsequently circulated on the instructions of the President. It contains, in the appendix, the joint statement issued at the end of the July 1994 high-level talks and an assessment of how the process of establishing ongoing monitoring and verification was proceeding at that time.

system. The remaining elements should be in place shortly.

II. *Concept of operations*

3. The attachment to document S/1994/341 outlined the Commission's operational concept for implementing its plan for ongoing monitoring and verification as contained in document S/22871/Rev.1. In brief, the concept is based on regular inspection of facilities of concern, on an inventory of all dual-purpose items (i.e. those which have permitted uses but which could be used for the acquisition of banned weapons) and on following the fate of all inventoried items. Underpinning the inspections and the establishment and maintenance of accurate inventories will be a full array of interlocking activities: aerial surveillance with a variety of sensors, remote sensors, tags and seals, a variety of detection technologies, information obtained from other sources, and, when sanctions on the dual-purpose items are lifted, notifications under the export/import control mechanism. No one of those elements on its own would suffice to provide confidence in the system but together they should constitute the most comprehensive international monitoring system ever established in the sphere of arms control. Confidence in its effectiveness will rely, *inter alia*, on the following:

(a) Possession by the Commission of a full picture of Iraq's past programmes and full accounting of the facilities, equipment, items and materials associated with those past programmes, in conjunction with full knowledge of the disposition of dual-purpose items currently available to Iraq. That information provides the baseline data from which ongoing monitoring and verification proceeds. Uncertainties relating to the accuracy or completeness of those data will feed through into uncertainties as to whether the ongoing monitoring and verification system is indeed monitoring all the items that should be monitored. This, in turn, would entail more inspections to obtain the data required to provide confidence in the system. This information is primarily obtained from Iraq's declarations, required under resolutions 687 (1991), 707 (1991) and 715 (1991), and through the Commission's inspection and analysis activities. Iraq is required to update its declarations on its dual-purpose activities and capabilities every six months;

(b) Completion of comprehensive monitoring and verification protocols for each site at which monitoring will be conducted as a consequence of the dual-purpose items present or activities undertaken there. These protocols are the product of the baseline inspection process, that is, inspections for the purposes of familiarization, tagging and inventorying, sensor installation and protocol-building as necessary. They provide the basis for future ongoing monitoring and verification activities at the specified site;

(c) Successful testing of the system of ongoing monitoring and verification in order to:

(i) Establish a clear understanding and practice of how the elements of the system, including the actions required of Iraq, should operate;

(ii) Evaluate the effectiveness of its elements both individually and as a whole.

While the system is premised on the provision by Iraq of accurate and complete declarations of its dual-purpose activities and capabilities and cannot be operated at its most effective and least intrusive without such full declarations, it has also been designed to be robust. Experience has shown that, even when initially presented with inadequate declarations, the Commission has been able, through the deployment of its various resources and the exercise of its inspection rights, to elicit the information required for the system to be established. However, should Iraq seek systematically to block the work of the Commission by, for example, preventing access to sites, the Commission would not be able to provide the Security Council with the assurances it seeks concerning Iraq's compliance with the terms of paragraph 10 of resolution 687 (1991). If such a case were to arise, the Commission would immediately inform the Council.

4. Once the sanctions imposed on Iraq under resolution 661 (1990) are eased or lifted in accordance with paragraph 21 of resolution 687 (1991) to the extent that the export to Iraq of dual-purpose items is again permitted, a further essential element of the overall monitoring of Iraq's dual-purpose capabilities will be the export/import mechanism envisaged under paragraph 7 of resolution 715 (1991).

III. *Actions to implement the plan*

5. Implementation of the plan is predicated on the Commission's obtaining full accounting for Iraq's past capabilities and full information on current dual-purpose activities and capabilities in Iraq. However, until 26 November 1993, Iraq failed to acknowledge its obligations under resolution 715 (1991) and the plans for ongoing monitoring and verification approved thereunder and, until that time, made no declarations in accordance with the requirements of the plans. It also impeded or blocked certain activities it deemed to be of a monitoring nature. Thus, in the circumstances that prevailed until Iraq's acknowledgement, while the Commission undertook much preparatory work, it was in no position to initiate its plan.

6. Once Iraq's formal acceptance of the resolution, adopted on 11 October 1991, was obtained on 26 No-

vember 1993, the Commission, while continuing efforts to elucidate all aspects of Iraq's past programmes, immediately reallocated the bulk of its resources to the establishment, as soon as feasible, of the system of ongoing monitoring and verification. In addition, the Commission added substantially to its staff in New York in order to ensure that personnel restrictions did not become a significant delaying factor in this process. This reallocation and increase of resources is amply demonstrated by the fact that, in the 30 months to November 1993, the Commission conducted 44 inspections, whereas, in the 10 months since then, the Commission conducted or initiated 29 inspections, of which all but 5 were directly related to the establishment of ongoing monitoring and verification.

7. The concept of operations and the numbers of inspections conducted show that establishment of the ongoing monitoring and verification system is a complex and large undertaking. It has entailed inspection of entire categories of sites and industries not previously visited by Commission personnel. This has required the Commission to adapt as follows:

(a) The new inspections called for expertise not previously used by the Commission and not available to it from amongst its own staff. Consequently, the Commission drew upon the resources of a large number of Member States to ensure that it was able to conduct its operations to the highest standards. Even so, in several areas the expertise could not be found from amongst the employees of supporting Governments and so had to be obtained through the recruitment of specialists from private industry;

(b) New methods needed to be developed for the conduct of baseline inspections and to assess the feasibility of monitoring methods;

(c) New applications of technologies had to be developed to serve the monitoring needs identified in the baseline inspection process.

8. The specific steps undertaken to establish and operate the system of ongoing monitoring and verification since 26 November 1993 are described in detail in annex I to document S/1994/489 and in annex I to the present report. The following paragraphs summarize the current status of those activities.

A. *Knowledge about past programmes*

9. The Commission's understanding of Iraq's past programmes has grown considerably during the past six months as a result of improvements in Iraq's declarations and of the inspection and analytical efforts of the Commission. As a result, the Commission is approaching a full understanding of those past programmes.

10. A full picture of Iraq's past programmes in relation to proscribed weapons is important as it provides a crucial part of the baseline information from which ongoing monitoring and verification proceeds. It is essential to verify Iraq's declarations if one is to have confidence in those baseline data and hence in the system built on them. Efforts to verify the information provided by Iraq, particularly that concerning foreign supplies, are ongoing. Given that Iraq has provided only limited documentation (claiming all documentation relating to its past programmes has been destroyed), those efforts have had to rely on the Commission's inspection activities, on interrogation of Iraqi personnel involved in the programmes and on contacts with the Governments of the declared or presumed suppliers. Through that process, the Commission has obtained additional information, which itself needed further investigation, including data concerning the disposition of production equipment and the acquisition and use of items and materials for the programmes, some of which revealed inconsistencies in Iraq's declarations. While those efforts helped to close gaps in Iraq's declarations of its past programmes and to verify other aspects declared but not previously supported by corroborating evidence, further actions are required by Iraq to provide all the necessary data. In that regard, follow-through on Iraq's commitment, expressed on numerous occasions, to cooperate in providing further complementary information and clarifications concerning its past programmes is essential in arriving at the full picture of those programmes referred to above and thus in building full confidence in the monitoring system.

B. *Iraq's declarations on current capabilities*

11. The situation is much improved from that which prevailed in November 1993 when Iraq, upon accepting the terms of resolution 715 (1991), announced that its previous reports entitled "Information and data related to the ongoing monitoring and verification plan" should be "considered to have been made and submitted in conformity with the provisions of resolution 715 (1991) and the plans approved thereunder". The Commission at that time responded that those previous reports were deficient in many regards and could not be considered as initial declarations under the plans, nor did they constitute a sufficient basis for the proper planning and implementation of ongoing monitoring and verification.

12. The Commission has since obtained a great deal of information about Iraq's dual-purpose activities and capabilities, enough to commence ongoing monitoring and verification. However, some of Iraq's declarations in this regard are still incomplete. Iraq needs to improve these declarations. There are gaps and discrep-

ancies in each area, which the Commission has endeavoured to resolve. Great difficulties were faced in obtaining the necessary data, particularly in the biological area. The process being pursued by the Commission to overcome them is illustrative of the process pursued in the other areas. Chapter III of annex I describes this in detail.

13. During the discussions in New York in September 1994 between the Commission and a high-level Iraqi delegation led by the Deputy Prime Minister of Iraq, Mr. Tariq Aziz, the Commission indicated areas where further information was required in this regard. Subsequent follow-up action is continuing in Iraq at the expert level in the course of inspection and ongoing monitoring and verification activities. Methods have been suggested by the Commission whereby information required for monitoring could be obtained. The Commission has received assurances that the missing information will be provided.

14. The complexity and size of the task of establishing the system of ongoing monitoring and verification is reflected in the difficulties encountered by the Commission in obtaining and by Iraq in gathering the required information. In large part, these difficulties can be ascribed to the fact that the Commission's ongoing monitoring and verification activities are taking it to sites it has not visited before and hence into contact with Iraqi personnel who have not previously had to deal with the Commission. Further efforts, primarily by Iraq, whose obligation it is to provide complete declarations, but also by the Commission in clarifying the requirements of the plan, are required to educate the Iraqi officials concerned. This should rectify the situation in the coming months.

C. *Baseline inspections*

15. The purpose of baseline inspections is to assess whether a site requires monitoring and, if so, to make recommendations on how monitoring should be conducted at the sites in question, on the items to be tagged and on the installation of monitoring devices. The end product of the baseline process, after decisions have been made on these recommendations, are site monitoring and verification protocols for each site to be monitored. Such protocols contain all information about the site and its contacts with other organizations of relevance to the Commission's monitoring activities.

16. A total of 27 inspection teams, in addition to numerous visits by smaller groups of specialists in sensor technologies, have conducted activities related to the acquisition of the baseline information. While that process will never be complete, in that the system will evolve continually in response to changes in Iraq's industrial base and developments in relevant technologies (e.g. development of new processes for the production of banned

items or materials or of new monitoring technologies), the Commission now has the information necessary to prepare usable monitoring and verification protocols for all the sites to be subjected to regular monitoring.

17. In the missile area, that process is most advanced. All the protocols currently envisaged have been prepared, that is, for some 30 sites. In the chemical area, the baseline inspections have been completed and the Commission's staff in New York are currently using the data from those inspections to prepare some 50 protocols. Those for the most important sites have already been completed. In the biological area, while gaps remain in the information provided about dual-purpose capabilities and further inspections are planned to address the matter, the Commission has completed its protocol-building inspections and hopes soon to have sufficient information to prepare the protocols currently envisaged, that is, some 75 protocols.

D. *Installation of sensors and tags*

18. The conduct of baseline inspections has given the Commission the information it requires to make decisions on the types of tags and monitoring sensors to be used in the ongoing monitoring and verification system in general and on how many and where they should be deployed. Tagging of all identified dual-purpose items and permitted short-range missiles and installation of sensors has been completed in the missile area. In the chemical area, four chemical air-sampling devices have been installed at one site. There are plans to install a further 20 such samplers in addition to monitoring cameras and flow meters. All identified relevant dual-purpose items in the chemical area have been tagged. In the biological area, tagging of all identified items is still proceeding—a team is currently in Iraq to pursue this. A comprehensive plan for the installation and operation of remote-controlled monitoring cameras at key biological sites has been prepared by a team sent to Iraq to study the feasibility of remote-controlled sensors in biological facilities. The Commission has identified funds and equipment to proceed with the plan, which it intends to do shortly. In its efforts to install sensors and tags, the Commission has received considerable assistance and support from Iraq.

E. *Baghdad Monitoring and Verification Centre*

19. Upon initiating the process of establishing the ongoing monitoring and verification system, it became apparent that the Commission would need to create a centre in Baghdad to operate the system. The intention to do so was reported to the Security Council in March and April 1994 (S/1994/341 and S/1994/489). Since that time,

the Commission has undertaken a feasibility study for such a centre; identified a site; obtained the agreement of the Government of Iraq to the use of that site as the Centre; drawn up architectural and engineering plans for the reconstruction of the building concerned to conform with the requirements of the Centre; accepted the Iraqi Government's offer to perform the reconstruction; supervised the construction work; conducted a security review upon the completion of the construction work undertaken by the Government of Iraq and produced a security programme for the Centre; identified major components of the security system (doors, locks, railings and surveillance cameras); acquired much of the furniture and equipment required for the Centre; and started the process of installing the communications and other equipment required for the Centre. The Commission notes Iraq's contribution to and cooperation in the construction works required to establish the monitoring system. These efforts, particularly those to construct a communications mast and to renovate the building to be used for the Baghdad Monitoring and Verification Centre, have significantly expedited the process of establishing the system. Full details are contained in annex II.

20. When the Centre is fully operational, it will comprise the following: offices of the Director and Deputy Director; monitoring experts in each of the areas to be monitored (missile, chemical, biological and—from IAEA—nuclear); export/import control experts; biological and chemical laboratories; the aerial inspection team with their photographic laboratory and imagery library; communications with New York, Vienna and all the remote-controlled sensors installed by inspection teams; equipment for reviewing the product of the remote-controlled monitoring cameras; medical and logistics support, including helicopter and ground transport; and interpretation and translation services. It is expected that, once fully operational, the Centre will have a total complement of approximately 80 persons.

21. Recruitment of personnel for this Centre is proceeding. For the monitoring, aerial inspection and export/import control experts, the Commission is setting up a pool of experts whom supporting Governments would make available to serve for a minimum of 90 days at the Centre. The aim is to rotate staff on a three- or six-month basis, with experts returning for several tours at the Centre, so as to benefit both from fresh perspectives and from continuity of experience.

22. In the missile area, the first monitoring group of experts arrived and commenced work on 17 August 1994. The first rotation is due on 14 October 1994. The first chemical team arrived in Iraq on 2 October 1994 to commence operations immediately. The first biological team is to arrive in the near future. The aerial inspection team has been operating in Iraq since June 1992. Export/import control experts will be recruited as and when it becomes evident that sanctions imposed by Security Council resolution 661 (1990) are due to be eased or lifted in accordance with paragraph 21 of resolution 687 (1991).

F. *National implementation measures*

23. Paragraphs 20 and 21 of the Commission's monitoring plan require Iraq to adopt the measures necessary to implement its obligations under section C of resolution 687 (1991), resolution 707 (1991) and the plan itself. Those measures are to include a prohibition and penal legislation forbidding all national and legal persons under Iraq's jurisdiction or control from undertaking anywhere any activity prohibited for Iraq by resolution 687 (1991) and all other related resolutions.

24. Iraq has forwarded to the Special Commission and IAEA the draft of a decision by the Revolutionary Command Council intended to give effect to those requirements. The Commission has discussed the draft decision informally with the competent Iraqi officials and has made certain suggestions. The Commission has drawn attention to the need to provide for prompt action in respect of any changes in the items prohibited or controlled under the annexes to the Commission's plan, as these annexes may be updated and revised from time to time. It would seem preferable to embody the lists of such materials and equipment in administrative regulations rather than the law itself. The Iraqi side has undertaken to review this aspect of the draft decree, which had annexed the lists of items to the decree itself, before being presented to the Revolutionary Command Council for adoption.

25. The Commission has also indicated the desirability that the legislation should make it clear that cooperation by natural or legal persons in Iraq with the Commission in carrying out its tasks is required and that such cooperation would not *per se* be the subject of any legal or other punitive measures.

IV. *Export/import monitoring mechanism*

26. As mentioned in the last report (S/1994/489), the Special Commission and IAEA prepared, pursuant to paragraph 7 of resolution 715 (1991), a concept paper outlining their proposal for an export/import mechanism for monitoring any future sales or supplies by other countries to Iraq of items relevant to the implementation of section C of resolution 687 (1991) and other related resolutions. The concept paper sets out procedures for notifications to the Commission and IAEA of exports of dual-purpose items to Iraq. Such notifications would be made both by the exporting country and by Iraq for the

items referred to in the relevant annexes to the plans of the Commission and IAEA for ongoing monitoring and verification already approved by resolution 715 (1991).

27. On 13 May 1994, the Executive Chairman of the Commission addressed a letter to the Chairman of the Committee established under resolution 661 (1990) (i.e. the "Sanctions Committee"), transmitting to him the concept paper for consideration and approval by that Committee. It will be recalled that paragraph 7 of resolution 715 (1991) had requested that the Sanctions Committee, the Commission and the Director General of IAEA develop "in cooperation" the export/import mechanism for approval by the Council.

28. In his letter of transmission, the Executive Chairman pointed out that paragraph 7 envisioned a system of monitoring that was to be of indefinite duration. It was thus understood that paragraph 7 of resolution 715 (1991) was intended to make provision for the monitoring of sales or supplies by other countries to Iraq of relevant dual-purpose items after the general sanctions imposed by resolution 661 (1990) on those items had been lifted, pursuant to paragraph 21 of resolution 687 (1991).

29. In order to avoid confusion between the sanctions regime and the monitoring mechanism, the Executive Chairman proposed that the two regimes should be kept entirely separate. The role of the Sanctions Committee would have priority for as long as items covered by the plans for ongoing monitoring and verification remained subject to the general sanctions under resolution 661 (1990). Any requests for their sale to Iraq, as essential for civilian needs, would continue to be addressed in accordance with existing procedures to the Sanctions Committee. Once the sanctions under resolution 661 (1990) on any dual-purpose items or categories of items were lifted, those items would become subject to the proposed export/import mechanism.

30. The joint Commission/IAEA concept paper, together with the Executive Chairman's letter of transmittal, were submitted by the Chairman of the Sanctions Committee to that Committee. Informal discussions in the Sanctions Committee appeared to reveal that a consensus could be arrived at on the proposal contained in the concept paper. However, before going to the Security Council with the required tripartite proposal for the export/import mechanism, the members of the Committee preferred to see a more detailed list of items to be reported than already appeared in the relevant annexes to the Commission's plan for ongoing monitoring and verification.

31. In the light of this, the Commission decided to prepare revisions to the annexes in its plan to provide therein more detailed information and lists on the items

to be covered by the reporting procedures. These revised lists have now been completed, and informal expert discussions will shortly be held to determine the adequacy of the revisions for purposes of implementing an export reporting procedure. Those discussions should be completed in the near future, after which the proposed revisions to the annexes will be made available to the Sanctions Committee and will be reported to the Security Council. It will be recalled that the plans of the Commission and IAEA for ongoing monitoring and verification permit the Commission and IAEA to update and revise the annexes to their plans based on information and experience gained in the implementation of resolutions 687 (1991) and 707 (1991) and of the plans, after informing the Council of such revisions. This is, therefore, the procedure that will be followed. The Commission and IAEA hope that it will be possible then to submit to the Security Council an agreed proposal by the Sanctions Committee, the Commission and IAEA, for the export/import mechanism.

V. *Future operations*

A. *Finance*

32. The monitoring and other activities of the Special Commission and of IAEA, undertaken pursuant to the relevant Council resolutions, are to be of indefinite duration and have to be planned on the assumption that there will be a sufficient, guaranteed, long-term source of funds to finance those activities. At the present time, as described in detail in annex III to the present report, financial restraints under the legal and other arrangements now pertaining have come very close to delaying the acquisition of all items and supplies required to have the monitoring system "up and running". Quite apart from this consideration, the constant need to seek contributions in cash and in-kind from various Governments is proving to be a time-consuming and onerous responsibility for the executive management of the Commission, diverting resources that could otherwise be devoted to operations. At the end of 1994, the funds for financing the operations of the Commission and IAEA will be exhausted and, at the time of writing, there is no firm undertaking that those funds will be replenished. The Council needs to address the issue of both short- and long-term financing at an early date if it is to have an assured and effective monitoring system.

B. *Operations and organization*

33. Funds permitting and unforeseen obstacles not intervening, the Commission expects to have installed all the tags and sensors currently envisaged and to have the Baghdad Monitoring and Verification Centre fully

equipped and staffed by the end of 1994. Work there will then focus on the conduct of ongoing monitoring and verification activities, which have already been initiated. In New York, while there will be further efforts to resolve outstanding issues in relation to Iraq's past programmes and to complete the installation of the currently envisaged elements of the ongoing monitoring and verification system, there will be a further redeployment of resources from efforts to establish ongoing monitoring and verification towards the organization and analysis of data being obtained from the monitoring process and preparations for the operation of the export/import control mechanism.

34. It is envisaged that, until the implementation of the export/import control mechanism, ongoing monitoring and verification activities will comprise primarily the following types of activities:

(a) Inspections to verify the completeness of the list of sites monitored and of the inventories, to verify declarations as to the activities conducted at sites, or to pursue any information obtained that might question Iraq's compliance with its obligations under paragraph 10 of resolution 687 (1991);

(b) Aerial surveillance, from both the Commission's high-altitude surveillance aircraft (the U-2) and its helicopters;

(c) Maintenance of the site-monitoring and verification protocols by the monitoring experts at the Baghdad Monitoring and Verification Centre;

(d) Monitoring activities conducted by experts dispatched to Iraq for that specific purpose because either the expertise required for the activity is not available among the staff of the Centre or because the scope of the activity is too great for the staff of the Centre to undertake without additional assistance;

(e) Review and analysis of the product of the sensors installed at the various sites.

C. Revisions to the annexes

35. In the course of operations in Iraq, it has become evident that some revisions to the annexes to the Commission's plan for ongoing monitoring and verification are in order. This is in response to a number of factors:

(a) As indicated in chapter IV above, discussions with the Sanctions Committee on the export/import control mechanism concept paper have shown that exporting States will require greater specification in technical terms of what constitutes a dual-purpose item and hence the export of which to Iraq would be subject to notification

to the joint Commission/IAEA unit provided for in the concept paper;

(b) Experience gained by the Commission during its inspection activities and in the course of establishing the system of ongoing monitoring and verification;

(c) Iraqi requests that provisions of the annexes to the Commission's plan be specified in greater technical detail to assist Iraq in understanding what is covered by the plans.

36. As noted above, revisions to the annexes have been prepared by the Commission. These should facilitate the performance by all concerned of their obligations under the Commission's plan and the export/import monitoring mechanism, thereby contributing to the increased effectiveness of the overall regime to monitor Iraq's compliance with paragraph 10 of resolution 687 (1991).

VI. Conclusions

37. The establishment of the system for ongoing monitoring and verification was a highly complex and sizeable undertaking, achieved not without difficulty. The Commission believes that the basic elements for a thorough system are now in place. There are plans to introduce in the immediate future technical additions to the system to improve its efficiency and convenience. In the light of the progress reported above, the Commission's system of ongoing monitoring and verification is now provisionally operational. The testing of the thoroughness and efficacy of the system has begun.

38. Enough operating experience will have to be gained to demonstrate that the integrated system will provide the Council with the assurance that Iraq's obligations not to re-acquire proscribed weapons can indeed be verified. After the lifting of the sanctions, the system, if it is to be effective and to endure, will have to be a dynamic one, refined and augmented in the light of experience, of technological developments and of the growth of Iraq's economy.

39. An essential condition for the effective operation of the system will be Iraq's actions in compliance with its obligations in accordance with the plans approved under resolution 715 (1991). If Iraq extends to the operation of ongoing monitoring and verification the same level of cooperation that it has to date in its establishment, there can be cause for optimism. The Executive Chairman will keep the Security Council informed each month in his oral reports on the working of the system so that the Council can draw the necessary conclusions at the appropriate time.

Annex I
Ongoing monitoring and verification activities

I. *Missile monitoring*

1. Since the last report, intensive efforts have been made to put into operation ongoing monitoring and verification of Iraq's missile-related activities and dual-purpose capabilities. Those efforts resulted in putting in place the essential elements of the system, including the creation of a group of resident expert monitors in the Commission's Baghdad Monitoring and Verification Centre. Protocols for missile-related facilities have been completed and serve as guidelines for ongoing monitoring and verification activities at the specified facilities. They also form an information source on Iraq's past and present activities. Iraq's declarations submitted under the plan for ongoing monitoring and verification, including the required biannual declarations received in July 1994, were assessed on a continuous basis. In parallel, the Commission continued its investigations into Iraq's past prohibited missile programmes and its compliance with resolution 687 (1991).

A. *Activities to establish monitoring*

1. UNSCOM 71/BM22

2. After Iraq's initial declaration under the plan for ongoing monitoring and verification had been received in January 1994 and analysed by the Commission, the Commission was able to proceed to the preparation of monitoring and verification protocols for identified missile-related facilities. UNSCOM 71/BM22 was tasked with that mission. The team carried out its activities in Iraq from 30 March to 20 May 1994. It visited more than 30 facilities to verify on site Iraq's declarations concerning those facilities and to identify focal points for future monitoring activities.

3. UNSCOM 71/BM22 prepared monitoring and verification protocols for each facility with specific recommendations for monitoring arrangements and inspection modalities. Depending on the nature of facilities and activities, different regimes of monitoring were envisaged. These included, *inter alia*, modalities for the collection of information, installation of cameras and other sensors, tagging and on-site checks of missile-related and dual-purpose equipment. The protocols also contain outlines for on-site inspection programmes for each facility. Successful completion of UNSCOM 71/BM22 marked a critical step towards the creation, in the missile area, of an ongoing monitoring and verification system covering research, development, modification, production, testing and other facilities, and missile-specific and dual-purpose items.

2. UNSCOM 79/BM23 and UNSCOM 80/BM24

4. Ongoing monitoring and verification provides for monitoring of missiles designed for use, or capable of being modified for use, in a surface-to-surface role with a range greater than 50 kilometres. UNSCOM 80/BM24 was given the task of tagging a number of operational missile systems to be monitored. The purpose of the tagging is to assist the Commission in effective monitoring of non-modification of missile systems and in keeping a reliable missile inventory control.

5. UNSCOM 80/BM24 conducted its mission in Iraq from 10 to 24 June 1994. In total, the team tagged more than 1,300 missiles of different types in a manner that would preclude undetected modifications of missiles to achieve proscribed ranges. All missiles were tagged by Commission inspectors, with Iraq's authorities providing preparations and support necessary for safe and efficient operations. UNSCOM 80/BM24 also visited a number of missile sites to ascertain that they were not suitable for prohibited modification activities.

6. After completion of the baseline activities related to operational missiles, the Commission will request Iraq, up to three times per year, to assemble a limited number of tagged missiles for purposes of inspecting them and making sure that they have not been modified to enable those missiles to reach a range greater than 150 kilometres. The Commission will select for each inspection up to 10 per cent of the quantity of tagged missiles. The first inspection of that kind will take place shortly.

7. Tagging operations with live missiles required extensive preparations, personnel training and elaboration of appropriate inspection modalities and safety procedures. UNSCOM 79/BM23 was in Iraq from 23 to 28 May 1994 to conduct preparations for UNSCOM 80/BM24 activities. UNSCOM 79/BM23 checked on-site work areas for tagging operations and other preparatory work done by the Iraqi authorities. Prime attention was paid to the safety aspects of working with live missiles. Special operational procedures, commensurate with the unique character of tagging activities, were established by the Commission.

8. UNSCOM 79/BM23 also compiled a technical reference baseline for Iraq's missile systems of interest to the Commission. Reference data for each missile system were obtained to include measurements and photography of major parts and components. The data collected will be used to establish "official" missile configurations for each missile system for use in future inspections and to support automated processing of data collected from the monitoring cameras.

3. UNSCOM 81/BM25

9. UNSCOM 81/BM25 was in Iraq from 14 to 22 June 1994. The objectives of the team were twofold: to

present to Iraq's experts definitions under elaboration by the Commission of the dual-purpose items and technologies contained in annex IV of the plan for ongoing monitoring and verification and to discuss certain aspects of past prohibited activities in Iraq, including missile production, modification projects and foreign supplies. As a special task related to verification of Iraq's compliance with resolution 687 (1991), the team was requested to investigate the alleged use of a tracking radar to support launches of prohibited missiles in December 1990. Iraq's officials strongly denied that the radar had been used during those tests or even had been intended to be used in any activities related to prohibited missiles. Those denials are contrary to information obtained by the Commission, which is currently pursuing its investigations in order to arrive at a final determination of the disposition of this radar.

4. UNSCOM 82/BM26

10. The Commission decided to use cameras and other sensors to increase the effectiveness of monitoring activities at a number of missile-related facilities selected by it for monitoring. Through efforts of several inspection teams, including UNSCOM 66, 69 and 71, specific areas were identified where hardware or technology essential for acquiring crucial elements of proscribed capabilities were present. Furthermore, the suitability of camera surveillance for monitoring activities at those areas was assessed. Over all, some 30 areas at 13 facilities were selected for camera monitoring.

11. UNSCOM 82/BM26 was mandated to carry out actual installation of monitoring camera systems. A typical system with constant data-collection capability consisted of the following: camera(s) with trigger sensors (if necessary), a controller, a recorder, a power unit and a transmitter at the monitored site; and a receiver, a controller computer and a recorder at the Baghdad Monitoring and Verification Centre. Each system is self-sufficient, with built-in redundancy and security controls. Interlinking communications are accomplished through a specifically designed system.

12. The team operated in Iraq from 3 to 28 July 1994 and installed more than 50 cameras with associated equipment. The team also placed tags and inventory labels on equipment identified for monitoring. The team used tamper-proof tags, specially designed to provide for high security, durability and effective inventory control.

13. After a period of initial operation of camera systems, a special sensor-testing team was dispatched to Iraq from 8 to 16 August 1994. The team's mission was to validate operational capabilities of the camera-monitoring systems (through tests of sensor and communication technologies), operation and maintenance procedures and processing modalities. The team provided recommendations for improved use of sensor-monitoring systems in the missile area.

14. As of now, a system for data collection from the camera systems and data analysis is provisionally operational.

5. UNSCOM 85/BM27

15. The team was in Iraq from 15 to 24 July 1994 with the primary mission of updating Iraq's information and the Commission's assessments of missile research and development activities in Iraq. Such research and development updates, based on the declarations and special reports by Iraq and data collected by inspection teams, are carried out by the Commission on a biannual basis. UNSCOM 85/BM27 was the second team to perform such a task.

16. Extensive discussions were held with Iraq's officials and missile experts to obtain information relevant to the team's mission. Iraq submitted a detailed report of its current missile programmes relevant to surface-to-surface missiles with a range greater than 50 kilometres. The team reaffirmed limitations established by the Commission on some missile design features so as to preclude the production of missiles that might achieve the proscribed range.

17. UNSCOM 85/BM27 was also mandated to investigate a number of issues related to research and development activities carried out by Iraq for the past proscribed missile programmes.

6. MG1

18. Upon completion of the baseline process in the missile area, the Commission decided to dispatch the first missile group of resident inspectors to the Baghdad Monitoring and Verification Centre. Such groups will operate continuously from the Centre and will be a core element in the ongoing monitoring and verification system. They are to perform a variety of important ongoing monitoring and verification missions, including:

(a) Execution of monitoring inspections on a regular basis at all missile-related sites under monitoring;

(b) Checks of the tagged operational missiles;

(c) Initial assessment and verification of Iraq's declarations and reports;

(d) Upkeep of a current inventory of items under monitoring;

(e) Supervision of the operation of the sensor-monitoring system and initial screening of the system output.

19. The first monitoring group arrived in Iraq on 17 August. The group is composed of four experts. The group's personnel will be rotated every three months, with the first rotation to take place on 14 October 1994. So far, MG1 has conducted more than 40 visits to facili-

ties being monitored and has presented a number of monitoring reports to the Commission.

B. *Past prohibited missile-related activities*

20. To establish a solid and verified baseline for ongoing monitoring and verification, the Commission needs to have a full and comprehensive picture of Iraq's missile-related capabilities, both present and past. As stipulated in Security Council resolutions 687 (1991), 707 (1991) and 715 (1991), Iraq is required to provide full, final and complete disclosure of all aspects of its proscribed programmes and to respond fully, completely and promptly to questions and requests from the Commission. Through its inspection activities, lengthy technical discussions with Iraq's authorities and in-depth analyses, the Commission now possesses a much fuller and more accurate picture of Iraq's past prohibited programmes, as compared with that presented by Iraq in its official "Full, final and comprehensive report" submitted in May 1992.

21. The Commission has continued its investigations into issues related to the past proscribed missile programmes. Special emphasis has been placed on verification of information provided by Iraq on foreign acquisition of proscribed missiles, their components and related production capabilities. Verification of this and other information provided by Iraq has been pursued by the Commission energetically.

22. Issues related to past programmes were also discussed with Iraq during the rounds of high-level talks in April and September 1994. During the reporting period, several inspection teams also addressed the relevant issues with Iraq's officials. While Iraq has not volunteered information, neither has it declined to provide answers to the Commission's specific requests. In general, information thus provided by Iraq agreed with that obtained by the Commission from other sources. Some explanations and clarifications from Iraq are still pending.

C. *Current monitoring programme*

23. The current monitoring programme in the missile area constitutes a multilayered system to accomplish the tasks of the plan for ongoing monitoring and verification in an efficient and practical manner. It covers, *inter alia*:

(a) A variety of sites and facilities, both currently engaged in missile activities and having relevant capabilities. At the present moment, the number of such facilities under monitoring exceeds 30;

(b) Activities crucial to re-acquiring prohibited missiles. Special modes of monitoring, that is, camera systems, were established. Such focal points for monitor-

ing include missile-propellant mixers/extruders, equipment for liquid engine production and gyro balancing, missile/warhead assembly lines, wind tunnel and static test stands;

(c) Specialized and dual-purpose equipment. Appropriate inventory control was established. For example, nearly 200 items have been tagged by the Commission. Many more are covered by facility protocols;

(d) Operational missiles designed for use, or capable of being modified for use, in a surface-to-surface role with a range greater than 50 kilometres. More than 1,300 missiles have been tagged by the Commission and will be regularly checked for non-modification.

24. Under its current monitoring programme, the Commission will use a variety of inspection modalities, including:

(a) Resident monitors (missile groups) in the Baghdad Monitoring and Verification Centre to perform a number of monitoring and verification tasks. It is envisaged that missile groups would carry out more than 150 inspection visits per year to facilities under monitoring;

(b) Camera and sensor monitoring of specific areas to collect on a continuous basis data on activities under observation;

(c) Special inspection teams to address specific issues, for example, research and development activities and static and flight missile tests;

(d) Compliance inspection teams to investigate Iraq's compliance with the relevant provisions of resolution 687 (1991);

(e) Missile monitoring activities to be supported by aerial inspections and surveillance carried out by the Commission.

25. It should be noted that the key to implementation of missile-related provisions of ongoing monitoring and verification will be transparency on Iraq's part concerning its activities to be monitored under the plan.

26. In summary, elements of monitoring and verification have been put in place and are operational.

II. *Chemical monitoring*

27. Since the last report, the Commission has worked in four areas to implement the chemical-monitoring aspects of the plan. Firstly, the Commission continues to investigate past Iraqi chemical weapons activities using seminars and question-and-answer sessions with competent Iraqi officials. A thorough understanding of Iraq's technical capabilities, manufacturing equipment and precursor suppliers, and past chemical weapons production activities are necessary prerequisites for the successful design and implementation of the ongoing monitoring and verification system. Secondly, the

Commission conducted a site sweep and hand-over of the Muthanna State Establishment. That facility was the hub of Iraq's past chemical weapons programmes. As such, it contained the bulk of the declared and discovered chemical agents, filled munitions and munitions production and filling equipment. The site survey and hand-over teams established that the site was free of prohibited materials and that all dual-use equipment at the site was properly tagged and inventoried. Thirdly, three chemical protocol-building missions have been conducted at a variety of sites. Finally, the chemical group has arrived in Iraq as part of the Baghdad Monitoring and Verification Centre and started its monitoring activities.

A. Activities to establish monitoring

1. UNSCOM 67/CW13 and UNSCOM 70/CW14

28. The inventory and protocol testing activities of UNSCOM 67/CW13 and the chemical air sampler installation by UNSCOM 70/CW14 have been described fully in chapter II.2.B, annex I of S/1994/489.

2. UNSCOM 75/CW16

29. The first series of chemical baseline inspections was carried out by UNSCOM 75/CW16 from 25 May to 5 June 1994. The team's task was to conduct baseline inspections and build protocols for the chemical sites known to have been associated with Iraq's past chemical weapons programmes or to have dual-purpose capabilities of specific concern for the future ongoing monitoring and verification system.

30. The team generated protocols for 14 sites. The protocols include data on the layout of the site, the chemical processes used, precursors utilized and waste materials produced. The team was able to make recommendations on the frequency of monitoring inspections for the 14 sites. They were also able to refine the baseline data requirements established by UNSCOM 67/CW13.

3. UNSCOM 76/CW17

31. The destruction of declared and discovered chemical weapons and related equipment and materials took place at the Muthanna State Establishment beginning in the summer of 1992. The work of the chemical destruction group was completed in the spring of 1994. Because the Muthanna site had been used as both Iraq's main chemical weapons production facility and as a collection point for prohibited items awaiting destruction, a team was dispatched to the site to certify the successful completion of destruction operations.

32. From 31 May to 12 June 1994, UNSCOM 76/CW17 surveyed the Muthanna site. The team conducted extensive chemical sampling and analysis operations in order to be able to declare the site free of chemical weapons hazards. During their survey operations, the team noted the existence of several pieces of equipment and other materials on which the Commission needed to take a decision as to their disposition. A complete description of those items was passed to the hand-over team.

4. UNSCOM 77/CW18

33. In addition to the work of the site survey team, a second mission (UNSCOM 77/CW18) reviewed the environmental analysis report of the survey team. The team, *inter alia*, tagged several pieces of relevant chemical-manufacturing equipment and dual-use metal working tools.

34. On 13 June 1994, a formal meeting was held at Iraq's National Monitoring Directorate at Baghdad. A protocol describing Commission actions at Muthanna and future Iraqi obligations with respect to the site was signed by representatives of Iraq and the Commission. This inspection ended the Commission's two-year control of the facility.

5. UNSCOM 89/CW19

35. This team operated in Iraq from 10 to 23 August 1994. Its task was to build protocols for 22 chemical facilities associated with the oil and petrochemical industry. Those sites were of interest because of the potential presence of either equipment or raw chemicals that could be used in the production of chemical warfare agents or equipment that could be used to store such chemicals.

36. The team verified declared equipment and activities, for example, the hydrofluoric acid catalysed alkylation of olefin to produce detergents, at the sites, which indicated that they should be subjected to monitoring. It collected the information required for the building of protocols for each of the sites and undertook much of the work to create the protocols.

6. UNSCOM 91/CW20

37. This team conducted its activities in Iraq from 13 to 24 September 1994. Its principal task was to conduct protocol-building inspections for 12 sites associated primarily with Iraq's chemical fertilizer industry in order to identify possible dual-purpose equipment, equipment or facility redundancies, plant capacity and normal utilization, unusual chemical processes and waste disposal methods, and to resolve anomalies in Iraq's declarations about those sites. The team obtained the information required to build protocols for these sites.

7. CG1

38. The first chemical monitoring group (CG1), arrived in Iraq on 2 October 1994 and comprised four experts. The team immediately initiated chemical monitoring. The experience of the team will be used to refine chemical monitoring and to refine further the information

requirements for monitoring and verification protocols and baseline.

39. Under the guidance of the Commission's staff in New York, the chemical group at Baghdad will:

(a) Draft and revise site monitoring and verification protocols;

(b) Conduct inspections of research, development and university facilities;

(c) Tag and monitor dual-use chemical-processing equipment;

(d) Conduct inspections of sites of potential relevance to the chemical-monitoring regime;

(e) Collect, assess and record monitoring sensor data;

(f) Provide technical expertise to the export/import monitoring group.

B. *Iraq's past chemical weapons programme*

40. As indicated throughout the present report, full knowledge and accounting for Iraq's past programmes is essential for confidence in the baseline information from which ongoing monitoring and verification will be conducted. The Commission has continued its efforts to fill in gaps in Iraq's declarations of its past chemical weapons programmes, particularly those relating to suppliers and quantities of items and materials supplied, as well as to find ways to verify independently Iraq's accounting of the past programme.

41. At the high-level political talks held in New York in November 1993 between the Commission and representatives of Iraq, it was suggested that seminar-style meetings between former officials involved in Iraq's chemical weapons programmes and Commission experts be held. The goal of those seminars would be to develop a more complete, accurate and detailed view of the past chemical weapons programmes.

42. A major breakthrough in that regard was made in April 1994, when a team (UNSCOM 74/CW15), sent to Iraq specifically to address that set of issues, obtained a hand-written list of the letters of credit authorized for the import of items in support of the chemical weapons programmes. Iraq claims that the list covers its entire procurement activities, which used letters of credit for its past chemical weapons programmes. Verification of the newly revealed Iraqi procurement data is complicated by the sometimes overly generalized descriptions of procured items associated with each letter of credit. Also complicating the assessment of this new data is the difficulty of obtaining corroborating information from the alleged supplier Governments. The Commission continues to pursue vigorously its efforts to refine and verify this new, and potentially valuable, information. With this information verified, it should prove possible to have a

firm understanding of the capabilities acquired by Iraq and hence to account for the materials and equipment supplied. This, in turn, will allow the Commission to be certain that it is indeed monitoring all the dual-purpose items in the chemical area that should be subjected to monitoring. Another inspection is planned for the second half of October 1994 to pursue the matter further.

C. *Current chemical-monitoring activities*

43. In addition to conducting ongoing monitoring and verification activities at sites for which monitoring and verification protocols have been prepared, the chemical monitoring teams (CG1) will also conduct visits to various institutions at which chemical research is undertaken but which might not need to be subject to regular monitoring. The aim of such visits would be to have an understanding of the direction and level of Iraq's basic research into chemistry and chemical processes that might also be useful for the production of chemical warfare agents or their precursor chemicals.

44. The team will also seek to clarify outstanding anomalies in Iraq's declarations concerning its dual-purpose capabilities. Minor adjustments have been made by the Commission to the formats under which Iraq reports such capabilities in order to facilitate both the collection of data by Iraq and its analysis by the Commission. The team will explain those changes to its Iraqi counterparts and provide such further clarifications as are required for Iraq to provide full and consistent declarations.

45. In support of ongoing monitoring and verification in the chemical area, the Commission intends to install further sensors. An additional 20 air-sampling devices are envisaged for installation at various chemical production facilities of special interest. At least one site will have flow meters installed at key points in the production equipment and several sites will be monitored by remote-controlled cameras.

46. Analysis of the samples taken by the air samplers will initially be conducted in laboratories outside Iraq. However, with the completion of the equipping of the Baghdad Centre, it is intended that analysis of those samples should be conducted at the chemical laboratory in the Centre. Only the samples that deviate from the normal background levels will be sent to approved international laboratories in order to obtain a cross-check from an independent laboratory. From time to time, calibrating exercises will be undertaken to ensure the accuracy of analysis at the various laboratories.

III. *Biological monitoring*

47. In preparation for the monitoring of Iraq's biological activities, UNSCOM has proceeded with the evaluation of the sites or facilities concerned, by assessing

the various elements that constitute Iraq's capability. Iraq's declarations form the basis for that work and are verified by the Commission for completeness and accuracy, after which the Commission is able to conduct a full analysis of Iraq's biological capabilities of concern to ongoing monitoring and verification.

A. *Baseline data on Iraq's capabilities*

48. Following discussions held in Baghdad and New York during the autumn of 1993, formats for reporting under the plan were established and presented to Iraq in December 1993. These were designed to facilitate the task of providing information concerning dual-purpose sites or facilities, activities, equipment, import or export and technical expertise. Iraq returned to the Commission formats for 35 biological sites in January 1994, but these did not contain complete responses to all the questions in the formats and hence did not furnish a full picture of the sites' capabilities.

49. Following discussions in February 1994 regarding the scope of Iraq's reporting on biological issues, the Commission presented Iraq, in March 1994, with a revised format for reporting to facilitate the task of gathering the information required and to incorporate questions to cover the information missing from the previous Iraqi response. In two subsequent inspections (UNSCOM 72/BW4 and UNSCOM 78/BW5, in April and May 1994, respectively), Commission teams visited sites declared by Iraq to familiarize themselves with the sites in preparation for later protocol-building and in order to tag and inventory declared dual-purpose items. During the course of those inspections, further discussions were held with Iraq on the information required. Further information was obtained, but also undeclared dual-purpose items, which should have been declared, were found and inconsistencies between the various sets of Iraqi declarations were noted. In short, the information contained in the total set of declarations remained incomplete.

50. Consequently, a team (UNSCOM 86/BW7) was dispatched to Iraq in June 1994 specifically to address the question of the gaps, inconsistencies and anomalies in the Iraqi declarations. As a result of those talks, Iraq was requested to provide supplementary information on 24 sites with biological activities and capabilities. Discussions focused on university laboratories, production facilities, breweries, import facilities and factories for the manufacture in Iraq of equipment that could be used in the production of biological agents.

51. Even so, the next inspection team (UNSCOM 84/BW6) in June 1994, with the task of inspecting a combination of declared and undeclared sites to assess how and whether they should be monitored, concluded that eight of the undeclared sites visited required monitoring because of the presence at the sites of items or activities subject to declaration. Iraq was again asked to provide missing information and clarifications to its earlier declarations. The issue was pursued further during technical talks held in New York in July 1994.

52. The next stage was to write the monitoring and verification protocols during a two-month long protocol-building inspection (UNSCOM 87/BW8) in July-September 1994. During the course of the inspection, more undeclared sites were inspected and found to require declarations and further inconsistencies were noted between previous declarations and the situation observed at the sites by the team, to include the discovery of undeclared equipment and activities that should have been declared. A follow-up inspection (UNSCOM 92/BW10) in September 1994 was organized to address issues not satisfactorily resolved during the protocol-building inspection. The results of the mission were pursued further during discussions in New York in September 1994. At that time, the Commission informed the high-level Iraqi delegation of the various steps taken in order to obtain the data required for monitoring and the difficulties encountered in doing so, while acknowledging Iraqi cooperation in facilitating access to sites. It was agreed that a further team (UNSCOM 96/BW12) should be dispatched to Iraq to present a list of additional information required. This team held discussions with Iraq's National Monitoring Directorate from 23 to 26 September 1994, stressing the link between full knowledge of Iraq's past programmes and in monitoring as well as the need for a full inventory of dual-purpose items. It suggested ways in which Iraq might assist the Commission in indirectly substantiating its account of its past programmes and accurately reporting its dual-purpose activities and capabilities in order to expedite the Commission's fulfilment of its mandate. Iraq reiterated its willingness to cooperate and, upon receipt of the list of additional information required, promised to respond promptly to all the questions.

B. *Activities to establish monitoring*

53. From April to October 1994, a total of nine inspections have been conducted in the biological field. They focused on the analytical work required to establish effective and efficient monitoring.

1. Initial inspection of undeclared sites (UNSCOM 72/BW4)

54. The team conducted its activities in Iraq from 8 to 26 April 1994. Its objective was to assess the information supplied by Iraq concerning the 35 sites declared by Iraq in January 1994 and 2 sites designated by the

Commission. The inspection sites included university laboratories, laboratories for routine control in medical diagnosis, veterinary diagnosis and food control, breweries and alcohol production facilities, and production facilities for vaccines, single-cell protein, fertilizers, pesticides and castor oil.

55. As noted in paragraph 49 above, the team also held discussions with Iraq on the content of its declarations. Just before the team left Baghdad and at the team's request, Iraq submitted copies of the declarations, information and data sent to the United Nations pursuant to the agreements on confidence-building measures for the year 1994 in accordance with document BWC/Conf.III/23/II and its annex on confidence-building measures.

2. UNSCOM 78/BW5

56. The purpose of the inspection was to identify and inventory equipment subject to declaration under the plan. This included equipment declared by Iraq or observed sites during UNSCOM 72/BW4. The inventory data is subsequently processed in a computer database, where it can be readily analysed and accessed by future inspectors.

57. UNSCOM 78/BW5 carried out its duties in Iraq from 28 May to 7 June 1994. It visited some 31 sites, at which 330 pieces of equipment were identified, described in detail, tagged and photographed.

58. In addition to the preparation of inventories, the team discussed with Iraq the issue of changes to the configuration of dual-purpose equipment. During discussions held with Iraq, it was stressed that the monitoring of dual-purpose equipment was a crucial element in the monitoring regime for a site and that the Commission needed to be aware of any changes of the location of and modification to such equipment. The team prepared a procedure for 30-day prior notification of transfer or modification of inventoried equipment. Iraq was informed that notification would be processed by the Commission on a no-objection basis. No such notification has yet been received.

3. UNSCOM 86/BW7

59. Biological technical talks (UNSCOM 86/BW7) were held at Baghdad from 5 to 8 June 1994. The purpose was to try to clarify inconsistencies and anomalies in declarations of the biological area submitted by Iraq in January and April 1994. The results of the mission were noted in paragraph 50 above.

4. UNSCOM 84/BW6

60. UNSCOM 84/BW6 had the task of conducting initial inspections at an additional 35 biological sites, either for initial inspection or in preparation for proto-col-building. The objective of the inspection was to assess activities conducted and to identify the equipment present at the sites in order to assess whether those sites, activities and equipment should be subject to declaration and hence to monitoring. UNSCOM 84/BW6 carried out its tasks from 24 June to 9 July 1994. In addition, and with a view to facilitating subsequent protocol-building at the biological sites to be monitored, protocols were built for four sites in order to test the viability of the draft protocol for such sites. The sites chosen for the testing had been visited previously. They represented four different activity areas: vaccine production, supplier company, research and development laboratory and single-cell protein production.

5. UNSCOM 87/BW8

61. The team's objective was to establish protocols for sites identified as requiring ongoing monitoring and verification. The main focus of this inspection was to establish guidelines, questionnaires and detailed instructions to be followed by the monitoring inspectors to be based at the Baghdad Monitoring and Verification Centre.

62. The team conducted its activities in Iraq from 25 July to 8 September 1994. It was planned that the inspection would prepare protocols for 55 sites. The team made three trips to Iraq (for a period of 10 days each) and visited facilities designated by the Commission. Each of the trips to Iraq was followed by a six-day protocol-drafting session at the Field Office in Bahrain.

63. Prior to the inspection, the team was provided by the Commission with a great deal of background information prepared from previous declarations and special reports, inspection findings and assessment work by the Commission's experts. However, the team had to gather much additional information in order to be in a position to prepare the protocols, given the inconsistencies between the situation it found on the ground and the information declared (see para. 52 above). Site plans and organizational charts requested during previous inspections but not received were provided by Iraq during the inspection.

6. UNSCOM 88/BW9

64. The team's objectives were to perform a feasibility study of remote monitoring in the biological area and, for the sites where this was deemed feasible, to establish the scope, foundations and requirements for the installation of remote monitors at biological sites.

65. It carried out its tasks in Iraq from 20 to 25 August 1994 and visited five biological facilities. It concluded that, at those sites, remote monitoring equipment could constitute an effective means of supplementary on-site inspections.

7. UNSCOM 92/BW10

66. The team's objectives were to visit sites falling under two main categories:

(a) Initial inspection of additional sites in order to assess activities at those sites and to identify dual-purpose equipment present there, with a view to subsequent protocol-building;

(b) Follow-up inspections of declared sites in order to complete the protocols for the sites.

67. The team carried out its tasks in Iraq from 29 August to 3 September 1994. During that time, the team visited a total of seven sites, acquiring further or new knowledge of them. The information is currently being analysed by the Commission's staff in New York.

8. UNSCOM 96/BW12

68. Further biological technical talks (UNSCOM 96/BW12) were held at Baghdad from 23 to 26 September 1994. The results of those talks are recorded in paragraph 52 above.

C. *Past military biological programmes*

69. The verification of Iraq's account of its past military biological programme has been rendered difficult by the claimed lack of supporting documentation. The areas where full verification remains pending include various aspects of the programme, such as storage of equipment, storage of organisms, personnel, relationships between the declared biological warfare research site and other organizations and facilities, and the acquisition of biotechnology. Additional information has been obtained on many of those areas in the course of the baseline inspection process, but more is required. The Commission continues to pursue the matter vigorously in all its contacts with Iraq.

D. *Current biological monitoring activities*

70. UNSCOM 94/BW11 was dispatched to Iraq on 29 September 1994. Its main objective is to continue the inventory and tagging of dual-purpose biological equipment started in May 1994 with UNSCOM 78/BW5. Owing to the receipt of additional information, including the new findings of declarable equipment during inspections since the first inventory, it has been necessary to perform a further inventory at approximately 50 sites. The team will also try to establish the circumstances that gave rise to the damage to or loss of tags noted during recent inspections, with a view to remedying the problem. The team is expected to operate in Iraq for approximately two weeks, covering a variety of sites falling in the categories of research and development facilities (such as universities and research institutes) and industrial facilities (such as vaccine production and pharmaceutical plants).

71. Once the process of preparing the protocols for each of the sites to be monitored in the biological area is complete, which should be in the near future, monitoring in the biological area will be conducted along the same lines as missile and chemical monitoring, with a resident team of experts based in the Baghdad Centre. Currently, it is envisaged that the team will comprise four experts.

IV. *Nuclear monitoring*

72. The Director General of IAEA is reporting separately on the activities of the action team set up to implement paragraphs 12 and 13 of resolution 687 (1991) and the IAEA plan for ongoing monitoring and verification approved under resolution 715 (1991).

73. The Special Commission continues, in accordance with paragraph 9 (b) (iii) of resolution 687 (1991) and paragraph 4 (b) of resolution 715 (1991), to provide its assistance and cooperation to the IAEA action team through the provision of special expertise and logistical, informational and other operational support for the carrying out of the IAEA plan for ongoing monitoring and verification. In accordance with paragraph 9 (b) (i) of the same resolution and paragraph 4 (a) of resolution 715 (1991), it continues to designate sites for inspection. In accordance with paragraph 3 (iii) of resolution 707 (1991), it continues to receive and decide on requests from Iraq to move or destroy any material or equipment relating to its nuclear weapons programme or other nuclear activities. Furthermore, it continues, in accordance with paragraph 4 (c) of resolution 715 (1991), to perform such other functions, in cooperation in the nuclear field with the Director General of IAEA, as may be necessary to coordinate activities under the plans for ongoing monitoring and verification, including making use of commonly available services and information to the fullest possible extent, in order to achieve maximum efficiency and optimum use of resources.

74. In conformity with its obligations to designate sites for inspection, the Commission, in late 1993, conducted a second aerial survey of gamma radiation over certain locations in Iraq. The results of the analysis of the survey were discussed at a meeting in September 1994 in New York. The assessment of the system for detecting gamma emissions and surveying gamma radiation levels concluded that the equipment could be of great potential use to the Commission in the performance of its mandate to support the work of the IAEA action team.

V. *Aerial inspections*

75. The aerial inspection team continues to undertake aerial inspections at sites being monitored and at new facilities considered to be of possible relevance to the

Commission's mandate. Where required, the team also provides support to ground inspections. All aerial inspections continue to be conducted on a no-notice basis. To date, some 500 aerial inspections have been undertaken by the team.

76. In response to the evolving requirements of ongoing monitoring and verification, the aerial inspection team is in the process of making a number of changes to its method of operations. As the expert monitoring groups become established at the Baghdad Centre, members of the groups are accompanying the aerial inspection team on relevant aerial missions. This allows the experts to advise the aerial inspectors to focus on particular areas or activities of importance at the facilities.

77. The aerial inspection team's photographic library will shortly be moved from its present location in the Commission's Bahrain Field Office to the Baghdad Centre. The library contains copies of all imagery and reports prepared by the team since the commencement of aerial inspections in June 1992. Immediate access to this historical imagery will enhance the aerial and ground teams' operations by allowing them to study sites in advance of inspections and thus readily to detect any external changes that have taken place at a facility since the previous inspection. In addition to the library, the aerial inspection team's photographic processing laboratory will also be moved into the Centre, thus permitting rapid access to the product from the aerial missions. During the course of the next three months, additional equipment will be procured for the team to assist in refining and improving the product from the aerial inspections.

78. The Commission's high-altitude surveillance aircraft, the U-2, continues to undertake an average of one or two flights a week. To date, 224 missions have been flown. The imagery obtained through those missions is crucial to the Commission's analysis of Iraq's capabilities and the Commission's operational planning. The Commission's photographic interpretation abilities have further improved during the period under review.

Annex II
Baghdad Monitoring and Verification Centre

I. *Preparatory efforts*

1. The concept of a Centre to support the ongoing monitoring and verification programme became an operational goal in early 1994. At the request of the Executive Chairman, the Chief of the Commission's Field Office at Baghdad undertook a study of alternative means to achieve a secure area for the collection of data from the ballistic-missile-monitoring camera system. On 7 February 1994, the Chief submitted a report in which the

United Nations offices at the Canal Hotel at Baghdad were the recommended site. On 7 March 1994, the Executive Chairman formally approved the site selection and a detailed plan of action to acquire 15 rooms on the second floor of the hotel.

2. The Canal Hotel was donated for exclusive use of the United Nations in the mid-1980s. It had been operated as a training hotel since 1978 in conjunction with a hotel management school that continues to operate in an adjacent compound. The facility is managed by the United Nations Administrative Unit, Baghdad, for a variety of United Nations agencies, including the Special Commission. The compound is guarded by a small contingent of the Iraqi Army. The main gate and immediate perimeter are guarded by Administrative Unit guards, all of whom are local nationals approved for United Nations employment by the Ministry of Foreign Affairs of Iraq. The Commission's efforts focused upon providing for facilities for a continuous presence in Iraq (beyond the presence of the small logistics support, medical and communications contingent within the Commission's Field Office), and within those offices to provide a secure area for sensitive information acquired from monitoring and from inspections.

3. By mid-April 1994, the Executive Chairman received a final report from a technical team addressing the design and installation of missile-monitoring cameras at (then) 14 sites in Iraq, connecting the cameras to the Centre and transmitting data to and from New York, Vienna and supporting analytical facilities. The technical team also conducted further assessment of the communications and security requirements for the Centre. Plans were completed for the transition of the Commission's Field Office facilities in the Ishtar Sheraton Hotel to the Centre.

4. In May 1994, via an exchange of letters, the Minister of Foreign Affairs of Iraq accepted a proposal by the Executive Chairman to designate the Canal Hotel as the Baghdad Centre. The Chairman also selected Rear Admiral (retired) Göran Wallén of Sweden to be the first Director of the Centre. On 20 May 1994, the Commission presented its requirements for personnel and equipment to the representatives of 20 permanent missions to the United Nations, and requested that interested Member States respond with an expression of support no later than 1 July 1994.

5. Including the small cadre of United Nations international staff members assigned to the Commission's Field Office, the Centre would support monitoring groups and technical support staff, totalling approximately 50 personnel. The staff would be recruited from contributing Governments for a minimum period of 90 days. Ideally, the Commission looked for national com-

mitments to staff certain positions during specific cycles or on a constant basis. Some Governments quickly affirmed their support, such as that of New Zealand, which is providing medical and some communications personnel. Including the Commission's helicopter unit, provided by the German army at Al-Rasheed Air Base, within the Centre's resources, the total complement for the Centre would be approximately 80 staff. While Governments evaluated the Commission requirements of 20 May 1994, the Commission's New York staff commenced active recruitment from contributing Governments of persons known for their expertise and, in many instances, their experience during previous inspections. In the course of that process, several Governments commenced personnel contributions to the Commission by offering experts in a variety of disciplines for service in the Centre and on inspection teams.

6. As the Commission prepared its equipment requirements for ongoing monitoring and verification, several contributing Governments made available computer and communications systems, chemical air-sampling stations, cameras and associated detection equipment, along with technical experts to install and initially operate the equipment at remote sites and within the Centre. One Government, for example, provided intrusion detection and surveillance cameras for interior Centre areas. Another Government donated over 50 cameras for remote site monitoring. Yet another Government paid for the purchase of computer equipment for use within the Centre.

7. In June 1994, the Administrative Unit staff assisted the Commission with preliminary assessments of the types of renovations required to provide for the varied operations within the Centre. To achieve greater efficiencies with the available floor space, for example, the Unit experimented with the removal of bathroom walls within several rooms. Every room included a bathroom. It was determined that removing the bathrooms increased the available space by 27 per cent in each room. Based on this and other considerations, initial allocations of space within the Centre indicated that more rooms would be required than the original conception of 15. Requirements for IAEA monitors were incorporated into the Centre. Studies also indicated the need for the Commission to secure the services of civil engineers to evaluate facility electrical, heating and air-conditioning systems, and to oversee renovation construction work.

8. The Administrative Unit, the Commission's Field Office, and other United Nations agencies resident in the Canal Hotel developed a plan for the reallocation of floor space to accommodate the expanding needs of the Commission. By mid-July, the Commission was granted an area encompassing most of the second floor, with the potential for future expansion if needed.

9. The Government of Iraq offered to construct a 92-metre antenna mast near the Centre to support the Commission's communications requirements and to eliminate the need for remote transmission via an antenna on the Ishtar Sheraton Hotel roof. The mast was erected within two weeks, from 13 to 25 June 1994, and was quickly put into service by the Commission. The height of the antenna fully supported Commission requirements for transmissions from remote locations. Further, the size of the mast platforms (approximately every two metres) affords great capacity for the addition of system equipment for the Commission and other United Nations agencies.

10. The pace of building the Centre accelerated with the joint announcement by the Commission, IAEA and the Government of Iraq on 5 July 1994 that the Centre should be provisionally operational during September 1994. In mid-July 1994, the Executive Chairman accepted the Iraqi Government's offer to perform the larger renovation tasks within the Centre area as a further step to meet the September date. The Government designated the Al-Fao Construction Bureau to design and implement the renovations to meet Centre requirements. The demolition and construction was performed beginning 8 August 1994 and terminated on 17 September 1994. The extensive renovation was accomplished under the supervision of construction engineers from a supporting Government.

II. *Centre staffing and early operations*

11. As the construction efforts were being arranged, the Centre staff was moving into the Canal Hotel building. On 31 July 1994, the staff of the operations room in the Ishtar Sheraton Hotel ceased functioning and relocated to the Canal Hotel building. On 1 August 1994, the Director assumed responsibility for the Commission's operations in Baghdad. The Chief of the former Field Office was designated Chief of Logistics within the Centre.

12. The first resident monitoring group for the Centre arrived at Baghdad on 17 August. This four-person team, the missile monitoring experts (designated MG1), was soon followed by the nuclear monitoring group (NMG 94-01), a two-person team, on 22 August 1994. (NMG 94-01 expanded to three persons on 29 September.) On 2 October, the first chemical group members arrived at Baghdad. The first biological group members are expected to arrive in the near future.

13. Missile group and nuclear monitoring group personnel commenced monitoring activities at various

sites throughout Iraq. Remote camera monitoring systems were tested and the Commission's and the IAEA's tags were checked for tampering or damage from movement of equipment. Several inspection teams used the temporary facilities within the Centre.

14. As the staff assembled, preparatory activities continued to move the Centre offices and functions to their permanent areas. The Centre security doors controlled access to 49 rooms on the Canal Hotel second floor. Furniture was being donated for the Centre from the Australian and American Embassy compounds. Office furniture was also acquired from the former Economic and Social Commission for Western Asia (ESCWA) at Baghdad.

15. In the final days of the present reporting period, a special team of security experts conducted an extensive survey of the facility to recommend measures for the Centre. Commitments from several contributing Governments were made to donate equipment, materials and technicians to ensure that the security programme was an integral function of Centre operations. Those commitments include ongoing maintenance, repair and renovation resources to sustain the Centre for as long as its operations are required.

Annex III
Administrative and financial issues

I. *Finance*

1. The financing of the operations of the Commission and IAEA under section C of Security Council resolution 687 (1991) and other relevant resolutions continues to be a matter of the most serious concern. Council resolution 699 (1991) explicitly provides that Iraq "shall be liable for the full costs of carrying out the tasks authorized by section C". However, the only Iraqi funds made available for financing the operations concerned are Iraqi frozen assets provided by Member States, under paragraph 1 of resolution 778 (1992), to the United Nations escrow account established pursuant to Council resolution 706 (1991). To the extent that those assets have not been sufficient to meet all the requirements of the Compensation Commission, the Special Commission and IAEA, and other United Nations operations in Iraq under the Council's resolutions, the financing of all those activities has had to be on the basis of voluntary contributions from States. In that regard, it will be recalled that resolution 699 (1991), in addition to laying down Iraq's obligations, encouraged "the maximum assistance, in cash and in kind, from all Member States to ensure that activities under section C of resolution 687 (1991) are undertaken effectively and expeditiously". The Council

augmented that request in its resolution 715 (1991), approving the plans of the Commission and IAEA for ongoing monitoring and verification, by calling for such assistance "in carrying out [their] activities under the plans approved by the present resolution, without prejudice to Iraq's liability for the full costs of such activities".

2. The Council's calls for such assistance have been generously responded to by a number of Governments, which have provided cash, equipment, services and personnel. However, it cannot be expected that the generosity of Governments will continue indefinitely or that funds in the escrow account will be sufficient, for even the immediate future, to meet the requirements of the various activities that are financed from that account, the Compensation Commission's Fund having the priority in that respect.

3. By the end of 1994, the Special Commission and IAEA will have spent a total of $81.5 million for their operations, including the costs of the contracts for the removal of fresh and irradiated nuclear fuel. A total of $71.4 million was provided through the escrow account and $9.4 million from direct contributions and loans. The operational budget of the Commission under long-term monitoring will in essence be for travel and mission subsistence allowance of experts and for the salary of the administrative and support staff provided by the United Nations. The Commission and IAEA will require an estimated $25 million in 1995 in support of their operations. This forecast assumes that Governments will pay for the salary of the experts and technical staff and that the monitoring equipment, that is, cameras, sensors, data-processing and analysis equipment will be provided by donor countries. However, the present funds earmarked for the Commission in the escrow account will be depleted at the end of 1994 if further funds earmarked for the Commission are not provided to the escrow account by Member States.

4. Contributions in cash and in kind from Governments may be either donations or subject to reimbursement of the costs involved when adequate Iraqi funds are available. Accordingly, the Special Commission, acting under the Security Council resolutions, has sought contributions directly from Governments for services, equipment and personnel needed to carry out its mandate. It has also given the necessary undertakings to Governments regarding reimbursement of their costs, if they indicate their intention to seek such reimbursement under the terms of the Council's resolutions, when Iraqi oil funds are available. That direct procedure, under the Council's authorization, is essential to a timely performance of the Commission's mandate, and the Commission will continue to act on it.

II. *Organization*

5. The establishment of ongoing monitoring and verification required a new infrastructure within the Commission to reflect its expanded activities. The operations of the Commission will now focus on monitoring activities while maintaining the ability to respond to any new information that might be obtained on Iraq's proscribed weapons programmes. The new organizational structure will eventually also have the additional mandate of implementing the export/import control mechanism required under paragraph 7 of resolution 715 (1991).

6. The following paragraphs contain a review of how the structure of the Commission has evolved or will evolve in order to respond to the changed circumstances in which it is now operating.

A. *Headquarters of the Special Commission*

7. At the headquarters of the Commission, the focus of effort shifted to the building of protocols, the development of relevant databases and the analysis of information—written and visual. Additional technical expertise was requested from Governments in order to boost the Commission's ability to cope with the additional workload. The total number of technical experts was increased from 12 at the end of 1993 to 23 by early September 1994. The most dramatic change occurred in the biological area. The Commission had only one biological expert in October 1993: it now has five.

8. The development of a custom-designed computer database in support of data gathering and analysis has been made possible thanks to the generosity of various Governments who contributed equipment, specifically designed software and training. Funds were allocated from the operational budget to improve the satellite link between New York and Baghdad and to increase the number of lines to allow the smooth and secure transmission of data.

B. *Office of the Special Commission at Baghdad*

9. The functions of the Office of the Special Commission at Baghdad, which previously had comprised essentially logistic support for inspections, were revised to respond to the additional requirements of ongoing monitoring and verification. The Executive Chairman decided that the Office would be replaced by a Baghdad Monitoring and Verification Centre, headed by a Director who would act as his personal representative in Iraq. Details of developments in that regard are contained in annex II.

Annex IV
Inspection schedule
(in-country dates)

Nuclear

15-21 May 1991	IAEA1/UNSCOM 1
22 June-3 July 1991	IAEA2/UNSCOM 4
7-18 July 1991	IAEA3/UNSCOM 5
27 July-10 August 1991	IAEA4/UNSCOM 6
14-20 September 1991	IAEA5/UNSCOM 14
22-30 September 1991	IAEA6/UNSCOM 16
11-22 October 1991	IAEA7/UNSCOM 19
11-18 November 1991	IAEA8/UNSCOM 22
11-14 January 1992	IAEA9/UNSCOM 25
5-13 February 1992	IAEA10/UNSCOM 27
7-15 April 1992	IAEA11/UNSCOM 33
26 May-4 June 1992	IAEA12/UNSCOM 37
14-21 July 1992	IAEA13/UNSCOM 41
31 August-7 September 1992	IAEA14/UNSCOM 43
8-18 November 1992	IAEA15/UNSCOM 46
5-8 December 1992	IAEA16/UNSCOM 47
25-31 January 1993	IAEA17/UNSCOM 49
3-11 March 1993	IAEA18/UNSCOM 52
30 April-7 May 1993	IAEA19/UNSCOM 56
25-30 June 1993	IAEA20/UNSCOM 58
23-28 July 1993	IAEA21/UNSCOM 61
1-15 November 1993	IAEA22/UNSCOM 64
4-11 February 1994	IAEA23/UNSCOM 68
11-22 April 1994	IAEA24/UNSCOM 73
21 June-1 July 1994	IAEA25/UNSCOM 83
22 August-2 September 1994	IAEA26/UNSCOM 90
3-29 September 1994	NMG 94-01
29 September-21 October 1994	NMG 94-02
14-21 October 1994	IAEA27/UNSCOM 93

Chemical

9-15 June 1991	CW1/UNSCOM 2
15-22 August 1991	CW2/UNSCOM 9
31 August-8 September 1991	CW3/UNSCOM 11
31 August-5 September 1991	CW4/UNSCOM 12
6 October-9 November 1991	CW5/UNSCOM 17
22 October-2 November 1991	CW6/UNSCOM 20
18 November-1 December 1991	CBW1/UNSCOM 21
27 January-5 February 1992	CW7/UNSCOM 26
21 February-24 March 1992	CD1/UNSCOM 29
5-13 April 1992	CD2/UNSCOM 32
15-29 April 1992	CW8/UNSCOM 35
18 June 1992-14 June 1994	CDG/UNSCOM 38
26 June-10 July 1992	CBW2/UNSCOM 39
21-29 September 1992	CW9/UNSCOM 44
6-14 December 1992	CBW3/UNSCOM 47

6-18 April 1993	CW10/UNSCOM 55
27-30 June 1993	CW11/UNSCOM 59
19-22 November 1993	CW12/UNSCOM 65
1-14 February 1994	CW13/UNSCOM 67
20-26 March 1994	CW14/UNSCOM 70
18-22 April 1994	CW15/UNSCOM 74
25 May-5 June 1994	CW16/UNSCOM 75
31 May-12 June 1994	CW17/UNSCOM 76
8-14 June 1994	CW18/UNSCOM 77
10-23 August 1994	CW19/UNSCOM 89
13-24 September 1994	CW20/UNSCOM 91
2 October- 1994 (ongoing)	CG1

Biological

2-8 August 1991	BW1/UNSCOM 7
20 September-3 October 1991	BW2/UNSCOM 15
11-18 March 1993	BW3/UNSCOM 53
8-26 April 1994	BW4/UNSCOM 72
28 May-7 June 1994	BW5/UNSCOM 78
24 June-8 July 1994	BW6/UNSCOM 84
5-8 June 1994	BW7/UNSCOM 86
25 July-8 September 1994	BW8/UNSCOM 87
20-25 August 1994	BW9/UNSCOM 88
29 August-3 September 1994	BW10/UNSCOM 92
29 September-14 October 1994	BW11/UNSCOM 94
23-26 September 1994	BW12/UNSCOM 96

Ballistic missiles

30 June-7 July 1991	BM1/UNSCOM 3
18-20 July 1991	BM2/UNSCOM 10
8-15 August 1991	BM3/UNSCOM 8
6-13 September 1991	BM4/UNSCOM 13
1-9 October 1991	BM5/UNSCOM 18
1-9 December 1991	BM6/UNSCOM 23
9-17 December 1991	BM7/UNSCOM 24
21-29 February 1992	BM8/UNSCOM 28
21-29 March 1992	BM9/UNSCOM 31
13-21 April 1992	BM10/UNSCOM 34
14-22 May 1992	BM11/UNSCOM 36
11-29 July 1992	BM12/UNSCOM 40A+B
7-18 August 1992	BM13/UNSCOM 42
16-30 October 1992	BM14/UNSCOM 45
25 January-23 March 1993	IMT1a/UNSCOM 48
12-21 February 1993	BM15/UNSCOM 50
22-23 February 1993	BM16/UNSCOM 51
27 March-17 May 1993	IMT1b/UNSCOM 54
5-28 June 1993	IMT1c/UNSCOM 57
10-11 July 1993	BM17/UNSCOM 60
24 August-15 September 1993	BM18/UNSCOM 62
28 September-1 November 1993	BM19/UNSCOM 63
21-29 January 1994	BM20/UNSCOM 66
17-25 February 1994	BM21/UNSCOM 69

30 March-20 May 1994	BM22/UNSCOM 71
23-28 May 1994	BM23/UNSCOM 79
10-24 June 1994	BM24/UNSCOM 80
14-19 June 1994	BM25/UNSCOM 81
3-28 July 1994	BM26/UNSCOM 82
15-24 July 1994	BM27/UNSCOM 85
17 August-9 October 1994	MG1
3-6 October 1994	BM28/UNSCOM 98A
21-31 October 1994	BM28/UNSCOM 98B
14 October- 1994 (ongoing)	MG2
14-19 October 1994	MG2A

Computer search

12 February 1992	UNSCOM 30

Special missions

30 June-3 July 1991
11-14 August 1991
4-6 October 1991
11-15 November 1991
27-30 January 1992
21-24 February 1992
17-19 July 1992
28-29 July 1992
6-12 September 1992
4-9 November 1992
4-8 November 1992
12-18 March 1993
14-20 March 1993
19-24 April 1993
4 June-5 July 1993
15-19 July 1993
25 July-5 August 1993
9-12 August 1993
10-24 September 1993
27 September-1 October 1993
1-8 October 1993
5 October-16 February 1994
2-10 December 1993
2-16 December 1993
21-27 January 1994
2-6 February 1994
10-14 April 1994
24-26 April 1994
28-29 May 1994
4-6 July 1994
8-16 August 1994
15-19 September 1994
21-25 September 1994
23-26 September 1994
3-6 October 1994

Document 194

Statement by the President of the Security Council concerning cooperation by Iraq with UNSCOM and reports of movements of Iraqi troops

S/PRST/1994/58, 8 October 1994

The Security Council notes with grave concern the statement issued on 6 October 1994 by the Revolutionary Command Council of Iraq. It underlines the complete unacceptability of the implication therein that Iraq may withdraw cooperation from the United Nations Special Commission. The Security Council emphasizes the necessity of full implementation of all its relevant resolutions, including full cooperation by Iraq, without interference, with the United Nations Special Commission's vital mission.

The Security Council has also received with grave concern reports that substantial numbers of Iraqi troops, including units of the Iraqi Republican Guard, are being redeployed in the direction of the border with Kuwait.

The Security Council therefore requests the Secretary-General to ensure that the United Nations Iraq-Kuwait Observation Mission (UNIKOM) redoubles its vigilance and reports immediately any violation of the demilitarized zone established under resolution 687 (1991) or any potentially hostile action.

The Security Council reaffirms its commitment to the sovereignty and territorial integrity of Kuwait. It underlines Iraq's full responsibility to accept all the obligations contained in all its relevant resolutions and to comply fully therewith.

Document 195

Sixth report of the Director General of the IAEA on the implementation of the Agency's plan for future ongoing monitoring and verification of Iraq's compliance with paragraph 12 of Security Council resolution 687 (1991)

S/1994/1151, 10 October 1994

Note by the Secretary-General

The Secretary-General has the honour to transmit to the members of the Security Council the attached communication dated 6 October 1994, which he has received from the Director General of the International Atomic Energy Agency (IAEA).

Annex
Letter dated 6 October 1994 from the Director General of the International Atomic Energy Agency addressed to the Secretary-General

Paragraph 8 of resolution 715 (1991), adopted by the Security Council on 11 October 1991, requests the Director General of the International Atomic Energy Agency to submit to the Security Council reports on the implementation of the Agency's plan for future ongoing monitoring and verification of Iraq's compliance with paragraph 12 of resolution 687 (1991). These reports are to be submitted when requested by the Security Council and, in any event, every six months after the adoption of resolution 715.

Accordingly, I am requesting you kindly to transmit to the President of the Security Council the enclosed sixth biannual report on the implementation of the Plan. I remain available for any consultations you or the Council may wish to have.

(Signed) Hans BLIX

Sixth report of the Director General of the International Atomic Energy Agency on the implementation of the IAEA's plan for future ongoing monitoring and verification of Iraq's compliance with paragraph 12 of resolution 687 (1991)

I. *Introduction*

1. On 11 October 1991, the Security Council adopted resolution 715 (1991) which, *inter alia,* ap-

proved the plan submitted in document S/22872/Rev.1/Corr.1 by the Director General of the International Atomic Energy Agency (IAEA) for future ongoing monitoring and verification of Iraq's compliance with paragraph 12 of Part C of Security Council resolution 687 (1991) and with the requirements of paragraphs 3 and 4 of resolution 707 (1991). In paragraph 8 of resolution 715, the Security Council requested the Director General of the IAEA to submit to it reports on the implementation of the plan when requested by the Security Council and, in any event, at least every six months after the adoption of resolution 715. The Director General has submitted thus far five reports, circulated on 15 April 1992, as S/23813; 28 October 1992, as S/24722; 19 April 1993, as S/25621; on 3 November 1993, as S/26685; and on 22 April 1994, as S/1994/490.

2. The Director General submits herewith the sixth six-month report on implementation of the plan for ongoing monitoring and verification related to Iraq's nuclear capabilities (hereinafter referred to as the Plan).

3. In addition to providing a semi-annual report on the implementation of the Plan, this document also summarizes the past three years of the IAEA activities in phasing in its Plan, activities which coincided with the continuing implementation by the IAEA of its mandate under the relevant Security Council resolutions to identify Iraq's nuclear weapons program.

II. *High-level technical talks*

4. Since the last report by the IAEA on the implementation of its Plan, two more rounds of high-level technical talks have been held between the IAEA and the United Nations Special Commission, on the one hand, and Iraq, on the other hand. These discussions were continuations of the talks initiated by a visit of Chairman Ekéus to Baghdad in July 1993 and focused on the implementation of the IAEA and the Special Commission plans for ongoing monitoring and verification and on the resolution of outstanding issues between Iraq and the two organizations. The ensuing series of high-level technical talks marked a turning point in the level of cooperation and support extended by the Iraqi authorities to IAEA and the Special Commission. This change in the Iraqi attitude has enabled the inspectors' work to be conducted effectively and has contributed significantly to expediting the process of establishing ongoing monitoring and verification, as called for in the Security Council resolutions. The substantive results of the last two rounds of high-level technical talks are summarized below. Reports on the high-level technical talks have been circulated as Security Council documents as identified in appendix A of this report.

5. From 24 to 26 April 1994, the two sides—the IAEA and the United Nation Special Commission, on the one hand, and Iraq, on the other hand—met in Baghdad to discuss issues relating to the implementation of resolutions 687 and 715 (1991). The two sides reviewed the considerable progress made in this regard since the last round of high-level talks, held in New York from 14 to 19 March 1994. It was noted that many actions had been undertaken during that period, including inspections to establish the baseline for implementing ongoing monitoring and verification. Iraq assured the Special Commission and the IAEA that it would respect their rights and privileges established under the Plans. For their part, the Special Commission and the IAEA reiterated their commitment to exercise these rights and privileges in a manner that respected Iraq's legitimate concerns relating to sovereignty, independence, security and dignity in accordance with the Charter of the United Nations, and to conduct their activities in the least intrusive manner consistent with effective monitoring and verification.

6. A further round of high-level technical talks took place in Baghdad on 4 and 5 July 1994. Discussions focused upon the parties' respective assessments of the stages which had been reached in connection with the two principal responsibilities of the Special Commission and the IAEA: the identification and destruction, removal or rendering harmless of Iraq's capabilities for weapons of mass destruction; and the putting in place and operation of an effective system of monitoring and verification as approved by the Security Council resolution 715 (1991). The Special Commission and the IAEA agreed that the first of these tasks was almost complete, with the destruction, removal or rendering harmless of declared and otherwise identified prohibited weapons and capabilities. As regards the second of these tasks, the Special Commission, the IAEA, and Iraq noted that substantial progress had been made in all the areas covered by the plans for ongoing monitoring and verification.

7. In the nuclear area, the IAEA indicated that the system for environmental monitoring was now well established and anticipated its ongoing development. Having received from Iraq the supplementary information required under the IAEA Plan, the IAEA was in possession of adequate information to support its monitoring activities. The Special Commission and the IAEA indicated that the plans for the installation of sensors were well advanced, and that it was the objective of the Special Commission and the IAEA to have the monitoring system operational in September 1994.

8. The Iraqi delegation stresses the view that it had completed all actions contemplated in the relevant provisions of section C of resolution 687 (1991) and that, consequently, the Security Council should immediately

apply paragraph 22 of the said resolution without any restrictions or further conditions.

9. The Special Commission, the IAEA, and Iraq agreed to continue the dialogue to further the execution of the relevant provisions of the Security Council's resolutions.

10. In addition to the two rounds of high-level technical talks, a meeting was held on 9 May 1994 at IAEA headquarters in Vienna between an Iraqi delegation headed by the Iraqi Deputy Prime Minister, Mr. Tariq Aziz, and an IAEA team headed by the Director General of the IAEA. The actions taken thus far in implementing many elements of the IAEA's Plan for ongoing monitoring and verification were reviewed. Confidence was expressed that continued cooperation would contribute to the implementation of the remaining elements in accordance with the tentative schedule envisaged during the March 1994 round of high-level technical talks.

11. In the course of the May meeting, the importance of the establishment in the Middle East of a zone free from weapons of mass destruction, as referred to in paragraph 14 of Security Council resolution 687 (1991), was also stressed by both sides. The Director General stated that the IAEA was doing its best to inform States which may negotiate such an agreement, of the Agency's expertise in the field of verification and of the modes of verification which might be employed.

12. During this meeting, the Iraqi delegation raised the issue of provision by the IAEA of technical assistance in the areas of medical and agricultural applications of radioisotopes and radiation. The IAEA agreed to examine the extent to which technical cooperation might be accommodated within the constraints of the relevant Security Council resolutions.

III. Inspection activities

13. Since the last report of 22 April 1994 to the Security Council on the implementation of the Plan, the IAEA has conducted two additional inspection missions in Iraq, bringing the total to twenty-six. The report on the results of IAEA-25 has been brought to the attention of the Security Council in document S/1994/1001; the IAEA-26 report is in preparation. The results of these two inspections are summarized below.

14. The twenty-fifth IAEA inspection mission in Iraq took place from 21 June to 1 July 1994. This inspection was principally directed towards ongoing monitoring and verification activities. Sites covered during this inspection included a number of sites with no known connection to the past nuclear program, but which were judged to have capabilities useful to a reconstituted nuclear program. No activity relevant to those proscribed under resolution 687 (1991) was identified. A

video surveillance system was installed and commissioned in the flow-forming machine workshop at Nassr (Taji), and a third video unit was added to the two units already installed in the milling and boring machine workshop at Um Al Ma'arik.

15. During the course of IAEA-25, several meetings were held with the Iraqi counterpart with a view to securing missing information and remedying inadequacies in the Iraqi declarations. In addition, the current activities at a number of sites were reviewed and the non-proscribed use of equipment declared in accordance with annex 3 of the Plan was confirmed. Follow-up activities from the previous inspections were also completed, including the transfer of irradiated beryllium components from the IRT reactor storage to Location C and the characterization of the different batches of uranium.

16. The twenty-sixth IAEA inspection mission in Iraq took place from 22 August to 7 September 1994. One of the main objectives of this inspection was to investigate Iraq's former activities in laser isotope separation (LIS) as a follow-up of information received in May 1994 from Member States indicating that Iraq had invested significant resources in this area. The subject of LIS-relevant activities had been addressed first during the seventh IAEA inspection mission, carried out in October 1991. At that time, the IAEA received two written statements from a senior Iraqi official denying the existence in Iraq of any LIS activities and, as a consequence, of any scientist or engineer who had been involved in such activities.

17. The investigation carried out by the IAEA-26 inspection team, which included five experts in LIS technology, resulted in a statement by the Iraqi side that the Laser Division of the Department of Physics of Tuwaitha "had received, in 1981, an objective from the Atomic Energy Commission to work in Laser Isotope Separation...we started in two lines; one which is looking after the molecular and the other, the atomic direction." Inspectors were informed that when the achievements of the Laser Division were assessed in 1987, it was decided to downgrade the project to a "watching brief" and to transfer a number of key personnel to other activities.

18. Thus, as finally acknowledged by Iraq, a specific task to explore the feasibility of LIS as a means of producing enriched uranium had, indeed, existed in Iraq. The task appears to have been poorly focused; its declared limited achievements are consistent with the equipment, personnel resources and expertise available, and with the analysis of confiscated Iraqi documents. The team of LIS experts unanimously agreed that the information which had been gathered was consistent with a loosely coordinated and largely empirical approach, but not consistent with achievement to substantial progress in what is a

highly complex technology. In the opinion of these experts, nothing was found to contradict the statement by the Iraqi side that they never achieved isotopic separation of uranium either in the metallic or the molecular form. A parallel investigation by the IAEA of suppliers of laser equipment supports, thus far, the conclusion that Iraq was unable to procure critical pieces of equipment, most notably copper vapour laser systems, from these suppliers.

19. In the course of IAEA-26, the IAEA team also conducted inspections of Iraq's current activities and of the utilization of machine-tools, non-nuclear materials and other equipment, at 15 facilities, installations, and sites.

IV. Assessment of results achieved in 26 inspection missions

20. At the completion of IAEA-26 a total of over 2,500 inspector days had been spent in Iraq since the beginning of inspection activities in May 1991. This involved the deployment of several hundred inspectors and support staff, comprising 35 nationalities. This inspection included 634 visits to 151 different sites, installations, and facilities. Reports of the inspection missions circulated so far as Security Council documents are identified in appendix B.

A. Identification of the secret Iraqi nuclear program

21. The first task assigned to the IAEA under resolution 687 (1991), namely the identification of the various elements of the clandestine Iraqi nuclear program, was largely completed by the end of September 1991, i.e., six months after the adoption by the Security Council of resolution 687. Charting the map of this program has entailed a number of difficulties, including sometimes dramatic confrontations between Iraqi authorities and the IAEA inspection teams. During this phase of the inspection process, the Iraqi Government employed a strategy of obstruction and delay in its efforts to conceal the real nature of its nuclear projects, while, on the other hand, demonstrating a level of cooperation in some less sensitive areas.

22. The secret Iraqi nuclear program appears to have commenced in 1981, under the code name of "Petrochemical Project 3" or "PC3" 1/. PC3 consisted of a diversified and well-financed approach to developing multiple techniques for the production of highly enriched uranium (HEU). At a later stage, a program to investigate all the practical elements of designing and building a nuclear weapon was added to PC3. In the course of PC3, several techniques for producing HEU were explored, including gaseous diffusion, electromagnetic separation (EMIS), and separation by centrifuge. Preliminary experi-

ments were also conducted in the area of laser isotope separation (LIS) and, later on, around the end of 1987, laboratory-scale research was started on a fifth uranium enrichment method, based on chemical enrichment through ion-exchange and liquid-liquid extraction.

23. In May 1987, as revealed in documents seized by IAEA inspectors, Iraqi activities concentrated on two methods, EMIS and centrifuge, which, in the assessment of the Iraqi scientists and engineers, were the most promising for industrial scale operation in Iraq.

24. A large construction program of industrial-scale facilities for EMIS was launched in 1987, followed in 1989 by the construction of a large plant for the mass production of centrifuges. The establishment of an organized structure to carry out weapon-design-related research and development activities dates from April 1988.

25. The Iraqi secret nuclear program was carried out at nine dedicated sites. Fifteen other sites in Iraq (mainly industrial State establishments) supported the PC3 project by providing services of various kinds and manufacturing components to be used in HEU production. The Gulf War stopped this HEU production effort well before any significant amount of such material was produced. At the time of the Gulf War, a significant amount of HEU in the form of fresh (i.e., unirradiated) reactor fuel was in Iraq under IAEA safeguards. Additionally other HEU, in the form of irradiated fuel, was present, also under IAEA safeguards. All safeguarded HEU has been accounted for by post-war IAEA inspections and has been removed from Iraq.

26. The rapid identification of the secret Iraqi nuclear program is due, in no small measure, to the continuous support of the UN Security Council and to the assistance extended to the IAEA by its Member States through the provision of intelligence information and of experts who expanded the competence of the IAEA teams in particular areas.

27. The identification of the main components of the secret Iraqi nuclear program was followed by a lengthy process of verification aimed at consolidating the inspection findings. Important details had to be clarified in areas such as the procurement of sensitive materials and equipment and the sources of foreign advice in sensitive technologies, with the objective of arriving at a consistent and reasonably complete picture of PC3. It is the considered opinion of the IAEA, based on the results of the twenty-six inspection missions, the analyses of thousands of samples, the analysis of documents confiscated in Iraq, the assessment of procurement and other information obtained from Member States of the IAEA,

---

1/ In the course of IAEA-6, IAEA inspectors confiscated in Iraq 2348 documents totaling 54,922 pages. The dates of these documents range from 1979 to 1991. All of the PC3 documents seized were stamped "Top Secret", the earliest of which bears the date 23 December 1981.

that the essential components of the clandestine Iraqi nuclear program have been identified and that the scope of the program is well understood. Although still lacking in some detail, the picture appears complete and consistent.

B. *Destruction, removal and rendering harmless operations*

28. The second main task given to the IAEA by resolution 687 (1991) concerns the destruction, removal or rendering harmless of the essential elements of the Iraqi nuclear weapons development program, including the nuclear-weapons-usable material known to have been in Iraq in the form of safeguarded reactor fuel.

29. Extensive destruction of the Iraqi nuclear installations occurred during the Gulf Was as a result of air raids by Coalition forces. Additional destruction of equipment and material was carried out by the Iraqi army at the end of the war and prior to the start of the IAEA inspections, in an attempt to remove evidence of its secret program.

30. Since September 1991, i.e., when the scope of the clandestine Iraqi nuclear program came into focus, the IAEA has supervised the systematic destruction of facilities, technical buildings, equipment and other items proscribed under Security Council resolution 687 which had escaped destruction during the war or which had been only slightly damaged. The IAEA teams ordered and supervised the destruction of over 1,900 individual items as well as 600 tons of specialty alloys useful in a nuclear weapons program or in uranium enrichment activities. At nuclear-dedicated sites, specialized process buildings covering a surface area of some 32,500 square metres were demolished with explosives, entailing as well the destruction of a large amount of high quality equipment which had been installed or stored at those sites.

31. With the completion of the destruction, removal and rendering harmless activities to date, the IAEA is satisfied that there remain no practical capabilities in Iraq for the production of nuclear weapons or of nuclear-weapons-usable material (i.e., HEU or plutonium). Should additional prohibited items be located, these items would also be subject to destruction, removal or rendering harmless.

32. As to the quantities of weapons-usable nuclear material (HEU in the form of reactor fuel elements) which were in Iraq under IAEA safeguards, these were found untouched and have been fully accounted for and removed, as referred to above. The operation for removing the special nuclear material, including a few grams of separated plutonium, has entailed, *inter alia*, a complex technical effort to clear part of the enriched fuel elements from the rubble of a bombed research reactor.

33. Reports on the status of destruction, removal and rendering harmless activities have been circulated semi-annually as Security Council documents and are listed in appendix C.

V. *Procurement-related information*

34. Under the IAEA plan, Iraq is required to declare to the IAEA all items listed in annex 3 of the Plan. These items fall into two general categories:

- Items prohibited under resolution 687
  Any items falling in this list must be destroyed, removed from Iraq or otherwise rendered harmless.

- Items of relevance under resolution 687
  These are items which could be used to implement activities prohibited under resolution 687, but which may also serve other non-prohibited purposes. The utilization in Iraq of such dual-use items must be monitored.

35. In order to ensure the completeness of the Iraqi declarations, and to ensure the destruction, removal and rendering harmless of all items falling within the first category, verification of the information provided by Iraq on the procurement of key materials, equipment and instrumentation needed in their secret nuclear program is essential. Verification of this information is a prerequisite for establishing a meaningful Plan. This is a lengthy process, requiring identification of the manufacturers and suppliers which in turn calls for the cooperation of the concerned Member States. The inquiries conducted so far by the IAEA in this delicate matter involve 172 companies and governmental institutions in 27 countries.

36. Since the last report on implementation of the Plan, two outstanding issues, related to procurement, have been resolved through independent verification. These issues concerned the quantities of natural uranium oxide which Iraq had procured from Brazil, and the amount and origin of the maraging steel which, according to Iraqi statements, had been procured through a UK-based intermediary. Both issues were important, since the first concerned the completeness of the inventory of nuclear material existing in Iraq, i.e., the nuclear material balance, and the second related to the amount of stock material that Iraq planned to use for the mass production of centrifuges.

VI. *Implementation of the IAEA ongoing monitoring and verification plan*

37. With the approval of the Plan by the Security Council in November 1991 in resolution 715, the IAEA began phasing in activities relevant to ongoing monitoring and verification, such as material accountancy and

containment measures. These measures have included the establishment of the inventories of nuclear material and other nuclear-related items, the application of seals and the tagging of equipment subject to the Plan.

38. In 1992, a periodic radiometric survey of the main surface water bodies of Iraq (rivers, lakes, and canals) was instituted. The radiometric survey of Iraqi water bodies is now routinely conducted, twice a year. Samples of water, sediment, and biota are collected at 45 pre-established sampling points and shipped out of Iraq for analysis. This technique is sensitive enough to detect radio-active and other chemical signatures which would reveal the existence of undeclared nuclear activities, for example, the operation of a nuclear reactor or a reprocessing plant.

39. The provision by Iraq of detailed information concerning sites, facilities, and installations subject to the Plan, using reporting forms developed by the IAEA has been completed recently. These forms, which cover all the reporting requirements under the Plan, were developed in such a way as to facilitate the electronic processing and updating of the information.

40. On-site inspections are the backbone of IAEA monitoring and verification activities. The value of visual observations and information gathering by experienced inspectors and experts cannot be overemphasized in terms of ensuring the IAEA's ability to respond immediately to developing situations. The procedures for conducting routine and no-notice inspections at sites, facilities or installations subject to the Plan have been thoroughly tested and have proved to be operational. The continuous presence in Iraq of nuclear inspectors, as of the end of August 1994, will facilitate the conduct of no-notice inspections at all sites.

41. The deployment of video surveillance systems to monitor the usage of dual-use equipment, such as high precision computer numerically controlled (CNC) machine-tools, was also begun in mid-1993. The installations are now complete and all of the equipment is operational.

42. Practical arrangements have been made with the Special Commission to coordinate the IAEA's activities in areas of overlapping responsibility, such as video surveillance and no-notice inspection of certain dual-use equipment.

43. Arrangements with the Special Commission have also been made to secure office space in the Baghdad Monitoring and Verification Centre (BMVC), which is now nearing completion, and to share the support services that BMVC will provide, such as aerial photography, high altitude imagery, transportation, communications, interpretation and medical services.

44. On 26 November 1993, Iraq formally accepted Security Council resolution 715 (1991). As underlined in the course of the high-level technical talks, this acceptance by Iraq of the resolution represented a major step towards Iraq's fulfilment of its obligations under the Security Council resolutions.

45. As required in paragraph 7 of resolution 715 (1991), the IAEA, the Special Commission and the Sanctions Committee have developed a mechanism for monitoring future sales and supplies by other countries to Iraq. It is expected that the Security Council will, in the near future, approve this jointly-developed mechanism, which will form an integral part of the IAEA's ongoing monitoring and verification activities in Iraq.

46. At the beginning of 1994, the Iraqi authorities established the National Monitoring Directorate (NMD), which will be responsible for implementing all actions required of Iraq under the provisions of resolution 715 (1991) and the Plans of the IAEA and the Special Commission. An Iraqi document outlining the NMD functions and responsibilities is contained in appendix D. Iraq is also developing comprehensive procedures to assist its personnel in the implementation of these functions and responsibilities.

47. The Iraqi authorities have also provided to the IAEA and the Special Commission a draft decision, to be promulgated by the Revolutionary Command Council, intended to address paragraphs 34 and 35 of the IAEA's Plan, as well as paragraph 20 of the Special Commission's Plan, which require Iraq to adopt legal measures necessary to implement its obligations under the terms of the relevant resolutions.

48. To implement the Plan effectively, the IAEA requires on a continuing basis updated information on sites, facilities, or installations which might harbour activities or utilize items prohibited under resolution 687. In this context, the IAEA has gathered and continues to gather much information of its own from its verification activities. It also acquires information through in-depth analyses of media reports and other open literature. In the future, it will secure information from detailed reports by States on exports to Iraq of nuclear-related material and equipment. Finally, the IAEA also receives information from its Member States collected through national intelligence means. No information, whatever its provenance, may be ignored, but all information must be critically analyzed to determine its credibility.

VII. Conclusion

49. It can be concluded that, with the establishment at the end of August of the IAEA continuous presence in Iraq, all elements of the IAEA's Plan are now in place. Monitoring and verification measures will evolve as technical needs arise and as advanced technologies become available. The implementation of the ongoing monitoring and verification plan does not foreclose the exercise by the IAEA of its right to investigate any aspect of Iraq's

former nuclear weapons program, in particular, through the follow-up of any new information developed by the IAEA or provided by Member States, and assessed as warranting further investigation.

Appendix A
High-level technical talks and related reports

Date	Location	Report in document	Dated
31 August-9 September 1993	New York	S/26451	6 September 1993
2-8 October 1993	Baghdad	S/26571	12 October 1993
15-30 November 1993	New York	S/26825	1 December 1993
2-5 February 1994	Baghdad	S/1994/151	29 April 1994
14-19 March 1994	New York	S/1994/341	24 March 1994
24-26 April 1994	Baghdad	S/1994/520	29 April 1994
4-5 July 1994	Baghdad	S/1994/86	20 July 1994

Appendix B
IAEA's inspections in Iraq and related reports

Inspection	Dates of inspection		Report	Dated
1	15-19 May	1991	S/22788	12 July 1991
2	22 June-3 July	1991	S/22788	12 July 1991
3	7-18 July	1991	S/22837	25 July 1991
4	27 July-10 August	1991	S/22986 and Corr. 1	28 August 1991
5	14-20 September	1991	S/23112	4 October 1991
6	22-30 September	1991	S/23122	8 October 1991
7	11-22 October	1991	S/23215	14 November 1991
8	11-18 November	1991	S/23283	12 December 1991
9	11-14 January	1992	S/23505	30 January 1992
10	5-13 February	1992	S/23644	26 February 1992
11	7-15 April	1992	S/23947	22 May 1992
12	26 May-4 June	1992	S/24223	2 July 1992
13	13-21 July	1992	S/24450	16 August 1992
14	31 August -7 September	1992	S/24593	28 September 1992
15	8-18 November	1992	S/24981	17 December 1992
16	5-8 December	1992	S/25013	24 December 1992
17	25-31 January	1993	S/25411	13 March 1993
18	3-11 March	1993	S/25666	26 April 1993
19	30 April-7 May	1993	S/25982	21 June 1993
20	25-30 June	1993	S/26333	20 August 1993
21	24-27 July	1993	S/26333	20 August 1993
22	1-15 November	1993	S/1994/31	14 January 1994
23	4-11 February	1994	S/1994/355	25 March 1994
24	11-21 April	1994	S/1994/650	1 June 1994
25	21 June-1 July	1994	S/1994/1001	26 August 1994
26	22 August-7 September	1994	in preparation	1994

Appendix C

IAEA semi-annual reports on destruction, removal and rendering harmless, pursuant
to United Nations Security Council resolution 699 (1991)

Document	Dated
S/23295	17 December 1991
S/24110	17 June 1992
S/24988	17 December 1992
S/25983	21 June 1993
S/26897	20 December 1993
S/1994/793	5 July 1994

Appendix D

Establishment of a national monitoring directorate in Iraq
(Iraqi document handed over to the IAEA on 4 July 1994)

THE TASKS OF A NATIONAL IRAQI MONITORING DIRECTORATE

1. Implementation of SCR 715 (1991) and its provision regarding prohibited activities.

2. The coordination and following-up with different Iraqi sectors and role liaison officers in the different sectors and facilities (F/I/S).

3. The coordination with the Ministry of Foreign Affairs and other concerned Ministries in implementing SCR 715 (1991).

4. The coordination and support for the different UNSCOM and IAEA teams in carrying out their tasks in the OMV process.

5. The coordination and support for the different UNSCOM teams in carrying out their task in the aerial survey.

6. Following-up of the operation of different sensors installed in different (F/I/S) and give whatever logistical support needed by UNSCOM and the IAEA teams to ensure the normal operation of these sensors.

7. The monitoring of import and export of machines, equipment and material in accordance with agreed upon import export mechanism.

8. The implementation of the roles and provision of different annexes of the OMV plan (UNSCOM and IAEA).

9. The coordination of different activities with Baghdad Monitoring Centre (UNSCOM and IAEA).

10. The assurance in the proper implementation of Iraqi legislative provisions regarding prohibited activities in accordance with pertinent Security Council resolutions.

11. Monitoring and control of movement of equipment and materials covered by the different annexes to resolution 715.

RELATIONSHIP BETWEEN THE NMD AND THE DIFFERENT FACILITIES INSTALLATION AND SITES

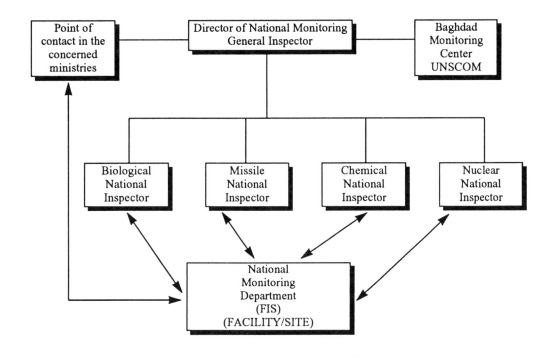

NATIONAL MONITORING DIRECTORATE

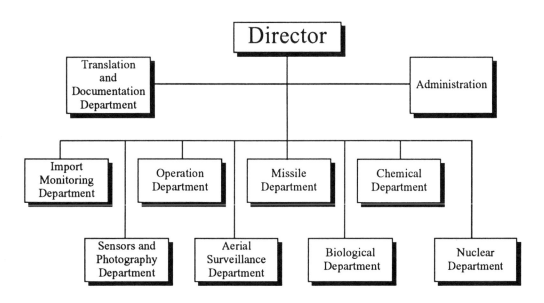

Document 196

Security Council resolution concerning military deployments by Iraq in the direction of the border with Kuwait

S/RES/949 (1994), 15 October 1994

The Security Council,

Recalling all its previous relevant resolutions, and *reaffirming* resolutions 678 (1990) of 29 November 1990, 686 (1991) of 2 March 1991, 687 (1991) of 3 April 1991, 689 (1991) of 9 April 1991 and 833 (1993) of 27 May 1993, and in particular paragraph 2 of resolution 678 (1990),

Recalling that Iraq's acceptance of resolution 687 (1991) adopted pursuant to Chapter VII of the Charter of the United Nations forms the basis of the cease-fire,

Noting past Iraqi threats and instances of actual use of force against its neighbours,

Recognizing that any hostile or provocative action directed against its neighbours by the Government of Iraq constitutes a threat to peace and security in the region,

Welcoming all diplomatic and other efforts to resolve the crisis,

Determined to prevent Iraq from resorting to threats and intimidation of its neighbours and the United Nations,

Underlining that it will consider Iraq fully responsible for the serious consequences of any failure to fulfil the demands in the present resolution,

Noting that Iraq has affirmed its readiness to resolve in a positive manner the issue of recognizing Kuwait's sovereignty and its borders as endorsed by resolution 833 (1993), but *underlining* that Iraq must unequivocally commit itself by full and formal constitutional procedures to respect Kuwait's sovereignty, territorial integrity and borders, as required by resolutions 687 (1991) and 833 (1993),

Reaffirming the commitment of all Member States to the sovereignty, territorial integrity and political independence of Kuwait and Iraq,

Reaffirming its statement of 8 October 1994 (S/1994/PRST/58),

Taking note of the letter from the Permanent Representative of Kuwait of 6 October 1994 (S/1994/1137), regarding the statement by the Revolution Command Council of Iraq of 6 October 1994,

Taking note also of the letter from the Permanent Representative of Iraq of 10 October 1994 (S/1994/1149), announcing that the Government of Iraq had decided to withdraw the troops recently deployed in the direction of the border with Kuwait,

Acting under Chapter VII of the Charter of the United Nations,

1. *Condemns* recent military deployments by Iraq in the direction of the border with Kuwait;

2. *Demands* that Iraq immediately complete the withdrawal of all military units recently deployed to southern Iraq to their original positions;

3. *Demands* that Iraq not again utilize its military or any other forces in a hostile or provocative manner to threaten either its neighbours or United Nations operations in Iraq;

4. *Demands* therefore that Iraq not redeploy to the south the units referred to in paragraph 2 above or take any other action to enhance its military capacity in southern Iraq;

5. *Demands* that Iraq cooperate fully with the United Nations Special Commission;

6. *Decides* to remain actively seized of the matter.

Document 197

Letter from the Representatives of Iraq and of the Russian Federation transmitting the text of a joint communiqué containing Iraq's announcement that it had withdrawn its troops to rearguard positions on 12 October 1994

S/1994/1173, 15 October 1994

Letter dated 14 October 1994 from the representatives of Iraq and the Russian Federation to the United Nations addressed to the President of the Security Council

Upon instructions from our respective Governments, we have the honour to enclose herewith the text of a Joint Communiqué issued by the Iraqi and Russian sides on Thursday, 13 October 1994, after the meeting held between H.E. Mr. Saddam Hussein, President of the Republic of Iraq and H.E. Mr. Andrei Kozyrev, Minister for Foreign Affairs of the Russian Federation.

We should be grateful if you would have this letter and its annex circulated as a document of the Security Council.

(*Signed*) Nizar HAMDOON
Permanent Representative of the Republic of Iraq

(*Signed*) Vasiliy S. SIDOROV
Chargé d'affaires a.i.
First Deputy Permanent Representative of the
Russian Federation

Annex
Joint communiqué on the outcome of the meeting in Baghdad

On 13 October 1994, Mr. Saddam Hussein, President of Iraq, received Mr. Andrei Kozyrev, Minister for Foreign Affairs of the Russian Federation, who had come to Iraq on the instructions of the President of the Russian Federation, Mr. Boris Yeltsin.

In the course of the meeting, the situation in the Gulf region and the current state of Russian-Iraqi relations were discussed.

The Russian Federation advocated the adoption of decisive measures to prevent an escalation of the tension and to resume the political and diplomatic efforts that would ultimately bring security and real stability to the region, the lifting of the sanctions against Iraq and the establishment of good-neighbourly relations between Iraq and Kuwait.

A number of specific measures to build confidence among the States of the region, removing mutual suspicion and creating a climate of trust, were discussed.

Iraq announced officially that at 2100 hours on 12 October it had completed the withdrawal of its troops to rearguard positions. The Russian Federation expressed its warm appreciation of this step on the part of Iraq.

Iraq affirmed its readiness to resolve in a positive manner the issue of recognizing Kuwait's sovereignty and borders, as laid down in Security Council resolution 833 (1993).

Following Iraq's official recognition of Kuwait's sovereignty and borders, the Russian Federation will support the official start of the long-term monitoring provided for in Security Council resolution 715 (1991) and the simultaneous initiation of a limited test period, which in the Russian Federation's opinion should not exceed six months, to verify the effectiveness of the monitoring, after which the Security Council will take a decision concerning the implementation of paragraph 22 of Security Council resolution 687 (1991) in its entirety, without imposing further conditions. The Russian Federation affirms that, subject to Iraq's implementation of the relevant Security Council resolutions, it will advocate the lifting of other sanctions.

Iraq confirmed its willingness to continue its cooperation with the International Committee of the Red Cross in investigating the fate of missing Kuwaiti nationals. Mr. Kozyrev indicated the special interest of the Russian Federation in this humanitarian issue.

Document 198

Letter dated 13 November 1994 from the Permanent Representative of Iraq transmitting the declaration of the National Assembly (10 November 1994) and decree of the Revolution Command Council No. 200 (10 November 1994) affirming Iraq's recognition of the sovereignty, territorial integrity and political independence of Kuwait and of its international boundaries as endorsed by the Security Council in its resolution 833 (1993)

S/1994/1288, 14 November 1994

Letter dated 13 November 1994 from the Permanent Representative of Iraq to the United Nations addressed to the Secretary-General

On instructions from my Government, I have the honour to transmit to you herewith a letter dated 12 November 1994 from Mr. Mohammed Said Al-Sahaf, Minister for Foreign Affairs of the Republic of Iraq, together with three enclosures.

I should be grateful if you would have the letter and its annex circulated as a document of the Security Council.

(*Signed*) Nizar HAMDOON
Ambassador
Permanent Representative

Annex
Letter dated 12 November 1994 from the Minister for Foreign Affairs of Iraq addressed to the Secretary-General

I should like at the outset to refer to the three sets of identical letters dated 8 March 1991, 21 March 1991 and 22 March 1991 from the Permanent Representative of Iraq to the United Nations addressed to the Secretary-General and the President of the Security Council (S/22342, S/22370 and S/22396 respectively) concerning fulfilment by the relevant Iraqi authorities of the obligations set forth in Security Council resolution 686 (1991).

An an expression of the desire of the Republic of Iraq for respect for the Charter of the United Nations and for international law, in keeping with its commitment to comply fully with all the relevant resolutions of the United Nations Security Council, and as a demonstration of Iraq's peaceful intentions and of its resolve to strive for the maintenance of peace, security and stability in the region and the establishment of relations of good-neighbourliness based on the principles of mutual respect for security, sovereignty and legitimate interests, I have the honour to transmit to you herewith the texts of the

Declaration issued by the National Assembly on 10 November 1994 and of Decree No. 200 of the Revolution Command Council of the Republic of Iraq together with a copy of the issue of *Alwaqai Aliraqiya*, the Government's official gazette, in which the Declaration and Decision were published. The two documents affirm Iraq's recognition of the sovereignty, territorial integrity and political independence of Kuwait and of its international boundaries as endorsed by the provisions of Security Council resolution 833 (1993).

Iraq proceeds from the premise that the Security Council will operate in accordance with the legal interpretation of the resolutions it adopts and that it will follow in their implementation the principles of justice and fairness principally through the lifting of the comprehensive embargo and, as a first step, the implementation of paragraph 22 of resolution 687 (1991) in full and without further restrictions or conditions.

I request you to have this letter and its enclosure circulated to the members of the Security Council.

(Signed) Mohammed Said AL-SAHAF
Minister for Foreign Affairs of the Republic of Iraq

Enclosure I
Declaration of the National Assembly

The National Assembly held an extraordinary session on 6 Jamada al-Thani 1415 corresponding to 10 November 1994. Having discussed the relationship between Iraq and the Security Council, and in order to affirm Iraq's peaceful intentions and its keenness for the maintenance of peace, security and stability in the region in accordance with the Charter of the United Nations and international law, and the establishment of good neighbourly relations on the basis of mutual respect for security, sovereignty and legitimate interests,

The National Assembly declares its support of the recognition by the Republic of Iraq of the sovereignty of the State of Kuwait, its territorial integrity and political independence, and its support for, in compliance with

United Nations Security Council resolution 833 (1993), the recognition by the Republic of Iraq of the international boundary between the Republic of Iraq and the State of Kuwait as demarcated by the United Nations Iraq-Kuwait Boundary Demarcation Commission established in pursuance to paragraph 3 of resolution 687 (1991), and its respect for the inviolability of the said boundary.

Sa'adi Mehdi SALEH
Speaker of the National Assembly
6 Jamada al-Than
10 November 1994

Enclosure II
Decree of the Revolution Command Council No. 200 on 10/11/1994

In expressing the desire to respect the Charter of the United Nations and international law; in conformity with the obligation of the Republic of Iraq to comply fully with all relevant resolutions of the United Nations Security Council; as evidence of Iraq's peaceful intentions; due to the determination to work for maintenance of peace, security and stability in the region and the establishment of good neighbourly relations on the basis of the rules of mutual respect to security, sovereignty and legitimate interests; reaffirming the Revolution Command Council Decision No. 55 of 5 March 1991, taking into consideration the Decision of the National Assembly adopted at its special meeting of 20 March 1991; taking into account the Declaration of the National Assembly of 10 November 1994; and, pursuant to the provisions of Article 42 (a) of the Constitution;

The Revolution Command Council has decided as follows:

1. The Republic of Iraq recognizes the sovereignty of the State of Kuwait, its territorial integrity and political independence.

2. The Republic of Iraq, in compliance with the United Nations Security Council resolution 833 (1993), recognizes the international boundary between the Republic of Iraq and the State of Kuwait as demarcated by the United Nations Iraq-Kuwait Boundary Demarcation Commission established in pursuance to paragraph 3 of resolution 687 (1991), and respects the inviolability of the said boundary.

3. The competent ministries and authorities shall undertake the implementation of this Decision.

4. This Decision shall take effect as of the Tenth of the month of November 1994, and it shall be published in the Official Gazette.

Saddam HUSSEIN
Chairman of the Revolution Command Council

Enclosure III
LAW

Decree No. 113
Date: 16 Rabii al-Awal 1415 H.
23 August 1994 A.D.

In accordance with the provisions of Para. (A) of Article 42 of the Constitution.

The Revolution Command Council has decided to promulgate the following Law:

Law No. 12 of 1994
Amending the Law of the Wounded Medal No. 33 of 1983

Article 1 of the Law of the Wounded Medal No. 33 of 1983 shall be deleted and substituted by the following:

Article 1:

1. A medal in the name of (The Wounded Medal) shall be created.

2. The medal shall be granted to the wounded persons from the military commander officers or commanders or commanding units being wounded in the battle during performing their military duties perfectly.

3. The medal shall be granted to the civil wounded persons who are wounded in the national battles.

Article 2:

This Law shall come into force from the date of its promulgation.

Saddam HUSSEIN
Chairman of the Revolution Command Council

(Published in Alwaqai Aliraqiya
(Ar. Edit.) No. 3526 of 5-9-1994.)

DECLARATION OF THE
NATIONAL ASSEMBLY
REPUBLIC OF IRAQ
THE NATIONAL ASSEMBLY

The National Assembly held an extraordinary session on 6 Jamada al-Akhira 1415 corresponding to 10 November 1994. Having discussed the relationship between Iraq and the Security Council, and in order to affirm Iraq's peaceful intentions and its keenness for the maintenance of peace, security and stability in the region in accordance with the Charter of the United Nations and international law, and the establishment of good neighbourly relations on the basis of mutual respect for security, sovereignty and legitimate interests.

The National Assembly declares its support of the recognition by the Republic of Iraq of the sovereignty of the State of Kuwait, its territorial integrity and political independence, and its support for, in compliance with United Nations Security Council resolution 833 (1993), the recognition by the Republic of Iraq of the international boundary between the Republic of Iraq and the State of Kuwait as demarcated by the United Nations Iraq-Kuwait Boundary Demarcation Commission established in pursuance to paragraph 3 of resolution 687 (1991), and its respect for the inviolability of the said boundary.

Sa'adi Mehdi SALEH
Speaker of the National Assembly
6 Jamada al-Akhira 1415 H.
10 November 1994

DECREE OF THE REVOLUTION COMMAND COUNCIL

IN THE NAME OF GOD THE COMPASSIONATE, THE MERCIFUL

REPUBLIC OF IRAQ

Decree No. 200
Date: 6 Jamada al-Akhira, 1415 H.
10 November 1994 A.D.

In expressing the desire to respect the Charter of the United Nations and international law; in conformity with the obligation of the Republic of Iraq to comply fully with all relevant resolutions of the United Nations Security Council; as evidence of Iraq's peaceful intentions; due to the determination to work for maintenance of peace, security and stability in the region and the establishment of good neighbourly relations on the basis of the rules of mutual respect to security, sovereignty and legitimate interests; reaffirming the Revolution Command Council Decision No. 55 of 5 March 1991; taking into consideration the Decision of the National Assembly adopted at its special meeting of 20 March 1991; taking into account the Declaration of the National Assembly of 10 Novem-

ber 1991; and, pursuant to the provisions of Article 42 (a) of the Constitution;

The Revolution Command Council has decided as follows:

1. The Republic of Iraq recognizes the sovereignty of the State of Kuwait, its territorial integrity and political independence.

2. The Republic of Iraq, in compliance with the United Nations Security Council resolution 833 (1993), recognizes the international boundary between the Republic of Iraq and the State of Kuwait as demarcated by the United Nations Iraq-Kuwait Boundary Demarcation Commission established in pursuance to paragraph 3 of resolution 687 (1991), and respects the inviolability of the said boundary.

3. The competent ministries and authorities shall undertake the implementation of this Decision.

4. This Decision shall take effect as of 10 November 1994, and it shall be published in the Official Gazette.

Saddam HUSSEIN
Chairman of the Revolution Command Council

CONTENTS

LAW

DECLARATION

DECREE

Document 199

Statement by the President of the Security Council concerning Iraq's recognition of the sovereignty, territorial integrity and political independence of Kuwait and of its international boundaries as endorsed by the Security Council in its resolution 833 (1993)

S/PRST/1994/68, 16 November 1994

The Security Council has received the letter addressed to the President of the Security Council by the Foreign Minister of Iraq dated 12 November 1994 1/ enclosing copies of Revolution Command Council decision No. 200 of 10 November 1994, signed by its President,

Mr. Saddam Hussein, and the declaration of the Iraqi National Assembly, also of 10 November 1994, which

1/ A similar communication, which was addressed to the Secretary-General with a request that it be circulated as a document of the Security Council, has been circulated under the symbol S/1994/1288.

confirm Iraq's irrevocable and unqualified recognition of the sovereignty, territorial integrity and political independence of the State of Kuwait, and of the international boundary between the Republic of Iraq and the State of Kuwait as demarcated by the United Nations Iraq-Kuwait Boundary Demarcation Commission, and confirm Iraq's respect for the inviolability of that boundary, in accordance with Security Council resolution 833 (1993).

The Security Council welcomes this development and the President of the Security Council has written to the Permanent Representative of Iraq accordingly, in a letter dated 16 November 1994 (S/1994/1297). The Council notes that Iraq has taken this action in compliance with Security Council resolution 833 (1993) and has

unequivocally committed itself by full and formal constitutional procedures to respect Kuwait's sovereignty, territorial integrity and borders, as required by Security Council resolutions 687 (1991), 833 (1993) and 949 (1994).

The Security Council considers this decision by Iraq to be a significant step in the direction towards implementation of the relevant Security Council resolutions. In the above-mentioned letter, the President of the Security Council informed the Government of Iraq that the members of the Security Council will follow closely Iraq's implementation of its decision; they will also continue to keep under review Iraq's actions to complete its compliance with all the relevant Security Council resolutions.

Document 200

Eighth report of the Executive Chairman of UNSCOM

S/1994/1422 and addendum, S/1994/1422/Add.1, 15 December 1994

Note by the Secretary-General

The Secretary-General has the honour to transmit to the Security Council a report submitted by the Executive Chairman of the Special Commission established by the Secretary-General, pursuant to paragraph 9 (b) (i) of Security Council resolution 687 (1991).

Annex
Eighth report of the Executive Chairman of the Special Commission established by the Secretary-General pursuant to paragraph 9 (b) (i) of Security Council resolution 687 (1991), on the activities of the Special Commission

I. INTRODUCTION

1. The present report is the eighth on the activities of the Special Commission established by the Secretary-General pursuant to paragraph 9 (b) (i) of Security Council resolution 687 (1991), submitted to the Security Council by the Executive Chairman of the Commission. It is the seventh such report provided in accordance with paragraph 3 of Security Council resolution 699 (1991). It covers the period from 10 June to 9 December 1994, and is further to the reports contained in documents S/23165, S/23268, S/24108 and Corr.1, S/24984, S/25977, S/26910 and S/1994/750.

2. As noted in the report contained in document S/1994/1138 and Corr.1 submitted under Council resolution 715 (1991), during the six months to October 1994, the Commission allocated the bulk of its

resources to the establishment of the ongoing monitoring and verification system. Since the time of that report, the Commission has been forced to redirect more of its total resources to resolving outstanding issues in relation to the past programmes and to the establishment of the export/import mechanism required under paragraph 7 of Security Council resolution 715 (1991). Even so, a large part of the developments to be covered in the present report have already been addressed in the October report. Consequently, there is considerable overlap between the two reports.

II. DEVELOPMENTS

A. General

3. Much has been achieved in the period under review. The Commission has moved on from the initial stages of establishing the system of ongoing monitoring and verification to a stage where the system is provisionally operational and its efficacy is being tested. Interim monitoring in the biological area began in December 1994. In addition, the Commission has advanced its understanding of the past programmes and has pursued the establishment of an export/import mechanism for dual-purpose items as defined by the plans for ongoing monitoring and verification. The political dialogue between the Commission and Iraq has continued; high-level meetings, both general and technical, were held in New York in July, September, October and November and in Baghdad in July, October and November 1994.

4. The emphasis of the Commission's efforts in this period was clearly to establish the ongoing monitoring and verification system. This required the collation and analysis of data about Iraq's dual-purpose capabilities, the preparation of monitoring and verification protocols for each site to be monitored, the inventorying and tagging of identified dual-purpose items, the installation of sensors, the establishment of the Baghdad Monitoring and Verification Centre and communications with remote-controlled sensors, and the dispatch of resident monitoring groups to Iraq to serve in the Centre.

5. Concurrent with this major effort, the Commission followed through on the understanding reached with Iraq in October 1993 to resolve outstanding issues related to Iraq's past proscribed programmes in parallel with the establishment of ongoing monitoring and verification. In this regard, further discussions were held with Iraq, Iraqi personnel were interviewed, the Commission obtained some limited additional documentation from Iraq and further inspections were conducted. Furthermore, the Commission intensified greatly its contacts with supporting and supplier Governments as part of its efforts to corroborate, in the absence of direct supporting evidence from Iraq itself, Iraqi accounts of its imports for the past programmes. Analysis of the data available to the Commission from all these sources has indicated new avenues of investigation to pursue in order to obtain an independently verified account. In many instances, new information obtained by the Commission contradicted the accounts given by Iraq. Detailed, complete and accurate data on previous imports of prohibited and dual-purpose items is necessary to fulfil the mandate to account fully for Iraq's past proscribed capabilities and to ensure a comprehensive ongoing monitoring and verification system covering all of Iraq's dual-purpose capabilities.

6. Considerable effort was also expended on another aspect of the Commission's work, completion of which is a prerequisite for fulfilling the terms for the lifting of the sanctions—development of the concept and operational plan for the export/import mechanism required under paragraph 7 of Security Council resolution 715 (1991). Further seminars were held with international experts to elaborate the items to be covered by the mechanism and to create a practical, effective and durable system.

7. Iraq was, during the period under report, generally cooperative in the Commission's efforts to establish the physical aspects of ongoing monitoring and verification. Access was provided to all sites designated by the Commission for inspection and to personnel involved. Iraq provided much support for the installation of monitoring sensors, for the inventorying and tagging of dual-purpose items, for the construction of the Baghdad Monitoring and Verification Centre and for the establishment of communications between the Centre and the remote-controlled sensors.

8. However, Iraq's attitude to the provision of data and supporting evidence still fell far short of its obligation to provide full, final and complete disclosures of its past proscribed programmes and of its current and recent dual-purpose capabilities subject to ongoing monitoring and verification. It appears that many of Iraq's declarations are incomplete and sometimes contradictory. The Commission has both direct and indirect evidence that Iraq is still failing to declare equipment and materials acquired for and capable of use in proscribed programmes and that its accounts of certain of its projects do not reflect their true purpose and their role as part of now proscribed weapons programmes. In general, in relation to the past programmes, Iraq has not volunteered information and has shown marked lack of transparency, disclosing information only when confronted with evidence by the Commission. Iraq maintains its claim, not believed by the Commission, that it has destroyed all documentation related to these programmes and that no other tangible proofs exist to support its accounts. Indeed, events of the past six months have strengthened the Commission's conviction that important documentation still exists and that the Iraqi authorities have taken the conscious decision not to release it freely to the Commission. In any case, Iraq has not fulfilled its undertaking to resolve all outstanding issues in relation to the past programmes in parallel with the establishment of ongoing monitoring and verification. The importance of doing so has been repeatedly impressed upon Iraq at each of the high-level meetings referred to above, as has the need for Iraq to provide documentation and supporting evidence.

9. The situation is better in relation to declarations required under the plan for ongoing monitoring and verification. Generally, despite omissions and inconsistencies, these declarations have been sufficient to permit the initiation of ongoing monitoring and verification. However, early in the reporting period, major problems continued in the biological area, where incomplete declarations, the failure to declare all equipment and materials which should be monitored, together with a failure to declare movement, repair or modification of equipment between inspections, resulted in a situation where the establishment of reliable baseline data from which to start monitoring was not possible. This, clearly, delayed the initiation of ongoing monitoring and verification in the biological area. However, in November 1994, Iraq presented new declarations in the biological area and has undertaken to work with the Commission to continue to improve these declarations. As a result of these develop-

ments, interim monitoring in the biological area has now started.

10. Initially, a delaying factor was that managers and senior personnel at sites being monitored were not sufficiently aware of the nature of ongoing monitoring and verification and of the Commission's rights to conduct it. However, the situation appears to be improving significantly as Iraq gains greater experience in ongoing monitoring and verification and so understands the need to educate key personnel at monitored sites.

11. There have been fewer problems in the exercise of the Commission's privileges and immunities during the period under review, with fewer challenges as to whether the Commission's activities are indeed related to resolution 715 (1991) (i.e. covered by the mandate to conduct ongoing monitoring and verification), only a few minor attempts to restrict or delay access to sites or personnel, and limited instances of tampering with tags. Harassment of Commission personnel has all but stopped and, while minor problems arose in relation to the operation of the aerial inspections, there have been no attempts to prevent the Commission from taking the photographs it is instructed to obtain.

12. However, in the autumn, the Iraqi authorities created a serious crisis with regard to the implementation of resolution 687 (1991). On 22 September 1994, the Iraqi authorities started to make threats to block the work of the Commission. In an effort to normalize the situation, the Executive Chairman visited Baghdad early in October 1994. In meetings with the Foreign Minister of Iraq and other officials on 4 and 5 October 1994, the Iraqi side rejected all appeals by the Chairman to withdraw those threats. At this time, Iraqi troop movements in the direction of Kuwait had already started.

13. On 6 October 1994, a joint meeting of Iraq's Revolution Command Council and the Iraqi Command of the Ba'ath Party indicated that, unless the Security Council's consideration of the Commission's biannual report on the implementation of ongoing monitoring and verification (S/1994/1138 and Corr.1) to take place on or about 10 October 1994 were favourable to Iraq, Iraq might withdraw its cooperation with the Commission. This was rejected by the Council on 8 October 1994 in a statement by its President on behalf of the Council (S/PRST/1994/58). On 15 October, the Security Council adopted resolution 949 (1994), demanding "that Iraq cooperate fully with the Commission" and the withdrawal of "all military units recently deployed to southern Iraq to their original positions".

14. Subsequently, it became clear that Iraq did not follow through on its threats and, throughout the events surrounding the troop movements of October 1994, the Commission was able to continue its operations as usual.

These developments served to underline the need continuously to watch Iraq's intentions and actions closely in relation to the work of the Commission. Any change in Iraq's current attitude towards the Commission will be reported to the Council immediately.

B. *Missiles*

15. In the missile area, the Commission has a fuller account of Iraq's past programmes but the issue of verification remains. Areas of particular concern relate to accounting for known imports of components and production equipment. Efforts to address these concerns have focused on increased contacts with supporting and supplier Governments and further discussions with Iraq. However, on several occasions, Iraq has not declared the full facts when issues have first been raised. A prime example relates to the import of a high-precision instrumentation radar which the Commission has firm evidence was imported for proscribed ballistic missile programmes and was used as part of the testing of proscribed missiles. Iraq denied this outright and has presented numerous different and conflicting explanations of the use and purpose of this radar. On 14 December 1994, the Commission informed Iraq by letter of its decision that the radar must be destroyed, stating:

> "The Commission's investigations into and judgements on this matter have relied on information obtained from a variety of different sources and on your authorities' own statements. From Iraq's own declarations, the radar was used around the time of two Al Abbas missile launches on 28 December 1990. Iraq subsequently acknowledged that the radar was installed at the testing site in Basrah on 26 December 1990, that adjustment and initial operations began on 27 December 1990, that testing activity and adjustment continued on 28 December 1990, and that the radar was disassembled and packaged on 29 December 1990. Most recently, Iraq further acknowledged that the radar was operating and the radar dish was pointed in the direction of the missiles during the two test launches.

> "The Commission has, on the basis of all the information available to it, concluded that the radar was indeed involved in the tracking of proscribed missile systems on 28 December 1990. Consequently, the radar is an item which is proscribed under paragraph 8 of Security Council resolution 687 (1991). The radar and associated equipment has therefore to be disposed of in accordance with that paragraph."

16. Ongoing monitoring and verification has proceeded well in this area. Monitoring and verification

protocols have been completed for the sites to be monitored and all missiles, components and equipment identified for monitoring have been tagged and inventoried. Fifty monitoring cameras have been installed at 15 sites and the missile monitoring group is proceeding with monitoring activities. In general, Iraq's declarations for missile monitoring have been adequate, although there have been some omissions, such as failure to declare stored dual-purpose equipment. These shortcomings are being addressed in the course of monitoring activities.

C. *Chemical weapons*

17. Similar problems exist in the chemical area regarding past programmes. The list of letters of credit obtained from Iraq in April 1994, while neither accurate nor complete, has provided the Commission with much new data and new avenues for further investigations. However, the Commission cannot yet be certain that it has accounted fully for all the precursors and production equipment imported. These uncertainties, coupled with a lack of substantiation of the disposition of chemical munitions, renders a full material balance for the chemical weapons programmes impossible for the moment.

18. Ongoing monitoring and verification is also proceeding well in this area, although it is less advanced than in the missile area. Monitoring and verification protocols have been completed for all the key sites and the key items have been tagged and inventoried. A chemical monitoring group is in Iraq operating out of the Baghdad Monitoring and Verification Centre. It is completing the protocol-building and tagging process at sites of secondary importance, such as universities, while conducting ongoing monitoring and verification of key sites. Four chemical sensors have been installed at one site and a further 20 should be installed at other sites in January 1995. Monitoring cameras and flow meters should be installed by the same date. A small chemical laboratory will be installed at the Centre in February 1995.

19. The Commission will experiment with a number of different configurations for the disposition of the chemical sensors, some being placed inside buildings and others outside, to assess the best combination of sensors, given the chemical processes and number of buildings involved and the prevailing wind conditions. These experiments should take about six to eight weeks to complete.

D. *Biological weapons*

20. The Commission faces its greatest problems in accounting for Iraq's past biological programme. Iraq's account is minimal and has no inherent logic. While access has been provided to interview the personnel in-volved in the declared programme, interviewees refused to answer questions relating to the programme, providing only incomplete and misleading information. While Iraq maintains that the programme was in the early research stages and would be defensively oriented, the indications all point to an offensive programme. In these circumstances, the Commission cannot yet provide a material balance for this programme.

21. The Commission has also faced greater problems in seeking to establish ongoing monitoring and verification in the biological area than it did in the other areas. Iraq's declarations of dual-purpose items were, until recently, often largely incomplete, inconsistent with each other and with the findings of inspection teams, and not updated with notifications of movement of declared items from one site to another.

22. To redress this situation, the Commission requested that Iraq provide new and complete declarations for all the sites to be monitored and instructed Iraq on how these declarations should be formatted. New declarations were submitted in November 1994. Currently, Iraq is working with inspection teams in Iraq to improve these declarations. In addition, an interim monitoring group has been dispatched to Iraq to obtain for the key sites the information that Iraq should have declared and which is required to create monitoring and verification protocols for those sites. Thereafter, this group will monitor these key sites. However, as this procedure is time- and resource-intensive, it cannot be followed for each of the numerous biological sites to be monitored.

23. In the meantime, the Commission has identified, inventoried and tagged a large number of dual-purpose items which will need to be monitored. A second round of inventorying has been necessitated by Iraq's failure to declare all such equipment and to notify movement of it and because of damage to tags already installed. Plans are in hand to install monitoring cameras at a number of sites to monitor activity levels and to install a biological laboratory at the Baghdad Monitoring and Verification Centre.

E. *Aerial surveillance*

24. Aerial surveillance, both by helicopter and by high-altitude aircraft, continues to be key to the efficacy of the Commission's overall ongoing monitoring and verification effort. Without these assets, the Commission's ability to identify undeclared facilities of potential interest for ongoing monitoring and verification would be greatly diminished. Furthermore, the efficiency with which the Commission could monitor the large number of declared sites would also be greatly reduced. It is worrying, in this regard, that Iraq still objects to each

flight of the Commission's high-altitude surveillance aircraft.

25. The aerial inspection team continues to perform a valuable task of obtaining close-up photography of monitored sites. Furthermore, with the arrival of the monitoring groups resident in Iraq, joint aerial inspections, with inspectors from the aerial inspection team and the weapons experts from one or more monitoring group, are creating new synergy and efficiency in monitoring. The contribution by the Government of Germany of three CH-53G helicopters, crew and maintenance staff is key to the performance of this and other essential tasks. It has been of the greatest importance in the implementation of the mandates of the Commission and the International Atomic Energy Agency (IAEA), particularly in areas remote from Baghdad. The Commission's aerial assets are currently fully utilized and it is envisaged that monitoring efforts will increasingly rely on their use.

F. *Baghdad Monitoring and Verification Centre*

26. Work continues to complete the installation of the equipment for the Baghdad Monitoring and Verification Centre. Some installation work in the period under review had to be delayed and rescheduled because of the lack of funding. Recent assurances as to new financial contributions have permitted the resumption of the work involved, and it is hoped that the Centre will be fully equipped and staffed by the end of February 1995. Thereafter, only minor adjustments to its staffing would be envisaged in the light of experience until the addition of an export/import control group to supplement the monitoring groups.

G. *Data handling*

27. The Commission's activities generate a large amount of data. The Commission, with the help of a supporting Government, has developed and is continuing to develop software for a single relational database to allow easy and full analysis of the data obtained from all sources. In addition, another Government is helping with customizing a second, compatible database specifically for handling the export/import data. This system should be installed by the end of February 1995.

H. *Export/import mechanism*

28. The Commission has conducted further seminars with international experts to develop further the export/import mechanism. There appears to be general agreement in the Sanctions Committee on the underlying concept of the paper submitted to it by the Commission

and IAEA in May 1994. The Commission hopes to reconvene its seminar of international experts in early January 1995 and so to be able to submit a final version of the concept paper to the Sanctions Committee towards the end of January 1995. It is envisaged that the paper would be forwarded to the Security Council for its consideration soon after. Revised annexes to the plans of the Commission and IAEA for ongoing monitoring and verification will also be brought to the Council's attention before they are implemented. These revised annexes will contain the comprehensive listing of items to be reported by exporting Governments under the mechanism.

III. ISSUES AND PRIORITIES FOR THE FUTURE

29. Iraq must provide credible accounts for all its past proscribed programmes and capabilities and supporting evidence to enable the Commission independently to verify its declarations so that the Commission can achieve a material balance for the past programmes and thereby have confidence that its ongoing monitoring and verification system is proceeding from a sound basis. Without such confidence, the Commission cannot be certain that it is indeed monitoring all the facilities and items in Iraq which should be monitored if the requirements of the Security Council are to be fulfilled. Furthermore, failure by Iraq to provide full and transparent accounting of its past programmes can only undermine confidence in its intentions and in the completeness of its declarations in this regard. The speed with which this issue can be resolved is primarily dependent on Iraq's openness and honesty, although supplier Governments can also play a significant role in responding to the Commission's requests for assistance in verifying Iraq's accounts of its imports. The absence of such responses can only delay the Commission's efforts to obtain a credible material balance for Iraq's past programmes. Certain supplier Governments have been very forthcoming and the Commission is pursuing its efforts with those which have still to reply.

30. Iraq should also provide complete data on all its current dual-purpose capabilities as defined in the plan for ongoing monitoring and verification contained in document S/22871/Rev.1. While, in the absence of full Iraqi declarations, the Commission could conduct intrusive inspections at all relevant facilities to uncover all such capabilities, this would be neither an efficient use of the Commission's resources nor the quickest means of implementing the terms of paragraph 22 of Security Council resolution 687 (1991).

31. Iraq has also yet to adopt the necessary legal and administrative measures to give effect to its obligations under the plan for ongoing monitoring and verifi-

cation, although it is known to be working on the necessary legislation.

32. Efforts to establish an effective ongoing monitoring and verification system are well-advanced. The system is provisionally operational and testing of it has begun. With the installation of further elements of the system, the Commission will gain experience in operating and confidence in the efficacy of the system. By the end of February 1995, the Baghdad Monitoring and Verification Centre should be fully staffed for its current operations.

33. An increasing share of the Commission's resources will in the future be devoted to the establishment and, upon the easing of the sanctions in accordance with paragraph 21 of Security Council resolution 687 (1991), operation of the export/import mechanism. The export/import mechanism is a fundamental element in the overall ongoing monitoring and verification system. Without it, once Iraq is able to import dual-purpose items, the system could not be expected to be effective. It is essential that this mechanism be operational prior to the easing of sanctions to the extent that Iraq is able to import such items. The Commission is pressing to have all the legal and practical elements adopted as soon as possible.

34. A major concern facing the Commission at this stage is financing. Activities to equip the Baghdad Monitoring and Verification Centre have already been delayed because of the lack of guaranteed funds to pay for the materials required. Furthermore, while the short-term financial crisis reported in October 1994 appears to have been addressed through the promise of funds from Kuwait and the United States of America, the Commission only has promises of funding until the end of March 1995. Insecure medium-term funding limits the Commission's ability to conduct long-term planning and hence will inevitably create inefficiencies. It may, in the worst case, adversely affect the effectiveness of the Commission's ongoing monitoring and verification regime or even endanger continuous operations. A long-term solution to the issue of the Commission's financing is necessary to ensure the fulfilment of the mandate contained in section C of Security Council resolution 687 (1991).

IV. CONCLUSION

35. While the preceding paragraphs inevitably dwell on outstanding issues where further work remains, much progress has been made during the period under review towards the fulfilment of the Commission's mandate. All items verified as being proscribed have now been destroyed. The ongoing monitoring and verification system is provisionally operational. The major elements for chemical and missile monitoring are in place. Interim monitoring in the biological area is about to commence. Testing of the system has begun, and a mechanism for monitoring Iraq's trade in dual-purpose items (the export/import mechanism) has been elaborated and appears to meet with approval.

Addendum (S/1994/1422/Add.1, 15 December 1994) Note by the Secretary-General

The Secretary-General has the honour to transmit to the Security Council an addendum to the report submitted by the Executive Chairman of the Special Commission established by the Secretary-General, pursuant to paragraph 9 (b) (i) of Security Council resolution 687 (1991), issued as document S/1994/1422, annex.

Annex
Addendum to the eighth report of the Executive Chairman of the Special Commission, established by the Secretary-General pursuant to paragraph 9 (b) (i) of Security Council resolution 687 (1991), on the activities of the Special Commission

APPENDIX I

A. *Missiles*

1. The Special Commission has continued its activities in the missile area under the mandate established by Security Council resolutions 687 (1991), 707 (1991) and 715 (1991). During 1994, the Commission will have conducted 15 missile inspections, more than the combined number of inspections undertaken in 1992 and 1993.

2. In order to provide the Council with an assessment of Iraq's compliance with the obligations set out under section C of resolution 687 (1991), the Commission intensified its endeavours to resolve outstanding issues in respect of Iraq's past prohibited missile programmes. In parallel, major efforts have been exerted to establish ongoing monitoring and verification of Iraq's missile-related activities and dual-purpose capabilities. As a result of these efforts, the essential elements of the monitoring system were in place as from the middle of August 1994. The system has been declared provisionally operational and is currently undergoing testing for thoroughness, reliability and the integrated operation of the system's components.

1. *Past programmes*
   (a) *Information*

3. Iraq is required, under the terms of Security Council resolutions 687 (1991), 707 (1991) and 715 (1991), to provide full, final and complete disclosures on all aspects of its proscribed programmes and to respond fully, completely and promptly to questions and requests from the Commission. As a result of inspections, lengthy discussions with Iraq's authorities and other bodies and detailed analysis, the Commission now possesses a much fuller and more accurate picture of Iraq's past prohibited missile programmes than that presented by Iraq in its official "full, final and comprehensive report" submitted in May 1992.

4. During the reporting period, the Commission has intensified its investigations into issues related to past proscribed missile programmes. Special emphasis has been placed on verification of information provided by Iraq concerning foreign acquisition of proscribed missiles, their components and related production capabilities. Validation of this, and other information provided by Iraq, has been energetically pursued by the Commission. Specific assistance to facilitate this process has been requested from a number of countries. While some Governments were unable or unwilling to confirm or deny details of supplies of equipment or assistance given to Iraq prior to the imposition of sanctions, the Commission has received many positive responses. Some 14 different bilateral meetings have been held during the reporting period on this matter.

5. The resulting information obtained from Governments and the Commission's own intensive analysis has, in some cases, revealed contradictions or highlighted omissions in Iraq's declarations. This has necessitated new rounds of discussions with Iraq in order to establish the true facts. Major issues related to past programmes were discussed with Iraqi representatives during a round of high-level talks in September 1994. Several inspection teams addressed in detail relevant issues with Iraqi officials and experts. However, there continues to be a proclivity for Iraq to fail to volunteer information and to confirm specific information only when a preponderance of evidence is produced by the Commission. This inevitably undermines the confidence the Commission can have in the completeness of Iraq's declarations. Furthermore, in some instances repeated statements by Iraq that equipment was not procured for proscribed programmes have proved to be incorrect. Iraq's continued insistence that all documents related to its past proscribed activities have been destroyed has also proved to be incorrect.

6. Some explanations and clarifications from Iraq are, as a consequence, still pending. The major outstanding issues relating to past proscribed missile programmes include accounting for certain missile components; identification of all equipment and items procured for, or used

in, proscribed activities; and full disclosure of foreign assistance received by Iraq from a number of countries. The resolution of these and other remaining issues would be greatly expedited if Iraq provided documentation or other supporting evidence which would allow independent verification. The Commission has repeatedly called upon Iraq to adopt an attitude of full openness and cooperation on matters relating to its past programmes consistent with its obligations under relevant Security Council resolutions.

(b) *Inspection activities*
  BM25/UNSCOM 81

7. BM25/UNSCOM 81 was in Iraq from 14 to 22 June 1994. The objectives of this team were twofold. First, to discuss unresolved issues related to past prohibited activities in Iraq, including missile production, modification projects and foreign supplies. Secondly, to elaborate, to Iraq's experts, definitions of the dual-purpose items and technologies contained in annex IV to the plan for ongoing monitoring and verification.

8. As a special task, related to verification of Iraq's compliance with resolution 687 (1991), the team was requested to continue investigation into the alleged use of a high-precision tracking radar to support launches of prohibited missiles in December 1990. Iraq's officials strongly denied that the radar had been used during those tests, or that it had been procured to support activities related to prohibited missiles. These denials contradicted information available to the Commission which indicated that the radar had been used in proscribed activities.

9. The Commission recently informed Iraq that, unless specific evidence were provided to prove clearly that the radar was not used in support of proscribed activities, the Commission, in accordance with its mandate to destroy or render harmless items prohibited under resolution 687 (1991), would proceed with the destruction of the radar. In response, Iraq has now acknowledged that the radar was intended to be used in both proscribed and non-proscribed activities. At the time of the writing of this report, discussions on this matter were continuing.

  BM28/UNSCOM 98

10. The mission of BM28/UNSCOM 98 was to begin the process of compiling, in a single document, a coherent and detailed description of past proscribed missile programmes based on Iraq's statements and declarations. This mission was necessitated by the fragmentary nature of Iraq's declarations concerning its past missile programmes. It is using information obtained by the Commission from its own inspection activities and other sources. The effort was initiated by the Commission to assist Iraq in clarifying its reporting on past activities. It

does not relieve Iraq of its obligations to provide to the Commission a full, final and complete accounting of its proscribed programmes as required by relevant Security Council resolutions.

11. BM28/UNSCOM 98 visited Iraq from 2 to 6 October and from 23 to 28 October 1994 to present to Iraq's experts the Commission's draft papers on past programmes. During its visits, the team reviewed these drafts with Iraq's authorities and interviewed a number of persons responsible for relevant activities. A follow-up team, BM30/UNSCOM 102, in Iraq from 9 to 16 December 1994, is continuing this effort.

12. This task will continue until the past programmes are clearly understood and properly documented. The Commission will evaluate all data obtained from Iraq with information obtained from a number of other sources in order to gain confidence, through analysis, in the completeness of Iraq's declarations.

2. *Ongoing monitoring and verification*
    (a) *Inspection activities*

13. The current monitoring programme in the missile area constitutes a multi-layered system to accomplish the tasks of the plan for ongoing monitoring and verification in an efficient and practical manner. It covers, *inter alia*:

(a) A variety of sites and facilities currently engaged in missile activities or having relevant capabilities. At this moment, more than 30 facilities are being monitored;

(b) Activities crucial to reacquiring prohibited missiles. The focal points for monitoring include missile propellant mixers/extruders, equipment for liquid engine production and gyroscope balancing, missile/warhead assembly lines, a wind tunnel and static test stands. Special modes of monitoring, i.e., camera systems, were established to monitor these activities. The cameras' recordings are analysed to extract information relevant for monitoring objectives;

(c) Specialized and dual-purpose equipment. Appropriate inventory control was established to monitor these items. For example, nearly 200 items have been tagged by the Commission. Many more are covered by facility protocols. Iraq's use of this equipment is checked by monitoring teams;

(d) Operational missiles designed for use, or capable of being modified for use, in a surface-to-surface role with a range greater than 50 kilometres. More than 1,300 missiles have been tagged by the Commission and are regularly checked for non-modification. In some instances, subsystems or components have been separately tagged.

BM26/UNSCOM 82

14. The Commission decided to use cameras and other sensors to increase the effectiveness of monitoring activities at a number of missile-related facilities. The task of BM26/UNSCOM 82 was to install the monitoring camera systems. The team operated in Iraq from 3 to 28 July 1994, and installed some 50 cameras with associated equipment at 15 sites being monitored. The team also placed tags and inventory labels on equipment identified for monitoring.

15. After a period of initial operation of the camera systems, a special sensor testing team was dispatched to Iraq from 8 to 16 August 1994. The team's mission was to validate the operational capabilities of the camera monitoring systems (through tests of sensor and communication technologies), operation and maintenance procedures, and processing modalities. The team provided recommendations for improved use of sensor monitoring systems in the missile area.

16. The product from the missile monitoring cameras is reviewed in three stages. First, each site is called up on a daily basis to check that the link is working. Secondly, the tape is reviewed by the resident missile monitoring team. Thirdly, the tape is dispatched for detailed expert analysis. The tapes are retained by the Commission for future comparative work.

BM27/UNSCOM 85

17. This team was in Iraq from 15 to 24 July 1994 with the primary mission of collecting updated information on and, by extension, updating the Commission's assessments of missile research and development activities in Iraq. Such updates are based on Iraq's declarations, special reports by Iraq and data collected by inspection teams. They are undertaken by the Commission on a biannual basis. BM27/UNSCOM 85 was the second team to perform such a task.

18. Extensive discussions were held with Iraqi officials and missile experts to obtain information relevant to the team's mission. Iraq submitted a detailed report on current missile programmes relevant to surface-to-surface missiles with a range greater than 50 kilometres. The team reaffirmed limitations established by the Commission on some missile design features so as to preclude any development of missiles capable of exceeding a range of 150 kilometres.

19. BM27/UNSCOM 85 also continued investigations into a number of issues related to research and development activities carried out by Iraq relating to past proscribed missile programmes.

Missile monitoring group 1

20. Upon completion of the baseline process in the missile area, in August 1994 the Commission dispatched the first missile monitoring group of resident inspectors to the Baghdad Monitoring and Verification Centre. Such groups now operate continuously from the Centre and are a core element in the ongoing monitoring and verification system in Iraq. Monitoring groups have to perform a variety of missions, including:

(a) Execution of monitoring inspections on a regular basis at all missile-related sites being monitored;

(b) Checks of the tagged operational missiles;

(c) Initial assessment and verification of Iraq's declarations and reports;

(d) Maintaining a current inventory of items being monitored;

(e) Initial screening of the output of the sensor monitoring system;

(f) Specific short-notice tasks as directed by the Commission.

21. The first monitoring group (MG1) arrived in Iraq on 17 August and completed its mission on 9 October 1994. The group was composed of four experts specializing in various areas of missile development and production. During the mission, the group carried out 48 inspections of sites on a no-notice or short-notice basis. The group provided detailed reports on the progress of permitted missile programmes in Iraq and Iraq's current use of its dual-purpose capabilities.

Missile monitoring group 2

22. The second monitoring group (MG2) entered Iraq on 14 October 1994, and is scheduled to maintain the continuous missile monitoring presence until early February 1995. The personnel on the team will be rotated at staggered times to ensure that an experienced cadre of personnel remain in Iraq during the turnover to the next monitoring team in February. As at 8 December 1994, the second monitoring group had conducted 60 visits to facilities being monitored.

Missile monitoring groups 2A and 2B

23. Special groups (MG2A and MG2B) were sent to Iraq to supplement the expertise of monitoring group 2 to verify the non-modification of operational missiles covered by the plan for ongoing monitoring and verification, which were originally tagged by UNSCOM 80 in June 1994. Monitoring group 2A was in Iraq from 19 to 22 October 1994 and monitoring group 2B carried out its mission from 2 to 6 December 1994. Iraq brought forward all the missiles requested for verification by the Commission. The teams verified all tags and compared the operational missiles with technical reference material to ensure that Iraq had performed no modifications to increase the range of those missiles.

(b) Ongoing monitoring and verification declarations

24. In general, declarations in respect of ongoing monitoring and verification have been adequate in the missile area over the reporting period, most anomalies having been detected and corrected during the earlier baseline inspections. Nevertheless, omissions continue to be discovered, but it is anticipated that these will be corrected during the current phase of monitoring.

B. Chemical weapons

25. Since the last report on its activities the Commission has pursued in tandem the development of chemical monitoring and its implementation. At the same time, clarification of outstanding aspects of the past chemical weapons programmes continues to be a major concern.

1. Past programmes
(a) Information

26. Full knowledge and accounting of Iraq's past programmes is the key to ensuring that proscribed programmes have been eliminated and to confirming that the monitoring regime encompasses all equipment, technology and material in Iraq with potential for use for chemical weapons purposes.

27. The Commission has continued its efforts to fill gaps in Iraq's declarations on its past chemical weapons programmes, particularly those relating to suppliers and quantities of items and materials imported. In addition, strenuous attempts have been made to find ways to verify independently Iraq's accounting of the past programmes. During the reporting period, some 10 bilateral discussions with supporting Governments have taken place and a considerable amount of data on Iraq's imports has been obtained by the Commission.

28. The Commission considered that a major breakthrough had been achieved in verifying Iraq's declaration on imports of proscribed materials as a result of the CW15/UNSCOM 74 inspection in April 1994. That team was sent to Iraq specifically to address the issue of verification of past imports. During the inspection, the team was given a list of letters of credit which the Iraqi side claimed to cover all items imported in support of the chemical weapons programmes. The Commission energetically pursued this issue with the Governments of the suppliers concerned in order to verify the quantities supplied and the dates of supply. However, as a result of detailed analysis of the list of letters of credit and of the information from supporting Governments, the Commission has concluded that the list is not complete and

contains errors. The consequence of the inconsistencies is that uncertainties remain, *inter alia*, about the amount of chemical agent produced, the amount of precursors imported and consumed, and the amount of production equipment imported. The Commission is actively endeavouring to resolve these inconsistencies and uncertainties with Iraq and supplier Governments.

(b) *Inspection activities*
CW21/UNSCOM 95

29. CW21/UNSCOM 95 was sent to Iraq from 23 to 27 October 1994 to address anomalies in the list of letters of credit and outstanding information from Iraq on its past programmes. It also sought to collect such data as it could in order to improve the Commission's understanding of the past chemical weapons programmes.

30. During initial discussions, Iraq maintained that the list of letters of credit was complete. However, the team cited general examples of areas of omissions in Iraq's declarations. The incomplete nature of the list was further underlined during interviews with persons associated with the past programmes who referred to imported items of equipment not included in declarations.

31. In the course of the discussions and questioning, the team collected sufficient information and evidence to conclude that Iraq's previous declarations contained significant inconsistencies concerning purchases of precursor chemicals and equipment, equipment utilization and supplier companies. Iraq admitted that the list of letters of credit was not 100 per cent complete, but claimed that it was 90 to 95 per cent complete. The resultant uncertainties, together with other information available to the Commission, potentially translate into several hundred tons of unaccounted-for chemical warfare agents.

32. Iraq has therefore been asked to supply a new full, final and complete declaration, with supporting evidence for its past programmes. Once this has been received, the Commission will undertake a further verification exercise. In order to clarify inconsistencies in Iraq's declarations referring to chemical weapons-related munitions, an inspection will take place in January to address this particular issue.

2. *Ongoing monitoring and verification*

33. Monitoring in the chemical area has been addressed in four interrelated ways. The first is through the Commission's continued investigations into past Iraqi chemical weapons programmes. A complete understanding of Iraq's technical capabilities, manufacturing equipment, precursor suppliers and past chemical weapon production activities are essential if the Commission is to be confident that it is monitoring from a solid

base. Secondly, the Commission conducted a site sweep and hand-over of the Muthanna State Establishment which is now being monitored. This facility was the hub of Iraq's past chemical weapons programmes, and contained the bulk of the declared and discovered chemical agent, filled munitions, and munition case production and filling equipment. The site survey and hand-over teams established that the site was free of prohibited materials and that all dual-use equipment at the site had been destroyed or properly tagged and recorded. Thirdly, protocol-building missions were conducted at a variety of chemical sites. Finally, the chemical monitoring group was established in Iraq as part of the Baghdad Monitoring and Verification Centre and commenced monitoring activities.

(a) *Inspection activities*
CW19/UNSCOM 89

34. The second chemical protocol-building team operated in Iraq from 10 to 23 August 1994. Its task was to build protocols for 22 chemical facilities associated with the oil and petrochemical industry. These sites are of relevance to the monitoring regime because of the potential presence of either equipment or raw chemicals which could be used in the production of chemical warfare agents, or equipment which could be used to store such chemicals.

35. The team verified declared equipment and activities at the sites declared for monitoring. It also collected the information required for the building of protocols for each of the sites.

CW20/UNSCOM 91

36. This team conducted its activities in Iraq from 13 to 24 September 1994. Its principal task was to conduct protocol-building inspections at 12 sites associated primarily with Iraq's chemical fertilizer industry. The inspections were undertaken in order to identify possible dual-purpose equipment, facility or equipment redundancies, plant capacity and normal utilization, unusual chemical processes, and waste disposal methods and to resolve anomalies in Iraq's declarations concerning the sites. In the course of the inspection, the team was able to obtain the information required to build protocols.

Chemical monitoring group 1

37. The first chemical monitoring group (CG1), comprising four chemical experts, arrived in Iraq on 2 October 1994. As the first monitoring team in the chemical area, it is refining the chemical monitoring process and the information requirements for facility protocols and baseline inspections.

38. Under the guidance of the Commission in New York, the chemical group undertakes the following tasks:

(a) Revision of site protocols;

(b) Tagging and monitoring of dual-use chemical processing equipment;

(c) Conducting inspections of newly declared and undeclared sites of potential relevance to the chemical monitoring regime;

(d) Collection, assessments and recording of monitoring sensor data;

(e) No-notice tasks as directed by the Commission.

39. In addition to conducting inspections at sites for which monitoring and verification protocols have been prepared, the monitoring group will visit various chemical-related organizations to assess their relevance to ongoing monitoring and verification.

40. The team also investigates outstanding anomalies in Iraq's declarations concerning its current dual-purpose capabilities. Minor adjustments have been made by the Commission to the formats under which Iraq reports such capabilities in order to facilitate both the collection of data by Iraq and its analysis by the Commission. The team explains these changes to its Iraqi counterparts and provides further clarifications, as necessary, to enable Iraq to provide full and consistent declarations.

41. In support of future ongoing monitoring and verification in the chemical area, the Commission intends to install further sensors. A team is currently in the country preparing for the installation in January of an additional 20 air-sampling devices at four additional chemical production facilities of particular importance to the monitoring regime. In addition, it is planned to install flow meters at key points in the production equipment at at least one site. Several sites will be monitored by remote-controlled cameras.

42. Analysis of the samples taken by air samplers is currently being conducted in laboratories outside Iraq. However, when the Baghdad Monitoring and Verification Centre has been completely equipped, it is intended that analysis of the samples will be undertaken at the chemical laboratory in the Centre. Only those samples which deviate from the normal background levels will be sent to approved international laboratories in order to obtain a cross-checking result from an independent source. From time to time, calibrating exercises will be undertaken to ensure the accuracy of analysis at the various laboratories. The presence of this analytical equipment will also enable other analytical questions to be dealt with at the Centre.

(b) *Ongoing monitoring and verification declarations*

43. Information provided by Iraq in respect of ongoing monitoring and verification in the chemical field has generally been reasonably accurate. Thus far no major inconsistencies have been encountered during the reporting period.

C. *Biological weapons*

1. *Past programmes*

44. Iraq has declared having undertaken biological research for military purposes at the Salman Pak site operated by Iraq's Technical Research Centre. During the first biological inspection in 1991, Iraq stated that the research could be used for defensive or offensive purposes, and concentrated on three agents, namely, *Bacillus anthracis* (anthrax), *Clostridium botulinum* (botulinum toxin) and *Clostridium perfringens* (gas gangrene).

45. Owing to the lack of supporting data, verification of Iraq's accounting for the storage and disposal of equipment, storage of organisms, personnel, relationships between the declared biological weapon research site and other organizations, and the acquisition of biotechnology has proved difficult. An accurate and verified account of these is essential if the Commission is to be certain that it is indeed monitoring the full extent of Iraq's dual-purpose biological capabilities. Furthermore, it will enable the Commission to focus its main monitoring efforts on key sites. The Commission has therefore continued to investigate past programme-related activities. Given the claimed destruction of all documentation related to the programme, verification of Iraq's account has, as in other areas, had to rely in large measure on interviews with personnel directly involved in the programme and indirect means of substantiation.

BW15/UNSCOM 104

46. BW15/UNSCOM 104 took place from 15 to 22 November 1994. Its prime activity was the interviewing of Iraqi officials who may have been associated with the past programme, in order to clarify the following points:

(a) Links between the Salman Pak site and other organizations;

(b) The logic of the programme, including doctrine, practice, priorities, achievements, acquisition of biotechnology and know-how, protection and medical aspects, storage and rationale for location of the programme;

(c) A material balance for equipment, cell stocks and complex media acquired by Salman Pak or the programme;

(d) The real extent and intentions of the programme.

47. During the inspection, the team held discussions with 28 persons, many of whom had never been in contact with the Commission's experts before, including 9 of the 10 employees at Salman Pak. Access to personnel,

whose identity had not previously been disclosed, therefore, constituted a major step forward. While the Commission remains unconvinced that Iraq's account of its past programme is either complete or accurate, this team did obtain new information, the significance of which requires further examination.

48. UNSCOM 104 continued the discussions with Iraq initiated during UNSCOM 96 on various direct and indirect means to substantiate Iraq's accounts in the absence of supporting documents or proof. Iraq agreed to try to provide such substantiation shortly after UNSCOM 104 left the country. In addition, various outstanding questions related to ongoing monitoring and verification declarations were addressed. Revised declarations were submitted, as requested by UNSCOM 96, and were further revised in the light of the team's comments.

2. *Ongoing monitoring and verification*

49. In preparation for the monitoring of Iraq's biological activities, the Commission has proceeded with the evaluation of the sites or facilities concerned by assessing the various elements which constitute Iraq's capability.

BW7/UNSCOM 86

50. Biological technical talks (BW7/UNSCOM 86) were held in Baghdad from 5 to 8 June 1994. The purpose was to try to clarify inconsistencies and anomalies between declarations concerning biological issues submitted by Iraq in January and April 1994 and the findings of BW4/UNSCOM 72, which visited many of the sites covered by their declarations for the first time.

51. During those talks, Iraq agreed to provide declarations and supplementary information regarding 24 sites. With respect to declarations, discussions focused on universities, breweries, facilities indigenously producing or modifying declarable equipment and import facilities. It was reiterated to Iraq that it was required to provide declarations for all dual-purpose capabilities covering the period from January 1986 to February 1994, including any facility related in any way to biological weapons activities. The form for 30-day prior notification of movement or modification of dual-use equipment, discussed during an earlier inspection, was provided to the Iraqi side. No such notification has yet been received by the Commission.

BW6/UNSCOM 84

52. BW6/UNSCOM 84 was in Iraq from 25 June to 5 July 1994. Its task was to survey 35 biological sites, some of which had not been declared by Iraq, in order to assess whether they should be monitored. Several sites were selected to test the practicality of the concept of the draft biological protocol. The sites chosen had been visited previously and covered four different activity areas, namely vaccine production, supplier company, research and development laboratory and single-cell production facility.

53. Eight of the undeclared sites were determined by the team to require monitoring as dual-purpose equipment was present or because of the nature of the activities conducted.

54. The team provided Iraq with a format for the provision of additional information required to complete the protocols and reiterated previous unfulfilled requests for information.

BW8/UNSCOM 87

55. BW8/UNSCOM 87 was in Iraq from 25 July to 7 September 1994 to create protocols for 55 sites which had been identified for monitoring.

56. However, the team observed inconsistencies and anomalies between its findings and those of previous inspection teams and the information contained in Iraq's various declarations. These related largely to equipment which had either been moved to the sites since the previous inspection or not been previously declared as being at those sites. Information on personnel, previously absent from declarations, was obtained during this inspection. None the less, queries concerning personnel present at sites, relationships between sites, and relationships to the past military biological programme were not fully clarified. During the course of the inspection, Iraq declared to the team the names of further sites at which biological equipment or activities were present, and the team inspected those sites.

Technical talks held in New York in July

57. Technical talks held in New York during July 1994 concentrated upon the full provision of information requested during BW7/UNSCOM 86 and which remained outstanding, such as documentation concerning the import of biological materials by import company and information on relevant university activities.

BW9/UNSCOM 88

58. The team was in Iraq from 20 to 25 August 1994 and visited five biological facilities. Its objectives were to perform a feasibility study of remote monitoring in the biological area and, for the sites where this was deemed feasible, to establish the scope, foundations and requirements for the installation of remote monitors at biological sites. It concluded that, at those sites, remote monitoring equipment could constitute an effective means of supplementary on-site inspections.

59. The team was in Iraq from 29 August to 3 September 1994. Its objectives were to complete the protocol-building process at certain sites and to inspect additional sites in order to assess whether they should be monitored.

60. The team visited a total of seven sites. On the basis of its results, two further sites were deemed as requiring monitoring.

BW11/UNSCOM 94

61. BW11/UNSCOM 94 was in Iraq from 29 September to 14 October 1994. Its main objective was to continue the inventorying and tagging of dual-use biological equipment started in May 1994 with BW5/UNSCOM 78 in order to address the anomalies in the equipment inventories observed during BW8/UNSCOM 87. UNSCOM 94 also determined the reasons for damage to or loss of tags noted during past inspections.

Technical talks held in New York in September

62. The discussions held in New York in September were in preparation for BW12/UNSCOM 96. They covered activities since 1986, monitoring, and Iraq's biological capability. The Commission presented the various steps taken so far in preparation for monitoring, and the difficulties encountered in certain areas in gathering the information required, especially in the field of research. It was agreed that a list of additional information required would be discussed and provided during BW12/UNSCOM 96.

BW12/UNSCOM 96

63. BW12/UNSCOM 96 held discussions with Iraqi officials at the National Monitoring Directorate from 23 to 26 September 1994. The main topics of discussion were discrepancies between inspection findings and declarations; the difficulties encountered in reconciling information from both sources; declarations or additional sites previously requested; movement or modification of equipment; indigenous production of fermenters; import activities; the relationship between various biological sites; storage of equipment; work with certain micro-organisms; damaged or lost tags; management structure at the sites; future biological activities; declarations for activities conducted between January 1986 and February 1994; and past biological weapons work.

64. During the discussions, the scope of the monitoring effort and of the reporting requirements under the plan was reiterated, and the link between past activities and ongoing monitoring and verification outlined. Throughout the discussions, examples of indirect means of substantiation were explored as an alternative to the provision of supporting documentation, given Iraq's claim to have destroyed all relevant documentation. The need for the site managers to be familiarized with their reporting obligations was also addressed.

BW13/UNSCOM 99

65. BW13/UNSCOM 99 started its activity in Iraq on 2 December 1994. Its main purpose is to continue the inventorying of research, development and production equipment recently declared by Iraq.

BW16/UNSCOM 105

66. This inspection, which started on 2 December 1994, initiated interim monitoring of a key production site. The interim monitoring will, in the first instance, undertake an in-depth analysis of the activities of the site in order to redress the inadequacy of and inconsistencies in Iraq's previous declarations concerning this site.

67. By actively pursuing the data through interim monitoring, the Commission is relying less on Iraq's openness and more on inspection findings to obtain the baseline information for this site. However, this is a very time-consuming process and so can only be performed for a limited number of sites. The interim monitoring process does not remove the requirement for Iraq to declare accurately all its relevant dual-purpose biological activities.

D. *Nuclear*

68. The Director-General of the International Atomic Energy Agency (IAEA) is reporting separately on the activities of the action team set up to implement paragraphs 12 and 13 of resolution 687 (1991).

69. The Commission continues, in accordance with paragraph 9 (b) (iii) of resolution 687 (1991) and paragraph 4 (b) of resolution 715 (1991), to assist and cooperate with the IAEA action team through the provision of special expertise and logistical, informational and other operational support for the carrying out of the IAEA plan for ongoing monitoring and verification. In accordance with paragraph 9 (b) (i) of resolution 687 (1991) and paragraph 4 (a) of resolution 715 (1991), it continues to designate sites for inspection. In accordance with paragraph 3 (c) of resolution 707 (1991), it continues to receive and decide on requests from Iraq to move or destroy any material or equipment relating to its nuclear weapons programme or other nuclear activities. Furthermore, it continues, in accordance with paragraph 4 (c) of resolution 715 (1991), to perform such other functions, in cooperation in the nuclear field with the Director-General of IAEA, as may be necessary to coordinate activities under the plans for ongoing monitoring and verification, including making use of commonly available services and information to the fullest possible extent, in

order to achieve maximum efficiency and optimum use of resources.

Gamma survey

70. A presentation on the final results of the gamma surveys undertaken in September and December 1993 was made to the Commission on 22 September 1994. The capability of the helicopter-borne detection system has been discussed not only as a means of detecting previously undeclared sites for designation by the Commission but also in respect of its future use as a major tool in the ongoing monitoring and verification regime in Iraq.

71. The results of the gamma missions have shown the ability of the system to provide the Commission and IAEA with the capability to conduct survey missions for detection of certain nuclear activities through the detection of trace radioactive materials over designated sites and to execute current monitoring missions over declared sites. The system is also useful in mapping the level and isotope distribution of radioactive sources over a significant surface area. Use of the gamma mapping in association with the current environmental sampling being undertaken by IAEA could improve detection capabilities significantly and strengthen the overall monitoring system.

72. For some sites the results of the gamma mission have shown unidentified radioactive emissions from unidentified sources which will be investigated during future inspections.

Status of nuclear fuel removal

73. In the period under review, the reprocessing of the irradiated nuclear fuel assemblies removed from Iraq under the contract between IAEA and CIR Minatom has been completed at the Mayak facility in the Russian Federation. The uranium oxide resulting from the reprocessing is being moved to the Elektrostahl facility, also in the Russian Federation, where it will be placed under IAEA safeguards. Vitrification of the waste resulting from the reprocessing is also near completion. In Vienna, at the beginning of December, preliminary discussions were held between the IAEA action team and CIR Minatom regarding procedures for the sale of the reprocessed uranium oxide. As operations under the fuel removal and reprocessing contract are nearly complete, the final payments due from the United Nations under contract in the amount of some US$3,900,000 will have to be made early in 1995. This will constitute a further drain on the funds available to the Commission and IAEA in the carrying out of their mandates.

E. Aerial surveillance

74. The aerial inspection team continues to undertake aerial inspections at sites being monitored and at new facilities considered to be of possible relevance to the Commission's mandate. Where required, the team also provides support to ground inspections. All aerial inspections continue to be conducted on a no-notice basis, utilizing the Commission's three CH-53G helicopters. To date over 500 aerial inspections have been undertaken by the team.

75. In response to the evolving requirements of ongoing monitoring and verification, the aerial inspection team has made a number of changes to its method of operations. As the expert monitoring groups have become established at the Baghdad Monitoring and Verification Centre, members of those groups are accompanying the aerial inspection team on relevant aerial missions. This allows the experts to advise the aerial inspectors to focus on particular areas or activities of importance at the facilities.

76. It is planned to move the aerial inspection team's film development laboratory from its present location in the Commission's Bahrain field office to the Baghdad Monitoring and Verification Centre. The team's photographic library will also move. This contains copies of all imagery and reports prepared by the team since the commencement of aerial inspections in June 1992. Immediate access to this historical imagery will enhance the aerial and ground teams' operations by allowing them to study sites in advance of inspections and thus readily to detect any external changes which have taken place at a facility since the previous inspection. Additional equipment has also been procured for the team to assist in refining and improving the product from the aerial inspections.

77. The Commission's high altitude surveillance aircraft, the U-2, continues to undertake an average of one to two flights a week. As at 6 December 1994, 229 missions have been flown. The imagery obtained from these missions is crucial to the Commission's operational planning.

APPENDIX II

A. Export/import monitoring mechanism

1. During the period covered by the present report* progress has been made towards the presentation to the Security Council of a proposal for a mechanism for monitoring any future sales or supplies by other countries to Iraq of items relevant to the implementation of section C of resolution 687 (1991) and other relevant resolutions once the sanctions on those items have been lifted. Paragraph 7 of Council resolution 715 (1991) requires such a

*For developments up to mid-June 1994, see S/1994/750, paragraphs 26 to 28. For developments from mid-June to the beginning of October 1994, see S/1994/1138, paragraphs 26 to 31.

mechanism to be developed in cooperation between the Security Council Committee established under resolution 661 (1990) (the Sanctions Committee), the Special Commission and the Director-General of IAEA.

2. A concept paper for the mechanism, prepared by the Commission and IAEA, has been submitted to the Sanctions Committee. Informal discussions in that Committee appeared to reveal that a consensus could be reached on the proposal in the paper, once the Sanctions Committee had before it a more detailed list of items to be reported under the mechanism by exporting Governments and Iraq than was available in the annexes to the Commission's and IAEA's plans for ongoing monitoring and verification.

3. Accordingly, revisions to the annexes in the chemical, biological and missile areas were prepared, and these were submitted, together with the previously revised annex in the nuclear area (S/24300), to an informal meeting of international experts, held in New York on 18 and 19 October 1994, in order to determine the adequacy of the revisions for purposes of implementing an export reporting procedure. While the lists were in large measure approved, proposals were made for some further changes. These changes have now been made and the lists circulated to the participants in the meeting for comments, most of which have been received. It is intended to reconvene the informal meeting at the end of the first week of January 1995, to receive the final drafts of the lists, to consider the draft reporting forms to be submitted by Governments pursuant to the mechanism, and to discuss the practical implementation of the mechanism. Immediately after that meeting, it is hoped to be able to resubmit to the Sanctions Committee the concept paper, with the draft revised annexes to the plans for ongoing monitoring and verification. When the concurrence of the Sanctions Committee is obtained in the course of January 1995, the proposal for the mechanism will be put before the Security Council for approval in a resolution to be adopted under Chapter VII of the Charter. The revisions to the annexes to the plans will also be brought to the attention of the Council, in accordance with the procedures for revision of the annexes already approved by the Council and contained in the Commission's and IAEA's plans for ongoing monitoring and verification (S/22871/Rev.1 and S/22871/Rev.2 and Corr.1, paras. 26 and 41).

B. *Resource implications*

4. The number of personnel and material resources required to support the export/import mechanism derives from the volume of data which the mechanism will generate. This figure, in turn, is derived from the volume

of dual-use items which will be imported by Iraq. The Commission is currently engaged in analytical studies to acquire broad outline figures for the likely level of reportable items.

5. Dual-use items imported into Iraq before the imposition of sanctions should have been either destroyed or consumed, or should be currently subjected to the monitoring regime. In the missile, chemical, biological and nuclear fields, the numbers of items of dual-use equipment destroyed under United Nations supervision or currently being monitored ranges from 500 to 1,000 separate pieces. Assuming that these items were imported during a period of approximately two to five years, the number of shipments of dual-use items could be expected not to exceed 2,000 during a normal year. Assessments of export patterns from Western countries into countries similar to Iraq confirm these figures. Further analysis and refinement of the figures will take place over the coming months as further data becomes available.

6. Notwithstanding the absence of precise figures relating to the volume of material anticipated under the export/import mechanism, the broad framework under which the regime will operate is currently being established. When operational, the export-import mechanism will constitute one of the main pillars of the ongoing monitoring and verification regime, and the Commission and IAEA's experts in New York, Vienna and Baghdad will be heavily involved in reviewing and assessing the information provided by Iraq and exporting Governments under the mechanism.

7. To administer the mechanism there will be export/import units staffed by customs experts and data entry personnel in Baghdad and New York. These units will be responsible for receiving the notification forms, ensuring their timely and efficient processing by the Commission's and IAEA's experts as may be the case, and the dissemination of information. In Iraq, the customs experts, in conjunction with the monitoring experts, will also undertake no-notice inspections at, *inter alia*, points of entry into Iraq, in order to verify that all relevant items are being declared. In view of the commercial sensitivity of data supplied under the export/import regime, special measures will be taken to ensure the security of this data.

8. On the basis of the figures set out above, the Commission currently envisages recruiting six to eight additional experts for its New York staff to process and analyse the data generated by the mechanism.

APPENDIX III
INFORMATION ASSESSMENT UNIT

The Information Assessment Unit is in the process of developing a new computer system which will form the key analytical tool for ongoing monitoring and verification and future export/import operations and analysis. The system will hold computerized versions of the site protocols, including declarations, inspection reports, imagery and maps. Work has already begun on creating a database to support export/import operations, which will be linked to the computerized site protocols, thus allowing the analysts to review items on order or being imported for each facility being monitored. In addition, the database will permit manipulation of information to allow assessments to be made on the total volume of items, such as dual-use chemicals, being imported into Iraq. In this manner, experts will at any time be able to make assessments about Iraq's potential capabilities to produce banned items, either at an individual site or throughout Iraq, and so will be better able to direct the Commission's monitoring of sites and imports to focus on the most significant issues.

APPENDIX IV
BAGHDAD MONITORING AND VERIFICATION CENTRE

A. *Concept and background information*

1. On 1 August 1994, the Commission established the Baghdad Monitoring and Verification Centre. In part, its establishment enabled the Executive Chairman to declare the ongoing monitoring and verification system provisionally operational.

2. The Centre provides offices, laboratories, and operational support for Commission and IAEA resident inspectors. The resident staff includes professional specialists in biological, chemical, and nuclear issues; missiles; aerial photography and interpretation and camera and other sensor technology. In the near future, it will include experts in export/import control of dual-use items. The resident and visiting inspectors are supported by a small staff led by the Director of the Centre. It should be noted that the Centre not only offers office space and common support for the inspectors, but also affords the opportunity for inter-disciplinary analysis of the data available to experts. This opportunity has become increasingly evident during inspections conducted in November and December 1994.

3. The Centre is located in the Canal Hotel, a building made available by the Government of Iraq for the exclusive use of the United Nations in the mid-1980s. The facility is managed by the United Nations Administrative Unit, Baghdad, for a variety of United Nations organizations. At the proposal of the Executive Chairman of the Commission, Iraq agreed that the Canal Hotel should serve as the Baghdad Monitoring and Verification Centre.

B. *Engineering support*

4. Immediately prior to the beginning of the reporting period, the Commission undertook a survey of the engineering support required to reconfigure the designated area in the Canal Hotel in a manner suitable for the tasks of the Centre.

5. The survey also indicated that the Centre would require extensive engineering support in a number of areas:

    (a) Reconfiguration of a large number of the rooms;

    (b) Rewiring of the electrical circuits and repair of the plumbing for the offices;

    (c) Physical barriers and control points needed to be installed at the numerous access points to ensure the security of the Centre.

6. In mid-July, the Al-Fao Construction Bureau was designated to perform the work. The indifferent quality of the workforce, the lack of qualified supervisors and the need for remedial repairs delayed the completion of the work.

7. The Iraqi renovation project was observed by construction engineers provided by a contributing Government. Their assessment of the facility and of the many requirements within the Centre indicated that the scope of engineering support must be enlarged to correct the deficiencies of the initial renovation and to engage in other projects to complete the facility. At the same time, efforts were made to arrange for engineering support for the long term. A fundamental consideration for these arrangements was the establishment and maintenance of a secure facility. This important factor made it necessary for the Commission to approach several Member States for both near- and long-term engineering support.

8. As the current reporting period closes, contributing Governments have provided craftsmen in response to specific requests for assistance, namely, installing locks; surveying the electric power system; completing a two-stage electric rewiring project; building the work surfaces and shelving in the operations room, the aerial inspection team offices and the laboratories; and designing the electrical system for the biological laboratory.

C. *Security measures*

9. Concerns about Centre security arise from many sources. Security of information, analyses and deliberations within the Centre is an essential element of the efficacy of ongoing monitoring and verification. Information security must encompass not only the findings of inspectors, but also the proprietary data of the notifications submitted to the Commission by Iraq and by the exporting Governments concerning dual-use items. Physical security must provide assurance of control over

all possible access points. A number of contributing Governments have made available technical experts and equipment to assist the Commission with its security programme.

D. *Equipment and furniture donations*

10. Contributing Governments of four States and the Economic and Social Commission for Western Asia (ESCWA) have provided, and continue to provide equipment, including furniture, for the Centre. Two Governments donated furniture and expendable supplies from their former embassy compounds in Baghdad. ESCWA is lending large quantities of office furniture, which was in storage at the former ESCWA headquarters in Baghdad. A third Government is providing the internal security camera system, an important component to the security programme for the Centre, and a fourth Government has donated computers and associated equipment for use in Baghdad.

11. The monitoring systems that have been installed at sites selected for that purpose and that support the efforts of the resident and visiting inspectors have been donated by a Member State, and installed and maintained by its technicians with assistance from technicians from other Governments. Most of the camera systems include real-time transmission from the remote sites so that the Centre may monitor system performance. It is expected that all remote cameras will incorporate this feature in the coming months. The Centre also receives data from associated sensors and from alarm devices that record interference with the monitoring. The contributing Governments have established an initial, periodic maintenance schedule, continually to ensure that the remote site systems are in working order.

E. *Personnel of the Centre*

12. The establishment of the Centre on 1 August was signified by the arrival of the first Director. The continuous presence of inspectors from a variety of disciplines has created new, and in many ways unforeseen, opportunities to enhance the Commission's capabilities and performance.

13. The Centre provides support for approximately 50 personnel in residence as well as support for a 31-person detachment of the German Army brigade that operates the Commission's three CH-53G helicopters. The number of resident experts will increase with the advent of the export/import mechanism. Visiting teams will temporarily expand the presence of the Commission and IAEA.

14. Recruitment of personnel for the Centre takes a variety of forms. Some Member States have made an ongoing commitment to make available a particular expertise. Most of the monitoring group inspectors are recruited through the Permanent Missions in New York. This continuous process of recruitment commenced formally with a presentation to over 20 Member States in late May 1994, and has worked well to provide personnel for all required positions in a timely manner during the reporting period.

F. *Future developments*

15. The complete establishment of the Centre will be but one factor in the full implementation of ongoing monitoring and verification. Plans are in hand to install all the currently envisaged equipment and laboratories required to support the full operation of the Centre by the end of February 1995. When the staff arrives to operate and maintain the new equipment, the Centre should be fully staffed and equipped. Adjustments to staffing levels will be made in line with requirements and in the light of experience gained in operating the ongoing monitoring and verification regime. The prime expansion currently envisaged will be the arrival of export/import experts at the appropriate time, in preparation for the operation of the export/import mechanism.

APPENDIX V
ADMINISTRATIVE AND FINANCIAL ISSUES

A. *Organizational and administrative issues*

1. Since the last report, there have been no further changes in the composition of the Special Commission.

2. The organizational structure remains essentially as reported previously. Currently there are 41 staff in the office of the Executive Chairman, 23 in the Bahrain field office, and 69 in the Baghdad field office.

3. Governments have continued to support the operation of the Commission through the contribution of personnel, services and equipment. These contributions have been essential to the work of the Commission in every area.

B. *Status, privileges and immunities*

4. The status, privileges and immunities of the Commission, IAEA and the specialized agencies involved in the implementation of Security Council resolution 687 (1991) continue to be regulated by the relevant agreements and Council resolutions and decisions.

5. The Commission and IAEA on the one hand and the Government of Bahrain on the other have extended for a further six months, until 31 March 1995, the agreement provided for in the earlier exchanges of letters relating to the facilities, privileges and immunities of the Commission and IAEA in Bahrain.

C. *Finance*

6. A full account of the financial difficulties which have confronted the Commission is contained in annex III to the report contained in S/1994/1138 and Corr. 1. The financial situation of the Commission remains an area of great concern in view of the difficulties in ensuring proper funding for the operations in a planned manner. At this time, the only commitments received from Member States for additional contributions have been $2.5 million from Kuwait and $40,000 from Switzerland. Other Member States in the Gulf region have expressed their continuing support for the work of the Commission and it is hoped that cash contributions will follow. It is also expected, as was the case in the past, that a portion of the matching transfer of frozen Iraqi assets from the United States of America to the escrow account will be made available to the Commission to cover some of its 1995 requirements. In the best possible circumstances, at this point, funds can be identified only for the first three months of 1995. Beyond that, there are no identified funds in the escrow account to cover the Commission's operations. Obviously, if further funds are not identified in the near future, the incremental shut-down of the Commission's operations, as indicated in the Commission's letter to the President of the Security Council of 3 November 1994, will ensue.

APPENDIX VI

INSPECTION SCHEDULE

(In-country dates)

Nuclear

15-21 May 1991	IAEA1/UNSCOM 1
22 June-3 July 1991	IAEA2/UNSCOM 4
7-18 July 1991	IAEA3/UNSCOM 5
27 July-10 August 1991	IAEA4/UNSCOM 6
14-20 September 1991	IAEA5/UNSCOM 14
21-30 September 1991	IAEA6/UNSCOM 16
11-22 October 1991	IAEA7/UNSCOM 19
11-18 November 1991	IAEA8/UNSCOM 22
11-14 January 1992	IAEA9/UNSCOM 25
5-13 February 1992	IAEA10/UNSCOM 27
7-15 April 1992	IAEA11/UNSCOM 33
26 May-4 June 1992	IAEA12/UNSCOM 37
14-21 July 1992	IAEA13/UNSCOM 41
31 August-7 September 1992	IAEA14/UNSCOM 43
8-19 November 1992	IAEA15/UNSCOM 46
6-14 December 1992	IAEA16/UNSCOM 47
22-27 January 1993	IAEA17/UNSCOM 49
3-11 March 1993	IAEA18/UNSCOM 52
30 April-7 May 1993	IAEA19/UNSCOM 56
25-30 June 1993	IAEA20/UNSCOM 58
23-28 July 1993	IAEA21/UNSCOM 61

1-9 November 1993	IAEA22/UNSCOM 64
4-11 February 1994	IAEA23/UNSCOM 68
11-22 April 1994	IAEA24/UNSCOM 73
21 June-1 July 1994	IAEA25/UNSCOM 83
22 August-2 September 1994	IAEA26/UNSCOM 90
7-29 September 1994	NMG 94-01
14-21 October 1994	IAEA27/UNSCOM 93
29 September-21 October 1994	NMG 94-02
21 October-9 November 1994	NMG 94-03
8-29 November 1994	NMG 94-04
29 November-16 December 1994	NMG 94-05
16 December 1994-13 January 1995	NMG 94-06

Chemical

9-15 June 1991	CW1/UNSCOM 2
15-22 August 1991	CW2/UNSCOM 9
31 August-8 September 1991	CW3/UNSCOM 11
31 August-5 September 1991	CW4/UNSCOM 12
6 October-9 November 1991	CW5/UNSCOM 17
22 October-2 November 1991	CW6/UNSCOM 20
18 November-1 December 1991	CBW1/UNSCOM 21
27 January-5 February 1992	CW7/UNSCOM 26
21 February-24 March 1992	CD1/UNSCOM 29
5-13 April 1992	CD2/UNSCOM 32
15-29 April 1992	CW8/UNSCOM 35
18 June 1992-14 June 1994	CDG/UNSCOM 38
26 June-10 July 1992	CBW2/UNSCOM 39
21-29 September 1992	CW9/UNSCOM 44
6-14 December 1992	CBW3/UNSCOM 47
6-18 April 1993	CW10/UNSCOM 55
27-30 June 1993	CW11/UNSCOM 59
19-22 November 1993	CW12/UNSCOM 65
1-14 February 1994	CW13/UNSCOM 67
20-26 March 1994	CW14/UNSCOM 70
18-22 April 1994	CW15/UNSCOM 74
25 May-5 June 1994	CW16/UNSCOM 75
31 May-12 June 1994	CW17/UNSCOM 76
8-14 June 1994	CW18/UNSCOM 77
10-23 August 1994	CW19/UNSCOM 89
13-24 September 1994	CW20/UNSCOM 91
2 October 1994-15 January 1995	CG 1
23-27 October 1994	CW21/UNSCOM 95

Biological

2-8 August 1991	BW1/UNSCOM 7
20 September-3 October 1991	BW2/UNSCOM 15
11-18 March 1993	BW3/UNSCOM 53
8-26 April 1994	BW4/UNSCOM 72
28 May-7 June 1994	BW5/UNSCOM 78
24 June-5 July 1994	BW6/UNSCOM 84
5-8 June 1994	BW7/UNSCOM 86
25 July-7 September 1994	BW8/UNSCOM 87

Biological (continued)

20-25 August 1994	BW9/UNSCOM 88
29 August-3 September 1994	BW10/UNSCOM 92
29 September-14 October 1994	BW11/UNSCOM 94
23-26 September 1994	BW12/UNSCOM 96
15-22 November 1994	BW15/UNSCOM 104
2-10 December 1994	BW16/UNSCOM 105 (IMT)
2-14 December 1994	BW13/UNSCOM 99 (IMT)
9-19 December 1994	BW17/UNSCOM 106 (IMT)
28 December 1994-	
31 January 1995	IBG 1

Ballistic missiles

30 June-7 July 1991	BM1/UNSCOM 3
18-20 July 1991	BM2/UNSCOM 10
8-15 August 1991	BM3/UNSCOM 8
6-13 September 1991	BM4/UNSCOM 13
1-9 October 1991	BM5/UNSCOM 18
1-9 December 1991	BM6/UNSCOM 23
9-17 December 1991	BM7/UNSCOM 24
21-29 February 1992	BM8/UNSCOM 28
21-29 March 1992	BM9/UNSCOM 31
13-21 April 1992	BM10/UNSCOM 34
14-22 May 1992	BM11/UNSCOM 36
11-29 July 1992	BM12/UNSCOM 40A+B
7-18 August 1992	BM13/UNSCOM 42
16-30 October 1992	BM14/UNSCOM 45
25 January-23 March 1993	IMT1a/UNSCOM 48
12-21 February 1993	BM15/UNSCOM 50
22-23 February 1993	BM16/UNSCOM 51
27 March-17 May 1993	IMT1b/UNSCOM 54
5-28 June 1993	IMT1c/UNSCOM 57
10-11 July 1993	BM17/UNSCOM 60
24 August-15 September 1993	BM18/UNSCOM 62
28 September-1 November 1993	BM19/UNSCOM 63
21-29 January 1994	BM20/UNSCOM 66
17-25 February 1994	BM21/UNSCOM 69
30 March-20 May 1994	BM22/UNSCOM 71
20 May-8 June 1994	BM23/UNSCOM 79
10-24 June 1994	BM24/UNSCOM 80
14-22 June 1994	BM25/UNSCOM 81
3-28 July 1994	BM26/UNSCOM 82
15-24 July 1994	BM27/UNSCOM 85
17 August-9 October 1994	MG 1
2-6 October 1994	BM28/UNSCOM 98A
23-28 October 1994	BM28/UNSCOM 98B
14 October 1994-2 February 1995	MG 2
19-22 October 1994	MG 2A
2-6 December 1994	MG 2B
1-6 December 1994 ⎫	
9-14 December 1994 ⎭	BM29/UNSCOM 101
9-16 December 1994	BM30/UNSCOM 102

Computer search

12 February 1992	UNSCOM 30

Special missions

30 June-3 July 1991
11-14 August 1991
4-6 October 1991
11-15 November 1991
27-30 January 1992
21-24 February 1992
17-19 July 1992
28-29 July 1992
6-12 September 1992
4-9 November 1992
4-8 November 1992
12-18 March 1993
14-20 March 1993
19-24 April 1993
4 June-5 July 1993
15-19 July 1993
25 July-5 August 1993
9-12 August 1993
10-24 September 1993
27 September-1 October 1993
1-8 October 1993
5 October-16 February 1994
2-10 December 1993
2-16 December 1993
21-27 January 1994
2-6 February 1994
10-14 April 1994
24-26 April 1994
28-29 May 1994
4-6 July 1994
8-16 August 1994
15-19 September 1994
21-25 September 1994
23-26 September 1994
3-6 October 1994
4-20 November 1994
7-12 November 1994
14-17 November 1994
4-18 December 1994
14-20 December 1994

Document 201

Seventh semi-annual report (for the period 18 June to 17 December 1994) on the implementation by the IAEA of the plan for the destruction, removal or rendering harmless of items listed in paragraph 12 of Security Council resolution 687 (1991)

S/1994/1438, 22 December 1994

Note by the Secretary-General

The Secretary-General has the honour to transmit to the Security Council the attached communication which he has received from the Acting Director General of the International Atomic Energy Agency (IAEA).

Annex
Letter dated 16 December 1994 from the Acting Director General of the International Atomic Energy Agency addressed to the Secretary-General

In its resolution 699 (1991) of 17 June 1991, the Security Council requests, *inter alia*, the Secretary-General to submit to the Security Council progress reports on the implementation of the plan for the destruction, removal or rendering harmless of the items specified in paragraph 12 of resolution 687 (1991). Such reports are to be submitted every six months after the adoption of resolution 699 (1991). The next report is therefore due on 17 December 1994.

Please find attached an outline of the activities carried out by the International Atomic Energy Agency during the past six months under the plan for destruction, removal or rendering harmless, which you might find useful for the preparation of your report.

(*Signed*) Boris SEMENOV
Acting Director General

Appendix
Seventh semi-annual report (covering the period from 18 June to 17 December 1994) on the implementation by the International Atomic Energy Agency of the plan for the destruction, removal or rendering harmless of items listed in paragraph 12 of Security Council resolution 687 (1991)

Introduction

1. By resolution 699 (1991) of 17 June 1991, the Security Council approved the plan submitted by the International Atomic Energy Agency (IAEA), through the Secretary-General, for the destruction, removal or rendering harmless of all items listed in paragraph 12 of Security Council resolution 687 (1991). Resolution 699 (1991) also called

for the Secretary-General to submit every six months a progress report on the implementation of the plan.

2. The first six reports were circulated by the Secretary-General to the members of the Security Council in document S/23295, dated 17 December 1991; S/24110, dated 17 June 1992; S/24988, dated 17 December 1992; S/25983, dated 21 June 1993; S/26897, dated 20 December 1993; and S/1994/793, dated 5 July 1994.

3. This is the seventh semi-annual report on the implementation by IAEA of the plan for destruction, removal or rendering harmless covering the period from 18 June to 17 December 1994. During this period, IAEA, with the assistance and cooperation of the Special Commission of the United Nations, conducted three on-site inspections in Iraq (IAEA/25, IAEA/26 and IAEA/27). Detailed reports of IAEA/25 and IAEA/26 have been distributed to the Security Council in documents S/1994/1001, dated 26 August 1994, and S/1994/1206, dated 22 October 1994. The report of IAEA/27 is in preparation.

4. In addition, as from August 1994, IAEA has established a continuous presence in Iraq as an element of its plan for ongoing monitoring and verification of Iraq's compliance with relevant Security Council resolutions. IAEA will include in its semi-annual reports on the implementation of the plan summaries of the inspection activities being carried out by IAEA under the plan.

Present status

5. As of 17 December 1994, IAEA has carried out 27 inspection missions in Iraq. In the course of those inspections, IAEA has been able to destroy, render harmless or remove from Iraq all items which have been located and identified as associated with Iraq's clandestine nuclear weapons programme. Should IAEA uncover any additional items not previously discovered or declared which are subject to such destruction, rendering harmless or removal from Iraq, IAEA will carry out such activities.

Nuclear material

6. As previously reported to the Security Council, the task of removing all special fissionable material from

Iraq has been completed with the removal of the remaining spent fuel to the Russian Federation under contract with the Russian Ministry of Atomic Energy (MINATOM). As provided for in the contract, MINATOM has reprocessed the spent fuel and downgraded the content of the U-235 isotope to slightly below 20 per cent. The recovered material, amounting to a total quantity of 141 kilograms of uranium (metal equivalent), with an average enrichment of $19.8 + 0.15$ per cent in U-235 isotope, was shipped from the Mayak reprocessing plant to the designated storage site at Electrostal, where it arrived on 6 December 1994. On 14 and 15 December 1994, IAEA safeguards inspectors visited Electrostal to verify the material and take samples for analysis. In order to complete its contractual obligations, MINATOM will now proceed with the conditioning—through vitrification—of the radioactive wastes, including small amounts of plutonium, resulting from the reprocessing of the Iraqi fuel and to the permanent disposal of the conditioned waste in the final repository at Mayak. It is expected that this operation will be completed by March 1995.

7. With the assistance of the Brazilian authorities, IAEA has finished its verification of the completeness and has assessed the correctness of the information provided by the Iraqi authorities regarding the amount of natural uranium oxide of Brazilian origin exported to Iraq.

8. All of the nuclear material remaining in Iraq, which consists of low enriched, natural and depleted uranium, has been consolidated in one site (Location C) and will continue to be monitored by IAEA.

Release of material and equipment

9. In response to a request by Iraq, IAEA, in consultation with the Special Commission, agreed to the release of several hundred tons of shielding lead for use in lead-acid battery production. As this lead is to be recovered from equipment associated with Iraq's hot cells, utilized in the building 22 (LAMA Laboratories) at Tuwaitha, its continued non-proscribed use will be subject to Agency monitoring. Accordingly, IAEA's agreement to the release of the shielded cells was granted subject to the following conditions: the dismantling of the cells will be verified by IAEA; the viewing windows of the hot cells are to be stored in Tuwaitha/Al Shakili and kept available for ongoing monitoring; the lead blocks are to be moved to the Falluja factory under IAEA supervision; the melting of the lead is to be verified by IAEA; and periodic visits will be made by IAEA to the battery factory at which the lead is to be utilized.

10. A second Iraqi request, concerning the release of conventional chemical equipment to be salvaged from the destroyed Al Qaim yellow cake production plant, was disposed of in September 1994 in consultation with the Special Commission. While authorizing the release, IAEA has reserved its full right to verify the use of the equipment as part of its monitoring and verification activity.

Establishment of an export/import monitoring mechanism

11. As provided for in Security Council resolution 715 (1991), IAEA, the Special Commission and the Security Council Committee established under resolution 661 (1990) are developing for the approval of the Security Council a mechanism for monitoring any future sales or supplies by other countries to Iraq of items relevant to the implementation of section C of resolution 687 (1991) and other relevant resolutions, and the plans for ongoing monitoring and verification approved under resolution 715 (1991). As a part of this exercise, IAEA is in the process of revising annex 3 of its plan, with a view to establishing a single list of items subject to reporting by Iraq and subject, at the same time, to reporting under the export/import mechanism by suppliers to Iraq.

Future actions

12. Verification of the correctness and assessment of the completeness of the list updates of items submitted by the Iraqi authorities pursuant to annex 3 of the plan for ongoing monitoring and verification will continue.

13. Consultations with the Special Commission concerning additional Iraqi requests for the release of dual-use equipment and materials will also continue.

Document 202

General Assembly resolution concerning the situation of human rights in Iraq

A/RES/49/203, 23 December 1994

The General Assembly,

Guided by the principles embodied in the Charter of the United Nations, the Universal Declaration of Human Rights 1/ and the International Covenants on Human Rights, 2/

Reaffirming that all Member States have an obligation to promote and protect human rights and fundamental freedoms and to fulfil the obligations they have undertaken under the various international instruments in this field,

Mindful that Iraq is a party to the International Covenants on Human Rights and to other international human rights instruments,

Recalling its resolution 48/144 of 20 December 1993, in which it expressed its deep concern at flagrant violations of human rights by the Government of Iraq,

Recalling also Security Council resolution 688 (1991) of 5 April 1991, in which the Council demanded an end to the repression of the Iraqi civilian population and insisted that Iraq cooperate with humanitarian organizations and ensure that the human and political rights of all Iraqi citizens were respected,

Recalling in particular Commission on Human Rights resolution 1991/74 of 6 March 1991, 3/ by which the Commission requested its Chairman to appoint a special rapporteur to make a thorough study of the violations of human rights by the Government of Iraq, based on all information the special rapporteur might deem relevant, including information provided by intergovernmental and non-governmental organizations and any comments and material provided by the Government of Iraq,

Recalling the pertinent resolutions of the Commission on Human Rights condemning the flagrant violations of human rights by the Government of Iraq, including its most recent resolution, 1994/74 of 9 March 1994, 4/ in which the Commission decided to extend the mandate of the Special Rapporteur for a further year and requested him to submit an interim report to the General Assembly at its forty-ninth session and a final report to the Commission at its fifty-first session,

Recalling also Security Council resolutions 687 (1991) of 3 April 1991, 706 (1991) of 15 August 1991, 712 (1991) of 19 September 1991 and 778 (1992) of 2 October 1992,

Deeply concerned by the deterioration of the overall human rights situation in Iraq and the continued massive and grave violations of human rights by the Government of Iraq, such as summary and arbitrary executions, torture and other cruel, inhuman or degrading treatment, enforced or involuntary disappearances, arbitrary arrests and detentions, lack of due process and the rule of law, and of freedom of thought, of expression, of association and of access to food and health care,

Deeply concerned also by the forced displacement of hundreds of thousands of Iraqi civilians and by the destruction of Iraqi towns and villages, as well as by the fact that tens of thousands of displaced Kurds have had to take refuge in camps and shelters in the north of Iraq,

Deeply concerned further by the increasingly severe and grave violations of human rights by the Government of Iraq against the civilian population in southern Iraq, in particular in the southern marshes, where the combination of massive drainage projects and wide-ranging military operations on the part of the Government has forced residents of the marshes to flee in large numbers, many of whom have sought refuge on the border between Iraq and the Islamic Republic of Iran,

Welcoming the decision to deploy a team of human rights monitors to such locations as would facilitate improved information flows and assessment and help in the independent verification of reports on the situation of human rights in Iraq,

Regretting that the Government of Iraq has not seen fit to respond to requests for a visit of the Special Rapporteur or to cooperate with him, in particular by failing to reply to his inquiries about acts being committed by the Government that are incompatible with the international human rights instruments that are binding on that country,

1. *Takes note with appreciation* of the interim report on the situation of human rights in Iraq submitted by the Special Rapporteur of the Commission on Human Rights 5/ and the observations, conclusions and recommendations contained therein;

1/ Resolution 217 A (III).
2/ Resolution 2200 A (XXI), annex.
3/ See *Official Records of the Economic and Social Council, 1991, Supplement No. 2* (E/1991/22), chap. II, sect.A.
4/ Ibid., *1994, Supplement No. 4* and corrigendum (E/1994/24 and Corr.1), chap.II, sect.A.
5/ A/49/651, annex.

2. *Expresses its strong condemnation* of the massive violations of human rights of the gravest nature, for which the Government of Iraq is responsible and to which the Special Rapporteur has referred in his recent reports, in particular:

(a) Summary and arbitrary executions, orchestrated mass executions and burials, extrajudicial killings, including political killings, in particular in the northern region of Iraq, in southern Shiah centres and in the southern marshes;

(b) The widespread routine practice of systematic torture in its most cruel forms;

(c) The enactment and implementation of recent decrees prescribing cruel and unusual punishment, namely, mutilation as a penalty for certain offences and the abuse and diversion of medical care services for the purposes of such legalized mutilations;

(d) Enforced or involuntary disappearances, routinely practised arbitrary arrest and detention, including arrest and detention of women, the elderly and children, and consistent and routine failure to respect due process and the rule of law;

(e) Suppression of freedom of thought, expression and association and violations of property rights;

(f) The unwillingness of the Government of Iraq to honour its responsibilities as regards the economic and social rights of the population, especially with regard to the rights to food and health;

3. *Condemns* the repression of the Iraqi civilian population in general, and of the political opposition in particular,

4. *Deplores* the refusal of Iraq to cooperate in the implementation of Security Council resolutions 706 (1991) and 712 (1991), which provide for the sale of oil in return for humanitarian aid, and its resultant failure to provide the Iraqi population with access to adequate food and health care;

5. *Calls upon* the Government of Iraq to resolve the cases of disappearances of Kuwaitis and nationals of other States by providing detailed information on all persons deported from or arrested in Kuwait between 2 August 1990 and 26 February 1991 and on those who were executed or died in detention during or after that period, as well as on the location of their graves, and also calls upon the Government of Iraq in particular:

(a) To release immediately all Kuwaitis and nationals of other States who may still be held in detention;

(b) To improve substantially its cooperation with international humanitarian organizations in an effort to resolve the cases of Kuwaitis and national of other States who have disappeared;

(c) To pay appropriate compensation to the families of such persons who died while in the custody of Iraqi authorities or for whom the Government of Iraq is responsible and has so far failed to account, through the mechanism established by Security Council resolution 692 (1991) of 20 May 1991;

6. *Calls once again upon* Iraq, as a State party to the International Covenant on Economic, Social and Cultural Rights 6/ and to the International Covenant on Civil and Political Rights, 6/ to abide by its obligations freely undertaken under the Covenants and under other international instruments on human rights and, particularly, to respect and ensure the rights of all individuals, irrespective of their origin, within its territory and subject to its jurisdiction;

7. *Recognizes* the importance of the work of the United Nations in providing humanitarian relief to the people of Iraq, and calls upon Iraq to allow unhindered access of the United Nations humanitarian agencies throughout the country, including ensuring the safety of United Nations personnel and humanitarian workers, *inter alia*, through the continued implementation of the Memorandum of Understanding signed by the United Nations and the Government of Iraq;

8. *Expresses special alarm* at the repressive practices directed against the Kurds, which continue to have an impact on the lives of the Iraqi people as a whole;

9. *Also expresses special alarm* at the grave violations of human rights in southern Iraq, and urges the Government of Iraq to implement without further delay the recommendations made by the Special Rapporteur, including, *inter alia*, the immediate halting and reversal of the draining of the marshes and the cessation of its military activities against the marsh Arabs, whose survival as a community is endangered;

10. *Welcomes* the sending of human rights monitors to the border between Iraq and the Islamic Republic of Iran, and calls upon the Government of Iraq to allow immediate and unconditional stationing of human rights monitors throughout the country, especially the southern marsh area;

11. *Once again expresses its special alarm* at the continuation of all internal embargoes, which permit no exceptions for humanitarian needs and which prevent the equitable enjoyment of basic foodstuffs and medical supplies, and calls upon the Government of Iraq, which has sole responsibility in this regard, to remove them and to take steps to cooperate with international humanitarian agencies in the provision of relief to those in need throughout Iraq and to act to take advantage of the "food for oil" formula as set forth in Security Council resolutions 706 (1991) and 712 (1991);

6/ See resolution 2200 A (XXI), annex.

12. *Regrets* the failure of the Government of Iraq to provide satisfactory replies concerning the violations of human rights brought to the attention of the Special Rapporteur, and calls upon it fully to cooperate and to reply without delay in a comprehensive and detailed manner so as to enable the Special Rapporteur to formulate the appropriate recommendations to improve the situation of human rights in Iraq;

13. *Requests* the Secretary-General to provide the Special Rapporteur with all necessary assistance in carrying out his mandate and to approve the allocation of sufficient human and material resources for the sending of human rights experts to such locations as would facilitate improved information flow and assessment and help in the independent verification of reports on the situation of human rights in Iraq;

14. *Decides* to continue its consideration of the situation of human rights in Iraq during its fiftieth session under the item entitled "Human rights questions" in the light of additional elements provided by the Commission on Human Rights and the Economic and Social Council.

Document 203

United Nations Consolidated Inter-Agency Humanitarian Programme in Iraq for the period from April 1995 to March 1996 (extract)

21 March 1995

Overview

Current Situation

Despite four consecutive years of stability and somewhat improved living conditions as a result of effective and continuing support from the international community, the current humanitarian situation in Iraq remains extremely precarious. Approximately 1.3 million people—representing 35 percent of the population—are dependent on some form of humanitarian aid (target beneficiaries: 750,000 in the three northern governorates and 550,000 in the centre and south). Moreover, Iraq hosts an estimated refugee population of 121,000 persons, essentially comprised of Kurds of Iranian and Turkish origin, Iranians of Persian and Arab origin, Palestinians and Eritreans, who are in need of varying degrees of external relief.

The continuing depreciation of the Iraqi dinar has caused hyperinflation. During the period December 1993-December 1994 alone, food commodities in the central and southern governorates increased by a staggering 616 percent, putting the procurement of food far beyond the reach of low- and middle-class households. A recent UNICEF study indicates that, as a result of this chronic situation, combined with other factors (such as the recent reduction, by 33 percent since October 1994, in the Government's food entitlement programme), nutritional vulnerability is likely to affect 3.6 million people, of whom 2.5 million are children and pregnant and lactating women.

In the three northern governorates, a recent household survey funded by USAID/OFDA and ODA-UK, confirmed a dramatic deterioration in the social and economic sectors and an increasing trend of destitute and vulnerable people in urban areas who can hardly afford to purchase food and other essential items. During the period June 1994-December 1994 alone, food prices rose by an estimated 93 percent.

In terms of health facilities, the past twelve months have witnessed a resurgence of vaccine-preventable diseases, due to the continuing acute shortage of vaccines. This situation has been compounded by the fact that the local pharmaceutical industry has stopped producing vaccines, along with antibiotics and life-saving drugs because of lack of raw materials. Most maternity hospitals continue to suffer greatly from a lack of basic equipment and medicines. Mothers suffering from severe anemia, hypertension or diabetes have no proper antenatal care or safe delivery conditions.

Due to the fact that the state of water and sanitation is critical, the quality of water available is poor and frequently contaminated. The deterioration of environmental sanitation and the low quality of water have facilitated the explosion of parasitic infestations and increased occurrence of water borne diseases which only serve to add to the already chronic health situation.

The educational sector also continues to experience an acute shortage of basic materials such as exercise books, textbooks, pencils and blackboards. The majority of schools are in physical need of repair and maintenance work, with broken windows and doors, an all too common feature of most classrooms. In fact, such unfavourable conditions have led to an increase in the school drop-out rate to an estimated 17 percent.

Additionally, due to the widespread problem of land-mines, particularly in the northern governorates, school-age children are particularly exposed when playing in mine-affected areas. Mine awareness materials have already been distributed in primary schools by NGOs in some of the affected areas. Clearly, however, much still needs to be done to tackle this problem.

In terms of the energy needs of the population, the supply of electricity in rural and urban areas is critical. Due to a lack of spare and replacement parts, a large number of electric installations remain unserviceable or operate below normal capacity. In the north, electricity provided from Mosul to the Dohuk governorate was interrupted in August 1993, thereby affecting the health infrastructure (in particular hospitals) and the supply of potable water to local inhabitants. As a result, thousands of families from Aqrah region left the area, placing greater strain on the humanitarian programme. To alleviate this situation, a number of power generators have been purchased and were installed in selected hospitals, social institutions and water stations. In the Erbil and Suleimaniyah governorates, (limited) electricity supply is available from local power sources. Over and above, the lack of an assured source of energy has limited urban growth, employment opportunities and the creation of small industries in the region.

From a housing and transport point of view, much still needs to be done in these two areas particularly in the three northern governorates. Although some repair work has been carried out on major roads in northern Iraq, many sections of secondary roads still require substantial work.

Where housing is concerned the needs continue to be great. In northern Iraq alone, an estimated 75,000 units are needed. The combined humanitarian efforts of international organisations, donors and NGOs to assist the population in northern Iraq in meeting their housing needs, particularly those of the internally displaced and returnees, resulted in the construction of a yearly average of 12,000 permanent shelter units in 1992/93. At the same time, there are thousands of returnees and displaced families in immediate need of urban shelter who for the time being are currently occupying former factories, unfinished buildings and abandoned army barracks, which are basically unfit for all but emergency human shelter.

Despite the vast problems Iraq has experienced so far, some positive results have been obtained in various sectors covered by the Programme towards self-sufficiency and reducing the amount and the cost of relief rehabilitation assistance.

It is none the less clear that the support of the international donor community continues to be urgently required for the implementation of priority activities set forth in the present Appeal.

The humanitarian programme
The United Nations Inter-Agency Programme was established on 18 April 1991 with the signing of the first Memorandum of Understanding between the United Nations and the Government of Iraq. Its principal aim has been to provide humanitarian assistance to vulnerable groups and to help the country move from the emergency relief situation which has affected most of the population since the Gulf crisis towards one of sustainable development. The endorsement of an extension to the programme on 22 October 1992 continues to cover the cooperation arrangements between the United Nations and the Government of Iraq in their joint efforts towards achieving the primary objectives of the agreement.

The Humanitarian Programme is coordinated by the United Nations Department of Humanitarian Affairs (UNDHA) and implemented by the participating UN agencies and NGOs, in close cooperation with the Government of Iraq and the relevant local authorities. It is funded through voluntary contributions made by donors directly to the individual UN agencies and NGOs, and through an Escrow Account of the United Nations in New York, which receives voluntary contributions for humanitarian assistance as well as "matching" funds released from frozen Iraqi assets held in the United States (for further details, see Annex I on "United Nations SCR 778 Escrow Account" [not reproduced here]).

The impact of external assistance provided under the umbrella of the United Nations Humanitarian Programme can be described as crucial to the basic survival of the most vulnerable groups of the population. The Humanitarian Programme's main objectives under the previous Appeal have focused on food and kerosene distribution, medicines and health care, nutrition as well as the provision of essential commodities such as water purification chemicals, potable water, shelter materials, sanitation equipment, agricultural/veterinary support, and resettlement assistance to returnees. In the northern governorates, the population has greatly benefitted from food and kerosene distributions during the four previous winters.

Capacity-building in support of the most vulnerable groups such as refugees, internally displaced, destitutes, hospital in-patients and persons placed in social institutions is an important feature of the Programme. Approximately two thirds of the assistance received so far has been channelled in the three northern governorates. However, due to a lack of funding and a deteriorating security situation, relief and rehabilitation activities have been particularly affected and reduced in the past few months.

An essential component to the Programme remains the provision of security coverage to UN and NGO relief personnel. Since May 1991, a United Nations Guards Contingent in Iraq (UNGCI) has been deployed (mainly in the three northern governorates). The number of Guards has varied between 500 and the current level of 85.

Despite the increased need for humanitarian assistance, response to the previous Appeal (April 1994-March 1995) has been inadequate with approximately 50 percent (US$146 million) of overall programme requirements (US$288.5 million) covered by allocations of "matching" funds, voluntary contributions and by carry-over from the previous phase. From this amount, funding to UN-directed humanitarian activities amounted to 92.5 million while contributions made available to humanitarian NGOs and other direct/bilateral programmes (including IFRC) amounted to US$53.5 million.

. . .

With diminishing contributions to the Programme over the last two years, UN agencies in Iraq are reducing personnel, including UN Guards, and downsizing their activities. As at 1 March 1995, there were 153 UN international staff (including UNGCI) and 147 international NGO staff working in Iraq.

Programme strategy

This Appeal is geared towards preserving the health of the Iraqi population as the main focus for humanitarian assistance, representing the highest priority for donor funding. The Appeal, totalling about US$183 million, constitutes an extremely conservative estimate of only essential needs towards this goal. It includes about US$130 million for UN Agencies programmes, and US$53 million for NGOs activities. It should be stressed that the country's needs are enormous and that they cannot be met solely through humanitarian assistance programmes. However, the amount appealed for will contribute towards alleviating the suffering of selectively targeted beneficiaries.

The three main components for preserving health are clean water, adequate food and nutrition, and appropriate health care including immunization and life-saving medicines. However, adequate food cannot be secured for the vulnerable population without essential inputs towards food production by subsistence farmers and resettling families and other vulnerable groups. The only "mechanized" assistance envisaged is the spraying against pests of date-palm plantations and wheat crops, the major sources of affordable cereal and energy for the lowest-income groups.

Education as a basic right of every child is addressed through rehabilitation of schools and provision of essential learning supplies. Shelter, resettlement and rehabilitation of communities will be addressed mainly with the help of NGOs and by encouraging and mobilizing communities in self-help schemes.

Other very pressing needs include provision of spare parts and further inputs for basic agriculture, rehabilitation of irrigation systems, water and sewage treatment plants, hospitals and schools, provision of energy, maintenance of roads and demining.

Humanitarian assistance to northern Iraq will consist of limited food relief, clean water supply, essential health services, resettlement, education materials and essential farming and veterinary inputs. With respect to the central and southern parts of the country, where the humanitarian situation has deteriorated the greatest during the past twelve months, the focus is still on emergency assistance in the following areas: food and nutrition, essential health services, maintaining supply of clean water, educational inputs and essential agricultural and veterinary inputs.

Refugees, returnees and internally displaced people also feature strongly under the Appeal. While UN-HCR budgets its assistance to refugees separately, food assistance for 65,000 refugees is included in WFP's programme. The needs of internally displaced persons are considered under all other proposed activities.

The humanitarian role of the international and national non-governmental organisations continues to be significant. The majority of the NGOs operate in northern Iraq. Some important project proposals from CARE International and OXFAM in support of activities in the central and southern parts of the country have been included in this Appeal. The implementation of NGO activities has been made possible through contractual arrangements with UN Agencies and through direct donor grants.

The volatile security situation in northern Iraq continues to justify maintaining the presence of the UNGCI. Their deployment remains a precondition to security and safety of UN and NGO international staff and for humanitarian operations in northern Iraq. The plan for a reduced number of UN Guards will require increased training of local security personnel by the UNGCI, to fill vital security roles related to the humanitarian programme.

The one-year duration of the current Programme, divided into two six-month periods, is for planning purposes only. The first period (April-September 1995) focuses on priority emergency requirements for the summer season, while the second (October 1995-March 1996) provides a general orientation as to the type of activities to be undertaken during the winter months. However, the extension of the Humanitarian Programme does not prejudice the possibility to terminate or expand the Programme at any time depending on the need for humanitarian assistance, the availability of financial resources to fund such assistance, or in the light of other developments affecting the situation in Iraq.

Document 204

Report of the Secretary-General on UNIKOM for the period 7 October 1994 to 31 March 1995

S/1995/251, 31 March 1995

I. *Introduction*

1. By paragraph 5 of its resolution 687 (1991) of 3 April 1991, the Security Council established a demilitarized zone (DMZ) along the Iraq-Kuwait boundary and decided to set up an observer unit with the following tasks: to monitor the Khawr Abd Allah waterway and the DMZ; to deter violations of the boundary through its presence in and surveillance of the DMZ; and to observe any potentially hostile action mounted from the territory of one State into the other. By its resolution 689 (1991) of 9 April 1991, the Security Council approved the report of the Secretary-General on the implementation of the above provisions (S/22454). Furthermore, by its resolution 806 (1993), the Council expanded the tasks of the United Nations Iraq-Kuwait Observation Mission (UNIKOM) to include the capacity to take physical action to prevent or redress small-scale violations of the DMZ or the boundary.

2. By its resolution 689 (1991), the Security Council noted that UNIKOM could be terminated only by a decision of the Council and decided to review the question of the termination or continuation as well as the modalities of the Mission every six months. The purpose of the present report is to provide the Security Council, prior to its forthcoming review, with an overview of UNIKOM's activities during the last six months.

II. *Organizational matters*

3. Major-General Krishna N. S. Thapa (Nepal) continued as Force Commander. The composition and strength of the Mission is detailed below:

Military observers

Argentina	7	Malaysia	7
Austria	7	Nigeria	6
Bangladesh	9	Pakistan	7
Canada	5	Poland	6
China	15	Romania	7
Denmark	6	Russian Federation	15
Fiji	6	Senegal	6
Finland	6	Singapore	6
France	15	Sweden	6
Ghana	6	Thailand	6
Greece	7	Turkey	6
Hungary	7	United Kingdom of Great	
India	6	Britain and Northern	
Indonesia	6	Ireland	15
Ireland	7	United States of America	15
Italy	6	Uruguay	6
Kenya	7	Venezuela	2
		Total	244

Infantry battalion (Bangladesh)	775

Support units

Engineers (Argentina)	50
Logistic unit (Denmark)	44
Total	94
Total, military personnel	1 113

Civilian personnel

International staff	81
Locally recruited staff	133
Total, civilian personnel	214

4. On 31 December 1994, the Government of Switzerland discontinued its voluntary contribution of two fixed-wing aircraft. UNIKOM's air assets now consist of two chartered helicopters and one chartered fixed-wing aircraft.

5. The Governments of Austria and Bangladesh withdrew their medical units at the end of February 1995. It has been difficult to obtain a replacement and, as a provisional measure, a small medical team has been contracted locally.

6. UNIKOM's headquarters remains in Umm Qasr. It also maintains liaison offices in Baghdad and Kuwait City. Its logistic base in Doha was moved at the end of January 1995 to a support centre in Kuwait City.

III. *Financial aspects*

7. The General Assembly, by its resolution 48/242 of 5 April 1994, authorized me to enter into commitments up to the amount of $5.5 million gross ($5,312,800 net) per month, for the maintenance of UNIKOM for the period from 1 November 1994 to 31 March 1995, subject to the review by the Security Council of the mandate of the Mission and to the prior concurrence of the Advisory Committee on Administrative and Budgetary Questions. This amount is inclusive of the two-thirds share to be met through voluntary contributions from the Government of Kuwait. On 11 November 1994, the Advisory Committee concurred in my entering into commitments of up to $27,400,700 gross ($26,333,700 net) for the maintenance of UNIKOM for the same period. One third of the amount authorized for this period has been assessed on Member States and two thirds has been received as a voluntary contribution from the Government of Kuwait.

8. It is estimated that the total cost of maintaining UNIKOM for the period from 1 November 1994 to 30 June 1995 will amount to $43,718,300 gross ($41,997,500 net). For the period from 1 July 1995 to 30 June 1996, the total cost is estimated at $63,912,000 gross ($61,298,000 net).

9. As at 22 March 1995, unpaid assessed contributions to the Special Account for UNIKOM for the period since the inception of the Mission amounted to $27,882,900. The total unpaid assessed contributions for all peace-keeping operations amounted to $1.7 billion.

IV. *Concept of operations*

10. For operational purposes, the DMZ remains divided into three sectors (North, Central and South), as shown on the attached map [not reproduced here]. UNIKOM's concept of operations has been based on surveillance, control, investigation and liaison. Surveillance of the DMZ is based on patrol and observation bases, ground and air patrols and observation points. Control operations include static checkpoints, random checks and maintenance of a force mobile reserve. Investigation teams are maintained at the level of both sector and UNIKOM headquarters, and continuous liaison is carried out at all levels.

11. The military observers perform UNIKOM's main patrol, observation, investigation and liaison activities. The infantry battalion carries out armed patrols, operates checkpoints and provides security for UNIKOM's easternmost position on the shore of the Khawr Abd Allah. The battalion forms UNIKOM's reserve. Its main camp is located south of Umm Qasr, with a company camp at Al-Abdaly and one platoon camp each located in Sectors Central and South.

V. *Situation in the DMZ*

12. The overall situation in the DMZ remained generally calm, although there was a period of tension in October 1994 in connection with reports about the deployment of Iraqi troops north of the DMZ. There was only a limited number of incidents and violations of the DMZ. These involved mainly overflights by military aircraft and the carrying or firing of weapons other than sidearms. Two civilians, one on each side of the border, lost their lives in shooting incidents. UNIKOM investigated all ground violations and communicated its findings to the parties. It also investigated a total of eight written complaints, four each from Iraq and Kuwait.

13. An incident occurred on the night of 28/29 December 1994 when a UNIKOM patrol vehicle came under automatic fire on the Kuwaiti side of the DMZ, just south of the border near the Al-Abdaly crossing-point. About 50 rounds were fired from a range of about 50 to 100 metres. The vehicle was struck by six rounds. One military observer was wounded in the leg by two bullets. UNIKOM carried out an extensive investigation but has been unable to determine who carried out the attack.

14. On 13 March 1995 two United States citizens mistakenly crossed the border from Kuwait into Iraq, where they were apprehended by the Iraqi police. On their way to the border they crossed a Kuwaiti checkpoint at the edge of the DMZ, as well as a UNIKOM checkpoint at the border, which is marked by a berm and trench constructed by the Kuwaiti authorities. They were allowed to pass the UNIKOM checkpoint because, with darkness having just fallen, the sentries on duty mistook the white vehicle for one belonging to the United Nations. The procedures at the checkpoint have since been tightened. Efforts are being made by the United Nations to have the two men released.

15. UNIKOM continued to provide administrative and logistic support for other United Nations agencies in Iraq and Kuwait.

VI. *Observations*

16. During the period under review, calm has generally prevailed along the border and in the demilitarized zone between Iraq and Kuwait. UNIKOM maintained a high level of vigilance and, through its patrols and liaison activities, has significantly contributed to the reduction of tension and the maintenance of calm in its area of operation. In the performance of its functions, UNIKOM has enjoyed the effective cooperation of the Iraqi and Kuwaiti authorities. I recommend that the Mission be maintained.

17. In conclusion, I wish to pay tribute to Major-General Thapa and the men and women under his command for the manner in which they have discharged their responsibilities. Their discipline and bearing have been of a high order, reflecting credit on themselves, on their countries and on the United Nations.

Document 205

Seventh report of the Secretary-General on the status of the implementation of the plan for the ongoing monitoring and verification of Iraq's compliance with relevant parts of section C of Security Council resolution 687 (1991)

S/1995/284, 10 April 1995

Note by the Secretary-General

The Secretary-General has the honour to transmit to the Security Council a report submitted by the Executive Chairman of the Special Commission established by the Secretary-General pursuant to paragraph 9 (b) (i) of Security Council resolution 687 (1991).

Annex
Report of the Secretary-General on the status of the implementation of the Special Commission's plan for the ongoing monitoring and verification of Iraq's compliance with relevant parts of section C of Security Council resolution 687 (1991)

I. INTRODUCTION

1. The present report is the seventh submitted pursuant to paragraph 8 of Security Council resolution 715 (1991) of 11 October 1991, by which the Council requested the Secretary-General to submit a report to the Security Council every six months on the implementation of the Special Commission's Plan for ongoing monitoring and verification of Iraq's compliance with relevant parts of section C of Security Council resolution 687 (1991). It updates the information contained in the first six reports (S/23801, S/24661, S/25620, S/26684, S/1994/489 and S/1994/1138 and Corr.1).

2. Further information concerning developments relating to the implementation of the plan is contained in the report to the Security Council of 15 December 1994 (S/1994/1422 and Add.1), the seventh report provided in accordance with paragraph 3 of resolution 699 (1991), the addendum to which covers in detail the array of ongoing monitoring and verification activities undertaken by the Commission in the period from June to December 1994.

II. CONCEPT OF OPERATIONS

3. The basic elements of the ongoing monitoring and verification system are regular inspections of relevant facilities, inventories of dual-purpose items 1/ and accounting for all inventoried items until they are consumed, disposed of or no longer operable. The inspections and the establishment and maintenance of accurate inventories will be underpinned by a full array of interlocking activities: aerial surveillance with a variety of sensors, remote sensors, tags and seals, a variety of detection technologies, information obtained from other sources and, when sanctions on the dual-purpose items are lifted, notifications under the export/import control mechanism. No one of these elements on its own would suffice to provide confidence in the system, but together they should constitute the most comprehensive international monitoring system ever established in the sphere of arms control. Confidence in its effectiveness will rely, *inter alia*, on the following:

(a) Possession by the Commission of a full picture of Iraq's past programmes and a full accounting of the facilities, equipment, items and materials associated with

---

1/ I.e., those which have permitted uses but which could be used for the acquisition of banned weapons.

those past programmes, in conjunction with full knowledge of the disposition of dual-purpose items currently available to Iraq, the technologies acquired by Iraq in pursuing the past programmes, and the supplier networks it established to acquire those elements of the programmes that it could not acquire indigenously. This information provides the baseline data from which ongoing monitoring and verification proceeds;

Knowledge of the level of technology attained by Iraq, of the production and acquisition methods it used and of the materials and equipment it had available are all key to designing a system of monitoring that addresses issues of concern and focuses monitoring effort where it would be most effective and efficient. For example, within Iraq, the system should focus more of its efforts on those technologies and production methods that Iraq is known to have mastered than on technologies and methods that Iraq is known not to have mastered, whereas, for the export/import monitoring regime, the converse would be true, with effort focusing on those items that Iraq would have to import in order to reactivate a proscribed weapons programme. Clearly, knowing where to focus effort requires knowledge of what Iraq achieved in its past programmes;

Similarly, knowledge of the procurement methods and routes used by Iraq for its past programmes is key to the design of an effective and efficient export/import monitoring regime. This system should be designed to be effective against the procurement routes and methods that Iraq is known to have used in the past. Testing whether it is, is predicated on knowing those routes and methods;

Full accounting for the materials, items and equipment associated with the past programmes is directly related to what assets should be monitored under the system. Dual-purpose materials, items and equipment from the past programmes must be monitored, along with other dual-purpose capabilities available to Iraq. Uncertainties relating to the accuracy or completeness of this accounting will consequently lead to uncertainties as to whether the ongoing monitoring and verification system is indeed monitoring all the materials, items and equipment which should be monitored;

Under Security Council resolutions 687, 707 and 715 (1991), Iraq is obliged to provide the above information, which the Commission then verifies through its inspection and analysis activities. Iraq is required to update its declarations on its dual-purpose activities and capabilities every six months;

(b) Completion of comprehensive monitoring and verification protocols for each site at which monitoring will be conducted as a consequence of the dual-purpose items present or activities undertaken there. These protocols are the product of the baseline inspection process, i.e., inspections for the purposes of identifying all dual-purpose capabilities requiring monitoring, tagging and inventorying, sensor installation and protocol-building as necessary. They collate all the information required for future ongoing monitoring and verification of, and contain recommendations as to the conduct of such monitoring at, the specified site;

(c) Successful testing of the system of ongoing monitoring and verification in order to:

– Establish a clear understanding and practice of how the elements of the system, including the actions required of Iraq, should operate;

– Evaluate the effectiveness of its elements, both individually and as a whole;

(d) Continuing reassessment of the operation of the system of ongoing monitoring and verification in order to make adjustments necessary in the light of Iraq's industrial development and of any further information which becomes available on Iraq's past programmes. Because of the scale of those past programmes, the damage caused during the Gulf war and Iraq's own actions in allegedly destroying material evidence, in particular documentation, elements could remain unclear for a long time. While these elements, except where otherwise indicated in the present report, are not such as to call into question the effectiveness and comprehensive nature of the monitoring system, the Commission will continue to seek out the information to clear them up. The entire process of verification of Iraq's declarations has been rendered both difficult and prolonged as a result of Iraq's refusal or inability to produce the documentation relating to its past programmes and Iraq's providing the Commission with frequently changing accounts of certain elements of its programmes. This has required the Commission to undertake more intensive investigations than would otherwise have been necessary. It has also had to seek information from other Governments of former suppliers to Iraq's programmes. This has consumed considerable periods of time. This procedure is still ongoing and will be vigorously pursued by the Commission. The full responsibility for the delays lies with Iraq. In addition to unclear elements of the nature referred to above, new information may become available to the Commission requiring investigation in the future. Iraq clearly understands this to be the case and the Deputy Prime Minister has on several occasions provided explicit assurances that Iraq will in no way hinder or interfere with such investigations.

While the system is premised on the provision by Iraq of accurate and complete declarations of its dual-purpose activities and capabilities and cannot be operated at its most effective and least intrusive without such full declarations, it has also been designed to be robust. Experience has shown that, even when initially presented with inadequate declarations, the Commission has been able, through the deployment of its various resources and the exercise of its inspection rights, to elicit the information required for the system to be established. The Commission recognizes that it has received full cooperation from Iraq in setting up and now in operating the monitoring system. It has also received assurances from Iraq, at the highest levels, that this cooperation will continue as the Security Council takes decisions in respect of easing or lifting sanctions and the oil embargo. However, should Iraq seek systematically at any time in the future to block the work of the Commission by, for example, preventing access to sites, the Commission would not be able to provide the Security Council with the assurances it seeks concerning Iraq's compliance with the terms of paragraph 10 of resolution 687 (1991). If such a case were to arise, the Commission would immediately inform the Council.

4. Once the sanctions imposed on Iraq under resolution 661 (1990) are eased or lifted, in accordance with paragraph 21 of resolution 687 (1991), to the extent that the export to Iraq of dual-purpose items is again permitted, a further essential element of the overall monitoring of Iraq's dual-purpose capabilities will be the export/import mechanism envisaged under paragraph 7 of resolution 715 (1991).

III. ACTIONS TO IMPLEMENT THE PLAN

A. *Ongoing monitoring and verification operations*

1. *Missile activities*

Summary

5. The Commission has essentially completed the accounting of facilities, equipment and materials used in the past proscribed missile programmes of Iraq. The Commission must complete its verification of certain elements of Iraq's account to ensure that all items subject to ongoing monitoring and verification are indeed included in the monitoring programme. The Commission is still waiting for responses to requests for information from a number of countries from which Iraq acquired or sought to acquire items for proscribed purposes about those transactions. In most cases, the remaining outstanding issues do not involve the receipt by Iraq of prohibited items, but deal with the technological level attained during, and the intended direction of, Iraq's past missile activities. Consequently, their resolution is required to ensure the right focus of ongoing monitoring and verification efforts.

6. The Commission completed the baseline survey of Iraq's permitted missile and related dual-purpose capabilities in May 1994. Installation of sensors and tags for monitored missiles and production equipment and related dual-purpose items was completed in July 1994 and the resident missile monitoring team began its monitoring activities in August 1994. Since then, the Commission has established a viable mechanism for monitoring Iraq's design, testing and production of permitted missile systems and related dual-purpose items. Iraq has provided support to ensure the proper operation of the monitoring system. The missile monitoring is now operational.

Past programmes

7. The lack of precision in the initial information provided by Iraq on its past ballistic missile programmes and the alleged destruction of documents by Iraq in late 1991 have made obtaining a complete understanding of Iraq's past ballistic missile programmes extremely difficult. The Commission has exerted considerable efforts to verify the information provided in Iraq's "Full, final and comprehensive report on ballistic missile activity", received in 1992. However, parts of the information provided have proved confusing, misleading or inaccurate. The Commission, therefore, embarked on an effort to seek corroborating information from a variety of sources to provide the verification required by the Security Council. Many of the details of those programmes have been elucidated. However, several issues remain to be resolved. These issues do not, in general, involve the delivery to or possession by Iraq of prohibited items, but bear directly on the technology level attained by Iraq. The Commission's understanding of this is important for the design and operation of the monitoring system.

8. Iraq's ballistic missile programme was initially centred around the single-stage, liquid-engine 8K14 (SCUD B) missile, for which it first received missiles and mobile launchers, together with associated support equipment, starting in 1974. Iraq has stated that in 1987 it started a programme to extend the range of these missiles and to reverse-engineer the system. In total, Iraq imported 819 such missiles and 11 mobile launchers for them. In addition, it produced indigenously 8 mobile launchers and constructed or was in the process of constructing 60 fixed launch sites for these missiles. The Commission has supervised or verified the destruction, and accounted for the expenditure, of the above assets.

9. The Commission has received numerous reports of the importation by Iraq of SCUD systems from countries other than the supplier of the 819 missiles described above. No evidence has been found of such imports. The Commission assesses that no additional missiles of this type or support equipment were indeed supplied to Iraq.

10. In its efforts to extend the range of the imported SCUD B missiles, Iraq used simple techniques which did

not add significantly to its missile technology base. However, its reverse-engineering efforts included the acquisition of sophisticated production machinery and technology as well as the acquisition from various suppliers of components for missile systems. In particular, Iraq gained expertise in missile propulsion systems and their propellants, guidance and control and airframe production technologies, and acquired the hardware for high-precision machining. The above notwithstanding, Iraq was not successful in its efforts to acquire an indigenous capability to produce indigenously entire missile systems through its reverse-engineering efforts.

11. Beginning in 1985, Iraq started a cooperative effort with other countries to develop a high-technology, two-stage missile system designed for a range of around 1,000 km, called the BADR 2000 in Iraq. In this effort, Iraq constructed sophisticated production facilities and imported high-technology production equipment for the fabrication of the first solid-propellant stage of this system. The Commission assesses, however, that no complete BADR 2000 missiles were produced by Iraq. The Commission has supervised and verified the destruction of all known items, production equipment and infrastructure directly associated with that programme. The Commission currently believes that Iraq did not acquire any technology or equipment for the production of any other aspects or components of that system, e.g., guidance and control and launchers.

12. The Commission believes that it has a broad understanding of the achievements of Iraq's past missile programmes and of the level of technological development of Iraq in this area. It further believes that it has accounted for the majority of the materials, items and equipment associated with these past programmes. Investigations into the disposition of some remaining items, particularly related to the former missile reverse-engineering project, are continuing. The Commission believes it has been able to design a reasonable monitoring system based on this level of technology and that all the physical assets that should be monitored are indeed being monitored.

13. However, there are still aspects of Iraq's past programmes, regarding the direction of its research and development efforts, that require further clarification. The Commission has, over the past six months, requested and received information on Iraq's past activities from many supporting nations. The information provided, in most cases, corroborates information provided by Iraq in its subsequent declarations. A few cases require continued investigation by the Commission to eliminate any possibility that they present potential loopholes in the ongoing monitoring and verification mechanism. The following cases exemplify such issues.

14. *Supersonic parachute recovery system.* In 1988, Iraq initiated the development of a supersonic parachute recovery system for the Al Hussein missile warhead. The programme continued through 1990. Iraq approached at least three different companies for the development, production and supply of the system. However, no systems were provided to Iraq. The Commission is currently investigating and verifying the programme's purpose and scope. Information available to the Commission from the potential suppliers does not corroborate Iraq's current declarations about the programme.

15. *Unsymmetrical dimethyl hydrazine (UDMH).* UDMH is a liquid fuel which can improve the performance of liquid-propellant rocket engines. In 1987, Iraq began inquiring about and procuring facilities, equipment, training and materials concerning every aspect of the use and production of UDMH and related systems in missiles. The programme continued until January 1991. Iraq declared that it had unilaterally destroyed 10.5 tons of UDMH in May 1991. The Commission has been unable to verify this. Further, Iraq declared that no experiments were performed using UDMH. The Commission has information which contradicts this statement. If Iraq mastered the technologies required for UDMH rocket engine design, the Commission would need to modify the ongoing monitoring and verification regime in the missile area to take account of Iraq's access to these technologies. The Commission is continuing to investigate this issue to ensure that it has an accurate account of Iraq's past activities in this regard.

Baseline data

16. The monitoring system in the missile area has been designed by assessing the critical aspects of each stage of the production of permitted missile systems to ensure that no components are produced or diverted for use in proscribed missile systems. Consequently, monitoring focuses on Iraq's non-proscribed missile research, development, testing and production activities, facilities and equipment. In addition, the system also monitors other facilities with related dual-purpose technologies and items and high-precision engineering manufacturing capabilities which could be used to support a clandestine effort to produce proscribed missiles.

17. The Commission completed the baseline survey of all of Iraq's declared missile and related research, development, test and production facilities in May 1994. Thirty-two baseline inspections were conducted during UNSCOM 71/BM 22. The baseline process included identifying the critical technologies and equipment, recommending the appropriate level of monitoring for the same and creating the detailed protocols necessary for conducting inspections at each site.

18. The Commission completed the installation of 41 monitoring cameras at 15 sites related to missiles or associated dual-use technology in July 1994. These cameras were tested during August 1994 and the system became operational in September 1994. The Commission completed the tagging and inventorying of 182 items of missile-related equipment in July 1994. The Commission completed a technical baseline survey of missile systems to be subject to monitoring in June 1994, and the tagging of all relevant operational missiles in Iraq in July 1994. The resident missile monitoring team initiated its inspection activities in August 1994.

Ongoing monitoring and verification apparatus

19. The plan for ongoing monitoring and verification of Iraq's compliance with relevant parts of section C of Security Council resolution 687 (1991), approved by the Security Council in its resolution 715 (1991), states that facilities, equipment, other items and technologies which could be used for the development, construction, modification or acquisition of ballistic missiles with a range greater than 150 kilometres should be subject to monitoring and verification. The Commission has undertaken to fulfil this requirement of the Security Council by designing a multi-level, comprehensive monitoring system covering Iraq's missile research, development, testing and production facilities as well as facilities with related dual-use capabilities. The monitoring system provides for: the periodic no-notice inspection of facilities by the Baghdad resident missile monitoring group; camera surveillance of critical areas and key production machines; inventory control, by tagging and regular inspection, of items and machinery located at key, related and dual-use facilities; special inspection teams to address specific issues (e.g., research and development activities); inspections to verify Iraq's compliance with existing resolutions; and aerial inspections and surveillance.

20. In order to accomplish the above tasks, the Commission has undertaken inspections of research, development, testing, production and modification activities and facilities. Inspection of research and development facilities establishes the technological capabilities of Iraq and helps identify any modifications necessary for the current monitoring regime. Inspection of testing facilities, including the witnessing of testing activity, provides assurance that current missile systems and those under development do not exceed the constraints established by the resolutions. Inspection of production and modification facilities guarantees that all missiles produced are accounted for and that no proscribed missile systems are produced. This is backed up by inspections of sites not currently under monitoring to ensure that no activities requiring monitoring are conducted at the site in ques-

tion, thereby ensuring, through a programme of such inspections, the comprehensiveness of the monitoring system (i.e., that all that should be is monitored). Finally, the verification inspections of the operational missile ensures that no modification to extend the maximum range of these missile systems will go undetected.

21. The resident missile monitoring teams have conducted 178 inspections since the last report. These inspections have established the effectiveness of the monitoring regime in verifying the current status of Iraq's non-proscribed missile programmes and related technology. The resident team is entrusted with the inspection of Iraq's missile and related facilities to ensure that there is no research or development into or production of missile systems exceeding the specifications of the resolutions, that all declared equipment is accounted for and that records agree with information on research, development and production available from other sources. Further, regular collection and review of video coverage of missile-related activities in critical areas and key equipment is conducted to guarantee that the Commission accounts for and tags all produced missiles subject to monitoring and that no production of proscribed missile systems occurs.

22. Since the last report the Commission has conducted three inspections of the tagged operational missiles to ensure that Iraq has not modified any missile to extend its range beyond that allowed by the resolutions. These inspections are conducted on a random sample of 10 per cent of the operational missile force three times per annum. No modifications of missiles under monitoring were detected.

23. The Commission has conducted, on a regular basis, research and development update inspections to confirm that current missile designs will not exceed the limits established by the resolutions. Such inspections are designed to review the technical details of the design, development and testing of missile systems and missile-related technological developments twice per annum. These inspections are designed to identify any requirement to modify the monitoring regime to assure its continued effectiveness. The Commission conducted its latest research and development update inspection in March 1995.

2. Chemical activities

Summary

24. During the high-level talks held at Baghdad in February 1995, Iraq promised to present a new full, final and complete declaration of its past chemical warfare activities in order to comply with the requirements of resolution 707 (1991). This it did on 25 March 1995, during the most recent visit of the Executive Chairman to

Baghdad. The new information provided is now being verified, in particular the claim that significantly reduced quantities of chemical warfare agents were produced.

25. The chemical monitoring system in Iraq is now operational, with the installation of its monitoring equipment almost complete. The additions and modifications to the system which are in the course of being made are not such as to undermine the effectiveness of the overall regime. Together with an efficient export/import monitoring regime, this system is expected to preclude Iraq from resuming prohibited chemical activities.

Past programmes

26. In order to resolve outstanding issues relating to its past chemical weapons programmes, Iraq provided on 25 March 1995 a new "full, final and complete" declaration of all aspects of its past chemical weapons programmes. This declaration contains new information on: the history and organizational structure of the past programmes; the weaponization of chemical weapons agents; the procurement of chemical weapons-related materials; and the material balance for precursor chemicals and chemical weapons agents produced and weaponized. Iraq has agreed to provide additional information and clarifications concerning these new declarations as required and upon the Commission's request. Any such additional information will be attached as an addendum to the new declaration.

27. In the new declaration, Iraq has revised some of the data previously provided. The most significant change relates to the quantities of chemical warfare agents produced. Iraq now declares that it produced 290 tons of chemical weapons agents less than previously stated. The declaration also indicated that, in 1985, certain biological activities were undertaken at Iraq's principal chemical weapons site, Muthanna. The Commission has started the process of verifying this new information. Verification of the statement relating to biological activities at Muthanna is dependent on full verification of Iraq's declarations concerning its biological activities in this time-frame.

28. On the basis of this new information, the Commission's understanding of Iraq's past chemical weapons programmes is as follows.

Agent production

29. Iraq started research into the production of chemical weapons agents in the 1970s and started batch production of agents in the early 1980s. At that stage, production was heavily reliant on the import of precursor chemicals from foreign suppliers.

30. In 1981, Iraq started producing the blister agent mustard (HD). Iraq's earlier declarations of 3,080 tons produced have been reduced in the latest disclosure to 2,850 tons. The quality of the mustard agent was good (not less than 80 per cent pure) and was such that the agent could be stored for long periods, either in bulk or in weaponized form. Even years after its production, the mustard agent analysed by the Commission was found to be in good and usable condition.

31. Production of the nerve gases tabun (GA) and sarin (GB) started in 1984 and the method of production changed over time in order to resolve stabilization problems. Iraq's latest declarations have reduced the stated amount of tabun produced from 250 tons to 210 tons and of sarin produced from 812 tons to 790 tons.

32. The tabun produced was poor, being of a maximum purity of 60 per cent. As a result, the agent did not store well and could only be stored for a limited period. Furthermore, Iraq experienced problems in the production of tabun owing to salt blockages forming in pipes during synthesis. Because of these problems, Iraq refocused its nerve agent research, development and production efforts on sarin (GB/GF).

33. The sarin produced was also of poor quality (maximum purity of 60 per cent when solvent is taken into account) and so too could only be stored for short periods. In order to overcome this problem, Iraq resorted to a binary approach to weaponization: the precursor chemicals for sarin (DF 2/ and the alcohols cyclohexanol and isopropanol) were stored separately for mixing in the munitions immediately prior to use to produce a mixture of two G-series nerve agents, GB and GF. Given that the locally manufactured DF had a purity of more than 95 per cent and the alcohols were imported and of 100 per cent purity, this process could be expected to yield relatively pure sarin.

34. Over the period from June 1992 to June 1994, the Commission's Chemical Destruction Group destroyed 30 tons of tabun, 70 tons of sarin and 600 tons of mustard agent, stored in bulk and in munitions.

35. Research into the production of CS was initiated at the Salman Pak site in the late 1970s and early 1980s for the purposes of riot control. It was conducted under the auspices of the Committee for National Security, not the Armed Forces. A few tons were produced at this site. In the early 1980s, military scale production of CS was started at the Muthanna site. The Commission has been unable to establish how much CS was produced in total. It is known that RPG-7 rocket-propelled grenades, 250- and 500-gauge bombs and 82mm and 120mm mortar shells were filled with CS, but again the quantity of munitions so filled cannot be established.

2/ Methyl phosphonyl difluoride.

Consequently, the Commission is unable to establish any kind of material balance for Iraq's CS-related activities.

36. Iraq also had a research and development programme for the production of a further nerve agent, VX. According to Iraq's account, VX was the focus of its research efforts in the period after September 1987. Iraq has stated that between late 1987 and early 1988, a total of 250 tons of phosphorous pentasulphide and 200 tons of di-isopropylamine were imported, these being two key precursors required for the production of VX. For the other precursors required, Iraq claims to have used only approximately 1 ton of methyl phosphonyl chloride (MPC) from a total of 660 tons produced indigenously. The remaining MPC is claimed to have been used to produce DF, then used in GB/GF production. The fourth precursor required for VX, ethylene oxide, was generally available, being a multi-purpose chemical.

37. Iraq states that it produced a total of only 10 tons of choline from the di-isopropylamine and ethylene oxide and approximately 3 tons of methyl thiophosphonyl dichloride from the phosphorous pentasulphide and methyl phosphonyl chloride. From this, Iraq states that it produced experimental quantities of VX (recently increased to 260 kg from 160 kg). Iraq has recently admitted that three 250-gauge aerial bombs had been filled with VX for experimental purposes.

38. Iraq claims that further attempts to produce VX were unsuccessful and the programme was finally abandoned in September 1988. According to Iraq's account, the remaining choline from the 10 tons was burned in early 1988 and the remaining 247 tons of phosphorous pentasulphide was discarded in 1991 by scattering it over an area of land and putting it in pits. Iraq also claims that 213 tons of di-isopropylamine was destroyed by bombing during the Gulf war. However, while the Commission has found traces of these chemicals at the sites at which Iraq states their destruction occurred, it has not been able to verify the quantities destroyed. Thus, precursors for the production of at least 200 to 250 tons of VX cannot be definitively accounted for.

39. The Commission has supervised the destruction, or verified Iraq's unilateral destruction, of 125 250-gauge bombs and several thousands 120mm mortar shells. In its new declaration, Iraq declared an additional 350 500-gauge and 100 250-gauge aerial bombs filled with CS in 1987.

Precursor chemical production

40. In the early stages of its chemical weapons programme, Iraq imported all its precursor chemicals. Over time, however, Iraq sought to obtain the capability to produce indigenously all the precursors required for the production of the agents noted above. Iraq acknowledges that it had or was on the brink of having the capability to produce in quantity the precursors for tabun (GA): D4 and phosphorous oxychloride ($POCl_3$), the sarin/cyclosarin (GB/GF) precursors: methylphosphonyl difluoride (DF), methyl phosphonyl dichloride (MPC), dimethylmethyl phosphonate (DMMP), trimethyl-phosphite (TMP), hydrogen fluoride (HF), phosphorous trichloride (PCl_3) and thionyl chloride ($SOCl_2$). Phosphorous trichloride and thionylchloride are also the main precursors for the production of mustard (HD).

41. Iraq also had the capability to produce, at least at laboratory scale, sodium sulphide (Na_2S) and thiodiglycol (both for sulphur mustard agent production), methyl benzilate (for BZ production), triethanol amine (for nitrogen-mustard agent production) and potassium bifluoride and ammonium bifluoride (for GB/GF production). In addition, Iraq had the capability to produce the VX precursors choline, methyl thiophosphonyl dichloride (MPS) at the least at pilot-plant scale.

42. Clearly, any ongoing monitoring and verification system in the chemical area will need to address these capabilities.

Equipment

43. For its past chemical weapons programme, Iraq had equipment for research and for production purposes, both of which need to be covered by the monitoring system. Iraq claims that all the laboratory equipment used for research purposes was destroyed during the Gulf war. However, the Commission has been unable to verify this independently and hence cannot definitively account for all the equipment of concern.

44. Of the production equipment, the Commission tagged and inventoried 240 key pieces, of which 40 were subsequently destroyed under the Commission's supervision. This equipment includes reaction vessels, heat exchangers, distillation columns and corrosion-resistant fittings. It is estimated that a further 50 key pieces of equipment, known to have been imported by Iraq, were destroyed during the Gulf war.

45. Iraq has the capability to produce certain of this dual-purpose equipment indigenously, at welding and heavy engineering plants. However, Iraq is still reliant on imports of corrosion-resistant metal alloys to do so.

46. The chemical component of the ongoing monitoring and verification system has been designed to ensure monitoring of all the appropriate laboratory and production equipment identified and the facilities where this equipment could be manufactured indigenously.

Munitions

47. Iraq has declared that it weaponized for chemical weapons purposes the following munitions: RPG-7 rocket-propelled grenades and 82 mm and 120 mm mortar shells exclusively for CS; 130 mm and 155 mm artillery shells for mustard agent; 250- and 500-gauge aerial bombs for mustard, tabun, sarin and CS; 122 mm rockets, R-400 and DB-2 aerial bombs for sarin and mixtures of GB/GF; and Al Hussein missile warheads for sarin. Of these, Iraq acquired the capability to produce all of the aerial bomb types listed and the Al Hussein missile warheads and chemical containers for 122 mm rockets. It was reliant on imports of the other empty munitions but had the capability to empty conventional artillery shells and aerial bombs for subsequent refill with chemical-weapons agent.

48. While the Commission can verify and confirm with Governments of suppliers the declared quantities of munitions imports, it cannot yet be sure that the declarations are comprehensive in this regard. However, the Commission's main efforts to establish a material balance for the chemical-weapons programmes as a whole rely more on material balances for agents and precursor chemicals than for munitions.

49. The major part of Iraq's chemical-weapons production and weaponization facilities has been destroyed. Identified chemical production equipment of dual-use character has been tagged. After the completion of the destruction of the relevant facilities, stockpiles and approximately 40 pieces of production equipment, the Commission's attention focused on Iraq's dual-purpose chemical capabilities in its non-proscribed industries.

Baseline data

50. The above indicates the technologies mastered by Iraq, chemicals, materials, items and equipment available to it and activities undertaken by it. The Commission clearly has to monitor these if it is to assure the Security Council that it is effectively monitoring Iraq's compliance not to reacquire chemical weapons. In addition, in order to ensure that it designed an effective and comprehensive monitoring system in the chemical area, the Commission had to conduct a survey of Iraq's non-proscribed chemical industries to assess the following: the level of research and development which could be applied to the production of chemical weapons agents and their precursors, either in laboratory or production quantities; the ability of Iraq to purify, stabilize and store either chemical weapons agents or their precursor chemicals; Iraq's capability to produce dual-use equipment which could be used to produce chemical weapons agents and precursors and its mastery of technologies, such as production of corrosion-resistant alloys and special welding technologies,

required to manufacture such equipment; and Iraq's capability to develop, produce, fill or store munitions which could be used for chemical weapons purposes (e.g., white-phosphorous-filled 155 mm shells, multi-purpose aerial bombs, etc.). Such capabilities are found in the organophosphorous and organohalide industries (such as pesticides, insecticides and fertilizers), the petrochemical industry, chemical laboratories, leather tanning, military munitions and heavy engineering plants, and hence the Commission conducted baseline inspections of these industries in order to assess which sites and facilities required monitoring.

51. In 1994, the Commission completed baseline inspections of 57 chemical sites, and monitoring and verification protocols were prepared for those sites related to production and storage of chemicals of concern and for sites involved in the manufacture of chemical production equipment.

52. In January and February 1995, baseline inspections were conducted at 17 universities, colleges and research institutions to assess their potential and hence their relevance for monitoring. In addition, five military storage depots were visited because of their potential to store munitions for chemical weapons (empty or filled). Unless other dual-purpose facilities come to the attention of the Commission, this completed the process of preparing monitoring and verification protocols for the sites to be monitored. However, it is expected that the number of chemical sites to be monitored by the Commission will increase along with the development of Iraq's chemical industry.

53. With the exception of two facilities in Iraq related to pesticide formulation, none of the chemical sites currently monitored has the capability to produce banned items. In addition, the research laboratories inspected currently have no potential for conducting significant chemical weapons-related research and development.

Ongoing monitoring and verification apparatus

54. In addition to the monitoring capabilities shared across the disciplines, such as aerial surveillance, chemical monitoring is centred around visits by the monitoring group to sites to be monitored, tagging and inventorying of key materials and equipment, collection and analysis of air samples using automatic air samplers located at certain of these sites, and monitoring of key items of equipment by remote-controlled cameras. In the future, flow meters and seals may also be deployed at certain production facilities.

55. On 2 October 1994, the first chemical monitoring team (CG-1) started its monitoring activities from its base in the Baghdad Monitoring Centre. Currently, the third chemical monitoring group (CG-3) is in Iraq. The

chemical monitoring groups have conducted 70 inspections to date. Beyond conducting ongoing monitoring and verification activities at sites for which monitoring and verification protocols have been prepared, the groups also visit chemical facilities which are currently not monitored, as part of a programme to ensure that such sites have not in fact acquired any capabilities which would require monitoring. If the group does identify a site at which monitoring should be conducted, it will establish procedures for regular monitoring of the site.

56. By the end of January 1995, all the sensor systems had been installed at the sites of interest. At six sites, 30 remote-controlled cameras were emplaced. At eight sites, 15 computer-controlled air samplers were installed. Sites so monitored include those capable of the production of precursors, dual-use equipment and pesticides.

57. At the end of February 1995, a chemical laboratory was installed at the Baghdad Monitoring Centre. The Centre now has the capability to analyse all types of chemical samples, including the samples from the air-sampling devices. The laboratory has a highly sensitive analytical capability using instruments and wet chemistry, providing sensitivity to parts per billion.

58. Minor adjustments are being made to the air-sampling devices to increase their reliability. These adjustments will be completed in May 1995. Meanwhile, manual-transportable air samplers will be made available to the chemical monitoring group. This will enable the group to take random air samples at sites during inspections. By the end of May 1995, the group will also be equipped with personal detection and protection equipment suitable for protection against all possible occupational and industrial hazards that might be encountered at Iraq's chemical facilities.

3. Biological activities

Summary

59. The task of establishing ongoing monitoring and verification in the biological area has taken longer than in other areas for two reasons: the nature and scope of the task made it a more difficult proposition; and Iraq's declarations about its dual-use capabilities were initially far from complete and the data contained in them varied from declaration to declaration to the point of contradiction. These difficulties notwithstanding, through the activities of its inspection teams, the Commission has been able to establish sufficient baseline data on key sites for it to commence monitoring. All the apparatus for biological monitoring is now in place and monitoring is proceeding.

60. However, Iraq has not provided an account of its past biological warfare programme and a new full,

final and complete declaration recently received from Iraq does not redress the problem. It is unable to account definitively for all the materials and items that may have been used in such a programme and are known to have been acquired by Iraq. The Commission assesses that Iraq obtained or sought to obtain all the items and materials required to produce biological warfare agents in Iraq. With Iraq's failure to account for all these items and materials for legitimate purposes, the only conclusion that can be drawn is that there is a high risk that they had been purchased and in part used for proscribed purposes—the production of agents for biological weapons. In these circumstances, the Commission cannot conclude that its biological monitoring is comprehensive in coverage and properly focused, i.e., that it is monitoring all biological facilities, activities, materials and items that should be subject to monitoring.

Past programmes

61. Iraq maintains that it had no biological weapons-related activities, only a basic military biological research programme. This programme, declared to have been conducted solely at the Salman Pak site, is stated by Iraq to have been initiated in 1986 and discontinued in 1990. It is stated to have employed 10 persons and to have produced only 10 basic research papers on various aspects of three bacteria (B. anthracis, Cl. botulinum and Cl. perfringens). It is further claimed that no decision had been taken as to the longer-term direction of the programme until the programme's discontinuation in autumn 1990. In its declarations, Iraq fails to explain or account for various aspects of its procurement or construction activities in the biological area in this timeframe.

Complex growth media

62. Iraq acknowledges that it procured, through the Technical and Scientific Materials Import Division (TSMID), 3/ very large quantities of complex growth media 4/ in 1988 but has failed to provide an accounting for the purposes of this importation and for the use of a significant portion of it.

63. Iraq claims that, while the media was imported by TSMID, the import was on behalf of the Ministry of Health for the purposes of hospital diagnostic laboratories. This importation of media by types, quantities and

3/ The Technical and Scientific Materials Import Division, the purchasing arm of the Technical Research Centre that was, within the Military Industrialization Corporation, directly responsible for Iraq's military biological programme.

4/ Complex growth media constitute the substrate on or in which bacteria or viruses are grown. Types imported by Iraq can be used in hospitals or laboratories as a diagnostic tool or for large-scale production of bacteria and viruses, be it for biological weapons purposes or civilian use, e.g., vaccine production.

packaging is grossly out of proportion to Iraq's stated requirements for hospital use. Iraq explains the excessive quantities imported and the inappropriate size of the packaging as being a one-of-a-kind mistake and attempts to justify the import as appropriate and required for medical diagnostic purposes.

64. However, for hospital diagnostic purposes, only small quantities are needed. According to Iraq's declarations, which are imprecise and changing, over the period 1987-1994 Iraq's total hospital consumption of all such media was less than 200 kg per annum. But in 1988 alone, TSMID imported nearly 39,000 kg of such media, which has a manufacturer's guarantee of 4 to 5 years. A further incongruity is that, of all the types of media required for hospital use, only a select few were "mistakenly" imported by TSMID in large quantities. These did not include those most frequently used in hospitals.

65. Furthermore, the packaging of TSMID imports is inconsistent with declared hospital usage: diagnostic assays use very small quantities of media and so, because the media deteriorates rapidly once a package has been opened, media for diagnostic purposes is normally distributed in 0.1-1 kg packages. However, the media imported by Iraq in 1988 was packaged in 25-100 kg drums. This style of packaging is consistent with the large-scale usage of media associated with the production of biological agents. The types of media imported are suitable for the production of anthrax and botulinum, known biological warfare agents researched by Iraq in its declared biological military programme.

66. The Special Commission has only accounted for some 22 tons of the 39 tons of complex media imported by TSMID in 1988. The media accounted for is still stored in Iraq (in large packages) and is under the Commission's monitoring regime. However, some 17 tons remain unaccounted for. Iraq claims that this quantity was distributed in original packages to numerous hospitals in 1989 but that it was all destroyed (along with documentation concerning its distribution, storage and consumption in hospitals) during riots that occurred in the aftermath of the Gulf war. It is claimed that no media was distributed to hospitals in regions where no riots occurred, e.g., in the Baghdad region. No attempts were made by Iraq to resupply the affected regions or hospitals to compensate for losses, although large amounts of the same imported media in good condition were still available in Iraq.

67. Iraq initially presented a set of documents in an attempt to prove that media had been received by a Ministry of Health storage site and was partly distributed to certain regional health centres. Iraq subsequently admitted that these documents had in fact been "recreated"

and now claims that all originals have been destroyed, misplaced or lost.

68. The Commission has information that, in addition to media delivered to Iraq in 1988, quantities of media were also purchased by Iraq in 1989 and 1990. Evidence of additional supplies in large packages was found in Iraq. This undermines Iraq's explanation that the TSMID purchases in 1988 were a one-of-a-kind mistake as to types and packaging of media imported, as does the fact that the Ministry of Health continued, through its own import division, its regular small-quantity purchases of media consistent with its diagnostic requirements throughout the period, including the purchase of kilogram quantities of two growth media only months after TSMID purchased 2-1/4 tons of the same media.

69. Iraq's current accounting of media importation and disposal is not acceptable. Full and substantial accounting by Iraq for the media, eminently suitable for production of biological agents, is an essential task if the Commission is to have any confidence that there was no production of biological agent for weapons purposes and that Iraq's dual-use capabilities are sufficiently monitored to ensure that Iraq cannot clandestinely reacquire biological weapons.

Equipment

70. Iraq has not provided satisfactory explanations for some other significant procurement efforts by TSMID related to the acquisition of dual-purpose biological equipment and supplies critical to a biological warfare capability. The following illustrates some issues of concern.

71. When confronted by the Commission with evidence, Iraq acknowledged the purchase by TSMID in 1989 of four filling machines, ostensibly for a biopesticide project at the Salman Pak site. Until this acknowledgement, Iraq, while declaring Salman Pak to be the site of its biological military research programme, had not declared any biopesticide activity there. Filling machines, while having many uses, are required for filling bacterial warfare agent into munitions or containers. Full accounting for these machines is therefore a requirement. Iraq claims that these four machines were destroyed by bombing in the Gulf war. No evidence (e.g., scrap) has been provided to support this claim. Furthermore, before describing this loss of the filling machines, Iraq had previously declared that all equipment at Salman Pak had been dispersed prior to the commencement of the air war in order to protect it from bombing and that no equipment had been destroyed at Salman Pak.

72. TSMID procured a spray dryer in 1989. Again, it is claimed that this was for the above-mentioned bio-

pesticide project at Salman Pak. This spray dryer has technical specifications which provide a capability of drying the bacterial slurry resulting from the fermentation process to produce dry matter with particle sizes in the range of 1 to 10μ. This particle size is associated with efficient dispersion of biological warfare agents, not with the production of biopesticides. Furthermore, dry bacterial matter is easier to store for longer periods. Such spray dryers, therefore, would be a crucial component in acquiring an indigenous capability to produce viable and durable biological weapons.

73. TSMID attempted to order various named and virulent anthrax strains, known to be particularly appropriate for biological warfare purposes. Iraq flatly denies this, despite confirmation to the Commission by the potential supplier.

Construction of biological facilities

74. As noted above, in addition to Iraq's procurement activities, its construction activities for biological purposes are also a matter of concern. In particular, the production facility at the Al Hakam site has long raised concerns relating to its original intent, as opposed to its current use. Iraq claims that this facility is and always was intended only as a single-cell protein (SCP) plant for the production of animal feed. However, certain design features of the Al Hakam facility were superfluous to the requirements of an SCP plant, and more consistent with the requirements of a biological warfare agent facility. Some examples follow.

75. The original design for Al Hakam had many costly features associated with work with toxic or infectious materials. Production of SCP does not involve the use of such materials and so would not require such safety features. An example of these features was the sophisticated air filtration system, using HEPA filters, 5/ for both input and output air on the declared animal house. Iraq argues that this system was required to prevent the spread of animal diseases. If, as claimed, the building were to house only animals for feeding, there would be no requirement for such safety features. On the other hand, such an air filtration system would be desirable if the building were planned for animal experiments involving infectious agents. According to information available to the Commission from the potential supplier, Iraq also ordered a similar air filtration system for another building at Al Hakam, housing laboratories. Iraq denies that such an order was made. When asked to present an air ventilation design plan for the building, Iraq stated that that particular page of the plans for the Al Hakam facility had been lost.

76. The layout of Al Hakam and the security arrangements there were more consistent with a military facility or a facility to produce toxic or pathogenic material than with a commercial SCP plant. The facility was constructed and equipped under conditions of great secrecy, akin to those used in Iraq's other proscribed programmes. No documents are available which identified Al Hakam, at the time of construction, as a purely civilian production project. Iraq could not provide any public announcements that were made about what it has since claimed was intended to be one of the world's largest SCP plants. No foreign contractors or suppliers ever visited the site. Iraq falsified the information on an end-user certificate for a fermenter purchased for Al Hakam, claiming that it would be installed at another site and under the management and supervision of another organization. It similarly falsified information for the import of spare parts for equipment available at Al Hakam.

Baseline data

77. While monitoring activities, by definition, concentrate on current dual-purpose biological capabilities and require comprehensive and verified baseline data on these capabilities, designing efficient and effective monitoring also necessitates a full understanding of Iraq's past biological programme. For example, knowledge of Iraq's past procurement methods for currently proscribed items or information on Iraq's past programme priorities provides important indicators in identifying choke points (either in terms of physical assets or in terms of technologies) in Iraq's ability to reacquire banned capabilities and hence for identifying where monitoring efforts can most profitably be focused.

78. In preparation for monitoring Iraq's biological activities, the Commission evaluated those dual-purpose technologies, activities, materials, items and equipment which could contribute to a biological warfare capability and proceeded to identify those sites or facilities in Iraq which, through the possession of same, contribute to such a capability. The basis for the above was Iraq's declarations of its dual-purpose capabilities, in turn verified by the Commission, and information obtained by the Commission in the course of its inspections of sites and facilities in Iraq.

79. The previous report submitted pursuant to Security Council resolution 715 (1991) (S/1994/1138) detailed the problems encountered by the Commission in establishing complete and accurate baseline data for Iraq's dual-purpose biological capabilities: incomplete and inaccurate initial declarations submitted by Iraq, inconsistencies in the data contained in Iraq's various

---

5/ These filters are of the sort used to create clean environments or to ensure that contaminants are not released from a workplace into the surrounding environment. They are therefore associated with work requiring high containment, such as work on pathogens or toxins.

declarations and between them and the findings of inspection teams, and undeclared movement of items to be monitored between inspections so that inconsistencies arose between the findings of inspection teams. All this made it impossible for the Commission to establish firm baseline data from which to start its monitoring of Iraq's biological activities.

80. The difficulties in obtaining reliable, accurate and complete declarations on biological sites necessitated a more radical and intensive approach to obtaining the baseline information required. The already intense schedule of biological inspections was further intensified with the initiation in December 1994 of a coordinated series of intrusive inspections. Interim biological monitoring began on 1 December 1994, comprising a Baghdad-based monitoring team that, in concert with special ad hoc teams of experts, sought to establish the baseline data necessary for the commencement of monitoring. Biological audits were conducted at 10 priority sites for which the information supplied by Iraq and obtained by earlier inspection teams was the most disparate.

81. The aim of these inspections was: to obtain information not yet provided but required for monitoring purposes; to assess Iraq's ability to produce indigenously key dual-purpose biological equipment; to examine records at organizations involved in the import and maintenance of such equipment; to prepare a full inventory of dual-use equipment in Iraq; and, through technical talks and interviews, to obtain a complete understanding of Iraq's past military biological programme. For sites of particular concern for the monitoring regime, the teams sought to obtain an in-depth understanding of the current activities and plans with regard to personnel, chain of command, reporting structure, operations and production, research and development activities, and production capability.

82. By pursuing interim monitoring as a means of obtaining the baseline data required for monitoring, the Commission was relying less on Iraq's openness and more on inspection findings than originally intended. This approach required a greater outlay of resources and so could only be applied to a few sites. The interim monitoring process did not obviate the need for Iraq to report accurately all its biological activities which required declaration under the plan for ongoing monitoring and verification.

Ongoing monitoring and verification apparatus

83. Given the nature of biological weapons, effective monitoring in the biological area necessitates a broader monitoring effort than is required in the other areas. The Commission will monitor Iraq's basic biological research potential, its stocks of micro-organisms and complex growth media, its biological production capacity (i.e., fermenters and incubators), its ability to isolate micro-organisms from fermenter slurry (i.e., spray and drum dryers) and to create particles of a size appropriate for biological warfare (milling machines), its ability to fill containers with biological materials and its ability to disperse such material.

84. These capabilities can be found in the following types of institutions in Iraq (hence monitoring efforts will take the Commission's teams to such facilities): biological laboratories (found in hospitals, universities and the food industry), biological production facilities (e.g., single-cell protein production, vaccine production, drug formulation and production, breweries and distilleries), and agricultural crop sprayers. In all, monitoring of Iraq's biological activities covers some 80 sites.

85. Monitoring is based on maintaining a comprehensive and accurate inventory of dual-purpose items and activities in Iraq, primarily through on-site inspections, i.e., by updating the baseline data contained in the monitoring and verification protocols. This involves the identification of any sites not yet subject to ongoing monitoring and verification which acquire dual-purpose capabilities requiring monitoring, the identification of newly acquired dual-use equipment, the inventorying and tagging of such equipment and assessment of its intended use and the assessment of how such newly acquired capabilities increase Iraq's overall biological warfare capabilities. Monitoring modalities include: on-site inspections (with or without prior notice); aerial surveillance; interviews with key personnel at monitored sites; examination of site records; updating of inventories; continuous flow monitoring and sensor-activated camera monitoring; sample taking; notifications of transfers within Iraq of inventoried items; and notification of modification, import or other acquisition of dual-purpose biological research and production equipment of dual-use character.

86. Monitoring efforts have resulted in the installation of 24 cameras at 5 key sites and locations (16 of them at 3 locations at the Al Hakam site) and the initiation of monitoring at those sites for which monitoring and verification protocols were ready. A total of 13 biological inspections were undertaken in the period from October 1994 to March 1995. The interim monitoring groups conducted 51 visits to 20 sites. A biological room has been installed at the Baghdad Monitoring Centre for the processing, packaging and onward transmission of biological samples taken during the course of monitoring.

87. Monitoring and verification protocols have now been completed for all the key biological sites in Iraq identified to date and monitoring of them is now proceeding. However, the failure of Iraq to disclose fully all aspects of its past biological military research programme

means that the Commission cannot be certain that its monitoring programme in the biological area is covering all the sites, facilities and capabilities that require monitoring under the terms of the plan approved by the Security Council.

4. Nuclear activities

88. The Commission, in accordance with paragraph 9 (b) (iii) of resolution 687 (1991), and paragraph 4 (b) of resolution 715 (1991), provides assistance and cooperation to the IAEA 687 Action Team set up to implement provisions of those resolutions pertaining to nuclear weapons. This includes the designation of undeclared sites to be inspected. The Commission provides expertise for logistical, information and other operational support for the Action Team's conduct of ongoing monitoring and verification. Monitoring activities in Iraq are coordinated across disciplines, including the nuclear area, not only to ensure the most effective and efficient use of resources, but also to benefit from the synergies ensuing from a multidisciplinary approach to the monitoring of sites of interest to more than one discipline.

89. During the period under review, the Commission has: provided comments on Iraqi requests to relocate nuclear-related, dual-use materials and equipment within Iraq; participated in inspections and monitoring teams of the International Atomic Energy Agency (IAEA); provided fixed-wing (C-160) and rotating wing (CH-53g) aircraft for the transport of IAEA inspectors into Iraq from Bahrain, and between points within Iraq; and provided the IAEA 687 Action Team with logistic support for its inspection activities through the Baghdad Monitoring Centre.

90. Iraqi requests to relocate materials, items and machine tools of potential nuclear application are approved only after two technical evaluations are concluded. The first evaluation, provided by IAEA, checks significance to past nuclear programmes, or potential value to a renewed nuclear programme. The Commission, in turn, looks for significance to all weapon programmes, including ballistic missiles and chemical and biological weapons. It provides its decision on request as required under paragraph 3 (c) of Security Council resolution 707 (1991). Close coordination between IAEA and the Commission is particularly important in the management and control of machine tool movements within Iraq. For example, flow-forming machines are under the monitoring of both the Commission and IAEA.

91. During the period since the last report, the Commission's nuclear experts have participated in several IAEA monitoring and inspection teams. Such joint operations have resulted in an increase in operating effi-

ciency and improved decision-making on such issues as site designation and equipment movement.

92. In addition to routine transport of IAEA inspectors from Bahrain to Habbaniyah by C-160 fixed-wing aircraft, helicopter support has proved invaluable in facilitating long-haul monitoring campaigns by IAEA environmental-sampling experts. Water sampling sites range from as far north as Zakho close to the Turkish border, to a western site on the Euphrates just west of Al Qa'im, to far south at several sites near Al Basrah. Without helicopter support, an effective widespread water sampling programme would be rendered difficult. In addition to supporting the surface-water sampling programme, the Commission has recently approved fitting its helicopters with air samplers. The helicopter-borne air samplers will complement IAEA's ability to investigate nuclear contaminant transport throughout the surface-water system and thus provide a more fully integrated and effective environmental sampling programme.

5. Aerial surveillance

93. The Commission's aerial inspection assets, the high-altitude surveillance aircraft (U2) and the Baghdad-based Aerial Inspection Team, continue to play an important role in the monitoring regime.

94. Both of the above assets continue to conduct aerial surveillance of sites under monitoring in Iraq, at the direction of the Commission, on a regular basis. With the advent of the permanent monitoring teams in Iraq, experts from the teams now accompany the team in order to assist it in focusing on particular areas of relevance at sites. The results obtained from these aerial missions is an important part of the overall inspection process in Iraq.

95. Both aerial assets will also continue to undertake missions at new sites in Iraq to ensure that the monitoring regime continues to encompass all activities and facilities within Iraq of relevance to the monitoring regime.

96. To date some 243 missions have been undertaken by the U2 and 550 missions by the Aerial Inspection Team.

B. Export/import mechanism

Summary

97. The proposal for the export/import mechanism prepared by the Commission and IAEA is now before the Sanctions Committee for appropriate action to co-sponsor the proposal so that it may be submitted to the Security Council for approval. The revised annexes to the Commission's and the IAEA's plans for ongoing monitoring and verification, which list the items to be notified under the mechanism, have been circulated to the Council and made available to the Sanctions Committee.

98. Planning continues for the setting up by the Commission and IAEA of a Joint Unit to process notifications received under the mechanism, and for taking all other actions necessary to put the mechanism into effect when the Council so decides.

1. *Actions to establish the mechanism*

99. Under paragraph 7 of resolution 715 (1991) the Security Council requested the Commission, in cooperation with the Committee established under resolution 661 (1990) (the Sanctions Committee) and the Director General of IAEA "to develop ... a mechanism for monitoring any future sales or supplies by other countries to Iraq of items relevant to the implementation of section C of resolution 687 and other relevant resolutions, including the present resolution and the plans approved hereunder".

100. The Commission and IAEA therefore undertook to prepare a proposal outlining a mechanism which, in their view, would fulfil these requirements. The mechanism envisaged rested on a system of notifications, made by Iraq and the Governments of exporters, concerning the supply of dual-purpose items to Iraq, dual-purpose in this context being those items referred to in the relevant annexes to the plans of the Commission and IAEA for ongoing monitoring and verification approved by the Council in resolution 715 (1991). 6/ The mechanism also envisaged the provision of information by Governments on any attempts by Iraq to procure items prohibited to it under the Council resolutions.

101. In February 1994, a seminar of invited export control experts was convened at the Commission's offices in New York, in order to explain the principles of the mechanism envisaged and to obtain views on how it might be implemented in practice. The seminar was attended by representatives of IAEA and experts from those Governments which had wide experience of exporting goods to Iraq, prior to the imposition of sanctions, which would now need to be notified under the mechanism. On 28 and 29 May 1994, the Executive Chairman of the Commission met senior representatives of the Government of Iraq, in order to explain the principles of the mechanism, and an agreed summary of that meeting was signed by both sides.

102. On 13 May 1994, the Executive Chairman wrote to the Sanctions Committee Chairman, transmitting the proposal for consideration and approval by the Committee. The Executive Chairman noted that paragraph 7 of resolution 715 (1991) was intended to make provision for the monitoring of sales or supplies by other countries to Iraq of relevant dual-purpose items after the general sanctions imposed by resolution 661 (1990) on those items had been lifted, pursuant to paragraph 21 of resolution 687 (1991). In order to avoid confusion between the sanctions regime and the monitoring mechanism, the Executive Chairman proposed that the two regimes should be kept entirely separate. The role of the Sanctions Committee would have priority for as long as items covered by the plans for ongoing monitoring and verification remained subject to the general sanctions under resolution 661 (1990). Once the sanctions under resolution 661 (1990) on any dual-purpose items or categories of items were lifted or whenever the Committee allowed Iraq to input such items under an exemption from the general sanctions, those items would become subject to the proposed export/import mechanism.

103. Informal discussions in the Sanctions Committee appeared to reveal that a consensus could be arrived at on the mechanism contained in the proposal. However, before going to the Security Council with the required tripartite proposal for the export/import mechanism, the members of the Committee preferred to see a more detailed list of items to be notified than already appeared in the relevant annexes to the Commission's plan for ongoing monitoring and verification. Such a list would provide greater specification, in technical terms, of what constituted a dual-purpose item and hence the export of which to Iraq would be subject to notification. A general requirement to revise the annexes had already become apparent during the course of inspections in Iraq and the establishment of the ongoing monitoring and verification regime. Iraq had also requested that provisions of the annexes to the Commission's plan be specified in greater detail.

104. The Commission's plan, as approved by the Security Council in its resolution 715 (1991), lays down in its paragraph 26 the following procedure for revising the annexes: "The Special Commission, may, however after informing the Security Council, update and revise the annexes in the light of information and experience gained in the course of implementation of resolutions 687 (1991) and 707 (1991) and of the plan. The Special Commission shall inform Iraq of any such changes."

105. In October 1994, the Commission convened a further informal seminar of international experts to review the proposed changes to the annexes. While these lists were in large measure accepted, proposals were made for further changes. In January 1995, a third seminar was held to review the draft of the final versions of the lists, to consider the draft notification forms to be completed by Governments pursuant to the mechanism, and to discuss the practical implementation of the mechanism.

6/ S/22871/Rev.1 and S/22872/Rev.1 and Corr.1, amended by S/1995/208 and S/1995/215, respectively.

106. The final version of the revised annexes to the Commission's Plan were submitted to the Security Council on 17 March 1995 (S/1995/208) and to the IAEA's plan on 23 March 1995 (S/1995/215).

107. The joint proposal by the Commission and IAEA was resubmitted to the Sanctions Committee on 15 February 1995. The mechanism, upon receiving the concurrence of the Sanctions Committee, will be transmitted to the Council for approval. It is anticipated that this will be done in the very near future.

2. Actions to implement the mechanism

108. The mechanism envisages the creation of a Joint Unit, staffed by personnel from the Commission and IAEA. The Joint Unit will be represented by staff in New York and in the Monitoring Centre in Baghdad.

109. Measures to establish these offices and the practical procedures to implement the mechanism began some 18 months ago with the recruitment of expert personnel to the Commission to focus primarily on the export/import mechanism, in the context of the overall ongoing monitoring and verification regime. These experts are also preparing the documentation which will explain, in detail, the workings of the mechanism in respect of the notification requirements levied on Iraq and the exporting Governments. These documents will be transmitted to Governments in a circular note. A customized computer database is also being developed at the Commission's office in New York, in order to ensure the swift processing of notification data and to support analytical requirements.

110. The Joint Units in New York and Baghdad will be staffed by customs experts and data-entry clerks. They will be responsible for receiving and processing, in manual and computerized format, the notifications provided by Iraq and exporting Governments. The notifications will also be analysed by experts of the Commission and IAEA and appropriate actions taken on the basis of their recommendations.

111. In Iraq, Joint Unit personnel, in conjunction with the resident monitoring team experts, will be responsible for inspecting notified items and associated paperwork, on their arrival in Iraq. They will also undertake no-notice inspections at points of entry into Iraq and other sites, in order to verify that all notifiable items are being declared.

112. As further preparation for the implementation of the export/import mechanism, the Commission has undertaken studies to ascertain the likely volume of data which the mechanism will generate. The results of these internal studies, and others undertaken by outside bodies, indicate that the number of shipments of dual-use goods could be expected not to exceed 2,000 during a normal year. Plans to acquire personnel and equipment to support this volume of shipments are being put into effect.

113. The Commission has also begun a dialogue with Iraq, in order to gain a full understanding of the existing customs and import systems in place in the country and so better to plan operations associated with the mechanism. In addition, the Commission will also shortly conduct baseline inspections of points of entry into Iraq as further preparation with the aim of foreshortening the time required to have a fully operational mechanism after its adoption and the easing or lifting of sanctions.

C. National implementation measures

114. Paragraphs 20 and 21 of the Commission's monitoring plan require Iraq to adopt the measures necessary to implement its obligations under section C of resolution 687 (1991), resolution 707 (1991) and the plan itself, to include a prohibition and penal legislation forbidding all natural and legal persons under Iraq's jurisdiction from undertaking anywhere any activity prohibited for Iraq by resolution 687 (1991) and all other related resolutions.

115. Iraq has consulted the Commission on the draft of a decision by the Revolution Command Council intended to give effect to those requirements. The Commission made certain suggestions to the Iraqi authorities concerning the need for such legislation to follow closely the language of the Council's resolutions. Attention was also drawn to the need for such legislation promptly to incorporate any changes to the lists of controlled items contained in the annexes to the plans for ongoing monitoring and verification and to the need to provide assurances to those who might cooperate with the Commission and IAEA in the performance of their tasks that such cooperation *per se* would not be the subject of any legal or other punitive measures.

116. It is the Commission's understanding that a revised draft now stands before the Revolution Command Council for adoption and, during the most recent high-level discussions in Baghdad in March 1995, the Iraqi authorities gave assurances that such adoption could be anticipated early in April 1995. The Commission has also been provided with a copy of regulations which the National Monitoring Directorate will issue to give full effect to the Revolution Command Council's decision. These regulations have now been translated from Arabic into English at United Nations Headquarters. They are available to any interested delegations in the Office of the Executive Chairman.

D. *Organization*

1. *Executive Office, New York*

117. In order to respond to changing priorities and tasks, the organization and equipping of the Executive Office of the Special Commission in New York has undergone substantial changes since Iraq accepted Security Council resolution 715 (1991) in November 1993. The increase in the number of staff to cope with the increased workload has resulted in acute overcrowding of the office space available to the Commission. If this issue is not resolved, it is bound to affect adversely the work performance of the staff.

118. Under the terms of the plan approved under resolution 715 (1991), Iraq is required to produce a substantial volume and range of declarations on a regular basis. Thus the immediate requirement for the Commission was to increase the number of staff in New York, in order to handle the additional data. However, in addition to further experts specialized in proscribed weapons systems, there was also a necessity to recruit from supporting Governments individuals with knowledge of relevant civil industries in which dual-use items and equipment might be used and others to assist the experts in the processing, handling and storage of the data.

119. Assistance was also required to collate much of the material required for the creation of the site protocols and to update those protocols in the light of declarations from Iraq and reports from the inspection teams conducting baseline inspections in Iraq. At the conclusion of the baseline process it also became apparent that such assistance would continue to be central to the successful maintenance of the monitoring system as the Commission established a multi-layered system with the introduction of sensors, primarily cameras and air-sampling equipment, at sites under monitoring in Iraq. The product from these sensors is an integral part of the monitoring regime and, as such, must be collated and analysed in the context of overall knowledge of the functions of sites under monitoring.

120. As noted in section B above, describing preparations for the export/import mechanism, the Commission began preparations for establishing the mechanism some 18 months ago with the recruitment of staff specialized in customs procedures. In 1994, in the light of the highly specialized requirements of administering such a mechanism, further staff were recruited. In the event of a modification to the existing sanctions regime, additional staff will be recruited to administer the export/import mechanism and to oversee the conduct of operations in Iraq. Analysis of the notifications provided by Iraq and Governments of exporters under the mechanism will be undertaken by the existing expert staff.

121. To support the above change of emphasis in mission focus, the Commission has made major upgrades to its automated data-processing equipment. This has involved an upgrade to the Commission's local area network (LAN) system and individual workstations. Many of these upgrades have been undertaken by donations of equipment by supporting Governments. The Commission has also been able to take advantage of existing computerized systems developed in other forums in support of other arms-control efforts.

122. To support the export/import mechanism, a dedicated, customized database is being created, modelled on the export control computer database used by a supporting Government. One prime concern in respect of handling the notifications received under the mechanism will be to ensure the security of such data, recognizing its commercial sensitivity. The computer equipment required to sustain the export/import database will also be donated by supporting Governments.

2. *Baghdad Monitoring and Verification Centre*

123. Preparations for the establishment of the Baghdad Monitoring and Verification Centre, its staffing and early operations, are described in annex II to the Commission's report of 7 October 1994 (S/1994/1138), which briefly describes the current operational status of the Centre.

124. The Commission plans to complete its initial projects for the Centre facilities during this summer. A principal delaying factor has been the lack of funding to purchase materials and supplies for renovation and construction. Several contributing Governments have made direct donations of materials, equipment and supplies so that seconded craftsmen and technicians could accomplish their work. The remaining projects are not essential for effective ongoing monitoring and verification but will, once completed, contribute to the improved efficiency of the Centre.

125. The Centre currently provides: space for an operations room, supporting radio and telephone (voice and facsimile) communications and real-time monitoring of sites through 107 remote-controlled cameras; offices for the aerial inspection team, and the biological, chemical, missile and nuclear monitoring groups (the latter group is staffed by IAEA); aerial photography, biological and chemical laboratories; a medical clinic; and offices for the Director and his support staff. The Centre staff also includes a German army detachment with three CH-53G helicopters at Al-Rasheed air base, deployed to support the operations of inspection teams and monitoring groups throughout Iraq. Approximately 80 staff are assigned to the Centre.

126. The next development within the Centre will be preparations to support an export/import mechanism

at the appropriate time. The Centre includes adequate space for this purpose, and specific facility modifications for the group are anticipated to be minimal.

127. The operation of the Centre is supported by the United Nations Administrative Unit-Baghdad which, *inter alia*, provides maintenance for the Commission's vehicles. Air transportation to support the Centre continues to be provided from Bahrain by a German air-force detachment with two C-160 Transall aircraft. This function, and all arrangements for the movement of experts and technicians as well as for cargoes of supplies, materials and equipment, is managed by the Commission's field office in Bahrain.

IV. FUTURE OPERATIONS

A. *Financial status of the Special Commission*

128. In order to plan for future monitoring and verification activities, including those related to export/import, the Commission needs secure long-term funding, rather than the ad hoc funding of the present situation. Lack of secure long-term funding has complicated the Commission's task of implementing its mandate and planning future operations.

129. Funds have only been identified for the first half of 1995 and are being received piecemeal. At present, there is no indication that additional funds will be made available to the Commission to cover operations for the remainder of 1995. An additional $13 million is required to support the Commission's operations until the end of 1995.

130. If further funds are not identified in the near future, the incremental shut-down of the Commission's operations, as indicated in the Commission's letter to the President of the Security Council of 3 November 1994, will ensue.

Status of finance of the Special Commission as at 31 March 1995

	United States dollars
Total funds provided through loans/contributions	9 405 500
Designation of 778 funds	82 190 000
Total available for operations	91 595 500
Expenditures from inception to 31 December 1993	55 230 704
1994 expenditures (estimated)	24 390 000
1995 projected requirements	25 000 000
Estimated total requirements from inception to 31 December 1995	104 620 704
Surplus/(deficit) against available funds	(13 025 204)

B. *Operations and organization*

131. As indicated in chapter III above, the main focus of the Commission's activities in Iraq is currently the operation of the system of ongoing monitoring and verification. Funding permitting, the Commission expects this to continue to be the case. Further effort will continue to be devoted to clarifying and resolving the remaining outstanding issues in relation to the past programmes and, once the export/import mechanism has been adopted, also as indicated above, a greater share of resources will be devoted to the operation of the mechanism.

132. It is envisaged that, until the implementation of the export/import mechanism, ongoing monitoring and verification activities will comprise primarily the following types of activities:

(a) Inspection to verify the completeness of the list of sites monitored and of the inventories, to verify declarations as to the activities conducted at sites or to pursue any information obtained that might question Iraq's compliance with its obligations under paragraph 10 of resolution 687 (1991);

(b) Aerial surveillance, from both the Commission's high-altitude surveillance aircraft (the U-2) and its helicopters;

(c) Maintenance of the site monitoring and verification protocols by the monitoring experts at the Baghdad Monitoring Centre;

(d) Monitoring activities conducted by experts dispatched to Iraq for a specific purpose because either the expertise required for the activity is not available amongst the staff of the Centre or because the scope of the activity is too great for the staff of the Centre to undertake without additional assistance;

(e) Review and analysis of the product of the sensors installed at the various sites.

V. CONCLUSIONS

133. The elements of ongoing monitoring and verification are now in place and the system is operational. Over time, additional elements may be added or existing elements may be adapted in the light of experience in order better to focus monitoring efforts, to respond to developments in Iraq's industrial base and to increase the level of assurance it provides that Iraq is not reacquiring banned capabilities. The Commission wishes to place on record that it has received full cooperation from Iraq in the setting up and operation of the monitoring system. Some issues, however, still remain.

134. There must be confidence that the system is comprehensive in its coverage of all that needs to be monitored. Accounting by Iraq for the materials, items and equipment acquired for past programmes and the use to which they have been put is thus required. An under-

standing of the levels of technologies attained by Iraq in its past programmes is also required if the Commission's efforts are to be correctly focused. If this accounting and understanding is not credibly provided by Iraq, the Commission will not be able to state with confidence that its monitoring is comprehensive and correctly focused, as is now illustrated by the situation in the biological area.

135. As described elsewhere in the present report, the Commission has continued its investigation in all areas of the past proscribed weapons activities in Iraq and its verification of Iraq's declarations. The Commission has come to the conclusion that Iraq has not provided a full and comprehensive disclosure of its past military biological programme or accounted for items and materials acquired for that programme. With Iraq's failure to account for the use of these items and materials for legitimate purposes, the only conclusion that can be drawn is that there is a high risk that they had been purchased and used for a proscribed purpose—acquisition of biological warfare agent. The Commission will continue its intensive efforts to elucidate all such outstanding issues arising from this and the other past programmes. It notes that, if Iraq decided to provide full, accurate and verifiable information, such matters could be resolved expeditiously.

136. An essential element of the system of ongoing monitoring and verification will be the export/import mechanism. The Commission and IAEA have completed work on all the components of the mechanism and it is now for the Sanctions Committee and the Security Council to consider and take action on the proposal for the mechanism prepared by the Commission and IAEA. The monitoring system, under Security Council resolution 715 (1991), will not be complete until the Council has acted on this matter.

Appendix
Inspection schedule
(in-country dates)

Nuclear

15 May-21 May 1991	IAEA1/UNSCOM 1
22 June-3 July 1991	IAEA2/UNSCOM 4
7 July-18 July 1991	IAEA3/UNSCOM 5
27 July-10 August 1991	IAEA4/UNSCOM 6
14 September-20 September 1991	IAEA5/UNSCOM 14
21 September-30 September 1991	IAEA6/UNSCOM 16
11 October-22 October 1991	IAEA7/UNSCOM 19
11 November-18 November 1991	IAEA8/UNSCOM 22
11 January-14 January 1992	IAEA9/UNSCOM 25
5 February-13 February 1992	IAEA10/UNSCOM 27
7 April-15 April 1992	IAEA11/UNSCOM 33
26 May-4 June 1992	IAEA12/UNSCOM 37

14 July-21 July 1992	IAEA13/UNSCOM 41
31 August-7 September 1992	IAEA14/UNSCOM 43
8 November-19 November 1992	IAEA15/UNSCOM 46
6 December-14 December 1992	IAEA16/UNSCOM 47
22 January-27 January 1993	IAEA17/UNSCOM 49
3 March-11 March 1993	IAEA18/UNSCOM 52
30 April-7 May 1993	IAEA19/UNSCOM 56
25 June-30 June 1993	IAEA20/UNSCOM 58
23 July-28 July 1993	IAEA21/UNSCOM 61
1 November-9 November 1993	IAEA22/UNSCOM 64
4 February-11 February 1994	IAEA23/UNSCOM 68
11 April-22 April 1994	IAEA24/UNSCOM 73
21 June-1 July 1994	IAEA25/UNSCOM 83
22 August-2 September 1994	IAEA26/UNSCOM 90
7 September-29 September 1994	NMG 94-01
14 October-21 October 1994	IAEA27/UNSCOM 93
29 September-21 October 1994	NMG 94-02
21 October-9 November 1994	NMG 94-03
8 November-29 November 1994	NMG 94-04
29 November-16 December 1994	NMG 94-05
16 December 1994-13 January 1995	NMG 94-06
12 January-2 February 1995	NMG 95-01
2 February-28 February 1995	NMG 95-02
28 February-16 March 1995	NMG 95-03
16 March-6 April 1995	NMG 95-04
6 April-26 April 1995	NMG 95-05

Chemical

9 June-15 June 1991	CW1/UNSCOM 2
15 August-22 August 1991	CW2/UNSCOM 9
31 August-8 September 1991	CW3/UNSCOM 11
31 August-5 September 1991	CW4/UNSCOM 12
6 October-9 November 1991	CW5/UNSCOM 17
22 October-2 November 1991	CW6/UNSCOM 20
18 November-1 December 1991	CBW1/UNSCOM 21
27 January-5 February 1992	CW7/UNSCOM 26
21 February-24 March 1992	CD1/UNSCOM 29
5 April-13 April 1992	CD2/UNSCOM 32
15 April-29 April 1992	CW8/UNSCOM 35
18 June 92-14 June 94	CDG/UNSCOM 38
26 June-10 July 1992	CBW2/UNSCOM 39
21 September-29 September 1992	CW9/UNSCOM 44
6 December-14 December 1992	CBW3/UNSCOM 47
6 April-18 April 1993	CW10/UNSCOM 55
27 June-30 June 1993	CW11/UNSCOM 59
19 November-22 November 1993	CW12/UNSCOM 65
1 February-14 February 1994	CW13/UNSCOM 67
20 March-26 March 1994	CW14/UNSCOM 70
18 April-22 April 1994	CW15/UNSCOM 74
25 May-5 June 1994	CW16/UNSCOM 75
31 May-12 June 1994	CW17/UNSCOM 76
8 June-14 June 1994	CW18/UNSCOM 77
10 August-23 August 1994	CW19/UNSCOM 89

13 September-24 September 1994	CW20/UNSCOM 91
2 October 1994-14 January 1995	CG 1
23 October-27 October 1994	CW21/UNSCOM 95
11 January-21 January 1995	CW23/UNSCOM108
16 January-22 January 1995	CW22/UNSCOM107
14 January-15 April 1995	CG 2
16 April-4 July 1995	CG 3

Biological

2 August-8 August 1991	BW1/UNSCOM 7
20 September-3 October 1991	BW2/UNSCOM 15
11 March-18 March 1993	BW3/UNSCOM 53
8 April-26 April 1994	BW4/UNSCOM 72
28 May-7 June 1994	BW5/UNSCOM 78
24 June-5 July 1994	BW6/UNSCOM 84
5 June-8 June 1994	BW7/UNSCOM 86
25 July-7 September 1994	BW8/UNSCOM 87
20 August-25 August 1994	BW9/UNSCOM 88
29 August-3 September 1994	BW10/UNSCOM 92
29 September-14 October 1994	BW11/UNSCOM 94
23 September-26 September 1994	BW12/UNSCOM 96
15 November-22 November 1994	BW15/UNSCOM104
2 December-10 December 1994	BW16/UNSCOM105 (IMT)
2 December-13 December 1994	BW13/UNSCOM 99 (IMT)
9 December-18 December 1994	BW17/UNSCOM106 (IMT)
28 December 1994-31 January 1995	IBG 1
10 January-22 January 1995	BW18/UNSCOM109
20 January-6 February 1995	BW19/UNSCOM110
23 January-3 February 1995	BW22/UNSCOM113
3 February-17 February 1995	BW20/UNSCOM111
3 February-17 February 1995	BW21/UNSCOM112
12 March-18 March 1995	BW23/UNSCOM115
24 March-6 April 1995	BW24/UNSCOM116
1 February-3 April 1995	IBG 2
4 April-9 July 1995	BG 1

Ballistic missiles

30 June-7 July 1991	BM1/UNSCOM 3
18 July-20 July 1991	BM2/UNSCOM 10
8 August-15 August 1991	BM3/UNSCOM 8
6 September-13 September 1991	BM4/UNSCOM 13
1 October-9 October 1991	BM5/UNSCOM 18
1 December-9 December 1991	BM6/UNSCOM 23
9 December-17 December 1991	BM7/UNSCOM 24
21 February-29 February 1992	BM8/UNSCOM 28
21 March-29 March 1992	BM9/UNSCOM 31
13 April-21 April 1992	BM10/UNSCOM 34
14 May-22 May 1992	BM11/UNSCOM 36
11 July-29 July 1992	BM12/UNSCOM 40A+B

7 August-18 August 1992	BM13/UNSCOM 42
16 October-30 October 1992	BM14/UNSCOM 45
25 January-23 March 1993	IMT1a/UNSCOM 48
12 February-21 February 1993	BM15/UNSCOM 50
22 February-23 February 1993	BM16/UNSCOM 51
27 March-17 May 1993	IMT1b/UNSCOM 54
5 June-28 June 1993	IMT1c/UNSCOM 57
10 July-11 July 1993	BM17/UNSCOM 60
24 August-15 September 1993	BM18/UNSCOM 62
28 September-1 November 1993	BM19/UNSCOM 63
21 January-29 January 1994	BM20/UNSCOM 66
17 February-25 February 1994	BM21/UNSCOM 69
30 March-20 May 1994	BM22/UNSCOM 71
20 May-8 June 1994	BM23/UNSCOM 79
10 June-24 June 1994	BM24/UNSCOM 80
14 June-22 June 1994	BM25/UNSCOM 81
3 July-28 July 1994	BM26/UNSCOM 82
15 July-24 July 1994	BM27/UNSCOM 85
17 August-9 October 1994	MG 1
2 October-6 October 1994	BM28/UNSCOM 98A
23 October-28 October 1994	BM28/UNSCOM 98B
14 October 1994-21 February 1995	MG 2
19 October-22 October 1994	MG 2A
2 December-6 December 1994	MG 2B
9 December-14 December 1994	BM29/UNSCOM101
9 December-16 December 1994	BM30/UNSCOM102
27 January-31 January 1995	MG 2C
22 February- ... 1995	MG 3
6 March-14 March 1995	UNSCOM103/BM31

Computer search

12 February 1992	UNSCOM 30

Special missions

30 June-3 July 1991
11 August-14 August 1991
4 October-6 October 1991
11 November-15 November 1991
27 January-30 January 1992
21 February-24 February 1992
17 July-19 July 1992
28 July-29 July 1992
6 September-12 September 1992
4 November-9 November 1992
4 November-8 November 1992
12 March-18 March 1993
14 March-20 March 1993
19 April-24 April 1993
4 June-5 July 1993
15 July-19 July 1993
25 July-5 August 1993
9 August-12 August 1993
10 September-24 September 1993

27 September-1 October 1993	7 November-12 November 1994
1 October-8 October 1993	14 November-17 November 1994
5 October-16 February 1994	4 December-18 December 1994
2 December-10 December 1993	14 December-20 December 1994
2 December-16 December 1993	7 January-31 January 1995
21 January-27 January 1994	7 January-21 January 1995
2 February-6 February 1994	13 January-26 January 1995
10 April-14 April 1994	13 January-16 March 1995
24 April-26 April 1994	12 January-28 January 1995
28 May-29 May 1994	23 January-14 February 1995
4 July-6 July 1994	25 January-4 February 1995
8 August-16 August 1994	19 February-23 February 1995
15 September-19 September 1994	22 February-28 February 1995
21 September-25 September 1994	28 February-18 March 1995
23 September-26 September 1994	16 March-29 March 1995
3 October-6 October 1994	24 March-27 March 1995
4 November-20 November 1994	

Document 206

Seventh report of the Director General of the IAEA on the implementation of the Agency's plan for future ongoing monitoring and verification of Iraq's compliance with paragraph 12 of Security Council resolution 687 (1991)

S/1995/287, 11 April 1995

Note by the Secretary-General

The Secretary-General has the honour to transmit to the members of the Security Council the attached communication, dated 5 April 1995, which he has received from the Director General of the International Atomic Energy Agency (IAEA).

Annex
Letter dated 5 April 1995 from the Director General of the International Atomic Energy Agency to the Secretary-General

Paragraph 8 of resolution 715 (1991), adopted by the Security Council on 11 October 1991, requests the Director General of the International Atomic Energy Agency to submit to the Security Council reports on the implementation of the Agency's plan for future ongoing monitoring and verification of Iraq's compliance with paragraph 12 of resolution 687 (1991). These reports are to be submitted when requested by the Security Council and, in any event, at least every six months after the adoption of resolution 715 (1991).

Accordingly, I am requesting you kindly to transmit to the President of the Security Council the enclosed seventh six-month report on the implementation of the

Plan. I remain available for any consultations you or the Council may wish to have.

(Signed) Hans BLIX

Appendix
Seventh report of the Director General of the International Atomic Energy Agency on the implementation of the Agency's plan for future ongoing monitoring and verification of Iraq's compliance with paragraph 12 of Resolution 687 (1991)

I. *Introduction*

1. On 11 October 1991, the Security Council adopted resolution 715 (1991) approving, *inter alia*, the plan submitted in document S/22872/Rev.1 and S/22872/Rev.1/Corr.1 by the Director General of the International Atomic Energy Agency (IAEA) for future ongoing monitoring and verification of Iraq's compliance with paragraph 12 of Part C of Security Council resolution 687 (1991) and with the requirements of paragraphs 3 and 5 of resolution 707 (1991). In paragraph 8 of resolution 715, the Security Council requested the Director General of the IAEA to submit to it reports on the implementation of the plan when requested by the Secu-

rity Council and, in and any event, at least every six months after the adoption of resolution 715.

2. The Director General submits herewith the seventh six-month report 1/ on implementation of the plan for ongoing monitoring and verification related to Iraq's nuclear capabilities (hereinafter referred to as the Plan).

3. It will be recalled that in the previous six-month report a detailed account was given of the IAEA's inspection activities which led to the identification and neutralization of the past covert Iraqi nuclear programme. In that report it was concluded that, with the establishment at the end of August 1994 of the IAEA's continuous presence in Iraq—the Nuclear Monitoring Group (NMG)—all elements of the Plan were in place, thus indicating that the Plan was operational. It was also concluded that (i) monitoring and verification measures would evolve as technical needs arose and as advanced technologies became available, and that (ii) the implementation of the Plan did not foreclose the exercise by the IAEA of its right to investigate any aspect of Iraq's former nuclear weapons programme through the follow-up of any new result or new information which in the IAEA's judgement warranted further investigation.

4. With the NMG in place at the Baghdad Monitoring and Verification Centre (BMVC), most of the future activities of the IAEA in Iraq, be they monitoring and verification of existing data or follow-up of new results or new information, will be carried out by that group in cooperation, where necessary, with the other resident teams of the Special Commission. This will not preclude the possibility of sending specialized inspection teams to Iraq, as has been done in the past.

5. Information has recently appeared in the media suggesting the existence in Iraq of a secret project which could be related to a nuclear weapons programme. The details are discussed further below.

II. *Iraq's past nuclear weapons programme*

6. As indicated in the previous six-month report, the IAEA is confident that the essential components of Iraq's past clandestine nuclear programme have been identified and have been destroyed, removed or rendered harmless, as appropriate. The IAEA is also confident that the scope of the past programme is well understood. Areas of residual uncertainty have been progressively reduced to a level of detail, the full knowledge of which is not likely to affect the overall picture.

7. This assessment is based not only on the verification of Iraqi statements, which may be presumed to be biased and incomplete, but also on information gathered during inspections and information provided by suppliers and Member States and, to a great extent, on analyses of the large quantity of original Iraqi documentation rele-

vant to the covert programme which was seized in Iraq in September—October 1991 by the teams of the sixth and seventh IAEA inspection missions.

8. The cache of original Iraqi documentation consists of a total of 54,9222 pages, comprising 2,348 individual documents, 1,138 of which had been stamped by the Iraqi authorities as secret or top secret. All of the documents have been abstracted and 325 have been fully translated. Of the 2,348 documents, 564 (about one quarter of the total) have no date; the remaining 1,784 cover a period of thirteen years, from 1979 through 1991. The distribution of documents by year of issue is shown as a bar-chart in the Attachment. As can be seen from this chart, 41% of the seized documents relate to the period 1988-1991. Documents stamped "Petrochemical Project 3" or "PC3", which was the code name of the covert Iraqi nuclear programme, tend to occur more frequently in the later years.

9. These seized documents contain a wealth of detailed information regarding the following areas of activity of the covert nuclear programme:
- electromagnetic isotope separation (EMIS) for the production of enriched uranium;
- chemical enrichment of uranium by liquid-liquid extraction and solid-liquid ion exchange;
- gaseous diffusion enrichment of uranium, abandoned in 1987;
- research aimed at lithium-6 production;
- design of facilities to handle large amounts of tritium; and
- weaponization 2/.

10. The documents also provide detailed information regarding matters such as:
- the organizational structure of PC3 and the staff assigned to the various project operations;
- the code numbers and description of the technical tasks assigned to each PC3 unit;
- achievement and failures in the execution of the various technical tasks;
- the identification and coding of eight dedicated sites directly associated with PC3 activities (Tuwaitha, Al Atheer, Tarmiya, Al Sharqat, Al Qaim, Al Jezira, Al Rabiya and Dijla); and
- procurement and foreign suppliers.

11. The IAEA believes that some of the documents seized by its inspectors in the course of the sixth inspection mission at the premises of the Engineering Design

1/ The Director General has so far submitted six reports, circulated on 15 April 1992, as S/23813; on 28 October 1992, as S/24722; on 19 April 1993, as S/25621; on November 1993, as S/26685; on 22 April 1994, as S/1994/490; and on 10 October 1994, as S/1994/1151.
2/ Weaponization refers to knowledge, techniques, technologies and engineering activities required to construct a nucleaar explosive device capable of being delivered to a target and of achieving a nuclear yield, assuming that fissile material is available.

Attachment

Distribution by date of issuance of 2348
documents confiscated in Iraq by IAEA-6 and IAEA-7

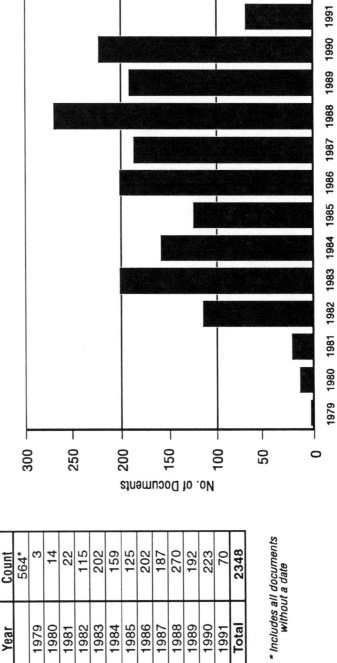

Year	Count
1979	564*
1980	3
1981	14
1982	22
1983	115
1984	202
1985	159
1986	125
1987	202
1988	187
1989	270
1990	192
1991	223
	70
Total	**2348**

* Includes all documents
without a date

Centre and then forcibly taken from them were not returned. To the IAEA's repeated requests for their return Iraq has consistently responded that no documents were withheld and that, in any event, no programme documents were any longer available as all of them had been destroyed. This response is not credible, but the IAEA has neither information on the location of such documents, nor any means to retrieve them.

12. Detailed analyses of the seized Iraqi documents have led to the following general conclusions:

- These documents provide a detailed account of the achievements and failures of PC3 from its inception until mid-1990 (i.e. shortly before Iraq's invasion of Kuwait). The most recent technical report among them is dated 11 November 1990 3/ and describes the progress in weaponization during the period 1 January 1990 - 31 May 1990. The absence of more recent documentation gives rise to uncertainties regarding PC3 activities in the several months which preceded the Gulf war, i.e. between June 1990 and January 1991.

- None of the seized documents contains information on gas centrifuge research and development, but there are indications that it was started in mid-1987, when the gaseous diffusion project was abandoned. There is evidence in at least two documents that in mid-1987 a complement of 150 staff who were working on gaseous diffusion were transferred to gas centrifuge enrichment, responsibility for which was transferred from the Iraqi Atomic Energy Commission (IAEC) to another organisation. The documents do not mention which organisation assumed responsibility, but other sources indicate that it was the Ministry of Industry and Military Industrialisation (MIMI).

13. This leaves two questions open: the first concerns the progress made by PC3 from June 1990 to January 1991; the second concerns the completeness of the IAEA's knowledge regarding gas centrifuge enrichment—nothing concerning this project was found in the seized documentation.

14. As to the first question, the Iraqi authorities assert that the invasion of Kuwait brought all Iraqi Atomic Energy Commission (IAEC) activities to a virtual halt; the sanctions imposed by Security Council resolution 661 of 6 August 1990 interrupted the flow of equipment and material needed for completing the industrial installations associated with the project and efforts had concentrated on measures to protect existing facilities from the threat posed by air raids—for instance the moving of foreign nationals who had been taken hostage to potential targets (this certainly happened in the case of Tuwaitha). The IAEA has no evidence to contradict these assertions. In fact, the absence of technical reports documenting progress after May 1990 could be an indication that the situation had become chaotic.

15. As to the second question, the Iraqi authorities maintain that, before the commencement of IAEA inspections in Iraq under resolution 687 (1991), orders were received from a senior government level requiring them to collect all sensitive documents and to surrender them to the Iraqi army for destruction. They also maintain that the IAEA's ability to get hold of documents in the course of the sixth inspection mission was due to negligence for which those responsible were punished. One of the seized documents records the fact that a considerable amount of documentation had been brought to the "previously agreed place" on 6 June 1991—in the interval between the first and second inspection missions. There is, however, no corroboration that this documentation was subsequently destroyed, nor is it considered credible that a complete master set of such documentation has not been retained.

16. The absence of original Iraqi documentation describing the progress of Iraq's gas centrifuge programme has compelled the IAEA to concentrate considerable effort on the independent verification of the correctness and completeness of the declarations concerning this programme contained in Iraq's "Full, Final and Complete Report" and in other statements. 4/ This independent verification has included investigations through suppliers (from whom the IAEA has obtained copies of original drawings of the Iraqi gas centrifuge components) and the assistance of a group of centrifuge technology experts. The consensus of these experts is that the picture of the centrifuge design and manufacturing activities carried out in Iraq is coherent, with no obvious gaps, and essentially complete.

17. The importance of verifying what materials and equipment subject to control and monitoring under the Plan has actually been imported by Iraq, is not limited to the centrifuge area. As discussed in the previous six-month report, the verification process is a lengthy one, calling for cooperation from concerned Member States and various suppliers. To date this investigation has entailed enquiries involving 186 companies in 28 countries.

3/ As already mentioned the date-spread of seized documents included the year 1991. However, the documents dated 1991 were mostly of an administrative nature.

4/ When the "Full, Final and Complete Report" (FFCR) was handed over by the Iraqi authorities, in July 1992, the IAEA was informed that the FFRC was not a free-standing document and that it had to be assessed together with a number of "Annexes". These "Annexes" were the written replies by Iraq to the detailed questions asked in the course of inspections, the documents supplied in the course of the "seminars" held on the different projects including the gas centrifuge project and the thousands of seized documents.

III. *Media reports on possible non-compliance*

18. A recently published article in the British press reports that an Iraqi scientist formerly employed by the Iraqi Atomic Energy Commission informed a British journalist that Iraq had resumed its nuclear weapons programme and was attempting to conceal it. According to this article, before his disappearance, the Iraqi scientist provided to the journalist copies of documents to support his contentions.

19. The IAEA has received and reviewed the documents in question. 5/ If genuine, they could suggest that theoretical computer-based studies related to nuclear weapons design are being conducted in Iraq. Initial analysis could not establish the documents' authenticity. Iraqi authorities deny the existence of such a programme, and challenge the authenticity of the documents pointing to many inconsistencies in content and in form. The IAEA is pursuing this matter with a view to determining the authenticity and clarifying the substance of these documents.

20. The IAEA will keep the Security Council informed on the outcome of its investigation.

IV. *Implementation of the plan*

A. *Inspection activities*

21. Since the issuance of the previous six-month report on 10 October 1994, the IAEA has carried out one inspection mission in Iraq, the twenty-seventh. The detailed report on this inspection is contained in document S/1994/1443, dated 22 December 1994. As indicated in that document, the report was the last of the series of mission-specific reports. With the establishment of the continuous presence in Iraq of the NMG, the IAEA's activities in Iraq will henceforth be described in semi-annual reports to the Security Council on the implementation of the Plan. The main focus of the twenty-seventh inspection mission was the implementation of activities associated with the Plan.

B. *Ongoing monitoring and verification activities*

22. The activities involved in ongoing monitoring and verification include: inspections at facilities, installations and sites; environmental monitoring; verification of the use of items described in Annex 3 of the Plan; verification of information provided by Iraq in accordance with paragraph 22 and Annex 2 of the Plan; verification of information acquired from Member States, from aerial surveillance and from open sources and assessed to warrant further investigation; and interviews with Iraqi personnel who were connected with Iraq's former nuclear programme.

23. When the NMG was established in August 1994, the conversion of the section of the Canal Hotel which was to accommodate the BMVC was in its early stages. The conversion is now practically complete and the internal structure has been modified to provide office, laboratory and storage space for each of the monitoring groups and centralised facilities for the communications, medical and administrative units. The normal complement of the NMG is three to four persons; they are accompanied on inspections by personnel from the Iraqi National Monitoring Directorate (NMD). In most instances the NMD escorts are not given prior notice of the location to be visited.

24. When the need arises, additional persons with particular expertise are assigned to the NMG to carry out specific tasks—e.g. the twice-yearly hydrological survey of the watersheds of the Tigris and Euphrates. The fifth such survey, carried out during the twenty-seventh inspection mission, involved the collection of samples of water, sediment and biota at 16 locations selected from the 52 locations for which baseline date had been established in the original survey, completed in November 1992. This part of the IAEA's environmental monitoring programme is a powerful and proven technique for the detection of activities such as the operation of nuclear reactors or of facilities for the extraction of plutonium from irradiated nuclear material.

25. This environmental monitoring programme also includes aerial and ground-based gamma radiation surveys, the collection of airborne particulate matter and the sampling—by the well-established "smear" technique—of materials deposited on surfaces.

26. Seals with unique verifiable signatures are attached by the IAEA to critical items of equipment in order to provide confirmation that such items are still at their respective declared locations. Seals are also used to prevent the undetected use of controlled equipment. A few cases of unauthorised removals of seals have occurred in the past two years, but in each case it was possible to verify that the identity and integrity of the equipment from which the seal had been removed had not been compromised.

27. IAEA video surveillance and recording equipment installed in two major engineering establishments has, with the assistance of the Special Commission, been modified in order to enable television signals to be transmitted from monitored locations to the BMVC. This capability provided the NMG with the opportunity to observe, at any time, activities in the areas under video surveillance. As the activities in some Iraqi engineering establishments are of interest both to the NMG and to

---

5/ The documents consist of a single page memorandum in Arabic and a single page excerpt from a memorandum in Arabic.

the Ballistic Missile Group, the relevant video signals are routed to both groups regardless of which group had installed the video surveillance system.

28. Since the establishment of the IAEA's continuous presence in Iraq 23 facilities have been inspected for the first time: three facilities identified by Iraq as the recipients of monitored items for which it had requested release or change of use; two facilities where previously undeclared items of dual-use equipment (coordinate measuring machines) were located; 16 facilities declared as having a means of power supply greater than 10MWe; one facility at which radioisotopes are used or stored; and one facility which was inspected on the basis of information obtained from Member States. The inspections at facilities in the Basrah area having a means of power supply greater than 10MWe revealed shortcomings in the inventory of such facilities declared by Iraq; information was obtained through the inspection process on an additional sixteen such facilities. The Iraqi NMD has been requested to prepare a correct declaration of the inventory of such facilities.

29. An inspection carried out on the basis of information received from Member States was conducted at a facility directly across the Tigris River from Tarmiya, the primary production-scale EMIS uranium enrichment plant. The inspection, which was unannounced, showed the facility to be a water purification plant which had been Iraq's largest producer of bottled drinking water. The facility was closed down in 1994 owing to a lack of process chemicals and of materials for making plastic bottles.

30. The level of practical cooperation by Iraqi counterparts in facilitating the carrying out of IAEA field activities continues to be high. The Iraqi personnel accompanying IAEA inspectors are usually punctual and helpful, and have been effective in locating the appropriate contact persons at facilities being inspected. Similarly, the facility personnel have proved willing and effective in providing materials and services required for the installation of video surveillance systems.

C. Provision of information by Iraq

31. Since the acceptance by Iraq, on 26 November 1993, of its obligations under Security Council resolution 715 (1991), Iraq has made three semi-annual declarations of, *inter alia*, the inventories of all facilities, installations and sites where nuclear activities of any kind have been or are carried out, or which are suitable for carrying out such activities, and of all material, equipment and items in Iraq identified in Annex 3 of the Plan.

32. To facilitate the preparation of these declarations, the IAEA prepared a series of forms (with detailed guidance for their completion) setting out the information requirements (detailed in paragraph 22 and Annex 2 of the Plan) with respect to: facilities, installations and sites; nuclear and non-nuclear material; equipment, isotopes, and existing and proposed programmes of nuclear activities. These forms have since been revised and reproduced in computer database format, which has led to significantly improved efficiency both in Iraq's production of the required declarations and in their evaluation by the IAEA.

33. In ongoing discussions the IAEA is seeking Iraq's cooperation in improving the quality and completeness of this information and particularly in producing a consolidated declaration which will bring together all of the information provided in the three semi-annual declarations. Iraq has given an assurance that the necessary work is in progress and has also agreed to provide computer-generated site and building plans to improve the quality of the drawings so far provided.

D. Release, relocation and change of use of equipment, materials and facilities

34. Requests for the release of—or for permission to relocate—equipment and material are processed in consultation with the Special Commission, as are requests for permission to change the use of monitored buildings. Items for which release, relocation or change of use is approved remain subject to ongoing monitoring and verification at a frequency commensurate with their significance.

E. Nuclear material accountancy

35. As previously reported, all weapons-usable nuclear material has been removed from Iraq—the final shipment, to the Russian Federation, having taken place in February 1994. This material, which comprises the fresh and irradiated fuel from the Tuwaitha research reactors and had been subject to routine verification under the safeguards agreement with Iraq, is fully accounted for and is under IAEA safeguards at its storage location in the Russian Federation. The irradiated fuel removed from Iraq has been reprocessed, and the recovered uranium has been mixed with natural uranium to reduce its enrichment in uranium 235 to less than 20%. The nuclear material remaining in Iraq comprises 1.8 tonnes of low-enriched uranium, 6 tonnes of depleted uranium and 540 tonnes of natural uranium, in a variety of physical and chemical forms, in sealed storage under IAEA control. The IAEA has carried out a detailed assessment of Iraq's procurement, production and usage of nuclear material and, taking into account the declared usage, considers that the inventory is correct, within the normal limits of accuracy.

F. *Data analysis and processing centre*

36. Over a year ago the IAEA established a Data Analysis and Processing Centre to support its ongoing activities in Iraq. This Centre maintains a computerised information system for the management, analysis and retrieval of information. The databases which make up the computerised information system contain—*inter alia*–textual, photographic and sensor data collected during inspections, data obtained from a variety of open sources, seized Iraqi documents, information provided by Member States, overhead imagery, Iraqi declarations, and other data on projects and sites in Iraq. The system, which currently contains the equivalent of some twenty thousand pages of text, is used in the preparation and support of field activities and provides the capability to record, process, search and retrieve data both at Headquarters and in the field. The data cover all relevant activities, facilities, materials and equipment known to exist in Iraq.

37. Information from Member States, overhead imagery, taken by U-2 and helicopter-based cameras (obtained and interpreted with the assistance and cooperation of the Special Commission), environmental monitoring data, and information gathered from inspections, are analyzed and correlated to identify sites which should be further investigated.

V. *Mechanism for monitoring exports and imports*

38. In paragraph 7 of resolution 715 (1991), the Security Council requested the "Committee established under resolution 661 (1990)", 6/ the Special Commission and the Director General of the IAEA "to develop in cooperation a mechanism for monitoring any future sales or supplies by other countries to Iraq of items relevant to the implementation of section C of resolution 687 (1991) and other relevant resolutions, including the present resolution and the plans approved hereunder".

39. The export/import monitoring mechanism is an important element of the Plan for ongoing monitoring and verification of Iraq's undertaking not to acquire proscribed nuclear weapons capabilities. Such monitoring is of indefinite duration and is to continue until the Security Council decides that it should be terminated.

40. To develop this mechanism, the Special Commission and the IAEA held a number of informal consultations with the Sanctions Committee and a group of international experts. On 15 February 1995, a report setting out the envisaged mechanism was formally submitted to the Sanctions Committee for its consideration and approval and for subsequent transmission to the Security Council.

VI. *Revision of Annex 3 of the Plan*

41. Before submitting to the Security Council the tripartite proposal referred to in Section V above, the Sanctions Committee expressed the opinion that a more detailed list of items to be reported under the export/import monitoring mechanism should be developed.

42. Accordingly, the IAEA has, in consultation with international experts in export control, revised Annex 3 of the Plan. Under cover of a letter dated 17 March 1995, the Director General transmitted the revised Annex 3 to the United Nations Secretary-General for translation and subsequent presentation to the Security Council. 7/ The revised Annex 3 will also be made available to the Sanctions Committee for its information.

43. The revision of Annex 3 of the Plan had three main objectives:

(a) *The identification of items prohibited to Iraq under paragraph 12 of resolution 687 (1991):*

The Plan provides that the existence in Iraq of any items in this category must be declared by Iraq. Pursuant to paragraph 12 of resolution 687, the IAEA may dispose of such items through destruction, removal or rendering harmless as appropriate. The transfer to Iraq of any item in this category and of technology directly associated with—or required for—the development, production or use of the item is prohibited. The prohibited items also include some of the dual-use commodities listed in the Annexes of the "Guidelines for Transfers of Nuclear-Related Dual-Use Equipment, Material, and Related Technology" 8/.

(b) *The identification of items which are directly relevant to research and development activities in the area of peaceful applications of nuclear energy and which are not prohibited to Iraq under paragraph 12 of resolution 687 (1991):*

Such items—which include nuclear materials, dedicated-use nuclear equipment, research and power reactors and components thereof, nuclear-fuel-cycle-related plants, components thereof and related technology—must be declared by Iraq to the IAEA under the provisions of the Plan. While resolution 687 (1991) does not prohibit the conduct of non-weapons-related nuclear activities by Iraq, paragraph 3 (vi) of resolution 707 (1991) currently restricts nuclear activities in Iraq to the "use of isotopes for medical,

6/ Referred to as the Sanctions Committee.
7/ The IAEA may, after informing the Security Council, revise the Annexes of the Plan in the light of information and experience gained in the implementation of resolutions 687 and 707 and of the Plan.
8/ See IAEA documents INFCIRC/254/Rev.1/Part 1 (issued in July 1992), INFCIRC/254/Rev.1/Part 2 (issued in July 1992), and INFCIR C/254/Rev.1/Part 1/Mod.2, (issued in April 1994).

agricultural or industrial purposes". This restriction is to remain operative until such time as "the Security Council determines that Iraq is in full compliance with this resolution [707 (1991)] and paragraphs 12 and 13 of resolution 687 (1991), and the IAEA determines that Iraq is in full compliance with its safeguards agreement with the Agency".

Until the restriction is lifted, the transfer to Iraq of items in this category is prohibited—except for those items related to the non-proscribed nuclear applications in medicine, agriculture and industry. Items in this category which are located in Iraq are controlled by the IAEA under its Plan to verify Iraq's compliance with this restriction. When the restriction is lifted, such items will be released for use by Iraq, their use being monitored under the Plan.

The transfer to Iraq of items for use in non-proscribed nuclear activities (i.e. the use of isotopes for medical, agricultural or industrial purposes) continues to be circumscribed by the sanctions imposed on Iraq by the Security Council in resolutions 661 (1990) and 670 (1991).

(c) *The identification of dual-use material, equipment and related technology which could be of significant value in the pursuit of a nuclear weapons programme or of nuclear fuel cycle activities prohibited under resolution 687 (1991):*

As indicated in sub-paragraph (a) above, some such items are prohibited to Iraq, notwithstanding their dual-use nature. Non-prohibited dual-use items present in Iraq at the end of the Gulf war are required to be declared to the IAEA under the Plan and their use is monitored by the IAEA. Until the sanctions provided for in resolutions 661 (1990) and 670 (1990) are lifted, the transfer to Iraq of dual-use items for essential civilian needs is regulated by the sanction. Subsequently, it will be covered by the export/import monitoring mechanism.

VII. *Resumption of technical assistance and cooperation in areas not prohibited by Security Council resolutions*

44. As indicated in the previous report on the implementation of the Plan, the IAEA has agreed to examine the extent to which technical assistance and cooperation might be accommodated within the constraints of the relevant Security Council resolutions. In so doing the IAEA took into account the practice followed by other United Nations organizations in securing the concurrence of the Sanctions Committee with the provi-

sion to Iraq of assistance which involves the transfer of funds, equipment or material.

45. The IAEA has identified five technical assistance projects approved by the Board of the Governors which, in the view of the IAEA, fall outside the proscription of the conduct of nuclear activities by Iraq imposed by resolutions 687 (1991) and 707 (1991). Of the five projects, three relate to agriculture (mutation techniques for crop protection; immunoassay techniques for rinderpest diagnosis; improvement of soil fertility) and two relate to nuclear medicine (rehabilitation of nuclear medicine services; rehabilitation of radiotherapy services for cancer).

46. As these projects involve the provision by the IAEA of experts, equipment and fellowships and—in two cases—the funding of visits by Iraqi scientists to foreign laboratories, the IAEA has requested, and recently received from, the Sanctions Committee its concurrence that the provision of the assistance in question falls within the limited exceptions to the sanctions provided for in resolution 661 (1990) and for approval of the start of project implementation.

VI. *Summary and conclusions*

47. As indicated in the previous six-month report, the IAEA is confident that the essential components of Iraq's clandestine nuclear programme have been identified and have been destroyed, removed or rendered harmless and that the scope of the past programme is well understood. This assessment is based not only on the verification of Iraqi statements, which may be presumed to be biased and incomplete, but also on information gathered during inspections, on information provided by suppliers and Member States and, to a great extent, on an analysis of the large cache of original Iraqi documentation which was seized in Iraq by the teams of the sixth and seventh IAEA inspection missions. Despite the absence in this cache of original Iraqi documentation regarding its gas centrifuge programme and the suspected withholding by Iraq of some documents from the cache, the areas of residual uncertainty, regarding Iraq's former nuclear weapons programme, have been progressively reduced to a level of detail, the full knowledge of which is not likely to affect the overall picture.

48. The IAEA's extensive knowledge of the scope of Iraq's past nuclear weapons programme has facilitated the design and implementation of a credible and sustainable plan for the ongoing monitoring and verification of Iraq's compliance with its obligations under the relevant Security Council resolutions.

49. The Plan has been operational since the end of August 1994, when the continuous presence of IAEA inspectors in Iraq—the Nuclear Monitoring Group—was established. The refurbishing and modification of the

Canal Hotel in Baghdad to accommodate the Baghdad Monitoring and Verification Centre is practically complete and the Centre provides adequate facilities for the implementation of the Plan.

50. During the period under review the Nuclear Monitoring Group has conducted more than 160 inspectors at some 70 facilities, including 23 facilities not previously inspected.

51. A number of requests for the release, relocation and change of use of equipment material and facilities, to be used in non-nuclear activities, have been approved, with the concurrence of the Special Commission and in compliance with the provisions of paragraph 3 (iii) of Security Council resolution 707 (1991).

52. Progress has been made in developing the export/import monitoring mechanism called for in paragraph 7 of resolution 715 (1991) to monitor any future sale or supply to Iraq of items relevant to the implementation of section C of resolution 687 (1991), to the temporary restriction on nuclear activities in Iraq pursuant to paragraph 3 (iv) of resolution 707 (1991) and to the Plan approved in resolution 715 (1991).

53. At the suggestion of the Sanctions Committee and in accordance with the procedures for amending the Annexes provided for in the Plan, the IAEA has revised

Annex 3 thereof with the assistance of international experts on export control. The revised version reflects the need to provide customs and export control authorities with a more detailed description of items subject to notification.

54. The Plan provided a sound basis for the ongoing monitoring and verification of Iraq's compliance with the requirements of the relevant Security Council resolutions in the area of nuclear weapons and will continue to be developed as technical needs arise and as advanced technologies become available.

55. The implementation of the Plan does not foreclose the exercise by the IAEA of its right to investigate any aspect of Iraq's former nuclear weapons programme. Indeed, vigorous exercise of the right—provided in the Plan—to immediate, unconditional and unrestricted access to any and all areas, facilities, equipment, records and means of transportation represents an important confidence-building measure.

56. Recent information made available through the media suggesting the existence of a secret project which, *prima facie*, could be related to a nuclear weapons programme, requires further investigation to verify its authenticity.

Document 207

Security Council resolution concerning sales of Iraqi petroleum and petroleum products

S/RES/986 (1995), 14 April 1995

The Security Council,

Recalling its previous relevant resolutions,

Concerned by the serious nutritional and health situation of the Iraqi population, and by the risk of a further deterioration in this situation,

Convinced of the need as a temporary measure to provide for the humanitarian needs of the Iraqi people until the fulfilment by Iraq of the relevant Security Council resolutions, including notably resolution 687 (1991) of 3 April 1991, allows the Council to take further action with regard to the prohibitions referred to in resolution 661 (1990) of 6 August 1990, in accordance with the provisions of those resolutions,

Convinced also of the need for equitable distribution of humanitarian relief to all segments of the Iraqi population throughout the country,

Reaffirming the commitment of all Member States to the sovereignty and territorial integrity of Iraq,

Acting under Chapter VII of the Charter of the United Nations,

1. *Authorizes* States, notwithstanding the provisions of paragraphs 3 (a), 3 (b) and 4 of resolution 661 (1990) and subsequent relevant resolutions, to permit the import of petroleum and petroleum products originating in Iraq, including financial and other essential transactions directly relating thereto, sufficient to produce a sum not exceeding a total of one billion United States dollars every 90 days for the purposes set out in this resolution and subject to the following conditions:

(a) Approval by the Committee established by resolution 661 (1990), in order to ensure the transparency of each transaction and its conformity with the other provisions of this resolution, after submission of an application by the State concerned, endorsed by the Government of Iraq, for each proposed purchase of Iraqi petroleum and petroleum products, including details of the purchase price at fair market value, the export route, the opening of a letter of credit payable to the escrow account to be established by the Secretary-General for the purposes of this resolution, and of any other directly related financial or other essential transaction;

(b) Payment of the full amount of each purchase of Iraqi petroleum and petroleum products directly by the purchaser in the State concerned into the escrow account to be established by the Secretary-General for the purposes of this resolution;

2. *Authorizes* Turkey, notwithstanding the provisions of paragraphs 3 (a), 3 (b) and 4 of resolution 661 (1990) and the provisions of paragraph 1 above, to permit the import of petroleum and petroleum products originating in Iraq sufficient, after the deduction of the percentage referred to in paragraph 8 (c) below for the Compensation Fund, to meet the pipeline tariff charges, verified as reasonable by the independent inspection agents referred to in paragraph 6 below, for the transport of Iraqi petroleum and petroleum products through the Kirkuk-Yumurtalik pipeline in Turkey authorized by paragraph 1 above;

3. *Decides* that paragraphs 1 and 2 of this resolution shall come into force at 00.01 Eastern Standard Time on the day after the President of the Council has informed the members of the Council that he has received the report from the Secretary-General requested in paragraph 13 below, and shall remain in force for an initial period of 180 days unless the Council takes other relevant action with regard to the provisions of resolution 661 (1990);

4. *Further decides* to conduct a thorough review of all aspects of the implementation of this resolution 90 days after the entry into force of paragraph 1 above and again prior to the end of the initial 180 day period, on receipt of the reports referred to in paragraphs 11 and 12 below, and *expresses its intention*, prior to the end of the 180 day period, to consider favourably renewal of the provisions of this resolution, provided that the reports referred to in paragraphs 11 and 12 below indicate that those provisions are being satisfactorily implemented;

5. *Further decides* that the remaining paragraphs of this resolution shall come into force forthwith;

6. *Directs* the Committee established by resolution 661 (1990) to monitor the sale of petroleum and petroleum products to be exported by Iraq via the Kirkuk-Yumurtalik pipeline from Iraq to Turkey and from the Mina al-Bakr oil terminal, with the assistance of independent inspection agents appointed by the Secretary-General, who will keep the Committee informed of the amount of petroleum and petroleum products exported from Iraq after the date of entry into force of paragraph 1 of this resolution, and will verify that the purchase price of the petroleum and petroleum products is reasonable in the light of prevailing market conditions, and that, for the purposes of the arrangements set out in this resolution, the larger share of the petroleum and petroleum products is shipped via the Kirkuk-Yumurtalik pipeline and the remainder is exported from the Mina al-Bakr oil terminal;

7. *Requests* the Secretary-General to establish an escrow account for the purposes of this resolution, to appoint independent and certified public accountants to audit it, and to keep the Government of Iraq fully informed;

8. *Decides* that the funds in the escrow account shall be used to meet the humanitarian needs of the Iraqi population and for the following other purposes, and *requests* the Secretary-General to use the funds deposited in the escrow account:

(a) To finance the export to Iraq, in accordance with the procedures of the Committee established by resolution 661 (1990), of medicine, health supplies, foodstuffs, and materials and supplies for essential civilian needs, as referred to in paragraph 20 of resolution 687 (1991) provided that:

(i) Each export of goods is at the request of the Government of Iraq;

(ii) Iraq effectively guarantees their equitable distribution, on the basis of a plan submitted to and approved by the Secretary-General, including a description of the goods to be purchased;

(iii) The Secretary-General receives authenticated confirmation that the exported goods concerned have arrived in Iraq;

(b) To complement, in view of the exceptional circumstances prevailing in the three Governorates mentioned below, the distribution by the Government of Iraq of goods imported under this resolution, in order to ensure an equitable distribution of humanitarian relief to all segments of the Iraqi population throughout the country, by providing between 130 million and 150 million United States dollars every 90 days to the United Nations Inter-Agency Humanitarian Programme operating within the sovereign territory of Iraq in the three northern Governorates of Dihouk, Arbil and Suleimaniyeh, except that if less than one billion United States dollars' worth of petroleum or petroleum products is sold during any 90 day period, the Secretary-General may provide a proportionately smaller amount for this purpose;

(c) To transfer to the Compensation Fund the same percentage of the funds deposited in the escrow account as that decided by the Council in paragraph 2 of resolution 705 (1991) of 15 August 1991;

(d) To meet the costs to the United Nations of the independent inspection agents and the certified public accountants and the activities associated with implementation of this resolution;

(e) To meet the current operating costs of the Special Commission, pending subsequent payment in full of the costs of carrying out the tasks authorized by section C of resolution 687 (1991);

(f) To meet any reasonable expenses, other than expenses payable in Iraq, which are determined by the Committee established by resolution 661 (1990) to be directly related to the export by Iraq of petroleum and petroleum products permitted under paragraph 1 above or to the export to Iraq, and activities directly necessary therefor, of the parts and equipment permitted under paragraph 9 below;

(g) To make available up to 10 million United States dollars every 90 days from the funds deposited in the escrow account for the payments envisaged under paragraph 6 of resolution 778 (1992) of 2 October 1992;

9. *Authorizes* States to permit, notwithstanding the provisions of paragraph 3 (c) of resolution 661 (1990):

(a) The export to Iraq of the parts and equipment which are essential for the safe operation of the Kirkuk-Yumurtalik pipeline system in Iraq, subject to the prior approval by the Committee established by resolution 661 (1990) of each export contract;

(b) Activities directly necessary for the exports authorized under subparagraph (a) above, including financial transactions related thereto;

10. *Decides* that, since the costs of the exports and activities authorized under paragraph 9 above are precluded by paragraph 4 of resolution 661 (1990) and by paragraph 11 of resolution 778 (1991) from being met from funds frozen in accordance with those provisions, the cost of such exports and activities may, until funds begin to be paid into the escrow account established for the purposes of this resolution, and following approval in each case by the Committee established by resolution 661 (1990), exceptionally be financed by letters of credit, drawn against future oil sales the proceeds of which are to be deposited in the escrow account;

11. *Requests* the Secretary-General to report to the Council 90 days after the date of entry into force of paragraph 1 above, and again prior to the end of the initial 180 day period, on the basis of observation by United Nations personnel in Iraq, and on the basis of consultations with the Government of Iraq, on whether Iraq has ensured the equitable distribution of medicine, health supplies, foodstuffs, and materials and supplies for essential civilian

needs, financed in accordance with paragraph 8 (a) above, including in his reports any observations he may have on the adequacy of the revenues to meet Iraq's humanitarian needs, and on Iraq's capacity to export sufficient quantities of petroleum and petroleum products to produce the sum referred to in paragraph 1 above;

12. *Requests* the Committee established by resolution 661 (1990), in close coordination with the Secretary-General, to develop expedited procedures as necessary to implement the arrangements in paragraphs 1, 2, 6, 8, 9 and 10 of this resolution and to report to the Council 90 days after the date of entry into force of paragraph 1 above and again prior to the end of the initial 180 day period on the implementation of those arrangements;

13. *Requests* the Secretary-General to take the actions necessary to ensure the effective implementation of this resolution, authorizes him to enter into any necessary arrangements or agreements, and *requests* him to report to the Council when he has done so;

14. Decides that petroleum and petroleum products subject to this resolution shall while under Iraqi title be immune from legal proceedings and not be subject to any form of attachment, garnishment or execution, and that all States shall take any steps that may be necessary under their respective domestic legal systems to assure this protection, and to ensure that the proceeds of the sale are not diverted from the purposes laid down in this resolution;

15. *Affirms* that the escrow account established for the purposes of this resolution enjoys the privileges and immunities of the United Nations;

16. *Affirms* that all persons appointed by the Secretary-General for the purpose of implementing this resolution enjoy privileges and immunities as experts on mission for the United Nations in accordance with the Convention on the Privileges and Immunities of the United Nations, and *requires* the Government of Iraq to allow them full freedom of movement and all necessary facilities for the discharge of their duties in the implementation of this resolution;

17. *Affirms* that nothing in this resolution affects Iraq's duty scrupulously to adhere to all of its obligations concerning servicing and repayment of its foreign debt, in accordance with the appropriate international mechanisms;

18. *Also affirms* that nothing in this resolution should be construed as infringing the sovereignty or territorial integrity of Iraq;

19. *Decides* to remain seized of the matter.

Document 208

Letter from the Director General of the IAEA concerning implementation by the IAEA of the plan for the destruction, removal or rendering harmless of items listed in paragraph 12 of Security Council resolution 687 (1991)

S/1995/481, 13 June 1995

Note by the Secretary-General

The Secretary-General has the honour to transmit to the members of the Security Council the attached communication, dated 13 June 1995, which he has received from the Director General of the International Atomic Energy Agency (IAEA).

Annex

Letter dated 13 June 1995 from the Director General of the International Atomic Energy Agency addressed to the Secretary-General

Security Council resolution 699 (1991), approved on 17 June 1991, requests, *inter alia*, the Secretary-General to submit to the Security Council progress reports on the implementation of the plan for the destruction, removal or rendering harmless of the items specified in paragraph 12 of resolution 687 (1991). Such reports are to be submitted every six months after the adoption of resolution 699 (1991). The next report is therefore due on 17 June 1995.

During the period under review, from 17 December 1994 to 17 June 1995, no development is to be reported relevant to the destruction, removal or rendering harmless of the items specified in paragraph 12 of resolution 687 (1991), nor in any other area of IAEA's activities in Iraq beyond what was reported to the Council in document S/1995/287 of 11 April 1995.

The implementation of the IAEA's ongoing monitoring and verification plan continues. A detailed report on these activities will be submitted, as requested in resolution 715 (1991), by 17 October 1995.

Kindly bring the content of this letter to the attention of the Council.

(Signed) Hans BLIX

Document 209

Letter dated 1 June 1995 from the Secretary-General to the President of the Security Council concerning resolution 986 (1995)

S/1995/495, 19 June 1995

I have the honour to refer to paragraph 13 of Security Council resolution 986 (1995) by which the Council requested me to take the actions necessary to ensure the effective implementation of that resolution and to report to it when I had done so.

On 15 May 1995 I received His Excellency Mr. Mohammed Al-Sahaf, Minister for Foreign Affairs of Iraq, who informed me that his Government would not implement resolution 986 (1995) because it objected, *inter alia*, to the proportion of petroleum to be exported via the Kirkuk-Yumurtalik pipeline and to the modalities for distribution of humanitarian relief in three northern governorates. I expressed my regret at that decision and urged the Government to reconsider it. I also stated the Secretariat's readiness to enter into discussions with Iraq on practical arrangements for implementing the resolution.

After undertaking a thorough review of the steps required to implement the resolution, I have concluded that cooperation from the Government of Iraq is an essential prerequisite. I believe it appropriate, therefore, to postpone preparation of the report required of me under paragraph 13 of resolution 986 (1995) until further progress has been made in discussions on the subject with Iraq.

I would be grateful if you would bring this information to the attention of the members of the Security Council.

(Signed) Boutros BOUTROS-GHALI

Document 210

Ninth report of the Executive Chairman of UNSCOM

S/1995/494, 20 June 1995

Note by the Secretary-General

The Secretary-General has the honour to transmit to the Security Council a report submitted by the Executive Chairman of the Special Commission established by the Secretary-General pursuant to paragraph 9 (b) (i) of Security Council resolution 687 (1991).

Annex
Ninth report of the Executive Chairman of the Special Commission established by the Secretary-General pursuant to paragraph 9 (b) (i) of Security Council resolution 687 (1991), on the activities of the Special Commission

I. *Introduction*

1. The present report is the ninth on the activities of the Special Commission established by the Secretary-General pursuant to paragraph 9 (b) (i) of Security Council resolution 687 (1991), submitted to the Council by the Executive Chairman of the Special Commission. It is the eighth such report provided in accordance with paragraph 3 of Security Council resolution 699 (1991). It covers the period from 10 December 1994 to 16 June 1995, and is further to reports contained in documents S/23165, S/23268, S/24108 and Corr.1, S/24984, S/25977, S/26910, S/1994/750 and S/1994/1422 and Add.1.

2. The work of the Special Commission in the reporting period has covered the whole range of activities envisaged by section C of Security Council resolution 687 (1991). However, the focus has been to ensure that the Commission is henceforth in a position to monitor Iraq's compliance with its obligations not to use, retain, possess, develop, construct or otherwise acquire those weapon capabilities banned to it under resolution 687 (1991). For the Commission's monitoring to proceed from a comprehensive and accurate base requires that the Commission be able to account, as far as possible, for the disposal or current location of Iraq's capabilities, both past and present, which could be used for banned weapons purposes. Consequently, a large part of the developments to be covered in the present report has already been addressed in the report submitted on 10 April 1995 under Security Council resolution 715 (1991) (S/1995/284).

II. *Developments*

A. *General*

3. The Commission has continued to be extremely active in the period under review. Investigations to elucidate fully all aspects of Iraq's past programmes have continued apace with analytical work being conducted at the Commission's headquarters in New York, inspection and investigation teams being dispatched to Iraq, inquiries on specific matters being addressed to supporting Governments and the responses to those inquiries being fed back into the analytical and investigative work. Seminars with international experts on relevant issues have been convened in New York under the auspices of the Special Commission in order to assist in the analytical process. Further work has been undertaken on the proposal for an export/import monitoring mechanism called for by the Security Council in paragraph 7 of its resolution 715 (1991). This proposal is currently with the Sanctions Committee established under Security Council resolution 661 (1990) for its approval, prior to onward transmission to the Council for adoption. A more detailed assessment of the status of the Commission's work in each area is given below.

4. During the period from 14 to 17 May 1995, the Deputy Executive Chairman of the Special Commission visited Baghdad with a group of chemical weapon experts. The primary purpose of that visit was to address issues arising from the analysis, by the Commission, of Iraq's amended full, final and complete disclosure of its past chemical weapons programmes, submitted on 25 March 1995. Its secondary purpose was to press Iraq to respond to the Commission's concerns relating to Iraq's past biological warfare programme. The mission obtained agreement by Iraq that significant questions did exist and that Iraq would address the chemical issues in written form during the Executive Chairman's next visit to Iraq. On biological matters, Iraq indicated that it could resolve the Commission's concerns, but only after the Commission had agreed that all other areas were closed.

5. Over the period from 29 May to 1 June 1995, the Executive Chairman of the Special Commission visited Baghdad for high-level talks with Iraq. During that time, the Executive Chairman had separate discussions with Iraq's Deputy Prime Minister, Mr. Tariq Aziz, and with the Director of Iraq's Military Industrialization Corporation, General Amer Mohammad Rasheed al

Ubeidi. The aim of the visit was threefold: to continue the high-level dialogue initiated in July 1993; to seek to push forward the process of clarifying outstanding issues, particularly in the biological weapons area; and to prepare, through the discussions, for the writing of the present report. Technical talks were also held on chemical weapons, during which some significant progress was made, and on ballistic missiles. However, Iraq refused to engage in efforts to resolve, with the specialists accompanying the Executive Chairman for that purpose, the biological weapon issues referred to in the Commission's last report of April 1995 to the Council.

6. During the meeting with the Deputy Prime Minister, he stated that Iraq's sole reason for cooperating with the Special Commission and the International Atomic Energy Agency (IAEA) was that it sought reintegration into the international community through the lifting of the sanctions and embargo, that is, through the fulfilment of the terms and implementation of paragraphs 21 and 22 of Security Council resolution 687 (1991), leading to the normalization of relations with Member States. If there were no prospect of such reintegration, it would be difficult for Iraq to justify the expense and the effort involved in such cooperation. However, because Iraq wanted full reintegration into the international community, it was prepared to make the necessary sacrifices as long as there was a prospect that such sacrifices would bear fruit.

7. Mr. Aziz stated that, for Iraq, prospects for the desired reintegration would only look good if the Special Commission and IAEA reported clearly to the Security Council that the essential provisions of Council resolutions 687 (1991) and 715 (1991), that is, those required for the implementation of paragraph 22 of the former resolution, had been implemented. He described those essential provisions as being the elimination of Iraq's weapons of mass destruction and ballistic missiles with a range greater than 150 kilometres and the operation of an effective ongoing monitoring and verification system to ensure Iraq's compliance with its obligations not to reacquire such weapons. At the present stage, Iraq required statements, on the one hand from the Special Commission that the chemical weapons and missile files were closed and the ongoing monitoring and verification system was operational, and on the other from IAEA that the nuclear file was closed. If Iraq thus deemed the prospects of reintegration to be positive, it would be ready in late June 1995 to address to the Special Commission's satisfaction the sole outstanding issue of significance, the biological issue. If the prospects were not good, it would have to assess the situation again.

8. In response to this, the Executive Chairman stated that much had been achieved in the implementation of paragraphs 8 to 10 of Security Council resolution 687 (1991)—indeed, the bulk of what was required. However, those provisions were not confined to the elimination of the named weapons, but also of associated major parts, subsystems and components of such weapons and of facilities for their research, development and production. The latter had, because of Iraq's incomplete and late declarations, taken longer to identify and eliminate than had the weapons. Nevertheless, while there remained a major issue in the biological area concerning the extent of Iraq's past programmes and hence the comprehensiveness of monitoring in the biological area, most of the work was now done. A system of ongoing monitoring and verification was operational in all areas. The export/import monitoring mechanism was available for early adoption and implementation.

9. The Chairman stated that, in the missile and chemical areas, while technical issues remained outstanding, they related more to the level of technical expertise achieved by Iraq or to accounting for components or materials than to weapons themselves or to an operational weapons production capability. Uncertainties arising from such issues (as mentioned in the report to the Security Council contained in document S/1995/284) had been reduced by Iraq during discussions with the Commission. They were no longer significant, in his view, for the evaluation of the fulfilment of the terms of paragraphs 8 to 10 of Security Council resolution 687 (1991), namely the assessment of whether Iraq's proscribed ballistic missile and chemical weapon capabilities had been eliminated and that current dual-purpose capabilities were being adequately monitored. However, he insisted that those issues still needed to be resolved and the Commission would continue to use its rights to do so under the relevant resolutions, the plan for ongoing monitoring and verification and the agreement contained in the Exchange of Letters of 7 and 14 May 1991 between the Secretary-General and the Foreign Minister of Iraq, regardless of what action the Security Council took on the implementation of paragraph 22 of resolution 687 (1991).

10. In that regard, the Executive Chairman welcomed the Deputy Prime Minister's pledge, made in October 1993 and reaffirmed during the meeting, to cooperate with such efforts and with future inspection teams investigating matters relating to past programmes, even after any decision by the Security Council to ease or lift the sanctions and the embargo.

B. *Missiles*

11. As reported in April 1995 (S/1995/284), the Commission has essentially completed the accounting of proscribed ballistic missile capabilities, that is, ballistic

missiles with a range greater than 150 kilometres and related major parts, and repair and production facilities associated with Iraq's past programmes in that area. Furthermore, as also noted in the report, missile monitoring was now operational. Further progress has since been made in the Commission's investigations, in the disposal of certain missile-related items and in clarifying the direction of Iraq's missile research and development efforts. Additional responses to the Commission's requests for information from some former suppliers would be of great assistance in the early completion of the verification process in this area. Investigations will continue until the Commission is satisfied that it has obtained as detailed a picture as possible of all aspects of Iraq's past programmes and current capabilities. However, the Commission considers that final elucidation of these outstanding matters should not materially affect its current assessment, as contained in the conclusions of the present report, of the overall extent of Iraq's past missile programmes.

C. *Chemical weapons*

12. As stated in its reports of June 1994 and April 1995 (S/1994/750 and S/1995/284), the Commission has completed the destruction of Iraq's identified chemical weapon facilities, stockpiles and production equipment and the Commission's chemical monitoring system in Iraq is now operational. Destruction activities were extensive, lasting two years and resulting in the destruction of over 480,000 litres of chemical warfare agents, over 28,000 chemical munitions and nearly 1,800,000 litres, over 1,040,000 kilograms and 648 barrels, of some 45 different precursor chemicals for the production of chemical warfare agents. Ongoing monitoring and verification, together with an effective export/import monitoring mechanism, is designed to preclude Iraq from resuming prohibited chemical activities.

13. The Commission has actively pursued its investigations to clarify those issues raised in the April report: completing the material balance for imported precursors and agent production; accounting for production equipment and munitions; and fully elucidating the extent of Iraq's achievements in research, development and production of the nerve agent VX. In that regard, it has held a seminar in New York of international experts on chemical weapons and, in the absence of documentary evidence from Iraq, has had further contacts with several supporting Governments to obtain verification of the quantities and types of chemical weapon-related items supplied by companies operating in their territories. This has resulted in the receipt of a large number of documents, which the Commission is continuing to analyse. The discussions held at Baghdad in May 1995 with Iraqi experts and inspection activities since the April report have provided more information and led to some important clarifications.

14. Iraq, at the Commission's request, has provided additional information on its procurement and disposition of precursor chemicals acquired for VX production and the reason for the cancellation of the project. This included original documentary evidence to support Iraq's declarations concerning its procurement of certain precursor chemicals. It also included details of the location of the sites at which Iraq disposed of one of the three key VX precursor chemicals, which enabled the Commission's resident chemical monitoring group to verify the Iraqi account. By taking samples at the sites concerned, the group verified that quantities of the pure chemical were indeed present and that the size of the pits in which the chemical was buried was consistent, in general terms, with the quantities of the chemical Iraq declared to be buried there. Iraq also gave the Commission information, pertaining to the second VX precursor, that the chemical monitoring group will verify in the coming weeks in order to confirm the disposition of the major portion of Iraq's declared imports of the precursor. On other issues related to the VX project, Iraq has promised that it will continue its efforts to obtain facts that will enable the Commission to verify Iraq's account. It has followed up on this undertaking and is continuing to send more information to the Commission.

15. During the discussions in May 1995, the Commission received additional information on quantities of various munitions acquired by Iraq and the purpose for their acquisition, particularly as it related to the chemical weapon programme. Iraq reaffirmed in writing that all of the munition types investigated by the Commission in relation to the chemical weapon programme were indeed acquired solely for chemical-fill purposes. While accounting fully for such munitions remains an important task, in the light of the Commission's current knowledge of the disposition of Iraq's stocks of chemical agents and their precursors, the significance of the issue of empty munitions in terms of chemical warfare capabilities is much diminished. Iraq further stated that it would address, in the framework of future biological discussions, the Commission's concern that these munitions might be or might have been used for the weaponization of biological warfare agents.

16. The Commission is now confident that it has a good overall picture of the extent of Iraq's past chemical weapons capabilities and that the essential elements of it have been destroyed. Remaining issues, which centre by and large on verification of Iraq's revised declarations, can be resolved satisfactorily given continued cooperation on the part of Iraq and assistance from supporting

Governments on supplies to Iraq. These issues will be pursued until the Commission considers that all avenues for investigation have been exhausted.

D. *Biological weapons*

17. The situation in the biological area remains blocked by Iraq's refusal to address the Commission's concerns. The evidence available to the Commission establishes that Iraq obtained or sought to obtain all the items and materials required to produce biological warfare agents in Iraq. With Iraq's failure to account for all those items and material for legitimate purposes, the only conclusion that can be drawn is that there is a high risk that Iraq purchased them and used them at least in part for proscribed purposes—the production of agents for biological weapons. Indeed, since the Commission's last report to the Security Council, it has received additional documentary evidence from supporting Governments that lends further weight to that conclusion. While all the elements of the system for biological monitoring are in place and monitoring is proceeding, the Commission cannot be certain that monitoring is comprehensive in coverage because it has been unable to obtain a credible account of Iraq's past military biological activities.

18. Since April 1995, Iraq has responded to the Commission's concerns in that regard only by assuring the Commission that Iraq could be prepared to address the matter in late June 1995. In the meantime, Iraq has stated that it is not responding to the Commission's questions concerning the scope of Iraq's military biological activities or any other issue relating to Iraq's proscribed biological programme. This has had the additional detrimental effect of delaying the completion of investigations and assessments of certain missile and chemical issues. Iraq's failure to account for its military biological programme leaves one of its essential obligations unfulfilled.

E. *National implementation measures*

19. There have been no new developments since the Commission's report in April 1995 regarding the national implementation measures Iraq is required to take under the plans for ongoing monitoring and verification. Iraq's anticipated enactment of those measures in the course of April has not materialized. The Commission will continue to pursue the matter and to press for the adoption of the necessary legislation so that this positive development can be reported to the Council.

F. *Aerial inspections*

20. The Commission's aerial inspection assets, the high-altitude surveillance aircraft (U2) and the Baghdad-based Aerial Inspection Team, continue to make an important contribution to the overall effort to ensure that all relevant activities and facilities within Iraq are encompassed by the monitoring regime.

21. Both assets continue to conduct aerial surveillance of sites under monitoring in Iraq and designated sites, at the direction of the Commission. Experts from the resident monitoring teams accompany the team in order to assist it in focusing on particular areas of relevance at sites. The results obtained from aerial missions are an important part of the overall inspection process in Iraq.

22. As at the end of May 1995, 250 missions have been undertaken by the U2 and 580 missions by the Aerial Inspection Team.

G. *Baghdad Monitoring and Verification Centre*

23. A full description of the status of the Centre is contained in paragraphs 123 to 127 of the April report. In addition, on 30 May 1995, the Executive Chairman of the Special Commission inaugurated the biological room in the Centre and, in May and June, the security camera system was upgraded. All of the Centre's planned facilities are now operational.

H. *Export/import mechanism*

24. As stated in the April report, a proposal for a mechanism, required under paragraph 7 of Security Council resolution 715 (1991), to monitor the sales to Iraq by other countries of dual-purpose items has been prepared and submitted jointly by the Special Commission and IAEA to the Sanctions Committee established pursuant to Security Council resolution 661 (1990) for the latter's consideration. The Committee has twice considered the proposal since it was resubmitted in February 1995, but, while it appears that there is no objection to the text and that all delegations have expressed support for the principles contained in it, formal agreement to submit it to the Security Council, in the name of all three bodies as required by resolution 715 (1991), has yet to be reached.

25. In the meantime, the Special Commission has continued its efforts to prepare for the implementation of the mechanism after its adoption by the Council: dedicated software for a transaction-based database is being developed for installation on the Commission's computer network; supporting documents and notification forms have been further refined; a preparatory inspection of Iraq's principal points of entry for traded goods has been undertaken to ensure that the Commission has full knowledge of Iraq's import procedures and facilities; and Iraq's legislation relevant to import and export has been

obtained for study. Through such preparations, the Commission aims to be in a position to implement its obligations under the mechanism immediately upon the Security Council taking appropriate action to adopt the mechanism and to bring it into effect.

III. Conclusions

26. The Government of Iraq has stated that, for it to see value in cooperating with the Special Commission and IAEA, it needed to be convinced that there was a prospect of paragraphs 21 and 22 of Security Council resolution 687 (1991) being implemented. It, therefore, demanded that the Special Commission and IAEA report to the Council that it had met the terms laid down in paragraph 22.

27. The Commission has repeatedly assured Iraq that its endeavours have been directed to bringing about, as soon as possible, a situation where paragraph 22 can be implemented. This, however, requires that the Commission be able to report to the Council that, based on its technical assessment, Iraq has met the requirements of paragraphs 8 to 10 of resolution 687 (1991). The Commission must be satisfied that the proscribed items have been disposed of, that it has as complete a picture as possible of Iraq's past programmes and that a comprehensive system of monitoring is operational.

28. Paragraph 22 states that:

"*The Security Council,*

"...

"*Decides* ... that ... upon Council agreement that Iraq has completed all actions contemplated in paragraphs 8 to 13 above, the prohibitions against the import of commodities and products originating in Iraq and the prohibitions against financial transactions related thereto ... shall have no further force or effect".

The Special Commission is responsible for reporting on the implementation of paragraphs 8 to 10 and the Director-General of IAEA on the implementation of paragraphs 11 to 13. The actions contemplated of Iraq in paragraphs 8 to 10 are as follows:

"8. ... Iraq shall unconditionally accept the destruction, removal, or rendering harmless, under international supervision, of:

(a) All chemical and biological weapons and all stocks of agents and all related subsystems and components and all research, development, support and manufacturing facilities related thereto;

(b) All ballistic missiles with a range greater than one hundred fifty kilometres, and related major parts and repair and production facilities;

"9. ... (*a*) Iraq shall submit to the Secretary-General ... a declaration on the locations, amounts and types of all items specified in paragraph 8 and agree to urgent, on-site inspection ... ;

"9. ... (*b*) (ii) The yielding by Iraq of possession to the Special Commission for destruction, removal or rendering harmless ... of all items specified under paragraph 8 (a), including items at the additional locations designated by the Special Commission ... and the destruction by Iraq, under the supervision of the Special Commission, of all its missile capabilities, including launchers, as specified in paragraph 8 (b);

"...

"10. *Decides further* that Iraq shall unconditionally undertake not to use, develop, construct or acquire any of the items specified in paragraphs 8 and 9, and requests the Secretary-General, in consultation with the Special Commission, to develop a plan for the future ongoing monitoring and verification of Iraq's compliance with the present paragraph ...".

Paragraph 5 of Security Council resolution 715 (1991), itself an elaboration of paragraph 10 of resolution 687 (1991), adds:

"*The Security Council,*

"...

"5. *Demands* that Iraq meet unconditionally all its obligations under the plans [for the future ongoing monitoring and verification of Iraq's compliance with paragraph 10 of resolution 687 (1991)] approved by the present resolution and cooperate fully with the Special Commission ... in carrying out the plans".

29. Clearly, Iraq has not met all these terms, given the absence of credible accounting for its military biological activities. In the ballistic missile and chemical weapon areas, the Commission is now confident that it has a good overall picture of the extent of Iraq's past programmes and that the essential elements of its proscribed capabilities have been disposed of. While there are still some issues to be resolved in those two areas, the uncertainties arising from them do not present a pattern consistent with efforts to conceal a programme to retain acquired proscribed weapons. These remaining issues are not of a magnitude that would affect the assessment as to whether Iraq has completed the substantive actions required of it under paragraphs 8 to 10 of Security Council resolution 687 (1991) to eliminate its proscribed ballistic missile and

chemical weapon and related facilities and to permit effective monitoring of its compliance in those areas.

30. The Commission has pursued, and is continuing to pursue, all means available to it to identify and verify every aspect of Iraq's past programmes. It realizes, however, that conditions have been such, particularly where the acquisition and disposal of items is concerned, that a verified accounting of each and every element of the past programmes is beyond the realm of possibility, given the various hostilities in which Iraq has been engaged and the unilateral actions by Iraq to destroy weapons, equipment, supplies and documentation. The Commission is, however, satisfied that, in the missile and chemical fields, it has achieved such a level of knowledge and understanding of Iraq's past programmes that it can have confidence that Iraq does not now have any significant proscribed capability. It is also confident that the comprehensiveness of its ongoing monitoring and verification activities, while those activities continue, is such that the Commission would detect any attempt to reconstitute a proscribed capability in those areas. Verification of the latest information obtained by the Commission in the missile and chemical fields can be carried out satisfactorily during the Commission's ongoing monitoring and verification operations, using the rights and privileges available to it under the relevant resolutions, the Exchange of Letters and the plan for ongoing monitoring and verification. As noted in paragraph 10 above, the Commission welcomes Iraq's pledge to cooperate with these efforts, even after any decision by the Security Council to ease or lift the sanctions and the embargo.

31. As regards paragraph 10 of resolution 687 (1991), it will be recalled that, by identical letters of 6 April 1991 to the Secretary-General and to the President of the Security Council (S/22456), Iraq indicated its acceptance of that resolution, and by further identical letters of 11 June 1991 to the same addressees (S/22689), Iraq confirmed that it had unconditionally undertaken not to use, develop, construct or acquire any of the items specified in the resolution. By a letter dated 26 November 1993 from the Minister for Foreign Affairs to the President of the Council (S/26811), the Government of Iraq stated that it had decided to accept the obligations set forth in resolution 715 (1991) and to comply with the provisions of the plans for monitoring and verification as contained therein.

32. On 7 October and again on 15 December 1994 (see S/1994/1138 and Corr.1 and S/1994/1422), the Commission reported to the Council that the ongoing monitoring and verification system was provisionally operational and that testing of the system had begun. In its report to the Council of 10 April 1995 (S/1995/284), it reported that the elements of ongoing monitoring and verification were now in place and the system was operational and that it had received full cooperation from Iraq in setting up and operation of the monitoring system. To ensure the comprehensiveness of the system as far as Iraq's obligations are concerned, Iraq needs to respond satisfactorily to the Commission's concerns regarding its past biological weapons programme. Furthermore, as the plan for ongoing monitoring and verification notes (S/22871/Rev.1, para. 10), the efficacy of the provisions of the plan will be enhanced when they are complemented by an export/import monitoring mechanism that combines transparency with timely information on future sales or supplies to Iraq of relevant dual-use items. Presently, the Commission is satisfied that Iraq's cooperation in carrying out the monitoring plan has been of a degree that satisfies the provisions of paragraph 5 of Security Council resolution 715 (1991).

Document 211

Follow-up to the seventh report of the Director General of the IAEA on the implementation of the Agency's plan for future ongoing monitoring and verification of Iraq's compliance with paragraph 12 of Security Council resolution 687 (1991)

S/1995/604, 21 July 1995

Note by the Secretary-General

The Secretary-General has the honour to transmit to the members of the Security Council the attached communication, dated 17 July 1995, which he has received from the Acting Director General of the International Atomic Energy Agency (IAEA).

Annex
Letter dated 17 July 1995 from the Acting Director General of the International Atomic Energy Agency (IAEA) addressed to the Secretary-General

I refer to section III of the IAEA's seventh semi-annual report (document S/1995/287 dated 11 April 1995) on the implementation of the IAEA's plan for ongoing monitoring and verification of Iraq's compliance with the relevant obligations specified in UNSC resolutions 687 (1991) and 715 (1991).

This section addressed the implications of two, single page, documents which were represented as official Iraqi correspondence, generated in April/May 1994, suggesting the reconstitution of a nuclear weapons programme.

As indicated in paragraph 20 of that report, the IAEA undertook to keep the Security Council informed of the outcome of the IAEA's investigation into this matter.

Accordingly, I am requesting you kindly to transmit the enclosed report on the IAEA's investigation into this matter to the Security Council.

The Director General and his staff are available for any consultations you or the Council may wish to have.
(*Signed*) QIAN JIHUI
Acting Director General

Appendix
Follow-up to the Seventh Report of the Director General of the International Atomic Energy Agency on the Implementation of the Agency's Plan for Ongoing Monitoring and Verification of Iraq's Compliance with Paragraph 12 of United Nations Security Council Resolution 687 (1991)

Section III of the IAEA's seventh semi-annual report (document S/1995/287 dated 11 April 1995) on the implementation of the IAEA's plan for ongoing monitoring and verification of Iraq's compliance with the relevant obligations specified in UNSC resolutions 687 (1991) and 715 (1991), addressed the implications of two, single page, documents which were represented as official Iraqi correspondence, generated in April/May 1994, suggesting the reconstitution of a nuclear weapons programme.

As first indicated in an article published in the London *Sunday Times* on 2 April 1995, the documents had been received by the newspaper in late February from an anonymous sender. Copies of the documents were obtained by the IAEA on 4 April 1995.

As indicated in S/1995/287, the IAEA had initiated an investigation with the aim of determining the authenticity and clarifying the substance of these documents.

On 5 May 1995, as this investigation was nearing completion, an additional set of three documents was received by the IAEA. This second set had been received by a journalist in another Member State around the same time as the first set of documents had been received in the United Kingdom. The second set was clearly related to the same subject and it was quickly determined that both sets originated from the same source.

The task of the IAEA remained unchanged, though somewhat expanded, namely to determine the authenticity of the documents and of the information contained therein—the additional documents providing a broader base on which to make that determination.

The IAEA has now completed its investigation which has entailed a detailed analysis of the form and content of the documents—including their comparison with the extensive database of documents seized in Iraq during the sixth IAEA inspection; an in-depth analysis of current and past correspondence and records provided by Iraq; interviews with Iraqi personnel allegedly involved, or known to have relevant technical competence; interviews with private Iraqi civilians not employed by the Government; interviews with journalists associated with the documents; and the carrying out of on-site inspection activities, including environmental monitoring, using the most sensitive analytical techniques.

Based on the results of these activities and the IAEA's extensive knowledge of Iraq's past programme and present situation, a large number of errors and inconsistencies have been identified in the documents, typified by the following:

- Linguistic correctness and conformity with Iraqi practice:
  These documents contain technical wording which differs from that found in the IAEA's extensive database of seized Iraqi documents and terms which are not in conformance with standard Iraqi usage.

- Conformity of layout and construction of documents with established Iraqi practices:
  The layout of the documents is not consistent with contemporary Iraqi usage. In addition, the documents reveal errors in construction, suggesting poor adaptation of authentic Iraqi documents.

- Scientific validity:
  Some technical elements of the programme, inferred from the documents, have been assessed as unlikely by experts from Nuclear Weapon States. Some of those elements are also inconsistent with available information on the status of Iraq's clandestine programme during the last years of the programme.

- Accuracy:
  Significant inaccuracies in qualifications, titles and names of individuals, as well as in technical and administrative organizational structures, have been clearly established.

The investigation undertaken by the IAEA and the basis for its conclusions have been comprehensively documented. In view, however, of the sensitive nature of the subject and of the process, it is considered prudent to keep this documentation confidential.

As a result of this investigation, the IAEA has reached the conclusion that, on the basis of all evidence available, these documents are not authentic. Furthermore, no credible evidence was found to suggest that the activities reported in these documents were or are being carried out in Iraq.

It should be noted that the IAEA will continue, under its ongoing monitoring and verification plan, to actively pursue any evidence that might point to the conduct of activities proscribed under the relevant Security Council resolutions.

Document 212

Report of the Secretary-General on UNIKOM for the period from 1 April to 30 September 1995

S/1995/836, 2 October 1995

I. *Introduction*

1. The present report gives an account of the activities of the United Nations Iraq-Kuwait Observation Mission (UNIKOM) in pursuance of the mandate entrusted to it by the Security Council in resolutions 687 (1991), 689 (1991) and 806 (1993).

II. *Activities of the United Nations Iraq-Kuwait Observation Mission and the situation in the demilitarized zone*

2. During the period under review, the situation in the demilitarized zone (DMZ) was calm. There were very few violations of the DMZ and those that occurred were minor, mainly overflights by unidentified aircraft. UNIKOM received six formal complaints: two from Iraq and four from Kuwait. None of these could be confirmed.

3. During the fishing season from May to July, Iraqi fishing boats were frequently observed operating close to the shore in Kuwaiti waters. After UNIKOM raised the issue with the Iraqi authorities, this activity diminished greatly.

4. The Kuwaiti authorities erected a barbed-wire fence running parallel to the trench and the berm from the coast to the Abdaly crossing.

5. UNIKOM monitored the DMZ from patrol and observation bases and observation points and through ground and air patrols. It also operated checkpoints and carried out investigations. It maintained liaison with the two sides at all levels. The deployment of UNIKOM is shown on the attached map [not reproduced here].

6. UNIKOM continued to act in coordination with the authorities of Iraq and Kuwait in cases of unauthorized border crossings and when responding to requests to facilitate repatriation. The Mission also exchanged information and closely cooperated on such matters with the Office of the United Nations High Commissioner for Refugees (UNHCR) and the International Committee of the Red Cross (ICRC).

7. At the request of ICRC, UNIKOM provided the venue and support for meetings of the Technical Subcommittee on Military and Civilian Missing Prisoners of War and Mortal Remains on 29 and 30 August and 26 and 27 September 1995.

8. In my last report (S/1995/251, para. 14), I reported the apprehension and detention by the Iraqi authorities of two United States citizens who had mistakenly crossed the border on 13 March 1995. The two men were released on 16 July 1995.

III. *Organizational matters*

9. As of September 1995, the overall strength of UNIKOM was 1,331, as follows:

(a) 244 military observers from Argentina (7), Austria (7), Bangladesh (9), Canada (5), China (15), Denmark (6), Fiji (6), Finland (6), France (15), Ghana (6), Greece (7), Hungary (7), India (6), Indonesia (6), Ireland (7), Italy (6), Kenya (7), Malaysia (7), Nigeria (6), Pakistan (7), Poland (6), Romania (7), the Russian Federation (15), Senegal (6), Singapore (6), Sweden (6), Thailand (6), Turkey (6), the United Kingdom of Great Britain and Northern Ireland (15), the United States of America (15), Uruguay (6) and Venezuela (2);

(b) An infantry battalion of 775 from Bangladesh;

(c) An engineer unit of 50 from Argentina;

(d) A logistics unit of 35 from Denmark;

(e) 227 civilian staff, of whom 80 were recruited internationally.

Major-General Krishna N. S. Thapa (Nepal) continued as Force Commander.

10. UNIKOM was supported by a chartered helicopter and a chartered fixed-wing aircraft. The former is currently being replaced by a unit from Bangladesh.

11. Medical services were provided on a temporary basis by a contractor. Germany has now offered to provide a civilian medical unit. Germany would thus become

a new contributor to UNIKOM. I propose to accept this offer, with the concurrence of the Security Council.

12. The headquarters of UNIKOM remains in Umm Qasr. The Mission also maintains liaison offices in Baghdad and Kuwait City. The latter was moved in March and is now collocated with UNIKOM's support centre in Kuwait City.

IV. *Financial aspects*

13. The General Assembly, by its resolution 49/245 of 12 July 1995, authorized me to enter into commitments for the period ending 30 June 1996 in the amount of $1,811,900 gross ($1,594,100 net) per month, equivalent to one third of the maintenance of UNIKOM, in addition to the two-thirds share of $3,188,100 per month to be met through voluntary contributions from the Government of Kuwait. This authorization is subject to review by the Security Council with regard to the mandate of the Mission. Assessments on Member States have been made for the period ending 31 October 1995 and the Government of Kuwait has paid its voluntary contributions for the period ending 31 October 1995.

14. As at 22 September 1995, unpaid assessed contributions to the Special Account for UNIKOM for the period since the inception of the Mission amounted to $37,283,547. The total unpaid assessed contributions for all peace-keeping operations amounted to $2.4 billion.

V. *Observations*

15. During the period under review, the Iraq-Kuwait border and the DMZ have been generally calm. Through its presence and activities, UNIKOM continued to contribute significantly to the calm that prevailed in the area of operation. In carrying out its tasks, UNIKOM enjoyed the effective cooperation of the Iraqi and Kuwaiti authorities. I recommend that the Mission be maintained.

16. In conclusion, I wish to pay tribute to Major-General Thapa and the men and women under his command for the manner in which they have discharged their responsibilities. Their discipline and bearing have been of a high order, reflecting credit on themselves, on their countries and on the United Nations.

Document 213

Eighth report of the Director General of the IAEA on the implementation of the Agency's plan for future ongoing monitoring and verification of Iraq's compliance with paragraph 12 of resolution 687 (1991)

S/1995/844, 6 October 1995

Note by the Secretary-General

The Secretary-General has the honour to transmit to the members of the Security Council the attached communication, dated 6 October 1995, which he has received from the Director General of the International Atomic Energy Agency (IAEA).

Annex
Letter dated 6 October 1995 from the Director General of the International Atomic Energy Agency to the Secretary-General

Paragraph 8 of resolution 715 (1991), adopted by the Security Council on 11 October 1991, requests the Director General of the International Atomic Energy Agency to submit to the Security Council reports on the implementation of the Agency's plan for future ongoing monitoring and verification of Iraq's compliance with paragraph 12 of resolution 687 (1991). These reports are to be submitted when requested by the Security Council

and, in any event, at least every six months after the adoption of resolution 715.

Accordingly, I am requesting you kindly to transmit to the President of the Security Council the enclosed eighth six-month report on the implementation of the Plan. I remain available for any consultations you or the Council may wish to have.

(*Signed*) Hans BLIX

Appendix
Eighth report of the Director General of the International Atomic Energy Agency on the implementation of the Agency's plan for future ongoing monitoring and verification of Iraq's compliance with paragraph 12 of Resolution 687 (1991)

I. *Introduction*

1. On 11 October 1991, the Security Council adopted resolution 715 (1991) approving, *inter alia*, the

plan submitted in document S/22872/Rev.1 and S/22872/Rev.1/Corr.1 by the Director General of the International Atomic Energy Agency (IAEA) for future ongoing monitoring and verification of Iraq's compliance with paragraph 12 of Part C of Security Council resolution 687 (1991) and with the requirements of paragraphs 3 and 5 of resolution 707 (1991). In paragraph 8 of resolution 715, the Security Council requested the Director General of the IAEA to submit to it reports on the implementation of the plan when requested by the Security Council and, in any event, at least every six months after the adoption of resolution 715.

2. The Director General submits herewith the eighth six-month report 1/ on implementation of the plan for ongoing monitoring and verification related to Iraq's nuclear capabilities (hereinafter referred to as the Plan).

II. *Iraq's past nuclear weapons programme*

3. As indicated in paragraph 12 of the latest report of the Director General to the Security Council, 2/ a detailed analysis of the documents seized in Iraq in September 1991 in the course of the sixth IAEA inspection revealed the absence of documentation concerning the progress of Iraq's covert nuclear programme—Petrochemical Project 3 (PC3)—post-dating the progress report for the period 1 January - 31 May 1990 of the Al Atheer project. This, gave rise to uncertainties regarding PC3 activities in the period which preceded the Gulf war, i.e. between June 1990 and mid-January 1991. Furthermore, none of the seized documents contained information on gas centrifuge enrichment research and development, except for indications that it had been started in mid-1987 with the transfer to gas centrifuge enrichment programme of staff who had been working on gaseous diffusion.

4. Until recently, the Iraqi explanation for the absence of relevant documentation on these two aspects was that the invasion of Kuwait had brought all IAEC activities to a virtual halt and that the centrifuge enrichment project was outside PC3 and its documentation handling would have been separated.

5. As discussed below, recent events have led to the provision by Iraq of hundreds of thousands of pages of documents relating to activities of PC3 and to Iraq's centrifuge enrichment programme, as well as to the other aspects of its covert nuclear weapons programme.

6. Following the arrival in Jordan on 8 August 1995 of General Hussein Kamel, the former Iraqi Minister of Industry and Military Industrialisation, the Director General of the IAEA was invited by the Iraqi Government to come to Baghdad or to send an IAEA delegation in order to receive information concerning Iraq's past nuclear programme, allegedly previously withheld at the instruction of General Hussein Kamel.

7. An IAEA delegation travelled to Baghdad and held talks with the Iraqi authorities from 17 to 20 August. In addition to providing new details on some aspects of their past nuclear programme, Iraqi officials provided information and supporting documents on a hitherto undisclosed project said to have been ordered by General Hussein Kamel shortly after the invasion of Kuwait in August 1990. According to Iraqi officials, the project consisted of a crash programme which was launched in September 1990 to extract and further enrich the highly enriched uranium (HEU) contained in safeguarded research reactor fuel at the Tuwaitha site and thus to accelerate the availability of weapons-grade material for the fabrication of a nuclear device. Had the programme been completed, this operation could have provided enough material for such a device in a shorter time than would have been necessary under Iraq's covert programme to enrich natural uranium.

8. With a view to delaying as long as possible detection by the IAEA of the diversion of the safeguarded fuel, the extraction operation had been ordered to start immediately after the twice-yearly safeguards inspection, the next of which was scheduled for November 1990 and was to be concluded before the next inspection, which was expected to take place six months later. The Iraqi officials stated that the manufacturing, assembling and testing of the equipment needed to extract the uranium from the safeguarded fuel was completed in late January 1991. As it turned out, the extraction process itself was never begun. The damage caused by the coalition air raids on Tuwaitha and other relevant facilities made further work on the project impossible. The first post-war inspection mission in Iraq in May 1991 fully accounted for the safeguarded reactor fuel, confirming that none of the HEU contained in the research reactor fuel was used for the recently declared crash programme.

9. In addition to disclosing the existence and scope of the crash programme, information was provided to the IAEA by Iraq in August 1995 concerning activities of PC3 in the second half of 1990, as well as details on other aspects of their past nuclear programme, as described below:

a. An oral description was given of the progress made by the weaponization team of PC3, responsible for the design and fabrication of nuclear weapons, during the second half of 1990. This included

1/ The Director General has so far submitted seven reports, circulated on 15 April 1992, as S/23813; on 28 October 1992, as S/24722; on 19 April 1993, as S/25621; on 3 November 1993, as S/26685; on 22 April 1994, as S/1994/490; on 10 October 1994, as S/1994/1151; and on 11 April 1995, as S/1995/287, supplemented on 21 July, with S/1995/604.
2/ See document S/1995/287 of 11 April 1995.

an explanation of the contribution by the Al Qa Qaa State Establishment in the development of the implosive package. To substantiate their statements, Iraqi officials provided a copy of the progress report of the weaponization team, covering the period from 1 June 1990 to 7 June 1991, which had been issued on 10 September 1991. This detailed document of 198 pages is particularly important since it relates to a period of time not covered by the documents seized by the sixth IAEA inspection team in September 1991 (see paragraph 3 above). The report, which has already been translated, indicates that work on weaponization in Al Atheer and in Tuwaitha continued through mid-January 1991, and that post-war activities were concentrated on the salvaging of equipment.

b. Iraqi officials finally confirmed, as the IAEA has long believed, that the centrifuge enrichment program had been carried out in the so-called Engineering Design Centre (Rashdiya), located in the northern suburbs of Baghdad, and not in Tuwaitha as previously declared. It was also stated that some limited work had continued, at Rashdiya during 1988/1989 which had led to the successful development of a gas diffusion barrier. This latter activity—said to have been discontinued in 1989—is unlikely to have had any practical consequence for the nuclear weapons programme, but is indicative of the capabilities of Iraqi scientists and engineers and of their perseverance in the face of repeated failures.

10. On 20 August 1995, just prior to the departure of the IAEA delegation from Baghdad, Iraqi authorities announced the discovery of thousands of documents, and several tons of metals and other materials, on a farm said to be owned by the family of General Hussein Kamel. The documents were transferred to the premises of the Baghdad Monitoring and Verification Centre (BMVC), where a joint IAEA/UNSCOM team, composed of linguists and experts in the various disciplines, completed in three weeks an inventory of all of the documents, sorted, according to their subject, into four categories—nuclear, chemical, biological and missiles. The documentary material, which included technical records, drawings, suppliers catalogues and extracts from scientific and technical publications, amounted to some 680,000 pages, of which some 80% related to Iraq's past nuclear programme. After having been inventoried, the nuclear-related documents were removed from the BMVC to IAEA Headquarters in Vienna. In order to facilitate their evaluation all documents are being transferred onto computer compatible media to allow for computer-assisted analysis of the text. The transfer is expected to be completed by the end of October 1995. Although it has not

yet been physically possible to conduct more than a cursory review of these documents, they touch upon many aspects of the covert nuclear weapons programme, including numerous technical reports on the centrifuge enrichment programme which are of particular interest to the IAEA to verify the completeness of the IAEA's knowledge in this area (see paragraph 3 above). 3/

11. The metals and other material were also transported to the BMVC, where samples were taken; analyses to assess their relevance to Iraq's programmes for weapons of mass destruction are now under way.

12. Following the talks in Baghdad the IAEA team travelled to Jordan to meet with General Hussein Kamel. His detailed description of the past covert nuclear weapons programme provided useful information. The possibility of further contacts and discussion was left open.

13. The sheer magnitude of the documentation provided by Iraq makes it impossible, at this stage, to draw definitive conclusions as to their content and implications. It is only possible to say that, of the information which has been reviewed and analysed to date, nothing suggests that a change is warranted in the IAEA's conclusion that Iraq's nuclear weapons programme has been, for all practical purposes, destroyed, removed or rendered harmless.

14. However, it is clear even at this stage that Iraq's crash programme to extract weapons-grade material from safeguarded reactor fuel constitutes an additional violation of its safeguards agreement with the IAEA. Equally, Iraq's failure until now to declare this crash programme and other weapons-related activities and to turn over to the IAEA all nuclear-related documents and materials clearly constitute violations of Iraq's obligations under the relevant Security Council resolutions.

III. *Implementation of the plan*

A. *Inspection activities*

15. As a consequence of the events described in paragraphs 5-14 above, an ad hoc inspection mission—IAEA-28—of IAEA inspectors, assisted by experts in centrifuge and weapon technologies provided by Member States, was sent to Iraq from 9 to 19 September 1995 to follow up on the new information received by the IAEA.

3/ As indicated in paragraph 11 of the previous report to the Council (S/1995/287), the IAEA has never accepted as credible repeated Iraqi statements that no documents relevant to the past nuclear weapons programme, other than those confiscated during IAEA-6, were any longer available as all of them had been destroyed. While the large amount of documents provided by Iraqi authorities on 20 August 1995 proves the corectness of the IAEA confictions, the IAEA continues to be persuaded that complete documentation of Iraq's past nuclear weapons programme still exists somewhere in Iraq. Efforts will therefore continue to obtain access to all documents relevant to the programme, as required under paragraph 3 (ii) of the Security Council resolution 707 (1991) and paragraph 3 and 5 of resolution 715 (1991).

A detailed report on IAEA-28 is being prepared and will be transmitted to the Council as soon as possible. However, the following provides highlights of the IAEA-28 mission's findings:

a. For the first time, it was acknowledged by Iraq that the activities carried out at first at Tuwaitha and later at Al Atheer had been aimed at the production of a nuclear device and not only to the definition of what was required to produce it, as had previously been asserted by Iraq. Key documentation on Iraq's design of a nuclear device was provided to the IAEA.

b. The involvement of the Al Qa Qaa State Establishment in support of the development of the implosion package was for the first time acknowledged by Iraq, and declared to have begun in 1987.

c. The crash programme which was initiated in the late summer of 1990 had been planned to comprise the chemical processing of both unirradiated and irradiated research reactor fuel to recover the highly enriched uranium (HEU) from the fuel; the re-enrichment of part of the HEU through the use of a 50-machine centrifuge cascade which was to have been specially constructed for the purpose; the conversion of the HEU chemical compounds to metal. Had the HEU recovery and enrichment process been successful, it could have resulted in the availability by the end of 1991 of a quantity of HEU sufficient to manufacture a single low-yield nuclear device.

d. Also planned were measures such as the fabrication of the implosion package and the selection and construction of a test site and studies of a delivery system. Assembly of the device could not have been possible, according to the estimate of the Iraqi scientists, before the end of 1992. The validity of this estimate was one of the issues addressed during IAEA-28 and is currently under assessment by the IAEA with the assistance of nuclear weapons experts.

e. Detailed explanations were provided by Iraqi authorities of centrifuge related activities in the buildings of the Engineering Design Centre (Rashdiya), but no convincing rationale was offered for Iraq's continued concealment, even after the commencement in July 1993 of the high-level technical talks, of the role played by the Engineering Design Centre in the covert nuclear programme.

f. No evidence has as of yet been found of practical progress towards the establishment of the 50-machine centrifuge enrichment cascade, although it appears that external assistance was to have been relied upon for the procurement and production of the carbon fibre cylinder components of the centrifuge rotors.

g. Wide ranging information was obtained which provided clarification and confirmation of various aspects of the procurement network established to support the centrifuge enrichment project.

h. In spite of the obvious progress in openness and transparency shown by a number of Iraqi staff participating in the technical discussions, there is still a tendency to misrepresent the expertise and competence of Iraqi scientists and engineers both in the areas of programme coordination and in some specific R & D activities.

i. Initial indications do not appear to conflict with the IAEA's assessment of the scope and status of Iraq's clandestine programme to acquire nuclear weapon capability, as set out in the IAEA's seventh semi-annual report. However, it would be premature to draw any definitive conclusions pending analysis of the recently acquired documentation, samples and other information.

B. Ongoing monitoring and verification

16. Events described in paragraphs 5-14 above, although commanding a shift in priority of other activities, did not detract from the full implementation of the IAEA Plan. In the period under review, resident inspectors of the Nuclear Monitoring Group (NMG) have continued their work in the field according to schedule, with the support of the staff of the Baghdad Monitoring and Verification Centre (BMVC) and in coordination with the chemical, biological and missiles groups of the Special Commission. 105 inspections—most of these unannounced—have been conducted at some 51 sites/facilities, 11 of which were visited for the first time.

17. The sixth radiometric survey of Iraq's main water bodies was completed in April 1995. Samples of water, sediment and biota were taken at 15 sites selected from the 52 locations for which baseline data had been established in the original survey completed in November 1992. Twelve additional locations along the Euphrates watercourse, close to the Al Qaim phosphate fertilizer plant were sampled. The Al Qaim phosphate plant was the facility where large quantities of uranium were extracted from uranium bearing Iraqi phosphate ores originating from Iraq's mine at Akashat. The uranium extraction and concentration plant was totally destroyed during the war. The analysis of water and sediment samples taken along the river in the proximity of the Al Qaim works will be used to determine the practical capability to detect a facility of this kind and verify how far downstream signatures from the plant persist. It will also provide a baseline against which future analyses at this specific site will be compared to verify the absence of uranium activity associated with phosphate fertilizer production.

18. The level of practical cooperation by Iraqi counterparts in facilitating and expediting IAEA's field work continues to be high.

C. *Provision of information by Iraq*

19. The reporting requirements stipulated in paragraph 22 and Annex 2 of the Plan are being fulfilled regularly at six-month intervals by the Iraqi authorities.

20. In July the semi-annual update was provided on facilities, installations and sites where nuclear activities of any kind have been carried out or which in IAEA's judgement could be suitable to host nuclear activities. The update is also required to include sites and facilities where material and equipment identified in the Annex 3 of the IAEA's Plan are located. In their July report the Iraqi authorities provided detailed information on 29 additional facilities bringing the total number of sites declared by Iraq under paragraph 22 of the Plan to 169. The large number of documents provided by Iraq on 20 August 1995 may contain information on hitherto undeclared sites and facilities which had been connected with the covert nuclear programme. In this case, Iraq will have to submit detailed information and the IAEA will decide if the inclusion of these sites or facilities in the monitoring regime is warranted.

D. *Release, relocation and change of the use of equipment, materials and facilities*

21. Through the channel of the Iraqi National Monitoring Directorate (NMD) the IAEA receives requests for the release of—or for the permission to relocate—equipment and materials, as well as requests for permission to change the use of monitored buildings. All NMD requests are processed in consultation with the Special Commission. Since the start of the implementation of the IAEA Plan (August 1994) some 20 such requests have been received and, in the period under review, 12 have been approved. Items for which release, relocation or change of use is approved remain subject to ongoing monitoring and verification at a frequency commensurate with their significance.

IV. *Summary*

22. The IAEA Plan for monitoring and verification of Iraq's compliance with the relevant Security Council resolutions continues to be implemented by resident inspectors of the Nuclear Monitoring Group with the assistance of, and in full coordination with, the Special Commission. During the period under review the Nuclear Monitoring Group conducted 105 inspections at some 51 facilities, 11 facilities of which were not previously inspected.

23. Shortly after the arrival in Jordan of General Hussein Kamel, the former Minister of Industry and Military Industrialisation, an IAEA delegation was invited to Baghdad to receive information on the past Iraqi covert nuclear programme, allegedly withheld at the instruction of General Hussein Kamel. Following this invitation a series of technical meetings were held in Baghdad with the Iraqi authorities from 17 to 20 August 1995 and information and supporting documents were given by the Iraqi authorities to the IAEA delegation. The most important information concerned the progress made in Iraq in their covert nuclear programme during the period immediately preceding the Gulf war, i.e. from June 1990 to the outbreak of the conflict (17 January 1991).

24. According to Iraqi officials a crash programme was launched in September 1990 to extract and further enrich the enriched uranium contained in the safeguarded research reactor fuel at the Tuwaitha site and to use the weapon-grade material resulting from this crash programme to accelerate the development of a nuclear device. Had this programme been completed, it could have provided enough material for a nuclear device in a shorter time than would have been necessary under Iraq's covert programme to enrich natural uranium. As it turned out, the chemical operations to extract the enriched uranium from the research reactor fuel was never begun since the equipment assembled to implement the programme was destroyed by coalition air raids in the first days of the war. All of the safeguarded research reactor fuel was accounted for by the inspectors of the IAEA-1 in May 1991.

25. Information was also provided by Iraq along with supporting documents on the progress made in the same time period by the weaponization team in Al Atheer. Assessment of the documents is under way.

26. On 20 August prior to the departure of the IAEA delegation from Baghdad, Iraqi authorities announced the discovery of thousands of documents and several tons of metals and other materials on a farm said to be owned by the family of General Hussein Kamel. The documents and materials were removed to the Baghdad Monitoring and Verification Centre where, in the course of three following weeks, a joint IAEA/UNSCOM team completed a preliminary scanning of all documents, sorting them according to their subject into four categories—nuclear, biological, chemical, and missiles. After this preliminary inventory the nuclear-related documents were removed to IAEA Headquarters in Vienna for review and analysis. At the same time, samples of metals and other material were taken and their analysis is under way.

27. Following talks in Baghdad, the IAEA team met in Jordan with General Hussein Kamel. His state-

ments on Iraq's past nuclear weapons programme provided useful information.

28. A follow-up inspection mission—IAEA-28—took place from 9 to 19 September 1995 with the participation of experts in centrifuge and weapons-related technologies provided by Member States. The report of this inspection is in preparation.

29. Clearly, given the sheer magnitude of the documentation provided in August by Iraq it would be premature at this stage to draw conclusions as to their detailed content and implications. There is no certainty, of course,

that all nuclear relevant documents have been delivered even now.

30. What is clear at this stage is that Iraq's crash programme to extract weapons-grade material from the safeguarded reactor fuel constitutes an additional violation of its safeguards agreement with the IAEA and Iraq's failure, until now, to declare this programme and other weapons-related activities and to turn over to the IAEA all nuclear-related documents and materials constitutes a violation of Iraq's obligations under the relevant Security Council resolutions.

Document 214

Eighth report of the Secretary-General on the status of the implementation of the plan for the ongoing monitoring and verification of Iraq's compliance with relevant parts of section C of Security Council resolution 687 (1991)

S/1995/864, 11 October 1995

Note by the Secretary-General

1. The Secretary-General has the honour to transmit to the Security Council a report submitted by the Executive Chairman of the Special Commission established by the Secretary-General pursuant to paragraph 9 (b) (i) of Security Council resolution 687 (1991).

2. The present report is the eighth submitted under paragraph 8 of Security Council resolution 715 (1991) of 11 October 1991, by which the Council requested the Secretary-General to submit a report to the Security Council every six months on the implementation of the Special Commission's plan for ongoing monitoring and verification of Iraq's compliance with the relevant parts of section C of Security Council resolution 687 (1991). It updates the information contained in the first seven reports (S/23801, S/24661, S/25620, S/26684, S/1994/489, S/1994/1138 and Corr.1 and S/1995/284).

3. Further information concerning developments since the last report submitted under resolution 715 (1991) is contained in the report to the Security Council of 20 June 1995 (S/1995/494), the ninth report provided in accordance with paragraph 3 of resolution 699 (1991).

Annex
Report of the Secretary-General on the status of the implementation of the Special Commission's plan for the ongoing monitoring and verification of Iraq's compliance with relevant parts of section C of Security Council resolution 687 (1991)

I. *Introduction*

1. The six months which have elapsed since the last report submitted to the Security Council under paragraph 8 of resolution 715 (1991) have been among the most eventful in the history of the Special Commission, both in respect of relations with the Government of Iraq and of the progress made in obtaining information regarding Iraq's programmes for production of weapons of mass destruction and missiles with a range greater than 150 kilometres. While the present report is submitted pursuant to resolution relating to ongoing monitoring and verification, the Commission has repeatedly pointed out that a full understanding of all aspects of Iraq's programmes for weapons of mass destruction is essential to the planning and the operation of an effective system of monitoring to ensure Iraq's compliance with its undertaking not to use, develop, construct or acquire any of the

items proscribed to it under paragraphs 8 and 9 of resolution 687 (1991), namely "(a) all chemical and biological weapons and all stocks of agents and all related subsystems and components and all research, development, support and manufacturing facilities related thereto; (b) all ballistic missiles with a range greater than 150 kilometres, and related major parts and repair and production facilities".

2. While describing the developments which have taken place in the conduct and strengthening of monitoring operations since April 1995, the present report contains a detailed account of the new information obtained regarding Iraq's prohibited programmes and its probable impact on the monitoring system. In the period under review, Iraq has taken important decisions to acknowledge its offensive biological weapons programme and documents are being obtained in all areas. However, much of the new information contradicts earlier declarations by Iraq and some assessments made by the Commission now must be revised. A more enduring and coherent explanation of past activities must be provided by Iraq in the new full, final and complete disclosures which it is to submit in all areas, as described more fully elsewhere in this report.

3. The Commission's report in April 1995 (S/1995/284) contained, in its paragraphs 3 and 4, a comprehensive description of the concept of operations underlying the Commission's monitoring system. It is worthwhile, in the light of developments in the last six months, to recall the sections in that description which explain the importance of a full knowledge of Iraq's prohibited programmes for the monitoring system and for confidence in its effectiveness and comprehensiveness. These require:

"Possession by the Commission of a full picture of Iraq's past programmes and a full accounting of the facilities, equipment, items and materials associated with those past programmes, in conjunction with full knowledge of the disposition of dual-purpose items currently available to Iraq, the technologies acquired by Iraq in pursuing the past programmes, and the supplier networks it established to acquire those elements of the programmes that it could not acquire indigenously. This information provides the baseline data from which ongoing monitoring and verification proceeds;

"Knowledge of the level of technology attained by Iraq, of the production and acquisition methods it used and of the materials and equipment it had available are all key to designing a system of monitoring that addresses issues of concern and focuses monitoring effort where it would be most effective

and efficient. For example, within Iraq, the system should focus more of its efforts on those technologies and production methods that Iraq is known to have mastered than on technologies and methods that Iraq is known not to have mastered, whereas, for the export/import monitoring regime, the converse would be true, with effort focusing on those items that Iraq would have to import in order to reactivate a proscribed weapons programme. Clearly, knowing where to focus effort requires knowledge of what Iraq would have achieved in its past programmes;

"Similarly, knowledge of the procurement methods and routes used by Iraq for its past programmes is key to the design of an effective and efficient export/import monitoring regime. This system should be designed to be effective against the procurement routes and methods that Iraq is known to have used in the past. Testing whether it is, is predicated on knowing those routes and methods;

"Full accounting for the materials, items and equipment associated with the past programmes is directly related to what assets should be monitored under the system. Dual-purpose materials, items and equipment from the past programmes must be monitored, along with other dual-purpose capabilities available to Iraq. Uncertainties relating to the accuracy or completeness of this accounting will consequently lead to uncertainties as to whether the ongoing monitoring and verification system is indeed monitoring all the materials, items and equipment which should be monitored". (ibid., para. 3 (a))

4. Under Security Council resolutions 687, 707 and 715 (1991), Iraq is obliged to provide the above information, which the Commission then verifies through its inspection, monitoring and analysis activities. Iraq is required to update its declarations on its dual-purpose activities and capabilities every six months.

5. The description in the present report of the new information received from Iraq in the period under review is intended to assist in assessing the extent to which such information, together with that previously obtained, contributes to meeting the criteria set out above. This, in turn, will bear upon the assessment of the effectiveness and comprehensiveness of the monitoring system and the extent to which it may have to be further modified and augmented to take account of recent developments. Because of the challenges to the monitoring system implied in the new revelations, this report contains, under each separate weapons heading, a detailed description of the operations of the newly designed monitoring system.

6. The present report, after summarizing relations with Iraq in the period under review, contains chapters

on the various areas of responsibility of the Special Commission, namely those relating to missiles with a range greater than 150 kilometres and to chemical and biological weapons. Further chapters cover the Commission's support and other responsibilities in the nuclear area; other activities, such as those in relation to the export/import mechanism; and finance, organization and air support. The final chapter contains the conclusion of the Commission on the developments which have occurred in the last six months.

II. Relations with Iraq: developments: visits by the Executive Chairman to Iraq

A. Summary of the Executive Chairman's visits

7. During the period under review, the Executive Chairman has paid five visits to Baghdad to maintain contact with the most senior levels of the Iraqi Government and to seek to expedite the work of the Commission, particularly in relation to Iraq's prohibited programmes, by pressing the Government to follow a policy of complete and frank disclosure. This was specially important in respect of Iraq's biological weapons programme, which the Commission's experts had determined to be of very significant proportions, despite Iraq's constant denials that it had done anything more than limited research.

8. The Executive Chairman's visits took place as follows: 29 May to 1 June, 30 June to 2 July, 4 to 6 August, 17 to 20 August and 29 September to 1 October 1995. Two visits were also paid to Baghdad by the Deputy Executive Chairman, from 14 to 17 May and 17 to 20 September 1995, to address issues relating to Iraq's prohibited programmes. Information on those visits, from April to 1 June 1995, will be found in the Commission's June 1995 report (S/1995/494, paras. 4-10).

B. Cooperation, ultimatum and disclosures

9. The visits listed above illustrate the rocky road of cooperation between Iraq and the Commission in the period under review, where indications that Iraq was contemplating ceasing such cooperation culminated in an ultimatum, early in August 1995, that such cooperation would cease if, by 31 August 1995, no progress was made in the Security Council in the direction of easing or lifting the sanctions and the oil embargo. However, the ultimatum was withdrawn following the departure of General Hussein Kamel Hassan from Baghdad and his receipt of asylum in Jordan. The General had, among a large number of important responsibilities, been in charge, over considerable periods of time, of Iraq's programmes in the areas now proscribed to it. Since his departure, the Deputy Prime Minister, Mr. Tariq Aziz, has stated that Iraq has adopted a new policy of complete cooperation and

transparency with the Commission and the International Atomic Energy Agency (IAEA), without any time-limit.

10. In the first of the Executive Chairman's visits, at the end of May 1995, the Deputy Prime Minister of Iraq sounded a warning that, if no prospect appeared for reintegrating Iraq into the international community through the easing or lifting of sanctions and the oil embargo, it would be difficult for Iraq to justify the expense and the effort involved in cooperation with the Commission and IAEA. Iraq required statements from the Commission that the chemical weapons and missile files were closed and the monitoring system was operational, and from IAEA that the nuclear file was closed. If Iraq received such assurances and thus judged the prospects for reintegration to be positive, it would, in late June, address the one outstanding issue of significance, the biological issue. In response, and subsequently in his June 1995 report to the Security Council (S/1995/494), the Chairman stated that the bulk of what was required to implement paragraphs 8 to 10 of Security Council resolution 687 (1991) with regard to chemical weapons and missiles had been achieved. However, in view of Iraq's late and incomplete declarations, a longer period had been needed to identify all aspects of Iraq's programmes than might otherwise have been required. Furthermore, the major area of Iraq's biological weapons programme remained non-disclosed. Monitoring was operational in all areas. Those uncertainties which remained in the missile and chemical areas needed to be resolved and in order to do so the Commission would continue to use its rights under the relevant Security Council resolutions and the exchange of letters of 7 and 14 May 1991 on the facilities, privileges and immunities of the Commission in Iraq.

11. Upon the Executive Chairman's arrival in Baghdad on 30 June 1995, Deputy Prime Minister Tariq Aziz said that his Government had reviewed carefully the Commission's report of June 1995. While it had found the report to contain both negative and positive elements, it had concluded that the positive elements were such that Iraq would now address the issue of its biological weapons programme. The following day, on 1 July 1995, Iraq made a brief oral presentation in the course of which it acknowledged an offensive biological weapons programme, including the production of a number of biological agents, but denied the weaponization of such agents. The Chairman welcomed this disclosure but expressed the view that it needed to be augmented, particularly as regards weaponization, and had to be presented to the Commission in the form of a full, final and complete disclosure as required by Security Council resolution 707 (1991). A fuller account of this and subsequent

disclosures relating to Iraq's biological weapons programme will be found in chapter V of the present report.

12. Iraq's decision to disclose its offensive biological weapons programme appeared to indicate that it was moving away from its warning of non-cooperation, expressed by Mr. Tariq Aziz during the Executive Chairman's preceding visit to Baghdad. However, this situation was abruptly reversed in the course of July 1995. On 17 July, President Saddam Hussein made a speech in Baghdad in which he indicated that his Government would cease cooperation with the Security Council if there were no progress in the Council towards the lifting of sanctions and the oil embargo. No deadline was given by the President for such progress. However, a few days later, in Cairo, the Foreign Minister of Iraq, Mr. Mohammed Saeed Al-Sahaf, made a speech in which he stated that 31 August 1995 was the deadline.

13. The Executive Chairman arrived in Baghdad for the third of his visits in the period under review on 4 August 1995. Iraq delivered to him what it stated to be its full, final and complete disclosure of its biological weapons programme, still denying that any of the agents produced had been weaponized. In a meeting with the Deputy Prime Minister, Mr. Tariq Aziz, on 5 August, the latter stressed to the Chairman that Iraq would cease cooperation with the Security Council and the Commission if there were no progress, by 31 August 1995, towards lifting sanctions and the oil embargo. The Deputy Prime Minister asked the Chairman to convey this information to the Security Council upon his return to United Nations Headquarters. The Chairman reached New York on 7 August, and immediately thereafter received a message from Mr. Tariq Aziz, through the Permanent Representative of Iraq to the United Nations, that the deadline was serious and that the Chairman should inform the Council accordingly. The Chairman did so, in an oral briefing to the Council on 10 August.

14. Three days previously, on 7 August 1995, General Hussein Kamel Hassan had left Baghdad, arriving in Amman the following day. On 13 August, the Executive Chairman received a letter from General Amer Rashid al-Ubeidi, Minister of Oil and former Director of the Military Industrialization Corporation (MIC), inviting him to return to Baghdad. In the letter, it was stated that the Government had ascertained that General Hussein Kamel Hassan had been responsible for hiding important information on Iraq's prohibited programmes from the Commission and IAEA by ordering the Iraqi technical personnel not to disclose such information and also not to inform Mr. Tariq Aziz or General Amer of these instructions. An identical letter was addressed to the Director General of IAEA. In a message to the Chairman

on 14 August, Mr. Tariq Aziz stated that the deadline was no longer in effect.

15. The Executive Chairman and the Leader of the IAEA Action Team, in response to the invitations from Iraq, arrived in Baghdad on 17 August 1995. On the evening of that day, a plenary meeting was held with an Iraqi delegation led by the Deputy Prime Minister, and including the Foreign Minister, Mr. Al-Sahaf, the Minister of Oil, General Amer, the Under-Secretary of the Foreign Ministry, Dr. Riyadh Al-Qaysi, and other senior officials. Mr. Tariq Aziz made an initial statement in the course of which he repeated that General Hussein Kamel Hassan had, unbeknown to the senior levels of the Iraqi leadership, hidden information on the prohibited programmes which Iraq would now disclose to the Commission and IAEA. Iraq had decided on a policy of cooperation and full transparency with the Commission and IAEA, without imposing any time-limit, and also of cooperation and good-neighbourliness with the States of the region and elsewhere and of economic development in Iraq itself. Following on the plenary meeting, in a meeting devoted to Iraq's biological weapons programme, Iraq for the first time disclosed a much more extensive programme than that contained in its full, final and complete disclosure of early August 1995, admitting weaponization immediately prior to the outbreak of the Gulf war, including the filling of biological warfare agents into 166 bombs and 25 Al Hussein missile warheads.

16. In the course of the following two days, Iraq made further disclosures in regard to other prohibited programmes, including indigenous production of Scud-type missile engines, assembled from both imported and locally produced parts, and the testing of such engines. The significance of this, and its consequences for Iraq's previous statements regarding unilateral destruction of proscribed materials, is discussed in paragraphs 21, 22 and 44 below.

17. On 20 August 1995, at the conclusion of the Executive Chairman's visit, a considerable cache of documents and other materials was located and taken possession of by the Commission, as described in paragraphs 24 to 27 below.

18. The Executive Chairman returned to New York through Jordan, thus affording the opportunity to meet General Hussein Kamel Hassan and to discuss with him Iraq's programmes in the proscribed fields. Useful information was obtained.

19. Both during and after the Executive Chairman's mid-August visit to Baghdad, expert teams in all areas of the Special Commission's responsibility held discussions with their Iraqi counterparts. The missile and biological teams obtained much valuable information, indicating programmes larger or more advanced in every

dimension than previously declared. In the chemical field, after being confronted with evidence found by the chemical team in the new documentation, Iraq acknowledged a much larger and more advanced programme than hitherto admitted for the production and storage of the chemical warfare agent VX. In this regard, the Deputy Executive Chairman visited Baghdad from 17 to 20 September 1995, in the course of which he pointed out to Iraqi officials, at senior levels, the gravity of the clear deception of Iraq in its spring 1995 declarations to the Commission concerning the VX nerve agent in particular. This had been reported to the Security Council in June 1995 and the intentional deception would have to be underscored in the current report.

20. On 29 September 1995, the Executive Chairman arrived in Baghdad, for his last visit in the period under review, to assess with the Iraqi authorities the situation resulting from the recent disclosures, following on the departure of General Hussein Kamel Hassan. The Chairman expressed the view, in the various meetings which he held, that it was in Iraq's best interests to provide everything now, rather than to drag out the uncovering of information which would have an increasingly negative impact. Iraq undertook to do its best, and the Deputy Prime Minister, Mr. Tariq Aziz, pledged his Government's cooperation and full openness with regard to the implementation of Security Council resolution 687 (1991).

C. Some consequences of recent disclosures

1. Unilateral destruction by Iraq

21. Iraq's decision in 1991 to undertake, in violation of Security Council resolution 687 (1991), the unilateral destruction of various elements of its prohibited programmes has had the most severe consequences in delaying, and in rendering much more complicated, any determination by the Commission that it has a complete picture of those programmes and has accounted for all the significant components thereof. This destruction has been stated by Iraq to cover all three areas of proscribed missiles and chemical and biological programmes. Unilateral destruction of weapons, equipment and materials, including agent and precursors, has made verification, particularly of the quantities involved, extremely difficult. The Commission has thus pressed for any documentation Iraq may have relating to such destruction, including the orders to carry it out and field reports on how those orders were executed.

22. The picture is further complicated by certain recent disclosures which show that Iraq has used alleged unilateral destruction to cover up elements of its prohibited programmes which it wished to keep concealed. Possibly the most important example of this, uncovered

to date, relates to the missile field. Iraq declared in 1992 that it had unilaterally destroyed 89 Scud/Al Hussein missiles. Recent analysis by the Commission's experts, and admissions by Iraq, now reveal that only 83 missiles were so destroyed in 1991. The figure was inflated by Iraq to 89, in order to conceal its indigenous production of engines for Scud-type missiles, as reported in paragraphs 43 and 44 of the present report. This example will require the Commission to take a new look at all Iraq's declarations on unilateral destruction and for it to press for documentation and any other means of verification of such declarations.

2. Documentation

23. The Commission has, on every available occasion, stressed to Iraq that the handing over of documentation relating to its prohibited programmes is the best and quickest means for the Commission to verify Iraq's declarations relating to the programmes. Iraq, however, has sought to maintain that, some time in 1991, it issued an order to destroy all documentation on those programmes. The Commission's attempts to obtain evidence of such an order, and to ascertain precisely when it was issued, have been unsuccessful. The Commission has remained sceptical that any such wholesale destruction ever took place. It has so told Iraq on numerous occasions. It was not conceivable that all evidence would be destroyed of major and very costly scientific research and engineering undertakings, representing billions of dollars in investment and countless man-hours of work.

24. On 20 August 1995, at the conclusion of the Executive Chairman's visit to Baghdad (17-20 August), the Chairman, in a public statement, complained that, while very significant new information had been provided, not a single document, which could help in verifying that information, had been handed over. Shortly after that statement was made, and while the Chairman's team was preparing for departure to the Habbaniyah airfield, General Amer Rashid al-Ubeidi contacted the Chairman and requested that, on his way to the airfield, he visit a farm which the General stated to have belonged to General Hussein Kamel Hassan, where items of great interest to the Commission could be found. On arrival at the farm, in addition to a number of shipping containers with miscellaneous equipment in them, the Chairman and his team found, in a locked chicken house, numerous metal and wooden boxes which were packed with documentation, together with microfiches, computer diskettes, videotapes, photographs and prohibited hardware components. Orders were immediately issued to the Commission's personnel, who had been brought to the site, to secure this material and transfer it to the Baghdad Monitoring and Verification Centre.

25. Examination of the contents of the boxes at the Centre revealed well over half a million pages of documentation. While most of this related to the nuclear area, a large amount concerned the chemical, biological and missile areas. This documentation has now been inventoried and is being arranged, after scanning, on a priority basis for examination. The initial assessment of the Commission is that the bulk of the material in the missile, chemical and biological fields comes from a number of the sites where Iraq's proscribed programmes had been carried out. The amount of material varies from area to area, being more comprehensive in certain areas than in others. However, documentation from the Headquarters of the Military Industrialization Corporation (MIC) is not included, nor are the relevant archives of the Ministry of Defence. From recent statements made by senior Iraqi officials, the Ministry's records are still intact and detailed.

26. Since the discovery of the documents, Iraq has admitted to the Commission's personnel that, in the summer of 1991, orders were issued by a "high authority" to the directors of the sites involved in Iraq's proscribed programmes to protect "important documents"—which was understood to relate to the technology of production—by packing them, in a very brief period of time, and delivering them on demand to representatives from the special security organizations. This delivery is said to have taken place without written orders or the provision of receipts by the representatives of those organizations when they collected the packed documents. Iraq's original claim that all documentation was destroyed is thus patently false.

27. The Commission doubts that the materials obtained are all those which were gathered under the protection order issued in 1991. More such documentation must still exist, particularly in certain significant areas such as production records, Iraq's procurement networks and sources of supply. Also, the relevant MIC headquarters documentation and archives of the Ministry of Defence are missing. These are materials which must be handed over if the Commission is to be able to undertake a speedy and thorough verification of Iraq's declarations regarding its prohibited programmes. The Commission, nevertheless, acknowledges that the materials already obtained, together with the admission that the relevant documentation was not all destroyed, is one of the most significant breakthroughs in the four years of its operations in Iraq, and will provide an invaluable source of verification material. What has been started should be completed by handing over the missing documentation identified above.

3. Rationale for Iraq's biological and chemical weapons

28. Iraq's intentions with regard to the operational use of its biological and chemical weapons have been subject to conflicting presentations by the Iraqi authorities in the period under review. On the one side, it was explained that the biological and chemical weapons were seen by Iraq as a useful means to counter a numerically superior force; on the other, they were presented as a means of last resort for retaliation in the case of a nuclear attack on Baghdad. Certain documentation supports the contention that Iraq was actively planning and had actually deployed its chemical weapons in a pattern corresponding to strategic and offensive use through surprise attack against perceived enemies. The known pattern of deployment of long-range missiles (Al Hussein) supports this contention. Iraq stated, during visits of both the Chairman and the Deputy Chairman, that authority to launch biological and chemical warheads was pre-delegated in the event that Baghdad was hit by nuclear weapons during the Gulf war. This pre-delegation does not exclude the alternative use of such a capability and therefore does not constitute proof of only intentions concerning second use. It is evident that the Commission must have a complete understanding of the concept behind each stage of the development of all proscribed weapons systems, together with their intended and actual deployment plans.

III. Missile activities

A. The monitoring system

29. Pursuant to the plan for ongoing monitoring and verification, approved by the Security Council in resolution 715 (1991), the Commission has established a multi-layered monitoring system in the missile area. The system is designed to cover essential elements of Iraq's missile and related research, development, testing and manufacturing facilities and non-proscribed missiles with ranges less than 150 kilometres as defined by the plan. The system is designed to compensate the limitations of one layer of the system with the strengths of other layers. The current monitoring system includes, inter alia:

30. On-site monitoring inspections. Such inspections are carried out without advance notice by a resident expert team based at the Commission's Baghdad Monitoring and Verification Centre (BMVC). These inspections include verification of Iraq's declarations under the plan, review of related facility documentation, inspection of items produced and production techniques, and inspection of all areas and buildings at each facility. Currently, over 30 different facilities are inspected on a routine basis, with the frequency of visits dependent on the nature of activities at the specific sites.

31. Continuous sensor monitoring. This is directed at critical areas of missile-related activities and dual-

purpose machines. On-site cameras are connected to and can be viewed remotely from the BMVC. Furthermore, the BMVC staff collect videotapes from the monitored facilities every 30 days, or more frequently if required, for detailed analysis. Tamper-proof tags and labels are used to positively identify important equipment at the facilities to assist in the monitoring of their use, movement or disposal. Currently, over 120 pieces of missile-related equipment carry UNSCOM tags and labels. The Commission regularly reviews the need to upgrade, replace or add additional sensors to improve its missile monitoring.

32. *Special inspections.* Special inspection teams are tasked to address specific issues, for example, assessing non-proscribed ongoing missile research and development activities. These teams are staffed by highly qualified experts in specific fields who advise the Commission of potential modifications to the monitoring regime.

33. *Compliance inspections.* Such inspection teams are used to verify information available to the Commission on Iraq's activities. These teams are also used to determine if new facilities should be included in the monitoring regime.

34. *Aerial surveillance.* The Commission uses both helicopter and high-level surveillance assets to monitor activities and the infrastructure of relevant facilities throughout Iraq.

35. After completion of the baseline process for each site being monitored, the Commission began operating the ongoing monitoring and verification system for Iraq's missile and related facilities on 17 August 1994. Since that time, the Commission has performed over 450 inspections at a variety of missile facilities and has installed over 40 video cameras at 16 facilities monitored for missile production-related activities. Iraq has continued to provide the support requested by the Commission in the conduct of these inspections, including, *inter alia*, access to production, quality control and inventory records; access to buildings, facilities or equipment located at the sites; installation of cameras and tags; and the provision of technical experts to explain designs, tests and production activities to the monitoring and inspection teams.

36. During the reporting period, the Commission conducted the second annual verification of Iraq's non-proscribed operational missiles as defined by Security Council resolutions 687 (1991) and 715 (1991), i.e. missiles with ranges less than 150 kilometres that are designed for use, or capable of being modified for use, in a surface-to-surface role with a range greater than 50 kilometres. The Commission uses tags to confirm that all such missiles are identified in Iraq and to ensure that these missile systems are not modified to ranges prohibited by

the Security Council. The Commission has established modalities pursuant to which Iraq is required to present 10 per cent of its missiles, three times per year, to the Commission for its verification. The Commission selects the missiles for Iraq to present and the timing of these inspections. In accordance with the established procedures, Iraq submitted the requested number of missiles for verification by the inspection team during the second annual verification. No modifications of these missiles were detected.

37. The Commission has recently obtained information that Iraq has resumed its acquisition efforts in support of its missile facilities. Iraq placed a number of orders, both directly and indirectly (through middlemen and front companies), for the purchase of equipment, technologies, supplies and material for both missile- and non-missile-related activities at these facilities. Iraq explained that many of these efforts were in direct support of its Ababil-100 programme for indigenous development and production of surface-to-surface missiles with ranges between 100 and 150 kilometres. During the period since the last report in April 1995, Iraq has acknowledged these procurement activities, including the actual import, without notifications to the United Nations Sanctions Committee established under Security Council resolution 661 (1990), of equipment and materials. In most cases, Iraq has wrongly asserted that such equipment and materials were purchased within Iraq.

B. *Destruction of proscribed items*

38. In April 1995, the Commission completed an investigation of Iraq's acquisition and use of equipment for Project 1728 (production of liquid-propellant rocket engines) prior to the Gulf war. On 21 April, the Commission sent a letter to Iraq outlining measures that needed to be taken for the disposal of this equipment, including the destruction of five key pieces of production and testing equipment purchased specifically for proscribed missile activities. Iraq was also informed that all work must cease on equipment requiring destruction. The personnel in the facilities where this equipment was located apparently disregarded these instructions and continued to operate the machinery to produce parts for current missile programmes. The Commission detected the continued operation of this equipment, in contravention of the Commission's instructions, through several elements of its monitoring system, primarily the monitoring cameras. Iraq also tried to delay the destruction of the equipment. The relevant developments were reported by the Executive Chairman to the Security Council on 2 July 1995. Shortly thereafter, Iraq agreed to comply with the Commission's decision and the destruction of the equipment was completed by the end of July 1995.

C. *Proscribed programme*

39. During the period since the report in April 1995, the Commission has continued its investigations of Iraq's proscribed former missile activities. These investigations concentrated on the unresolved issues mainly connected with Iraq's past research and development activities. The Commission sought additional data from Iraq and its explanations concerning work on a number of undeclared missile designs or components, missile fuels and the connections between the missile programme and other proscribed activities. These issues were addressed during the rounds of high-level talks from May until early August 1995 and additionally by the inspection team UNSCOM 122/BM 33. At that time, Iraq provided some answers to the Commission's requests, but mainly limited its admissions to cases where the Commission had evidence of Iraq's activities. However, in the majority of cases in the period prior to mid-August 1995, Iraq tried to mislead the Commission by withholding information or by attributing the case on which information was requested to some other activity. Thus, Iraq specifically denied the existence of any biological warheads, test activity with chemical warheads, any work on advanced liquid-propellant missile systems, using new materials for missile airframes (like aluminium), and missile fuels (like UDMH). Iraq also continued, in the period indicated, to falsify its accounting of missiles, warheads and supporting/auxiliary equipment.

40. During the Executive Chairman's visit to Baghdad from 17 to 20 August 1995, following on the events described in paragraph 14 above, Iraq, in contradistinction to its attitude prior to that time, disclosed substantial new information related to its proscribed missile programme. Iraq acknowledged for the first time work on advanced rocket engines, including those with increased thrust or using UDMH fuel. Iraq also admitted to the production of proscribed rocket engines made of indigenously produced or imported parts and without cannibalization of the imported Soviet-made Scud engines. Iraq further admitted that the number and the purpose of static and flight tests of proscribed missiles had previously been misrepresented.

41. As described in paragraphs 24 to 27 above, the Commission obtained boxes with documents and materials including, in addition to written documentation, videotapes, films, microfiches and computer diskettes related to missile activities. Some prohibited missile components were also found in the boxes. Apparently these documents had at one time belonged to projects that were engaged in activities such as project 144 (modification and production of missile systems), the Karama project (production of missile guidance and control systems), project 1728 (production of liquid-propellant rocket en-

gines) and Badr-2000 (two-stage solid-propellant missile). The Iraqi representatives who had worked on these projects explained that they had been ordered to prepare a selection of the most important documents and to hand them over to the special security organizations. In the view of the Commission, the boxes obtained by it do not contain the full record of proscribed missile activities or a complete set of documentation which could be expected to be found at such facilities. The Commission intends to exploit fully available documents in the verification process, while continuing to press for the handing over of all the relevant documents.

42. During the Executive Chairman's visit to Baghdad from 29 September to 1 October, and the UNSCOM 123/BM 34 inspection (27 September-1 October), the Iraqi authorities provided additional information on previously undisclosed activities. It appeared that Iraq considered this to be critical and essential information on its prohibited activities and it was therefore withheld from the Commission for more than four years. At the end of September 1995, the Commission obtained new information on Iraq's testing activity, including both static and flight testing of Scud variant missile systems; several new designs of longer-range missile systems; development and testing of new liquid-propellant engine designs; development and successful testing of a warhead separation system; an indigenous design of a 600 mm diameter supergun system; and three separate flight tests of chemical warheads. Some of the previously undisclosed designs included missiles that could reach targets at ranges of up to 3,000 kilometres. The Commission also obtained information of a special missile under design for delivery of a nuclear explosive device. Since these and previous declarations substantially change the scope of Iraq's missile programme, the Commission has requested, and Iraq has agreed to provide, a new full, final and complete disclosure (FFCD) for its proscribed missile activities.

43. New Iraqi disclosures, including production of indigenous rocket engines, have a severe impact on the Commission's accounting of proscribed weapons and equipment used in the missile programmes prohibited by Security Council resolution 687 (1991). So far Iraq has failed to provide conclusive evidence on the quantity of engines produced by Iraq. Thus, the Commission has no firm basis for establishing at this time a reliable accounting of Iraq's proscribed missiles.

44. Another serious complicating factor in establishing a new accounting of proscribed weapons and items in Iraq is associated with unilateral destruction allegedly carried out by Iraq in the summer of 1991 to which reference has already been made in paragraphs 21 and 22 above. The destruction of large quantities and varieties of proscribed items carried out at that time was

disclosed by Iraq to the Commission only in March 1992. However, the Commission has come to the conclusion that this March declaration and Iraq's original FFCD of May 1992 had been intentionally falsified to cover activities that Iraq intended to withhold from the Commission at that time. For example, Iraq declared that 89 proscribed operational missiles were destroyed in summer 1991, although only 83 such missiles were actually destroyed. In this case, the inflated number seems to have been put forward by Iraq to cover undeclared static and flight test activities and its efforts to produce its own missiles. Iraq later presented an incorrect accounting of missile warheads—both imported and indigenously produced—to hide its projects involving unconventional and separating warheads. Iraq presented false figures on the quantity of destroyed imported missile components and other items. Iraq has agreed to provide a new declaration on the material balance of proscribed weapons and other prohibited items, in the new FFCD, to correct these and other false or misleading disclosures. Until it verifies Iraq's new declaration, the Commission will not be able to provide a definite accounting of weapons (missiles, launchers and supporting/auxiliary equipment) as well as equipment and materials used in the proscribed missile programme of Iraq.

45. As may be seen from the above, during much of the reporting period, Iraq has continued to withhold information related to its proscribed missile programme. For the most part, Iraq has provided new data only when there were clear indications that the Commission possessed information from other sources. However, after the Executive Chairman's visit in mid-August, Iraq volunteered some important new information and in several cases supported these disclosures with additional documents. Nevertheless, based on the totality of the information available to it, the Commission believes that Iraq has not yet disclosed fully and completely its proscribed missile activities. The information to be included in the forthcoming FFCD will be crucial for the Commission's verification of Iraq's compliance with its obligations. For this reason, Iraq needs to provide accurate and substantiated data, including documentary evidence to support its statements, and to make suggestions for speedy and effective verification.

46. The Commission intends to continue its intensive inspection and investigation missions under resolution 687 (1991), including application of new verification methods, in order to obtain a full and complete picture of Iraq's proscribed missile activities. Iraq's cooperation, including the provision of accurate information and supporting documentation, access to personnel involved in the relevant activities and support of the Commission's inspection and monitoring efforts will be required, on a continuous basis, in order to enable the Commission to achieve this objective in a speedy and efficient manner.

IV. *Chemical activities*

A. *The monitoring system*

47. During the period under review, four additional baseline inspections were completed in the chemical area. Monitoring and verification protocols were prepared for one research institute and three chemical storage and production sites. These activities were conducted by the chemical monitoring team stationed at the Baghdad Monitoring and Verification Centre. The Commission has thus completed baseline inspections of 62 chemical sites and 18 universities, colleges and research institutes. Over 200 monitoring inspections have been undertaken by the chemical monitoring team to date. Some site protocols will be re-evaluated in the light of recent findings that sites outside of the Muthanna State Establishment were also involved in Iraq's chemical weapons programme, a fact which has been denied until very recently. It is anticipated that information from the documents obtained on 20 August 1995 will lead to inspections at newly identified sites not yet visited.

48. During monitoring inspections in June and July 1995, the chemical monitoring team detected the unauthorized movement and use of four major items of tagged equipment at two sites under monitoring. Iraq was immediately instructed to replace the equipment in its original position. This was done. The seriousness of this unauthorized activity and the attendant considerations of possible destruction of the equipment was underlined to Iraq at the highest level.

49. In addition to the monitoring tools and modalities described in paragraphs 30 to 34 of the chapter on missile activities in the present report, the Commission's chemical monitoring apparatus also includes 19 air samplers installed at 6 chemical production sites in Iraq. From 2 to 11 July 1995, a technical support team performed a retrofit of these samplers and reviewed their locations in order to optimize their use. As a result, several samplers were moved and some added or removed from sites. The upgraded samplers are now better equipped to withstand difficult conditions, such as humidity and chemical extremes.

50. Ten sampling pumps and supporting calibration equipment have been provided to the chemical monitoring team. This gives the team the capability to take air samples at any location in Iraq. An infrared spectrometer and a melting-point determination apparatus are currently under procurement to enlarge the range of samples which can be analysed.

51. A reverse osmosis water purification system and a complete air filtration system for the chemical fume hood has been installed in the chemical laboratory at the

Baghdad Monitoring and Verification Centre. These will enhance the health and safety of personnel working in the laboratory. To ensure the health and safety of monitoring personnel in the field, protective equipment has also been procured, including HEPA filters, a variety of respirators and pressed air suits.

B. *Proscribed programme*

52. The new information obtained by the Commission in August and September 1995 clearly shows that Iraq's full, final and complete disclosure presented on 25 March 1995, the attachment of 27 March 1995 and the addenda to the attachment, received on 29 May 1995, are incorrect and incomplete. The new information was gathered initially from material obtained in Iraq on 20 August 1995 and subsequently admitted by Iraq during the course of technical talks undertaken by the UNSCOM 124/CW 25 inspection team. The material includes documents, videotapes, microfiches and microfilm records and computer discs spanning a large part of Iraq's chemical weapons programme.

53. In response to the Commission's statements that the March 1995 FFCD was no longer adequate, on 7 October 1995, Iraq provided the Commission with a number of revised chapters. The revised chapters, however, cover only those areas already raised by UNSCOM 124/CW 25 as examples of shortcomings in the existing FFCD. The March 1995 FFCD omitted information on major militarily significant chemical weapons capabilities, such as additional types of warfare agents, advanced agent and precursor production, stabilization and storage technologies, new types and numbers of munitions and field trials and additional sites involved in the programme.

54. During the technical talks held in Baghdad in September 1995, it became clear that Iraq was continuing to withhold important information on the extent and technical depth of its chemical weapons programme. Iraq officially stated that the March 1995 FFCD was complete and accurate and that there was no additional information available. Only belatedly did it admit shortcomings in its latest FFCD.

55. Of greatest concern are new revelations concerning the timing, extent and success of Iraq's programme for the production of the nerve agent VX. In the March 1995 Iraqi FFCD and its amendments, it was asserted that the VX programme existed only from April 1987 to September 1988, conducted only laboratory-scale production and had been abandoned because of poor agent quality and instability.

56. Based on the new findings, it is now clear that the VX programme began at least as early as May 1985 and continued without interruption until December 1990. The Commission has concluded that VX was produced on an industrial scale. Precursor and agent storage and stabilization problems were solved. Furthermore, one of Iraq's documents on this subject, dated 1989, proposes "the creation of strategic storage of the substance (VX-hydrochloride, one step from conversion into VX) so it can be used at any time if needed".

57. Significant in this context is Iraq's admission, in September 1995, of the production in 1990 of 65 tonnes of choline, a chemical used exclusively for the production of VX. This amount would be sufficient for the production of approximately 90 tonnes of VX. Furthermore, Iraq had, *inter alia*, over 200 tons each of the precursors phosphorous pentasulphide and di-isopropylamine. These quantities would be sufficient to produce more than 400 tonnes of VX. At present, there is no conclusive evidence to support Iraq's claims concerning the complete disposal of these two precursors and the choline.

58. Iraq's recent declarations concerning the weaponization of biological agents has rendered invalid the current material balance for chemical munitions and the quantities of weaponized chemical agents. This derives from the fact that the munitions, including missile warheads, declared as being used for biological agents had previously been declared as used for chemical weapons purposes.

59. Iraq has also admitted the development of prototypes of binary sarin-filled artillery shells, 122 mm rockets and aerial bombs. However, the new documentation shows production in quantities well beyond prototype levels. Iraq has also admitted three flight tests of long-range missiles with chemical warheads, including one, in April 1990, with sarin.

60. Iraq admitted that it had received significant assistance from abroad. This support included, at a minimum, the provision of munitions specifically designed for chemical weapons fill, technical support for the development of a VX precursor manufacturing process and the provision of technical personnel directly to the Muthanna State Establishment (MSE).

61. The recently obtained documentation contains significant information on procurement and financing for MSE. These records indicate that at least $100 million in procurement remains undeclared. This finding contradicts Iraqi statements that all MSE procurement had been declared.

62. The new information on Iraq's proscribed chemical weapons programme will require appropriate follow-up action, including technical analysis of the documents and expert seminars. The documentation shows Iraq's efforts to produce indigenously key precursors for chemical weapons, for example, the synthesis of cyclo-

hexanol (a GF precursor) from phenol and the synthesis of di-isopropylamine (a VX precursor) from ammonia and acetone. In the light of this, certain proposals by Iraq to construct new facilities with dual-use capabilities will have to be considered very carefully by the Commission and the monitoring system adjusted accordingly.

63. The new information invalidates material balances provided in the March 1995 FFCD and subsequent amendments. At the present time also the Commission cannot exclude the potential existence of stocks of VX, its direct precursors and undeclared munitions in Iraq. In these circumstances, the Commission is requiring a new full, final and complete disclosure from Iraq which will give a coherent and true account of its chemical weapons programme.

V. Biological activities

A. The monitoring system

64. Monitoring in the biological area began in full on 4 April 1995, preceded by a four-month interim monitoring phase. The scope of activities and sites to be encompassed by the monitoring needs to be broad because of the inherent dual-use nature of biological technology and the ease with which civilian facilities can be converted for biological weapons purposes. The Commission has been compelled to cast a wider net in the biological field because of Iraq's incomplete disclosure of the full extent of its past biological warfare activities. In actively seeking to establish an understanding of such a programme, the Commission has had to rely less on Iraq's openness and more on its own findings.

65. Currently, 79 sites throughout Iraq are included in the biological monitoring and verification regime. These sites are comprised of:

(a) Five sites currently known to have played a significant role in Iraq's past biological weapons programme;

(b) Five vaccine or pharmaceutical facilities;

(c) Thirty-five research and university sites which have significant technology or equipment;

(d) Thirteen breweries, distilleries and dairies with dual-purpose capabilities;

(e) Eight diagnostic laboratories;

(f) Five acquisition and distribution sites of biological supplies/equipment;

(g) Four facilities associated with biological equipment development;

(h) Four product development organizations.

Of these sites, 9 are category A (most intense monitoring), 15 are category B, 10 category C and 45 category D.

66. The monitoring concept that has been implemented by the Commission includes: equipment inventory at all sites where dual-purpose equipment is located;

notifications by Iraq of transfer, modification and acquisition of such equipment; placement of cameras at selected sites to observe change in activity or use of equipment; routine inspections of sites by a Baghdad-based monitoring team, primarily on a no-notice basis, and on a variable frequency; and identification of factors related to "break-out" scenarios at sites and of their possible role in proscribed activities. These monitoring activities from the Baghdad Monitoring and Verification Centre are reinforced by special inspections where investigations by most experienced specialists are desired. Key aspects of the baseline process, including identification of additional sites of interest and their capability, identification of undeclared dual-use equipment, assessment of their present and future use, are also ongoing activities that are incorporated into the monitoring process.

67. During the reporting period since 10 April 1995, over 150 inspections or visits to different sites have been made by the biological monitoring team, including over 20 inspections of the Al Hakam facility. At three sites, including Al Hakam, video monitoring, using a total of 22 cameras, supplement the other monitoring efforts. Both realtime images and recorded videotapes are analysed and the information is incorporated into the monitoring process.

B. Proscribed programme

68. While ongoing monitoring concentrates mainly on dual-use biological capabilities in Iraq, an efficient and effective monitoring is not possible without a full understanding of Iraq's proscribed biological activities. In its report to the Security Council last April (S/1995/284), the Commission stated that "it has come to the conclusion that Iraq has not provided a full and comprehensive disclosure of its past military biological programme or accounted for items and materials for that programme".

69. Up to the middle of the reporting period, Iraq continued to deny having ever had any offensive biological weapons programme or activities. It should be recalled that, in March 1995, Iraq officially submitted a new full, final and complete disclosure in the biological area which, like its original FFCD in May 1992, and other declarations since the adoption of resolution 687 (1991), adhered to the position that Iraq had had only a very small defensive biological research programme conducted by 10 people from 1985 until the autumn of 1990. The March 1995 FFCD was so contrary to the information in the Commission's possession that the Commission saw no merit in initiating verification of the document. Essentially a stalemate developed between Iraq and the Commission. The Commission continued to collect information related to Iraq's biological weapons programme while, in parallel, trying to persuade Iraq,

through a dialogue, to present a true declaration covering its biological weapons activities.

70. In April and May 1995, Iraq continued to display an uncooperative attitude. During the Executive Chairman's visit to Iraq (29 May-1 June), Iraq refused even to meet with the biological experts accompanying the Chairman. The stalemate continued through June, but with promises from Iraq of information about its biological weapons programme to be provided only in late June or early July, if Iraq at that time concluded that there were indications that progress was being made towards the reintegration of Iraq into the international community (see para. 10 above).

71. On 1 July 1995, during the Executive Chairman's visit to Iraq (see para. 11 above), Iraq did provide an oral overview of its past programme, admitting for the first time that it indeed had had an offensive biological weapons programme from April 1986 to September 1990. But while acknowledging an offensive programme that included the production of large quantities of two warfare agents at the Al Hakam facility, the overview, nevertheless, firmly denied weaponization of these or any other biological warfare agents. During technical discussions that followed this oral presentation, the Commission's experts indicated that several major issues related to Iraq's biological weapons programme—for example weaponization, earlier initiation date of the programme, larger involvement of Iraq's other establishments, and the material balance of supplies and agents—were still outstanding and urged Iraq to address those issues in a new FFCD that Iraq undertook to submit to the Commission.

72. In the second half of July, Iraq prepared a draft FFCD and the UNSCOM 121/BW 26 team was sent to Iraq to review the draft together with Iraqi personnel in order to assist them in the preparation of a document that would be amenable to speedy and effective verification.

73. The July draft declaration contained many areas in which Iraq's disclosures were inconsistent with the Commission's information or where information was missing or unclear. These deficiencies followed a pattern: they appeared to be designed to deny information that would either provide evidence of weaponization or reveal military connections with the biological weapons programme. There was also a strong suspicion that Iraq's new accounts of agent production and complex growth media consumption were manipulated to provide what Iraq hoped would pass as a credible accounting for the missing media, as previously described by the Commission in its April 1995 report (S/1995/284, paras. 62-69). The UNSCOM 121/BW 26 team strongly advised Iraq not to submit a deficient declaration.

74. Nevertheless, on 4 August 1995, Iraq officially submitted its FFCD to the Executive Chairman. This new FFCD was consistent with Iraq's oral presentation of 1 July and the July draft and ignored the Commission's suggestions. Because of the acknowledgement that Iraq's programme was offensive in nature, it was considered a breakthrough in the stalemate that had existed between the Commission and Iraq. The Commission initiated verification efforts, including analysis by the Commission's and visiting experts of various portions of Iraq's declaration; inquiries with States concerning supplier information; detailed assessment of the new FFCD and correlation with information available to the Commission.

75. On 17 August 1995, after the events described in paragraph 14 above, Iraq informed the Executive Chairman that the full, final and complete disclosure of 4 August should not be considered valid. Iraq then presented to the Chairman a vastly different account of Iraq's past biological warfare programme that included weaponization, additional agents and additional sites involved in the programme. Iraq undertook to submit to the Commission a new FFCD. During this visit, some documents were obtained which related to the proscribed biological weapons programme. On 22 August 1995, a biological expert team (UNSCOM 125/BW 27) visited Baghdad in order to collect detailed information and clarifications on the revelations which had been presented during the Chairman's visit. A summation of the most recent revelations of Iraq's biological weapons programme follows. It should be stressed that it is solely based on declarations made by Iraq since mid-August, which remain subject to verification. At this time, therefore, the Commission can give no assurances as to the correctness and comprehensiveness of that information:

(a) Iraq stated that, in 1974, the Government had adopted a policy to acquire biological weapons. In 1975, a research and development biological weapons programme was established under the Al Hazen Ibn Al Haytham Institute at a site located in Al Salman. The work was poorly directed. Coupled with a lack of appropriate facilities and equipment, it was said the Institute achieved little and it closed in 1978;

(b) The failure of the Al Hazen Institute was claimed to be a severe setback for the programme and the following years are alleged to be devoid of any biological weapons-related activity. In the early period of the Iran/Iraq war (perhaps in 1982 or 1983), a prominent Iraqi microbiologist wrote a report expressing his concerns on scientific developments relating to biological warfare agents and suggesting that research in this subject be commenced in Iraq. It is still uncertain whether this report was followed up, but in 1985 the Muthanna State Establishment, Iraq's main facility for chemical weapons research and development, production and weaponization, recommended the commencement of a biological weapons programme. In May or June 1985, Muthanna sought and obtained endorsement from the Ministry of Defence for this programme. It was anticipated that the biological weapons research would be production-oriented and thus, in addition to laboratory-scale equipment, a pilot plant in the form of one 150-litre fermenter was purchased by Muthanna. Throughout 1985, personnel were recruited by Muthanna and by the end of the year, a staff of 10 was working on biological weapons research;

(c)   Initial work at Muthanna was said to focus on literature studies, until April 1986, when bacterial strains were received from overseas. Research then concentrated on the characterization of *Bacillus anthracis* (anthrax) and *Clostridium botulinum* (botulinum toxin) to establish pathogenicity, growth and sporulation conditions, and their storage parameters. (Anthrax is an acute bacterial disease of animals and humans that can be incurred by ingestion or inhalation of the bacterial spores or through skin lesions. It produces an infection resulting in death in days to weeks after exposure. Botulinum toxin produces an acute muscular paralysis resulting in death of animals or humans.) As claimed by Iraq, there was no production of agents and the imported fermenters at Muthanna were not used. However, Muthanna was still looking ahead to biological warfare agent production and wrote a report to the Ministry of Defence recommending that the former single-cell protein plant at Taji be taken over by Muthanna for the production of botulinum toxin. The Ministry of Defence agreed but, in early 1987, before the plan could be implemented, the proposal went into abeyance for a short time owing to administrative reasons;

(d)   In May 1987, the biological weapons programme was transferred from Muthanna to Al Salman. The reason for this was said to be that the biological work interfered with the (presumably higher-priority) chemical weapons programme at Muthanna. At Al Salman, the biological weapons group administratively came under the Forensic Research Department of the Technical Research Centre (TRC) of the Military Industrialization Corporation. After a slow beginning, it appeared that the biological weapons programme flourished at Al Salman. Equipment, including the fermenters, was transferred from Muthanna, new equipment was acquired, and new staff joined the biological weapons group to bring the workforce up to about 18. The research at Al Salman shifted to issues related more to the application of the agents as biological weapons. The effects on larger animals, including sheep, donkeys, monkeys and dogs, were studied within the laboratory and inhalation chamber, as well as in the field. Initial weapons field trials were

conducted in early 1988. Studies of scale-up production were initiated on botulinum toxin and anthrax;

(e)   The earlier proposal for the acquisition of a biological weapons production site was revived and the former single-cell protein plant at Taji was taken over by TRC in mid-1987. The plant was said to be in a run-down condition and it was not until early in 1988 that it was made operational. With a workforce of eight people, and using one 450-litre fermenter, production of botulinum toxin commenced in February or March 1988 and continued until September/October of that year. Production of botulinum toxin also was carried out at Al Salman in flasks or laboratory fermenters;

(f)   Initial production fermentation studies with anthrax at Al Salman used 7- and 14-litre laboratory-scale fermenters at the end of 1988. From the beginning of 1989, the 150-litre fermenter transferred from Muthanna was used to produce *Bacillus subtilis*, a simulant for anthrax as a biological warfare agent. After five or six runs of producing subtilis, anthrax production began at Al Salman around March 1989. About 15 or 16 production runs were performed, producing up to 1,500 litres of anthrax, which was concentrated to 150 litres. Additional production with the laboratory fermenters was also accomplished;

(g)   Towards the end of 1987, a report on the success of biological weapons work by TRC was submitted to MIC. This resulted in a decision to enter the full-scale production phase for a biological weapons programme;

(h)   In March 1988, a new site for biological weapons production was selected at a location now known as Al Hakam. The project was given the designator "324". The design philosophy for the Al Hakam plant was taken from the chemical weapons research and production facility at Muthanna: the buildings were to be well separated, research areas were segregated from production areas and the architectural features of Muthanna buildings copied where appropriate. The plan for the new facility at Al Hakam envisaged research and development, production and storage of biological warfare agents, but not munitions filling. Construction of the production buildings at the northern end of the Al Hakam site was largely complete by September 1988 after which work commenced on erection of the laboratory buildings;

(i)   In 1988, a search for production equipment for the biological weapons programme was conducted in Iraq. Two 1,850-litre and seven 1,480-litre fermenters from the Veterinary Research Laboratories were transferred to Al Hakam in November 1988. The 450-litre fermenter line at Taji, which was at the time used in the production of botulinum toxin, was also earmarked for transfer to Al Hakam and was relocated there in October

1988. From mid-1988, large fermenters were also sought from abroad, but after Iraq completed a contract for a 5,000-litre fermenter, an export licence was not granted;

(j) At Al Hakam, production of botulinum toxin for weapons purposes began in April 1989 and anthrax in May 1989. Initially much of the fermentation capacity for anthrax was used for the production of anthrax simulant for weapons field trials. Production of anthrax itself, it is claimed, began in earnest in 1990. In total, about 6,000 litres of concentrated botulinum toxin and 8,425 litres of anthrax were produced at Al Hakam during 1990;

(k) From the early period of the biological weapons programme at Al Salman, there was interest in other potential biological warfare agents beyond anthrax and botulinum toxin. It became the policy to expand the biological weapons programme into these other fields. Thus, from the design phase of Al Hakam as a biological weapons research, production and storage facility, there were plans for such diversification, including facilities to work on viruses and laboratory space for genetic engineering studies;

(l) In April 1988, in addition to anthrax and botulinum toxin, a new agent, *Clostridium perfringens* (gas gangrene), was added to the bacterial research work at Al Salman. (*Clostridium perfringens* produces a condition known as gas gangrene, so named because of the production of gaseous rotting of flesh, common in war casualties requiring amputation of limbs.) In August 1989, work on perfringens was transferred from Al Salman to Al Hakam;

(m) In May 1988, studies were said to be initiated at Al Salman on aflatoxin. (Aflatoxin is a toxin commonly associated with fungal-contaminated food grains and is known for its induction of liver cancers. It is generally considered to be non-lethal in humans but of serious medical concern because of its carcinogenic activity.) Later research was also done on trichothecene mycotoxins such as T-2 and DAS. (Tricothecene mycotoxins produce nausea, vomiting, diarrhoea and skin irritation and, unlike most microbial toxins, can be absorbed through the skin.) Research was conducted into the toxic effects of aflatoxins as biological warfare agents and their effect when combined with other chemicals. Aflatoxin was produced by the growth of the fungus aspergillus in 5-litre flasks at Al Salman;

(n) In 1989, it was decided to move aflatoxin production for biological weapons purposes to a facility at Fudaliyah. The facility was used for aflatoxin production in flasks from April/May 1990 to December 1990. A total of about 1,850 litres of toxin in solution was declared as having been produced at Fudaliyah;

(o) Another fungal agent examined by Iraq for its biological weapons potential was wheat cover smut. (Wheat cover smut produces a black growth on wheat and other cereal grains; contaminated grain cannot be used as foodstuff.) After small production at Al Salman, larger-scale production was carried out near Mosul in 1987 and 1988 and considerable quantities of contaminated grain were harvested. The idea was said not to have been further developed; however, it was only sometime in 1990 that the contaminated grain was destroyed by burning at the Fudaliyah site;

(p) Another toxin worked for weapons application was ricin. (Ricin is a protein toxin derived from castor bean plants that is highly lethal to humans and animals. When inhaled, ricin produces a severe diffuse breakdown of lung tissue resulting in a haemorrhagic pneumonia and death.) It appears that work started in 1988 at Al Salman. The first samples of ricin were supplied from the Sammarra drug factory and after some initial toxicological tests in conjunction with Muthanna, the quantity required for a weapons test was determined. Ten litres of concentrated ricin were prepared. A weapons trial was conducted with the assistance of Muthanna using artillery shells. The test was considered to be a failure. The project was said to have been abandoned after this;

(q) Work on virus for biological weapons purposes started at Al Salman in July 1990. Shortly thereafter, a decision was taken to acquire the Foot and Mouth Disease facility at Daura and it was taken over for biological weapons purposes, in addition to the continued production of vaccines. It was decided that the Daura plant within the biological weapons programme would include facilities for bacteriology, virology and genetic engineering. Three viral agents for the biological weapons programme were obtained from within Iraq: haemorrhagic conjunctivitis virus, a rotavirus and camel pox virus. (Haemorrhagic conjunctivitis is an acute disease that causes extreme pain and temporary blindness. Rotavirus causes acute diarrhoea that could lead to dehydration and death. Camel pox causes fever and skin rash in camels; infection of humans is rare.) It was stated that very little work had been done on these viruses and none had been produced in quantity;

(r) Early in 1988, efforts began in the weaponization of biological warfare agents and some of the senior scientists involved in the biological weapons programme at TRC were sent to Iraq's munitions factories to familiarize themselves with this aspect. At about the same time, TRC first discussed with the Muthanna State Establishment weaponization of biological warfare agents and it was agreed that, because of Muthanna's experience in the weaponization of chemical agents, the Establishment would also provide the necessary assistance for the selection of weapons types for warfare agents and the conduct of field trials;

(s) The first field trials of biological weapons were said to have been conducted in March 1988 at Muthanna's weapons test range, Muhammadiyat. Two tests were done on the same day, one using the anthrax simulant, *Bacillus subtilis*, and the other using botulinum toxin. The munitions chosen for the tests were aerial bombs positioned on adjacent stands. The effects were observed on test animals (for botulinum toxin) or on Petri dishes (for subtilis). The first tests of both agents were considered failures. The agents in both cases did not spread far enough. Later in March, the second field trial with the same weapons systems was said to have been conducted and it was considered successful;

(t) No further weapons field trials were claimed to have been carried out for the next 18 months. In November 1989, further weaponization trials for anthrax (again using subtilis), botulinum toxin and aflatoxin were conducted, this time using 122 mm rockets, again at Muhammadiyat. These tests were also considered a success. Live firings of filled 122 mm rockets with the same agents were carried out in May 1990. Trials of R400 aerial bombs with *Bacillus subtilis* were first conducted in mid-August 1990. Final R400 trials using subtilis, botulinum toxin and aflatoxin followed in late August 1990;

(u) After 2 August 1990, the date of Iraq's invasion of Kuwait, Iraq's biological weapons programme was drastically intensified: the emphasis was shifted to production and later to weaponization of produced biological warfare agents. The foot and mouth disease plant at Daura was converted to biological weapons production. The six vaccine fermenters with ancillary equipment at the plant were used for production of botulinum toxin from November 1990 until 15 January 1991, by which time about 5,400 litres of concentrated toxin had been produced. It was decided that there was an additional requirement for anthrax production and the fermenters at Al Hakam that had been previously used for the production of botulinum toxin there were modified to meet the requirements for increased anthrax production. Production of perfringens for biological weapons purposes also began at Al Hakam in August 1990 using the 150-litre fermenter which had been relocated from Al Salman. A total of 340 litres of concentrated perfringens was produced;

(v) In December 1990, a programme was initiated to develop an additional delivery means, a biological weapons spray tank based on a modified aircraft drop tank. The concept was that tanks would be fitted either to a piloted fighter or to a remotely piloted aircraft to spray up to 2,000 litres of anthrax over a target. The field trials for both the spray tank and the remotely piloted

vehicle were conducted in January 1991. The test was considered a failure and no further effort towards further development was said to have been made. Nevertheless, three additional drop tanks were modified and stored, ready for use. They are said to have been destroyed in July 1991. The prototype spray tank used for trials was claimed to have been destroyed during the Gulf war bombing;

(w) Weaponization of biological warfare agents began on a large scale in December 1990 at Muthanna. As declared, the R400 bombs were selected as the appropriate munition for aerial delivery and 100 were filled with botulinum toxin, 50 with anthrax and 16 with aflatoxin. In addition, 25 Al Hussein warheads, which had been produced in a special production run since August 1990, were filled with botulinum toxin (13), anthrax (10) and aflatoxin (2). These weapons were then deployed in early January 1991 at four locations, where they remained throughout the war;

(x) In summary, Iraq has declared the production of at least 19,000 litres of concentrated botulinum toxin (nearly 10,000 litres were filled into munitions), 8,500 litres of concentrated anthrax (some 6,500 litres were filled into munitions) and 2,200 litres of concentrated aflatoxin (1,580 litres were filled into munitions);

(y) Iraq declared that it had decided to destroy biological munitions and the remaining biological warfare bulk agent after the Gulf war. An order for destruction was claimed to have been given orally, and no Iraqi representative seems to be able to recall an exact date for the order or the dates of destruction operations. The order was said to have been given some time in May or June 1991. All filled biological bombs were relocated to one airfield and deactivation chemicals added to agent fill. The bombs were then explosively destroyed and burnt, and the remains buried. A similar disposal technique was used for the missile warheads at a separate site. In late August 1995, Iraq showed to an UNSCOM team a location which it claimed to be a warhead destruction site. However, later on, Iraq changed its story and was unable to identify with any degree of certainty the exact location of warheads destruction operations;

(z) Of the bacterial bulk agent stored at Al Hakam, Iraq stated that a similar deactivation procedure had been adopted. The detoxified liquid was emptied into the facility's septic tank and eventually dumped at the site. About 8,000 litres of concentrated botulinum toxin, over 2,000 litres of concentrated anthrax, 340 litres of concentrated perfringens and an unspecified quantity of aflatoxin, according to Iraq's declaration, were destroyed at Al Hakam.

76. Iraq's biological weapons programme as described to the Commission embraced a comprehensive

range of agents and munitions. Agents under Iraq's biological weapons programme included lethal agents, e.g. anthrax, botulinum toxin and ricin, and incapacitating agents, e.g. aflatoxin, mycotoxins, haemorrhagic conjunctivitis virus and rotavirus. The scope of biological warfare agents worked on by Iraq encompassed both anti-personnel and anti-plant weapons. The programme covered a whole variety of biological weapons delivery means, from tactical weapons (e.g. 122 mm rockets and artillery shells), to strategic weapons (e.g. aerial bombs and Al Hussein warheads filled with anthrax, botulinum toxin and aflatoxin) and "economic" weapons, e.g. wheat cover smut. Given the Iraqi claim that only five years had elapsed since its declared inception in 1985, the achievements of Iraq's biological weapons programme were remarkable.

77.   The achievements included the production and actual weaponization of large quantities of bacterial agents and aflatoxin and research on a variety of other biological weapons agents. A special dedicated facility, Al Hakam, for biological weapons research and development as well as large-scale production was under construction, with most essential elements completed at the time of the Gulf war and production and storage capabilities operational. A number of other facilities and establishments in Iraq provided active support for the biological weapons programme. The programme appears to have a degree of balance suggesting a high level of management and planning that envisioned the inclusion of all aspects of a biological weapons programme, from research to weaponization. It is also reasonable to assume that, given that biological weapons were considered as strategic weapons and were actually deployed, detailed thought must have been given to the doctrine of operational use for these weapons of mass destruction.

78.   It appears that, until August 1990, the biological weapons programme had been developing at a steady pace, continuing to expand and diversify. In August 1990, a "crash" programme was launched and the imperatives of production and weaponization took over.

79.   The documentation on Iraq's biological weapons programme obtained by the Commission in August 1995 appears to represent a fraction of all the documents generated under the programme. For example, studies were described orally by Iraq to the Commission that are not included in any of the documentation. Some of the studies referred to in the documents differ significantly from those described to the Commission. Information available to the Commission from other sources does not correspond in important aspects to the information provided by Iraq.

80.   In spite of the substantial new disclosures made by Iraq since mid-August, the Commission does not believe that Iraq has given a full and correct account of its biological weapons programme. The Commission intends to continue its intensive inspection, verification and analytical efforts with the objective of presenting to the Security Council, as soon as possible, its assessments of Iraq's compliance with the biological weapons-related provisions of Security Council resolution 687 (1991). Success will depend on Iraq's cooperation with these efforts and its complete openness, including provision to the Commission of all documentation and of a truly full, final and complete disclosure of Iraq's proscribed biological weapons programme.

VI. *Nuclear activities*

81.   The Director General of IAEA is reporting separately on the activities of the UNSC 687 Action Team set up to implement paragraphs 12 and 13 of Security Council resolution 687 (1991) and the IAEA plan for ongoing monitoring and verification approved under resolution 715 (1991) (S/22872/Rev.1 and Corr.1).

82.   The Special Commission continues, in accordance with paragraph 9 (b) (iii) of resolution 687 (1991) and paragraph 4 (b) of resolution 715 (1991), to provide its assistance and cooperation to the IAEA Action Team through the provision of special expertise and logistical, informational and other operational support for the carrying out of the IAEA plan for ongoing monitoring and verification. In accordance with paragraph 9 (b) (i) of resolution 687 (1991) and paragraph 4 (a) of resolution 715 (1991), it designates sites for inspection. In accordance with paragraph 3 (iii) of resolution 707 (1991), it decides on requests from Iraq to move or destroy any material or equipment relating to its nuclear weapons programme or other nuclear activities. Furthermore, it continues, in accordance with paragraph 4 (c) of resolution 715 (1991), to perform such other functions, in cooperation in the nuclear field with the Director General of IAEA, as may be necessary to coordinate activities under the plans for ongoing monitoring and verification, including making use of commonly available services and information to the fullest extent possible, in order to achieve maximum efficiency and optimum use of resources.

83.   During the current reporting period, the Commission has reviewed and concurred with a number of IAEA evaluations of Iraqi requests to relocate materials and equipment within Iraq, participated with IAEA teams during routine inspections, provided, through the German Government, fixed-wing (C-160) and rotating-wing (CH-53G) aircraft for the transport of IAEA inspectors into Iraq from Bahrain and between points within Iraq and provided the UNSC 687 Action Team with working

room and supporting facilities at the Baghdad Monitoring and Verification Centre.

84. Close coordination between IAEA and the Commission is already ongoing in the management and control of machine tool movements within Iraq, and a better integration between the IAEA and UNSCOM systems of survey has been implemented, for example for machines located at the Nassr State Establishment, which are under both missile and nuclear monitoring. Cross-disciplinary inspections have been more frequent in order to increase the information flow and develop cross-fertilization between the specialized teams. IAEA and the Commission also cooperated in the initial assessment of the documents obtained in Iraq on 20 August 1995.

85. The Commission's nuclear experts will participate in certain inspections decided by the Action Team during the coming months. Regular meetings are now scheduled, alternatively in New York and Vienna, to exchange information from all sources and to plan cross-disciplinary inspections. Commission experts regularly visit Vienna to update the IAEA photo library. The Commission's experts are continuing to participate in IAEA's negotiations with the Russian Federation regarding the sale of the nuclear materials removed from Iraq and reprocessed in Russia.

VII. Other activities

A. Export/import mechanism

86. As mentioned in the April 1995 report, the joint proposal prepared by the Special Commission and IAEA for the export/import mechanism called for in paragraph 7 of Security Council resolution 715 (1991) was submitted to the Sanctions Committee in February 1995. Upon receipt of the concurrence of that Committee, it is to be transmitted to the Council for its approval.

87. In the course of the consideration of the proposal by the Sanctions Committee, certain delegations requested information on the modalities which would be followed by the Special Commission and IAEA when implementing the mechanism in Iraq. On 17 July 1995, the Executive Chairman of the Commission sent a letter to the Chairman of the Sanctions Committee responding to this request. In that letter, the Chairman pointed out that the Security Council had on several occasions confirmed that the sole responsibility for carrying out their mandates in Iraq rested with the Commission and IAEA. Nevertheless, the Commission and IAEA had kept the Council fully informed of their activities and their modus operandi. In keeping with that practice, it was useful to indicate the general principles which would be followed in implementing the mechanism in Iraq.

88. In his letter, the Executive Chairman explained that an office of export/import specialists would be estab-

lished in the Baghdad Monitoring and Verification Centre which would serve as an administrative clearing house for communications from Iraq regarding the notification forms which it would be required to submit. That office and the Centre would also implement inspections within Iraq to ensure that the mechanism was being complied with. These inspections would be as vigorous as necessary to ensure that no violations of the export/import regime would occur. In this regard, the Commission and the IAEA intended to rely on their full rights under the relevant Security Council resolutions (including resolutions 687 (1991), 707 (1991) and 715 (1991), the plans for ongoing monitoring and verification (S/22871/Rev.1 and S/22872/Rev.1 and Corr.1), the privileges and immunities as set forth in the exchange of letters between the United Nations and Iraq of 6 and 17 May 1991 and the decision to be taken by the Security Council approving the mechanism.

89. The letter further stated that inspections under the mechanism would take place not only at the declared end-user sites where notified items would be tagged, as appropriate, and entered into the site protocols, but would also be conducted anywhere else in Iraq, including points of entry into Iraq, where there was reason to believe that notified items or dual-use items in respect of which there should have been notification might be found. To ensure Iraqi compliance the monitoring activities would be carried out in whatever ways yielded the most effective results, whether by monitoring end-user sites, or border crossings, or other locations.

90. The Executive Chairman proposed, when the Sanctions Committee was in a position to forward the proposal for the mechanism to the Security Council, as the tripartite proposal called for in paragraph 7 of resolution 715 (1991), that it should be accompanied, for purposes of information, by his letter setting out in general terms the modalities which it was intended would be followed in implementing the mechanism.

91. On 20 July 1995, the Sanctions Committee resumed consideration of the Special Commission's and IAEA's joint proposal for the export/import mechanism, together with the Executive Chairman's letter of 17 July. The Committee approved the proposal and the suggestion of the Executive Chairman that its transmission to the Council should be accompanied by the letter of 17 July. Because of a request, formal transmission to the Council has been postponed. Transmission is expected to take place as soon as all members indicate the concurrence of their Governments.

92. In the meantime, the Special Commission has continued its efforts to prepare for the implementation of the mechanism after its adoption by the Security Council

so as to be able to put it into effect as of such time as the Council directs.

B. *National implementation measures*

93. There have been no new developments since the Commission's reports in April and June 1995 regarding the national implementation measures which Iraq is required to take under the plans for ongoing monitoring and verification. The Commission has continued to pursue the matter and to press for the adoption of the necessary legislation. On each occasion that the matter has been raised, the Iraqi representatives have stated that the legislation is with the Office of the Presidency and that no problems were foreseen in its adoption. Assurances that such adoption would be forthcoming in a matter of days or weeks have not been fulfilled. The absence of this legislation, almost four years after the adoption of resolution 715 (1991) approving the plans for ongoing monitoring and verification, is of great concern to the Commission. There is no doubt that the enactment of this legislation, *inter alia*, prohibiting Iraqi citizens from engaging in activities proscribed by resolution 687 (1991), would be regarded as an indication of Iraq's will to comply fully with the requirements of the resolution.

C. *Aerial surveillance*

94. The aerial imagery provided by the Commission's high-altitude surveillance aircraft (U-2) and the Baghdad-based aerial inspection team continues to be an essential tool for the monitoring regime and for the investigation of new sites. To date, over 600 missions have been undertaken by the aerial inspection team and 269 missions by the U-2.

95. The establishment of the photographic development laboratory in the Monitoring Centre in Baghdad has facilitated the swift processing and review of the aerial photographic product. The capability to process photography at the Centre has also proved a useful asset for ground inspection teams.

VIII. *Finance, organization and air support*

96. The financial situation of the Special Commission is more precarious than ever. Funds, either from frozen Iraqi assets or provided as contributions to the Commission, have been trickling into the escrow account established under Security Council resolution 778 (1992) on a very irregular basis. While funding has been secured for the remainder of 1995, funds have yet to be identified for 1996. The level of operational expenditures of the Commission from its inception in May 1991 until the end of 1995 will have reached $100 million. The operational budget of the Commission, under the current rate of activities, will be around $20 million for the next year.

97. The above figures only reflect the operational budget of the Commission, which has greatly benefited from the assistance of supporting Governments through the direct provision of services, staff and equipment. Such Governments may seek reimbursement when adequate funds are obtained from Iraq, which has responsibility for all costs incurred under section C of Security Council resolution 687 (1991).

98. The number of the Special Commission's experts in New York has been increased over the last few months to cope with the growing workload. All additional experts have been provided by Member States at their own cost.

99. The Commission is strengthening its communications system between New York and Baghdad and is acquiring an improved voice and fax data system which will enable the transmission of data in a highly secure manner.

100. The office space situation of the Commission in New York is becoming more difficult. It will be impossible to accommodate, within the currently available space, the additional documents obtained in August which are now arriving in New York. A special request has been made for additional secure space for this purpose.

101. The Commission has described the establishment, preparations and resources of the Baghdad Monitoring and Verification Centre in earlier reports (S/1994/1138 and S/1995/284). All the projects planned to renovate the Canal Hotel facilities for the Centre, in part using Iraqi labour and materials, are now completed. This effort has taken up much of the last year and could not have been finished without the generous contributions of personnel, equipment and materials from supporting States.

102. The field office in Bahrain continues to support the operations of the Commission and the activities of the Baghdad Monitoring and Verification Centre. The Commission wishes to place on record its gratitude to the Government of Bahrain for its great generosity and unstinting support in the establishment and maintenance of the field office in Bahrain. This has constituted one of the most important contributions to the work of the Commission and has considerably expedited that work.

103. Recently, the Secretary-General noted the substantial contributions of air support from the Government of Germany for the operations of the Special Commission and IAEA in Iraq (A/50/1, para. 701). Indeed, without the C-160 transport aircraft and the CH-53G helicopters, the Commission would not have accomplished its work and could not meet the requirements of

the Security Council in carrying out ongoing monitoring and verification and its other responsibilities in Iraq.

104. The airlift support provided by Germany has been of the highest quality. One measure of the success of this effort is that the helicopter unit recently achieved 3,000 accident-free flying hours in Iraq under the difficult and complex flight conditions existing there. The C-160 Transall aircraft has flown over 10,000 passengers into and out of Iraq. Another measure is the outstanding logistical support from the contributing Government to its forward-deployed units in Bahrain and in Iraq. Air support will continue to be critical to Commission and IAEA operations in Iraq.

105. Helicopter support in Iraq has been and will continue to be vital for the independence of the operations of the Commission and IAEA. Indeed, with the lifting of sanctions and the resumption of international trade, the requirement for helicopter support will increase significantly. Helicopters will provide efficient transportation for inspection teams to travel to border crossings and points of entry. At the same time, the current requirements will remain for low-altitude aerial inspection photography; medical evacuation; rapid, no-notice movement of inspection teams; and airlift for vehicles. These many needs are met with the CH-53G, which appears to be the most efficient aircraft currently available for this purpose. The Commission remains profoundly grateful to the Government of Germany for its unique and vital contribution in carrying out the Security Council's mandate in Iraq under section C of Security Council resolution 687 (1991).

IX. *Conclusion*

106. During the period under review and since the Special Commission's report in June 1995, very important developments have taken place in all areas, and a considerable amount of information has become available to the Commission concerning Iraq's proscribed programmes. The Commission's preliminary analysis of this information reveals that Iraq has been concealing proscribed activities and that, consequently, some of the assessments in the Commission's earlier reports have to be revised.

107. Iraq has been misleading the Commission by withholding information that, before the Gulf war, it had secretly produced Scud-type missile engines and carried out research and development on a variety of projects on missiles of prohibited ranges. Furthermore, Iraq's efforts to conceal its biological weapons programme, its chemical missile warhead flight tests and work on the development of a missile for the delivery of a nuclear device led it to provide incorrect information concerning certain of its missile activities. The new revelations cast into doubt

the veracity of Iraq's previous declarations in the missile area, including the material balance for proscribed weapons and items. Consequently, Iraq has agreed to provide a new declaration with a full, final and complete disclosure in the missile area.

108. In the chemical weapons area, the Special Commission's investigations have led to disclosure of activities aiming at the acquisition of a considerable capability for the production of the advanced nerve agent VX. Whether Iraq still keeps precursors in storage for immediate VX use has not been fully clarified. The revelations also shed new light on the scope and ambition of Iraq's chemical weapons programme. The Commission must adjust the direction of some of its monitoring activities, especially to prevent Iraq from using its chemical compounds, equipment and activities for secret acquisition of chemical weapons. Further destruction of some Iraqi chemical assets has to be contemplated. The Commission has requested Iraq to provide a new declaration comprising a full, final and complete disclosure of its capabilities with regard to chemical weapons.

109. The Special Commission has detected and identified a hitherto secret offensive biological weapons programme in Iraq comprising a large-scale production of biological warfare agents, the filling and deployment of missile warheads and aerial bombs with agents, as well as biological weapons research and development activities of considerable width and depth. As late as August of this year, Iraq presented to the Commission a formal, but essentially false, declaration on its biological weapons activities. Consequently, the Commission has requested again—and Iraq has agreed to provide—a full, final and complete disclosure of its biological weapons programme in the form of a new declaration. Much remains to be verified with regard to these weapons, in particular the destruction of munitions and bulk agents.

110. Given the new disclosures, the Special Commission is obliged to consider, in accordance with paragraph 8 of Security Council resolution 687 (1991), the possible destruction of facilities and items which were used in the production of biological weapons.

111. For the fulfilment of the Special Commission's tasks, it needs a complete understanding of the concept behind each stage of the development of all proscribed weapons. A special concern of the Commission in this respect is the matter of the deployment of Iraq's proscribed missiles with non-conventional warheads for strategic and offensive use.

112. The increased flow of data, whether originating in Iraq's new admissions or in recently obtained documents and other types of documentation, has opened up new possibilities for a solid and credible account of the proscribed weapons and weapons capabilities. With

these new developments, the prospects for the full implementation of the weapons chapter of Security Council resolution 687 (1991) have improved.

113. Further exploration and investigation are necessary to verify that Iraq's new statements and the declarations in all the weapons areas requested by the Commission are true representations of the facts. The large amount of documentation obtained will be of use in this regard. The Special Commission will concentrate its personnel and technical resources in order to achieve a complete and reliable account as fast as possible.

114. The system for ongoing monitoring and verification is now in place and has been tested for some time. It is as much in the interests of Iraq as of the Commission that the ongoing monitoring and verification system functions without any flaws. Even if the new revelations have led to adjustments, redirection and augmentation of activities, the system has already proved to be robust and fundamentally sound. Indeed, it was during the build-up of the monitoring structures that the Commission's scientists and analysts were able to detect Iraq's concealment of its hitherto secret biological weapons programme. Likewise, as mentioned above, Iraqi efforts to circumvent the control arrangements in the missile and chemical areas have been detected before any serious damage has occurred. The Commission also detected undeclared efforts by Iraq to establish a covert procurement network for activities under monitoring.

115. In this report, the Commission has outlined its concerns in all areas of its responsibility. Questions can still be raised about the intentions of Iraq as regards possible remnants of its proscribed programmes. In the coming months, the Government of Iraq must present three new declarations comprising full, final and complete disclosures of all its proscribed capabilities. Iraq must at the same time hand over the weapons documentation still in its hands. Access to and control of all relevant documentary evidence is necessary for the Commission to be able quickly and effectively to verify Iraq's declarations and ascertain that all Iraq's proscribed weapons capabilities have indeed been disposed of. If the requested declarations and actions by Iraq fulfil the requirements of the Security Council, a solid base will be laid for the full implementation of all aspects of section C of Security Council resolution 687 (1991). With an effective and proven monitoring and verification system in place, the Commission should be able to confirm that Iraq would have no capability to project any threat with proscribed weapons against its neighbours.

116. A necessary prerequisite for a comprehensive solution is that Iraq demonstrate a full openness and a manifest willingness to cooperate in all its dealings with the Special Commission. Iraq's stated preparedness to provide such cooperation is a hopeful sign. The true character of Iraq's expressed political intent will soon be tested by the Commission in its inspections and analytical activity. If Iraq were genuinely to translate its statements into action, there would be a real hope for the completion of the task entrusted to the Special Commission within a reasonable time-frame.

Appendix
Inspection schedule
(in-county dates)

Nuclear

15 May-21 May 1991	IAEA 1/UNSCOM 1
22 June- 3 July 1991	IAEA 2/UNSCOM 4
7 July- 18 July 1991	IAEA 3/UNSCOM 5
27 July- 10 August 1991	IAEA 4/UNSCOM 6
14 September-20 September 1991	IAEA 5/UNSCOM 14
21 September-30 September 1991	IAEA 6/UNSCOM 16
11 October-22 October 1991	IAEA 7/UNSCOM 19
11 November-18 November 1991	IAEA 8/UNSCOM 22
11 January-14 January 1992	IAEA 9/UNSCOM 25
5 February-13 February 1992	IAEA 10/UNSCOM 27
7 April-15 April 1992	IAEA 11/UNSCOM 33
26 May-4 June 1992	IAEA 12/UNSCOM 37
14 July-21 July 1992	IAEA 13/UNSCOM 41
31 August-7 September 1992	IAEA 14/UNSCOM 43
8 November-19 November 1992	IAEA 15/UNSCOM 46
6 December-14 December 1992	IAEA 16/UNSCOM 47
22 January-27 January 1993	IAEA 17/UNSCOM 49
3 March-11 March 1993	IAEA 18/UNSCOM 52
30 April-7 May 1993	IAEA 19/UNSCOM 56
25 June-30 June 1993	IAEA 20/UNSCOM 55
23 July-25 July 1993	IAEA 21/UNSCOM 61
1 November-9 November 1993	IAEA 22/UNSCOM 64
4 February-11 February 1994	IAEA 23/UNSCOM 65
11 April-22 April 1994	IAEA 24/UNSCOM 73
21 June-1 July 1994	IAEA 25/UNSCOM 53
22 August-2 September 1994	IAEA 26/UNSCOM 90
7 September-29 September 1994	NMG 94-01
14 October-21 October 1994	IAEA 27/UNSCOM 93
29 September-21 October 1994	NMG 94-02
21 October-9 November 1994	NMG 94-03
8 November-29 November 1994	NMG 94-04
29 November-16 December 1994	NMG 94-05
16 December 1994-13 January 1995	NMG 94-06
12 January-2 February 1995	NMG 95-01
2 February-28 February 1995	NMG 95-02
28 February-16 March 1995	NMG 95-03
16 March-6 April 1995	NMG 95-04
6 April-26 April 1995	NMG 95-05
27 April-10 May 1995	NMG 95-06
11 May-30 May 1995	NMG 95-07
31 May-20 June 1995	NMG 95-08

Nuclear (continued)

21 June-9 July 1995	NMG 95-09
10 July-30 July 1995	NMG 95-10
31 July-10 August 1995	NMG 95-11
11 August-29 August 1995	NMG 95-12
30 August-11 September 1995	NMG 95-13
9 September-19 September 1995	IAEA 28/UNSCOM 131
12 September-3 October 1995	NMG 95-14
4 October-...	NMG 95-15

Chemical

9 June-15 June 1991	CW 1/UNSCOM 2
15 August-22 August 1991	CW 2/UNSCOM 9
31 August-8 September 1991	CW 3/UNSCOM 11
31 August-5 September 1991	CW 4/UNSCOM 12
6 October-9 November 1991	CW 5/UNSCOM 17
22 October-2 November 1991	CW 6/UNSCOM 20
18 November-1 December 1991	CBW 1/UNSCOM 21
27 January-5 February 1992	CW 7/UNSCOM 26
21 February-24 March 1992	CD 1/UNSCOM 29
5 April-13 April 1992	CD 2/UNSCOM 32
15 April-29 April 1992	CW 8/UNSCOM 35
18 June 1992-14 June 1994	CDG / UNSCOM 38
26 June-10 July 1992	CBW 2/UNSCOM 39
21 September-29 September 1992	CW 9/UNSCOM 44
6 December-14 December 1992	CBW 3/UNSCOM 47
6 April-18 April 1993	CW 10/UNSCOM 55
27 June-30 June 1993	CW 11/UNSCOM 59
19 November-22 November 1993	CW 12/UNSCOM 65
1 February-14 February 1994	CW 13/UNSCOM 67
20 March-26 March 1994	CW 14/UNSCOM 70
18 April-22 April 1994	CW 15/UNSCOM 74
25 May-5 June 1994	CW 16/UNSCOM 75
31 May-12 June 1994	CW 17/UNSCOM 76
8 June-14 June 1994	CW 18/UNSCOM 77
10 August-23 August 1994	CW 19/UNSCOM 89
13 September-24 September 1994	CW 20/UNSCOM 91
2 October 1994-14 January 1995	CG 1
23 October-27 October 1994	CW 21/UNSCOM 95
11 January-21 January 1995	CW 23/UNSCOM 108
16 January-22 January 1995	CW 22/UNSCOM 107
14 January-15 April 1995	CG 2
16 April-26 September 1995	CG 3
16 September-20 September 1995	CW 25/UNSCOM 124
27 September 1995- ...	CG 4

Biological

2 August-8 August 1991	BW 1/UNSCOM 7
20 September-3 October 1991	BW 2/UNSCOM 15
11 March-18 March 1993	BW 3/UNSCOM 53
8 April-26 April 1994	BW 4/UNSCOM 72
28 May-7 June 1994	BW 5/UNSCOM 78
24 June-5 July 1994	BW 6/UNSCOM 84

5 June-8 June 1994	BW 7/UNSCOM 86
25 July-7 September 1994	BW 8/UNSCOM 87
20 August-25 August 1994	BW 9/UNSCOM 88
29 August-3 September 1994	BW 10/UNSCOM 92
29 September -14 October 1994	BW 11/UNSCOM 94
23 September-26 September 1994	BW 12/UNSCOM 96
15 November-22 November 1994	BW 15/UNSCOM 104
2 December-10 December 1994	BW 16/UNSCOM 105 (IMT)
2 December-13 December 1994	BW 13/UNSCOM 99 (IMT)
9 December-16 December 1994	BW 17/UNSCOM 106 (IMT)
28 December 1994-31 January 1995	IBG 1
10 January-22 January 1995	BW 18/UNSCOM 109
20 January-6 February 1995	BW 19/UNSCOM 110
23 January-3 February 1995	BW 22/UNSCOM 113
3 February-17 February 1995	BW 20/UNSCOM 111
3 February-17 February 1995	BW 21/UNSCOM 112
12 March-18 March 1995	BW 23/UNSCOM 115
24 March-6 April 1995	BW 24/UNSCOM 116
1 February-3 April 1995	IBG 2
4 April-7 August 1995	BG 1
27 April-16 May 1995	BW 25/UNSCOM 118
15 July-26 July 1995	BW 26/UNSCOM 121
19 August- 3 Septmber 1995	BW 27/UNSCOM 125
27 September-11 October 1995	BW 28/UNSCOM 126
8 August 1995- ...	BG2

Ballistic missiles

30 June-7 July 1991	BM 1/UNSCOM 3
18 July-20 July 1991	BM 2/UNSCOM 10
8 August-15 August 1991	BM 3/UNSCOM 8
6 September-13 September 1991	BM 4/UNSCOM 13
1 October-9 October 1991	BM 5/UNSCOM 18
1 December-9 December 1991	BM 6/UNSCOM 23
9 December-17 Decmber 1991	BM 7/UNSCOM 24
21 February-29 February 1992	BM 8/UNSCOM 28
21 March-29 March 1992	BM 9/UNSCOM 31
13 April-21 April 1992	BM 10/UNSCOM 34
14 May-22 May 1992	BM 11/UNSCOM 36
11 July-29 July 1992	BM 12/UNSCOM 40A+B
7 August-18 August 1992	BM 13/UNSCOM 42
16 October-30 October 1992	BM 14/UNSCOM 45
25 January-23 March 1993	IMT1a/UNSCOM 48
12 February-21 February 1993	BM 15/UNSCOM 50
22 February-23 February 1993	BM 16/UNSCOM 51
27 March-17 May 1993	IMT1b/UNSCOM 54
5 June-28 June 1993	IMT1c/UNSCOM 57
10 July-11 July 1993	BM 17/UNSCOM 60
24 August-15 September 1993	BM 18/UNSCOM 62
28 September-1 November 1993	BM 19/UNSCOM 63
21 January-29 January 1994	BM 20/UNSCOM 66
17 February-25 February 1994	BM 21/UNSCOM 69
30 March-20 May 1994	BM 22/UNSCOM 71

Ballistic missiles (continued)

20 May-8 June 1994	BM 23/UNSCOM 79
10 June-24 June 1994	BM 24/UNSCOM 80
14 June-22 June 1994	BM 25/UNSCOM 81
3 July-28 July 1994	BM 26/UNSCOM 82
15 July-24 July 1994	BM 27/UNSCOM 85
17 August-9 October 1994	MG 1
2 October-6 October 1994	BM 28/UNSCOM 98A
23 October-28 October 1994	BM 28/UNSCOM 98B
14 October 1994-21 February 1995	MG 2
19 October-22 October 1994	MG 2A
2 December-6 December 1994	MG 2B
9 December-14 December 1994	BM 29/UNSCOM 101
9 December-16 December 1994	BM 30/UNSCOM 102
27 January-31 January 1995	MG 2C
22 February-30 May 1995	MG 3
6 March-14 March 1995	BM 31/UNSCOM 103
25 May-1 June 1995	BM 32/UNSCOM 100
30 May-27 August 1995	MG 4
25 July-30 July 1995	BM 33/UNSCOM 122
20 August-24 August 1995	MG 4A
27 August 1995- ...	MG 5
27 September-1 October 1995	BM 34/UNSCOM 123

Computer search

12 February 1992	UNSCOM 30

Export/import mission

22 April-6 May 1995	UNSCOM 119

Special missions

30 June-3 July 1991
11 August-14 August 1991
4 October-6 October 1991
11 November-15 November 1991
27 January-30 January 1992
21 February-24 February 1992
17 July-19 July 1992
28 July-29 July 1992
6 September-12 September 1992
4 November-9 November 1992
4 November-8 November 1992
12 March-18 March 1993
14 March-20 March 1993
19 April-24 April 1993
4 June-5 July 1993
15 July-19 July 1993
25 July-5 August 1993
9 August-12 August 1993

10 September-24 September 1993
27 September-1 October 1993
1 October-8 October 1993
5 October-15 February 1993
2 December-10 December 1993
2 December-16 December 1993
21 January-27 January 1994
2 February-6 February 1994
10 April-14 April 1994
24 April-26 April 1994
28 May-29 May 1994
4 July-6 July 1994
8 August-16 August 1994
15 September-19 September 1994
21 September-25 September 1994
23 September-26 September 1994
3 October-6 October 1994
4 November-20 November 1994
7 November-12 November 1994
14 November-17 November 1994
4 December-18 December 1994
14 December-20 December 1994
7 January-31 January 1995
7 January-21 January 1995
13 January-26 January 1995
13 January-16 March 1995
12 January-28 January 1995
23 January-14 February 1995
25 January-4 February 1995
19 February-23 February 1995
22 February-28 February 1995
28 February-18 March 1995
16 March-29 March 1995
24 March-27 March 1995
4 May-23 May 1995
14 May-17 May 1995
29 May-1 June 1995
19 June-22 June 1995
22 June-2 July 1995
30 June-2 July 1995
2 July-10 July 1995
4 August-6 August 1995
7 August-12 August 1995
17 August-20 August 1995
24 August-2 September 1995
24 August-18 September 1995
5 September-14 September 1995
17 September-20 September 1995
29 September-1 October 1995

Document 215

Decision 32 taken by the Governing Council of the United Nations Compensation Commission: Payment of parts 1 and 2 of the second instalment of claims for serious personal injury or death (category B claims)

S/AC.26/Dec.32 (1995), 12 October 1995

Decision Concerning the Payment of Parts 1 and 2 of the second installment of claims for serious personal injury or death (category B claims) taken by the Governing Council of the United Nations Compensation Commission at its 55th meeting held on 11 October 1995 at Geneva

The Governing Council,

Decides, that the amount of US$8,252,500.00 be paid with respect to those awards as listed and as previously approved by the Governing Council in Decision 26 [S/AC.26/Dec.26 (1994)] and in Decision 27 [S/AC.26/Dec.27 (1995)].

Document 216

Report on the situation of human rights in Iraq prepared by the Special Rapporteur of the Commission on Human Rights on the situation of human rights in Iraq (extract)

A/50/734, 8 November 1995

Note by the Secretary-General

The Secretary-General has the honour the transmit to the members of the General Assembly the attached interim report prepared by Mr. Max van der Stoel, Special Rapporteur of the Commission on Human Rights on the situation of human rights in Iraq, in accordance with paragraph 14 of Commission on Human Rights resolution 1995/76 of 8 March 1995 and Economic and Social Council decision 1995/286 of 25 July 1995.

Annex
Interim report on the situation of human rights in Iraq, prepared by Mr. Max van der Stoel, Special Rapporteur of the Commission on Human Rights, in accordance with Commission resolution 1995/76 and Economic and Social Council decision 1995/286

I. *Introduction*

1. In accordance with paragraph 15 of Commission on Human Rights resolution 1995/76 of 8 March 1995, as approved by Economic and Social Council decision 1995/286 of 25 July 1995, the present report constitutes the interim report of the Special Rapporteur on the situation of human rights in Iraq. The final report will be submitted to the Commission on Human Rights at its fifty-second session.

2. In carrying out his mandate, the Special Rapporteur has again examined a wide range of information pertaining to general and specific allegations submitted through testimony and in documentary form, including script, photographs and video recordings. However, direct access to locations within Iraq has again not been possible owing to the Government's refusal so far to cooperate with the United Nations in receiving a return visit of the Special Rapporteur to Iraq or to accept the stationing of human rights monitors throughout Iraq pursuant to resolutions of the General Assembly and the Commission on Human Rights.

3. In implementation of paragraph 12 of Commission on Human Rights resolution 1995/76 regarding the sending of human rights monitors "to such locations as would facilitate improved information flows and assessment and would help in the independent verification of reports on the situation of human rights in Iraq", and taking into account the Government of Iraq's refusal to cooperate in the placement of human rights monitors inside Iraq, the Special Rapporteur requested the sending of staff members of the Centre for Human Rights to Kuwait and Lebanon. These locations were chosen because of the possibility of obtaining relevant information from persons there who claim to be victims of, or eyewitnesses to, human rights violations committed by the Government of Iraq.

4. The first mission referred to above took place from 22 to 30 June 1995, when two staff members from the Centre for Human Rights travelled to Kuwait in order to follow up on the Special Rapporteur's continuing concern for Kuwaiti and third-country nationals who disappeared in the custody of Iraqi authorities during the illegal occupation of Kuwait in 1990 and 1991 (see, in particular, A/49/651, paras. 12-33 and 99) and, at the same time, in order to meet with Iraqi citizens who had recently fled from Iraq to Kuwait. During the visit to Kuwait, the staff members met with a wide range of persons and received testimony, together with supplementary information in documentary and photographic form. Section III of the present report describes the results of the mission based on information received prior to and during the visit to Kuwait.

5. The second fact-finding mission took place from 24 to 30 July 1995, when two staff members from the Centre for Human Rights travelled to Lebanon in order to interview Iraqi citizens who had recently arrived in that country. Three days were spent in the town of Chtaura towards the Lebanese border with the Syrian Arab Republic in order to meet with recently arrived Iraqi citizens living in the Syrian Arab Republic. Section IV of the present report describes the results of the mission based upon information received prior to and during the visit to Lebanon.

6. On 4 September 1995, the Special Rapporteur submitted his first periodic report to the Commission on Human Rights pursuant to Commission resolution 1995/76 (E/CN.4/1996/12), in which he studied the texts of two recent decrees of the Revolution Command Council that were reported to grant amnesty to specified categories of persons. A summary of the report, highlighting the Special Rapporteur's analysis and comments with regard to the importance of the decrees and their impact is reproduced in section II of the present report.

7. Among the most visible and disturbing policies of the Government of Iraq, affecting virtually the entire population, are those that concern the rights to food and health. In section V of the present report, the Special Rapporteur addresses the deteriorating situation regarding these most vital of economic rights and offers his conclusions as to the responsibilities of the Government of Iraq.

8. In section VI of the present report, the Special Rapporteur reports upon the referendum held in Iraq on 15 October 1995. In his analysis, he applies the international human rights standards to which Iraq has voluntarily ascribed in the area of civil and political rights.

9. Aside from the matters addressed below, it is again to be observed that there are no signs of improvement in the general situation of human rights in Iraq. The

details of this overall assessment of the situation of human rights in Iraq, taking into account ongoing developments, will be given in the Special Rapporteur's report to the Commission on Human Rights at its fifty-second session.

II. *Revolution Command Council decrees Nos. 61 and 64*

10. On 28 July 1995, the Government of Iraq transmitted, through a note verbale from its Permanent Mission in Geneva addressed to relevant special rapporteurs and working groups of the Commission on Human Rights, the text of Revolution Command Council decree No. 61 dated 22 July 1995, which "remits the remainder of the sentences of Iraqi prisoners and detainees, commutes death sentences to life imprisonment and pardons persons liable to the penalty of amputation of the hand or the auricle of the ear". By a second note, dated 2 August 1995 from the Permanent Mission of the Republic of Iraq to the United Nations Office at Geneva addressed to the Centre for Human Rights, the Government of Iraq transmitted the text of Revolution Command Council decree No. 64 (bearing the signature of Saddam Hussein as Chairman of the Council and entering into force on 30 July 1995), which was said to grant "a general amnesty to Iraqis living in or outside Iraq in respect of the penalties imposed on them following their conviction for political reasons". The full texts of decrees Nos. 61 and 64 are reproduced in the annex to the Special Rapporteur's first periodic report (E/CN.4/1996/12).

11. The decrees introduce considerable opportunity for arbitrariness and abuse at the hands of undoubtedly biased persons. For example, paragraph II of decree No. 61 stipulates that reductions of sentences will apply only in such cases where the relatives of those imprisoned "undertake to ensure their good conduct" and "provided that the said undertaking is endorsed by a member of the Arab Baath Socialist Party". Similarly, paragraph VI gives an advantage to those who have "obtained an understanding of the revolutionary course of action", while paragraph VIII, subparagraph 3, effectively conditions exemption from applicable amputation decrees upon repentance. For example, in terms of the independent and impartial administration of the criminal justice system normally required, one may wonder on what basis members of the Arab Baath Socialist Party are to play a determinative role.

12. If careful consideration is given to the many conditions and exclusions contained in the decrees, it will be seen that large numbers of persons apparently addressed by the decrees would not in fact enjoy any benefit. For example, the decrees apply only to persons "convicted" or "sentenced", presumably in a formal juridical sense, subsequent to court proceedings and orders. Yet

large numbers of persons remain detained in Iraq, and are subject to punishment, in the absence of formal or proper convictions or sentences. These persons would not enjoy the benefit of the decrees.

13. Another limiting aspect of decree No. 64 is that it expressly applies only to "citizens" and "Iraqis" rather than anyone having been found guilty of commission of the offences irrespective of nationality. The application of paragraphs II and III of the decree are thus discriminatory in so far as they exclude non-nationals, whilst the Government has previously stripped hundreds of thousands of persons of their "Iraqi" nationality by asserting their "Persian ancestry".

14. Regarding the explicit exclusions to be found in the decrees, persons convicted of "espionage" are excluded from application of the decrees. This is a particularly important exclusion in the case of Iraq because so many laws refer to "espionage" and because the crime applies to a wide variety of behaviour.

15. Finally, there are evident shortcomings within decree No. 61 as regards the continuing effects of decrees prescribing amputations and branding. Specifically, paragraph III of decree No. 61 exempts from the penalty of amputation only those persons who have served two years in custody or detention; presumably, those having served less than two years will be subject to amputation, which normally is applicable upon conviction. In addition, since paragraph VIII.3 effectively exempts from amputation of the auricle of the ear only persons who have given themselves up "repentantly", presumably those who refuse to make such a declaration will still suffer the inhuman and degrading punishment.

16. The most important context for analysing the recent amnesty decrees is that of the overall legal and political order prevailing in Iraq. It is precisely the existence of several repressive Iraqi laws that quells freedom of thought, information, expression, association and assembly through fear of arrest, imprisonment and other sanctions. This repression will not be affected by the latest amnesty decrees. So long as powers of arbitrary arrest, detention and imprisonment exist, "amnesties" will inspire little confidence. This is especially so for "political" offences, while decrees such as No. 840 of 4 November 1986 continue to make critics and insulters of the President, the Baath Party and the institutions of government subject to the death penalty and Baath Party members are granted impunity for any harm done to property or persons (including death) while pursuing opponents of the Government. Simply, while there is no effective rule of law in Iraq, there will be little confidence in the reliability of "amnesty" decrees.

17. It is for this reason that the Special Rapporteur has previously called for the abrogation of such repressive laws as those establishing the offence of "insulting" the leadership and institutions of government and the Baath Party, the granting of impunity for those causing harm to the person of property of "subversives", "saboteurs" and other perceived opponents of the Government or the Baath Party and the inhuman punishments of amputation and disfigurement examined by the Special Rapporteur in previous reports (see in particular, E/CN.4/1995/56).

III. The mission to Kuwait

A. The fate of persons missing as a result of the Iraqi occupation of Kuwait

18. As noted in paragraph 4 above, two staff members from the Centre for Human Rights, acting as human rights monitors in the framework of Commission resolution 1995/76, undertook a visit to Kuwait from 22 to 30 June 1995. During their stay in Kuwait, the monitors met with a wide variety of persons of special relevance to the continuing problem of Kuwaiti and third-country nationals who disappeared during or subsequent to their alleged arrest and detention by Iraqi forces occupying Kuwait between 2 August 1990 and 26 February 1991. Among those interviewed were representatives of the Kuwaiti National Committee for Missing and Prisoner of War Affairs and family members of the Kuwaitis who had disappeared.

19. The fate of Kuwaitis and other persons who disappeared during Iraq's occupation of Kuwait forms part of the mandate of the Special Rapporteur as a result of paragraph 4 of Commission resolutions 1992/71 and 1993/74, paragraph 5 of Commission resolution 1994/74 and paragraph 3 of Commission resolution 1995/76. The Special Rapporteur briefly addressed this aspect of the mandate in two reports to the Commission (E/CN.4/1993/45, para. 49, and E/CN.4/1994/58, para. 32) and more extensively in his last report to the General Assembly (A/49/651, paras. 12-33 and 99).

20. As previously stated by the Special Rapporteur (see A/49/651, paras. 31 and 32), there can be no doubt that many persons disappeared during or subsequent to the Iraqi occupation of Kuwait. In so far as the disappearances occurred during the Iraqi occupation of Kuwait, there can also be no doubt of the general responsibility of Iraq under international law for the fate of these persons and the effects on their families. Detailed testimonies and other corroborative evidence further establishes the specific responsibility of Iraqi forces and authorities in relation to many individual cases. However, from the point of view of the relations of those who disappeared, the preoccupying question is the present whereabouts of their loved ones: are these persons still detained in Iraq, as has been claimed, or, in the event that they have been released or have perished, what details can

be communicated to the distraught families regarding the release or death of former detainees?

21.   Certainly, the human tragedy of this continuing matter is enormous both in terms of any remaining detainees who are no doubt suffering untold emotional anguish and possibly enduring physical hardship and in terms of the relatives of the missing persons who are suffering severe mental distress because they are without knowledge of the whereabouts and condition of their loved ones. The relatives of the missing persons also report that they are regularly subjected to extortion attempts that play upon their desires to learn anything of those missing. As a result of the never-ending uncertainty and the unresolvable pain and depression, the social lives, employment performance and personal relationships of family members are all damaged.

22.   In accordance with the applicable rules of international law, Iraq must account for those who were arrested by its forces. If Iraq were still to be holding prisoners of war (POWs) and civilian internees, a premise the Iraqi authorities deny, several obligations arising under international humanitarian law and international human rights law would be breached.

23.   In addition, the Government of Iraq has, to the knowledge of the Special Rapporteur, failed to demonstrate a genuine concern for those who are still missing in so far as it has yet to participate fully and in a cooperative spirit with both Governments and international humanitarian organizations that are seeking to resolve the cases on behalf of the next of kin. In particular, the Government of Iraq failed for a period of two years even to attend the meetings of the Tripartite Committee established pursuant to the cease-fire agreement that ended the armed conflict following the liberation of Kuwait.

24.   However, as from July 1994, the Government of Iraq renewed its participation in the framework of the Tripartite Committee, as well as in the framework of a Technical Subcommittee that was established by the Tripartite Committee on 8 December 1994, and has undertaken to conduct the detailed technical work relating to investigations and inquiries concerning the missing persons. As of 7 April 1995, the Technical Subcommittee had processed 168 dossiers, on which the Government of Iraq had provided preliminary replies based on intermediate investigations regarding 70 individual files. In addition, the mortal remains of one missing person were repatriated to the Kuwaiti authorities.

25.   For almost all cases to which the Government of Iraq has so far responded, it is reported to have provided evasive replies regarding the individual files. Indeed, based upon information received during the mission, despite the Iraqi authorities admitting to having arrested and detained some of the missing Kuwaitis, the Government of Iraq claims to be ignorant of the specifically relevant authority or military unit operating at the time and place where the person disappeared; the Government claims that the files that could have been useful to determine the fate of the missing persons were destroyed during the retreat of the Iraqi authorities from Kuwait and that many of these units were subsequently dissolved, with many of their members having retired from the armed forces. Therefore, the Government of Iraq maintains, upon information collected verbally by the responsible officers after the 1991 uprising in the south of Iraq, that the detainees escaped by exploiting the confusion that prevailed in the southern governorates at the time.

26.   Based upon information received by the Special Rapporteur, the specific military units responsible in the areas where the arrests and disappearances occurred have now resorted to *pro forma* responses, admitting only to having arrested and detained some of the still missing Kuwaitis. Some have also participated in initial investigations into some of the cases.

27.   Noting that the Government of Iraq is showing to a certain extent its willingness at long last to collaborate with the Tripartite Committee, the Special Rapporteur stresses that Iraq is under an obligation to provide substantive replies on the individual files without further delay. It is to be recalled in this connection that, in its resolution 46/135 of 17 December 1991, the General Assembly called upon Iraq in the following specific terms to cooperate in the search for those who had disappeared:

> "4. ... to provide information on all Kuwaiti persons and third-country nationals deported from Kuwait between 2 August 1990 and 26 February 1991 who may still be detained and ... to release these persons without delay;

> "5. ... to provide ... detailed information on persons arrested in Kuwait between 2 August 1990 and 26 February 1991 who may have died during or after that period while in detention, as well as on the site of their graves;

> "6. ... to search for the persons still missing and to cooperate with international humanitarian organizations, such as the International Committee of the Red Cross, in this regard;

> "7. ... to cooperate and facilitate the work of international humanitarian organizations, notably the International Committee of the Red Cross, in their search for and eventual repatriation of Kuwaiti and third-country national detainees and missing persons."

28. Notwithstanding Iraq's recent but limited steps towards full cooperation in this tragic matter, the Special Rapporteur cannot avoid noting that Iraq failed:

(a) To inform families about the whereabouts of persons arrested in Kuwait, or to give arrested persons the right to contact their families;

(b) To provide information about death sentences imposed on POWs and civilian detainees, as required by articles 101 and 107 of the Third Geneva Convention of 12 August 1949 and articles 74 and 75 of the Fourth Geneva Convention of 12 August 1949;

(c) To issue death certificates for deceased POWs and civilian internees and to provide information about graves in accordance with articles 120 and 121 of the Third Geneva Convention of 12 August 1949 and articles 129 to 131 of the Fourth Geneva Convention of 12 August 1949;

To comply at least with this, the Government of Iraq faces a heavy burden of doing everything within its powers to explain the fate of the hundreds of persons who still remain missing as a result of its illegal occupation of Kuwait.

B. Information regarding other violations of human rights

29. Other information (mainly testimonies from asylum-seekers) received in Kuwait by the monitors assisting the Special Rapporteur paints an even grimmer picture of life in southern Iraq. Testimonies focused upon the climate of oppression and the dire economic and social situation in the south of the country. The second of these issues will be taken up in section V below.

30. According to testimonies received, penal amputations continued to be enforced in southern Iraq in the spring and early summer of 1995. Military deserters who had escaped to Kuwait stated that they saw many soldiers with their ears cut off. Two young men who were interviewed had suffered the penalties themselves: one had both his ears entirely amputated in a rough fashion and had a "-" sign scar in the middle of his forehead, which he stated was the result of a surgical cut applied at the time of the amputation of his ears, while the other young man had a large and dark "‡" sign branded between his eyebrows and had large inflamed scars running up and down his arms and on his body from battery acid that had been poured on him by military officers as an alternative to cutting off his ears; the officers had also fractured the skull of the second soldier with a metal pipe, resulting in a speech impediment and recurring dizzy spells. The deserter who had had both his ears amputated testified that he had been given a general anaesthetic in a prison hospital where the operation was performed and where he had remained without medicine for weeks

afterward; his bandages were changed only every two weeks. He further testified that he was among several hundreds of others who had been brought from throughout Amarah, Nassiriyah and Basrah governorates in order to have their ears cut off in the prison hospital. While some were said also to receive the surgical cut across the forehead as had the witness, others were said to have been branded on the forehead with an "X". Many were said to have acquired infections, received no treatment and died. Another soldier who claimed to have had access to military detention centres as part of his work testified to having seen at least 30 soldiers in various places who had had their ears cut off, stating that they were bandaged and bleeding, with some having acquired infections for which they were prohibited treatment and for which, in any event, there were no medicines available. These testimonies were supported by that of a medical doctor who had fled from Basrah, where he confirmed that many young men had been brought to the hospitals to have their ears cut off: one ear for the first desertion, both ears for a second offence, and branding of the foreheads for all. While anaesthetics were used for the operations, which were described as an irregular cut followed by a suture, post-operative treatment was forbidden; one victim was said to have died of septicemia. For the brandings, the technique employed was a cauterized "-" sign across the forehead. The doctor stated that he had heard from other doctors that a total of 150 amputations were performed in January 1995. The doctor also confirmed that they were forced to perform the operations or receive heavy penalties for refusal: one doctor who refused was arrested by the Mukhabarat for two days and returned compliant, while another disappeared.

31. The testimonies concerning amputations confirm what the Special Rapporteur had reported in his last report to the General Assembly (A/49/651, paras. 44-71 and 99 (j)). They also demonstrate the arbitrary and irregular fashion in which the barbaric decrees have been implemented.

32. Other testimonies indicated that arbitrary arrests and detentions remained widespread in southern Iraq. Several witnesses testified that, upon arrest, they had been beaten and badly mistreated. All witnesses testified that they had fled because of the constant fear in which they lived and that the economic deterioration had increased the arbitrary interference of security and Baath Party officials in the daily lives of the citizenry. Bribery and corruption were also said to be rife. There was said to be no rule of law.

33. The witnesses were unanimous that the food and health situation, and the socio-economic situation in general, had become precarious. Most stated that they were preoccupied in their daily lives with achieving a

subsistence-level existence. The medical doctor who was interviewed confirmed that protein and calorie deficiencies were common among children, as were cases of anaemia and related diseases. The doctor lamented the unavailability of many medicines and the emergence of a flourishing, but very expensive, black market for drugs. Although the doctor had seen no deaths as a result of malnutrition, he stressed that the situation was deteriorating day by day prior to his departure in the spring.

34. In general terms, one witness described Iraq as "one huge prison" where all within huddled in fear. Another witness pleaded that the United Nations should ignore the Government of Iraq and "take food and medicine directly to the people". All felt that Iraqi society was shattered.

IV. *The mission to Lebanon*

35. The testimonies received in Lebanon were mainly from refugees who had recently fled from the central part of Iraq. All gave testimony about a general state of repression and fear throughout Iraq and all indicated that the overall socio-economic situation was poor, with dire consequences for the most vulnerable in terms of access to food and health care.

36. In general, life was said to be harsh and expensive. Government ration cards were said to be good for only 10 days in early 1995. Two witnesses claimed to have seen food aid from the United Nations being sold on the black market; one witness testified to having seen United Nations Children's Fund (UNICEF) and World Food Programme (WFP) trucks in Najaf and Karbala offloading at government distribution points only to see some of the food appear on the black market later. Expired goods (including milk and medications) were also said to be distributed through the Government of Iraq with the Government accusing the United Nations of dumping the goods on a desperate people.

37. Two witnesses testified to having seen army deserters who had had an ear cut off and had been branded on the forehead. The desertions were blamed on the extremely low pay for conscripted soldiers, which had forced many to desert in order to help their families to survive. Now many have been disfigured, while others are said to have died as a result of the initial traumas or subsequent untreated infections. Those who survive are said to hide in shame. One witness said that some victims and their families had sought revenge for the disfigurements by trying to kill the doctors and Baath Party officials who had performed or ordered the amputations; several such incidents were said to have taken place in Nassiriyah.

38. Many witnesses testified about the general breakdown in law and order: bribery, corruption and thievery were said to be the main problems. Matters of corruption ranged from petty to issues of life and death. One witness stated that "even if you kill someone, you can still buy your freedom by paying the judge". Another witness testified that higher education had become completely corrupt with professors, who were very poor, readily accepting bribes to change grades, to give out the questions to examinations in advance or just to grant a passing grade to a student who had already answered all the questions correctly. Admissions are said to be controlled by the Baath Party and the children of important Baathists are said to get privileged entrances and advancements throughout the system: easier admissions, easier passes and better grades. Another witness stated that the problem of bribery had reached such a stage that those who were to be executed could buy their freedom from the executioner, but then someone else had to be executed in their stead to ensure that a body was surrendered by the executioner as per instructions. The general decay in order, parallelled by an increase in corruption, has resulted in a confused and thoroughly arbitrary system where it is said to be a regular occurrence that the wrong people are arrested, detained, tortured and even executed—without apology or consequence.

39. Arbitrary arrests were said still to be common throughout the country, with people still being taken directly from their homes. The Mukhabarat is said to be still preoccupied with trying to find everyone who participated in the March-April 1991 uprisings.

40. Upon arrest, cruel tortures and gross mistreatment still occur. Two witnesses gave testimony, corroborated by their own scars and disabilities, about terrible tortures that they suffered over long periods of time. One witness testified that, during three and one half years of arbitrary detention (first in the General Directorate of Security in Baghdad and then in Radwaniyah prison) prior to his release in the spring of last year, he was regularly hanged from his hands, which were bound behind his back, with someone pulling down on his body so that his rotator cups were destroyed and he can now rotate his arms backwards over his head but he can carry hardly any weight. In addition, he was badly beaten on his back, causing some of his vertebrae to become displaced and resulting in a serious curvature of the spine: he is now deeply bowed when he stands. Further, he was forced on several occasions to sit on a bottle for minutes at a time causing bleeding and rectal damage that required medical treatment and, on one occasion, he suffered electric shocks to his tongue and genitals. The second witness claimed to have been imprisoned and brutally tortured over a 12-year period in the Mukhabarat office in Baghdad, Fadhliyah detention centre and Badush prison in Mosul. Among the astounding number and

variety of tortures he claims to have suffered are the following: he was hanged by his feet from a rotating fan and beaten with cables by Mukhabarat officers; he was forced to sit on bottles of varying sizes for various periods of time; he was once made to stand in a large tub of filthy waste water up to his nose so he could hardly breath; he was once sprinkled with sulphuric acid from a syringe during an interrogation; during another interrogation, he had a heavy acidic oil poured on one arm; he was administered electric shocks on different occasions, once while sitting in a chair with his feet in a shallow bucket of water, causing his feet to inflame and making it difficult to walk; he once had a small leather strap tied around his penis to prevent him from urinating while, at the same time, he was forced to drink large quantities of sugared water; he was several times forced to crouch for long periods in a tiny box; and he was raped numerous times. Having been sentenced to life imprisonment for espionage and membership in the Islamic movement, the witness claims to have been liberated during an uprising by the al-Jabouri clan in Mosul in 1994 and subsequently fled the country. The witness bears numerous scars and suffers disabilities that are consistent with his testimony.

V. *The rights to food and health*

41. The Special Rapporteur has commented upon the rights to food and health in all but one of his previous reports to the Commission on Human Rights and to the General Assembly (A/46/647, annex, paras. 52-55 and 95-98; E/CN.4/1992/31, paras. 81-83, 138, 143 (w), 145 (o) and (p) and 158; A/47/367, para. 14; A/47/367/Add.1, paras. 6-14, 56 (a)-(c) and 58 (a)-(c); E/CN.4/1993/45, paras. 67-72 and 185; A/48/600, annex, paras. 33-42, 44-46, 58-59 and 62-88; E/CN.4/1994/58, paras. 72-79, 152 and 186; A/49/651, annex, paras. 89-98; and E/CN.4/1995/56, paras. 44-47, 54, 67 (m) and 68 (c)). Since his initial appointment in June 1991, the Special Rapporteur has observed the constantly deteriorating situation of the population. This dire situation has met with the steadfast refusal of the Government of Iraq to take advantage of resources available to alleviate the suffering of the people—as the Government is obliged to do under international law. As such, there can be no doubt that the policy of the Government of Iraq is directly responsible for the physical and mental pain, including long-term disabilities, of millions of people and the death of many thousands more.

42. Since the Special Rapporteur's last report to the Commission on Human Rights (E/CN.4/1995/56), the Security Council adopted resolution 986 (1995) of 14 April 1995, which affords Iraq the opportunity of selling oil up to the amount of US$1 billion every 90 days, on a renewable basis, in order to purchase essential food

and medical supplies for humanitarian purposes. As was the case with the "food-for-oil" formula presented pursuant to Security Council resolutions 706 (1991) and 712 (1991), the Government of Iraq has rejected the offer made in resolution 986 (1995), despite the fact that the total available annual sale would be US$4 billion, i.e. about one quarter of Iraq's total export sales prior to its invasion of Kuwait and the imposition of United Nations economic sanctions. The United Nations offer received unfavourable responses from the Government from its inception and was turned down completely by both the Iraqi Cabinet of Ministers and the National Assembly. It is interesting to note that, immediately after Security Council resolution 986 (1995) was adopted, market prices of essential food and other commodities improved significantly and the free market value of the United States dollar dropped by 50 per cent against the Iraqi dinar from ID 1,200 to ID 600. Such a sustained drop in prices would have had the effect of making more food and other essential commodities available to those in need. However, the drop in prices and exchange rates was shortlived following the negative response from the Government and the appearance of several Ministers and other top officials on television who categorically decried and rejected resolution 986 (1995) on unspecified grounds of "sovereignty infringement and interference in the internal affairs of Iraq". Senior officials also argued that the new initiative was designed to prolong the sanctions—an assertion that flies in the face of the fact that it is for Iraq alone to comply fully with the terms of the relevant Security Council resolutions and end the sanctions regime forthwith.

43. As a consequence of the Government of Iraq's intransigence on the "food-for-oil" formula, the economic situation continued to deteriorate and prices of essential food items and basic living commodities fell even further beyond the reach of a large part of the population. According to the Department of Humanitarian Affairs mid-term review of the United Nations consolidated inter-agency humanitarian cooperation programme for Iraq, dated 21 September 1995, in the last six months "the humanitarian situation deteriorated in all sectors, particularly in the areas of nutrition and health. Living conditions remain precarious for at least an estimated 4 million persons". Essential food prices have continued to escalate drastically, especially after the release of the last reports of the United Nations Special Commission monitoring the dismantling of Iraq's nuclear, chemical and biological capacities; prices of wheat flour, rice, vegetable oil and sugar increased between 30 and 50 per cent on the free market. For example, the price of vegetable oil jumped from ID 800 to ID 1,200 per kilogram, the increase accounting alone for 15 per cent of the

monthly salary of an average government employee. These large increases in the prices of food commodities must also be viewed in relation to the oppressive 616 per cent increase in the central and southern governorates in 1994, as reported by the Department of Humanitarian Affairs (see *DHA News* special edition, "1994 in review", p. 111). At the same time, the Department of Humanitarian Affairs reported in the same mid-term review, that the "purchasing power of the population has deteriorated further because of the continued depreciation of the Iraqi dinar from 1,000 to the dollar in April to 2,000 ID in September 1995" such that the "salaries of civil servants (averaging ID 5,000 per month after 50-70 per cent increments in August 1995) are inadequate for the purchase of basic food commodities".

44. The Government has continued distribution of its subsidized food basket at reduced levels for four essential food items, namely, wheat flour, rice, vegetable oil and sugar. In October 1994, the basket was reduced by 37 per cent in terms of calorie intake, with the shortfall of over 50 per cent remaining unbridgeable for a large percentage of the population in view of the prohibitive food prices on the free market. This situation prevailed until just recently when, in celebration of his "endorsement" as President in the national referendum held on 15 October 1995, President Saddam Hussein was reported to have increased the rations. It is not clear how long this celebratory increase will continue. Prior to it, government rations met only 30 per cent of people's food needs with the Department of Humanitarian Affairs reporting that "an FAO-led crop and nutrition status assessment mission confirmed that the situation in Iraq was demonstrating pre-famine conditions".

45. The economic hardship affecting the population is being manifested in various ways. More and more families have been cramming roadways around Baghdad and other cities to sell personal belongings, furniture and even parts of their homes (e.g. doors, windows and cement blocks) in order to buy food. Child beggars and small-time traders are now a common sight in the capital and prostitution is said to be rising all over the country. Media reports also point to a flourishing trade in human organs as the desperate line up to sell a kidney in order to help their families to survive.

46. Although the number of privileged groups and persons appears to be declining, certain groups remain privileged by comparison to others, e.g. high-ranking military officers and Baath Party elite. This privilege is to be observed not only in the fact that the average salary of a civil servant is one half that of a military officer, but more importantly in the fact that members of the Baath Party and military officers enjoy their own food distribution network through cooperatives and they receive spe-

cial salary allowances depending on their relationships with their supervisors and the extent of their support for the official policies of the Government. Of course, this is to say nothing of the bribes and "gifts" that government and Baath Party officials may obtain by virtue of the important administrative positions to which they may be assigned. Moreover, the inner circle of the leadership does not appear touched by any economic hardships affecting their access to food or health care.

47. It is also evident that there is discrimination within the country on a regional basis. The central cities of Iraq, especially Tikrit, Samara and parts of Baghdad, continue to enjoy preferred distribution of limited resources; while the infrastructure (including water purification and sewage systems) of Baghdad was rebuilt almost immediately after the war, that of the southern cities has continued to lag far behind. For example, according to a survey conducted by government agencies with the full support of UNICEF in April 1995 and released in July 1995, 50 per cent of the rural population in the central/southern part of Iraq have no access to potable water supplies. More distressingly, the same survey found that 90 per cent of the rural population in the southern governorate of Thiqar had no access to potable water supplies. An erratic electric power supply and a shortage of water has had a negative impact on public health, with adverse effects on vulnerable groups, especially children. One hospital in Najaf was found without water for three consecutive days. In addition, commodity prices in the southern governorates are much higher than in the central governorates, owing to the deteriorating modes of transport and the cost of distribution. In the northern governorate of Dohuk, which was cut off from the national power grid in August 1993 and had been receiving 12 MW of power per day from Turkey over the past few months, there has been almost no electricity since 23 June when, for technical reasons, the Turkish source of power was also cut off. The resulting non-availability of power during the summer months created enormous problems in the health and water sectors. According to the *DHA News* special edition, "1994 in review" (p. 112), severe shortages of electricity also "prompted significant movement of people, placing greater strain on the humanitarian programme" last year.

48. Among the related health problems are the increasing levels of contaminated water as recorded by the ongoing UNICEF-sponsored water quality control programme. As a result, the number of cases of water-borne and diarrhoeal disease was seen to increase. Initial investigations by UNICEF had indicated that water was not being chlorinated as required, and subsequent follow-up revealed that UNICEF's chlorine powder had been put on sale in the market for domestic use—available in

well-designed, locally printed packets and tins. This increase in corruption affecting the health and well-being of the population derives from the continuing economic pressures and the inability of the authorities to ensure proper use of humanitarian assistance.

49. In the face of the continuing deterioration of the food and health situation in Iraq in the last year, to say nothing of other forms of repression, many Iraqis sought to travel abroad to obtain food, health care or refuge. In response, the Government increased by 150 per cent the exit tax on all Iraqis travelling abroad; the fee was increased from ID 40,000 to ID 100,000 (i.e. almost two years' pay for an average government employee). In addition, skilled persons such as engineers, architects and doctors are required to post a guarantee of return in the amount of ID 1 million in the form of cash in a bank account or fixed property. This prohibitive exit tax forces many people to remain in Iraq to the detriment of their health and well-being.

50. Beyond the Government of Iraq's refusal to cooperate with the United Nations according to Security Council resolution 986 (1995), which proposes an increased sale of "oil for food", beyond the Government's restrictions on access to food and health in certain parts of the country and beyond the severe restrictions on exit from the country, the Special Rapporteur has received credible allegations that Iraqi forces have continued their attacks on the farming communities (with destruction of their crops and livestock) located along the internal frontier with the region of northern Iraq, from which the Government withdrew its administration in 1991. Similar allegations have been received concerning some attacks against farmers in the south of the country, resulting in the destruction of wheat and barley crops and livestock. These attacks negatively affect the internal food resources available for the rest of the population.

51. According to the Department of Humanitarian Affair's mid-term review and the assessment mission of the Food and Agriculture Organization of the United Nations (FAO), both referred to above, Iraq's "overall food requirements" in 1995/96 amount to "about US$2.7 billion". To keep alive 2.15 million of the most vulnerable people through 1996, a WFP *News Update* of 26 September 1995 states that US$122.5 million is required. An earlier United Nations consolidated interagency humanitarian cooperation programme for Iraq appealed for a total of US$135 million for the current six-month period (i.e. 1 October 1995-31 March 1996). The Special Rapporteur cannot help but underscore that the stated amounts are far below the resources available through Security Council resolution 986 (1995), even should the Government of Iraq finally take advantage of the opportunity to sell some oil for the good of the Iraqi

people. Indeed, it is entirely within the means of the Government of Iraq to respond immediately to the dire food and health needs of the people of Iraq either through full compliance with the Security Council resolutions establishing the sanctions or by cooperation with the United Nations pursuant to resolution 986 (1995).

VI. *The referendum of 15 October 1995*

52. On 15 October 1995, a national referendum was held in Iraq on the question: "Are you in favour of Saddam Hussein assuming the post of President of the Republic of Iraq?" In order to analyse and understand the process and significance of the referendum in terms of applicable international human rights standards, it is necessary to consider the political context in which the referendum was held. In this connection, the Special Rapporteur refers to his previous comments on the rights pertaining to democratic governance in Iraq (E/CN.4/1994/58, paras. 80-86) and to the structure and abuse of power in the country (E/CN.4/1994/58, paras. 159-184).

53. The applicable international standards by which the 15 October 1995 referendum is to be assessed are those contained principally in article 21 of the Universal Declaration of Human Rights and article 25 of the International Covenant on Civil and Political Rights, to which Iraq is a party. Both article 21 of the Universal Declaration and article 25 of the Covenant stress the free expression of the will of the people as the basis for determining the legitimate representatives of the people. However, for the will of the people to be freely formed and expressed, a variety of other freedoms must be respected, in particular the freedoms of thought, conscience, religion and belief (as guaranteed under article 18 of the Covenant); opinion, expression and information (as guaranteed under article 19 of the Covenant); assembly (as guaranteed under article 21 of the Covenant); and association (as guaranteed under article 22 of the Covenant). One could easily also add other freedoms such as that of movement and respect for personal integrity and privacy rights. In other words, the possibility of non-manipulated and unimpaired formation of views and also the uninfluenced expression of those views must be guaranteed.

54. As the Special Rapporteur has previously commented in detail (see E/CN.4/1994/58, paras. 80-86 and 159-184), the conditions necessary to ensure that the free will of the people is the basis of the authority of government do not exist in the present legal and political order of Iraq. More specifically, the almost total control of information coupled with an all-pervasive and generalized fear among the population of severe sanctions for non-support of the prevailing order, maintained through

abuses of power and facilitated by the absence of the rule of law in the country, combine to undermine and distort apparent expressions of the "will of the people" totally. While the Government purports that the referendum of 15 October 1995 was "free", the Special Rapporteur does not believe that the mere mechanical conduct of the formal process of voting can be equated with a genuine expression of the will of the people in Iraq. This is because the risk of being found in opposition to the President and the prevailing order is literally life-threatening: according to Revolution Command Council decree No. 840 of 4 November 1986, any person insulting the President of the Republic, the Revolution Command Council, the National Assembly, the Government or the Baath Party is subject to severe penalties, including death. This kind of law placed in the hands of a totally intrusive security apparatus, unconstrained by any respect for the rule of law, means that virtually no citizen would risk demonstrating any opposition to the presidency or Government—or would do so at his mortal peril. Indeed, this conclusion is logical as long as there exists in Iraq such coercive forces as decree No. 840 or political attacks against, and killings of, perceived oppositional leaders (see, e.g., A/49/651, paras. 72-88).

55. Given the prevailing legal and political order in Iraq, the national referendum of 15 October 1995 confirmed nothing except the fact that, even amid heavy economic pressures, the government authorities are capable of organizing such an event in a period of only three weeks and achieving, according to Iraqi television, a 99.96 per cent "approval" of the President from a staggering participation rate of 99.467 per cent of the 8,402,321 eligible voters. Perhaps more noteworthy is the fact that the overwhelming results were achieved without the President once having to address the people, appear in public, make a single promise or in any sense campaign to win the approval of the electorate. The extremely high turn-out also indicates that the population was already fully identified and listed by voting district at the time the referendum was announced. This fact underlines the degree to which the government authorities are in control of the movement and activities of people within the country.

56. Regarding the conduct of the referendum, all eligible voters were reportedly sent a two-part ballot card prior to the referendum with the first part of the card requiring detailed personal identification and with the second part, detachable from the first, constituting the ballot itself. At the polling stations, voters were to present to the referendum administrators, in the presence of various Iraqi security forces and Baath Party officials, the first part of the ballot card together with official papers verifying their identity and eligibility, whereupon voters

were directed to complete the second part of the card in a separate booth and then to place their completed ballots into an opaque sealed box. In the light of the overall political order in Iraq, but also in the light of the specific process at the polling stations, it may be appreciated that few if any voters would have felt confident to express their views against the President just after having formally presented themselves to security forces and Baath Party officials. Indeed, this may to a large extent explain the remarkable fact that not one person voted against the President in the governorates of Karbala, Najaf, Misan, Muthana or Dhi Qar, while only 18 voted against in Basrah, i.e. virtually no one voted against the President in the southern governorates that had been the scene of bloody uprisings in April 1991. However, this seemingly paradoxical voting result may well be an entirely rational result based on fear resulting from the harsh repression of April 1991 and its aftermath; the population has now been totally subdued, made to conform, become economically exhausted and totally dependent. In such circumstances, it would appear natural to follow one's basic survival instincts and vote rationally in favour of the President, although this "rational" vote could hardly be construed as an expression of the genuine will of the people.

57. One important fact is that the participating voters hardly represented the totality of the relevant Iraqi population. To begin with, between 2 and 3 million eligible voters in the northern governorates of Arbil, Dohuk and Suleimaniyah did not participate because the central authorities withdrew from the region in October 1991, leaving it to its own local administration. A second group of about 2 million Iraqis also was not taken into account by the referendum: these persons fled or were expelled from Iraq and now live outside their country precisely because of President Saddam Hussein and his policies; for the most part, these people voted against Saddam Hussein with their feet.

58. In trying to understand the significance of the referendum, which is, in fact, the first time in Saddam Hussein's presidency that he has ever gone directly to the people, the Special Rapporteur notes the remarks of Deputy Prime Minister Tariq Aziz, as reported by the Iraqi News Agency in Baghdad on 17 October 1995, who stated that the referendum was part of a process of moving "from revolutionary to constitutional legitimacy". Without fully understanding the notion of "revolutionary legitimacy" as it applies to a Government that has prevailed for well over a quarter century, the Special Rapporteur understands from Mr. Aziz's remarks that Iraq is certainly not a State with constitutional legitimacy, i.e. Iraq is not a State under the rule of law. Certainly, this admission by Mr. Aziz only confirms what the Special Rapporteur has observed since he first took up his

mandate: in so far as the prevailing legal and political order in Iraq does not respect the rule of law, Iraq is in violation of its international obligations in the field of human rights law. However, in relation to the internal political regime within Iraq, it would appear that the logic of the present "revolutionary legitimacy" would not have required Saddam Hussein to relinquish the presidency even if he had not succeeded in obtaining an "endorsement" from the people: he could simply have continued to lead the revolution as he had been doing so far. If this means that the referendum had no legal implication within the State, then what was the motivation for the event? By this analysis, it would appear that the referendum had little to do with domestic legitimacy or respect for human rights (indeed, it was a mockery of international human rights standards), but more to do with an external political agenda. In the view of the Special Rapporteur, this was the significance of the referendum of 15 October 1995.

VII. Conclusions

59. From his analysis of Revolution Command Council decrees Nos. 61 and 64, the Special Rapporteur concludes that their heavily conditioned nature greatly reduces their possible value to the addressees. Moreover, in the absence of far greater change in the legal and political order of Iraq, especially the abrogation of repressive laws quelling freedoms of thought, information, expression, association and assembly, decrees Nos. 61 and 64 merit virtually no confidence. In the light of the legal system and political situation that prevail in Iraq, and barring the abrogation of existing laws, the effect of the so-called "amnesty" decrees cannot be considered a step towards liberalization of the government system in accordance with the obligations undertaken by the Government of Iraq.

60. With respect to the several hundred persons who still remain missing as a result of the illegal Iraqi occupation of Kuwait in 1990 and 1991, the Special Rapporteur reaffirms his opinion that the Government of Iraq is fully responsible for the fate of these persons and must take every step to assist in determining their exact whereabouts or fates. The Special Rapporteur concludes that the Government's resumption of participation in the Tripartite Commission is a positive step that needs to be followed up by full, open and energetic cooperation aimed at resolving the outstanding cases without any further delay.

61. On the subject of the amputation decrees, which are still in force within Iraq notwithstanding decrees Nos. 61 and 62, the Special Rapporteur concludes that they remain gross violations of human rights and an offence to the population as a whole and, in particular, to the individuals who must endure their cruel and unusual punishments.

62. With regard to the rights to food and health, the Special Rapporteur emphasizes again the responsibility of Iraq, pursuant to article 2 of the International Covenant on Economic, Social and Cultural Rights, to which Iraq is a party, "to take steps, individually and through international assistance and cooperation, especially economic and technical, to the maximum of its available resources" to alleviate the suffering of the people.

63. As concerns the national referendum of 15 October 1995, the Special Rapporteur concludes that the result in no way reflects the genuine will of the people as required by article 21 of the Universal Declaration of Human Rights and article 25 of the International Covenant on Civil and Political Rights. To the contrary, in the prevailing legal and political order in Iraq with life-threatening laws applicable to persons expressing any opposition to the Government, the conduct of the referendum made a mockery of relevant international human rights standards.

VIII. Recommendations

64. The Government of Iraq should immediately abrogate any and all decrees that prescribe cruel and unusual punishment or treatment.

65. The Government of Iraq should immediately take every necessary step to abolish the practices of torture and cruel and unusual punishments and treatment.

66. The Government of Iraq should step up its cooperation with the Tripartite Commission aiming to discover the whereabouts or resolve the fate of the several hundred Kuwaitis and third-country nationals who disappeared under the illegal Iraqi occupation of Kuwait in 1990 and 1991.

67. The Government of Iraq should immediately cooperate with the United Nations to organize a sale of oil in order to purchase desperately needed humanitarian goods as authorized by Security Council resolution 986 (1995).

68. The Government of Iraq should immediately abrogate all laws penalizing the free expression of competing views and ideas and should take all necessary steps to ensure that the genuine will of the people is the basis of the authority in the State.

Document 217

Letter from the Chairman of the Sanctions Committee to the President of the Security Council forwarding a proposal for a mechanism to monitor Iraq's exports and imports of dual-purpose capabilities

S/1995/1017, 7 December 1995

I have the honour to refer to paragraph 7 of Security Council resolution 715 (1991), by which the Council:

> "*Requests* the Security Council Committee established under resolution 661 (1990) concerning the situation between Iraq and Kuwait, the Special Commission and the Director General of the [International Atomic Energy] Agency to develop in co-operation a mechanism for monitoring any future sales or supplies by other countries to Iraq of items relevant to the implementation of section C of resolution 687 (1991) and other relevant resolutions, including the present resolution and the plans approved hereunder;".

I am transmitting herewith, with the concurrence of the Executive Chairman of the Special Commission and the Director General of the International Atomic Energy Agency (IAEA), a report prepared by the Committee established by Security Council resolution 661 (1990), the Special Commission and the Director General of IAEA that contains the provisions for the mechanism for export/import monitoring under paragraph 7 of Security Council resolution 715 (1991) of 11 October 1991.

The report is also accompanied by the text of a letter, dated 17 July 1995, which was addressed to me by the Executive Chairman of the Special Commission. This indicates the general principles that will be followed in implementing the export/import mechanism in Iraq and it is transmitted to the Council for purposes of information.

It is hoped that it will be possible for the Council to take an early decision on the report transmitted herewith, so that preparations, as necessary, may be pursued at the national level for the implementation, at the appropriate time, of the export/import mechanism. Such a decision will also allow the Special Commission and IAEA, which the report proposes be mandated to implement the mechanism, to proceed with those preparations which, until now, it has not yet undertaken, pending a mandate.

(*Signed*) Tono EITEL
Chairman of the Security Council Committee
established by resolution 661 (1990)
concerning the situation between
Iraq and Kuwait

Annex I
Provisions for the mechanism for export/import monitoring under paragraph 7 of Security Council resolution 715 (1991) of 11 October 1991

Report prepared by the Committee established by Security Council resolution 661 (1990), the Special Commission and the Director General of the International Atomic Energy Agency

I. *Objective*

1. By paragraph 7 of its resolution 715 (1991) of 11 October 1991, the Security Council:

> "*Requests* the Security Council Committee established under resolution 661 (1990) concerning the situation between Iraq and Kuwait, the Special Commission and the Director General of the [International Atomic Energy] Agency, to develop in co-operation a mechanism for monitoring any future sales or supplies by other countries to Iraq of items relevant to the implementation of section C of resolution 687 (1991) and other relevant resolutions, including the present resolution and the plans approved hereunder".

The present report is submitted to the Security Council pursuant to that request.

2. The export/import mechanism (hereafter "the mechanism") is one element of the Special Commission's and IAEA's plans (S/22871/Rev.1 and S/22872/Rev.1 and Rev.1/Corr.1), approved by Security Council resolution 715 (1991), for ongoing monitoring and verification of Iraq's undertaking not to reacquire proscribed weapons capabilities. Such monitoring is of indefinite duration and is to continue until the Security Council decides that it should be terminated.

3. Paragraph 7 of resolution 715 (1991) makes provision for the monitoring of sales or supplies by other countries to Iraq of items covered by the two plans after the sanctions imposed by resolution 661 (1990) on those items have been reduced or lifted pursuant to paragraph 21 of resolution 687 (1991). The mechanism should provide important data, which will serve as one of the main tools for ensuring that Iraq does not reconstitute its weapons of mass destruction programmes. It

is evident, therefore, that the mechanism must be in place before any decisions are taken by the Security Council to reduce or lift sanctions on items covered by the relevant resolutions and the plans.

4. It follows that there will be a period of time after the Security Council adopts the mechanism before it reduces or lifts sanctions on items covered by the mechanism. For as long as these items remain subject to the sanctions under resolution 661 (1990), the Committee established under that resolution shall continue to perform its present functions, and any requests for the sale of such items to Iraq, as essential for civilian needs, should be addressed in accordance with existing procedures. The Committee shall seek the advice of the Commission or IAEA, as the case may be, on the disposition of the request. If authorization is granted by the Committee, the Commission and IAEA will be so informed to enable them to make the necessary arrangements to monitor the items in Iraq.

5. The mechanism takes account of the requirements of paragraph 7 of resolution 715 (1991), and of certain elements in the plans approved under that resolution including a requirement for timely information about any sale or supply to Iraq by other States of items covered by the plans. The mechanism also takes account of the continued embargo on the sale or supply to Iraq of items prohibited by paragraphs 8 and 12 of resolution 687 (1991).

6. The mechanism is not a regime for international licensing, but rather for the timely provision of information by States in which companies are located which are contemplating sales or supplies to Iraq of items covered by the plans. 1/ Iraq's obligations, comprehensively spelled out in the plans, are further detailed in the mechanism.

7. Even without inspecting every import into Iraq, it is feasible to establish an effective and credible mechanism. It must be robust enough to deter Iraq and suppliers 2/ from potential breaches. The mechanism must also be augmented by the ability of the Commission and IAEA to conduct unrestricted inspections throughout Iraq. No other existing export/import control has such supplementary ground inspection rights. Nevertheless, to be workable, the mechanism must also be sufficiently simple so as not to place an undue reporting burden on Governments. The aim is to encourage companies and Governments to report all of interest, while keeping data volume manageable for all concerned.

8. Each Government shall determine what measures it has to take to give effect internally to the notification requirements under the mechanism (e.g. requiring national licences). Each Government shall remain free to enact prohibitions or controls on exports that go beyond the requirements of the Security Council resolutions and the mechanism.

9. The mechanism aims to secure timely notification of the export to Iraq of any items identified in the plans for ongoing monitoring and verification. Both Iraq and the Governments of suppliers shall provide these notifications in advance of shipment. These notifications shall identify the supplier, give a description of the item or items (including technology) and provide the name of the end-user or consignee and the expected date of dispatch/shipping. Other information, when available to the Government of the supplier, which should assist in administering the mechanism, shall also be included in the standardized notification forms referred to in paragraph 14 below. The notifications are imperative, as they make it possible to monitor the supply to Iraq of all items covered by the plans, both non-proscribed dedicated-use items and dual-use items (i.e. those items that can be used for either permitted or proscribed purposes). Iraq shall also report the export of items subject to the plans, whether such items are in the original or modified form, so that the Commission and IAEA can maintain full accounting for all monitored items.

10. If an item, the import of which should have been notified under the mechanism but was not, is found in Iraq, the import would constitute a case of non-compliance with the monitoring regime established by the plans for ongoing monitoring and verification. The steps to be taken in cases of non-compliance are defined in paragraphs 22 to 24 of the Special Commission's plan and paragraphs 36 to 39 of the IAEA plan. The strong presumption would be that the item had been procured for prohibited purposes and so, as such, would be subject to disposal in accordance with the measures provided for in paragraphs 8 and 12 of Security Council resolution 687 (1991).

II. *Scope*

11. The annexes to the plans for ongoing monitoring and verification, and any appendices thereto, identify the items and technologies which Iraq, as importer, and the Government of the supplier, as exporter, shall notify. A compendium of definitions of terms used in the annexes shall be provided to Governments. This compendium shall have the same status as the annexes.

12. For purposes of monitoring within Iraq and reporting by Iraq, such monitoring and reporting covers all items and technologies provided for in the plans and

---

1/ Both the Commission's and IAEA's plans, however, envisage special cases where the import by Iraq of clearly defined items requires prior consent; see paras. 24 and 25.
2/ Any entity involved in a transaction covered by the mechanism which becomes aware that the ultimate destination of a controlled item is Iraq.

their annexes, including appendices, whether identified generically or specifically.

13. For Governments of suppliers, their notification obligations shall be limited to the items and technologies that are specifically identified. 3/ The annexes also identify items the export of which to Iraq is prohibited under the Security Council's resolutions. The procedures to be followed in respect of such items are contained in paragraphs 24 and 25 below.

14. Standardized export/import notification forms shall be made available by the Commission and IAEA to Governments. Supplementary information and clarifications regarding completion of the forms and other aspects of the monitoring regime shall be provided by the Commission and IAEA to Governments in circular notes of an advisory character. These notes shall be used to give, for example, details on the practical implementation of the mechanism, such as the timing for submission of notifications.

15. Should experience over time demonstrate the need, or new technologies so require, the annexes may be amended in accordance with the plans, after appropriate consultations with interested States and, as laid down in the plans, notification to the Security Council.

III. Characteristics of the mechanism

16. Resolution 715 (1991) foresees a unified monitoring mechanism, under the Security Council. A single address for communications from Governments, including the completed notification forms, would greatly simplify the task of Governments. A joint unit, constituted by the Commission and IAEA, shall be established at United Nations Headquarters in New York, where the largest number of Governments are represented. This Unit shall receive, for action by the Commission or IAEA, as the case may be, all communications from Governments. Action by the Commission and IAEA shall be coordinated closely, especially where the items concerned come under the provisions of both plans for ongoing monitoring and verification, and any following correspondence on such items shall be shared between the Commission and IAEA. The notifications Iraq is required to submit shall be delivered to the Baghdad Monitoring and Verification Centre, which shall serve both the Commission and IAEA, for onward transmission to the Joint Unit in New York.

17. In all relevant areas, a comprehensive exchange of information between the Commission and IAEA shall take place. The capability to draw on the resources of the Commission and IAEA in their respective spheres of competence may be essential, in certain instances, for the determination of the potential uses of a particular item subject to notification and thus of its correct charac-

terization under the plans and the mechanism. It is important that the Commission and IAEA have this independent capability in order to avoid any possible claims of partiality. In a similar vein, recognizing that information provided in notifications may, in certain instances, be proprietary and sensitive for commercial reasons, the information provided shall be treated as confidential and restricted to the Commission and IAEA, to the extent that this is consistent with their respective responsibilities under Security Council resolution 715 (1991), other relevant resolutions and the plans.

18. The information provided shall be stored both manually and electronically and collated with other information derived from inspections and declarations, in order to assess the extent of Iraq's compliance. It is important for implementation of the overall monitoring process as it:

(a) Provides information on denied exports, thereby acting as a means of identifying possible proscribed activities;

(b) Allows inspectors to tag notified equipment as it is imported into the country;

(c) Allows inspectors to verify the location of imported materials;

(d) Alerts inspectors to the locations of new facilities relevant to monitoring;

(e) Monitors the quantities of materials imported, in order to identify any increase in import which may be out of proportion to commercial and other nonproscribed requirements.

The information shall also provide an essential tool for the designation of sites, facilities, activities, materials and other items in Iraq for inspection purposes.

19. The notification procedure must be swift and, as far as possible, while being consistent with the terms set down by the Security Council, not impede Iraq's legitimate right to import or export items for nonproscribed uses. To that end, these notification forms shall apply to transactions involving any type of reportable item (dual-use items or proscribed and nonproscribed dedicated-use items, as determined under the Council's resolutions). Two separate sets of forms are envisaged: one for Iraq to complete and the other for the Government of the supplier to complete. Each transaction shall have a unique designator number assigned by the

---

3/ These items and technologies are identified in the March 1995 revision of the annexes to the Commission's plan as follows: chemical, in paras. 1, 2, 10, 12 and 13 of annex II; biological, in the appendix to annex III; and, missiles, in paras. 1 and 2 of annex IV. In the nuclear area, they are identified in the March 1995 revision of annex III of the IAEA plan. If, in the future, the annexes are revised, in accordance with the procedures in para. 15 of the present report, and such revisions involve a renumbering of the paragraphs just indicated, the renumbering will be communicated to all States by means of a circular note.

Joint Unit, to be used where available in all correspondence. This obviates the requirement to repeat information. Substantive changes to earlier statements shall be transmitted to the Joint Unit by Iraq and the Government of the supplier as those changes become known to them.

20. Each form shall be in two parts, with an acknowledgement section. Iraq should facilitate the process by filing notifications as early as possible in the transaction. The onus shall be on Iraq to ensure that a supplier understands its part in the notification process. In this regard, Iraq shall inform the supplier of the unique designator number assigned by the Joint Unit on the basis of Iraq's initial notification. This would help to avoid confusion arising, for example, from differing descriptions of the exported item by Iraq and by the supplier.

21. The forms themselves shall be developed by the Commission and IAEA, bearing in mind standardized international practice in respect of commodity description and coding in international trade. The forms shall be available in English and French and shall be submitted to the Joint Unit in either one of these languages so as to facilitate and expedite the processing of the forms.

22. In order to facilitate the work of the Joint Unit and monitoring inspections, Iraq shall maintain files with the relevant documentation (e.g. contracts, shipping documents, letters of credit, etc.) for imports of all items subject to notification by it. These files shall be available to the Commission or IAEA, as the case may be, upon request. Full files shall be kept at the points of entry and by the Iraqi National Monitoring Directorate. Copies of relevant documentation shall accompany each item as it is transported between its point of entry and the site of end-use. Relevant technical documentation shall also be available at the end-use site for inspection by the Commission or IAEA, as the case may be.

23. In the event that a difference arises between the Commission or IAEA and the Government of a supplier on whether a particular export is subject to notification, or whether it is prohibited under the plans or on any other substantive matter arising in the course of implementing the mechanism, every effort shall be made to settle the difference through confidential consultations between the Commission or IAEA, on the one hand, and the Government, on the other. In the event that such consultations do not resolve the difference, the matter may be referred by the Commission or IAEA, or the Government concerned, to the Security Council or the Sanctions Committee, as appropriate.

IV. *Special cases*

24. The Commission's plan for ongoing monitoring and verification identifies items, the acquisition of which by Iraq is prohibited save for certain limited exceptions 4/ with respect to which Iraq must obtain prior consent from the Commission. Where such consent is obtained, Iraq must communicate that consent to the supplier, to be attached to the notification by the Government of the supplier referred to in paragraph 9 above. A special case relates to the emergency import of vaccines, where such import by Iraq may take place with simultaneous notification to the Commission. In such circumstances, the Commission shall notify the supplier, the name of which must be provided to the Commission by Iraq in its simultaneous notification, of its consent. In cases where these requirements are not met, Governments shall be obliged to provide to the Joint Unit, referred to in paragraph 16 above, any information notified to them, by a supplier located on their territories, concerning attempts by Iraq to acquire from that supplier items prohibited under the plans. Governments will be encouraged also to provide any other information they may have on such attempts.

25. The IAEA plan for ongoing monitoring and verification, as approved by the Security Council, requires both Iraq and exporting States to secure prior approval from IAEA or the Sanctions Committee, as the case may be, of transfers to Iraq, in particular prior to the lifting of sanctions. 5/ Once sanctions are lifted, these provisions would be superseded by this mechanism.

26. Attempts might be made to supply Iraq with items subject to the plans in total circumvention of the mechanism. In this respect, Governments may have at their disposal national information concerning unauthorized exports to Iraq which should have been notified under the mechanism. The Commission and IAEA shall exercise their rights, under the relevant Security Council resolutions and the plans, to conduct no-notice on-site inspections at any Iraqi point of entry or elsewhere in Iraq and to require Iraq, where necessary, to impound items until such time as the unopened consignment can be inspected.

27. There may also be attempts to supply Iraq with such items clandestinely through transshipment. By this method, goods could leave the country of origin without the supplier showing Iraq as the final destination. Goods under transshipment are usually deemed for customs purposes to be transit goods; they are not considered to have been imported into the country of transshipment. In order to close this possible loophole, the country of transshipment shall take action in the event that it receives information that Iraq has become indicated as the final destination after the goods were exported from their country of origin. Where this has occurred, the transshipment country shall notify the Joint Unit of all shipments of such items.

4/ See S/22871/Rev.1, sect. C, Provisions related to chemical items, para. 32, and sect. D, Provisions related to biological items, para. 38.
5/ See S/22872/Rev.1 and Rev.1/Corr.1, Introduction, para. 9 and sect. C, Obligations of Iraq, paras. 23, 25 and 26.

28. Where it comes to the attention of a Government that the destination of goods subject to notification, which are located in a bonded warehouse on its territory, has been changed to Iraq, that Government shall inform the Joint Unit accordingly.

29. Data available to the Commission and to IAEA may, in some cases, indicate that Iraq is importing dual-use items in amounts in excess of that required for non-proscribed internal consumption or export. Likewise, such data may indicate the import of items of a quality and nature that is not justified for use in Iraq's non-proscribed programmes. In such cases the Commission and IAEA, shall, in the first instance, inform the Government of Iraq, through the Joint Unit, of its findings and call upon it to cease entering into any arrangements for procurement of these items. Thereafter, the Joint Unit shall, by a circular note to all States, recommend that they not enter into any new commitments to provide Iraq with the items in question until further notice. Should it prove necessary and in order to decide upon appropriate measures, the Commission or IAEA, as appropriate, shall enter into confidential consultations with the Governments of suppliers with outstanding contracts to provide such items.

Annex II
Letter dated 17 July 1995 from the Executive Chairman of the United Nations Special Commission addressed to the Chairman of the Security Council Committee established by resolution 661 (1990) concerning the situation between Iraq and Kuwait

I have the honour to refer to the proposal for the mechanism for export/import monitoring under paragraph 7 of Security Council resolution 715 (1991), which has been submitted to the Sanctions Committee by the Special Commission and by the International Atomic Energy Agency (IAEA), and which is currently under consideration by it. In connection with that proposal, certain delegations have requested information on the modalities that will be followed by the Special Commission and IAEA in Iraq when implementing that mechanism in Iraq.

The Security Council has, on a number of occasions, confirmed that sole responsibility for carrying out their mandates in Iraq rests with the Special Commission and IAEA (e.g. statement to the press by the President of the Council of 24 September 1991 and statement by the President of the Council of 28 February 1992 (S/23663)). Nevertheless, the Commission and IAEA have kept the Council fully informed of their activities and their *modus operandi*. In keeping with this practice, it may be useful to indicate the general principles that would be followed in implementing the mechanism in Iraq.

An Office of export/import specialists will be established in the Baghdad Monitoring and Verification Centre and will serve as an administrative clearing-house for communications from Iraq regarding the notification forms that it is required to submit. This Office and the Centre will also implement inspections within Iraq to ensure that the mechanism is being complied with. These inspections will be as vigorous as is necessary to ensure that no violations of the export/import regime occur. In this regard, the Commission and IAEA intend to rely on their full rights under the relevant Security Council resolutions, including resolutions 687 (1991), 707 (1991) and 715 (1991), the plans for ongoing monitoring and verification (S/22871/Rev.1 and S/22872/Rev.1 and Rev.1/Corr.1), the privileges and immunities as set forth in the exchange of letters between the United Nations and Iraq of 6 and 17 May 1991 and the decision to be taken by the Security Council approving the mechanism.

Inspections under the mechanism will take place not only at the declared end-user sites, where notified items will be tagged, as appropriate, and entered into the site protocols, but will also be conducted anywhere else in Iraq where there is reason to believe that notified items or dual-use items in respect of which there should have been notification may be found. To ensure Iraqi compliance, the monitoring will be carried out in whatever ways yield the most effective results, whether by monitoring end-user sites, or border crossings or other locations. For example, if information available to the Commission and experience proves this to be effective, the Commission may station its personnel at key points, including points of entry and of customs inspection in Iraq. The extent to which various inspection rights will be exercised in Iraq will depend, *inter alia*, on the degree of Iraqi cooperation in carrying out the mechanism and the findings of the Commission and IAEA regarding the Iraqi customs and import procedures.

I believe that, when the Sanctions Committee is in a position to forward the proposal for the mechanism to the Security Council, as the tripartite proposal called for in paragraph 7 of resolution 715 (1991), it should be accompanied, for purposes of information, by this letter setting out, in general terms, the modalities which it is intended will be followed in implementing the mechanism.

(*Signed*) Rolf EKÉUS
Executive Chairman of the
United Nations Special Commission

Document 218

Decision 34 taken by the Governing Council of the United Nations Compensation Commission concerning the third instalment of claims for serious personal injury or death (category B claims) (extract)

S/AC.26/Dec.34 (1995), 13 December 1995

...

The Governing Council,

Having received, in accordance with article 37 of the Provisional Rules for Claims Procedure, the fourth report of the Panel of Commissioners appointed to review individual claims for serious personal injury or death, covering 1055 individual recommendations,

1. *Approves* the recommendations made by the Panel of Commissioners and accordingly,

2. *Decides,* pursuant to article 40 of the Rules, to approve the amounts of the recommended awards totaling US$2,450,000.00 concerning the 719 claims listed in the annexes to the report;

3. *Decides* that the following amounts be paid with respect to those awards as listed below:

...

4. *Recalls* that when payments are made in accordance with Decision 17 (S/AC.26/Dec.17 (1994)] and pursuant to the terms of Decision 18 (S/AC.26/Dec.18 (1994)], Governments and international organizations shall distribute amounts received in respect of approved awards within six months of receiving payment, and shall, not later than three months after the expiration of this time limit, provide information on such distribution;

5. *Decides* that no compensation is awarded concerning the 311 claims referred to in paragraph 23 of the report;

6. *Notes* the transfer by the Executive Secretary of the 18 claims referred to in paragraph 23 of the report to the Panel of Commissioners appointed for category "C" claims;

7. *Notes* that no recommendation has been made at this stage for the seven claims referred to in paragraph 23 of the report;

8. *Requests* that the Executive Secretary provides copies of the report and the pertinent annexes to the report to the Secretary-General and to respective Governments and international organizations, and reminds these Governments and international organizations of their obligation to take the appropriate measures to preserve the confidentiality of the annexes.

Document 219

Letter dated 14 December 1995 from the Director General of the IAEA to the Secretary-General concerning implementation by the IAEA of the plan for the destruction, removal or rendering harmless of items listed in paragraph 12 of Security Council resolution 687 (1991)

S/1995/1040, 18 December 1995

Note by the Secretary-General

The Secretary-General has the honour to transmit to the members of the Security Council the attached communication, dated 14 December 1995, which he has received from the Director General of the International Atomic Energy Agency (IAEA).

Annex
Letter dated 14 December 1995 from the Director General of the International Atomic Energy Agency addressed to the Secretary-General

Security Council resolution 699 (1991), approved on 17 June 1991, *inter alia,* requests, the Secretary-General to submit to the Security Council progress reports on the implementation of the plan for the destruction, removal or rendering harmless of the items specified in paragraph 12 of resolution 687 (1991). Such reports are to be submitted every six months after the adoption of resolution 699 (1991). The next report is therefore due on 17 December 1995.

As you will recall, in August 1995, IAEA was invited by the Government of Iraq to visit Baghdad for technical talks. During these discussions, IAEA was informed of a crash programme, established by Iraq in the late summer/early fall of 1990, to divert for use in Iraq's clandestine nuclear weapons programme, the highly enriched uranium contained in research reactor fuel that was subject to IAEA safeguards. In the course of these discussions, a number of documents were handed over to IAEA. At the close of the discussions, Iraqi officials also advised IAEA of a cache of documents, materials and fabricated items relating to Iraq's programme for weapons of mass destruction that had been concealed on property declared to belong to the family of General Hussein Kamel (the Haidar House Farm). This cache of documents, along with those handed over during the technical talks, have been catalogued, and the portion relating to Iraq's clandestine nuclear weapons programme, including almost a million pages of documents, have been transferred to IAEA headquarters in Vienna, where analysis is in progress.

During follow-up inspections, conducted in September and October 1995, the Iraqi Government handed over a number of additional technical documents relating to the former nuclear weapons programme. These documents have also been removed from Iraq and are the subject of urgent detailed evaluation.

Among the latter documents were detailed lists of equipment and materials utilized in the clandestine nuclear programme that had been salvaged during and after the Gulf war and removed to other locations. The lists indicate the presence in Iraq of hitherto undeclared items that could fall in the categories of those proscribed to Iraq under resolution 687 (1991). IAEA is in the process of locating, identifying and analysing the characteristics of such items. This process may result in the need to destroy, remove or render harmless part of the items contained in the lists. IAEA will keep the Security Council informed on this matter.

Kindly bring the content of this letter to the attention of the Council.

(Signed) Hans BLIX

Document 220

Tenth report of the Executive Chairman of UNSCOM

S/1995/1038, 17 December 1995

Note by the Secretary-General

1. The Secretary-General has the honour to transmit to the Security Council a report submitted by the Executive Chairman of the Special Commission established by the Secretary-General pursuant to paragraph 9 (b) (i) of Security Council resolution 687 (1991).

2. It is the tenth such report provided in accordance with paragraph 9 (b) (i) of Security Council resolution 687 (1991) and paragraph 3 of Council resolution 699 (1991). It covers the period from 17 June to 17 December 1995 and is further to the reports contained in documents S/23165, S/23268, S/24108 and Corr.1, S/24984, S/25977, S/26910, S/1994/750, S/1994/1422 and Add.1 and S/1995/494.

3. In addition, eight reports have been submitted to the Security Council under paragraph 8 of resolution 715 (1991). These reports are contained in documents S/23801, S/24661, S/25620, S/26684, S/1994/489, S/1994/1138 and Corr.1, S/1995/284 and S/1995/864.

Annex
Tenth report of the Executive Chairman of the Special Commission established by the Secretary-General pursuant to paragraph 9 (b) (i) of Security Council resolution 687 (1991), and paragraph 3 of resolution 699 (1991) on the activities of the Special Commission

I. *Introduction*

1. The work of the Special Commission in the reporting period, 17 June to 17 December 1995, has covered the whole range of activities envisaged by section C of Security Council resolution 687 (1991). Further information concerning developments since the last report submitted under Council resolution 699 (1991) is contained in the report to the Council of 11 October 1995

(S/1995/864), the eighth report provided in accordance with paragraph 8 of resolution 715 (1991).

2. Since its report to the Council in October, the Commission has stepped up its activities in following up on and seeking to verify the very large amount of new information on Iraq's proscribed programmes that has continued to be obtained since August 1995. The Commission has also followed up on a growing concern regarding ongoing activities in Iraq in areas prohibited since the adoption of resolution 687 (1991), in particular in the missile area, where recent evidence indicates that activities have been or are being pursued that go beyond what is permitted under the resolution.

II. Developments

A. Developments in Iraq

3. The new information obtained since August 1995—in particular Iraq's long-delayed admission of its full-scale offensive biological weapons programme and its advances in the production of the chemical agent VX—confirmed what the Commission had for a considerable time believed on the basis of its own analytical work and its inspection and monitoring activities. These disclosures, on the one hand, gave rise to great concern in the Security Council and among Member States in general as to both the scope and advanced degree of development of Iraq's now proscribed programmes and the grave dangers that they have posed to the peoples of the region and to international peace and security during the Gulf war and since. On the other hand, Iraq's disclosures represented a great step forward in the work of the Commission and of the International Atomic Energy Agency (IAEA) in uncovering, subject to verification still, the remaining elements of Iraq's programmes.

4. The new information has greatly expedited the work of the Commission in accomplishing its tasks under resolution 687 (1991). Without Iraq's admissions, elucidation of the Commission's concerns would have taken up considerable periods of time in conducting inspection missions and in investigation of Iraq's procurement abroad and of information from other sources. The documents obtained on 20 August 1995 at the Haidar Farm near Baghdad, at the conclusion of a visit by the Executive Chairman to Iraq (see S/1995/864, paras. 23-27), have provided materials both for verifying some aspects of Iraq's disclosures and for indicating other avenues that require further investigation.

5. Far from delaying the process of completing the picture of Iraq's proscribed programmes and of verifying its declarations on those programmes, this documentation has considerably speeded up these activities. The Commission has catalogued and assigned priorities for the examination of all the documentation and continues intensive work on the translation and analysis of those that appear to be of the most immediate importance and significance. Analytical work of this nature has been accompanied by further investigation missions to follow up with Iraq on its new declarations. A special concern, in this regard, has been the need to determine the full extent of Iraq's programmes and to seek verification of Iraq's claims to have destroyed all proscribed weapons, in particular its stocks of agent VX and its precursors, operational missile systems, all of its biological warfare agent and all of the aerial bombs and missile warheads that Iraq states it filled with various chemical and biological agents in the period immediately preceding the Gulf war.

6. In response to the Commission's request, Iraq has recently submitted new declarations, containing "full, final and complete disclosures" relating to its chemical, biological and missile programmes. It will be recalled that such disclosures are required under Security Council resolution 687 (1991) and paragraph 3 (i) of resolution 707 (1991). The Commission concluded that new declarations were required because the radical nature of the latest information rendered the previous declarations completely out of date. Two of these declarations, in the chemical and biological areas, were delivered in draft form, thus inviting the Commission's comments. Experts from the Commission in both these areas have visited Baghdad and discussed the declarations with their Iraqi counterparts.

7. During these discussions, various shortcomings were brought to the attention of the Iraqi experts. Iraq has undertaken to redraft the declarations substantially to meet the Commission's requirements. The declaration on missiles was presented in final, not draft form. The declaration is now being analysed in New York. Further information on all these declarations will be found in the sections below dealing with missiles, chemical weapons and biological weapons respectively. While there is some disappointment that the new declarations are not close to meeting the Commission's requirements, the stated readiness of Iraq to meet these requirements is a welcome sign of Iraq's undertakings to cooperate, without time-limits, which were given to the Executive Chairman by Deputy Prime Minister Mr. Tariq Aziz in Baghdad in August 1995 and which were repeated in New York in December 1995.

B. Executive Chairman's visit to Baghdad

8. Since the October 1995 report, the Executive Chairman has paid one further visit to Baghdad, from 27 to 29 November 1995. Immediately prior to the visit, there had been disquieting press reports that the Foreign Minister of Iraq, Mr. Mohammed Saeed Al-Sahaf, had

made some remarks calling upon the Commission to set an early time-limit for the completion of its work. This remark could be understood as coming perilously close to the ultimatum given by Iraq in July and August 1995, when it had called upon the Council to commence a move to lift sanctions and the oil embargo by 31 August 1995 or Iraq would cease its cooperation. Had Iraq not withdrawn that ultimatum, a most serious crisis would have occurred. Furthermore, when the Chairman met with the Deputy Prime Minister of Iraq on 28 November 1995, Mr. Aziz affirmed that Iraq would continue its cooperation without time-limits.

9. Immediately prior to his meeting with the Deputy Prime Minister, the Chairman held two meetings with the leaders of Iraq's technical teams, including General Amer Mohammed Rashid al Ubeidi, now Minister of Oil, General Ahmed Mutharda, now Minister of Transport and Communications, and General Amer Saadi, now in the Office of the President of Iraq. The three Generals all played leading roles in the weapons programmes now proscribed to Iraq. In the course of these meetings, the Chairman outlined certain continuing concerns of the Commission. While remaining issues had probably been narrowed down, it was vital for these to be cleared up completely. Issues such as the numbers of missiles, biological and chemical weapons produced and the verification of the unilateral destruction by Iraq of its operational missile systems, chemical and biological weapons, agent stocks and precursors remained to be addressed. Similar concerns related to Iraq's indigenous production of SCUD-type missile engines and components and to the need for Iraq to revise its previous accounting for the disposition of all of Iraq's long-range missiles. The original accounting had related to the 819 SCUD missiles obtained from the former Soviet Union, before the Commission had been aware that Iraq had successfully produced and tested similar missiles of its own.

10. During the two technical meetings, the Iraqi delegation handed over a personal diary relating to destruction of certain of Iraq's chemical and biological bombs, which had been provided by a junior military engineer. General Amer Rashid believed it would help considerably in the verification of Iraq's claims to have destroyed its chemical and biological weapons.

11. The Chairman welcomed the receipt of the diary, and of a document listing an inventory of chemical agents and precursors that was also delivered to him. When authenticated, these documents could assist in the verification process. He also welcomed the continuing provision of documents by Iraq. However, he indicated that the Commission was convinced that certain of the most important documentation had not yet been handed over, namely documentation in the possession of the central authorities, including the Military Industrialization Corporation and the Ministry of Defence.

12. The Chairman also drew attention to the Commission's concern that the various levels of the Iraqi establishment still found it difficult to cooperate fully in the voluntary provision of information. The Commission's experts were encountering instances where particular Iraqi counterparts would deny knowledge until confronted with evidence that the Commission already had data to the contrary. This attitude had to change to one of full transparency and a readiness to volunteer all relevant information, if the resolution of the remaining issues was to be expedited. The steps Iraq has taken in this direction are positive.

13. In his meeting with the Deputy Prime Minister, in addition to mentioning the concerns he had raised in the technical meetings, the Chairman referred to the requirements of resolution 687 (1991), regarding the destruction, removal or rendering harmless of all chemical and biological weapons and all stocks of agents and all related subsystems and components and all research, development, support and manufacturing facilities. The disclosure of Iraq's biological weapons programme, and the facilities involved therein, gave rise to new issues. The Commission was undertaking an assessment of those facilities to determine what should be done. The Deputy Prime Minister recognized that, in principle, some destruction might be necessary, but he appealed for it to be deferred for as long as possible. He looked forward to the development of a new environment, in which the Commission and Iraq's Government could work together to finalize all issues in a smooth, cooperative and professional manner, without scepticism or exaggeration. Such an environment would contribute to a careful and thorough consideration of those outstanding matters, taking account of Iraq's observations. The Chairman indicated that he would proceed with the assessment to which he had referred, seeking the advice of international experts. After that, decisions would be taken and carried out. The Commission had to carry out the terms of its mandate in full.

14. Mr. Aziz stressed that the leadership of Iraq had no interest in concealing information, weapons or materials for weapons, and that the objective was to finish with all issues relating to proscribed weapons of mass destruction so as to "see paragraph 22 of Security Council resolution 687 (1991) implemented". The Chairman welcomed that declaration.

C. *Visit to New York by the Deputy Prime Minister of Iraq*

15. In addition to the Executive Chairman's visit to Baghdad, the Deputy Prime Minister of Iraq paid a visit to New York in December. Mr. Aziz met the Chairman

on 12 December. The first meeting was confined to an issue that had just arisen concerning the admission to Iraq of an UNSCOM mission, including members of the German Bundestag responsible for matters relating to the Commission, in order to review all aspects of German air support for the Commission and to make recommendations thereon, including the future of such support. The mission was to visit Iraq from 13 to 16 December 1995. The Commission considered that the assessment of its air operations and the future thereof, by persons invited by the Commission, formed an integral part of the Commission's activities.

16. Iraq, however, on 11 December 1995, informed the Commission that the mission would be admitted to Iraq only on the basis of a bilateral arrangement arrived at between Germany and Iraq, and not under the aegis of the Commission. The Chairman requested an early meeting on 12 December with the Deputy Prime Minister to ask that the mission be allowed to proceed as originally planned. A negative answer from Iraq would be seen as a failure in cooperation, with likely adverse effects. The Deputy Prime Minister, however, maintained the position taken by Iraq. Iraq did not accept that the mission, as composed, came within its understanding of the persons Iraq was required to admit to its territory under the arrangements relating to the Commission. In the light of this, the mission's visit to Iraq did not take place, the Commission maintaining its original position regarding the correctness of the mission as planned.

17. At a later meeting on 12 December between the Deputy Prime Minister and the Chairman, a discussion took place on the latest developments. The Chairman indicated that the December report could not contain definitive findings as the current situation was a highly mobile one where new information and disclosures changed the picture almost daily. The period since the Commission's October report had been one of intensive developments. Some of them had been positive, such as the receipt of the new declarations in the chemical, biological and missile areas. As regards the chemical and biological areas, both sides had agreed upon the need for them to be reworked by Iraq. The Chairman hoped that, as a result of that reworking, the confused situation around the number and eventual disposition of biological and chemical weapons could be cleared up. In addition to the positive elements, however, recent information received from both inside and outside Iraq gave rise to serious concern that, after the adoption of resolution 687 (1991), Iraq had continued to acquire components from abroad for its missile programmes and had conducted a clandestine programme on missiles capable of reaching beyond the 150-kilometre range, the limit laid down in Security Council resolution 687 (1991). None of these

particular matters were included in the new full, final and complete disclosures on Iraq's missile programmes. That declaration, which had been said to be in final form, would have to be corrected.

18. The Deputy Prime Minister said that, since August 1995, Iraq had made a tremendous effort to clarify all issues and to provide the necessary documentary proof. He was convinced that Iraq would fill any gaps that still remained. Even if the Commission did not yet believe that it had a clear picture, that did not shake Iraq's confidence regarding the statement the Deputy Prime Minister had made in August 1995 that all weapons were destroyed. Mr. Aziz repeatedly affirmed Iraq's intentions to cooperate fully and in a transparent manner with the Commission, without limits, until all issues were settled. He gave his personal commitment to work to that end. He asked that the Commission not rush to judgement on matters of serious concern outlined by the Chairman. In that context, he invited the Chairman to send an expert team to Baghdad, after the Deputy Prime Minister's return there, to investigate in full the issues of serious concern that the Chairman had raised. Iraq was already investigating some of them, and the early clarification of all of them was in Iraq's best interests.

19. The Chairman agreed to send the requisite team of missile experts to Baghdad as soon as all the necessary expertise and information could be assembled.

D. *Visit to the States members of the Gulf Cooperation Council*

20. Immediately prior to going to Baghdad at the end of November 1995, the Executive Chairman visited the capitals of the States members of the Gulf Cooperation Council (Bahrain, Kuwait, Oman, Qatar, Saudi Arabia and United Arab Emirates). He did so in order to explain to them the activities of the Commission and its future plans. Much concern had been created in the region following on the disclosures of August 1995 and later regarding Iraq's biological and chemical weapons and its missile activities. The Chairman wished to provide assurances that the Commission would carry out the measures necessary to ensure that Iraq did not possess banned weapons and could not resume their production so as to pose a threat to its neighbours with such weapons. He also wanted to seek the political and financial support of the States concerned in order for the Commission to carry out the mandates of the Security Council. He was met with understanding in every capital he visited, where he found that the work of the Commission was followed with the greatest attention. At a meeting of the Gulf Cooperation Council, held at the level of heads of State in Muscat, at the beginning of December 1995, a communiqué was adopted which, *inter alia*, expressed sup-

port for the work of the Commission and promised political and financial backing for its work.

E. Material and financial support for the Special Commission

21. In the period under review, the Commission has had to devote much time to the issue of the provision to it of the contributions in kind and of the financial resources needed for it to carry out its activities. It is only because of the great generosity of many Governments that the Commission has been able to discharge its mandate outside of obligatory assessments and of the regular budget of the United Nations. Under resolution 699 (1991), Governments will be able eventually to claim reimbursement, if they so wish, for their contributions, when the embargo on the export of Iraqi oil is lifted, but until such time resources will have to be made available by Governments at their own cost. This is immeasurably less than would be the cost to the international community of dealing with the situation that could arise if Iraq were able to reactivate its proscribed programmes on any scale because the Commission has had to cease operations for lack of resources.

22. The Commission estimates that contributions in kind from various Member States have covered about two thirds of the total cost of its operations. The remaining third has been provided through direct financial contributions to the Commission. Its cash costs to date have amounted to around $20 to $25 million per year: a total of $100 million between 1991 and 1995. These funds, while small compared to the size of Member States' support in kind, are essential to the viability of the Commission. They have been covered mainly from frozen Iraqi assets made available through the escrow account established under Security Council resolution 778 (1992) and also from voluntary contributions from Kuwait, Saudi Arabia and Qatar.

23. In the period under review, the Commission has been seeking a more assured means of securing the financing needed for its operations. The amount of frozen Iraqi assets to be made available under resolution 778 (1992) is almost exhausted and the Commission is having to look elsewhere for future financial support. In this regard, it has been engaged with a wide range of countries to secure the financial future of the Commission.

24. Contributions in kind have come through the secondment of experts and other personnel to serve with the Commission and by, *inter alia*, the donation of vehicles, laboratories, computers, monitoring cameras and detection and communications equipment. All members of the European Union have provided support to the Commission, as have Australia, New Zealand, the Russian Federation, Switzerland, the United States of Amer-

ica, and a number of countries in Latin America. New Zealand, for example, has continuously supported the Commission and IAEA since 1991 through the provision of a medical team. It has also provided a specialized communications team.

25. Of particular importance has been the provision of air support by Germany and by the United States and of ground facilities by the Government of Bahrain for the Commission's Field Office in Muharraq. Germany has to date, from the early months of the Commission's activities, provided all the aircraft for transportation into and out of Iraq from Bahrain and for transportation and other air services within Iraq.

26. This air support has been invaluable in the conduct of the operations of the Commission and of IAEA. The air assets operate in difficult and potentially dangerous conditions that require the utmost professionalism. This is ably demonstrated by the German crews who are stationed in Iraq and Bahrain. The Commission and IAEA remain grateful to the Government of Germany for this support.

27. The three CH-53 helicopters play an essential part in the long-term monitoring system of the Commission and IAEA. They are involved in the low—altitude aerial inspection activity (providing a platform for photography), surveillance of large inspection sites during inspections (to ensure that all activity at the site can be monitored simultaneously), the rapid transport of expert teams carrying out no-notice inspections and with the transport of vehicles and equipment throughout Iraq. The independence of operation brought about by these helicopters is fundamental to the Commission and IAEA. Without such a capability, the monitoring system as presently constituted would not work.

28. The two Transall aircraft are the sole means for the Commission and IAEA to fly their experts and equipment in and out of Iraq and thus sustain all the operations in Iraq. In addition, the helicopters and C-160 Transall aircraft provide the Commission and IAEA with essential medical evacuation capabilities.

29. Following almost four years of continuous support, the Government of Germany has announced, with effect from 1 January 1996, there would be a reduction in the number of aircraft provided to the Commission and IAEA. Germany has informed the Commission of its intention to reduce to one the number of transport aircraft stationed at Bahrain and the number of helicopters stationed in Iraq to two until 30 June 1996. The Commission believes that any diminution in the number of aircraft, either fixed-wing or helicopter, will deal a serious blow to the operations of the Commission and IAEA in Iraq.

30. The Commission believes that, as a result of the cutbacks and potential delays with the provision of back-up aircraft, it will be unable to adhere to a firm plan of operations. This would have serious consequences for the Commission and IAEA. Activities would have to be curtailed to a point where the ability of the Commission and IAEA to carry out their mandate could be called into question. The Commission has been actively pursuing replacement air support for over six months. It is hoped that the present level of air support can be maintained in the interim. If this proves not to be the case, the Commission will have to request the Council to address the issue in the immediate future.

31. The U-2 aircraft made available to the Commission by the United States is another key component in the air surveillance required to identify new sites for inspection and to follow activities that should be investigated to ascertain their legitimate character or otherwise. It will remain one of the most important tools in ensuring the completeness and efficacy of the Commission's monitoring system.

32. The facilities made available by the Government of Bahrain in Muharraq, at the Government's expense, for the Commission's Field Office, have been vital as they serve as the single staging area for all the Commission's movements into and out of Iraq. The offices, situated in a hangar within the secure environment of the airport at Muharraq, could not be improved on from the point of view of convenience and safety. Immediate access is accorded to the Commission's aircraft and the Commission's staff is also immediately available to meet experts and other personnel arriving in Bahrain. Equipment and other material can be stored safely and moved efficiently into and out of Iraq. Expert teams are assembled and trained in the Field Office.

33. The Commission is aware that the Government of Bahrain could have other important uses for the facilities it has provided and thus the Commission is doubly grateful for the priority the Government has given to the requirements of the Commission. This is a demonstration of Bahrain's dedication to the United Nations. Bahrain thus continues to make a most significant contribution to the maintenance of international peace and security not only in the Gulf but in the international community as a whole.

34. The Field Office functions under an Agreement between the United Nations and the State of Bahrain that is subject to renewal every six months. The Chairman has assured the Government that its contribution and assistance in carrying out the relevant resolutions of the Security Council is recognized and appreciated as one of the first rank.

III. Missiles

35. This latest reporting period has been very important for the Commission's investigations of Iraq's prohibited missile activities. The Commission described some of the more significant events in its October report to the Security Council. Iraq has admitted that it had been withholding important information on its missile programmes. The Commission requested Iraq to provide a new full, final and complete disclosure as required by resolutions 687 (1991) and 707 (1991).

36. On 16 November 1995, Iraq submitted to the Commission such a declaration consisting of more than 2,500 pages. This declaration has clarified a number of outstanding and unresolved issues. Iraq included in its submission, at the Commission's request, documents to support many of its statements such as contracts, offers, orders and minutes of meetings related to Iraq's dealings with its main foreign suppliers in the missile area. The Commission welcomes this new approach by Iraq, a clear departure from the past practice when Iraq claimed that documents related to proscribed activities had been destroyed.

37. Of interest in this new information is Iraq's confirmation of the use in proscribed activities of the large radar destroyed under protest by Iraq a year ago. Iraq had claimed that the radar had nothing to do with proscribed activities and the Commission was acting improperly. This matter had been brought to the attention of the Council in the Commission's report of 15 December 1994 and in oral briefings to the Council describing Iraq's initial refusal to implement the Commission's decision.

38. The Commission had suggested, in a spirit of cooperation, that Iraq should initially submit a draft version so that appropriate ways and means could be discussed to facilitate subsequent efficient and speedy verification of a formal full, final and complete disclosure. However, Iraq stated that the document of 16 November was presented as a final version of its disclosure and that no substantive additions or corrections would be made to it.

39. The Commission has begun its analysis of Iraq's declaration. Establishing a definite and verifiable material balance for proscribed weapons is a fundamental requirement for the Commission to be able to assess Iraq's compliance with the missile-related provisions of resolution 687 (1991). Iraq's accounting in the November full, final and complete disclosures does not appear to constitute a firm basis for this.

40. While some relevant documentation was submitted by Iraq in its November full, final and complete disclosures, it did not provide original documents to account for the expenditure of all imported proscribed missile systems. There is no evidence to support Iraq's

declaration on the indigenous production of missile engines or on their disposal. The Commission's last report indicated that Iraq had acknowledged the production of major parts of proscribed rocket engines. The recent disclosure provided more information on these indigenously produced rocket engines. According to Iraq, some 80 major subsystems of SCUD-type engines had been produced. Fifty-three had been rejected as unfit. Seventeen had been disposed of in testing. Iraq claims to have unilaterally destroyed the remaining 10. Iraq's statements in this respect remain to be verified.

41. Currently, Iraq's account concerning missile warheads, including those for the delivery of weapons of mass destruction, lacks consistency and the necessary evidence for verification. For example, Iraq has not provided any evidence to support its claims that only 120 indigenous warheads were produced. There are significant gaps in Iraq's accounting for such major components for operational missiles as guidance and control systems, liquid propellant fuels and ground support equipment. In October 1995, Iraq handed over to the Commission 18 gyro-instruments for proscribed missiles, without offering a satisfactory explanation for their continuous holding up to that time. It admitted, however, that in late 1993 an order had been issued to one of its missile facilities to start work on prohibited gyro-instruments. The Commission is still studying the full, final and complete disclosures with respect to the material balance in other areas such as imported and indigenously manufactured missile components and tooling and equipment for production activities.

42. The Commission's preliminary review of Iraq's full, final and complete disclosures has also shown several areas where the Commission possesses reliable information that contradicts that disclosure or indicates that Iraq's declarations are incomplete. The declaration has not addressed, in a comprehensive and detailed manner, a number of Iraq's missile projects. Iraq's current declarations on the relation of missile programmes to other proscribed activities in the chemical, biological and nuclear weapons areas fails to meet the Commission's requirements. The Commission believes that Iraq is still withholding important documents related to proscribed activities and has not provided them in the new disclosure.

43. In view of these major deficiencies in the full, final and complete disclosures, Iraq's insistence that the document submitted on 16 November is the final and formal disclosure will complicate the verification process. The Commission is disappointed that Iraq chose to provide its declaration in final form and did not avail itself of the opportunity to resolve major discrepancies through discussion. The Commission will, however, work as

quickly as possible, without sacrificing thoroughness, to carry out verification of Iraq's declaration.

44. In its October report (S/1995/864, para. 37), the Commission informed the Security Council that it had obtained information that Iraq had resumed its acquisition efforts from foreign sources in support of its missile activities. The Commission has kept this matter under close scrutiny.

45. The Government of Jordan recently intercepted a large shipment of high-grade missile components destined for Iraq. Iraq has denied that it had sought to purchase these components, although it has recently acknowledged that some of them are currently in Iraq. The Commission has launched an investigation into this matter in order to determine the exact nature of the missile components involved, their source, the procurement network used and the end-user in Iraq. There is evidence that this acquisition is for long-range missiles and thus further indicates continued activities in Iraq in the area of proscribed missiles.

46. Iraq has recently admitted that, after the adoption of resolution 687 (1991), it conducted a covert programme to develop and produce a surface-to-surface missile. Iraq carried out a number of tests with modified surface-to-air missiles for this project. This missile would be capable of prohibited ranges. These activities were not disclosed by Iraq in its full, final and complete disclosures nor in its declarations required under the plan for ongoing monitoring and verification. If further investigation proves this information to be correct, there would have been a clear violation of the provisions of resolution 687 (1991).

47. Since its October report, the Commission has continued its efforts to monitor Iraq's research, development, testing and production of non-proscribed missiles and their components. Between 9 and 15 December, the Commission conducted its regular research and development update inspection mission (UNSCOM 130/BM 35). Such missions are designed to perform an in-depth technical analysis of Iraq's ongoing efforts to develop and manufacture non-proscribed missile systems, i.e. with a range of less than 150 kilometres. The team was also tasked to study the monitoring arrangements to ensure that they are meeting the requirements of the Commission at the current level of Iraq's missile-related activities.

IV. *Chemical weapons*

48. The new information obtained by the Commission since August 1995 clearly shows that Iraq's chemical weapons programme was more developed and wider in scope than had previously been admitted. Thus the March 1995 chemical full, final and complete disclosure and

subsequent amendments were rendered invalid and the Commission requested that Iraq submit a new disclosure, as required under resolutions 687 (1991) and 707 (1991).

49. A draft chemical weapons full, final and complete disclosure was provided by Iraq on 5 November 1995. As it was in draft form, the Commission's experts were able to review it and to identify those areas that required amendment, in order for the necessary changes to be incorporated by Iraq into the final form of the document.

50. The Commission's chemical experts held talks with Iraq's representatives in Baghdad from 29 November to 2 December 1995. During these talks, the Commission's experts explained that the draft full, final and complete disclosure still lacked important information, contained incorrect information and was internally inconsistent. It was also emphasized that, while Iraq had begun to provide some documentation to support its declarations, further material must be provided, in order to allow the Commission to verify the declarations definitively.

51. The Iraqi side accepted all the comments and recommendations made by the Commission's experts concerning the additional information to be included in the final version of the full, final and complete disclosures. Overall, these discussions were productive and the presence of senior Iraqi officials from the Military Industrialization Corporation proved helpful.

52. One area discussed at length concerned Iraq's account of its activities in relation to the V class of highly toxic chemical warfare agents. In the draft full, final and complete disclosures, Iraq acknowledged that it had produced more VX agent than had previously been declared. Earlier declarations had stated that only 260 kilogrammes were produced in 1988. In the draft, Iraq admitted that 1.8 tonnes had been produced in that year and a further 1.5 tonnes in 1990. It has stated that purity and stabilization problems caused the programme to be abandoned in 1990, in favour of the production of Sarin and Cyclosarin.

53. While noting the revised account of VX activities, the Commission's experts repeated the importance attached to providing a means of verifying the information. This was particularly significant, in view of the fact that, at the beginning of 1989, Iraq had in its possession the necessary quantities of precursors for the large-scale production of V-agents. The evidence currently available to the Commission in respect of the disposal by Iraq of those precursors is far from conclusive. Until such evidence is provided, Iraq's VX activities will continue to be of particular concern to the Commission, since it is unable to confirm that stocks of VX, large quantities of its precursors and appropriate weapons do not remain in

Iraq. Iraq undertook to provide necessary evidence, in order to substantiate its declarations.

54. The Commission's experts also underlined other areas where the draft was deficient and contradictory. These include the overall material balance, where there continue to be major inconsistencies. This assessment was accepted and it was agreed that a completely new material balance would be provided by Iraq. This would be based on documents and not simply on the recollection of those involved.

55. The issue of chemical munitions was also discussed. Here the Commission's experts noted that the accounting for such munitions procured and indigenously produced was not complete. This included the chemical warheads for ballistic missiles. Based on information available to it, the Commission believes that there were further activities relating to the development of chemical munitions that have still not been disclosed, including foreign assistance. Iraq agreed to complete this chapter of the full, final and complete disclosures and to provide appropriate documents.

56. It was also emphasized on several occasions during the meetings that the full, final and complete disclosures should include all of Iraq's institutions involved in the proscribed chemical weapons activities and all contacts and activities that had taken place with foreign entities.

57. Several additional documents were provided to the Commission both during and subsequent to the November discussions in Baghdad. Iraq has undertaken to continue to search for more documentation requested by the Commission. This includes production records, procurement documents, storage inventories and destruction certificates of chemical weapons and their components. The Commission strongly believes that such documentation still exists in Iraq.

58. The ongoing monitoring activities in the chemical field were explained in detail in the Commission's last report. Of note is the recent admission by Iraq of its 1988 plans to relocate the production of chemical precursors to civilian chemical facilities, which has confirmed the Commission's approach taken with respect to its monitoring system. The Commission's monitoring team continues to discover non-declared dual-use equipment in Iraq. Under the monitoring plan, Iraq is required to declare all such dual-use chemical manufacturing equipment. Iraq is still unable to provide complete semi-annual declarations required by the monitoring plan in the chemical field.

59. Since its October report, the Commission has conducted its first night-time inspection of a chemical site. Additional steps have been undertaken to refine the monitoring system to take account of increasing monitoring

requirements and tasks to be performed in the light of Iraq's disclosures in August 1995 and subsequently. This will include, for example, the expansion of the chemical analytical capabilities of the Baghdad Monitoring and Verification Centre in the near future. In addition, the permanent chemical monitoring team will be reinforced by additional personnel. Currently initial tests with temporary mobile monitoring cameras are being carried out by the Commission's chemical monitoring team in Iraq.

V. *Biological weapons*

60. The Commission's main findings and assessments of Iraq's proscribed biological weapons activities were outlined in its last report to the Security Council (S/1995/864). In particular, the Commission concluded that it did not believe that Iraq had given a full and correct account of its biological weapons programme. Thus, Iraq was requested to resubmit its full, final and complete disclosure, a declaration required from Iraq under resolutions 687 (1991) and 707 (1991).

61. Iraq submitted a draft declaration in the biological weapons area to the Commission on 5 November. This document was provided in a draft form so that the Commission could make its preliminary comments on the structure and contents of the document. This was meant to give Iraq an opportunity to improve its declaration to meet the Commission's requirements. Such a process is intended to facilitate subsequent verification by the Commission of the accuracy of the Iraqi declaration once a formal disclosure is provided.

62. The draft full, final and complete disclosures of November was Iraq's third official declaration in the biological weapons area submitted this year. The November document encompasses the disclosures made by Iraq since August 1995, primarily its admission of a comprehensive and well-advanced offensive biological weapons programme, ranging from research and development on a variety of bacteriological agents, viruses and toxins through the production, weaponization and military deployment of biological and toxin weapons. The draft also describes involvement of a number of facilities, in particular at Al Hakam and Dawrah. In some cases, Iraq provided, in response to the Commission's requirements, documentary support of its declarations that were helpful in establishing some milestones in its biological weapons programme and the scope of related activities. Iraq continues to find additional documents, which it is providing to the Commission to substantiate its declarations. The Government of Iraq has assigned high-ranking officials from its biological weapons programme to lead and participate in discussions with the Commission's representatives.

63. Notwithstanding the above positive steps, the November draft contains major deficiencies in structure and content. Serious gaps and omissions exist in the declaration and in the documentary support, especially related to biological warfare agent and munition production, munition filling and the destruction of weaponized and bulk agents. In a number of cases, Iraq's declarations appear to downgrade the scope and the results of research, development and production efforts related to certain biological warfare agents.

64. Through recent high-level political talks and expert discussions, the Commission has pointed to the serious deficiencies in the November draft. Evidence available to the Commission establishes that the biological weapons programme was more extensive than has been admitted by Iraq in its November document. Moreover, information contained in it does not match, in a number of important aspects, the current findings by the Commission based on inspections, analytical work and information provided to it from supporting Governments. The documentation provided by Iraq in its draft, together with other Iraqi documentation obtained by the Commission, constitute only a fraction of the documents generated under the biological weapons programme. The Commission continues to believe that important documents are still being withheld by Iraq, despite assurances of full cooperation from the Government of Iraq.

65. The Commission is especially concerned by Iraq's continuing failure to provide definite figures on amounts of biological weapons agents and munitions produced, weaponized and destroyed. In the absence of such figures, accompanied by supporting documentation, it is not possible to establish a material balance of proscribed items, nor is it possible for the Commission to provide an assessment to the Security Council that Iraq does not retain biological weapons agents and munitions.

66. Security Council resolution 687 (1991) requires that Iraq unconditionally accept the destruction, removal or rendering harmless under Commission's supervision of all biological weapons and all stocks of agents and related substances and components and all research, development, support and manufacturing facilities. The Commission needs to identify what equipment, material and facilities should be subjected to the provisions of the resolution. The first team (UNSCOM 127/BW 29) sent to Iraq for this purpose has just completed its mission and will report its findings to the Executive Chairman for review and final decision. Meanwhile, the Commission has requested Iraq to cease all activities at the facilities in question that have made a major contribution to the biological weapons programme and still have significant equipment present. Iraq has begun to do so.

67. The next major step is for Iraq to submit its formal full, final and complete disclosures of its proscribed biological weapons activities. This will allow the Commission to pursue the verification process. Iraq has undertaken to do so. The Commission intends to continue its inspection activities and analytical efforts with a view to conducting verification in an effective, efficient and speedy manner. The Commission reaffirms that Iraq's full cooperation and complete openness will be the essential element in this process.

68. Monitoring in the biological area through resident inspection teams, aerial surveillance and camera/sensor detection continues, covering a variety of sites and activities in Iraq. On a number of occasions, the biological monitoring group in the Baghdad Monitoring and Verification Centre was also tasked to investigate specific issues related to the proscribed activities in order to expedite fact-finding efforts by the Commission.

VI. *Nuclear weapons*

69. The Director General of IAEA is reporting separately on the activities of the action team set up to implement paragraphs 12 and 13 of resolution 687 (1991) and the IAEA plan for ongoing monitoring and verification approved under Security Council resolution 715 (1991) (S/22872/Rev.1 and Corr.1).

70. In accordance with relevant Security Council resolutions the Commission continues:

(a) To provide information, special expertise, logistical and other operational support, for the implementation of the IAEA plan for ongoing monitoring and verification;

(b) To designate sites for inspection and to receive and advise on requests from Iraq to move or destroy any material or equipment relating to its nuclear weapons programme or other nuclear activities; and

(c) To perform such other functions, in cooperation in the nuclear field with the Director General of IAEA, as may be necessary to coordinate activities under the plan for ongoing monitoring and verification, including making use of commonly available services and information to the fullest possible extent, in order to achieve maximum efficiency and optimum use of resources.

71. The Commission's nuclear experts participated in the IAEA 28/UNSCOM 131 and IAEA 29/UNSCOM 132 inspections conducted between September and October 1995. In particular, the links between the missile and the nuclear areas were investigated. The report of the first of these inspections was submitted to the Security Council on 1 December 1995 (see S/1995/1003, annex).

72. The Commission's experts are continuing to participate in the IAEA negotiations with the Russian Federation regarding the sale of the nuclear materials removed from Iraq and reprocessed in the Russian Federation. The Russian side is required to assist in the disposition of the materials under the original contract for removal and reprocessing. So far these negotiations have failed to produce results because of certain conditions that the Russian side is insisting on, in particular substantial prepayments, which the Commission and IAEA are not in a position to meet and which, in their view, go beyond the normal commercial practice in this regard.

VII. *Radiological weapons*

73. During the reporting period Iraq has acknowledged the existence of a programme related to radiological weapons. On 29 August 1995, a biological inspection team (UNSCOM 125) was given a brief account by the Iraqi authorities of an experiment in the radiological weapons field conducted at the end of 1987 by the Muthanna State Establishment. According to Iraq's statements, the purpose of this experiment was to study the military effectiveness of using irradiated materials. A number of lead-shielded metal containers with irradiated zirconium oxide were exploded at a chemical weapons test site. Each container, which weighed about 1 ton (because of extensive shielding), had from 0.5 to 1 kilogramme of irradiated zirconium oxide. Taking into account the poor test results and safety problems with the handling and transportation of irradiated materials, this project was purportedly shelved at the end of 1987. In total, only a few kilogrammes of zirconium oxide had been irradiated in the research reactor in Tuwaitha for the purpose of this project. The team was told that no special weapons system was created.

74. However, in its draft full, final and complete disclosures on the chemical weapons programme, Iraq mentioned the production of 100 empty casings of LD-250 aerial chemical bombs (known as "Muthanna-4") in 1987. These casings were modified at the request of the Al-Qa'qa State Establishment and the Iraqi Atomic Energy Commission (IAEC). Iraq stated that 75 bombs were delivered to the Al-Qa'qa State Establishment and 25 bombs were destroyed unilaterally by Iraq in the summer of 1991. On 2 December 1995, the Commission's chemical expert team asked the Iraqi authorities to clarify the purpose of the production of these munitions. The Iraqi representatives admitted that these aerial bombs had been modified for the purpose of radiological weapons. Iraq promised to provide all information related to its efforts in the area of radiological weapons in Iraq's next disclosure covering its nuclear programme. Iraq also agreed to provide in its new chemical disclosure all information concerning munitions modified and produced by the Muthanna State Establishment and other

establishments for the purpose of radiological weapons. Such information is important to reconcile the material balance of munitions in other areas, e.g. chemical weapons.

75. On 4 December 1995, additional information on this project was given by Iraq to representatives of the nuclear and chemical monitoring teams. They were told that, around the end of 1987, the Military Industrialization Corporation gave orders to the Nuclear Research Centre at Tuwaitha to explore radiological weapons as a means of "area denial" to be used in the final stages of the Iran/Iraq war. Three prototypes were made based on modified "Nasser 28" aerial bombs. These prototypes had a gross weight of 1,400 kilogrammes and had a radioactive content of some two curies deriving mainly from the hafnium impurity present in the zirconium oxide that had been irradiated in the IRT5000 research reactor at Tuwaitha. All three bombs were exploded at test sites. One bomb had been detonated as a ground-level static test, while the other two bombs had been fitted with impact fuses and were dropped from an aircraft at a testing range.

76. The Commission/IAEA team was told that the results of these tests were disappointing in that the majority of the radioactive material concentrated on the crater with a sharp decline in the radiation level at a relatively short distance away. Concurrently with the "Nasser 28" experiments, development of an alternative design based on a derivative of the Muthanna-3 chemical bomb casing—renumbered Muthanna-4 for the project—was undertaken. This version weighed about 400 kilogrammes and, since it could be accommodated in the aircraft bomb bays, more weapons could be carried by one aircraft. In order to cover the possibility that a decision be taken to go ahead with the deployment of radiological weapons, 80 Muthanna-4 casings were prepared. These casings are lost.

77. According to Iraq, at this stage in the development, mid-1988, a progress report was made to the Military Industrialization Corporation. The report was reviewed by the Corporation, which then presented a "pros and cons" summary to the leadership. The leadership did not pursue the option of the radiological weapon and the project was shelved. The question of documentation was raised and the Iraqi counterparts were asked to seek out drawings and reports that could be used to corroborate their explanation of the radiological weapons project. The Iraqi authorities undertook to do so, but stated that the report on the project had been at the Military Industrialization Corporation at the time when all the documentation was surrendered to the special security organizations (see S/1995/864, para. 26). It was confirmed by the Iraqi authorities that IAEA will be provided with a comprehensive account of the radiological weapons project in the nuclear full, final and complete disclosures currently under preparation by Iraq.

VIII. *Aerial inspections*

78. The aerial imagery provided by the Commission's high-altitude surveillance aircraft (U-2) and the Baghdad-based aerial inspection team continues to be an essential tool for the monitoring regime and for the investigation of new sites. To date over 600 missions have been undertaken by the aerial inspection team and 277 missions by the U-2.

79. If the reduction in the number of CH-53 helicopters, mentioned above, takes place, it will have a major impact on the operational effectiveness of the aerial inspection team. By curtailing the number of missions that it is able to undertake, the team will be unable to fulfil the helicopter-borne aerial requirements of the monitoring regime.

IX. *Export/import mechanism*

80. The Commission's October 1995 report contained a detailed account of the proceedings in the Sanctions Committee regarding the export/import mechanism. The mechanism was approved in that Committee on 20 July 1995. However, its formal transmission to the Security Council, as the tripartite proposal by the Sanctions Committee, the Special Commission and the Director General of IAEA called for under paragraph 7 of resolution 715 (1991), was postponed pending indications of the concurrence of their Governments from all members of the Committee. On 6 December 1995, the Sanctions Committee, having obtained such concurrence, authorized its Chairman to address a letter to the President of the Security Council, transmitting the mechanism for approval by the Council. This transmission, as approved by the Sanctions Committee in July, was accompanied, for purposes of information, by a letter of 17 July 1995 from the Executive Chairman of the Special Commission, regarding the modalities envisaged for implementing the mechanism in Iraq. The mechanism and the letters were circulated to the Security Council on 8 December 1995 (S/1995/1017).

X. *National implementation measures*

81. In the report it submitted to the Council in October 1995, the Commission expressed its grave concern at the failure of Iraq to adopt and implement the national implementation measures it is required to take under the plans for ongoing monitoring and verification. As pointed out in several previous reports, when Iraq is pressed on this matter, its representatives have stated that the legislation would be promulgated shortly. This has not proved to be the case, to the detriment of Iraq's

assurances of full compliance with the relevant Security Council resolutions and of its intentions to forego entirely any activities connected with the weapons programmes now proscribed to it. The Commission can do no more than press Iraq to act promptly and keep the Council informed of developments in relation to an action that Iraq is still required to take under the Council's resolutions. The matter was raised with the Deputy Prime Minister on 12 December 1995, and he has repeated the assurances that the necessary legislation will be enacted.

XI. *Conclusion*

82. The period from 17 June to 17 December 1995 has been one in which the most significant developments have taken place, particularly with regard to the disclosure of Iraq's proscribed programmes. Iraq's attitude towards cooperation with the Commission and the Security Council has also changed from one where ultimatums with deadlines were delivered to one of promises of complete cooperation and transparency, without time-limits. Iraq admits that it has not taken all actions required of it under paragraph 22 of Security Council resolution 687 (1991), but insists that now its declared policy is to do so as fast as possible so that that paragraph can be implemented. Iraq has also admitted that, as late as August 1995, it had been withholding important information from the Commission, but is now in the course of disclosing what had been concealed. After having maintained for a number of years that all documentation relating to its proscribed programmes had been destroyed, Iraq has, during the period under review, provided the Commission and IAEA with substantial quantities of documentation, and is continuing to do so. All of these are positive developments.

83. The amount of new information that has become available both from inside Iraq and from other sources in the recent past, and which requires further investigation and verification, is such that it is not possible at the present time to give a firm assessment of the extent to which full disclosure of all elements of Iraq's proscribed programmes has been made. While there has been substantial progress, there are areas where the picture is still far from complete and further actions are required by Iraq. The Commission believes that, while a great volume of documentation has been made available, many of the most important documents remain and are still being withheld from the Commission. When this documentation is made available, it should provide the most certain and the speediest way of clearing up vital issues such as the quantities of proscribed weapons, items or materials produced or acquired and the disposition thereof. It should also help in determining the extent to which Iraq has continued activities, particularly in the missile area, in circumvention of the provisions of resolutions 687 (1991) and 715 (1991).

84. While the Commission welcomes the repeated assurances which it has received from the Deputy Prime Minister Tariq Aziz, on behalf of the leadership of Iraq, regarding Iraq's full cooperation, instances continue to be encountered, at all levels, where full disclosure is not made and misleading statements are put forward. Likewise, information that should have been volunteered in support of a policy of complete transparency is not provided. The issue thus remains whether there are two policies being pursued, one calling for full cooperation and the other for concealing proscribed activities as long as possible. The Commission can only hope that the first of these will prevail and that the second will be completely abandoned.

85. If the problems just indicated can be speedily resolved by Iraq, the Commission believes that it should be possible to clear up what remains in the near future. These issues must be credibly settled before the Commission's mandate will have been discharged.

Document 221

General Assembly resolution concerning the situation of human rights in Iraq

A/RES/50/191, 22 December 1995

The General Assembly,

Guided by the Charter of the United Nations, the Universal Declaration of Human Rights 1/ and the International Covenants on Human Rights, 2/

Reaffirming that all Member States have an obligation to promote and protect human rights and fundamental freedoms and the duty to fulfil the obligations they have undertaken under the various international instruments in this field,

1/ Resolution 217 A (III).
2/ Resolution 2200 A (XXI).

Mindful that Iraq is a party to the International Covenants on Human Rights and to other international human rights instruments,

Recalling its resolution 49/203 of 23 December 1993, in which it expressed its strong condemnation of the massive violations of human rights of the gravest nature in Iraq,

Recalling also Commission on Human Rights resolution 1991/74 of 6 March 1991, by which the Commission requested its Chairman to appoint a Special Rapporteur to make a thorough study of the violations of human rights by the Government of Iraq, based on all information the Special Rapporteur might deem relevant, including information provided by intergovernmental and non-governmental organizations and any comments and material provided by the Government of Iraq,

Recalling further the pertinent resolutions of the Commission on Human Rights condemning the flagrant violations of human rights by the Government of Iraq, including its most recent resolution 1995/76 of 8 March 1995, by which the Commission extended the mandate of the Special Rapporteur for a further year and requested him to submit an interim report to the General Assembly at its fiftieth session and a final report to the Commission at its fifty-second session,

Bearing in mind Security Council resolution 668 (1991) of 5 April 1991, in which the Council demanded an end to the repression of the Iraqi civilian population and insisted that Iraq cooperate with humanitarian organizations and ensure that the human and political rights of all Iraqi citizens were respected,

Recalling Security Council resolutions 687 (1991) of 3 April 1991, 706 (1991) of 15 August 1991, 712 (1991) of 19 September 1991 and 778 (1992) of 2 October 1992,

Recalling also Security Council resolution 986 (1995) of 14 April 1995, which authorized States to permit imports of Iraqi oil up to the amount of 1 billion United States dollars every ninety days, on a renewable basis, in order to purchase essential food and medical supplies for humanitarian purposes,

Deeply concerned by the persisting massive and grave violations of human rights by the Government of Iraq, of which there are no signs of improvement, such as summary and arbitrary executions, the enactment and implementation of decrees prescribing cruel and inhuman punishments, torture and other cruel, inhuman or degrading treatment, arbitrary arrests and detentions, lack of due process, non-respect for the rule of law and the suppression of freedom of thought, of expression and of association, as well as the persistence of specific discrimination within the country as regards access to food and

health care, which amounts to a violation of the economic and social rights of Iraqis,

Deeply disturbed by the observation by the Special Rapporteur that Iraqi armed forces have continued their attacks on the farming communities throughout the region adjoining northern Iraq and in the south of the country, resulting in the destruction of their crops and livestock,

Deeply disturbed also by reports about the climate of oppression and the dire economic and social situation in the south of Iraq,

Noting the responsibility of the Iraqi authorities with regard to persons missing and detained as a result of the Iraqi occupation of Kuwait and also that Iraq has recently renewed its participation in the Tripartite Commission established pursuant to the cease-fire agreement of 1991,

Deploring the refusal of the Government of Iraq to cooperate with the United Nations human rights mechanisms, in particular by receiving a return visit of the Special Rapporteur to Iraq and allowing the stationing of human rights monitors throughout Iraq pursuant to the relevant resolutions of the General Assembly and the Commission on Human Rights,

1. *Takes note with appreciation* of the interim report on the situation of human rights in Iraq 3/ submitted by the Special Rapporteur of the Commission on Human Rights and the observations, conclusions and recommendations contained therein;

2. *Expresses its strong condemnation* of the massive and extremely grave violations of human rights for which the Government of Iraq is responsible, resulting in an all-pervasive order of repression and oppression which is sustained by broad-based discrimination and widespread terror;

3. *Expresses its condemnation* with regard to the violations of human rights and international humanitarian law, in particular of:

(a) Summary and arbitrary executions, including political killings;

(b) The widespread routine practice of systematic torture in its most cruel forms;

(c) The enactment and implementation of decrees prescribing cruel and unusual punishment, namely mutilation, as a penalty for certain offences and the abuse and diversion of medical-care services for the purpose of such mutilations;

(d) Enforced or involuntary disappearances, routinely practised arbitrary arrests and detention and consistent and routine failure to respect due process and the rule of law;

3/ A/50/734.

(e) Suppression of freedom of thought, information, expression, association and assembly, through fear of arrest, imprisonment and other sanctions, including the death penalty, as well as harsh limitations to freedom of movement;

4. *Urges* the Government of Iraq to cooperate with the United Nations with a view to arranging for the export of oil in order to purchase essential food and medical supplies for humanitarian purposes, as authorized by Security Council resolution 986 (1995);

5. *Strongly condemns* the continued refusal of the Government of Iraq to take advantage of resources available to alleviate the suffering of the people, which includes long-term disabilities, of millions of people and the death of many thousands more;

6. *Again expresses its special alarm* at the policies of the Government of Iraq, which discriminate between regions and prevent the equitable enjoyment of basic foodstuffs and medical supplies, and calls upon Iraq, which has sole responsibility in this regard, to take steps to cooperate with international humanitarian agencies in the provision of relief to those in need throughout Iraq;

7. *Calls once again upon* Iraq, as a State party to the International Covenant on Economic, Social and Cultural Rights and to the International Covenant on Civil and Political Rights, to abide by its freely undertaken obligations under the Covenants and under other international instruments on human rights, and particularly to respect and ensure the rights of all individuals, irrespective of their origin, within its territory and subject to its jurisdiction;

8. *Demands* that the Government of Iraq restore the independence of the judiciary and abrogate all laws granting impunity to specified forces or persons killing or injuring individuals for any purpose beyond the administration of justice under the rule of law as prescribed by international standards;

9. *Demands* that the Government of Iraq abrogate any and all decrees that prescribe cruel and inhuman punishment or treatment and take every step necessary to ensure that the practices of torture and cruel and unusual punishments and treatment no longer occur;

10. *Urges* the Government of Iraq to abrogate all laws and procedures, including Revolution Command Council Decree No. 840, of 4 November 1986, that penalize the free expression of competing views and ideas and to ensure that the genuine will of the people shall be the basis of authority in the State;

11. *Also urges* the Government of Iraq to improve its cooperation with the Tripartite Commission with a view to establishing the whereabouts or resolving the fates of the remaining several hundred missing persons and prisoners of war, Kuwaitis and third-country nationals, victims of the illegal Iraqi occupation of Kuwait;

12. *Requests* the Secretary-General to provide the Special Rapporteur with all necessary assistance in carrying out his mandate and to approve the allocation of sufficient human and material resources for the sending of human rights monitors to such locations as would facilitate improved information flow and assessment and help in the independent verification of reports on the situation of human rights in Iraq;

13. *Decides* to continue its consideration of the situation of human rights in Iraq during its fifty-first session under the item entitled "Human rights questions" in the light of additional elements provided by the Commission on Human Rights and the Economic and Social Council.

Document 222

Letter dated 18 January 1996 from the Secretary-General to the Deputy Prime Minister of Iraq inviting Iraq to enter into discussions on implementation of Security Council resolution 986 (1995)

Not issued as a United Nations document

I am writing to you to express my growing concern over the increasing humanitarian suffering of the Iraqi people as reported to me by several United Nations programmes and agencies.

In this regard and in the context of our continuing discussions and based on the mandate given to the Secretary-General of the United Nations in accordance with Security Council's resolution 986 (1995), I invite Iraq to enter into discussion's with the Secretariat of the United Nations in order to reach arrangements to be agreed upon between the two parties for implementing the oil for food formula.

While I extend this invitation to you, I hope that the Iraqi Government will respond to it positively.

Please accept, Excellency, the assurances of my highest regards.

(*Signed*) Boutros BOUTROS-GHALI

Document 223

Letter dated 19 January 1996 from the Deputy Prime Minister of Iraq to the Secretary-General agreeing to enter into discussions with the United Nations on implementation of Security Council resolution 986 (1995)

Not issued as a United Nations document

I am in receipt of your letter addressed to me on 18 January 1996.

I wish to inform you of the acceptance of the Iraqi Government to enter into discussions with the Secretariat of the United Nations concerning the issue of oil for food.

I am awaiting your proposal on the date and venue of these discussions.

Please accept, Excellency, the assurances of my highest consideration.

(*Signed*) Tariq AZIZ
Deputy Prime Minister

V   Subject index to documents

[This subject index to the documents reproduced in this book should be used in conjunction with the index on pages 838-844. A complete listing of the documents indexed below appears on pages 139-154.]

A

Abductions.
– Document 14
See also: Detained persons. Disappearance of persons. Hostages. Terrorism.

Administrative records.
– Document 18

Aggression.
See: International security. Invasion of Kuwait. Regional security. Self-defence (international law).

Agreed Minutes Between the State of Kuwait and the Republic of Iraq Regarding the Restoration of Friendly Relations, Recognition and Related Matters (1963).
– Documents 4, 35, 38-39, 48, 100, 128, 158, 161, 167

Agriculture.
– Documents 31, 34, 44-45, 51, 66, 93, 99, 144, 160
See also: Livestock industry.

Aid coordination.
– Documents 44, 51
See also: Coordination within UN System. Inter-agency cooperation. Technical cooperation.

Aid financing.
– Documents 51, 78, 81
See also: Oil-for-food.

Aid programmes.
– Documents 44, 99, 207
See also: Economic assistance. Emergency relief. Food aid. Humanitarian assistance. Inter-agency cooperation. Refugee assistance. Technical cooperation.

Air transport.
– Documents 16, 34, 44-45, 57-58, 74, 76, 141, 146-148, 151, 155, 165

Aircraft.
– Documents 16, 26, 58, 74, 76-77, 80, 85-86, 88, 92, 102, 115, 127, 146, 148, 151, 155

Airports.
– Documents 16, 45, 79, 88, 92, 102, 113, 141, 151

Airspace.
– Documents 155, 198-199
See also: Sovereignty.

"All necessary means" provision.
– Documents 19, 21

Annexation of territory.
– Documents 8, 11, 16, 18, 26, 46

Arab-Israeli conflict.
See: Middle East situation.

Archives.
– Document 157

Armaments.
See: Ballistic missiles. Biological weapons. Chemical weapons. Nuclear weapons. On-site inspections. Verification. Weapons destruction. Weapons of mass destruction.

Armed conflicts.
– Documents 22-23, 26, 30, 45
See also: Armed incidents. Human rights in armed conflicts. Invasion of Kuwait.

Armed forces.
See: Military personnel. Troop withdrawal.

Armed incidents.
– Documents 14, 63-64, 75, 77, 86, 92, 113, 124, 147-148, 154, 175, 186
See also: Military activity.

Arms embargo.
– Documents 7, 35, 39, 58, 62, 69, 80, 82, 88-89
See also: Oil embargo.

Arms limitation.
See: Disarmament agreements. Nuclear non-proliferation. Weapons destruction.

Assets.
See: Frozen assets.

Auditing.
– Document 207

B

Bacteriological weapons.
See: Biological weapons.

Baghdad Monitoring and Verification Centre (BMVC).
– Documents 193, 200, 205, 210, 214

Ballistic missiles.
– Documents 35, 39, 52, 73-74, 88, 92-93, 102, 105, 108, 114, 134, 137, 141, 155, 165, 179, 187, 189, 193, 200, 205, 210, 214
See also: Nuclear weapons.

Bangladesh—Military personnel.
– Document 171

Banking.
– Document 45

Basic needs.
– Documents 13, 17, 20, 28, 31-32, 34, 44, 51, 66, 78, 81, 98, 101, 103, 111, 126-127, 129, 135, 201-203, 216, 221

Biological products.
– Document 88

Biological weapons.
– Documents 26, 35, 39, 52, 61, 73, 82, 88, 92-93, 100, 102, 107, 114, 118, 137, 141, 151, 165, 187, 189, 193, 200, 205, 210, 213-214, 220
See also: Chemical weapons.

Blockade.
– Documents 12, 103, 106
See also: Arms embargo. Sanctions.

Borders.
See: Boundaries.

Border incidents.
See: Armed incidents. Military activity.

Boundaries.
– Documents 1-2, 4, 35, 38-39, 48, 70, 74, 77, 86, 100, 107-108, 120, 123, 128, 131, 137, 140, 147-149, 152, 154, 157-158, 160-163, 167, 170-171, 175, 178, 181, 183, 186, 192, 194, 196-199, 202, 204, 212
See also: Maritime boundaries. UN. Iraq-Kuwait Boundary Demarcation Commission.

Boutros-Ghali, Boutros.
– Documents 21, 33-34, 38, 43, 48-50, 52-53, 56-58, 60, 65, 70, 75, 77-79, 86, 88, 113-114, 123, 126, 131, 134, 140, 149, 154-155, 157, 160, 170-171, 181-182, 187, 191-193, 205, 209, 212

Budget contributions.
See: Financing.

C

Cease-fires.
– Documents 26-27, 30, 35-36, 39, 41-42, 73, 79, 86, 92, 100, 122, 141, 164, 167
See also: Truce supervision.

Charter of the United Nations (1945).
– Documents 6-7, 9, 21, 26, 35, 37, 47, 54-55, 58, 61-62, 71-72, 80, 88-90, 92, 96-96, 100, 102, 114, 118, 128, 132, 143, 151-152, 157-158, 161-162, 178, 183, 202, 207, 221

Chemicals.
– Documents 88, 193, 205
See also: Explosives. Petroleum products.

Chemical and biological warfare.
See: Biological weapons. Chemical weapons.

Chemical plants.
– Documents 35, 43, 52, 61, 73-74, 88-89, 92-93, 104, 114, 118, 134, 141, 165, 179, 189, 205

Chemical weapons.
– Documents 26, 35, 39, 52, 61, 64-65, 73-74, 88, 92-93, 100, 102, 107, 114, 118, 134, 137, 141, 151, 164-165, 179, 193, 200, 205, 210, 214, 220
See also: Biological weapons. Weapons destruction.

Chemical-weapon-free zones.
– Document 35
See also: Chemical weapons.

Chicago Convention on International Civil Aviation (1944).
– Document 16

Children.
– Documents 13, 20, 28, 44, 55, 57, 66, 78-79, 96, 103, 143, 160, 178, 202

Civil and political rights.
– Documents 37, 96, 103, 143, 178, 202
See also: Due process of law.

Civil registration.
– Document 18

Civil unrest.
– Documents 31, 66

Civilians.
– Documents 20, 32, 37, 44-46, 51, 57, 66, 72, 78-79, 81, 86, 88, 90, 93, 96-98, 100-102, 107-108, 132, 135, 137, 143, 178, 202, 207, 216
See also: Human rights in armed conflicts.

Claims.
– Documents 67, 107, 110, 121, 184-185, 215
See also: Compensation. UN. Compensation
Commission.

Commissions of inquiry.
– Documents 143, 178
See also: Fact-finding missions. Special missions.

Communication systems.
– Documents 31, 34, 44-45, 66, 82

Compensation.
– Documents 17, 26-27, 35, 45, 49, 54-56, 65, 67-68,
  71-72, 74, 78-79, 90-91, 106-108, 110-111, 121,
  132, 137, 145, 160, 181-185, 202, 215
See also: UN. Compensation Commission.

Compliance with Security Council resolutions.
– Documents 7, 12, 17, 19, 21, 25-27, 39, 59, 82,
  100-101, 107, 134, 136, 155-156, 172, 176,
  187-188, 193-195, 205-206, 211, 213-214

Confidence-building measures.
– Document 197
See also: Negotiation. Verification.

Confiscations.
– Documents 46, 103, 182

Consultations.
– Documents 15, 38, 81, 87, 109, 112, 117, 130,
  150, 153, 168
See also: Negotiation.

Consumer goods.
– Document 207

Conventions.
See: International conventions. International
covenants. Treaties.

Convention for the Suppression of Unlawful Acts
against the Safety of Civil Aviation (1971).
– Document 59

Convention for the Suppression of Unlawful Seizure
of Aircraft (1970).
– Document 59

Convention on International Civil Aviation (1944).
– Document 16

Convention on Offences and Certain Other Acts
Committed on Board Aircraft (1963).
– Document 59

Convention on the Privileges and Immunities of the
United Nations (1946).
– Documents 48-49, 81, 88

Convention on the Privileges and Immunities of the
Specialized Agencies.
– Document 88

Convention on the Prohibition of the Development,
Production and Stockpiling of Bacteriological
(Biological) and Toxin Weapons and on Their
Destruction (1972).
– Documents 35, 39, 74

Cooperation between organizations.
– Document 127
See also: Inter-agency cooperation.

Coordination within UN System.
– Documents 93, 99
See also: Aid coordination. Aid programmes.
Inter-agency cooperation.

D

Data collection and analysis.
– Documents 17, 82, 88, 102, 155, 172, 187, 193,
  200, 206, 213

Debt.
See: External debt.

Demilitarized zones.
– Documents 38-39, 50, 60, 77, 86, 100, 108, 113,
  128, 131, 137, 147-148, 154, 157-158, 170, 186,
  191-192, 204

Demographic records.
– Documents 17-18
See also: Population composition.

Deportation.
– Documents 97, 202
See also: Expulsions.

Detained persons.
– Documents 20, 26, 35, 46, 79, 96-97, 100-101,
  103, 143, 178, 202
See also: Abductions. Disappearance of persons.
Extralegal executions. Prisoner treatment. Torture
and other cruel treatment.

Diplomacy.
See: Consultations. Good offices. Negotiation.

Diplomatic and consular services.
– Documents 11, 14, 16-17, 46
See also: Embassies.

Diplomatic privileges and immunities.
See: Privileges and immunities.

Diplomatic protection.
– Documents 11, 14

Diplomats' security.
– Documents 14, 17
See also: Staff security.

Disappearance of persons.
– Documents 20, 46, 79, 96-96, 100, 103, 143, 178, 197, 202, 216
See also: Abductions. Detained persons. Extralegal executions. Human rights violations. Torture and other cruel treatment.

Disarmament.
See: Biological weapons. Chemical weapons. Disarmament agreements. Nuclear weapons. On-site inspection. Verification. Weapons destruction. Weapons of mass destruction.

Disarmament agreements.
– Documents 35, 73, 82, 88
See also: On-site inspection. Verification. Weapons destruction.

Displaced persons.
– Documents 34, 44, 46, 51, 57, 66, 86, 103
See also: Humanitarian assistance. Refugees.

Domestic trade.
– Document 45

Drinking water.
See: Water supply.

Dual-purpose capabilities.
– Documents 35, 58, 63-64, 73, 82, 88, 95, 114, 119, 134, 136, 155, 187, 190, 205-206, 211, 213, 217

Due process of law.
– Documents 96, 103, 143, 178, 202
See also: Civil and political rights.

E

Economic assistance.
– Documents 15, 47
See also: Aid programmes. Humanitarian assistance. Reconstruction.

Economic conditions.
– Documents 31, 45
See also: Living conditions. Social conditions.

Economic, social and cultural rights.
– Documents 20, 103, 143, 178, 202

Education.
– Document 45

Elderly.
– Documents 13, 20, 44, 57, 66, 96, 178, 202

Elections.
– Document 216

Electric power.
– Document 45
See also: Energy resources.

Embargo.
See: Arms embargo. Blockade. Oil embargo. Sanctions.

Embassies.
– Documents 14, 17
See also: Diplomatic and consular services.

Emergency relief.
– Documents 51, 57, 93, 202, 207
See also: Humanitarian assistance.

Emigration.
See: Expulsion. Refugees. Repatriation.

Energy resources.
– Documents 31, 34, 66
See also: Electric power.

Environmental impact.
– Documents 34, 39, 45, 54-55, 66, 74, 99, 144

Environmental protection.
– Documents 34, 99, 144

Equipment and supplies.
– Document 207
See also: Medical supplies.

Escrow account.
– Documents 65, 78, 81, 90, 141, 160, 191

European Community (EEC).
– Document 47

Exiles.
See: Expulsions. Refugees. Repatriation.

Experts.
– Documents 43, 48, 52, 155, 157, 202, 207

Explosives.
– Document 26
See also: Chemicals.

Exports.
– Documents 207, 209
See also: Petroleum exports.

Export restrictions.
– Documents 78, 205
See also: Arms embargo. Import restrictions. Oil embargo. Oil-for-food. Sanctions.

Expulsions.
– Documents 16-17, 46
See also: Deportation.

External debt.
– Documents 35, 54, 56, 74, 207

Extralegal executions.
– Documents 20, 96, 103, 143, 178, 202
See also: Detained persons. Disappearance of persons. Summary executions. Torture and other cruel treatment.

F

Fact-finding missions.
– Documents 45-46, 63-64, 92, 96, 103, 158
See also: Commissions of inquiry. Special missions.

Factories.
– Documents 45, 100, 141-142
See also: Chemical plants. Manufacturing.

Financial assistance.
See: Aid financing. Economic assistance.

Financing.
– Documents 38, 66, 113, 141, 149, 154, 160, 165, 170, 179, 186, 189, 192, 204-205, 212
See also: Aid financing. Funds.

Fisheries.
– Document 45

Food aid.
– Documents 13, 34, 51, 93, 103, 132, 160
See also: Humanitarian assistance.

Food and Agriculture Organization of the United Nations (FAO).
– Documents 31, 34, 51, 216

Food distribution.
– Documents 13, 103, 123, 216
See also: Food supply.

Food relief.
See: Food aid.

Food supply.
– Documents 13, 16-17, 26, 31-32, 34-35, 66, 72, 74, 81, 87, 90, 98, 101, 112, 143, 160, 178, 202, 207
See also: Food distribution.

Foreigners.
See: Third-State nationals

Frontiers.
See: Boundaries.

Frozen assets.
– Documents 16, 65-66, 132, 137, 160, 165, 207

Funds.
– Documents 7, 35, 81, 110, 121, 132, 160
See also: Aid financing. Financing. Intergovernmental bodies. Trust funds.

G

Geneva Convention Relative to the Protection of Civilian Persons in Time of War (1949).
– Documents 13, 16-17, 20, 46, 79, 97, 100

Geneva Convention Relative to the Treatment of Prisoners of War (1949).
– Documents 26, 79, 97, 100

Gold reserves.
See: Monetary reserves.

Good offices.
– Documents 13, 16-17, 21, 154, 157

Guards Contingent.
See: UN Guards Contingent.

Guidelines.
– Documents 35, 58, 62, 67, 80

Guidelines to Facilitate Full International Implementation of Paragraphs 24, 25 and 27 of Security Council Resolution 687 (1991).
– Documents 62, 67, 80

H

Health conditions.
– Document 31, 34, 45, 51, 55, 66, 72, 74, 216

Health services.
– Documents 31, 34, 51, 143, 160, 178, 202

Hospitals.
– Documents 17, 66
See also: Health services.

Hostages.
– Documents 17, 67, 96, 103, 221
See also: Abductions. Terrorism.

Housing.
See: Living conditions. Shelter.

Human rights.
– Documents 20, 37, 46, 55, 66, 81, 96-96, 103, 143, 161, 167, 178, 202, 207, 216
See also: Civil and political rights. Economic, social and cultural rights.

Human rights in armed conflicts.
– Documents 13, 17, 20, 26, 46, 97, 103, 110, 216, 221
See also: Armed conflicts. Civilian persons. Demilitarized zones. Prisoners of war.

Human rights violations.
– Documents 20, 96-97, 103, 143, 178, 202, 216
See also: Disappearance of persons. Extralegal executions. Religious intolerance. Summary executions. Torture and other cruel treatment.

Humanitarian assistance.
– Documents 13, 20, 26, 28, 31-32, 34-38, 44, 51, 57, 66, 72, 78, 81, 87, 93, 96-98, 101, 107, 123, 126-127, 129, 132, 135, 137, 143, 160, 178, 202-203, 207, 209
See also: Displaced persons. Economic assistance. Emergency relief. Food aid. Refugee assistance. Special missions.

I

Imports.
See: Petroleum imports.

Import restrictions.
– Document 205
See also: Arms embargo. Export restrictions. Sanctions.

Independence of Kuwait.
– Document 4

Industrial sector.
See: Manufacturing.

Information systems.
– Documents 45-46
See also: Communication systems.

Information centres.
– Document 206

Information exchange.
– Document 207

Infrastructure.
– Documents 31, 34, 45, 66, 74

Inter-agency cooperation.
– Documents 51, 82, 86, 107, 127, 129
See also: Aid coordination. Aid programmes. Coordination within UN system. Humanitarian assistance. Technical cooperation.

Inter-Agency Humanitarian Programme for Iraq, Kuwait and the Iraq/Turkey and Iraq/Iran Border Areas.
– Documents 51, 66, 78, 123, 127, 129, 135, 160, 203, 207

Intergovernmental bodies.
– Document 35
See also: Funds.

Intergovernmental organizations.
– Documents 57, 121
See also: Non-governmental organizations.

International Atomic Energy Agency (IAEA).
– Documents 35, 39, 43, 52-53, 61, 63-65, 73, 76, 82, 89, 92-94, 100, 107-108, 114, 116, 118-119, 134, 136-138, 141-142, 146, 155-158, 160, 164-166, 168, 172-173, 176-177, 187-190, 195, 200-201, 206, 208, 210-211, 213-214, 219

IAEA. Director General.
– Documents 82, 88-89, 94, 104, 116, 118, 135, 142, 151, 156, 166, 172, 210, 217

International Committee of the Red Cross (ICRC).
– Documents 13, 20, 26, 28, 31-32, 35, 44, 51, 66, 72, 74, 79, 93, 97, 100, 107-108, 113, 137
See also: Repatriation.

International Convention against the Taking of Hostages (1979).
– Documents 35, 59

International Convention on the Prevention and Punishment of the Crime of Genocide (1948).
– Document 103

International Court of Justice (ICJ).
– Document 55

International Covenant on Civil and Political Rights (1966).
– Documents 46, 66, 96, 103, 143, 178, 202, 216

International Covenant on Economic, Social and Cultural Rights (1966).
– Documents 66, 103, 143, 178, 202, 221

International Covenants on Human Rights (1966).
– Documents 20, 96, 143, 178, 202, 221

International humanitarian law.
– Document 13

International Maritime Organization (IMO).
– Documents 99, 144

International Monetary Fund (IMF).
– Documents 100, 107

International obligations.
– Documents 14, 16, 65, 73, 102, 105, 175
See also: Treaties.

International Organization for Migration (IOM).
– Documents 51, 93

International organizations.
See: Intergovernmental organizations.
Non-governmental organizations.

International security.
– Documents 6, 37
See also: Regional security.

Invasion of Kuwait.
– Documents 5-7, 12, 17-18, 20, 55, 100, 107

Inventories.
– Documents 94, 116, 119, 136, 142, 156, 166, 172, 188, 190, 193, 195, 206, 211, 213, 219

Iran (Islamic Republic of)
– Documents 37, 51, 66, 178, 202-200

K

Khawr 'Abd Allah waterway.
– Documents 86, 100, 113, 131, 157-158, 161, 170, 192

Kurds.
– Documents 37, 44, 51, 66, 96, 103, 107, 143, 178, 202

L

Land mines.
– Documents 26, 34, 45, 47, 66, 86
See also: Mine clearance.

League of Arab States.
– Documents 6, 107

Legitimacy of governments.
– Documents 7, 18, 29
See also: Sovereignty.

Liability.
– Documents 17, 26, 39, 49, 54-55, 64
See also: Compensation.

Livestock industry.
– Document 45
See also: Agriculture.

Living conditions.
– Document 20
See also: Economic conditions. Shelter.
Social conditions.

Loss of life.
– Documents 45-46, 55, 66-67

M

Malnutrition.
See: Nutrition.

Manufacturing.
– Documents 31, 45
See also: Factories.

Maps.
– Documents 35, 157-158

Marine environment.
– Document 144
See also: Environmental impact.

Marine pollution.
See: Environmental impact. Oil pollution.

Maritime boundaries.
– Documents 161-162, 167

Maritime enforcement of sanctions.
– Documents 12, 58
See also: Arms embargo. Oil embargo. Sanctions.

Marsh Arabs
– Documents 103, 202-203, 221

Mediation.
See: Consultations. Good offices. Negotiation.

Medical services.
– Documents 31, 34, 44, 66
See also: Health services.

Medical supplies.
– Documents 13, 16, 20, 26, 28, 31-32, 34-35, 66, 72, 81, 90, 98, 143, 178, 202, 207

Memoranda of Understanding between the Government of Iraq and the United Nations.
– Documents 44, 51, 57, 72, 93, 123, 126-127, 143, 178, 202

Middle East—Regional security.
– Document 35

Middle East situation.
– Documents 21, 33, 39, 55

Middle East—Weapon-free zones.
– Documents 35, 39, 63-64

Military action pursuant to Security Council resolution 678 (1990).
– Documents 22-23, 26-27

Military activity.
– Documents 110, 115, 194, 196-197, 202
See also: Armed incidents. Invasion of Kuwait.
Military occupation.

Military assistance.
– Document 9

Military occupation.
– Documents 5-9, 11-12, 15-22, 25-26, 29, 34-36,
  39, 45-46, 55, 67, 79, 107-108, 110, 145
See also: Compensation. Military activity. Troop
withdrawal.

Military personnel.
– Documents 70, 113, 124, 127, 129, 131, 149, 171,
  204, 212

Mine clearance.
– Documents 47, 66, 86
See also: Land mines.

Minorities.
– Document 103

Missing persons.
See: Disappearance of persons. International
Committee of the Red Cross. Repatriation.

Missions.
See: Commissions of inquiry. Fact-finding missions.
Special missions.

Monetary reserves.
– Documents 72, 100, 107

Mothers.
– Documents 13, 66
See also: Women.

Municipal services.
– Document 45
See also: Police.

N

Negotiation.
– Documents 6, 33, 39, 42, 44, 51, 59, 70, 123, 126-127,
  140, 162, 172, 176, 197-198, 210-211, 217
See also: Consultations. Good offices.

No-objection procedure.
– Document 32

Non-governmental organizations.
– Documents 31, 44-46, 51, 66, 93, 127, 129

Notification.
– Document 151

Nuclear facilities.
– Documents 35, 43, 52-53, 61, 63-64, 73-74, 76,
  82-85, 88-89, 92-95, 104-105, 114, 116, 118-119,
  134, 136-137, 141-142, 151, 155-156, 164-167,
  172-173, 177, 179, 187-190, 193, 195, 200-201,
  205-206, 210-211, 213-214, 220
See also: On-site inspection.

Nuclear materials.
– Documents 35, 52-53, 61, 63-64, 73, 76, 82, 88-89,
  95, 100, 104, 108, 114, 116, 118-119, 136, 142,
  156, 165-166, 172, 177, 187-188, 190, 193, 195,
  200-201, 205-206, 210, 213-214, 219-220

Nuclear non-proliferation.
– Documents 35, 73, 82, 92

Nuclear safeguards.
– Documents 35, 73, 76, 82, 100

Nuclear technology.
– Documents 82, 89, 108, 116, 136-137, 141, 165

Nuclear weapons.
– Documents 35, 39, 52-53, 61, 73-74, 88, 92-95,
  100, 107, 114, 119, 134, 141, 151, 155, 164-165,
  173, 187, 189, 206, 213, 219-220

Nuclear-weapon-free zones.
See: Nuclear non-proliferation. Nuclear weapons.

Nutrition.
– Documents 28, 66, 72
See also: Food aid.

O

Oil embargo.
– Documents 10, 12, 49, 54-55, 100, 132, 160, 191
See also: Petroleum exports. Sanctions.

Oil-for-food.
– Documents 78, 90, 101, 103, 123

Oil pollution.
– Documents 34, 45
See also: Environmental impact. Petroleum.

On-site inspection.
– Documents 35, 43, 52-53, 61, 63-64, 73-74, 76,
  82-85, 88-89, 92-95, 100, 102, 104-105, 108, 114,
  116, 118-119, 122-123, 133-134, 136-137, 141-142,
  146, 151, 155-156, 164-166, 172-173, 176-177,
  179, 187-190, 193, 195, 200-201, 205-206, 208,
  210-211, 213-214
See also: Chemical plants. Disarmament agreements.
Nuclear facilities. Weapons destruction.

P

Palestinians.
See: Middle East situation.

"Pause of goodwill" clause.
– Document 19

Payments.
– Documents 72, 81, 91, 108, 111, 181, 183-185, 207, 215
See also: Compensation. Oil-for-food. Repatriation. UN. Compensation Commission.

Peace-keeping operations.
– Documents 35, 38, 40, 50, 70, 74-75, 77, 86, 113, 124, 131, 140, 148-149, 152, 154, 170-171, 186, 192, 194, 204, 212
See also: Truce supervision. UN Iraq-Kuwait Observation Mission.

Pérez de Cuéllar, Javier
– Documents 7, 11-13, 16-18, 21, 33-34, 37, 40, 43, 45-50, 52-54, 56-58, 60-62, 65, 70-75, 77-79, 81-82, 86, 88-90, 92-95, 98-99

Petroleum.
– Documents 31, 34, 45, 49, 55, 66, 78, 90, 132, 207, 209
See also: Oil embargo. Oil pollution. Pipelines.

Petroleum exports.
– Documents 54, 56, 65-67, 71-72, 74, 78, 81, 90-91, 101, 111, 132, 137, 160, 191, 202

Petroleum imports.
– Documents 31, 54, 72, 81, 191, 207

Petroleum products.
– Documents 49, 55, 132, 160, 191, 207, 209

Pipelines.
– Documents 10, 45, 78, 207, 209
See also: Petroleum.

Police.
– Documents 60, 77, 128, 137, 140, 154

Political opposition.
– Documents 22-23, 34, 46, 51, 66, 103, 178, 202, 216

Political prisoners.
See: Detained persons. Extralegal executions. Freedom of thought. Prisoner treatment. Torture and other cruel treatment.

Political rights.
See: Civil and political rights.

Pollution.
See: Environmental impact. Oil pollution.

Population composition.
– Documents 18, 34, 45-46
See also: Demographic records.

Ports.
See: Shipping.

Prisoner treatment.
– Document 103
See also: Detained persons. Torture and other cruel treatment.

Prisoners of war.
– Documents 20, 26, 46, 79, 97, 216
See also: Human rights in armed conflicts.

Privileges and immunities.
– Documents 14, 17, 47, 49, 63, 73-74, 76, 81, 83-84, 88, 91-92, 100, 118, 132, 141, 165, 179, 189, 207

Programme implementation.
– Documents 127, 134-135, 156, 187

Project preparation.
– Document 51

Property.
– Documents 103, 107, 140, 143, 178, 202
See also: Return of property.

Protocol for the Prohibition of the Use in War of Asphyxiating, Poisonous or Other Gases, and of Bacteriological Methods of Warfare (1925).
– Documents 35, 39, 74

Public health.
– Documents 28, 31

R

Radiation protection.
– Document 53

Recognition (international law).
– Documents 4, 7-8

Reconstruction.
– Documents 26, 33-34, 45, 51
See also: Economic assistance.

Refugees.
– Documents 31, 37, 44, 51, 57, 66, 93, 103, 216
See also: Displaced persons. Repatriation.

Refugee assistance.
– Documents 34, 37, 44, 51, 66
See also: Humanitarian assistance.

Staffing.
– Documents 86, 204

Summary executions.
– Documents 20, 96, 103, 143, 178, 202
See also: Extralegal executions. Torture and other cruel treatment.

T

Technical cooperation.
– Document 206
See also: Aid coordination. Aid programmes. Coordination within UN system. Inter-agency cooperation.

Telecommunications.
See: Communications systems.

Terrorism.
– Documents 35, 59, 74, 100, 107
See also: Abductions. Hostages.

Third-State nationals
– Documents 11, 14, 17, 20, 25, 34-35, 45-46, 72, 79, 97, 100, 107-108, 137
See also: Deportation. Expulsions.

Threats to international peace and security.
See: Charter of the United Nations.

Torture and other cruel treatment.
– Documents 20, 34, 46, 96, 103, 143, 178, 202, 216
See also: Detained persons. Disappearance of persons. Extralegal executions. Prisoner treatment. Summary executions.

Trade boycotts.
– Documents 7, 35, 145

Transit countries.
– Documents 78, 207

Transportation.
– Documents 16, 31, 34, 44-45, 57, 66, 73, 82
See also: Air transport.

Treaties.
– Documents 4, 13-14, 16-17, 20, 26, 35, 38, 48, 73, 81-82, 96-97, 143, 178
See also: Disarmament agreements. International obligations. Verification.

Treaty on the Non-Proliferation of Nuclear Weapons (1968).
– Documents 35, 39, 73-74, 82, 100, 107

Troop-contributing States.
– Documents 38, 50, 60, 70, 77, 86, 147, 152, 154, 170-171, 186, 192, 204, 212
See also: Military personnel. Peace-keeping operations.

Troop withdrawal.
– Documents 6-7, 17, 19, 21, 24, 27, 29-30, 35, 39, 196-197
See also: Military occupation.

Truce supervision.
– Documents 35, 38, 40, 50, 60, 70, 74-75, 77, 86, 113, 131, 149, 152, 154
See also: Cease-fires.

Trust funds.
– Documents 181, 186
See also: Financing. Funds. Special accounts.

Turkey—Humanitarian assistance.
– Documents 51, 66, 78, 203

Turkey—Pipelines.
– Documents 78, 207

Turkey—Refugee assistance.
– Document 51

Turkey—Transit countries.
– Document 207

U

UN. Administrative Committee on Coordination (ACC).
– Document 47

UN. Centre for Human Rights.
– Document 216

UN. Commission on Human Rights.
– Documents 20, 96, 103, 108, 143, 178, 216, 221

UN. Commission on Human Rights. Special Rapporteur on the situation of human rights in Iraq.
– Documents 96, 103, 108, 143, 178, 202, 216, 221

UN. Commission on Human Rights. Special Rapporteur on the situation of human rights in Kuwait under Iraqi occupation.
– Documents 97, 107

UN. Compensation Commission (UNCC).
– Documents 35, 49, 54-55, 65, 67-68, 91, 106-107, 110, 121, 132, 145, 160, 184-185, 215

UN. Compensation Fund.
– Documents 35, 49, 54-56, 65, 67, 72, 81, 91, 132, 184-185, 207

UN. Economic and Social Council (ECOSOC).
– Documents 96, 99, 143, 202, 216

UN. General Assembly—Resolutions.
– Documents 3, 96-97, 99, 143-144, 178, 202, 216

UN. Iraq-Kuwait Boundary Demarcation
Commission.
– Documents 48, 70, 74, 77, 86, 113, 120, 123, 128,
131-132, 137-138, 152, 157-158, 160-163, 167,
199

UN. Military Staff Committee.
– Document 12

UN. Secretariat.
– Documents 92, 151, 182, 216

UN. Secretary-General.
– Documents 7, 11-13, 16-18, 21, 33-34, 37, 40, 43,
45-50, 52-54, 56-58, 60-62, 65, 70-75, 77-79, 81-82,
86, 88-90, 92-95, 98-102, 104-105, 107, 113-114,
116, 118, 123, 126-127, 131-132, 134, 136, 140,
142, 147, 149, 151, 154-155, 157-158, 160, 165-166,
170-171, 179, 181-182, 187, 191-193, 205, 207,
209, 212

UN. Secretary-General—Representatives of.
– Documents 20, 31-32, 34-35, 39, 44-46, 51, 57,
66, 99, 144

UN. Security Council.
– Documents 3, 5-6, 10, 15, 21, 25, 27, 30-34, 36,
39, 41-42, 47, 54-55, 58-59, 63-64, 66, 74, 76,
78-80, 82-86, 88, 90, 92, 95, 98-101, 103-107,
109, 111-114, 116, 119, 132, 154-157

UN. Security Council—Maintenance of sanctions.
– Documents 5, 25, 87, 117, 138, 150, 168

UN. Security Council—Resolutions.
– Documents 6-8, 11-19, 26, 35-37, 40, 54, 61-62,
71-73, 81, 89, 92, 128, 132, 152, 155, 161, 183,
196, 207

UN. Security Council—Statements by the President.
– Documents 28, 47, 63, 69, 83-85, 87, 98, 101,
104-105, 108-109, 111-112, 115, 117, 120, 122,
124-125, 129-130, 133, 137-139, 146, 148, 150,
153, 159, 164, 167-169, 174-175, 180, 194, 199

UN. Security Council Committee Established by
Resolution 661 (1990) (Sanctions Committee).
– Documents 7, 12-13, 15-16, 58, 62, 80-81, 88-89,
138, 207
See also: Sanctions. Sanctions—Exceptions to.
Sanctions—Requests for assistance under Article 50
of the Charter.

UN. Special Commission Established under Security
Council Resolution 687 (1991) (UNSCOM).
– Documents 35, 43, 52, 61, 63-65, 73-74, 82-85,
88-89, 92-93, 100, 102, 104-105, 107, 114-115,
118, 122-123, 126-127, 133, 137-138, 141, 146,
148, 151, 155, 160, 164-165, 173, 179, 187,
189-190, 193-194, 196, 200, 205, 210, 214

UN. Special Commission Established under
Security Council Resolution 687 (1991)
(UNSCOM)—Financing.
– Documents 65, 92-93, 141, 165, 179, 189, 205,
214

UN Guards Contingent.
– Documents 57, 66, 93, 124, 127, 129

UN Iraq-Kuwait Observation Mission (UNIKOM).
– Documents 38, 40, 50, 60, 70, 74-75, 77, 86, 100,
107, 113, 131, 140, 146-149, 152, 154, 157-158,
161, 170-171, 175, 181, 186, 192, 194, 204, 212

UN Iraq-Kuwait Observation Mission
(UNIKOM)—Budget contributions.
– Documents 38, 131

UN Iraq-Kuwait Observation Mission
(UNIKOM)—Financing.
– Documents 38, 113, 131, 154, 157, 186, 192, 204,
212

UN Iraq-Kuwait Observation Mission
(UNIKOM)—Mandate.
– Documents 35, 38, 40, 154
See also: Troop-contributing States.

UN membership.
– Document 3

UN system.
– Document 29

United Nations Children's Fund (UNICEF).
– Documents 28, 31, 34, 51, 66, 107, 127, 160

United Nations Development Programme (UNDP).
– Documents 31, 34, 51, 66

United Nations Disaster Relief Organization.
(UNDRO).
– Documents 31, 34

United Nations Educational, Scientific and Cultural
Organization (UNESCO).
– Documents 45, 144

United Nations Environment Programme (UNEP).
– Documents 34, 45, 99, 144

United Nations High Commissioner for Refugees, Office of (UNHCR).
– Documents 31, 34, 51, 66, 107

United Nations Relief and Works Agency for Palestine Refugees in the Near East (UNRWA).
– Document 33

Universal Declaration of Human Rights.
– Documents 20, 46, 66, 96-97, 143, 178, 202, 216, 221

Urban areas.
– Document 45

V

Verification.
– Documents 35, 52-53, 73, 82, 88, 100, 107-108, 114, 116, 118, 134, 136, 141, 155-156, 164-165, 172-173, 176, 179, 187-189, 193, 195, 200, 202, 206, 210, 213-214
See also: Confidence-building measures. On-site inspection. Treaties.

Vienna Convention on Consular Relations (1963).
– Documents 14, 17

Vienna Convention on Diplomatic Relations (1961).
– Documents 14, 17

W

War damage compensation.
See: Claims. Compensation. Military occupation.

Water supply.
– Documents 17, 28, 31, 34, 45, 51, 66
See also: Sanitation.

Weapons destruction.
– Documents 35, 39, 52-53, 61, 65, 73, 76, 88, 92-95, 102, 105, 108, 114, 118-119, 132, 141-142, 147-148, 151, 155-156, 160, 164-166, 177, 179, 188-190, 195, 200-201, 210, 214, 219
See also: Ballistic missiles. Biological weapons. Chemical weapons. Nuclear weapons. On-site inspections.

Weapons of mass destruction.
– Documents 63-64, 73-74, 89, 92-93, 100-103, 105, 108, 114, 118-119, 132, 137, 141, 147, 165, 189, 210, 214
See also: Biological weapons. Chemical weapons. Nuclear weapons.

Women.
– Documents 20, 44, 51, 78-79, 96, 103, 143, 160, 178, 202
See also: Mothers.

World Food Programme (WFP).
– Documents 34, 51, 66, 107, 127, 216

World Health Organization (WHO).
– Documents 28, 31, 34-35, 45, 51-52, 66, 88, 92, 107, 127

Z

Zones of peace.
See: Chemical-weapon-free zones.

VI Index

[The numbers following the entries refer to paragraph numbers in the Introduction.]

Petroleum companies, 327
Petroleum exports, 11, *95*, 222, 323, 330.
  See also Kirkuk-Yumurtalik pipeline; Oil embargo; Oil-for-food
Preventive diplomacy, 356, 360.
  See also Pause of goodwill; Peace plans
Prisoners of war, 78, 83, 187-188, 192-194, 220, 340.
  See also Detained persons
Privileges and immunities, 234, 236, 249
Proscribed capabilities, 237, 240, 268

Q

Qatar
  attacks on, 72

R

Ratqah oil field, 134, 161
Reconstruction
  Iraq, 111-113, 173, 180
  Kuwait, 111-113, 117-118, , 204
  Persian Gulf region, 111, 203
Refugee assistance, 125, 171.
  See also Displaced persons; Humanitarian assistance; Iraqi refugees
Regional Organization for the Pro-tection of the Marine Environment (ROPME), 203-204
Regional security
  Persian Gulf region, 1-2, 65, 105, 74-75, 87, 96-97, 179, 244
Repatriation, 11, 15, 46-47, 50, 97, 164, 169, 173, 185, 187-189, 192, 194
Return of property, 128, 164, 196-199, 201-202
  financing, *95*, 197-198
Revolution Command Council, Iraq, 36, 85, 167, 287
Rules for Claims Procedure, 213
  Art. 16, 217
  Art. 36, 218

Rumaila oil field, 35

S

Safwan, 145, 156
Sanctions, 2, 13-14, 16, 39, 50, 55-56, 60, 67, 76, 81, 100, 106, 114-115, 167, 171, 239, 241-242, 244, 291, 294-295, 311, 313, 318, 321, 326, 329, 342-346, 349-354, 366.
  See also Arms embargo; Oil embargo
  guidelines, 114-115, 341
  impact of, *50-52*, 222, 329, 349-350, 354
  review, 96, 342-346, 349-354
Saudi Arabia, 4, 21, 30, 36, 40-41, 70, 77, 191, 207, 324
  attacks on, 71
  detained persons, 188-189, 194
Scud missiles, 245, 300, 302.
  See also Surface-to-surface missiles
Self-defence, 40-41, 70, 129
Shiites, 336, 339
  humanitarian assistance, 171
Shipping, 44, 55, 145
Southern Iraq, 136, 140, 188, 270, 287, 336
Southern Rhodesia, 60
Sovereignty, independence and territorial integrity
  Kuwait, 1, 5, 13, 33, 36, 88, 109, 167
Soviet Union,
  See Union of Soviet Socialist Republics
Special missions, 54, 111, 317
Special Rapporteurs on the situation of human rights
  See UN. Special Rapporteur
Staff security, 11, 174, 180.
  See also UN Guards Contingent
Suleimaniyah governorate, 175, 178
Surface-to-surface missiles, 71, 300.
  See also Scud missiles

T

Technical Subcommittee on Military and Civilian Missing Prisoners of War and Mortal Remains, 192
Terrorism, 98, 224-225
Third River Project, 336
Third-State nationals, 15, 43, 46-49, 57, 79, 97, 122, 169, 185-187.
  See also Migrant workers
Treaty on the Non-Proliferation of Nuclear Weapons (1968), 93, 244, 361
Tripartite Commission on Repatriation, 192-193, 195
  See also Technical Subcommittee
Troop withdrawal
  Coalition States, 65, 129, 174
  Iraq, 4, 37, 67, 147
Troop-contributing countries
  Coalition, 4, 35, 65, 68, 70, 77, 123
  UNIKOM, 144
Trust funds, 165

U

Umm Qasr, 129, 133, 135, 137, 139, 144, 156, 161
Union of Soviet Socialist Republics, 26, 28, 31, 37, 44, 61, 76, 229, 370
  & res. 678 (1990), 61
  & res. 687 (1991), 103
UN & international security, 1-2, 355-359, 373-374
UN Convention on the Law of the Sea (1982), 157
UN Humanitarian Centres (UNHUCS), 173
UN Iraq-Kuwait Observation Mission (UNIKOM), 7, 17, 127-148, 158, 161-162, 166, 169
  Chief Military Observer, 136, 162
  mandate, 127-128, 132, 142, 148, 162
  military personnel, 129-130, 136, 143-144, 146, 148

United Nations publications of related interest

The following UN publications may be obtained from the addresses indicated below, or at your local distributor:

An Agenda for Peace
Second edition, 1995
By Boutros Boutros-Ghali,
Secretary-General of the United Nations
E.95.I.15   92-1-100555-8   155 pp. $7.50

An Agenda for Development
By Boutros Boutros-Ghali,
Secretary-General of the United Nations
E.95.I.16   92-1-100556-6   132 pp. $7.50

Confronting New Challenges, 1995
Annual Report on the Work of the Organization
By Boutros Boutros-Ghali,
Secretary-General of the United Nations
E.95.I.47   92-1-100595-7   380 pp. $7.50

New Dimensions of Arms Regulation and
Disarmament in the Post–Cold War Era
By Boutros Boutros-Ghali,
Secretary-General of the United Nations
E.93.IX.8   92-1-142192-6   53 pp. $9.95

Basic Facts About the United Nations
E.95.I.31   92-1-100570-1   341 pp. $7.50

World Economic and Social Survey 1995
E.95.II.C.1   92-1-109130-6   245 pp. $55.00

Yearbook of the United Nations, Vol. 47
E.94.I.1   0-7923-3077-3   1993   1,428 pp. $150.00

Yearbook of the United Nations, Special Edition,
UN Fiftieth Anniversary, 1945-1995
E.95.I.50   0-7923-3112-5   1995   443 pp. $95.00

The United Nations Blue Books Series

The United Nations and Apartheid, 1948-1994
E.95.I.7   92-1-100546-9   565 pp. $29.95

The United Nations and Cambodia, 1991-1995
E.95.I.9   92-1-100548-5   352 pp. $29.95

The United Nations and Nuclear Non-Proliferation
E.95.I.17   92-1-100557-4   199 pp. $29.95

The United Nations and El Salvador, 1990-1995
E.95.I.12   92-1-100552-3   611 pp. $29.95

The United Nations and Mozambique, 1992-1995
E.95.I.20   92-1-100559-0   321 pp. $29.95

The United Nations and the Advancement of Women, 1945-1995
E.95.I.29   92-1-100567-1   689 pp. $29.95

The United Nations and Human Rights, 1945-1995
E.95.I.21   92-1-100560-4   536 pp. $29.95

The United Nations and Somalia, 1992-1996
E.96.I.8   92-1-100566-3   516 pp. $29.95

United Nations Publications
2 United Nations Plaza, Room DC2-853
New York, NY 10017
United States of America
Tel.: (212) 963-8302; 1 (800) 253-9646
Fax: (212) 963-3489

United Nations Publications
Sales Office and Bookshop
CH-1211 Geneva 10
Switzerland
Tel.: 41 (22) 917-26-13;
      41 (22) 917-26-14
Fax: 41 (22) 917-00-27